AF265202

BUNYAN'S DIVINE EMBLEMS.
24
II.   The Lark & the Fowler
III. The Vine Tree
IV.   The Frog
V.   Fowls flying in the Air
VI.   The Lord's Prayer
VII. The ... in the Water
X.   The ... in the Water
XVIII. The Sinner & the Spider
XXI. The Cuckoo
XXV. The Rising of the Sun
XXVII. The Child & Bird
XXIX. The Rose Bush
XXXI. The Frog
XXXV. The Horse & his Rider
XXXIX. The Looking Glass
XLII. The Hour Glass
XLIII. The Candle
XLIV. The Skilful Player on an Instrument

The Works of John Bunyan

VOL. IV.

Christian meeting with Evangelist

BIBLIOTHECA·BODLEIANA

THE

ENTIRE WORKS

OF

JOHN BUNYAN,

AUTHOR OF "THE PILGRIM'S PROGRESS."

EDITED,

WITH ORIGINAL INTRODUCTIONS, NOTES, AND MEMOIR OF THE AUTHOR,

BY HENRY STEBBING, D.D., F.R.S.,

RECTOR OF ST. MARY SOMERSET WITH ST. MARY MOUNTHAW, UPPER THAMES STREET, LONDON.

Illustrated with Engrabings on Steel and Wood.

IN FOUR VOLUMES.

VOL. IV.

LONDON:

JAMES S. VIRTUE, CITY ROAD AND IVY LANE.

1860.

CONTENTS OF VOLUME IV.

PREFATORY REMARKS

ON

THE LIFE AND DEATH OF MR. BADMAN.

THIS is an ingenious and pathetic fiction. The chief character looks at us with a living and truthful expression. We tremble to see how he entangles himself in crime and wretchedness. His horrible folly blinding him to the future, becomes, by turns, the object of our pity and detestation. It seems as if we were with a real man, and that it would give us comfort to shout in his ear, and bid him look at the pit of destruction yawning just before him.

It is in the breadth and rude force of the delineations, that the merit of this remarkable narrative consists. The name of "Badman" shows that there is to be no attempt at any nicety of drawing or development. It tells us, at once and plainly, with what kind of a personage we are to become acquainted, and what sort of incidents we may look for in his life. There is more of honesty than art in this outset of a story. Some readers will feel that they can too readily picture to themselves the career of such a character to be interested in it. A man who, we are forewarned, can only be bad from first to last, will appear too entirely destitute of modifying qualities to be an object of sympathy. Nor are such objections without reason. To some minds the following narrative will present much which is repulsive: to others it will appear cold and harsh, the usual alternations of natural feeling being lost under the dismal sway of all-prevailing, desperate wickedness. Most persons largely and profoundly acquainted with human character, love to speak of its wonderful combinations of light and darkness—of good and evil; some traces, at least, of the former remaining even in the most deplorable instances of helpless, unresisting depravity. This is not a mere notion; or the result of a proud, philosophic desire to vindicate human virtue. It is in accordance with reason and Scripture, that a man may be lost, though there be still large remnants of good in him, even to the moment of his ruin; but it agrees with neither to suppose that man, in his present state, can be finally and absolutely destitute of moral feeling.

Thus, whenever either artist or writer depicts a form invested in gloom, and fails to introduce some light to relieve it, the work is regarded as an unskilful production, and simply because it is not in accordance with the true, the natural, and the actual. The darkest human soul has some light about it, if not in it, and quickening it. Human nature is mainly made up of instincts. Each of these bears traces of good, and these can only be entirely obliterated by the extinction of the instinct. When this takes place through the whole series, reprobation has done its work, and the wretched victim of sin is banished into the outer darkness. Such a condition even as this, may possibly be described with wholesome, as well as startling effect, by a vigorous pen; but it does not seem to have been Bunyan's intention to enter into the more gloomy depths of human iniquity to find a subject for his purpose. He meant to set before his readers an ordinary victim of the world's temptations, and inbred evil. Hence the feeling, that his object would have been better effected had he not begun by stamping the character, through which his moral was to be wrought, with the invariable and ineffaceable brand-mark of unmixed depravity.

But whatever the notions of a delicate and cultivated mind in respect to this fiction, there can be little doubt that to the class of readers for whom it was originally intended, it spoke with terrifying force. In Bunyan's days, such persons had not been taught to look for nicely contrived plots; to study the progress of a story, carefully conducted, step by step, to a startling conclusion; or to make themselves acquainted with the working of passions, properly opposed to each other, and explained by motives as skilfully adjusted and counterbalanced. Unprepared for the study of fiction by models of this kind, the purchasers of Bunyan's history would, probably, have turned with distaste from a delineation of character, intended for Mr. Badman, had it not been given in the broad, plain details of Mr. Badman's own wicked dispositions and actions. It was enough for them to have such a personage himself before them. The more simply his deeds and his fate were described the better. They needed no addition to the stimulant which the history itself afforded, to feel themselves sufficiently excited, whether for amusement or instruction. A tract intended for the humblest class of readers, at this time, would scarcely obtain circulation, if not written with more regard to art and propriety than this narrative. But to Bunyan's contemporaries any rude materials for a story, just put into shape by an active fancy, were an acceptable boon.

There is one species of excellence in the work which mere literary ability would have failed, in any age, to give it. Bunyan had closely observed the workings and results of vice in all its lower grades. Not only was its open-faced, daring progress familiar to him; he knew how it came to be so daring. The cradle in which it was rocked, and the den where it lay in its last struggles, had fixed his notice from the moment of his awakening to a terrible sense of his own danger. Had he not been influenced in all he wrote by the call of practical duty, he might have composed a work coloured with the deepest tints of sombre romance. But this would not have served his purpose. What he saw on the open, high-road of common life, was better fitted for the lesson which he wished to teach, than what either his imagination or his more secret experience might have furnished. Mr. Badman, therefore, is but the representative of a class everywhere to be found, and easily recognised by the ordinary expression of baseness and audacity. It required no mental training, no particular effort of thought, to enable a reader to understand what was meant when such a picture was drawn: and Bunyan intended to make its moral thus directly intelligible. When he wrote *Grace Abounding*, he provided instruction for a class of readers whose experience might render it applicable to themselves, or whose habits of thinking might make it interesting as a profound explanation of great religious phenomena. In *The Pilgrim's Progress* he furnished a far more numerous class with subjects for thought: curiosity, sympathy, and a crowd of hopes and fears, stood obedient to every stroke of his pen, as he traced line after line of that wonderful story. But simple as it is in style, it must be looked into, before the events and characters become thoroughly clear to apprehension. Readers of very humble mental endowments may enter quickly into its whole meaning; but then they must have the will to do so,—it does not stare them in the face, force them to take an interest in it, and compel them to blush and tremble.

Thus there was still a class for which Bunyan had not yet contributed just what was needed. Neither *Grace Abounding*, nor *The Pilgrim's Progress*, nor *The Holy War*, was the kind of narrative that would gain the attention of the rough and idle multitude. Ability and holiness make men systematic in their labours. It is not to be supposed, therefore, that a mere accident, or capricious impulse only, led Bunyan to describe the career of Mr. Badman. Something was needed to complete his narrative writings, so that, by one or the other, he might reach each of the classes towards whose edification he was anxious to minister. By this history, he began with that which might be considered the lowest in moral apprehension, or the least willing to become interested in the counsels or warnings of piety. The homeliness, consequently, of the style, the very little invention employed either about the characters, or the incidents, may be attributed not to any failure of ingenuity in the author, but to his steadiness of purpose to make the real Mr. Badman recognise the likeness, and repent.

H. S.

THE LIFE AND DEATH OF MR. BADMAN,

PRESENTED TO THE WORLD IN

A FAMILIAR DIALOGUE BETWEEN MR. WISEMAN AND MR. ATTENTIVE.

THE AUTHOR TO THE READER.

COURTEOUS READER,—As I was considering with myself what I had written concerning the Progress of the Pilgrim from this world to glory, and how it had been acceptable to many in this nation, it came again into my mind to write, as then, of him that was going to heaven, so now, of the life and death of the ungodly, and of their travel from this world to hell. The which in this I have done, and have put it, as thou seest, under the name and title of Mr. Badman, a name very proper for such a subject. I have also put it in the form of a dialogue, that I might with more ease to myself, and pleasure to the reader, perform the work.

And although, as I said, I have put it forth in this method, yet have I as little as may be gone out of the road of mine own observation of things. Yea, I think I may truly say that to the best of my remembrance, all the things that here I discourse of, I mean as to matter of fact, have been acted upon the stage of this world, even many times before mine eyes.

Here therefore, courteous reader, I present thee with the life and death of Mr. Badman indeed: yea, I do trace him in his life, from his childhood to his death; that thou mayest, as in a glass, behold with thine own eyes the steps that take hold of hell; and also discern, while thou art reading of Mr. Badman's death, whether thou thyself art treading in his path thereto.

And let me entreat thee to forbear quirking and mocking, for that Mr. Badman is dead; but rather gravely inquire concerning thyself by the word, whether thou art one of his lineage or no: for Mr. Badman has left many of his relations behind him; yea, the very world is overspread with his kindred. True, some of his relations, as he, are gone to their place and long home, but thousands of thousands are left behind; as brothers, sisters, cousins, nephews, besides innumerable of his friends and associates.

I may say, and yet speak nothing but too much truth in so saying, that there is scarce a fellowship, a community, or fraternity of men in the world, but some of Mr. Badman's relations are there. Yea, rarely can we find a family or household in a town, where he has not left behind him a brother, nephew, or friend.

The butt therefore, that at this time I shoot at, is wide; and it will be as impossible for this book to go into several families, and not to arrest some, as for the king's messenger to rush into an house full of traitors, and find none but honest men there.

I cannot but think that this shot will light upon many, since our fields are so full of this game; but how many it will kill to Mr. Badman's course, and make alive to the Pilgrim's Progress, that is not in me to determine; this secret is with the Lord our God only, and he alone knows to whom he will bless it to so good and so blessed an end. However, I have put fire to the pan, and doubt not but the report will quickly be heard.

I told you before that Mr. Badman had left many of his friends and relations behind him, but if I survive them (as that's a great question to me), I may also write of their lives: however, whether my life be longer or shorter, this is my prayer at present, that God will stir up witnesses against them, that may either convert or confound them; for wherever they live, and roll in their wickedness, they are the pest and plague of that country.

England shakes and totters already, by reason of the burden that Mr. Badman and his friends have wickedly laid upon it: yea, our earth reels and staggereth to and fro like a drunkard, the transgression thereof is heavy upon it.

Courteous reader, I will treat thee now, even at the door and threshold of this house, but only with this intelligence, that Mr. Badman lies dead within. Be pleased therefore (if thy leisure will serve thee) to enter in, and behold the state in which he is laid, betwixt his death-bed and the grave. He is not buried as yet, nor doth he stink, as is designed he shall, before he lies down in oblivion.

Now as others have had their funerals solemnized, according to their greatness and grandeur in the world, so likewise Mr. Badman, (forasmuch as he deserveth not to go down to his grave with silence,) has his funeral state according to his deserts.

Four things are usual at great men's funerals, which we will take leave, and I hope without offence, to allude to, in the funeral of Mr. Badman.

First. They are sometimes, when dead, presented to their friends, by their completely wrought images, as lively as by cunning men's hands they can be; that the remembrance of them may be renewed to their survivors, the remembrance of them and their deeds: and this I have endeavoured to answer in my discourse of Mr. Badman, and therefore I have drawn him forth in his features and actions from his childhood to his grey hairs. Here, therefore, thou hast him lively set forth as in cuts: both as to the minority, flower, and seniority of his age, together with those actions of his life, that he was most capable of doing, in and under those present circumstances of time, place, strength; and the opportunities that did attend him in these.

Second. There is also usual at great men's funerals, those badges and escutcheons of their honour, that they have received from their ancestors, or have been thought worthy of for the deeds and exploits they have done in their life; and here Mr. Badman has his, but such as vary from all men of worth, but so much the more agreeing with the merit of his doings. They all have descended in state, he only as an abominable branch. His deserts are the deserts of sin, and therefore the escutcheons of honour that he has, are only that he died without honour, "and at his end became a fool." "Thou shalt not be joined with them in burial." "The seed of evil doers shall never be renowned." (Isa. xiv. 20.)

The funeral pomp therefore of Mr. Badman, is to wear upon his hearse the badges of a dishonourable and wicked life; since "his bones are full of the sin of his youth, which shall lie down," as Job says, "with him in the dust." Nor is it fit that any should be his attendants, now at his death, but such as with him conspired against their own souls in their life—persons whose transgressions have made them infamous to all that have or shall know what they have done.

Some notice therefore I have also here in this little discourse given the reader, of them who were his confederates in this life, and attendants at his death; with a hint, either of some high villany committed by them, as also of those judgments that have overtaken and fallen upon them from the just and revenging hand of God. All which are things either fully known by me, as being eye and ear-witness thereto, or that I have received from such hands, whose relation as to this I am bound to believe. And that the reader may know them from other things and passages herein contained, I have pointed at them in the margin, as with a finger thus: ☞

Third. The funerals of persons of quality have been solemnized with some suitable sermon at the time and place of their burial; but that I am not come to as yet, having got no further than to Mr. Badman's death; but forasmuch as he must be buried, after he hath stunk out his time before his beholders, I doubt not but some such that we read are appointed to be at the burial of Gog, will do this work in my stead; such as shall leave him neither skin nor bone above ground, but shall set a sign by it till the buriers have buried it in the valley of Hamon-gog. (Ezek. xxxix.)

Fourth. At funerals there does use to be mourning and lamentation, but here also Mr. Badman differs from others; his familiars cannot lament his departure, for they have not sense of his damnable state; they rather ring him, and sing him to hell in the sleep of death, in which he goes thither. Good men count him no loss to the world, his place can well be without him, his loss is only his own, and it is too late for him to recover that damage or loss by a sea of bloody tears, could he shed them. Yea, God has said, he will laugh at his destruction; who then shall lament for him, saying, "Ah! my brother." He was but a stinking weed in his life; nor was he better at all in his death. Such may well be thrown over the wall without sorrow, when once God has plucked them up by the roots in his wrath.

Reader, if thou art of the race, lineage, stock or fraternity of Mr. Badman, I tell thee before thou readest this book, thou wilt neither brook the author nor it, because he hath writ of Mr. Badman as he has. For he that condemneth the wicked that die so, passeth also the sentence upon the wicked that live. I therefore expect neither credit of, nor countenance from thee, for this narration of thy kinsman's life.

For thy old love to thy friend, his ways, doings, &c., will stir up in thee enmity rather, in thy very heart, against me. I shall therefore incline to think of thee, that thou wilt rend, burn, or throw it away in contempt; yea, and wish also, that for writing so notorious a truth, some mischief may befall me. I look also to be loaded by thee with disdain, scorn and contempt; yea, that thou shouldst railingly and villifyingly say I lie, and am a bespatterer of honest men's lives and deaths. For Mr. Badman, when himself was alive, could not abide to be counted a knave, though his actions, told all that went by, that indeed he was such an one. How then should his brethren that survive him, and that tread in his very steps, approve of the sentence that by this book is pronounced against him? Will they not rather imitate Korah, Dathan, and Abiram's friends,—even rail at me for condemning him, as they did at Moses for doing execution?

I know it is ill puddling in the cockatrice's den, and that they run hazards that hunt the wild boar. The man also that writeth Mr. Badman's life had need be fenced with a coat of mail, and with the staff of a spear, for that his surviving friends will know what he doth: but I have adventured to do it, and to play, at this time, at the hole of these asps; if they bite, they bite—if they sting, they sting. Christ sends his lambs in the midst of wolves, not to do like them, but to suffer by them for bearing plain testimony against their bad deeds. But had one not need to walk with a guard, and to have a sentinel stand at one's door for this? Verily, the flesh would be glad of such help; yea, a spiritual man, could he tell how to get it. (Acts xxiii.) But I am stript naked of these, and yet am commanded to be faithful in my service for Christ. Well then, I have spoken what I have spoken, and now come on me what will. (Job xiii. 13.) True, the text says, Rebuke a scorner, and he will hate thee: and that he that reproveth a wicked man getteth himself a blot and shame. But what then? Open rebuke is better than secret love, and he that receives it shall find it so afterwards.

So then, whether Mr. Badman's friends shall rage or laugh at what I have writ, I know the better end of the staff is mine. My endeavour is to stop an hellish course of life, and to "save a soul from death," (James v.;) and if for so doing I meet with envy from them from whom in reason I should have thanks, I must remember the man in the dream, that cut his way through his armed enemies, and so got into the beauteous palace: I must, I say, remember him, and do myself likewise.

Yet four things I will propound to the consideration of Mr. Badman's friends, before I turn my back upon them.

1. Suppose that there be an hell in very deed; not that I do question it any more than I do whether there be a sun to shine; but I suppose it for argument sake with Mr. Badman's friends: I say, suppose there be an hell, and that too such an one as the Scripture speaks of, one at the remotest distance from God and life eternal, one where the worm of a guilty conscience never dies, and where the fire of the wrath of God is not quenched: suppose, I say, that there is such an hell, prepared of God (as there is indeed) for the body and soul of the ungodly world after this life to be tormented in: I say, do but with thyself suppose it, and then tell me, is it not prepared for thee, thou being a wicked man? Let thy conscience speak, I say, is it not prepared for thee, thou being an ungodly man? And dost thou think, wast thou there now, that thou art able to wrestle with the judgment of God? Why, then, do the fallen angels tremble there? Thy hands cannot be strong, nor can thy heart endure, in that day when God shall deal with thee. (Ezek. xxii. 14.)

2. Suppose that some one that is now a soul in hell for sin, was permitted to come hither again to dwell; and that they had a grant also, that upon amendment of life, next time they die, to change that place for heaven and glory. What sayest thou, O wicked man? Would such an one, thinkest thou, run again into the same course of life as before, and venture the damnation that for sin he had already been in? Would he choose again to lead that cursed life that afresh would kindle the flames of hell upon him, and that would bind him up under the heavy wrath of God? O! he would not, he would not; the 16th of Luke insinuates it; yea, reason itself, awake, would abhor it, and tremble at such a thought.

3. Suppose again, that thou that livest and rollest in thy sin, and that as yet hast known nothing but the pleasure thereof, shouldst be by an angel conveyed to some place where, with convenience, from thence thou mightest have a view of heaven and hell—of the joys of the one, and the torments of the other; I say, suppose that from thence thou mightest have such a view thereof as would convince thy reason that both heaven and hell are such realities as by the word they are declared to be; wouldst thou, thinkest thou, when brought to thy home again, choose to thyself thy former life—to wit, to return to thy folly again? No; if belief of what thou sawest remained with thee, thou wouldst eat fire and brimstone first.

4. I will propound again. Suppose that there was amongst us such a law, (and such a magistrate to inflict the penalty,) that for every open wickedness committed by thee, so much of thy flesh should with burning pincers be plucked from thy bones; wouldst thou then go on in thy open way of lying, swearing, drinking, and whoring, as thou with delight doest now? Surely, surely, no. The fear of the punishment would make thee forbear; yea, would make thee tremble, even then when thy lusts were powerful, to think what a punishment thou wast sure to sustain, so soon as the pleasure was over. But oh! the folly, the madness, the desperate madness that is in the hearts of Mr. Badman's friends, who in despite of the threatenings of an holy and sin-revenging God, and of the outcries and warnings of all good men, yea, that will in despite of the groans and torments of those that are now in hell for sin, (Luke xvi. 24, 28,) go on in a sinful course of life; yea, though every sin is also a step of descent down that infernal cave. O how true is that saying of Solomon, "The heart of the sons of men is full of evil, and madness is in their heart while they live, and after that they go to the dead." (Eccles. ix. 3.) To the dead! that is, to the dead in hell, to the damned dead; the place to which those that have died bad men are gone, and that those that live bad men are like to go to, when a little more sin, like stolen waters, hath been imbibed by their sinful souls.

That which has made me publish this book is—

1. For that wickedness like a flood is like to drown our English world. It begins already to be above the tops of the mountains; it has almost swallowed up all; our youth, our middle age, old age, and all, are almost carried away of this flood. O debauchery, debauchery, what hast thou done in England! Thou hast corrupted our young men, hast made our old men beasts; thou hast deflowered our virgins, and hast made our matrons bawds. Thou hast made our earth to reel to and fro like a drunkard; it is in danger to be removed like a cottage, yea it is, because transgression is so heavy upon it, like to fall and rise no more. (Isa. xxiv. 20.)

O! that I could mourn for England, and for the sins that are committed therein, even while I see that, without repentance, the men of God's wrath are about to deal with us, each having his "slaughtering weapon in his hand." (Ezek. ix. 1, 2.) Well, I have written, and by God's assistance shall pray that this flood may abate in England; and could I but see the tops of the mountains above it, I should think that these waters were abating.

2. It is the duty of those that can, to cry out against this deadly plague, yea, to lift up their voice as with a trumpet against it; that men may be awakened about it, fly from it, as from that which is the greatest of evils. Sin pulled angels out of heaven, pulls men down to hell, and overthroweth kingdoms. Who, that sees an house on fire, will not give the alarm to them that dwell therein? Who, that sees the land invaded will not set the beacons on a flame? Who, that sees the devils, as roaring lions, continually devouring souls, will not make an outcry? But above all, when we see sin, sinful sin, a-swallowing up a nation, sinking of a nation, and bringing its inhabitants to temporal, spiritual, and eternal ruin, shall we not cry out, and cry, "They are drunk, but not with wine; they stagger, but not with strong drink; they are intoxicated with the deadly poison of sin, which will, if its malignity be not by wholesome means allayed, bring soul and body, and estate, and country, and all, to ruin and destruction?"

3. In and by this my outcry I shall deliver myself from the ruins of them that perish; for a man can do no more in this matter—I mean as man in my capacity—than to detect and condemn the wickedness, warn the evil doer of the judgment, and fly therefrom myself. But O! that I might not only deliver myself! Oh that many would hear, and turn at this my cry, from sin! that they may be secured from the death and judgment that attend it.

Why I have handled the matter in this method, is best known to myself; and why I have concealed most of the names of the persons whose sins or punishments I here and there in this book make relation of, is,

(1.) For that neither the sins nor judgments were all alike open; the sins of some were committed, and the judgments executed for them only in a corner. Not to say that I could not learn some of their names; for could I, I should not have made them public for this reason,

(2.) Because I would not provoke those of their relations that survive them; I would not justly provoke them; and yet, as I think, I should, should I have entailed their punishment to their sins, and both to their names, and so have turned them into the world.

(3.) Nor would I lay them under disgrace and contempt, which would, as I think, unavoidably have happened unto them had I withal inserted their names.

As for those whose names I mention, their crimes or judgments were manifest—public almost as anything of that nature that happeneth to mortal men. Such, therefore, have published their own shame by their sin, and God, his anger, by taking of open vengeance. As Job says, "God has struck them as wicked men in the open sight of others." (Job xxxiv. 26.) So that I cannot conceive, since their sin and judgment was so conspicuous, that my admonishing the world thereof, should turn to their detriment: for the publishing of these things are, so far as relation is concerned, intended for remembrances; that they may also bethink themselves, repent and turn to God, lest the judgments for their sins should prove hereditary. For the God of heaven hath threatened to visit the iniquity of the fathers upon the children, if they hate him, to the third and fourth generation. (Exod. xx. 5.)

Nebuchadnezzar's punishment for his pride being open—for he was for his sin driven from his kingly dignity, and from among men too, to eat grass like an ox, and to company with the beasts—Daniel did not stick to tell Belshazzar, his son, to his face thereof; nor to publish it that it might be read and remembered by the generations to come. The same may be said of Judas and Ananias, &c., for their sin and punishment were known to all the dwellers at Jerusalem. (Acts i.; v.)

Nor is it a sign but of a desperate impenitence and hardness of heart, when the offspring or relations of those who have fallen by open, fearful, and prodigious judgments, for their sin, shall overlook, forget, pass by, or take no notice of such high out-goings of God against them and their house. Thus Daniel aggravates Belshazzar's crime, for that he hardened his heart in pride, though he knew that for that very sin and transgression his father was brought down from his height, and made to be a companion for asses. "And thou his son, O Belshazzar," says he, "hast not humbled thine heart, though thou knewest all this." (Dan. v. 22.) A home reproof, indeed; but home reproof is most fit for an open and a continued in transgression.

Let those, then, that are the offspring or relations of such, who by their own sin, and the dreadful judgments of God, are made to become a sign, (Deut. xvi. 9, 10,) having been swept, as dung, from off the face of the earth, beware, lest when judgment knocks at their door, for their sins, as it did before at the door of their progenitors, it falls also with as heavy a stroke as on them that went before them: lest, I say, they in that day, instead of finding mercy, find for their high, daring, and judgment-affronting sins, judgment without mercy.

To conclude: let those that would not die Mr. Badman's death, take heed of Mr. Badman's ways; for his ways bring to his end. Wickedness will not deliver him that is given to it, though they should cloak all with a profession of religion.

If it was a transgression of old for a man to wear a woman's apparel, surely it is a transgression now for a sinner to wear a Christian profession for a cloak. Wolves in sheeps' clothing swarm in England this day; wolves both as to doctrine, and as to practice too. Some men make a profession, I doubt, on purpose that they may twist themselves into a trade; and thence into an estate; yea, and if need be, into an estate knavishly, by the ruins of their neighbour. Let such take heed, for those that do such things have the greater damnation.

Christian, make thy profession shine by a conversation according to the gospel, or else thou wilt damnify religion, bring scandal to thy brethren, and give offence to the enemies; and it would be better that a millstone was hanged about thy neck, and that thou, as so adorned, was cast into the bottom of the sea, than so to do.

Christian, a profession according to the gospel, is, in these days, a rare thing; seek, then, after it, put it on, and keep it without spot, and, as becomes thee, white, and clean, and thou shalt be a rare Christian.

The prophecy of the last times, is, that professing men—for so I understand the text—shall be, many of them, base, (2 Tim. iii.;) but continue thou in the things that thou hast learned, not of wanton men, nor of licentious times, but of the word and doctrine of God; that is, according to godliness, and thou shalt walk with Christ in white.

Now, God Almighty give his people grace, not to hate or malign sinners, nor yet to choose any of their ways, but to keep themselves pure from the blood of all men, by speaking and doing according to that name and those rules that they profess to know and love, for Jesus Christ's sake.

JOHN BUNYAN.

THE LIFE AND DEATH OF MR. BADMAN.

WISEMAN. Good morrow, my good neighbour, Mr. Attentive; whither are you walking so early this morning? Methinks you look as if you were concerned about something more than ordinary. Have you lost any of your cattle, or what is the matter?

ATTENTIVE. Good sir, good morrow to you; I have not as yet lost aught: but yet you give a right guess of me, for I am, as you say, concerned in my heart, but it is because of the badness of the times. And, sir, you, as all our neighbours know, are a very observing man, pray, therefore, what do you think of them?

Wise. Why, I think, as you say, to wit, that they are bad times, and bad they will be, until men are better: for they are bad men that make bad times; if men, therefore, would mend, so would the times. It is a folly to look for good days so long as sin is so high, and those that study its nourishment so many. God bring it down, and those that nourish it, to repentance, and then, my good neighbour, you will be concerned, not as you are now: now you are concerned because times are so bad, but then you will be so because times are so good: now you are concerned so as to be perplexed, but then you will be concerned so as to lift up your voice with shouting; for, I dare say, could you see such days, they would make you shout.

Atten. Ay, so they would: such times I have prayed for, such times I have longed for; but I fear they will be worse before they be better.

Wise. Make no conclusions, man; for he that hath the hearts of men in his hand can change them from worse to better, and so bad times into good. God give long life to them that are good, and especially to those of them that are capable of doing him service in the world. The ornament and beauty of this lower world, next to God and his wonders, are the men that spangle and shine in godliness.

Now, as Mr. Wiseman said this, he gave a great sigh.

Atten. Amen, amen. But why, good sir, do you sigh so deeply? Is it for aught else than that for the which, as you have perceived, I myself am concerned?

Wise. I am concerned with you for the badness of the times; but that was not the cause of that sigh, of the which, as I see, you take notice. I sighed at the remembrance of the death of that man for whom the bell tolled at our town yesterday.

Atten. Why, I trow, Mr. Goodman, your neighbour, is not dead. Indeed, I did hear that he had been sick.

Wise. No, no; it is not he. Had it been he, I could not but have been concerned; but yet not as

I am concerned now. If he had died, I should only have been concerned for that the world had lost a light: but the man that I am concerned for now was one that never was good, therefore such an one who is not dead only, but damned. He died that he might die, he went from life to death, and then from death to death, from death natural to death eternal.

And as he spake this, the water stood in his eyes.

Atten. Indeed, to go from a death-bed to hell is a fearful thing to think on. But, good neighbour Wiseman, be pleased to tell me who this man was, and why you conclude him so miserable in his death?

Wise. Well, if you can stay, I will tell you who he was, and why I conclude thus concerning him.

Atten. My leisure will admit me to stay, and I am willing to hear you out; and I pray God your discourse may take hold on my heart, that I may be bettered thereby.

So they agreed to sit down under a tree. Then Mr. Wiseman proceeded as followeth.

Wise. The man that I mean is one Mr. Badman; he has lived in our town a great while, and now, as I said, he is dead. But the reason of my being so concerned at his death, is, not for that he was at all related to me, or for that any good conditions died with him, for he was far from them, but for that, as I greatly fear, he hath, as was hinted before, died two deaths at once.

Atten. I perceive what you mean by two deaths at once; and to speak truth, it is a fearful thing thus to have ground to think of any: for although the death of the ungodly and sinners is laid to heart but of few, yet to die in such a state is more dreadful and fearful than any man can imagine. Indeed if a man had no soul, if his state was not truly immortal, the matter would not be so much; but for a man to be so disposed of by his Maker, as to be appointed a sensible being for ever, and for him too to fall into the hands of revenging justice, that will be always, to the utmost extremity that his sin deserveth, punishing of him in the dismal dungeon of hell, this must needs be unutterably sad, and lamentable.

Wise. There is no man, I think, that is sensible of the worth of one soul, but must, when he hears of the death of unconverted men, be stricken with sorrow and grief: because, as you said well, that man's state is such, that he has a sensible being for ever. For it is sense that makes punishment heavy. But yet sense is not all that the damned have, they have sense and reason too; so then, as sense receiveth punishment with sorrow, because it feels, and bleeds under the same, so by reason, and the exercise thereof, in the midst of torment, all present affliction is aggravated, and that three manner of ways:—1. Reason will consider thus with himself. For what am I thus tormented? and will easily find it is for nothing but that base and filthy thing, sin; and now will vexation be mixed with punishment, and that will greatly heighten the affliction. 2. Reason will consider thus with himself. How long must this be my state? And will soon return to himself this answer: This must be my state for ever and ever. Now this will greatly increase the torment. 3. Reason will consider thus with himself. What have I lost more than present ease and quiet by my sins that I have committed? And will quickly return himself this answer: I have lost communion with God, Christ, saints, and angels, and a share in heaven and eternal life: and this also must needs greaten the misery of poor damned souls. And this is the case of Mr. Badman.

Atten. I feel my heart even shake at the thoughts of coming into such a state. Hell! Who knows that is yet alive, what the torments of hell are? This word *hell* gives a very dreadful sound.

Wise. Ay, so it does in the ears of him that has a tender conscience. But if, as you say, and that truly, the very name of hell is so dreadful, what is the place itself, and what are the punishments that are there inflicted, and that without the least intermission, upon the souls of damned men for ever and ever.

Atten. Well, but passing this; my leisure will admit me to stay, and therefore pray tell me what it is that makes you think that Mr. Badman is gone to hell.

Wise. I will tell you. But first do you know which of the Badmans I mean?

Atten. Why was there more of them than one?

Wise. O yes, a great many, both brothers and sisters, and yet all of them the children of a godly parent, the more a great deal is the pity.

Atten. Which of them therefore was it that died?

Wise. The eldest, old in years, and old in sin; but the sinner that dies an hundred years old shall be accursed.

Atten. Well, but what makes you think he is gone to hell?

Wise. His wicked life, and fearful death, especially since the manner of his death was so corresponding with his life.

Atten. Pray let me know the manner of his death, if yourself did perfectly know it.

Wise. I was there when he died; but I desire not to see another such man while I live die in such sort as he did.

Atten. Pray therefore let me hear it.

Wise. You say you have leisure and can stay, and therefore, if you please, we will discourse even orderly of him. First, we will begin with his life, and then proceed to his death: because a relation of the first may the more affect you, when you shall hear of the second.

Atten. Did you then so well know his life?

Wise. I knew him of a child. I was a man, when he was but a boy, and I made special observation of him from first to last.

Atten. Pray then let me hear from you an account of his life; but be as brief as you can, for I long to hear of the manner of his death.

Wise. I will endeavour to answer your desires, and first, I will tell you that from a child he was very bad; his very beginning was ominous, and presaged that no good end was, in likelihood, to follow thereupon. There were several sins that he was given to, when but a little one, that manifested him to be notoriously infected with original corruption; for I dare say he learned none of them of his father and mother; nor was he admitted to go much abroad among other children that were vile, to learn to sin of them: nay, contrariwise, if at any time he did get abroad amongst others, he would be as the inventor of bad words, and an example in bad actions. To them all he used to be, as we say, the ringleader, and master-sinner from a child.

Atten. This was a bad beginning indeed, and did demonstrate that he was, as you say, polluted, very much polluted with original corruption.

Original sin is the root of actual transgression.

For to speak my mind freely, I do confess, that it is mine opinion, that children come polluted with sin into the world, and that ofttimes the sins of their youth, especially while they are very young, are rather by virtue of indwelling sin, than by examples that are set before them by others. Not but that they learn to sin by example too, but example is not the root, but rather the temptation unto wickedness. The root is sin within; "for from within, out of the heart of man," proceedeth sin. (Mark vii. 21.)

Wise. I am glad to hear that you are of this opinion, and to confirm what you have said by a few hints from the word. Man in his birth is compared to an ass, (an unclean beast,) and to a wretched infant in its blood. (Job xi. 12. Ezek. 16.) Besides, all the first-born of old that were offered unto the Lord, were to be redeemed at the age of a month, and that was before they were sinners by imitation. The scripture also affirmeth, that by the sin of one, judgment came upon all; and renders this reason, "for that all have sinned." (Rom. v. 12.) Nor is that objection worth a rush, that Christ by his death hath taken away original sin. First, because it is scriptureless. Secondly, because it makes them incapable of salvation by Christ: for none but those that in their own persons are sinners, are to have salvation by him. Many other things might be added, but between persons so well agreed as you and I are, these may suffice at present. But when an antagonist comes to deal with us about this matter, then we have for him often other strong arguments, if he be an antagonist worth the taking notice of.

Atten. But, as we hinted before, he used to be the ringleading sinner, or the master of mischief among other children; yet these are but generals: pray therefore tell me in particular which were the sins of his childhood.

Wise. I will so. When he was but a child, he was so addicted to lying, that his parents scarce knew when to believe he spake true; yea, he would invent, tell, and stand to the lies that he invented and told, and that with such an audacious face, that one might even read in his very countenance, the symptoms of an hard and desperate heart this way.

Badman addicted to lying from a child.

Atten. This was an ill beginning indeed, and argueth that he began to harden himself in sin betimes. For a lie cannot be knowingly told and stood in, (and I perceive that this was his manner of way in lying,) but he must as it were force his own heart unto it. Yea, he must make his heart hard, and bold to do it. Yea he must be arrived to an exceeding pitch of wickedness thus to do, since all this he did against that good education, that before you seemed to hint he had from his father and mother.

A lie knowingly told demonstrates that the heart is desperately hard.

Wise. The want of a good education, as you have intimated, is many times a cause why children do so easily, so soon, become bad; especially when there is not only a want of that, but bad examples enough, as, the more is the pity, there is in many families; by virtue of which poor children are trained up in sin, and nursed therein for the devil and hell. But it was otherwise with Mr. Badman, for to my knowledge, this his way of lying, was a great grief to his parents, for their hearts were much dejected at this beginning of their son; nor did there want counsel and correction from them to him, if that would have made him better. He wanted not to be told, in my hearing, and that over and over, that "all liars should have their part in the lake which burneth with fire and brimstone;" and that "whosoever loveth and maketh a lie," should not have any part in the new and heavenly Jerusalem. (Rev. xxi. 8, 27; xxii. 15.) But all availed nothing with him; when a fit, or an occasion to lie came upon him, he would invent, tell, and stand to his lie as steadfastly as if it had been the biggest of truths that he told, and that with that hardening of his heart and face, that it would be to those who stood by, a wonder. Nay, and this he would do when under the rod of correction, which is appointed by God for parents to use, that thereby they might keep their children from hell. (Prov. xxii. 15; xxiii. 13, 14.)

The liar's portion.

Atten. Truly it was, as I said, a bad beginning, he served the devil betimes; yea he became nurse to one of his brats, for a spirit of lying is the devil's brat, "for he is a liar, and the father of it." (John viii. 44.)

The devil's brat.

Wise. Right, he is the father of it indeed. A lie is begot by the devil as the father, and is brought forth by the wicked heart, as the mother: wherefore another scripture also saith, "Why hath Satan filled thine heart to lie," &c. (Acts v. 3, 4.) Yea, he calleth the heart that is big with a lie, an heart that hath conceived, that is, by the devil. "Why hast thou conceived this thing in thy heart? thou hast not lied unto men, but unto God." True, his lie was a lie of the highest nature, but every lie *The father and mother of a lie.* hath the same father and mother as had the lie last spoken of. "For he is a liar, and the father of it." A lie then is the brat of hell, and it cannot be in the heart before the person has committed a kind of spiritual adultery with the devil. That soul therefore that telleth a known lie, has lien with, and conceived it by lying with the devil, the only father of lies. For a lie has only one father and mother—the devil and the heart. No marvel, therefore if the hearts that hatch and bring forth lies, be so much of complexion with the devil. Yea, no marvel, though God and Christ have so bent their word against liars. A liar is wedded to the devil himself.

Atten. It seems a marvellous thing in mine eyes, that since a lie is the offspring of the devil, and since a lie brings the soul to the very den of devils, to wit, the dark dungeon of hell, that men should be so desperately wicked as to accustom themselves to so horrible a thing.

Wise. It seems also marvellous to me, especially when I observe for how little a matter some men will study, contrive, make, and tell a lie. You shall have some that will lie it over and over, and *Some will tell a lie for a penny profit.* that for a penny profit. Yea, lie and stand in it, although they know that they lie. Yea, you shall have some men that will not stick to tell lie after lie, though themselves get nothing thereby. They will tell lies in their ordinary discourse with their neighbours; also their news, their jests, and their tales must needs be adorned with lies, or else they seem to bear no good sound to the ear, nor show much to the fancy of him to whom they are told. But, alas! what will these liars do, when, for their lies, they shall be tumbled down into hell, to that devil that did beget those lies in their heart, and so be tormented by fire and brimstone, with him, and that for ever and ever, for their lies?

Atten. Can you not give one some example of God's judgments upon liars, that one may tell them to liars when one hears them lie, if perhaps they may by the hearing thereof be made afraid, and ashamed to lie.

Wise. Examples! why, Ananias and his wife *An example for liars.* are examples enough to put a stop, one would think, to a spirit addicted thereto, for they both were stricken down dead for telling a lie, and that by God himself, in the midst of a company of people. (Acts v.) But if God's threatening of liars with hell-fire, and with the loss of the kingdom of heaven, will not prevail with them to leave off to lie and make lies, it cannot be imagined that a relation of temporal judgments that have swept liars out of the world heretofore, should do it. Now, as I said, this lying was one of the first

sins that Mr. Badman was addicted to, and he could make them and tell them fearfully.

Atten. I am sorry to hear this of him, and so much the more, because, as I fear, this sin did not reign in him alone; *A spirit of lying accompanied with other sins.* for usually one that is accustomed to lying, is also accustomed to other evils besides; and if it were not so also with Mr. Badman, it would be indeed a wonder.

Wise. You say true, the liar is a captive slave of more than the spirit of lying; *Badman given to pilfer.* and therefore this Mr. Badman, as he was a liar from a child, so he was also much given to pilfer and steal, so that what he could, as we say, handsomely lay his hands on, that was counted his own, whether they were the things of his fellow children, or if he could lay hold of anything at a neighbour's house, he would take it away; you must understand me of trifles—for being yet but a child, he attempted no great matter, especially at first. But yet, as he grew up in strength and ripeness of wit, so he attempted to pilfer and steal things still of more value than at first. He took at last great pleasure in robbing of gardens and orchards; and, as he grew up, to steal pullen from the neighbourhood. Yea, what was his father's could not escape his *Badman would rob his father.* fingers, all was fish that came to his net, so hardened, at last, was he in this mischief also.

Atten. You make me wonder more and more. What, play the thief too! What, play the thief so soon! He could not but know, though he was but a child, that what he took from others was none of his own. Besides, if his father was a good man, as you say, it could not be but he must also hear from him, that to steal was to transgress the law of God, and so to run the hazard of eternal damnation.

Wise. His father was not wanting to use the means to reclaim him, often urging, as I have been told, that saying in the law of Moses, "Thou shalt not steal." (Exod. xx. 15.) And also that, "This is the curse that goeth forth over the face of the whole earth, for every one that stealeth shall be cut off," &c. (Zech. v. 3.) The light of nature also, though he was little, must needs show him that what he took from others was not his own, and that he would not willingly have been served so himself. But all was to no purpose; let father and conscience say what they would to him, he would go on, he was resolved to go on in his wickedness.

Atten. But his father would, as you intimate, sometimes rebuke him for his wickedness; pray how would he carry it then?

Wise. How! why, like to a thief that is found. He would stand gloating, and hang- *How Badman did use to carry it when his father used to chide him for his sins.* ing down his head in a sullen, pouching manner, (a body might read, as we use to say, the picture of ill-luck in his face,) and when his father did demand his answer to such questions concerning his villany, he would grumble and mutter at him, and that should be all he could get.

Atten. But you said that he would also rob his father, methinks that was an unnatural thing.

Wise. Natural or unnatural, all is one to a thief. Besides, you must think that he had likewise companions to whom he was, for the wickedness that he saw in them, more firmly knit than either to father or mother. Yea, and what had he cared, if father and mother had died for grief for him. Their death would have been, as he would have counted, great release and liberty to him : for the truth is, they and their counsel were his bondage ; yea, and if I forget not, I have heard some say, that when he was, at times, among his companions, he would greatly rejoice to think that his parents were old, and could not live long, and then, quoth he, I shall be mine own man, to do what I list, without their control.

Atten. Then it seems he counted that robbing of his parents was no crime.

Wise. None at all; and therefore he fell directly under that sentence, " Whoso robbeth his father or his mother, and saith it is no transgression, the same is the companion of a destroyer." (Prov. xxviii. 24.) And for that he set so light by them as to their persons and counsels, it was a sign that at present he was of a very abominable spirit, and that some judgment waited to take hold of him in time to come. (1 Sam. ii. 25.)

Atten. But can you imagine what it was, I mean in his conceit, (for I speak not now of the suggestions of Satan, by which doubtless he was put on to do these things,) I say what it should be in his conceit, that should make him think that this, his manner of pilfering and stealing, was no great matter.

Wise. It was for that the things that he stole were small; to rob orchards and gardens, and to steal pullen, and the like, these he counted tricks of youth, nor would he be beat out of it by all that his friends could say. They would tell him that he must not covet, or desire (and yet to desire is less than to take) even anything the least thing that was his neighbour's ; and that if he did, it would be a transgression of the law ; but all was one to him ; what through the wicked talk of his companions, and the delusion of his own corrupt heart, he would go on in his pilfering course, and where he thought himself secure, would talk of, and laugh at it when he had done.

Atten. Well, I heard a man once, when he was upon the ladder, with the rope about his neck, confess (when ready to be turned off by the hangman) that that which had brought him to that end was his accustoming of himself, when young, to pilfer and steal small things. To my best remembrance he told us, that he began the trade of a thief by stealing of pins and points ; and therefore did forewarn all the youth that then were gathered together to see him die, to take heed of beginning, though but with little sins ; because by tampering at first with little ones, way is made for the commission of bigger.

Wise. Since you are entered upon stories, I also will tell you one ; the which, though I heard it not with mine own ears, yet my author I dare believe. It is concerning one old Tod, that was hanged about twenty years ago, or more, at Hertford, for being a thief. The story is this :—At a summer assizes holden at Hertford, while the judge was sitting upon the bench, comes this old Tod into the court, clothed in a green suit, with his leathern girdle in his hand, his bosom open, and all on a dung sweat, as if he had run for his life ; and being come in, he spake aloud as follows : " My lord," said he, " here is the veriest rogue that breathes upon the face of the earth. I have been a thief from a child : when I was but a little one, I gave myself to rob orchards, and to do other such like wicked things, and I have continued a thief ever since. My lord, there has not been a robbery committed these many years, within so many miles of this place, but I have either been at it or privy to it." The judge thought the fellow was mad, but after some conference with some of the justices, they agreed to indict him ; and so they did of several felonious actions ; to all which he heartily confessed guilty, and so was hanged, with his wife at the same time.

Atten. This is a remarkable story indeed, and you think it is a true one.

Wise. It is not only remarkable, but pat to our purpose. This thief, like Mr. Badman, began his trade betimes ; he began too where Mr. Badman began, even at robbing of orchards, and other such things, which brought him, as you may perceive, from sin to sin, till at last it brought him to the public shame of sin, which is the gallows. As for the truth of this story, the relater told me that he was at the same time himself in the court, and stood within less than two yards of old Tod, when he heard him aloud to utter the words.

Atten. These two sins of lying and stealing were a bad sign of an evil end.

Wise. So they were, and yet Mr. Badman came not to his end like old Tod ; though I fear to as bad, nay, worse than was that death of the gallows, though less discerned by spectators. But more of that by and by. But you talk of these two sins as if these were all that Mr. Badman was addicted to in his youth. Alas! alas! he swarmed with sins, even as a beggar does with vermin, and that when he was but a boy.

Atten. Why, what other sins was he addicted to, I mean while he was but a child ?

Wise. You need not ask to what other sins was he, but to what other sins was he not addicted ;

that is, of such as suited with his age : for a man may safely say that nothing that was vile came amiss to him, if he was but capable to do it. Indeed some sins there be that childhood knows not how to be tampering with; but I speak of sins that he was capable of committing, of which I will nominate two or three more. And, first, he could *Badman could not abide the Lord's day.* not endure the Lord's day because of the holiness that did attend it; the beginning of that day was to him as if he was going to prison except he could get out from his father and mother, and lurk in byholes among his companions, until holy duties were over. Reading the Scriptures, hearing sermons, godly conference, repeating of sermons and prayer, were things that he could not away with; and therefore if his father on such days (as often he did, though sometimes, notwithstanding his diligence, he would be sure to give him the slip) did keep him strictly to the observation of the day, he would plainly show by all carriages that he was highly discontented therewith. He would sleep at duties, would talk vainly with his brothers, and as it were, think every godly opportunity seven times as long as it was, grudging till it was over.

Atten. This his abhorring of that day, was not, *Why Badman could not abide the Lord's day.* I think, for the sake of the day itself : for as it is a day, it is nothing else but as other days of the week. But I suppose that the reason of his loathing of it was, for that God hath put sanctity and holiness upon it; also because it is the day above all the days of the week that ought to be spent in holy devotion, in remembrance of our Lord's resurrection from the dead.

Wise. Yes, it was therefore that he was such an enemy to it; even because more restraint was laid upon him on that day, from his own ways, than were possible should be laid upon him on all others.

Atten. Doth not God, by instituting of a day unto holy duties, make great proofs how the hearts and inclinations of poor people do stand to holiness of heart, and a conversation in holy duties.

Wise. Yes, doubtless; and a man shall show his *God proves the heart by instituting the Lord's day.* heart and his life what they are, more by one Lord's day than by all the days of the week besides : and the reason is, because on the Lord's day there is a special restraint laid upon man as to thoughts and life, more than upon other days of the week besides. Also, men are enjoined on that day to a stricter performance of holy duties, and restraint of worldly business, than upon other days they are; wherefore, if their hearts incline not naturally to good, now they will show it, now they will appear what they are. The Lord's day is a kind of an emblem of the heavenly Sabbath above, and it makes manifest how the heart stands to the perpetuity of holiness, more than to be found in a transient duty does. On other days

a man may be in and out of holy duties, and all in a quarter of an hour; but now, the Lord's day is, as it were, a day that enjoins to one perpetual duty of holiness : "Remember that thou keep holy the Sabbath day;" which by Christ is not abrogated, but changed into the first of the week, not as it was given in particular to the Jews, but as it was sanctified by him from the beginning of the world, (Gen. ii. 2. Exod. xxxi. 13—17. Mark xvi. 1; xxvii. 28. Acts xx. 7. Cor. xvi. 1, 2. Rev. i. 10;) and therefore is a greater proof of the frame and temper of a man's heart, and does more make manifest to what he is inclined than doth his other performance of duties: therefore God puts great difference between them that truly call and walk in this day as holy, and count it honourable, upon the account that now they have an opportunity to show how they delight to honour him; in that they have not only an hour, but a whole day to show it in. (Isa. lviii. 13.) I say he puts great difference between these, and that other sort that say, " When will the Sabbath be gone, that we may be at our worldly business." (Amos viii. 5.) The first he calleth a blessed man, but brandeth the other for an unsanctified worldling. And, indeed, to delight ourselves in God's service upon his holy days gives a better proof of a sanctified nature than to grudge at the coming, and to be weary of the duties of such days, as Mr. Badman did.

Atten. There may be something in what you say, for he that cannot abide to keep one day holy to God, to be sure he hath given a sufficient proof that he is an unsanctified man ; and as such what should he do in heaven ? That being the place where a perpetual Sabbath is to be kept to God ; I say to be kept for ever and ever. (Heb. iv. 9.) And for aught I know, one reason why one day in seven had been by our Lord set apart unto holy duties for men, may be to give them conviction that there is enmity in the hearts of sinners to the God of heaven, for he that hateth holiness hateth God himself. They pretend to love God, and yet love not a holy day, and yet love not to spend that day in one continued act of holiness to the Lord. They had as good say nothing as to call him " Lord, Lord," and yet not do the things that he says. And this Mr. Badman was such an one : he could not abide this day, nor any of the duties of it. Indeed, when he could get from his friends, and so spend it in all manner of *How Badman did use to spend the Lord's day.* idleness and profaneness, then he would be pleased well enough : but what was this but a turning the day into night, or other than taking an opportunity, at God's forbidding, to follow our callings, to solace and satisfy our lusts and delights of the flesh. I take the liberty to speak thus of Mr. Badman, upon a confidence of what you, sir, have said of him is true.

Wise. You need not to have made that apology for your censuring Mr. Badman, for all that knew him will confirm what you say of him to be true. He could not abide either that day, or anything else that had the stamp or image of God upon it. Sin, sin, and to do the thing that was naught, was that which he delighted in, and that from a little child.

Atten. I must say again I am sorry to hear it, and that for his own sake, and also for the sake of his relations, who must needs be broken to pieces with such doings as these. For, for these things' sake comes the wrath of God upon the children of disobedience, (Eph. v. 6,) and doubtless he must be gone to hell if he died without repentance ; and to beget a child for hell is sad for parents to think on.

Wise. Of his dying, as I told you, I will give you a relation anon, but now we are upon his life, and upon the manner of his life in his childhood, even of the sins that attended him then, some of which I have mentioned already; and indeed I have mentioned but some, for yet there are more to follow, and those not at all inferior to what you have already heard.

Atten. Pray what were they ?

Wise. Why he was greatly given, and that while a lad, to grievous swearing and cursing : yea, he then made no more of swearing and cursing than I do of telling my fingers. Yea, he would do it without provocation thereto. He counted it a glory to swear and curse, and it was as natural to him as to eat, and drink, and sleep.

Badman given to swearing and cursing.

Atten. Oh, what a young villain was this! here is, as the apostle says, a yielding of members as instruments of unrighteousness unto sin, indeed! This is proceeding from evil to evil with a witness. This argueth that he was a black-mouthed young wretch indeed.

Wise. He was so ; and yet, as I told you, he counted above all this kind of sinning to be a badge of his honour : he reckoned himself a man's fellow when he had learnt to swear and curse boldly.

Swearing his badge of honour.

Atten. I am persuaded that many do think, as you have said, that to swear is a thing that does bravely become them, and that it is the best way for a man, when he would put authority or terror in his words, to stuff them full of the sin of swearing.

Wise. You say right, else, as I am persuaded, men would not so usually belch out their blasphemous oaths as they do : they take a pride in it ; they think that to swear is gentleman-like ; and having once accustomed themselves unto it, they hardly leave it all the days of their lives.

Atten. Well, but now we are upon it pray show me the difference between swearing and cursing ; for there is a difference ; is there not ?

Difference betwixt swearing and cursing.

Wise. Yes, there is a difference between swearing and cursing. Swearing, vain swearing, such as young Badman accustomed himself unto. Now vain and sinful swearing is a light and wicked calling of God, &c., to witness to our vain and foolish attesting of things, and those things are of two sorts. 1. Things that we swear are, or shall be done. 2. Things so sworn to, true or false.

What swearing is.

1. Things that we swear are, or shall be done. Thou swearest thou hast done such a thing, that such a thing is so, or shall be so ; for it is no matter which of these it is that men swear about, if it be done lightly, and wickedly, and groundlessly it is vain, because it is a sin against the third commandment, which says, " Thou shalt not take the name of the Lord thy God in vain." (Exod. xx. 7.) For this is a vain using of that holy and sacred name, and so a sin for which, without sound repentance, there is not, nor can be rightly expected, forgiveness.

Atten. Then it seems, though as to the matter of fact, a man swears truly, yet if he sweareth lightly and groundlessly, his oath is evil, and he by it under sin.

Wise. Yes, a man may say, " The Lord liveth," and that is true, and yet in so saying " swear falsely ;" because he sweareth vainly, needlessly, and without a ground. (Jer. v. 2.) To swear groundedly and necessarily, which then a man does when he swears as being called thereto of God, that is tolerated by the word. But this was none of Mr. Badman's swearing, and therefore that which now we are not concerned about.

A man may sin in swearing to the truth.

Atten. I perceive by the prophet, that a man may sin in swearing to the truth. They therefore must needs most horribly sin that swear to confirm their jests and lies ; and as they think, the better to beautify their foolish talking.

Wise. They sin with a high hand ; for they presume to imagine that God is as wicked as themselves, to wit, that he is an avoucher of lies to be true. For, as I said before, he that swears to swear, is to call God to witness ; and to swear to a lie, is to call God to witness that that lie is true. This, therefore, must needs offend ; for it puts the highest affront upon the holiness and righteousness of God, therefore his wrath must sweep them away. (Zech. v. 3.) This kind of swearing is put in with lying, and killing, and stealing, and committing adultery ; and, therefore, must not go unpunished. (Jer. vii. 9. Hos. iv. 2, 3.) For if " God will not hold him guiltless that taketh his name in vain," which a man may do when he swears to a truth, as I have showed before, how can it be imagined, that he should hold such guiltless, who, by swearing, will appeal to God, if lies be not true, or that swear out of their frantic and bedlam madness. It would grieve and provoke a sober man to wrath, if one should swear to a notorious lie, and avouch that that man would attest it for a truth ; and yet thus do men deal with the holy God. They tell their jestings, tales,

He that swears to a lie concludes that God is as wicked as himself.

and lies, and then swear by God that they are true. Now this kind of swearing was as common with young Badman, as it was to eat when he was an hungered, or to go to bed when it was night.

Atten. I have often mused in my mind, what it should be that should make men so common in the use of the sin of swearing, since those that be wise, will believe them never the sooner for that.

Wise. It cannot be anything that is good, you may be sure; because the thing itself is abominable. 1. Therefore it must be from promptings Six causes of vain swearing. of the spirit of the devil within them. 2. Also it flows sometimes from hellish rage, when the tongue hath set on fire of hell even the whole course of nature. 3. But commonly swearing flows from that daring boldness that biddeth defiance to the law that forbids it. 4. Swearers think also that by their belching of their blasphemous oaths out of their black and polluted mouths, they show themselves the more valiant men. 5. And imagine also that by these outrageous kind of villanies they shall conquer those that at such a time they have to do with, and make them believe their lies to be true. 6. They also swear frequently to get gain thereby, and when they meet with fools they overcome them this way. But if I might give advice in this matter, no buyer should lay out one farthing with him that is a common swearer in his calling; especially with such an oath-master that endeavoureth to swear away his commodity to another, and that would swear his chapman's money into his own pocket.

Atten. All these causes of swearing, so far as I can perceive, flow from the same root as do the oaths themselves—even from a hardened and desperate heart. But pray show me now how wicked cursing is to be distinguished from this kind of swearing.

Wise. Swearing, as I said, hath immediately to do with the name of God; and it calls upon him to be witness of the truth of what is said; that is, if they that swear, swear by him. Some, indeed, swear by idols, as by the mass, by our lady, by saints, beasts, birds, and other creatures; but the usual way of our profane ones in England, is to swear by God, Christ, faith, and the like; but, however, or by whatever they swear, cursing is distinguished from swearing thus :—To curse, to Of cursing, what it is. curse profanely, it is to sentence another or ourself, for, or to evil; or to wish that some evil might happen to the person or thing under the curse, unjustly. It is to sentence for, or to evil, that is without a cause. Thus Shimei cursed David : he sentenced him for and to evil unjustly, when he said to him, " Come out, come out, thou bloody man, and thou man of Belial. The Lord hath returned upon thee all the blood of the house of Saul, in whose stead thou hast reigned : and the Lord hath delivered the kingdom into the hand of Absalom thy son : and,

behold, thou art taken in thy mischief, because thou art a bloody man." (2 Sam. xvi. 7, 8.) This David calls a grievous curse. " And, behold," saith he to Solomon his son, " thou hast with thee Shimei, a Benjamite, which cursed me with a grievous curse in the day when I went to Mahanaim." (1 Kings ii. 8.) But what was this curse ? Why, first, it was a wrong sentence past upon David. Shimei called him a bloody man, a man of Belial, when he was not; secondly, he sentenced him to the evil that at present was upon him for being a bloody man (that is, against the house of Saul), when that present evil overtook David, for quite another thing. And we may thus apply it to the profane ones of our own times, who, in their rage and envy, have little else in their mouths but a sentence against their neighbour for and to evil unjustly. How common is it with many, when they are but a little How the profane ones of our time curse. offended with one, to cry, " Hang him ! " " Damn him ! " " Rogue ! " This is both a sentencing of him for and to evil, and is in itself a grievous curse. 2. The other kind of cursing is to wish that some evil might happen to, and overtake this or that person or thing. And this kind of cursing Job counted a grievous sin. " I have not suffered," says he, " my mouth to sin, by wishing a curse to his soul;" or consequently to body or estate. (Job xxxi. 30.) This, then, is a wicked cursing, to wish that evil might either befall another or ourselves. And this kind of cursing young Badman accustomed himself unto. 1. He would wish that evil might befall others ; he would Badman's way of cursing. wish their necks broken, or that their brains were out, or that the pox or the plague was upon them, and the like. All which is a devilish kind of cursing, and is become one of the common sins of our age. 2. He would also as often wish a curse to himself, saying, " Would I might be hanged, or burned, or that the devil might fetch me, if it be not so," or the like. We count the damn-me-blades to be great swearers, but when in their hellish fury thy say, " God damn me," " God perish me," or the like, they rather curse than swear ; yea, curse themselves, and that with a wish that damnation might light upon themselves ; which wish and curse of theirs in a little time, they will see accomplished upon them, even in hell-fire, if they repent them not of their sins.

Atten. But did this young Badman accustom himself to such filthy kind of language ?

Wise. I think I may say that nothing was more frequent in his mouth, and that upon the least provocation. Yea, he was so versed in such kind of language, that neither father, nor mother, nor brother, nor sister, nor servant, Badman would curse his father, &c. no, nor the very cattle that his father had, could escape these curses of his. I say that even the brute beasts, when he drove them or rid upon them, if they pleased not his humour, they must be sure to partake of his curse. He would wish their necks broke, their legs broke, their guts out, or that the devil might fetch them, or the like; and no marvel, for he that is so hardy to wish damnation, or other bad curses to himself, or dearest relations, would not stick to wish evil to the silly beast in his madness.

Atten. Well, I see still that this Badman was a desperate villain. But pray, sir, since you have gone thus far, now show me whence this evil of cursing ariseth, and also what dishonour it bringeth to God; for I easily discern that it doth bring damnation to the soul.

Wise. This evil of cursing ariseth, in general, from the desperate wickedness of the heart, but particularly from, 1. Envy, which is, as I apprehend, the leading sin to witchcraft. *Four causes of swearing.* 2. It also ariseth from pride, which was the sin of the fallen angels. 3. It ariseth, too, from scorn and contempt of others. 4. But for a man to curse himself, must needs arise from desperate madness. The dishonour that it bringeth to God, is this:—It taketh away from him his authority, *The dishonour it brings to God.* in whose power it is only to bless and to curse; not to curse wickedly, as Mr. Badman, but justly, and righteously, giving, by his curse to those that are wicked, the due reward of their deeds. Besides, these wicked men, in their wicked cursing of their neighbour, &c., do even curse God himself in his handiwork. (James iii. 9.) Man is God's image; and to curse wickedly the image of God, is to curse God himself. Therefore, as when men wickedly swear, they rend, and tear God's name, and make him, as much as in them lies, the avoucher and approver of all their wickedness; so he that curseth and condemneth in this sort his neighbour, or that wisheth him evil, curseth, condemneth, and wisheth evil to the image of God, and, consequently, judgeth and condemneth God himself. Suppose that a man should say with his mouth, I wish that the king's picture was burned, would not this man's so saying render him as an enemy to the person of the king? Even so it is with them that, by cursing, wish evil to their neighbour, or to themselves—they contemn the image, even the image, of God himself.

Atten. But do you think that the men that do thus, do think that they do so vilely, so abominably?

Wise. The question is not what men do believe concerning their sin, but what God's word says of it. If God's word says that swearing and cursing are sins, though men should count them for virtues, their reward will be a reward for sin, to wit, the damnation of the soul. To curse another, and to swear vainly and falsely, are sins *Swearing and cursing are sins against the light of nature.* against the light of nature. 1. To curse is so, because whoso curseth another, knows, that at the same time he would not be so served himself. 2. To swear, also, is a sin against the same law; for nature will tell me, that I should not lie, and, therefore, much less swear, to confirm it. Yea, the heathens have looked upon swearing to be a solemn ordinance of God, and, therefore, not to be lightly or vainly used by men, though to confirm a matter of truth. (Gen. xxxi. 43—55.)

Atten. But I wonder, since cursing and swearing are such evils in the eyes of God, that he doth not make some examples to others, for their committing such wickedness.

Wise. Alas! so he has, a thousand times twice told, as may be easily gathered by any observing people in every age and country. I could present you with several myself; but waving the abundance that might be mentioned, I will here present you with two: one was that dreadful judgment of God upon one N— P— at Wimbledon in Surrey; who, after a horrible fit of swearing *Examples of God's anger against them that swear and curse.* at and cursing of some persons that did not please him, suddenly fell sick, and in little time died raving, cursing, and swearing. But above all, take that dreadful story of Dorothy Mately, an inhabitant of Ashover, in the county of Derby. This Dorothy Mately, saith the relater, was noted by the people of the town to be a great swearer, and curser, and liar, and thief, just like Mr. Badman. And the labour that she did usually follow, was to wash the rubbish that came forth of the lead mines, and there to get sparks of lead ore; and her usual way of asserting of things, was with these kind of imprecations: I would I might sink into the earth if it be not so; or, I would God would make the earth open and swallow me up. Now upon the 23rd of March, 1660, this Dorothy was washing of ore upon the top of a steep hill, about a quarter of a mile from Ashover, and was there taxed by a lad for taking of two single pence out of his pocket, for he had laid his breeches by, and was at work in his drawers; but she violently denied it; wishing, that the ground might swallow her up if she had them: she also used the same wicked words on several other occasions that day. Now one George Hodgkinson, of Ashover, a man of good report there, came accidentally by where this Dorothy was, and stood still awhile to talk with her, as she was washing her ore; there stood also a little child by her tub side, and another a distance from her, calling aloud to her to come away; wherefore the said George took the girl by the hand to lead her away to her that called her. But behold, they had not gone above ten yards from Dorothy, but they heard her crying out for help; so, looking back, he saw the woman, and her tub and sieve, twisting round, and sinking into the ground. Then said the man, "Pray to God to pardon thy sin, for thou art never to be seen alive any longer." So she and her tub twirled round and round, till they sunk about three yards into the earth, and then for a while stayed. Then she called for help again; thinking, as she said, she should stay there. Now the man, though greatly amazed, did begin to think which way to help her; but immediately a great stone which appeared in the earth, fell upon her head, and broke her skull, and then the earth fell in upon her and covered her. She was afterwards digged up, and found about four yards within ground, with the boy's two single pence in her pocket, but her tub and sieve could not be found.

Atten. You bring to my mind a sad story, the which I will relate unto you. The thing is this:

About a bow-shot from where I once dwelt, there was a blind ale-house, and the man that kept it had a son whose name was Edward. This Edward was, as it were, a half fool, both in his words and manner of behaviour. To this blind ale-house certain jovial companions would once or twice a week come, and this Ned, for so they called him, his father would entertain his guests withal—to wit, by calling for him to make them sport by his foolish words and gestures. So when these boon blades came to this man's house, the father would call for Ned. Ned therefore would come forth; and the villain was devilishly addicted to cursing, yea, to cursing his father and mother, and any one else that did cross him. And because, though he was an half fool, he saw that his practice was pleasing, he would do it with the more audaciousness. Well, when these brave fellows did come at their times to this tippling-house, as they call it, to fuddle and make merry, then must Ned be called out; and because his father was best acquainted with Ned, and best knew how to provoke him, therefore he would usually ask him such questions, or command him such business, as would be sure to provoke him indeed. Then would he, after his foolish manner, curse his father most bitterly, at which the old man would laugh, and so would the rest of the guests, as at that which pleased them best, still continuing to ask, that Ned still might be provoked to curse, that they might still be provoked to laugh. This was the mirth with which the old man did use to entertain his guests. The curses wherewith this Ned did use to curse his father, and at which the old man would laugh, were these, and such like—the devil take you, the devil fetch you; he would also wish him plagues and destructions many. Well, so it came to pass, through the righteous judgment of God, that Ned's wishes and curses were in a little time fulfilled upon his father; for not many months passed between them after this manner, but the devil did indeed take him, possess him, and also in few days carried him out of this world by death; I say, Satan did take him and possess him; I mean, so it was judged by those that knew him, and had to do with him in that his lamentable condition. He could feel him like a live thing go up and down in his body; but when tormenting time was come, as he had often tormenting fits, then he would lie like an hard

bump in the soft place of his chest, I mean I saw it so, and so would rent and tear him, and make him roar till he died away. I told you before, that I was an ear and eye-witness of what I here say; and so I was. I have heard Ned in his roguery, cursing his father, and his father laughing thereat most heartily; still provoking of Ned to curse, that his mirth might be increased. I saw his father also, when he was possessed, I saw him in one of his fits, and saw his flesh, as it was thought, by the devil, gathered up on an heap, about the bigness of half an egg, to the unutterable torment and affliction of the old man. There was also one Freeman, who was more than an ordinary doctor, sent for, to cast out this devil; and I was there when he attempted to do it; the manner thereof was this:—They had the possessed into an out-room, and laid him on his belly upon a form, with his head hanging over the form's end; then they bound him down thereto; which done, they set a pan of coals under his mouth, and put something therein which made a great smoke, by this means, as it was said, to fetch out the devil. There therefore they kept the man till he was almost smothered in the smoke, but no devil came out of him; at which Freeman was somewhat abashed, the man greatly afflicted, and I made to go away wondering and fearing. In a little time, therefore, that which possessed the man, carried him out of the world, according to the cursed wishes of his son. And this was the end of this hellish mirth.

Wise. These were all sad judgments.

Atten. These were dreadful judgments indeed.

Wise. Ay, and they look like the threatening of that text, though chiefly it concerned Judas, " As he loved cursing, so let it come unto him; as he delighted not in blessing, so let it be far from him. As he clothed himself with cursing like as with a garment, so let it come into his bowels like water, and like oil into his bones." (Ps. cix. 17, 18.)

Atten. It is a fearful thing for a youth to be trained up in a way of cursing and swearing.

Wise. Trained up in them! that I cannot say Mr. Badman was, for his father hath ofttimes in my hearing bewailed the badness of his children, and of this naughty boy in particular. I believe that the wickedness of his children made him, in the thoughts of it, go many a night with heavy heart to bed, and with as heavy a one to rise in the morning. But all was one to his graceless son, neither wholesome counsel, nor fatherly sorrow, would make him mend his manners. There are some indeed that do train up their children to swear, curse, lie, and steal, and great is the misery of such poor children whose hard hap it is *A grievous thing to bring up children wickedly.* to be ushered into the world by, and to be under the tuition too, of such ungodly parents. It had been better for such parents, had they not begat them, and better for such children had they not been born. O! methinks for a father or mother to train up a child in that very way that leadeth to hell and damnation, what thing so horrible! But Mr. Badman was not by his parents so brought up.

Atten. But methinks, since this young Badman would not be ruled at home, his father should have tried what good could have been done of him abroad, by putting him out to some man of his acquaintance, that he knew to be able to command him, and to put him pretty hard to some employ: so should he, at least have been prevented of time to do those wickednesses that could not be done without time to do them in.

Wise. Alas, his father did so; he put him out betimes to one of his own acquaint-ance, and entreated of him all love, that he would take care of his son, and keep him from extravagant ways. His trade also was honest and commodious; he had besides a full employ therein, so that this young Badman had no vacant seasons, nor idle hours yielded him by his calling, therein to take opportunities to do badly: but all was one to him, as he had begun to be vile in his father's house, even so he continued to be when he was in the house of his master.

Atten. I have known some children, who, though they have been very bad at home, yet have altered much when they have been put out abroad; especially when they have fallen into a family, where the governors thereof have made conscience of maintaining of the worship and service of God therein; but perhaps that might be wanting in Mr. Badman's master's house.

Wise. Indeed some children do greatly mend, when put under other men's roofs; but, as I said, this naughty boy did not so; nor did his badness continue, because he wanted a master that both could and did correct it; for his master was a very good man, a very devout person; one that frequented the best soul-means, that set up the worship of God in his family, and also that walked himself thereafter. He was also a man very meek and merciful, one that did never over-drive young Badman in business, nor that kept him at it at unseasonable hours.

Atten. Say you so! This is rare. I, for my part, can see but few that can parallel, in these things, with Mr. Badman's master.

Wise. Nor I neither; yet Mr. Badman had such an one; for, for the most part, masters are now-a-days such as mind nothing but their worldly concerns, and if apprentices do but answer their commands therein, soul and religion may go whither they will. Yea, I much fear, that there have been many towardly lads put out by their parents to such masters, that have quite undone them as to the next world.

Atten. The more is the pity. But pray, now you have touched upon this subject, show me how many ways a master may be the ruin of his poor apprentice.

Wise. Nay, I cannot tell you of all the ways, yet some of them I will mention. Suppose, then,

that a towardly lad be put to be an apprentice with one that is reputed to be a godly man, yet that lad may be ruined many ways; that is, if his master be not circumspect in all things that respect both God and man, and that before his apprentice. 1. If he be not moderate in the use of his apprentice; if he drives him beyond his strength; if he holds him to work at unseasonable hours; if he will not allow him convenient time to read the word, to pray, &c. This is the way to destroy him; that is, in those tender beginnings of good thoughts, and good beginnings about spiritual things. 2. If he suffers his house to be scattered with profane and wicked books, such as stir up to lust, to wantonness, such as teach idle, wanton, lascivious discourse, and such as have a tendency to provoke to profane drollery and jesting; and lastly, such as tend to corrupt and pervert the doctrine of faith and holiness. All these things will eat as doth a canker, and will quickly spoil, in youth, &c., those good beginnings that may be putting forth themselves in them. 3. If there be a mixture of servants, that is, if some very bad be in the same place, that's a way also to undo such tender lads; for they that are bad and sordid servants will be often—and they have an opportunity, too, to be—distilling and fomenting of their profane and wicked words and tricks before them, and these will easily stick in the flesh and minds of youth, to the corrupting of them. 4. If the master have one guise for abroad, and another for home; that is, if his religion hangs by in his house as his cloak does, and he be seldom in it, except he be abroad; this, young beginners will take notice of, and stumble at. We say, hedges have eyes, and little pitchers have ears; and indeed, children make a greater inspection into the lives of fathers, masters, &c., than ofttimes they are aware of: and therefore should masters be careful, else they may soon destroy good beginnings in their servants. 5. If the master be unconscionable in his dealing, and trades with lying words; or if bad commodities be avouched to be good, or if he seeks after unreasonable gain, or the like; his servant sees it, and it is enough to undo him. Eli's sons being bad before the congregation, made men despise the sacrifices of the Lord. (1 Sam. ii.) But these things by the by, only they may serve for a hint to masters to take heed that they take not apprentices to destroy their souls. But young Badman had none of these hindrances; his father took care, and provided well for him, as to this. He had a good master, he wanted not good books, nor good instruction, nor good sermons, nor good examples, no, nor good fellow servants neither; but all would not do.

Atten. 'Tis a wonder, that in such a family, amidst so many spiritual helps, nothing should take hold of his heart! What! not good books, nor good instructions, nor good sermons, nor good examples, nor good fellow-servants, nor nothing do him good!

Wise. You talk, he minded none of these things; nay, all these were abominable to him. 1. For good books, they might lie in his master's house till they rotted for him, he would not regard to look into them; but contrariwise, would get all the bad and abominable books that he could, as beastly romances, and books full of ribaldry, even such as immediately tended to set all fleshly lusts on fire. True, he durst not be known to have any of these to his master; therefore would he never let them be seen by him, but would keep them in close places, and peruse them at such times as yielded him fit opportunities thereto. 2. For good instructions, he liked that much as he liked good books; his care was to hear but little thereof, and to forget what he heard as soon as it was spoken. Yea, I have heard some that knew him then, say, that one might evidently discern by the show of his countenance and gestures, that good counsel was to him like little ease, even a continual torment to him; nor did he ever count himself at liberty, but when farthest off of wholesome words. He would hate them that rebuked him, and count them his deadly enemies. 3. For good example, which was frequently set him by his master, both in religious and civil matters; these young Badman would laugh at, and would also make a byword of them, when he came in place where he with safety could. 4. His master, indeed, would make him go with him to sermons, and that where he thought the best preachers were, but this ungodly young man, what shall I say, was, I think, a master of art in all mischief; he had these wicked ways to hinder himself of hearing, let the preacher thunder never so loud. (1.) His way was, when come into the place of hearing, to sit down in some corner, and then to fall fast asleep. (2.) Or else to fix his adulterous eyes upon some beautiful object that was in the place, and so, all sermon-while, therewith be feeding his fleshly lusts. (3.) Or, if he could get near to some that he observed would fit his humour, he would be whispering, giggling, and playing with them, till such time as sermon was done.

Atten. Why, he was grown to a prodigious height of wickedness.

Wise. He was so, and that which aggravates all was, this was his practice as soon as he was come to his master; he was as ready at all these things as if he had, before he came to his master, served an apprenticeship to learn them.

Atten. There could not but be added, as you relate them, rebellion to his sin. Methinks it is as if he had said, I will not hear, I will not regard, I will not mind good, I will not mend, I will not turn, I will not be converted.

Wise. You say true, and I know not to whom more fitly to compare him than to that man who, when I myself rebuked him for his wickedness, in this great huff replied, " What would the devil do for company, if it was not for such as I?"

Atten. Why, did you ever hear any man say so?

Wise. Yes, that I did; and this young Badman was as like him as an egg is like an egg. Alas! the Scripture makes mention of many that, by their actions, speak the same. " They say unto God, Depart from us, for we desire not the knowledge of thy ways." (Job xxi. 14.) Again, " They refused to hearken, and pulled away the shoulder, and stopped their ears; yea, they made their hearts as an adamant-stone, lest they should hear the law, and the words which the Lord of hosts hath sent." (Zech. vii. 11, 12.) What are all these but such as Badman, and such as the young man but now mentioned? That young man was my playfellow when I was solacing myself in my sins: I may make mention of him to my shame; but he has a great many fellows.

Atten. Young Badman was like him indeed, and he trod his steps, as if his wickedness had been his very copy; I mean, as to his desperateness: for had he not been a desperate one, he would never have made you such a reply, when you was rebuking of him for his sin. But when did you give him such a rebuke?

Wise. A while after God had parted him and I, by calling of me, as I hope, by his grace, still leaving him in his sins; and, so far as I could ever gather, as he lived, so he died, even as Mr. Badman did: but we will leave him, and return again to our discourse.

Atten. Ha! poor obstinate sinners! Do they think that God cannot be even with them?

Wise. I do not know what they think, but I know that God hath said, " That as he cried, and they would not hear, so they cried, and I would not hear, saith the Lord of hosts." (Zech. vii. 13.) Doubtless there is a time a-coming when Mr. Badman will cry for this.

Atten. But I wonder that he should be so expert in wickedness so soon! Alas, he was but a stripling; I suppose he was, as yet, not twenty.

Wise. No, nor eighteen neither: but, as with Ishmael, and with the children that mocked the prophet, (Gen. xxi. 9, 10. 2 Kings ii. 23, 24,) the seeds of sin did put forth themselves betimes in him.

Atten. Well, he was as wicked a young man as commonly one shall hear of.

Wise. You will say so, when you know all.

Atten. All I think here is a great all; but if there is more behind, pray let us hear it.

Wise. Why, then I will tell you, that he had not been with his master much above a year and a half, but he came acquainted with three young villains, who here shall be nameless, that taught him to add to his sin much of like kind; and he as aptly received their instructions. One of them was chiefly given to uncleanness, another to drunkenness, and the third to purloining, or stealing from his master.

Atten. Alas! poor wretch, he was bad enough before; but these, I suppose, made him much worse.

Wise. That they made him worse you may be sure of, for they taught him to be an arch, a chief one in all their ways.

Atten. It was an ill hap that he ever came acquainted with them.

Wise. You must rather word it thus :—It was A sign of the judgment of God that he did; God's anger. that is, he came acquainted with them through the anger of God. He had a good master, and before him a good father: by these he had good counsel given him for months and years together; but his heart was set upon mischief: he loved wickedness more than to do good, even until his iniquity came to be hateful; therefore from the anger of God it was that these companions of his and he did at last so acquaint together. Says Paul, " They did not like to retain God in their knowledge;" and what follows? wherefore " God gave them over," or up to their own hearts' lusts. (Rom. i. 28.) And again, "As for such as turn aside to their own crooked ways, the Lord shall lead them forth with the workers of iniquity." (Ps. cxxv. 5.) This, therefore, was God's hand upon him that he might be destroyed, be damned, because he received not the love of the truth, that he might be saved. He chose his delusions and deluders for him, even the company of base men, of fools, that he might be destroyed.

Atten. I cannot but think, indeed, that it is a great judgment of God for a man to be given up The devil's to the company of vile men; for decoys. what are such but the devil's decoys, even those by whom he draws the simple into his net? A whoremaster, a drunkard, a thief, what are they but the devil's baits, by which he catcheth others?

Wise. You say right; but this young Badman was no simple one, if by simple you mean one uninstructed; for he had often good counsel given him; but, if by simple you mean him that is a fool as to the true knowledge of, and faith in Christ, then he was a simple one indeed: for he chose death rather than life, and to live in continual opposition to God, rather than to be reconciled unto him, according to that saying of the wise man: " The fools hated knowledge, and did not choose the fear of the Lord." (Prov. i. 29.) And what judgment more dreadful can a fool be given up to, than to be delivered into the hands of such men, that have skill to do nothing but to ripen sin, and hasten its finishing unto damnation? And, therefore, men should be afraid of offending God, because he can in this manner punish them for their sins. I knew a man that once was, as I thought, hopefully awakened about his condition; yea, I knew two that were so awakened; but in time they began to draw back, and to incline again to their lusts: wherefore God gave them up to the company of three or four men, that in less than three years' time brought them roundly to the This was gallows, where they were hanged done at like dogs, because they refused to Bedford. live like honest men.

Atten. But such men do not believe that thus to be given up of God is in judgment and anger; they rather take it to be their liberty, and do count it their happiness; they are glad that their cord is loosed, and that the reins are on their neck; they are glad that they may sin without control, and that they may choose such company as can make them more expert in an evil way.

Wise. Their judgment is, therefore, so much the greater, because thereto is added blindness of mind, and hardness of heart in a wicked way. They are turned up to the way of death, but must not see to what place they are going: they must go as the ox to the slaughter, " and as the fool to the correction of the stocks, till a dart strikes through his liver," not knowing that it is for his life. (Prov. vii. 22, 23.) This, I say, makes their judgment double, they are given up of God, for a while to sport themselves with that which will assuredly make them " mourn at the last, when their flesh and their body are consumed." (Prov. v. 11.) These are those that Peter speaks of that shall utterly perish in their own corruptions; these, I say, who count it pleasure to riot in the day-time, and that sport themselves with their own deceivings, are as natural brute beasts, made to be taken and destroyed.

Atten. Well, but I pray now concerning these three villains that were young Badman's companions. Tell me more particularly how he carried it then.

Wise. How he carried it! why, he did as they. I intimated so much before, when I said, they made him an arch, a chief one in their ways. First, he became a frequenter of taverns and tippling-houses, and would stay Badman there until he was even as drunk frequents as a beast. And if it was so that taverns. he could not get out by day, he would, be sure, get out by night. Yea, he became so common a drunkard at last, that he was taken notice of to be a drunkard even by all.

Atten. This was swinish, for drunkenness is so beastly a sin, a sin so much against nature, that I wonder that any that have but the appearance of men can give up themselves to so beastly—yea, worse than beastly—a thing.

Wise. It is a swinish vanity indeed. I will tell you another story. There was a A story for a gentleman that had a drunkard to drunkard. be his groom, and coming home one night very much abused with beer, his master saw it — "Well," quoth his master within himself, "I will let thee alone to-night, but to-morrow morning I will convince thee that thou art worse than a beast, by the behaviour of my horse." So, when morning was come, he bids his man go and water his horse, and so he did; but, coming up to his master, he commands him to water him again; so the fellow rid into the water the second time, but his master's horse would now drink no more, so the fellow came up and told his master. Then said his master, "Thou drunken sot, thou art far worse than my horse; he will drink but to satisfy nature, but thou wilt drink to the abuse of nature; he will drink but to refresh himself, but thou to thy hurt and damage; he will drink, that he may be more serviceable to his master, but thou till thou art incapable of serving either God or man. Oh, thou beast, how much art thou worse than the horse that thou ridest on."

Atten. Truly I think that his master served him right; for, in doing as he did, he showed him plainly, as he said, that he had not so much government of himself as his horse had of himself; and, consequently, that his beast did live more according to the law of his nature by far than did his man. But pray go on with what you have further to say.

Wise. Why, I say, that there are four things, which, if they were well considered, would make Evils attending drunkenness to be abhorred in the drunkenness. thoughts of the children of men. 1. It greatly tendeth to impoverish and beggar a man. "The drunkard," says Solomon, "shall come to poverty." (Prov. xxiii. 21.) Many that have begun the world with plenty, have gone out of it in rags, through drunkenness. Yea, many children that have been born to good estates, have yet been brought to a flail and a rake, through this beastly sin of their parents. 2. This sin of drunkenness it bringeth upon the body many, great, and incurable diseases, by which men do in little time come to their end, and none can help them. So, because they are overmuch wicked, therefore they die before their time. 3. Drunkenness is a sin that is oftentimes attended with abundance of other evils—"Who hath woe? who hath sorrow? who hath contentions? who hath babbling? who hath wounds without cause? who hath redness of eyes? They that tarry long at the wine, they that go to seek mixed wine," (Prov. xxiii. 29, 30;) that is, the drunkard. 4. By drunkenness men do oftentimes shorten their days; go out of the ale-house drunk, and break their necks before they come home. Instances not a few might be given of this, but this is so manifest, a man need say nothing.

Atten. But that which is worse than all is, it The worst also prepares men for everlasting evil. burnings.

Wise. Yea, and it so stupifies and besots the soul, that a man that is far gone in drunkenness

is hardly ever recovered to God. Tell me, when did you see an old drunkard converted? No, no; such an one will sleep till he dies, though he sleeps on the top of a mast; let his dangers be never so great, and death and damnation never so near, he will not be awaked out of his sleep. So that if a man have any respect either to credit, health, life, or salvation, he will not be a drunken man. But the truth is, where this sin gets the upper hand, men are, as I said before, so intoxicated and bewitched with the seeming pleasures and sweetness thereof, that they have neither heart nor mind to think of that which is better in itself; and would, if embraced, do them good.

Atten. You said that drunkenness tends to poverty, yet some make themselves rich by drunken bargains.

Wise. I said so, because the word says so. And as to some men's getting thereby, that is indeed but rare and base; yea, and base will be the end of such gettings. The word of God is against such ways, and the curse of God will be the end of such doings. An inheritance may sometimes thus be hastily gotten at the beginning, but the end thereof shall not be blessed. Hark what the prophet saith, "Woe to him that coveteth an evil covetousness, that he may set his nest on high." (Hab. ii. 9.) Whether he makes drunkenness, or aught else, the engine and decoy to get it; for that man doth but consult the shame of his own house, the spoiling of his family, and the damnation of his soul; for that which he getteth by working of iniquity, is but a getting by the devices of hell; therefore he can be no gainer neither for himself or family, that gains by an evil course. But this was one of the sins that Mr. Badman was addicted to after he came acquainted with these three fellows, nor could all that his master could do break him of this beastly sin.

Atten. But where, since he was but an apprentice, could he get money to follow this practice; for drunkenness, as you have intimated, is a very costly sin.

Wise. His master paid for all; for, as I told you before, as he learned of these three villains to be a beastly drunkard, so he learned of them to pilfer and steal from his master. Sometimes Badman's master's purse paid for his drunkenness. he would sell off his master's goods, but keep the money, that is, when he could; also, sometimes he would beguile his master by taking out of his cash-box; and when he could do neither of these, he would convey away of his master's wares, what he thought would be least missed, and send or carry them to such and such houses, where he knew they would be laid up to his use; and then appoint set times there, to meet and make merry with these fellows.

Atten. This was as bad, nay, I think, worse than the former; for by thus doing he did not only run himself under the wrath of God, but has endangered the undoing of his master and his family.

Wise. Sins go not alone, but follow one the other as do the links of a chain; he that will be a drunkard, must have money either of his own, or of some other man's; either of his father's, mother's, master's, or at the highway, or some way.

Atten. I fear that many an honest man is undone by such kind of servants.

Wise. I am of the same mind with you, but this should make the dealer the more wary what kind of servants he keeps, and what kind of apprentices he takes. It should also teach him to look well to his shop himself; also to take a strict account of all things that are bought and sold by his servants. The master's neglect herein may embolden his servant to be bad, and may bring him too in short time to rags and a morsel of bread.

Atten. I am afraid that there is much of this kind of pilfering among servants in these bad days of ours.

Wise. Now, while it is in my mind, I will tell you a story. When I was in prison, there came a woman to me that was under a great deal of trouble. So I asked her, she being a stranger to me, what she had to say to me. She said, she was afraid she should be damned. I asked her the cause of those fears. She told me that she had some time since lived with a shopkeeper at Wellingborough, and had robbed his box in the shop several times of money, to the value of more than now I will say; and pray, says she, tell me what I shall do. I told her I would have her go to her master, and make him satisfaction. She said she was afraid. I asked her why? She said she doubted he would hang her. I told her that I would intercede for her life, and would make use of other friends too to do the like; but she told me she durst not venture that. Well, said I, shall I send to your master, while you abide out of sight, and make your peace with him, before he sees you; and with that, I asked her master's name. But all that she said in answer to this, was, "Pray let it alone till I come to you again." So away she went, and neither told me her master's name nor her own. This is about ten or twelve years since, and I never saw her again. I tell you this story for this cause; to confirm your fears, that such kind of servants too many there be; and that God makes them sometimes like old Tod, of whom mention was made before, through the terrors that he lays upon them, to betray themselves. I could tell you of another, that came to me with a like relation concerning herself, and the robbing of her mistress; but at this time let this suffice.

Atten. But what was that other villain addicted to; I mean young Badman's third companion.

Wise. Uncleanness: I told you before, but it seems you forgot.

Atten. Right, it was uncleanness. Uncleanness is also a filthy sin.

Wise. It is so; and yet it is one of the most reigning sins in our day.

Atten. So they say, and that too among those that one would think had more wit, even among the great ones.

Uncleanness the reigning sin.

Wise. The more is the pity; for usually examples that are set by them that are great and chief, spread sooner, and more universally, than do the sins of other men; yea, and when such men are

Sins of great men dangerous.

at the head in transgressing, sin walks with a bold face through the land. As Jeremiah saith of the prophets, so it may be said of such, "From them is profaneness gone forth into all the land," (Jer. xxiii. 15;) that is, with bold and audacious face.

Atten. But pray let us return again to Mr. Badman and his companions. You say one of them was very vile in the commission of uncleanness.

Wise. Yes, so I say; not but that he was a drunkard and also thievish, but he was most arch in this sin of uncleanness: this roguery was his masterpiece, for he was a ringleader to them all in the beastly sin of whoredom. He was also best acquainted with such houses where they were, and so could readily lead the rest of his gang unto them. The strumpets also, because they knew this young villain, would at first discover themselves in all their whorish pranks to those that he brought with him.

Atten. That is a deadly thing: I mean, it is a deadly thing to young men, when such beastly queans, shall, with words and carriages that are openly tempting, discover themselves unto them; it is hard for such to escape their snare.

Wise. That is true, therefore the wise man's counsel is the best: "Come not near the door of her house;" for they are, as you say, very tempting, as is seen by her in the Proverbs: "I looked," says the wise man, "through my casement, and behold among the simple ones, I discerned a young man void of understanding, passing through the streets near her corner, and he went the way to her house, in the twilight, in the evening, in the black and dark night. And behold, there met him a woman with the attire of an harlot, and subtle of heart; (she is loud and stubborn; her feet abide not in her house. Now she is without, now

Signs of a whore.

she is in the street, and lieth in wait at every corner.) So she caught him, and kissed him, and with an impudent face, said unto him, I have peace-offerings with me; this day have I paid my vows. Therefore came I forth to meet thee, diligently to seek thy face, and I have found thee. I have decked my bed with coverings of tapestry, with carved works, with fine linen of Egypt. I have perfumed my bed with myrrh, aloes, and cinnamon. Come, let us take our fill of love until the morning; let us solace ourselves with loves."

(Prov. vii. 6—18.) Here was a bold beast. And, indeed, the very eyes, hands, words, and ways of such, are all snares and bands to youthful, lustful fellows. And with these was young Badman greatly snared.

Atten. This sin of uncleanness is mightily cried out against both by Moses, the prophets, Christ, and his apostles; and yet, as we see, for all that, how men run headlong to it!

The sin of uncleanness decried.

Wise. You have said the truth, and I will add, that God, to hold men back from so filthy a sin, has set such a stamp of his indignation upon it, and commanded such evil effects to follow it, that were not they that use it bereft of all fear of God, and love to their own health, they could not but stop and be afraid to commit it. For besides the eternal damnation that doth attend such in the next world, for these have no " inheritance in the kingdom of Christ and of God," (Ephes. v. 5,) the evil effects thereof in this world are dreadful.

Atten. Pray show me some of them, that as occasion offereth itself, I may show them to others for their good.

Wise. So I will. 1. It bringeth a man as was said of the sin before, to want and poverty; "for by means of a whorish woman, a man is brought to a piece of bread." (Prov. vi. 26.) The reason is, for that an whore will not yield without hire; and men when the devil and lust is in them, and God and his fear far away from them, will not stick, so they may accomplish their desire, to lay their signet, their bracelets, and their staff to pledge, rather than miss of the fulfilling of their lusts. 2. Again, by this sin men diminish their strength, and bring upon themselves, even upon the body, a multitude of diseases. This King Lemuel's mother warned him of. " What, my son ?" said he, " and what the son of my womb? And what the son of my vows? Give not thy strength unto women, nor thy ways to that which destroyeth kings." (Prov. xxxi. 2, 3.) This sin is destructive to the body.

The evils attending it.

A story for unclean persons to take notice of.

Give me leave to tell you another story. I have heard of a great man that was a very unclean person, and he had lived so long in that sin that he had almost lost his sight. So his physicians were sent for, to whom he told his disease; but they told him that they could do him no good, unless he would forbear his women. " Nay then," said he, " farewell sweet sight." Whence observe, that this sin, as I said, is destructive to the body; and also, that some men be so in love therewith, that they will have it, though it destroy their body.

Atten. Paul says also, that he that sins this sin, sins against his own body. But what of that, he that will run the hazard of eternal damnation to his soul, but he will commit this sin, will for it run the hazard of destroying his body. If young Badman feared not the damnation of his soul, do you think that the consideration of impairing of his body would have deterred him therefrom?

Wise. You say true. But yet, methinks, there are still such bad effects follow, often, upon the commission of it, that if men would consider them. it would put, at least, a stop to their career therein.

Atten. What other evil effects attend this sin ?

Wise. Outward shame and disgrace, and that in these particulars:—First. There often follows this foul sin, the foul disease, now called by us the pox. A disease so nauseous and stinking, so infectious to the whole body, and so entailed to this sin, that hardly are any common with unclean women, but they have more or less a touch of it to their shame.

Atten. That is a foul disease indeed! I knew a man once that rotted away with it; and another that had his nose eaten off, and his mouth almost quite sewed up thereby.

Wise. It is a disease, that where it is, it commonly declares that the cause thereof is uncleanness. It declares to all that behold such a man, that he is an odious, a beastly, unclean person. This is that strange punishment that Job speaks of, that is appointed to seize on these workers of iniquity.

Atten. Then it seems you think that the strange punishment that Job there speaks of, should be the foul disease.

Wise. I have thought so indeed, and that for this reason: we see that this disease is entailed, as I may say, to this most beastly sin, nor is there any disease so entailed to any other sin as this to this. That this is the sin to which the strange punishment is entailed, you will easily perceive when you read the text. " I made a covenant with mine eyes," said Job, " why should I think upon a maid? For what portion is there (for that sin) from above, and what inheritance of the Almighty from on high?" And then he answers himself, " Is not destruction to the wicked, and a strange punishment to the workers of iniquity?" This strange punishment is the pox. Also I think this foul disease is that which Solomon intends, when he saith, speaking of this unclean and beastly creature, " A wound and dishonour shall he get, and his reproach shall not be turned away." (Prov. vi. 33.) A punishment Job calls it; a wound and dishonour, Solomon calls it: and they both do set it as a remark upon this sin; Job calling it a " strange punishment," and Solomon, a " reproach that shall not be turned away" from them that are common in it.

Atten. What other things follow upon the commission of this beastly sin ?

Wise. Why, oftentimes it is attended with murder —with the murder of the babe begotten on the defiled bed. How common it is for the bastard-getter and bastard-bearer to consent together to murder their children, will be better known at the day of judgment; yet something is manifest now. I will tell you another story. An ancient man, one of mine acquaintance, a man of good credit in our country, had a mother that was a midwife, who was mostly employed in laying great persons. To this woman's house, upon a time, comes a brave young gallant on horseback, to fetch her to lay a young lady. So she addresses herself to go with him; wherefore, he takes her up behind him, and away they ride in the night. Now they had not rid far, but the gentleman, alighting from his horse, took the old midwife in his arms from the horse, turned round with her several times, and then set her up again; then he got up, and away they went till they came to a stately house, into which he had her, and so into a chamber where the young lady was in her pains. He then bid the midwife do her office, and she demanded help, but he drew out his sword, and told her, if she did not make speed to do her office without, she must look for nothing but death. Well, to be short, this old midwife laid the young lady, and a fine sweet babe she had. Now, there was made in a room hard by a very great fire: so the gentleman took up the babe, went and drew the coals from the stock, cast the child in, and covered it up, and there was an end of that. So when the midwife had done her work, he paid her well for her pains, but shut her up in a dark room all day, and when night came, took her behind him again, and carried her away, till she came almost at home; then he turned her round and and round, as he did before, and had her to her house, set her down, bid her farewell, and away he went: and she could never tell who it was. This story the midwife's son, who was a minister, told me; and also protested that his mother told it him for a truth.

Atten. Murder doth often follow indeed, as that which is the fruit of this sin. But sometimes God brings even these adulterers and adulteresses to shameful ends. I heard of one, I think a doctor of physic, and his whore, who had three or four bastards betwixt them, and had murdered them all, but at last themselves were hanged for it, in or near Colchester. It came out after this manner: the whore was so afflicted in her conscience about it, that she could not be quiet until she had made it known. Thus God many times makes the actors of wickedness their own accusers, and brings them by their own tongues to condign punishment for their own sins.

Wise. There has been many such instances, but we will let that pass. I was once in the presence of a woman, a married woman, that lay sick of the sickness whereof she died; and, being smitten in her conscience for the sin of uncleanness, which she had often committed with other men, I heard her, as she lay upon her bed, cry out thus: "I am a whore, and all my children are bastards, and I must go to hell for my sin; and look! there stands the devil at my bed's feet, to receive my soul when I die."

Atten. These are sad stories, tell no more of them now, but, if you please, show me yet some other of the evil effects of this beastly sin.

Wise. This sin is such a snare to the soul, that unless a miracle of grace prevents, it unavoidably perishes in the enchanting and bewitching pleasures of it. This is manifest by these and such-like texts—"The adulteress will hunt for the precious life." (Prov. vi. 26.) "Whoso committeth adultery with a woman lacketh understanding, and he that doth it destroyeth his own soul." (Prov. vi. 31.) "A whore is a deep ditch, and a strange woman is a narrow pit." (Prov. xxiii. 27.) "Her house inclineth unto death, and her paths unto the dead. None that go in unto her return again, neither take they hold of the path of life." (Prov. ii. 18, 19.) "She hath cast down many wounded; yea, many strong men have been slain by her. Her house is the way to hell, going down to the chambers of death." (Prov. vii. 26, 27.)

Atten. These are dreadful sayings, and do show the dreadful state of those that are guilty of this sin.

Wise. Verily so they do. But yet that which makes the whole more dreadful is, that men are given up to this sin because they are abhorred of God, and because abhorred, therefore they shall fall into the commission of it, and shall live there. "The mouth," that is, the flattering lips, "of strange women is a deep pit, he that is abhorred of the Lord shall fall therein." (Prov. xxii. 14.) Therefore it saith again of such, that they have none "inheritance in the kingdom of Christ and of God." (Eph. v. 5.)

Atten. Put all together, and it is a dreadful thing to live and die in this transgression.

Wise. True. But suppose, that instead of all these judgments, this sin had attending of it all the felicities of this life, and no bitterness, shame, or disgrace mixed with it, yet one hour in hell will spoil all. O! this hell, hell-fire, damnation in hell, it is such an inconceivable punishment, that were it but thoroughly believed, it would nip this sin, with others, in the head. But here is the mischief, those that give up themselves to these things do so harden themselves in unbelief and atheism about the things, the punishments that God hath threatened to inflict upon the committers of them, that at last they arrive to almost an absolute and firm belief that there is no judgment to come hereafter: else they would not, they could not, no, not attempt to commit this sin by such abominable language as some do. I heard of one that should say to his miss, when he tempted her to the committing of this sin, "If thou wilt venture thy body, I will venture my soul." And I myself heard another say, when he was tempting of a maid to commit uncleanness with him,—it was in Oliver's days,—that if she did prove with child, he would tell her how she might

Desperate words.

escape punishment (and that was then somewhat severe), "Say," saith he, "when you come before the judge, that you are with child by the Holy Ghost." I heard him say thus, and it greatly afflicted me; I had a mind to have accused him for it before some magistrate; but he was a great man, and I was poor and young, so I let it alone, but it troubled me very much.

Atten. It was the most horrible thing that ever I heard in my life. But how far off are these men from that spirit and grace that dwelt in Joseph.

Wise. Right: when Joseph's mistress tempted him, yea, tempted him daily; yea, she laid hold on him, and said, with her whore's forehead, "Come, lie with me," but he refused; he hearkened not to lie with her, or to be with her. Mr. Badman would have taken the opportunity. And a little to comment upon this of Joseph. 1. Here is a miss, a great miss, the wife of the captain of the guard, some beautiful dame, I'll warrant you. 2. Here is a miss won, and in her whorish affections come over to Joseph, without his speaking of a word. 3. Here is her unclean desire made known, "Come, lie with me," said she. 4. Here was a fit opportunity, there was none of the men of the house there within. 5. Joseph was a young man full of strength, and therefore the more in danger to be taken. 6. This was to him a temptation from her that lasted days. 7. And yet Joseph refused, (1,) her daily temptation; (2,) her daily solicitation; (3,) her daily provocation, heartily, violently, and constantly. For when she caught him by the garment, saying, "Lie with me," he left his garment in her hand, and gat him out. Ay, and although contempt, treachery, slander, accusation, imprisonment, and danger of death followed (for an whore careth not what mischief she does, when she cannot have her end), yet Joseph will not defile himself, sin against God, and hazard his own eternal salvation.

Atten. Blessed Joseph! I would thou hadst more fellows!

Wise. Mr. Badman has more fellows than Joseph, else there would not be so many whores as there are: for though I doubt not but that *that* sex is bad enough this way, yet I verily believe that many of them are made whores at first by the flatteries of Badman's fellows. Alas! there is many a woman plunged into this sin at first even by promises of marriage. I say, by these promises they are flattered, yea, forced into a consenting to these villanies, and so being in, and growing hardened in their hearts, they at last give themselves up, even as wicked men do, to act this kind of wickedness with greediness. But Joseph, you see, was of another mind, for the fear of God was in him. I will, before I leave this, tell you here two notable stories; and I wish Mr. Badman's companions may hear of them. They are found in "Clark's Looking-Glass for Sinners," and are

these. Mr. Cleaver, says Mr. Clark, reports of one whom he knew that had committed the act of uncleanness, whereupon he fell into such horror of conscience that he hanged himself, leaving it thus written in a paper: "Indeed," saith he, "I acknowledge it to be utterly unlawful for a man to kill himself, but I am bound to act the magistrate's part, because the punishment of this sin is death." Clark doth also make mention of two more, who, as they were committing adultery in London, were immediately struck dead with fire from heaven, in the very act. Their bodies were so found, half burnt up, and sending out a most loathsome savour.

Atten. These are notable stories indeed.

Wise. So they are, and I suppose they are as true as notable.

Atten. Well, but I wonder, if young Badman's master knew him to be such a wretch, that he would suffer him in his house.

Wise. They liked one another even as fire and water do. Young Badman's ways were odious to his master, and his master's ways were such as young Badman could not endure. Thus in these two was fulfilled that saying of the Holy Ghost: "An unjust man is an abomination to the just; and he that is upright in the way is abomination to the wicked." (Prov. xxix. 27.) The good man's ways Mr. Badman could not abide, nor could the good man abide the bad ways of his base apprentice. Yet would his master, if he could, have kept him, and also have learnt him his trade.

Atten. If he could! Why he might if he would, might he not?

Wise. Alas, Badman ran away from him once and twice, and would not at all be ruled. So the next time he did run away from him he did let him go indeed. For he gave him no occasion to run away, except it was by holding of him as much as he could (and that he could do but little) to good and honest rules of life. And had it been one's own case, one should have let him go. For what should a man do, that had either regard to his own peace, his children's good, or the preservation of the rest of his servants from evil, but let him go? Had he stayed, the house of correction had been most fit for him, but thither his master was loath to send him, because of the love that he bore to his father. An house of correction, I say, had been the fittest place for him, but his master let him go.

Atten. He ran away, you say, but whither did he run?

Wise. Why, to one of his one trade, and also like himself. Thus the wicked joined hand in hand, and there he served out his time.

Atten. Then, sure, he had his heart's desire, when he was with one so like himself.

Wise. Yes. So he had, but God gave it to him in his anger.

Atten. How do you mean?

Wise. I mean as before, that for a wicked man to be by the providence of God turned out of a good man's doors into a wicked man's house to dwell, A sign of God's anger upon him. is a sign of the anger of God. For God by this, and such judgments, says thus to each an one: " Thou wicked one, thou lovest not me, my ways, nor my people; thou castest my law and good counsel behind thy back. Come, I will dispose of thee in my wrath; thou shalt be turned over to the ungodly, thou shalt be put to school to the devil, I will leave thee to sink and swim in sin, till I shall visit thee with death and judgment." This was therefore another judgment that did come upon this young Badman.

Atten. You have said the truth, for God by such a judgment as this, in effect says so indeed; for he takes them out of the hand of the just, and binds them up in the hand of the wicked, and whither they then shall be carried, a man may easily imagine.

Wise. It is one of the saddest tokens of God's anger that happens to such kind of persons: and that for several reasons. 1. Such an one, by this judgment, is put out of the way, and from under the means which ordinarily are made use of to do good to the soul. For a family where godliness is professed and practised is God's ordinance, the place which he has appointed to teach young ones the way and fear of God. Now, to be put out of such a family into a bad, a wicked one, as Mr. Badman was, must needs be in judgment, and a sign of the anger of God. For in ungodly families men learn to forget God, to hate goodness, and to estrange themselves from the ways of those that are good. 2. In bad families, they have continually fresh examples, and also incitements to evil, and fresh encouragements to it too. Yea, moreover, in such places evil is commended, praised, well-spoken of, and they that do it are applauded; and this, to be sure, is a drowning judgment. 3. Such places are the very haunts and walks of the infernal spirits, who are continually poisoning the cogitations and minds of one or other of such families, that they may be able to poison others. Therefore observe it, usually in wicked families some one, or two, are more arch for wickedness than are any other that are there. Now such are Satan's conduit-pipes; for by them he conveys of the spawn of hell, through their being crafty in wickedness, into the ears and souls of their companions. Yea, and when they have once conceived wickedness they travail with it as doth a woman with child, till they have brought it forth; " Behold, he travaileth with iniquity, and hath conceived mischief, and brought forth falsehood." (Ps. vii. 14.) Some men, as here is intimated in the text, and as was hinted also before, have a kind of mystical, but hellish, copulation with the devil, who is the father, and their soul the mother of wickedness; and they, so soon as they have conceived by him, finish, by bringing forth sin, both it, and their own damnation. (James i. 15.)

Atten. How much then doth it concern those parents that love their children, to see, that if they go from them they It concerns parents to put their children into good families. be put into such families as be good, that they may learn there betimes to eschew evil, and to follow that which is good?

Wise. It doth concern them indeed, and it doth also concern them that take children into their families to take heed Masters should also beware what servants they entertain. what children they receive; for a man may soon, by a bad boy, be damaged both in his name, estate, and family, and also hindered in his peace and peaceable pursuit after God and godliness; I say by one such vermin as a wicked and filthy apprentice.

Atten. True, for one sinner destroyeth much good, and a poor man is better than a liar. But many times a man cannot help it, for such as at the beginning promise very fair, are by a little time proved to be very rogues, like young Badman.

Wise. That is true also, but when a man has done the best he can to help it, he may with the more confidence expect the blessing of God to follow, or he shall have the more peace, if things go contrary to his desire.

Atten. Well, but did Mr. Badman and his master agree so well? I mean his last master, since they were birds of a feather, I mean since they were so well met for wickedness.

Wise. This second master was, as before I told you, bad enough; but yet he would often fall out with young Badman Young Badman and his second master cannot agree. his servant, and chide, yea, and sometimes beat him too for his naughty doings.

Atten. What! for all he was so bad himself! This is like the proverb, " the devil corrects vice."

Wise. I will assure you 'tis as I say. For you must know, that Badman's ways suited not his master's gains. Could he have done as the damsel that we read of (Acts xvi.) did, to wit, fill his master's purse with his badness, he had certainly been his white-boy, but it was not so with young Badman; and therefore, though his master and he did suit well enough in the main, yet in this and that point they differed. Young Badman was for neglecting of his mas- Reasons of their disagreeing. ter's business, for going to the whore-house, for beguiling of his master, for attempting to debauch his daughters, and the like; no marvel then if they disagreed in these points. Not so much for that his master had an antipathy against the fact itself, for he could do so when he was an apprentice; but for that his servant by his sin made spoil of his commodities, &c., and so damnified his master. Had, as I said before, young Badman's wickedness only a tendency to his master's advantage—as could he have sworn, lied, cozened, cheated, and defrauded customers for his master—and, indeed, sometimes he did so—but had that been all that he had done, he had not had, no not a wry word from his master; but this was not always Mr. Badman's way.

Atten. That was well brought in, even the maid that we read of in the Acts, and the distinction was as clear betwixt the wickedness, and wickedness of servants.

Wise. Alas! men that are wicked themselves, yet greatly hate it in others, not simply because it is wickedness, but because it opposeth their interest. Do you think that that maid's master would have been troubled at the loss of her, if he had not lost, with her, his gain? No, I'll warrant you; she might have gone to the devil for him; but when her master saw "that the hope of his gain was gone," then he fell to persecuting Paul. But Mr. Badman's master did sometimes lose by Mr. Badman's sins, and then Badman and his master were at odds.

Atten. Alas, poor Badman! Then it seems thou couldst not at all times please thy like.

Wise. No, he could not, and the reason I have told you.

Atten. But do not bad masters condemn themselves in condemning the badness of their servants.

Wise. Yes; in that they condemn in another which they either have, or do allow in themselves. And the time will come, when that very sentence that hath gone out of their own mouths against the sins of others, themselves living and taking pleasure in the same, shall return with violence upon their own pates. The Lord pronounced judgment against Baasha, as for all his evils in general, so for this in special, because he was "like the house of Jeroboam," and yet "killed him." (1 Kings xvi. 7.) This is Mr. Badman's master's case; he is like his man and yet he beats him. He is like his man, and yet he rails at him for being bad.

Atten. But why did not young Badman run away from this master, as he ran away from the other?

Wise. He did not. And if I be not mistaken, the reason why was this. There was godliness in the house of the first, and that young Badman could not endure. For fare, for lodging, for work, and time, he had better, and more by this master's allowance, than ever he had by his last; but all this would not content, because godliness was promoted there. He could not abide this praying, this reading of scriptures, and hearing and repeating of sermons; he could not abide to be told of his transgressions in a sober and godly manner.

Atten. There is a great deal in the manner of reproof; wicked men both can and cannot abide to hear their transgressions spoken against.

Wise. There is a great deal of difference indeed. This last master of Mr. Badman would tell Mr. Badman of his sins in Mr. Badman's own dialect; he would swear, and curse, and damn, when he told him of his sins, and this he could bear better than to be told of them after a godly sort. Besides, that last master would, when his passions and rage were over, laugh at and make merry with the sins of his servant Badman: and that would please young Badman well. Nothing offended Badman but blows, and those he had but few of now, because he was pretty well grown up. For the most part when his master did rage and swear, he would give him oath for oath, and curse for curse, at least secretly, let him go on as long as he would.

Atten. This was hellish living.

Wise. 'Twas hellish living indeed: and a man might say, that with this master, young Badman completed himself yet more and more in wickedness, as well as in his trade; for by that he came out of his time, what with his own inclination to sin, what with his acquaintance with his three companions, and what with this last master, and the wickedness he saw in him, he became a sinner in grain. I think he had a bastard laid to his charge before he came out of his time.

By what means Badman came to be completed in wickedness.

Atten. Well, but it seems he did live to come out of his time, but what did he then?

Wise. Why, he went home to his father, and he, like a loving and tender-hearted father, received him into his house.

Atten. And how did he carry it there?

Wise. Why, the reason why he went home, was, for money to set up for himself; he stayed but a little at home, but that little while that he did stay, he refrained himself as well as he could, and did not so much discover himself to be base, for fear his father should take distaste, and so should refuse, or for a while forbear to give him money. Yet even then he would have his times, and companions, and the fill of his lusts with them, but he used to blind all with this, he was glad to see his old acquaintance, and they as glad to see him, and he could not in civility but accommodate them with a bottle or two of wine, or a dozen or two of drink.

He refrains himself for money.

Atten. And did the old man give him money to set up with?

Wise. Yes, above two hundred pounds.

Atten. Therein, I think, the old man was out. Had I been his father, I would have held him a little at staves-end, till I had had far better proof of his manners to be good; for I perceive that his father did know what a naughty boy he had been, both by what he used to do at home, and because he changed a good master for a bad, &c. He should not therefore have given him money so soon. What if he had pinched a little, and gone to journey-work for a time, that he might have known what a penny was by his earning of it? Then, in all probability, he had known better how to have spent it: yea, and by that time, perhaps, have better considered with himself, how to have lived in the world. Ay, and who knows but he might have come to himself with the prodigal, and have asked God and his father forgiveness for the villanies that he had committed against them.

Wise. If his father could also have blessed this manner of dealing to him, and have made it effectual for the ends that you have propounded, then I should have thought as you. But alas, alas, you talk as if you never knew, or had at this present forgot what the bowels and compassions of a father are. Why, did you not serve your own son so? But 'tis evident enough that we are better at giving good counsel to others, than we are at taking good counsel ourselves. But, mine honest neighbour, suppose that Mr. Badman's father had done as you say, and by so doing had driven his son to ill courses, what had he bettered either himself or his son in so doing?

We are better at giving than taking good counsel.

Atten. That's true, but it doth not follow, that if the father had done as I said, the son would have done as you suppose. But if he had done as you have supposed, what had he done worse than what he hath done already?

Wise. He had done bad enough, that is true. But suppose his father had given him no money, and suppose that young Badman had taken a pet thereat, and in an anger had gone beyond sea, and his father had neither seen him nor heard of him more. Or suppose that of a mad and headstrong stomach he had gone to the highway for money, and so had brought himself to the gallows, and his father and family to great contempt, or if by so doing he had not brought himself to that end, yet he had added to all his wickedness such and such evils besides. And what comfort could his father have had in this? Besides, when his father had done for him what he could, with desire to make him an honest man, he would then, whether his son had proved honest or no, have laid down his head with far more peace than if he had taken your counsel.

Atten. Nay, I think I should not have been forward to have given advice in the cause; but truly you have given me such an account of his villanies, that the hearing thereof has made me angry with him.

Wise. In an angry mood we may soon outshoot ourselves, but poor wretch as he is, he is gone to his place. But, as I said, when a good father hath done what he can for a bad child, and that child shall prove never the better, he will lie down with far more peace than if through severity he had driven him to inconveniences. I remember that I have heard of a good woman, that had, as this old man, a bad and ungodly son, and she prayed for him, counselled him, and carried it motherly to him for several years together; but still he remained bad. At last, upon a time, after she had been at prayer, as she was wont, for his conversion, she comes to him, and thus, or to this effect, begins again to ad-

A good mother, and a bad son.

monish him. "Son," said she, "thou hast been and art a wicked child, thou hast cost me many a prayer and tear, and yet thou remainest wicked. Well, I have done my duty, I have done what I can to save thee; now I am satisfied that if I shall see thee damned at the day of judgment, I shall be so far off from being grieved for thee, that I shall rejoice to hear the sentence of thy damnation at that day:" and it converted him. I tell you that if parents carry it lovingly towards their children, mixing their mercies with loving rebukes, and their loving rebukes with fatherly and motherly compassions, they are more likely to save their children, than by being churlish and severe towards them: but if they do not save them, if their mercy do them no good, yet it will greatly ease them at the day of death, to consider; I have done by love as much as I could to save and deliver my child from hell.

Atten. Well, I yield. But pray let us return again to Mr. Badman. You say, that his father gave him a piece of money that he might set up for himself.

Wise. Yes, his father did give him a piece of money, and he did set up, and almost as soon set down again; for he was not long set up, but by his ill managing of his matters at home, together with his extravagant expenses abroad, he was got so far in debt, and had so little in his shop to pay, that he was hard put to it to keep himself out of prison. But when his creditors understood that he was about to marry, and in a fair way to get a rich wife, they said among themselves, "We will not be hasty with him. If he gets a rich wife, he will pay us all."

Mr. Badman sets up for himself.

Atten. But how could he so quickly run out, for I perceive 'twas in little time, by what you say?

Wise. 'Twas in little time indeed, I think he was not above two years and a half in doing of it. But the reason is apparent, for he being a wild young man, and now having the bridle loose before him, and being wholly subjected to his lusts and vices, he gave himself up to the way of his heart, and to the sight of his eye, forgetting that for all these things God would bring him to judgment; and he that doth thus, you may be sure, shall not be able long to stand on his legs. Besides, he had now an addition of new companions —companions, you must think, most like himself in manners, and so such that cared not who sunk, if they themselves might swim. These would be often haunting of him, and of his shop too when he was absent. They would commonly egg him to the ale-house, but yet make him Jack-pay-for-all; they would also be borrowing money of him, but take no care to pay again, except it was with more of their company, which also he liked very well; and so his poverty came like "one that travelleth, and his want as an armed man." (Prov. vi. 11.) But all the while they

The reason of his running out.

New associates.

studied his temper—he loved to be flattered, praised, and commended for wit, manhood, and personage; and this was like stroking him over the face. Thus they colleagued with him, and yet got more and more into him, and so, like horse-leeches, they drew away that little that his father had given him, and brought him quickly down, almost to dwell next door to the beggar.

Atten. Then was the saying of the wise man fulfilled, "He that keepeth company with harlots, and a companion of fools, shall be destroyed." (Prov. xxix. 3; xii. 20.)

Wise. Ay, and that too, "A companion of riotous persons shameth his father," (Prov. xxviii. 7;) for he, poor man, had both grief and shame, to see how his son (now at his own hand) behaved himself in the enjoyment of those good things, in and under the lawful use of which he might have lived to God's glory, his own comfort, and credit among his neighbours. "But he that followeth after vain persons, shall have poverty enough." (Prov. xxviii. 19.) The way that he took, led him directly into this condition; for who can expect other things of one that follows such courses. Besides, when he was in his shop, he could not abide to be doing; he was naturally given to idleness. He loved to live high, but his hands refused to labour; and what else can the end of such an one be but that which the wise man saith? "The drunkard and the glutton shall come to poverty, and drowsiness shall clothe a man with rags." (Prov. xxiii. 21.)

Atten. But now, methinks, when he was brought thus low, he should have considered the hand of God that was gone out against him, and should have smote upon the breast, and have returned.

Wise. Consideration, good consideration, was far from him, he was as stout and proud now, as ever in all his life, and was as high too in the pursuit of his sin, as when he was in the midst of his fulness; only he went now like a tired jade, the devil had rid him almost off his legs.

His behaviour under his decays.

Atten. Well, but what did he do when all was almost gone?

Wise. Two things were now his play. 1. He bore all in hand by swearing, and cracking, and lying, that he was as well to pass as he was the first day he set up for himself, yea, that he had rather got than lost; and he had at his beck some of his companions that would swear to confirm it as fast as he.

Atten. This was double wickedness, 'twas a sin to say it, and another to swear it.

Wise. That's true, but what evil is that that he will not do, that is left of God, as I believe Mr. Badman was?

Atten. And what was the other thing?

Wise. Why, that which I hinted before, he was for looking out for a rich wife: and now I am come to some more of his invented, devised, designed, and abominable

Badman is for a rich wife.

roguery, such that will yet declare him to be a most desperate sinner. The thing was this : a wife he wanted, or rather money; for as for a woman, he could have whores enough at his whistle. But, as I said, he wanted money, and that must be got by a wife or no way; nor could he so easily get a wife neither, except he became an artist at the way of dissembling; nor would dissembling do among that people that could dissemble as well as he. But there dwelt a maid not far from him that was both godly and one that had a good portion, but how to get her, there lay all the craft. Well, he calls a council of some of his most trusty and cunning companions, and breaks his mind to them; to wit, that he had a mind to marry; and he also told them to whom : but, said he,

He calls his companions together, and they advise him how to get her.

how shall I accomplish my end, she is religious, and I am not? Then one of them made reply, saying, "Since she is religious, you must pretend to be so likewise, and that for some time before you go to her. Mark therefore whither she goes daily to hear, and do you go thither also; but there you must be sure to behave yourself soberly, and make as if you liked the word wonderful well; stand also where she may see you, and when you come home, be sure that you walk the street very soberly, and go within sight of her; this done for awhile, then go to her, and first talk of how sorry you are for your sins, and show great love to the religion that she is of, still speaking well of her preachers, and of her godly acquaintance, bewailing your hard hap, that it was not your lot to be acquainted with her and her fellow professors sooner; and this is the way to get her. Also you must write down sermons, talk of Scriptures, and protest that you came a-wooing to her only because she is godly, and because you should count it your greatest happiness if you might but have such a one. As for her money, slight it, it will be never the further off, that's the way to come soonest at it, for she will be jealous at first that you come for her money; you know what she has, but make not a word about it. Do this, and you shall see if you do not entangle the lass." Thus was the snare laid for this poor honest maid, and she was quickly catched in his pit.

Atten. Why, did he take this counsel?

Wise. Did he ! yes, and after awhile, went as boldly to her, and that under a vizard of religion, as if he had been for honesty and godliness, one of the most sincere and upright-hearted in England. He observed all his points, and followed the advice of his counsellors, and quickly obtained her, too; for natural parts he had, he was tall, and fair, and had plain, but very good clothes on his back; and his religion was the more easily attained, for he had seen something in the house of his father, and first master, and so could the more readily put himself into the form and show thereof. So he appointed his day, and went to her, as that he might easily do, for she had neither father nor mother to oppose. Well, when he was come, and had given her a civil compliment, to let her understand why he was come, then he began and told her, that he had found in his heart a great deal of love to her person, and that of all the damsels in the world he had pitched upon her, if she thought fit, to make her his beloved wife. The reasons, as he told her, why he had pitched upon her were, her religious and personal excellencies; and therefore entreated her to take his condition into her tender and loving consideration. "As for the world," quoth he, "I have a very good trade, and can maintain myself and family well, while my wife sits still on her seat; I have got thus and thus much already, and feel money come in every day, but that is not the thing that I aim at; it is an honest and godly wife." Then he would present her with a good book or two, pretending how much good he had got by them himself. He would also be often speaking well of godly ministers, especially of those that he perceived she liked, and loved most. Besides, he would be often telling of her what a godly father he had, and what a new man he was also become himself; and thus did this treacherous dealer deal with this honest and good girl, to her great grief and sorrow, as afterwards you shall hear.

Badman's compliment—his lying compliment.

Atten. But had the maid no friend to look after her?

Wise. Her father and mother were dead, and that he knew well enough, and so she was the more easily overcome by his naughty lying tongue. But if she had never so many friends, she might have been beguiled by him. It is too much the custom of young people now, to think themselves wise enough to make their own choice, and that they need not ask counsel of those that are older, and also wiser than they; but this is a great fault in them, and many of them have paid dear for it. Well, to be short, in little time Mr. Badman obtains his desire, gets this honest girl, and her money, is married to her, brings her home, makes a feast, entertains her royally, but her portion must pay for all.

Neglect of counsel about marriage dangerous.

Badman obtains his desire, is married, &c.

Atten. This was wonderful deceitful doings—a man shall seldom hear of the like.

Wise. By this his doing, he showed how little he feared God, and what little dread he had of his judgments. For all this carriage, and all these words were by him premeditated evil; he knew he lied, he knew he dissembled; yea, he knew that he made use of the name of God, of religion, good men, and good books, but as a stalking-horse, thereby the better to catch his game. In all this his glorious pretence of religion, he was but a glorious painted hypocrite, and hypocrisy is the highest sin that a poor carnal wretch can attain unto; it is also a sin that most dareth God, and that also bringeth the greater damnation. Now was he a whited wall, now was he a painted sepulchre, now was he a grave that appeared not, (Matt. xxiii. 27;) for this poor, honest, godly damsel little thought that both her peace and comfort, and estate, and liberty, and person, and all, were going to her burial, when she was going to be married to Mr. Badman: and yet so it was, she enjoyed herself but little afterwards; she was as if she was dead and buried to what she enjoyed before.

Atten. Certainly some wonderful judgment of God must attend and overtake such wicked men as these.

Wise. You may be sure that they shall have judgment to the full, for all these things, when the day of judgment is come. But as for judgment upon them in this life, it doth not always come—no, not upon those that are worthy thereof. "They that tempt God are delivered, and they that work wickedness are set up." (Mal. iii. 15.) But they are reserved to the day of wrath; and then, for their wickedness, God will repay them to their faces. "The wicked is reserved to the day of destruction; they shall be brought forth to the day of wrath. Who shall declare his way to his face? and who shall repay him what he hath done? Yet shall he be brought to the grave, and shall remain in the tomb." (Job xxi. 30—32.) That is, ordinarily they escape God's hand in this life, save only a few examples are made, that others may be cautioned, and take warning thereby: but at the day of judgment they must be rebuked for their evil with the lashes of devouring fire.

Atten. Can you give me no examples of God's wrath upon men that have acted this tragical wicked deed of Mr. Badman.

Wise. Yes; Hamor and Shechem, and all the men of their city, for attempting to make God and religion the stalking-horse to get Jacob's daughters to wife, were together slain with the edge of the sword—a judgment of God upon them, no doubt, for their dissembling in that matter. All manner of lying and dissembling is dreadful, but to make God and religion a disguise, therewith to blind thy dissimulation from other's eyes, is highly provoking to the divine Majesty. I knew one that dwelt not far off from our town, that got him a wife as Mr. Badman got his; but he did not enjoy her long, for one night, as he was riding home from his companions, where he had been at a neighbouring town, his horse threw him to the ground, where he was found dead at break of day, frightfully and lamentably mangled with his fall, and besmeared with his own blood.

Atten. Well, but pray return again to Mr. Badman. How did he carry it to his wife, after he was married to her?

Wise. Nay, let us take things along as we go. He had not been married but a little while, but his creditors came upon him for their money. He deferred them a little while, but at last things were come to

His creditors require payment.

that point that pay he must, or must do worse; so he appointed them a time, and they came for their money, and he paid them down with her money, before her eyes, for those goods that he had profusely spent among his whores long before (besides the portion that his father gave him), to the value of two hundred pounds.

Atten. This beginning was bad; but what shall I say? It was like Mr. Badman himself. Poor woman! this was but a bad beginning for her; I fear it filled her with trouble enough, as I think such a beginning would have done one perhaps much stronger than she.

Wise. Trouble, aye, you may be sure of it, but now it was too late to repent; she should have looked better to herself when being wary would have done her good; her harms may be an advantage to others, that will learn to take heed thereby; but for herself, she must take what follows, even such a life now as Mr. Badman her husband will lead her, and that will be bad enough.

Atten. This beginning was bad, and yet I fear it was but the beginning of bad.

Wise. You may be sure that it was but the beginning of badness, for other evils came on apace; as for instance :—It was but a little while after he was married, but he hangs his religion upon the hedge, or rather dealt with it as men deal with their old clothes, who cast them off, or leave them to others to wear; for his part he would be religious no longer. Now therefore he had pulled off his vizard, and began to show himself in his old shape, a base, wicked, debauched fellow; and now the poor woman saw that she was betrayed indeed; now also his old companions begin to flock about him, and to haunt his house and shop as formerly. And who with them but Mr. Badman? And who with him again but they? Now, those good people that used to company with his wife, began to be amazed and discouraged; also he would frown and glout upon them, as if he abhorred the appearance of them; so that in little time he drove all good company from her, and made her sit solitary by herself. He also began to go out a-nights to those drabs who were his familiars before, with whom he would stay sometimes till midnight, and sometimes till almost morning, and then would come home as drunk as a swine; and this was the course of Mr. Badman. Now, when he came home in this case, if his wife did but speak a word to him, about where he had been, and why he had abused himself, though her words were spoken in never so much meekness and love, then she was whore, and bitch, and jade! and it was well if she missed his fingers and heels. Sometimes also he would bring his punks home to his house, and woe be to his wife when they were gone, if she did not entertain them with all varieties possible, and also carry it lovingly to them. Thus this good woman was made by Badman, her husband, to possess

He drives good company from his wife.

He goes to his whores.

nothing but disappointments, as to all that he had promised her, or that she hoped to have at his hands. But that that added pressing weight to all her sorrow, was, that, as he had cast away all religion himself, so he attempted, if possible, to make her do so too. He would not suffer her to go out to the preaching of the word of Christ, nor to the rest of his appointments, for the health and salvation of her soul. He would now taunt at and reflectingly speak of her preachers; and would receive, yea, raise scandals of them, to her very great grief and affliction. Now, she scarce durst go to an honest neighbour's house, or have a good book in her hand; especially when he had his companions in his house, or had got a little drink in his head. He would also, when he perceived that she was dejected, speak tauntingly, and mockingly to her in the presence of his companions, calling of her his religious wife, his demure dame, and the like; also he would make a sport of her among his wanton ones abroad. If she did ask him (as sometimes she would) to let her go out to a sermon, he would in a currish manner reply, "Keep at home, keep at home, and look to your business, we cannot live by hearing of sermons." If she still urged that he would let her go, then he would say to her, "Go if you dare." He would also charge her with giving of what he had to her ministers, when, vile wretch, he had spent it on his vain companions before. This was the life that Mr. Badman's good wife lived, within few months after he had married her.

He seeks to force his wife from her religion.

Atten. This was a disappointment indeed.

Wise. A disappointment indeed, as ever I think poor woman had. One would think that the knave might a little let her have had her will, since it was nothing but to be honest, and since she brought him so sweet, so lumping a portion, for she brought hundreds into his house: I say, one would think he should have let her had her own will a little, since she desired it only in the service and worship of God. But could she win him to grant her that? No, not a bit, if it would have saved her life. True, sometimes she would steal out when he was from home, or on a journey, or among his drunken companions, but with all privacy imaginable; and, poor woman, this advantage she had, she carried it so to all her neighbours, that, though many of them were but carnal, yet they would not betray her, or tell of her going out to the word, if they saw it, but would rather endeavour to hide it from Mr. Badman himself.

Atten. This carriage of his to her was enough to break her heart.

Wise. It was enough to do it indeed, it did effectually do it. It killed her in time, yea, it was all the time a killing of her. She would often-times, when she sat by herself, thus mournfully bewail her condition: "Woe is me that I sojourn in Mesech, that I dwell in the tents of Kedar! My

Her repentance and complaint.

soul hath long time dwelt with him that hateth peace." "What shall be given unto thee, thou deceitful tongue? or what shall be done unto thee, thou false tongue?" (Ps. cxx.) "I am a woman grieved in spirit, my husband has bought me and sold me for his lusts. It was not me, but my money that he wanted: O that he had had it, so I had had my liberty!" This she said, not of contempt of his person, but of his conditions; and because she saw that by his hypocritical tongue, he had brought her not only almost to beggary, but robbed her of the word of God.

Atten. It is a deadly thing, I see, to be un-equally yoked with unbelievers.

The evil of being un-equally yoked together.

If this woman had had a good husband, how happily might they have lived together! Such an one would have prayed for her, taught her, and also would have encouraged her in the faith, and ways of God. But now, poor creature, instead of this, there is nothing but the quite contrary.

Wise. It is a deadly thing indeed, and there-fore, by the word of God his people are forbid to be joined in marriage with them. "Be ye not," saith it, "unequally yoked together with un-believers: for what fellowship hath righteousness with unrighteousness? and what communion hath light with darkness? and what concord hath Christ with Belial? or what part hath he that believeth with an infidel? and what agreement hath the temple of God with idols?" (2 Cor. vi. 14—16.) There can be no agreement where such matches are made; even God himself hath declared the contrary, from the beginning of the world. "I," says he, "will put enmity between thee and the woman, between thy seed and her seed." (Gen. iii. 15.) Therefore he saith in another place, they can mix no better than iron and clay. (Dan. ii. 43.) I say, they cannot agree, they cannot be one, and therefore they should be aware at first, and not lightly receive such into their affections. God has often made such matches bitter, especially to his own. Such matches are, as God said of Eli's sons that were spared, "to consume the eyes, and to grieve the heart." Oh! the wailing and lamentation that they have made that have been thus yoked, especially if they were such as would be so yoked, against their light and good counsel to the contrary.

Atten. Alas! he deluded her with his tongue, and feigned reformation.

Wise. Well, well; she should have gone more warily to work. What if she had

Counsel to those godly maids that are to marry.

acquainted some of her best, most knowing, and godly friends there-with? What if she had engaged a godly minister or two to have talked with Mr. Badman? Also, what if she had laid wait round about him, to espy if he was not otherwise behind her back than he was before her face? And besides, I verily think (since in the multitude of counsellors there is safety) that if she had ac-quainted the congregation with it, and desired them to spend some time in prayer to God about it, and if she must have had him, to have received him as to his godliness, upon the judgment of others, rather than her own (she knowing them to be godly and judicious, and unbiassed men,) she had had more peace all her life after, than to trust to her own poor, raw, womanish judgment, as she did. Love is blind, and will see nothing amiss, where others may see a hundred faults. Therefore I say, she should not have trusted to her own thoughts in the matter of his goodness. As to his person, there she was fittest to judge, because she was to be the person pleased; but as to his godliness, there the word was the fittest judge, and they that could best understand it, because God was therein to be pleased. I wish that all young maidens will take heed of being beguiled with flatter-ing words, with feigning and lying

A caution to young maidens.

speeches, and take the best way to preserve them-selves from being bought and sold by wicked men, as she was; lest they repent with her, when (as to this) repentance will do them no good, but for their unadvisedness go sorrowing to their graves.

Atten. Well, things are past with this poor woman, and cannot be called back; let others be-ware, by her misfortunes, lest they also fall into her distress.

Wise. That is the thing that I say, let them take heed, lest for their unadvisedness they smart, as this poor woman has done. And ah! methinks, that they that yet are single persons, and that are tempted to marry to such as Mr. Badman, would, to inform and warn themselves in this matter, before they entangle themselves, but go to some that are already in the snare, and ask them how it is with them, as to the suitable or unsuitableness of their marriage, and desire their advice. Surely they would ring such a peal in their ears about the unequality, unsuitableness, disadvantages, and disquietments, and sins that attend such marriages, that would make them beware as long as they live. But the bird in the air knows not the notes of the bird in the snare, until she comes thither herself. Besides, to make up such marriages, Satan, and carnal reason, and lust, or at least inconsiderateness, has the chiefest hand; and where these things bear sway, designs, though never so destructive, will go headlong on: and therefore I fear that but little warning will be taken by young girls, at Mr. Badman's wife's affliction.

Atten. But are there no dissuasive arguments to lay before such, to prevent their future misery?

Wise. Yes—there is the law of God, that for-biddeth marriage with unbelievers. These kind of marriages also are condemned even by irrational creatures. 1. It is forbidden by the law of God, both in the Old Testament and in the New. (1.) In the Old:—"Thou shalt not make marriages with them; thy daughter thou shalt not give unto his son, nor his daughter shalt thou take unto thy son." (Deut. vii. 3.) 2. In the New Testament it is forbidden—"Be ye not unequally yoked together with unbelievers; let them marry to whom they will," only, "in the Lord." (2 Cor. vi. 14—16. 1 Cor. vii. 39.) Here now is a prohibition, plainly *Rules for those that are to marry.* forbidding the believer to marry with the unbeliever, therefore they should not do it. Again, these unwarrantable marriages are, as I may so say, condemned by irrational creatures, who will not couple but with their own sort: will the sheep couple with a dog, the partridge with a crow, or the pheasant with an owl? No, they will strictly tie up themselves to those of their own sort only. Yea, it sets all the world a wondering when they see or hear the contrary. Man only is most subject to wink at, and allow of these unlawful mixtures of men and women; because man only is a sinful beast, a sinful bird, therefore he, above all, will take upon him by rebellious actions to answer, or rather to oppose and violate, the law of his God and Creator; nor shall these or other interrogatories, What fellowship? what concord? what agreement? what communion can there be in such marriages? be counted of weight, or thought worth the answering by him. But further, the dangers that such do commonly run themselves into, should be to others a dissuasive argument to stop them from doing the like: for besides the distresses of Mr. Badman's wife, many that have had very hopeful beginnings for heaven, have, by virtue of the mischiefs that have attended these unlawful marriages, miserably and fearfully miscarried. Soon after such marriages, conviction, the first step towards heaven, hath ceased; prayer, the next step towards heaven, hath ceased; hungerings and thirstings after salvation, another step towards the kingdom of heaven, hath ceased. In a word, such marriages have estranged them from the word, from their godly and faithful friends, and have brought them again into carnal company, among carnal friends, and also into carnal delights, where, and with whom they have in conclusion both sinfully abode and miserably perished. And this is one reason why God hath forbidden this kind of unequal marriages. "For they," saith he, meaning the ungodly, "will turn away thy son from following me, that they may serve other gods; so will the anger of the Lord be kindled against you, and destroy you suddenly." (Deut. vii. 4.) Now mark, there were some in Israel that would, notwithstanding this prohibition, venture to marry to the heathens and unbelievers. But what followed? "They served their idols, yea, they sacrificed their sons and their daughters unto devils. Thus were they defiled with their own works, and went a whoring with their own inventions: therefore was the wrath of the Lord kindled against his people, insomuch that he abhorred his own inheritance." (Ps. cvi. 36—40.)

Atten. But let us return again to Mr. Badman; had he any children by his wife?

Wise. Yes, seven.

Atten. I doubt they were but badly brought up.

Wise. One of them loved its mother dearly, and would constantly hearken to her voice. Now that child she had the *Badman's children that he had by this good woman.* opportunity to instruct in the principles of the Christian religion, and it became a very gracious child. But that child Mr. Badman could not abide, he would seldom afford it a pleasant word, but would scold and frown upon, speak churlishly and doggedly to it, and though as to nature it was the most feeble of the seven, yet it oftenest felt the weight of its father's fingers. Three of his children did directly follow his steps, and began to be as vile as, in his youth, he was himself. The others that remained became a kind of mongrel professors, not so bad as their father, nor so good as their mother, but were betwixt them both. They had their mother's notions and their father's actions, and were much like those that you read of in the Book of Nehemiah—"These children were half of Ashdod, and could not speak in the Jews' language, but according to the language of each people." (Neh. xiii. 24.)

Atten. What you say in this matter is observable, and if I take not my mark amiss, it often happeneth after this manner where such unlawful marriages are contracted.

Wise. It sometimes doth so, and the reason, with respect to their parents, is this: where the one of the parents is godly, and the other ungodly and vile, though they can agree in begetting of children, yet they strive for their children when they are born. The godly parent strives for the child, and by prayers, counsel, and good examples, labours to make it holy in body and soul, and so fit for the kingdom of heaven; but the ungodly would have it like himself, wicked, and base, and sinful; and so they both give instructions accordingly. Instructions did I say? yea, and examples too, according to their minds. Thus the godly, as Hannah, is presenting her Samuel unto the Lord; but the ungodly, like them that went before them, are for offering their children to Moloch, to an idol, to sin, to the devil, and to hell. Thus one hearkeneth to the law of their mother, and is preserved from destruction, but as for the other, as their father did, so do they. Thus did Mr. Badman and his wife part some of their children betwixt them; but as for the other three, that were as it were mongrels, betwixt both, they were like unto those that you read of in Kings—"They heard the Lord, but served their own idols." (2 Kings xvii.) They had, as I said, their mother's motions, and, I will add, profession too; but their father's lusts, and something of his life. Now, their father did not like them because they had their mother's tongue; and the mother did not like them because they had still their father's heart and life; nor were they indeed fit company for good or bad. The good would not trust them because they were bad, the bad would not trust them because they were good—viz., the good would not trust them because they were bad in their lives, and the bad would not trust them because they were good in their words. So they were forced with Esau to join in affinity with Ishmael; to wit, to look out a people that were hypocrites, like themselves, and with them they matched, and lived, and died.

Atten. Poor woman, she could not but have much perplexity.

Wise. Yea, and poor children, that ever they were sent into the world as the fruit of the loins, and under the government of such a father as Mr. Badman.

Atten. You say right, for such children lie almost under all manner of disadvantages; but we must say nothing, because this also is the sovereign will of God.

Wise. We may not by any means object against God; yet we may talk of the advantages and disadvantages that children have, by having for their parents such as are either godly or the contrary.

Atten. You say right, we may so, and pray now, since we are about it, speak something in brief unto it, that is, unto this—what advantage those children have above others that have for their parents such as indeed are godly.

Wise. So I will, only I must first premise these two or three things. 1. They have not the advantage of election for their fathers' sakes. 2. They are born as others, the *children of wrath*, though come of godly parents. 3. Grace comes not unto them as an inheritance, because they have godly parents. These things premised, I shall now proceed. 1. The children of godly parents are the children of many prayers—they are prayed for before, and prayed for after they are born; and the prayer of a godly father and godly mother doth much. 2. They have the advantage of what restraint is possible, from what evils their parents see them inclinable to, and that is a second mercy. 3. They have the advantage of godly instruction, and of being told which be, and which be not the right ways of the Lord. 4. They have also those ways commended unto them, and spoken well of in their hearing, that are good. 5. Such are also, what may be kept out of evil company, from evil books, and from being taught the way of swearing, lying, and the like, as Sabbath-breaking, and mocking at good men, and good things, and this is a very great mercy. 6. They have also the benefit of a godly life set before them doctrinally by their parents, and that doctrine backed with a godly and holy example: and all these are very great advantages. Now all these advantages, the children of ungodly parents want, and so are more in danger of being carried away with the error of the wicked;

for ungodly parents neither pray for their children, nor do, nor can they heartily instruct them; they do not after a godly manner restrain them from evil, nor do they keep them from evil company. They are not grieved at, nor yet do they forewarn their children to beware of such evil actions that are abomination to God, and to all good men. They let their children break the Sabbath, swear, lie, be wicked, and vain. They commend not to their children an holy life, nor set a good example before their eyes. No, they do in all things contrary: estranging of their children what they can from the love of God and all good men, so soon as they are born. Therefore it is a very great judgment of God upon children to be the offspring of base and ungodly men.

Atten. Well, but before we leave Mr. Badman's wife and children, I have a mind if you please, to inquire a little more after one thing, the which I am sure you can satisfy me in.

Wise. What is that?

Atten. You said a while ago, that this Mr. Badman would not suffer his wife to go out to hear such godly ministers as she liked, but said if she did, she had as good never come home any more. Did he often carry it thus to her?

Wise. He did say so, he did often say so. This I told you then, and had also then told you more, but that other things put me out.

Atten. Well said, pray therefore now go on.

Wise. So I will. Upon a time, she was on a Lord's day for going to hear a sermon, and Mr. Badman was unwilling she should; but she at that time, as it seems, did put on more courage than she was wont; and therefore after she had spent upon him a great many fair words and entreaties, if perhaps she might have prevailed by them, but all to no purpose at all. At last she said she would go, and rendered this reason for it. I have a husband, but also a God; my God has commanded me, and that upon pain of damnation, to be a continual worshipper of him, and that in the way of his own appointments. I have a husband, but also a soul, and my soul ought to be more unto me than all the world besides. This soul of mine I will look after, care for, and, if I can, provide it an heaven for its habitation. You are commanded to love me, as you love your own body, and so do I love you; but I tell you true, I prefer my soul before all the world, and its salvation I will seek. At this, first he gave her an ugly wish, and then fell into a fearful rage, and swore moreover that if she did go, he would make both her and all her damnable brotherhood, for so he was pleased to call them, to repent their coming thither.

Atten. But what should he mean by that?

Wise. You may easily guess what he meant: he meant he would turn informer, and so either weary out those that she loved, from meeting together to worship God; or make them pay

D

dearly for their so doing; the which if he did, he knew it would vex every vein of her tender heart.

Atten. But do you think Mr. Badman would have been so base?

Wise. Truly he had malice and enmity enough in his heart to do it, only he was a tradesman; also he knew that he must live by his neighbours, and so he had that little wit in his anger, that he refrained himself, and did it not. But, as I said, he had malice and envy enough in his heart to have made him to do it, only he thought it would worst him in his trade; yet these three things he would be doing. 1. He would be putting of others on to molest and abuse her friends. 2. He would be glad when he heard that any mischief befell them. 3. And would laugh at her, when he saw her troubled for them. And now I have told you Mr. Badman's way as to this.

Atten. But was he not afraid of the judgments of God, that did fly about at that time?

Wise. He regarded not the judgment nor mercy of God, for had he at all done that, he could not have done as he did. But what judgments do you mean?

Atten. Such judgments that if Mr. Badman himself had taken but sober notice of, they might have made him hung down his ears.

Wise. Why, have you heard of any such persons that the judgments of God have overtaken?

Atten. Yes, and so, I believe, have you too, though you make so strange about it.

Wise. I have so indeed, to my astonishment and wonder.

Atten. Pray therefore, if you please, tell me what it is, as to this, that you know; and then, perhaps, I may also say something to you of the same.

Wise. In our town there was one W. S., a man of a very wicked life; and he, when there seemed to be countenance given to it, would needs turn informer. Well, so he did, and was as diligent in his business as most of them could be; he would watch of nights, climb trees, and range the woods of days, if possible, to find out the meeters, for then they were forced to meet in the fields; yea, he would curse them bitterly, and swear most fearfully what he would do to them when he found them. Well, after he had gone on like a bedlam in his course awhile, and had done some mischiefs to the people, he was stricken by the hand of God, and that in this manner. 1. Although he had his tongue naturally at will, now he was taken with a faultering in his speech, and could not for weeks together speak otherwise than just like a man that was drunk. 2. Then he was taken with a drawling, or slabbering at his mouth, which slabber sometimes would hang at his mouth well nigh half way down to the ground. 3. Then he had such a weakness in the back sinews of his neck, that ofttimes he could not look up before him, unless he clapped his hand

hard upon his forehead, and held up his head that way, by strength of hand. 4. After this his speech went quite away, and he could speak no more than a swine or a bear. Therefore, like one of them, he would gruntle and make an ugly noise, according as he was offended or pleased, or would have anything done, &c. In this posture he continued for the space of half a year, or thereabouts, all the while otherwise well, and could go about his business, save once that he had a fall from the bell as it hangs in our steeple, which it was a wonder it did not kill him. But after that he also walked about, until God had made a sufficient spectacle of his judgment for his sin, and then on a sudden he was stricken, and died miserably. And so there was an end of him and his doings. I'll tell you of another. About four miles from St. Neots, there was a gentleman had a man, and he would needs be an informer, and a lusty young man he was. Well, an informer he was, and did much distress some people, and had perfected his informations so effectually against some, that there was nothing further to do, but for the constables to make distress on the people, that he might have the money or goods; and as I heard, he hastened them much to do it. Now while he was in the heat of his work, as he stood one day by the fireside, he had, it should seem, a mind to a sop in the pan, for the spit was then at the fire, so he went to make one; but behold, a dog—some say his own favourite dog—took distaste at something, and immediately bit his master by the leg; the which bite, notwithstanding all the means that was used to cure him, turned, as was said, to a gangrene. However, that wound was his death, and that a dreadful one too: for my relater said, that he lay in such a condition by this bite, at the beginning, till his flesh rotted from off him before he went out of the world. But what need I instance in particular persons; when the judgment of God against this kind of people was made manifest, I think I may say, if not in all, yet in most of the counties in England where such poor creatures were. But I would, if it had been the will of God, that neither I nor anybody else, could tell you more of these stories: true stories, that are neither lie nor romance.

Atten. Well, I also heard of both these myself, and of more too, as remarkable in their kind as these, if I had any list to tell them; but let us leave those that are behind to others, or to the coming of Christ, who then will justify or condemn them, as the merit of their work shall require; or if they repented, and found mercy, I shall be glad when I know it, for I wish not a curse to the soul of mine enemy.

Wise. There can be no pleasure in the telling of such stories, though to hear of them may do us a pleasure. They may put us in mind that there is a God that judgeth in the earth, and that doth not always forget nor defer to hear the cry of the destitute; they also carry along with them both caution and counsel to those that are the survivors of such. Let us tremble at the judgments of God, and be afraid of sinning against him, and it shall be our protection. It shall go well with them that fear God, that fear before him.

Atten. Well, sir, as you have intimated, so I think we have in this place spoken enough about these kind of men; if you please, let us return again to Mr. Badman himself, if you have any more to say of him.

Wise. More! we have yet scarce thoroughly begun with anything that we have said. All the particulars are in themselves so full of badness, that we have rather only looked in them, than indeed said anything to them: but we will pass them, and proceed. You have heard of the sins of his youth, of his apprenticeship, and how he set up, and married, and what a life he hath led his wife; and now I will tell you some more of his pranks. He had the very knack of knavery;

New discourse of Mr. Badman.

had he, as I said before, been bound to serve an apprenticeship to all these things, he could not have been more cunning, he could not have been more artificial at it.

Atten. Nor perhaps so artificially neither. For as none can teach goodness like to God himself, so concerning sin and knavery, none can teach a man it like the devil, to whom, as I perceive, Mr. Badman went to school from his childhood to the end of his life. But pray, sir, make a beginning.

Wise. Well, so I will. You may remember that I told you what a condition he was in for money before he did marry, and how he got a rich wife, with whose money he paid his debts. Now when he had paid his debts, he having some money left, he sets up again as briskly as ever, keeps a great shop, drives a great trade, and runs again a great way into debt; but now not into the debt of one or two, but into the debt of many, so that at last he came to owe some thousands of pounds; and thus he went on for a long time.

Mr. Badman plays a new prank.

And to pursue his ends the better, he began now to study to please all men, and to suit himself to any company; he could now be as they, say as they, that is, if he listed; and then he would list, when he perceived that by so doing, he might either make them his customers or creditors for his commodities. If he dealt with honest men, as with some honest men he did, then he would be as they, talk as they, seem to be sober as they, talk of justice and religion as they, and against debauchery as they; yea, and would, too, seem to show a dislike of them that said, did, or were otherwise than honest. Again, when he did light among those that were bad, then he would be as they, but yet more close and cautiously, except he was sure of his company. Then he would carry it openly, be as they; say, damn them and sink them, as they. If they railed on good men, so

could he; if they railed on religion, so could he; if they talked beastly, vainly, idly, so would he; if they were for drinking, swearing, whoring, or any the like villanies, so was he.

Mr. Badman's perfections.

This was now the path that he trod in, and could do all artificially as any man alive. And now he thought himself a perfect man, he thought he was always a boy till now. What think you now of Mr. Badman?

Atten. Think! why, I think he was an atheist; for no man but an atheist can do this. I say, it cannot be but that the man that is such as this Mr. Badman, must be a rank and stinking atheist; for he that believes that there is either God or devil, heaven or hell, or death, and judgment after, cannot do as Mr. Badman did: I mean, if he could do these things without reluctancy and check of conscience; yea, if he had not sorrow and remorse for such abominable sins as these.

Wise. Nay, he was so far off from reluctances and remorse of conscience for these things, that he counted them the excellency of his attainments, the quintessence of his wit, his rare and singular virtues, such as but few besides himself could be the masters of. Therefore, as for those that made boggle and stop at things, that could not in conscience, and for fear of death and judgment, do such things as he, he would call them fools, and noddies, and charge them for being frighted with the talk of unseen bugbears; and would encourage them, if they would be men indeed, to labour after the attainment of this his excellent art. He would oftentimes please himself with the thoughts of what he could do in this matter, saying within himself, " I can be religious, and irreligious, I can be anything, or nothing; I can swear, and speak against swearing; I can lie, and speak against lying; I can drink, wench,

How Mr. Badman came to enjoy himself.

be unclean, and defraud, and not be troubled for it. Now I enjoy myself, and am master of mine own ways, and not they of me. This I have attained with much study, great care, and more pains." But this his talk should be only with himself, to his wife, who he knew durst not divulge it; or among his intimates, to whom he knew he might say anything.

Atten. Did I call him before an atheist? I may call him now a devil, or a man possessed with one, if not with many. I think that there cannot be found in every corner such an one as this. True, it is said of King Ahaz, that he sinned more and more; and of Ahab, that he sold himself to work wickedness; and of the men of Sodom, that they were sinners exceedingly before the Lord.

Wise. An atheist he was no doubt, if there be such a thing as an atheist in the world; but for all his brags of perfection, and security in his wickedness, I believe that at times God did let down fire from heaven into his conscience. True, I believe he would quickly put it out again, and grow more desperate and wicked afterward, but this also turned to his destruction, as afterward you may hear.

But I am not of your mind, to think that there are but few such in the world; except you mean as to the degree of wickedness unto which he had attained. For otherwise, no doubt, there is abundance of such as he; men of the same mind, of the same principles, and of the same conscience too, to put them into practice. Yea, I believe that there are many that are endeavouring to attain to the same pitch of wickedness, and all them are such as he, in the judgment of the law, nor will their want of hellish wit to attain thereto, excuse them at the day of judgment. You know that in all science some are more arch than some; and so it is in the art as well as in the practice of wickedness; some are two-fold, and some seven-fold more the children of hell than others (and yet all the children of hell) else they would all be masters, and none scholars in the school of wickedness. But there must be masters, and there must be learners; Mr. Badman was a master in this art, and therefore it follows that he must be an arch and chief one in that mystery.

There are abundance like Mr. Badman.

Atten. You are in the right, for I perceive that some men, though they desire it, cannot be so arch in the practice thereof as others, but are, as I suppose they call them, fools and dunces to the rest, their heads and capacities will not serve them to act and do so wickedly. But Mr. Badman wanted not a wicked head to contrive, as well as a wicked heart to do his wickedness.

Wise. True, but yet I say such men shall at the day of judgment, be judged, not only for what they are, but also for what they would be. For if the thought of foolishness is sin, doubtless the desire of foolishness is more sin: and if the desire be more, the endeavour after it must needs be more and more. (Ps. xxiv. 9.) He then that is not an artificial atheist and transgressor, yet if he desires to be so, if he endeavoureth to be so, he shall be judged and condemned to hell for such an one. For the law judgeth men, as I said, according to what they would be. He that " looketh upon a woman to lust after her, hath committed adultery with her already in his heart." (Matt. v. 28.) By the same rule, he that would steal, doth steal; he that would cheat, doth cheat; he that would swear, doth swear; and he that would commit adultery, doth do so. For God judgeth men according to the working of their minds, and saith, " As he thinketh, so is he." (Prov. xxiii. 7.) That is, so is he in his heart, in his intentions, in his desires, in his endeavours; and God's law, I say, lays hold of the desires, intentions, and endeavours, even as it lays hold of the act of wickedness itself. (Matt. v. Rom. vii. 7.) A man then that desires to be as bad as Mr. Badman—and desires to be so wicked have many in their hearts—though he never attains to that proficiency in wickedness as he, shall yet be judged for as bad a man as he, because it was in his desires to be such a wicked one.

Atten. But this height of wickedness in Mr. Badman, will not yet out of my mind. This hard, desperate, or, what shall I call it, diabolical frame of heart, was in him a foundation, a groundwork to all acts and deeds that were evil.

Wise. The heart, and the desperate wickedness of it, is the foundation and groundwork of all. Atheism, professed and practical, spring both out of the heart, yea and all manner of evils besides. For they be not bad deeds that make a bad man, but he *A bad heart makes a bad man.* is already a bad man that doth bad deeds. A man must be wicked before he can do wickedness. "Wickedness proceedeth from the wicked." (1 Sam. xxiv. 13.) It is an evil tree that bears evil fruit. Men gather no grapes of thorns; the heart therefore must be evil, before the man can do evil, and good before the man doth good. (Matt. vii. 16—18.)

Atten. Now I see the reason why Mr. Badman was so base as to get a wife by dissimulation, and to abuse her so like a villain when he had got her; it was because he was before, by a wicked heart, prepared to act wickedness.

Wise. You may be sure of it, " For from within, out of the heart of men, proceed evil thoughts, adulteries, fornications, murders, thefts, covetousness, wickedness, deceit, lasciviousness, an evil eye, blasphemy, pride, foolishness : all these evil things come from within, and defile a man." (Mark vii. 21—23.) And a man, as his naughty mind inclines him, makes use of these, or any of these, to gratify his lust, to promote his designs, to revenge his malice, to enrich, or to wallow himself in the foolish pleasures and pastimes of this life. And all these did Mr. Badman do, even to the utmost, if either opportunity, or purse, or perfidiousness, would help him to the obtaining of his purpose.

Atten. Purse ! why he could not but have a purse to do almost what he would, having married a wife with so much money.

Wise. Hold you there; some of Mr. Badman's sins were costly, as his drinking, and whoring, and keeping other bad company; though he was a man that had ways too many to get money, as well as ways too many to spend it.

Atten. Had he then such a good trade, for all he was such a bad man ? Or, was his calling so gainful to him, as always to keep his purse's belly full, though he was himself a great spender?

Wise. No, it was not his trade that did it, though he had a pretty trade too. He had another way to get money, and that by hatfuls and pocketfuls at a time.

Atten. Why I trow he was no highwayman, was he ?

Wise. I will be sparing in my speech as to that; though some have muttered as if he could ride out now and then, about nobody but himself knew what, over night, and come home all dirty and weary next morning. But that is not the thing I aim at.

Atten. Pray let me know it, if you think it convenient that I should.

Wise. I will tell you: it was this,—he had an art to break, and get hatfuls of money by breaking.

Atten. But what do you mean by Mr. Badman's breaking? You speak mystically, do you not?

Mr. Badman had an art to break, and to get money that way.

Wise. No, no, I speak plainly. Or, if you will have it in plainer language, it is this:—When Mr. Badman had swaggered and whored away most of his wife's portion, he began to feel that he could not much longer stand upon his legs in this course of life, and keep up his trade and repute, such as he had, in the world, but by the new engine of breaking. Wherefore, upon a time, he gives a great and sudden rush into several men's debts, to the value of about four or five thousand pounds, driving at the same time a very great trade, by selling many things for less than they cost him, to get his custom, therewith to blind his creditors' eyes. His creditors, therefore, seeing that he had a great employ, and dreaming that it must needs at length turn to a very good account to them, trusted him freely without mistrust, and so did others too, to the value of what was mentioned before. Well, when Mr. Badman had well feathered his nest with other men's goods and money, after a little time he breaks. And by and by it is noised abroad that

He breaks.

Mr. Badman had shut up shop, was gone, and could trade no longer. Now, by that time his breaking had come to his creditors' ears, he had by craft and knavery made so sure of what he had, that his creditors could not touch a penny. Well, when he had done, he sends his mournful, sugared letters to his creditors, to let them understand what had happened unto him, and desired them not to be severe with him, for he bore towards all men an honest mind, and would pay so far as he was able. Now, he sends his letters by a man confederate with him, who could make both the worst and best of Mr. Badman's case—the best for Mr. Badman, and the worst for his creditors. So when he comes to them, he both bemoans them and condoles Mr. Badman's condition, telling them that, without a speedy bringing of things to a conclusion, Mr. Badman would be able to make them no satisfaction; but at present he both could and would, and that to the utmost of his power, and to that end, he desired that they would come over to him. Well, his creditors appoint him a time, and come over; and he, meanwhile, authorizes another to treat with them, but will not be seen himself, unless it was on a Sunday, lest they should snap him with a writ. So his deputed friend treats with them about their concern with Mr. Badman, first telling them of the great care that Mr. Badman took to satisfy them and all men for whatsoever he owed, as far as in him lay, and how little he thought a while since to be in this low condition. He pleaded also the greatness of his charge, the greatness of taxes, the badness of the times, and the great losses that he had by many of his customers; some of which died in his debt, others were run away, and for many that were alive, he never expected a farthing from them. Yet nevertheless he would show himself an honest man, and would pay as far as he was able; and if they were willing to come to terms, he would make a composition with them, for he was not able to pay them all. The creditors asked what he would give? It was replied, Half-a-crown

What Mr. Badman propounds to his creditors.

in the pound. At this they began to huff, and he to renew his complaint and entreaty; but the creditors would not hear, and so for that time their meeting without success broke up. But after his creditors were in cool blood, and admitting of second thoughts, and fearing lest delays should make them lose all, they admit of a second debate, come together again, and by many words and great ado, they obtained five shillings in the pound. So the money was produced, releases and discharges drawn, signed, and sealed, books crossed, and all

Mr. Badman gains by breaking.

things confirmed; and then Mr. Badman can put his head out of doors again, and be a better man than when he shut up shop, by several thousands of pounds.

Atten. And did he do thus indeed?

Wise. Yes, once and again. I think he broke twice or thrice.

Atten. And did he do it before he had need to do it?

Wise. Need! What do you mean by need? There is no need at any time for a man to play the knave. He did it of a wicked mind, to defraud and beguile his creditors: he had wherewithal of his father, and also by his wife, to have lived upon,

There is no plea for his dishonesty.

with lawful labour, like an honest man. He had also, when he made this wicked break, though he had been a profuse and prodigal spender, to have paid his creditors their own to a farthing. But had he done so, he had not done like himself, like Mr. Badman; had he, I say, dealt like an honest man, he had then gone out of Mr. Badman's road. He did it therefore of a dishonest mind, and to a wicked end; to wit, that he might have wherewithal, howsoever unlawfully gotten, to follow his cups and queans, and to live in the swing of his lusts, even as he did before.

Atten. Why this was a mere cheat.

Wise. It was a cheat indeed. This way of breaking is nothing else but a more neat way of thieving, of picking of pockets, of breaking open of shops, and of taking from men what one has nothing to do with. But though it seems easy, it is hard to learn; no man that has conscience to God or man, can ever be his crafts-master in this hellish art.

Atten. Oh, sir! What a wicked man was this!

Wise. A wicked man indeed. By this art he could tell how to make men send their goods to his shop, and then be glad to take a penny for that which he had promised, before he came thither, to give them a groat; I say, he could make them glad to take a crown for a pound's worth, and a thousand for that for which he had promised before to give them four thousand pounds.

Atten. This argueth that Mr. Badman had but little conscience.

Wise. This argued that Mr. Badman had no conscience at all; for conscience, the least spark of a good conscience, cannot endure this.

Atten. Before we go any further in Mr. Badman's matters, let me desire you, if you please, to give me an answer to these two questions :— 1. What do you find in the word of God against such a practice as this of Mr. Badman's is? 2. What would you have a man to do that is in his creditor's debt, and can neither pay him what he owes him, nor go on in a trade any longer?

Wise. I will answer you as well as I can. And first, to the first of your questions; to wit, What I find in the word of God against such a practice, as this of Mr. Badman's is. The word of God doth forbid this wickedness; and to make it the more odious in our eyes, it joins it with theft and robbery. "Thou shalt not," says God, "defraud thy neighbour, neither rob him." (Lev. xix. 13.) Thou shalt not defraud, that is, deceive or beguile. Now thus to break, is to defraud, deceive and beguile; which is, as you see, forbidden by the God of heaven : "Thou shalt not defraud thy neighbour, neither rob him." It is a kind of theft and robbery, thus to defraud and beguile. It is a vilely robbing of his shop, and picking of his pocket; a thing odious to reason and conscience, and contrary to the law of nature. It is a designed piece of wickedness, and therefore a double sin. A man cannot do this great wickedness on a sudden, and through a violent assault of Satan. He that will commit this sin, must have time to deliberate, that by invention he may make it formidable, and that with lies and high dissimulations. He that commits this wickedness, must first hatch it upon his bed, beat his head about it, and lay his plot strong; so that to the completing of such a wickedness, there must be adjoined many sins, and they too must go hand in hand until it be completed. But what saith the scripture? Let "no man go beyond, and defraud his brother in any matter, because the Lord is the avenger of all such." (1 Thess. iv. 6.) But this kind of breaking is a going beyond my brother; this is a compassing of him about, that I may catch him in my net; and as I said, an art to rob my brother, and to

pick his pocket, and that with his consent; which doth not therefore mitigate, but so much the more greaten, and make odious the offence. For men that are thus wilily abused, cannot help themselves —they are taken in a deceitful net. But God will here concern himself, he will be the avenger, he will be the avenger of all such either here or in another world. And this the apostle testifies, where he saith, "But he that doth wrong shall receive for the wrong which he hath done; and there is no respect of persons." (Col. iii. 25.) That is, there is no man, be he what he will, if he will be guilty of this sin, of going beyond, of beguiling of, and doing wrong to his brother, but God will call him to an account for it, and will pay him with vengeance for it too; for there is no respect of persons. I might add, that this sin of wronging, of going beyond, and defrauding of my neighbour, it is like that first prank that the devil played with our first parents, as the altar that Uriah built for Ahaz, was taken from the fashion of that that stood at Damascus, to be the very pattern of it. "The serpent beguiled me," says Eve; Mr. Badman beguiles his creditors. The serpent beguiled Eve with lying promises of gain; and so did Mr. Badman beguile his creditors. The serpent said one thing and meant another, when he beguiled Eve; and so did Mr. Badman when he beguiled his creditors. That man, therefore, that doth thus deceive and beguile his neighbour, imitateth the devil; he taketh his examples from him, and not from God, the word, or good men. And this did Mr. Badman. And now to your second question : to wit, what I would have a man do that is in his creditor's debt, and that can neither pay him, nor go on in a trade any longer? First of all, if this be his case, and he knows it, let him not run one penny further in his creditors' debt. For that cannot be done with good conscience. He that knows he cannot pay and yet will run into debt, does knowingly wrong and defraud his neighbour, and falls under that sentence of the word of God, "The wicked borroweth, and payeth not again." (Ps. xxxvii. 21.) Yea, worse, he borrows, though at the very same time he knows that he cannot pay again. He doth also craftily take away what is his neighbour's. That is, therefore, the first thing that I would propound to such; let him not run any farther into his creditors' debt. Secondly. After this, let him consider, how, and by what means he was brought into such a condition that he could not pay his just · debts. To wit, whether it was by his own remissness in his calling, by living too high in diet or apparel, by lending too lavishingly that which was none of his own, to his loss; or whether by the immediate hand and judgment of God. If by searching, he finds that this is come upon him through remissness in his calling, extravagances in his family, or the like; let him labour for a sense of his sin and wickedness, for

How those that are bankrupts should deal with their consciences.

he has sinned against the Lord: first, in his being slothful in business, and in not providing, to wit, of his own, by the sweat of his brow, or other honest ways, for those of his own house; and secondly, in being lavishing in diet and apparel in the family, or in lending to others that which was none of his own. This cannot be done with good conscience: it is both against reason and nature, and therefore must be a sin against God. I say, therefore, if thus this debtor hath done, if ever he would live quietly in conscience, and comfortably in his condition for the future, let him humble himself before God, and repent of this his wickedness. For "he also that is slothful in his work is brother to him that is a great waster." (Prov. xviii. 9.) To be slothful and a waster too is to be as it were a double sinner. But again, as this man should inquire into these things, so he should also into this. How came I into this way of dealing, in which I have now miscarried? Is it a way that my parents brought me up in, put me apprentice to, or that by providence I was first thrust into? Or is it a way into which I have twisted myself, as not being contented with my first lot, that by God and my parents I was cast into? This ought duly to be considered; and if, upon search, a man shall find that he is out of the place and calling into which he was put by his parents, or the providence of God, and has miscarried in a new way, that through pride and dislike of his first state he has chose rather to embrace, his miscarriage is his sin, the fruit of his pride, and a token of the judgment of God upon him for his leaving of his first state. And for this he ought, as for the former, to be humble and penitent before the Lord. But if by search he finds that his poverty came by none of these, if by honest search he finds it so, and can say with good conscience, I went not out of my place and state in which God by his providence had put me, but have abode with God in the calling wherein I was called, and have wrought hard, and fared meanly, been civilly apparelled, and have not directly, nor indirectly made away with my creditors' goods; then has his fall come upon him by the immediate hand of God, whether by visible or invisible ways. For sometimes it comes by visible ways, to wit, by fire, by thieves, by loss of cattle, or the wickedness of sinful dealers, &c. And sometimes by means invisible, and then no man knows how; we only see things are going, but cannot see by what way they go. Well, now, suppose that a man, by an immediate hand of God, is brought to a morsel of bread, what must he do now? I answer, his surest way is still to think that this is the fruit of some sin, though possibly not sin in the management of his calling, yet of some other sin. "God casteth away the substance of the wicked." (Prov. x. 3.) Therefore let him still humble himself before his God, because his hand is upon him, and say, "What sin is this, for which the hand of God is upon me?" And let him be diligent to find it out, for some sin is the cause of this judgment; for

God "doth not afflict willingly nor grieve the children of men." (Lam. iii. 33.) Either the heart is too much set upon the world, or religion is too much neglected in thy family, or something. There is a snake in the grass, a worm in the gourd; some sin in thy bosom, for the sake of which God doth thus deal with thee. Thirdly. This thus done, let that man again consider thus with himself: perhaps God is now changing of my condition and state in the world; he has let me live in fashion, in fulness, and abundance of worldly glory; and I did not to his glory improve, as I should, that his good dispensation to me. But when I lived in full and fat pasture, I did there lift up the heel. Therefore he will now turn me into hard commons, that with leanness, and hunger, and meanness, and want, I may spend the rest of my days. But let him do this without murmuring, and repining; let him do it in a godly manner, submitting himself to the judgment of God. "Let the rich rejoice in that he is made low." (James i. 9, 10.) This is duty, and it may be privilege to those that are under this hand of God. And for thy encouragement to this hard work, (for this is a hard work,) consider of these four things. 1. This is right lying down under God's hand, and the way to be exalted in God's time. When God would have Job embrace the dunghill, he embraces it, and says, "The Lord gave, and the Lord hath taken away, blessed be the name of the Lord." (Job i. 21.) 2. Consider, that there are blessings also that attend a low condition, more than all the world are aware of. A poor condition has preventing mercy attending of it. The poor, because they are poor, are not capable of sinning against God as the rich man does. 3. The poor can more clearly see himself preserved by the providence of God than the rich, for he trusteth in the abundance of his riches. 4. It may be God has made thee poor, because he would make thee rich. "Hearken, my beloved brethren, hath not God chosen the poor of this world, rich in faith, and heirs of the kingdom which God hath promised to them that love him?" (James ii. 5.) I am persuaded if men upon whom this hand of God is, would thus quietly lie down and humble themselves under it, they would find more peace, yea, more blessing of God attending them in it, than the most of men are aware of. But this is an hard chapter, and therefore I do not expect that many should either read it with pleasure, or desire to take my counsel. Having thus spoken to the broken man, with reference to his own self, I will now speak to him as he stands related to his creditors. In the next place, there- Honest dealing fore, let him fall upon the most with creditors. honest way of dealing with his creditors, and that I think must be this—First, let him timely make them acquainted with his condition, and also do to them these three things. 1. Let him heartily and unfeignedly ask them forgiveness for the wrong that he has done them. 2. Let him proffer them *all*, and the whole *all* that ever he has in the world; let him hide nothing, let him strip himself to his raiment for them; let him not keep a ring, a spoon, or anything from them. 3. If none of these two will satisfy them, let him proffer them his body, to be at their dispose, to wit, either to abide imprisonment at their pleasure, or to be at their service, till by labour and travel he hath made them such amends as they in reason think fit, only reserving something for the succour of his poor and distressed family out of his labour, which in reason, and conscience, and nature, he is bound also to take care of. Thus shall he make them what amends he is able, for the wrong that he hath done them in wasting and spending their estates. By thus doing, he submits himself to God's rod, commits himself to the dispose of his providence. Yea, by thus doing, he casteth the lot of his present and future condition into the lap of his creditors, and leaves the whole dispose thereof to the Lord, even as he shall order and incline their hearts to do with him. And let that be either to forgive him; or to take that which he hath for satisfaction; or to lay his body under affliction, this way or that, according to law; can he, I say, thus leave the whole to God, let the issue be what it will, that man shall have peace in his mind afterwards. And the comforts of that state (which will be comforts that attend equity, justice, and duty) will be more unto him, because more according to godliness, than can be the comforts that are the fruits of injustice, fraudulency, and deceit. Besides, this is the way to engage God to favour him by the sentence of his creditors, for *he* can entreat them to use him kindly, and he will do it when his ways are pleasing in his sight. When a man's ways please the Lord, his enemies shall be at peace with him. And surely, for a man to seek to make restitution for wrongs done to the utmost of his power, by what he is, has, and enjoys in this world, is the best way, in that capacity, and with reference to that thing, that a man can at this time be found active in. But he that doth otherwise, abides in his sin, refuses to be disposed of by the providence of God, chooseth an high estate, though not attained in God's way; when God's will is that he should descend into a low one. Yea, he desperately saith in his heart and actions, I will be mine own chooser, and that in mine own way, whatever happens or follows thereupon.

Atten. You have said well, in my mind. But suppose now that Mr. Badman was here, could he not object as to what you have said, saying, "Go and teach your brethren, that are professors, this lesson, for they, as I am, are guilty of breaking; yea, I am apt to think, of that which you call my knavish way of breaking, to wit, of breaking before they have need to break. But if not so, yet they are guilty of neglect in their calling, of living higher both in fare and apparel than their trade or income will maintain. Besides, that they do break

all the world very well knows, and that they have the art to plead for a composition is very well known to men; and that it is usual with them to hide their linen, their plate, their jewels, and, it is to be thought, sometimes money and goods besides, is as common as four eggs a-penny." And thus they beguile men, debauch their consciences, sin against their profession, and make, it is to be feared, their lusts in all this, and the fulfilling of them, their end. I say, if Mr. Badman was here to object thus unto you, what would be your reply?

Wise. What? Why, I would say, I hope no good man, no man of good conscience, no man that either feareth God, regardeth the credit of religion, the peace of God's people, or the salvation of his own soul, will do thus. Professors such, perhaps, there may be, and who upon earth can help it? Jades there be of all colours. If men will profess, and make their profession a stalking-horse to beguile their neighbours of their estates, as Mr. Badman himself did, when he beguiled her that now is with sorrow his wife, who can help it? The churches of old were pestered with such, and therefore no marvel, if these perilous difficult times be so. But mark how the apostle words it: "Nay, ye do wrong, and defraud, and that your brethren. Know ye not that the unrighteous shall not inherit the kingdom of God? Be not deceived, neither fornicators, nor idolaters, nor adulterers, nor effeminate, nor abusers of themselves with mankind, nor thieves, nor covetous, nor drunkards, nor revilers, nor extortioners shall inherit the kingdom of God." (1 Cor. vi. 8—10.) None of these shall be saved in this state, nor shall profession deliver them from the censure of the godly, when they shall be manifest such to be. But their profession we cannot help: how can we help it, if men should ascribe to themselves the title of holy ones, godly ones, zealous ones, self-denying ones, or any other such glorious titles? and while they thus call themselves, they should be the veriest rogues for all evil, sin, and villany imaginable, who could help it? True, they are a scandal to religion, a grief to the honest-hearted, an offence to the world, and a stumbling-stone to the weak, and these offences have come, do come, and will come, do what all the world can; but woe be to them through whom they come. Let such professors therefore be disowned by all true Christians, and let them be reckoned among those base men of the world which by such actions they most resemble. They are Mr. Badman's kindred. For they are a shame to religion, I say these slithy, rob-shop, pickpocket men, they are a shame to religion, and religious men should be ashamed of them. God puts such an one among the fools of the world, therefore let not Christians put them among those that are wise for heaven. "As the partridge sitteth on eggs, and hatcheth them not, so he that getteth riches, and not by right, shall leave them in the midst of his days, and at his end shall be a fool." (Jer. xvii. 11.) And the man under consideration is one of these, and therefore must look to fall by this judgment. A professor! and practise such villanies as these! such an one is not worthy to bear that name any longer. We may say to such as the prophet spake to their like, to wit, to the rebellious that were in the house of Israel: "Go ye, serve every man his idols," (Ezek. xx. 39,) if ye will not hearken to the law and testament of God, to lead your lives hereafter; "but pollute God's holy name no more with your gifts, and with your idols." Go, professors, go; leave off profession, unless you will lead your lives according to your profession. Better never profess, than to make profession a stalking-horse to sin, deceit, to the devil, and hell. The ground and rules of religion allow not any such thing: "Receive us," says the apostle, "we have wronged no man, we have corrupted no man, we have defrauded no man." (2 Cor. vii. 2.) Intimating that those that are guilty of wronging, corrupting, or defrauding of any, should not be admitted to the fellowship of saints, no, nor into the common catalogue of brethren with them. Nor can men, with all their rhetoric and eloquent speaking, prove themselves fit for the kingdom of heaven, or men of good conscience on earth. O that godly plea of Samuel: "Behold here I am," says he, "witness against me, before the Lord, and before his anointed, whose ox have I taken? or whose ass have I taken? or whom have I defrauded? whom have I oppressed?" &c. (1 Sam. xii. 3.) This was to do like a man of good conscience indeed. And in this his appeal he was so justified in the consciences of the whole congregation, that they could not but with one voice, as with one mouth, break out jointly and say, "Thou hast not defrauded us, nor oppressed us." A professor, and defraud. Away with him! A professor should not owe any man anything but love. A professor should provide things, not of other men's, but of his own, of his own honest getting, and that not only in the sight of God, but of all men; that he may adorn the doctrine of God our Saviour in all things.

Atten. But suppose God should blow upon a professor in his estate and calling, and he should be run out before he is aware, must he be accounted to be like Mr. Badman, and lie under the same reproach as he?

Wise. No: if he hath dutifully done what he could to avoid it. It is possible for a ship to sink at sea, notwithstanding the most faithful endeavour of the most skilful pilot under heaven. And thus, as I suppose, it was with the prophet, that left his wife in debt, to the hazarding the slavery of her children by the creditors. (2 Kings iv. 1, 2.) He was no profuse man, nor one that was given to defraud, for the text says, he "feared God;" yet, as I said, he was run out more than she could pay. If God would blow upon a man, who can help it? and he will do so sometimes, because he will change

dispensations with men, and because he will try their graces; yea, also because he will overthrow the wicked with his judgments; and all these things are seen in Job. But then the consideration of this should bid men have a care God does sometimes blow upon his own people. that they be honest, lest this comes upon them for their sin. It should also bid them beware of launching further into the world, than in an honest way by ordinary means they can godlily make their retreat; for the further in, the greater fall. It should also teach them to beg of God his blessing upon their endeavours, their honest and lawful endeavours. And it should put upon them a diligent looking to their steps, that if in their going they should hear the ice crack, they may timely go back again. These things considered, and duly put in practice, if God will blow upon a man, then let him be content, and with Job embrace the dunghill: let him give unto all their dues, and not fight against the providence of God, but humble himself rather under his mighty hand, which comes to strip him naked and bare: for he that doth otherwise, fights against God; and declares that he is a stranger to that of Paul; "I know both how to be abased, and I know how to abound; everywhere, and in all things, I am instructed both to be full, and to be hungry, both to abound, and to suffer need." (Phil. iv. 12.)

Atten. But Mr. Badman would not, I believe, have put this difference betwixt things feigned, and those that fall of necessity.

Wise. If he will not, God will, conscience will; and that not thine own only, but the consciences of all those that have seen the way, and that have known the truth of the condition of such an one.

Atten. Well: let us at this time leave this matter, and return again to Mr. Badman.

Wise. With all my heart will I proceed to give you a relation of what is yet behind of his life, in order to our discourse of his death.

Atten. But pray do it with as much brevity as you can.

Wise. Why, are you weary of my relating of things?

Atten. No: but it pleases me to hear a great deal in few words.

Wise. I profess myself not an artist that way, but yet, as briefly as I can, I will pass through what of his life is behind; and again I shall begin with his fraudulent dealing, as before I have showed with his creditors, so now, with his customers, and those that he had otherwise to deal withal. He dealt by deceitful weights and measures. He kept weights to buy by, and weights to sell by; measures to buy by, and measures to sell by; those he bought by were too big, those that he sold by were too little. Besides he could use a More of Mr. Badman's fraudulent dealing. He used deceitful weights and scales. thing called sleight of hand, if he had to do with other men's weights and measures, and by that means make them whether he did buy or sell, yea though his customer or chapman looked on, turn to his own advantage. Moreover, he had the art to misreckon men in their accounts whether by weight, or measure, or money, and would often do it to his worldly advantage, and their loss. What say you to Mr. Badman now? And if a question was made of his faithful dealing, he had his servants ready, that to his purpose he had brought up, that would avouch and swear to his book, or word. This was Mr. Badman's practice. What think you of Mr. Badman now?

Atten. Think! Why I can think no other but that he was a man left to himself, a naughty man; for these, as his other, were naughty things; if the tree, as indeed it may, ought to be judged, what it is, by its fruits, then Mr. Badman must needs be a bad tree. But pray, for my further satisfaction, show me now by the word of God, the evil of this his practice: and first of his using false weights and measures.

Wise. The evil of that! Why the evil of that appears to every eye. The heathens, that live like beasts and brutes in many things, do abominate and abhor such wickedness as this. Let a man but look upon these things as he goes by; and he shall see enough in them from the light of nature to make him loathe so base a practice, although Mr. Badman loved it.

Atten. But show me something out of the word against it, will you?

Wise. I will willingly do it. And first, look into the Old Testament: "Ye shall," saith God there, "do no unrighteousness in judgment, in meteyard, in weight, or in measure. Just balances, just weights, a just ephah, and a just hin shall ye have." (Lev. xix. 35, 36.) This is the law of God, and that which all men, according to the law of the land, ought to obey. So again: "Ye shall have just balances, and a just ephah," &c. (Ezek. xlv. 10.) Now having showed you the law, I will also show you how God takes swerving therefrom. "A false balance is not good," (Ps. x. 23;) "a false balance is abomination to the Lord." (Prov. xi. 1.) Some have just weights, but false balances; and by virtue of these false balances, by their just weights, they deceive the country. Wherefore, God first of all commands that the balance be made just. A just balance shalt thou have; else they may be, yea are, deceivers, notwithstanding their just weights. Now, having commanded that men have a just balance, and testifying that a false one is an abomination to the Lord, he proceedeth also unto weight and measure. "Thou shalt not have in thy bag divers weights, a great and a small," (Deut. xxv. 13;) that is, one to buy by, and another to sell by, as Mr. Badman had. "Thou shalt not have in thine house divers measures, a great and a small (and these had Mr. Badman also). But thou shalt have a perfect and a just weight; a perfect

and just measure shalt thou have, that thy days may be lengthened in the land which the Lord thy God giveth thee. For all that do such things (that is, that use false weights and measures) and all that do unrighteously, are an abomination unto the Lord thy God." (Deut. xxv. 14—16.) See now both how plentiful and how punctual the Scripture is in this matter. But perhaps it may be objected that all this is old law, and therefore hath nothing to do with us under the New Testament. Not that I think you, neighbour, will object thus. Well, to this foolish objection, let us make an answer. First, he that makes this objection, if he doth it to overthrow the authority of those texts, discovereth The law commands men to be honest in their weights and measures. that himself is first cousin to Mr. Badman: for a just man is willing to speak reverently of those commands. That man therefore hath, I doubt, but little conscience, if any at all that is good, that thus objecteth against the text. But let us look into the New Testament, and there we shall see how Christ confirmeth the same. Where he commandeth that men make to others good measure, including also that they make good weight; telling such that do thus, or those that do it not, that they may be encouraged to do it: "Good measure, pressed down, and shaken together, and running over, shall men give into your bosom; for with the same measure that ye mete withal, it shall be measured to you again," (Luke vi. 38;) to wit, both from God and man. For as God will show his indignation against the false man, by taking away even that he hath, so he will deliver up the false man to the oppressor, and the extortioner shall catch from him, as well as he hath catched from his neighbour; therefore another scripture saith, "When thou shalt make an end to deal treacherously, they shall deal treacherously with thee." (Isa. xxxiii. 1.) That the New Testament also hath an inspection into men's trading, yea, even with their weights and measures, is evident from these general exhortations, "Defraud not;" "lie not one to another;" "let no man go beyond his brother in any matter, for the Lord is the avenger of all such:" "whatsoever ye do, do it heartily, as unto the Lord," "doing all in his name," "to his glory;" and the like. All these injunctions and commandments do respect our life and conversation among men, with reference to our dealing, trading, and so consequently they forbid false, deceitful, yea, all doings that are corrupt. Having thus in a word or two showed you that these things are bad, I will next, for the conviction of those that use them, show you where they are to be found. 1. They are not to be found in the house of the good and godly man, for he, as his God, abhors them; but they are to be found in the house of evil doers, such as Mr. Badman's is. "Are there," saith the prophet, "yet the treasures of wickedness in the house of the wicked, and the scant measure that is abominable?" (Micah vi. 10.) Are they there yet, notwithstanding God's forbidding, notwithstanding God's tokens of anger against those that do such things!—O how loth is a wicked man to let go a sweet, a gainful sin, when he hath hold of it! They hold fast deceit, they refuse to let it go. 2. These deceitful weights and measures are not to be found in the house of the merciful, but in the house of the cruel; in the house of them that love to oppress. "The balances of deceit are in his hand; he loveth to oppress." (Hos. xii. 7.) He is given to oppression and cruelty, therefore he useth such wicked things in his calling. Yea, he is a very cheat, and, as was hinted before, concerning Mr. Badman's breaking, so I say now, concerning his using these deceitful weights and measures, it is as bad, as base, as to take a purse, or pick a pocket, for it is a plain robbery; it takes away from a man that which is his own, even the price of his money. 3. The deceitful weights and measures are not to be found in the house of such as relieve the belly, and that cover the loins of the poor, but of such as indeed would swallow them up. "Hear this, O ye that swallow up the needy, even to make the poor of the land to fail, saying, When will the new moon be gone, that we may sell corn? and the Sabbath, that we may set forth wheat, making the ephah small, and the shekel great (making the measure small, and the price great), and falsifying the balances by deceit. That we may buy the poor for silver, and the needy for a pair of shoes, and sell the refuse of the wheat. The Lord hath sworn by the excellency of Jacob, Surely I will never forget any of their works." (Amos viii. 4—7.) So detestable and vile a thing is this in the sight of God. 4. God abominates the thoughts of calling of those that use false weights and measures by any other term than that they be impure ones, or the like: "Shall I count them pure," saith he, "with the wicked balances, and with the bag of deceitful weights?" (Micah vi. 11.) No, by no means; they are impure ones; their hands are defiled; deceitful gain is in their houses. They have gotten what they have by coveting an evil covetousness, and, therefore, must and shall be counted among the impure, among the wicked of the world. Thus you see how full and plain the word of God is against this sin, and them that use it. And, therefore, Mr. Badman, for that he used by these things thus to rook and cheat his neighbours, is rightly rejected from having his name in and among the catalogue of the godly.

Atten. But I am persuaded that the using of these things, and the doing by them thus deceitfully, is not counted so great an evil by some.

Wise. Whether it be counted an evil or a virtue by men it mattereth not. You see by the Scriptures the judgment of God upon it. It was not counted an evil by Mr. Badman, nor is it by any that still are treading in his steps. But I say it is no matter how men esteem of things, let us adhere to the judgment of God. And the rather because, when we ourselves have done weighing and measuring to others, then God will weigh and measure both us and our actions. And when he doth so, as he will do shortly, then woe be to him to whom, and of whose actions, it shall be thus said by him, "Tekel, thou art weighed in the balances, and art found wanting." (Dan. v. 27.) God will then recompense their evil of deceiving upon their own head, when he shall shut them out of his presence, favour, and kingdom for ever and ever.

Atten. But it is a wonder, that since Mr. Badman's common practice was to do thus, that some one or more did not find him out, and blame him for this his wickedness.

Wise. For the generality of people he went away clever with his knavery; for what with his balance, his false balance, and good weight, and what with his sleight-of-hand to boot, he beguiled sometimes a little, and sometimes more, most that he had to deal with. Besides, those that use this naughty trade are either such as blind men with a show of religion, or by hectoring the buyer out by words. I must confess Mr. Badman was not so arch at the first, that is, to do it by show of religion; for now he began to grow threadbare—though some of his brethren are arch enough How Mr. Badman did cheat, and hide his cheating. this way, yea, and of his sisters, too, for I told you at first that there were a great many of them, and never a one of them good: but for hectoring, for swearing, for lying, if these things would make weight and measure, they should not be wanting to Mr. Badman's customers.

Atten. Then it seems he kept good weights and a bad balance. Well, that was better than that both should be bad.

Wise. Not at all. There lay the depth of his deceit: for if any at any time found fault that he used them hardly, and that they wanted their weight of things, he would reply, Why, did you not see them weighed? will you not believe your own eyes? If you question my weights, pray carry them whither you will; I will maintain them to be good and just. The same he Good weights and a bad balance a deep piece of knavery. would say of his scales. So he blinded all by his balance.

Atten. This is cunning indeed; but, as you say, there must be also something done or said to blind therewith, and this I perceive Mr. Badman had.

Wise. Yes, he had many ways to blind, but he was never clever at it by making a show of religion, though he cheated his wife therewith; for he was, especially by those that dwelt near him, too well known to do that, though he would bungle at it as well as he could. But there are some that are arch villains this way: they shall to view live a whole life religiously, and yet shall be guilty of these most horrible sins. And yet religion in itself is never the worse, nor yet the true professors of it. But, as Luther says, in the name of God begins all mischief. For hypocrites have no other way to bring their evils to maturity but by using and mixing the name of God and religion therewith. Thus they become whited walls; for by this white, the white of religion, the dirt of their actions is hid. Thus, also, they become graves that appear not; and they that go over them that have to do with them are not aware of them, but suffer themselves to be deluded by them. Yea, if there shall, as there will sometimes, rise a doubt in the heart of the buyer about the weight and measure he should have, why he suffereth his very senses to be also deluded by recalling of his chapman's religion to mind, and thinks verily that not his good chapman, but himself is out; for he dreams not that his chapman can deceive. But if the buyer shall find it out, and shall make it apparent that he is beguiled, then shall he be healed by having amends made, and perhaps fault shall be laid upon servants, &c., and so Master Cheat shall stand for a right honest man in the eye of his customer, though the next time he shall pick his pocket again. Some plead custom for their cheat, as if that could acquit them before the tribunal of God; and others say, it came to them for so much, and, therefore, another must take it for so much, though there is wanting both as to weight and measure: but in all these things there are juggles, or, if not, such must know that "that which is altogether just," (Deut. xvi. 20,) they must do. Suppose that I be cheated myself with a brass half-crown, must I, therefore, cheat another therewith? If this be bad in the whole, it is also bad in the parts. Therefore, however thou art dealt withal in thy buying, yet thou must deal justly in selling, or thou sinnest against thy soul, and art become as Mr. Badman. And know that a pretence to custom is nothing worth. It is not custom, but good conscience that will help at God's tribunal.

Atten. But I am persuaded that that which is gotten by men this way doth them but little good.

Wise. I am of your mind for that, but this is not considered by those thus minded; for if they can get it, though they get, as we say, the devil and all by their getting, yet they are content, and count that their getting is much. Little good! why do you think they consider that? No; no more than they consider what they shall do in the judgment, at the day of God Almighty, for their wrong getting of what they get, and that is just nothing at all. But to give you a more direct answer. This kind of getting is so far off from doing them little good that it doth them no good at all, because thereby they lose their own souls: "What shall it profit a man, if he shall gain the whole world, and lose his own soul?" (Mark viii. 36.) He loseth, then, he loseth greatly that

getteth after this fashion. This is the man that is penny-wise and pound-foolish; this is he that loseth his good sheep for a halfpenny-worth of tar; that loseth a soul for a little of the world. And then what doth he get thereby but loss and damage? Thus he getteth, or rather loseth, about the world to come. But what doth he get in this world more than travail and sorrow, vexation of spirit, and disappointment? Men aim at blessedness in getting, I mean, at temporal blessedness; but the man that thus getteth shall not have that. For though an inheritance after this manner may be hastily gotten at the beginning, yet the end thereof shall not be blessed. They gather it indeed, and think to keep it too, but what says Solomon? God casteth it away. "The Lord will not suffer the soul of the righteous to famish, but he casteth away the substance of the wicked." (Prov. x. 3.)

The time, as I said, that they do enjoy it, it shall do them no good at all; but long, to be sure, they must not have it. For God will either take it away in their lifetime, or else in the generation following, according to that of Job: "He (the wicked) may prepare it, but the just shall put it on, and the innocent shall divide the silver." (Job xxvii. 17.) Consider that also that is written in Proverbs: "A good man leaveth an inheritance to his children's children, and the wealth of the sinner is laid up for the just." (Prov. xiii. 22.) What then doth he get thereby, that getteth by dishonest means? Why, he getteth sin and wrath, hell and damnation: and now tell me how much he doth get. This, I say, is his getting; so that as David says, we may be bold to say too: I beheld the wicked in great prosperity, and presently I cursed his habitation, for it cannot prosper with him. (Ps. lxxiii. 3.) Fluster and huff, and make ado for awhile he may, but God hath determined that both he and it shall melt like grease, and any observing man may see it so. Behold, the unrighteous man, in a way of injustice, getteth much, and loadeth himself with thick clay, but anon it withereth, it decayeth, and even he, or the generation following, decline, and return to beggary. And this Mr. Badman, notwithstanding his cunning and crafty tricks to get money, did die, nobody can tell whether worth a farthing or no.

Atten. He had all the bad tricks, I think, that it was possible for a man to have, to get money; one would think that he should have been rich.

Wise. You reckon too fast, if you count these all his bad tricks to get money; for he had more besides. If his customers were in his books, as it should go hard but he would have them there,—at least, More of Mr. Badman's bad tricks. if he thought he could make any advantage of them then,—then would he be sure to impose upon them his worst, even very bad commodity, yet set down for it the price that the best was sold at: like those that sold the refuse wheat, or the worst of the wheat; making the shekel great, yet hoisting up the price: this was Mr. Badman's way. *Another art to cheat withal.* He would sell goods that cost him not the best price by far, for as much as he sold his best of all for. He had also a trick to mingle his commodity, that that which was bad might go off with the least mistrust. Besides, if his customers at any time paid him money, let them look to themselves, and to their acquittances, for he would usually attempt to call for that payment again, especially if he thought that there were hopes of making a prize thereby, and then to be sure if they could not produce good and sufficient ground of the payment, a hundred to one but they paid it again. Sometimes the honest chapman would appeal to his servants for proof of the payment of money, but they were trained up by him to say after his mind, right or wrong; so that, relief that way, he could get none.

Atten. It is a bad, yea, an abominable thing, for a man to have such servants. For by such means a poor customer may be undone, and not know how to help himself. Alas! if the master be so unconscionable, as I perceive Mr. Badman was, to call for his money twice, and if his servant will swear that it is a due debt, where is any help for such a man? He must sink, there is no remedy.

Wise. This is very bad, but this has been a practice, and that hundreds of years ago. But what saith the word of God? I will "punish all *Servants, observe these words.* those that leap upon the threshold, which fill their masters' houses with violence and deceit." (Zeph. i. 9.) Mr. Badman also had this art: could he get a man at advantage, that is, if his chapman durst not go from him, or if the commodity he wanted could not for the present be conveniently had elsewhere, then let him look to himself, he would surely make his purse-strings crack; he would exact upon him without any pity or conscience.

Atten. That was extortion, was it not? I pray let me hear your judgment of extortion, what it is, and when committed?

Wise. Extortion is a screwing from men more than by the law of God or men is right; and it is *Of extortion.* committed sometimes by them in office, about fees, rewards, and the like: but it is most commonly committed by men of trade, who without all conscience, when they have the advantage, will make a prey of their neighbour. And thus was Mr. Badman an extortioner; for although he did not exact, and force away, as bailiffs and clerks have used to do, yet he had his opportunities, and such cruelty to make use of them, that he would often, in his way, be extorting and forcing of money out of his neighbour's pocket. For every man that makes a prey of his advantage upon his neighbour's necessities, to force from him more than in reason and conscience, according to the present prices of things such commodity is worth, may very well be called

an extortioner, and judged for one that hath no inheritance in the kingdom of God.

Atten. Well, this Badman was a sad wretch.

Wise. Thus you have often said before. But now we are in discourse of this, give me leave a little to go on. We have a great many people in the country too that live all their days in the practice, and so under the guilt of extortion; people, alas! that think scorn to be so accounted. As for example: there is a poor body that dwells, we will suppose, so many miles from the market; and this man wants a bushel of *Who are extortioners.* grist, a pound of butter, or a cheese for himself, his wife, and poor children; but dwelling so far from the market, if he goes thither, he shall lose his day's work, which will be eightpence or tenpence damage to him, and that is something to a poor man. So he goeth to one of his masters or dames for what he wanteth, and asks them to help him with such a thing. Yes, say they, you may have it; but withal they will give him a gripe, perhaps make him pay as much, or more, for it at home, as they can get when they have carried it five miles to a market, yea, and that too for the refuse of their commodity. But in this the women are especially faulty, in the sale of their butter and cheese, &c. Now this is a kind of extortion, it is a making a prey of the necessity of the poor, it is a grinding of their faces, a buying and selling of them. But above all, your hucksters, that buy up the *Of hucksters.* poor man's victuals by wholesale, and sell it to him again for unreasonable gains, by retail, and as we call it, by piecemeal, they are got into a way, after a stinging rate, to play their game upon such by extortion: I mean such who buy up butter, cheese, eggs, bacon, &c., by wholesale, and sell it again, as they call it, by pennyworths, two pennyworths, a halfpennyworth, or the like, to the poor, all the week after the market is past. These, though I will not condemn them all, do, many of them, bite and pinch the poor by this kind of evil dealing. These destroy the poor because he is poor, and that is a grievous sin. "He that oppresseth the poor to increase his riches, and that giveth to the rich, shall surely come to want." (Prov. xxii. 16.) Therefore he saith again, "Rob not the poor because he is poor, neither oppress the afflicted in the gate; for the Lord will plead their cause, and spoil the soul of those that spoiled them." (Prov. xxii. 22, 23.) Oh, that he that gripeth and grindeth the face of the poor, would take notice of these two scriptures! Here is threatened the destruction of the estate, yea, and of the soul too, of them that oppress the poor. Their soul we shall better see where, and in what condition that is in, when the day of doom is come; but for the estates of such, they usually quickly moulder; and that sometimes all men, and sometimes no man knows how. Besides, these are usurers, yea, they take usury for victuals, which thing the Lord has forbidden. And because they cannot so well do it on the market-day, therefore they do it, as I said, when the market is over; for then the poor fall into their mouths, and are necessitated to have, as they can, for their need, and they are resolved they shall pay soundly for it. Perhaps some will find fault for my meddling thus with other folks' matters, and for my thus prying into the secrets of their iniquity. But to such I would say, since such actions are evil, it is time they were hissed out of the world. For all that do such things, offend against God, wrong their neighbour, and, like Mr. Badman, do provoke God to judgment.

Atten. God knows there is abundance of deceit in the world!

Wise. Deceit! ay, but I have not told you the thousandth part of it; nor is it my business now to rake to the bottom of that dunghill. What would you say, if I should anatomize some of those vile wretches called pawnbrokers, that lend money and goods to poor people, who are by necessity forced to such an inconvenience; and will make, by one trick or other, the interests of what they so lend amount to thirty, forty, yea, sometimes fifty pound by the year; notwithstanding the principal is secured by a sufficient pawn; which they will keep too at last, if they can find any shift to cheat the wretched borrower.

Atten. Say! Why such miscreants are the pest and vermin of the commonwealth, not fit for the society of men; but methinks by some of those things you discoursed before, you seem to import that it is not lawful for a man to make the best of his own.

Wise. If by making the best you mean to sell for as much as by hook or by crook he can get for his commodity, then I say it is not lawful. And if I should say the contrary, I should justify Mr. Badman and all the rest of that gang; but that I never shall do, for the word of God condemns them. But that it is not lawful for a man at all times to sell his commodity for as much as he can, I prove by these reasons. First, if it be lawful for me always to sell my commodity as dear, or for as much as I can, then it is lawful for me to lay aside in my dealing with others good conscience to them, and to God; but it is not lawful for me, in my dealings with others, to lay aside good conscience, &c. Therefore it is not lawful for me always to sell my commodity as dear, or for as much as I can. That it is not lawful to lay aside good conscience in our dealings has already been proved in the former part of our discourse: but that a man must lay it aside that will sell his commodity always as dear, or for as much as he can, is plainly manifest thus. 1. He that will, as is mentioned afore, sell his commodity as dear as he can, must sometimes make a prey of the ignorance of his chapman: but that he cannot do with a good conscience, for that is to overreach, and to go beyond my chapman,

Good conscience must be used in selling.

and is forbidden. (1 Thess. iv. 6.) Therefore he that will sell his commodity, as afore, as dear, or for as much as he can, must of necessity lay aside a good conscience. 2. He that will sell his commodity always as dear as he can, must needs sometimes make a prey of his neighbour's necessity; but that he cannot do with a good conscience, for that is to go beyond and defraud his neighbour, contrary to 1 Thess. iv. 6. Therefore he that will sell his commodity, as afore, as dear, or for as much as he can, must needs cast off and lay aside a good conscience. 3. He that will, as afore, sell his commodity as dear, or for as much as he can, must, if need be, make a prey of his neighbour's fondness; but that a man cannot do with a good conscience, for that is still a going beyond him, contrary to 1 Thess. iv. 6. Therefore he that will sell his commodity as dear, or for as much as he can, must needs cast off, and lay aside a good conscience. The same also may be said for buying; no man may always buy as cheap as he can, but must also use good conscience in buying; the

We must use good conscience in buying.

which he can by no means use and keep, if he buys always as cheap as he can, and that for the reasons urged before. For such will make a prey of the ignorance, necessity, and fondness of their chapman, the which they cannot do with a good conscience. When Abraham would buy a burying-place of the sons of Heth, thus he saith unto them: "Intreat for me to Ephron the son of Zohar, that he may give me the cave of Machpelah, which he hath in the end of his field; for as much money as it is worth shall he give it me." (Gen. xxiii. 8, 9.) He would not have it under foot, he scorned it, he abhorred it: it stood not with his religion, credit, nor conscience. So also when David would buy a field of Ornan the Jebusite, thus he said unto him, "Grant me the place of this threshing-floor, that I may build an altar therein unto the Lord; thou shalt grant it me for the full price." (2 Chron. xxi. 22.) He also, as Abraham, made conscience of this kind of dealing: he would not lie at catch to go beyond, no, not the Jebusite, but will give him his full price for his field. For he knew that there was wickedness, as in selling too dear, so in buying too cheap, therefore he would not do it. There ought therefore to be good conscience used, as in selling so in buying; for it is also unlawful for a man to go beyond, or to defraud his neighbour in buying; yea, it is unlawful to do it in any matter, and God will plentifully avenge that wrong; as I also before have warned and testified. (Lev. xxv. 14.) But, secondly, if it be lawful for me always to sell my commodity as dear, or for as much as I can, then it is lawful for me to deal with my neighbour

Charity must be used in our dealings.

without the use of charity. But it is not lawful for me to lay aside, or to deal with my neighbour without the use of charity, therefore it is not lawful for me always to sell my commodity to my neighbour for as much as I can. A man in dealing should as really design his neighbour's good, profit, and advantage as his own; for this is to exercise charity in his dealing. That I should thus use, or exercise charity towards my neighbour in my buying and selling, &c., with him is evident from the general command, "Let all your things be done in charity." (1 Cor. xvi. 14.) But that a man cannot live in the exercise of charity that selleth as afore, as dear, or that buyeth as cheap as he can, is evident by these reasons:—1 He that sells his commodity as dear, or for as much money always as he can, seeks himself, and himself only. But charity seeketh not her own, not her own only; so then, he that seeks himself, and himself only, as he that sells, as afore, as dear as he can, does, maketh no use of, nor doth he exercise charity in his so dealing. 2. He that selleth his commodity always for as much as he can get, hardeneth his heart against all reasonable entreaties of the buyer; but he that doth so cannot exercise charity in his dealing; therefore it is not lawful for a man to sell his commodity, as afore, as dear as he can. 3. If it be lawful for me to sell my commodity, as afore, as dear as I can, then there can be no sin in my trading, how unreasonably soever I manage my calling, whether by lying, swearing, cursing, cheating; for all this is but to sell my commodity as dear as I can.

There may be, and is, sin in trading. But that there is sin in these is evident; therefore I may not sell my commodity always as dear as I can. 4. He that sells, as afore, as dear as he can, offereth violence to the law of nature, for that saith, "Do unto all men, even as ye would that they should do unto you." (Matt. vii. 12.) Now, was the seller a buyer, he would not that he of whom he buys should sell him always as dear as he can; therefore he should not sell so himself when it is his lot to sell and others to buy of him. 5. He that selleth, as afore, as dear as he can, makes use of that instruction that God hath not given to others, but sealed up in his hand, to abuse his law, and to wrong his neighbour withal, which indeed is contrary to God. God hath given thee more skill, more knowledge and understanding in thy commodity than he hath given to him that would buy of thee. But what! canst thou think that God has given thee this that thou mightest thereby make a prey of thy neighbour? that thou mightest thereby go beyond and beguile thy neighbour? No, verily, but he hath given thee it for his help; that thou mightest in this be eyes to the blind, and save thy neighbour from that damage that his ignorance, or necessity, or fondness would betray him into the hands of. 6. In all that a man does he should have an eye to the glory of God, but that he cannot have that sells his commodity always for as much as he can, for the reasons urged before. 7. All that a man does he should do in the name of the Lord Jesus Christ, that is, as being commanded and authorised to do

it by him; but he that selleth always as dear as he can, cannot so much as pretend to this without horrid blaspheming of that name, because commanded by him to do otherwise. 8. And lastly, in all that a man does he should have an eye to the day of judgment, and to the consideration of how his actions will be esteemed of in that day. Therefore there is not any man can, or ought to sell always as dear as he can, unless he will, yea, he must say, in so doing, I will run the hazard of the trial of that day. "If thou sell ought unto thy neighbour, or buyest ought of thy neighbour, ye shall not oppress one another." (Lev. xxv. 14.)

Atten. But why do you put in those cautionary words—They must not sell always as dear, nor buy always as cheap as they can? Do you not thereby intimate that a man may sometimes do so?

Wise. I do indeed intimate that sometimes the seller may sell as dear, and the buyer buy as cheap as he can; but this is allowable only in these cases: when he that sells is a knave and lays aside all good conscience in selling; or when the buyer is a knave, and lays aside all good conscience in buying. If the buyer therefore lights of a knave, or if the seller lights of a knave, then let them look to themselves; but yet so as not to lay aside conscience, because he that thou dealest with doth so; but how vile or base soever the chapman is, do thou keep thy commodity at a reasonable price: or, if thou buyest, offer reasonable gain for the thing thou wouldest have; and if this will not do with the buyer or seller, then seek thee a more honest chapman. If thou objectest, But I have not skill to know when a pennyworth is before me, get some that have more skill than thyself in that affair, and let them in that matter dispose of thy money. But if there were no knaves in the world these objections need not be made. And thus, my very good neighbour, have I given you a few of my reasons why a man that hath it should not always sell too dear, nor buy as cheap as he can, but should use good conscience to God and charity to his neighbour in both.

Atten. But were some men here to hear you, I believe they would laugh you to scorn.

Wise. I question not that at all, for so Mr. Badman used to do when any man told him of his faults; he used to think himself wiser than any, and would count, as I have hinted before, that he was not arrived to a manly spirit, that did stick or boggle at any wickedness. But let Mr. Badman and his fellows laugh, I will bear it, and still give them good counsel. But I will remember, also, for my further relief and comfort, that thus they that were covetous of old served the Son of God himself. It is their time to laugh now, that they may mourn in time to come. And, I say again, when they have laughed out their laugh, he that useth not good conscience to God, and charity to his neighbour in buying and selling, dwells next door to an infidel, and is near of kin to Mr. Badman.

Atten. Well, but what will you say to this question? You know that there is no settled price set by God upon any commodity that is bought or sold under the sun, but all things that we buy and sell do ebb and flow, as to price, like the tide; how, then, shall a man of a tender conscience do, neither to wrong the seller, buyer, nor himself, in buying and selling of commodities?

Wise. This question is thought to be frivolous by all that are of Mr. Badman's way; it is also difficult in itself, yet I will endeavour to shape you an answer, and that first to the matter of the question—to wit, how a tradesman should, in trading, keep a good conscience, a buyer or seller either; secondly, how he should prepare himself to this work, and live in the practice of it. For the first, he must observe what hath been said before, to wit, he must have conscience to God, charity to his neighbour, and, I will add, much moderation in dealing. Let him, therefore, keep within the bounds of the affirmative of those eight reasons that before were urged to prove that men ought not in their dealing but to do justly and mercifully betwixt man and man, and then there will be no great fear of wronging the seller, buyer, or himself. But particularly to prepare or instruct a man to this work :—1. Let the tradesman or others consider that there is not that in great gettings, and in abundance, which the most of men do suppose; for all that a man has over and above what serves for his present necessity and supply serves only to feed the lusts of the eye. For "what good is there to the owners thereof, save the beholding of them with their eyes?" (Eccles. v. 11.) Men also, many times, in getting of riches, get therewith a snare to their soul: but few get good by getting of them. But this consideration Mr. Badman could not abide. 2. Consider that the getting of wealth dishonestly—as he does that getteth it without good conscience and charity to his neighbour—is a great offender against God. Hence he says, "I have smitten mine hand at thy dishonest gain, which thou hast made." (Ezek. xxii. 13.) It is a manner of speech that shows anger in the very making of mention of the crime. 3. Consider, therefore, that a little honestly gotten, though it may yield thee but a dinner of herbs at a time, will yield more peace therewith than will a stalled ox ill gotten. "Better is a little with righteousness than great revenues without right." (Prov. xvi. 8.) 4. Be thou confident that God's eyes are upon all thy ways, and that he pondereth all thy goings, and also that he marks them, writes them down, and seals them up in a bag against the time to come. 5. Be thou sure that thou rememberest that thou knowest not the day of thy death. Remember, also, that when death comes, God will give thy

substance, for the which thou hast laboured, and for the which perhaps thou hast hazarded thy soul, to one thou knowest not who, nor whether he shall be a wise man or a fool. And, then, "What profit hath he that laboureth for the wind?" (Eccles. v. 16.) Besides, thou shalt have nothing that thou mayest so much as carry away in thine hand. Guilt shall go with thee, if thou hast got it dishonestly; and they, also, to whom thou shalt leave it, shall receive it to their hurt. These things, duly considered, and made use of by thee to the preparing of thy heart to thy calling of buying or selling, I come, in the next place, to show thee how thou shouldst live in the practical part of this art. Art thou to buy or sell? 1. If thou sellest, do not commend; if thou buyest, do not dispraise, any otherwise but to give the thing that thou hast to do with its just value and worth, for thou canst not do otherwise knowingly, but of a covetous and wicked mind. Wherefore else are commodities overvalued by the seller, and also undervalued by the buyer. "It is naught, it is naught, saith the buyer: but, when he has gone his way, then he boasteth." (Prov. xx. 14.) What hath this man done now but lied in the dispraising of his bargain? And why did he dispraise it but of a covetous mind to wrong and beguile the seller? 2. Art thou a seller, and do things grow dear? Set not thy hand to help, or hold them up higher: this cannot be done without wickedness neither; for this is a making of "the shekel great." (Amos viii. 5.) Art thou a buyer, and do things grow dear? use no cunning or deceitful language to pull them down, for that cannot be done but wickedly too. What, then, shall we do, will you say? Why, I answer, leave things to the providence of God, and do thou with moderation submit to his hand. But since, when they are growing dear, the hand that upholds the price is, for the time, more strong than that which would pull it down, that being the hand of the seller, who loveth to have it dear, especially if it shall rise in his hand: therefore I say, do thou take heed, and have not a hand in it; the which thou mayest have to thine own and thy neighbour's hurt these three ways :—(1.) By crying out scarcity, scarcity beyond the truth and state of things; especially take heed of doing this by way of a prognostic for time to come. It was for this for which he was trodden to death in the gate of Samaria that you read of in the book of Kings. (2 Kings vii. 17.) This sin has a double evil in it: it belieth the present blessing of God among us, and it undervalueth the riches of his goodness, which can make all good things to abound towards us. (2.) This wicked thing may be done by hoarding up when the hunger and necessity of the poor calls for it. Now, that God may show his dislike against this, he doth, as it were, license the people to curse such an hoarder up: "He that withholdeth corn, the people shall curse him; but blessing shall be upon the head of him that selleth it." (Prov. xi. 26.) (3.) But if things will rise, do thou be grieved; be also moderate in all thy sellings, and be sure let the poor have a penny-worth, and sell thy corn to those in necessity: which then thou wilt do when thou showest mercy to the poor in thy selling to him, and when thou, for his sake, because he is poor, undersellest the market. This is to buy and sell with good conscience: thy buyer thou wrongest not; thy conscience thou wrongest not; thyself thou wrongest not, for God will surely recompense thee. I have spoken concerning corn; but thy duty is to let thy moderation in all things " be known unto all men. The Lord is at hand." (Phil. iv. 5.)

Atten. Well, sir, now I have heard enough of Mr. Badman's naughtiness; pray, now, proceed to his death.

Wise. Why, sir, the sun is not so low; we have yet three hours to-night.

Atten. Nay, I am not in any great haste; but I thought you had even now done with his life.

Wise. Done! no; I have yet much more to say.

Atten. Then he has much more wickedness than I thought he had.

Wise. That may be. But let us proceed. This Mr. Badman, added to all his wickedness this: he was a proud man—a very proud man. He was exceeding proud and haughty in mind. He looked that what he said ought not, must not, be contradicted or opposed. He counted himself as wise as the wisest in the country, as good as the best, and as beautiful as he that had most of it. He took great delight in praising of himself, and as much in the praises that others gave him. He could not abide that any should think themselves above him, or that their wit or personage should by others be set before his. He had scarce a fellowly carriage for his equals; but for those that were of an inferior rank, he would look over them in great contempt, and if at any time he had any remote occasion of having to do with them, he would show great height, and a very domineering spirit. So that in this it may be said that Solomon gave a characteristical note of him when he said, " Proud and haughty scorner is his name who dealeth in proud wrath." (Prov. xxi. 24.) He never thought his diet well enough dressed, his clothes fine enough made, or his praise enough refined.

Atten. This pride is a sin that sticks as close to nature, I think, as most sins. There is uncleanness and pride, I know not of any two gross sins that stick closer to men than they. They have, as I may call it, an interest in nature; it likes them because they most suit its lusts and fancies: and, therefore, no marvel though Mr. Badman

was tainted with pride, since he had so wickedly given up himself to work all iniquity with greediness.

Wise. You say right. Pride is a sin that sticks close to nature, and is one of the first follies wherein it shows itself to be polluted. For even in childhood, even in little children, pride will first of all show itself. It is a hasty, an early appearance of the sin of the soul. It, as I may say, is that corruption that strives for predominancy in the heart, and, therefore, usually comes out first. But, though children are so incident to it, yet, methinks, those of more years should be ashamed thereof. I might at the first have begun with Mr. Badman's pride, only I think it is not the pride in infancy that begins to make a difference betwixt one and another, as did and do those wherewith I began my relation of his life: therefore I passed it over; but now, since he had no more consideration of himself and of his vile and sinful state but to be proud when come to years, I have taken the occasion, in this place, to make mention of his pride.

Atten. But pray, if you can remember them, tell me of some places of Scripture that speak against pride. I the rather desire that, because that pride is now a reigning sin; and I happen sometimes to fall into the company of them that, in my conscience, are proud very much; and I have a mind, also, to tell them of their sin. Now, when I tell them of it, unless I bring God's word, too, I doubt they will laugh me to scorn.

Wise. Laugh you to scorn! the proud man will laugh you to scorn, bring to him what text you can, except God shall smite him in his conscience by the word. Mr. Badman did use to serve them so that did use to tell him of his. And, besides, when you have said what you can, they will tell you they are not proud, and that you are rather the proud man, else you would not judge, nor so malapertly meddle with other men's matters as you do. Nevertheless, since you desire it, I will mention two or three texts. They are these:—" Pride and arrogancy do I hate." (Prov. vii. 13.) " A man's pride shall bring him low." (Prov. xxix. 23.) " And he shall bring down their pride." (Isa. xxv. 11.) " And all the proud, yea, and all that do wickedly, shall be stubble, and the day that cometh shall burn them up, saith the Lord of hosts." (Mal. iv. 1.) This last is a dreadful text. It is enough to make a proud man shake. God, saith he, will make the proud ones as stubble; that is, as fuel for the fire: and the day that cometh shall be like a burning oven, and that day shall burn them up, saith the Lord. But Mr. Badman could never abide to hear pride spoken against, nor that any should say of him, he is a proud man.

Atten. What should be the reason of that?

Wise. He did not tell me the reason; but I

suppose it to be that which is common to all vile persons. They love this vice, but care not to bear its name. The drunkard loves the sin, but loves not to be called a drunkard; the thief loveth to steal, but cannot abide to be called a thief; the whore loveth to commit uncleanness, but loveth not to be called a whore: and so Mr. Badman loved to be proud, but could not abide to be called a proud man. The sweet of sin is desirable to polluted and corrupted man, but the name thereof is a blot in his escutcheon.

Atten. It is true that you have said; but pray how many sorts of pride are there?

Wise. There are two sorts of pride; pride of spirit and pride of body. The first of these is thus made mention of in the Scriptures: " Every one that is proud in heart is an abomination to the Lord." (Prov. xvi. 5.) " An high look, and a proud heart, and the ploughing of the wicked is sin." (Prov. xxi. 4.) " The patient in spirit is better than the proud in spirit." (Eccles. vii. 8.) Bodily pride the Scriptures mention: " In that day the Lord will take away the bravery of their tinkling ornaments about their feet, and their cauls and their round tires like the moon, the chains, and the bracelets, and the mufflers, the bonnets, and the ornaments of the legs, and the headbands, and the tablets, and the earrings, the rings, and nose-jewels, the changeable suits of apparel, and the mantles, and the wimples, and the crisping pins, the glasses, and the fine linen, and the hoods and the vails." (Isa. iii. 18—23.) By these expressions it is evident that there is a pride of body, as well as a pride of spirit, and that both are sin, and so abominable to the Lord. But these texts Mr. Badman could never abide to read, they were to him as Micaiah was to Ahab, they never spake good of him, but evil.

Atten. I suppose that it was not Mr. Badman's case alone, even to malign those texts that speak against their vices; for I believe that most ungodly men, where the Scriptures are, have a secret antipathy against those words of God that do most plainly and fully rebuke them for their sins.

Wise. That is out of doubt; and by that antipathy they show that sin and Satan are more welcome to them than are the more wholesome instructions of life and godliness.

Atten. Well, but not to go off from our discourse of Mr. Badman. You say he was proud; but will you show me now some symptoms of one that is proud?

Wise. Yes, that I will. And first I will show you some symptoms of pride of heart. Pride of heart is seen by outward things, as pride of body in general is a sign of pride of heart; for all proud gestures of the body flow from pride of heart. Therefore Solomon saith, " There is a generation, O how lofty are their eyes, and their

eyelids are lifted up." (Prov. xxx. 13.) And again, " There is that exalteth his gait," (Prov. xvii. 19,) his going. Now these lofty eyes, and this exalting of the gait, is a sign of a proud heart; for both these actions come from the heart. For out of the heart comes pride, in all the visible appearances of it. But more particularly:—1. Heart pride is discovered by a stretched out neck, and by mincing as they go. For the wicked, the proud, have a proud neck, a proud foot, a proud tongue, by which this their going is exalted. This is that which makes them look scornfully, speak ruggedly, and carry it huffingly among their neighbours. 2. A proud heart is a persecuting one: " The wicked in his pride doth persecute the poor." (Ps. x. 2.) 3. A prayerless man is a proud man. (Ps. x. 4.) 4. A contentious man is a proud man. (Ps. xiii. 10.) 5. The disdainful man is a proud man. (Ps. cxix. 51.) 6. The man that oppresses his neighbour is a proud man. (Ps. cxix. 122.) 7. He that hearkeneth not to God's word with reverence and fear is a proud man. (Jer. xiii. 15, 17.) 8. And he that calls the proud happy, is, be sure, a proud man. All these are proud in heart, and this, their pride of heart, doth thus discover itself. (Jer. xliii. 2. Mal. iii. 15.) As to bodily pride, it is discovered, that is something of it, by all the particulars mentioned before; for though they are said to be symptoms of pride of heart, yet they are symptoms of that pride, by their showing of themselves in the body. You know diseases that are within, are seen ofttimes by outward and visible signs, yet by these very signs even the outside is defiled also. So all those visible signs of heart pride are signs of bodily pride also. But to come to more outward signs. The putting on of gold, and pearls, and costly array, the plaiting of the hair, the following of fashions, the seeking by gestures to imitate the proud, either by speech, looks, dresses, goings, or other fool's baubles, of which at this time the world is full, all these, and many more, are signs as of a proud heart, so of bodily pride also. But Mr. Badman would not allow, by any means, that this should be called pride, but rather neatness, handsomeness, comeliness, cleanliness, &c.; neither would he allow that following of fashions was anything else, but because he would not be proud, singular, and esteemed fantastical by his neighbours.

Atten. But I have been told that when some have been rebuked for their pride, they have turned it again upon the brotherhood of those by whom they have been rebuked, saying, " Physician, heal thy friends, look at home, among your brotherhood, even among the wisest of you, and see if you yourselves be clear, even your professors; for who is prouder than your professors? scarce the devil himself."

Wise. My heart aches at this, because there is

too much cause for it. This very answer would Mr. Badman give his wife, when she, as she would sometimes, reprove him for his pride. We shall have, says he, great amendments in living now, for the devil is turned a corrector of vice ; for no sin reigneth more in the world, quoth he, than pride among professors. And who can contradict him ? Let us give the devil his due ; the thing is too apparent for any man to deny. And I doubt not but the same answer is ready in the mouths of Mr. Badman's friends ; for they may and do see pride display itself in the apparel and carriages of professors, one may say, almost as much as among any people in the land, the more is the pity. Ay, and I fear that even their extravagances in this hath hardened the heart of many an one, as I perceive it did somewhat the heart of Mr. Badman himself. For my own part, I have seen many myself, and those church-members too, so decked and bedaubed with their fangles and toys,—and that when they have been at the solemn appointments of God, in the way of his worship,—that I have wondered with what face such painted persons could sit in the place where they were without swooning. But certainly the holiness of God, and also the pollution of themselves by sin, must need be very far out of the minds of such people, what profession soever they make. I have read of "a whore's forehead," (Jer. iii. 3,) and I have read of Christian shamefacedness, (1 Tim. ii. 9,) I have read of costly array, and of that which becometh women professing godliness, with good works, (1 Pet. iii. 1—3 ;) but if I might speak, I know what I know, and could say, and yet do no wrong, that which would make some professors stink in their places, (Jer. xxiii. 15 ;) but now I forbear.

Atten. Sir, you seem greatly concerned at this, but what if I shall say more ? It is whispered that some good ministers have countenanced their people in their light and wanton apparel, yea, have pleaded for their gold and pearls, and costly array.

Wise. I know not what they have pleaded for, but it is easily seen that they tolerate, or at leastwise wink and connive at such things, both in their wives and children. And so "from the prophets of Jerusalem is profaneness gone forth into all the land." (Jer. xxiii. 15.) And when the hand of the rulers are chief in a trespass, who can keep their people from being drowned in that trespass ?

Atten. This is a lamentation, and must stand for a lamentation.

Wise. So it is, and so it must. And I will add, it is a shame, it is a reproach, it is a stumbling-block to the blind ; for though men be as blind as Mr. Badman himself, yet they can see the foolish lightness that must needs be the bottom of all these apish and wanton extravagances. But many have their excuses ready—to wit, their parents, their

Professors guilty of the sin of pride.

Pride in professors a stumbling-block.

husbands, and their breeding calls for it, and the like ; yea, the examples of good people prompt them to it : but all these will be but the spider's web, when the thunder of the word of the great God shall rattle from heaven against them, as it will at death or judgment ; but I wish it might do it before. But alas! these excuses are but bare pretences, these proud ones love to have it so. I once talked with a maid by way of reproof, for her fond and gaudy garment. But she told me the tailor would make it so ; when alas, poor proud girl, she gave order to the tailor so to make it. Many make parents, and husbands, and tailors, &c., the blind to others; but their naughty hearts, and their giving of way thereto, that is the original cause of all these evils.

Atten. Now you are speaking of the cause of pride, pray show me yet further why pride is now so much in request.

Wise. I will show you what I think are the reasons of it. 1. The first is, because such persons are led by their own hearts, rather than by the word of God. I told you before, that the original fountain of pride is the heart. For out of the heart comes pride : it is, therefore, because they are led by their hearts, which naturally tends to lift them up in pride. This pride of heart tempts them, (Obad. 3,) and by its deceits overcometh them ; yea, it doth put a bewitching virtue into their peacock's feathers, and then they are swallowed up with the vanity of them. 2. Another reason why professors are so proud—for those we are talking of now—is because they are more apt to take example by those that are of the world, than they are to take example of those that are saints indeed. Pride is of the world : "For all that is in the world, the lust of the flesh, the lust of the eyes, and the pride of life, is not of the Father, but of the world." (1 John ii. 16.) Of the world, therefore, professors learn to be proud. But they should not take them for example. It will be objected, "No, nor your saints neither, for you are as proud as others ;" well, let them take shame that are guilty. But when I say, professors should take example for their life by those that are saints indeed, I mean as Peter says, they should take example of those that were in old time the saints : for saints of old time were the best, therefore to these he directed us for our pattern. Let the wives' conversation be chaste, and also coupled with fear. "Whose adorning," saith Peter, "let it not be that outward adorning of plaiting the hair, and of wearing of gold, or of putting on of apparel ; but let it be the hidden man of the heart, in that which is not corruptible, even the ornament of a meek and quiet spirit, which is, in the sight of God, of great price. For after this manner, in the old time, the holy women also, who trusted in God, adorned themselves, being in subjection unto their own husbands." (1 Pet. iii. 3—5.) 3. Another reason is, because

Why pride is in such request.

they have forgotten the pollution of their nature: for the remembrance of that must needs keep us humble, and being kept humble, we shall be at a distance from pride. The proud and the humble are set in opposition; "God resisteth the proud, but giveth grace unto the humble." And can it be imagined that a sensible Christian should be a proud one; sense of baseness tends to lay us low, not to lift us up with pride; not with pride of heart, nor pride of life. But when a man begins to forget what he is, then he, if ever, begins to be proud. Methinks it is one of the most senseless and ridiculous things in the world, that a man should be proud of that which is given him on purpose to cover the shame of his nakedness with. 4. Persons that are proud have gotten God and his holiness out of their sight. If God was before them, as he is behind their back, and if they saw him in his holiness, as he sees them in their sins and shame, they would take but little pleasure in their apish knacks. The holiness of God makes the angels cover their faces, crumbles Christians, when they behold it, into dust and ashes. And as his majesty is, such is his word; therefore they abuse it, that bring it to countenance pride. Lastly, but what can be the end of those that are proud in the decking of themselves after their antic manner? Why are they for going with their bull's foretops, with their naked shoulders, and paps hanging out like a cow's bag? Why are they for painting their faces, for stretching out their neck, and for putting of themselves unto all the formalities which proud fancy leads them to? Is it because they would honour God? because they would adorn the gospel? because they would beautify religion, and make sinners to fall in love with their own salvation? No, no; it is rather to please their lusts, to satisfy their wild and extravagant fancies; and I wish none doth it to stir up lust in others, to the end they may commit uncleanness with them. I believe whatever is their end, this is one of the great designs of the devil: and I believe also, that Satan has drawn more into the sin of uncleanness by the spangling show of fine clothes than he could possibly have drawn unto it without them. I wonder what it was that of old was called the attire of an harlot; certainly it could not be more bewitching and tempting than are the garments of many professors this day.

Atten. I like what you say very well, and I wish that all the proud dames in England that profess were within the reach and sound of your words.

Wise. What I have said, I believe is true; but as for the proud dames in England that profess, they have Moses and the prophets, and if they will not hear them, how then can we hope that they should receive good by such a dull-sounding ram's horn as I am? However, I have said my mind; and now, if you will, we will proceed to some other of Mr. Badman's doings.

Atten. No; pray, before you show me anything else of Mr. Badman, show me yet more particularly the evil effects of this sin of pride.

Wise. With all my heart, I will answer your request. 1. Then, it is pride that makes poor man so like the devil in hell, that he cannot in it be known The evil effects of pride. to be the image and similitude of God. The angels, when they became devils, it was through their being lifted, or puffed up with pride. It is pride also that lifteth or puffeth up the heart of the sinner, and so makes him to bear the very image of the devil. 2. Pride makes a man so odious in the sight of God, that he shall not, must not, come nigh his majesty. "Though the Lord be high, yet hath he respect unto the lowly, but the proud he knoweth afar off." (Ps. cxxxviii. 6.) Pride sets God and the soul at a distance; pride will not let a man come nigh God, nor God will not let a proud man come nigh unto him. Now this is a dreadful thing. 3. As pride sets, so it keeps God and the soul at a distance. "God resisteth the proud," (James iv. 6;) resists, that is, he opposes him, he thrusts him from him, he contemneth his person and all his performances. Come into God's ordinances the proud man may; but come into his presence, have communion with him, or blessing from him, he shall not. For the high God doth resist him. 4. The word saith that "the Lord will destroy the house of the proud." He will destroy his house; it may be understood, he will destroy him and his. So he destroyed proud Pharaoh, so he destroyed proud Korah, and many others. 5. Pride, where it comes, and is entertained, is a certain forerunner of some judgment that is not far behind. When pride goes before, shame and destruction will follow after. "When pride cometh, then cometh shame." (Prov. xi. 2.) "Pride goeth before destruction, and an haughty spirit before a fall." (Prov. xvi. 18.) 6. Persisting in pride makes the condition of a poor man as remediless as is that of the devils themselves. And this I fear was Mr. Badman's condition, and that was the reason that he died so as he did; as I shall show you anon. But what need I thus talk of the particular actions, or rather the prodigious sins of Mr. Badman, when his whole life, and all his actions, went as it were to A general character of Mr. Badman. the making up of one massy body of sin? Instead of believing that there was a God, his mouth, his life, and actions, declared that he believed no such thing. "The transgressions of the wicked saith within my heart, that there is no fear of God before his eyes." (Ps. xxxvi. 1.) Instead of honouring of God, and of giving glory to him for any of his mercies, or under any of his good providences towards him,—for God is good to A brief relation of Mr. Badman's ways. all, and lets his sunshine and his rain fall upon the unthankful and the unholy,—he would ascribe the glory to other causes. If they were mercies, he would ascribe them—if the open face of the providence did not give him the lie—to his own wit, labour, care, industry, or the like. If they were crosses, he would ascribe them, or count them the offspring of fortune, ill luck, chance, the ill management of matters, the ill will of neighbours, or to his wife's being religious, and spending, as he called it, too much time in reading, praying, or the like. It was not in his way to acknowledge God —that is, graciously—or his hand in things. But, as the prophet saith, " Let favour be showed to the wicked, yet will he not learn righteousness." (Isa. xxvi. 10.) And again, "The people turneth not unto him that smiteth them, neither do they seek the Lord of hosts." (Isa. ix. 13.) This was Mr. Badman's temper; neither mercies nor judgment would make him seek the Lord. Nay, as another scripture says, he would not see the works of God, nor regard the operations of his hands, either in mercies or in judgments. But further, when by providence he has been cast under the best means for his soul,—for, as was showed before, he having had a good master, and before him a good father, and after all a good wife, and being sometimes upon a journey, and cast under the hearing of a good sermon, as he would sometimes for novelty's sake go to hear a good preacher,—he was always without heart to make use thereof. " In this land of righteousness he would deal unjustly, and would not behold the majesty of the Lord." (Isa. xxvi. 10.) Instead of

Mr. Badman's judgment of the Scriptures.

reverencing the word, when he heard it preached, read, or discoursed of, he would sleep, talk of other business, or else object against the authority, harmony, and wisdom of the Scriptures—saying, " How do you know them to be the word of God? how do you know that these sayings are true?" The Scriptures, he would say, were as a nose of wax, and a man may turn them whithersoever he lists. One scripture says one thing, and another says the quite contrary; besides, they make mention of a thousand impossibilities; they are the cause of all dissensions and discords that are in the land. Therefore you may, would he say, still think what you will, but in my mind, they are best at ease that have least to do

Good men Mr. Badman's song.

with them. Instead of loving and honouring of them that did bear in their foreheads the name, and in their lives the image of Christ, they should be his song, the matter of his jests, and the objects of his slanders. He would either make a mock at their sober deportment, their gracious language, quiet behaviour, or else desperately swear that they did all in deceit and hypocrisy. He would endeavour to render godly men as odious and contemptible as he could. Any lies that were made by any, to their disgrace, those he would avouch for truth, and would not endure to be controlled. He was much like those that the prophet speaks of, that would sit and slander his mother's son; yea, he would speak reproachfully of his wife, though his conscience told him, and many would testify, that she was a very virtuous woman. He would also raise slanders of his wife's friends himself, affirming that their doctrine tended to lasciviousness, and that in their assemblies they acted and did unbeseeming men and women, that they committed uncleanness, &c. He was much like those that affirmed the apostle should say, " Let us do evil that good may come." (Rom. iii. 8.) Or like those of whom it is thus written, " Report, say they, and we will report it." (Jer. xx. 10.) And if he could get anything by the end that had any scandal in it, if it did but touch professors, how falsely soever reported, oh! then he would glory, laugh, and be glad, and lay it upon the whole party, saying, " Hang them rogues, there is not a barrel better herring of all the holy brotherhood of them. ' Like to like,' quoth the devil to the collier, this is your precise crew." And then he would send all home with a curse.

Atten. If those that make profession of religion be wise, Mr. Badman's watchings and words will make them the more wary, and careful in all things.

The markings of the wicked should make us careful.

Wise. You say true. For when we see men do watch for our halting, and rejoice to see us stumble and fall, it should make us the more careful. I do think it was as delightful to Mr. Badman to hear, raise, and tell lies, and lying stories of them that fear the Lord, as it was for him to go to bed when a weary. But we will at

Badman delights in lying.

this time let these things pass. For as he was in these things bad enough, so he added to these many more the like. He was an angry, wrathful, envious man, a man that knew not what meekness or gentleness meant, nor did he desire to learn.

Badman an angry, envious man.

His natural temper was to be surly, huffy, and rugged, and worse; and he so gave way to his temper, as to this, that it brought him to be furious and outrageous in all things, especially against goodness itself, and against other things too, when he was displeased.

Atten. Solomon saith, he is a fool that rageth. (Prov. xiv. 16.)

Wise. He doth so; and says moreover, that " anger resteth in the bosom of fools." (Eccles. vii. 9.) And, truly, if it be a sign of a fool to have anger rest in his bosom, then was Mr. Badman, notwithstanding the conceit that he had of his own abilities, a fool of no small size.

Atten. Fools are mostly most wise in their own eyes.

Wise. True: but I was a saying, that if it be a sign that a man is a fool, when anger rests in his bosom, then what is it a sign of, think you, when malice and envy rest there? For, to my knowledge, Mr. Badman was as malicious and as envious a man as commonly you can hear of.

Atten. Certainly, malice and envy flow from pride and arrogance, and they again from ignorance, and ignorance from the devil. And I thought, that since you spake of the pride of Mr. Badman before, we should have something of these before we had done.

Wise. Envy flows from ignorance indeed. And this Mr. Badman was so envious an one, where he set against, that he would swell with it as a toad, as we say, swells with poison. He whom he maligned might at any time even read envy in his face wherever he met with him, or in whatever he had to do with him. His envy was so rank and strong, that if it at any time turned its head against a man, it would hardly ever be pulled in again. He would watch over that man to do him mischief, as the cat watches over the mouse to destroy it; yea, he would wait seven years, but he would have an opportunity to hurt him, and when he had it, he would make him feel the weight of his envy. Envy is a devilish thing, the scripture intimates that none can stand before it: "A stone is heavy, and the sand weighty; but a fool's wrath is heavier than them both. Wrath is cruel, and anger is outrageous; but who can stand before envy?" (Prov. xvii. 3, 4.) This envy, for the foulness of it, is reckoned among the foulest villanies that are, as adultery, murder, drunkenness, revellings, witchcrafts, heresies, seditions, &c.; yea, it is so malignant a corruption, that it rots the very bones of him in whom it dwells: "A sound heart is the life of the flesh; but envy the rottenness of the bones." (Prov. xiv. 30.)

Atten. This envy is the very father and mother of a great many hideous and prodigious wickednesses. I say, it is the very father and mother of them; it both begets them, and also nourishes them up, till they come to their cursed maturity in the bosom of him that entertains them.

Wise. You have given it a very right description, in calling of it the father and mother of a great many other prodigious wickednesses; for it is so venomous and vile a thing, that it puts the whole course of nature out of order, and makes it fit for nothing but confusion, and a hold for every evil thing: "For where envying and strife is, there is confusion, and every evil work." (James iii. 16.) Wherefore, I say, you have rightly called it the very father and mother of a great many other sins. And now for our further edification, I will reckon up of some of the births of envy. 1. Envy, as I told you before, it rotteth the very bones of him that entertains it. And, 2. As you have also hinted, it is heavier than a stone, than sand; yea, and I will add, it falls like a millstone upon the head. Therefore, 3. It kills him that throws it, and him at whom it was thrown. "Envy slayeth the silly one." (Job v. 2.) That is, him in whom it resides, and him who is its object. 4. It was that also that slew Jesus Christ himself; for his adversaries persecuted him through their envy.

5. Envy was that, by virtue of which Joseph was sold by his brethren into Egypt. 6. It is envy that hath the hand in making of variance among God's saints. 7. It is envy in the hearts of sinners, that stirs them up to thrust God's ministers out of their coasts. 8. What shall I say? It is envy that is the very nursery of whisperings, debates, backbitings, slanders, reproaches, murders, &c. It is not possible to repeat all the particular fruits of this sinful root. Therefore, it is no marvel that Mr. Badman was such an ill-natured man, for the great roots of all manner of wickedness were in him, unmortified, unmaimed, and untouched.

Atten. But it is a rare case, even this of Mr. Badman, that he should never in all his life be touched with remorse for his ill-spent life.

Wise. Remorse, I cannot say he ever had, if by remorse you mean repentance for his evils. Yet twice I remember he was under some trouble of mind about his condition: once when he broke his leg as he came home drunk from the alehouse; and another time when he fell sick, and thought he should die. Besides these two times, I do not remember any more.

Atten. Did he break his leg, then?

Wise. Yes; once as he came home drunk from the alehouse.

Atten. Pray how did he break it?

Wise. Why upon a time he was at an alehouse, that wicked house about two or three miles from home, and having there drank hard the greatest part of the day, when night was come, he would stay no longer, but calls for his horse, gets up, and, like a madman, as drunken persons usually ride, away he goes, as hard as horse could lay legs to the ground. Thus he rid, till coming to a dirty place, where his horse flouncing in, fell, threw his master, and with his fall broke his leg; so there he lay. But you would not think how he swore at first. But after awhile, he coming to himself, and feeling by his pain, and the uselessness of his leg, what case he was in, and also fearing that this bout might be his death, he began to cry out after the manner of such, "Lord, help me! Lord, have mercy upon me! Good God, deliver me!" and the like. So there he lay, till some came by, who took him up, carried him home, where he lay for some time, before he could go abroad again.

Atten. And then you say he called upon God.

Wise. He cried out in his pain, and would say, "O God," and "O Lord, help me!" But whether it was that his sin might be pardoned, and his soul saved, or whether to be rid of his pain, I will not positively determine; though I fear it was but for the last; because when his pain was gone, and he had got hopes of mending, even before he could go abroad, he cast off prayer, and began his old game; to wit, to be as bad as he was before. He then would send for his old companions; his sluts also would come to his house to see him, and with them he would be, as well as he could for his lame leg, as vicious as they could be for their hearts.

Atten. It was a wonder he did not break his neck.

Wise. His neck had gone instead of his leg, but that God was long-suffering towards him; he had deserved it ten thousand times over. There have been many, as I have heard, and as I have hinted to you before, that have taken their horses when drunk as he; but they have gone from the pot to the grave; for they have broken their necks betwixt the alehouse and home. One hard by us also drunk himself dead; he drank, and died in his drink.

Atten. It is a sad thing to die drunk.

Wise. So it is. But yet I wonder that no more do so. For considering the hei-
How many sins do accompany drunkenness. nousness of that sin, and with how many other sins it is accompanied, as with oaths, blasphemies, lies, re-vellings, brawlings, &c., it is a wonder to me, that any *that* live in that sin should escape such a blow from heaven, that should tumble them into their graves. Besides, when I consider also how, when they are as drunk as beasts, they, without all fear of danger, will ride like bedlams and madmen, even as if they did dare God to meddle with them' if he durst, for their being drunk: I say, I won-der that he doth not withdraw his protecting pro-vidences from them, and leave them to those dangers and destructions that by their sin they have deserved, and that by their bedlam madness they would rush themselves into. Only I consider again, that he hath appointed a day wherein he will reckon with them, and doth also commonly make examples of some, to show that he takes notice of their sin, abhors their way, and will count with them for it at the set time.

Atten. It is worthy of our remark, to take notice how God, to show his dislike of the sins of men, strikes some of them down with a blow; as the breaking of Mr. Badman's leg, for doubtless that was a stroke from heaven.

Wise. It is worth our remark indeed. It was an open stroke, it fell upon him while he was
An open stroke. in the height of his sin: and it looks much like to that in Job. "Therefore he knoweth their works, and over-turneth them in the night, so that they are destroyed. He striketh them as wicked men in the open sight of others," (Job xxxiv. 25, 26,) or, as the margin reads it, "in the place of beholders." He lays them with his stroke in the place of beholders. There was Mr. Badman laid, his stroke was taken notice of by every one. His broken leg was at this time the town talk. "Mr. Badman has broke his leg," says one. "How did he break it?" says another. "As he came home drunk from such an alehouse," says a third. "A judgment of God upon him," said a fourth. This his sin, his shame, and punishment, are all made conspicuous to all that are about him. I will here

tell you another story or two. I have read in Mr. Clark's "Looking-glass for Sinners," that upon a time, a certain drunken fellow boasted in his cups, that there was neither heaven nor hell; also he said, he believed that man had no soul, and that for his own part, he would sell his soul to any that would buy it. Then did one of his companions buy it of him for a cup of wine, and presently the devil, in man's shape, bought it of that man again at the same price; and so in the presence of them all laid hold on the soul-seller and carried him away through the air, so that he was never more heard of. He tells us also, that there was one at Salisbury, in the midst of his health-drinking and carousing in a tavern, and he drank a health to the devil, saying, that if the devil would not come and pledge him, he would not believe that there was either God or devil. Whereupon his companions, stricken with fear, hastened out of the room: and presently after, hearing a hideous noise, and smelling a stinking savour, the vintner ran up into the chamber, and coming in, he missed his guest, and found the window broken, the iron bar in it bowed, and all bloody: but the man was never heard of after-wards. Again, he tells us of a bailiff of Hedley, who upon a Lord's day being drunk at Melford, got upon his horse to ride through the streets, saying, that his horse would carry him to the devil; and presently his horse threw him, and broke his neck. These things are worse than the breaking of Mr. Badman's leg, and should be a caution to all of his friends that are living, lest they also fall by their sin into these sad judgments of God. But, as I said, Mr. Badman quickly forgot all; his conscience was choked, before his leg was healed. And therefore, before he was well of the fruit of one sin, he tempts God to send another judgment to seize upon him: and so he did quickly after. For not many Mr. Badman fallen sick. months after his leg was well, he had a very dangerous fit of sickness, insomuch that now he began to think he must die in very deed.

Atten. Well, and what did he think and do then?

Wise. He thought he must go to hell; this I know, for he could not forbear but say so. To my best remembrance, he lay crying His conscience is wounded. out all one night for fear, and at times he would so tremble, that he would make the very bed shake under him. But oh! how the thoughts of death, of hell-fire, and of eternal judgment, did then wrack his conscience. Fear might be seen in his face, and in his tossings to and fro: it might also be heard in his words, and be understood by his heavy groans. He would often cry, I am undone, I am undone; my vile life has undone me.

Atten. Then his former atheistical thoughts and principles were too weak now to support him from the fears of eternal damnation.

Wise. Ay! they were too weak indeed. They may serve to stifle conscience when a man is in the midst of his prosperity, and to harden the heart against all good counsel when a man is left of God, and given up to his reprobate mind; but alas! atheistical thoughts, notions, and opinions, must shrink and melt away when God sends, yea, comes with sickness to visit the soul of such a sinner for his sin. There was a man dwelt about twelve miles off from us, that had so trained up himself in his atheistical notions, that at last he attempted to write a book against Jesus Christ, and against the divine authority of the Scriptures; but I think it was not printed. Well, after many days God struck him with sickness, whereof he died. So, being sick, and musing upon his former doings, the book that he had written came into his mind, and with it such a sense of his evil in writing of it, that it tore his conscience as a lion would tear a kid. He lay therefore upon his death-bed in sad case, and much affliction of conscience; some of my friends also went to see him: and as they were in his chamber one day, he hastily called for pen, ink, and paper, which when it was given him, he took it, and writ to this purpose: I, such a one, in such a town, must go to hell-fire, for writing a book against Jesus Christ, and against the holy Scriptures: and would also have leaped out of the window of his house to have killed himself, but was by them prevented of that: so he died in his bed, such a death as it was. It will be well if others take warning by him.

His atheism will not help him now.

Atten. This is a remarkable story.

Wise. It is as true as remarkable. I had it from them that I dare believe, who also themselves were eye and ear witnesses; and also that catched him in their arms, and saved him when he would have leaped out of his chamber window, to have destroyed himself.

Atten. Well, you have told me what were Mr. Badman's thoughts now, being sick, of his condition; pray tell me also what he then did when he was sick?

Wise. Did? He did many things, which I am sure he never thought to have done, and which, to be sure, was not looked for of his wife and children. In this fit of sickness, his thoughts were quite altered about his wife; I say his thoughts, so far as could be judged by his words and carriages to her. For she was his good wife, his godly wife, his honest wife, his duck and dear, and all. Now he told her that she had the best of it, she having a good life to stand by her, while his debaucheries and ungodly life did always stare him in the face. Now he told her the counsel that she often gave him was good, though he was so bad as not to take it. Now he would hear her talk to him, and he would lie sighing by her while she so did. Now he would bid her pray for him, that he might be delivered from hell. He would also now consent, that some of her good ministers might come to him to com-

What Mr. Badman did more when he was sick.

fort him; and he would seem to show them kindness when they came, for he would treat them kindly with words, and hearken diligently to what they said, only he did not care that they should talk much of his ill-spent life, because his conscience was clogged with that already. He cared not now to see his old companions, the thoughts of them were a torment to him; and now he would speak kindly to that child of his that took after its mother's steps, though he could not at all abide it before. He also desired the prayers of good people, that God of his mercy would spare him a little longer, promising that if God would but let him recover this once, what a new, what a penitent man he would be toward God, and what a loving husband he would be to his wife; what liberty he would give her, yea, how he would go with her himself to hear her ministers, and how they should go hand in hand in the way to heaven together.

Atten. Here was a fine show of things. I'll warrant you, his wife was glad for this.

Wise. His wife? Ay, and a many good people besides. It was noised all over the town what a great change there was wrought upon Mr. Badman; how sorry he was for his sins, how he began to love his wife, how he desired good men should pray to God to spare him; and what promises he now made to God in his sickness, that if ever he should raise him from his sick-bed to health again, what a new penitent man he would be towards God, and what a loving husband to his good wife. Well, ministers prayed, and good people rejoiced, thinking verily that they now had gotten a man from the devil; nay, some of the weaker sort did not stick to say that God had begun a work of grace in his heart; and his wife, poor woman, you cannot think how apt she was to believe it so; she rejoiced, and she hoped as she would have it. But, alas! alas! in little time things all proved otherwise. After he had kept his bed awhile, his distemper began to abate, and he to feel himself better, so he in a little time was so finely mended, that he could walk about the house, and also obtained a very fine stomach to his food; and now did his wife and her good friends stand gaping to see Mr. Badman fulfil his promise of becoming new towards God, and loving to his wife; but the contrary only showed itself. For so soon as ever he had hopes of mending, and found that his strength began to renew, his trouble began to go off his heart, and he grew as great a stranger to his frights and fears, as if he had never had them. But verily, I am apt to think, that one reason of his no more regarding, or remembering of his sick-bed fears, and of being no better for them, was, some words that the doctor that supplied him with physic said to him when he was mending. For as soon as Mr. Badman began to mend, the doctor comes and sits him down by him in his house, and there fell into discourse with him

Mr. Badman recovers, and returns to his old course.

about the nature of his disease; and among other things they talked of Badman's trouble, and how he would cry out, tremble, and express his fears of going to hell when his sickness lay pretty hard upon him. To which the doctor replied, that those fears and outcries did arise from the height of his distemper; for that disease was often attended with lightness of the head, by reason the sick party could not sleep, and for that the vapours disturbed the brain. "But you see, sir," quoth he, "that so soon as you got sleep and betook yourself to rest, you quickly mended, and your head settled, and so those frenzies left you." "And was it so indeed," thought Mr. Badman; "were my troubles only the effects of my distemper, and because ill vapours got up into my brain? Then surely, since my physician was my saviour, my lust again shall be my god." So he never minded religion more, but betook him again to the world, his lusts, and wicked companions. And there was an end of Mr. Badman's conversion.

Atten. I thought, as you told me of him, that this would be the result of the whole; for I discerned, by your relating of things, that the true symptoms of conversion were wanting in him, and that those that appeared to be anything like them were only such as the reprobates may have.

Wise. You say right, for there wanted in him, when he was most sensible, a sense of the pollution of his nature; he only had guilt for his sinful actions; the which Cain, and Pharaoh, and Saul, and Judas, those reprobates, have had before him. Besides, the great things that he desired were, to be delivered from going to hell, (and who would willingly?) and that his life might be lengthened in this world. We find not, by all that he said or did, that Jesus Christ the Saviour was desired by him, from a sense of his need of his righteousness to clothe him, and of his spirit to sanctify him. His own strength was whole in him, he saw nothing of the treachery of his own heart; for had he, he would never have been so free to make promises to God of amendment. He would rather have been afraid, that if he had mended, he should have turned with the dog to the vomit, and have begged prayers of saints, and assistance from heaven upon that account, that he might have been kept from doing so. It is true he did beg prayers of good people, and so did Pharaoh of Moses and Aaron, and Simon Magus of Simon Peter. His mind also seemed to be turned to his wife and child; but, alas! it was rather from conviction that God had given him concerning their happy estate over his, than for that he had any true love to the work of God that was in them. True, some shows of kindness he seemed to have for them, and so had rich Dives when in hell, to his five brethren that were yet in the world; yea, he had such love as to wish them in heaven, that they might not come thither to be tormented.

Atten. Sick-bed repentance is seldom good for anything.

Wise. You say true, it is very rarely good for anything indeed. Death is unwelcome to nature, and usually when sickness and death visit the sinner—the first taking of him by the shoulder, and the second standing at the bed-chamber door, to receive him—then the sinner begins to look about him, and to bethink with himself, "These will have me away before God; and I know that my life has not been as it should, how shall I do to appear before God!" Or, if it be more the sense of the punishment of sinners, that also is startling to a defiled conscience, now roused by death's lumbering at the door. And hence usually is sick-bed repentance, and the matter of it; to wit, to be saved from hell, and from death, and that God will restore them again to health till they mend, concluding that it is in their power to mend, as is evident by their large and lavishing promises to do it. I have known many that, when they have been sick, have had large measures of this kind of repentance, and while it has lasted, the noise and the sound thereof has made the town to ring again. But, alas! how long has it lasted? ofttimes scarce so long as until the party now sick has been well. It has passed away like a mist or a vapour—it has been a thing of no continuance. But this kind of repentance is by God compared to the howling of a dog. "And they have not cried unto me with their heart, when they howled upon their beds." (Hosea vii. 14.)

Atten. Yet one may see by this the desperateness of man's heart; for what is it but desperate wickedness to make promise to God of amendment if he will but spare them, and yet so soon as they are recovered, or quickly after, fall to sin as they did before, and never to regard their promise more.

Wise. It is a sign of desperateness indeed; yea, of desperate madness. For, surely, they must needs think, that God took notice of their promise, that he heard the words that they spake, and that he hath laid them up against the time to come; and will then bring out, and testify to their faces, that they flattered him with their mouth, and lied unto him with their tongue, when they lay sick, to their thinking, upon their death-bed, and promised him that if he would recover them they would repent and amend their ways. But thus, as I have told you, Mr. Badman did. He made great promises that he would be a new man, that he would leave his sins, and become a convert, that he would love, &c., his godly wife, &c. Yea, many fine words had Mr. Badman in his sickness, but no good actions when he was well.

Atten. And how did his good wife take it when she saw that he had no amendment, but that he returned with the dog to his vomit, to his old courses again?

Wise. Why, it broke her heart, it was a worse disappointment to her than the cheat that he gave her in marriage—at least she laid it more to heart, and could not so well grapple with it. You must think that she had put up many a prayer to God for him before, even all the time that he had carried it so badly to her, and now, when he was so affrighted in his sickness, and so desired that he might live and mend, poor woman, she thought that the time was come for God to answer her prayers; nay, she did not let [hinder] with gladness, to whisper it out amongst her friends, that it was so. But when she saw herself disappointed by her husband turning rebel again, she could not stand up under it, but falls into a languishing distemper, and in a few weeks gave up the ghost.

Mr. Badman's wife's heart is broken.

Atten. Pray, how did she die?

Wise. Die? She died bravely; full of comfort of the faith of her interest in Christ, and by him, of the world to come. She had many brave expressions in her sickness, and gave to those that came to visit her many signs of her salvation; the thoughts of the grave, but especially of her rising again, were sweet thoughts to her. She would long for death, because she knew it would be her friend. She delivered herself like to some that were making of them ready to go meet their bridegroom. "Now," said she, "I am going to rest from my sorrows, my sighs, my tears, my mournings and complaints. I have heretofore longed to be among the saints, but might by no means be suffered to go, but now I am going, and no man can stop me, to the great meeting, 'to the general assembly and church of the first-born, which are written in heaven.' (Heb. xii. 23.) There I shall have my heart's desire; there I shall worship without temptation or other impediment; there I shall see the face of my Jesus, whom I have loved, whom I have served, and who now I know will save my soul. I have prayed often for my husband, that he might be converted, but there has been no answer of God in that matter. Are my prayers lost? are they forgotten? are they thrown over the bar? No; they are hanged upon the horns of the golden altar, and I must have the benefit of them myself, that moment that I shall enter into the gates, in at which the righteous nation that keepeth truth shall enter. I say, I shall have the benefit of them. I can say as holy David; I say, I can say of my husband, as he could of his enemies: 'As for me, when they were sick, my clothing was of sackcloth; I humbled my soul with fasting, and my prayer returned into mine own bosom.' (Ps. xxxv. 13.) My prayers are not lost, my tears are yet in God's bottle; I would have had a crown, and glory for my husband, and for those of my children that follow his steps; but so far as I can see yet, I must rest in the hope of having all myself."

Her Christian speech.

Her talk to her friends.

Atten. Did she talk thus openly?

Wise. No: this she spake but to one or two of her most intimate acquaintance, who were permitted to come and see her, when she lay languishing upon her death-bed.

Atten. Well, but pray go on in your relation, this is good; I am glad to hear it, this is a cordial to my heart while we sit thus talking under this tree.

Wise. When she drew near her end, she called for her husband, and when he was come to her, she told him, that now he and she must part, and said she, "God knows, and thou shalt know, that I have been a loving, faithful wife unto thee; my prayers have been many for thee; and as for all the abuses that I have received at thy hand, those I freely and heartily forgive, and still shall pray for thy conversion, even as long as I breathe in this world. But, husband, I am going thither, where no bad man shall come, and if thou dost not convert, thou wilt never see me more with comfort: let not my plain words offend thee; I am thy dying wife, and of my faithfulness to thee, would leave this exhortation with thee. Break off thy sins, fly to God for mercy while mercy's gate stands open; remember that the day is coming, when thou, though now lusty and well, must lie at the gates of death, as I do. And what wilt thou then do; if thou shalt be found with a naked soul, to meet with the cherubims with their flaming swords? Yea, what wilt thou then do, if death and hell shall come to visit thee, and thou in thy sins, and under the curse of the law?"

Her talk to her husband.

Atten. This was honest and plain: but what said Mr. Badman to her?

Wise. He did what he could to divert her talk, by throwing in other things; he also showed some kind of pity to her now, and would ask her what she would have? and with various kind of words put her out of her talk: for when she saw that she was not regarded, she fetched a deep sigh, and lay still. So he went down, and then she called for her children, and began to talk to them. And first she spake to those that were rude, and told them the danger of dying before they had grace in their hearts. She told them also, that death might be nearer than they were aware of; and bid them look when they went through the churchyard again, if there was not little graves there. And "Ah, children," said she, "will it not be dreadful to you if we only shall meet at the day of judgment, and then part again, and never see each other more?" And with that she wept, the children also wept; so she held on her discourse. "Children," said she, "I am going from you, I am going to Jesus Christ, and with him there is neither sorrow, nor sighing, nor pain, nor tears, nor death. Thither would I have you go also, but I can neither carry you, nor fetch you

He diverts her discourse.

Her speech to her children that were rude.

thither; but if you shall turn from your sins to God, and shall beg mercy at his hands by Jèsus Christ, you shall follow me, and shall, when you die, come to the place where I am going, that blessed place of rest: and then we shall be for ever together, beholding the face of our Redeemer, to our mutual and eternal joy." So she bid them remember the words of a dying mother when she was cold in her grave, and themselves were hot in their sins, if perhaps her words might put a check to their vice, and that they might remember and turn to God. Then they all went down but her darling, to wit, the child that she had most love for, because it followed her ways. So she ad-

Her speech to her darling. dressed herself to that. "Come to me," said she, "my sweet child, thou art the child of my joy. I have lived to see thee a servant of God; thou shalt have eternal life. I, my sweet heart, shall go before, and thou shalt follow after; if thou shalt 'hold the beginning of thy confidence stedfast unto the end.' (Heb. iii. 14.) When I am gone, do thou still remember my words: love thy Bible, follow my ministers, deny ungodliness still, and if troublesome times shall come, set a higher price upon Christ, his word and ways, and the testimony of a good conscience, than upon all the world besides. Carry it kindly and dutifully to thy father, but choose none of his ways. If thou mayest, go to service, choose that rather than to stay at home; but then be sure to choose a service where thou mayest be helped forwards in the way to heaven; and that thou mayest have such a service, speak to my minister, he will help thee, if possible, to such a one. I would have thee also, my dear child, to love thy brothers and sisters, but learn none of their naughty tricks. 'Have no fellowship with the unfruitful works of darkness, but rather reprove them.' (Eph. v. 11.) Thou hast grace, they have none. Do thou therefore beautify the way of salvation before their eyes, by a godly life and comformable conversation to the revealed will of God, that thy brothers and sisters may see, and be the more pleased with the good ways of the Lord. If thou shalt live to marry, take heed of being served as I was; that is, of being beguiled with fair words; and the flatteries of a lying tongue. But first be sure of godliness; yea, as sure as it is possible for one to be in this world. Trust not thine own eyes, nor thine own judgment: I mean as to that person's godliness that thou art invited to marry. Ask counsel of good men, and do nothing therein, if he lives, without my minister's advice. I have also myself desired him to look after thee." Thus she talked to her children, and gave them counsel, and after she had talked to this a little longer, she kissed it, and bid it go down. Well, in short, her time drew on, and the day that she must die. So

Her death. she died with a soul full of grace, a heart full of comfort, and by her death ended a life full of trouble. Her husband made a funeral for her, perhaps because he was glad he was rid of her, but we will leave that to be manifest at Judgment.

Atten. This woman died well. And now we are talking of the dying of Christians, I will tell you a story of one that died some time since in our town. The man was a godly old Puritan, for so the godly were called in time past. This man, after a long and godly life, fell sick of the sickness whereof he died. And as he lay drawing on, the woman that looked to him thought she heard music, and that the sweetest that she heard in her life, which also continued until he gave up the ghost. Now, when his soul departed from him, the music seemed to withdraw, and to go further and further off from the house, and so it went until the sound was quite gone out of hearing.

Wise. What do you think that might be?

Atten. For aught I know, the melodious notes of angels that were sent of God to fetch him to heaven.

Wise. I cannot say but that God goes out of his ordinary road with us poor mortals sometimes. I cannot say this of this woman, but yet she had better music in her heart than sounded in this woman's ears.

Atten. I believe so; but pray tell me did any of her other children harken to her words, so as to be bettered in their souls thereby?

Wise. One of them did, and became a very hopeful young man; but for the rest I can say nothing.

One of her children converted by her dying words.

Atten. And what did Mr. Badman do after his wife was dead?

Wise. Why, even as he did before, he scarce mourned a fortnight for her, and his mourning then was, I doubt, more in fashion than in heart.

Atten. Would he not sometimes talk of his wife when she was dead?

Wise. Yes, when the fit took him, and could commend her too extremely, saying she was a good, godly, virtuous woman. But this is not a thing to be wondered at. It is common with wicked men to hate God's servants while alive, and to commend them when they are dead. So served the Pharisees the prophets—those of the prophets that were dead they commended, and those that were alive they condemned.

Atten. But did not Mr. Badman marry again quickly?

Wise. No, not for a good while after; and when he was asked the reason, he would make this slight answer: "Who would keep a cow of their own that can have a quart of milk for a penny?" Meaning,

Mr. Badman's base language.

who would be at the charge to have a wife, that can have a whore when he listeth? So villanous, so abominable did he continue after the death of his wife. Yet, at last, there was one was too hard for him. For, getting of him to her upon a time, and making of him sufficiently

He marries again, and how he got his last wife.

drunk, she was so cunning as to get a promise of marriage from him, and so held him to it, and forced him to marry her. And she, as the saying is, was as good as he at all his vile and ranting tricks. She had

What she was, and how they lived.

her companions as well as he had his, and she would meet them too at the tavern and alehouse more commonly than he was aware of. To be plain, she was a very whore, and had as great resort came to her, where time and place was appointed, as any of them all. Ay, and he smelt it too, but could not tell how to help it; for if he began to talk, she could lay in his dish the whores that she knew he haunted, and she could fit him also with cursing and swearing, for she would give him oath for oath, and curse for curse.

Atten. What kind of oaths would she have?

Wise. Why damn her, and sink her, and the like.

Atten. These are provoking things.

Wise. So they are; but God doth not altogether let such things go unpunished in this life. Something of this I have showed you already, and will here give you one or two instances more. There lived, saith one, in the year 1551, in a city of Savoy, a man who was a monstrous curser and swearer, and though he was often admonished and blamed for it, yet would he by no means mend his manners. At length a great plague happening in the city, he withdrew himself into a garden, where being again admonished to give over his wickedness, he hardened his heart more, swearing, blaspheming God, and giving himself to the devil: and immediately the devil snatched him up suddenly, his wife and kinswoman looking on, and carried him quite away. The magistrates advertised hereof, went to the place and examined the women, who justified the truth of it. Also at Oster, in the duchy of Magapole, saith Mr. Clark, a wicked woman used in her cursing to give herself body and soul to the devil, and being reproved for it, still continued the same, till, being at a wedding-feast, the devil came in person, and carried her up into the air, with most horrible outcries and roarings: and in that sort carried her round about the town, that the inhabitants were ready to die for fear. And by and by he tore her in four pieces, leaving her four quarters in four several highways, and brought her bowels to the marriage-feast, and threw them upon the table before the mayor of the town, saying, " Behold these dishes of meat belong to thee, whom the like destruction waiteth for, if thou dost not amend thy wicked life."

Atten. Though God forbears to deal thus with all men that thus rend and tear his name, and that immediate judgments do not overtake them, yet he makes their lives by other judgments bitter to them, does he not?

Wise. Yes, yes, and for proof, I need go no further than to this Badman and his wife, for their railing, and cursing, and swearing ended not in words. They would fight and fly at each other, and that like cats and dogs. But it must be looked upon as the hand and judgment of God upon him for his villany. He had an honest woman before, but she would not serve his turn, and therefore God took her

He is punished in his last wife for his bad carriages towards his first.

away, and gave him one as bad as himself. Thus that measure that he meted to his wife this last did mete to him again. And this is a punishment wherewith sometimes God will punish wicked men. So said Amos to Amaziah : " Thy wife shall be an harlot in the city." (Amos vii. 17.) With this last wife Mr. Badman lived a pretty while, but, as I told you before, in a most sad and hellish manner. And now he would bewail his first wife's death, not of love that he had to her godliness, for that he could never abide, but for that she used always to keep at home, whereas this would go abroad. His first wife was also honest, and true to that relation, but this last was a whore of her body. The first woman loved to keep things together, but this last would whirl them about as well as he. The first would be silent when he chid, and would take it patiently when he abused her, but this would give him word for word, blow for blow, curse for curse, so that now Mr. Badman had met with his match : God had a mind to make him see the baseness of his own life in the wickedness of his wife's. But all would not do with Mr. Badman, he would be Mr. Badman still. This judgment did not work any reformation upon him, no, not to God nor man.

Atten. I warrant you that Mr. Badman thought when his wife was dead, that next time he would match far better.

Wise. What he thought I cannot tell, but he could not hope for it in this match. For here he knew himself to be catched, he knew that he was by this woman entangled, and would therefore have gone back again, but could not. He knew her, I say, to be a whore before, and therefore could not promise himself a happy life with her. For he or she that will not be true to their own soul, will neither be true to husband nor wife. And he knew that she was not true to her own soul, and therefore could not expect she would be true to him. But Solomon says, " A whore is a deep pit," and Mr. Badman found it true. For when she had caught him in her pit, she would never leave him till she had got him to promise her marriage; and when she had taken him so far, she forced him to marry indeed; and after that, they lived that life that I have told you.

Atten. But did not the neighbours take notice of this alteration that Mr. Badman had made?

Wise. Yes; and many of his neighbours, yes, many of those that were carnal, said,

None did pity him.

" It is a righteous judgment of God upon him for his abusive carriage and language to his other wife ;" for they were all convinced that she was a virtuous woman, and that he, vile wretch, had killed her, I will not say *with*, but with the *want* of, kindness.

Atten. And how long, I pray, did they live together?

Wise. Some fourteen or sixteen years, even until (though she also brought something with her) they had sinned all away, and parted as poor as owlets.

Badman and his last wife part as poor as owlets.

And, in reason, how could it be otherwise? he would have his way, and she would have hers; he among his companions, and she among hers; he with his whores, and she with her rogues; and so they brought their noble to ninepence.

Atten. Pray, of what disease did Mr. Badman die, for now I perceive we are come up to his death?

Wise. I cannot so properly say that he died of one disease, for there were many

Mr. Badman's sickness and diseases of which he died.

that had consented, and laid their heads together to bring him to his end. He was dropsical, he was consumptive, he was surfeited, was gouty, and, as some say, he had a tang of the pox in his bowels. Yet the captain of all these men of death that came against him to take him away was the consumption, for it was that that brought him down to the grave.

Atten. Although I will not say but the best men may die of consumption, a dropsy, or a surfeit,—yea, that these may meet upon a man to end him,—yet I will say again that many times these diseases come through man's inordinate use of things. Much drinking brings dropsies, consumptions, surfeits, and many other diseases; and I doubt, that Mr. Badman's death did come by his abuse of himself in the use of lawful and unlawful things. I ground this my sentence upon that report of his life that you at large have given me.

Wise. I think verily that you need not call back your sentence; for it is thought by his cups and his queans he brought himself to this his destruction. He was not an old man when he died, nor was he naturally very feeble, but strong and of a healthy complexion. Yet, as I said, he moultered away, and went, when set a going, rotten to his grave. And that which made him stink when he was dead—I mean that made him stink in his name and fame—was, that he died with a spice of the foul disease upon him: a man whose life was full of sin, and whose death was without repentance.

Atten. These were blemishes sufficient to make him stink indeed.

Wise. They were so, and they did do it. No

Badman's name stinks when he is dead.

man could speak well of him when he was gone. His name rotted above ground as his carcase rotted under. And this is according to the saying of the wise man: "The memory of the just is blessed, but the name of the wicked shall rot." (Prov. x. 7.) This text, in both the parts

of it, was fulfilled upon him and the woman that he married first. For her name still did flourish, though she had been dead almost seventeen years; but his began to stink and rot before he had been buried seventeen days.

Atten. That man that dieth with a life full of sin, and with a heart void of repentance, although he should die of the most golden disease, if there were any that might be so called, I will warrant him his name shall stink, and that in heaven and earth.

Wise. You say true; and therefore doth the name of Cain, Pharaoh, Saul, Judas, and the Pharisees, though dead thousands of years ago, stink as fresh in the nostrils of the world, as if they were but newly dead.

Atten. I do fully acquiesce with you in this. But, sir, since you have charged

That Mr. Badman died impenitent is proved.

him with dying impenitent, pray let me see how you will prove it: not that I altogether doubt it, because you have affirmed it, but yet I love to have a proof of what men say in such weighty matters.

Wise. When I said he died without repentance, I meant, so far as those that knew him could judge, when they compared his life, the word, and his death together.

Atten. Well said; they went the right way to find out whether he had, that is, did manifest that he had repentance or no. Now then show me how they did prove he had none.

Wise. So I will. And first, this was urged to prove it. He had not in all the time of his sickness, a sight and sense of his sins, but was as secure, and as much at quiet, as if he had never sinned in all his life.

Atten. I must needs confess that this is a sign he had none. For how can a man repent of that of which he hath neither sight nor sense? But it is strange that he had neither sight nor sense of sin now, when he had such a sight and sense of his evil before: I mean when he was sick before.

Wise. He was, as I said, as secure now as if he had been as sinless as an angel, though all men knew what a sinner he was, for he carried his sins in his forehead. His debauched life was read and known of all men; but his repentance was read and known of no man; for, as I said, he had none. And, for aught I know, the reason why he had no sense of his sins now, was because he profited not by that sense that he had of them before. He liked not to retain that knowledge of God then, that caused his sins to come to remembrance. Therefore God gave him up now to a reprobate mind, to hardness and stupidity of spirit; and so was that scripture fulfilled upon him, "He hath blinded their eyes," (Isa. vi. 10;) and that, "Let their eyes be darkened that they may not see." (Rom. xi. 10.) Oh! for a man to live in sin; and to go out of the world without repentance for it, is the saddest judgment that can overtake a man.

Atten. But, sir, although both you and I have

consented that without a sight and sense of sin there can be no repentance, yet that is but our bare say so; let us therefore now see if by the Scripture we can make it good.

Wise. That is easily done. The three thousand that were converted, (Acts ii.,) repented not till they had sight and sense of their sins; Paul repented not till he had sight and sense of his sins, (Acts ix.;) the jailer repented not till he had sight and sense of his sins, (Acts xvi.;) nor could they. For of what should a man repent? The answer is, Of sin. What is it to repent of sin? The answer is, To be sorry for it, to turn from it. But how can a man be sorry for it that has neither sight nor sense of it? David did not only commit sins, but abode impenitent for them until Nathan the prophet was sent from God to give him a sight and sense of them; and then, but not till then, he indeed repented of them. (2 Sam. xii.) Job, in order to his repentance, cries unto God, "Show me wherefore thou contendest with me." (Job x. 2.) And again, "That which I see not teach thou me: I have borne chastisement, I will not offend any more." (Job xxxiv. 32.) That is, not in what I know, for I will repent of it; nor yet in what I know not, when thou shalt show me it. Also Ephraim's repentance was after he was turned to the sight and sense of his sins, and after that he was instructed about the evil of them. (Jer. xxxi. 18—20.)

Atten. These are good testimonies of this truth, and do, if matter of fact, with which Mr. Badman is charged, be true, prove indeed that he did not repent, but as he lived so he died in his sin; for without repentance a man is sure to die in his sin; for they will lie down in the dust with him, rise at the judgment with him, hang about his neck like cords and chains when he standeth at the bar of God's tribunal, and go with him too, when he goes away from the judgment-seat, with a "Depart from me, ye cursed, into everlasting fire, prepared for the devil and his angels," (Matt. xxv. 41;) and there shall fret and gnaw his conscience, because they will be to him a never-dying worm.

Wise. You say well, and I will add a word or two more to what I have said. Repentance, as it is not produced without a sight and sense of sin, so every sight and sense of sin cannot produce it: I mean every sight and sense of sin cannot produce that repentance—that is repentance unto salvation—repentance never to be repented of. For it is yet fresh before us, that Mr. Badman had a sight and sense of sin in that fit of sickness that he had before, but it died without procuring any such godly fruit; as was manifest by his so soon returning with the dog to his vomit. Many people think also that repentance stands in confession of sin only, but they are very much mistaken; for repentance, as was said before, is a being sorry for, and returning from transgression to God by Jesus Christ. Now, if this be true,

that every sight and sense of sin will not produce repentance, then repentance cannot be produced there where there is no sight and sense of sin. That every sight and sense of sin will not produce repentance, to wit, the godly repentance that we are speaking of is manifest in Cain, Pharaoh, Saul, and Judas, who all of them had sense, great sense of sin, but none of them repentance unto life. Now I conclude that Mr. Badman did die impenitent, and so a death most miserable.

Atten. But pray, now, before we conclude our discourse of Mr. Badman, give me another proof of his dying in his sins.

Wise. Another proof is this, he did not desire a sight and sense of his sins that he might have repentance for them. Did I say he did not desire it? I will add, he greatly desired to remain in his security. And that I shall prove by that which follows:—First, he could not endure that any man now should talk to him of his sinful life, and yet that was the way to beget a sight and sense of sin, and so of repentance from it, in his soul. But, I say, he could not endure such discourse. Those men that did offer to talk unto him of his ill-spent life, they were as little welcome to him in the time of his last sickness, as was Elijah when he went to meet with Ahab, as he went down to take possession of Naboth's vineyard. "Hast thou found me," said Ahab, "O mine enemy?" (1 Kings xxi. 20.) So would Mr. Badman say in his heart to and of those that thus did come to him, though, indeed, they came even of love, to convince him of his evil life, that he might have repented thereof, and have obtained mercy.

Atten. Did good men then go to see him in his last sickness?

Wise. Yes; those that were his first wife's acquaintance, they went to see him, and to talk with him, and to him, if perhaps he might now, at last, bethink himself, and cry to God for mercy.

Atten. They did well to try now at last if they could save his soul from hell. But, pray, how can you tell that he did not care for the company of such?

Wise. Because of the differing carriage that he had towards them from what he had when his old carnal companions came to see him. When his old companions came to see him, he would stir up himself as much as he could, both by words and looks, to signify they were welcome to him; he would also talk with them freely, and look pleasantly upon them, though the talk of such could be none other but such as David said carnal men would offer to him when they came to visit him in his sickness. "If he come to see me," says he, "he speaketh vanity: his heart gathereth iniquity to itself." (Ps. xli. 6.) But these kind of talks, I say, Mr. Badman better brooked than he did the company of better men. But I will more particularly give you a character of his carriage to good men, and good talk, when they came to see him. 1. When they were come, he would seem to fail in his spirits at the sight of them. 2. He

How Badman carried it to good men when they came to visit him in his last sickness.

would not care to answer them to any of those questions that they would at times put to him to feel what sense he had of sin, death, hell, and judgment ; but would either say nothing, or answer them by way of evasion, or else by telling of them he was so weak and spent that he could not speak much. 3. He would never show forwardness to speak to or talk with them, but was glad when they held their tongues. He would ask them no question about his state and another world, or how he should escape that damnation that he had deserved. 4. He had got a haunt [habit] at last to bid his wife and keeper, when these good people attempted to come to see him, to tell them that he was asleep or inclining to sleep, or so weak for want thereof, that he could not abide any noise. And so they would serve them time after time, till at last they were discouraged from coming to see him any more. 5. He was so hardened now, in this time of his sickness, that he would talk, when his companions came unto him, to the disparagement of those good men, and of their good doctrine too, that of love did come to see him, and that did labour to convert him. 6. When these good men went away from him, he would never say, " Pray when will you be pleased to come again, for I have a desire to more of your company, and to hear more of your good instruction ? " No, not a word of that, but when they were going would scarce bid them drink, or say, " Thank you for your good company and good instruction." 7. His talk in his sickness with his companions would be of the world, as trades, houses, lands, great men, great titles, great places, outward prosperity, or outward adversity, or some such carnal thing. By all which I conclude that he did not desire a sense and sight of his sin, that he might repent and be saved.

Atten. It must needs be so as you say, if these things be true that you have asserted of him. And I do the rather believe them, because I think you dare not tell a lie of the dead.

Wise. I was one of them that went to him, and that beheld his carriage and manner of way ; and this is a true relation of it that I have given you.

Atten. I am satisfied. But, pray, if you can, show me now by the word what sentence God doth pass upon such men ?

Wise. Why, the man that is thus averse to repentance, that desires not to hear of his sins that he might repent and be saved, is said to be a man that saith unto God, " Depart from me, for I desire not the knowledge of thy ways." (Job xxi. 14.) He is a man that says in his heart, and with his actions, " I have loved strangers " (sins), " and after them will I go." (Jer. ii. 25.) He is a man that shuts his eyes,

stops his ears, and that turneth his spirit against God. Yea, he is the man that is at enmity with God, and that abhors him with his soul.

Atten. What other sign can you give me that Mr. Badman died without repentance ?

Wise. Why, he did never heartily cry to God for mercy all the time of his affliction. True, when sinking fits, stitches, or pains took hold upon him, then he would say, as other carnal men used to do, " Lord, help me ! Lord, strengthen me ! Lord, deliver me ! " and the like ; but to cry to God for mercy, that he did not, but lay, as I hinted before, as if he never had sinned.

Atten. That is another bad sign, indeed, for crying to God for mercy is one of the first signs of repentance. When Paul lay repenting of his sin upon his bed, the Holy Ghost said of him, " Behold, he prayeth." (Acts ix. 11.) But he that hath not the first signs of repentance, it is a sign he hath none of the other, and so, indeed, none at all. I do not say but there may be crying where there may be no sign of repentance. " They cried," says David, " to the Lord, but he answered them not," (Ps. xviii. 41,) but that he would have done if their cry had been the fruit of repentance. But, I say, if men may cry, and yet have no repentance, be sure they have none that cry not at all. It is said in Job, " They cry not when he bindeth them," (Job xxxvi. 13 ;) that is, because they have no repentance : no repentance, no cries ; false repentance, false cries ; true repentance, true cries.

Wise. I know that it is as possible for a man to forbear crying that hath repentance, as it is for a man to forbear groaning that feeleth deadly pain. He that looketh into the book of Psalms, where repentance is most lively set forth, even in its true and proper effects, shall there find that crying, strong crying, hearty crying, great crying, and incessant crying, hath been the fruits of repentance ; but none of this had this Mr. Badman, therefore he died in his sins.

That crying is an inseparable effect of repentance is seen in these scriptures :—" Have mercy upon me, O God, according to thy loving-kindness : according unto the multitude of thy tender mercies blot out all my transgressions." (Ps. li. 1.) " O Lord, rebuke me not in thine anger, neither chastise me in thy hot displeasure. Have mercy upon me, O Lord, for I am weak : O Lord, heal me, for my bones are vexed. My soul is also sore vexed : but thou, O Lord, how long ? Return, O Lord, deliver my soul : O save me for thy mercies' sake." (Ps. vi. 1—4.) " O Lord, rebuke me not in thy wrath : neither chastise me in thy hot displeasure. For thy arrows stick fast in me, and thy hand presseth me sore. There is no soundness in my flesh because of thine anger, neither is there any rest in my bones because of my sin. For mine iniquities are gone over mine head : as an heavy burden they are too heavy for me.

My wounds stink, and are corrupt because of my foolishness. I am troubled; I am bowed down greatly; I go mourning all the day long. For my loins are filled with a loathsome disease! and there is no soundness in my flesh. I am feeble, and sore broken: I have roared by reason of the disquietness of my heart." (Ps. xxxviii. 1—8.) I might give you a great number more of the holy sayings of good men, whereby they express how they were, what they felt, and whether they cried or no, when repentance was wrought in them. Alas, alas! it is as possible for a man, when the pangs of guilt are upon him, to forbear praying, as it is for a woman when pangs of travail are upon her, to forbear crying. If all the world should tell me that such a man hath repentance, yet if he is not a praying man, I should not be persuaded to believe it.

Atten. I know no reason why you should, for there is nothing can demonstrate that such a man hath it. But pray, sir, what other sign have you by which you can prove that Mr. Badman died in his sins, and so in a state of damnation?

Wise. I have this to prove it. Those who were his old sinful companions in the time of his health were those whose company and carnal talk he most delighted in in the time of his sickness. I did occasionally hint this before, but now I make it an argument of his want of grace: for where there is indeed a work of grace in the heart, that work doth not only change the heart, thoughts, and desires, but the conversation also; yea, conversation and company too. When Paul had a work of grace in his soul, he essayed to join himself to the disciples: he was for his old companions in their abominations no longer; he was now a disciple, and was for the company of disciples. "And he was with them, coming in and going out at Jerusalem." (Acts ix. 28.)

Atten. I thought something when I heard you make mention of it before. Thought I, this is a shrewd sign that he had not grace in his heart. Birds of a feather, thought I, will flock together. If this man was one of God's children, he would herd with God's children; his delight would be with, and in the company of, God's children. As David said, "I am a companion of all them that fear thee, and of them that keep thy precepts." (Ps. cxix. 63.)

Wise. You say well, for what fellowship hath he that believeth with an infidel? And although it be true, that all that join to the godly are not godly, yet they that shall inwardly choose the company of the ungodly and open profane, rather than the company of the godly, as Mr. Badman did, surely are not godly men, but profane. He was, as I told you, out of his element, when good men did come to visit him; but then he was where he would be, when he had his vain companions about him. Alas! grace, as I said, altereth all—heart, life, company, and all; for by it the heart and man is made new. And a new heart and a new man must have objects of delight that are new, and like himself: "Old things are passed away." Why? For "all things are become new." (2 Cor. v. 17.) Now if all things are become new, to wit, heart, mind, thoughts, desires, and delights, it followeth by consequence that the company must be answerable: hence it is said, that they "that believed were together;" that "they went to their own company;" that they were "added to the church;" that they "were of one heart and of one soul;" and the like. Now if it be objected, that Mr. Badman were sick, and so could not go to the godly, yet he had a tongue in his head, and could, had he had a heart, have spoken to some to call or send for the godly to come to him. Yea, he would have done so; yea, the company of all others, especially his fellow sinners, would, even in every appearance of them, before him, have been a burden and a grief unto him. His heart and affection standing bent to good, good companions would have suited him best. But his companions were his old associates, his delight was in them, therefore his heart and soul were yet ungodly.

Atten. Pray how was he when he drew near his end? for I perceive that what you say of him now hath reference to him and to his actions at the beginning of his sickness. Then he could endure company, and much talk; besides, perhaps then he thought he should recover and not die, as afterwards he had cause to think, when he quite wasted with pining sickness, when he was at the grave's mouth. But how was he, I say, when he was, as we say, at the grave's mouth, within a step of death? when he saw and knew, and could not but know, that shortly he must die, and appear before the judgment of God?

Wise. Why there was not any other alteration in him, than what was made by his disease upon his body. Sickness, you know, will alter the body, also pains and stitches will make men groan; but for his mind he had no alteration there. His mind was the same, his heart was the same. He was the selfsame Mr. Badman still, not only in name but conditions, and that to the very day of his death; yea, so far as could be gathered to the very moment in which he died. *How Mr. Badman was when near his end.*

Atten. Pray how was he in his death? Was death strong upon him? or did he die with ease, quietly?

Wise. As quietly as a lamb. There seemed not to be in it, to standers by, so much as a strong struggle of nature; and as for his mind, it seemed to be wholly at quiet. Pray why do you ask me this question?

Atten. Not for mine own sake, but for others. For there is such an opinion as this among the ignorant: that if a man dies, as they call it like a lamb, that is, quietly, and without that consternation of mind that others show in *The opinion of the ignorant about his manner of dying.*

their death, they conclude, and that beyond all doubt, that such a one is gone to heaven, and is certainly escaped the wrath to come.

Wise. There is no judgment to be made by a quiet death, of the eternal state of him that so dieth. Suppose one man should die quietly, another should die suddenly, and a third should die under great consternation of spirit, no man can judge of their eternal condition by the manner of any of these kinds of deaths. He that dies quietly, suddenly, or under consternation of spirit, may go to heaven, or may go to hell; no man can tell whither a man goes, by any such manner of death. The judgment therefore that we make of the eternal condition of man, must be gathered from another consideration: to wit, did the man die in his sins? did he die in unbelief? did he die before he was born again? then he is gone to the devil and hell, though he died never so quietly. Again, was the man a good man? had he faith and holiness? was he a lover and a worshipper of God by Christ, according to his word? Then he *is* gone to God and heaven, how suddenly, or in what consternation of mind soever he died; but Mr. Badman was naught, his life was evil, his ways were evil, evil to his end. He therefore went to hell and to the devil, how quietly soever he died. Indeed there is, in some cases, a judgment to be made of a man's eternal condition by the manner of the death he dieth. As suppose now a man should murder himself, or live a wicked life, and after that die in utter despair; these men without doubt do both of them go to hell. And here I will take an occasion to speak of two of Mr. Badman's brethren, for you know I told you before that he had brethren, and of the manner of their death. One of them killed himself, and the other after a wicked life died in utter despair. Now I should not be afraid to conclude of both these, that they went by, and through their death to hell.

Atten. Pray tell me concerning the first, how he made away with himself?

Wise. Why, he took a knife and cut his own throat, and immediately gave up the ghost and died. Now what can we judge of such a man's condition; since the scripture saith, "No murderer hath eternal life," &c., but that it must be concluded that such a one is gone to hell. He was a murderer, a self-murderer; and he is the worst murderer, one that slays his own body and soul. Nor do we find mention made of any but cursed ones that do such kind of deeds. I say, no mention made in holy writ of any others, but such that murder themselves. And this is a sore judgment of God upon men, whom God shall for the sins of such give them up to be their own executioners, or rather to execute his judgment and anger upon themselves. And let me earnestly give this caution to sinners: take heed, sirs, break off your sins, lest God serves you as he served Mr. Badman's brother; that is, lest he gives you up to be your own murderers.

Atten. Now you talk of this; I did once know a man, a barber, that took his own razor, and cut his own throat, and then put his head out of his chamber window, to show the neighbours what he had done, and after a little while died.

Wise. I can tell you a more dreadful thing than this; I mean as to the manner of doing the fact. There was about twelve years since, a man that lived at Brafield, by Northampton, named John Cox, that murdered himself. The manner of his doing of it was thus. He was a poor man, and had for some time been sick, and the time of his sickness was about the beginning of hay-time; and taking too many thoughts how he should live afterwards, if he lost his present season of work, he fell into deep despair about the world, and cried out to his wife the morning before he killed himself, saying, "We are undone." But quickly after, he desired his wife to depart the room, because, said he, I will see if I can get any rest; so she went out: but he, instead of sleeping, quickly took his razor, and therewith cut up a great hole in his side, out of which he pulled and cut off some of his guts, and threw them, with the blood, up and down the chamber. But this not speeding of him so soon as he desired, he took the same razor, and therewith cut his own throat. His wife then hearing of him sigh and fetch his wind short, came again into the room to him, and seeing what he had done, she ran out and called in some neighbours, who came to him where he lay in a bloody manner, frightful to behold. Then said one of them to him, "Ah! John, what have you done? Are you not sorry for what you have done?" He answered roughly, "It is too late to be sorry." Then said the same person to him again, "Ah! John, pray to God to forgive this bloody act of thine." At the hearing of which exhortation, he seemed much offended, and in angry manner, said, "Pray!" and with that flung himself away to the wall, and so, after a few gasps, died desperately. When he had turned him of his back to the wall, the blood ran out of his belly as out of a bowl, and soaked quite through the bed to the boards, and through the chinks of the boards it ran pouring down to the ground. Some said, that when the neighbours came to see him, he lay groping with his hand in his bowels, reaching upward, as was thought, that he might have pulled or cut out his heart. It was said also, that some of his liver had been by him torn out and cast upon the boards, and that many of his guts hung out of the bed on the side thereof; but I cannot confirm all particulars; but the general of the story, with these circumstances above mentioned, is true. I had it from a sober and credible person, who himself was one that saw him in this bloody state, and that talked with him, as was hinted before. Many other such dreadful things might be told you, but these are enough, and too many too, if God in his wisdom had thought necessary to prevent them.

Atten. This is a dreadful story. And I would to God that it might be a warning to others to instruct them to fear before God, and pray, lest he gives them up to do as John Cox hath done. For surely self-murderers cannot go to heaven; and therefore, as you have said, he that dieth by his own hands is certainly gone to hell. But speak a word or two of the other man you mentioned.

Wise. What? Of a wicked man dying in despair?

Atten. Yes, of a wicked man dying in despair.

Wise. Well, then, this Mr. Badman's other brother was a very wicked man, both in heart and life: I say in heart, because he was so in life, nor could anything reclaim him; neither good men, good books, good examples, nor God's judgments. Well, after he had lived a great while in his sins, God smote him with a sickness of which he died. Now, in his sickness his conscience began to be awakened, and he began to roar out of his ill-spent life, insomuch that the town began to ring of him. Now, when it was noised about, many of the neighbours came to see him, and to read by him, as is the common way with some; but all that they could do, could not abate his terror, but he would lie in his bed gnashing of his teeth, and wringing of his wrists, concluding upon the damnation of his soul, and in that horror and despair he died, not calling upon God, but distrusting in his mercy, and blaspheming of his name.

Atten. This brings to my mind a man that a friend of mind told me of. He had been a wicked liver; so when he came to die, he fell into despair; and having concluded that God had no mercy for him, he addressed himself to the devil for favour, saying, "Good devil, be good unto me."

Wise. This is almost like Saul, who being forsaken of God, went to the witch of Endor, and so to the devil for help. But alas, should I set myself to collect these dreadful stories, it would be easy in little time to present you with hundreds of them. But I will conclude as I began; they that are their own murderers, or that die in despair, after they have lived a life of wickedness, do surely go to hell. And here I would put in a caution: Every one that dieth under consternation of spirit—that is, under amazement and great fear, do not therefore die in despair; for a good man may have this for his bands in his death, and yet go to heaven and glory. For, as I said before, he that is a good man, a man that hath faith and holiness, a lover and worshipper of God by Christ, according to his word, may die in consternation of spirit: for Satan will not be wanting to assault good men upon their death-bed, but they are secured by the word and power of God; yea, and are also helped, though with much agony of

spirit, to exercise themselves in faith and prayer, the which he that dieth in despair, can by no means do. But let us return to Mr. Badman, and enter further discourse of the manner of his death.

Atten. I think you and I are both of a mind; for just now I was thinking to call you back to him also. And pray now, since it is your own motion to return again to him, let us discourse a little more of his quiet and still death.

Wise. With all my heart. You know we were speaking before of the manner of Mr. Badman's death; how that he died still and quietly; upon which you made observation, that the common people conclude that if a man dies quietly, and as they call it, like a lamb, he is certainly gone to heaven; when alas, if a wicked man dies quietly, if a man that has all his days lived in notorious sin, dieth quietly, his quiet dying is so far off from being a sign of his being saved, that it is an uncontrollable proof of his damnation. This was Mr. Badman's case, he lived wickedly even to the last, and then went quietly out of the world; therefore Mr. Badman is gone to hell. *(margin: Further discourse of Mr. Badman's death.)*

Atten. Well, but since you are upon it, and also so confident in it, to wit, that a man that lives a wicked life till he dies, and then dies quietly, is gone to hell; let me see what show of proof you have for this your opinion.

Wise. My first argument is drawn from the necessity of repentance. No man can be saved except he repents, nor can he repent that sees not, that knows not that he is a sinner; and he that knows himself to be a sinner, will, I warrant him, be molested for the time by that knowledge. This, as it is testified by all the scriptures, so it is testified by Christian experience. He that knows himself to be a sinner, is molested, especially if that knowledge comes not to him until he is cast upon his death-bed—molested, I say, before he can die quietly. Yea, he is molested, dejected, and cast down, he is also made to cry out, to hunger and thirst after mercy by Christ, and if at all he shall indeed come to die quietly—I mean with that quietness that is begotten by faith and hope in God's mercy, to the which Mr. Badman and his brethren were utter strangers—his quietness is distinguished, by all judicious observers, by what went before it, by what it flows from, and also by what is the fruit thereof. I must confess I am no admirer of sick-bed repentance, for I think verily it is seldom good for anything; but I *(margin: Sick-bed repentance seldom good for anything.)* say, he that hath lived in sin and profaneness all his days, as Mr. Badman did, and yet shall die quietly, that is, without repentance steps in betwixt his life and death, he is assuredly gone to hell, and is damned.

Atten. This does look like an argument indeed; for repentance must come, or else we must go to hell-fire; and if a lewd liver shall—I mean that so continues till the day of his death—yet go out of the world quietly, it is a sign that he died without repentance, and so a sign that he is damned.

Wise. I am satisfied in it for my part, and that from the necessity and nature of repentance. It is necessary, because God calls for it, and will not pardon sin without it: "Except ye repent, ye shall all likewise perish." (Luke xiii. 5.) This is that which God hath said, and he will prove but a foolhardy man that shall yet think to go to heaven and glory without it. Repent, for "now also the axe is laid unto the root of the trees; therefore every tree that bringeth not forth good fruit" (but no good fruit can be where there is no sound repentance) "is hewn down, and cast into the fire." (Matt. iii. 10.) This was Mr. Badman's case, he had attending of him a sinful life, and that to the very last, and yet died quietly, that is, without repentance; he is gone to hell and is damned. For the nature of repentance, I have touched upon that already, and showed, that it never was where a quiet death is the immediate companion of a sinful life; and therefore Mr. Badman is gone to hell. My second argument is drawn from that blessed word of Christ, "While the strong man armed keeps the house, his goods are in peace, till a stronger than he comes." But the strong man armed kept Mr. Badman's house—that is, his heart, and soul, and body—for he went from a sinful life quietly out of this world. The stronger did not disturb by intercepting with sound repentance betwixt his sinful life and his quiet death; therefore Mr. Badman is gone to hell. The strong man armed is the devil, and quietness is his security. The devil never fears losing of the sinner, if he can but keep him quiet: can he but keep him quiet in a sinful life, and quiet in his death, he is his own. Therefore he saith his goods are in peace; that is, out of danger. There is no fear of the devil's losing such a soul, I say, because Christ, who is the best judge in this matter, saith his goods are at peace, in quiet, and out of danger.

Atten. This is a good one too; for, doubtless, peace and quiet with sin, is one of the greatest signs of a damnable state.

Wise. So it is; therefore, when God would show the greatness of his anger against sin and sinners in one word, he saith, They are "joined to idols; let them alone." (Hos. iv. 17.) "Let them alone," that is, disturb them not; let them go on without control; let the devil enjoy them peaceably, let him carry them out of the world unconverted quietly. This is one of the sorest of judgments, and bespeaketh the burning anger of God against sinful men. See, also, when you come home, the fourteenth verse of the fourth chapter of Hosea, "I will not punish your daughters when they commit whoredom." I will let them alone, they shall live and die in their sins. But my third argument is drawn from that saying of Christ, "He hath blinded their eyes, and hardened

their heart; that they should not see with their eyes, nor understand with their heart, and be converted, and I should heal them." (John xii. 40.) There are three things that I will take notice of from these words. The first is, that there can be no conversion to God where the eye is darkened, and the heart hardened. The eye must first be made to see, and the heart to break and relent under and for sin, or else there can be no conversion. "He hath blinded their eyes, and hardened their hearts lest they should see, and understand, and" so "be converted." And this was clearly Mr. Badman's case, he lived a wicked life, and also died with his eyes shut, and heart hardened, as is manifest in that a sinful life was joined with a quiet death; and all for that he should not be converted, but partake of the fruit of his sinful life in hell-fire. The second thing that I take notice of from these words is, that this is a dispensation and manifestation of God's anger against a man for his sin. When God is angry with men, I mean, when he is so angry with them, this among many is one of the judgments that he giveth them up unto, to wit, to blindness of mind, and hardness of heart, which he also suffereth to accompany them till they enter in at the gates of death. And then and there, and not short of then and there, their eyes come to be opened. Hence it is said of the rich man mentioned in Luke, "He died, and in hell he lifted up his eyes," (Luke xvi. 22,) implying that he did not lift them up before; he neither saw what he had done, nor whither he was going, till he came to the place of execution, even into hell. He died asleep in his soul; he died besotted, stupified, and so consequently for quietness like a child or lamb, even as Mr. Badman did. This was a sign of God's anger; he had a mind to damn him for his sins, and therefore would not let him see nor have an heart to repent for them, lest he should convert; and his damnation, which God had appointed, should be frustrate: "Lest they should be converted, and I should heal them." The third thing I take notice of from hence, is, that a sinful life, and quiet death annexed to it, is the ready, the open, the beaten, the common highway to hell; there is no surer sign of damnation than for a man to die quietly after a sinful life. I do not say that all wicked men that are molested at their death with a sense of sin and fears of hell, do therefore go to heaven, for some are also made to see, and are left to despair, not converted by seeing, that they might go roaring out of this world to their place. But I say there is no surer sign of a man's damnation than to die quietly after a sinful life; than to sin and die with his eyes shut; than to sin and die with an heart that cannot repent. "He hath blinded their eyes and hardened their heart, that they should not see with their eyes, nor understand with their heart," (John xii. 40;) no not so long as they are in this world, "lest they should see with their eyes, and hear with their ears, and understand with their heart, and should be converted, and I should heal them." (Acts xxviii. 27.) God has a judgment for wicked men, God will be even with wicked men, God knows how to reserve the ungodly to the day of judgment to be punished; and this is one of his ways by which he doth it. Thus it was with Mr. Badman. Fourthly, it is said in the book of Psalms, concerning the wicked, "There are no bands in their death, but their strength is firm." (Ps. lxxiii. 4.) By no bands, he means no troubles, no gracious chastisements, no such corrections for sin as fall to be the lot of God's people for theirs; yea, that many times falls to be theirs, at the time of their death. Therefore he adds concerning the wicked, they are "not in trouble" then "as other men, neither are they plagued like other men;" but go as securely out of the world as if they had never sinned against God, and put their own souls into danger of damnation. "There are no bands in their death." They seem to go unbound, and set at liberty out of this world, though they have lived notoriously wicked all their days in it. The prisoner that is to die at the gallows for his wickedness, must first have his irons knocked off his legs; so he seems to go most at liberty, when indeed he is going to be executed for his transgressions. Wicked men also have no bands in their death, they seem to be more at liberty when they are even at the wind-up of their sinful life, than at any time besides. Hence you shall have them boast of their faith and hope in God's mercy, when they lie upon their death-bed; yea, you shall have them speak as confidently of their salvation as if they had served God all their days; when the truth is, the bottom of this their boasting is because they have no bands in their death. Their sin and base life comes not into their mind to correct them, and bring them to repentance; but presumptuous thoughts, and an hope and faith of the spider's (the devil's) making, possesseth their soul, to their own eternal undoing. Hence wicked men's hope is said to die, not before, but with them: they give up the ghost together. And thus did Mr. Badman. His sins and his hope went with him to the gate, but there his hope left him, because it died there; but his sins went in with him, to be a worm to gnaw him in conscience for A frivolous ever and ever. The opinion, thereopinion. fore, of the common people concerning this kind of dying is frivolous and vain; for Mr. Badman died like a lamb, or as they call it, like a chrisom-child, quietly and without fear. I speak not this with reference to the struggling of nature with death, but as to the struggling of the conscience with the judgment of God. I know that nature will struggle with death. I have seen a dog and sheep die hardly: and thus may a wicked man do, because there is an antipathy betwixt nature and death. But even while, even then, when death and nature are struggling for mastery, the soul, the conscience, may be as be-

sotted, as benumbed, as senseless and ignorant of its miserable state, as the block or bed on which the sick lies; and thus they may die like a chrisom-child in show, but indeed like one who by the judgment of God is bound over to eternal damnation; and that also by the same judgment is kept from seeing what they are, and whither they are going, till they plunge down among the flames. And as it is a very great judgment of God on wicked men that so die—for it cuts them off from all possibility of repentance, and so of salvation—so it is as great a judgment upon those that are their companions that survive them, for by the manner of their death, they dying so quietly, so like unto chrisom-children, as they call it, they are hardened, and take courage to go on in their course. For comparing their life with their death, their sinful, cursed lives with their childlike, lamb-like death, they think that all is well, that no damnation has happened to them; though they lived like devils incarnate, yet they died like harmless ones. There was no whirlwind, no tempest, no band nor plague in their death: they died as quietly as the most godly of them all, and had as great faith and hope of salvation, and would talk as boldly of salvation, as if they had assurance of it. But as was their hope in life, so was their death; their hope was without trial, because it was none of God's working, and their death was without molestation, because so was the judgment of God concerning them. But I say, at this their survivors take heart to tread their steps, and to continue to live in the breach of the law of God; yea, they carry it stately in their villanies; for so it follows in the psalm: "There are no bands in their death, but their strength is firm, &c. Therefore pride compasseth them (the survivors) about as a chain, violence covereth them as a garment." (Ps. lxxiii. 4, 6.) Therefore they take courage to do evil, therefore they pride themselves in their iniquity. Therefore, wherefore? Why, because their fellows died, after they had lived long in a most profane and wicked life, as quietly and as like to lambs, as if they had been innocent. Yea, they are bold, by seeing this to conclude, that God either does not or will not take notice of their sins. They "speak wickedly, they speak loftily." (Ps. lxxiii. 8.) They speak wickedly of sin, for that they make it better than by the word it is pronounced to be. They speak wickedly concerning oppression, that they commend, and count it a prudent act. They also speak loftily; "They set their mouth against the heavens," &c. (Ps. lxxiii. 9.) "And they say, How doth God know? and is there knowledge in the most High?" (Ps. lxxiii. 11.) And all this, so far as I can see, ariseth in their hearts from the beholding of the quiet and lamb-like death of their companions. "Behold these are the ungodly who prosper in the world, (that is, by wicked ways;) they increase in riches." (Ps. lxxiii. 12.) This therefore is a great judgment of God, both upon that man that dieth in his sins, and also upon his companion that beholdeth him so to die. He sinneth, he dieth in his sins, and yet dieth quietly. What shall his companions say to this? What judgment shall he make how God will deal with him, by beholding the lamb-like death of his companion? Be sure he cannot, as from such a sight, say, "Woe be to me," for judgment is before him: he cannot gather that sin is a dreadful and a bitter thing, by the child-like death of Mr. Badman; but must rather, if he judgeth according to what he sees, or according to his corrupted reason, conclude with the wicked ones of old, that "Every one that doeth evil is good in the sight of the Lord, and he delighteth in them; or, Where is the God of judgment?" (Mal. ii. 17.) Yea, this is enough to puzzle the wisest man. David himself was put to a stand by beholding the quiet death of ungodly men. "Verily," says he, "I have cleansed my heart in vain, and washed my hands in innocency." (Ps. lxxiii. 13.) They, to appearance, fare better by far than I: "their eyes stand out with fatness," they have more than heart can wish; but all the day long have I been plagued, and chastened every morning. This, I say, made David wonder, yea, and Job and Jeremiah too: but he goeth into the sanctuary, and then he understands their end, nor could he understand it before. "I went into the sanctuary of God." What place was that? Why, there where he might inquire of God, and by him be resolved of this matter: "Then," says he, "understood I their end." Then I saw, that "thou hast set them in slippery places," and that "thou castest them down to destruction." Castest them down, that is, suddenly, or as the next words say, "as in a moment they" are "utterly consumed with terrors;" which terrors did not seize them on their sick-bed, for they had no bands in their death. The terrors, therefore, seized them there, where also they are holden in them for ever. This he found out, I say, but not without great painfulness, grief, and pricking in his reins; so deep, so hard, and so difficult did he find it, rightly to come to a determination in this matter. And, indeed, this is a deep judgment of God towards ungodly sinners; it is enough to stagger a whole world: only the godly that are in the world have a sanctuary to go to, where the oracle and word of God is, by which his judgments, and a reason of many of them, are made known to, and understood by them.

Atten. Indeed, this is a staggering dispensation. It is full of the wisdom and anger of God. And I believe, as you have said, that it is full of judgment to the world. Who would have imagined, that had not known Mr. Badman, and yet had seen him die, but that he had been a man of an holy life and conversation, since he died so stilly, so quietly, so like a lamb or a chrisom-child? Would they not, I say, have concluded that he was a righteous man? or that if they had known him and his life, yet to see him die so quietly, would they not have concluded that he had made his peace with God?

Nay, further, if some had known that he had died in his sins, and yet that he died so like a lamb, would they not have concluded that either God doth not know our sins, or that he likes them, or that he wants power, or will, or heart, or skill to punish them, since Mr. Badman himself went from a sinful life so quietly, so peaceable, and so like a lamb as he did?

Wise. Without controversy this is an heavy judgment of God upon wicked men; one goes to hell in peace, another goes to hell in trouble; one goes to hell, being sent thither by the hand of his companion; one goes thither with his eyes shut, and another goes thither with his eyes open; one goes thither roaring, and another goes thither boasting of heaven and happiness all the way he goes; one goes thither like Mr. Badman himself, and others go thither as did his brethren. But above all, Mr. Badman's death, as to the manner of dying, is the fullest of snares and traps to wicked men; therefore they that die as he are the greatest stumble to the world: they go, and go, they go on peaceably from youth to old age, and thence to the grave, and so to hell, without noise: "They go as an ox goeth to the slaughter, or as a fool to the correction of the stocks;" that is, both senselessly and securely. Oh, but being come at the gates of hell! Oh, but when they see those gates set open for them! Oh, but when they see that that is their home, and that they must go in thither, then their peace and quietness flies away for ever: then they roar like lions, yell like dragons, howl like dogs, and tremble at their judgment as do the devils themselves. Oh, when they see they must shoot the gulf and throat of hell! when they shall see that hell hath shut her ghastly jaws upon them! when they shall open their eyes, and find themselves within the belly and bowels of hell! Then they will mourn, and weep, and hack, and gnash their teeth for pain. But this must not be, or if it must, yet very rarely, till they are gone out of the sight and hearing of those mortals whom they do leave behind them alive in the world.

Atten. Well, my good neighbour Wiseman, I perceive that the sun grows low, and that you have come to a conclusion with Mr. Badman's life and death; and, therefore, I will take my leave of you. Only, first, let me tell you, I am glad that I have met with you to-day, and that our hap was to fall in with Mr. Badman's state. I also thank you for your freedom with me, in granting of me your reply to all my questions, I would only beg your prayers that God will give me much grace, that I may neither live nor die as did Mr. Badman.

Wise. My good neighbour Attentive, I wish your welfare in soul and body; and if aught that I have said of Mr. Badman's life and death may be of benefit unto you, I shall be heartily glad; only I desire you to thank God for it, and to pray heartily for me, that I with you may be kept by the power of God through faith unto salvation.

Atten. Amen. Farewell.

Wise. I wish you heartily farewell.

NOTES.

Note 1. p. 8.—"*He hath died two deaths at once.*]—This expression may remind some readers of the double night, the night of natural darkness, and the night of the soul, in which, says one of the old divines, all men sleep who lie down on their beds prayerless.

Note 2, p. 10.—"*Examples! Why, Ananias and his wife.*"]—It might be objected, that in this case it was especially said, "Thou hast not lied unto men, but unto God:" but to such a remark it may be answered, that it would be very difficult for a person addicted to falsehood to draw a boundary-line between the lie to man and the lie to God. Ananias, apparently, only addressed himself to Peter; but he was, in reality, attempting to deceive the Holy Ghost. In so far as the same blessed Spirit may be abiding in a man, and may be directing his words and actions, falsehood addressed or practised upon that man must seem, at least, to approach the sin committed by Ananias and his wife. Neither the careless nor the practised liar can be always on his guard against the danger to which he is thus exposed; nor, if he were, would he be able, under strong temptation, to resist the force of habit. He would plunge headlong beyond the line which he had thought never to pass.

Note 3, p. 18.—"*Young Badman was like him, indeed.*"]—The merit of this part of the story is found in the acute analysis of vices, and their origin. It would be difficult for any irreligious reader, however little inclined to reflection, to avoid discovering some resemblance to his own sins and follies, in the sharp, well-delineated outlines of this singular portrait-gallery.

Note 4, p. 29.—"*That is, ordinarily, they escape God's hand in this life.*"]—To many, even thoughtful persons, it is a perplexing mystery, that so comparatively small a number of wicked men are openly punished for their evil deeds. But their surprise would be lessened were they to know the actual amount of punishment inflicted, even in the present world, on the corrupt, the violent, and the profane. Though the number of public, startling visitations for sin is small; the instances of suffering arising from it, by the appointment of God's providence,—by the ordained and foreseen operation of his laws,—are numerous beyond calculation. Then, again, it should always be borne in mind, that while some wicked men are spared, that they may be converted and live; others are sustained in health and strength, and are suffered to enjoy a long prosperity, not for their own sakes, but for the sake of others. As the world at present exists, there must be a close interweaving of interests, and even of many natural affections, bringing the best and the worst of human beings, for a time, into intimate relationships. Were the tie to be suddenly broken, pious and amiable individuals would often be exposed to the most distressing sufferings, and society itself would become more or less disorganized. The better God's ways are understood, the fuller and clearer the justification of his wisdom.

Note 5, p. 34.—"*Truly he had malice and enmity enough in his heart to do it, only he was a tradesman.*"]—This passage is a quiet but bitter satire on a numerous class of persons in Bunyan's times. By a little latitude of interpretation, it is applicable to the men of any age, whose ready malice is restrained by other selfish passions still stronger than malice.

Note 6, p. 39.—"*This thus done, let that man again consider thus with himself.*"]—It would be difficult to find any teacher of the practical duties of life more acute than Bunyan. The instructions here given to men suffering from embarrassed circumstances are admirably drawn up. Each case is met by its appropriate remedy. No one finds himself consigned to hopelessness; but all are taught to survey, with strict self-justice, the circumstances through which they have fallen into distress. Viewed in these particular and incidental lessons, and without regard to Mr. Badman himself, Bunyan's wisdom and experience deserve the most earnest respect.

Note 7, p. 45.—"*But, above all, your hucksters, that buy up the poor man's victuals by wholesale,*" *&c.*]—The little village of Elstow, and even Bedford itself, no doubt furnished abundant examples of the species of extortion which it is Bunyan's purpose to denounce. Poverty, except in very large cities, is always subject to frauds like those here described. Hence, whatever the other vices of populous towns, the humbler classes have less to dread in them from the dishonesty of dealers than elsewhere. Both competition, and the general knowledge of the value of things, are their defence against a thousand petty impositions practised in remote parts of the country. Even there, the state of things has undergone a vast improvement since the seventeenth century.

Note 8, p. 57.—"*We find not, by all that he said or did, that Jesus Christ, the Saviour, was desired by him,*" *&c.*]—Repentance is here very properly tried by its only sufficient test. The mere anxiety to escape from punishment is no more repentance than any other wish to avoid pain. It is the transfer of the affections from one class of objects to another of a totally different kind, which can alone prove that change of will which constitutes repentance. A sick-bed is not to be undervalued as favourable to such a change. Separation from the world, the forced discovery of the frailty of the body, time for reflection, are all helps to a more humble frame of mind. If prayer follows, discoveries may be made not only of divine justice, but of divine goodness; and should the soul happily continue its contemplations till the grandeur of these discoveries win upon its affections, it will exercise repentance, and will bring forth enduring fruits answerable to the change.

Note 9, p. 68.—"*Yea, you shall have them speak as confidently of their salvation as if they had served God all their days.*"]—The whole account of Mr. Badman's death affords a triumphant proof of Bunyan's thorough knowledge of practical as well as doctrinal Christianity.

THE SAINT'S KNOWLEDGE OF CHRIST'S LOVE.

However ready we may be to credit the reports of a person's benevolence, the impression which they leave can never equal that made by the benevolence itself. If our hearts have grown warm at the recital of some noble act of charity, the rising sense of distress in ourselves immediately mixes the feeling of admiration with doubts and questionings. We wonder whether the same charity would meet our case. The answer given to such an inquiry is the test to us of what the supposed benevolence is worth.

This is a consideration not to be neglected in any view of Christianity. The great Author and Finisher of our faith is revealed to us as a Saviour, a friend, and benefactor, whose goodness, and means for its exercise, are equally inexhaustible. We learn the attributes of his character from unerring records of his life and doctrine; and a promise is given, in his own word, that all who hear that word, and accept it, shall be partakers of his bounty.

It is only when the mind has ceased to feel the force of truth, using its arguments on the grandest themes, that these appeals founded on the word and character of the Saviour fail altogether of effect. They have some influence on men of the most worldly character; not, indeed, a converting or sanctifying influence, but one sufficiently powerful to touch the affections, and occasionally create a wish to show respect by the lighter instances of obedience. If some higher degree of sensibility exists, the name of Jesus becomes suggestive of thoughts which readily take the form of devotion; and a feeling is created which so far resembles faith that it urges the mind to dwell on the promises of the New Testament as a possible resource in trouble.

But with all this supposed knowledge and approach to faith, there is no conviction in the heart of sufficient strength to endure any actual trial. The reason is evident. He is seen through the medium of description only. Belief in Him extends only to the verbal account given of his work or suffering. This even is more than many ever possess, and often serves as a means employed by divine grace itself to carry the soul forward to a higher state. But as no description of the sun will give warmth to a wretch perishing with cold,—as images of crystal streams are powerless to allay the traveller's thirst in the desert,—so it is with Christ as a Redeemer, and all his other characters of Saviour. The purposes, nature, and effects of redemption admit of many forcible representations. They may be set forth in expressions full of pathos and attractive beauty. When they are so exhibited, the understanding by its ordinary operations takes a ready part in the defence of their reasonableness, and thus there is a conquest over prejudice—an acquisition of knowledge, which, if knowledge were always power, would of itself fill the soul with a sense of unutterable gratitude. But to create this feeling the love of Christ must have been proved in the efficacious working of his grace. Whatever may be the sentiments produced by reading or contemplation, if they fall short of that apprehensive faith which justifies, the love of Christ is but a name. The saint's " knowledge of Christ's love" expresses a reality, and by those who have earnestly sought it, the reality is felt in regard both to the knowledge and the love. As this is the case with the blessings, so it is with the restriction of their enjoyment to a particular class. It is as certain that the actual knowledge of Christ's love is the possession of the saints alone, as it is that such a knowledge and such a love are not a shadow of something else, but as real an endowment in themselves as reason, or any of the other gifts of God bestowed upon our race. The love of Christ is itself so great a reality that on it depends whatever peace or happiness man, in his present condition, can enjoy. It constitutes, by its wonderful and mysterious connection with the whole system of God's government, the source of power and energy in every case of man's conquest over evil. Viewed under any of these aspects, if there be a felt participation in the blessings offered, the knowledge of the mystery is also of the highest and truest kind, involving, by its application to all the wants and capabilities of the soul, the elements of a universal wisdom.

But that neither the love itself, nor the knowledge of it can be enjoyed without holiness, is a necessity arising from their very nature. The love spoken of gives the first proof of its existence by taking possession of the heart, and there working those wonderful changes which are described as a new creation. It is in the fact that divine love has made him a hopeful, happy, and holy being, that the saint recognises its true character. Where it does not produce this effect, it has no reality for the individual. The knowledge of it is the experience of its power ; in this experience consists the life of the saint : and such a knowledge of Christ's love is that only which properly deserves the name.

Any fair and cautious examination of spiritual virtues will show that they are, one and all, the offspring of Christ's love, beginning with him, flowing from him, and then reverting to him as the one object concentrating all its energies. Whatever may be the effort of human nature to attain to a sense of freedom, it is never reached except through the medium of redemption—the first result of Christ's love. Affections released from the oppressive burden of innate tendencies to evil, give token by their fresh and healthful movements of a truer life—another effect of this same regenerating love. These general consequences of its power may be traced in numberless minute ramifications of individual feeling : its presence and action are discovered in the gaze fixed on heaven, in the movement of the lips uttering praise, and by an habitual conformity to the example of Christ in common incidents of outward conduct and inward temper.

It is only from a love, seated in the consciousness of life itself, that these instinctive sympathies with the blessed Saviour can arise. But where they exist there is the knowledge which, to be viewed rightly, must be regarded as a collateral effect of grace—as a gift treasured in the love, not as an independent achievement of the understanding. In every other respect but this of experience, the love of Christ " surpasses knowledge."

Contemplating these special endowments of holiness as the riches of those " who are called to be saints," our individual experience becomes a sure and definite test of spiritual life. To love Christ is the privilege of the holy, the essence and the concentration of the graces of the holy. He, therefore, who has this sublime affection has within himself the surest of all proofs that he is a child of God.

H. S.

THE SAINTS' KNOWLEDGE OF CHRIST'S LOVE;

OR,

THE UNSEARCHABLE RICHES OF CHRIST.

" That ye may be able to comprehend, with all saints, what is the breadth, and length, and depth, and height; and to know the love of Christ, which passeth knowledge."—Eph. iii. 18, 19.

The apostle having, in the first chapter, treated of the doctrine of election, and in the second, of the reconciling of the Gentiles with the Jews to the Father, by his Son, through the preaching of the gospel, comes in the third chapter to show that that also was, as that of election, determined before the world began. Now, lest the afflictions that attend the gospel should, by its raging among these Ephesians, darken the glory of these things unto them, therefore he makes here a brief repetition and explanation, to the end they might be supported and made live above them. He also joins thereto a fervent prayer for them, that God would let them see in the spirit and faith, how they, by God and by Christ, are secured from the evil of the worst that might come upon them: " For this cause I bow my knees to the Father of our Lord Jesus Christ, of whom the whole family in heaven and earth is named; that he would grant you according to the riches of his glory, to be strengthened with might by his Spirit in the inner man, that Christ may dwell in your hearts by faith; that ye, being rooted and grounded in love, may be able to comprehend with all saints, what is the breadth, and length, and depth, and height, and to know the love of Christ, which passeth knowledge," &c., knowing that their deep understanding what good by these were reserved for them, they would never be discouraged, whatever troubles should attend their profession.

Breadth, and *length*, and *depth*, and *height* are words that in themselves are both ambiguous, and to wonderment: ambiguous, because unexplained, and to wonderment, because they carry in them an inexpressible something; and that something that which far outgoes all those things that can be found in this world. The apostle here was under a spiritual surprise; for, while meditating and writing, he was caught: the strength and glory of the truths that he was endeavouring to fasten upon the people to whom he wrote, took him away into their glory, beyond what could to the full be

uttered. Besides, many times things are thus expressed, on purpose to command attentions, a stop and pause in the mind about them; and divert, by their greatness, the heart from the world, unto which they naturally are so inclined. Also, truths are often delivered to us, like wheat in full ears, to the end we should rub them out before we eat them, and take pains about them, before we have the comfort of them.

Breadth, length, depth, and *height.*—In my attempting to open these words, I will give you some that are of the same kind, and then show you the reasons of them; and then also something of their fulness.

First, *those of the same kind* are used sometimes to show us the power, force, and subtilty of the enemies of God's church, (Dan. iv. 11. Rom. viii. 38, 39;) but, secondly, most properly to show us the infinite and unsearchable greatness of God. (Job xi. 7—9. Rom. xi. 33.)

They are here to be taken in this second sense, that is, to suggest unto us the unsearchable and infinite greatness of God, who is a *breadth* beyond all breadths, a *length* beyond all lengths, a *depth* beyond all depths, and a *height* beyond all heights, and that in all his attributes. He is an eternal being, an everlasting being, and in that respect he is beyond all measures, whether they be of breadth, or length, or depth, or height. In all his attributes he is beyond all measure, whether you measure by words, by thoughts, or by the most enlarged and exquisite apprehension; his greatness is unsearchable; his judgments are unsearchable. (Job v. 9.) He is infinite in wisdom. " O the depth of the riches both of the wisdom and knowledge of God!" (Rom. xi. 33.) "If I speak of strength, lo, he is strong," (Job ix. 19;) yea, " the thunder of his power who can understand?" (Job xxvi. 14.) "There is none holy as the Lord," (1 Sam. ii. 2,) " and his mercy is from everlasting to everlasting, upon them that fear him." (Ps. ciii. 17.) The greatness of God, of the God and Father of our Lord Jesus Christ, is that, if rightly considered, which will support the spirits of those of his people that are frighted with the greatness of their adversaries. For here is a greatness against a greatness. Pharaoh was great, but God more great—more great in power, more great in wisdom, more great in every way for the help of his people; wherein they dealt proudly, he was above them. These words, therefore, take in for this people, the great God who, in his immensity and infinite greatness, is beyond all beings. But to come to the reason of the words—

First. They are made use of to show to the Ephesians that God, with what he is in himself, and with what he hath in his power, is all for the use and profit of the believers, else no great matter is held out to them thereby. But this God is our God! there is the comfort. For this cause, therefore, he presenteth them with this description of him—to wit, by breadth, and length, and depth, and height. As who should say, the high God is yours; the God that fills heaven and earth is yours; the God whom the heaven of heavens cannot contain is yours; yea, the God whose works are wonderful, and whose ways are past finding out, is yours. Consider, therefore, the greatness that is for you, that taketh part with you, and that will always come in for your help against them that contend with you. It is my support; it is my relief; it is my comfort in all my tribulations, and I would have it yours—and so it will when we live in the lively faith thereof. Nor should we admit of distrust in this matter from the consideration of our own unworthiness, either taken from the finiteness of our state, or the foulness of our ways. For now, though God's attributes, several of them in their own nature, are set against sin and sinners,—yea, were we righteous, are so high that needs they must look over us, for it is to him a condescension to behold things in heaven (how much more, then, to open his eyes upon such as we!)—yet, by the passion of Jesus Christ, they harmoniously agree in the salvation of our souls. Hence God is said to be love. (1 John iv.) God is love, might some say, and justice too; but his justice is turned, with wisdom, power, holiness, and truth, to love—yea, to love those that be found in his Son; forasmuch as there is nothing fault-worthy in his righteousness which is put upon us. So, then, as there is in God's nature a *length*, and *breadth*, and *depth*, and *height* that is beyond all that we can think, so we should conclude that all this is love to us for Christ's sake; and then dilate with it thus in our minds, and enlarge it thus in our meditations, saying still to our low and trembling spirits, "It is as high as heaven; what canst thou do? deeper than hell; what canst thou know? The measure thereof is longer than the earth, and deeper than the sea." (Job xi. 8, 9.)

But we will pass generals, and more particularly speak something of their fulness, as they are fitted to suit and answer to the whole state and condition of a Christian in this life. The words are boundless. We have here a breadth, a length, a depth, and height made mention of; but *what* breadth, *what* length, *what* depth, *what* height is not so much as hinted. It is, therefore, infiniteness suggested to us, and that has engaged for us. For the apostle conjoins therewith, "And to know the love of Christ which passeth knowledge." Thus, therefore, it suits and answers a Christian's condition while in this world, let that be what it will. If his afflictions be broad, here is a breadth; if they be long, here is a length; if they be deep, here is a depth; and if they be high, here is a height. And I will say, there is nothing that is more helpful, succouring, or comfortable to a Christian while in a state of trial and temptation, than to know that there is a breadth to answer a breadth, a length to answer a length, a depth to answer a depth, and a height to answer a height. Wherefore this is that the apostle prayeth for—namely, that the Ephesians might have understanding in these things, "that ye may know what is the breadth, and length, and depth, and height."

Of the largeness of the apostle's heart in praying for his people, to wit, "that they might be able to comprehend with all saints," what, &c., of that we shall speak afterwards.

But, first, to speak to these four expressions, "breadth," "length," "depth," and "height."

1. What is the breadth? This word is to show that God is all over everywhere spreading of his wings, stretching out his goodness to the utmost bounds, for the good of those that are his people. (Deut. xxxii. 11, 12. Gen. xlix. 26.)

In the sin of his people there is a breadth—a breadth that spreadeth over all wheresoever a man shall look. The sin of the saints is a spreading leprosy. (Lev. xiii. 12.) Sin is a scab that spreadeth; it is a spreading plague; it knows no bounds, (Lev. xiii. 57;) or, as David saith, "I have seen the wicked spreading himself." (Ps. xxxvii. 35.) Hence it is compared to a cloud, to a thick cloud that covereth or spreadeth over the face of all the sky. Wherefore here is a breadth called for, a breadth that can cover all, or else what is done is to no purpose. Therefore, to answer this, here we have a breadth, a spreading breadth: "I spread my skirt over thee." But how far? Even so far as to cover all: "I spread my skirt over thee, and covered thy nakedness." (Ezek. xvi. 8.) Here, now, is a breadth according to the spreading nature of the sin of this wretched one; yea, a superabounding spreading; a spreading beyond, a spreading to cover. "Blessed is he whose sin is covered," (Ps. xxxii. 1,) " whose spreading sin is covered by the mercy of God through Christ." (Rom. iv. 4—7.) This is the spreading cloud, whose spreadings none can understand: "He spread a cloud for a covering, and fire to give light in the night." (Ps. cv. 39.)

This breadth that is in God, it also overmatcheth that spreading and overspreading rage of men, that is sometimes as if it would swallow up the whole church of God. You read of the rage of the king of Assyria, that there was a breadth in it, an overflowing breadth, to the filling of "the breadth of thy land, O Immanuel." (Isa. viii. 8.) But what follows? "Associate yourselves, O ye people, (ye Assyrians,) and ye shall be broken to pieces: and give ear all ye of far countries; gird yourselves, and ye shall be broken to pieces. Take counsel together, and it shall come to nought; speak the word, and it shall not stand, for God is with us." (Isa. viii. 9, 10.) God will over-match and go beyond you.

Wherefore this word *breadth*, and *what is the breadth*. It is here expressed on purpose to succour and relieve, or to show what advantage, for support, the knowledge of the overspreading grace of God by Christ yieldeth unto those that have it, let their trials be what they will. Alas! the sin of God's children seemeth sometimes to overspread not only their flesh and the face of their souls, but the whole face of heaven. And what shall he do now, that is a stranger to *this* breadth made mention of in the text? Why he must despair, lie down and die, and shut up his heart against all comfort, unless he, with his fellow-Christians, can at least apprehend what is this breadth, or the breadth of mercy intended in this place. Therefore Paul, for the support of the Ephesians, prays that they may know "what is the breadth."

This largeness of the heart and mercy of God toward his people, is also signified by the spreading out of his hand to us in the invitations of the gospel. "I said," saith he, "Behold me, behold me, I have spread out my hands all the day to a rebellious people, to a people that provoketh me continually." (Isa. lxv. 1—3.)

"I have spread out my hands," that is, opened my arms as a mother affectionately doth, when she stoopeth to her child in the warm workings of her bowels, and claspeth it up in them, and kisseth, and putteth it into her bosom.

For by spreading out the hands or arms to embrace, is showed the breadth or largeness of God's affections; as by our spreading out our hands in prayer is signified the great sense that we have of the spreading nature of our sins, and of the great desires that are in us that God would be merciful to us. (Ezra ix. 5—15.)

This word also answereth to, or may fitly be set against, the wiles and temptations of the devil, who is that great and dogged leviathan that spreadeth his "sharp-pointed things upon the mire," (Job xli. 30;) for be the spreading nature of our corruptions never so broad, he will find sharp-pointed things enough to stick in the mire of them, for our affliction. These sharp-pointed things are those that in another place are called "fiery darts," (Eph. vi. 16;) and he has abun-dance of them, with which he can, and will, sorely prick and wound our spirits; yea, so sharp some have found these things to their souls, that they have pierced beyond expression: "When," said Job, "I say, my bed shall comfort me, my couch shall ease my complaint, then thou scarest me with dreams, and terrifiest me through visions, so that my soul chooseth strangling, and death, rather than my life." But now, answerable to the spreading of these sharp-pointed things, there is a super-abounding breadth in the sovereign grace of God, the which whoso seeth and understandeth, as the apostle doth pray we should, is presently helped; for he seeth that this grace spreadeth itself, and is broader than can be either our mire or the sharp-pointed things that he spreadeth thereupon for our vexation and affliction: "It is broader than the sea." (Job xi. 9.)

This therefore should be that upon which those that see the spreading nature of sin, and the leprosy and contagion thereof, should meditate, to wit, the broadness of the grace and mercy of God in Christ. This will poise and stay the soul; this will relieve and support the soul in and under those many misgiving and desponding thoughts unto which we are subject, when afflicted with the apprehensions of sin, and the abounding nature of it.

· Shall *another* man pray for this, one that knew the goodness and benefit of it, and shall not I meditate upon it? and shall not I exercise my mind about it? Yes surely, for it is my duty, it is my privilege and mercy so to do. Let this therefore, when thou seest the spreading nature of thy sin, be a memento to thee, to the end thou mayst not sink and die in thy soul.

2. What is the breadth and *length*. As there is a breadth in this mercy and grace of God by Christ, so there is a *length* therein, and this length is as large as the breadth, and as much suiting the condition of the child of God, as the other is. For, though sin sometimes is most afflicting to the conscience, while the soul beholdeth the over-spreading nature of it, yet here it stoppeth not, but ofttimes through the power and prevalency of it, the soul is driven with it, as a ship by a mighty tempest, or as a rolling thing before the whirlwind: driven, I say, from God, and from all hopes of his mercy, as far as the east is from the west, or as the ends of the world are asunder. Hence it is supposed by the prophet, that for and by sin they may be driven from God to the utmost part of heaven; and that is a sad thing; a sad thing, I say, to a gracious man: "Why," saith the prophet to God, "art thou so far from helping me, and from the words of my roaring?" (Ps. xxii. 1.) Sometimes a man, yea, a man of God, is, as he apprehends, so *far* off from God that he can neither *help* him, nor *hear* him; and this is a dismal state: "And thou hast removed my soul," said the church, "far off from peace; I forgot prosperity." (Lam. iii. 17.) This is the

state sometimes of the godly, and that not only with reference to their being removed by persecutors from the appointments and gospel-seasons which are their delight, and the desire of their eyes, but also with reference to their faith and hope in their God. They think themselves beyond the reach of his mercy. Wherefore, in answer to this conceit it is, that the Lord asketh, saying, "Is my hand shortened at all that I cannot redeem?" (Isa. l. 2.) And again, "Behold the Lord's hand is not shortened, that it cannot save, neither his ear heavy, that it cannot hear." (Isa. lix. 1.) Wherefore he saith again, "If any of thine be driven out unto the utmost parts of heaven, from thence will the Lord thy God gather thee, and from thence will he fetch thee." (Deut. xxx. 4. Neh. i. 9.) God has a long arm, and he can reach a great way further than we can conceive he can: when we think his mercy is clean gone, and that ourselves are free among the dead, and of the number that he remembereth no more, then he can reach us, and cause that again we stand before him. He could reach Jonah, though in the belly of hell, (Jonah ii. 2,) and reach thee, even then when thou thinkest thy way is hid from the Lord, and thy judgment passed over from thy God. There is a length to admiration, beyond apprehension or belief, in the arm of the strength of the Lord; and this is that which the apostle intended by this word *length*; namely, to insinuate what a reach there is in the mercy of God, how far it can extend itself: "If I take the wings of the morning," said David, "and dwell in the uttermost parts of the sea, even there shall thy hand lead me, and thy right hand shall hold me." (Ps. cxxxix. 9, 10.) I will gather them from ·the east, and from the west, and from the north, and from the south, saith he; that is, from the uttermost corners.

This therefore should encourage them that for the present cannot stand, but that do fly before their guilt. Them that feel no help nor stay, but that go, as to their thinking, every day by the power of temptation, driven yet farther off from God, and from the hopes of obtaining of his mercy to their salvation—poor creature, I will not now ask thee how thou camest into this condition, or how long this has been thy state; but I will say before thee, and I prithee hear me, O the length of the saving arm of God! As yet thou art within the reach thereof; do not thou go about to measure arms with God, as some good men are apt to do: I mean, do not thou conclude, that because thou canst not reach God by thy short stump, therefore he cannot reach thee with his long arm. Look again: "Hast thou an arm like God," (Job xl. 9,) an arm like his for length and strength? It becomes thee, when thou canst not perceive that God is within the reach of thy arm, then to believe that thou art within the reach of his; for it is long, and none knows how long.

Again, is there such a length—such a length in the arm of the Lord, that he can reach those that are gone away, as far as they could? then this should encourage us to pray, and hope for the salvation of any one of our backslidden relations, that God would reach out his arm after them: saying, "Awake, O arm of the Lord. Art thou not it that hath cut Rahab, and wounded the dragon? Art thou not it which hath dried the sea, the waters of the great deep; that hath made the depths of the sea a way for the ransomed to pass over?" (Isa. li. 9, 10.) Awake, O arm of the Lord, and be stretched out, as far as to where my poor husband is, where my poor child, or to where my poor backslidden wife or dear relation is, and lay hold, fast hold; they are gone from thee, but, O! thou the hope of Israel, fetch them again, and let them stand before thee. I say, there is in this word *length* matter of encouragement for us thus to pray; for if the length of the reach of mercy is so great, and if also this length is for the benefit of those that may be gone off far from God, (for they at present have no need thereof that are near,) then improve this advantage at the throne of grace for such, that they may come to God again.

8. As there is a breadth and length here, so there is a *depth*. What is the breadth, and length, and depth? And this depth is also put in here, on purpose to help us under a trial that is diverse from the two former. I told you that by the breadth, the apostle insinuates a remedy and succour to us when we see our corruptions spread like a leprosy; and by length he would show us that when sin has driven God's elect to the furthest distance from him, yet his arm is long enough to reach them, and fetch them back again.

But, I say, as we have here a breadth, and a length, so we have also a depth. That ye may know what is the depth, Christians have sometimes their sinking fits, and are as if they were always descending; or, as Heman says, "counted with them that go down into the pit." (Ps. lxxxviii. 4.) Now guilt is not to such so much a wind and a tempest, as a load and burthen. The devil and sin, and the curse of the law, and death, are gotten upon the shoulders of this poor man, and are treading of him down, that he may sink into, and be swallowed up of his miry place. "I sink," says David, "in deep mire, where there is no standing; I am come into deep waters, where the floods overflow me." (Ps. lxix. 2.) Yea, there is nothing more common among the saints of old, than this complaint. "Let neither the water-flood overflow me, neither let the deep swallow me up, neither let the pit shut her mouth upon me." (Ps. lxix. 14, 15.) Heman also saith, "Thou hast laid me in the lowest pit, in darkness, in the deeps. Thy wrath lieth hard upon me, and thou hast afflicted me with all thy waves." (Ps. lxxxviii. 6, 7.) Hence it is again that the Psalmist says, "Deep calleth unto deep at the noise of thy water-spouts; all thy waves and thy billows are gone over me." (Ps. xlii. 7.) "Deep calleth unto deep." What is that? Why, it is expressed in the verse before: "O God," says he, "my soul is cast down within me." (Ps. xlii. 6.) "Down;" that is, deep into the jaws of distrust and fear. And, Lord, my soul in this depth of sorrow calls for help to thy depth of mercy: for though I am sinking and going down, yet not so low but that thy mercy is yet underneath me. Do of thy compassion open those everlasting arms, (Deut. xxxiii. 27,) and catch him that has no help or stay in himself: for so it is with one that is falling into a well or dungeon.

Now mark, as there is in these texts the sinking condition of the godly man set forth—of a man whom sin and Satan is treading down into the deep; so in our text which I am speaking to at this time, we have a depth that can more than counterpoise these deeps, set forth with a hearty prayer, that we may know it. And although the deeps, or depths of calamity, into which the godly may fall, may be as deep as hell—and methinks they should be no deeper—yet this is the comfort, and for the comfort of them of the godly that are thus sinking, the mercy of God for them lies deeper: "It is deeper than hell; what canst thou know?" (Job xi. 8.) And this is that which made Paul that he was not afraid of this depth: "I am persuaded," said he, "that neither height nor depth shall be able to separate us from the love of God, which is in Christ Jesus our Lord." (Rom. viii. 38, 39.) But of this he could by no means have been persuaded, had he not believed that mercy lieth deeper for the godly to help them than can all other depths be to destroy them. This is it at which he stands and wonders, saying, "O the depth of the riches, both of the wisdom and knowledge of God," (Rom. xi. 33;) that is, to find out a way to save his people, notwithstanding all the deep contrivances that the enemy hath, and may invent to make us come short of home.

This is also that, as I take it, which is wrapped up in the blessing wherewith Jacob blessed his son Joseph: God "shall bless thee," saith he, "with blessings of heaven above, and blessings of the deep that lieth under," (Gen. xlix. 25;) a blessing which he had ground to pronounce, as well from his observation of God's good dealing with Joseph, as in a spirit of prophecy. For he saw that he lived and was become a flourishing bough, by a wall, after that the archers had done their worst to him. (Gen. xlix. 22—24.) Moses also blesseth God for blessing of Joseph thus, and blessed his portion to him, as counting of it sufficient for his help in all afflictions. "Blessed," saith he, "of the Lord, be his land, for the precious things of heaven, for the dew, and for the deep that coucheth beneath." (Deut. xxxiii. 13.)

I am not of belief that these blessings are confined to things temporal, or carnal, but to things spiritual and divine; and that they have most chiefly respect to soul and eternal good. Now mark, he tells us here, that the blessings of the

deep do couch beneath—"couch," that is, lie close, so as hardly to be discerned by him that willingly would see that himself is not below these arms that are beneath him. But that, as I said, is hard to be discerned by him that thus is sinking, and that has, as he now smartingly feels, all God's waves and his billows rolling over him. However, whether he sees or not—for this blessing lieth couched—yet there it is, and there will be, though one should sink as deep as hell. And hence they are said to be "everlasting arms" that are "underneath," (Deut. xxxiii. 27;) that is, arms that are long and strong, and that can reach to the bottom, and also beyond all the misery and distress that Christians are subject to in this life. Indeed mercy seems to be asleep when we are sinking, (Mark iv. 36—39;) for then we are as if all things were careless of us, but it is but as a lion couchant, it will awake in time for our help. (Ps. xliv. 22—26.) And forasmuch as this term is it which is applicable to the lion in his den, it may be to show that as a lion, so will God at the fittest season arise for the help and deliverance of a sinking people. Hence, when he is said to address himself to the delivering of his people, it is that he comes as a roaring lion. "The Lord shall go forth as a mighty man, he shall stir up jealousy like a man of war: he shall cry, yea roar; he shall prevail against his enemies." (Isa. xlii. 13.) However, here is a depth against the depth that is against us, let that depth be what it will: as, let it be the depth of misery, the depth of mercy is sufficient. If it be the depth of hellish policy, the depth both of the wisdom and knowledge of God shall go beyond it, and prevail.

This therefore is worthy of the consideration of all sinking souls—of the souls that feel themselves descending into the pit. There is such a thing as this experienced among the godly. Some, come to them (when tempted) when you will, they will tell you they have no ground to stand on,—their feet have slipped, their foundation is removed, and they feel themselves sinking, as into a pit that has no bottom. (Ps. xi. 3.) They inwardly sink, not for want of something to relieve the body, but for want of some spiritual cordial to support the mind. "I went down to the bottoms of the mountains," said Jonah, "the earth with her bars was about me for ever; my soul fainted within me." (Jonah ii. 6, 7.)

Now for such to consider that underneath them, even at the bottom, there lieth a blessing, or that in this deep whereinto they are descending, there lieth a delivering mercy couching to catch them, and to save them from sinking for ever, this would be a relief unto them, and help them to hope for good.

Again: as this, were it well considered by the sinking ones, would yield them stay and relief, so this is it by the virtue whereof they that have been sinking heretofore, have been lifted up, and above their castings down again. There are of those that have been in the pit, now upon Mount Zion, with the harps of God in their hands, and with the song of the Lamb in their mouths. But how is it that they are there? Why, David by his own deliverance shows you the reason: "For great is thy mercy toward me," saith he, "and thou hast delivered my soul from the lowest hell." (Ps. lxxxvi. 13.) And again: "He brought me up also out of an horrible pit, (a pit of noise, a pit wherein was the noise of devils, and of my heart answering them with distrust and fear,) out of the miry clay, (into which I did not only sink, but was by it held from getting up: but he brought me up,) and set my feet upon a rock, and established my goings. And he hath put a new song in my mouth, even praise unto our God." (Ps. xl. 2, 3.)

But let me here give, if it may be, a timely caution to them that think they stand upon their feet. Give not way to falling because everlasting arms are underneath, take heed of that: God can let thee fall into mischief, he can let thee fall, and not help thee up. Tempt not God, lest he cast thee away indeed. I doubt there are many that have presumed upon this mercy, that thus do couch beneath, and have cast themselves down from their pinnacles into vanity, of a vain conceit that they shall be lifted up again, whom yet God will leave to die there, because their fall was rather of wilfulness than weakness, and of stubbornness and desperate resolutions, than for want of means and helps to preserve them from it.

4. As there is a breadth, and length, and depth, in this mercy and grace of God through Christ towards his people, so there is also a *height*—"that ye may comprehend with all saints what is the breadth, and length, and depth, and height." There are things that are high, as well as things that are low; things that are above us, as well as things that are under, that are distressing to God's people. It is said when Noah was a preacher of righteousness, "there were giants in the earth in those days," (Gen. iv. 6;) and these, as I conceive, were some of the heights that were set against Noah; yea, they were the very dads and fathers of all that monstrous brood that followed in the world in that day. Of this sort were they who so frighted and terrified Israel, when they were to go to inherit the land of promise. The men that were tall as the cedars, and strong as the oaks, frighted them; they were in their own sight, when compared with these high ones, but as grasshoppers. This therefore was their discouragement. (Numb. xiii. 31—33. Deut. ii. 10; ix. 2.)

Besides, together with these, they had high walls—walls as high as heaven; and these walls were of purpose to keep Israel out of his possession. See how it is expressed: "The people is greater and taller than we; the cities are great, and walled up to heaven; and, moreover, we have seen the sons of the Anakims there." (Deut. i. 28.) One of these, to wit, Goliath by name, how did he fright the children of Israel in the days of Saul! How did the appearance of him make them scuttle together on heaps before him? (1 Sam. xvii.) By these giants, and by these high walls, God's children to this day are sorely distressed, because they stand in the cross ways to cut off Israel from his possession.

But now, to support us against all these, and to encourage us to take heart notwithstanding all these things, there is for us a height in God. He hath made his Son higher than the kings of the earth. (Ps. lxxxix. 26, 28.) His Word also is settled for ever in heaven, and therefore must needs be higher than their walls. (Ps. cxix. 89.) He also saith in another place, "If thou seest the oppression of the poor, and violent perverting of judgment and justice in a province, marvel not at the matter; for he that is higher than the highest, regardeth; and there be higher than they." (Eccles. v. 8.) It was this that made Paul, that he feared not the height; not things present, nor things to come. (Rom. viii. 89.)

But again, as there are these things standing or lying in our way, so there are another sort of heights that are more mischievous than these; and they are the fallen angels. These are called spiritual wickedness, or wicked spirits, in high places. For God has suffered them for a time, to take to themselves principality and power, and so they are become the rulers of the darkness of this world. By these we are tempted, sifted, threatened, opposed, undermined: also by these there are snares, pits, holes, and what not made, and laid for us, if peradventure by something we may be destroyed. Yea, and we should most certainly be so, were it not for the rock that is higher than they. But "he that cometh from above is above all." (John iii. 31.) These are they that our king has taken captive, and hath rid (in his chariots of salvation) in triumph over their necks. These are they, together with all others, whose most devilish designs he can wield, and turn, and make work together for his ransomed's advantage. There is a height—an infinitely over-topping height—in the mercy and goodness of God for us against them.

There are heights also that build up themselves in us, which are not but to be taken notice of; yea, there are a many of them, and they place themselves directly so that if possible they may keep the saving knowledge of God out of our hearts. These high things, therefore, are said to exalt themselves against the knowledge of God, (2 Cor. x. 5,) and do ofttimes more plague, afflict, and frighten Christian men and women, than anything besides. It is from these that our faith and spiritual understanding of God, and of his Christ. is opposed and contradicted; and from these also that we are so inclinable to swerve from right doctrine into destructive opinions. It is from these that we are so easily persuaded to call into question our former experience of the goodness of God towards us, and from these that our minds are so often clouded and darkened, that we cannot see afar off. These would betray us into the hands of fallen angels and men; nor should we by any means help or deliver ourselves, were it not for one that is higher. These are the dark mountains at which our feet would certainly stumble, and upon which we should fall, were it not for one who can leap and skip over these mountains of division, and come in to us. (Sol. Song ii. 8, 17.)

Further, there is a height also that is obvious to our senses, the which, when it is dealt withal by our corrupted reason, proves a great shaking to our mind, and that is the height and exceeding distance that heaven is off of us, and we off it. "Is not God in the height of heaven? and behold the height of the stars, how high they are." (Job xxii. 12.) Hence heaven is called the place for height. (Prov. xxv. 3.) Also when Ahaz is bid to ask with reference to heaven, he is bid to ask it, in the height, the height above. (Isa. vii. 11.) Now, saith reason, how shall I come thither? especially when a good man is at his furthest distance therefrom? which is, when he is in the grave. Now I say, every height is a difficulty to him that is loaden with a burden, especially the heaven of heavens, where God is, and where is the resting-place of his, to them that are oppressed with the guilt of sin. And, besides, the dispensation which happeneth to us last, to wit, death, as I said before, makes this heaven, in my thoughts, while I live, so much the more unaccessible. Christ indeed could mount up, (Acts i. 9;) but me, poor me, how shall I get thither? Elijah indeed had a chariot sent him to ride in thither, and went up by it into that holy place, (2 Kings ii. 11;) but I, poor I, how shall I get thither? Enoch is there, because "God took him," (Gen. v. 24;) but as for me, how shall I get thither? Thus some have mourningly said. And although distrust of the power of God, as to the accomplishing of this thing, is by no means to be smiled upon, yet methinks the unconcernedness of professors thereabout, doth argue that considering thoughts about that are wanting.

I know the answer is ready: Get Christ, and go to heaven. But methinks the height of the place, and the glory of the state that we are to enjoy therein, should a little concern us, at least so as to make us wonder in our thinking, that the time is coming that we must mount up thither. And since there are so many heights between *this* place, between *us* and *that*, it should make us admire at the heights of the grace and mercy of God, by which means is provided to bring us thither. And I believe that this thing, this very thing, is included here by the apostle, when he prays for the Ephesians, that they might know the height.

Methinks, how shall we get thither, will still stick in my mind. "I will ascend," says one, "above the heights of the clouds; I will be like the Most High." (Isa. xiv. 14.) And I, says another, will set my "nest among the stars" of heaven. (Obad. 4.) Well, but what of all this? If heaven has gates, and they shall be shut, how wilt thou go in thither? "Though they climb up to heaven, thence will I bring them down." (Amos ix. 2.) Still, I say, therefore, how shall we get in thither? Why, for them that are godly, there is the power of God, the merits of Christ, the help of angels, and the testimony of a good conscience, to bring them thither; and he that has not the help of all these, let him do what he can, shall never come thither. Not that all these go to the making up of the height that is intended in the text; for the height there, is what is in God through Christ to us alone. But the angels are the servants of God for that end, (Luke xvi. 32. Heb. i. 14;) and none with ill consciences enter in thither. (Ps. xv. 1; xxiv. 3, 4.) What, "know ye not that the unrighteous shall not inherit the kingdom of God? be not deceived," (1 Cor. vi. 9;) such have no inheritance in the kingdom of Christ and of God. (Eph. v. 5.)

This then should teach us, that in God is a power that is able to subdue all things to himself. In the completing of many things there seems to be an utter impossibility, as that a virgin should conceive in her womb, as a virgin, and bring a Son into the world: that the body that is turned into dust, should arise and ascend into the highest heaven. (Phil. iii. 21.) These things, with many more, seem to be utterly impossible: but there is that which is called the power of God, by the which he is able to make all things bend to his will, and to make all obstructions give place to what he pleases. God is high above all things, and can do whatever it pleaseth him. But since he can do so, why doth he suffer this and that thing, to appear, to act, and do so horribly repugnant to his word? I answer, he admits of many things, to the end he may show his wrath and make his power known; and that all the world may see how he checks and overrules the most vile and unruly things, and can make them subservient to his holy will. And how would the breadth and the length, and the depth and the height of the love and mercy of God in Christ to usward, be made to appear, so as in all things it doth, were there not admitted that there should be breadths, and lengths, and depths, and heights, to oppose? Wherefore, these oppositions are therefore suffered, that the greatness of the wisdom, the power, the mercy, and grace of God to us in Christ, might appear and be made manifest unto us.

This calls therefore upon Christians wisely to consider of the doings of their God. How many opposite breadths, and lengths, and depths, and heights did Israel meet with in their journey from

Egypt to Canaan, and all to convince them of their own weakness, and also of the power of their God! And they that did wisely consider of his doings there, did reap the advantage thereof. Come, behold the works of the Lord towards me, may every Christian say. He hath set a Saviour against sin, a heaven against a hell, light against darkness, good against evil; and the breadth, and length, and depth, and height of the grace that is in himself, for my good, against all the power, and strength, and subtilty of every enemy.

This also, as I hinted but just before, shows both the power of them that hate us, and the inability of us to resist. The power that is set against us none can crush and break but God: for it is the power of devils, of sin, of death, and of hell. But we, for our parts, are crushed before the moth, being a shadow, a vapour, and a wind that passeth away. (Job iv. 19.) Oh how should we, and how would we, were but our eyes awake, stand and wonder at the preservations, the deliverances, the salvations, and benefits with which we are surrounded daily; while so many mighty evils seek daily to swallow us up, as the grave! See how the golden psalm of David reads it: "Be merciful unto me, O God, for man would swallow me up: he fighting daily oppresseth me. Mine enemies would daily swallow me up; for they be many that fight against me, O thou Most High." (Ps. lvi. 1, 2.) This is at the beginning of it. And he concludes it thus: "Thou hast delivered my soul from death: wilt not thou deliver my feet from falling, that I may walk before God in the light of the living?" (Ps. lvi. 13.)

By this also we see the reason why it is so impossible for man or angel to persuade unbelievers to come in to, and close with Christ; why, there is a breadth that they cannot get over, a length that they cannot get beyond, a depth that they cannot pass, and heights that so hinder them of the prospect of glory, and the way thereto, that they cannot be allured thither. And that nothing can remove these, but those that are in God, and that are opposite thereto; even the breadth and length, and depth and height, that is in the text expressed, is to all awakened men an undoubted truth.

One item I would here give to him that loveth his own soul, and then we will pass on in pursuance of what is to come. Since there is an height obvious to sense, and that that height must be overcome ere a man can enter into life eternal, let thy heart be careful that thou go the right way to overpass that height, that thou mayest not miss of the delectable plains, and the pleasures that are above. Now there is nothing so high as to overtop this height, but Jacob's ladder, and that can do it; that ladder, when the foot thereof doth stand upon the earth, reacheth with its top to the gate of heaven. This is the ladder by which angels ascend thither; and this is the ladder by which thou mayest ascend thither. "And he

dreamed, and behold a ladder set upon the earth, and the top of it reached to heaven: and behold the angels of God ascending and descending on it." (Gen. xxviii. 12.)

This ladder is Jesus Christ, the Son of man, as is clear by the Evangelist John. (John i. 51.) And in that it is said to stand upon the earth, that is to show that he took hold of man who is of the earth, and therein laid a foundation for his salvation: in that it is said the top reached up to heaven, that is to show, that the divine nature was joined to the human, and by that means he was every way made a Saviour complete. Now, concerning this ladder, it is said, heaven was open where it stood, to show, that by him there is entrance into life; it is said also concerning this ladder, that the Lord stood there, at the top above it, saying, "I am the Lord God of Abraham," (Gen. xxviii. 13,) to show his hearty and willing reception of those that ascend the height of his sanctuary this way. All which Christ further explains by saying, "I am the way, and the truth, and the life, no man cometh to the Father but by me." (John xiv. 6.) Look to thyself, then, that thou do truly, and after the right manner, embrace this ladder, so will he draw thee up thither after him. (John xii. 32.) All the rounds of this ladder are sound, and fitly placed, not one of them is set further than that by faith thou mayest ascend step by step unto, even until thou shalt come to the highest step thereof, from whence, or by which thou mayest step in at the celestial gate, where thy soul desireth to dwell.

Take my caution, then, and be wary, no man can come thither but by him. Thither, I say, to be accepted; thither, there to dwell, and there to abide with joy for ever. "That ye may be able to comprehend with all saints, what is the breadth, and length, and depth, and height; and to know the love of Christ, which passeth knowledge."

Having thus spoken of the breadth, and length, and depth, and height that is in God's mercy by Christ to usward, we will now come more directly to the prayer of the apostle for these Ephesians, with reference thereunto; to wit, that they might be able to comprehend with all saints what they are.

And first, as to the ability that he prays for, to the end that they may be capable to do this thing.

I. *That ye may be able.*

The weakness that is here supposed to hinder their thus comprehending, &c., did, doubtless, lie in their grace, as well as in their nature: for in both, with reference to them that are Christians, there is great disability, unless they be strengthened mightily by the Holy Ghost. Nature's ability depends upon graces, and the ability of graces depends upon the mighty help of the Spirit of God. Hence, as nature itself, where grace is not, sees nothing, so nature by grace sees but weakly, if that grace is not strengthened with all might by the spirit of grace. The breadths, lengths, depths, and heights here made mention of, are mysteries, and in all their operations do work wonderfully mysteriously; insomuch that many times, though they are all of them busily engaged for this and the other child of God, yet they themselves see nothing of them. As Christ said to Peter, "What I do, thou knowest not now," (John xiii. 7;) so may it be said to many where the grace and mercy of God in Christ is working: they do not know, they understand not where it is, nor what will be the end of such dispensations of God towards them. Wherefore they also say as Peter to Christ, "Dost thou wash my feet? thou shalt never wash my feet," (John xiii. 6, 8;) yea, and when some light to convince of this folly breaks in upon them, yet if it be not very distinct and clear, causing the person to know the true cause, nature, and end of God's doing of this or that, they swerve with Peter as much on the other side. (Heb. iii. 10.) They have not known my ways and my methods with them in this world, were that that caused Israel always to err in their hearts and lie cross to all and each of these breadths, lengths, depths, and heights, whenever they were under the exercise of any of them in the wilderness. (John xiii. 9, 10.)

And the reason is, as I said before, for that they are very mysterious in their workings, for they work by, upon, and against oppositions; for, and in order to, the help and salvation of his people. Also, as was hinted a while since, that the power and glory of this breadth, and length, &c., of the mercy and grace of God, may the more show its excellency and sufficiency as to our deliverance, we by him seem quite to be delivered up to the breadths, lengths, and depths, and heights, that oppose, and that utterly seek our ruin; wherefore, at such times, nothing of breadths, lengths, depths, or heights can be seen, save by those that are very well skilled in those mysterious methods of God, in his gracious acting towards his people. "Who will bring me into the strong city? Wilt not thou, O God, which hadst cast us off? and thou, O God, which didst not go out with our armies?" is a lesson too hard for every Christian man to say over believingly. And what was it that made Jonah say, when he was in the belly of hell, "yet will I look again toward thy holy temple," (Jonah ii. 4,) but the good skill that he had in understanding of the mystery of these breadths, and lengths, and depths, and heights of God, and of the way of his working by them? Read the text at large:—"Thou hadst cast me into the deep, in the midst of the seas, and the floods compassed me about: all thy billows and thy waves passed over me. Then I said, I am cast out of thy sight; yet I will look again toward thy holy temple." (Jonah ii. 3, 4.)

These and such like sentences are easily played with by a preacher when in the pulpit, especially if he has a little of the notion of things; but of the difficulty and strait that those are brought into out of whose mouth such things or words are extorted by reason of the force of the labyrinths they are fallen into—of those they experience nothing, wherefore to those they are utterly strangers.

He, then, that is able to comprehend with all saints what is the breadth, and length, and depth, and height, must be a good expositor of providence, and must see the way and the workings of God by them. Now there are providences of two sorts, seemingly good and seemingly bad, and those do usually as Jacob did when he blessed the sons of Joseph, cross hands, and lay the blessing where we would not. "And when Joseph saw that his father laid his right hand upon the head of Ephraim, it displeased him." (Gen. xlviii. 17.) I say there are providences unto which we would have the blessings entailed, but they are not. And they are providences that smile upon the flesh, to wit, such as cast into the lap, health, wealth, plenty, ease, friends, and abundance of this world's good: because these, Manasseh, as his name doth signify, have in them an aptness to make us forget our toil, our low estate, and from whence we were: but the great blessing is not in them. There are providences, again, that take away from us whatever is desirable to the flesh; such is the sickness, losses, crosses, persecution, and affliction; and usually in these, though they make us shrink whenever they come upon us, blessing coucheth, and is ready to help us. For God, as the name of Ephraim signifies, makes us fruitful in the land of our affliction. (Gen. xli. 52.) He, therefore, in blessing of his people, lays his hands across, guiding them wittingly, and laying the chiefest blessing on the head of Ephraim, or on that providence that sanctifies affliction. Abel! what to the reason of Eve was he, in comparison of Cain? Rachael called Benjamin the son of her sorrow; but Jacob knew how to give him a better name. (Gen. xxxv. 18.) Jabez also, though his mother so called him, because, as it seems, she brought him forth with more than ordinary sorrow, was yet more honourable, more godly, than his brethren. (1 Chron. iv. 9, 10.) He that has skill to judge of providences aright has a great ability in him to comprehend with other saints what is the breadth, and length, and depth, and height; but he that has no skill as to discerning of them, is but a child in his judgment in those high and mysterious things. And hence it is that some shall suck honey out of that at which others tremble for fear it should poison them. I have often been made to say, "Sorrow is better than laughter, and the house of mourning better than the house of mirth." (Eccles. vii. 3, 5.) And I have more often seen that the afflicted are always the best sort of Christians. There is a man never well, never prospering, never but under afflictions, disappointments, and sorrows : why, this man, if he be a Christian, is one of the best of men. " They that go down to the sea in ships, that do business in great waters ; these see the works of the Lord, and his wonders in the deep." (Ps. cvii. 23, 24.) And it is from hence, for aught I know, that James admonishes the brother of high degree to rejoice in that he is made low; and he renders the reason of it, to wit, for that the fashion of the world perisheth ; the rich man fadeth away in his way ; but the tempted, and he that endureth temptation, is blessed. Now, I know these things are not excellent in themselves, nor yet to be desired for any profit that they can yield, but God doth use by these, as by a tutor or instructor, to make known to them that are exercised with them, so much of himself as to make them understand that riches of his goodness that is seldom by other means broken up to the sons of men. And hence it is said that the afterwards of affliction doth yield the peaceable fruits of righteousness to them that are exercised thereby. (Heb. xii. 11.)

The sum is, these breadths, and lengths, and depths, and heights of God, are to be discerned ; and some that are good do more, and some do less discern them, and how they are working, and putting forth themselves in every providence, in every change, in every turn of the wheel that passeth by us in this world. I do not question but that there are some that are alive, that have been able to say the days of affliction have been the best unto them, and that could, if it were lawful, pray that they might always be in affliction, if God would but do to them as he did when his hand was last upon them. For by them he caused his light to shine ; or, as Job has it, "Thou huntest me as a fierce lion ; and again thou showest thyself marvellously upon me." (Job x. 16.) See also the writing of Hezekiah, and read what profit he found in afflictions. (Isa. xxxviii.)

But again, these breadths, lengths, depths, and heights have in themselves naturally that glory that cannot be so well discerned or kept in view by weak eyes. He had need have an eye like an eagle that can look upon the sun, that can look upon these great things, and not be stricken blind therewith. You see how Saul was served when he was going to Damascus. (Acts ix.) But Stephen could stand and look up steadfastly into heaven ; and that, too, when with Jonah he was going into the deep. (Acts vii.) But I have done with this, and proceed.

II. That ye may be able to comprehend.

Although apprehending is included in comprehending, yet to comprehend is more. To comprehend is to know a thing fully, or to reach it all. But here we must distinguish, and say that there is a comprehending that is absolute, and a comprehending that is comparative. Of comprehending absolutely or perfectly, we are not here to speak ; for that the apostle could not, in this place, as to the thing prayed for, desire ; for it is utterly impossible perfectly to know whatsoever is in the breadths, lengths, depths, and heights here spoken of, whether you call them mercies, judgments, or the ways of God with men : " How unsearchable are his judgments, and his ways past finding out !" (Rom. xi. 33.) Or, if you take them to signify his love, unto which you see I am inclined, why, that you read of in the same place, to be it which passes knowledge. Wherefore should the apostle, by this term, conclude or insinuate that what he calls here breadths, lengths, depths, or heights, might be fully or perfectly understood and known, he would not only contradict other scriptures, but himself, in one and the selfsame breath. Wherefore it must be understood comparatively ; that is, and that he says, with, or as much as others, as any, even with all saints, "that ye may be able to comprehend with all saints, what is the breadth, and length, and depth, and height." I would ye were as able to understand, to know, and to find out these things, as ever any were ; and to know with the very best of saints " the love of Christ, which passeth knowledge." There are, as has before been hinted, degrees of knowledge of these things; some know more, some less ; but the apostle prays that these Ephesians might see, know, and understand as much thereof as the best, or as any under heaven.

First. And this, in the first place, shows us the love of a minister of Jesus Christ. A minister's love to his flock is seen in his praying for them; wherefore Paul commonly, by his epistles, either first or last, or both, gives the churches to understand that he did often heartily pray to God for them. (Rom. xvi. 20, 24. 1 Cor. xvi. 23. Gal. vi. 18. Eph. i. 16. Phil. i. 4. Col. i. 3. 1 Thess. i. 2. 1 Tim. vi. 21. 2 Tim. iv. 22.) And not only so, but also specifies the mercies, and blessings, and benefits which he earnestly begged for them of God. (2 Cor. xiii. 7. 2 Thess. i. 11.)

Second. But, secondly, this implies that there are great benefits accrue to Christians by the comprehending of these things : yea, it implies, that something very special is ministered to us by this knowledge of these. And here to touch upon a few of them :—

1. He that shall arrive to some competent knowledge of these things, shall understand more thoroughly the greatness, the wisdom, the power, &c., of the God that is above. For by these expressions are the attributes of God set forth unto us. And although I have discoursed of them hitherto under the notion of grace and mercy, yet it was not for that I concluded they excluded the expressing of his other attributes,

but because they all, as it were, turn into loving methods in the wheel of their heavenly motion towards the children of God. Hence it is said, "God is love," (1 John iv. 16 ;) "God is light." (1 John i. 5.) God is what he is for his own glory, and the good of them that fear him. God? Why God in the breadth, length, depth, height that is here intended, comprehends the whole world, (Col. i. 17;) the whole world is in him, for he is before, above, beyond, and round about all things. Hence it is said, the heavens for breadth are but his span; that he gathered the wind in his fists, (Prov. xxx. 4,) measureth the waters in the hollow of his hand, weigheth the mountains in scales, and the hills in a balance. (Isa. xl. 32.) Yea, that all nations before him are as nothing, and they are counted to him less than nothing and vanity. (Isa. xl. 17.) Hence we are said to live and move in him, (Acts xvii. 28,) and that he is beyond all search.

I will add one word more, notwithstanding there is such a revelation of him in his word, in the book of creatures, and in the book of providences, yet the scripture says, "Lo, these are part of his ways: but how little a portion is heard of him ?" (Job xxvi. 14.) So great is God above all that we have read, heard, or seen of him, either in the Bible, in heaven, or earth, the sea, or what else is to be understood. But now that a poor mortal, a lump of sinful flesh, or, as the scripture phrase is, poor dust and ashes, should be in the favour, in the heart, and wrapped up in the compassions of such a God! O amazing! O astonishing consideration! And yet "This God is our God for ever and ever; and he will be our guide even unto death." (Ps. xlviii. 14.)

It is said of our God, that "he humbleth himself when he beholds things in heaven;" how much more then when he openeth his eyes upon man, but most of all when he makes it, as one may say, his business to visit him every morning, and to try him every moment, having set his heart upon him, being determined to set him also among his princes. "The Lord is high above all nations, and his glory above the heavens, who is like to the Lord our God, who dwelleth on high, who humbleth himself to behold the things that are in heaven, and in the earth? He raiseth up the poor out of the dust, and lifteth the needy out of the dunghill; that he may set him with princes, even with the princes of his people." (Ps. cxiii. 4—8.)

2. If this God be our God; or if our God be such a God, and could we but attain to that knowledge of the breadth, and length, and depth, and height that is in him, as the apostle here prays, and desires we may, we should never be afraid of anything we shall meet with, or that shall assault us in this world. The great God, the former of all things, taketh part with them that fear him, and that engage themselves to walk in his ways, of love and respect they bear unto him; so that such may boldly say, "The Lord is my helper, and I will not fear what man shall do unto me." (Heb. xiii. 6.) Would it not be amazing should you see a man encompassed with chariots and horses, and weapons for his defence, yet afraid of being sparrow-blasted, or overrun by a grasshopper? Why "it is he that sitteth upon the circle of the earth," and to whom "the inhabitants thereof are as grasshoppers," (Isa. xl. 22,) that is the God of the people that are lovers of Jesus Christ; therefore we should not fear them. To fear man is to forget God; and to be careless in a time of danger, is to forget God's ordinance. What is it then? Why, let us fear God, and diligently keep his way, with what prudence and regard to our preservation, and also the preservation of what we have, we may. And if, we doing this, our God shall deliver us and what we have into the hands of them that hate us, let us laugh, be fearless and careless, not minding now to do anything else but to stand up for him against the workers of iniquity; fully concluding that both we and our enemies are in the hand of him that loveth his people, and that will certainly render a reward to the wicked, after that he has sufficiently tried us by their means. "The great God that formed all things, both rewardeth the fool and rewardeth transgressors." (Prov. xxvi. 10.)

3. Another thing that the knowledge of what is prayed for of the apostle, if we attain it, will minister to us, is, an holy fear and reverence of this great God in our souls; both because he is great, and because he is wise and good, (Jer. x. 7;) "Who shall not fear thee, O Lord, and glorify thy name?" (Rev. xv. 4.)

Greatness should beget fear, greatness should beget reverence. Now, who so great as our God? and so, who to be feared like him? He also is wise, and will not be deceived by any. "He will bring evil, and not call back his words, but will rise against the house of evil doers, and against the help of them that work iniquity." (Isa. xxxi. 2.) Most men deal with God as if he were not wise; as if he either knew not the wickedness of their hearts and ways, or else knew not how to be even with them for it: when, alas! he is wise in heart, and mighty in power; and although he will not, without cause, afflict, yet he will not let wickedness go unpunished. This therefore should make us fear. He also is good, and this should make us serve him with fear. Oh! that a great God should be a good God— a good God to an unworthy, to an undeserving, and to a people that continually do what they can to provoke the eyes of his glory; this should make us tremble. He is fearful in service, fearful in praises.

The breadth, and length, and depth, and height of his outgoing towards the children of men, should also beget in us a very great fear and dread of his majesty. When the prophet saw the height of the wheels, he said they were dreadful, (Ezek. i.

18,) and cried unto them, O wheel! (Ezek. x. 13.) His judgments also are a great deep, (Ps. xxxvi. 6;) nor is there any "searching of his understanding." (Isa. xl. 28.) He can tell how to bring his wheel upon us, and to make our table a snare, a trap, and a stumbling-block unto us. (Isa. viii. 14. Rom. xi. 8—10.) He can tell how to make his Son to us a rock of offence, and his gospel to be a savour of death unto death, unto us. (2 Cor. ii. 15, 16.) He can tell how to choose delusions for us, (Isa. lxvi. 4. 2 Thess. ii. 11,) and to lead us forth with the workers of iniquity. (Ps. cxxv. 5.) He can outwit, and outdo us, and prevail against us for ever, (Job xiv. 20;) and therefore we should be afraid and fear before him, for our good, and the good of ours for ever; yea, it is for these purposes, with others, that the apostle prayeth thus for his people: for the comprehending of these things do poise and keep the heart in an even course. This yields comfort, this gives encouragement, this begets fear and reverence in our hearts of God.

4. This knowledge will make us willing that he should be our God; yea, will also make us abide by that willingness. Jacob said with a vow, "If God will be with me, and will keep me in this way that I go, and will give me bread to eat, and raiment to put on; so that I come again to my father's house in peace; then shall the Lord be my God. And this stone which I have set for a pillar, shall be God's house; and of all that thou shalt give me, I will surely give the tenth unto thee." (Gen. xxviii. 20—22.) Thus he considered the greatness of God, and from a supposition that he was what he had heard him, of his father, to be; he concluded to choose him for his God, and that he would worship him, and give him that honour that was due to him as God. How did the king of Babylon set him above all gods, when but some sparkling rays from him did light upon him! He calls him "a God of gods," (Dan. ii. 47,) prefers him above all gods, charges all people and nations that they do nothing amiss against him. (Dan. iii. 28, 29.) He calls him "the Most High" God, the God that liveth for ever; and confesses, that he doth whatsoever he will in heaven and earth; and concludes with praising and extolling of him. (Dan. iv.) We naturally love greatness; and when the glorious beauty of the King of glory shall be manifest to us, and we shall behold it, we shall say as Joshua did: Let all men do as seems them good; "but as for me and my house, we will serve the Lord." (Josh. xxiv. 15.)

When the Apostle Paul sought to win the Athenians to him, he sets him forth before them with such terms as bespeaks his greatness; calling of him, (and that rightly,) God that made the world, and all things; the Lord of heaven and earth; one that giveth to all life and breath, and all things; one that is nigh to every one; "he in whom we live, and move, and have our being;" God that hath made of one blood all nations of men, and that hath determined the times before appointed, and the bounds of their habitation, &c. (Acts xvii. 24—28.) These things bespeak the greatness of God, and are taking to considering men. Yea, these very Athenians, while ignorant of him, from those dark hints that they had by natural light concerning him, erected an altar to him, and put this singular inscription upon it—

TO THE UNKNOWN GOD,

to show, that according to their mode, they had some kind of reverence for him: but how much more when they came to know him, and to believe that God, in all his greatness, had engaged himself to be theirs, and to bring them to himself, that they might in time be partakers of his glory.

5. The more a man knows or understands of the greatness of God towards him, expressed here by the terms of unsearchable breadth, length, depth, and height, the better will he be able in his heart to conceive of the excellent glory and greatness of the things that are laid up in the heavens for them that fear him. They that know nothing of this greatness, know nothing of them; they that think amiss of this greatness, think amiss of them; they that know but little of this greatness, know but little of them: but he that is able to comprehend with all saints what is the breadth, and length, and depth, and height, he is best able to conceive of, and consequently to make a judgment concerning the due worth and blessed glory of them.

This is both evident to reason; also experience confirmeth the same: for as for those dark souls that know nothing of his greatness, they have in derision those who are, through the splendour of the glory, captivated and carried away after God. Also, those whose judgments are corrupted, and themselves thereby made as drunkards, to judge of things foolishly, they, as it were, step in the same steps with the other, and vainly imagine thereabout. Moreover we shall see those little-spirited Christians, though Christians indeed, that are but in a small measure acquainted with this God, with the breadths, and lengths, and depths, and heights that are in him, taken but little with the glory and blessedness that they are to go to when they die; wherefore they are neither so mortified to this world, so dead to sin, so self-denying, so delighted in the book of God, nor so earnest in desires to be acquainted with the heights and depths that are therein. No, this is reserved only for those who are devoted thereto; who have been acquainted with God in a measure beyond that which your narrow-spirited Christians understand. There doth want as to these things, enlargings in the hearts of the most of saints, as there did in those of Corinth, and also in those at Ephesus. Wherefore, as Paul bids the one, and prays that the other may be enlarged, and have great knowledge thereabout; so we should, to answer such love, through desire, separate ourselves from terrene things, that we may seek and intermeddle with all wisdom. Christ says, if any man will do his will, he shall know of the doctrine. Oh! that we were indeed enlarged as to these breadths, and lengths, and depths, and heights of God, as the apostle desired the Ephesians might.

6. Then those great truths, the coming of Christ, the resurrection of the dead, and eternal judgment, would neither seem so like fables, nor be so much off our hearts as they do, and are; for the thorough belief of them depends upon the knowledge of the abilities that are in God to perform what he has said thereabout: and hence it is that your inferior sort of Christians live so like as if none of these things were at hand; and hence it is again that they so soon are shaken in mind about them, when tempted of the devil, or briskly assaulted by deceivers. But this cometh to pass that there may be fulfilled what is written, "While the bridegroom tarried, they all slumbered and slept." (Matt. xxv. 5.) Surely the meaning is, they were asleep about his coming, the resurrection, and the judgment, and consequently had lost much of that knowledge of God, the which, if they had retained, these truths, with power, would have been upon their hearts. The Corinthians were horribly decayed here, though some more than others. Hence Paul, when he treats of this doctrine, bids them awake to righteousness, and not to sin, telling them that some among them had not the knowledge of God. (1 Cor. xv. 34.) To be sure, they had not such a knowledge of God as would keep them steady in the faith of these things. (1 Cor. xv. 51.)

Now, the knowledge of the things above mentioned, to wit, this comprehending knowledge, will greaten these things, bring them near, and make them to be credited, as are the greatest of God's truths; and the virtue of the faith of them is to make one die daily. Therefore,

7. Another advantage that floweth from this knowledge, is, that it makes the next world desirable, not simply as it is with those lean souls, that desire it only as the the thief desireth the judge's favour, that he may be saved from the halter, but out of love such have to God and to the beauties of the house he dwells in, and that they may be rid of this world, which is to such as a dark dungeon. The knowledge of God that men pretend they have, may easily be judged of, by the answerableness or unanswerableness of their hearts and lives thereto. Where is the man that groans earnestly to be gone to God, that counts this life a strait unto him—that saith as a sick man of my acquaintance did, when his friend at his bed-side prayed to God to spare his life, No, no, said he, pray not so; for it is better to be dissolved and be gone? Christians should show the world how they believe; not by words on paper, not by gay and flourishing notions, but by those desires they have to be gone, and the proof that these desires

are true, is a life in heaven while we are on earth. I know words are cheap, but a drachm of grace is worth all the world. But where, as I said, shall it be found? not among carnal men, not among weak Christians, but among those, and those only, that enjoy a great measure of Paul's wish here. But to come to

"And to know the love of Christ which passeth knowledge." These words are the second part of the text, and they deal mainly about the love of Christ, who is the Son of God. We have spoken already briefly of God, and therefore now we shall speak also of his Son. These words are a part of the prayer aforementioned, and have something of the same strain in them. In the first part, he prays that they might comprehend that which cannot absolutely by any means be comprehended; and here he prays that that might be known, which yet in the same breath he saith, "passeth knowledge," to wit, the love of Christ: "And to know the love of Christ, which passeth knowledge."

In the words we are to take notice of three things:

I. Of the love of Christ.

II. Of the exceeding greatness of it.

III. Of the knowledge of it.

I. *The love of Christ.*

I. We will begin with the first of these, to wit, Of the love of Christ. Now, for the explication of this we must inquire into three things.

First. Who Christ is.

Second. What love is.

Third. What the love of Christ is.

First. Christ is a person of no less quality than is he of whom we treated before, to wit, very God. So I say, not titularly, not nominally, not so counterfeitly, but the self-same in nature with the Father. (John i. 1, 2. 1 John v. 7. Phil. ii. 5.) Wherefore what we have under consideration, is so much the more to be taken notice of; namely, that a person so great, so high, so glorious, as this Jesus Christ was, should have love for us that passes knowledge. It is common for equals to love, and for superiors to be beloved; but for the King of princes, for the Son of God, for Jesus Christ to love man thus, this is amazing, and that so much the more, for that man, the object of this love, is so low, so mean, so vile, so undeserving, and so inconsiderable, as by the Scriptures everywhere he is described to be.

But to speak a little more particularly of this person.

1. He is called God. (John i. 1.)

2. The King of glory, (Ps. xxiv. 10,) and Lord of glory. (1 Cor. ii. 8.)

3. The brightness of the glory of his Father. (Heb. i. 3.)

4. The head over all things. (Eph. i. 22.)

5. The Prince of life. (Acts iii. 15.)

6. The Creator of all things. (Col. i. 16.)

7. The upholder of all things. (Heb. i. 3.)

8. The disposer of all things. (Matt. xxviii. 18.)

9. The only beloved of the Father. (Matt. xi.)

But the persons of him beloved are called transgressors, sinners, enemies, dust and ashes, fleas, worms, shadows, vapours; vile, sinful, filthy, unclean, ungodly fools, madmen. And now is it not to be wondered at? and are we not to be affected herewith, saying, And wilt thou set thine eye upon such an one? but how much more when he will set his heart upon us? and yet this great, this high, this glorious person, verily, verily, loveth such!

Second. We now come to the second thing, namely, to show *what is love;* not in a way of nice distinction of words, but in a plain and familiar discourse, yet respecting the love of the person under consideration.

Love ought to be considered with reference to the subject, as well as to the object of it.

The subject of love in the text is Christ; but forasmuch as love in him is diverse from the love that is in us, therefore it will not be amiss if a little difference be made appear.

1. Love in us is a passion of the soul, and being such, is subject to ebb and flow, and to be extreme both ways. For whatever is a passion of the soul, whether love or hatred, joy or fear, is more apt to exceed or come short, than to keep within its due bounds. Hence, ofttimes that which is loved to-day is hated to-morrow; yea, and that which should be loved with bounds of moderation, is loved to the drowning of both soul and body in perdition and destruction.

2. Besides, love in us is apt to choose to itself undue and unlawful objects, and to reject those that, with leave of God, we may embrace and enjoy; so unruly, as to the laws and rules of divine government, ofttimes is this passion of love in us.

3. Love in us requires that something pleasing and delightful be in the object loved, at least so it must appear to the lust and fancy of the person loving, or else love cannot act; for the love that is in us, is not of power to set itself on work, where no allurement is in the thing to be beloved.

4. Love in us decays, though once never so warm and strongly fixed, if the object falls off, as to its first alluring provocation; or disappointeth our expectation with some unexpected reluctancy to our fancy or our mind.

All this we know to be true from nature, for every one of us are thus; nor can we refuse, or choose as to love, but upon, and after the rate, and the working thus of our passions. Wherefore our love, as we are natural, is weak, unorderly, fails, and miscarries, either by being too much or too little; yea, though the thing which is beloved be allowed for an object of love, both by the law of nature and grace. We therefore must put a vast difference betwixt love as found in us, and love as found in Christ, and that both as to the nature, principle, or object of love.

Love in Christ is not love of the same nature, as is love in us; love in him is essential to his being, (1 John iv. 16;) but in us it is not so, as has been already showed. God is love, Christ is God; therefore Christ is love, love naturally. Love therefore is essential to his being. He may as well cease to be, as cease to love. Hence therefore it follows, that love in Christ floweth not from so low and beggarly a principle as doth love in man; and consequently is not, nor can be attended with those infirmities or defects that the love of man is attended with.

(1.) It is not attended with those unruly or uncertain motions that ours is attended with; here is no ebbing, no flowing, no going beyond, no coming short, and so nothing of uncertainty. "Having loved his own which were in the world, he loved them unto the end." (John xiii. 1.)

True, there is a way of manifesting of this love, which is suited to our capacities as men, and by that we see it sometimes more, sometimes less; also it is manifested to us as we do, or do not walk with God in this world. (John xiv. 23.) I speak now of saints.

(2.) Love in Christ pitcheth not itself upon undue or unlawful objects; nor refuseth to embrace what by the eternal covenant is made capable thereof. It always acteth according to God; nor is there at any time the least shadow of swerving as to this.

(3.) Love in Christ requireth no taking beauteousness in the object to be beloved, as not being able to put forth itself without such attracting allurements. (Ezek. xvi. 6—8.) It can act of and from itself, without all such kind of dependencies. This is manifest to all who have the least true knowledge of what that object is in itself, on which the Lord Jesus has set his heart to love them.

(4.) Love in Christ decays not, nor can be tempted so to do by anything that happens, or that shall happen hereafter in the object so beloved. But as this love at first acts by and from itself, so it continues to do until all things that are imperfections are completely and everlastingly subdued. The reason is, because Christ loves to make us comely, not because we are so. (Ezek. xvi. 9—14.)

Object. But all along Christ compareth his love to ours. Now, why doth he so, if they be so much unlike?

Ans. Because we know not love but by the passions of love that work in our hearts; wherefore he condescends to our capacities, and speaketh of his love to us, according as we find love to work in ourselves to others. Hence he sets forth his love to us, by borrowing from us instances of our love to wife and children. (Eph. v. 25.) Yes, he sometimes sets forth his love to us, by calling to mind how sometimes a man loves a woman that is a whore. " Go," saith God to the prophet, " love a woman beloved of her friend, yet an adulteress according to the love of the Lord toward the children of Israel, who look to other gods, and love flagons of wine." (Hos. iii. 1.) But then, these things must not be understood with respect to the nature, but the dispensations and manifestations of love; no, nor with reference to these either, any further than by making use of such suitable similitudes, thereby to commend his love to us, and thereby to beget in us affections to him for the love bestowed upon us.

Wherefore Christ's love must be considered both with respect to the essence, and also as to the divers workings of it. For the offence thereof, it is, as I said, natural with himself, and as such, it is the root and ground of all those actions of his, whereby he hath showed that himself is loving to sinful man. But now, though the love that is in him is essential to his nature, and can vary no more than God himself, yet we see not this love but by the fruits of it, nor can it otherwise be discerned. " Hereby perceive we the love of God, because he laid down his life for us." (1 John iii. 16.) We must then betake ourselves to the discoveries of this love, of which there are two sorts :—

1. Such as are the foundations.

2. Such as are the consequences of those fundamental acts.

Those which I call the foundations, are they upon which all other discoveries of his goodness depend, and they are two : 1. His dying for us. 2. His improving of his death for us at the right hand of God.

Third. And this leads me to the third particular, to wit, to show you *what the love of Christ is*, namely, in the discovery of it.

And to know the love of Christ. The love of Christ is made known unto us, as I said,

First. By his dying for us.

Second. By his improving of his dying for us.

First. His dying for us appears,

1. To be wonderful in itself.

2. In his preparations for that work.

1. It appears to be wonderful in itself, and that both with respect to the nature of that death, as also with respect to the persons for whom he so died.

The love of Christ appears to be wonderful by the death he died, in that he died such a death. It was strange love in Christ that moved him to die for us : strange, because not according to the custom of the world. Men do not use in cool blood deliberately to come upon the stage or ladder, to lay down their lives for others ; but this did Jesus Christ, and that too for such, whose qualification, if it be duly considered, will make this act of his far more amazing. He laid down his life for his enemies, and for those that could

not abide him ; yea, for those, even for those that brought him to the cross, not accidentally, or because it happened so, but knowingly, designedly, (Zech. xii. 10,) he knew it was for those he died, and yet his love led him to lay down his life for them. I will add, that those very people for whom he laid down his life, though they by all sorts of carriages did what they could to provoke him to pray to God his Father, that he would send and cut them off by the flaming sword of angels, would not be provoked, but would lay down his life for them. Nor must I leave off here. We never read that Jesus Christ was more cheerful in all his life on earth, than when he was going to lay down his life for them—now he thanked God, (Luke xxii. 19,) now he sang. (Matt. xxvi. 30.)

But this is not all. He did not only die, but died such a death, as indeed cannot be expressed. He was content to be counted the sinner ; yea, to be counted the sin of the sinner ; nor could this but be odious to so holy a Lamb as he was, yet willing to be this and thus for that love that he bare to men.

This being thus, it follows, that his sufferings must be unconceivable ; for that, what in justice was the proper wages of sin and sinners, he must undergo ; and what that was can no man so well know as he himself, and damned spirits ; for the proper wages of sin, and of sinners for their sin, is that death which layeth pains, such pains which it deserveth, upon the man that dieth so. But Christ died so, and consequently was seized by those pains not only in body, but in soul. His tears, his cries, his bloody sweat, (Luke xxii. 44,) the hiding of his Father's face ; yea, God's forsaking of him in his extremity, (Matt. xxvii. 46,) plainly enough declares the nature of the death he died. (Mark xv. 39.) For my part, I stand amazed at those that would not have the world believe that the death of Jesus Christ was, in itself, so terrible as it was.

I will not stand here to discourse of the place called hell, where the spirits of the damned are ; we are discoursing of the nature of Christ's sufferings. And I say, if Christ was put into the very capacity of one that must suffer what in justice ought to be inflicted for sin, then, how can we so diminish the greatness of his sufferings, as some do, without undervaluing of the greatness of his love, I know not ; and how they will answer it, I know not. And on the contrary, what if I should say that the soul of Christ suffered as long as his body lay in the grave, and that God's loosing of the pains of death at Christ's resurrection, must not so much be made mention of with reference to his body, as to his soul, if to his body at all. For what pain of death was his body capable of, when his soul was separate from it? (Acts ii. 24 ;) and yet God's loosing the pains of death, seems to be but an immediate antecedent to his rising from the dead. And this sense Peter doth indeed seem to pursue, saying, "For David speaketh concerning him, I foresaw the Lord always before my face, for he is on my right hand, that I should not be moved. Therefore did my heart rejoice, and my tongue was glad; moreover, also, my flesh shall rest in hope, because thou wilt not leave my soul in hell, neither wilt thou suffer thine Holy One to see corruption." (Acts ii. 25—27.) This, saith Peter, was not spoken of David, but he being a prophet, and knowing that God had sworn with an oath, that of the fruit of his loins, according to the flesh, he would raise up Christ to sit on his throne. (Acts ii. 29, 30.) He seeing this before, spake of the resurrection of Christ, that his soul was not left in hell, neither did his flesh see corruption. (Acts ii. 31.) "Thou wilt not leave my soul in hell." His soul was not left in hell. Of what use are these expressions, if the soul of Christ suffered not, if it suffered not when separated from the body? for of that time the Apostle Peter seems to treat. Besides, if it be not improper to say, that soul was not left there, that never was there, I am at a loss. Thou wilt not leave; his soul was not left there; *ergo*, it was there, seems to be the natural conclusion. If it be objected that by hell is meant the grave, it is foolish to think that the soul of Christ lay there while his body lay dead therein. But again, the apostle seems clearly to distinguish between the places where the soul and body of Christ was, counting his body to be in the grave, and his soul, for the time, in hell. If there be objected what was said by him to the thief upon the cross, (Luke xxiii. 43,) I can answer, Christ might speak that with reference to his Godhead, and if so, that lies as no objection to what hath been insinuated. And why may not that be so understood, as well as where he said, when on earth, "The Son of man which is in heaven," (John iii. 13,) meaning himself. For the personality of the Son of God —call him Son of man, or what other term is fitting—resideth not in the human, but in the divine nature of Jesus Christ. However, since hell is sometimes taken for the place, (Acts i. 25,) sometimes for the grave, sometimes for the state, (Ps. cxvi. 3,) and sometimes but for a figure of the place where the damned are tormented, (1 Pet. iii. 19,) I will not strictly assign to Christ the place, the prison where the damned spirits are, (Jonah ii. 2,) but will say, as I said before, that he was put into the place of sinners, into the sins of sinners, and received what by justice was the proper wages of sin both in body and soul; as is evident from that 53rd of Isaiah. This soul of his I take to be that which the inwards and the fat of the burnt sacrifices were a figure or shadow of: "And the fat and the inwards were burnt upon the altar, whilst the body was burned for sin without the camp." (Exod. xxix. 13, 14. Lev. viii. 14—17.)

And now, having said this much, wherein have I derogated from the glory and holiness of Christ? Yea, I have endeavoured to set forth something of the greatness of his sorrows, the odiousness of sin, the nature of justice, and the love of Christ. And be sure, by how much the sufferings of the Son of God abounded for us, by so much was this unsearchable love of Christ made manifest. Nor can they that would, before the people, pare away, and make but little these infinite sufferings of our Lord, make his love to be so great as they ought, let them use what rhetoric they can. For their objecting the odious names and place of hell, accounting it not to be fit to say, that so holy a person as the Son of God was there, I answer, though I have not asserted it, yet let me ask, which is more odious, hell or sin? Or whether such think that Christ Jesus was subject to be tainted by the badness of the place, had he been there? Or whether, when the scripture says, God is in hell, it is any disparagement to him? (Ps. cxxxix. 8.) Or if a man should be so bold as to say so, whether by so saying, he confined Christ to that place for ever? And whether by so thinking he has contradicted that called the apostles' creed?

2. Having thus spoken of the death and sufferings of Christ, I shall in the next place speak of his preparations for his so suffering for us; and by so doing, yet show you something more of the greatness of his love.

Christ, as I have told you, was, even before his sufferings, a person of no mean generation, being the Son of the Eternal God. Neither had his Father any more such sons but he; consequently he of right was heir of all things, and so to have dominion over all worlds. For, "for by him were all things created." And hence all creatures are subject to him; yea, the angels of God worship him. Wherefore, as so considered, he augmented not his state by becoming lower than the angels for us; for what can be added to him who is naturally God? Indeed he did take, for our sakes, the human nature into union with himself, and so began to manifest his glory, and the kindness that he had for us before all worlds began now eminently to show itself. Had this Christ of God, our friend, given all he had to save us, had not his love been wonderful? But when he shall give for us himself, this is more wonderful. But this is not all; the case was so betwixt God and man, that this Son of God could not, as he was before the world was, give himself a ransom for us, he being altogether incapable so to do, being such an one as could not be subject to death, the condition that we by sin had put ourselves into.

Wherefore that which would have been a death to some, to wit, the laying aside of glory, and becoming, of the King of princes, a servant of the meanest form, this he of his own goodwill was heartily content to do. Wherefore, he that once was the object of the fear of angels, is now become a little creature, a worm, an inferior one, (Ps. xxii. 6;) born of a woman, brought forth in a stable, laid in a manger, (Luke ii. 7;) scorned of men, tempted of devils, (Luke iv. 2. Matt. iv. 1—11;) was beholden to his creatures for food, for raiment, for harbour, and a place wherein to lay his head when dead. In a word, he "made himself of no reputation, took upon him the form of a servant, and was made in the likeness of men," (Phil. ii. 7;) that he might become capable to do this kindness for us. And it is worth your noting, that all the while that he was in the world, putting himself upon those other preparations, which were to be antecedent to his being made a sacrifice for us, no man, though he told what he came about to many, had, as we read of, an heart once to thank him for what he came about. No, they railed on him, they degraded him, they called him devil, they said he was mad, and a deceiver, a blasphemer of God, and a rebel against the state : they accused him to the governor ; yea, one of his disciples sold him, another denied him, and they all forsook him, and left him to shift for himself in the hands of his horrible enemies ; who beat him with their fists, spat on him, mocked him, crowned him with thorns, scourged him, made a gazing stock of him, and finally, hanged him up by the hands and the feet alive, and gave him vinegar to increase his affliction, when he complained that his anguish had made him thirsty. And yet all this could not take his heart off the work of our redemption. To die he came, die he would, and die he did, before he made his return to the Father, for our sins, that we might live through him.

Nor may what we read of in the word concerning those temporal sufferings that he underwent be overlooked, and passed by without serious consideration ; they being a part of the curse that our sin had deserved. For all temporal plagues are due to our sin while we live, as well as the curse of God to everlasting perdition, when we die. Wherefore this is the reason why the whole life of the Lord Jesus was such a life of affliction and sorrow, he therein bare our sicknesses, and took upon him our deserts : so that now the curse in temporals, as well as the curse in spirituals, and of everlasting malediction, is removed by him away from God's people ; and since he overcame them, and got to the cross, it was by reason of the worthiness of the humble obedience that he yielded to his Father's law in our flesh; for his whole life, as well as his death, was a life of merit and purchase, and desert. Hence it is said, he increased in favour with God, (Luke ii. 52,) for his works made him still more acceptable to him; for he standing in the room of man, and becoming our reconciler to God, by the heavenly Majesty he was counted as such, and so got for us what he earned by his mediatory works; and also partook thereof, as he was our head himself. And was there not in all these things love, and love that was infinite ? Love which was not essential to his divine nature,

could never have carried him through so great a work as this : passions here would have failed, would have retreated, and have given the recoil ; yea, his very humanity would have flagged and fainted, had it not been managed, governed, and strengthened by his eternal Spirit. Wherefore it is said, that "through the eternal Spirit he offered himself without spot to God," (Heb. ix. 14;) and that he was declared to be the Son of God with so doing, and by the resurrection from the dead. (Rom. i. 4.)

Second. We come now to the second thing propounded, and by which his love is discovered, and that is his improving of his dying for us. But I must crave pardon of my reader, if he thinks that I can discover the ten hundred thousandth part thereof, for it is impossible ; but my meaning is, to give a few hints what beginnings of improvement he made thereof, in order to his further progress therein.

1. Therefore, this his death for us was so virtuous, that in the space of three days and three nights it reconciled to God, in the body of his flesh, as a common person, all, and every one, of God's elect. Christ, when he addressed himself to die, presented himself to the justice of the law, as a common person, standing in the stead, place, and room of all that he undertook for. He gave "his life a ransom for many," (Matt. xx. 28;) "he came into the world to save sinners," (1 Tim. i. 15.) And as he thus presented himself, so God, his Father, admitted him to this work ; and therefore it is said, "The Lord hath laid on him the iniquity of us all." (Isa. liii. 6.) And again, "Surely he hath borne our griefs, and carried our sorrows." (Isa. liii. 4.) Hence it unavoidably follows, that whatever he felt, and underwent, in the manner or nature, or horribleness of the death he died, he felt and underwent all as a common person ; that is, as he stood in the stead of others ; therefore it is said, "He was wounded for our transgressions, he was bruised for our iniquities ; the chastisement of our peace was upon him." (Isa. liii. 5.) And again, the just died for the unjust. (1 Pet. iii. 18.)

Now then, if he presented himself as a common person to justice, if God so admitted and accounted him, if also he laid the sins of the people, whose persons he represented, upon him, and under that consideration punishes him with those punishments and death that he died, then Christ, in life and death, is concluded by the Father to live and die as a common or public person, representing all in this life and death, for whom he undertook thus to live, and thus to die. So then it must needs be, that what next befalls this common person, it befalls him with respect to them in whose room and place he stood and suffered. Now, the next that follows is, that he is justified of God; that is, acquitted and discharged from this punishment, for the sake of the worthiness of his death and merits ; for that must be before he could be raised from the dead. (Acts ii. 24.) God raised him not up as guilty, to justify him afterwards: his resurrection was the declaration of his precedent justification. He was raised from the dead, because it was neither in equity or justice possible that he should be holden longer there, his merits procured the contrary.

Now he was condemned of God's law, and died by the hand of justice, he was acquitted by God's law, and justified of justice; and all as a common person; so, then, in his acquitting, we are acquitted, in his justification we are justified: and, therefore, the apostle applieth God's justifying of Christ to himself, and that rightly. (Isa. l. 8. Rom. ii. 33, 34.) For if Christ be my undertaker, will stand in my place, and do for me, it is but reasonable that I should be a partaker. Wherefore we are also said to be quickened together with him, (Eph. ii. 5;) that is, when he was quickened in the grave, raised up together, and made to sit together in heavenly places in Christ Jesus. Therefore another scripture saith, "Hath he quickened you together with him, having forgiven you all trespasses." (Col. ii. 13.) This quickening must not be understood of the renovation of our hearts, but of the restoring of Jesus Christ to life after he was crucified; and we are said to be quickened together with him, because we were quickened in him at his death, and were to fall or stand by him quite through the three days' and three nights' work; and were to take, therefore, our lot with him. Wherefore it it said again, that his resurrection is our justification, (Rom. iv. 25;) that by one offering he has purged our sins for ever, (Heb. x. 12;) and that by his death he hath delivered us from the "wrath to come." (1 Thess. i. 10.) But I say, I would be understood aright. This life resideth yet in the Son, and is communicated from him to us, as we are called to believe his word. Meanwhile we are secured from wrath and hell, being justified in his justification, quickened in his quickening, raised up in his resurrection, and made to sit already together in heavenly places in Christ Jesus.

And is not this a glorious improvement of his death, that after two days the whole body of the elect, in him, should be revived, and that in the third day we should live in the sight of God, in and by him? (Heb. vi. 18—20.)

2. Another improvement of his death for us was this: by that he slew for us our infernal foes; by it he abolished death, (2 Tim. i. 1;) by death he destroyed him that had the power of death, (Heb. ii. 14;) by death he took away the sting of death, (1 Cor. xxv. 55, 56;) by death he made death a pleasant sleep to saints, and the grave for a while an easy house and home for the body.

By death he made death such an advantage to us that it is become a means of translating of the souls of them that believe in him to life. And all this is manifest; for that death is ours, a blessing to us, as well as Paul and Apollos, the world, and life itself. (1 Cor. iii. 22.) And that all this is done for us by his death is apparent, for that his person is where it is, and that by himself as a common person he has got the victory for us. For though as yet all things are not put under our feet, yet we see Jesus crowned with honour and glory, who, by the grace of God, tasted death for every man: " For it became him," [God,] " for whom are all things, and by whom are all things, in bringing many sons unto glory, to make the captain of their salvation perfect through sufferings." (Heb. ii. 10.) It became him, that is, it was but just and right he should do so, if there was enough in the virtuousness of his death and blood to require such a thing. But there was so. Wherefore God has exalted him, and us in him, above these infernal foes. Let us, therefore, see ourselves delivered from death first by the exaltation of our Jesus; let us behold him, I say, as crowned with glory and honour, as, or because, he tasted death for us; and then we shall see ourselves already in heaven by our Head, our undertaker, our Jesus, our Saviour.

3. Another improvement that has already been made of his death for us is thus—he hath, at his entrance into the presence of God, for his worthiness' sake, obtained that the Holy Ghost should be given unto him for us, that we by that might, in all things yet to be done, be made meet to be partakers personally in ourselves, as well as virtually by our head and forerunner, of the inheritance of the saints in light. Wherefore the abundant pourings out of that was forborn until the resurrection and glorification of our Lord Jesus. " For the Holy Ghost was not yet given, because that Jesus was not yet glorified." (John vii. 39.) Nor was it given so soon as received: for he received it upon his entering into the holy place, when he had sprinkled the mercy-seat with the blood of sprinkling; but it was not given out to us till some time after, (Acts iv:) however, it was obtained before. (Acts ii. 33.) And it was meet that it should in that infinite immeasurableness in which he received it, first abide upon him, that his human nature, which was the first-fruits of the election of God, might receive by its abidings upon him, that glory for which it was ordained; and that we might receive, as we receive all other things—first by our head and undertaker—sanctification in the fulness of it. Hence it is written, that as he is made unto us of God, wisdom, and righteousness, and redemption, so sanctification too, (1 Cor. i. 30:) for first we are sanctified in his flesh, as we are justified by his righteousness. Wherefore he is that Holy One that setteth us, in himself, a holy lump before God, not only with reference to justification and life, but with reference to sanctification and holiness: for we that are elect, are all considered in him as he has received that, as well as in that he has taken pos-

session of the heaven for us. I count not this all the benefit that accrueth to us by Jesus his receiving the Holy Ghost, at his entrance into the presence of God for us. For we also are to receive it ourselves from him, according as by God we are placed in the body at the times appointed of the Father; that we, as was said, may receive personal quickening, personal renovation, personal sanctification, and, in conclusion, glory. But, I say, for that he hath received this Holy Spirit to himself, he received it as the effect of his ascension, which was the effect of his resurrection, and of the merit of his death and passion. And he received it as a common person, as a head and undertaker for the people.

4. Another improvement that has been made of his death, and of the merits thereof for us, is, that he has obtained to be made of God the chief and high Lord of heaven for us, (all this while we speak of the exaltation of the human nature, in, by, and with which the Son of God became capable to be our reconciler unto God): "All things," saith he, "are delivered unto me of my Father: and all power in heaven and earth is given unto me;" and all this because he died. "He humbled himself, and became obedient unto death, even the death of the cross: wherefore God hath highly exalted him, and given him a name above every name, that at the name of Jesus every knee shall bow, of things in heaven, of things in earth, and things under the earth; and that every tongue should confess that Jesus Christ is Lord, to the glory of God the Father." (Phil. ii. 8—11.) And all this is, as was said afore, for our sakes. He has given him to be head over all things to the church. (Eph. i. 22.)

Wherefore, whoever is set up on earth, they are set up by our Lord: "By me," saith he, "kings reign, and princes decree justice. By me princes rule, and nobles, even all the judges of the earth." (Prov. viii. 15, 16.) Nor are they, when set up, left to do, though they should desire it, their own will and pleasure. The *Metheg-Ammah* (the bridle) is in his own hand, and he giveth reins, or check, even as it pleaseth him. (2 Sam. viii. 1.) He has this power for the well-being of his people. Nor are the fallen angels exempted from being put under his rebuke. He is the only potentate, (1 Tim. vi. 15,) and in his times will show it. Peter tells us, He "is gone into heaven, and is on the right hand of God; angels, and authorities, and powers being made subject unto him." (1 Pet. iii. 22.)

This power, as I said, he has received for the sake of his church on earth, and for her conduct and well-being among the sons of men. Hence, as he is called the King of nations, in general, (Jer. x. 7,) so the King of saints, in special, (Rev. xv. 3;) and as he is said to be Head over all things in general, so to his church in special. (1 Cor. xii. 28—30.)

5. Another improvement that he hath made of his death for us, is, he hath obtained, and received into his own hand, sufficiency of gifts to make ministers for his church withal. I say, to make and maintain, in opposition to all that would hinder, a sufficient ministry. "Wherefore he saith, When he ascended up on high, he led captivity captive, and gave gifts unto men. And he gave some, apostles; and some, prophets; and some, evangelists; and some, pastors and teachers; for the perfecting of the saints, for the work of the ministry, for the edifying of the body of Christ. Till we all come in the unity of the faith, and knowledge of the Son of God, unto a perfect man, unto the measure of the stature of the fulness of Christ." (Eph. iv. 8, 11—13.) Many ways has Satan devised to bring into contempt this blessed advantage that Christ has received of God for the benefit of his church; partly while he stirs up persons to revile the sufficiency of the Holy Ghost, as to this thing; partly while he stirs up his own limbs and members to broach his delusions in the world in the name of Christ, and, as they blasphemously call it, by the assistance of the Holy Ghost; partly while he tempteth novices in their faith to study and labour in nice distinctions, and the affecting of uncouth expressions, that vary from the form of sound words, thereby to get applause, and a name, a forerunner of their own destruction. (John iii. 6.)

But, notwithstanding all this, "wisdom is justified of her children," (Matt. xi. 19;) and at the last day, when the outside and inside of all things shall be seen and compared, it will appear that the Son of God has so managed his own servants in the ministry of his word, and so managed his word while they have been labouring in it, as to put in his blessing by that, upon the souls of sinners, and has blown away all other things as chaff. (James i. 18.)

6. Another improvement that the Lord Christ has made of his death for his, is the obtaining and taking possession of heaven for them. "By his own blood he entered in once into the holy place, having obtained eternal redemption for us." (Heb. ix. 12.) This heaven, who knows what it is? This glory, who knows what it is? It is called God's throne, God's house, (John xiv. 2,) God's habitation, paradise, (2 Cor. xii. 4,) the kingdom of God, the high and holy place, (Isa. lvii. 15,) Abraham's bosom, (Luke xvi. 22,) and the place of heavenly pleasures. (Ps. xvi. 11.) In this heaven is to be found, *the face of God for ever*, (Ps. xli. 12,) immortality, the person of Christ, the prophets, the angels, the revelation of all mysteries, the knowledge of all the elect, *eternity*.

Of this heaven, as was said afore, we are possessed already, we are in it, we are set down in it, and partake already of the benefits thereof, but all by our head and undertaker; and it is fit that we should believe this, rejoice in this, talk of this, tell one another of this, and live in the expectation of our own personal enjoyment of it. And as we should do all this, so we should bless and praise the name of God, who has put over this house, this kingdom, and inheritance, into the hand of so faithful a friend; yea, a Brother, a Saviour, and blessed Undertaker for us. And, lastly, since all these things already mentioned are the fruit of the sufferings of our Jesus, and his sufferings the fruit of that love of his that passeth knowledge, how should we bow the knee before him, and call him tender Father! yea, how should we love and obey him, and devote ourselves unto his service, and be willing to be also sufferers for his sake, to whom be honour and glory for ever! And thus much of the love of Christ in general.

I might here add many other things, but, as I told you before, we would under the head but now touched upon, treat about the fundamentals, or great and chief parts thereof, and then the exceeding greatness of it more particularly. Wherefore of that we must say something now.

II. *The exceeding greatness of Christ's love.*

To know the love of Christ, which passeth knowledge. In that it is said to pass knowledge, it is manifest it is exceeding great, or greatly going beyond what can be known: for to exceed is to go beyond, be above, or to be out of the reach of what would comprehend that which is so. And since the expression is absolutely indefinite, and respecteth not the knowledge of this or the other creature only, it is manifest that Paul, by his thus saying, challengeth all creatures in heaven and earth to find out the bottom of this love, if they can—" the love of Christ, which passeth knowledge." I will add, that forasmuch as he is indefinite also about the knowledge, as well as about the persons knowing, it is out of doubt that he here engageth all knowledge, in what enlargements, attainments, improvements, and heights soever it hath, or may for ever attain unto. " It passeth knowledge."

Of the same import also is that other passage of the apostle, a little above, in the self-same chapter: I preach, saith he, "among the Gentiles the unsearchable riches of Christ," (Eph. ii. 8;) or those riches of Christ that cannot by searching be found out in the all of them: *the riches*, the riches of his love and grace; the riches of his love and grace towards us. " For ye know the grace of our Lord Jesus Christ, that though he was rich, yet for your sakes he became poor, that ye through his poverty might be rich." (2 Cor. viii. 9.) Ye know the grace, that is so far, and so far every believer knows it; for that his leaving heaven and taking upon him flesh, that he might bring us thither, is manifest to all. But yet, all the grace that was wrapped up in that amazing condescension, knoweth none, nor can know; for if that might be, that possibility would be a flat contradiction to the text—" The love of Christ, which passeth knowledge." Wherefore the riches of this love, in the

utmost of it, is not, cannot be known by any, let their understanding and knowledge be heightened and improved what it may; yea, and being heightened and improved, let what search there can by it be made into this love and grace—" That which is afar off, and exceeding deep, who can find out ?" (Eccles. vii. 24.) And that this love of Christ is so, shall anon be made more apparent. But at present we will proceed to particular challenges for the making out of this, and then we will urge those reasons that will be for the further confirmation of the whole.

First. This love passes the knowledge of the *wisest* saint: we now single out the greatest proficient in this knowledge; and to confirm this, I need go no further than to the man that spake these words, to wit, Paul, for in his conclusion, he includes himself—" The love of Christ, which passeth knowledge," even my knowledge. As who should say, though I have waded a great way in the grace of Christ, and have as much experience of his love as any he in all the world, yet I confess myself short, as to the fulness that is therein, nor will I stick to conclude of any other, that " he knows nothing yet as he ought to know." (1 Cor. viii. 2; xiii. 12.)

Second. This love passeth the knowledge of all the saints, were it all put together. We—we all, and every one—did we each of us contribute for the manifesting of this love, what it is, the whole of what we know, it would amount but to a broken knowledge; we know but in part, (1 Cor. xiii. 9,) we see darkly, (1 Cor. xiii. 12,) we walk not by sight, but faith. (2 Cor. v. 7.) True, now we speak of saints on earth.

Third. But we will speak of saints in heaven; they cannot to the utmost know this love of Christ. For though they know more thereof than saints on earth, because they are more in the open visions of it, and also are more enlarged, being spirits perfect, than we on earth, yet, to say no more now, they do not see the rich and unsearchable runnings out thereof unto sinners here on earth. Nor may they there measure that to others, by what they themselves knew of it here. For sins, and times, and persons, and other circumstances, may much alter the case; but were all the saints on earth, and all the saints in heaven, to contribute all that they know of this love of Christ, and to put it into one sum of knowledge, they would greatly come short of knowing the utmost of this love, for that there is an infinite deal of this love yet unknown by them. It is said plainly, that they on earth do not yet know what they shall be. (1 John iii. 2.) And as for them in heaven, they are not yet made perfect as they shall be. (Heb. xi. 39, 40.) Besides, we find the souls under the altar, how perfect now soever, when compared with that state they were in when with the body, (Isa. lxiii. 16,) yet are not able in all points, though in glory, to know, and so to govern themselves there without directions, (Rev. vi. 9—11;)

I say, they are not able, without directions and instructions, to know the kinds and manner of workings of the love of Christ towards us that dwell on earth.

Fourth. We will join with these, the angels, and when all of them, with men, have put all and every whit of what they know of this love of Christ together, they must come far short of reaching to, or of understanding, the utmost bound thereof. I grant that angels do know, in some certain parts of knowledge of the love of Christ, more than saints on earth can know while here; but then again, I know that even they do also learn many things of saints on earth, which shows that themselves know also but in part, (Eph. iii. 10;) so then, all, as yet, as to this love of Christ, and the utmost knowledge of it, are but as so many imperfects, (1 Pet. i. 12;) nor can they all, put all their imperfects together, make up a perfect knowledge of this love of Christ; for the texts do yet stand where they did, and say, " his riches are unsearchable, and his love that which passeth knowledge."

We will come now to show you, besides what has been already touched on, the reason why this riches is unsearchable, and that love such as passeth knowledge; and the first is, because it is eternal: all that is eternal has attending of it, as to the utmost knowledge of it, a fourfold impossibility :—

1. It is without beginning.
2. It is without end.
3. It is infinite.
4. It is incomprehensible.

1. *It is without beginning :*—That which was before the world was, is without a beginning; but the love of Christ was before the world.

This is evident from Proverbs viii. His delights, before God had made the world, are there said to be with the sons of men; not that we then had being, for we were as yet uncreated; but though we had not beings created, we had being in the love and affections of Jesus Christ. Now this love of Christ must needs—as to the fulness of it, as to the utmost of it—be absolutely unknown to man. Who can tell how many heart-pleasing thoughts Christ had of us before the world began? Who can tell how much he then was delighted in that being we had in his affections, as also in the consideration of our beings, believings, and being with him afterwards?

In general, we may conclude it was great; for there seems to be a parallel betwixt his Father's delights in him, and his delights in us: "I was daily his delight, and my delights were with the sons of men." (Prov. viii. 30, 31.) But, I say, who can tell, who can tell altogether, what and how much the Father delighted in his Son before the world began? Who can tell what kind of delight the Father had in the Son before the world began? Why, there seems to be a parallel betwixt the Father's love to Christ, and Christ's love to us; the Father's delight in Christ, and his

delight in us. Yea, Christ confirms it, saying, " As the Father hath loved me, so have I loved you, continue ye in my love." (John xv. 9.) I know that I am not yet upon the nature of the word eternal; yet since, by eternal, we understand, before the world began, as well as forward to an endless for ever, we may a little inquire of folks as they may read, if they can tell the kind or measure of the love wherewith Christ then loved us. I remember the question that God asked Job. " Where," saith he, " wast thou when I laid the foundation of the earth? declare if thou hast understanding," (Job xxxviii. 4:) thereby insinuating, that because it was done before he had his being, therefore he could not tell how it was done. Now, if a work so visible, as the creation is, is yet as to the manner of the workmanship thereof, wholly unknown to them that commenced in their beings afterwards, how shall that which has, in all the circumstances of it, been more hidden and inward, be found out by them that have intelligence thereof by the ear, and but in part, and that in a mystery, and long afterwards? But to conclude this, that which is eternal is without all beginning. This was presented to consideration before, and therefore it cannot to perfection be known.

2. That which is eternal is *without end,* and how can an endless thing be known? that which has no end has no middle, wherefore it is impossible that the one half of the love that Christ has for his church should ever by them be known. I know that those visions that the saved shall have in heaven of this love, will far transcend our utmost knowledge here, even as far as the light of the sun at noon goes beyond the light of a blinking candle at midnight. And hence it is, that when the days of those visions are come, the knowledge that we now have shall be swallowed up: " When that which is perfect is come, then that which is in part shall be done away." (1 Cor. xiii. 10.) And although he speaks here of perfections, " when that which is perfect is come," &c., yet even that perfection must not be thought to be such as is the perfection of God; for then should all that are saved be so many eternals, and so many infinites, as he is infinite. But the meaning is, we shall then be with the eternal, shall immediately enjoy him with all the perfection of knowledge, as far as is possible for a creature, when he is brought up to the utmost height that his created substance will bear to be capable of. But for all that, this perfection will yet come short of the perfection of him that made him, and consequently, short of knowing the utmost of his love: since that in the root is his very essence and nature. I know it says also that we should " be known even as we are known." But yet this must not be understood, as if we should know God as fully as he knows us. It would be folly and madness so to conclude; but the meaning is, we are known for happiness; we are known of God, for heaven and felicity; and when that which is perfect is come, then shall we per-

fectly know, and enjoy that for which we are now known of God. And this is that which the apostle longed for, namely, if by any means he might apprehend that for which he was also apprehended of Christ Jesus, (Phil. iii. 12;) that is, know, and see that, unto the which he was appointed of God, and apprehended of Christ Jesus. It is said again, "We shall be like him, for we shall see him as he is." (1 John iii. 2.) This text has respect to the Son, as to his humanity, and not as to his divinity; and not as to his divinity simply or distinctly considered; for as to that, it is as possible for a spirit to drink up the sea, as for the most enlarged saint that is, or ever shall be in glory, so to see God as to know him altogether, to the utmost, or throughout. But the humanity of the Son of God, we shall see throughout, in all the beauty and glory that is upon him; and that was prepared for him before the foundation of the world. And Christ will that we see this glory, when he takes us up in glory to himself, (John xvii. 24;) but the utmost boundlessness of the divine majesty, the eternal deity of the Son of God, cannot be known to the utmost, or altogether. I do not doubt but that there will then in him—I mean in Christ—and in us, break forth these glorious rays and beams of the eternal majesty, as will make him in each of us admirable one to another, (2 Thess. i. 10;) and that then, that of God shall be known of us, that now never entered into our hearts to think of. But the whole is not, cannot, shall never be fully known of any. And therefore the love of Christ, it being essential to himself, cannot be known, because of the endlessness that is in it. I said before, that which has no end has no middle, how then shall those that shall be in heaven eternally, ever pass over half the breadth of eternity? True, I know that all enjoyments there will be enjoyments eternal: yea, that whatever we shall there embrace, or what embraces we shall be embraced with, shall be eternal; but I put a difference betwixt that which is eternal, as to the nature, and that which is so as to the durableness thereof. The nature of eternal things we shall enjoy, so soon as ever we come to heaven, but the duration of eternal things, them we shall never be able to pass through, for they are endless. So then the eternal love of Christ, as to the nature of it, will be perfectly known of saints, when they shall dwell in heaven; but the endlessness thereof they shall never attain unto. And this will be their happiness. For could it be that we should in heaven ever reach the end of our blessedness, (as we should, could we reach to the end of this love of Christ,) why then, as the saying is, " We should be at the land's end, and feel the bottom of all our enjoyments." Besides, whatsoever has an end, has a time to decay, and to cease to be, as well as to have a time to show forth its highest excellences. Wherefore from all these considerations it is most manifest, that the love of Christ is unsearchable, and that it passes knowledge.

3 and 4. Now the other two things follow of course, to wit, that this love is *infinite* and *incomprehensible*. Wherefore here is that that still is above and beyond even those that are arrived to the utmost of their perfections. And this, if I may so say, will keep them in an employ, even when they are in heaven: though not an employ that is laboursome, tiresome, burthensome, yet an employ that is dutiful, delightful, and profitable; for although the work and worship of saints in heaven is not particularly revealed as yet, and so " it doth not yet appear what we shall be," yet in the general we may say, there will be that for them to do, that has not yet by them been done; and by that work which they shall do there, their delight will be delight unto them. The law was the shadow, and not the very image of heavenly things. (Heb. x. 1.) The image is an image, and not the heavenly things themselves, (Heb. ix. 23,) (the heavenly things they are saints,) there shall be worship in the heavens. Nor will this at all derogate from their glory. The angels now wait upon God, and serve him, (Ps. ciii. 20;) the Son of God is now a minister, and waiteth upon his service in heaven, (Heb. viii. 1, 2;) some saints have been employed about service for God, after they have been in heaven, (Luke ix. 29—32,) and why we should be idle spectators when we come thither, I see not reason to believe. It may be said, "They there rest from their labours." True, but not from their delights. All things then that once were burthensome, whether in suffering or service, shall be done away, and that which is delightful and pleasureable shall remain. But then will be a time to receive, and not to work. True, if by work you mean such as we now count work; but what if our work be there, to receive and bless? The fishes in the sea do drink, swim, and drink. But for a further discourse of this, let that alone till we come thither. But to come down again into the world, for now we are talking of things aloft:

Second. This love of Christ must needs be beyond our knowledge, because we cannot possibly know the utmost of our sin. Sin is that which sets out, and off, the knowledge of the love of Christ. There are four things that must be spoken to for the clearing of this:

1. The nature of sin.
2. The aggravations of sin.
3. The utmost tendencies of sin.
4. And the perfect knowledge of all this.

1. Before we can know this love of Christ, as afore, we must necessarily know the nature of sin, that is, what sin is, what sin is in itself. But no man knows the nature of sin to the full; not what sin in itself is to the full. The apostle saith, "That sin," that is in itself, "is exceeding sinful." (Rom. vii. 13.) That is, exceeding it as to its filthiness, goes beyond our knowledge. But this is seen by the commandment. Now the reason why none can, to the full, know the horrible nature of sin, is because none, to the full, can

know the blessed nature of the blessed God. For sin is the opposite to God. There is nothing that seeketh absolutely, and in its own nature to overcome, and to annihilate God, but sin: and sin doth so. Sin is worse than the devil; he therefore that is more afraid of the devil than of sin, knows not the badness of sin as he ought, nor but little of the love of Jesus Christ. He that knows not what sin would have done to the world, had not Christ stepped betwixt those harms and it, how can he know so much as the extent of the love of Christ in common? And he that knows not what sin would have done to him in particular, had not Christ the Lord stepped in and saved, cannot know the utmost of the love of Christ to him in particular. Sin therefore, in the utmost evil of it, cannot be known of us: so consequently the love of Christ, in the utmost goodness of it, cannot be known of us.

Besides, there are many sins committed by us, dropping from us, and that pollute us, that we are not at all aware of. How then should we know that love of Christ by which we are delivered from them? "Lord, who can understand his errors?" said David. (Ps. xix. 12.) Consequently, who can understand the love that saves him from them? Moreover, he that knows the love of Christ to the full, must also know to the full that wrath and anger of God, that like hell itself, burneth against sinners for the sake of sin: but this knows none. "Lord, who knows the power of thine anger?" said Moses. (Ps. xc. 11.) Therefore none knows this love of Christ to the full. The nature of sin is to get into our good, to mix itself with our good, to lie lurking many times under the formality and show of good; and that so close, so cunningly, and invisibly, that the party concerned embraces it for virtue, and knows not otherwise to do; and yet from this he is saved by the love of Christ; and therefore, as was hinted but now, if a man doth not know the nature of his wound, how should he know the nature and excellency of the balsam that hath cured him of his wound?

2. There are the due aggravations that belong to sin, which men are unacquainted with; it was one of the great things that the prophets were concerned with from God towards the people, (Jer. ii.;) (as to show them their sins, so,) to show them what aggravations did belong thereto. (Jer. iii. Ezek. xvi.)

There are sins against light, sins against knowledge, sins against love, sins against learning, sins against threatenings, sins against promises, vows, and resolutions, sins against experience, sins against examples of anger, and sins that have great, and high, and strange aggravations attending of them; the which we are ignorant of, though not altogether, yet in too great a measure. Now if these things be so, how can the love that saveth us from them be known or understood to the full?

Alas, our ignorance of these things is manifest by our unwillingness to abide affliction, by our secret murmuring under the hand of God; by our wondering why we are so chastised as we are, by our thinking long that the affliction is no sooner removed.

Or, if our ignorance of the vileness of our actions is not manifest this way, yet it is in our lightness under our guilt, our slight thoughts of our doings, our slovenly doing of duties, and asking of forgiveness after some evil or unbecoming actions. It is to no boot to be particular; the whole course of our lives doth too fully make it manifest that we are wonderful short in knowing both the nature, and also the aggravations of our sins: and how then should we know that love of Christ in its full dimensions, by which we are saved and delivered therefrom?

3. Who knows the utmost tendencies of sin?— I mean, what the least sin driveth at, and what it would unavoidably run the sinner into? There is not a plague, a judgment, an affliction, an evil under heaven, that the least of our transgressions has not called for at the hands of the great God: nay, the least calleth for all the distresses that are under heaven, to fall upon the soul and body of the sinner at once. This is plain, for that the least sin deserveth hell; which is worse than all the plagues that are on earth.

But I say, who understandeth this? And I say again, if one sin, the least sin, deserveth all these things, what thinkest thou do all thy sins deserve? how many judgments! how many plagues! how many lashes with God's iron whip dost thou deserve! besides there is hell itself, the place itself, the fire itself, the nature of the torments, and the durableness of them, who can understand?

But this is not all; the tendencies of thy sins are to kill others. Men, good men, little think how many of their neighbours one of their sins may kill. As, how many good men and good women do unawares, through their uncircumspectness, drive their own children down into the deep? (Ps. cvi. 6, 7.) We will easily count them very hard-hearted sinners, that used to offer their children in sacrifice to devils, when it is easy to do worse ourselves; they did but kill the body, but we body and soul in hell, if we have not a care.

Do we know how our sins provoke God? how they grieve the Holy Ghost? how they weaken our graces? how they spoil our prayers? how they weaken faith? how they tempt Christ to be ashamed of us? and how they hold back good from us? And if we know not every one of all these things to the full, how shall we know to the full the love of Christ, which saveth us from them all?

4. Again, fourthly, but who has the *perfect knowledge* of all these things? I will grant that some good souls may have waded a great way in some one or more of them; but I know that there

is not any that thoroughly know them all. And yet the love of Christ doth save us from all, notwithstanding all the vileness and soul-damning virtue that is in them. Alas! how short are we of the knowledge of ourselves, and of what is in us. How many are there that do not know that man consisteth of a body made of dust, and of an immortal soul? yea, and how many be there of those that confess it, that know not the constitution of either? I will add, how many are there that profess themselves to be students of these two parts of man, that have oftentimes proved themselves to be but fools as to both? And I will conclude, that there is not a man under heaven that knoweth it altogether; for man is "fearfully and wonderfully made," (Ps. cxxxix. 14:) nor can the manner of the union of these two parts be perfectly found out. How much more then must we needs be at loss as to the fulness of the knowledge of the love of Christ?

Third. But, thirdly, he that altogether knoweth the love of Christ, must, precedent to that, know not only all the wiles of the devil, but also all the plottings, contrivings, and designs and attempts of that wicked one; yea, he must know all the times that he hath been with God, together with all the motions that he has made that he might have leave to fall upon us as upon Job and Peter, to try if he might swallow us up. (Job i., ii. Luke xxii. 31.) But who knows all this? No man, no angel. For if the heart of man be so deep that none, by all his actions, save God, can tell the utmost secrets that are therein, how should the heart of angels, which in all likelihood are deeper, be found out by any mortal man? And yet this must be found out before we can find out the utmost of the love of Christ to us. I conclude therefore, from all these things, that the love of Christ passeth knowledge, or that by no means the bottom, the utmost bounds thereof, can be understood.

Fourth. He that will presume to say this love of Christ can be to the utmost known by us, must presume to say that he knoweth the utmost of the merits of his blood, the utmost exercise of his patience, the utmost of his intercession, the utmost of the glory that he has prepared and taken possession of for us. But I presume that there is none that can know all this, therefore I may without any fear assert, there is none that knows, that is, that knows to the full the other.

III. *The knowledge of Christ's love attainable in this world.*

We come now more particularly to speak of the knowledge of the love of Christ. We have spoken of the love of Christ, to wit, of the exceeding greatness of it, and now we come to speak of the knowledge of it; that is to say, we will show what knowledge of it is attainable in this world, under these three heads. As to this,

First. It may be known as to the nature of it.

Second. It may be known in many of the degrees of it.

Third. But the greatest knowledge that we can have of it here, is to know that it passes knowledge.

First. We may know it in the *nature* of it; that is, that it is love, free, divine, heavenly, everlasting, incorruptible. And this no love is but the love of Christ; all other love is either love corruptible, transient, mixed, or earthly. It is divine, for it is the love of the holy nature of God. It is heavenly, for that it is from above: it is everlasting, for that it has no end: it is immortal, for that there is not the appearance of corruptibleness in it, or likelihood of decay.

This is general knowledge, and this is common among the saints, at leastwise in the notion of it. Though I confess it is hard in time of temptation practically to hold fast the soul to all these things. But as I have said already, this love of Christ must be such, because love in the root of it is essential to his nature; as also I have proved now, as is the root, such are the branches; and as is the spring, such are the streams, unless the channels in which those streams do run, should be corrupted, and so defile it: but I know no channels through which this love of Christ is conveyed unto us, but those made in his side, his hands, and his feet, &c., or those gracious promises that dropped like honey from his holy lips, in the day of his love in which he spake them; and seeing his love is conveyed to us, as through those channels, and so by the conduit of the holy and blessed Spirit of God, to our hearts, it cannot be that it should hitherto be corrupted. I know the cisterns, to wit, our hearts, into which it is conveyed, are unclean, and may take away much, through the damp that they may put upon it, of the native savour and sweetness thereof. I know also, that there are those that tread down and muddy those streams with their feet, (Ezek. xxxiv. 18, 19;) but yet neither the love, nor the channels in which it runs, should bear the blame of this. And I hope those that are saints indeed, will not only be preserved to eternal life, but nourished with this that is incorruptible unto the day of Christ.

I told you before, that in the hour of temptation it will be hard for the soul to hold fast to these things—that is, to the true definition of this love—for then, or at such seasons, it will not be admitted that the love of Christ is either transient or mixed: but we count that we cannot be loved long, unless something better than yet we see in us, be found there, as an inducement to Christ to love, and to continue to love our poor souls. (Isa. lxiv. 6.) But these the Christian at length gets over; for he sees by experience he hath no such inducement, (Deut. ix. 5;) also that Christ loves freely, and not for or because of such poor, silly, imaginary enticements. (Ezek. xvi. 60—62.) Thus therefore the love of Christ may be known, that is, in the nature of it: it may, I say, but not easily. (Ezek.

xxxvi. 25—33.) For this knowledge is neither easily got, though got, nor easily retained, though retained. There is nothing that Satan setteth himself more against than the breaking forth of the love of Christ in its own proper native lustre; for he knows it destroys his kingdom, which standeth in profaneness, in errors, and delusions, the only destruction of which is the knowledge of this love of Christ. (2 Cor. v. 14.) What mean those swarms of opinions that are in the world? What is the reason that some are carried about as clouds with a tempest? What mean men's waverings, men's changing, and interchanging truth for error, and one error for another? Why, this is the thing, the devil is in it. This work is his, and he makes this ado, to make a dust, and a dust to darken the light of the gospel withal. And if he once attaineth to that, then farewell the true knowledge of the love of Christ.

Also he will assault the spirits of Christians with divers and sundry cogitations, such as shall have in them a tendency to darken the judgment, delude the fancy, to abuse the conscience. He has an art to metamorphose all things; he can make God seem to be to us a most fierce and terrible destroyer, and Christ a terrible exactor of obedience, and most amazingly pinching of his love. He can make supposed sins unpardonable, and unpardonable ones appear as virtues. He can make the law to be received for gospel, and cause that the gospel shall be thrown away as a fable. He can persuade that faith is fancy, and that fancy is the best faith in the world. Besides, he can tickle the heart with false hope of a better life hereafter, even as if the love of Christ were there. But, as I said before, from all these things the true love of Christ, in the right knowledge of it, delivereth those that have it shed abroad in the heart by the Holy Ghost that he hath given. (Rom. v.) Wherefore it is for this purpose that Christ biddeth us to continue in his love, (John xv. 9,) because the right knowledge and faith of that to the soul, disperseth and driveth away all such fogs and mists of darkness, and makes the soul to sit fast in the promise of eternal life by him; yea, and to grow up into him who is the head " in all things."

Before I leave this head, I will present my reader with these things, as helps to the knowledge of the love of Christ; I mean the knowledge of the nature of it, and as *helps* to retain it.

First. Know, thyself, what a vile, horrible, abominable sinner thou art; for thou canst not know the love of Christ, before thou knowest the badness of thy nature. " O wretched man that I am," (Rom. vii. 24,) must be, before a man can perceive the nature of the love of Christ. He that sees himself but little, will hardly know much of the love of Christ; he that sees of himself nothing at all, will hardly ever see anything of the love of Christ. But he that sees most of what an abominable wretch he is, he is like to see most of what is the love of Christ. All errors in doctrine take

their rise from the want of this (I mean errors in doctrine as to justification). All the idolizing of men's virtues, and human inventions, riseth also from the want of this. So, then, if a man would be kept sure and steadfast, let him labour before all things to know his own wretchedness. People naturally think that the knowledge of their sins is the way to destroy them, when in very deed it is the first step to salvation. Now, if thou wouldst know the badness of thyself, begin in the first place to study the law, then thy heart, and so thy life. The law thou must look into, for that is the glass; thy heart thou must look upon, for that is the face; thy life thou must look upon, for that is the body of a man, as to religion. (James i. 25.) And without the wary consideration of these three, it is not to be thought that a man can come at the knowledge of himself, and consequently to the knowledge of the love of Christ. (James i. 26, 27.)

Second. Labour to see the emptiness, shortness, and the pollution that cleaveth to a man's own righteousness. This also must in some measure be known before a man can know the nature of the love of Christ. They that see nothing of the loathsomeness of man's best things will think that the love of Christ is of that nature as to be procured or won, obtained or purchased, by man's good deeds. And although so much gospel-light is broke forth as to stop men's mouths from saying this, yet it is nothing else but sound conviction of the vileness of man's righteousness that will enable men to see that the love of Christ is of that nature as to save a man without it; as to see that it is of that nature as to justify him without it,—I say without it, or not at all. There is shortness, there is hypocrisy, there is a desire of vain-glory, there is pride, there is presumption in man's own righteousness; nor can it be without these wickednesses when men know not the nature of the love of Christ. Now these defile it, and make it abominable. Yea, if there were no imperfection in it but that which I first did mention, to wit, shortness, how could it cover the nakedness of him that hath it, or obtain for the man, in whole or in part, that Christ should love, and have respect unto him?

Occasions many thou hast given thee to see the emptiness of man's own righteousness, but all will not do unless thou hast help from heaven: wherefore thy wisdom will be, if thou canst tell where to find it, to lie in the way of God, that when he comes to visit the men that wait upon him in the means of his own appointing, thou mayst be there; if perhaps he may cast an eye of pity upon thy desolate soul, and make thee see the things abovementioned, that thou mayst know the nature of the love of Christ.

Third. If thou wouldst know the nature of this love, be much in acquainting of thy soul with the nature of the law, and the nature of the gospel, (Gal. iii. 21;) the which, though they are not diametrically opposite one to another, yet do propound things so differently to man, that if he knows not where, when, and how to take them, it is impossible but that he should confound them, and in confounding of them lose his own soul. (Rom. x. 4.) The law is a servant both first and last to the gospel; when, therefore, it is made a Lord, it destroyeth; and then, to be sure, it is made a Lord and Saviour of, when its dictates and commands are depended upon for life.

Thy wisdom, therefore, will be to study these things distinctly and thoroughly; for, so far as thou art ignorant of the true knowledge of the nature of these, so far thou art ignorant of the true knowledge of the nature of the love of Christ. Read Paul to the Galatians; that epistle was indited by the Holy Ghost on purpose to direct the soul in and about this very thing.

Fourth. The right knowledge of the nature of the love of Christ is obtained and retained by keeping of these two doctrines at an everlasting distance as to the conscience, to wit, not suffering the law to rule but over my outward man, not suffering the gospel to be removed one hair's breadth from my conscience. When Christ dwells in my heart by faith, (Eph. iii. 17,) and the moral law dwells in my members, (Col. iii. 5,) the one to keep up peace with God, the other to keep my conversation in a good decorum, then am I right, and not till then.

But this will not be done without much experience, diligence, and delight in Christ. For there is nothing that Satan more desireth than that the law may abide in the conscience of an awakened Christian, and there take up the place of Christ and faith; for he knows if this may be obtained the veil is presently drawn over the face of the soul, and the heart darkened as to the knowledge of Christ; and being darkened, the man is driven into despair of mercy, or is put upon it to work for life. (2 Cor. iii. 13—15.) There is, therefore, as I say, much diligence required of him that will keep these two in their places assigned them of God. I say much diligent study of the word, diligent prayer, with diligence to walk with God in the world. But we will pass this, and come to the second head.

Second. As the love of Christ may be known in the nature of it, so it may be known in many *degrees* of it. That which is knowable admits of degrees of knowledge: the love of Christ is knowable. Again: that which is not possible to be known to the utmost is to be known we know not how much; and, therefore, they that seek to know it should never be contented or satisfied, to what degree of the knowledge of it soever they attain; but still should be reaching forward, because there is more to be known of it before them. "Brethren," said Paul, "I count not myself to have apprehended"—that is, to the utmost—"but this one thing I do, forgetting those things which are behind, and reaching forth unto those things which are before, I press towards the mark for the prize of the high calling of God in Christ Jesus." (Phil iii. 13, 14.)

I might here discourse of many things, since I am upon this head of reaching after the knowledge of the love of Christ, in many of the degrees of it. But I shall content myself with few.

1. He that would know the love of Christ in several degrees of it must begin at his person, for in him dwells all the treasures of wisdom and knowledge. Nay, more: "In him are hid all the treasures of wisdom and knowledge." (Col. ii. 3.) In him, that is, in his person; for the godhead of Christ and our nature to be united in one person is the highest mystery; and the first appearance of the love of Christ by himself to the world. (1 Tim. iii. 16.) Here, I say, lie hid the treasures of wisdom, and here, to the world, springs forth the riches of his love. (John i. 14.) That the eternal Word, for the salvation of sinners, should come down from heaven and be made flesh is an act of such condescension, a discovery of such love, that can never to the full be found out. Only here we may see love in him was deep, was broad, was long, and high; let us, therefore, first begin here to learn to know the love of Christ in the high degrees thereof.

(1.) Here, in the first place, we perceive love, in that the human nature, the nature of man, not of angels, is taken into union with God. Whoso could consider this, as it is possible for it to be considered, would stand amazed till he died with wonder. By this very act of the heavenly wisdom we have an unconceivable pledge of the love of Christ to man; for in that he hath taken into union with himself our nature, what doth it signify but that he intendeth to take into union with himself our persons? For this very purpose did he assume our nature. Wherefore we read that in the flesh he took upon him, in that flesh he died for us, the just for the unjust, that he might bring us to God. (1 Pet. iii. 18.)

(2.) As he was made flesh, so, as was said afore, he became a public or common person for us: and hereby is perceived another degree of his love; undertaking to do for his what was not possible they should do for themselves, perfecting of righteousness to the very end of the law, and doing for us to the reconciling of us unto his Father and himself. (Rom. x. 3, 4.)

(3.) Herein, also, we may attain to another degree of knowledge of his love by understanding that he has conquered, and so disabled our foes, that they cannot now accomplish their designed enmity upon us, (Rom. v. Eph. v. 26, 27 ;) but that when Satan, death, the grave, and sin, have done to this people whatever can by them be done, we shall be still more than conquerors, though on our side be many disadvantages, through him that loved us, over them. (Rom. viii. 37.)

(4.) By this also we may yet see more of his love, in that, as a forerunner he is gone into heaven to take possession thereof for us, (Heb. vi. 20,) there to make ready and to prepare for us our summer-houses, our mansions, dwelling-places; as if we were the lords and he the servant! (John xiv. 2, 3.) Oh, this love!

(5.) Also we may see another degree of his love, in this, that now in his absence he has sent the third person in the Trinity to supply his place as another comforter of us, (John xv. 26; xvi. 7,) that we may not think he has forgot us, nor be left destitute of a revealer of truth unto us. (John xiv. 16.) Yea, he has sent him to fortify our spirits, and to strengthen us under all adversity, and against our enemies of what account or degree soever. (Luke xxi. 15.)

(6.) In this also we may see yet more of the love of Christ, in that though he is in heaven, and we on earth, nothing can happen to his people to hurt them, but he feels it, is touched with it, and counteth it as done unto himself; yea, sympathises with them, and is afflicted and grieved in their griefs and their afflictions.

(7.) Another thing by which also yet more of the love of Christ is made manifest, and so may by us be known, is this: he is now, and has been ever since his ascension into glory, laying out himself as high-priest for us, (Heb. vii. 24—26,) that by the improving of his merits before the throne of grace, in way of intercession, he might preserve us from the ruins that our daily infirmities would bring upon us, (Heb. viii. 12;) yea, and make our persons and performances acceptable in his Father's sight. (Rom. v. 10. 1 Pet. ii. 5.)

(8.) We also see yet more of his love by this, that he will have us where himself is, that we may behold and be partakers of his glory. (John xvii. 24.) And in this degree of his love there are many loves.

(a) Then he will come for us as a bridegroom for his bride. (Matt. xxv. 6—10.)

(b) Then shall a public marriage be solemnized, and eternized betwixt him and his church. (Rev. xix. 6, 7.)

(c) Then she shall be wrapped up in his mantles and robes of glory. (Col. iii. 4.)

(d) Then they shall be separated, and separated from other sinners, and all things that offend shall be taken away from among them. (Matt. xxv. 31; xiii. 41.)

(e) Then shall they be exalted to thrones and power of judgment, and shall also sit in judgment on sinful men and fallen angels, acquiescing, by virtue of authority, with their king and head upon them. (1 Cor. vi. 2, 3.)

(f) Then, or from thenceforth for ever, there shall be no more death, sorrow, hidings of his face, or eclipsing of their glory for ever. (Luke xx. 36.)

(g) And thus you may see what rounds this our Jacob's ladder hath, and how by them we climb, and climb, even until we are climbed up to heaven. But now we are set again; for all the glories, all the benefits, all the blessings, and all the good things that are laid up in heaven for these, who can understand?

2. A second thing whereby the love of Christ in some degrees of it may be known, is this, that he should pass by angels and take hold of us. Whoso considereth the nature of spirits, as they are God's workmanship, must needs confess that as such they have a pre-eminence above that which is made of dust. This then was the disparity betwixt us and them, they being by birth far more noble than we. But now, when both are fallen, and by our fall both in a state of condemnation, that Jesus Christ should choose to take up us, the most inconsiderable, and pass by them, to their eternal perdition and destruction, O love! love in a high degree to man: for verily he took not hold of angels, but of the seed of Abraham he took hold. (Heb. ii. 16.) Yet this is not all. In all probability this Lord Jesus has ten times as much to do now he has undertaken to be our Saviour, as he would have had, had he stepped over us and taken hold on them.

(1.) He needed not to have stooped so low as to take flesh upon him; theirs being a more noble nature.

(2.) Nor would he, in all likelihood, have met with those contempts, those scorns, those reproaches and undervaluings from them, as he has all along received in this his undertaking, and met with from sinful flesh. For they were more noble than we, and would sooner have perceived the design of grace, and so, one would think, more readily have fallen in therewith than [those who were in] such darkness as we were, and still by sin are.

(3.) They would not have had those disadvantages as we, for that they would not have had a tempter, a destroyer, so strong and mighty as ours is. Alas! had God left us and taken them, though we should have been never so full of envy against their salvation, yet, being but flesh, what could we have done to them to have laid obstacles in the way of their faith and hope, as they can, and do, in ours?

(4.) They, it may fairly be presumed, had they been taken and we left, and made partakers in our stead, while we had been shut out as they are, would not have put Christ so to it, now in heaven (pray bear with the expression, because I want a better), as we by our imperfections have done, and do. Sin, methinks, would not have so hanged in their natures as it doth in ours, their reason, and sense, and apprehensions, being more quick, and so more apt to have been taken with this love of Christ, and by it more easily have been sanctified.

(5.) The law which they have broken being not so intricate as that against which we have offended, theirs being a commandment with faithfulness to abide in the place in which their Creator had set them; methinks, considering also the aptness of their natures as angels, would not have made their complete obedience so difficult.

(6.) Nor can I imagine but had they been taken they, as creatures excelling in strength, would have been more capable of rendering these praises and blessings to God for eternal mercies than such poor sorry creatures as we are could. But, "behold what manner of love the Father hath bestowed upon us that we should be called the children of God," (1 John iii. 1;) that we, not they, that we, notwithstanding all that they have, or could have done to hinder it, should be called the children of God.

This, therefore, is an high degree of the love of Jesus Christ to us, that when we and they are fallen, he should stoop and take up us, the more ignoble, and leave so mighty a creature in his sins to perish.

3. A third thing whereby the love of Christ, in some of the degrees of it, may be known, will be to consider more particularly the way and unwearied work that he hath with man, to bring him to that kingdom that by his blood he hath obtained for him.

(1.) Man, when the Lord Jesus takes him in hand to make him partaker of the benefit, is found an enemy to his Redeemer; nor doth all the intelligence that he has had of the grace and love of Christ to such, mollify him at all, to wit, before the day of God's power comes. (Rom. v. 7, 10.) And this is a strange thing. Had man, though he could not have come to Christ, been willing that Christ should have come to him, it had been something; it would have shown that he had taken his grace to heart, and considered of it; yea, and that he was willing to be a sharer in it. But verily here is no such thing; man, though he has free will, yet is willing by no means to be saved God's way, to wit, by Jesus Christ, before (as was said before) the day of God's power comes upon him. When the good shepherd went to look for his sheep that was lost in the wilderness, and had found it, did it go one step homewards upon its own legs? did not the shepherd take her, and lay her upon his shoulder, and bring her home rejoicing? (Luke xv.) This then is not love only, but love to degree.

(2.) When man is taken, and laid under the day of God's power; when Christ is opening his ear to discipline, and speaking to him, that his heart may receive instruction, many times that poor man is, as if the devil had found him, and not God. How frenzily he imagines! how crossly he thinks! how ungainly he carries it under convictions, counsels, and his present apprehension of things! I know some are more powerfully dealt withal, and more strongly bound at first by the word; but others more in an ordinary manner, that the flesh and reason may be seen to the glory of Christ. Yea, and where the will is made more quickly to comply with its salvation, it is no thanks to the sinner at all. (Job iv. 18.) It is the day of the power of the Lord that has made the work so soon to appear. Therefore count

this an act of love, in the height of love; love in a great degree. (John xv. 16.)

(3.) When Christ Jesus has made this madman to come to himself, and persuaded him to be willing to accept of his salvation, yet he may not be trusted, nor left alone, for then the corruptions that still lie scattering up and down in his flesh will tempt him to it, and he will be gone. Yea, so desperately wicked is the flesh of saints, that should they be left to themselves but a little while, none knows what horrible transgressions would break out. Proof of this we have to amazement, plentifully scattered here and there in the word. Hence we have the patience of God, and his gentleness, so admired, (2 Chron. xxxii. 21;) for through that it is that they are preserved: He that keepeth Israel, neither slumbers nor sleeps, (Ps. cxx. 4;) but watches for them, and over them every moment, for he knows else they will be hurt. (Isa. xxvii. 3.)

(4.) Yea, notwithstanding this, how often are saints found playing truant, and lurking like thieves in one hole or other; now in the guilt of backsliding by the power of this, and then in filth by the power of that corruption. (Jer. ii. 26.) Yea, and when found in such decayings, and under such revoltings from God, how commonly do they hide their sin with Adam, and David, even until their Saviour fireth out of their mouths a confession of the truth of their naughtiness. "When I kept silence," said David, (and yet he chose to keep silence after he had committed his wickedness,) "my bones waxed old through my roaring all the day long. For day and night thy hand was heavy upon me, my moisture is turned into the drought of summer." (Ps. xxxii. 3, 4.) But why didst thou not confess what thou hadst done then? So I did, saith he, at last, and thou forgavest the iniquity of my sin. (Ps. xxxii. 5.)

(5.) When the sins of saints are so visible and apparent to others, that God, for the vindication of his name and honour, must punish them in the sight of others—yea, must do it as he is just—yet then, for Christ's sake, he waveth such judgments, and refuseth to inflict such punishments, as naturally tend to their destruction, and chooseth to chastise them with such rods and scourges, as may do them good in the end, and that they may not be condemned with the world. (1 Cor. xi. 31, 32.) Wherefore the Lord loves them, and they are blessed, whom he chasteneth and teacheth out of his law. (Heb. xii. 5, 8. Ps. xciv. 12.) And these things are love to a degree.

(6.) That Christ should supply out of his fulness the beginnings of grace in our souls, and carry on that work of so great concern; and that which at times we have so little esteem of, is none of the least of the aggravations of the love of Christ to his people. And this work is as common as any of the works of Christ, and as necessary to our salvation, as is his righteousness, and the imputation thereof to our justification; for else how could we hold out to the end? (Matt. xxiv. 13,) and yet none else can be saved.

(7.) And that the love of Christ should be such to us, that he will thus act, thus do to, and for us, with gladness, (as afore is manifest by the parable of the lost sheep,) is another degree of his love towards us; and such an one too, as is none of the lowest rate. I have seen hot love soon cold; and love that has continued to act, yet act towards the end, as the man that by running, and has run himself off his legs, pants, and can hardly run any longer: but I never saw love like the love of Christ, who as a giant, and bridegroom coming out of his chamber, and as a strong man, rejoiceth to run his race, (Ps. xix. 5;) loving higher and higher, stronger and stronger, I mean as to the lettings out of love, for he reserveth the best wine even till the last. (John ii. 10.)

(8.) I will conclude with this, that his love may be known in many degrees of it, by that sort of sinners whose salvation he most rejoiceth in, and that is, in the salvation of the sinners that are of the biggest size: great sinners, Jerusalem sinners, Samaritan sinners, publican sinners. I might urge, moreover, how he hath proportioned invitations, promises, and examples of his love, for the encouragement and support of those whose souls would trust in him; by which also great degrees of his love may be understood. But we will come now to the third thing that was propounded.

Third. But the greatest attainment that, as to the understanding of the love of Christ, we can arrive to here, is to *know that it passes knowledge:* "And to know the love of Christ that passeth knowledge."

This truth discovereth itself—

1. By the text itself: for the apostle here, in this prayer of his for the Ephesians, doth not only desire that they may know, but describeth that thing which he prays they may know, by this term, "It passeth knowledge:" "And to know the love of Christ which passeth knowledge." As our reason and carnal imagination will be rudely and unduly tampering with anything of Christ, so more especially with the love and kindness of Christ: judging and concluding that just such it is, and none other, as may be apprehended by them; yea, and will have a belief that just so, and no otherwise, are the dimensions of this love; nor can it save beyond our carnal conceptions of it. Saying to the soul, as Pharaoh once did to Israel in another case, "Let the Lord be with you as I shall (judge it meet he should) let you go." We think Christ loves us no more than we do think he can, and so conclude that his love is such as may by us be comprehended, or known to the utmost bounds thereof. But these are false conceptions; and this love of Christ that we think is such, is indeed none of the love of Christ, but a false image thereof, set before our eyes. I speak

not now of weak knowledge, but of foolish and bold conclusions. A man, through unbelief, may think that Christ has no love for him, and yet Christ may love him with a love that passeth knowledge. But when men, in the common course of their profession, will be always terminating here, that they know how, and how far Christ can love, and will thence be bold to conclude of their own safety, and of the loss and ruin of all that are not in the same notions, opinions, formalities, or judgments as they,—his is the worst and greatest of all. The text therefore, to rectify those false and erroneous conclusions, says, "It is a love that passeth knowledge."

And it will be worth our observation to take notice that men, erroneous men, do not put these limits so commonly to the Father and his love, as the Son and his. Hence you have some that boast that God can save some who have not the knowledge of the person of the Mediator Jesus Christ the righteous; as the heathens that have, and still do, make a great improvement of the law and light of nature; crying out with disdain against the narrowness, rigidness, censoriousness, and pride of those that think the contrary: being not ashamed all the while to eclipse, to degrade, to lessen and undervalue the love of Jesus Christ; making of him, and his under-kings, to offer himself a sacrifice to appease the justice of God for our sins, but a thing indifferent, and in its own nature but as other smaller matters.

But all this while the devil knows full well at what game he plays, for he knows that without Christ, without faith in his blood, there is no remission of sins. Wherefore, saith he, let these men talk what they will of the greatness of the love of God as Creator, so they slight and undervalue the love of Christ as Mediator. And yet it is worth our consideration, that the greatness of the love of God is most expressed in his giving of Christ to be a Saviour, and in bestowing his benefits upon us, that we may be happy through him.

But to return: the love of Christ that is so indeed, is love that passeth knowledge; and the best and highest of our knowledge of it is, that we know it to be such.

2. Because I find that at this point the great men of God, of old, were wont to stop, be set, and beyond which they could not pass. It was this that made Moses wonder, (Deut. iv. 31—34;) it was this that made David cry out, How great and wonderful are the works of God? "Thy thoughts to usward, they cannot be reckoned up in order unto thee: If I would declare and speak of them, they are more than can be numbered." (Ps. xl. 5.) And again, "How precious also are thy thoughts unto me, O God! how great is the sum of them! If I should count them, they are more in number than the sand." (Ps. cxxxix. 17, 18.) And a little before, "Such knowledge is too wonderful for me." (Ps. cxxxix. 6.) Isaiah saith there hath

not entered into the heart of man what God has prepared for them that wait for him. (Isa. lxiv. 4.) Ezekiel says, this is the river that cannot be passed over. (Ezek. xlvii. 5.) And Micah to the sea, (Micah vii. 29,) and Zechariah to a fountain, (Zech. xiii. 1,) hath compared this unsearchable love. Wherefore the apostle's position, " that the love of Christ is that which passeth knowledge," is a truth not to be doubted of: consequently, to know this, and that it is such, is the farthest that we can go. This is to justify God, who has said it, and to magnify the Son, who has loved us with such a love. And the contrary is to dishonour him and lessen him, and to make him a deficient Saviour. For suppose this should be true, that thou couldest to the utmost comprehend this love; yet unless, by thy knowledge, thou canst comprehend beyond all evil of sin, or beyond what any man's sins, who shall be saved, can spread themselves or infect, thou must leave some pardonable man in an unpardonable condition; for that thou canst comprehend this love, and yet canst not comprehend that sin. This makes Christ a deficient Saviour. Besides, if thou comprehendest truly, the word that says, " it passeth knowledge," has lost its sanctity, its truth.

It must therefore be, that this love passeth knowledge, and that the highest pitch that a man by knowledge can attain unto, as to this, is to know that it passeth knowledge. My reason is, for that all degrees of love, be they never so high, or many, and high, yet, if we can comprehend them, rest in the bowels of our knowledge: for that only which is beyond us, is that which passeth knowledge. That which we can reach, cannot be the highest: and if a man thinks there is nothing beyond what he can reach, he has no more knowledge as to that; but if he knows that together with what he hath already reached, there is that which he cannot reach before, then he has a knowledge for that also, even a knowledge that it passeth knowledge. It is true a man that thus knoweth, may have divers conjectures about that thing that is beyond his knowledge, yea, in reason it will be so, because he knows that there is something yet before him: but since the thing itself is truly beyond his knowledge, none of his conjectures about that thing may be counted knowledge. Or suppose a man that thus conjectureth, should hit right as to what he now conjectures, his right hitting about that thing may not be called knowledge: it is as yet to him but as an uncertain guess, and is still beyond his knowledge.

Quest. But may some say, what good will it do a man to know that the love of Christ passeth knowledge? One would think that it should do one more good to believe that the knowledge of the whole love of Christ might be attainable.

Ans. That there is an advantage in knowing that the love of Christ passeth knowledge, must not be questioned, for the apostle saith it doth. (2 Tim. iii. 16.) For to know what the holy word affirms,

is profitable; nor would he pray that we might know that which passeth knowledge, were there not by our knowing of it some help to be administered. But to show you some of the advantages that will come to us by knowing that the love of Christ passeth knowledge.

(1.) By knowing of this a child of God has in reserve for himself, at a day, when all that he otherwise knows, may be taken from him through the power of temptation. Sometimes a good man may be so put to it, that all that he knows comprehensively may be taken from him, to wit, the knowledge of the truth of his faith, or that he has the grace of God in him, or the like; this, I say, may be taken from him. Now if at this time he knows the love of Christ that passeth knowledge, he knows a way in all probability to be recovered again: for if Christ Jesus loves with a love that passeth knowledge, then saith the soul that is thus in the dark, he may love me yet, for aught I know; for I know that he loves with a love that passeth knowledge, and therefore I will not utterly despond. Yea, if Satan should attempt to question whether ever Christ Jesus will look upon me or no? The answer is, if I know the love that passes knowledge. But he may look upon me, (Satan,) yea, and love, and save me too, for aught I poor sinner know; for he loves with a love that passeth knowledge. If I be fallen into sin that lies hard upon me, and my conscience fears that for this there is no forgiveness: the help for a stay from utter despair is at hand; but there may, say I, for Christ loves with a love that passeth knowledge. If Satan would dissuade me from praying to God, by suggesting as if Christ would not regard the stammering and chattering prayer of mine: the answer is ready, but he may regard for aught I know; for he loves with a love that passeth knowledge. If the tempter doth suggest, that thy trials, and troubles, and afflictions, are so many that it is to be thought thou shalt never get beyond them: the answer is near, but for aught we know, Christ may carry me through them all; for he loves with a love that passeth knowledge. Thus, I say, is relief at hand, and a help in reserve for the tempted, let their temptations be what they will. This therefore is the weapon that will baffle the devil when all other weapons fail: for aught I know, Christ may save me; for he loves with a love that passeth knowledge. Yea, suppose he should drive me to the worst of fears, and that is to doubt that I neither have nor shall have for ever the grace of God in my soul: the answer is at hand, but I have, or may have it; for Christ loves with a love that passeth knowledge. Thus therefore you may see, that in this prayer of Paul there is a great deal of good. He prays, when he prays that we might know the love of Christ that passeth knowledge, that we may have a help at hand, and relief against all the horrible temptations of the devil. For this is a help at hand, a help that is ready to fall in with us, if there be yet remaining with us but the least grain of right reasoning according to the nature of things: for if it be objected against a man that he is poor, because he has but a groat in his pocket; yet if he has an unknown deal of money in his trunks, how easy is it for him to recover himself from that slander, by returning the knowledge of what he has upon the objector. This is the case, and thus it is, and will be with them that know the love of Christ that passeth knowledge. Wherefore,

(2.) By this knowledge room is made for a Christian, and liberty is ministered unto him, to turn himself every way in all spiritual things. This is the Christian's *rehoboth*, that well for which the Philistines have no heart to strive, and that which will cause that we be fruitful in the land. (Gen. xxvi. 22.)

If Christians know not with this knowledge, they walk in the world as if they were pinioned, or as if fetters were hanged on their heels. But this enlarges their steps under them. (2 Sam. xxii. 37.) By the knowledge of this love they may walk at liberty, and their steps shall not be straitened. This is that which Solomon intends when he saith, "Get wisdom, and get understanding," (Prov. iv. 5;) then, "when thou goest, thy steps shall not be straitened, and when thou runnest, thou shalt not stumble." (Prov. iv. 12.) A man that has only from hand to mouth, is oft put to it to know how to use his penny, and comes off also, many times, but with an hungry belly; but he that has not only that, but always over and to spare, he is more at liberty, and can live in fulness, and far more like a gentleman. There is a man has a cistern, and that is full of water; there is another also that has his cistern full, and withal his spring in his yard; but a great drought is upon the land in which they dwell. I would now know which of these two have the most advantage to live in their own minds at liberty, without fear of wanting water; why this is the case in hand. There is a Christian that knows Christ in all these degrees of his love that are knowable, but he knoweth Christ nothing in his love that passeth knowledge. There is another Christian, and he knows Christ, as the first, but withal, he also knows him as to his love that passeth knowledge. Pray now tell me, which of these two is likeliest to live most like a Christian, that is like a spiritual prince, and like him that possesseth all things? which has most advantage to live in godly largeness of heart, and is most at liberty in his mind? which of these two has the greatest advantage to believe, and the greatest engagements laid upon him to love the Lord Jesus? which of these has also most in readiness to resist the wiles of the devil, and to subdue the power and prevalency of corruptions? It is this that makes men fathers in Christianity: "I write unto you, fathers, because ye have known; I have written unto you, fathers, because ye have known," (1 John ii. 13, 14;) why have not others known? not so as the fathers.

The fathers have known, and known. They have known the love of Christ in those degrees of love which are knowable, and have also known the love of Christ to be such which passeth knowledge. In my father's house is bread enough, and to spare, was that that fetched the prodigal home. (Luke xxv. 17.) And when Moses would speak an endless all to Israel for the comfort and stay of their souls, he calls their God "the fountain of Jacob upon a land of corn and wine." (Deut. xxxiii. 28.)

(3.) By this knowledge, or knowledge of the love of Christ which passeth knowledge, there is begot in Christians a greater desire to press forwards to that which is before them. (Phil. iii. 12—21.) What is the reason of all that sloth, carnal contentedness, and listlessness of spirit in Christians, more than the ignorance of this? For he that thinks he knows what can be known, is beyond all reason that should induce him to seek yet after more. Now the love of Christ may be said not to be knowable upon a threefold account:—

(*a*) For that my knowledge is weak.

(*b*) For that my knowledge is imperfect.

(*c*) Or for that, though my knowledge be never so perfect, because the love of Christ is eternal.

There is love that is not to be apprehended by weak knowledge. Convince a man of this, and then if the knowledge of what he already has be truly sweet to his soul, (Prov. ii. 10,) it will stir him up with great heartiness to desire to know what more of this is possible.

There is love beyond what he knows already, who is endowed with the most perfect knowledge, that man here may have. Now, if what this man knows already of this love is indeed sweet unto him, then it puts him upon hearty desires that his soul may yet know more. And because there is no bounds set to man, how much he may know in this life thereof, therefore his desires, notwithstanding what he has attained, are yet kept alive, and in the pursuit after the knowledge of more of the love of Christ. And God in old time has taken it so well at the hands of some of his, that their desires have been so great, that when, as I may say, they have known as much on earth as is possible for them to know, (that is, by ordinary means,) he has come down to them in visions and revelations, or else taken them up to him for an hour or two into paradise, that they might know, and then let them down again.

But this is not all; there is a knowledge of the love of Christ that we are by no means capable of until we be possessed of the heavens. And I would know, if a man indeed loveth Christ, whether the belief of this be not one of the highest arguments that can be urged to make such an one weary of this world, that he may be with him. To such an one "to live is Christ, and to die is gain." (Phil. i. 21.) And to such an one it is difficult to bring his mind to be content to stay here a longer time, except he be satisfied that Christ has still work for him here to do.

I will yet add, there is a love of Christ I will not say that cannot be known, but I will say that cannot be enjoyed ; no, not by them now in heaven (in soul) until the day of judgment. And the knowledge of this, when it has possessed even men on earth, has made them choose a day of judgment before a day of death, that they might know what is beyond that state and knowledge which even the spirits of just men made perfect now do enjoy in heaven. (2 Cor. v. 4.) Wherefore, as I said at first, "to know the love of Christ that passeth knowledge," is advantageous upon this account— it begetteth in Christians a great desire to reach, and press forward to, that which is before.

One thing more, and then, as to this reason, I have done. Even that love of Christ that is absolutely unknowable, as to the utmost bound thereof, because it is eternal, will be yet in the nature of it sweet and desirable, because we shall enjoy or be possessed of it so. This, therefore, if there were no more, is enough, when known, to draw away the heart from things that are below to itself.

(4.) The "love that passeth knowledge." The knowledge of that is very fruitful knowledge. It cannot be, but it must be fruitful. Some knowledge is empty and alone, not attended with that good, and with those blessings wherewith this knowledge is attended. Did I say it is fruitful ? I will add, it is attended with the best fruit ; it yieldeth the best wine ; it fills the soul with all the fulness of God. "And to know the love of Christ which passeth knowledge, that ye may be filled with all the fulness of God." God is in Christ, and makes himself known to us by the love of Christ. Whosoever transgresseth, and abideth not in the doctrine of Christ, hath not God, for God is not to be found nor enjoyed but in him, consequently he that hath, and abideth in, the doctrine of Christ, hath both the Father and the Son. (2 John 9.) Now, since there are degrees of knowledge of this doctrine, and since the highest degree of the knowledge of him is to know that he has a "love that passeth knowledge," it follows, that if he that has the least saving knowledge of this doctrine, hath God, he that hath the largest knowledge of it has God much more, or, according to the text, is filled with all the fulness of God. What this fulness of God should be, is best gathered from such sayings of the Holy Ghost, as come nearest to this in language, filled,

Full of goodness. (Rom. xv. 14.)
Full of faith. (Acts vi. 5.)
Full of the Holy Ghost. (Acts vii. 55.)
Full of assurance of faith. (Heb. x, 22.)
Full of assurance of hope. (Heb. vi. 11.)
Full of joy unspeakable, and full of glory. (1 Pet. i. viii.)
Full of joy. (1 John i. 4.)
Full of good works. (Acts xi. 36.)
Being filled with the knowledge of his will, (Col. i. 9.)
Being filled with the Spirit. (Eph. v. 18.)

Filled with the fruits of righteousness, which is by Jesus Christ to the glory and praise of God. (Phil. iv. 11.)

These things to be sure are included, either for the cause or effect of this fulness. The cause they cannot be ; for that is God's by his Holy Spirit. The effects, therefore, they are, for wherever God dwells in the degree intended in the text, there is shown, in an eminent manner by these things, "what is the riches of the glory of his inheritance in the saints." (Eph. i. 18.) But these things dwell not in that measure specified by the text, in any but those who "know the love of Christ which passeth knowledge."

But what a man is he that is filled with all these things ! or that is, as we have it in the text, "filled with all the fulness of God !" Such men are at this day wanting in the churches. These are the men that sweeten churches, and that bring glory to God and to religion. And knowledge will make us such, such knowledge as the apostle here speaketh of.

I have now done, when I have spoken something by way of use unto you, from what hath been said. And,

First. Is there such breadth, and length, and depth, and height in God for us ? And is there toward us love in Christ that passeth knowledge ? Then this shows us not only the greatness of the majesty of the Father and the Son, but the great goodwill that is in their hearts to them that receive their word.

God has engaged the breadth, and length, and depth, and height, of the love, the wisdom, the power, and truth that is in himself for us ; and Christ has loved us with a love that passeth knowledge. We may well say, "Who is like thee, O Lord, among the gods ?" (Exod. xv. 11.) Or, as another prophet has it, "Who is a God like unto thee, that pardoneth iniquity, and passeth by the transgression of the remnant of his heritage ? he retaineth not his anger for ever, because he delighteth in mercy." (Micah vii. 18.) Yea, no word can sufficiently set forth the greatness of this love of God and his Son to us poor miserable sinners.

Second. Is there so great a heart for love towards us both in the Father and in the Son ? then let us be much in the study and search after the greatness of this love. This is the sweetest study that a man can devote himself unto, because it is the study of the love of God and of Christ to man. Studies that yield far less profit than this, how close are they pursued by some who have adapted themselves thereunto ! Men do not use to count telling over of their money burdensome to them, nor yet the recounting of their grounds, their herds, and their flocks, when they increase. Why, the study of the unsearchable love of God in Christ to man is better in itself, and yields more sweetness to the soul of man, than can ten thousand such things as but now are mentioned. I know the wise men of this world, of whom there are many, will say, as to what I now press you unto, who can show us any good in it? But, Lord, lift thou up the light of thy countenance upon us. Thou hast put gladness in my heart more than in the time that their corn and their wine increaseth. David also said that his meditation on the Lord should be sweet. Oh! there is in God and in his Son that kindness for the sons of men, that, did they know it, they would like to retain the knowledge of it in their hearts. They would cry out, as she did of old, "Set me as a seal upon thy heart, as a seal upon thine arm: for love is strong as death." (Sol. Song viii. 6, 7.) Every part, crumb, grain, or scrap of this knowledge is to a Christian as drops of honey are to sweet-palated children, worth the gathering up, worth the putting to the taste to be relished. Yea, David says of the word, which is the ground of knowledge, It is sweeter than honey or the honeycomb. "More," said he, "to be desired are they than gold; yea, than much fine gold; sweeter also than honey and the honeycomb." (Ps. xix. 10.) Why, then, do not Christians devote themselves to the meditation of this so heavenly, so goodly, so sweet, and so comfortable a thing, that yieldeth such advantage to the soul? The reason is, these things are talked of, but not believed. Did men believe what they say when they speak so largely of the love of God, and the love of Jesus Christ, they would, they could not, but meditate upon it. There are so many wonders in it, and men love to think of wonders; there is so much profit in it, and men love to think of that which yields them profit. But, as I said, the belief of things are wanting. Belief of a thing will have strong effects, whether the ground for it be true or false. As suppose one of you should, when you are at a neighbour's house, believe that your own house is on fire whilst your children are fast asleep in bed, though indeed there were no such thing, I shall appeal to any of you if this belief would not make notable work with, and upon, your hearts. Let a man believe he shall be damned, though afterwards it is evident he believed a lie, yet what work did that belief make in the man's heart. Even so, and much more, the belief of heavenly things will work, because true and great, and most good; also, where they are indeed believed, their evidence is managed upon their spirit by the power and glory of the Holy Ghost itself. Wherefore let us study these things.

Third. Let us cast ourselves upon this love. No greater encouragement can be given us than what is in the text and about it. It is great, it is love that passeth knowledge. Men that are sensible of danger, are glad when they hear of such helps upon which they may boldly venture for escape. Why, such an help and relief the text helpeth trembling and fearful consciences to. Fear and trembling as to misery hereafter can flow but from what we know, feel, or imagine; but the text speaks of a love that is beyond that

we can know, feel, or imagine, even of a love that passeth knowledge, consequently of a love that goes beyond all these. Besides, the apostle's conclusion upon this subject plainly makes it manifest that this meaning which I have put upon the text is the mind of the Holy Ghost. "Now, unto him," saith he, "that is able to do exceeding abundantly above all that we ask or think, according to the power that worketh in us, unto him be glory in the church by Christ Jesus, throughout all ages, world without end. Amen." (Eph. iii. 20, 21.) What can be more plain? what can be more full? what can be more suitable to the most desponding spirit in any man? He can do more than thou knowest he will; he can do more than thou thinkest he can. What dost thou think? "Why, I think," saith the sinner, "that I am cast away." Well, but there are worse thoughts than these, therefore think again. "Why," saith the sinner, "I think that my sins are as many as all the sins of the world." Indeed, this is a very black thought, but there are worse thoughts than this, therefore, prithee, think again. "Why, I think," saith the sinner, "that God is not able to pardon all my sins." Ay, now thou hast thought indeed. For this thought makes thee look more like a devil than a man; and yet, because thou art a man, and not a devil, see the condescension and the boundlessness of the love of thy God. He is able to do above all that we think. Couldst thou, sinner, if thou hadst been allowed, thyself express what thou wouldst have expressed, the greatness of the love thou wantest, with words that could have suited thee better? For it is not said, he can do above what we think, meaning our thinking at present, but above all we can think; meaning, above the worst and most soul-dejecting thoughts that we have at any time. Sometimes the dejected have worse thoughts than at other times they have. Well, take them at their worst times, at times when they think, and think till they think themselves down into the very pangs of hell, yet this word of the grace of God is above them, and shows that he can yet recover and save these miserable people.

And, now I am upon this subject, I will a little further walk and travel with the desponding ones, and will put a few words in their mouths for their help against temptations that may come upon them hereafter. For as Satan follows such now, with charges and applications of guilt, so he may follow them with interrogatories and appeals; for he can tell how, by appeals as well as by charging of sin, to sink and drown the sinner whose soul he has leave to engage. Suppose, therefore, that some distressed man or woman should after this way be engaged, and Satan should with his interrogatories and appeals be busy with them to drive them to desperation, the text last-mentioned, to say nothing of the subject of our discourse, yields plenty of help for the relief of such an one. Says Satan, "Dost thou not know that thou hast horribly sinned?" "Yes," says the soul, "I do." Says Satan, "Dost thou not know that thou art one of the vilest in all the pack of professors?" "Yes," says the soul, "I do." Says Satan, "Doth not thy conscience tell thee that thou art and hast been more base than any of thy fellows can imagine thee to be?" "Yes," says the soul, "my conscience tells me so." "Well," saith Satan, "now will I come upon thee with my appeals. Art thou not a graceless wretch?" "Yes." "Hast thou an heart to be sorry for this wickedness?" "No, not as I should." "And, albeit," saith Satan, "thou prayest sometimes, yet is not thy heart possessed with a belief that God will not regard thee?" "Yes," says the sinner. "Why, then, despair, and go hang thyself," saith the devil. And now we are at the end of the thing designed and driven at by Satan. "But what shall I now do?" saith the sinner. I answer, "Take up the words of the text against him—'Christ loves with a love that passeth knowledge.'" And answereth him further, saying, "Satan, though I cannot think that God loves me, though I cannot think that God will save me, yet I will not yield to thee; for God can do more than I think he can. And, whereas, thou appealedst unto me, if whether when I pray, my heart is not possessed with unbelief that God will not regard me: that shall not sink me neither; for God can ' do abundantly above what I ask or think.'" Thus this text helpeth where obstructions are put in against our believing, and thereby casting ourselves upon the love of God in Christ for salvation.

And yet this is not all; for the text is yet more full: "He is able to do abundantly more," yea, "exceeding abundantly more," or "above all that we ask or think." It is a text made up of words picked and packed together by the wisdom of God; picked and packed together on purpose for the succour and relief of the tempted, that they may, when in the midst of their distresses, cast themselves upon the Lord their God. He can do abundantly more than we ask. "Oh!" says the soul, "that he would but do so much for me as I could ask him to do! how happy a man should I then be!" Why, what wouldst thou ask for, sinner? "You may be sure," says the soul, "I would ask to be saved from my sins; I would ask for faith in and love to Christ; I would ask to be preserved in this evil world, and ask to be glorified with Christ in heaven." He that asketh for all this doth indeed ask for much, and for more than Satan would have him believe that God is able or willing to bestow upon him. But mark, the text doth not say that God is able to do all that we can ask or think, but that he is able to do above all, yea, abundantly above all, yea, exceeding abundantly above all that we ask or think. What a text is this! What a God have we! God foresaw the sins of his people, and what work the devil would make with their hearts about them; and, therefore, to prevent their ruin by his tempta-

tion, he has thus largely, as you see, expressed his love by his word. Let us, therefore, as he has bidden us, make this good use of this doctrine of grace, to cast ourselves upon this love of God in the times of distress and temptation.

Fourth. Take heed of abusing this love. This exhortation seems needless; for love is such a thing, that one would think none could find in their heart to abuse. But for all that, I am of opinion that there is nothing that is more abused among professors this day, than is this love of God. There has of late more light about the love of Christ broke out than formerly: every boy now can talk of the love of Christ; but this love of Christ has not been rightly applied by preachers, or else not rightly received by professors. For never was this grace of Christ so turned into lasciviousness as now. Now it is a practice among professors to learn to be vile of the profane; yea, and to plead for that vileness: nay, we will turn it the other way, now it is so that the profane do learn to be vile of those that profess, (they teach the wicked ones their ways, Jer. ii. 23;) a thing that no good man should think on but with blushing cheeks.

Jude speaketh of these people, and tells us that they, notwithstanding their profession, deny the only Lord God, and our Saviour Jesus Christ. (Jude 4.) "They profess," saith Paul, "that they know God, but in works they deny him, being abominable and disobedient, and unto every good work reprobate." (Tit. i. 16.)

But I say, let not this love of God and of Christ be abused. It is unnatural to abuse love; to abuse love is a villany condemned of all, yea, to abuse love is the most inexcusable sin of all. It is next the sin of devils to abuse love, the love of God and of Christ.

And what says the apostle? "Because they received not the love of the truth that they might be saved. And for this cause, God shall send them strong delusion, that they should believe a lie, that they all might be damned, who believed not the truth, but had pleasure in unrighteousness." (2 Thess. ii. 10—12.) And what can such an one say for himself in the judgment, that shall be charged with the abuse of love? Christians, deny yourselves, deny your lusts, deny the vanities of this present life, devote yourselves to God; become lovers of God, lovers of his ways, and a people zealous of good works; then shall you show one to another, and to all men, that you have not received the grace of God in vain. (2 Cor. vi. 1.) Renounce therefore the hidden things of dishonesty, walk not in craftiness, nor handle God's word deceitfully, but by manifestation of the truth, commend yourselves to every man's conscience in the sight of God. Do this, I say, yea, and so endeavour such a closure with this love of God in Christ, as may graciously constrain you to do it, because, when all proofs of the right receiving of this love of Christ shall be produced, none will be found of worth enough to justify the simplicity of our profession, but that which makes us " zealous of good works." (Tit. ii. 14.) And what a thing will it be to be turned off at last, as one that abused the love of Christ : as one that presumed upon his lusts, this world and all manner of naughtiness, because the love of Christ to pardon sins was so great! What an unthinking, what a disingenuous one wilt thou be counted at that day ! yea, thou wilt be found to be the man that made a prey of love, that made a stalking-horse of love, that made of love a slave to sin, the devil and the world, and will not that be bad ?

Fifth. Is the love of God and of Christ so great? Let us then labour to improve it to the utmost for our advantage, against all the hindrances of faith.

To what purpose else is it revealed, made mention of, and commended to us ? We are environed with many enemies, and faith in the love of God and of Christ is our only succour and shelter. Wherefore our duty, and wisdom, and privilege is, to improve this love for our own advantage ; improve it against daily infirmities ; improve it against the wiles of the devil ; improve it against the threats, rage, death, and destruction, that the men of this world continually with their terror set before you. But how must that be done ? Why, set this love, and the safety that is in it, before thine eyes ; and behold it while these things make their assaults upon thee. These words, the faith of this, God loves me, will support thee in the midst of what dangers may assault thee. And this is that which is meant, when we are exhorted to rejoice in the Lord, (Phil. iii. 1 ;) to make our boast in the Lord, (Ps. xliv. 51 ;) to triumph in the Lord, (2 Cor. ii. 14 ;) and to set the Lord always before our face. (Ps. xvi. 8.) For he that can do this thing steadfastly, cannot be overcome. For in God there is more than can be in the world, either to help or hinder ; wherefore, if God be my helper, if God loves me, if Christ be my Redeemer, and has bestowed his love that passeth knowledge upon me, who can be against me ? (Heb. xiii. 6. Rom. viii. 31 ;) and if they be against me, what disadvantage reap I thereby, since even all this also worketh for my good ? This is improving the love of God, and of Christ for my advantage. The same course should Christians also take with the degrees of this love, even set it against all the degrees of danger ; for here deep calleth unto deep. There cannot be wickedness and rage wrought up to such or such a degree, as of which it may be said, there are not degrees in the love of God and of Christ to match it. Wherein Pharaoh dealt proudly against God's people, the Lord was above him, (Exod. xviii. 11 ;) did match and overmatch him ; he came up to him, and went beyond him ; he collared with him, overcame him, and cast him down. " The Lord is a man of war, the Lord is his name. Pharaoh's chariots and his hosts hath he cast into the sea—

they sank into the bottom as a stone." (Exod. xv. 5.) There is no striving against the Lord that hath loved us ; there is none that strive against him can prosper. If the shields of the earth be the Lord's, (Ps. xlvii. 9,) then he can wield them for the safeguard of his body, the Church ; or if they are become incapable of being made use of any longer in that way, and for such a thing, can he not lay them aside, and make himself new ones ? Men can do after this manner, much more God. But again, if the miseries or afflictions which thou meetest with, seem to thee to overflow, and to go beyond measure, above measure, and so to be above strength, and begin to drive thee to despair of life, (2 Cor. i. 8,) then thou hast also, in the love of God, and of Christ, that which is above, and that goes beyond all measure also, to wit, love unsearchable, unknown, and that " can do exceeding abundantly above all that we ask or think." Now God hath set them one against the other, and it will be thy wisdom to do so too, for this is the way to improve this love.

But though it be easy thus to admonish you to do, yet you shall find the practical part more difficult ; wherefore, here it may not be amiss, if I add to these another head of counsel.

1. First, then, wouldst thou improve this love of God and of Christ to thy advantage ? why, then, thou must labour after the knowledge of it. This was it that the apostle prayed for, for these Ephesians, as was said before, and this is that that thou must labour after, or else thy reading, and my writing, will, as to thee, be fruitless. Let me then say to thee, as David to his son Solomon. " And thou, Solomon, my son, know thou the God of thy father." (1 Chron. xxviii. 9.) Empty notions of this love will do nothing but harm, wherefore they are not empty notions that I press thee to rest in, but that thou labour after the knowledge of the savour of this good ointment, (Sol. Song i. 3,) which the apostle calleth " the savour of the knowledge of this Lord Jesus." (2 Cor. ii. 14.) Know it, until it becometh sweet or pleasant to thy soul, and then it will preserve and keep thee. (Prov. ii. 10, 11.) Make this love of God and of Christ thine own, and not another's. Many there are that can talk largely of the love of God to Abraham, to David, to Peter, and Paul. But that is not the thing ; give not over until this love be made thine own, until thou find and feel it to run warm in thy heart by the shedding of it abroad there, by the spirit that God hath given thee. (Rom. v. 5.) Then thou wilt know it with an obliging and engaging knowledge ; yea, then thou wilt know it with a soul-strengthening and soul-encouraging knowledge.

2. Wouldst thou improve this love ? then set it against the love of all other things whatsoever, even until this love shall conquer thy soul from the love of them to itself. This is Christian. Do it, therefore, and say, " Why should anything have

my heart but God, but Christ? He loves me with love that passeth knowledge. He loves me, and he shall have me: he loves me, and I will love him: his love stripped him of all for my sake; Lord, let my love strip me of all for thy sake. I am a son of love, an object of love, a monument of love, of free love, of distinguishing love, of peculiar love, and of love that passeth knowledge, and why should not I walk in love? in love to God, in love to men, in holy love, in love unfeigned?" This is the way to improve the love of God for thy advantage, for the subduing of thy passions, and for sanctifying of thy nature. It is an odious thing to hear men of base lives talking of the love of God, of the death of Christ, and of the glorious grace that is presented unto sinners by the word of the truth of the gospel. Praise is comely for the upright, not for the profane. Therefore let him speak of love that is taken with love, that is captivated with love, that is carried away with love. If this man speaks of it, his speaking signifies something; the powers and bands of love are upon him, and he shows to all that he knows what he is speaking of. But the very mentioning of love is, in the mouth of the profane, like a parable in the mouth of fools, or as salt unsavoury. Wherefore, Christian, improve this love of God as thou shouldst, and that will improve thee as thou wouldst. Wherefore,

3. If thou wouldst improve this love, keep thyself in it. "Keep yourselves in the love of God." (Jude 21.) This text looks as if it favoured the Socinians, but there is nothing of that in it. And so doth that, "If ye keep my commandments, ye shall abide in my love: even as I have kept my Father's commandments, and abide in his love." (John xv. 10.) The meaning, then, is this, that living a holy life is the way, after a man has believed unto justification, to keep himself in the savour and comfort of the love of God. And oh that thou wouldst indeed so do! And that because, if thou shalt want the savour of it, thou wilt soon want tenderness to the commandment, which is the rule by which thou must walk, if thou wilt do good to thyself, or honour God in the world. "To him that ordereth his conversation aright, I will show the salvation of God." (Ps. l. 23.) He that would live a sweet, comfortable, joyful life, must live a very holy life. This is the way to improve this love to thyself indeed.

4. To this end, you must take root and be grounded in love, that is, you must be well settled, and established in this love, if indeed you would improve it. You must not be shaken as to the doctrine and grounds of it. (Eph. iii. 17.) These you must be well acquainted with; for he that is but a child in this doctrine, is not capable as yet of falling in with these exhortations; for such waver and fear when tempted; and "he that feareth is not made perfect in love," (1 John iv. 18,) nor can he so improve it for himself and soul's good as he should.

5. And lastly, keep, to this end, those grounds and evidences that God hath given you of your call to be partakers of this love, with all clearness upon your hearts, and in your minds. For he that wants a sight of them, or a proof that they are true and good, can take but little comfort in this love. There is a great mystery in the way of God with his people. He will justify them without their works, he will pardon them for his Son's sake. But they shall have but little comfort of what he hath done, doth, and will do, for them that are careless, carnal, and not holy in their lives. Nor shall they have their evidences for heaven at hand, nor out of doubt with them, yea, they shall walk without the sun, and have their comforts by bits and knocks; while others sit at their Father's table, have liberty to go into the wine-cellar, rejoice at the sweet and pleasant face of their heavenly Father towards them, and know it shall go well with them at the end.

Something now for a conclusion should be spoken to the carnal world, who have heard me tell of all this love. But what shall I say unto them? If I should speak to them, and they should not hear; or if I should testify unto them, and they should not believe; or entreat them, and they should scorn me? all will but aggravate, and greaten their sin, and tend to their further condemnation. And therefore I shall leave the obstinate where I found him, and shall say to him that is willing to be saved, "Sinner, thou hast the advantage of thy neighbour, not only because thou art· willing to live, but because there are those that are willing thou shouldst, to wit, those unto whom the issues from death do belong," and they are the Father and the Son, to whom be glory, with the blessed Spirit of grace, world without end. Amen.

A DISCOURSE OF THE HOUSE OF THE FOREST OF LEBANON.

THE remarks made on *Solomon's Temple Spiritualized* may be generally applied to the present treatise. But boldly as Bunyan exercised his ingenuity in the former case, he has ventured a still freer employment of his fancy in the latter. Solomon's Temple had a definite typical character. Authority existed for an evangelical interpretation of the structure, its furniture, and ornaments. A commentator once put upon the path which, up to a certain point, is indisputably safe, may be allowed some liberty to pursue it farther, trusting to the fair conclusions of known principles and analogies. But even this latitude cannot, in all cases, be indulged without danger. The clue which Scripture affords must not be spun out too thin : if stretched beyond the intended length it will break, and every step we set without it will involve us more and more in a labyrinth of error.

Such is not unfrequently the consequence of too eager a pursuit of tracks which begin with Scripture. The ardent inquirer hopes, when he arrives at the last stage where they are visible, that his own earnest desires may keep him in the right direction, and that he may go on safely as long as his hope of discovering fresh truth continues to urge him forward. But if this be hazardous, though justified by a beginning with known Scripture, it is far more so when speculative ingenuity has, at the very commencement of interpretation, to constitute itself the authority and basis of the views to be displayed. Bunyan's two treatises are illustrative of this remark. In his discourse on Solomon's Temple, he took advantage of the authority given him by Scripture itself. With the reverence proper to his habits of thought, he followed upon the line of Scripture, as far as it went. A feeling that his own spiritual-mindedness could not fail him, while on such a track, encouraged his further meditation when the letter of Scripture could no longer be referred to. He reasoned and wrote according to what he believed to be the teaching of correspondent facts.

But the House of the Forest of Lebanon does not present the same encouragement to a scriptural commentator as the Temple. It would be difficult to find any sufficient authority, in Scripture itself, for treating it symbolically. A very little consideration will convince devout believers in revealed truth, that nothing can be more dangerous than to look for revelation where revelation is not afforded. To exalt tradition to an equality with revelation is one well known source of error ; but it is not the only source of mistakes and perversions in respect to religious opinion : the theoretical interpretation of Scripture may lead to at least as many errors as the belief in tradition. It is even a step in advance of this sort of interpretation, to make that a symbol which was never meant for a symbol—to convert into a type what we have no authority to suppose God ever intended to be a type.

An ingenious man may, with little difficulty, discover something in all human events analogous to mysteries of providence and grace. The building of a house on this or that kind of foundation is an authorized image of prudence, or the contrary. But it is far from the line of modest and humble inquiry to suppose that a house, though built by King Solomon himself, may be regarded as a monument of divine wisdom, constructed with especial reference to many awful truths and sublime mysteries, and intended to cast through every frame of its numberless windows some ray of light on the hearts of believers to remote generations.

The House of the Forest of Lebanon was built by Solomon for his own gratification and convenience. It had no dependence upon the Temple—no relation to any sacred or appointed purpose, Had it never been built, no prophecy or design would have been left unaccomplished by the failure, and every word of Scripture, which needed some building type for its fulfilment, would have found it provided in the Temple. It was, therefore, in the simple spirit of speculation that Bunyan chose to look upon the House of the Forest of Lebanon as a mystical edifice. The materials of which it was built, the doors, the windows, the architectural arrangements, might have been prefigured by some pattern shown in the Mount, or in a dream divinely sent : but we read of no such directions. Solomon raised the structure according to his own fancy ; and though, at the time, his mind may have been sufficiently devout to intermix some holy purpose with all his plans, we have no authority in this instance for a minute interpretation of his thoughts, or even for determining what his thoughts were.

Thus the following treatise, viewed aright, will be regarded not as a commentary on Scripture, but as the ingenious speculation of a spiritual mind, choosing at will the objects from which it might draw the largest amount of religious inferences. Always recollecting the distinction between themes set by divine authority, and those which only human wisdom and piety suggest, we may often study the latter with great comfort and profit. Bunyan's meditations on the House of the Forest of Lebanon are full of sweet and valuable suggestions. It would be an error to suppose that the structure, or its decorations, were absolutely intended to teach the truths which he derives from the account of them in history. But the truths themselves may be accepted with thankfulness; nor are these to be undervalued because suggested by objects chosen for contemplation by the mere individual taste or humour of the teacher. When once the line is fairly drawn between the divine and the human, and there is no danger of confounding the one with the other, any object may be adopted as the symbol of an argument. The cedars of Lebanon, or Lebanon itself, might have been selected for such a purpose. If happy and devout reflections followed upon the thought of either the one or the other, there would be reason for thankfulness that the writer, or preacher, had so contemplated the object. But if the pleasure or instruction thus afforded led to the notion that, because the object was named in Scripture, the lesson was taught in Scripture, this would be an opening to many errors, to errors from which pious commentators would be the first to guard their readers.

Bunyan's opinion that the House of the Forest of Lebanon was actually built on Mount Lebanon, has no support either from the text of Scripture, or from sound Biblical scholars. The latter, almost without exception, assert that it adjoined Solomon's other palace, or stood on some favourite spot at a small distance from Jerusalem. Josephus could hardly have failed to know the site of so celebrated a structure, and he speaks of it as seen by the Queen of Sheba in immediate connection with the other wonders of the royal residence.

These considerations may lead to others of a similar kind, and be not unprofitable in guarding the ardent and affectionate student against too ready a trust in allegorical expositions. A bold assumption in the interpretation of one portion of Scripture may seem to justify one equally so in the case of others; and the incautious reader may find that he has imperceptibly contracted a habit of resting the most precious burdens of truth on fictitious support. To be sufficiently guarded against this danger is to be placed in a condition for safely enjoying such a treatise as the following—for profiting by the holy sentiments and doctrines of the author, though questioning his method of introducing them.

H. S.

A DISCOURSE

OF

THE HOUSE OF THE FOREST OF LEBANON.

CHAPTER I.

INTRODUCTION.

As Solomon built a house for Pharaoh's daughter, and that called the temple of the Lord, so he built a house in Lebanon, called "the house of the forest of Lebanon." (1 Kings vii. 2.)

Some, I perceive, have thought that this house, called "the house of the forest of Lebanon," was none other than that called the temple at Jerusalem; and that that was called "the house of the forest of Lebanon," because built of the wood that grew there. But that Solomon built another than that, even one in Lebanon, called "the house of the forest of Lebanon," is evident, and that from these reasons.

First. That in the forest of Lebanon is mentioned as another, besides that called "the temple of the Lord;" and that too when the temple, and its finishing is spoken of; yea, it is mentioned with an also, as an additional house, besides the temple of the Lord.

"In the fourth year," saith the text, "was the foundation of the house of the Lord laid, in the month Zif; and in the eleventh year, in the month Bul, (which is the eighth month,) was the house finished throughout all the parts thereof, and according to all the fashion of it; so he was seven years in building it." "But Solomon was building his own house thirteen years, and he finished all his house. He built also the house of the forest of Lebanon," &c. (1 Kings vi. 37, 38; vii. 1, 2.)

Can there now be anything more plain? Is not here the house of the forest of Lebanon mentioned as another besides the temple?—he built the temple, he built his own house, he built also the house of the forest of Lebanon.

Second. It is evident by the difference of their measures and dimensions. The length of the temple was threescore cubits; but the length of the house of the forest of Lebanon was a hundred cubits: so that the house of the forest of Lebanon was forty cubits more than was that called Solomon's temple. The breadth of Solomon's temple was twenty cubits, but the breadth of the house of the forest of Lebanon was fifty cubits: and as there is odds between threescore and fivescore, so there is also between twenty and fifty.

As to their height, they were both alike; but equality in height can no more make them the same, than can a twenty years' age in two make them one and the same person.

Their porches also differed greatly; the porch of the temple was in length but twenty cubits, but the length of that of the house of the forest of Lebanon was fifty cubits. So that here also is thirty odds. The porch of the temple was but ten cubits broad, but the porch of the house of the forest of Lebanon thirty cubits. Now, I say, who that considereth these disproportions can conclude that the house of the forest of Lebanon was none other than that called the temple of Jerusalem? For all this compare 1 Kings vi. 2, 3, with chap. vii. 2, 6.

Third. If you add to these the different makes of the houses, it will sufficiently appear that they were not one. The house of the forest of Lebanon was built upon four rows of cedar pillars; but we read of no such pillars upon which the temple stood. The windows of the house of the forest of Lebanon stood in three rows, light against light; but we read of no such thing in the temple. The temple had two pillars before the door of its porch, but we read not of them before the door of the porch of the house of the forest of Lebanon.

In the sixth and seventh chapters of the first book of Kings, these two houses, as to their make, are exactly set forth; so that he that listeth may search and see if, as to this, I have not said the truth.

CHAPTER II.

OF WHAT THE HOUSE OF THE FOREST OF LEBANON WAS A TYPE.

That the house of the forest of Lebanon was a house significant, I think is clear; also, if it had not, we should not have had so particular an account thereof in the holy word of God : I read but of four buildings wherein, in a particular manner, the houses or fabrics are, as to their manner of building, distinctly handled : the tabernacle is one, the temple another ; the porch which he built for his throne, his throne for judgment ; and this house of the forest of Lebanon is the fourth. Now the three first—to wit, the tabernacle, the temple, the porch and throne—wise men will say are typical ; and therefore so is this.

I will therefore take it for granted, that the house of the forest of Lebanon is a significative thing, yea, a figure of the Church, as the temple at Jerusalem was, though not under the same consideration. The temple was a figure of the Church under the gospel, as she relateth to worship ; but the house of the forest of Lebanon was a figure of that Church, as she is assaulted for her worship, as she is persecuted for the same. Or take it more expressly thus : I take this house of the forest of Lebanon to be a type of the Church in the wilderness, or as she is in her sackcloth state.

We read before this house was built, that there was a Church in the wilderness ; and also after this house was demolished, that there would be a Church in the wilderness, (Acts vii. 38 ;) but we now respect that wilderness state that the Church of the New Testament is in, and conclude that this house of the forest of Lebanon was a type and figure of that, that is, of her wilderness state, (Rev. xii. 14.) And methinks the very place where this house was built does intimate such a thing ; for this house was not built in a town, a city, &c., as was that called the temple of the Lord ; but was built in a kind of a wood, a wilderness, it was built in the forest of Lebanon ; unto which that saying seems directly to answer. "And to the woman" (the Church) "were given two wings of a great eagle, that she might fly into the wilderness unto her place." (Rev. xii. 14.)

A wilderness state is a desolate, a tempted, an afflicted, a persecuted state. (Jer. ii. 6.) All which is more than intimated by the witnesses wearing of, and prophesying in, sackcloth, and also expressed of by that Rev. xii.

Answerable to this is that of the prophet concerning this house of the forest of Lebanon, where he says, "Open thy doors, O Lebanon ! that the fire may devour thy cedars." And again, "Howl, fir-tree, for the cedar is fallen." (Zech. xi. 1, 2.)

What can be more express ? The prophet here knocks at the very door of the house of the forest of Lebanon, and tells her, that her cedars are designed for fire ; unto which also most plainly answer the flames to which so many of the cedars of Lebanon—God's saints, I mean—for many hundred years, have been delivered for their profession ; and by which, as another prophet has it,

for many days they have fallen. (Dan. xi. 33.) Also when the King of Assyria came up with his army against Jerusalem, this was his vaunting, " I am come to the sides of Lebanon, and I will cut down the tall cedars thereof." (Isa. xxvii. 24.) What was this King of Assyria, but a type of the beast made mention of in the New Testament ? Now, saith he, I will cut down the cedars of Lebanon ; who are, in our gospel times, the tall ones of the Church of God. And I say again, in that he particularly mentions Lebanon, he intends that house which Solomon built there—the which was builded as a fortification to defend the religion of the temple, as the saints now in the wilderness of the people, are set for the defence of the gospel. But more of this anon.

This house, therefore, was builded to make assaults, and to be assaulted, as the Church in the wilderness is ; and hence the state of this house is compared to the condition of a woman in travail, struggling with her pains, as also we find the state of the Church in the wilderness is, " O inhabitant of Lebanon, that makest thy nest in the cedars, how gracious shalt thou be when pangs come upon thee, the pain as of a woman in travail !" (Jer. xxii. 23.) And again, Verily, verily, I say unto you, that ye shall weep and lament, and have sorrow, as a woman in travail, (John xvi. 20—22 :) much answering her case, who, in her travails, and while "pained to be delivered," was said, even in this case, to stand before the dragon, who with open mouth sought to destroy her fruit, so " soon as it was born." (Rev. xii. 1—6.)

Hence, again, when Christ calls his spouse out to suffer, he calls, or draws her out of his house in Lebanon, to look "from the lions' den, from the mountains of the leopards," (Sol. Song iv. 8,) to the things that are invisible ; even as Paul said when he was in affliction, " We look not at the things which are seen." (2 Cor. iv. 18.) He draws them out thence, I say, as sheep appointed for the slaughter ; yea, he goeth before them, and they follow him thither. Also, when the prophet foretells the affliction of the Church, he expresses it by the fall of the cedars of Lebanon, saying, the Lord shall cut down the thickets of the forest with iron ; a little afore called the axe and saw. And Lebanon shall fall by a mighty one. (Isa. x. 15, 24.) And again, "the earth mourneth and languisheth, Lebanon is ashamed and hewn down." (Isa. xxxiii. 9.)

Do we think that the prophet prophesieth here against trees, against the natural cedars of Lebanon ? No, no ; it is a prophecy touching the afflicted state of the Church in the wilderness, of which Lebanon—I mean this house of the forest of Lebanon—was a figure.

When God also threateneth the enemies of his Church in the wilderness with his judgments, for their cruel dealing with her in the day of her desertion, he calls those judgments the violence of

Lebanon: that is, by way of comparison, such as the violence done to Lebanon was. "The violence of Lebanon shall cover thee; and the spoil of beasts which made them [Lebanon] afraid: because of men's blood, and for the violence of the land, of the city, and of all that dwell therein." (Hab. ii. 17.) This is like that, "Reward her, even as she rewarded you; and double unto her double, according to her works." (Rev. xviii. 6.) This the Church doth by her prayers. "The violence done to me, and to my flesh, be upon Babylon, shall the inhabitant of Zion say; and my blood upon the inhabitants of Chaldea, shall Jerusalem say." (Jer. li. 35.) And then shall be fulfilled that which is written, look what they did unto Lebanon shall be done unto them. (Obad. 15. Ezek. xxxv. 14, 15.)

God has his time to return the evil that the enemies do to his Church, and he will do it when his time is come, upon their own head; and this return is called the covering of them with the violence of Lebanon, or that violence showed to her in the day of her distress.

It is yet further evident, that this house of the forest of Lebanon was a type of the Church in the wilderness.

First. For that she is called a tower, or place of fortification and defence; the same term that is given to the Church in a captivated state. (Sol. Song vii. 4. Micah iv. 8—10.) For, as the Church in the wilderness is compared to a woman in travail, to show her fruitfulness to God-ward in her most afflicted condition; so she is called a tower, to show her fortitude and courage, for God and his truth, against Antichrist. I say therefore, unto both these is she compared in that scripture last cited, the which you may peruse if you please. A tower is a place of receipt for the afflicted, and so is the Church under the rage of Antichrist; yea, and though it is the only place designed by the enemy for ruin and destruction, yet it is the only place of safety in the world.

Second. This tower, this house of the forest of Lebanon, it seems to be so built as to confront Damascus, the chief city of the King of Assyria; and in so doing, it was a most excellent type of the spirit and design of the Church in the wilderness, who is raised up, and built to confront Antichrist. Hence Christ calls some of the features of his Church, and compares them to this. "Thy neck," says he, "is as a tower of ivory; thine eyes like the fishpools in Heshbon, by the gate of Bath-rabbim; thy nose is as the tower of Lebanon, which looketh toward Damascus." (Sol. Song vii. 4.) Thy nose, that great ornament of thy lovely countenance, is as a tower looking that way; so set, as Christ says of his, as a flint. And this is a comely feature in the Church, that her nose stands like a tower, or as he says in another place, like a fenced brazen wall against Damascus, the metropolitan of her enemy: "for the head of Syria is Damascus." (Isa. vii. 8.)

And as Christ thus compares his Church, so she again returns, or compares the face of her Lord to the same, saying, "His legs are as pillars of marble set upon sockets of fine gold: his countenance is as Lebanon, excellent as the cedars." (Sol. Song v. 15.)

Thus, in Lebanon, in this brave house, is found the excellency of the Church, and the beauty of Christ, for that they are both as a rock, with glory and majesty, bended against the enemies of the truth. "The face of the Lord is against them that do evil." Pillars his legs are here compared to, and pillars were they that upheld this house, this tower, which thus bravely was builded with its face confronting the enemy's country.

That this house of the forest of Lebanon was a type of the Church in affliction, yet further appears, for that at the fall of Babylon, her cedars are said to rejoice in special. "The fir-trees rejoice at thee, and the cedars of Lebanon, saying, Since thou art laid down, no feller is come up against us." (Isa. xiv. 8.) This is at the destruction of Babylon, the type of that called Antichrist.

But why should Lebanon, the cedars in Lebanon, in an especial manner here, be said to rejoice at his downfall? Doubtless to show that as the enemy made his inroad upon Jerusalem, so in a particular manner Lebanon, and the house there, were made to smoke for it. (Isa. xxxvii. 24. Jer. xxii. 23. Zech. xi. 1.) This answereth to that, "Rejoice over her thou heaven, and ye holy apostles and prophets, for God hath avenged you of her." Hence again, when he speaks of giving glory to his afflicted Church, for all the sorrow which she hath sustained in her bearing witness for the truth against Antichrist, he calls it the glory of Lebanon: that is, as I take it, the glory that belongs to her, for the afflictions which she underwent for his name. "The glory of Lebanon shall be given unto it." (Isa. xxxv. 2.) And again, "The glory of Lebanon shall come unto thee." (Isa. lx. 13.)

These are promises to the Church for her suffering of affliction, and they are made unto her as she bears the name of Lebanon, who, or which was her type in those havocs made in it, when the enemy, as I said, assaulted the Church of old.

Thus by these few lines I have showed you that there was a similitude betwixt this house in the forest of Lebanon, and our gospel-church in the wilderness. Nor need we stumble because this word "house" is not subjoined in every particular place where this sorrow or joy of Lebanon is made mention of: for it is a usual thing with the Holy Ghost, when he directs his speech to a man, to speak as if he spake to a tree; and when he directs his voice to a king, to speak as if he intended the kingdom; so when he speaks of the house, to speak as to the forest of Lebanon. Instances many might be given.

CHAPTER III.

OF THE LARGENESS OF THE HOUSE OF THE FOREST OF LEBANON.

The house of the forest of Lebanon was forty cubits longer than was the temple at Jerusalem, to show that the Church in the wilderness would increase more, and be far larger than she that had peace and prosperity : and as it was forty cubits longer, so it was thirty cubits wider, still showing that every way she would abound. Hence they that came out of great tribulation, when compared with others, are said to be a numberless number, or a multitude which no man could number, of all nations, and kindreds, and people, and tongues. "These," saith one, " are they which came out of great tribulation, and have washed their robes, and made them white in the blood of the Lamb; therefore are they before the throne of God." (Rev. vii. 14, 15.)

The Church, as it respected temple-worship, was confined to the land of Canaan; but our New Testament persecuted one is scattered among the nations, as a flock of sheep are scattered in a wood or wilderness. Hence they are said to be in "the wilderness of the people," fitly answering to this house of the forest of Lebanon. (Ezek. xx. 35—37.)

But though the house exceeded in length and breadth the temple at Jerusalem, yet as to their height they were the same, to show that what acts that in the wilderness doth, above what they have been capable to do, that have not been in that condition; yet the nature of their grace is the same. (Rom. xv. 27. 1 Pet. i. 1.)

But, I say, as for length and breadth, the Church in the wilderness exceeds more than the house of Lebanon did that of the temple at Jerusalem, as it is written, "More are the children of the desolate, than the children of the married wife, saith the Lord." And again : "Thou shalt break forth on the right hand and on the left; and thy seed shall inherit the Gentiles, and make the desolate cities to be inhabited." (Isa. liv. 1—3.)

This is spoken of the Church in the wilderness, that was made up chiefly of the Gentiles, of which the house of the forest of Lebanon was a figure; and how she at last shall recover herself from the yoke and tyranny of Antichrist. And then she shall shoulder it with her adversary, saying, "Give place to me, that I may dwell." (Isa. xlix. 20.)

And I will add, it was not only thus magnificent for length and breadth, but for terror; it was compacted after the manner of a castle, or stronghold, as was said before. It was a tower built for an armoury; for Solomon put there his two hundred targets, and three hundred shields of gold. (2 Chron. ix. 15, 16.)

This place, therefore, was a terror to the heathen on that side of the Church especially, because she stood with her nose so formidable against Damascus : no marvel, therefore, if the implacable cried out against them, "Help, men of Israel, help!" and "Will ye rebel against the king ?" (Acts xxi. 28. Neh. ii. 19.)

For it is the terror, or majesty and fortitude, which God has put upon the Church in the wilderness, that makes the Gentiles so bestir them to have her under foot. Besides, they misapprehend concerning her, as if she were for destroying kings, for subverting kingdoms, and for bringing all to desolation; and so they set themselves against her, "crying, These that have turned the world upside down, are come hither also ; whom Jason hath received : and these all do contrary to the decrees of Cæsar, saying, that there is another King, one Jesus." (Acts xvii. 5—7.)

Indeed the very name of Jesus is the very tower of the Christian Church, and that by which she frights the world, but not designedly, but through their misunderstanding ; for neither she nor her Jesus is for doing them any hurt: however, this is that which renders her yet in their eye, "terrible as an army with banners." (Sol. Song vi. 10.)

How then could she escape persecution for a time; for it was the policy of Jeroboam, (1 Kings xii. 26—28,) and it is yet the policy of the nations to secure themselves against this their imagined danger, and therefore to use all means, as Pharaoh did, to keep this people low enough, saying, "Come on, let us deal wisely with them, lest they multiply, and it come to pass when there falleth out any war, they join also to our enemies, and fight against us, and so get them up out of the land." (Exod. i. 10.)

But could the house of Lebanon, though a fortified place, assault Damascus ? Could it remove from the place on which God had set it ? It only was a place of defence for Judah, or for the worship of the temple. And had the adversary let the temple-worship and worshippers alone, the shields and targets in the house of the forest of Lebanon had not been uncovered, had not been made bare against them. The same may now be said of the Church in the wilderness; she moveth no sedition, she abideth in her place. Let her temple-worshippers but alone, and she will be as if she were not in the world: but if you afflict her, "Fire proceedeth out of their mouth, and devoureth their enemies: and if any man will hurt them, he must in this manner be killed," (Rev. xi. 5;) and so die by the sword of the Spirit.

But because the weapons of the Church, though none of them are carnal, be so talked of in the world, the blind are yet more afraid of her than they in this manner are like to be hurt by her; and therefore they of old have peeled, and polled, and endeavoured to spoil her all along; sending their servants, and saying to their bailiffs and sheriffs, "Go to a nation scattered and peeled, to a people terrible from their beginning, a nation meted out and trodden down, whose land the rivers have spoiled." (Isa. xviii. 2.)

But this people shall prevail, though not by worldly force: her God will deliver her. And then, or at that time, shall the present be brought to the Lord of hosts, of a people scattered and peeled, and from a people terrible from their beginning hitherto, a nation meted out and trodden under foot, whose land the rivers have spoiled, to the place of the name of the Lord of hosts, the Mount Zion. (Isa. xviii. 7.)

Now thus did the house of the forest of Lebanon provoke; it was built defensively, it had a tower, it had armour; its tower confronted the enemy's land. No marvel, then, if the King of Assyria so threatened to lay his army on the sides of Lebanon, and to cut down the tall cedars thereof. (Isa. xxxvii. 24.)

The largeness, therefore, and prowess of the Church, by reason of her inherent fortitude, and the valorous acts that she hath done, by suffering, by prayer, by faith, and a constant enduring of hardship for the truth, doth force into the world a belief, through their own guilt and clamours of conscience against them for their debaucheries, that this house of the forest of Lebanon will destroy them all, when she shall be delivered from her servitude. "Come now, therefore," saith Balak to Balaam, "and curse me this people," if peradventure I may overcome them, when he might have let them pass peaceably by, and they would not have lift up a finger against him. Wherefore, from all these things it appears that the house of the forest of Lebanon was a type of the Church in the wilderness.

CHAPTER IV.

OF THE MATERIALS OF WHICH THE HOUSE OF THE FOREST OF LEBANON WAS MADE.

The foundation of the house of the forest of Lebanon was of the same great stones which were laid in the foundation of the temple of the Lord. (1 Kings vii. 2—11.)

And this shows that the Church in the wilderness has the same foundation and support, as had the temple that was at Jerusalem, though in a state of sackcloth, tears, and afflictions, the lot of the Church in the wilderness; for she, while there, is to howl. (Zech. xi. 2.)

Now, since the foundation is the same, what is it but to show also, that she, though in an afflicted condition, shall certainly stand; "the gates of hell shall not prevail against it." (Matt. xvi. 18.)

Her confronting idolatrous nations is therefore a sign of her troubles; not any prediction of a fall. Her rock is steadfast, not like the rock of her adversaries, the enemy being judges. (Deut. xxxii. 31.)

But that which in special I take notice of, is that I find, in a manner, in this house of the forest of Lebanon nothing but pillars and beams, great timber, and thick beams, and of those was the house builded; pillars to hold up, and thick beams to couple together, and thus was the house finished. I read not here of any garnishing, either of the pillars, beams, doors, posts, walls, or any part of the house; all was plain, without garnish, fitly representing the state of the Church in the wilderness, which was clothed with sackcloth, covered with ashes, wearing her mourning weeds, with her tears upon her cheeks, and a yoke or band about her neck. (Isa. lii. 1, 2; lxi. 3.)

By this kind of description we may also note with what kind of members this house, this Church is furnished. Here, as I said, that is, in the house of the forest of Lebanon, you find pillars, pillars; so in the Church in the wilderness. O the mighty ones of which this Church was compacted! They were all pillars, strong, bearing up the house against wind and weather; nothing but fire and sword could dissolve them. As therefore this house was made up of great timber, so this Church in the wilderness was made up of giants in grace. These men had the faces of lions: no prince, no king, no threat, no terror, no torment, could make them yield! They loved not their lives unto the death. They have laughed their enemies in the face, they have triumphed in the flames.

They were pillars, they were pillars of cedar: the cedar is the highest tree in the world; wherefore in that this house was made of cedar, it may be to denote that in the Church in the wilderness, however contemned by men, was the highest perfection of goodness, as of faith, love, prayer, holy conversation, and affection for God and his truth.

For indeed, none ever showed the like, none ever showed higher cedars than those that were in Lebanon. None ever showed higher saints than were they in the Church in the wilderness. Others talked, these have suffered; others have said, these have done: these have voluntarily taken their lives in their hands, for they loved them not to the death: and have fairly, and in cool blood, laid them down before the world, God, angels, and men, for the confirming of the truth, which they have professed. (Acts xv. 26. Rev. xii. 11.)

These are pillars, these are strong ones indeed: it is meet therefore, that the Church in the wilderness, since she was to resemble the house of the forest of Lebanon, should be furnished with these mighty ones.

Cedars! The same that the holiest of all in the temple was covered with within, (and that house was a figure of heaven,) to show that the Church of God in the wilderness, how base and low soever in the judgment of the world, is yet the only heaven that God hath among the children of men. Here are many nations, many kingdoms, many countries, and many cities; but the Church in the wilderness was but one, and she was the heaven that God has here : hence she is called, " Thou heaven." " Rejoice over her, thou heaven." (Rev. xviii. 20.)

And again, when the combustion for religion is in the Church in the wilderness, it is said to be in heaven—" And there was war in heaven. Michael and his angels fought against the dragon, and the dragon fought, and his angels." (Rev. xii. 7.)

The Church therefore loseth not all her titles of honour, no, not when at the lowest : she is God's heaven still. Though she may not be called now a crown of glory, yet she is still God's lily amongst thorns ; though she may not be called the Church of Jerusalem, yet she may the Church in the wilderness ; and though she may not be called Solomon's temple, yet she may the house of the forest of Lebanon.

Cedars ! Cedars are tall and sweet, and so are the members of the Church in the wilderness. Oh their smell, their scent, it hath been " as the wine of Lebanon." (Hosea xiv. 5—7.) They that have gone before, have left this smell still in the nostrils of their survivors, as that both fragrant and precious.

This house of the forest of Lebanon was builded " upon four rows of cedar pillars." (1 Kings vii. 2.) These four rows were the bottom pillars, those upon which the whole weight of the house did bear. The Holy Ghost saith here four rows, but says not how many were in a row. But we will suppose them to allude to the twelve apostles, or to the apostles and prophets, upon whose foundation the Church in the wilderness is said to be built. (Eph. ii. 20.) And if so, then it shows that as the house of the forest of Lebanon stood upon these four rows of pillars, as the names of the twelve tribes stood in four rows of precious stones upon Aaron's breastplate, when he went into the holiest, so this house, or Church in the wilderness, stands upon the doctrine of the apostles and prophets. (Ezek. xxviii. 17 ; xxxix. 10.)

But because it only saith it stood upon four rows, not specifying any number, therefore as to this we may say nothing certain, yet I think such a conjecture hath some show of truth in it ; however, I will leave it to wiser judgments.

" And it was covered with cedar above, upon the beams that lay on forty-five pillars, fifteen in a row." (1 Kings vii. 3.) These pillars, as the others, are such upon which the house did also bear ; this is clear, because the beams that lay upon the four rows of pillars afore-mentioned, lay also upon these forty-five.

It seems, therefore, that these four rows of pillars were they that were the more outside ones ; that is, two rows on this side of the house, and two rows also on that ; and that those forty-five pillars, fifteen in a row, stood in three rows more inward, and so did bear up with the other, the beams that were laid upon them, much like to those inner pillars that usually stand in our parish churches. If so, then the first four rows did seem to be a guard to these, for that as they stood more to the outsides of the house, so more to the weather, and nearer to the first approach of the enemy.

And this may show that the apostles, in their doctrine, are not only a foundation to the forty-five pillars, but a protection and defence : I say a protection and defence to all the pillars that ever were besides in the Church in the wilderness. And it is to be considered that the four rows are mentioned as placed first, and so were those upon which the thick beams that first were for coupling of the house were laid : the which most fitly teacheth that the office and the graces of the apostles were first in the Church in the wilderness, according to 1 Cor. xii. 18.

These forty-five pillars standing in the midst, by the others, may also be to show that in the time of the trouble of the Church in the wilderness state, there will be those that will stand by and maintain her apostolical doctrine, though for so doing they bear the burden of the whole.

But I read of no chambers for ease or rest in this house ; here is no room for chambering. They that were for being members in the Church in the wilderness must not look for rest until their Lord shall come. (Rom. xiii. 13, 14. 2 Thess. i. 5—9.)

Here, therefore, was but hard lodging ; the house of the forest of Lebanon was not made for tender skins, and for those that cannot lie out of down beds, but for those that were warlike men, and that were willing to endure hardness for that religion that God had set up in his temple ; and is fitly answered by that of the apostle : " Thou, therefore," my son, " endure hardness as a good soldier of Jesus Christ. No man that warreth entangleth himself with the affairs of this life, that he may please him who hath chosen him to be a soldier." (2 Tim. ii. 3, 4.)

Forty-five pillars ! It was forty-five years that the Church was of old in a bewildered and warlike condition before she enjoyed her rest in Canaan. (Josh. xiv. 10.) Now as there were forty-five years of trouble, so here are forty-five pillars for support ; perhaps to intimate that God will have in his Church in the wilderness a sufficient succession of faithful men that, like pillars, shall bear up the truth above water all the time of Antichrist's reign and rage.

The thick beams that lay over-thwart to couple this house of the forest of Lebanon together, did bear upon these forty-five pillars to show that by the burden-bearers that have and shall be in the Church of God in the wilderness, the unity of that house is through the Spirit maintained. And indeed, had it not been for these pillars, the sufferers, these burden-bearers in the Church, our house in the forest of Lebanon, or more properly our Church in the wilderness, had before this been but in a poor condition. Thus, therefore, this Church, which in her time is the pillar and ground of truth in the world, has been made to stand and abide it. " When the blast of the terrible ones is as a storm against the wall." (Isa. xxv. 4.) "Many a time have they afflicted me from my youth, may Israel now say: many a time have they afflicted me from my youth, yet they have not prevailed against me." (Ps. cxxix. 1, 2.)

Thus you see how the house of the forest of Lebanon was a type of the Church in the wilderness; and you see also by this the reason why the house of the forest of Lebanon had its inward glory lying more in great pillars and thick beams than in other ornaments. And, indeed, here had need be pillars and pillars, and beams and beams too, since it was designed for assaults to be made upon it; since it was set for a butt for the marksman, and to be an object for furious heathens to spend their rage against its walls.

The glory, therefore, of the temple lay in one thing, and the glory of this house lay in another: the glory of the temple lay in that she contained the true form and modes of worship; and the glory of the house of the forest of Lebanon lay in the many pillars and thick beams, by which she was made capable, through good management, to give check to those of Damascus, when they should attempt to throw down that worship.

And, as I said before, these pillars were sweet-scented pillars, for that they were made of cedar; but what cared the enemy for that, they were offensive to him, for that they were placed as a fortification against him. Nor is it any allurement to Satan to favour the mighty ones in the Church in the wilderness, for the fragrant smell of their sweet graces; nay, both he and his angels are the more bent to oppose them, because they are so sweet-scented.

The cedars, therefore, got nothing because they were cedars at the hands of the barbarous Gentiles, for they would burn the cedars, as the angels or pillars get nothing of favour at the hands of Antichrist, because they are pillars of, and angels for, the truth, yea, they so much the more by her are abhorred.

Well, but they are pillars for all that; yea, pillars to the Church in the wilderness, as the others were in the house of the forest of Lebanon, and pillars they will abide there, dead and alive, when the enemy has done what he can.

The pillars were set in three rows, for so are forty-five when they are set fifteen in a row. And they were set in three rows to bear. This manner also of their standing thus was also doubtless significant.

But, again, they, these pillars, may be set or placed thus in three rows in the house of the forest of Lebanon, to show that the three offices of Christ are the great things that the Church in the wilderness must bear up before the world.

The three offices of Christ, they are his priestly, his prophetical, and his kingly offices. These are those in which God's glory and the Church's salvation are most immediately concerned; and they that have been most opposed by the devil and his angels: all heresies, errors, and delusions, with which Christ's Church has been assaulted in all ages have bent themselves against some one or all of these. (Rev. xvi. 13, 16.)

Christ is a priest to save, a prophet to teach, and a king to rule his Church, (Isa. xxxiii. 22:) but this Antichrist cannot bear; therefore he attempts to get up into the throne himself, and to act as if he were one above all that is called God, or that is worshipped.

But behold! here are pillars in three rows, mighty pillars to bear up Christ in these his offices before the world, and against all falsehood and deceit.

Fifteen in a row, I can say no further than I can see; what the number of fifteen should signify I know not, God is wiser than man; but yet methinks their standing thus should signify a reserve: as, suppose the first three that the enemy comes at should be destroyed by their hands, there are three times fourteen behind: suppose, again, that they should serve the next three so, yet there is a reserve behind. When that fine one Jezebel, had done what she could against the afflicted Church in her time, yet there was left a reserve, a reserve of seven thousand that were true worshippers of God. (1 Kings xix. 18.)

Always when Antichrist made his inroads upon the Church in the wilderness to slay, to cut off, and to kill, yet some of the pillars stood, they were not all burnt in the fire, nor cut down. They said indeed, "Come and let us cut them off from being a nation, that the name of Israel may be no more in remembrance." (Ps. lxxxiii. 4.) But what then? there is a difference betwixt saying and doing; the bush was not therefore consumed because it was set on fire; the Church shall not be consumed although she be afflicted. (Exod. iii. 3.)

And this reason is because God has still his fifteens; therefore if Abel falls by the hand of Cain, Seth is put in his place, (Gen. iv. 25;) if Moses is taken away, Joshua shall succeed him, (Josh. i. 2, 3;) and if the devil break the neck of Judas, Matthias is at hand to take his office. (Acts i. 26.) God has, I say, a succession of pillars in his house; he has to himself a reserve.

Yet, again, methinks that there should be forty-five pillars, and besides them four rows of pillars, and all this to bear up an invisible burden, for we read of nothing upon the pillars but the heavens and roof. It should be to show that it is impossible that a carnal heart should conceive of the weight that truth lays upon the conscience of a believer: they see nothing, alas, nothing at all, but a beam, a truth; and say they, "Are you such fools to stand groaning to bear up that, or what is contained therein?" They, I say, see not the weight, the glory, the weight of glory that is in a truth of God; and therefore they laugh at them that will count it worth the while to endure so much to support it from falling to the ground.

Great pillars and beams, great saints, and great truths are in the Church of God in the wilderness; and the beams lie upon the pillars, or the truth upon the saints.

The tabernacle and ark formerly were to be borne upon men's shoulders, even as these great beams are borne up by these pillars: and as this tabernacle and ark were to be carried hither and thither, according to the appointment of God, so were these beams to be by these pillars borne up, that therewith the house might be girt together, kept uniform, and made to stand fast notwithstanding the wind and the storm.

CHAPTER V.

OF THE WINDOWS OF THE HOUSE OF THE FOREST OF LEBANON.

The house of the forest of Lebanon had many windows in it; "and there were windows in three rows, and light was against light in three ranks." (1 Kings vii. 4.)

Windows are to let the light in at, and the eye out at, to objects at a distance from the house, and from those that are therein.

The windows here are figures of the word of God, by which light the light of life is let into the heart; through that, the glass of these windows, the beams of the Sun of righteousness shine into the Church. Hence the word is compared to glass, through which the glorious face of Christ is seen. (2 Cor. iii. 18.) This, therefore, this house of the forest of Lebanon had; it had windows, a figure of that word of God, through, and by which, the Church in the wilderness sees the mind of God, and so what, while there, she ought to believe, do, and leave undone in the world.

This house had plenty of windows, three rows of windows on both sides the house. In three rows, by these windows in three rows, perhaps, was prefigured how into the Church in the wilderness was to shine the doctrine of the Trinity: yea, to signify that she was to be possessed with that in her most low state, and when under her greatest clouds. The doctrine of the Trinity! that is the substance, that is the ground and fundamental of all, (1 John ii. 22, 23; iv. 2—4. 2 John 9, 10;) for by this doctrine, and by this only, the man is made a Christian; and he that has not this doctrine, his profession is not worth a button.

You must know that sometimes the Church in the wilderness has but little light, but the diminution of her light is not then so much in or as to substantials, as it is as to circumstantial things; she has then the substantials with her in her darkest day, even windows in three rows.

The doctrine of the Trinity! You may ask me what that is? I answer, it is that doctrine that showeth us the love of God the Father in giving of his Son: the love of God the Son in giving of

himself; and the love of the Lord the Spirit, in his work of regenerating of us, that we may be made able to lay hold of the love of the Father by his Son, and so enjoy eternal life by grace. This doctrine was always let in at these windows into the Church in the wilderness for to make her sound in faith, and hearty in obedience; as also meek and patient in temptation and tribulation.

And as to the substance of Christianity, this doctrine is sufficient for any people, because it teacheth faith, and produceth a good moral life. These, therefore, if these doctrines shine upon us through these windows of heaven so as that we see them, and receive them, they make us fit to glorify God here, and meet to be glorified of and with him hereafter.

These lights, therefore, cause that the inhabitants of this Church in the wilderness see their way through the dark pitch night of this world: for as the house of the forest of Lebanon, this Church of God in the wilderness had always her lights or windows in these three rows to guide, to solace, and comfort her.

This house, therefore, is thus discriminated and distinguished from all other houses in the world; no house that we read of in the Bible was thus adorned with light, or had windows in three rows but this; and answerable hereunto no congregation or church but the true Church of God has the true antitype thereof.

Light! windows! A sufficiency of windows was of great use to a people that dwelt in a forest, or wood, as the inhabitants of the house of the forest of Lebanon did: but how solitary had this house been had it had no light at all! To be in a wood, and that without windows, is one of the worst of conditions.

This also is the relief that the Church in the wilderness had; true, she was in a wood, but had light, called in another place God's rod, or his word which giveth instruction. "Feed thy people with thy rod, the flock of thine heritage, which dwell solitary in the wood," &c. (Micah vii. 14.)

To be, as was said, in a wood, and without light too, is a condition very desolate: the Egyptians found it so, for all they were in their houses. (Exod. x. 21, 23.)

But how much more, then, is that people's case to be lamented that are under persecution, but have not light in three rows to guide them. But this is not the state of the Church in the wilderness—she has her windows in three rows—to wit, the light of the face of the Father, the light of the face of the Son, and the light of the face of the Holy Ghost; all shining through the windows or glass of the word to her comfort and consolation, though now in the forest of Lebanon.

"And light was against light in three ranks." This is an additional account of the windows that were in the house of the forest of Lebanon. Before he said she had windows in three rows but now he adds that there was light against light, light opposite to light, and that also in three ranks.

In that he saith, they were in ranks, he either means in order, or insinuates a military posture, for in both these ways is this word taken. (Numb. ii. 16, 24. 1 Chron. xii. 33, 38. Mark vi. 40.)

Nor need any smile because I say the lights were set in a military posture; we read of potsherds striving with potsherds, and why may it not as well be said, "light was against light." (Isa. xlv. 9.)

But we will pursue our design : here is opposition insinuated; in the margin it is "sight against sight;" wherefore the lights thus placed in the house of the forest of Lebanon give me another encouragement to think that this house was a type of the Church in the wilderness, and that she is the seat of spiritual war also. (Rev. xii. 7.)

For as this house of the forest of Lebanon was that which was the object of the rage of the King of Assyria, because it stood in his way to hinder his ruining Jerusalem, so the spirit and faithfulness of the Church of God in the wilderness stands in the way, and hinders Antichrist's bringing of the truth to the ground.

And as the enemy brake into Lebanon, and did set fire to her cedars, so the boar, the Antichrist, the dragon, and his angels got into the Church in the wilderness. (Ps. lxxx. 13. 2 Thess. ii. 4. Rev. xii. 7.)

This being so, here must needs be war; and since the war is not carnal, but spiritual, it must be made by way of controversy, contention, disputation, argument, reasonings, &c., which were the effect of opposite apprehensions, fitly set out in this house of the forest of Lebanon, for that there was "light against light," "sight against sight," in three ranks.

Wherefore in that he saith "light was against light" in three ranks, he suggesteth, to the life, how it would be in the Church in the wilderness.

And suppose they were the truly godly that made the first assault, can they be blamed? For who can endure a boar in a vineyard; a man of sin in a holy temple; or a dragon in heaven? What, then, if the Church made the first assault? Who bid the boar come there? What had he to do in God's house? The Church, as the house of the forest of Lebanon, would have been content with its own station; and bread and water will serve a man that may with peace enjoy his delights in other things. But when privilege, property, life, delight, heaven, and salvation comes to be intruded, no marvel if the woman, though but a woman, cries out, and set her light against them; had she seen the thief, and said nothing, she had been far worse.

I told you before that by the windows is meant the word, which is compared to glass. (1 Cor. xiii. 12. 2 Cor. iii. 18. James i. 23—25.)

What, then, is the word against the word?

No, verily; it is, therefore, not the word, but opposite apprehensions thereabout, that the Holy Ghost now intends; for he saith not, that window was against window, respecting the true sense of the word, but light was against light, respecting the divers notions and apprehensions that men of opposite spirits would have about the word.

Nor are we to take this word light, especially in the antitype, in a proper, but a metaphorical sense; that is, with respect to the judgment of both parties. Here is the true Church, and she has the true light; here also is the boar, the man of sin, and the dragon, and they see by their way; and yet, as I said, all by the selfsame windows. They that are the Church do, in God's light, see light; but they that are not, do, in their own way, see. And let a man and a beast look out at the same window, the same door, the same casement, yet the one will see like a man, and the other but like a beast. No marvel, then, though they have the same windows, that "light is against light," and sight against sight, in this house. For there are that know nothing but what they know naturally as brutes. (Ps. xcii. 6. Jer. x. 8; xiv. 21. Jude 10.)

No marvel, then, if there is here a disagreement; the beast can but see as a beast, but the Church is resolved not to be guided by the eye of a beast, though he pretends to have his light by that very window by which the Church has hers. The beast is moon-eyed, and puts darkness for light, yes, and hates the light that is so indeed; but the saints will not hear him, for they know the voice of their Lord. (Isa. v. 20. John iii. 20.)

How, then, can it be but that light should be against light in this house, and that in a military posture? And how can it be but that here "every battle of the warrior" should be "with confused noise, and garments rolled in blood." (Isa. ix. 5.)

And in that he saith "light was against light in three ranks," it shows their preparations one against another; also, that they on both sides are resolved to stand by their way. The Church is confident, the man of sin is confident; they both have the same windows to see by, and so they manage their matters; yet not so simply by the windows as by their divers judgments they make of that which shineth in at them. Each one, therefore, [who] hath the true and false profession will be confident of his own way; he that was right knew he was right, and he that was wrong thought he was right, and so the battle began. "There is a way which seemeth right unto a man, but the end thereof are the ways of death." (Prov. xiv. 12.)

Nor is it in man to help it; there has been reasoning, there has been disputing, there has blood also been spilt on both sides through the confidence that each had of the goodness of his own way; but no reconciliation is made; the enmity is set here of God; iron and clay cannot mix. (Gen. iii. 15. Dan. ii. 42, 43.) God will have things go on thus in the world till his words shall be fulfilled; "the deceived and the deceiver are his." (Job xii. 16.) Things, therefore, must have their course in the Church in the wilderness till the mystery of God shall be fulfilled. (Rom. xvii. 17.)

: Hence it is said, God will bring Gog against his people of Israel, "as a cloud to cover the land." (Ezek. xxxviii. 16.) But for what cause? Why, that he may contend awhile with them, and then fall by their light to the ground. Therefore he says also there, that he "will give unto Gog a place of graves in Israel, and it shall be called the valley of Hamon-gog." (Ezek. xxxix. 11.)

God will get himself great glory by permitting the boar, the man of sin, and the dragon to revel it in the Church of God; for they, by setting up and contending for their darkness, and calling of it the light, and by setting of it against that light, which is light in very deed, do not only prove the power of truth where it is, but illustrate it so much the more: for, as black sets off white, and darkness, light, so error sets off truth. He that calls a man a horse, doth in conclusion but fix the belief of his humanity so much the more in the apprehension of all rational creatures.

"Light against light in three ranks." The three ranks on the Church's side signify her light in the Trinity, as was said, and in the three offices of Christ: and the ranks against these three ranks be to signify the opposite apprehensions of the enemy. They differ also about the authority of the word, and ordinances, about the offices, officers, and executions of office, in the Church, &c. There is an opposition everywhere, even round about the house; there was "light against light in three ranks."

This house of the forest of Lebanon was therefore a significative thing, wisely built, and fit for the purpose which it was designed, which was to show what afterward would be the state of the Church in the wilderness. Nor could anything in the temple more aptly express itself in a typical way, as to any of the things concerning New Testament matters, than doth this house of the forest of Lebanon: as to the things designed to be signified thereby. It speaks, can we but hear: it points to things, as it were with a finger, have we but eyes to see.

It is not therefore to be wondered at, that we hear both parties plead so much for their authority, crying out against each other, as those that destroy religion. So doth the Church, so doth the man of sin. "The living child is mine," saith one; "Nay, but the dead child is thine, and the living child is mine," says the other. And thus they spake before the king. (1 Kings iii. 16—22.)

Now this could not be, were there not different apprehensions here: light against light then is the cause of all this; and here is "light against light in three ranks," and so will be until the beast is dead.

The Church will not give place, for she knows she has the truth; the dragon and his angels, they will not give place, but as beaten back by the power of the truth: for thus it is said of the dragon and his angels, they fought and prevailed not. Therefore there will, there must, there cannot but be a spiritual warfare here, and that until one of the two are destroyed, and their body given to the burning flame. (Dan. vii. 11. Rev. xix. 20.)

CHAPTER VI.

OF THE DOORS, AND POSTS, AND THEIR SQUARE, WITH THE WINDOWS OF THE HOUSE OF THE FOREST OF LEBANON.

"And all the doors and posts were square, with the windows." The doors, they were for entrance, the posts were the support of the doors, and the windows were, as was hinted before, for light. Now, here they are said to be all square; square is a note of perfection; but this word square may be taken two ways.

1. Either as to the fashion of the things themselves; or,

2. With reference to the uniform order of the whole.

In the first sense was the altar of burnt offering, the altar of incense, and the breast-plate of judgment, square, (Exod. xxvii. 1; xxviii. 16; xxx. 2:) and so also it is said of our New Testament New Jerusalem. (Rev. xxi. 16.)

But the square in the text is not thus to be understood, but if I mistake not, as is signified under the second head, that is, for an uniform order. The whole fabric, as the doors, posts, and windows, presented themselves to beholders in an exact uniform order, and so right delectable to behold. Hence we may gather, that this house of the forest of Lebanon was so exactly built, and consequently so complete to view, that it was alluring to the beholders; and that the more, for that so pretty a fabric should be found in a forest, or wood. A lily among thorns, a pearl on a dunghill, and beauty under a veil, will make one turn aside to look on it.

Answerable to this, the Church, even in the wilderness, or under persecution, is compared not only to a woman, but to a comely and delicate woman. And who that shall meet such a creature in a wood, unless he feared God, but would seek to ravish and defile her.

Therefore I say, that which is here said to be square must be understood to be so as to prospect and view, or right taking to the eye.

Thus, therefore, they are allured, and think to defile her in the bed of love, but coming to her, and finding of her chaste, and filled with nothing but armour, and men-at-arms, to maintain her chastity, *nolens volens*, their fleshly love is turned into cruel rage, and so they go to variance.

"I have likened," says God, "the daughter of

Zion to a comely and delicate woman." (Jer. vi. 2.) But where is she? O! she is in the field, in the forest among the shepherds. But what will they do with her? Why, because she complies not with their desires, they "prepare war against her," saying, "Arise, let us go up at noon. Arise, and let us go by night, and let us destroy her palaces." (Jer. vi. 4, 5.)

Wherefore the beauty of the house of the forest of Lebanon, as well as the fortitude thereof, was a temptation to the enemy to come to take it into their possession; especially since it stood, as it were, on the borders of Israel, and so faced the enemy's country.

Thus the church, though in her weeds of widowhood, is become the desire of the eyes of the nations; for indeed her features are such, considering who is her head, where mostly to the eye beauty lies, that whoso sees but the utmost glimpse of her is easily ravished with her beauties. See how the prophet words it—"Many nations are gathered together against thee, that say, Let her be defiled, and let our eye look upon Zion." (Micah iv. 11.)

The Church—the very name of the Church of God—is beautiful in the world; and, as among women, she that has beauty, has her head desired, if it might be, to stand upon another woman's shoulders, so this, and that, and every nation that beholds the beauty of the Church, would fain be called by that name.

The Church, one would think, was but in a homely dress when she was coming out of captivity; and yet then the people of the countries desired to be one with her: "Let us (said they to Zerubbabel, and to the fathers of the Church) build with you, for we seek your God as ye do." (Ezra iv. 2.)

The very name of the Church, as I said, is striven for of the world; but that is the Church which Christ has made so, her features also remain with herself, as this comely prospect of the house of the forest of Lebanon abode with it, whoever beheld or wished for it. The beauty, therefore, of this house, though it stood in the forest, was admirable; even as is the beauty of the Church in the wilderness, though in a bewildered state.

Hear the relation that the Holy Ghost gives of the intrinsic beauty of the church, when she was to go to be in a persecuted state. She was "clothed with the sun, and the moon under her feet, and upon her head a crown of twelve stars." (Rev. xii. 1.) And yet now the dragon stood by. (Rev. xii. 4.) But I say, Here is a woman! let who will attempt it, show such another in the world, if he can.

They, therefore, that have any regard to morality, civility, or to ceremonial comeliness, covet to be of the Church of God, or to appropriate that glorious title to themselves.

And here, indeed, Antichrist came in; she took this name to herself; and though she could not come at the sun, nor moon, nor stars, to adorn herself with them, yet she has found something that makes her comely in her followers' eyes. See how the Holy Ghost sets her forth. She "was arrayed in purple and scarlet colour, and decked with gold and precious stones, and pearls, having a golden cup in her hand," &c. (Rev. xvii. 4.) Hence she is called "the well-favoured harlot," (Josh. iii. 4,) "the lady of kingdoms," (Nah. iii. 4. Isa. xlvii. 5, 7,) &c.

But because the chaste matron, the spouse of Christ, would not allow this slut to run away with this name, therefore she gets upon the back of her beast, and by him pushes this woman into the dirt; but because her faith and love to her husband remains, she turns again, and pleads by her titles, her features, and ornaments, that she, and she only, is she whose square answereth to the square of her figure, and to the characters which her Lord hath given of his own, and so the game began.

For so soon as this mistress became a dame in the world, and found that she had her stout abettors, she attempts to turn all things topsy-turvy, and to set them, and to make of them what she lists. And now she will have an altar like that which was Tiglath-pileser's. Now must the Lord's brazen altar be removed from its place, the borders of the basis must be cut off, and the laver removed from off them; the molten sea must also now be took off the backs of the brazen oxen, where Solomon set it, and be set on a pavement of stone. (2 Kings xvi. 10—17.)

Solomon! alas, Solomon's nobody now; this woman is wiser in her own conceit than seven men that can render a reason. Now also the covert of the Sabbath must be turned to the use of the King of Assyria, &c. (2 Kings xvi. 18.)

Thus has the beauty of God's Church betrayed her into the hands of her lovers, who loved her for themselves, for the devil, and for the making of her a seat, a throne for the man of sin. And poor woman, all her struggling and striving, and crying out under the hands of these ravishers, has not, as yet, delivered her, though it has saved her life. (Deut. xxii. 25—27.)

But though thus it has been with Christ's true Church, and will be as long as his enemy Antichrist reigns, yet the days will come, when God will give her her ornaments, and her bracelets, and her liberty, and her joy, that she had in the day of her espousals.

CHAPTER VII.

OF THE REPETITION OF LIGHT AGAINST LIGHT IN THE HOUSE OF THE FOREST OF LEBANON.

To be sure it was not superfluously done of the Holy Ghost, to make repetition of these words. And light was against light in three ranks; therefore something is intended in the adding of them again, that was not intended by the first mentioning of them. (1 Kings vii. 4, 5.)

I have told you what I thought was intended by the first rehearsal of them, namely, to show how Antichrist got in with his sensuality, and opposed it to the true light of the word of God, exalting himself above God, and also above all divine revelation; this was his light against light. But, I say, why is it repeated? For he saith, "Light was against light in three ranks" again.

Truly, I think it is repeated, to show the evil effects the first antichristian opposition would have in the Church of God, towards the end of her wilderness state. For, "light against light" now, for that it is here repeated, is to show us some new thing, or, as far as wood and windows can speak, to let us understand what would be the consequence of those antichristian figments that were brought into the Church at first by him.

For, can it be imagined, but that, since so much confusion was brought into the Church, some of the truly godly themselves would be much damnified thereby? The apostle says, "Evil communications corrupt good manners." (1 Cor. xv. 33.) And that "their word will eat, as doth a canker." (1 Tim. ii. 17.) Mischief therefore must needs follow this ugly deed of the man of sin.

If a house be on fire, though it is not burnt down, the smell of the flame may long remain there; also we count it no wonder to see some of the effects upon the rafters, beams, and some of the principal posts thereof. The calf that was set up at Dan, defiled that people, until the captivity of the people. (Judges xviii. 30.)

And I say again, since light against light was so early in the Church in the wilderness, and has also been there so long; and again, since many in this Church were both born and bred there under these oppositions of light; it is easy to conclude, that something of the enemy's darkness might be also called light, by the sincere that followed after. For by antichristian darkness, though they might call it light, the true light was darkened, and so the eye made dim, even the eye of the truly godly. Also, the Holy Ghost did much withdraw itself from the Church; so the doctrines, traditions, and rudiments of the world took more hold there, and spread themselves more formidably over the face of that whole Church.

For after the first angel had sounded, and the star was fallen from heaven to the earth, and had received the key of the bottomless pit, and had opened the mouth thereof, the smoke came out amain. (Rev. ix. 1.) This angel was one of the first dads of Antichristianism; and this smoke was that which they call light, but it was "light against light." "And he opened the bottomless pit, and there arose a smoke out of the pit, as the smoke of a great furnace; and the sun and the air were darkened, by reason of the smoke of the pit." (Rev. ix. 2.)

The sun I take to be the gospel of God, and the air, a type of the breathings of the Holy Ghost. The smoke, I take to be the doctrines and traditions of Antichrist; that which was, as I said before, put for light against the true light of the word. Now, since the sun and the air were darkened, by this smoke,—yea, and so darkened, as that the sun, nor moon, nor stars, nor day, nor night, could shine for a third part of them,—no marvel though the true worshippers here were benighted, or at least, had but little light to walk by; yea, I have known some that have been born and bred up in smoky holes, that have been made both in smell and sight to carry the tokens of their so being bred about them.

And I say again, as to what is now under our consideration, no marvel if they that breathed in this Church in the wilderness, after the smoke came out of this pit, sucked in the smoke with the air, until it became natural to them. A house annoyed with smoke is a great offence to the eyes, whose light being thereby impaired, the judgment also, since that as to visibles is guided by the eye, must needs be in danger of being in part misled.

And this being the effect of light against light at first, is the cause of what to this day we see in the Church among the true brotherhood. For as a cause produceth an effect, so sometimes an effect sets on foot another cause.

Now therefore, we have light against light among the godly, as afore there was antichristian against the Christian light. Not that light against light is now godly in the all of it. It is antichristian that opposes the Christian light still. But, as before, the darkness that opposed the light was in the Antichristians, now that darkness is got into the Christians, and has set them against one another. Light, therefore, against light now is, in the Christians, truly pre-figured by that which was in the house of the forest of Lebanon. Witness the jars, the oppositions, the contentions, emulations, strifes, debates, whisperings, tumults, and condemnations, that like cannon-shot have so frequently on all sides been let fly against one another.

Shall I need to mention particular contests many years past, and presented to us in print? Words and papers now in print, as also the many petty divisions, and names amongst us, sufficiently make this manifest.

Wherefore light against light in this last place, or where it is thus repeated, cannot, I think, be more fitly applied than to that now under our consideration; that is to say, than to the opposite persuasions, different apprehensions, and thwart conclusions, that are constantly drawn from the same texts, to maintain a diverse practice. Though we are to acknowledge with thankfulness, that this opposition lies not so much in fundamentals, as in things of a lesser import.

The godly all hold the head, for there Antichrist could never divide them: their divisions therefore are, as I said, only about smaller things.

I do not say that the antichristian darkness has done nothing in the Church as to the hurting it in the great things of God; but, I say, it has not been able to do that which could sever their head from them: otherwise there appears even too much of the effect of his doings there. For even as to the offices of our Lord, some will have his authority more large, some more strait. Some confine his rules to themselves, and to their more outward qualification, and some believe they are extended further. Some will have his power in his Church purely spiritual, others again would have it mixed. Some count his word perfect and sufficient to guide in all religious matters, others again hold that an addition of something human is necessary. Some are for confining of his benefits, in the saving effects of them, only to the elect, others are for a stretching of them further. I might here multiply things; but that light against light is now among the godly, as light against light was in the house of the forest of Lebanon, is not at all to be questioned.

This therefore may stand for another argument, to prove that the house of the forest of Lebanon was a type of the Church in the wilderness. As to the number here, that is to say, in three ranks, it is also, as I think, to show that though, as was said afore, this darkness could not sever the true Church from her head, yet it has eclipsed the glory of things. By two lights a man cannot see this or that thing so exactly as by one single light: no, they both make all confused, though they make not all invisible. (Matt. vi. 22, 23.)

As, for instance, sunlight and moonlight together, firelight and sunlight together, candlelight and moonlight together, make things more obscure than to look on them by a single light.

The word reflecting upon the understanding, without the interposing of man's traditions, makes the mind of God to a man more clear than when attended with the other. How much more then when light shall be against light in three ranks!

Christ in his offices, blessed be God, is to this day known in his Church, notwithstanding there is yet with us light against light in three ranks. But in these things he is not so distinctly, fully, and completely known, as he was before the Church went into the wilderness. No, that knowledge is lost to "a third part of it," as was also showed before. (Rev. viii. 12.)

Things therefore will never be well in the Church of God, so long as there is thus light against light therein. When there is but one Lord among us, and his name One, and when divisions, by the consent of the whole, are banished,— I mean, not persecuted, but abandoned in all by a joint consent,—and when every man shall submit his own single opinion to those truths, that by their being retained, are for the health of all, then look for good days, and not until then. For this house of the forest of Lebanon, in which, as

you see, there is "light against light in three ranks," was not built to prefigure the Church in her primitive state, but to show us how we should be while standing before the face of the dragon, and while shifting for ourselves in the wilderness.

And although by her pillars, and beauty, and tower, ay, and by her facing the very metropolitan of her enemies, she showeth that the true grace of God is in her, and a strength and courage that is invincible, yet for that she has also affixed to her station, "light against light in three ranks," it is evident her eye is not so single, and consequently, that her body is not so full of light, as she will be when her sackcloth is put off, and as when she has put on her beautiful garments. For then it is that her moon is to shine as the sun, and that the light of her sun is to be sevenfold, even as the light of seven days; then, I say, "When the Lord bindeth up the breach of his people, and healeth the stroke of their wound." (Isa. xxx. 26.)

You know that a kingdom flourishes not so long as it is the seat of war, but when that is over, peace and prosperity flourishes. This house, as has been hinted, was a type of the Church in a wood, a forest, a wilderness.

CHAPTER VIII.

OF THE SHIELDS AND TARGETS THAT WERE IN THE HOUSE OF THE FOREST OF LEBANON.

As this house of the forest of Lebanon was that which, in the general, prefigured the state of the Church in the wilderness, so it was accoutred with such military materials as suited her in such a condition—that is to say, with shields and targets: consequently with other warlike things. "And King Solomon made two hundred targets of beaten gold, six hundred shekels of gold went to one target, and he made three hundred shields of beaten gold; three hundred shekels of gold went to one shield. And the king put them in the house of the forest of Lebanon." (1 Kings x. 16, 17. 2 Chron. ix. 15, 16.)

This supposes that the house of the forest of Lebanon would be attacked by the enemy. And good reason there was for such a supposition, since it was built for defence of that worship that was set up in the Church. Hence it is said, when the enemy used to come with his chariots and horsemen against them, that they "did look in that day to the armour of the house of the forest." (Isa. xxii. 7, 8.)

That was, to see how they were prepared at Lebanon, to make resistance against their foes, and to secure themselves and their religion from that destruction that by the enemy was designed should be made upon both. And thus again, or in this thing, the house of the forest of Lebanon shows that it was a figure of the Church of the wilderness: for she also is furnished with such weapons as were counted by the wisdom of God necessary for the security of the soul, and Christian religion—to wit, "the weapons of our warfare," "the whole armour of God." (2 Cor. x. 4.)

For, though this house of the forest of Lebanon was a place of defence, yet her armour is described and directed too, both as to matter and to measure. It was armour made of gold, such armour, and so much of it; and it was made by direction of Solomon, who was a type of Christ, by the power of whose grace and working, our armour is also provided for us, as in the texts afore mentioned may appear. By this description, therefore, of the armour of the house of the forest of Lebanon we are confined, that being a type to the armour of God, in the antitype thereto for the defence of the Christian religion. We then may make use of none but the armour of God for defence of our souls, and the worship of God. This alone is the golden armour provided by our Solomon, and put in the house of the forest of Lebanon, or rather in the Church in the wilderness, for her to resist the enemy withal.

Two hundred targets.—There is but little mention made of targets in the Bible, nor at all expressly how they were used, but once; and that was when Goliath came to defy Israel, he came, as, with other warlike furniture, so " with a target of brass between his shoulders." (1 Sam. xvii. 6.)

A target, that is, saith the margin, a gorget. A gorget is a thing wore about the neck, and it serveth in that place instead of a shield. Wherefore in some of your old Bibles, that which in one place is called a target, in another is called a shield; a shield for that part. This piece of armour, I suppose, was worn in old time by them that used spears, and it was to guard the upper part of the back and shoulders from the arrows of their enemies, that were shot into the air, to the intent they might fall upon the upper part of the body.

The shields were for them which drew bows, and they were to catch, or beat off those arrows that were levelled at them by the enemy before.

"Asa had," at one time, "an army of men that bare targets and spears, out of Judah three hundred thousand, and out of Benjamin that bare shields, and drew bows, two hundred and fourscore thousand." (2 Chron. xiv. 8.)

I cannot tell what the target should signify here, unless it was to show that those in the type were more weak and faint-hearted than those in the antitype: for in that this gorget was prepared for some back part of the body, it supposed the wearers subject to run away, to flee. But in the description of the Christian armour, we have no provision for the back: so our men in the Church in the wilderness are supposed to be more stout; their face is made strong against the face of their enemies, and their foreheads strong against their foreheads. (Ezek. iii. 8, 9.)

The shield was a type of the Christian faith, and so the apostle applies it. The which he also counteth a principal piece of our Christian armour, when he saith, "Above all, taking the shield of faith, wherewith ye shall be able to quench all the fiery darts of the wicked." (Eph. vi. 16.)

These targets and shields were made of gold, to show the excellent worth of this armour of God: to wit, that it is not carnal but spiritual, not human but divine; nor common or mean, but of an infinite value. Wherefore James, alluding to this, saith, "Hearken, my beloved brethren, hath not God chosen the poor of this world rich in faith?" (hath he not given them this golden shield?) " and made them heirs of that kingdom, which he hath promised to them that love him." (James ii. 5.)

Faith! Peter saith faith, in the very trial of it, is much more precious than is gold that perisheth: if so, then what is that worth, or value, that is in the grace itself? (1 Pet. i. 7.) This also is that which Christ intends when he says, "buy of me gold tried in the fire, that thou mayest be rich." (Rev. iii. 18.)

And methinks the apostles, and the Lord Jesus Christ, do in all these places allude to the shields, the shields of gold, that Solomon made, and put in the house of the forest of Lebanon: which house, as I have showed, was that which indeed prefigured the state of the Church in the wilderness; and these shields a type of faith.

Obj. 1. But here is mention made of nothing but shields and targets?

Answ. True; and that perhaps to show us that the war that the Church makes with Antichrist, is rather defensive than offensive: shields and targets are weapons defensive, weapons provided for self-preservation, not to hurt others with. A Christian also, if he can but defend his soul in the sincere profession of the true religion, doth what by duty, as to this, he is bound. Wherefore though the New Testament admits him to put on the whole armour of God, yet the whole and every part thereof is spiritual, and only defensive. True, there is mention made of the sword, but that sword " is the word of God," (Eph. vi. 17 :) a weapon that hurteth none, none at all but the devil and sin, and those that love it. Indeed it was made for Christians to defend themselves and their religion with, against hell and the angels of darkness.

These two pieces of armour, then, that Solomon the king did put into the house of the forest of Lebanon, were types of the spiritual armour that the Church in the wilderness should make use of. And as we read of no more that was put there— at least to be typical—so we read of, and must use no more than we are bid to put on by the apostle, for the defence of true religion.

Obj. 2. But he that shall use none other than this, must look to come off a loser.

Answ. In the judgment of the world, this is true: but not in the judgment of them that have skill, and an heart to use it. For this armour is not Saul's, which David refused, but God's, by which the lives of all those have been secured that put it on, and handled it well. You read of some of David's mighty men of valour, that their "faces were like the faces of lions," and that they "were as swift" of foot "as the roes upon the mountains," (1 Chron. xii. 8,) being expert in handling spear and shield.

Why, God's armour makes a man's face look thus, also it makes him that useth it more lively and active than before. God's armour is no burden to the body nor clog to the mind, but rather a natural, instead of an artificial fortification.

But this armour comes not to any but out of the king's hand: Solomon put these targets and shields into the house of the forest of Lebanon; so Christ distributeth his armour to his Church. Hence it is said, it is given to his to suffer for him. It is given to his by himself, and on his behalf. (Phil. i. 29.) That is, that they might with it fight those battles which he shall manage against Antichrist. Hence they are called the armies in heaven, and are said to follow their Lord "upon white horses clothed in fine linen, white and clean." (Rev. xix. 14.) But, as I said, still their war was but defensive. For, a little further, do but observe, and you shall find the beast fall upon him. "And I saw the beast, and the kings of the earth, and their armies gathered together, to make war against him that sat on the horse, and against his army." (Rev. xix. 19.)

It is they that fall on, it is they that pick the quarrel, and give the onset. Besides, the armour, as I said, is only spiritual; wherefore the slaughter must needs be spiritual also. Hence, as here it is said the Lamb did slay his enemies by the sword, spirit, or breath of his mouth, so his army also slays them by the fire that proceedeth out of his mouth. (Rev. i. 16; xix. 21.)

Here is therefore no man's person in danger by this war. And I say again, so far as any man's person is in danger, it is by wrong managing of this war. True, the persons of the Christians are in danger, but that is because of the bloody disposition of an antichristian enemy. But we speak now with reference to the Lamb and the army that follows him: and as to them, no man's person is in danger simply as such. Wherefore it is not men but sin; not men, but the man of sin, that wicked one, that the Son of God makes war against, in and by his Church. (2 Thess. ii. 8. Heb. xii. 4.)

Let us therefore state the matter right. No man needs be afraid to let Jesus Christ be chief in the world; he envies nobody, he designs the hurt of none: his kingdom is not of this world, nor doth he covet temporal matters; let but his wife, his Church alone, to enjoy her purchased privileges, and all shall be well. Which privileges of hers, since they are soul concerns, make no infringement upon any man's liberties. Let but

faith and holiness walk the streets without control, and you may be as happy as the world can make you. I speak now to them that contend with him.

But if seasonable counsel will not go down, if hardness of heart and blindness of mind, and so perishing from the way shall overtake you, it is but what you of old have been cautioned of. "Be wise now therefore, O ye kings, be instructed ye judges of the earth. Serve the Lord with fear, and rejoice with trembling. Kiss the Son, lest he be angry, and ye perish from the way, when his wrath is kindled but a little. Blessed are all they that put their trust in him." (Ps. ii. 10—12.)

Now let this also that has been said upon this head, be another argument to prove that the house of the forest of Lebanon was a type of the Church in the wilderness.

CHAPTER IX.

Solomon did also put vessels into the house of the forest of Lebanon. "And all King Solomon's drinking-vessels were of gold, and all the vessels of the house of the forest of Lebanon were of" gold, "pure gold, none were of silver; it was nothing accounted of in the days of Solomon." (1 Kings x. 21. 2 Chron. ix. 20.)

Since it is not expressed what those vessels of pure gold were which Solomon put in the house of the forest of Lebanon, therefore, as to the affirmative, no man can be absolute; vessels of gold, vessels of pure gold, the Holy Ghost says they were, and so leaves it to the prudent to make their conjectures: and although I may not put myself among the number of those prudent ones, yet let me take leave to say what I think in the case.

First then, negatively, they were not vessels ordained for divine worship; for, as that was confined to the temple, so the vessels, and materials, and circumstances for worship, was there.

I say, the whole uniform worship of the Jews now was confined to the temple. (2 Chron. ii. 4; vii. 12, 15, 16.) Wherefore the vessels here mentioned could not be such as was in order to set up worship here, for to Jerusalem they were to bring their sacrifices. True, they had synagogues where ordinary service was done; there the law was read, and there the priests taught the people how they should serve the Lord; but for that which stood in carnal ordinances, as sacrificings, washings, and using vessels for that purpose, that was performed at Jerusalem.

This house therefore—to wit, the house of the forest of Lebanon—was not built to slay, or to offer burnt-offerings or sacrifices in; but as that altar was which the two tribes and an half, built by Jordan, when they went each to their inheritance—namely, to be a witness of the people's resolutions to preserve true religion in the Church, to themselves, and to their posterity. (Josh. xxii. 21—29.)

Since this house therefore was designed for defensive war, it was not requisite that the formalities of worship should be there.

The Church in the wilderness also, so far as she is concerned in contention, so far she is not taken up in the practical parts of religion, (1 Thess. ii. 2;) for religion is not to be practised in the Church in the moments of contention. Let us practise then our religion in peace, and in all peaceable ways, and vindicate it by way of contention; that is, when asked or required, by opposites, to render a reason thereof. (Phil. i. 7, 17. Acts xxii. 1.)

But my contention must be, not in pragmatic languages, or in striving about words to no profit, but by words of truth and soberness, with all meekness and fear. (Acts xxvi. 24, 25. Tit. iii. 1, 2. 1 Pet. iii. 15.)

To practise and defend a practice, you know are two things: I practise religion in my closet, in my family, in the congregation; but I defend this practice before the magistrate, the king, and the judge. Now the temple was prepared for the practice of religion, and the house of the forest of Lebanon for defence of the same. (Rev. xi. 1.)

So far then as the Church in the wilderness worships, so far she is compared to the temple; and so far as she defends that worship, so far she is called an army, (Rev. xix. 14;)—an army terrible with banners. (Sol. Song vi. 4. Ps. lx. 4.) For God has given a banner to them that fear him, that it may be displayed, because of the truth. Hence she says to God, "We will rejoice in thy salvation, and in the name of our God we will set up our banners." (Ps. xx. 5.)

But here is in all this no hurt to the world; the kingdom, the worship, the war is spiritual, even as the armour is. I have spoken this to distinguish worship from contending for worship, and to make way for what is yet to be said.

If the vessels of the forest of Lebanon, or those put in that house, were not such as related to worship—to worship simply as such—then it should seem, these vessels, therefore, were for some other use than formal worship in the house of the forest of Lebanon. The best way then, that I know of, to find out what they were, is, first to consider to what they are joined in the mention of them. Now I find them joined in the mention of them with Solomon's drinking vessels; and since as they were made of fine or pure gold, I take them also to be vessels of the same kind—to wit, vessels to drink in. Now if we join to this the state of the Church in the wilderness, of which, as we have said, this house of the forest of Lebanon was a type, then we must understand that by these vessels were prefigured such draughts as the Church has when in a bewildered or persecuted state; and they are of two sorts, either—

First. Such as are exceeding bitter; or,

Second. Such as are exceeding sweet: for both these attend a state of war.

First. Such as are exceeding bitter: these are called cups of red wine, signifying blood; also, the cup of the Lord's fury, the cup of trembling, the cup of astonishment, &c. (Ps. lxxv. 8. Iss. li. 17, 22. Jer. xxv. 15. Ezek. xxiii. 33.)

Nor is there anything more natural to the Church, while in a wilderness condition, than such cups and draughts as these. Hence she, as there, is said to be clothed, as was said afore, in sackcloth, to mourn, to weep, to cry out, and to be in pain, as a woman in travail. See the Lamentations, and you will find all this verified. See also Rev. ii. 3; xii. 2.

And whoso considers what has already been said as to what the house of the forest of Lebanon met with, will find that what is here inferred, is not foreign but natural. For, can it be imagined that when the King of Assyria laid down his army by the sides of Lebanon, and when the fire was to devour her cedars; also, when Lebanon was to be cut down and languish, that these vessels, these cups, was not then put into her hand. And, I say again, since the Church in the wilderness, Lebanon's antitype, has been so persecuted, so distressed, so oppressed, and made the seat of so much war, so much blood, of so many murders of her children within her, &c., can it be imagined that she drank of none of these cups? yes, yes; she has drank the red wine at the Lord's hand, even the cup of blood, of fury, of trembling, and of astonishment; witness her own cries, sighs, tears, and tremblings; with the cries of the widows, children, and orphans within her. (Lam. i. 2, 4, 5.)

But why do I cite particular texts, since reason, histories, experience, anything that is intelligible, will confirm this for a truth; namely, that a people, whose profession is directly in opposition to the devil and Antichrist, and to all debauchery, inhumanity, profaneness, superstition, and idolatry, when suffered to be invaded by the dragon, the beast, the false prophet, and whore, must needs taste of these cups, and drink thereof to their astonishment.

But all these are of pure gold. They are of God's ordaining, appointing, filling, timing; and also sanctified by him for good to those of his that drink them. Hence Moses chose rather to drink a brimmer of these, "than to enjoy the pleasures of sin for a season." (Heb. xi. 25.)

The sourness, bitterness, and wormwood of them, therefore, is only to the flesh, that loveth neither God, nor Christ, nor grace. (Ps. lxxv. 8. Phil. i. 28.)

The afflictions, therefore, that the church in the wilderness hath met with, these cups of gold, are of more worth than are all the treasures of Egypt; they are needful, and profitable, and praiseworthy also, and tend to the augmenting of our glory, when the next world is come. (1 Thess. iii. 3. Rev. ii. 10. 1 Pet. i. 6.)

Besides they are signs, tokens, and golden marks of love ; and jewels that set off the beauty of the Church in the sight of God the more. (Gal. vi. 17. Rev. iii. 19. Heb. xii. 6.) They are also a means by which men are proved sound, honest, fruitful, and true lovers of God ; as also such whose graces are not counterfeit, feigned, or unsound, but true, and such as will be found to praise, and honour, and glory, at the appearing of Jesus Christ. (Isa. xxvii. 9. Heb. xii. 7—10. 1 Pet. ii. 19. 2 Cor. iv. 17, 18. 1 Thess. i. 5.)

And this has been the cause that the men of our Church in the wilderness have gloried in tribulation ; taking pleasure in reproaches, in necessities, in persecutions, and in distresses for Christ's sake. (Rom. v. 3. 2 Cor. xii. 9, 10.) Yea, this is the reason why they have bade one another rejoice, when they fell into divers temptations, saying happy is the man that endureth temptations ; and behold we count them happy that endure, (James i. 2, 12 ; v. 11 :) and again, "if ye be reproached for the name of Christ, happy are ye." (1 Pet. iv. 14.)

These therefore are vessels of pure gold, though they contain such bitter draughts, and though such as at which we make so many wry faces, before we can get their liquor down.

Do you think that a Christian, having even this cup in his hand to drink it, would change it for a draught of that which is in the hand of the woman that sits on the back of the scarlet-coloured beast? (Rev. xvii. 3, 4.) No, verily ; for he knows that her sweet is poison, and that his bitter is to purge his soul, body, life, and religion, of death. (2 Tim. ii. 11, 12.)

God sends his love-tokens to his Church two ways—sometimes by her friends, sometimes by her enemies. When they come by the hand of a friend, as by a minister, a brother, or by the Holy Ghost, then they come smoothly, sweetly, and are taken, and go down like honey ; but when these love-tokens come to them by the hand' of an enemy, then they are handed to them roughly : Pharaoh handed love-tokens to them roughly ; the King of Babylon handed these love-tokens to them roughly. They bring them of malice ; God sends them of love : they bring them, and give them to us, hoping they will be our death ; they give us them therefore with many a foul curse ; but God blesses them still. Did not Haman lead Mordecai in his state by the hand of anger ?

Nor is this cup so bitter but that our Lord himself drank deep of it, before it was handed to his Church : he did, as loving mothers do, drink thereof himself, to show us it is not poison, also to encourage us to drink it for his sake, and for our endless health. (Matt. xx. 22 ; xxvi. 39—42.)

And, as I told you before, I think I do not vary from the sense of the text, in calling them cups ;

because, though there they have no name, they are joined with King Solomon's drinking vessels ; and because as so joined in the type, so they are also joined here : therefore the cup here is called Christ's cup. "Are ye able to drink of the cup that I shall drink of ?" "Ye shall indeed drink of my cup." (Matt. xx. 22, 23.) Here you see they are joined in a communion in this cup of affliction, as the cups in one and the same breath are joined with those King Solomon drank in, which he put in the house of the forest of Lebanon.

Second. But these are not all the cups that belong to the house of the forest of Lebanon, or rather to the Church in the wilderness ; there is also a cup out of which at times is drunk what is exceeding sweet.

It is called the cup of consolation, the cup of salvation ; a cup in the which God himself is. (Ps. cxvi. 13. Jer. xvi. 7.) As he said, the Lord is the portion of my cup ; or rather, "the Lord is the portion of mine inheritance, and my cup." (Ps. xvi. 5.)

This cup they that are in the Church in the wilderness have usually for an after-draught to that bitter one that went before. Thus, as tender mothers give their children plums or sugar to sweeten their palate after they have drank a bitter potion, so God gives his the cups of salvation and consolation after they have suffered a while. " For as the sufferings of Christ abound in us, so our consolation also aboundeth by Christ." (2 Cor. i. 5.)

Hence the apostle assureth himself, concerning the affliction of them at Corinth ; yea, and also promiseth them that as they were partakers of the sufferings, so should they be of the consolation. (2 Cor. i. 7.)

Some of these cups are filled until they run over, as David said his did when the Valley of the Shadow of Death was before him. "Thou preparest a table before me," said he, "in the presence of mine enemies : thou anointest my head with oil ; my cup runneth over." (Ps. xxiii. 5.)

This is that which the apostle calls exceeding ; that is, that which is beyond measure. "I am," says he, "filled with comfort, I am exceeding joyful in all our tribulations." (2 Cor. vii. 4.)

Now he has one answering the other. Thou hast made summer and winter : thou hast made the warm beams of thy sun answerable to the cold of the dark night. This may be also yet signified by the building of this house, this type of the Church in the wilderness in so pleasant a place as the forest of Lebanon was. (Sol. Song iv. 8.) Lebanon ! Lebanon was one of the sweetest places in all the land of Canaan. Therefore we read of the fruit of Lebanon, of the streams from Lebanon, the scent, the smell, the glory of Lebanon ; and also of the wine and flowers of Lebanon. (Ps. lxxii. 16, Hos. xiv. 6, 7. Isa. xxv. 2, 6—13. Neh. i. 4.)

Lebanon ! That was one thing that wrought with Moses to desire that he might go over Jordan ;

namely that he might see that goodly mountain and Lebanon. The glory and excellent beauty of the Church, Christ also setteth forth, by comparing of her to Lebanon. "Thy lips, O my spouse," says he, "drop as the honeycomb; honey and milk are under thy tongue, and the smell of thy garments is like the smell of Lebanon." (Sol. Song iv. 11, 15.)

This house, therefore, being placed here, might be to show how blessed a state God could make the state of his Church by his blessed grace and presence, even while she is in a wilderness condition.

We will add to this for further demonstration, that letter of that godly man Pomponius Algerius, an Italian martyr, some of the words of which are these:—

"Let," saith he, "the miserable worldly man answer me; what remedy or safe refuge can there be unto him if he lack God, who is the life and medicine of all men? and how can he be said to fly from death when himself is already dead in sin? If Christ be the way, verity, and life, can there be any life then without Christ?

"The heat of the prison to me is coldness; the cold winter to me is a fresh spring in the Lord. He that feareth not to be burned in the fire, how will he fear the heat of weather? Or what careth he for the pinching frost which burneth with the love of the Lord?

"The place is sharp and tedious to them that be guilty, but to the innocent and guiltless it is mellifluous. Here droppeth the delectable dew; here floweth the pleasant nectar; here runneth the sweet milk; here is plenty of all good things. And although the place itself be desert and barren, yet to me it seemeth a large walk and a valley of pleasure; here to me is the better and more noble part of the world. Let the miserable worldling say, and confess, if there be any plot, pasture, or meadow, so delightful to the mind of man as here. Here I see kings, princes, cities, and people; here I see wars where some be overthrown, some be victors, some thrust down, some lifted up. Here is Mount Zion; here I am already in heaven itself. Here standeth first Christ Jesus in the front; about him stand the old fathers, prophets, and evangelists, apostles, and all the servants of God, of whom some do embrace and cherish me, some exhort me, some open the sacraments unto me, some comfort me, others are singing about me; and how then shall I be thought to be alone among so many, and such as these be, the beholding of whom is to me both solace and example? for here I see some crucified, some slain, some stoned, some cut asunder, and some quartered, some roasted, some broiled, some put in hot caldrons, some having their eyes bored through, some their tongues cut out, some their skin plucked over their heads, some their hands and feet chopped off, some put into kilns and furnaces, some cast down headlong and given to the beasts,

and fowls of the air to feed upon. It would," said he, "ask a long time if I should recite all.

"To be short, divers I see with divers and sundry torments excruciate, yet notwithstanding, all living and all safe. One plaster, one salve cureth all their wounds, which also giveth to me strength and life; so that I sustain all these transitory anguishes and small afflictions with a quiet mind, having a greater hope laid up in heaven. Neither do I fear mine adversaries which here persecute me and oppress me, for he that dwells in heaven shall laugh them to scorn, and the Lord shall deride them. I fear not ten thousands of people which compass me about. The Lord my God shall deliver me, my hope, my supporter, my comforter, who exalteth up my head. He shall smite all those that stand up against me without cause, and shall dash the teeth and jaws of sinners asunder, for he only is all blessedness and majesty.

"The rebukes for Christ make us jocund, for so it is written: if ye be rebuked and scorned for the name of Christ, happy be you, for the glory and spirit of God resteth upon you. (1 Pet. 4.) Be ye, therefore, certified (said he, by this his letter to his friends,) that our rebukes, which are laid upon us, redound to the shame and harm of the rebukers.

"In this world there is no mansion firm to me; and therefore I will travel up to the New Jerusalem which is in heaven, and which offereth itself to me, without paying any fine or income. Behold, I have entered already on my journey, where my house standeth for me prepared, and where I shall have riches, kinsfolks, delights, honours, never-failing.

"As for these earthly things here present, they are transitory shadows, vanishing vapours, and ruinous walls. Briefly, all is but very vanity of vanities, whereas hope and the substance of eternity to come are wanting, which the merciful goodness of the Lord hath given as companions to accompany me, and to comfort me; and now do the same begin to work, and to bring forth fruits in me. I have travelled hitherto, laboured and sweat early and late, walking day and night, and now my travels begin to come to effect. Days and hours I have bestowed upon my studies.

"Behold the true countenance of God is sealed upon me; the Lord hath given mirth in my heart, and therefore in the same will I lay me down in peace and rest. (Ps. iv.) And who, then, shall dare to blame this our age consumed; or say that our years be cut off? What man can now cavil that these our labours are lost, which have followed and found out the Lord and maker of the world, and which have changed death for life? My portion is the Lord, saith my soul, and therefore I will seek and wait for him.

"Now, then, if to die in the Lord be not to die, but to live most joyfully, where is this wretched worldly rebel which blameth us of folly for giving away our lives to death? O how delectable is this death to me! To taste the Lord's cup, which is an assured pledge of true salvation, for so hath the Lord forewarned us, saying, the same that they have done to me they will also do unto you.

"Wherefore let the doltish world, with his blind worldlings, (who in the bright sunshine yet go stumbling in darkness, being as blind as beetles,) cease thus unwisely to carp against us for our rash suffering, as they count it. To whom, thus, we answer again, with the holy apostle, that neither tribulation, nor anguish, nor hunger, nor nakedness, nor jeopardy, nor persecution, nor sword, shall be able ever to separate us from the love of Christ; we are slain all the day long; we are made like sheep ordained to the shambles. (Rom. viii.)

"Thus," saith he, " do we resemble Christ our Head, which said that the disciple cannot be above his master, nor the servant above his Lord." The same Lord hath also commanded that every one shall take up his cross and follow him. (Luke ix.)

" Rejoice, rejoice, my dear brethren and fellow-servants, and be of good comfort when ye fall into sundry temptations; let your patience be perfect in all parts. For so it is foreshowed us before, and is written, that they which shall kill you shall think to do God good service; therefore afflictions and death be as tokens and sacraments of our election and life to come.

"Let us then be glad and sing unto the Lord, when as we, being clear from all just accusations, are persecuted and given to death; for better it is that we in doing well do suffer, if it so be the will of God, than doing evil. (1 Pet. iii.) We have for our example Christ and the prophets which spake in the name of the Lord, whom the children of iniquity did quell and murder. And now we bless and magnify them that then suffered.

" Let us be glad and joyous in our innocency and uprightness; the Lord shall reward them that persecute us; let us refer all revengement to him.

"I am accused of foolishness, for that I do not shrink from the true doctrine, and knowledge of God, and do not rid myself out of these troubles, when with one word I may. O the blindness of man, which seeth not the sun shining, neither remembereth the Lord's words. Consider therefore what he saith, you are the light of the world. A city built on the hill cannot be hid; neither do men light a candle and put it under a bushel, but upon a candlestick, that it may shine and give light to them in the house. And in another place, he saith, you shall be led before kings and rulers. Fear ye not them which kill the body, but him which killeth both body and soul. Whosoever shall confess me before men, him will I also confess before my Father which is in heaven; and he that denieth me before men, him will I deny before my heavenly Father.

"Wherefore, seeing the words of the Lord be so plain, how, or by what authority, will this wise counsellor then approve this his counsel which he doth give? God forbid that I should relinquish the commandments of God to follow the counsels of

men. For, it is written, blessed is the man that hath not gone in the way of sinners, and hath not stood in the counsel of the ungodly, and hath not sit in the chair of pestilence. (Ps. i.) God forbid that I should deny Christ where I ought to confess him: I will not set more by my life than by my soul, neither will I exchange the life to come for this world here present. O how foolishly speaketh he which argueth me of foolishness!"

And a little farther he saith, "And now let this carnal, politic counsellor, and disputer of this world, tell wherein have they to blame me. If in mine examinations I have not answered so after their mind and affection as they required of me, seeing it is not ourselves that speak, but the Lord that speaketh in us, as he himself doth forewitness, saying, When you shall be brought before rulers and magistrates, it is not you yourselves that speak, but the Spirit of my Father that shall be in you. (Matt. x.) Wherefore, if the Lord be true and faithful of his word, as it is most certain, then there is no blame in me; for he gave the words that I did speak, and who was I that I could resist his will?

" If any man shall reprehend the things that I said, let him then quarrel with the Lord, whom it pleased to work so in me; and if the Lord be not to be blamed, neither am I herein to be accused, which did that I purposed not, and that I forethought not of. The things that there I did utter and express [he means when he was before the magistrates], if they were otherwise than well, let them show it, and then will I say that they were my words, and not the Lord's. But if they were good and approved, and such as cannot justly be accused, then must it needs be granted, spite of their teeth, that they proceeded of the Lord; and then who be they that shall accuse me? People of prudence? Or, who shall condemn me? Just judges? And though they so do, yet, nevertheless, the word shall not be frustrate; neither shall the gospel be foolish, or therefore decay; but rather the kingdom of God shall the more prosper and flourish to the Israelites, and shall pass the sooner unto the elect of Christ Jesus; and they which shall so do, shall prove the grievous judgment of God, neither shall they escape without punishment, that be persecutors and murderers of the just.

"My well-beloved," saith he, "lift up your eyes, and consider the counsels of God. He showed unto us of late an image of his plague, which was to our correction; and if we shall not receive him, he will draw out his sword, and strike with sword, pestilence, and famine, the nation that shall rise against Christ."

This, as I said, is part of a letter, writ by Pomponius Algerius, an Italian martyr, who, when he wrote it, was in prison, in, as he calls it, his delectable orchard, the prison of Leonine, 12 calend. August, anno 1555. As is to be seen in the second volume of the book of martyrs.

This man was, when he wrote this letter, in the

house of the forest of Lebanon, in the Church in the wilderness, in the place and way of contending for the truth of God, and he drank of both these bitter cups of which I spake before, to wit, of that which was exceeding bitter, and of that which was exceeding sweet; and the reason why he complained not of the bitter was because the sweet had overcome it; as his afflictions abounded for Christ, so did his consolations by him. So, did I say? they abounded much more.

But was not this man, think you, a giant—a pillar in this house? Had he not also, now, hold of the shield of faith? Yea, was he not now in the combat? And did he not behave himself valiantly? Was not his mind elevated a thousand degrees beyond sense, carnal reason, fleshly love, self concerns, and the desires of embracing temporal things? This man had got that by the end that pleased him; neither could all the flatteries, promises, threats, or reproaches, make him once listen to, or desire to inquire after, what the world, or the glory of it, could afford. His mind was captivated with delights invisible; he coveted to show his love to his Lord, by laying down his life for his sake; he longed to be there, where there shall be no more pain, nor sorrow, nor sighing, nor tears, nor troubles: he was a man of a thousand. (Eccles. vii. 28.)

But to return again to our text. You know we are now upon the vessels of the house of the forest of Lebanon, which, I have told you, could not be vessels for worship; for that worship that was ordained to be performed at the temple was also confined to that, and to the vessels that were there. Therefore, they must be, in all probability, the vessels that I have mentioned, the which you see how we have expounded and applied.

If I am out, I know it not; if others can give me better light here about, for it I will be thankful.

There was also added to this house of the forest of Lebanon, store-cities, chariot-cities, and cities of horsemen; unto which King Jotham added castles and towers. (2 Chron. viii. 4—6; xxvii. 3, 4.)

These might be to signify by what ways and means God would at times revenge the quarrel of his Church, even in this world, upon them that, without cause, should, for their faith and worship, set themselves against them. For here is a face of threatening revenge—they were store-houses, chariot-cities, cities of horsemen, with castles, and towers. And they stood on the same ground that this house was builded upon, even in the forest of Lebanon.

We know that in Israel God stirred up kings who at times suppressed idolatry there, and plagued the persecutors too, as Jehu, Hezekiah, Josiah, &c. And he has promised that, even in gospel times, "kings shall hate the whore, make her desolate and naked, and shall eat her flesh, and burn her with fire." (Rev. xvii. 12, 16.)

Here now are the store-houses, chariot-cities, cities of horsemen, with towers, and castles, for the help of the house of the forest of Lebanon, for the help of the Church in the wilderness, or, as you have it, in another place, as the serpent cast floods of water out of his mouth, after the woman, "that he might cause her to be carried away of the flood. And the earth helped the woman, and the earth opened her mouth, and swallowed up the flood, which the dragon cast out of his mouth." (Rev. xii. 15, 16.)

Thus the Medes and Persians helped to deliver the Church from the clutches and strong hand of the King of Babylon.

This Lebanon, therefore, was a place considerable, and a figure of great things; the countenance of the Lord Jesus is compared to it, and so is the face of his spouse, and also the smell of her garment. (Sol. Song iv. 11; v. 15; vii. 4.)

CHAPTER X.

OF THE PORCH OF THE HOUSE OF THE FOREST OF LEBANON.

Solomon also made a porch to this house of the forest of Lebanon. He made several porches, as, one for the temple, one for the house which he dwelt in, one for the throne of the kingdom, and this that was for the house of the forest of Lebanon; of all which, this last is that mentioned—"And he made a porch of pillars, the length thereof was fifty cubits, the breadth thereof thirty cubits; and the porch was before them, and the other pillars, and the thick beam were before them." (1 Kings vii. 6.) This porch was famous both for length, and breadth, and strength; it was able to contain a thousand men. It was like that of the tower of David, otherwise called the stronghold, the castle of Zion, which is the city of David. (2 Sam. v. 7. 1 Chron. xi. 5. Micah iv. 8.)

This tower of David was built for an armoury; whereon there hanged a thousand bucklers, all shields of mighty men. It was fifty cubits long, and thirty broad, a spacious place, a large receptacle for any that liked to take shelter there. It was made of pillars, even as the house within was, or it stood upon pillars. The pillars, you know, I told you before, were to show us what mighty men, or what men of mighty grace, God would have his Church in the wilderness furnished with. And it is worth your observing here also we have pillars, pillars. And he made the porch of pillars; that is, of pillars of cedar, as the rest of the pillars of the house were.

"And the porch was before them;" that is, as I take it, an entering porch, less than the space within: so that the pillars, neither as to number nor bigness, could be seen without, until, at least, they that had a mind to see entered the mouth of the porch.

And by this was fitly prefigured, how unseen the strength of the Church under persecution is of all that are without her. Alas! they think that she will be run down with a push; or, as they said, "What do these feeble Jews? will they fortify themselves? will they sacrifice? will they make an end in a day? will they revive the stones, out of the heaps of the rubbish, which are burnt?" Alas! "if a fox go up, he shall even break down their stone wall." (Neh. iv. 2, 3.)

But do you think these men saw the strength of the Jews now? No, no, their pillars were within, and so were shadowed from their eyes. David himself could not tell what judgment to make of the way of the world, against the people of God, until he went into the sanctuary of God. (Ps. lxxiii. 16, 17.)

How then can the world judge of the condition of the saints? Alas, had they known the Church's strength, surely they would not, as they have, so furiously assaulted the same. But what have they got by all they have done, either against the head or body of the same?

She yet has being in the world, and will have, shall have, though all the nations on earth should gather themselves together against it. Nor is it the cutting off of many that will make her cease to flourish. Alas! were she not sometimes pruned and trimmed, her boughs would stand too thick. Those, therefore, that are taken away with God's pruning-hooks are removed, that the under branches may grow the better.

But, I say, to extinguish her, it is in vain for any to hope for that. She stands upon pillars, on rocks, on the munition of rocks: stand therefore she must, whether the world believes it or no.

"And the other pillars were before them," or, as the margin has it, "according to them." The other pillars, that is, they more inward; those that were in the body of the house. Christ doth not as the poor world doth, that is, set the best leg before; the pillars that were more inward in the house, were as good as those in the front. It is true, some are appointed to death, to show to the world the strength of grace, not that he can help nobody to that strength but they. The most feeble of his flock, when Christ shall stand by and strengthen them, are able to do, and bear, what the strong have underwent. For so he saith.

And "the other pillars, and the thick beams, were," according to them: nay, "before them." Indeed, they that are left, seem weak and feeble, if compared to them that have already been tried with fire and sword, and all the tortures of men. But, that grace by which they were helped, that have done such mighty acts already, can help those who seem more weak, yet to go beyond them. God strengtheneth "the spoiled against the strong; so that the spoiled shall come against the fortress." Or, as another scripture has it, "The lame take the prey." (Isa. xxxiii. 23.) So that, you see, here is all substance. All here are pillars and thick beams, both in the house and in the porch.

The conclusion therefore is, the true members of the Church in the wilderness are strong, mighty, being made able by the grace of God for their standing; and being also coupled and compacted together with the biggest bands, or thickest beams, that the Holy Ghost puts forth to bind and hold this Church together.

And there is reason for it. The Church is God's tower, or battery, by which he beateth down Antichrist; or, if you will have it in the words of the prophet, "Thou art my battle-axe, and weapons of war; for with thee (saith God) will I break in pieces," &c. (Jer. li. 19, 20.) Wherefore, since the Church is set for defence of religion, and to be as a battery to beat down Antichrist, it is requisite that she should be made up of pillars of strong and staunch materials.

The largeness of the porch was commodious; it was the next shelter, or the place whereunto they of the house of the forest of Lebanon, when pursued, might resort or retreat with the less difficulty. Thus the Church in the wilderness has her porch, her place, her bosom, whereunto her discouraged may continually resort, and take up and be refreshed. As Abiathar thrust in to David and his men in the wilderness, in the day when Saul had slain his father, and of his brethren even "fourscore and five persons that did wear a linen ephod." (1 Sam. xxii. 17—23.)

When the apostles were persecuted, "they went to their own company," because the Lord was there. (Acts iv. 23.)

There we find the pillars, and have both solace and example. There, as Pomponius said of his person, stands Christ Jesus in the front as Captain of the Lord's host, and round about him the old fathers, prophets, apostles, and martyrs.

This porch, therefore, I take to be a figure of those cordial and large affections, which the Church in the wilderness has to all, and for all them that love the truth, and that suffer and are afflicted for the sincere profession thereof.

This porch was bigger than that which belonged to the temple, by much; to show that those that are made the objects of the enemy's rage most, are usually most prepared with affection for them that are in the same condition. Fellow-feeling is a great matter. It is said of the poor afflicted people that were in Macedonia, "in a great trial of affliction, the abundance of their joy, and their deep poverty, abounded unto the riches of their liberality; for to their power, yea, and beyond their power," they showed their charity to the destroyed Church of Jerusalem. (2 Cor. viii. 1—4.)

And a porch in a forest, or a bosom in a wilderness, is seasonable to them that in the wilderness are faint and weary.

Nabal shut up his doors against David, and therefore he died like a beast. Poor David! thou wast bewildered, but this churl had no compassion for thee. (1 Sam. xxv. 5—10, 25—39.)

Blest Obadiah, thou hadst a bosom, and bread, and hiding-places for the Church, when rent and torn by the fury of Jezebel, and thou hast for it thy reward in heaven. (1 Kings xviii. 3, 4. Matt. x. 42.)

Ebed-melech, because he had compassion on Jeremiah when he was in the dungeon, God did not only give him his life for a prey, but promised him the effects of putting his trust in the Lord. (Jer. xxxviii. 7—11; xxxix. 15—18.)

And he made a porch of pillars. The porch is but the entrance of the house, whither many go that yet step not into the house, but make their retreat from thence. But it is because they are non-residents, they only come to see; or else if they pretended more, it was not from the heart. "They went out from us," said John, "but they were not of us; for if they had been of us, they would, no doubt, have continued with us; but they went out, that they might be made manifest that they were not all of us." (1 John ii. 19.)

And, forasmuch, as this porch was fifty cubits long, men may take many a step straight forward therein, and be but in the porch yet. Even as we have seen men go, as one would think, till they are out of view in the porch of this Church in the wilderness; but presently you have them without the door again.

True, this porch was made of pillars; and so to every one at first entrance it showed the power of the place; the Church in the wilderness also is so builded, that men may see it is ordained for defence. Men also, at their first offer to step over the threshold there, with mouth profess that they will dwell as soldiers there. But words are but wind; when they see the storm a-coming they will take care to shift for themselves. This house, or Church in the wilderness, must see to itself, for all them.

As the house, therefore, is a figure of the Church in the wilderness, so, so great a porch belonging to it, may be also to show that numbers may there be entertained that, if need be, will quickly whip out again. Although, therefore, the porch was made of pillars, yet every one that walked there were not such. The pillars was to show them, not what they were, but what they should be that entered this house.

The Church also in the wilderness, even in her porch, or first entrance into it, is full of pillars, apostles, prophets, and martyrs of Jesus. There also hang up the shields that the old warriors have used, and are plastered upon the walls the brave achievements which they have done. There are also such encouragements there for those that stand, that one would think none that came thither with pretence to serve there, would for very shame attempt to go back again; and yet, not to their credit be it spoken, they will forsake the place without blushing; yea, and plead for this their so doing. But I have done with the explicatory part, and conclude that from these ten particulars thus handled in this book, the house of the forest of Lebanon was a type, or figure, of the Church in the wilderness.

Nor do I know, if this be denied, how so fitly to apply some of these texts which speak to the Church, to support her under her troubles, of the comforts that afterwards she shall enjoy, since they are presented to her under such metaphors as clearly denote she was once in a wilderness. For instance—

1. "Sing, O ye heavens, for the Lord hath done it, (that is, redeemed his servant Jacob from his sins, and from the hand of the enemy:) shout, ye lower parts of the earth, (or Church once trampled under foot;) break forth into singing, ye mountains, O forest, and every tree therein, (here is comfort for the Church, under the name of a forest, that in which the house we have been speaking of was built:) for the Lord hath redeemed Jacob, and glorified himself in Israel." (Isa. xliv. 23.)

To what, I say, can this text be more fitly applied, than to the Church in the wilderness, put here under the name of a forest, as well as under the title of heaven? Yea, methinks, it is cried here to her, "O forest," on purpose to intimate to us, that the house in the forest of Lebanon was the figure of the Church in this condition.

2. Again, "Is it not yet a very little while, and Lebanon shall be turned into a fruitful field, and the fruitful field shall be esteemed as a forest? And in that day shall the deaf hear the words of the book, and the eyes of the blind shall see out of obscurity, and out of darkness. The meek also shall increase their joy in the Lord, and the poor among men shall rejoice in the Holy One of Israel. For the terrible one is brought to nought, and the scorner is consumed, and all that watch for iniquity are cut off." (Isa. xxix. 17—20.) Lebanon was a forest, but now she must be a fruitful field. What means he here by Lebanon but the Church under persecution, and the fruitful field? Mistress Babylon shall become as a forest, that is, as the Church under distress. But when shall this be? Why, when the terrible one is brought low, and the scorner is consumed, &c.

What can be more plain than this to prove that Lebanon, even the house in the forest of Lebanon, (for that is here intended,) was a figure of the Church in the wilderness, or in a tempted and persecuted state. For to be turned into a fruitful field, signifies the recovering of the afflicted Church into a state most quiet and fruitful; fruitful fields are quiet because they are fenced, and so shall the Church be in that day.

3. "The wilderness and the solitary place shall be glad for them; and the desert shall rejoice, and blossom as the rose." (Isa. xxxv. 1.)

What are we to understand by these words, if they be not a prophecy of the flourishing state of Christ's kingdom, who, in the days of her persecution, is compared to a wilderness, to a desert, and to solitary places. And she "shall be glad for them." For what? For that she is rid of the dragons, wild beasts, satyrs, screech-owls, great owl, and vulture, types of the beasts and unclean birds of Antichrist. (Isa. xxxiv. 13—15.)

She shall be glad for them that they are taken away from her, and placed far away; for then no lion shall be there, nor any ravenous beast: yea, it is the habitation of dragons, where each lay, shall be grass with reeds and rushes, as it is. (Isa. xxxv.) And now, "the lame man shall leap as a hart, and the tongue of the dumb sing; for in the wilderness shall waters break out, and streams in the desert." Read the whole chapter.

For that the desert and wilderness is thus mentioned, and that to express the state of the Church in trouble by, it is clear that Lebanon is not excluded, nor the thing that is signified thereby, which, I say, is the Church in her low estate, in her forest, or wilderness condition.

4. "I will plant in the wilderness the cedar, the shittah-tree, and the myrtle, and the oil-tree; and I will set in the desert the fir-tree, and the pine, and the box-tree together." (Isa. xli. 19.)

Can any think that trees are the things taken care of here? They are the men that Antichrist has murdered in his heat and rage against Christ, the which God will restore again to his Church, when Antichrist is dead and buried in the sides of the pit's mouth.

And that you may the better understand he meaneth so, he expresseth again the state of the Church as like to a wilderness condition, and promiseth that in that very Church, now so like a wilderness, to plant it again with Christians, flourishing with variety of gifts and graces, signified by the various nature and name of the trees spoken of here.

5. "Behold, I will do a new thing; now it shall spring forth; shall ye not know it? I will even make a way in the wilderness, and rivers in the desert. The beast of the field shall honour me, the dragons and the owls, because I give waters in the wilderness, and rivers in the desert, to give drink to my people, my chosen." (Isa. xliii. 19, 20.)

Here God alludes to the condition of the children of Israel in the wilderness of old, and implies they shall be in a wilderness again; and as then he gave them water, and delivered them from serpents, cockatrices, vipers, dragons, so he will do now, now to his people, his chosen.

6. "The Lord shall comfort Zion, he will comfort all her waste places, and he will make her wilderness like Eden, and her desert like the garden of the Lord; joy and gladness shall be found therein, thanksgiving, and the voice of melody." (Isa. li. 3.)

See, here are Zion's waste places, Zion's wilderness, forest, or Lebanon. Next, here is a promise that he will comfort her; and what doth this suppose but that she was in her wilderness state, uncomfortable at least as to her outward peace, her liberty, and gospel privileges and beauties? Then here is the comparison, by which he illustrates his promise as to what degree and pitch he will comfort her. "He will make her wilderness like Eden, and her desert like the garden of the Lord." The effects of all which will be, she will have joy and gladness; she will be thankful, and be melodious in her voice, in her soul to the Lord. This, I say, will follow upon her deliverance from her desert, her wilderness, her desolate, and comfortless state: all which is more fully expressed by her repeated hallelujahs. (Rev. xix. 1—6.) Which hallelujahs there are the effect of her deliverance from the rage of the beast and great whore, of whose greatness and ruin you read in the two foregoing chapters.

Now, I say, since the Church was to be in a wilderness condition under the gospel; and since we have this house of the forest of Lebanon so particularly set forth in the Scriptures; and also since this house, its furniture, its troubles, and state, do so paint out this Church in this wilderness state, I take it to be for that very thing designed, that is to say, to prefigure this church in this, her so solitary and wilderness state.

CONCLUSION.

We will now, therefore, here make a brief conclusion of all.

First. This may inform us of the reason of the deplorable state of a professing people. It is allotted to them in this world to be so. The world, and men of the world, must have their tranquillity here, and must be possessed of all; this was foreshown in Esau, who had of his sons many that were dukes and kings before there was any king in Israel. (Gen. xxxvi. 31.) God so disposing of things that all may give place when his Son shall come to reign in Mount Zion, and before his ancients gloriously, which coming of his will be at the resurrection, and end of this world, and then shall his saints reign with him, "when Christ, who is our life, shall appear, then shall ye also appear with him in glory." (Col. iii. 4.)

Let not therefore kings, and princes, and potentates be afraid; the saints that are such indeed know their places, and are of a peaceable deportment; "the earth God hath given to the children of men," and his kingdom to the sons of God. (Ps. cxv. 16. Matt. xxv. 34. Luke xii. 32.)

I know there are extravagant opinions in the world about the kingdom of Christ, as if it consisted in temporal glory in part, and as if he would take it to him by carnal weapons, and so maintain it in its greatness and grandeur; but I confess myself an alien to these notions, and believe and profess the quite contrary, and look for the coming of Christ to judgment personally, and betwixt this and that, for his coming in Spirit, and in the power of his word to destroy Antichrist, to inform kings, and so to give quietness to his Church on earth; which shall assuredly be accomplished, when the reign of the beast, the whore, the false prophet, and of the man of sin is out. (2 Thess. ii. 8.

Isa. xlix. 23; lii. 15; lx. 3, 10, 11, 16; lxii. 2. Rev. xxi. 24.)

Second. Let this teach men not to think that the Church is cursed of God, because she is put in a wilderness state. Alas! that is but to train her up in a way of solitariness, to make her Canaan the more welcome to her. Rest is sweet to the labouring man. Yea, this condition is the first step to heaven; yea, it is a preparation to that kingdom. God's ways are not as man's. "I have chosen thee," saith he, "in the furnace of affliction."

When Israel came out of Egypt, they were led of God into the wilderness; but why? That he might have them to a land that he had espied for them, that he might bring them to a city of habitation. (Ezek. xx. 6. Ps. cvii. 1—7.)

The world know not the way of the Lord, nor the judgment of our God. Do you think that saints that dwell in the world, and that have more of the mind of God than the world, would, could so rejoice in God, in the cross, in tribulations and distresses, were they not assured that through many tribulations is the very roadway to heaven? (Acts xiv. 22.)

Let this then encourage the saints to hope, and to rejoice in hope of the glory of God, notwithstanding present tribulations. This is our seed-time, our winter, afflictions are to try us of what mettle we are made; yea, and to shake off worm-eaten fruit, and such as are rotten at core. Troubles for Christ's sake are but like the prick of an awl in the tip of the ear, in order to hang a jewel there.

Let this also put the saints upon patience: when we know that a trial will have an end, we are by that knowledge encouraged to exercise patience. I have a bad master, but I have but a year to serve under him, and that makes me serve him with patience. I have but a mile to go in this dirty way, and then I shall have my path pleasant and green, and this makes me tread the dirty way with patience.

I am now in my rags, but by that a quarter of a year is come and gone, two hundred a-year comes into my hand, wherefore I will wait, and exercise patience. Thus might I multiply comparisons. Be patient, then, my brethren. But how long? To the coming of the Lord. But when will that be? The coming of the Lord draws nigh.

"Be patient," my brethren, be long patient, even "unto the coming of the Lord. Behold, the husbandman waiteth for the precious fruit of the earth, and hath long patience for it, until he receive the early and latter rain. Be ye also patient; stablish your hearts: for the coming of the Lord draweth nigh." (James v. 7, 8.)

PREFATORY REMARKS

on

ANTICHRIST, AND HIS RUIN.

———————

The controversy respecting Antichrist has engaged minds of very different character. With some it has been a subject of interest because of its numerous and extensive historical associations. The grandest epochs in the world's progress, the most terrible revolutions, have appeared to many inquirers only as the circles of an eddy following the plunge of this great enemy of mankind into the stream of human life. Prophecy, for the same reason, has neither chapter nor verse viewed irrespectively of the awful being designated as Antichrist. His very title appals us. It is the embodiment in a name of the resolute, unceasing, universal activity of malice, opposing itself to the will of the most perfect benevolence. History teaches us, that of the two parties into which mankind have ever been divided, Antichrist was always either secretly or openly the leader of one. Prophecy reveals him working through a thousand channels, reviving old forces, or creating new: the events foreshadowed, whether more or less dimly, are the issue of the conflict between him and his invincible antagonist.

But, independent even of the profounder interest belonging to the subject, spiritually considered, a topic of this nature has points to which no mind of ordinary thoughtfulness can be quite indifferent. Not only is the existence of evil a fact, but it is also a fact that evil often appears in such a course of action, that it is almost impossible to avoid ascribing it to a distinct, intelligent agent. Whatever arguments may be opposed to this suggestion, men's natural feelings and instincts are too powerful to let mere reasoning prevail. In every case of unusual crime, and even whenever common immoralities have passed their ordinary measure, a degree of awe is created in the public mind, which has a far closer resemblance to the terror excited by some supernatural power, than to any species of natural alarm. This is practically the recognition of an Antichrist: of a personal, individual being, whose terrible will it is to resist, with gigantic might, the power which is working for man's salvation.

The growth of systems, intended to benefit the age in which they have arisen, seems to furnish even fresh provocatives to the malice of this antagonist. He is a mystery; but the more definite the plan through which good is to be promoted, the more easily may his course be traced. Against the increasing light of dawning truth, the outline of his dark, shadowy form, becomes more and more visible. The virtues and blessings seen and felt, are not greater realities than the existence of the adversary by which their diffusion is so often checked. It is not difficult, therefore, to understand, that a dispensation of grace and holiness was likely, above all others, to stimulate his further activity.

Apostles and evangelists were the first to detect his subtle agency, opposing itself on all sides to the influence of the gospel. It was to them that he first appeared sufficiently invested with form and substance to have a name given him. As Antichrist he became known to the infant churches; was detected and abhorred: his steps were traced by the tares which he sowed, and his presence recognised by the strange disturbance and unexpected troubles of faithful congregations. When defeated in one place, he began his work in another; when compelled to pause from his work by the ceaseless diligence of spiritual pastors, and prayerful churches, he waited for his revenge till another age. Thus it was that he stirred up the powers of the heathen world to successive persecutions; and the suffering church again knew him as Antichrist. The dark times which intervened between the triumphs of Christianity over the opposition of civil governments, and its revival at the beginning of the sixteenth century, were marked by circumstances of striking interest in regard to this subject. Antichrist, during a gloomy period of four or five hundred years, is supposed to have fought against Christianity under the emblazoned ensign of the cross. Ministers of the church spoke of other ministers of the gospel as furnishing him with the means of carrying on his unholy warfare. Two, and sometimes three, rival claimants to supreme power in the hierarchy, pointed to each other as the veritable Antichrist. Where he actually was, mankind at large seemed either unable or unwilling to determine. But if ever he exercised his art effectually to the retarding of the world's progress towards truth and holiness, it was in those ages of sloth and superstition.

It is no subject for surprise, that when men awakened from the torpor into which they had been cast, they should look around them with surprise, not unmingled with horror and indignation. An enemy had been among them. There was darkness where there should have been light; and the truths which were confessed as the gift of heaven, could scarcely be discerned for the errors and deceptions which crowded on all sides around them. This was the work of Antichrist; and that was Antichrist, whether man or system, the ruler of a state, the head of a church, or a church itself, to which, according to the aroused spirit of the times, the ruinous effects of superstition might be most readily attributed.

Thus the idea of Antichrist has changed with the changing events and temper of different ages. At first sight, this may seem to throw a doubt over the fact of his existence. But so far from doubting his being, or his individuality, because different generations have felt his presence haunting them under various shapes, we ought from this to be the more strongly convinced of his personal agency in all the events which agitate the world. It is the part of that particularizing, subtle power, which belongs, in our conception, to an individual only, to seize upon special opportunities for good or evil. To take advantage of changing seasons, to make instant use of means and instruments, there must be the ever watchful eye, and the answering strength. The work of Antichrist has in every season of his observed operations corresponded to this personal presence of a wise and daring enemy. He cannot be regarded as a mere abstraction. If the expressions of Scripture be fairly interpreted, they reveal to us a being who can avail himself of many shapes and channels of evil, without becoming identical, or confounding himself with any. A heresy may be an effectual instrument in his hands, but the heresy is not Antichrist. Modern luxury, science, literature, and infidelity, may enter into his plans, but though they, and all who promote them, should be combined in the fulfilment of his ends, they would not be Antichrist. That mention is made of "many antichrists," does not alter the important fact, that it is as a personal agent we are to regard him who has the first claim to that bad title and eminence. The false spirit, the human instrument of his will, is, doubtless, an antichrist, in an inferior degree. But it is an error to lose sight of the one governing Antichrist in any of these his ministers. In the highest seat of power to which the corruptions of the world, and their own pride and blasphemy may raise them, they only exist for his temporary purposes. The work of the season done, they are stripped of their pomp, and other subordinate antichrists supply their place. But the Antichrist to which they are subject, began his course with the beginning of the gospel; and will pursue it, unintermittingly, till he be finally overthrown.

H. S.

OF ANTICHRIST, AND HIS RUIN;

AND OF

THE SLAYING THE WITNESSES.

A PREMONITION TO THE READER.

AFTER that God had delivered Babylon and her king into the hands of the kings of the Medes and Persians, then began the liberty of the Jews from their long and tedious captivity; for though Nebuchadnezzar and his sons did tyrannically enslave, and hold them under, yet God so wrought with the hearts of these kings that succeeded them, that they made proclamation to them to go home and build their city, temple, &c., and worship their own God according to his own law. (2 Chron. xxx. 6. Ezra i.) But because I would not be tedious in enumerating instances for the clearing of this, therefore I will content myself with one, and with a brief note upon it. It is that in the seventh of Ezra, verse 26 :—" And whosoever will not do the law of thy God, and the law of the king, let judgment be executed speedily upon him, whether it be unto death, or to banishment, or to confiscation of goods, or to imprisonment." This is the conclusion of a letter that King Artaxerxes gave to Ezra the priest and scribe, when he granted his petition, and gave him leave to go to Jerusalem to build the temple, and to offer sacrifice there to the God whose house is in Jerusalem. And a conclusion it was, both comfortable and sharp—comfortable to Ezra and his companions, but sharp unto his enemies. I shall here present you with a copy of the letter at large :—

" 12. Artaxerxes, king of kings, unto Ezra the priest, a scribe of the law of the God of heaven, perfect peace, and at such a time.

" 13. I make a decree, that all they of the people of Israel, and of his priests and Levites, in my realm, who are minded of their own free will to go up to Jerusalem, go with thee.

" 14. Forasmuch as thou art sent of the king, and of his seven counsellors, to inquire concerning Judah and Jerusalem, according to the law of thy God which is in thine hand;

" 15. And to carry the silver and gold, which the king and his counsellors have freely offered unto the God of Israel, whose habitation is in Jerusalem,

" 16. And all the silver and gold that thou canst find in all the province of Babylon, with the free-will offering of the people, and of the priests, offering willingly for the house of their God, which is in Jerusalem:

" 17. That thou mayest buy speedily with this money bullocks, rams, lambs, with their meat-offerings and their drink-offerings, and offer them upon the altar of the house of your God which is in Jerusalem.

" 18. And whatsoever shall seem good to thee, and to thy brethren, to do with the rest of the silver and the gold, that do after the will of your God.

" 19. The vessels also that are given thee for the service of the house of thy God, those deliver thou before the God of Jerusalem.

" 20. And whatsoever more shall be needful for the house of thy God, which thou shalt have occasion to bestow, bestow it out of the king's treasure-house.

" 21. And I, even I, Artaxerxes the king, do make a decree to all the treasurers who are beyond the river, that whatsoever Ezra the priest, the scribe of the law of the God of heaven, shall require of you, it be done speedily,

" 22. Unto an hundred talents of silver, and to an hundred measures of wheat, and to an hundred baths of wine, and to an hundred baths of oil, and salt without prescribing how much.

" 23. Whatsoever is commanded by the God of heaven, let it be diligently done for the house of the God of heaven : for why should there be wrath against the realm of the king and his sons ?

" 24. Also we certify you, that touching any of the priests and Levites, singers, porters, Nethinims, or ministers of this house of God, it shall not be lawful to impose toll, tribute, or custom, upon them.

" 25. And thou, Ezra, after the wisdom of thy

God, that is in thine hand, set magistrates and judges, who may judge all the people that are beyond the river, all such as know the laws of thy God; and teach ye them that know them not.

"26. And whosoever will not do the law of thy God, and the law of the king, let judgment be executed speedily upon him, whether it be unto death, or to banishment, or to confiscation of goods, or to imprisonment."

This is the letter; and now for the scope thereof.

First. Generally.

Second. Particularly.

First. Generally.—The general scope of the letter is this: A grant given by the king to Ezra the scribe, to go to Jerusalem, and build there the temple of God, and offer sacrifice in it according to the law; with commissions annexed thereunto, to the king's lieutenants, treasurers, and governors on that side the river, to further the work with such things as by the king was commanded they should.

Second. Particularly.—But we will consider the matter particularly.

First. As to the manner of the grant which the king gave to Ezra and his brethren to go thither.

Second. As to the king's grant, with reference to their building, and way of worship.

Third. With reference to the king's liberality and gifts towards the building of the temple, and by what rules it was to be bestowed.

Fourth. As to the way that the king concluded they should be governed in their own land.

Fifth. With reference to the king's charge to his officers that were thereabout, not to hinder Ezra in his work.

Sixth. And lastly, with reference to the king's threat and commandment to do judgment if they should hinder it.

First. As to the manner of the grant that the king gave to Ezra and his brethren to go to build, it was such an one as forced none, but left every Jew to his own choice, whether he would go or forbear. The words are these: "Artaxerxes, king of kings, unto Ezra the priest, a scribe of the law of the God of heaven, perfect peace, and at such a time. I make a decree, that all they of the people of Israel, and of his priests and Levites in my realm, who are minded of their own free will to go up to Jerusalem, go with thee." (Ezra vii. 12, 13.)

Thus gracious, then, was the king: he made a decree, that all they of the captive Jews, their priests and Levites, that would return to their own land, to build their temple, and to sacrifice there, might: he would hinder none, force none, but left them free to do as they would.

Second. As to the king's grant, with reference to their building, and way of worship there, nothing was to be done therein, but according to the law of the God of Ezra, which was in his hand. (Ezra vii. 14.)   Hence, when he was come to Jerusalem, he was to inquire concerning Judah and Jerusalem; to wit, what was wanting in order to the temple and worship of God there, according to the law of his God, which was in his hand. Also when they went about to build, and to sacrifice, all was to be done according as was commanded by the God of heaven. (Ezra vii. 23.) Yea, this was granted by the king and his seven counsellors.

Third. As to the king's liberality towards the building of this house, &c., it was large. He gave silver, gold, bullocks, rams, lambs; with wheat, wine, oil, and salt, (Ezra vii. 17, 22;) but would by his royal power, give no orders how in particular things should be bestowed, but left all that to Ezra the priest, to do with it according to the will, word, or law of his God. (Ezra vii. 18.)

Fourth. As to the way that the king concluded they should be governed in their own land, it was by their own laws; yea, he did bid Ezra the priest, after the wisdom of his God that was in his hand, set magistrates and judges, who might judge all the people, &c., only he bid him make them such as did know the law of his God. Also the king added, that they should teach it to them that knew it not.

Fifth. As to the king's officers, he gave them a charge not to *hinder*, but *further* this work. To further this work, not by putting their hand thereto, (that was to be left to the Jews alone, especially to Ezra, according to the law of his God,) but that they should speedily give him such things which the king had commanded, to wit, silver, and wheat, and wine, and oil, and salt, for their encouragement; and to do therewith, as by the law of their God they should. Further, that they should not impose toll, tribute, or custom, upon the priests, Levites, singers, porters, Nethinims, or ministers.

Sixth. And now we come to the conclusion, to wit, the king's threat and command to do judgment on them that obeyed not the law of Ezra's God, and the king.

Considering what has been said before, I conclude—

1. That this king imposed no law, no priest, no people upon these Jews; but left them wholly to their own law, their own ministers, and their own people: all which were the laws of God, the priests of God, the people of God, as to their building of their temple, and the worship of their God.

2. He forced not THIS people, no, not to their land, their temple, nor their worship, by his or their law; but left them free to their own mind, to do thereabout as they would.

3. He added not any law therefore of his own, either to prescribe worship, or to enforce it upon the Jews.

But you will say, upon what then was the threatening and the command to punish grounded? I answer, upon a supposed breach of two laws.

He of the Jews that in Jerusalem rebelled against the law of the Lord, was in his own land left by the king to be punished by the same law, according to the penalties thereof: and he of the king's officers, that refused to do the king's laws, that refused to give the Jews such things as the king commanded, and that would yet exact such customs and tributes as the king forbade, should be punished by the king's laws, whether unto death, or unto banishment, or unto confiscation of goods, or to imprisonment.

And if all kings would but give such liberty, to wit, that God's people should be directed in their temple building and temple worship, as they find it in the law of their God, without the additions of man's inventions; and if all kings did but lay the same penalty upon them of their pretended servants that should hinder this work, which this brave King Artaxerxes laid upon his, how many of the enemies of the Jews, before this time, would have been hanged, banished, had their goods confiscated to the king, or their bodies shut up in prison! The which we desire not; we desire only that this letter of the king might be considered of, and we left to do as is there licensed and directed: and when we do the contrary, let us be punished by the law of God, as we are his servants, and by the law of the king, as we are his subjects; and we shall never complain.

Only I cannot but observe how prettily it is done of some, who urge this text to colour their malice, ignorance, and revenge withal, while they cry, "the law of God," and "the law of the king," when they will neither let, according to this scripture, the law of God, nor the law of the king take place: not the law of God; for that they will not leave us to that, to square and govern ourselves in temple-work, and sacrificing by. Nor will they do the law of the king, which has made void, *ipso facto*, whatever law is against the word of God; but because themselves can do, they will force us to do so too.

Before I leave this, I would touch once again upon the candour of this King Artaxerxes, who thus did: because he gave this leave and license to the Jews, contrary (if he had any) to his own national worship; yea, and also to the impairing of his own incomes. Methinks he should have a religion of his own; and that, not that of the Jews, because he was a Gentile; and not, as we read of, proselyted to the Jews' religion. Indeed, he spake reverently of the God of Israel, and of his temple worship, and sacrifices, as did also several other kings; but that will not prove that he was adapted to that religion.

That his incomes were impaired it is evident, because he took off toll, tribute, and custom for them of whom mention is made before; nor is it, I think, to be believed that he did exact it of their brethren. But we may see what the Lord can do; for thus to do was put into the heart of the king by the God of heaven. (Ezra vii. 27.) This,

therefore, ariseth not of nature: no more did the kindness of Cyrus or Darius, of whom we read in the beginning of this history. As God, therefore, did put it into the hearts of the wicked kings of Babylon to distress his Church and people for their sins, so he put it into the hearts of the kings of the Medes and Persians, who were to be, in a sense, their saviours: to ease them of those distresses, to take off the yoke, and let them go free. Indeed, there was an Artaxerxes that put a stop to this work of God, (Ezra iv.,) and he also was of the kings that had destroyed the Babylonians; for it doth not follow because God had begun to deliver his people that, therefore, their deliverance must be completed without stop or let. The Protestants in France had more favour formerly than from their prince they at this time have; yet I doubt not but that God will make that horn also one of them (in his time) that (indeed) shall hate the whore. As the sins of God's people brought them into captivity, so their sins can hold them there; yea, and when the time comes that grace must fetch them out, yet the oxen that draw this cart may stumble; and the way through roughness may shake it sorely. However, heaven rules and overrules; and, by one means and another, as the captivity of Israel did seem to linger, so it came out at the time appointed, in the way that best pleased God, most profited them, and that most confounded those that were their implacable enemies. This, therefore, should instruct those that yet dwell where the woman sitteth, to quietness and patience.

To quietness; for God rules, and has the dispose of things. Besides, it is a kind of arraigning of his wisdom to be discontent at that which at present is upon the wheel. Above all it displeases him that any should seek or go about to revenge their own injuries, or to work their own deliverances, for that is the work of God; and he will do it by the kings: nor is he weak, nor has he missed the opportunity; nor doth he sleep, but waketh, and waiteth to be gracious.

This also should teach them to be *patient*, and put them upon bearing what at present they may undergo, patiently. Let them wait upon God, patiently let them wait upon men, and patiently let them bear the fruits of their own transgressions, which, though they should be none other but a deferring of the mercy wished for, is enough to try, and crack, and break their patience, if a continual supply, and a daily increase thereof, be not given by the God of heaven.

And, before I do conclude this, let me also add one word more, to wit, to exhort them to look that they may see that which God at present may be doing among the Babylonians.

When God had his people into Babylon of old, he presented them with such rarities there as he never showed them in their own country. And is there nothing now to be seen by them that are not yet delivered from that oppression, that may give them occasion to stay themselves and wonder! What, is preservation nothing? What, is baffling and befooling the enemies of God's Church nothing? In the Maryan days here at home there was such sweet songs sung in the fire, such sweet notes answering them from prison, and such providences, that coals of burning fire still dropped here and there upon the heads of those that hated God, that it might, and doubtless did, make those that did wisely consider of God's doings, to think God was yet near, with, and for, a despised and afflicted people.

I conclude then, first with a word of counsel, and then with a word of caution.

First. Let us mend our pace in the way of reformation, that is the way to hasten the downfall of Antichrist; ministers need reforming, particular congregations need reforming, there are but few church members but need reforming. This twenty years we have been degenerating, both as to principles and as to practice; and have grown at last into an amazing likeness to the world, both as to religion and civil demeanour: yea, I may say, so remiss have churches been in instructing those that they have received into fellowship with them, and so careless have the received been of considering the grounds of their coming into churches, that most members, in some places, seem now to be at a loss; yea, and those churches stand with their fingers in their mouths, and are as if they would not, durst not, or could not help it.

My second is a word of caution.

First. Take heed of overlooking or of shutting your eyes upon your own guilt: " He that covereth his sins shall not prosper." It is incident to some men, when they find repentance is far from them, to shut their eyes upon their own guilt, and to please themselves with such notions of deliverance from present troubles as will stand with that course of sin which is got into their families, persons, and professions, and with a state of impenitence; but I advise you to take heed of this.

Second. Take heed in laying the cause of your troubles in the badness of the temper of governors. I speak not now with reflection upon any, excepting those concerned in this caution: God is the chief, and has the hearts of all, even of the worst of men, in his hand. Good-tempered men have sometimes brought trouble, and bad-tempered men have sometimes brought enlargement to the churches of God: Saul brought enlargement, (1 Sam. xiv. 28;) David brought trouble, (2 Sam. xii. 10;) Ahab brought enlargement, (1 Kings xxi. 29;) Jehoshaphat and Hezekiah did both sometimes bring trouble. (2 Chron. xix. 2; xx. 35; xxxii. 25.) Therefore the good or bad tempers of men sway nothing with God in this matter; they are the sins or repentance of his people that make the church either happy or miserable upon earth.

Take heed, I say, therefore, of laying of the trouble of the Church of God at the doors of governors; especially at the doors of kings, who seldom trouble churches of their own inclinations, (I say seldom, for some have done so, as Pharaoh;) but, I say, lay not the cause of your trouble there, for oftentimes they see with other men's eyes, hear with other men's ears, and act and do by the judgments of others;—thus did Saul when he killed the priests of the Lord, (1 Sam. xxii. 18;) and thus did Darius when he cast Daniel into the lions' den, (Dan. vi. 7;)—but rather labour to see the true cause of trouble, which is sin, and to attain to a fitness to be delivered out thence, and that is by repentance, and amendment of life. If any object that God ofttimes delivers his of mere grace, I answer, that is no thanks to them; besides, we must mind our duty. Further, when God comes to save his people, he can cut off such objectors, if they be impenitent, as the sinners of his people, and can save his Church without letting them be sharers in that salvation: so he served many in the wilderness; and, it is to be feared, so he will serve many at the downfall of Antichrist.

I shall say no more but to testify that my loyalty to my king, my love to my brethren, and service for my country has been the cause of this my present scribble. Farewell.

Thine in the Lord,

JOHN BUNYAN.

OF ANTICHRIST, AND HIS RUIN.

CHAPTER I.

OF ANTICHRIST AND HIS FIRST APPEARANCE.

ANTICHRIST is the adversary of Christ—an adversary really, a friend pretendedly; so, then, Antichrist is one that is against Christ, one that is for Christ, and one that is contrary to him—and this is that mystery of iniquity. (2 Thess. ii. 7.) Against him in deed, for him in word, and contrary to him in practice. Antichrist is so proud as to go before Christ, so humble as to pretend to come after him, and so audacious as to say that himself is he. Antichrist will cry up Christ; Antichrist will cry down Christ: Antichrist will proclaim that himself is one above Christ. Antichrist is the man of sin, the son of perdition; a beast that hath two horns like a lamb, but speaks as a dragon. (Rev. xiii. 11.)

Christ is the Son of God: Antichrist is the son of hell.

Christ is holy, meek, and forbearing: Antichrist is wicked, outrageous, and exacting.

Christ seeketh the good of the soul: Antichrist seeks his own avarice and revenge.

Christ is content to rule by his word: Antichrist saith the word is not sufficient.

Christ preferreth his Father's will above heaven and earth: Antichrist preferreth himself and his traditions above all that is written, or that is called God, or worshipped,

Christ has given us such laws and rules as are helpful and healthful to the soul: Antichrist seeketh to abuse those rules to our hurt and destruction.

Antichrist may be considered either more particularly or more generally.

1. More particularly: and so there are many Antichrists. (1 John ii. 18.)

2. More generally: and so the *many* maketh but *one* great Antichrist, one man of sin, one enemy, one great whore, one son of perdition. (2 Thess. ii. 3. Rev. xix. 2.)

Again: Antichrist must be distinguished with respect to his more *internal* and *external* parts, and so there is the *spirit, soul,* or *life,* (1 John iv. 3,) and also the *body* and *flesh* of Antichrist. (2 Thess. ii. 7.) The spirit, or soul, or life of Antichrist is *that* spirit of error, *that* wicked, *that* mystery of iniquity that, under colour and pretence of verity, draweth men from truth to falsehood. The *body* or flesh of Antichrist is that heap of men, that assembly of the wicked, that synagogue of Satan that is acted and governed by that spirit. But God will destroy both soul and body; he "shall consume the glory of his forest, and of his fruitful field, both soul and body," (or from the soul, even to the flesh,) "and they shall be" (both soul and body) "as when a standard-bearer fainteth." (Isa. x. 18.)

Antichrist, therefore, is a *mystical* man, so *made* or *begotten* of the devil, and sent into the world, himself being the chief and highest of him. Three things, therefore, go to the making up of Antichrist, the head, body, and soul. The devil, *he* is the head; the synagogue of Satan, *that* is the body; that wicked spirit of iniquity, *that* is the soul of Antichrist. Christ, then, is the head of his Church; the devil is the head of Antichrist; the elect are the body of Christ; the reprobate professors are the body of Antichrist; the Holy Ghost is the Spirit of life that actuateth Christ's body; that wicked spirit of iniquity is that which actuateth the body of Antichrist. Thus, therefore, are the two great mighties set forth before us, who are the heads of those two bodies; and thus are these two bodies set before us, who are to be actuated by these two spirits.

The reason why Christ came into the world, was, that he might destroy all the works of the head of Antichrist, and they which he endeavoureth to complete by his wicked spirit working in his body. And the reason why Antichrist came into the world, was, that the Church, which is the body of Christ, might be tried, and made white by suffering under his tyranny, and by bearing witness against his falsehoods. For, for the trial of the faithful, and for the punishment of the world, Antichrist was admitted to come: but when he came, he first appeared there where one would have thought there had been no place nor corner for his reception.

The devil then, made use of the Church of God to midwive this monster into the world, as the apostle plainly shows, there he first sat, *showing himself.* (2 Thess. ii. 4.) Here therefore was his first appearance, even in the Church of God: not that the Church of God did willingly admit him there to sit *as such;* he had *covered* his cloven-foot; he had *plums* in his dragon's mouth, and so came in by flatteries; promising to do for Christ and his Church, that which he never meant to perform. For he showed himself that he was God, and in appearance, set his heart to do as the heart of God. (Ezek. xxviii. 2—6.) And who could have found in their hearts to shut the door upon such an one? True, he came, when he came thither, out of the bottomless pit; but there came such a smoke out thence with him, and that smoke so darkened the light of the sun, of the moon, of the stars, and of the day, that had they been upon their watch, as they were not, they could not have perceived him from another man. Besides, there came with him so many *locusts* to usher him into the house of God, (Rev. ix. 2, 3,) and they so suited the flesh and reason of the godly of that day, that with good words and fair speeches, by their crafty and cunning sleights, whereby they lay in wait to deceive, they quite got him in, and set him up, and made him a *great one,* even the chief, before they were aware. Further, he quickly got him a *beast* to ride on, far, for sumptuous glory, beyond (though as to nature, as assish a creature as) that on which Balaam was wont to ride: and by this exaltation he became not only more stately, but the *horns* of the beast would push for him. (Rev. xvii. 3—6.)

Again, this man of sin, when he came into the world, had the art of metamorphosing, and could change himself, both in form and shape, into the likeness of a beast, a man, or woman; and the kings of the earth, with the inhabitants of the world, began then to love such women dearly; wherefore they went to her into the bed of love, and defiled themselves with the filthiness of her fornications, gave her their troth, and became her husbands, and beloved sons: took up helmet and shield, and stood to defend her; yea, though Christ himself, and some of the chief of his followers, cried out of her shame, and of the evil of their doings, yet would she be audacious.

Also this woman had now arrayed herself in

flesh-taking ornaments, of the colour of purple and scarlet, and was decked with gold, and precious stones, and pearls, after the manner or attire of harlots. Thus came she to them, and lay in their bosoms, and gave them out of her golden cup of the wine of her fornication; of the which they bibbed till they were drunken; and then, in requital, they also gave her of such liquors as they could, to wit, to drink of the blood of saints, and of martyrs of Jesus, till she, like these beasts, was drunken also.

Now when they were drunken, they did as drunkards do, revel, roar, and belch out their own shame, in the sight of them that were sober; wherefore they cried out upon such doings, and chose rather to die, than to live with such company. And so it is still with them where she yet sitteth and so will be till she shall fall into the hands of the strong Lord, who will judge her according to her ways. And that she must do, as is implied by this, that her fornications are in a cup; she has therefore but her cup to be drank out; wherefore when it is empty, then, whether she will or no, the Lord God will call her to such a reckoning, that all the clothes on her back, with what pearls and jewels she has, shall not be able to pay the shot.

CHAPTER II.

OF THE RUIN OF ANTICHRIST.

Antichrist, as was said, had a time to come into the world, and so must have a time to go out again : for although he saith that he is a God, yet must he be subject to the will of God, and must go as well as come according to that will. Nor can all the fallen angels, with all the members and limbs of Antichrist, cause that this their brat should abide so much as one day longer than our God's prefixed time. And this the head of Antichrist understandeth very well : wherefore the Holy Ghost saith, "Woe to the inhabiters of the earth, and of the sea; for the devil is come down unto you, having great wrath, because he knows he hath but a short time." (Rev. xii. 12.)

Besides, the text says plainly, the Lord shall destroy him, (2 Thess. ii. 8,) and that he goeth into perdition, (Rev. xvii. 11 ; xix. 26:) also the Church of God believes it, and the limbs of Antichrist fear it.

Now when, or as his time shall come to be destroyed, so he shall be made a hand of, and that with such instruments and weapons of God's indignation, as best shall be suited to his several parts.

Such weapons as are best for the destroying of his *soul*, shall be used for the destroying of it; and such weapons as are best for the destroying of his *body*, shall be made use of for the destroying of it.

I. *The destruction of the soul of Antichrist.*

And therefore, as to his *soul*, or that spirit of error that governs him in all his works of mischief, this must be consumed by the spirit of Christ's mouth, and be destroyed by the brightness of his coming.

This we have in the words of Paul: "For," says he, "the mystery of iniquity (the spirit of Antichrist) doth already work; only he who now letteth, will let, until he be taken out of the way. And then shall that wicked be revealed, whom the Lord shall consume with the spirit of his mouth, and shall destroy with the brightness of his coming." (2 Thess. ii. 7, 8.) The apostle here treateth of Antichrist, with reference to his more subtle and spiritual part, since that indeed is the chiefest of Antichrist : wherefore he calls it that *wicked;* not that wicked *one*, as referring to the whole, but that *wicked*, as referring to the *mystery* or *spirit of iniquity*, the heart and soul of Antichrist ; and tells us, that the Lord shall "consume him with the spirit of his mouth, and shall destroy him with the brightness of his coming."

Now, by the *spirit of his mouth*, I understand his *holy word*, which is called "the word and breath of his lips," (Isa. xi. 4,) and also, "the sword of his mouth." (Rev. ii. 16.) By "the brightness of his coming," I also understand not *only* his presence, but an *increase* of light by his presence, not only to help Christians to begin to bear witness against some parts and pieces of the errors of Antichrist, but until the *whole* is rooted out of the world. By this, I say, must the soul, spirit, or life of Antichrist be taken away. But how shall Christ by this rod, sword, or spirit of his mouth, consume this wicked, this *mystery of iniquity?* Not by himself immediately, but by his *spirit* and *word* in his Church; the which he will use, and so manage in this work, that they shall not rest till he by them has brought this beast to his grave. This beast is compared to the wild boar, and the beast that comes out of the wood to devour the Church of God, (as we read in the book of Psalms, lxxx. 13 :) but Christ, with the dogs that eat the crumbs of his table, will so hunt and scour him about, that albeit he may let out some of their bowels with the tushes of his chaps, yet they will not let him alone till they have his life : for the Church shall single him out from all beasts, and so follow him with cries, and pinch him with their voices, that he alone shall perish by their means. Thus shall Christ consume and wear him out by the spirit of his mouth, and destroy him with the brightness of his coming.

Hence you find again, that this *wicked* is to melt and consume away as grease : for the Lord Jesus shall consume him, and cause him to melt away ; not all at once, but *now* this part, and *then* that ; *now* his *soul*, and after that his *body*, even until soul and body are both destroyed.

And that you may be convinced of the truth of this thing, do but look back and compare Antichrist four or five hundred years ago with Antichrist as he is now, and you shall see what work the Lord Jesus has begun to make with him, even with the spirit, and soul, and life of Antichrist; both in confounding and blasting of it by this spirit of his mouth, as also by forcing of it to dishonourable retreats, and by making of it give up to him as the conqueror, not only some of his superstitious and diabolical rites and ceremonies to be destroyed, but many a goodly truth, which this vile one had taken from his Church, to be renewed to them. Nay, further, he hath also already began to take from him both kingdoms and countries, though as to some not so absolutely as he shall do by and by. And, in the meantime, this is the plague wherewith the Lord shall plague or smite the people that have fought against Jerusalem: "Their flesh shall consume away while they stand upon their feet, and their eyes shall consume away in their holes, and their tongue shall consume away in their mouth." (Zech. xiv. 12.) And how has this long ago been fulfilled here in England! as also in Scotland, Holland, Germany, France, Sweden, Denmark, Hungary, and other places! (Isa. xvii. 4—6.) Nor hath this spirit of Antichrist, with all his art and artifices, been able to reduce to Antichrist again, those people, nations, or parts of nations, that by the spirit of Christ's mouth, and "the brightness of his coming," have been made to forsake him, and to turn from him to Christ: the reason is, for that the Lord has not retreated, but is still going on in the spirit of his mouth, and his brightness, to make that conquest over him that is determined, in the way that is determined: of which more shall be spoken afterward; for the pathway that he goeth, is as the shining light, which shines more and more unto noon. True, the fogs of Antichrist, and the smoke that came with him out of the bottomless-pit, has darkened and eclipsed the glorious light of the gospel: but you know, in eclipses, when they are on the recovering hand, all the creatures upon the face of the earth cannot put a stop to that course, until the sun or the moon have recovered their glory. And thus it shall be now, the Lord is returned to visit the earth, and his people with his primitive lustre; he will not go back, nor slack his hand, until he has recovered what Antichrist has darkened of his. "The anger of the Lord shall not return, until he have executed, and till he have performed the thoughts of his heart; in the latter days ye shall consider it perfectly." (Jer. xxiii. 20.) Therefore he saith again, "The light of the moon shall be as the light of the sun (was in her eclipse;) and the light of the sun shall be sevenfold, as the light of seven days, in the day that the Lord bindeth up the breach of his people, and healeth the stroke of their wound," &c., as the verse before has it, "in the day when the towers fall."

For (as was said before) as to the recovery of the light of the gospel from under antichristian mists and fogs of darkness, Christ will do that, not by might nor power, but by the spirit of his mouth, and the brightness of his coming: wherefore the *soul* of Antichrist, or that spirit of wickedness by which this gospel-light hath been diminished, must be consumed and destroyed by that spirit also. Nor can any other way of conquest over that be thorough and lasting, because that spirit can by no other means be slain. The *body* of Antichrist may be destroyed by other instruments, but spirits cannot be killed but by spirits. The temporal sword then may kill the body, but after that it hath no more than it can do, wherefore the other must be dealt with by another kind of weapon: and here is one sufficient, the spirit against the spirit—the spirit and face of Christ against the spirit, that wicked, of Antichrist. And by this spirit of Christ's mouth, all the spirit that is in all the *trinkets* and *wash* of Antichrist shall also be destroyed; so that those trinkets, those rites, ceremonies, and ordinances of this man of sin shall be left as carrion upon the face of the earth, and shall stink in the noses of men, as doth the corrupted blood of a dead man.

II. *The Ordinances of Antichrist.*

Now, therefore, will the beauty of Antichrist fade like a flower, and fall as doth a leaf when the sap of the tree has left it; or as the beauty departeth from the body when the soul, or life, or spirit is gone forth. And as the body cannot be but unpleasant and unsavoury when under such a state, so the body of Antichrist will be to beholders when the Lord has slain the spirit thereof. It is the spirit of Antichrist that puts life into the body, and that puts lustre into the ordinances of Antichrist, as the light of the sun, and of the moon, and of the stars do put lustre upon the things of this visible world: wherefore, when this spirit and soul, and life of Antichrist is slain, then it will be with *him* as it would be with the *world* had it no light of the sun, of the moon, or of the stars.

And hence, as the loss of our natural life is compared to the loss of *these* lights, (Eccles. xii. 2,) so the loss of the life, soul, and spirit of Antichrist is compared to these things also. For the soul of Antichrist is compared to a heaven, and her ordinances and rites to the ordinances of heaven; wherefore, when the Lord comes to fight against her with the spirit of his mouth, he saith, The stars of the heaven thereof shall be darkened, and the constellations thereof shall not give their light, (Isa. xiii. 10,) because he will slay that spirit of Antichrist that is in them. (Isa. xxxiv. Rev. vi. 13, 14.)

Take things therefore more distinctly, thus: the Antichristians' spirit is the heaven of Antichristians; their sun, moon, and stars are their superstitious ordinances; their earth is the body or flesh of Antichrist, otherwise called the "Church and Synagogue of Satan." Now, as the earth cannot live and be desirable without the influences of the spirit of the heavens, so neither can Antichrist live when the Lord shall darken the light of his heaven, and shall slay the spirit thereof. Hence you read, as I touched before, that when his heaven shall be rolled together as a scroll " all the host thereof"—unto which I compared the ordinances of Antichrist—" shall fall down as the leaf falleth off from the vine, and as a falling fig from the fig-tree." (Isa. xxxiv. 4.) But how, or why doth the leaf or the fig fall from the tree? Why, because the spirit, or sap of the tree, is gone from them.

Therefore the first and chief proceeding of the Lord with the man of sin, is *to slay his soul*, that his *body* may also be consumed; and when the spirit of Antichrist shall be made to leave both the body and ordinances of Antichrist, it will be easy to deal both with the one and the other. And first, for the ordinances of Antichrist; because the spirit of error is in them, as well as in the body itself. When that spirit, as I said, has left them, they will of themselves even moulder away, and not be: as we have seen by experience here in England, as others also have seen in other countries. For as concerning his masses, prayers for the dead, images, pilgrimages, monkish vows, sinful fasts, and the beastly single life of their priests, though when the spirit of Antichrist was in them, they did bear some sway in the world, yet now of what esteem are they? or who has reverence for them? They are now blown together under hedges, as the dry leaves, for the mice and frogs to harbour in: yea, the locusts, too, camp in the hedges among the dry leaves in the cold day, and " when the sun arises they fly away." (Nahum iii. 15—17.) When it is a cold day for them in a nation, then they lurk in the hedges, though their ordinances lie there, as leaves that are dry and fallen down from the tree; but when the sun ariseth, and waxeth warm, they abide not, but betake them to their wings, and fly away. But one would think that fallen leaves should have no great nourishment in them: true, if you have respect to men, but with vermin anything will do. We speak then of them with reference to *men*, not with respect to the very members of Antichrist: and I say, as to *them*, when the spirit of Antichrist is gone out of these ordinances, they will be with them as dry leaves that nobody seeketh after. The ordinances therefore of Antichrist are not able to bear up themselves in the world, as the ordinances of the Lord Jesus are; for even the ordinances of Christ, where the spirit of Christ is not, are yet in some esteem with men: but these, when the spirit of delusion has left them, are abhorred, both skin and bones; for in themselves they are without any sense or rationality, (Ezek. xx. 25, 26;) yea, they look as parts of things which are used to conjure up devils with: these

were prefigured by the ordinances that were NOT good, and by the judgments whereby one *should not live*. For what is there or can there be, of the least dram of truth or profit in the things that are without the word, that being the only stamp by which one is distinguished from the other? I say what is there in any of them, to the man whose eyes are open, but delusion and deceit? Wherefore, as has been expressed already, when the Lord Christ, by the spirit of his mouth, &c., shall drive this mystery of iniquity from them, and strip them of that spirit of delusion that now by its craft puts bewitching excellence upon them, they will of themselves become such stinking rivers, ponds, and pools that flesh and blood will loath to drink of them; yea, as it was with the ponds and pools of Egypt, they will be fit for nought but to breed and hatch up frogs in.

Wherefore these ordinances shall be rejected, not one of them shall find favour with men on earth, when the Lord, " by the spirit of his mouth and the brightness of his coming," shall have separated their spirit from them.

Now by *ordinances* of Antichrist, I do not intend things that *only* respect matters of worship in Antichrist's kingdom, but those *civil laws* that impose and enforce *them* also; yea, that enforce *that* worship with pains and penalties, as in the Spanish inquisition: for these must, as the other, be overthrown by Christ, by the spirit of his mouth and the brightness of his coming: for these laws, as the other, took their being, and have their soul and life by the spirit of Antichrist,—yea, as long as there is life in them, it is because the spirit of that man of sin yet remaineth in them. Wherefore these are also great ordinances, though of another nature than are those mentioned before: *great*, I say, are they, forasmuch as neither the church of Antichrist, nor his instruments of worship, can either live or stand without them. Wherefore it was admitted to the image of the beast not only to *speak*, but to *cause*. To speak out his laws of worship, " and cause that as many as would not worship the image of the beast should be killed." (Rev. xiii. 15.) And mark, this is because that the life that was communicated to the image of the beast, was by him also communicated to his word and authority. Wherefore these laws must not be separated from those in which the spirit of Antichrist is; yea, they are the very pillars and sinews by which Antichristianism remains: and were these dispirited the whole building would quickly become a ruinous heap.

What could the King of Babylon's golden image have done had it not been for the burning fiery furnace that stood within view of the worshippers? (Dan. iii.) Yea, what could that horrible command to pray for thirty days to neither God nor man, but to the king, have done, had it not been for the dark den and the roaring lions there in readiness to devour those that disobeyed it? (Dan. vi.) As therefore the burning fiery furnace and the den of lions were the support of the horrible religion of the Babylonians of old, so popish edicts are the support of the religion of Antichrist now; and as long as there is spirit—that is *authority*—in them that are like to those now mentioned, the spirit of such laws is that that makes them dreadful: for as the furnace would have been next to nothing if void of fire, and the den as little frightful if destitute of lions, so these laws will be as insignificant when Christ has slain that spirit that is in them—that spirit that causes that as many as will not worship the image of the beast should be killed.

Nor can any sword reach *that* life of Antichrist that is in these, but the sword of Christ's mouth; therefore as all the religious rites and ceremonies of Antichrist are overthrown by his spirit working in *his* as Christians, so those antichristian laws will have their soul and their life taken from them also by this spirit of his mouth working in some of his, as magistrates, and no otherwise: for before kings and princes, &c., come to be enlightened about the evils that are in *such* edicts by the spirit of the living God, they will let this image of the beast both *speak* and *cause*, &c. But when they shall *see* they will say, Let it be decreed that this prop of Antichrist be taken down. It was decreed by Darius that they that prayed for thirty days to any God but him should be cast into the den of lions, (Dan. vi. 9;) but this was *before he saw*, but when he came to see, then he decreed again;—a decree that quite took away the power of that which he had decreed before. (Dan. vi. 26.)

Nor are we without instances of this kind nearer home: who is now afraid of the act for burning of those that papists call heretics, since by the king and parliament, as by the finger of God, the life and soul is taken out of it? I bring this to show you that as there is life in wicked antichristian penal laws, as well as in those that are superstitiously religious, so the life of these, of all these, must be destroyed by the same spirit working in those that are Christ's, though in a diverse way.

Nor will the life of these sinews, as I have called them, be taken away, but as God shall enlighten men to see the abominable filthiness of that which is antichristian worship; as would easily be made appear, if some that dwell in those countries where the beast and his image have been worshipped, would but take the pains to inquire into antiquity about it. As the noble king, King Henry VIII., did cast down the antichristian worship, so he cast down the laws that held it up; so also did the good King Edward, his son. The brave Queen Elizabeth also, the sister to King Edward, hath left of things of this nature, to her lasting fame behind her. And if one such law of Antichrist hath escaped the hand of one, another hath taken it, and done that

execution on it that their zeal and piety prompted them to.

There is yet another thing that the spirit of Antichrist is immediately concerned in, and that is the antichristian names of the men that worship the beast,—the names, I mean, that Antichrist hath baptized them into: for those names are breathed upon them by the very spirit of Antichrist; and are such as are absolutely names of blasphemy, or such as do closely border thereupon; some such as Elihu durst not for his life give unto men, only he calls them "flattering titles." (Job xxxii. 21, 22.) Now, therefore, of the danger (though not of the names themselves) you read sufficiently in the Scriptures; and perhaps the Holy Ghost has contented himself with giving of items that are general, that men might, as to them, be the more cautious of what names they give one to another, (Rev. xvii. 5;) but this is clear, they are worn by men of spiritual employ: but since they are but mentioned, and are not distinctly nominated, how should we know which are they, and which not? Verily, by searching the word of God, and by seeing by that what names we are allowed to give unto men, with reference to their offices, dignities, and places: for God has a quarrel with the *names*, as well as with the *persons* that wear them; and when his Son shall down with Antichrist, he will slay seven thousand names of men, as well as the persons of the worshippers of the beast.

But there are things as well as men, (Job xxii. 28;) and these also have been baptized into those names by the very spirit of Antichrist, and must be destroyed by Christ, the spirit of his mouth, and the brightness of his coming: "the idols he shall utterly abolish," (Isa. ii. 18;) and there are *men* that are idols as well as *things*. (Zech. xi. 17.) Wherefore let men have a care, as to shun the worship of idols, so that they bare not the name or stand in the place of one: and the reason of this caution is because *name* and *thing* are both abominable unto God.

To give you the number of these names that the spirit of Antichrist has baptized men into, (besides the *things* that do also wear such blasphemies upon them,) would be a task too great for me, and too wearisome for you. It shall satisfy then, that I give you notice that there are such *things* and *men* and *names;* and that I put you upon search to find out what they be. But whatsoever of the spirit, or soul, or life of Antichrist is in these names, men, or things, must be consumed by Christ, by the spirit of his mouth, and the brightness of his coming.

Another thing that I would touch upon is this; to wit, the lying legends and false miracles that Antichrist cries up: *these*, by the means of which such as dwell upon the earth are deceived, and made to adore and worship the beast,—these have their life and soul (as had those mentioned before) from the spirit of wickedness; and must be destroyed as they, namely, by Christ, the spirit of his mouth, and the brightness of his coming. For these are not of the body of Antichrist, but rather such implements, or whatever you will call them, by which the spirit and soul of Antichrist is conveyed into, and kept also alive in the body of Antichrist, which is the Church and Synagogue of Satan : you may call them organs and means by which that wicked [one] worketh in the mysteries of iniquity, for the begetting of and maintaining a lying and false belief of the religion of the beast. Nor can it be thought but that, as the antichristian statists of Antichrist, mentioned before, do put a dread and fear upon men that are worshippers of the beast and his image, to the holding of them still to his service, so these legends and miracles do, on the other hand, abridge and bind their consciences to that worship ; but all because of that spirit of Antichrist that is in them.

So then, here is the spirit of Antichrist diffusing itself into all the things pertaining to the kingdom of the beast ; for it dwells in the body of Antichrist, it dwells in the matters and things of worship of Antichrist, it dwells in the titles and names that are antichristian, and it dwells in the laws, legends, and miracles of Antichrist. And as it is the spirit of Antichrist, so it must be destroyed, not by sword, nor by bow, but by Christ, as fighting against it with the spirit of his mouth, and as conquering of it by the brightness of his coming.

III. *The destruction of the body of Antichrist.*

We come now to discourse of the *body* or flesh of Antichrist, and of the destruction of *that ;* for that must be destroyed also. Now the body of Antichrist is that church or synagogue in which the spirit of Antichrist dwells, or unto which the spirit of Antichrist is become a soul and life.

And this is to be destroyed, either as it is a body mystical, or under the more gross consideration.

First. As it is a body mystical, and so it is to be destroyed absolutely.

Second. As it is to be considered more grossly, and so it is to be destroyed conditionally. That is, if repentance doth not save the men that have gone to the making up of this body, and to the rejoicing in it.

As she is a body mystical, so she is to be destroyed the same way that the things of Antichrist, of which we discoursed before, were to be destroyed ; to wit, by Christ, the spirit of his mouth, and the brightness of his coming.

This then is the sum as to this : *that the church of Antichrist, as a church, shall be destroyed by the word and spirit of Christ.* Nor can anything in heaven prevent it, because the strong God has decreed it : " And a mighty angel took up a stone, like a great millstone, and cast it into the sea, saying, Thus with violence shall that great city Babylon be thrown down, and shall be found no

more at all." (Rev. xviii. 21.) This city, Babylon, is here sometimes considered in the *whole,* and sometimes as to the *parts* of it ; but always, whether in whole or in part, as *some,* or else as the *whole* of the antichristian church ; and as such, it must not be destroyed but by the means aforesaid. By which means her witchcrafts, spiritual whoredoms, spiritual murders, thefts, and blasphemies, shall be so detected and made manifest, so laid open, and so discovered, that the nations shall abhor her, flee from her, and buy her merchandise no more. (Rev. xviii. 11.) Hence her tempting things rot and moulder away ; for these will not keep, they are things not lasting, but that perish in the using : what then will they do when they are laid by ? Therefore it follows, " all things which were (thy) dainty and goodly (ones) are departed from thee, and thou shalt find them no more at all." (Rev. xviii. 14.) Now, if when she had things to trade with her dealers left her, how shall she think of a trade when she hath nothing to traffic with ? Her things are slain, and stink already, by the weapons that are made mention of before ; what then will her carcase do ? It follows then that as to her church-state, she must of necessity tumble : wherefore, from Rev. xviii. 22—24, you have the manner of her total ruin as a church, and something of the cause thereof.

But as she must, with reference to her body, be considered mystically as a church, so also she must be considered as a body of men, (this is that which I called more *grossly,*) and as such, against whom the wrath of God will burn, and against whom, if repentance prevent not, he will have indignation for ever. These, I say, are them ; to wit, as they are the body of the people that have been seduced by this spirit of Antichrist, that have been made use of to do all the mischiefs that have been done both to true religion and to the professors of it for this many hundred years ; wherefore these must not escape. Wherefore you find that after Antichrist, as to the spirit and mystery of Antichrist, is slain, that the body of Antichrist, or the heap of people that became her vassals, come next to be dealt withal.

Therefore the angel that standeth in the sun, makes a proclamation to all the fowls that fly in the midst of heaven, to gather themselves, and to come unto the supper of the great God ; that they may eat the flesh of the several sorts of the men that have been the lovers, the countenancers, the upholders and defenders of her antichristian state, worship, and falsehoods, (Rev. xix. 17, 18 :) for abundance of their hearts shall be hardened, and made yet more obdurate, that they may be destroyed for the wickedness that they have done.

Wherefore, you find (as did the enemies of the Church of old,) that they might revenge themselves for the loss of their idol, or antichristian state, begin a new war with the king, whose name is the Lord of hosts : " And I saw the beast, and the kings of the earth, and their armies, gathered together to make war against him that sat on the horse, and against his army." (Rev. xix. 19.)

Their implacable malice remained when their church-state was gone; wherefore they will now at last make another attempt upon the men that had been the instruments in Christ's hand to torment them that dwelt on the earth: of which more hereafter.

Now, therefore, is the last stroke of the batter, with reference to the destroying the body of Antichrist; only the head of this monster remains, and that is SATAN himself: wherefore the next news that we hear of is, that he is taken also— "And I saw an angel come down from heaven, having the key of the bottomless pit, and a great chain in his hand; and he laid hold on the dragon, that old serpent, which is the devil, and Satan, and bound him a thousand years, and cast him into the bottomless pit, and shut him up, and set a seal upon him, that he should deceive the nations no more till the thousand years should be fulfilled," &c. (Rev. xx. 1—3.)

IV. *Brave days when Antichrist is dead.*

Now, therefore, there will be nothing of Antichrist to be seen throughout the nations, but ruinous heaps, and desolate places. It is said of the army of the man of sin, when he came into the land of God's people, though it was before him "as the garden of Eden," yet behind him it would be as "a desolate wilderness," (Joel ii. 3;) such ruins would he make of the flock of God, and of all their ordinances and heavenly dainties. But when the days that I have spoken of shall come, it will be to him a time of retaliation; for it shall then be done unto Antichrist as he hath done to the Church of God: as he hath made women childless, so shall he be made childless; as he has made Zion sit upon the ground, so now must this wicked one come down and sit in the dust; yea, as he has made many churches desolations, so now shall he be also made a desolation. Wherefore, whoso will find his body, they must look for it in the side of the pit's mouth; and whoso will find his friends and companions, they must look for them there likewise. "They have set her a bed in the midst of the slain, with all her multitude: her graves are round about him, all of them uncircumcised, slain by the sword: though their terror was caused in the land of the living, yet have they borne their shame with them that go down to the pit; he is put in the midst of them that be slain. There is Meshech, Tubal, and all her multitude. There is Edom, her king, and all her princes, &c. There be the princes of the north, all of them," which, with their might, are laid "with them that are slain by the sword, and bare their shame with them that go down to the pit." (Ezek. xxxii. 25—30.) For, "as Babylon hath caused the slain of Israel to fall, so at Babylon shall fall the slain of all the earth." (Jer. li. 49.) The margin reads it thus: both Babylon is to fall, O ye slain of Israel! and with Babylon the slain of all the earth. Now, then, she is gone down, when all these things shall be fulfilled; and what remains now, but to talk of her, as folk use to do of them that are dead: for the day will come that the Church of God shall have no more of Antichrist, Babylon, or the mother of harlots, than only the remembrance of her; to wit, that there was such an enemy of God in the world, that there was such a superstitious, idolatrous, bloody people in the world. Wherefore the people that shall be born, that shall live to serve God in these happy days, they shall see Antichrist only in its ruins; they shall, like the sparrows, the little robins, and the wren, sit and sing, and chirrup one to another, while their eyes behold this dead hawk. "Here," shall they say, "did once the lion dwell; and there was once a dragon inhabited it; here did they live that were the murderers of the saints; and there another, that did use to set his throat against the heavens; but now in the places where these ravenous creatures lay, grows grass, with reeds and rushes," (Isa. xxxv. 7,)—or else, now their habitation is cursed, nettles grow, and so do thorns and brambles, where their palaces were wont to be. "And as no good was with them while they lived, so their name stinketh now they are dead; yea, as they wrought mischiefs, and lived like the wild beasts when they enjoyed their abundance, so now the wild beasts of the desert, yea, they of the desert, shall meet with the wild beasts of the island: and the satyr shall cry to his fellows, their houses shall be full of doleful creatures, even as devils and wicked spirits do haunt the desolate houses of the wicked, when they are dead." (Isa. xxxiv.) "And Babylon, the glory of kingdoms, the beauty of the Chaldees' excellency, shall be as when God overthrew Sodom and Gomorrah. It shall never be inhabited, neither shall it be dwelt in from generation to generation: neither shall the Arabian pitch tent there: neither shall the shepherds make their fold there." (Isa. xiii. 19, 20.)

A while after this, as was hinted before, the Christians will begin with detestation to ask what Antichrist was? where Antichrist dwelt? who were his members? and what he did in the world? and it shall be answered by them that shall have skill to consider his features by the word, by way of taunt and scorn, "Is this the man that made the earth to tremble, that did shake kingdoms; that made the world as a wilderness, and destroyed the cities thereof; that opened not the house of his prisoners? All the kings of the nations, even all of them lie in glory, every one in his own house. But thou art cast out of thy grave like an abominable branch; and as the raiment of those that are slain, thrust through with a sword, that go down to the stones of the pit, as a carcase trodden under feet." (Isa. xiv. 16—19.)

There will be a strange alteration when Antichrist is dead, and that both in the Church and in the world. The Church and the members of it then shall wear the name of their God in their foreheads; that is, they shall be bold in the profession of their king, and their God; yea, it shall be their glory to be godly; and carnal men shall praise them for it: the praise of the whole earth shall the Church of God be in those days.

Then there shall no more be a Canaanite in the house of the Lord: no lion shall be there; the unclean shall no more tread in the paths of God's people, but the ransomed of the Lord shall walk there.

Glory that has not been seen nor heard of by the people that need to walk in sackcloth shall now be set in the land of the living. For as it was said of Christ, with reference to his day, so it shall be said of saints, with reference to *this* day: many kings and righteous men have desired to see the things that will be seen then, and shall not see them: but without all doubt, the men that shall be born at this time will consider that these glories, and liberties, and privileges of theirs, cost the people that walked in the King of Babylon's fiery furnace, or that suffered the trials, troubles, and tyranny of the antichristian generation, more groans and hearty wishes than they did them that shall enjoy them. Thus, then, it will go; the afflicted prayed for them, and the possessors bless God for the enjoyment of them.

Oh! now shall the Church walk in the light of the Lord, and sit every man under his vine, and under his fig-tree, and none shall make him afraid.

"For the Lord will have mercy on Jacob, and will yet choose Israel, and set them in their own land, and the stranger shall be joined with them, and they shall cleave to the house of Jacob. And the people shall take them, and bring them to their place: and the house of Israel shall possess them in the land of the Lord, for servants and handmaids: and they shall take them captives whose captives they were, and they shall rule over their oppressors. And it shall come to pass in the day that the Lord shall give thee rest from thy sorrow, and from thy fear, and from the hard bondage wherein thou wast made to serve, that thou shalt take up this proverb against the king of Babylon, and say, How hath the oppressor ceased? the golden city (or the exactress of gold) ceased? The Lord hath broken the staff of the wicked, and the sceptre of the rulers. He who smote the people in wrath with a continual stroke; he that ruled the nations in anger, is persecuted, and none hindereth. The whole earth is at rest, and is quiet: they break forth into ringing. Yea, the fir-trees rejoice at thee, and the cedars of Lebanon, saying, Since thou art laid down, no feller is come up against us." (Isa. xiv. 1—8.)

Also the world will now be (as it were) another thing than it was in the days of Antichrist: now will kings, and princes, and nobles, and the whole commonalty be rid of that servitude and bondage which in former times (when they used to carry Bell and the Dragon upon their shoulders) they were subjected to. They were then a burthen to them, but now they are at ease. It is with the world, that are the slaves of Antichrist now, as it is with them that are slaves and captives to a whore: they must come when she calls, run when she bids, fight with and beat them that she saith miscall her, and spend what they can get by labour or fraud upon her, or she will be no more their whore, and they shall be no more her bosom ones. But now! Now it will be otherwise! Now they will have no whore to please! Now they will have none to put them upon persecuting of the saints! Now they shall not be made, as before, guilty of the blood of those against whom this gentleman shall take a pet. Now the world shall return and discern between the righteous and the wicked; yea, they shall cleave to, and countenance the people of God, being persuaded, as Laban was of Jacob, that the Lord will bless them for his people's sakes: for at this day, "the remnant of Jacob shall be (among the Gentiles) in the midst of many people, as a dew from the Lord, as the showers upon the grass, that tarrieth not for man, nor waiteth for the sons of men." (Micah v. 7.)

Also in these days men shall come flocking into the house of God, both kings and princes, and nobles, and the common people, as the doves do to their windows: and for that cause it is spoken to the Church, with reference to the latter days, saying, "Enlarge the place of thy tent, and let them stretch forth the curtains of thy habitations: spare not, lengthen thy cords and strengthen .thy stakes; for thou shalt break forth on the right hand, and on the left; and thy seed shall inherit the Gentiles, and make the desolate cities to be inhabited." (Isa. liv. 2, 3.)

Now will be broken up those prophecies and promises that to this day lie as under lock and key, and that cannot be opened until they be fulfilled. Now will the Spirit of God be poured forth abundantly, and our rivers shall be in high places; that is, shall break forth from the hearts of great ones; yea, then shall our waters be made deep: "And I will cause their rivers to run like oil, saith the Lord God." (Ezek. xxxii. 14.) Then shall the differences, the divisions, and debates that are among the godly cease; for men " shall see eye to eye, when the Lord shall bring again Zion," (Isa. lii. 8 :) yea, the watchmen of God's people shall do so; for it is for want of light *in them* that the lambs have so butted one another.

Now the Church of God shall read with great plainness the depths of providence, and the turnings and windings of all God's dark and intricate dispensations, through which she hath waded in the cloudy and dark day. Now, I say, they shall see there was an harmony in them, and that if one of them had been wanting, the work and way of her deliverance could not have been so full of the wisdom, and justice, and goodness of God: wherefore now will that song be sung with clearer notes than ever —" Great and marvellous are thy works, Lord God Almighty; just and true are thy ways, thou king of saints. Who shall not fear thee, O Lord, and glorify thy name? for thou only art holy: for all nations shall come and worship before thee; for thy judgments are made manifest." (Rev. xv. 3, 4.) And again, " For true and righteous are his judgments; for he hath judged the great whore which did corrupt the earth with her fornication, and hath avenged the blood of his servants at her hand." (Rev. xix. 2.)

CHAPTER III.

OF THE MANNER OF THE RUIN OF ANTICHRIST.

What Antichrist is, I have told you; and that as to his soul and body. I have also told you where, or in what things the spirit and life of Antichrist lieth, and how he shall reign for a time. I have, moreover, showed you that he shall be destroyed, and by what, and that with reference both to his soul and body. Wherefore, waving other things, I shall here only present you with a few short hints concerning the *manner* of his downfall.

There is the *downfall*, the *time* of the downfall, and the *manner* of the downfall of Antichrist.

The manner of the downfall of Antichrist may be considered either with respect to the *suddenness, unexpectedness, terribleness,* or *strangeness* thereof. It may also be considered with respect to the way of God's procedure with her, as to the *gradualness* thereof. As to the *suddenness* thereof, it is said to be in an *hour*. It is also to be, *when* by her *unexpected*; for then she saith, " I sit a queen." (Rev. xviii. 7.) For the terribleness of it, the nations shall shake at the sound of her fall. (Ezek. xxxi. 16, 17.) And for the *strangeness* thereof, it shall be to the wonder of the world, (Isa. xiv. 12;) it will be as when God overthrew Sodom.

But I shall not enlarge upon this method in my discourse, but shall show you the *manner* of the ruin of Antichrist, with respect to the *gradualness* thereof. (Ezek. xvi. 36—43. Rev. xviii. 8. Isa. xlvii. 9.)

Antichrist then shall be brought to ruin gradually; that is, by degrees—a part after a part; *here* a fenced city, and *there* a high tower, even until she is made to lie even with the ground. And yet all shall be within the compass of God's days, hours, or moments; for within the compass of these *limited* times Antichrist shall be destroyed.

Now, (as I said) he, she, Sodom, Egypt, Babylon, Antichrist, shall be destroyed, not all at once, after the way of our counting of time; but by step after step, piece after piece. And perhaps there may be in the words now following,

something that signifies this: they shall " show the king of Babylon that his city is taken at one end." (Jer. li. 31.) This is also showed by the vessels in which is contained the wrath of God for her, together with the manner of pouring of it out. The vessels in which it is contained are called VIALS; now a vial is that which letteth out what is contained in it by degrees, and not all at once.

There are also two things to be considered, as to the manner of its being poured out of them. The first respecteth the nature of the vial. The other, the *order* of the angels that poured forth this wrath.

For the first: the vial, as it letteth out what is in it by degrees, so it doth it with certain *gusts*, that are mixed with strength and violence, bolting it out with noise, &c.

As for the order of the angels, or that order that they observe, they plainly show that this enemy must come down by degrees; for that these vials are by them poured out one after another, each one working something of their own effects, before another is poured forth. The first is poured forth upon the antichristian *earth;* the second upon her *sea;* the third is poured forth upon her *rivers;* and the fourth upon her *sun;* the fifth is poured forth upon the *seat of the beast;* the sixth upon her *euphrates;* and the seventh into her *air.* (Rev. xvi. 2—17.) And, I say, they are poured forth not all at one time, but now one, and then another. Now, since by these vials Antichrist must fall, and since also they are poured forth successively, it is evident that this *man of sin*, this *son of perdition*, is to fall and die by degrees. He would not die at all, as is manifest by his wrestling with it; but he is a strong God that judges, and therefore he must come down: his friends also, with what cordials they can, will labour to lengthen out his tranquillity; but God hath set his bounds, and he cannot go beyond the time appointed.

We must also put a difference betwixt her being fought withal and wounded, and that of her dying the death. Michael and his angels have been holding of her in play a long season, but yet she is not dead, (Rev. xii.;) but, as I said, she shall descend in battle, and perish, and shall be found no more for ever.

I. *A tenth part of the city falls.*

To speak then to the manner of the ruin of this Antichrist, with respect to the gradualness thereof: it must piece after piece be overthrown, until at last every whit thereof is rolled down from the rocks as a burnt mountain.

And hence we read that this city falls first in a *tenth part* thereof, even while nine parts remain yet standing. Nor doth this tenth part, notwithstanding the faith and faithful testimony of the two witnesses, quite fall, until they are slain, and also raised again : for it is said, the same hour that the witnesses were raised, the tenth part of the city fell, (Rev. xi. 13 ;) the tenth part of that city that reigneth over the kings of the earth, which city is Sodom, Egypt, Babylon, or the great whore. (Rev. xvii. 18.)

By the city then, I understand the church of Antichrist in its utmost bounds; and so it reacheth as far as the beast with seven heads and ten horns hath dominion. Hence this city is also called cities, as one universe is called by the name of several countries, &c. And them cities also are called "the cities of the nations," (Rev. xvi. 19 ;) for as when they are put together they all make but one, so when they are considered apart they are found in number ten, and answer to the ten horns upon the heads of the (seven headed) beast that carries her, and do give her protection.

This then I take to be the meaning : that the antichristian church is divided into ten parts, and each part is put under one of the horns of the beast for protection ; but that aid and protection shall not help, when God shall come to execute judgment upon her: for it saith, "A tenth part of the city fell ;" that is, first, and as a forerunner of the fall of all the rest. Now where this tenth part is, or which of the ten parts must fall first, or whether indeed a tenth part is already fallen, that I will leave to those that are wiser than myself to determine.

But since I am speaking of the fall of a tenth part of Antichrist, a word or two about the means of the fall thereof.

The means of the fall of this tenth part, is an earthquake ; yet not such as is universal, over the face of all, but an earthquake in that tenth part where that city stood that should fall. Now by earthquakes here cannot be meant anything but such a shaking as unsettleth the foundations of this tenth part; but whether it shall be in this tenth part as a city, or in it as a state, that I shall not determine ; only my thoughts are, that it shall be an earthquake in that kingdom where this tenth part shall happen to be : an earthquake not to overthrow further than is appointed ; and that is the city which is called the tenth part of the great Antichrist. So far as that state is a state, so far then it is shaken for reformation, not for destruction ; for in the earthquake were slain seven thousand (names of) men ; and the remnant were affrighted, and gave glory to the God of heaven. But thus much for the first: great Babylon falleth first, in a tenth part of it.

II. *The other nine portions full.*

Again, the next step that the strong God taketh towards the utter overthrow of Antichrist, will be more sore upon the whole, though not at first universal neither, yet in conclusion, it shall throw down the nine parts that are left: for thus it is recorded—"And the cities of the nations fell :"

The *cities of the nations*, the antichristian churches, otherwise called the daughters of the mother of harlots, and abominations of the earth.

Now to show you the hand of God in this second stroke, wherewith the Lord will smite this enemy.

1. Here we have a great earthquake.

2. And then, the fall of the cities of the nations.

For the earthquake, it is said to be such as never was, "so mighty an earthquake, and so great," (Rev. xvi. 18 ;) for it extended itself as far as the other nine cities had any ground to stand on, for it shook the foundations of them all.

The fall of the cities was not immediately upon the shake that was made, but the earthquake produced an eruption, an eruption in the nine remaining parts of this city; and such an eruption as is of the worser sort, for it divided them into a three-headed division : "And the great city was divided into three parts"—the great city, to wit, the powers by which they were upheld. The meaning then is this : when God shall strike this man of sin the second time, he will not be so sparing as he was at first, when he struck but a tenth part to the ground ; but now he will so shake, so confound, so divide, so raise up Antichrist against himself, to wit, in the body and members of him, that they shall set to fighting, and to tearing one another in pieces, until they have consumed the whole of these nine parts. It was, saith the text, divided into three parts, which divisions are the worst of all : it will be therefore such a division as will bring them all to ruin. Hence it follows, "And the cities of the nations fell."

Wherefore, this three-cornered eruption will be the most dreadful to Antichrist that ever was : it will be like that that was in Jerusalem when she came to be laid even with the ground ; and like that that came upon the armies of the Gentiles, when they came up to fight against Jehoshaphat.

"For the children of Ammon and Moab stood up against the inhabitants of Mount Seir, utterly to slay and destroy them: and when they had made an end of the inhabitants of Seir, every one helped to destroy another." (2 Chron. xx. 23.) This, I say, is the division that this mighty earthquake shall make betwixt the horns that are left to these nine parts that remained, when the tenth part of the city fell. And this will come to pass through the increase of the heat of God's anger : for he is angry with the waters where the woman sitteth, because they have delivered up his beloved to the bloody whore ; wherefore, he now will give them blood to drink in fury.

Hence his beginning to deal with Antichrist is called, the beginning of revenges : "I will make," saith God, "mine arrows drunk with blood, and my sword shall devour flesh ; and that with the blood of the slain, and of the captives, from the beginning of revenges upon the enemy." (Deut.

xxxii. 42.) And therefore it is said again, that when God comes to do this work upon this Antichrist, it is because " it is the day of the Lord's vengeance, and the year of recompences for the controversy of Zion," (Isa. xxxiv. 8 :) " for the day of vengeance is in mine heart, and the year of my redeemed is come." (Isa. lxiii. 4.)

A peace, therefore, cannot be made among these cities when God has forbidden it : wherefore the effect of all is, the cities of the nations fall. There is therefore like to be no more good days for Antichrist after this earthquake has begun to shake her; no, nothing now is to be expected of her, but rumours, tumults, stirs, and uproars—" One post shall run to meet another, to show the king of Babylon that his city is taken at one end :" and again, " A rumour shall both come one year; and after that in another year shall come a rumour, and violence in the land, ruler against ruler," &c. (Jer. li. 31, 46.) So that this earthquake has driven away peace, shaken the foundations, and will cast the nine cities down to the ground

III. *The fall of Babylon the Great.*

And this is a second stroke that God will give this man of sin, and a third cometh quickly. Wherefore it follows upon the downfall of these cities of the nations, that great Babylon came into remembrance before God, to give unto her the cup of the wine of the fierceness of his wrath." Now then, have at great Babylon. *Great Babylon!* What is that ? Why, I take it to be the *mother*, the *metropolitan*, the *great whore herself*: for though sometimes, by the great whore, or great Babylon, we may understand, the church of Antichrist in general; yet by it is meant more properly the mother of the daughters, of whose overthrow we have spoken before. We are now then come to the threshold of the door of the house of the OLD one; to the door of the mother of harlots, and abomination of the earth. This, then, that but now is said to come into remembrance with God, is that which gave being to the cities destroyed before ; to wit, the mistress, the queen, the mother-church, as she calleth herself.

And this is the wisdom of God concerning her, that she should not be the first that should die; but that she should live to see the destruction of her daughters, and pine away under the sight and sense of that, even until judgment also shall overtake herself.

Thus Pharaoh and his chief ones did live to see the greatest part of Egypt destroyed before judgment overtook them, but at last it came to their doors also.

Zedekiah lived to see his children slain before his face, before judgment overtook him to his own personal destruction. (Jer. lii. 8—11.)

Babylon, also, when God sent the cup of his fury unto her, yet was to live to see the nations drink before her : " take the wine-cup of my fury,"

said God to the prophet, " and cause all the nations to whom I send thee, to drink it," (Jer. xxv. 15 :) to wit, all the kingdoms of the world which are upon the face of the earth. " And Sheshach shall drink after them." (Jer. xxv. 26.) But what was Sheshach ? may some say. I answer, it was Babylon, the princess of the world, and at that time the head of all those nations, (Dan. iv. 22,) as this queen is now the mother of harlots. Wherefore, the same prophet, speaking of the destruction of the same Sheshach, saith, " How is Sheshach taken ? and how is the praise of the whole earth surprised ? How is Babylon become an astonishment among the nations ?" (Jer. li. 41.)

Now, if this was the method of God's proceeding with his enemies in the way of his judgments of old, why may we not suppose that he will go the same way with his great enemy now: especially since those judgments mentioned before, were executed upon those, which, in some things, were figures of the great whore. Besides, we read here plainly, that when the cities of the nations were fallen, great Babylon came into remembrance before God, to give her to drink of the cup.

From all which I conclude, as I did before, that the mother, the metropolitan, the lady of kingdoms, shall live to see her daughters executed before her face : after which she shall come into consideration herself; for she must assuredly drink of the cup.

This destruction, therefore, must be last, for the reasons urged before, and also because she most deserves the bottom of the cup. The bottom is the dregs, the most bitter part, and that where the most heat, and fiercest wrath of God doth lie. (Ps. lxxv. 8 :) wherefore, although you find that by the first earthquake a great slaughter was made, and that a tenth part of the city fell, yet from that judgment some did escape ; " and the remnant were affrighted, and gave glory to the God of heaven." (Rev. xi. 13.) But now, this *earthquake*, by virtue of which the cities of the nations fall, and as an effect of which great Babylon is come into "remembrance before God," neither spares one of the daughters of this whore, nor any man that is a lover of them ; but it so is seconded by a " hailstorm," and that hailstorm worketh so in wrath, that not one escapes by repentance. Every hailstone was the weight of a talent, which some say is six pounds above half an hundred weight; by this, therefore, God shows, that now his anger was wrought up to the height. I know not wherewith so to compare these hailstones, as with the talent of lead that was laid over the mouth of the ephah, which was prepared to hold the woman, whose name was *wickedness*, this very whore of Babylon ; for that talent of lead was to keep down this mistress, that she might get no more out of the ephah, and these hailstones are to banish her out of the world. (Zech. v. 5—11.) Therefore it follows, that she must have the most heavy judgment, even the bottom of the cup.

"And great Babylon came into remembrance before God." To *remember* with God is to visit either with grace or wrath; God is said to remember Rachel, when he visited her with the blessing of a fruitful womb. (Gen. xxx. 22.) It is said, also, that God *remembered* Noah, when the time came on that he was to be delivered from the flood. (Gen. viii. 1.) Here, also, he is said to *remember* Babylon, that is, to visit her with his anger for the wickedness that she had committed: "To give unto her the cup of the wine of the fierceness of his wrath."

Now, then, is the time of iniquity, when it will be come to the full; and now also is the time of God's anger, when it will be come to the full; now, therefore, must the murders, and thefts, and blasphemies, and fornications, &c., belonging to this mother of harlots, be recompensed to the full, to wit, with the dregs of this cup; yet since the *hailstones* come by *weight*, and the wrath comes by *measure*, for so a talent and a cup imports, it follows, that the Almighty God, even in the midst of the heat of all this anger, will keep to the rules of justice and judgment while he is dealing with this enemy: he has not *passions* to carry him beyond rules of judgment; nor *weakness*, to cause him to fall short of doing justice: therefore he has, as was said, his judgments for her by weight, and his indignation by measure; but yet this weight and measure is not suited to her constitution, not with an intent to purge or refine her; but it is disposed according to the measure and nature of her iniquity, and comes to sweep her, as with the besom of destruction, until she is swept off from the face of all the earth.

And thus I have showed you the manner of the ruin of Antichrist; that is, that it will be gradual, part after part, until the whole be overthrown. And this truth may be applied both to the soul, as well as to the body of Antichrist; for the soul, spirit, or life of Antichrist must also after this manner be destroyed. And hence it is said to be consumed, that is, by degrees; for to consume, is to destroy by degrees: only this caution I would have the reader remember,—that much of the soul of Antichrist may be destroyed, when none of her daughters are; and that the destruction of her spirit is a certain forerunner of the destruction of her body in the manner that we have related.

Now since she is dying, let us ring her passing-bell; for when she is dead, we that live to see it, intend to *ring out*.

"For thus saith the Lord God; When I shall make thee a desolate city, like the cities that are not inhabited; when I shall bring up the deep upon thee, and great waters shall cover thee; when I shall bring thee down with them that descend into the pit, with the people of old time, and shall set thee in the low parts of the earth, in places desolate of old, with them that go down to the pit, that thou be not inhabited; and I shall set glory in the land of the living; I will make thee a terror, and thou shalt be no more: though thou be sought for, yet shalt thou never be found again, saith the Lord God." (Ezek. xxvi. 19—21.)

CHAPTER IV.

OF THE SIGNS OF THE APPROACH OF THE DOWN-FALL OF ANTICHRIST.

Having in the foregoing discourse spoken of Antichrist, his ruin, and the manner thereof, I now come to speak of the signs of the approach of her destruction. And whether I shall hit right, as to these, that I must leave to time to make manifest; and in the meanwhile to the wise in heart to judge.

That she shall fall there is nothing more certain; and when she is fallen, that she never shall rise again, is also as firmly decreed; yea, and showed too by him that cast the millstone into the sea, and said, "Thus with violence shall that great city, Babylon, be thrown down, and shall be found no more at all." (Rev. xviii. 21.) This is therefore her fate and destiny, from the mouth of the holy one; and is sealed up in the scriptures of truth, for the comfort of the people that have been afflicted by her.

True, the time of her fall is not certainly known by the saints, nor *at all believed by her;* wherefore, her plagues must come unlooked for by her. And as to the saints, their guesses as to the *time* of her ruin, must needs be *conjectural* and uncertain. For her part, she shall say, and that when she stands where she must suddenly fall, "I shall be a lady for ever." And as to the saints that would very willingly see her downfall, how often have they been mistaken as to the set time thereof.

Nor have I been without thought but that this mistake of the godly may become a snare to Antichrist, and a trap to her upholders. For what can be a greater judgment, or more effectually harden the hearts of the wicked, than for them to behold that the predictions, prophecies, expectation and hopes of their enemies (as to their ruin) should quite (as to the time) be frustrate, and made void.

Moses prophesied, and the people hoped that God would give Israel the land of Canaan; and yet the Canaanites beat them.

Jeremiah prophesied that the enemy should come and take the city of Jerusalem; but because he came once, and went back without doing it, how stout and hardened were the hearts of that people against all the rest of his prophetic sayings as to such a thing. Now the error lay not in these prophets, but in the people's mistaking the times: and if mistakes do so much harden the heart of the wicked, what will they do to such of them who make it their business to blind and harden their hearts against God, by abusing all truths? Surely, when men seek to harden their hearts by abusing of truth, they will do it to purpose when they have also the advantage of the weakness of their professed enemies to do it by: especially when their enemies shall say they speak by the word of the Lord, and time shall manifest it to be both a mistake and a falsehood.

It is to be bewailed, namely, the forwardness of some in this matter, who have predicted concerning the *time* of the downfall of Antichrist, to the shame of them and their brethren: nor will the wrong that such by their boldness have done to the Church of God, be ever repaired by them nor their works. But the judgments of God are a great deep; and therefore who can tell, since the enemy of God would not be convinced by the power of truth, and the virtuous lives of some, but that God might leave them to be snared, hardened and emboldened to run upon their unavoidable destruction, by the lies and lightness of others. They begin to vaunt it already, and to say, Where is the word of the Lord, as to this, let it come now. But when Agag said, "surely the bitterness of death is past," then was the time for him to be hewn in pieces. (1 Sam. xv. 32, 33.) I shall not therefore meddle with the times and seasons which the Father hath put in his own power; no, though they as to Antichrist's ruin are revealed; because by the Holy Ghost there is a challenge made, notwithstanding the time is set, and by the word related to the man of wisdom, to find it out if he can. (Rev. xiii. 18.)

If Samson's riddle was so puzzling, what shall we think of this? and though the angel hath intimated that this sealed matter shall be opened towards the time of the end, (Dan. xii. 9;) yet it is evident some have either been too hasty, or presumed too much upon their own abilities: for I am sure they have missed the mark, hardened the heart of the enemy, stumbled the weak, and shamed them that loved them.

But since the most high hath irreversibly determined her downfall also, let us see if we can have better success in discoursing upon the *signs*, than others have had who have meddled with the *timing* thereof.

I. *The First Sign.*

First then: the downfall and ruin of Antichrist draws near, *when the Church and people of God are driven from all those hiding-places that God has prepared for them in the wilderness.* The Church of God, when the dragon did his worst, had an hiding-place prepared her of God, that she might not utterly be devoured by him; and so shall have till the time of his end shall come.

Of this you read in the 12th of the Revelations, a place worthy to be noted for this. But now, when the time of the ruin of Antichrist draws on, then is the Church deprived of her shelter, and laid open, as one would think, to be utterly swallowed up for ever, having no more place in the wilderness—that is, among the nations—to hide herself from the face of the serpent. But how comes this to be a *sign* of the approach of the ruin of Antichrist? Why thus: the time of this beast's war with the Church of God, and the time that the Church shall have an hiding-place in the wilderness, are both of a length, the one continuing *forty-two months*, the other *a thousand two hundred and threescore days.* Now since the war that this beast makes with the woman and her seed, and the woman's hiding-place in the wilderness from his face, are for length of time the same, what hindereth but that when the woman and her seed can find no more shelter in the nations, the time that the beast hath allotted him to make war against her should be finished also? when we therefore shall see that plots and conspiracies, that designs for utter ruin, are laid against God's Church all the world over, and that none of the kings, princes, or mighty states of the world, will open their doors, or give them a city for refuge, then is the ruin of Antichrist at hand: for Haman's plot, though the most universal that ever yet was hatching, (being laid in a hundred and twenty-seven provinces,) did but presage the deliverance and exaltation of the Jews, and the hanging of Haman and his sons: yea, and I take it, that the very day that this great enemy had set for the utter overthrow of the Church, God made the day in which their deliverance began, and that from whence it was completed: and I take *that* to be a type of *this.*

There is but one thing that I can think of that can give matter of a show of doubt about this thing; and that is, though the time of this war against the saints, and that of the woman's shelter in the wilderness as to length be one and the same, yet whether they did commence together, and begin to take their rise, as men do that begin to run a race? a word, therefore, to this. I suppose they did commence much together; for else with whom should this beast make war, and how should the Church escape? Or, if the beast began his war before the woman began to have a hiding-place, why was she not swallowed up, since in the wilderness was her only place of shelter? Again, what needed the woman to have a place of shelter in the wilderness, when there was no war made against her? And yet this must be, if her thousand two hundred and threescore days began before the beast's forty-two months: but they ended both together; for the *beast* could not kill the *witnesses* before they had finished their testimony; which testimony of theirs lasted this full time that the beast had granted him to make war with them, to wit, one thousand two hundred and threescore days. Therefore their times went out together, as will be made appear, if you consider also that the witnesses were slain, by virtue, not of the old, but of a new war levied against them; and that, as it should seem, at the very time when her hiding-place was taken from her; for then indeed, for a little season, will the Church of God be overcome, as I shall show by and by.

Wherefore, let God's people consider and remember that when God's church is absolutely forlorn, and has no hiding-place any longer in the world, the kingdom of Antichrist will quickly begin to tumble. Nor is this the alone place from whence we may gather these conclusions.

The time of Pharaoh's tyranny, of his life, and of the deliverance of the children of Israel, came out much together; as any will discern that shall consider the history of them. (Gen. xv. 13.)

David, when Saul did sorely prosecute him, fled last into the wilderness to Achish, the King of Gath, a Philistine, for shelter; and he gave him Ziklag for his refuge. (1 Sam. xxvii. 5, 6.) And that place so continued to David until just about the time in which Saul must die; and then behold, David's Ziklag is burnt with fire, and himself stript naked of harbour! (1 Sam. xxx. 1.) But what matter! the time of Saul's life, as well as of David's Ziklag, was now upon expiring; for within three or four days after, David became King of Israel.

And thus also it was with the Babel-beast: his time expired when the captivity of Israel was upon the finishing; then was the time of his land come, and in that very night was Belshazzar, the King of the Chaldeans, slain. (Dan. v. 25—30.)

Thus, therefore, it will happen to the Church in the latter days: her place of shelter in the wilderness, her Ziklag will be taken from her, about the time that the war that the beast has to make upon the woman and her seed shall be finished. But now the Church is not therefore immediately delivered, when her Ziklag is taken from her; for after that the beast levieth a new war, to the overcoming and killing of the Church. I say, therefore, that this is a sign, not of the downfall of Antichrist, but of the approach thereof: for the Church's bondage shall continue but three days, and a little after this. Much like to this was that of David; for after he had lost his Ziklag, for two or three days he had sore distress; but lo, then came the kingdom to him.

Indeed, sense and reason saith it is a fearful thing for the Church of God to be exposed to the rage of her enemy all over the world at once; and that all nations should shut up their gates, let down their portcullises, bolt up their doors, and set open their flood-gates to destroy them: but so will be the dispensation of God, to the end deliverance may be the sweeter, and the enemies fall the more headlong, and the arm of God the more manifest, both *for* the one, and *against* the other. And in this will that scripture be fulfilled: " And there shall be a time of trouble, such as never was since there was a nation, and at that time thy people shall be delivered, every one that shall be found written in the book." (Dan. xii. 1.)

Let us gather up what has been said again; namely, that it is a sign of the approach of the ruin of Antichrist, when God's Church can find no more shelter in the wilderness, because when her Ziklag is burned, the time of the war that the beast is to make against her is finished. Wherefore, when she hath given one desperate struggle more, and laid the Church of God, or his witnesses, for dead, in the street of his great city, for three days and an half, then comes the kingdom, and the long long-looked-for rest and glory. Wherefore it remains, that an angel should stand in the sun, and make proclamation to all the fowls that fly in the midst of heaven, to gather themselves together to the supper of the great God: " That ye may eat the flesh of kings, and the flesh of captains, and the flesh of mighty men, and the flesh of horses, and of them that sit on them; and the flesh of all men, both free and bond, both small and great." (Rev. xix. 18.) This is to be after the forty-two months of the beast; and consequently, after the thousand two hundred and threescore days that the Church was to be in sackcloth; yea, after the resurrection of the witnesses, as is evident by that which follows: " And the beast was taken, (that is, after the second year,) and with him the false prophet that wrought miracles before him, with which he deceived them that had received the mark of the beast, and them that worshipped his image; these both were cast alive into a lake of fire burning with brimstone." (Rev. xix. 20.)

II. *The Second Sign.*

Another sign of the approach of the ruin of Antichrist is this: towards the end of her reign the nations will be made to see her baseness, and to abhor her and her ways. They will, I say, be made to see these things in order to her ruin: also, when they shall be made to see, her ruin will not be far off. For so long as the nations and their rulers shall continue in that dead sleep that she hath bewitched them into, by their drinking of the wine of her fornication, so long we have no ground to think that her ruin is at the door; but when God shall lay her before kings, and shall discover her nakedness to the nations, then be sure her destruction is at hand. Hence you read, that precedent to her downfall: An angel comes down from heaven and lightens the earth with his glory. [*The earth,*] that is, the kingdoms, countries, and nations where the woman sitteth, or they that border thereupon. [*Enlightened,*] to let them see the filthiness of the whore. [*With his glory,*] with the doctrine that he had commission to preach against her for the discovering of her lewdness to the earth. This also was the way that God took with backsliding Israel of old, (and she was a type of our religious Babel,) when he intended to bring her to judgment for her sins, (Ezek. xvi. 37;) and this is the way that God will take to destroy our religious Antichrist, when he comes to deliver his people out of her hand.

For though the people that suffer at her hand can do nothing against her but lay in prayers and tears against her before the God of heaven, and bear their witness against her before the gods of the earth, yet when kings shall come to be concerned—and they will count themselves concerned when they shall see how they have been deceived by her—then let her look to it.

"Behold, I am against thee, saith the Lord of hosts; and I will discover thy skirts upon thy face; and I will show the nations thy nakedness, and the kingdoms thy shame; and I will cast abominable filth upon thee, and make thee vile, and will set thee as a gazing-stock." And what follows? "And it shall come to pass, that all they that look upon thee shall flee from thee and say, Nineveh is laid waste: who will bemoan her? whence shall I seek comforters for thee?" (Nahum iii. 5, 6.)

Wherefore there wants nothing but that she be discovered to the nations and their kings, for did they but see her, though they lay yet in her bosom, they would rise up against her that she must die; wherefore it is written again, I will "bring forth a fire from the midst of thee; it shall devour thee: and I will bring thee to ashes upon the earth in the sight of all them that behold thee." (Ezek. xxviii. 18.)

The chief of the wisdom of Antichrist this day is laid out, if, perhaps, by it she may cover her nakedness, and keep it from the eyes of kings and their people. But God has said it shall not avail: "Thy nakedness shall be uncovered; yea, thy shame shall be seen: I will take vengeance; and I will not meet thee as a man." (Isa. xlvii. 3.) But how will he make her naked? Verily, by kings. But how shall kings do it? Why, by virtue of the glory of the angel; yea, they "shall make her desolate and naked, and shall eat her flesh, and burn her with fire." (Rev. xvii. 16.)

Let this, I pray, be considered, that Antichrist shall not down but by the hand of kings. The preacher then kills her soul, and the king kills her body. And why should not the kings have it granted unto them that she should fall by their hand? the kings are those that she has abused, that she has in the grossest manner abused, and has served herself of them; but the time of the end of Antichrist, mystery, Babylon, is coming, "and then many nations and great kings shall serve themselves of him." (Jer. xxvii. 7.)

Nor shall all the tricks, lies, and deceit under which formerly she used to shroud herself be able to prove a balm to her any longer; no, "in vain shalt thou use many medicines," for no cure shall be unto thee; "the nations have heard of thy shame." (Jer. xlvi. 11, 12.)

Babylon has for a long time been "a lady of kingdoms," and "a golden cup in the Lord's hand;" the nations also have largely drank of her cup, and the kings have committed fornication with her. (Rev. xviii. 3.) But now the angel is come down, and hath *enlightened the earth with his glory*. Wherefore now it follows immediately— "Babylon is fallen! is fallen!" that is, in the eyes and esteem of the nations as well as otherwise.

True, some of the kings will bewail her fall, and will cry, "Alas! alas!" when they see that they cannot help her; for that they shall see, as is evident, because they stand afar off to lament her, "afar off for the fear of her torment." The kings, therefore, into whose hands God shall deliver her, and who shall execute his judgments upon her, shall be more mighty and powerful to bring her down than shall be the whole world besides to uphold her.

And this observe further, that as the kings that shall hate her, shall hate her because in the light of the glory of the angel they are made able to see her filthiness, so the kings that shall bewail her are such as in judgment are left in the dark, and that shall be bewitched by her to the end. This, therefore, will let us see something of the meaning of God, in that he has drawn off from her some of the kings already, to wit, that he might train them up by the light of the gospel, that they may be expert, like men of war, to scale her walls, when the King of kings shall give out the commandment to them so to do.

There has been a great deal of talk in the countries about the ruin and destruction of Babylon, but could we see more of the kings engaged against her, we should hope groundedly that her fall was at the door. Well, blessed be God for what kings there are, and the Lord turn the hearts of many more to hate her.

Some, as I said before, have adventured to foretell the *time* of her downfall, but give me the *signs* thereof. This, therefore, is a sign, a sign that her downfall approaches, when God shall lay her nakedness before the nations, and put it into the hearts of kings to abhor her. The signs of the times the Lord Jesus would have us mind, and because the Jews neglected them, though as to the time they hit pretty right, yet they missed of the thing that the time brought forth.

III. *The Third Sign.*

A third sign of the approach of the ruin of Antichrist is this—"When Babylon is become the habitation of devils," &c., then the downfall thereof is upon us. True, Babylon was always an habitation for devils, but not an habitation *only* for them; Israel once dwelt there, and *our* Antichrist was sometimes a place of residence for good men. The meaning, then, is—When you shall see the Church and people of God so forsake her that she is in a manner left to herself and to her disciples, then she is to fall quickly: when you hear it proclaimed by them that are yet in her of God's people, "We would have healed Babylon, but she is not healed: forsake her, and let us go every one into his own country," (Jer.

li. 9,) then she will soon be hissed out of the world: for this is the way of the wisdom of God—namely, to bring his people out of a city or place when he intends the ruin of that place. When God was about to destroy the *old* world, he put his Noah into an ark; when God was about to destroy Sodom, he sent his Lot away thence to Zoar; when Christ was about to destroy Jerusalem, he bid his disciples flee from the midst of that; and when there shall be by God a hissing for his people, and when they shall hear him, and obey, and gather to him, then you shall see what will become of this enemy of Christ:—" I will hiss for them, and gather them, for I have redeemed them." (Zech. x. 8—12.)

I say, therefore, when Babylon shall become the habitation of devils, a hold for all foul spirits, and a cage for every unclean and hateful bird, then Babylon is fallen.

And thus the angel that lightened the earth with his glory, proclaimed—"Babylon the great is fallen! is fallen! and is become the habitation of devils, and a hold for every foul spirit, and a cage for every unclean and hateful bird." Wherefore it must be that by that her time is come that she should fall, God will have gleaned his people from the midst of her. And when God shall have gleaned his people from the midst of her, those that are left behind will appear more than ever to be what they are, to wit, devils, foul spirits, and hateful birds; wherefore now will Antichrist appear in his own most proper colours.

But to comment a little upon the words.

Babylon, mystery Babylon. The antichristian church.

Is fallen! is fallen! In the eyes and faith of the godly, by her dropping into the dregs of degeneracy, and so is become the habitation of devils, &c., in order to her falling into utter and unavoidable destruction for ever.

Is become. That is, through the labour of the fanners and winnowers that God hath sent to fan Babylon, and to fetch out his people, that she might be left to her chaff: " I will send" (saith God to Babylon) " fanners that shall fan her, and that shall empty her land" (of good men); " for in the day of trouble they shall be against her round about." (Jer. li. 2.)

An habitation of devils. Devils: not such by *nature*, but by *practice*. Incarnate devils. For when the time is come that Babylon must be destroyed, she shall be found to be an habitation for the most vile of the sons of men: for as devils have acted towards the world, so shall the sons of this sorceress, and this whore, act towards Christ and his members in the latter days. And perhaps the departing of Zion from the midst of her will blow her up into this spirit of devilism. Let God's people, therefore, when Antichrist is towards her end, look for nothing from her but what the devil in times past used to do, to wit, all sinful subtlety, malice, wrath, fraud, deceit, lying, murder, false

accusings, and implacable madness of spirit to do them mischief. (But, Lord God! think I, what will become of good men! and where will they be safe in such days? only I comfort myself by saying to myself again, this is a sign that the ruin of Antichrist is at the door.) But this, I say, he must needs be a *tuneable* man that shall be able in those days to sing this song to himself at all seasons: for this is to drive reason backward, and to set the cart before the horse. For what will the good man's reason say when it seeth all Babylonians are become devils, but that the Church of God will certainly be torn in pieces? But behold! the text and the Holy Ghost runs counter: " Babylon is fallen! is fallen! and" (or, for it) " is become the habitation of devils." These words for certain are the words of an holy angel, for it could not have entered into the heart of mere man to have conceived them.

An habitation. To be an habitation (for devils) is to be their house, their dwelling-place, their place of privilege, their place of rest and abode, or thither whither they have right to go. And thus will Babylon be; that is, an house, an habitation, a dwelling-place, and a place of rest, only for devilish-minded men; thither may such men come; for such her doors stand open, and there may such inhabit. When, therefore, you see good men come out thence, and all sorts of wicked men flock in thither, then know that Babylon is near her end.

And a hold for every foul spirit. Understand by spirit, either those that are devils by nature, or such as are such otherwise. But I think that the angel chiefly intends all manner of unclean and filthy spirits; and so the church and members of Babylon, their only place of safety: or if you understand it of the uncleanness of the spirits and minds of men, then the meaning is that they are called foul spirits, in allusion to those of devils which go by the same name. (Matt. ix. 25.) But, however, or which way soever taken, it seems Babylon is their *hold;* that is, their place of defence: for by an hold, we often understand a place of strength, a castle, a fort, a tower; so that these devils, these foul-spirited men, these Babylonians, will not only find house-room and harbour in Babel, but shelter, defence, and protection, when she is near her ruin: yea, they will find her an upholder to them, and a countenancer of them, in all their foul and devilish pranks; yea, such an hold shall she be to such foul spirits in such foul acts, that it shall not be possible that they should be driven from her, or from them : for an *hold* is often taken in the scriptures for a place that is impregnable, and must be so taken here. This intimates, then, that some faint opposition by the kings and nations will be made against these inhabiters, foul spirits, but to little purpose, until the time of her land shall come, (Jer. xxvii. 7;) for in their hold they still will be secured and defended from what reason, law, and scripture can or would do unto them. Thus when we see how Babel towards her end will be filled, and with what, to wit, with devils and foul spirits; yea, and that she will not only be an habitation, but a place of defence for such.

And a cage for every unclean and hateful bird. Those that before are called devils, and foul spirits, are also here called birds, unclean and hateful beasts. By the term [*birds,*] he may allude to that of the prophet Isaiah, where these unclean birds are mentioned. (Isa. xxxiv. 11—17.) And by *cage,* he may allude to the prophet Jeremiah, from whom, as I think, the Holy Ghost takes those words; but then we must put *men* in the place of *birds,* and the *Babylonian kingdom* for the *cage.* (Jer. v. 27.)

Every unclean bird. As was said before, a hold for *every* foul spirit. These unclean birds, therefore, are not all of one feather, or kind, but of *all* and *every* kind; and it intimates that the worst act of all professions shall be as in a cage, in Babylon, a little before her downfall. But, I say, if they will not be all of one feather, yet in their temper they will somewhat agree, being either in *shape,* monstrous; of *appetite,* ravenous; or of *inclination,* lovers of the night: for of all these sorts were the forbidden, or unclean birds, among the Jews. Now since these unclean birds are not all of one feather, or kind, it intimates that the basest of all sorts, sects, professions, and degrees, shall take shelter in Babylon towards her end; and that they shall there, in their temper, unanimously agree to show themselves monstrous, to devour and eat up the poor and needy, and to blow out the light of the gospel.

A cage. Not to imprison them in, but for them to sit and sing in, to confer their notes in, to make melodious music in, I mean, melodious to their own thinking; for the ass thinks that he sings full favouredly, and the owl endeavours to lift up her voice above all the birds of the wood : but it will be a prediction of her fall, and that her ruin is at the door.

Of these birds Zephaniah speaks, when he prophesies of the downfall of Nineveh, saying, " The cormorant and the bittern shall lodge in the uppermost lintels of it, their voice shall sing in the windows (when) desolation shall be in the thresholds." (Zeph. ii. 14.) An unseasonable time to sing in; for when death is coming in at the door. mourning should be in the chambers. But this is the judgment of God, that she should be a cage for every unclean bird to sing in, even then when her destruction and desolation cometh upon her.

To sing, as in a cage, doth also denote security, and that the heart is far from fear ; for she saith, I shall see no sorrow in that hour in which her judgment comes.

But is this a sign of the approach of the ruin of Antichrist? And must those that shall live to see those days rejoice when these things begin to come to pass? Are not these things rather a sign that the utter overthrow of the Church of God is at the door? Indeed, to sense it is, and reason will be apt to say so. But hark what the Holy Ghost saith : " She is fallen! is fallen now !"

When, therefore, we shall see men like devils; yea, every foul spirit, and hateful bird, flock to, and take shelter in Babylon; let us not be frighted or dejected, but pluck up our hearts, and say, this is one of the signs that the downfall of Babylon is near. Wherefore it follows, after that the prophet had told us that these birds should dwell in the land of the people of God's curse, (Isa. xxxiv.,) " that the wilderness and the solitary place shall be glad for them, (for that they are there,) and the desert shall rejoice, and blossom as the rose." (Isa. xxxv. 1.) *It shall blossom as a rose:* " it shall blossom," saith he, " abundantly, and rejoice even with joy and singing : the glory of Lebanon shall be given unto it, the excellency of Carmel and Sharon, they shall see the glory of the Lord, and excellency of our God." (Isa. xxxv. 2.) And to support the weak from those fears that in those days will be pulling of them down, he adds, " Strengthen ye the weak hands, and confirm the feeble knees. Say to them that are of a fearful heart, Be strong, fear not : behold, your God will come with vengeance, even God with a recompense, he will come and save you. Then the eyes of the blind shall be opened, and the ears of the deaf shall be unstopped. Then shall the lame man leap as an hart, and the tongue of the dumb sing : for in the wilderness shall waters break out, and streams in the desert. And the parched ground shall become a pool, and the thirsty land springs of water : in the habitation of dragons where each lay, shall be grass, with reeds and rushes. And an highway shall be there, and a way, and it shall be called the way of holiness; the unclean shall not pass over it ; but it shall be for those : the wayfaring men, though fools, shall not err therein. No lion shall be there, nor any ravenous beast shall go up thereon, it shall not be found there; but the redeemed shall walk there. And the ransomed of the Lord shall return, and come to Zion with songs and everlasting joy upon their heads : they shall obtain joy and gladness, and sorrow and sighing shall flee away." (Isa. xxxv. 3—10.)

What say ye now, ye sons of God! Will you learn to make a judgment of things according to the mystery of the wisdom of God, or will ye longer conclude according to sense and reason : " He turneth the shadow of death into the morning," (Amos v. 8 :) and commands ofttimes that the fairest day should succeed the foulest night. Wherefore, when we see these devils, foul spirits, and unclean birds in Babylon; yea, when we see good men leave her, and the vilest run in to her, then let us sing the angels' song, and say, " Babylon the great is fallen! is fallen, and is become the habitation of devils, and a hold for every foul spirit, and a cage for every unclean and hateful bird."

IV. *The Fourth Sign.*

Another sign of the approach of the ruin of Antichrist is, "The Slaying of the Witnesses:" for the witnesses are to be slain before the fall of Antichrist; and that by the hand of the beast, who shall manage the members of Antichrist, having qualified them before for that work, with those qualifications of which you read in the sign foregoing. For what can better fit a generation for such a work, than to be themselves all turned devils, and also succourers of all foul spirits. Wherefore, they must be the wickedest of men that shall do this: the very scum of the nations, and the very vilest of people. Nor is this a new notion: God threatened to give his sanctuary " into the hands of strangers for a prey, and to the wicked of the earth for a spoil," (Ezek. vii. 21:) to robbers, burglars, and they should defile it. (Ezek. vii. 22.) Again, saith God of his people, " I will bring the worst of the heathen, and they shall possess their houses." (Ezek. vii. 24.) For the truth is, this work is too bad for men either of reason or conscience to be found in the practice of. The hangman is usually none of the best. The witnesses are also to be slain; but not a man, but a beast must slay them; " a den of thieves, a hold of foul spirits," must do it.

That the witnesses must be slain before the fall of Babylon has been hinted already. Also, that their death is a forerunner of the ruin of Antichrist, has before been touched upon; but in this place I shall a little enlarge.

And therefore I proceed: " And when they shall have finished their testimony, the beast that ascendeth out of the bottomless pit shall make war against them, and shall overcome them, and kill them. And their dead bodies shall lie in the street of the great city, which spiritually is called Sodom and Egypt, where also our Lord was crucified. And they of the people, and kindreds, and tongues, and nations, shall see their dead bodies three days and an half, and shall not suffer their dead bodies to be put in graves." (Rev. xi. 7—9.) " And after three days and an half, the Spirit of life from God entered into them, and they stood upon their feet; and great fear fell upon them who saw them. And they heard a great voice from heaven, saying unto them, Come up hither: And they ascended up to heaven in a cloud, and their enemies beheld them." (Rev. xi. 11, 12.)

Thus you see their *death* is before their *deliverance*. Also their death is to be by the hand of the beast; to wit, by the men that have and hold his mark, and that of his image, and that are of the number of his name. You see also that their death is not only a forerunner of their deliverance, but a *sign* that their deliverance is at

the door; since the one is but three days and an half before the other.

And if a short comment upon this text will give a little light to the reader, I shall not count my labour lost.

And when they shall have finished their testimony. When, or about the time they have done their work of witness-bearing for God in the world: when they have made or are making an end of giving their testimony for Christ, and against the witchcrafts, idolatries, sorceries, fornications, thefts, murders, and wickedness of Antichrist; then, and not till then.

The beast that ascended out of the bottomless pit. The *beast:* the power that carrieth and beareth up Antichrist, the mother of harlots: the beast upon which the woman sitteth, and by the heads and horns of which she is protected and defended; he is said to ascend out of the bottomless pit: for that he manifesteth by his doings that he was born there, and came to do the work of the king thereof.

Shall make war against them. We read that he made war against them all the time of their prophesying in sackcloth, while they were bearing their testimony against his doing; and that his commission was, that he should have leave to make war so long. (Rev. xii. 6.) But here we read again, that when they had finished their testimony, and so consequently he had run out the time of his first commission for war, he makes war again. So that this war which now he raiseth against them seems to be another, a new war, and such as is grounded upon other, to wit, new arguments, besides those upon which his first war stood. By his first war he sought to beat down and overthrow *their testimony.* (Rev. xiii. 4.) By this war he seeketh to overthrow *themselves.* The first war he made was grounded upon a vain *confidence* of his ability to destroy their faith; but this last was grounded upon *madness* against them, because their testimony had prevailed against him: wherefore, *torment,* wherewith these witnesses by their testimony tormented him and his followers, was the cause of this last war. And this is insinuated when he saith, " they made merry for their victory over them, because these two prophets," (to wit, by their testimony,) " tormented them that dwelt on the earth." (Rev. xi. 10.)

The beast, therefore, will make a war against the witnesses all the time of their prophesying in sackcloth, which will be a thousand two hundred and threescore days. (Rev. xii. 6.) In all which time they shall give him the foil, and overcome by their faith and testimony; and be proclaimed more than conquerors over him, through the Christ that loved them. But now in this second war he overcomes them, " he overcomes them, and kills them."

Jezebel for a long time made war against Elias the prophet, seeking to overthrow the worship of God which he maintained, and to establish the religion of Baal: but when she saw that by all she could do she got nothing, but that the prophet got the day of her worship, priests and worshippers, (1 Kings xviii. 30—40,) she breaks out into a rage, as one tormented almost to death, and raises a new war; not now against his religion, but his person, and desperately swears by all the gods that she had, that by to-morrow that time the life of the prophet should be as the life of one of her priests whom he had slain for an idolater. (1 Kings xix. 2.) When the devil sees that he cannot do by argument, he will try if he can by blows.

When Zedekiah, the son of Chenanah, saw that with argument he could not overcome Micaiah, he steps to him, and takes him a box of the ear. (1 Kings xxii. 24.) This new war is a box of the ear which the beast will give the witnesses, because they overcame him by their faith and testimony, all the time that the first war lasted.

Now how long this second war will last, and what strugglings the witnesses will make before he shall overcome them, I know not: this I know, that the text saith, " By this war he shall overcome them."

And shall overcome them. Saints are not said to be overcome when they are imprisoned, banished, and killed for their faithful testimony: no, by these things *they* overcome. To overcome, then is to get the mastery, to subdue, to turn out of possession, to take and hold captive, to strip the subdued of power and privilege, as is sufficiently manifest both by scripture and reason: " For of whom a man is overcome, of the same he is brought in bondage." (2 Pet. ii. 19.)

So, then, when he is said to overcome them, it is meant he shall get the mastery of them, they shall grow faint before him, have no heart or spirit to bear up in their profession against him: *against him*, I say, as she did the thousand two hundred and three score days' war with him; for then they were overcomers, and did bear away the garland.

Nor do I, for my part, wonder at this, when I consider that these witnesses are a succession of good men; and that when Israel came out of Egypt of old, the feeble and weak-handed did come behind. (Deut. xxv. 17—19.) It will be the lot, therefore of the Church, in the latter end of the reign of the beast, to be feeble and weak in their profession, the valiant ones having gone before: these will come in when those that were able have bravely borne their testimony, or when they are upon finishing of that; in comparison of whom they that come after will be but like eggs to the cocks of the game; wherefore they must needs be crushed, cowed, and overcome. And then will the beast boast himself, as did his type of old, and say, " My hand hath found, as a nest, the riches of the people; and as one gathereth eggs that are left, have I gathered all the earth, and there was none that moved the wing, or opened the mouth, or peeped." (Isa. x. 14.)

A sad time, and it is to happen to the people that are left, to the latter end of the witness-bearers; and that, too, when they shall have finished their testimony.

Of this tyranny the cruelty of Amalek was a type, who, as was hinted before, smote the hindermost, the weak: but his judgment is, that " he shall perish for ever."

And shall overcome them. There are two ways of overcoming; to wit, by power and policy; and perhaps by both these ways they may be overcome. However, overcome they shall be; for so saith the holy word of God; yea, the beast shall overcome them. Wherefore the Church of God, at that day, will be under such a cloud as she never was since Christ's day. Now how long they shall thus be held captive before they are brought to execution—whether the beast will ride in triumph while they are in his bonds, or whether he will suddenly kill them—that time, and observation, and experience, must make manifest: but kill them he shall, that is certain, for so says the Holy Ghost.

And shall overcome them, and kill them. In this method, therefore, God will suffer the beast to proceed with the Church of God, after she has sufficiently borne her testimony for him in the world. He shall " war against them," but that is not all: he shall overcome them, but that is not all; he " shall overcome them, and kill them."

And kill them. Of their slaughter also I shall speak a word or two. But first I would note, as all know, that there is a difference to be put betwixt killing and overcoming; for though every one that is killed is overcome, yet every one that is overcome is not killed, (Acts xxi. 32 ;) men may be overcome and yet live, (Jer. xii. 11 ;) but when they are killed it is otherwise: there may be a cry heard from the mouth of them that are overcome, but not from the mouth of them that are killed, (Exod. xxxii. 18. Acts vii. 34 ;) they that are overcome may consult their own enlargement and deliverance, but they that are killed cannot do so. I do therefore distinguish betwixt being *killed* and *overcome*, because the text doth so : " He shall make war against them, and shall overcome them, and kill them."

And kill them. From these words, therefore, I will take occasion to inquire.

First. How they are to be considered as to this slaughter.

Second. What death they must die to accomplish this prophecy.

First. How they are to be considered?

I answer, not in a carnal or natural, but in a mystical sense. For, first, they are called witnesses; secondly, they are put under the number of two—" my two witnesses." (Rev. xi. 3.) Both which are to be mystically taken.

First. Because their testimony standeth not in their words only, but in their conversation; yea, in their suffering also; and that is a mystical witness-bearing.

Second. They go under the number of *two*, not because there were indeed two such men in the world, but because *two* are a sufficient number to bear witness, (Numb. xxxv. 30. Deut. xvii. 6; xix. 15;) and God's Church, in the most furious heat and rage of Antichrist, have been at least of such a number of professing saints, to proclaim against the beast and his worship in the name of God. To think that there have been two such men in the world is ridiculous, for these witnesses must continue to give their testimony for God against Antichrist a thousand two hundred and threescore years. Nor can they scripturally bear this title, "my two witnesses," but with respect to their prophesying so long. The witnesses, therefore, are nothing else but a successive Church or the congregation of God abiding for him against Antichrist, by reason of a continual succession of men that is joined by the special blessing of God unto it.

Second. What death they must die? I answer, not a corporeal one, but that which is mystically such. And I choose to understand it thus, because this suiteth best with their state and condition, which is mystical. Besides, thus did they (when they did overcome) slay their enemies, even with the fire or sword of their mouth: "If any man will hurt them, fire proceedeth out of their mouth and devoureth their enemies: and if any man will hurt them, he must in this manner be killed." (Rev. xi. 5.) As therefore they went about to kill their enemies, so their enemies will kill them: but they sought to kill their enemies by their testimony, as to their antichristian spirit and church-state; and their enemies will kill them as to their Christian heat and fervency of mind, and also as to their Christian Church-state. So that, (at least so I think,) there will be such ruins brought, both upon the spirit of Christianity and the true Christian Church-state before this Antichrist is destroyed, that there will for a time scarce be found a Christian spirit, or a true visible living Church of Christ in the world: nothing but the dead bodies of these will be to be seen of the nations; nor them neither, otherwise than as so many ruinous heaps. For the love that I bear to the Church of Christ, I wish, as to this, I may prove a false prophet; but this looks so like the text, and also so like the dispensations of God with his Church of old, that I cannot but think it will be so. For the text, I have spoken to that already, wherefore I will now present you with some things that look like parallel cases.

First. When the Church was coming out of Egypt, just before they were delivered from Pharaoh, they were in their own eyes, and in the eyes of their enemies, none other than dead; "It had been better," said they to Moses, "that we had served the Egyptians, than that we should die in this wilderness." (Exod. xiv. 12.) The people said so, Moses feared, and Pharaoh concluded they were all dead men. (Exod. xii. 33.) Also Paul tells us, "that they were baptized" (that is, buried) "unto Moses in the cloud, and in the sea." They were for the time, to use the expression, a *dead Church* both in the eyes of Pharaoh, in the eyes of Moses, and also in their own.

And it is to be taken notice of: as the witnesses in the text were slain but a little before the ruin of Antichrist began, so this Church was *baptized* in the sea but a little before great Pharaoh was *drowned* there.

Second. In the time of Elias, which time also was typical of this, what Church was there to be seen in Israel? None but what was under ground, buried in dens, and in caves of the earth: yea, the prophet could see none, and therefore he cried to God, and said, Lord, they have "digged down thine altars," and slain thy prophets, "and I am left alone, and they seek my life!" (1 Kings xix. 14.) What visible living Church was now in the land, I mean, either with reference to a godly spirit for it, or the form and constitution of it? What was, was known to God, but dead to every man alive.

Third. What was the *dry bones* that we read of in the 37th of Ezekiel, but the Church of God, and also a figure of what we are treating of? And why called *dry bones*, since the people were alive, with their substance, wives, and children, but to show, that that Church of God was now, as to their spirit and Church-state, accounted as *dead*, not only by themselves, but by the King of Babylon, and the nations round about? Babylon then was the valley, and the grave; and the Church of God were the bones—bones without flesh, sinews, or skin; bones exceeding dry; yea, so dry and dead were they, that the prophet himself could not tell whether ever they should live again. (Ezek. xxxvii. 1—3.)

Now this, as I said, was a state that was not to end with the Church of Israel, but to be acted over once again by the beast with the Church of the New Testament. Yea, it is an easy matter to make their witnesses in this their death, and the Church of Israel in this their grave, in many things to symbolize.

Fourth. Take another instance, or rather comparison, unto which the Church of God compared herself, when under the King of Babylon's tyranny: and that is, she counted herself as the dung that the beast lets fall to the ground from behind him. And doth this look like a visible Church-state? Or has it the smell or savour of such a thing? Nebuchadnezzar, (said she,) "hath swallowed me up like a dragon; he hath filled his belly with my delicates, he hath cast me out." (Jer. li. 34.) Pray, what would you think of a man, of whom one should tell you that he was eaten up of a dragon, made to fill the belly of a dragon, and cast out as the dung of a dragon? Would you think that such an one did all this while retain the shape, form, or similitude of a man? Why, thus the Church said she was, and thus the Church shall be again : for she is once more to be overcome, to be overcome and killed ; and that by the beast, the dragon's whelp, of which the King of Babylon was a type. And therefore I conclude the premises ; that is, that the beast will kill the Church that shall be in the latter days, as to her Christian spiritedness, and her Church-state. And I could further add, that if we hold they die corporeally, we must conclude, that their natural body being slain, shall lie three years and a half in the street ; yea, that their resurrection shall be corporeal, &c. But why we should think thus, as yet I can see no reason, since the persons are such mystically ; the beast mystically so ; the street in which they be, mystically such ; and the days of their unburied state, to be taken mystically likewise. But we will pass this, and descend to other things.

Fifth. I will yet add another thing. When Israel was coming out of Babylon,—yea, while they were building of the temple of God, which was a figure of our Church-state now under the gospel,—they were not only troubled, hindered, and molested in their work, but were made for a time to cease, and let the work lie still.

" Now (says the text) when the copy of King Artaxerxes' letter (which he sent to forbid the Jews in their work) was read before Rehum and Shimshai the scribe, and their companions, they went up in haste to Jerusalem unto the Jews, and made them to cease by force and power. Then ceased the work of the house of God which is at Jerusalem : so it ceased unto the second year of the reign of Darius, the King of Persia." (Ezra iv. 23, 24.)

And I pray, since their temple-worship was a type of a New Testament Church-state and worship, what doth their causing of that work to cease signify to us, but that we must have a time also to cease as they ? And since their temple-work was caused to cease before the house was finished, what face could there be at present thereupon, but that, to look to, it was like some deformed, battered, broken building, or as such an one that was begun by foolish builders ? Yea, and since the Jews left off to build God's house at the command of the heathens, what did that bespeak, but that they had lost their spirit, were quashed, and so as to their temple-work, killed, as it were, to all intents and purposes ? And thus it will be, a little before the Church of God shall be set free from the beast, and all his angels : for these things were writ for our admonition, to show us what shall be done thereafter ; yea, and whether we believe or disbelieve hereabout, time will bring it to pass.

I do not question but many good men have writ more largely of this matter : but as I have not seen their books, so I walk not by their rules. If I mistake, the mistakes are only mine ; and if I shall merit shame, I alone must bear it.

Some may think they have said enough, when they assert that for the witnesses to be killed, is to be *dead in law.* But I answer, that is not to be *overcome.* They are here said to be overcome ; and that is more than to be dead in law : for a man may be dead in law, and yet not be overcome ; and if so, then far enough off from being killed. So then, for as much as they are said to be overcome and killed, it must be more than to be dead in law. Besides, the text supposeth that they had yielded up, as dying men do their souls, their spirit of life into the hands of God : for it saith concerning them, that at their resurrection, the spirit of life from God entered *again* into them : into them, antecedent thereunto. " And after three days and an half, the spirit of life from God entered into them, and they stood upon their feet." (Rev. xi. 11.) Thus it was concerning the dry bones, of which mention was made before : " Then said he unto me, Prophesy unto the wind, prophesy son of man, and say to the wind, Thus saith the Lord God, Come from the four winds, O breath, and breathe upon these slain, that they may live." (Ezek. xxxvii. 9.) And thus much concerning their killing.

Now, as I said, since in death the body doth not only lie dead, but the spirit of life departs therefrom, it is to show that not only their bodies, their Church-state, shall die, (for *Churches* are called *bodies,* 1 Cor. xii. 27. Eph. iii. 6 ; iv. 12 ; v. 23. Col. i. 18.) but that spirit of life that acted those bodies, shall be taken up to God. There shall, for a time, be no living visible Church of Christ in the world : a Church but no living Church, as to Church-state ; a Church in ruins, but not a Church in order. Even as there was once a Christ, but no living Christ in the grave, yet the gates of hell shall not prevail to an utter overthrow thereof, no more than they prevailed to an utter overthrow of Christ ; but as one did, so shall the other, revive, and rise again, to the utter confusion and destruction of their enemies : yea, and as Christ, after his resurrection, was, as to his body, more glorious than he was before, so the witnesses, after their resurrection, shall be more spiritual, heavenly, and exact in all their ways, than they were before they were killed. Resurrections are always attended with new additions of glory ; and so shall the Church of God, as to her Church state, be in the latter days.

But yet the beast shall not altogether have his will, (if that at all was his will,) that these witnesses, in this second war, should be conquered to a compliance with Antichrist in his foolish and vain religion : for it is not with dead men to comply, but as they are dead to their own Church-state, so they are to his. When the Jews had killed Christ, it was beyond all the art of hell to cause that his body should see corruption ; so when the beast has killed the witnesses, he shall not be able to corrupt them with any of his vices.

Hence you find that not the witnesses, but the

dwellers upon the earth were them that danced after the devil's pipe, when he had fulfilled their murder.

Nor doth this murder, as to the fulfilling of it in those nations where the woman sitteth, seem to be a great way off, if all be true that from foreign parts some have said: for what a withdrawing of God and of his Spirit is there already in some of the Churches of God! The word worketh not that sound repentance which it was wont to do: preachers preach for little but to spend themselves, as men that are wounded do when with groans they let out their life. Where, say some, is the spirit and life of communion? And where that practical holiness that formerly used to be seen in the houses, lives, and conversations of professors? The whole head is sick, and the whole heart faint already; and how long will it be before churches die of the wound that the beast has given them, time must make appear: but die I perceive they must; for if the wound already given will not kill, repeated blows shall.

By all that I have said, I do not deny but that many of the people of God may die corporeally, by the hand of the beast, in this second war that shall be made by him against the witnesses: but should as many more die, that will not prove that that death will be that that by the killing of the witnesses is intended.

Something I would bestow upon the reader, for him to carry with him as a memorandum, while he reads this account of things: As,

First. This victory of the beast, is not to be until the witnesses have finished their testimony; and so by all that he shall do, he shall not hinder the revelation of any of the truths that they either were to bring to light, or to confirm by their witness-bearing.

Witnesses are not always bound to speak: there is a time "to keep silence," (Eccles. iii. 7,) and "thou shalt be dumb." (Ezek. iii. 26.) But how shall we know when this time is come?

1. When a sufficient testimony has been given for Christ, and against Antichrist, before the God of heaven; for he must be the judge.

2. When her enemies forbear to plead against her by argument, and rather betake themselves to blows. (Matt. x. 19.)

3. When the spirit of testimony-bearing is taken from the Church; for that is not essential to Christianity, but is given and taken away as there is occasion.

4. When testimony-bearing becomes a vain or needless repetition, when they have heard sufficiently of things before.

Second. This victory of the beast shall not invalidate or weaken their testimony; no, not in the eyes of the world; for they will still remember, and have a reverence for it. This is intimated by this, that "they of the people, and kindreds, and tongues, and nations," (that are neither the witnesses, nor they that in the next verse are called

the inhabiters, or they that dwell upon the earth,) "shall not suffer their dead bodies to be [buried, or be] put into graves." (Rev. xi. 9.)

Third. This shall not lengthen the reign and tranquillity of the antichristian kingdom; nor frustrate, drive back, (or cause to tarry,) the glorious freedom and liberty of the saints.

But some may say, this will be a SAD day.

So it will, and gloomy; but it will be but short, and "the righteous shall have dominion over them next morning." It will last but three days and a half; nor shall it come, but for the sins of churches and saints, and to hasten the downfall of the kingdom of the beast, and for the sweetening to the Church her future mercies. Christ Jesus, our Lord, in answer to the question of his disciples, about the destruction of Jerusalem, presented them with a relation of many sad things; but when he was come even to the hearts of men, and had told them "that they should fail for fear;" he said, "when these things begin to come to pass, then look up, and lift up your heads, for your redemption draweth nigh." (Luke xxi. 25—28.)

It is as ordinary as for the light to shine, for God to make black and dismal dispensations to usher in bright and pleasing: yea, and the more frightful that is which goes before, the more comforting is that which follows after. Instances in abundance might be given as to this, but at present let this suffice that is here upon the paper before us; namely, the state of the witnesses, with their glorious resurrection

V. *The Fifth Sign.*

Another sign of the approach of the ruin of Antichrist, will be this: the great joy that will be in her, and among her disciples, when they shall see that the witnesses are slain, and lie dead upon the spot: "And they that dwell upon the earth shall rejoice over them, and make merry, and send gifts one to another, because these two prophets tormented them that dwell on the earth." (Rev. xi. 10.) Babylon has been always a merry city, and her disciples merry men; but the poor Church of Christ has been solitary, and as a wife forsaken; her tears upon her cheeks bear her witness, and so doth her sackcloth-weed.

Hence our Babylon, under the name of Nineveh, is called "the rejoicing city." (Zech. ii. 15.) Only her joy is distinguished from that which is the joy of God's people, by these two things—either she rejoiceth in outward carnal glory, or else in the ruin of the Church of God. This last, to wit, the *supposed* ruin of the Church of God, is that which will be now the cause of her glorying. And this is the joy that God complaineth of, and for the which he said that he would punish Babylon: "Chaldea shall be a spoil; all that spoil her shall be satisfied, saith the Lord; because ye were glad, because ye rejoice, O ye destroyers of mine heritage," &c. (Jer. i. 10, 11.) The joy, therefore, of Babylon, Antichrist; the joy that she shall conceive in her heart upon the slaughter of the witnesses, is a sure sign of her unavoidable ruin and destruction. These two prophets tormented her; they were to Babylon as Mordecai was to Haman, a continual plague and eye-sore; as also was David to the wretched Saul: but now they are overcome, now they are killed; now she rejoiceth, and maketh merry. And this her joy was of old prefigured by them that in her spirit have gone before her: as,

1. When the Philistines had, as they thought, for ever overcome Samson, that Nazarite of God, how joyful were they of the victory! "Then the lords of the Philistines gathered them together for to offer a great sacrifice unto Dagon their god, and to rejoice: for they said, Our god hath delivered Samson our enemy into our hands. And when the people saw him (saw him in chains) they praised their god; for they said, Our god hath delivered into our hands our enemy, and the destroyer of our country, which slew many of us." Poor Samson! while thou hadst thy locks, thy liberty, and thine eyes, thou didst shake the pillar that did bear up their kingdom! But now they have conquered thee, how great is their joy! How great is their joy, and how near their downfall! This, therefore, is a joy that is like that we have under consideration, to wit, the joy of them that dwell upon the earth; for that the witnesses that did bear up the name of God in the world, were overcome and killed.

2. Like to this, is that which you read of in the first book of Samuel, concerning the men that had burnt David's Ziklag. Ziklag was poor David's place of safety; nor had he any else but that under the whole heaven: but the children of the east came upon it, and took it, set it on fire, and carried thence all David's substance, with his wives and his children. (Very ill done to a man in affliction; to a man that went always in fear of his life, because of the rage of his master Saul.) But how were they that had got the victory? Oh! joyful, and glad, and merry at heart at the thoughts of the richness of the booty? "Behold, they were spread abroad upon all the earth, eating, and drinking, and dancing, because of all the great spoil that they had taken out of the land of the Philistines (from Ziklag) and out of the land of Judah." (1 Sam. xxx. 16.) Here again you find a joy and merriment like these that we have under consideration, and that upon such like accounts. Nothing pleases the wicked more than to see the godly go down the wind; for their words, and lives, and actions are a plague and a torment to them: as it is said of these two prophets, "They tormented them that dwelt on the earth."

3. While the Church of God lay dead in Babylon, and as bones exceeding dry, what a trampling upon them was there by Belshazzar a little before his death! He called for his golden and silver vessels that his father Nebuchadnezzar had taken out of the temple of God that was at Jerusalem, (those holy vessels once dedicated to the worship and service of God) that his princes, his wives, and his concubines might drink therein. An high affront to heaven: "They drank wine, and praised the gods of gold, and of silver, of brass, of iron, of wood, and of stone," (Dan. v. 4,) and all to show what a conquest, as he thought, he had got over the God of heaven, and over his people that dwelt in Jerusalem, and over his ordinances and vessels used in his worship and service; yea, this he did with such joy that was not usual, as is intimated by his doing of it before a thousand of his lords, and that till he had drank himself drunken. But all this while, as was hinted before, the Church of God, as it were, lay dead at his feet; or, as the phrase is, "as bones exceeding dry." This, too, will be the joy of the beast and his followers in the latter days: they will make war with the witnesses; they shall overcome them, and kill them; and when that is done, they shall rejoice over them and make merry. But as Belshazzar soon after this saw the handwriting that made his *knees knock together*, and as he lived not to see the light of another day, so it will be with the beast and his followers: the next news that we hear upon this mirth and jollity, is, the tenth part of his kingdom falls, and so on till the whole is ruined.

4. Moab, also, in the day that Israel was taken captive by their enemies, could not forbear but *skip for joy*, so glad was he in his heart thereat. But what saith the jealous Lord? "Make ye him drunken, for he magnified himself against the Lord. Moab also shall be in derision; for was not Israel (saith God) a derision unto thee? Was he found among thieves? for since thou spakest of him thou skippest for joy." (Jer. xlviii. 26, 27.) Of all things, God cannot away with this: for when the wicked would rejoice that they have been suffered to make havoc of the Church of God, they deny the wisdom and power by which they were permitted to do this, and offer sacrifice to their own net and drag, (Hab. i. 16;) which provoketh the holiness of Israel: "Shall the axe boast itself against him that heweth therewith? or shall the saw magnify itself against him that shaketh it? As if the rod should shake itself against him that lift it up; or as if the staff should lift up itself, as if it were no wood." But what follows? Why, burning and consuming of soul and body of them that do such a thing. (Isa. x. 15—18.) And this text I the rather bring, because it is to be the portion of Antichrist.

And therefore let this be a caution to the men that wonder after the beast, to caution them to repentance, for he will assuredly go into perdition. What! shall the witnesses of God be killed? Shall the beast stand glorying over them while they are dead, with his feet in their neck, and shall none be angry at it? Let them that *love* themselves *look* to themselves: God will be concerned, and will assuredly for this quickly put a period to the kingdom and reign of Antichrist, (Jer. l. 13.)

And although this glorying mistress of iniquity, this Antichrist and Babylon, may say that her power is the hammer of the whole earth, yet God will cut him in sunder, and break him in pieces with his bout-hammers, with the Protestant kings of the earth, that he will use to do this work withal; that is, when this last sign is fulfilled. I call it the *last* sign; I find none that doth intervene betwixt the slaying of the witnesses, and the beginnings of the ruin of Antichrist but this.

But a little to comment upon their joy, as the Holy Ghost doth set it forth. The cause of their joy we have touched already; which was, for that they had slain their tormentors. For, as was showed you, the witnesses had been their tormentors: but when they shall overcome them and kill them, they rejoice, make merry, and send gifts one to another.

This *repeating*, and *repeating* with aggravation, doth manifest, and at that day their joy will be exceeding great: "they shall rejoice, and make merry," &c. They shall rejoice over them, over their slain, their enemies, their tormenting enemies. This joy, therefore, is a joy that flows from victory, from victory after a war that has lasted a thousand two hundred and threescore years. They shall rejoice, as they do that have a most potent, vexatious, and tormenting enemy lying dead at their foot, and as those that ride in triumph over them. They shall therefore rejoice as conquerors use to do, who make the slaughters of their spoiled enemies the *trophy* of their joy.

For the devil, that great deceiver of mankind, will so flush up and bewitch the men that wonder after the beast, with the victory that they shall get over the faithful witnesses for God and his Son, that they will think (it will never be day) that the victory is so complete, so universal, so thorough, that the conquest must be lasting. And from sense and reason they will have ground to think so, for who now is left in the world any more to make head against them? but here comes in that which will utterly spoil this joy; these conquered, killed, dead men must come to life again; and then what has become of their joy? "And great fear fell upon them which saw them." (Rev. xi. 11.) Wherefore this joy must fade and vanish; but, I say, the followers of the beast will be far from thinking so, for they will "rejoice over them, make merry, and send gifts one to another," concluding that these tormentors shall never torment them more. But Jacob's blessing upon his son Gad shall be fulfilled upon these witnesses: "Gad," saith he, "a troop shall overcome him; but he shall overcome at the last." (Gen. xlix. 19.) So, then, these conquerors must not always rejoice, though they will suppose they shall, and also make merry too.

And make merry. To make merry is more than to rejoice. To rejoice doth show the present act of the soul, but to make merry is to use the means as will keep this joy alive and on foot. Joy is one thing, and the continuance of it is another. Joy may be begotten by a conceit, a thought, but it cannot be maintained so, because deliberation will come in and spoil it, (Esther v. 4,) if sufficient means is not used to continue it; wherefore he adds, they rejoiced over them, "and made merry."

And there are five things that are usually made use of to keep up wicked joy—1. There is the merriment of music. (Luke xv. 25, 32.) 2. The merriment of feasting. (Judges xix. 6, 9.) 3. The merriment of laughter. (Eccles. x. 19.) 4. The merriment of fleshly solace. (Jer. xxxi. 4.) 5. Revenge upon a supposed enemy, (2 Sam. xiii. 28.) So, then, by these five things we see what is the way that sinful joy is maintained in the hearts of wicked men, and also by what means the limbs and brats of Antichrist will keep up that joy that at first will be conceived in their hearts at the thoughts that now they have killed their tormentors. (1.) They shall have music. (2.) They shall have feasting. (3.) They shall have laughter. (4.) They shall have fleshly solace. And (5.) They shall have their fill, for the time, of revenge. Thus, therefore, shall they rejoice over them, and make merry, all the time of that little *short everlasting* that they are to live in the world.

And make merry. To make merry, to make wicked mirth, there must be a continual fraternity or brotherhood in iniquity maintained among them, and that where none may come to interrupt; and that they will be capable of doing anywhere then, for that their tormentors will be dead. Wickedness shall walk with open face in those days, for then there will be none alive for God and his ways; wherefore the beast and his train may do what they will: now will be the time for men to live carelessly and wantonly, and to make their wantonness their joy, (after the manner of the Zidonians,) for there will be none to put them to shame.

And shall send gifts one to another. This is another token of their gladness, and also a means to buoy them up still: and it will be a sign that they have joined hand in hand to do this wickedness, not dreaming of the punishment that must follow. This sending of gifts to each other, and that after they have slain these two prophets, doth also declare that they will be far from repentance for the commission of so great an offence. Nay, it signifies further that they were resolved and determined to quench all manner of convictions one in another that might arise in their hearts for the sin which they had committed: for a gift blinds the eyes of the wise and perverts the judgment of the righteous: how much more, then, will it stifle and choke appearances of such upon the spirits of wicked men! I question not at all but many have been by the favours and gifts of wicked men drawn down into the belly of hell.

Now, what these gifts will be, either as to kind or quantity, that I can say nothing to; but, probably, whatever they will be, there will be but little of their own cost in them. Victors and conquerors do use to visit their friends with their spoils won in battle, with the spoil of the enemies of their God. (Ezra x. 7.)

And this was David's way after he had recovered the loss that he had sustained at the burning of his Ziklag; he sent to his friends of what he had taken from his enemies as token of victory: "David sent of the spoil" (says the text) "unto the elders of Judah, even to his friends, saying, Behold, a present for you of the spoils of the enemies of the Lord!" (1 Sam. xxx. 26.) And why may not those we have now under consideration do so to their god, and their friends also? Spoiling is like to be one of the last of the mischiefs that Antichrist shall do to the Church of God in this world; and, methinks, since the beast will have power to overcome, and to kill, he should also have power to take away. (Dan. xi. 33.) "Hast thou killed, and also taken possession?" said the prophet to wicked Ahab.

However, whatever their gifts may be, and at whose cost soever bought, it is a sign their hearts will be open, they shall send gifts one to another: their merry days will then be come, and their enemies will then be dead at their feet; wherefore now they will have nothing to do but to rejoice over them, and to make merry, and to send gifts one to another.

Thus, as to sense and reason, all shall be hush, all shall be quiet and still: the followers of the Lamb shall be down; the followers of the beast shall be up, cry peace and safety, and shall be as secure as an hard heart, false peace, and a deceitful devil can make them. But, behold! while they thus "sing in the windows," death is straddling over the threshold! (Zeph. ii. 14.) While they are crying peace and safety, sudden destruction cometh: by that they have well settled themselves at their table with Adonijah, (1 Kings i.,) they shall hear it proclaimed with sound of trumpet— the witnesses are risen again.

Now the Christians' pipes will go again: and surely the earth will be rent with the sound of their shouts and acclamations, while they cry with joyful sound—" The kingdoms of this world are become the kingdoms of our Lord, and of his Christ: and he shall reign for ever and ever." (Rev. xi. 15.)

But woe to the wicked, it shall be ill with them; for the Lord Jesus will now begin to show his jealousy, and to make known his indignation towards those that have thus cruelly slain his prophets, digged down his altars, and made such havoc of the afflicted Church of God. (Isa. lxvi. 14.) Now will he whet his *glittering sword*, and his hand shall take hold on vengeance, that he may render a recompence to his enemies, and repay them that hate him. (Deut. xxxii. 41.)

But this he will not do immediately by himself, but by such instruments as have been spoken of before, of which more particularly to treat, shall be that I shall next take in hand.

CHAPTER V.

OF THE INSTRUMENTS THAT GOD WILL USE TO BRING ANTICHRIST TO HIS RUIN.

Although I have hinted at this before, yet it may be convenient briefly to touch it again. Antichrist, as I have told you, consisteth of soul and body, and must be destroyed by such instruments as may most properly be applied to each. Further, as to the soul, spirit, or life of Antichrist and its destruction, of that we have also spoken already: it remains, then, that now we discourse of the ruin of his body and flesh.

I then take it, that the destruction of her flesh shall come by the sword, as managed in the hands of kings, who are God's ministers for the punishment of evil deeds, and the praise of them that do well. (Rom. xii.) Not that the Church, even as a church, shall be quite exempt, and have therein no hand at all; for she, even as such, shall, with her faith and prayers, help forward that destruction.

The Church, therefore, as a church, must use such weapons as are proper to her as such: and the magistrate, as a magistrate, must use such weapons as are proper to him as such. When the Church of Israel were prisoners in Babylon, they did not fight their way through their foes and the countries to Jerusalem, but waited in their captivated state with patience until the kings of the Medes and Persians came to deliver them. Nor is it to be slighted, but to be thought on seriously, that before there was an Israelite captive in Babylon, their deliverer Cyrus was prophesied of: which Cyrus did afterwards come and take Babylon, and deliver the captive, as it was foretold he should. He saith unto Cyrus, " He is my shepherd, and shall perform all my pleasure: even saying to Jerusalem, Thou shalt be built; and to the temple, Thy foundation shall be laid." (Isa. xliv. 28.) And again, "Thus saith the Lord to his anointed, to Cyrus, whose right hand I have holden to subdue nations before him," &c. " I have raised him up in righteousness: and I will direct all his ways: he shall build my city, and shall let go my captives, not for price nor reward, saith the Lord of hosts." (Isa. xlv. 1, 13.) And this accordingly he did, to wit, when the time was come; as may be seen in those holy records where these things are made mention of. Indeed, as I said, the Church is not excluded; she may and ought, with her faith and prayer and holy life, to second this work of kings. Wherefore when God speaks of bringing down the lofty city, and of laying it low in the dust by the Church, he saith they shall do it by their feet, and with their steps: "The foot shall tread it down, even the feet of the poor, and the steps of the needy." (Isa. xxvi. 6.)

By feet and steps I understand the good lives of the children of God: but now, when kings come to deal with her as kings, they serve her as Samuel served Agag, as a judge, "cut her in pieces with their swords:" or as you have it elsewhere, "They make her desolate and naked; they eat her flesh, and burn her with fire." The sword will be put into their hands for this very purpose. Thus, therefore, must their deliverance be begun.

It is also to be considered that after these first kings of the Medes and Persians had broken the yoke of the King of Babylon from off the neck of the captive Church, and had given her licence to go to her place to build her temple and city, and to sacrifice there according to the law of their God, (as both in Ezra and Nehemiah we read;) and when their work was hindered by under-officers, or they endeavoured so to do, they pleaded the licence that they received to build and sacrifice by the decree of the first kings, and so finished their deliverance: they went not on in headstrong manner, as if they regarded neither king nor Cæsar: "But Zerubbabel, and Joshua, and the rest of the chief of the fathers of Israel, said unto them" that sought to hinder their work, "Ye have nothing to do with us to build an house unto our God, but we ourselves will build unto the Lord God of Israel, as king Cyrus, the King of Persia hath commanded us." (Ezra iv. 3.) And as they said, so also they did: "the elders of the Jews builded, and they prospered, through the prophesying of Haggai the prophet, and Zechariah the son of Iddo. And they builded, and finished it, according to the commandment of the God of Israel, and according to the commandment of Cyrus, and Darius, and Artaxerxes, King of Persia." (Ezra vi. 14.) Yea, they did not only accept of the kindness of kings, but did acknowledge that kindness with thanksgiving, as a gift of the God of heaven: for the kings had commanded and given leave to the Jews to go to Jerusalem, to build their temple, and to do sacrifice there, according to the counsel of the priests that were at Jerusalem, and according to the law of God that they had in their hand. (Ezra vii. 13, 14.) For Artaxerxes sent Ezra the priest to inquire after the condition that Jerusalem and Judah was in, according to, or by, the law of God that was in his hand. (Ezra vii. 14.) And he had licence also further to do with the king's silver and gold, which he gave for the service of the house of the Lord, "according to the will, word, or law of his God." "And thou, Ezra," (says the king,) "after the wisdom of thy God," (that is, after his word,) "which is in thy hand, set magistrates and judges which may judge all the people that are beyond the river, all such as know the laws of thy God, and teach ye them that know them not. And

whosoever will not do the law of thy God," (that is, worship, and walk by the rule of his testament,) "and the law of the king," (that is, shall refuse to give Ezra such things as by the king was appointed for Ezra's help in the furthering of the worship of God, according to the law of his God,) "let judgment be executed speedily upon him, whether it be to death, or to banishment, or to confiscation of goods, or to imprisonment." (Ezra vii. 25, 26.) This was, therefore, a wonderful gracious licence that the king now gave to Ezra: he imposed nothing upon him or the Jews in matters of religion and worship, but left him and them wholly to the law, will, and word of God, only he laid check upon wicked and ungodly people: that if they did things contrary to the laws of Ezra's God, or did slight the king's law, as aforesaid, that then such penalties and pains should be inflicted upon them.

To the same purpose was the decree of Cyrus, and that of Darius to put it in execution. Also the penalty enacted against such offenders was full as sharp and severe: "Also I have made a decree (said the king) that whosoever shall alter this word, let timber be pulled down from his house; and being set up, let him be hanged thereon, and let his house be made a dunghill for this. And the God that hath caused his name to dwell there, destroy all kings and people that shall put to their hand to alter and to destroy this house of God, which is at Jerusalem: I Darius have made a decree, let it be done with speed." (Ezra vi. 11, 12.)

Indeed, sometimes a stop was put to this work by the king, and the Jews were made to cease by force and power, (Ezra iv. 23, 24,) the which the good people did bear with patience, (Ezra iv. 11—21;) also they waited to see their God go before them among the kings, who at length took away Artaxerxes, who for a time had put a stop to the work, and brought in another, who gave leave that with speed it should be set on foot again. (Ezra v.)

The Jews did also in these vacancies, or times in the which hindrances were put, carry it very tenderly and lovingly to those kings that at present they were under, submitting of their bodies and their goods to their will, and meekly endured the trial and affliction, serving them with all faithfulness, watching to save their lives from the hands of bloody men. Also when the king's laws, and the law of their God did at any time come in competition, they would indeed adhere to, and do the law of their God; yet with that tenderness to the king, his crown, and dignity, that they could at all times appeal to the righteous God about it. (Dan. vi. 22.) Nor did they lose by so doing; yea, they prospered; for by this means Mordecai was made a great man, and a saviour of his people. By this means also was Daniel made a great man, and helpful to his brethren. (Dan. v. 29.)

Kings, I say, must be the men that must down with Antichrist, and they shall down with her in God's time.

God hath begun to draw the hearts of some of them from her already, and he will set them, in time, against her round about. If, therefore, they do not that work so fast as we would have them, let us exercise patience and hope in God: it is a wonder that they go so fast as they do, since the concerns of whole kingdoms lie upon their shoulders, and that there are so many Sanballats and Tobiases to flatter with them, and misinform them concerning the people that are delivered but in part. See what an ugly account was given of Jerusalem by the enemies of the Jews, even then when they were in the hands of their deliverers: "Be it known unto the king, that the Jews which came up from thee to us, are come unto Jerusalem, building the rebellious and bad city, and have set up the walls thereof, and joined the foundations.— Be it known now unto the king, that if this city be builded, and the walls set up again, then will they not pay toll, tribute, and custom, and so thou shalt endamage the revenue of the kings." (Ezra iv. 12, 13.) Oh! what *be it known, be it known* is here! But were not these gentlemen more afraid of losing their own places and preferments than of the king's losing of his toll and custom? But the whole was a lie, though it hindered the work for a time, and the patience of the people, and their loyalty to the king, did conquer and overcome all.

I speak the more to this, because (as I have said) I believe that by magistrates and powers we shall be delivered and kept from Antichrist; and because God has already begun to do it by such, by which also she shall be destroyed: and I have a few things to present to good men, to be conversant in, in such a day as this.

Let the king have verily a place in your hearts, and with heart and mouth give God thanks for him; he is a better saviour of us than we be aware of, and may have delivered us from more deaths than we can tell how to think. We are bidden to "give thanks to God for all men, and, in the first place, for kings, and all that are in authority." (1 Tim. ii. 1, 2.)

Be not angry with them, no, not in thy thought; but consider, if they go not on in the work of reformation so fast as thou wouldest they should, the fault may be thine; know that thou also hast thy cold and chill frames of heart, and sittest still when thou shouldest be up and doing.

Pray for the kings to the God of heaven, who has the hearts of kings in his hand: and do it "without wrath, and doubting;" without *wrath*, because thy self is not perfect; and without *doubting*, because God governeth them, and has promised to bring down Antichrist by them.

Pray for the long life of the king.

Pray that God would always give wisdom and judgment to the king.

Pray that God would discover all plots and conspiracies against his person and government.

Pray also that God would make him able to drive away all evil, and evil men from his presence; and that he may be a greater countenancer than ever of them that are holy and good, and wait and believe, that God that has begun his quarrel with Babylon, Antichrist, the mother of Antichrist, the whore, would in his own time, and in his own way, bring her down by the means which he has appointed.

I do confess myself one of the old-fashion professors, that covet to fear God and honour the king. I also am for *blessing* of them that *curse* me, for *doing good* to them that *hate* me, and for *praying* for them that *despitefully use me, and persecute me*: and have had more peace in the practice of these things than all the world are aware of. I only drop this, because I would show my brethren that I also am one of them; and to set them right that have wrong thoughts of me as to so weighty matters as these.

Now these kings whose hearts God shall set to destroy Antichrist, shall do it without those inward reluctances that will accompany inferior men: they shall be stript of all pity and compassion. Hence they are compared to the mighty waves of the sea, (Jer. li. 42,) which saith, when the wrecked and dying mariners cry out for mercy for themselves, and for their children, I am a sea; "I travail not, nor bring forth children; neither do I nourish up young men, or bring up virgins." (Isa. xxxiii. 4, 5.) I have therefore no pity for these, or any of them: therefore they must be swallowed up of this sea, and sink like a stone in the midst of these mighty waters.

And thus much for the *means* by which God will destroy the body and flesh of Antichrist.

CHAPTER VI.

OF THE CAUSES OF THE RUIN OF ANTICHRIST.

Although the causes of the ruin of Antichrist be to some conspicuous enough, yet to some they may be otherwise: yea, and will to all kings and people whose eyes shall be held, that they may not see the judgment, in the reasonableness and equitableness thereof; and these shall wail when they see "the smoke of her torment;" and these shall cry, Alas! alas! (Rev. xviii. 10.) Wherefore, for further edification, as I have treated of the *man of sin* already, so will I now of the *causes* of his downfall. And,

I. *The First Cause.*

He must down, for that *he hath usurped, and taken the name and attributes of God upon himself:* he hath said, "I am God:" he hath sit in the temple of God, "showing himself that he is God;" yea, and that in contempt and scorn of any other, "exalting himself above all that is called God, or that is worshipped," (2 Thess. ii. ;) yea, hath cried down all gods but himself: wherefore it must needs be, that he be brought to judgment, that the truth of his saying may be proved. And for this cause he is threatened, under the name of the Prince of Tyrus: "Because thine heart is lifted up, (saith the Lord,) and thou hast said, I am a god, therefore I will bring strangers upon thee, the terrible of the nations: and they shall draw their swords against the beauty of thy wisdom, and they shall defile thy brightness. They shall bring thee down to the pit, and thou shalt die the deaths of them that are slain in the midst of the seas. Wilt thou yet say before him that slayeth thee, I am a god? but thou shalt be a man, and no god, in the hand of him that slayeth thee." (Ezek. xxviii. 2, 7—9.)

If God will not give his *name* or *glory* to another, be sure he will not be *under* another; but *this* to have, and *thus* to do, Antichrist has attempted. But how? In that he has been so bold as to prescribe and impose a worship besides, and without reverence of that which God has prescribed and imposed: for to do this is to make one's self a God. "Thou shalt have no other gods before me," (Exod. xx. 3,) is the first command. And the first, to enforce the second, "Thou shalt not make unto thee any graven image, or any likeness of any thing that is in heaven above, or that is in the earth beneath, or that is in the water under the earth: thou shalt not bow down thyself to them, nor serve them," (Exod. xx. 4, 5:) for he that doth thus is an idolater; and he that these things doth impose is one that shows himself a god. But this doth Antichrist do: and it is worth the noting, that God forbids not only images, but the *likeness of any thing:* books, altars, fancies, imaginations, or any thing in heaven above, or in the earth beneath, to bow down to, or to make them a means to worship or come to God by, if he has not commanded nor tolerated them in his holy word.

Thus saith the Lord: And, *I am the Lord,* is the *stamp,* the *seal,* and *sign* of all true rules of worship; and therefore it is so often repeated both in Moses, and in the prophets, where God commandeth worship to be performed, and imposeth the means and methods of it. Now this, *Thus saith the Lord,* Antichrist has rejected; and, *I am the Lord,* he hath assumed to himself: and therefore without the law, the word and commandment, hath framed and imposed a worship, exalting himself in the temple of God, although he is but the man of sin, above all that is called God, or that is worshipped.

Nor is he in this, his so foul a fact, without them that adore, worship his image, and wonder after him; yea, he hath got by this means almost the whole world to himself, who say, "Who is like unto the beast? Who is able to make war with him?" (Rev. xiii. 4.) And that they might show their resolvedness to stand by him, they receive his mark in their forehead, or in their hand: his MARK; that is, they either openly or seriously become his disciples, and worship him according to the rules, methods, and ways that he hath prescribed. Wherefore, these with him, are also to drink of the fierceness of the wrath of Almighty God: "If any man worship the beast, and his image, and receive his mark in his forehead, or in his hand, the same shall drink of the wine of the wrath of God, which is poured out without mixture into the cup of his indignation; and he shall be tormented with fire and brimstone, in the presence of the holy angels, and in the presence of the Lamb." (Rev. xiv. 9, 10.)

But, I say, for that Antichrist hath thus taken the *place of God,* prescribed and imposed a worship *as a god,* got the world to worship and wonder after him as *after a god,* therefore shall he die the death of the uncircumcised, both in the soul, spirit, body, or flesh of Antichrist; therefore will God enlighten, and gather, and set the kings and nations against him, that both he and his may be buried, and have their dolesome withdrawing-rooms from the world in the sides of the pit's mouth.

II. *The Second Cause.*

Antichrist must be destroyed, because *he hath set himself against the Son of God;* against the Father, and against the Son. He had a spite against the Son betimes, even then when he came forth but in little bits, when he attempted to deny that he was come in the flesh. (1 John iv. 1—4.) But seeing he could make no earnings of that, he hath changed his methods, and seeks to run him out and down by other means and ways: because therefore he hath set himself against the Son of God, the King, therefore he must die. That he hath set himself against the Son of God, is also evident; for he hath his name from thence: he is therefore called Antichrist. That he hath set himself against him is yet further evident; for that he hath endeavoured to take from him his headship *over,* and his offices *for* and *in* the Church, which is his body. He hath plainly endeavoured to be head, for that he hath striven to take his wife from him, and to cause that she should be called HIS: yea, he hath endeavoured by all inventions to prostrate her to his lusts, to deflower her, and to make her an adulteress. He has been worse than Pharaoh, who took Abraham's wife, (Gen. xii. :) and worse than Abimelech, who lusted after Isaac's, (Gen. xxiv. :) yea, worse than Phalti, who run away with David's, (1 Sam. xxiii. 44;) forasmuch as she is higher, beloved better, and cost more than did any of these. Would it not be counted an high affront, for a base inferior fellow, to call himself the head of the queen? Yet thus has Antichrist done, and worse; he has called himself the head of the Universal Church of God.

And as he has attempted to be head in his stead, so to be king, priest, and prophet.

1. He has attempted to wrest his sceptre and kingdom from him, in that he hath endeavoured to thrust himself into his throne, which is the

heart and conscience of his people. The *heart* and *conscience* is that which Christ claimeth for his own proper and peculiar seat: "My son, give me thy heart." "That Christ may dwell in your hearts by faith." (Eph. iii. 17.) In this therefore the Church is not to be for another man, so will he be for her; but this throne Antichrist has lusted for, attempted to take, and made war with Christ and his Church, because they would not yield up to him this glorious throne of his, and therefore he must die.

2. He hath intruded upon the priestly office of Christ, hath called himself *high-priest*, though the Lord hath said, "Because thou hast rejected knowledge, I will also reject thee, that thou shalt be no priest to me: seeing thou hast forgotten the law of thy God, I will also forget thy children." (Hosea iv. 6.) But he will make himself a *priest ;* he hath invented sacrifices for the *quick* and the *dead :* he hath put, as he presumes, merit and worth into these sacrifices; he hath commanded that those that worship, should have faith in, and expect benefit by these sacrifices, although he offereth to his God nought else but the flesh of the *hog*, and of the *mouse*, with the *broth* of his abominable things. (Isa. lxvi. 17.) Many and sundry ways he hath set himself up to be high-priest, though God knows no high-priest but one, though the Church ought to know no high-priest but one; yea, though no high-priest but one can approach God's mercy-seat, to do for us the necessary and desired work.

3. He hath intruded upon the prophetical office of Jesus Christ. What else means his pretences to *infallibility ?* And that too when he imposes unwritten verities, abominable traditions, blasphemous rites and ceremonies; and forbids or dispenseth with the holy commands of God. Yea, when he enforceth these his Omrian statutes, and doth impose the works of the house of Ahab, (Micah vi. 16,) he doth all in the name of the Lord Christ, when himself hath set himself in his place, and in his room. This is mystery Babylon, *the mystery of iniquity :* this is Antichrist's soul and body, and as such, must be destroyed. But,

III. *The Third Cause.*

Antichrist must be destroyed, because *he hath blasphemed against the Holy Ghost*, and so set himself above the Father, the Son, the Spirit; against *all* that is called God. The Holy Ghost is the Spirit of truth that Christ has promised to give unto his Church, to help her in the understanding of his holy word, and to enable her to believe, and walk humbly and holily before God and man. The spirit of Antichrist is that spirit of error that hath puffed up the false church into a conceit of herself, and unscriptural worship; and that hath made this false church, which is his body, to ascribe all the horrible things and acts thereof, to the wisdom, guidance, directions, or operations of the Holy Ghost: As,

1. In all her unscriptural councils, assemblies, and convocations, they blasphemously father what they do upon the Holy Ghost, and make him the inventor and approver thereof.

2. She also blasphemeth the Holy Ghost, in accusing and condemning the Holy Scriptures of insufficiency, for that she saith, though it is a rule, yet but an imperfect one; one deficient, one that is not able to make the man of God perfect in all things, without the traditions, inventions, and blasphemous helps of antichristian wisdom.

3. She hath also blasphemed the Holy Ghost, in that she hath set up her own church-government, offices, officers, and discipline: none of all which is the Church of Christ directed to by the wisdom of the Spirit of God in his testament.

4. She hath also sinned against the Holy Ghost, in that she hath, as it were, turned the Holy Ghost out of doors, in concluding that he, without the works of the flesh, is not sufficient to govern the hearts of worshippers, in the service and worship of God.

5. She hath also thus sinned, in that *she hath wrought many lying miracles* in the face of the world, and imposed them upon her disciples for the confirming of her errors and blasphemous opinions, to the confronting of the true miracles wrought by the Holy Ghost; and also to the concluding, that there was an insufficiency in those that were true, to confirm the truth without the addition of hers, which she has wrought by the power of Satan, and the spirit of delusion, only to confirm her lies.

6. She hath sinned against the Holy Ghost, in that she hath, with Jeroboam, the son of Nebat, striven against the judgments wherewith God hath punished her; to call her back from her wicked way, and persisted therein, to the effectual proving of herself to be the lewd woman. (2 Kings xiii. 4—7, 23, 24.)

7. She hath sinned by labouring to hide all her wickedness, by lies, dissimulations, and filthy equivocations of her priests, friars, Jesuits, &c. I say, her labouring to hide the wickedness that she hath committed against kings, countries, nations, kingdoms, and people. She hath hid these things by the means or persons made mention of before; as by the tail; for they indeed are the tail of the beast, that cover his most filthy parts: the prophet that speaketh lies, he is the tail. But,

IV. *The Fourth Cause.*

Antichrist must be destroyed, *for the horrid outrage, and villanous murders that she hath committed upon the bodies of the saints.* For there is none, as to these things, for cruelty, to be compared with the church of Antichrist, and her followers: for upon whom hath not her cruelty been showed; have they never so little stood in her way, though never so innocently and honestly by so doing, stood to the truth and verity of

God? Yea, the promoting of her own superstition, idolatry, and blasphemous rites and ceremonies, have been so pursued by her, that she has waded through a sea of innocent blood for the accomplishment thereof.

The poor Church of God is a sensible bleeding witness of this, and so has been for hundreds of years together—witness the chronicles of all nations where she hath had to do; yea, and the sackcloth and ashes, and tears, and widows, and fatherless children, and their cries, of all which the holy word of God is a sufficient confirmation; "and in her," when God shall come to make inquisition for blood, "will be found the blood of saints and prophets, and of all that were slain upon the earth." (Rev. xviii. 24.) And yet has she such a whore's forehead, such a blindness in her judgment, and such an hard and obdurate heart, that it is not possible she should ever repent. Murders have been so natural to her, and in them her hand has been so exercised, that it is now become a custom, a trade, a pastime to her, to be either in the act, or laying some foundation for murders: witness those plots, designs, conspiracies, and frequent attempts that are, one or other of them, continually on foot in the world for the commission of murders.

Nay, the text last mentioned seems to import, that blood is so natural to her, that she sticketh not at any condition, sex, age, or degree, so she may imbrue her hands in blood. In her was found the blood of saints and prophets, and of *all* other carnal, natural, ignorant, graceless men that have been slain upon the earth. It is she that sets kings and kingdoms at variance; it is she that sets parents and children at variance, by her abuse of the word of our Lord and Christ. And besides, is it not easy, if we do but consider those bloody massacres that have been committed by her hand, both in France, Ireland, Piedmont, and in several places besides, without wronging of her, to conclude, that the blood of thousands that have not known their right hand from their left in religion hath been shed to quench, if it might have been, her insatiate thirst after blood. Therefore for these things shall she be judged as women that shed blood are judged, because she is an adulteress, and blood is in her hands. (Ezek. xxiii. 45.) She hath been as a beast of prey: nay, worse; for they do but kill and tear for the hunger of themselves, and of their whelps; but she, to satisfy her wanton and beastly lusts. "They have cast lots for my people, (saith God,) and have given a boy for an harlot, and sold a girl for wine, that they might drink," (Joel iii. 3;) and therefore must Antichrist be destroyed. Forbearance is no payment, God's patience is not a sign that he *forgetteth* to take vengeance; but rather, that he waiteth till his own are come out of her, and until her iniquity is filled up; for then he will execute the judgment written, and will remember, as has been said, the Babylonians and all their ways.

V. *The Fifth Cause.*

Antichrist must be destroyed *because she hath put out of order and confounded the rule and government that God has set up in the world.* I say she has put it out of order, and confounded it in all places where she rules, so that it cannot accomplish the design of him that ordained it, to wit, to be a terror to evil works, and a praise to them that do well.

Wherefore we read, that those *horns* or *kings* where mystery Babylon sitteth, are upon the heads of that beast that carrieth her, which beast is her protector. Magistracy is God's ordinance, appointed for the good of society, and for the peace and safety of those that are good. But this Antichrist has, where she rules, put all out of order; and no wonder, for she has *bepuddled* the word of God: no wonder then, I say, if the foundations of the world be out of course. It is she that hath turned the sword of the magistrate against those that keep God's law: it is she that has made it the ruin of the good and virtuous, and a protection to the vile and base. Wherefore, when the Holy Ghost tells us that the time is coming in which God will count with the bloody-minded, for the murders that they have committed, he in a manner doth quite excuse the magistrate, saying, "Woe to the bloody city! it is full of lies and robbery; the prey departeth not: the noise of a whip, the noise of the rattling of wheels, and of the prancing horses, and of the jumping chariots. The horseman lifteth up both the bright sword and the glittering spear, and there is a multitude of slain, and a great number of carcasses, and there is no end of their corpses; they stumble upon their corpses." (Nahum iii. 1—3.) But what is the cause of all this slaying, and the reason of this abundance of corpses? Why, it is because of the unsatiable thirst of the bloody city after blood; and "because of the multitude of the whoredoms of the well-favoured harlot, the mistress of witchcrafts, that selleth nations through her whoredoms, and families through her witchcrafts." (Nahum iii. 4.) But doth this bloody city spill this blood by herself simply, as she is the adulterated whore? No, this church has found out a trick; that is to say, to quarrel with Christ in his members; and to persuade the powers where she rules to set ensnaring laws to catch them, and to execute the same upon them.

Thus when the synagogue of Satan, of old, had taken Christ, and accused him, they made Pontius Pilate to condemn and hang him. But God has begun to show to some of the kings this wickedness, and has prevailed with them to PROTEST against her. And in the meantime, for those that are yet in the bed of love with her, the Holy Ghost doth, in the text last mentioned, and in Rev. xviii. 24, much excuse them for the blood that they have shed, and for the injuries that they have done to his people, because they have not doue it of their mere inclinations, nor in the prosecution of their office, but through the whoredoms and witchcrafts of this well-favoured harlot, who hath with false doctrines, false promises, and causeless curses, prevailed on them to do it. And they have done it, rather of *fear* than *favour.* Some indeed have more doted upon her beauty, and have more thoroughly been devoted to her service ; but they also had not that aptness to do so of themselves, but have been forced to it by the power of her enchantments; therefore, I say, the main guilt shall be laid at her door, for that she in chief has deserved it. " Son of man (says God) take up a lamentation for the princess of Israel." Why ? Because their mother, the Church, was at that time adulterated, and become a lioness, had lain down with the heathen, and so brought forth young lions, that is, rulers : " And she brought up one of her whelps : it became a young lion ; and it learned to catch the prey ; it devoured men." (Ezek. xix. 1—3.) *It learnt, it learnt :* but of *who* but of its *dam,* or of the lioness to whom she had put it to learn to do such things? Therefore they are to be lamented and pitied, rather than condemned, and their mother made to bear the blame. Wherefore it follows, " She was pulled up in fury, she was cast down to the ground, and the east wind dried up her fruit : her strong rods .were broken and withered; the fire consumed them. And now she is planted in the wilderness, (in the provinces of Babylon,) in a dry and thirsty ground. And fire is gone out of a rod of her branches, which hath devoured her fruit, so that he hath no strong rod to be a sceptre to rule. This is a lamentation, and shall be for a lamentation." (Ezek. xix. 12—14.)

VI. *The Sixth Cause.*

Antichrist must be destroyed, because of *her exceeding covetousness.* Religion, such as it is, is the thing pretended to; but the great things of this world are the things really intended by her in all her seeming self-denials and devotions. And for this covetousness also it is that this destruction is to fall upon her : " Woe to him that coveteth an evil covetousness to his house, (to his church,) that he may set his nest on high," (Hab. ii. 9 ;) (for he could not do the one before he had obtained the other :) for then indeed they began to be high, when they had so inveigled Constantine, that he bestowed upon them much riches and honour ; and then it was cried by an angel, and the cry was heard in the city, Constantinople : " Woe ! woe ! woe ! this day is venom poured into the Church of God !" (as both my Lord Cobham and Mr. Fox witness in the book of " Acts and Monuments.")

Nor has any generation since the world began, been so insatiably greedy of gain, as these poor people have been : they have got kingdoms, they have got crowns, they have got, —— What have they not got ? They have got everything but grace and pardon. Did I say before that *religion* is their pretence ? Doth not the whole course of their way declare it to their face ? Every one of them, from the least even to the greatest, is given to covetousness, from the prophet even to the priest, every one dealeth falsely. (Jer. vi. 13; viii. 10.) *Money, money,* as the pedlar cries, broken or whole, is the sinews of their religion : and it is for that they set kingdoms, crowns, principalities, places, preferments, sacraments, pardons, prayers, indulgences, liberty ; yea, and souls and bodies of men, women, and children to sale. Yea, it is for this that they have invented so many places, offices, names, titles, orders, vows, &c. It is to get money, to rob countries, that they may make their nests on high : and indeed they have done it, to the amazement of all the world. They are clambered up above *kings* and *princes,* and *emperors:* they wear the *triple-crown :* they have made *kings* bow at their *feet,* and *emperors* stand bare-foot at their *gates :* they have *kicked* the crowns of princes from their heads, and *set* them on again with their *toes.* Thus their covetousness has set them high, even above the suns, moons, and stars of this world; but to what end ? That they may be cast down to hell.

VII. *The Seventh Cause.*

Antichrist must be destroyed, because *he standeth in the way of the setting up of the kingdom of Christ in the world.* Many princes were in Edom before there was a king in Israel; and Christ has suffered Antichrist to set up before him. And he standeth in his way, and has so overspread the world in all places with that which is directly contrary to him, that he cannot set up his kingdom, until that which is Antichrist's is tumbled down to the ground ; even as a man whose ground is full of thorns, and briars, and weeds, cannot sow in expectation of a crop until he has removed them. And these seeds has Antichrist sown where the kingdom of Christ should stand. " Upon the land of my people shall come up thorns and briars ; yea, upon all the houses of joy in the joyous city : because the palaces shall be forsaken, the multitude of the city shall be left ; the forts and towers shall be for dens for ever, a joy of wild asses, a pasture of flocks, (this is to happen to the Church of God,) until the Spirit be poured upon us from on high, and the wilderness be a fruitful field, and the fruitul field be counted for a forest." (Isa. xxxii. 13—15.) And the antichristian synagogue be turned into a wilderness.

When God came from Egypt with his people, to set up his kingdom in Canaan, he cast out the heathen before them in order thereunto ; " Thou hast brought a vine out of Egypt, thou hast cast out the heathen, and planted it." (Ps. lxxx. 8.) Wherefore, Antichrist must be removed and destroyed for this : for Antichrist is in flat opposition to Christ, as Tibni was to Omri, (1 Kings xvi. 21, 22 ;) wherefore Antichrist must die. The reason is, because Christ's kingdom shall be peaceable without molestation ; and glorious without the fumes and fogs of antichristian darkness : because also, as the world hath seen the manner of the reign of Antichrist, and how tyrannical and out-rageous a kingdom his is, so they shall see the reign of Christ, by his word and spirit in his people, how peaceable, how fruitful in blessedness and prosperity his kingdom is. And hence it is that God purposeth to bury Antichrist before he sets " glory in the land of the living," (Ezek. xxvi. 20, 21 ;) as also you read in the book of Revelations, for there you find the kingdom of Antichrist was destroyed before the New Jerusalem was set up. When men intend to build a new house, if in the place where the old one stood, they first pull down the old one, raze the foundation, and then they begin their new. Now God, as I said, will have his primitive Church-state set up in this world, (even where Antichrist has set up his ;) wherefore, in order to this, Antichrist must be pulled down, down stick and stone ; and, then, they that live to see it will behold the New Jerusalem come down from heaven, *as a bride* adorned for her husband.

New wine is not put into old bottles, nor a new piece into an old garment; nor shall any of the old antiscriptural ordinances, ceremonies, rites, or vessels of the man of sin be made use of, or ac-counted anything worth, in this day of the king-dom of Jesus Christ. And thus I have showed you something of Antichrist, of his ruin, and of the manner and signs of the approach thereof; together with the means and causes of his ruin : all which I leave to the judgment of the godly, and beg their instruction, where they see me to be out ; and shall conclude, after a short word of application.

First. Must Antichrist be destroyed? Then this informs us that a time is coming wherein there shall be no Antichrist to afflict God's Church any more. It is Antichrist, antichristians, and antichristianism, that is the cause of the troubles of Christians, *for being Christians.* And therefore it is from the consideration of this that it is said, men shall beat their swords into ploughshares, and their spears into pruning-hooks, and that they shall learn war no more, (Isa. ii. 4 ;) yea, it is from the consideration of this, that it is said the child shall play with venomous and destroying beasts, and that a little child shall lead the *wolf,* the *leopard,* and the *young lion,* and that the weaned child shall put his hand into the cockatrice's den, and catch no hurt thereby. (Isa. xi. 6—9.) For, as was said before, it is through the instigation of this spirit of error, that the governors of the world have heretofore done hurt to Zion, and I say now again, all things shall turn to their right course, and occupy their places, as do the bodies in the higher orbs,

Second. Is Antichrist to be destroyed, and must she have an end? Then this gives us to under-stand, that a day is coming when Antichrist shall be unknown, not seen nor felt by the Church of God. There are men to be born who shall not know Antichrist, but as they read in the word that such a thing has been. These shall talk of her, as Israel's children's children were to talk of Pharaoh, of his cruelty, of his tasks, of his pride, of the Red Sea, and how he was drowned there : they shall talk of them, as of those that have been long dead ; as of those who for their horrible wickedness are laid in the pit's mouth. This will be some of that sweet chat that the saints shall, at their spare hours, have in time to come. When God has pulled this dragon out of the sea, this leviathan out of his river, and cast his dead carcass upon the open field, then shall those whose ances-tors have been put into terrors by him, come flocking to see the monster ; and shall rejoice for all the mercy. In that day the Church of God shall say, " O Lord, I will praise thee : though thou wast angry with me, thine anger is turned away, and thou comfortest me. In that day shall ye say, Praise the Lord, call upon his name, declare his doings among the people," &c. (Isa. xii. 1, 4.) O how sweetly did David, and the Church in his day, sing of the ruins of the Egyptians, and the deliverances of their fathers, which had been in times of old ! (Ps. lxviii.) to wit, what God did in Egypt, what he did at the Red Sea, what he did to Sihon, to Og, and to the remnant of the giants ; how he divided the waters of Jordan, and gave the land of Canaan in its fruit-fulness among his people, (Ps. cv. ;) how that though Pharaoh and his horsemen and chariots were terrible *then,* yet *now* there is nothing left but their souls, their feet, and the palms of their hands ; nothing but that which can do no hurt ; nothing but what may minister an occasion of joyful remembrance of them. (Ps. cvi. ; cxxxii.)

Third. Is Antichrist to be destroyed? *Then this calls aloud to God's people to make haste to come out of her.* " Ho, ho," says the prophet, (he cries out as if the people were asleep,) " Come forth, and flee from the land of the north." (Zech. ii. 6.) The people of God in the latter days will want a heart to come out of her, with that fear of her plagues as they should : wherefore another says, " Come out of her, my people, that ye be not partakers of her sins, and that ye receive not of her plagues." (Rev. xviii. 4.) When Israel was carried into Babylon, it was not that they should dwell there for ever, though they were bid to build them houses, and beget them children there. But when they had built, planted vineyards, and got wives and children there, it was hard getting them from thence again ; for now they were as it were naturalized to the country, and to the man-ners of it. (Jer. xxix. 4—7.) But God will have them out, (but they must not think to carry thence their houses and vineyards on their backs,) or he will destroy them with those destructions wherewith he hath threatened to destroy Babylon itself. Flesh will hang behind, because it favoureth the things of the flesh, plenty of which there is in that country : but they that will live after the flesh must die. "Wherefore come out from among them, and be ye separate, and touch not the unclean thing, and I will receive you, and I will be a father unto you, and ye shall be my sons and daughters, saith the Lord Almighty." (2 Cor. vi. 17, 18.) But why (some may say) *must we come out?* I answer, because God has *temple-work* to do, *temple-worship* to do, *temple-sacrifices* to offer, and none of these things can by any means be done, but at Jerusalem. But if you still object, and say, "the Lord has raised us up prophets in Babylon," and we will not come out; you must not murmur if you feel what is to follow. And that such may know upon what bottom they stand, let them read the 29th chapter of Jeremiah, verses 15—19.

Fourth. Must Antichrist be destroyed? *Then what mean they who were to appearance once come out, but now are going thither again?* If it cost Lot's wife dear for but *looking* back, shall it not cost them much dearer that are *going* back, that are *gone* back again? and that *after* the angel had fled through the midst of heaven, preaching the gospel to those that dwell on the earth ? (Rev. xiv. 6—10.) They that received the mark of the beast at first, *before* this angel came forth, are, when compared with these, excusable, (Rev. xiii. 16, 17;) wherefore, they are not threatened with that smoking wrath, as are these which are here under consideration.

You dread that which is like *to* become of them that will be so mad to run into an house when fire is putting to the gunpowder barrel, in order to its blowing up; why thus do they, let their pretended cause be what it will, that are returning again to Babel. Are her plagues pleasant or easy to be borne? Or dost thou think that God is at play with thee, and that he threateneth but in jest? Her plagues are *death*, and *mourning*, and *famine*, and *fire*, (Rev. xviii. 8 ;) are these things to be overlooked? And they that, as before is hinted, shall receive the mark of the beast in their forehead, or in their hand, and shall worship him, they, "the same shall drink of the wine of the wrath of God." (Rev. xiv. 10.) And will this be a delightsome draught? Remember how ill God took it, that his people of old, in their hearts, though but in their hearts, went back again into Egypt. You may say, but I have *friends, relations,* and *concerns* in Babylon. And I answer, so had Lot in Sodom, (Gen. xix. 14—16;) but for all that he must either quickly come out, or run the hazard of being burned there with them. But methinks a people that belong to God should be willing to leave all to follow him; besides, his presence is promised at Jerusalem, there, also, will he accept thy offerings.

Fifth. Is Antichrist to be destroyed ? *Then let*

them that love God, his Son, and his Zion, cry to God that it may be hastened in its time. One of the songs of Zion is, that Babylon shall be destroyed ; the cries of the souls of them that were slain for the witness of Jesus is, that Babylon may be counted with, and that their blood may be revenged upon her : the promise is, that Babylon shall be destroyed ; and do we hold our tongues ? The Church of God will not flourish as it should, until Babylon is destroyed ; the world will never be in its right wits, until Babylon is destroyed ; the kingdom of Christ will never be set up, in and by his Church, as it ought, and shall, until Antichrist is destroyed : there will never be peace upon earth till Antichrist is destroyed ; and God has promised that there shall be peace and truth, and glory, when Babylon is destroyed ; and do we hold our peace ? Besides, your innocency in suffering; your honesty towards God, in your testimony for his truth ; the substantial ground which you have for the bottom of your faith, as to things controverted betwixt Antichrist and you, will never be manifested as it will then ; and so consequently, you never so brought out to the light, and your enemies never so put to shame as then : "Then shame shall cover her that said unto thee, Where is the Lord thy God ?" Wherefore, as I said, cry unto the Lord, keep not silence, give him no rest, let him not alone, until he has delivered his miserable people out of the mouth of this lion, and from the paw of this bear.

Sixth. Is Antichrist to be destroyed? *Then let us live in the expectation of it,* and let this be one of our songs in the house of our pilgrimage. God bids his people, while in Babylon, to let Jerusalem come into their mind, (Jer. li. 50,) and writes to them that then were in her, to acquaint them that he remembered them still, and would assuredly deliver them from that *place* and *state:* and wherefore doth he thus, but to beget an expectation in them of their salvation and deliverance ? (Jer. xxix. 13, 14.) The Lord is so pleased with the faith and expectation of his people, as to this, that they seldom are herein concerned as they should, but he steps in with them, and warms their hearts. The reason is, because the faith of God's people, as to the downfall of Babylon, stands upon as sure a foundation as doth the salvation of their souls ; and that next to that, God is as much delighted in what he has purposed to do against Babylon, as in anything else in the earth ; and therefore, if you consider it well, the great and glorious promises that are to be fulfilled on earth, are to be fulfilled when Antichrist is dead and buried : these *bits* are too good even for his children to have, so long as this dog is by, lest he should snatch at the crumbs thereof ; wherefore they are reserved until he is gone: for thus saith the Lord, "that after seventy years be accomplished at Babylon, I will visit you, and perform my good word towards you, in causing you to return to this place : for I know the thoughts that I think towards you, saith the Lord; thoughts of peace, and not of evil, to give you an expected end." This is in Jeremiah the twenty-ninth, (verses 10, 11;) and in chapter the thirty-first he adds, " therefore they shall come and sing in the height of Zion, and shall flow together to the goodness of the Lord for wheat, and for wine, and for oil, and for the young of the flock, and of the herd; their soul shall be as a watered garden, and they shall not sorrow any more at all. Then shall the virgin rejoice in the dance, both young men and old together: for I will turn their mourning into joy, and will comfort them, and make them rejoice from their sorrow: And I will satiate the soul of the priests with fatness, and my people shall be satisfied with my goodness, saith the Lord." (Verses 12 to 14.) Again, in the thirty-second chapter, still speaking of the same thing, he saith, " Yea, I will rejoice over them to do them good, and I will plant them in this land assuredly, with my whole heart, and with my whole soul." (Verse 41.)

I conclude this with that which I find in chapter the thirty-third—"And I will cleanse them from all their iniquity, whereby they have sinned against me, and I will pardon all their iniquities whereby they have sinned, and whereby they have transgressed against me. And it shall be to me a name of joy, a praise and an honour before all the nations of the earth, which shall hear of all the good that I do unto them: and they shall fear and tremble, for all the goodness, and for all the prosperity that I procure unto it." (Verses 8, 9.)

Seventh. Must Antichrist be destroyed? *Then this should make us glad, when we see the signs of his fall presenting themselves to our view.* Indeed, the signs of his fall, or those that forerun it, are terrible and amazing to behold: but what of that, since the wrinkles that are in their faces threaten not us, but them? A man is angry, and will punish; yea, and whets his sword, makes his rod, and he speaks not a word, but *blood, blood* is in it. Indeed, this should make them that are concerned in that anger be afraid (but the judgment is, they are fast asleep,) but what is in all this of terror to them, for the pleading whose cause he is so angry with the other. Nothing whereat the innocent should be afraid. Cold blasts in November are not received with that gentleness as are colder in March and April; for that these last cold ones are but the farewell notes of a piercing winter; they also bring with them the signs and tokens of a comfortable summer. Why, the Church is now at the rising of the year; let then the blasts at present, or to come, be what they will, Antichrist is assuredly drawing towards his downfall: and though the devil, knowing what is to be done to him, and to his kingdom, shall so blind his disciples, and fright the godly, do something like it upon the Church of Christ; yet we should look through these paper-winkers, and espy in all this, that fear, yea, certain terrible judgments are following of him at the heels, by which not only the soul, spirit, and life of Antichrist, but the body thereof; yea, body, and soul, and head, are quickly to go down thither, from whence they, as such, shall not arise again. Amen.

PREFATORY REMARKS

ON

THE HEAVENLY FOOTMAN.

A MIND disposed to thought rejoices in the infinite variety of suggestions and openings to reflection furnished by Scripture. Even in a state of lassitude the depression must be deep indeed, if some expression, some image, do not occur to break the lethargy, and excite interest and inquiry. A traveller, or a man engaged in a race; a benighted, homeless wanderer seeking shelter; a poor fugitive fleeing from the avenger, are objects which may awake sympathy in almost any heart, and so lead it to profitable meditation. Among the multitude of living forms, rising before us wherever we look into the great mirror of Scripture, these are very prominent, and comforting as well as solemn truths may be learnt by making our thoughts companions of their journey. There is, in this respect, an unnoticed appeal to reflection in the history of the prodigal son. He was a traveller. We may trace his steps from his father's house, from city to city, from one scene to another, till, at last, he is discovered lying famished on the sere leaves of a bare wood, unfed and unsheltered. His journey, on return, may suggest feelings of another kind. It is not to be supposed that he had only to say "I will arise, and go to my father," to find himself immediately at home. He had travelled long and far. A weary distance lay between him and the mansion of his father. With no provision for the way, bare and sore-footed, his mind harassed by doubts and questionings as to how he might be received, if received at all, his return presents some striking images of the state of a penitent, happily resolving to seek mercy, but having to pass through many tribulations before he dare hope to reach it.

The very words, " So run that ye may obtain," suggest thoughts of an ardent hope, fixed on some object of desire, and now directed to the means for securing success. Up to the very point of starting in the race, we may see the eager candidate subjecting himself to the severest discipline, trying his strength and fleetness, and continually calculating his prospects of success. Thus it is not only in the race itself that an image is presented to us of spiritual energy, tried to the uttermost, but we have thought upon thought awakened by the recollection that from the moment a noble design, an ardent wish, enters the mind of a man, indications are given that a change has been wrought in the entire state of his being.

A more exciting species of reflection is created by the supposed view of a wretched fugitive pursued by the avenger. The speed of him who is seen running in a race, with a crown, or some other prize in view, stimulates the noblest and most generous kind of sympathy. Very different is the feeling produced when the eye is fixed upon a man who, should his breath fail, or his foot slip, would the next instant perish by the sword. Anxiety, not unmixed with horror, is aroused at such a spectacle; and the mind which realizes to itself the spiritual lesson thus suggested, has in itself a warning to flee in time, from the wrath to come, not likely to be forgotten.

There still remains the more ordinary image of a traveller, his face towards home, but with a long, difficult, and laborious journey still before him. When the Christian wisely transfers the representation to himself, and so makes it a reality, he has occupation for his mind in ways the most interesting and profitable. A little effort, sincerely made, will give him the sense, the feelings, and emotions of a man actually requiring the foresight, the caution, diligence, courage, and other qualities of character corresponding to those so well known as the marks of a prudent traveller. Hence one of his first anxieties will be to determine whether he be on the right road. Obvious to common sense as the necessity for such caution must appear, it is equally certain that such caution is but little exercised by those who think themselves on the path of life. Assuredly no prudent traveller, in a case where error could be possible, would go so boldly and uninquiringly on his route, as many Christians take it for certain that they are on the road to heaven, though they have never either patiently or earnestly asked the way.

So again, the actual traveller, and his spiritual antitype, will not fail to consider what means of support and shelter they may look for in their progress. The hardiest constitution, the bravest spirit, cannot be sustained without due nourishment. Neglect in this respect has ruined many a Christian.

Sinking with exhaustion, inexperienced in the methods of seeking for help and support, the unhappy victim of his own thoughtlessness and presumption, falls prostrate under the first pressure of his unavoidable necessities and dangers. The man travelling on foot is especially exposed to hardships, and requires, accordingly, a large measure of both prudence and fortitude. But such a traveller is so far a truer and more lively representative of the Christian. No artificial means of conveyance, or support, can avail him on the path of salvation. He must make the journey in the strength of his own frame, except as that frame is supported from heaven, the power of Christ, and the life of the Spirit, operating upon it. But the support thus rendered still leaves him on foot. It does not take him out of the conditions of his own individual responsibility. As long as no sufferings, burdens, or temptations but such as are common to men, occur to prove his strength, he must wend his way by its proper exercise. Should a deluge be at hand, he will have an ark to bear him over the flood: if his work be done, and his journey at an end, there will be the chariot and the horses thereof, to bear him on high. But while he is still in the ordinary condition of humanity, it is as a simple, humble traveller on foot that he must pursue his way. His very weakness, his unostentatious state, is useful. It teaches him to beware of danger before it happen, and to pray for the unseen guardianship of heaven. The support which he needs, must be furnished him at every short stage of his route, or he will faint on the way. Hence a necessary dependence on the grace of God. Were he to regard himself as one travelling with horsemen, he might either suppose that he could hasten his course whenever he pleased, or that he might depend upon his own resources for the supply of necessities. But he wisely owns that, at the best, for some time to come, he must travel among those on foot; asking, not demanding shelter; confessing, not concealing poverty; patiently pursuing his way, looking for the end, but not supposing he has attained it, whenever weariness warn him that without farther help he can go no further.

The comparison, or parable, of a man on foot travelling towards heaven, will suggest to most thoughtful minds numberless lessons applicable to their own state and necessities.

H. S.

THE HEAVENLY FOOTMAN;

OR,

A DESCRIPTION OF THE MAN THAT GETS TO HEAVEN.

TOGETHER WITH THE WAY HE RUNS IN, THE MARKS HE GOES BY; ALSO, SOME DIRECTIONS HOW TO RUN SO AS TO OBTAIN.

"And it came to pass, when they had brought them forth abroad, that he said, Escape for thy life; look not behind thee, neither stay thou in all the plain : escape to the mountain, lest thou be consumed."—GEN. xix. 17.

AN EPISTLE TO ALL THE SLOTHFUL AND CARELESS PEOPLE.

FRIENDS,—— Solomon saith that "the desire of the slothful killeth him," (Prov. xxi. 25;) and if so, what will slothfulness itself do to those that entertain it? The proverb is, "He that sleepeth in harvest is a son that causeth shame." (Prov. x. 5.) And this I dare be bold to say, no greater shame can befall a man than to see that he hath fooled away his soul, and sinned away eternal life. And I am sure this is the next way to do it; namely, to be slothful,—slothful I say in the work of salvation. The vineyard of the slothful man, in reference to the things of this life, is not fuller of briars, nettles, and stinking weeds, than he that is slothful for heaven, hath his heart full of heart-choking and soul-damning sin.

Slothfulness hath these two evils: first, to neglect the time in which it should be getting of heaven; and by that means doth, in the second place, bring in untimely repentance. I will warrant you that he who should lose his soul in this world through slothfulness, will have no cause to be glad thereat when he comes to hell.

Slothfulness is usually accompanied with carelessness, and carelessness is for the most part begotten by senselessness; and senselessness doth again put fresh strength into slothfulness, and by this means the soul is left remediless.

Slothfulness shutteth out Christ; slothfulness shameth the soul. (Sol. Song v. 2—4. Prov. xii. 4.)

Slothfulness it is condemned even by the feeblest of all the creatures. "Go to the ant, thou sluggard, consider her ways and be wise." (Prov. vi. 6;) "The sluggard will not plough by reason of the cold," (Prov. xx. 4;) that is, he will not break up the fallow ground of his heart because there must be some pains taken by him that will do it;

"therefore shall he beg in harvest," that is, when the saints of God shall have their glorious heaven and happiness given to them; but the sluggard shall "have nothing," that is, be never the better for his crying for mercy, according to that in Matt. xxv. 10—12.

If you would know a sluggard in the things of heaven, compare him with one that is slothful in the things of this world. As,

I. He that is slothful is loth to set about the work he should follow: so is he that is slothful for heaven.

II. He that is slothful, is one that is willing to make delays: so is he that is slothful for heaven.

III. He that is a sluggard, any small matter that cometh in between, he will make it a sufficient excuse to keep him off from plying his works: so it is also with him that is slothful for heaven.

IV. He that is slothful doth his work by the halves : and so it is with him that is slothful for heaven. He may almost, but he shall never altogether, obtain perfection of deliverance from hell; he may almost, but he shall never, without he mend, be altogether a saint.

V. They that are slothful do usually lose the season in which things are to be done : and thus it is also with them that are slothful for heaven, they miss the seasons of grace. And therefore,

VI. They that are slothful have seldom or never good fruit : so also it will be with the soul-sluggard.

VII. They that are slothful they are chid for the same : so also will Christ deal with those that are not active for him. Thou wicked or slothful servant, out of thine own mouth will I judge thee; thou saidst I was thus, and thus, wherefore then gavest not thou my money to the bank, &c. (Luke

xix. 22.)   Take the unprofitable servant, and cast him into utter darkness, where shall be weeping and gnashing of teeth. (Matt. xxv. 26—30.)

1. What shall I say? time runs; and will you be slothful?

2. Much of your lives are past; and will you be slothful?

3. Your souls are worth a thousand worlds; and will you be slothful?

4. The day of death and judgment is at the door; and will you be slothful?

5. The curse of God hangs over your heads; and will you be slothful?

6. Besides the devils are earnest, laborious, and seek by all means every day, by every sin, to keep you out of heaven, and hinder you of salvation; and will you be slothful?

7. Also your neighbours are diligent for things that will perish; and will you be slothful for things that will endure for ever?

8. Would you be willing to be damned for slothfulness?

9. Would you be willing the angels of God should neglect to fetch your souls away to heaven when you lie a dying, and the devils stand by ready to scramble for them?

10. Was Christ slothful in the work of your redemption?

11. Are his ministers slothful in tendering this unto you?

12. And lastly, if all this will not move, I tell you God will not be slothful or negligent to damn you—whose damnation now of a long time slumbereth not—nor the devils will not neglect to fetch thee, nor hell neglect to shut its mouth upon thee.

Sluggard, art thou asleep still?   Art thou resolved to sleep the sleep of death?   Wilt neither tidings from heaven or hell awake thee?   Wilt thou say still, "Yet a little sleep, a little slumber," and "a little folding of the hands to sleep?" (Prov. vi. 10.)   Wilt thou yet turn thyself in thy sloth, as the door is turned upon the hinges?   O that I was one that was skilful in lamentation, and had but a yearning heart towards thee, how would I pity thee!   How would I bemoan thee!   O that I could with Jeremiah let my eyes run down with rivers of waters for thee!   Poor soul, lost soul, dying soul, what a hard heart have I that I cannot mourn for thee!   If thou shouldst lose but a limb, a child, or a friend, it would not be so much, but poor man it is *thy soul*; if it was to lie in hell but for a day, but for a year, nay, ten thousand years, it would (in comparison) be nothing.   But O it is for ever!   O this cutting *ever!*   What a soul-amazing word will that be, which saith, "Depart from me, ye cursed, into EVERLASTING fire!" &c.

Obj. But if I should set in, and run as you would have me, then I must run from all my friends, for none of them are running that way.

Ans. And if thou dost, thou wilt run into the bosom of Christ, and of God, and then what harm will that do thee?

Obj. But if I run this way then I must run from all my sins,

Ans. That is true indeed; yet if thou dost not, thou wilt run into hell-fire.

Obj. But if I run this way then I shall be hated, and lose the love of my friends and relations, and of those that I expect benefit from, or have reliance on, and I shall be mocked of all my neighbours.

Ans. And if thou dost not thou art sure to lose the love and favour of God and Christ, the benefits of heaven and glory, and be mocked of God for thy folly, "I also will laugh at your calamity; I will mock when your fear cometh:" and if thou wouldst not be hated and mocked, then take heed thou by thy folly dost not procure the displeasure and mockings of the great God; for his mocks and hatred will be terrible, because they will fall upon thee in terrible times, even when tribulation and anguish taketh hold on thee; which will be when death and judgment comes, when all the men in the earth, and all the angels in heaven, cannot help thee. (Prov. i. 26—28.)

Obj. But surely I may begin this time enough, a year or two hence, may I not?

Ans. First. Hast thou any lease of thy life; did ever God tell thee thou shalt live half a year, or two months longer?   Nay, it may be that thou mayest not live so long?   And therefore,

Secondly. Wilt thou be so sottish and unwise, as to venture thy soul upon a little uncertain time?

Thirdly. Dost thou know whether the day of grace will last a week longer or no?   For the day of grace is past with some before their life is ended: and if it should be so with thee, wouldest thou not say, O that I had begun to run before the day of grace had been past, and the gates of heaven shut against me.   But,

Fourthly. If thou shouldst see any of thy neighbours neglect the making sure of either house or land to themselves if they had it proffered to them, saying, Time enough hereafter, when the time is uncertain,—and besides, they do not know whether ever it will be proffered to them again, or no,—I say, wouldest thou not then call them fools?   And if so, then dost thou think that thou art a wise man to let thy immortal soul hang over hell by a thread of uncertain time, which may soon be cut asunder by death?

But to speak plainly, all these are the works of a slothful spirit.   Arise man, be slothful no longer; set foot, and heart, and all into the way of God, and run, the crown is at the end of the race; there also standeth the loving forerunner, even Jesus, who hath prepared heavenly provision to make thy soul welcome, and he will give it thee with a willinger heart than ever thou canst desire it of him.   O, therefore, do not delay the time any longer, but put into practice the words of the men of Dan to their brethren, after they had seen the goodness of the land of Canaan : "Arise," say they, &c., "for we have seen the land, and behold it is very good; and are ye still ?" (or do you forbear running ?) "Be not slothful to go, and to enter to possess the land." (Judges xviii. 19.) Farewell.

I wish our souls may meet with comfort at the journey's end.

JOHN BUNYAN.

THE CONTENTS OF THE WHOLE OF THIS BOOK.

THE HEAVENLY FOOTMAN.

1 COR. ix. 24.
"So run, that ye may obtain."

HEAVEN and happiness is that which every one desireth, insomuch that wicked Balaam could say, "Let me die the death of the righteous, and let my last end be like his." (Numb. xxiii. 10.) Yet for all this there are but very few that do obtain that ever-to-be desired glory, insomuch that many eminent professors drop short of a welcome from God into this pleasant place.

The apostle, therefore, because he did desire the salvation of the souls of the Corinthians, to whom he writes this epistle, layeth them down in these words such counsel, which, if taken, would be for their help and advantage.

First. Not to be wicked, and sit still, and wish for heaven, but *to run* for it.

Second. Not to content themselves with every kind of running; but, saith he, "*So run, that ye may obtain.*" As if he should say, Some, because they would not lose their souls, they begin to run betimes, (Eccles. xii. 1,) they run apace,

N 2

they run with patience, (Heb. xii. 1,) they run the right way. (Matt. xiv. 26.) Do YOU *so run*. Some run from both father, mother, friends, and companions, and thus that they may have the crown. Do YOU *so run*. Some run through temptations, afflictions, good report, evil report, that they may win the pearl. (1 Cor. iv. 13. 2 Cor. vi.) Do YOU *so run*. " So run, that ye may obtain."

These words, they are taken from men's running for a wager: a very apt similitude to set before the eyes of the saints of the Lord. " Know ye not that they which run in a race run all, but one receiveth the prize? So run, that ye may obtain." That is, do not only run, but be sure you win as well as run. " So run, that ye may obtain."

I shall not need to make any great ado in opening the words at this time, but shall rather lay down one doctrine that I do find in them; and in prosecuting that, I shall show you, in some measure, the scope of the words.

I. The Doctrine of the Text.

They that will have heaven must run for it; I say, they that will have heaven they must run for it. I beseech you to heed it well. " Know ye not that they which run in a race run all, but one receiveth the prize? So run ye." The prize is heaven, and if you will have it, you must run for it. You have another scripture for this in the 12th of the Hebrews, the 1st, 2nd, and 3rd verses. " Wherefore seeing we also," saith the apostle, " are compassed about with so great a cloud of witnesses, let us lay aside every weight, and the sin which doth so easily beset us, and let us run with patience the race that is set before us." And *let us run*, saith he.

Again, saith Paul, " I therefore so run, not as uncertainly, so fight I," &c.

II. The word RUN opened.

But before I go any farther :

1. *Fleeing.*

Observe, that this running is not an ordinary, or any sort of running, but it is to be understood of the swiftest sort of running : and therefore in the 6th of the Hebrews it is called " a fleeing;" that " we might have a strong consolation, who have fled for refuge, to lay hold upon the hope set before us." Mark, " who have fled." It is taken from that 20th of Joshua, concerning the man that was to flee to the city of refuge, when the avenger of blood was hard at his heels, to take vengeance on him for the offence he had committed; therefore it is a *running* or *fleeing* for one's life. A running with all might and main, as we use to say. So run.

2. *Pressing.*

Second. This running in another place is called a pressing. " I press toward the mark," (Phil. iii. 14,) which signifieth, that they that will have heaven, they must not stick at any difficulties they meet with, but press, crowd and thrust through all that may stand between heaven and their souls. So run.

3. *Continuing.*

Third. This running is called in another place, " a continuing in the way of life." " If ye continue in the faith grounded, and settled, and be not moved away from the hope of the gospel" of Christ. (Col. i. 23.) Not to run a little now and then, by fits and starts, or half way, or almost thither; but to run for my life, to run through all difficulties, and to continue therein to the end of the race, which must be to the end of my life. So run, that ye may obtain.

III. Several Reasons for Clearing this Doctrine.

And the reasons for this point are these :

First. Because all or every one that runneth doth not obtain the prize; there be many that do run, yea, and run far too, who yet miss of the crown that standeth at the end of the race. You know that all that run in a race do not obtain the victory; they all run, but one wins. And so it is here; it is not every one that runneth, nor every one that seeketh, nor every one that striveth for the mastery, that hath it. (Luke xiii.) Though a man do strive for the mastery, saith Paul, " yet he is not crowned except he strive lawfully ;" that is, unless he so run, and so strive, as to have God's approbation. (2 Tim. ii. 5.) What, do you think that every heavy-heeled professor will have heaven? What, every lazy one? Every wanton and foolish professor, that will be stopped by anything, kept back by anything, that scarce runneth so fast heavenward, as a snail creepeth on the ground? Nay, there are some professors do not go on so fast in the way of God, as a snail doth go on the wall, and yet these think that heaven and happiness is for them. But stay, there are many more that run than there be that obtain; therefore he that will have heaven must *run* for it.

Second. Because you know that though a man do run, yet if he do not overcome, or win, as well as run, what will they be the better for their running? They will get nothing. You know the man that runneth, he doth do it that he may win the prize; but if he doth not obtain it, he doth lose his labour, spend his pains and time, and that to no purpose; I say, he getteth nothing. And ah! how many such runners will there be found in the day of judgment! Even multitudes, multitudes that have run, yea, run so far as to come to heaven gates, and not able to get any further, but there stand knocking when it is too late, crying, " Lord, Lord," when they have nothing but rebukes for their pains. Depart from me, you come not here, you come too late, you run too lazily, the door is shut. "When once the master of the house is risen up," saith Christ, "and hath shut to the door, and ye begin to stand without and to knock at the door, saying, Lord, Lord, open unto us, I will say, I know ye not; depart," &c. (Luke xiii. 25.) O sad will the state of those be that run and miss; therefore if you will have heaven you must run for it; and "so run, that ye may obtain."

Third. Because the way is long, (I speak metaphorically,) and there is many a dirty step, many a high hill, much work to do, a wicked heart, world, and devil, to overcome; I say, there are many steps to be taken by those that intend to be saved, by running or walking in the steps of that faith of our father Abraham. Out of Egypt thou must go through the Red Sea; thou must run a long and tedious journey, through the vast howling wilderness, before thou come to the land of promise.

Fourth. They that will go to heaven they must run for it; because, as the way is long, so the time in which they are to get to the end of it is very uncertain; the time present is the only time; thou hast no more time allotted thee than that thou now enjoyest. "Boast not thyself of tomorrow, for thou knowest not what a day may bring forth." (Prov. xxvii. 1.) Do not say, I have time enough to get to heaven seven years hence: for I tell thee the bell may toll for thee before seven days more be ended; and when death comes, away thou must go, whether thou art provided or not: and therefore look to it; make no delays; it is not good dallying with things of so great concernment as the salvation or damnation of thy soul. You know he that hath a great way to go in a little time, and less by half than he thinks of, he had need *run* for it.

Fifth. They that will have heaven they must run for it, because the devil, the law, sin, death, and hell, followeth them. There is never a poor soul that is going to heaven, but the devil, the law, sin, death, and hell, makes after that soul. "Your adversary, the devil, as a roaring lion, walketh about, seeking whom he may devour." And I will assure you the devil is nimble, he can run apace, he is light of foot, he hath overtaken many, he hath turned up their heels, and hath given them an everlasting fall. Also the law, that can shoot a great way; have a care thou keep out of the reach of those great guns, the ten commandments. Hell also hath a wide mouth, it can stretch itself farther than you are aware of: and, as the angel said to Lot, Take heed, "look not behind thee, neither tarry thou in all the plain," (that is, anywhere between this and heaven,) "lest thou be consumed," (Gen. xix. 17,) so say I to thee, take heed, tarry not, lest either the devil, hell, death, or the fearful curses of the law of God, do overtake thee, and throw thee down in the midst of thy sins, so as never to rise and recover again. If this were well considered, then thou, as well as I, wouldst say, they that will have heaven must *run* for it.

Sixth. They that will go to heaven must run for it, because perchance the gates of heaven may be shut shortly. Sometimes sinners have not heaven gates open to them so long as they suppose; and if they be once shut against a man, they are so heavy, that all the men in the world, nor all the angels in heaven, are not able to open them. I shut, "and no man openeth," saith Christ. And how if thou shouldst come but one quarter of an hour too late? I tell thee it will cost thee an eternity to bewail thy misery in. Francis Spira can tell thee what it is to stay till the gate of mercy be quite shut; or to run so lazily, that they be shut before thou get within them. What, to be shut out! What, out of heaven! Sinner, rather than lose it, run for it; yea, and "so run, that thou mayest obtain."

Lastly. Because if thou lose, thou losest all—thou losest soul, God, Christ, heaven, ease, peace, &c. Besides, thou layest thyself open to all the shame, contempt, and reproach, that either God, Christ, saints, the world, sin, the devil, and all can lay upon thee. As Christ saith of the foolish builder, so will I say of thee, if thou be such a one who runs and missest; I say, even all that go by will begin to mock at thee, saying, This man began to run well, but was not able to finish. (Luke xiv. 28—30.) But more of this anon.

Quest. But how should a poor soul do to run? For this very thing is that which afflicteth me sore, (as you say,) to think that I may run, and yet fall short. Methinks to fall short at last, O it fears me greatly! Pray tell me, therefore, how I should run.

Ans. That thou mayest indeed be satisfied in this particular, consider these following things.

IV. Nine Directions how to Run.

The First Direction.

If thou wouldest so run as to obtain the kingdom of heaven, then be sure that thou get into the way that leadeth thither: for it is a vain thing to think that ever thou shalt have the prize, though thou runnest never so fast, unless thou art in the way that leads to it. Set the case that there should be a man in London that was to run to York for a wager; now, though he run never so swiftly, yet if he run full south, he might run himself quickly out of breath, and be never the nearer the prize, but rather the farther off. Just so is it here; it is not simply the runner, nor yet the hasty runner, that winneth the crown, unless he be in the way that leadeth thereto. I have observed, that little time which I have been a professor, that there is a great running to and fro, some this way, and some that way, yet it is to be feared most of them are out of the way; and then, though they run as swift as the eagle can fly, they are benefited nothing at all.

Here is one runs a quaking, another a ranting; one again runs after the Baptism, and another after the Independency: here's one for Free-will, and another for Presbytery, and yet possibly most of all these sects run quite the wrong way, and yet every one is for his life, his soul, either for heaven or hell.

If thou now say, Which is the way? I tell thee it is CHRIST THE SON OF MARY, THE SON OF GOD. Jesus saith, "I am the way, and the truth, and the life; no man cometh unto the Father but by me." (John xiv. 6.) So then thy business is, if thou wouldest have salvation, to see if Christ be thine, with all his benefits; whether he hath covered thee with his righteousness, whether he hath showed thee that thy sins are washed away with his heart-blood, whether thou art planted into him, and whether thou have faith in him, so as to make a life out of him, and to conform thee to him. That is, such faith as to conclude that thou art righteous, because Christ is thy righteousness, and so constrained to walk with him as the joy of thy heart, because he saveth thy soul. And for the Lord's sake take heed, and do not deceive thyself, and think thou art in the way upon too slight grounds; for if thou miss of the way, thou wilt miss of the prize; and if thou miss of that, I am sure thou wilt lose thy soul, even that soul which is worth more than the whole world.

But I have treated more largely on this in my book *Of the Two Covenants*, and therefore shall pass it now; only I beseech thee to have a care of thy soul, and that thou mayest so do, take this counsel :—

Mistrust thy own strength, and throw it away; down on thy knees in prayer to the Lord for the spirit of truth; search his word for direction; flee seducers' company; keep company with the soundest Christians. that have most experience of Christ; and be sure thou have a care of Quakers, Ranters, Free-willers: also do not have too much company with some Anabaptists, though I go under that name myself. I tell thee this is such a serious matter, and I fear thou wilt so little regard it, that the thoughts of the worth of the thing, and of thy too light regarding of it, doth even make my heart ache whilst I am writing to thee. The Lord teach thee the way by his Spirit, and then I am sure thou wilt know it. *So run.*

Only by the way let me bid thee have a care of two things, and so I shall pass to the next thing.

First. Have a care of relying on the outward obedience to any of God's commands, or thinking thyself ever the better in the sight of God for that.

Second. Take heed of fetching peace for thy soul from any inherent righteousness: but if thou canst believe, that as thou art a sinner, so thou art justified freely by the love of God, through the redemption that is in Christ; and that God, for Christ's sake, hath forgiven thee, not because he saw anything done, or to be done, in or by thee, to move him thereunto to do it; for that is the right way; the Lord put thee into it, and keep thee in it.

The Second Direction.

As thou shouldest get into the way, so thou shouldest also be much in studying and musing on the way. You know men that would be expert in any thing, they are usually much in studying of that thing, and so likewise is it with those that quickly grow expert in any way : this, therefore, thou shouldest do; let thy study be much exercised about Christ, which is the way; what he is, what he hath done, and why he is what he is, and why he hath done what is done; as why "he took upon him the form of a servant," why he was "made in the likeness of men," (Phil. ii. 7,) why he cried, why he died, why he bore the sin of the world, why he was made sin, and why he was made righteousness, why he is in heaven in the nature of man, and what he doth there. (2 Cor. v. 21;) be much in musing and considering of these things; be thinking also enough of those places which thou must not come near, but leave some on this hand, and some on that hand; as it is with those that travel into other countries, they must leave such a gate on this hand, and such a bush on that hand, and go by such a place, where standeth such a thing. Thus, therefore, thou must do : avoid such things which are expressly forbidden in the word of God. "Withdraw thy foot far from her, and come not nigh the door of her house, for her steps take hold on hell, going down to the chambers of death." (Prov. v. and vii.) And so of every thing that is not in the way, have a care of it, that thou go not by it, come not near it, have nothing to do with it. *So run.*

The Third Direction.

Not only thus, but in the next place, thou must strip thyself of those things that may hang upon thee, to the hindering of thee in the way to the kingdom of heaven, as covetousness, pride, lust, or whatever else thy heart may be inclining unto, which may hinder thee in this heavenly race. Men that run for a wager, if they intend to win as well as run, they do not use to encumber themselves, or carry those things about them that may be an hindrance to them in their running. "Every man that striveth for the mastery is temperate in all things," (1 Cor. ix. 25;) that is, he layeth aside everything that would be any ways a disadvantage to him; as saith the apostle, "Let us lay aside every weight, and the sin which doth so easily beset us, and let us run with patience the race that is set before us." (Heb. xii. 1.) It is but a vain thing to talk of going to heaven, if thou let thy heart be encumbered with those things that would hinder. Would you not say that such a man would be in danger of losing, though he run, if he fill his pockets with stones, hang heavy garments on his shoulders, and great lumpish shoes on his feet? So it is here; thou talkest of going to heaven, and yet fillest thy pocket with stones, *i.e.* fillest thy heart with this world lettest that hang on thy shoulders, with its profits and pleasures. Alas, alas, thou art widely mistaken! If thou intendest to win thou must strip, thou must lay aside every weight, thou must be temperate in all things. Thou must *so run*.

The Fourth Direction.

Beware of by-paths, take heed thou dost not turn into those lanes which lead out of the way. There are crooked paths, paths in which men go astray, paths that lead to death and damnation, but take heed of all those. (Isa. lxix. 8.) Some of them are dangerous because of practice, (Prov. vii. 25,) some because of opinion, but mind them not; mind the path before thee, look right before thee, turn neither to the right hand nor to the left, but let thine eyes look right on, even right before thee, (Prov. iii. 17;) "Ponder the path of thy feet, and let all thy ways be established. Turn not to the right hand, nor to the left. Remove thy foot far from evil." (Prov. iv. 26, 27.) This counsel being not so seriously taken as given, is the reason of that starting from opinion to opinion, reeling this way and that way, out of this lane into that lane, and so missing the way to the kingdom. Though the way to heaven be but one, yet there are many crooked lanes and by-paths shoot down upon it, as I may say. And again, notwithstanding the kingdom of heaven be the biggest city, yet usually those by-paths are most beaten, most travellers go those ways; and therefore the way to heaven is hard to be found, and as hard to be kept in, by reason of these. Yet nevertheless it is in this case, as it was with the harlot of Jericho, she had one scarlet thread tied in her window, by which her house was known. (Josh. ii. 18.) So it is here, the scarlet streams of Christ's blood run throughout the way to the kingdom of heaven; therefore mind that, see if thou do find the besprinkling of the blood of Christ in the way, and if thou do, be of good cheer, thou art in the right way; but have a care thou beguile not thyself with a fancy; for then thou mayest light into any lane or way; but that thou mayest not be mistaken, consider, though it seem never so pleasant, yet if thou do not find that in the very middle of the road there is writing with the heart-blood of Christ, that he came into the world to save sinners, and that we are justified, though we are ungodly, shun that way; for this it is which the apostle meaneth when he saith, we have "boldness to enter into the holiest by the blood of Jesus, by a new and living way which he hath consecrated for us, through the vail, that is to say, his flesh." (Heb. x. 19, 20.) How easy a matter is it in this our day for the devil to be too cunning for poor souls, by calling his by-paths the way to the kingdom! If such an opinion or fancy be but cried up by one or more, this inscription being set upon it by the devil, "This is the way of God," how speedily, greedily, and by heaps, do poor simple souls throw away themselves upon it; especially if it be daubed

over with a few external acts of morality, if so good! But this is because men do not know painted by-paths from the plain way to the kingdom of heaven. They have not yet learned the true Christ, and what his righteousness is, neither have they a sense of their own insufficiency; but are bold, proud, presumptuous, self-conceited. And therefore,

The Fifth Direction.

Do not thou be too much in looking too high in thy journey heavenwards. You know men that run a race do not use to stare and gaze this way and that, neither do they use to cast up their eyes too high, lest haply, through their too much gazing with their eyes after other things, they in the mean time stumble, and catch a fall. The very same case is this, if thou gaze and stare after every opinion and way that comes into the world; also if thou be prying overmuch into God's secret decrees, or let thy heart too much entertain questions about some nice foolish curiosities, thou mayest stumble and fall, as many hundreds in England have done, both in Ranting and Quakery, to their own eternal overthrow, without the marvellous operation of God's grace be suddenly stretched forth to bring them back again. Take heed, therefore, follow not that proud, lofty spirit, that, devil-like, cannot be content with his own station. David was of an excellent spirit, where he saith, "Lord, my heart is not haughty, nor mine eyes lofty, neither do I exercise myself in great matters, or things too high for me. Surely I have behaved and quieted myself as a child that is weaned of his mother: my soul is even as a weaned child." (Ps. cxxxi. 1, 2.) Do thou so *run*.

The Sixth Direction.

Take heed that you have not an ear open to every one that calleth after you as you are in your journey. Men that run, you know, if any do call after them, saying, I would speak with you, or go not too fast, and you shall have my company with you, if they run for some great matter, they use to say, Alas! I cannot stay, I am in haste, pray talk not to me now; neither can I stay for you, I am running for a wager; if I win I am made, if I lose I am undone, and therefore hinder me not. Thus wise are men when they run for corruptible things, and thus shouldest thou do; and thou hast more cause to do so than they, forasmuch as they run but for things that last not, but thou for an incorruptible glory. I give thee notice of this betimes, knowing that thou shalt have enough call after thee, even the devil, sin, this world, vain company, pleasures, profits, esteem among men, ease, pomp, pride, together with an innumerable company of such companions; one crying, Stay for me, the other saying, Do not leave me behind, a third saying, And take me along with you. What, will you go, saith the devil, without your sins, pleasures, and profits? Are you so hasty? Can you not stay and take these along with you? Will you leave your friends and companions behind you? Can you not do as your neighbours do, carry the world, sin, lust, pleasure, profit, esteem among men, along with you? Have a care thou do not let thine ear now be open to the tempting, enticing, alluring, and soul-entangling flatteries of such sink-souls as these are. "My son," saith Solomon, "if sinners entice thee, consent thou not." (Prov. i. 10.)

You know what it cost the young man which Solomon speaks of in the 7th of the Proverbs, that was enticed by a harlot, "With her much fair speech she" won him, and "caused him to yield, with the flattering of her lips she forced him," till he went after her "as an ox to the slaughter, or as a fool to the correction of the stocks;" even so far, "till the dart struck through his liver, and knew not that it was for his life. Hearken unto me now therefore," saith he, "O ye children, and attend to the words of my mouth, let not thine heart decline to her ways, go not astray in her paths, for she hath cast down many wounded, yea, many strong men have been slain by her" (that is, kept out of heaven). "Her house is the way to hell, going down to the chambers of death." Soul, take this counsel, and say, Satan, sin, lust, pleasure, profit, pride, friends, companions, and everything else, let me alone, stand off, come not nigh me, for I am running for heaven, for my soul, for God, for Christ, from hell and everlasting damnation: if I win, I win all, and if I lose, I lose all; let me alone, for I will not hear. So *run*.

The Seventh Direction.

In the next place, be not daunted though thou meetest with never so many discouragements in thy journey thither. That man that is resolved for heaven, if Satan cannot win him by flatteries, he will endeavour to weaken him by discouragements; saying, thou art a sinner, thou hast broke God's law, thou art not elected, thou comest too late, the day of grace is past, God doth not care for thee, thy heart is naught, thou art lazy, with a hundred other discouraging suggestions; and thus it was with David, where he saith, "I had fainted, unless I had believed to see the goodness of the Lord in the land of the living." (Ps. xxvii. 13, 14.) As if he should say, the devil did so rage, and my heart was so base, that had I judged according to my own sense and feeling, I had been absolutely distracted; but I trusted to Christ in the promise, and looked that God would be as good as his promise, in having mercy upon me, an unworthy sinner; and this is that which encouraged me, and kept me from fainting. And thus must thou do when Satan, or the law, or thy own conscience, do go about to dishearten thee, either by the greatness of thy sins, the wickedness of thy heart, the tediousness of the way, the loss of outward enjoyments, the hatred that thou wilt procure from the world, or the like; then thou must encourage

thyself with the freeness of the promises, the tender-heartedness of Christ, the merits of his blood, the freeness of his invitations to come in, the greatness of the sin of others that have been pardoned, and that the same God, through the same Christ, holdeth forth the same grace as free as ever. If these be not thy meditations thou wilt draw very heavily in the way to heaven, if thou do not give up all for lost, and so knock off from following any farther; therefore I say, take heart in thy journey, and say to them that seek thy destruction, "Rejoice not against me, O my enemy, for when I fall I shall arise, when I sit in darkness the Lord shall be a light unto me." (Micah vii. 8.) So *run*.

The Eighth Direction.

Take heed of being offended at the cross that thou must go by before thou come to heaven. You must understand (as I have already touched) that there is no man that goeth to heaven but he must go by the cross. The cross is the standing way-mark by which all they that go to glory must pass by. "We must through much tribulation enter into the kingdom of God." (Acts xiv. 22.) "Yea, and all that will live godly in Christ Jesus shall suffer persecution." (2 Tim. iii. 12.) If thou art in the way to the kingdom, my life for thine thou wilt come at the cross shortly—the Lord grant thou dost not shrink at it, so as to turn thee back again. "If any man will come after me," saith Christ, "let him deny himself, and take up his cross daily, and follow me." (Luke ix. 23.) The cross it stands, and hath stood, from the beginning as a way-mark to the kingdom of heaven. You know if one ask you the way to such and such a place, you, for the better direction, do not only say, this is the way, but then also say, you must go by such a gate, by such a stile, such a bush, tree, bridge, or such like. Why, so it is here: art thou inquiring the way to heaven? Why, I tell thee, Christ is the way, into him thou must get, into his righteousness, to be justified; and if thou art in him, thou wilt presently see the cross, thou must go close by it, thou must touch it, nay, thou must take it up, or else thou wilt quickly go out of the way that leads to heaven, and turn up some of those crooked lanes that lead down to the chambers of death.

How thou mayest know the cross by these six things :—

1. It is known in the doctrine of justification.
2. In the doctrine of mortification.
3. In the doctrine of perseverance.
4. In self-denial.
5. Patience.
6. Communion with poor saints.

1. In the doctrine of justification, there is a great deal of the cross in that; a man is forced to suffer the destruction of his own righteousness for the righteousness of another. This is no easy

matter for a man to do; I assure to you it stretcheth every vein in his heart before he will be brought to yield to it. What, for a man to deny, reject, abhor, and throw away all his prayers, tears, alms, keeping of sabbaths, hearing, reading, with the rest, in the point of justification, and to count them accursed, and to be willing in the very midst of the sense of his sins to throw himself wholly upon the righteousness and obedience of another man, abhorring his own, counting it as deadly sin, as the open breach of the law; I say, to do this in deed and in truth is the biggest piece of the cross; and, therefore, Paul calleth this very thing a suffering where he saith, "And I have suffered the loss of all things," which principally was his righteousness, "that I might win Christ, and be found in him, not having," but rejecting, "mine own righteousness." (Phil. iii. 8, 9.) That is the first.

2. In the doctrine of mortification is also much of the cross. Is it nothing for a man to lay hands on his vile opinions, on his vile sins, of his bosom sins, of his beloved, pleasant, darling sins, that stick as close to him as the flesh sticks to the bones? What, to lose all these brave things that my eyes behold, for that which I never saw with my eyes? What, to lose my pride, my covetousness, my vain company, sports, and pleasures, and the rest? I tell you this is no easy matter: if it were, what need of all those prayers, sighs, watchings? What need we be so backward to it? Nay, do you not see that some men, before they will set about this work, they will even venture the loss of their souls, heaven, God, Christ, and all? What means else all those delays and put-offs, saying, "Stay a little longer; I am loth to leave my sins while I am so young, and in health?" Again, what is the reason else that others do it so by the halves, coldly, and seldom, notwithstanding they are convinced over and over; nay, and also promise to amend, and yet all is in vain. I will assure you, to cut off right hands, and to pluck out right eyes, is no pleasure to the flesh.

3. The doctrine of perseverance is also cross to the flesh, which is not only to begin, but to hold out, not only to bid fair, and to say, "Would I had heaven, but so to know Christ, to put on Christ, and walk with Christ, so as to come to heaven." Indeed, it is no great matter to begin to look for heaven, to begin to seek the Lord, to begin to shun sin. Oh, but it is a very great matter to continue with God's approbation. "My servant Caleb," saith God, is a man of "another spirit, he hath followed me"—followed me always, he hath continually followed me—"fully, he shall possess the land." (Numb. xiv. 24.) Almost all the many thousands of the children of Israel in their generation fell short of perseverance when they walked from Egypt towards the land of Canaan. Indeed, they went to the work at first pretty willingly, but they were very short-winded, they were quickly out of breath, and in their hearts they turned back again into Egypt.

It is an easy matter for a man to run hard for a spurt, for a furlong, for a mile or two; oh, but hold out for a hundred, for a thousand, for ten thousand miles; that man that doth this, he must look to meet with cross, pain, and wearisomeness to the flesh, especially if, as he goeth, he meeteth with briars, and quagmires, and other encumbrances, that makes his journey so much the more painfuller.

Nay, do you not see with your eyes daily that perseverance is a very great part of the cross? why else do men so soon grow weary? I could point out a many that, after they have followed the ways of God about a twelvemonth, others, it may be, two, three, or four—some more, and some less—years, they have been beat out of wind, have taken up their lodging and rest before they have got half-way to heaven, some in this, and some in that sin, and have secretly, nay, sometimes openly said, that the way is too strait, the race too long, the religion too holy, and cannot hold out, I can go no further.

4, 5, 6. And so likewise of the other three, to wit, patience, self-denial, communion and communication with and to the poor saints. How hard are these things? It is an easy matter to deny another man, but it is not so easy a matter to deny one's self; to deny myself out of love to God, to his gospel, to his saints, of this advantage, and of that gain, nay, of that which otherwise I might lawfully do, were it not for offending them. That scripture is but seldom read, and seldomer put in practice, which saith, "I will eat no flesh while the world standeth, if it make my brother to offend." (1 Cor. viii. 13.) Again, "We that are strong ought to bear the infirmities of the weak, and not to please ourselves." (Rom. xv. 1.) But how froward, how hasty, how peevish, and self-resolved are the generality of the professors at this day! Also how little considering the poor, unless it be to say, "Be thou warmed and filled!" But to give is a seldom work; also especially to give to any poor. (Gal. vi. 10.) I tell you all things are cross to flesh and blood; and that man that hath but a watchful eye over the flesh, and also some considerable measure of strength against it, he shall find his heart in these things like unto a starting horse that is rid without a curbing bridle, ready to start at everything that is offensive to him; yea, and ready to run away too, do what the rider can.

It is the cross which keepeth those that are kept from heaven. I am persuaded, were it not for the cross, where we have one professor we should have twenty; but this cross, that is it which spoileth all.

Some men, as I said before, when they come at the cross they can go no further, but back again to their sins they must go. Others, they stumble at it, and break their necks; others, again, when they see the cross is approaching, they turn aside to the left hand, or to the right hand, and so think to get to heaven another way; but they will be deceived! "Yea, and all that will live godly in Christ Jesus shall"—mark, shall be sure to "suffer persecution." (2 Tim. iii. 12.) There are but few, when they come at the cross, cry, "Welcome cross," as some of the martyrs did to the stake they were burned at: therefore if you meet with the cross in thy journey, in what manner soever it be, be not daunted, and say, "Alas, what shall I do now!" But rather take courage, knowing that by the cross is the way to the kingdom. Can a man believe in Christ and not be hated by the devil? Can he make a profession of this Christ, and that sweetly and convincingly, and the children of Satan hold their tongue? Can darkness agree with light? or the devil endure that Christ Jesus should be honoured both by faith and a heavenly conversation, and let that soul alone at quiet? Did you never read, that "the dragon persecuteth the woman?" (Rev. xii.) And that Christ saith, "In the world ye shall have tribulation?" (John xvi. 33.)

The Ninth Direction.

Beg of God that he would do these two things for thee :—First, enlighten thine understanding; and, secondly, inflame thy will. If these two be but effectually done, there is no fear but thou wilt go safe to heaven.

One of the great reasons why men and women do so little regard the other world, it is, because they see so little of it : and the reason why they see so little of it is, because they have their understandings darkened ; and, therefore, saith Paul, "do not you believers walk as do other Gentiles, even in the vanity of their minds, having their understanding darkened, being alienated from the life of God through the ignorance," or foolishness, "that is in them, because of the blindness of their heart." (Eph. iv. 17, 18.) Walk not as those ; run not with them : alas, poor souls, they have their understandings darkened, their hearts blinded, and that is the reason they have such undervaluing thoughts of the Lord Jesus Christ and the salvation of their souls. For when men do come to see the things of another world, what a God, what a Christ, what a heaven, and what an eternal glory there is to be enjoyed; also when they see that it is possible for them to have a share in it, I tell you it will make them run through thick and thin to enjoy it. Moses having a sight of this, because his understanding was enlightened, he feared not the wrath of the king, but chose "rather to suffer affliction with the people of God, than to enjoy the pleasures of sin for a season." He refused to be called the son of the king's daughter; accounting it wonderful riches to be counted worthy of so much as to suffer for Christ with the poor despised saints ; and that was because he saw him who was invisible, and "had respect unto the recompence

of the reward." (Heb. xi. 24—27.) And this is that which the apostle usually prayeth for in his epistles for the saints—namely, "That they might know what is the hope of God's calling, and the riches of the glory of his inheritance in the saints." (Eph. i. 18.) And that they might "be able to comprehend with all saints what is the breadth, and length, and depth, and height, and to know the love of Christ, which passeth knowledge." (Eph. iii. 18, 19.) Pray, therefore, that God would enlighten thy understanding : that will be a very great help unto thee. It will make thee endure many a hard brunt for Christ; as Paul saith, "After ye were illuminated, ye endured a great fight of afflictions. You took joyfully the spoiling of your goods, knowing in yourselves that ye have in heaven a better and an enduring substance." (Heb. x. 32—34.) If there be never such a rare jewel lie just in a man's way, yet if he sees it not, he will rather trample upon it than stoop for it, and it is because he sees not. Why, so it is here, though heaven be worth never so much, and thou hast never so much need of it, yet if thou see it not—that is, have not thy understanding opened or enlightened to see—thou wilt not regard at all : therefore cry to the Lord for enlightening grace, and say, "Lord, open my blind eyes; Lord, take the veil off of my dark heart, show me the things of the other world, and let me see the sweetness, glory, and excellency of them for Christ his sake." This is the first.

Cry to God that he would inflame thy will also with the things of the other world. For when a man's will is fully set to do such or such a thing, then it must be a very hard matter that shall hinder that man from bringing about his end. When Paul's will was set resolvedly to go up to Jerusalem, though it was signified to him before what he should there suffer, he was not daunted at all; nay, saith he, "I am ready," or willing, "not to be bound only, but also to die at Jerusalem for the name of the Lord Jesus." (Acts xxi. 13.) His will was inflamed with love to Christ, and, therefore, all the persuasions that could be used wrought nothing at all.

Your self-willed people nobody knows what to do with them ; we used to say, He will have his own will, do all what you can. Indeed to have such a will for heaven is an admirable advantage to a man that undertaketh a race thither ; a man that is resolved, and hath his will fixed, saith he, I will do my best to advantage myself; I will do my worst to hinder my enemies ; I will not give out as long as I can stand ; I will have it or I will lose my life ; "though he slay me, yet will I trust in him." (Job xiii. 15.) "I will not let thee go except thou bless me." (Gen. xxxii. 26.) *I will, I will, I will,* O this blessed inflamed will for heaven! What is like it? If a man be willing, then any argument shall be matter of encouragement; but if unwilling, then any argument shall give discouragement: this is seen both in saints and sinners; in them that are the children of God, and also those that are the children of the devil. As,

1. The saints of old, they being willing and resolved for heaven, what could stop them? Could fire and faggot, sword or halter, stinking dungeons, whips, bears, bulls, lions, cruel rackings, stoning, starving, nakedness, &c.? "Nay, in all these things they were more than conquerors, through him that loved them," (Rom. viii. 37;) who had also made them "willing in the day of his power."

2. See again, on the other side, the children of the devil, because they are not willing, how many shifts and starting-holes will they have. I have married a wife, I have a farm, I shall offend my landlord, I shall offend my master, I shall lose my trading, I shall lose my pride, my pleasures, I shall be mocked and scoffed, therefore I dare not come. I, saith another, will stay till I am older, till my children are out, till I am got a little aforehand in the world, till I have done this, and that, and the other business; but alas, the thing is, they are not willing; for were they but soundly willing, these, and a thousand such as these, would hold them no faster than the cords held Samson, when he broke them like burnt flax. (Judges xv. 14.) I tell you the will is all; that is one of the chief things which turns the wheel either backwards or forwards; and God knoweth that full well, and so likewise doth the devil, and therefore they both endeavour very much to strengthen the will of their servants. God, he is for making of his a willing people to serve him; and the devil, he doth what he can to possess the will and affection of those that are his with love to sin; and therefore when Christ comes close to the matter indeed, saith he, "Ye will not come to me." (John v. 40.) "How often would I have gathered you as a hen doth her chickens, and ye would not." (Luke xiii. 34.) The devil had possessed their wills, and so long he was sure enough of them. O therefore cry hard to God to inflame thy will for heaven and Christ: thy will, I say, if that be rightly set for heaven, thou wilt not be beat off with discouragements; and this was the reason that when Jacob wrestled with the angel, though he lost a limb, as it were, and the hollow of his thigh was put out of joint as he wrestled with him, yet, saith he, "I will not"— mark, I WILL NOT—"let thee go except thou bless me." (Gen. xxxii. 24—26.) Get thy will tipped with the heavenly grace and resolution against all discouragements, and then thou goest full speed for heaven; but if thou falter in thy will, and be not found there, thou wilt run hobbling and halting all the way thou runnest, and also to be sure thou wilt fall short at last. The Lord give thee a will and courage.

Thus have I done with directing thee how to run to the kingdom; be sure thou keep in memory what I have said unto thee, lest thou lose thy way. But because I would have thee think of them, take all in short in this little bit of paper.

1. Get into the way.

2. Then study on it.

3. Then strip, and lay aside everything that would hinder.

4. Beware of by-paths.

5. Do not gaze and stare too much about thee, but be sure to ponder the path of thy feet.

6. Do not stop for any that call after thee, whether it be the world, the flesh, or the devil, for all these will hinder thy journey, if possible.

7. Be not daunted with any discouragements thou meetest with as thou goest.

8. Take heed of stumbling at the cross.

9. Cry hard to God for an enlightened heart, and a willing mind, and God give thee a prosperous journey.

Yet before I do quite take my leave of thee, let me give thee a few motives along with thee. It may be they will be as good as a pair of spurs to prick on thy lumpish heart in this rich journey.

V. Nine Motives to urge us on in the Way.

The First Motive.

Consider there is no way but this, thou must either win or lose. If thou winnest, then heaven, God, Christ, glory, ease, peace, life, yea, life eternal, is thine; thou shalt be made equal to the angels in heaven, thou shalt sorrow no more, sigh no more, feel no more pain; thou shalt be out of the reach of sin, hell, death, the devil, the grave, and whatever else may endeavour thy hurt. But contrariwise, and if thou lose, then thy loss is heaven, glory, God, Christ, ease, peace, and whatever else which tendeth to make eternity comfortable to the saints; besides, thou procurest eternal death, sorrow, pain, blackness, and darkness, fellowship with devils, together with the everlasting damnation of thy own soul.

The Second Motive.

Consider that this devil, this hell, death and damnation, followeth after thee as hard as they can drive, and have their commission so to do by the law, against which thou hast sinned, and therefore for the Lord's sake make haste.

The Third Motive.

If they seize upon thee before thou get to the City of Refuge, they will put an everlasting stop to thy journey. This also cries, "*Run* for it."

The Fourth Motive.

Know also, that now heaven gates, the heart of Christ, with his arms, are wide open to receive thee. O methinks that this consideration, that the devil followeth after to destroy, and that Christ standeth open-armed to receive, should make thee reach out and fly with all haste and speed. And therefore,

The Fifth Motive.

Keep thine eyes upon the prize, be sure that

thy eyes be continually upon the profit thou art like to get. The reason why men are so apt to faint in their race for heaven, it lieth chiefly in either of these two things :

First. They do not seriously consider the worth of the prize ; or else if they do, they are afraid it is too good for them : but most lose heaven for want of considering the prize and the worth of it. And therefore that thou mayest not do the like, keep thy eye much upon the excellency, the sweetness, the beauty, the comfort, the peace that is to be had there by those that win the prize. This was that which made the apostle run through anything ; good report, evil report, persecution, affliction, hunger, nakedness, peril by sea, and peril by land, bonds and imprisonments : also it made others endure to be stoned, sawn asunder, to have their eyes bored out with augurs, their bodies broiled on gridirons, their tongues cut out of their mouths, boiled in cauldrons, thrown to the wild beasts, burned at the stake, whipped at posts, and a thousand other fearful torments, " while they looked not at the things which are seen," as the things of this world, " but at the things which are not seen ; for the things which are seen are temporal ; but the things which are not seen are eternal." (2 Cor. iv. 18.) O this word eternal, that was it that made them, that when they might have had deliverance they would not accept of it, for they knew in the world to come they should have a better resurrection. (Heb. xi. 35.)

Second. And do not let the thoughts of the rareness of the place make thee say in thy heart, " This is too good for me ;" for I tell thee, heaven is prepared for whosoever will accept of it, and they shall be entertained with hearty good welcome. Consider, therefore, that as bad as thou have got thither ; thither went scrubbed, beggarly Lazarus, &c. Nay, it is prepared for the poor, " Hearken, my beloved brethren," saith James— take notice of it—" hath not God chosen the poor of this world rich in faith, and heirs of the kingdom ?" (James ii. 5.) Therefore, take heart and *run*, man. And,

The Sixth Motive.

Think much of them that are gone before. First, How really they got into the kingdom. Secondly, how safe they are in the arms of Jesus ; would they be here again for a thousand worlds ? Or if they were, would they be afraid that God would not make them welcome ? Thirdly, what they would judge of thee if they knew thy heart began to fail thee in thy journey, or thy sins began to allure thee, and to persuade thee to stop thy race ; would they not call thee a thousand fools ? and say, O that he did but see what we see, feel what we feel, and taste of the dainties that we taste of ! O if he were one quarter of an hour to behold, to see, to feel, to taste and enjoy, but the thousandth part of what we enjoy, what would he do ! what would he suffer ! what would

he leave undone ! Would he favour sin ? would he love this world below ? would he be afraid of friends, or shrink at the most fearful threatenings that the greatest tyrants could invent to give him ? Nay, those who have had but a sight of these things by faith, when they have been as far off from them as heaven from earth, yet they have been able to say with a comfortable and merry heart, as the bird that sings in the spring, that this and more shall not stop them from *running* to heaven. Sometimes, when my base heart hath been inclining to this world, and to loiter in my journey towards heaven, the very consideration of the glorious saints and angels in heaven, what they enjoy, and what low thoughts they have of the things of this world together, how they would befool me, if they did but know that my heart was drawing back, hath caused me to rush forward, to disdain these poor, low, empty, beggarly things, and to say to my soul, " Come, soul, let us not be weary ; let us see what this heaven is ; let us even venture all for it, and try if that will quit the cost." Surely Abraham, David, Paul, and the rest of the saints of God, were as wise as any are now, and yet they lost all for this glorious kingdom. O therefore throw away stinking lusts, follow after righteousness, love the Lord Jesus, devote thyself unto his fear, I'll warrant thee he will give thee a goodly recompence. Reader, what sayest thou to this ? Art thou resolved to follow me ? Nay, resolve if thou canst to get before me. " So run, that ye may obtain."

The Seventh Motive.

To encourage thee a little farther, set to the work, and when thou hast run thyself down weary. then the Lord Jesus will take thee up and carry thee. Is not this enough to make any poor soul begin his race ? Thou, perhaps, criest, " O but I am feeble, I am lame," &c. Well, but Christ hath a bosom ; consider, therefore, when thou hast run thyself down weary, he will put thee in his bosom : " He shall gather the lambs with his arms, and carry them in his bosom, and shall gently lead those that are with young." (Isa. xl. 11.) This is the way that fathers take to encourage their children, saying, " Run, sweet babe, while thou art weary, and then I will take thee up and carry thee." " He will gather his lambs with his arm, and carry them in his bosom." When they are weary they shall ride.

The Eighth Motive.

Or else he will convey new strength from heaven into thy soul, which will be as well. " The youths shall faint and be weary, and the young men shall utterly fall ; but they that wait upon the Lord shall renew their strength ; they shall mount up with wings as eagles, they shall run and not be weary, they shall walk and not faint." (Isa. xl. 30, 31.) What shall I say besides what hath already been said ? Thou shalt have good and easy lodging, good and wholesome diet, the bosom of Christ to lie in, the joys of heaven to feed on. Shall I speak of the satiety and of the duration of all these? Verily to describe them to the height is a work too hard for me to do.

The Ninth Motive.

Again, methinks the very industry of the devil, and the industry of his servants, &c., should make you that have a desire to heaven and happiness to run apace. Why, the devil, he will lose no time, spare no pains; also neither will his servants; both to seek the destruction of themselves and others: and shall not we be as industrious for our own salvation? Shall the world venture the damnation of their souls for a poor corruptible crown; and shall not we venture the loss of a few trifles for an eternal crown? Shall they venture the loss of eternal friends, as God to love, Christ to redeem, the Holy Spirit to comfort, heaven for habitation, saints and angels for company, and all this to get and hold communion with sin, and this world, and a few base, drunken, swearing, lying, covetous wretches like themselves? And shall not we labour as hard, run as fast, seek as diligently, nay, a hundred times more diligently, for the company of these glorious, eternal friends, though with the loss of such as these, nay, with the loss of ten thousand times better than these, poor, low, base, contemptible things? Shall it be said at the last day, that wicked men made more haste to hell than you did make to heaven? that they spent more hours, days, and that early and late, for hell, than you spent for that which is ten thousand thousand of thousands of times better? O let it not be so, but run with all might and main.

Thus you see I have here spoken something, though but little. Now I shall come to make some use and application of what hath been said, and so conclude.

VI. NINE USES OF THIS SUBJECT.
The First Use

You see here, that he that will go to heaven, he must *run* for it; yea, and not only run, but *so run*, that is, as I have said, to run earnestly, to run continually, to strip off everything that would hinder in his race, with the rest. Well then, do you so run?

1. And now let us examine a little. Art thou got into the right way? Art thou in Christ's righteousness? Do not say yes in thy heart, when in truth there is no such matter. It is a dangerous thing, you know, for a man to think he is in the right way, when he is in the wrong. It is the next way for him to lose his way, and not only so, but if he run for heaven, as thou sayest thou dost, even to lose that too. O this is the misery of most men! To persuade themselves that they run right, when they never had one foot in the way! The Lord give thee understanding here, or else thou art undone for ever. Prithee, soul, search when was it thou turned out of thy sins and righteousness, into the righteousness of Jesus Christ? I say, dost thou see thyself in him? And is he more precious to thee than the whole world? Is thy mind always musing on him? dost thou love to be talking of him, and also to be walking with him? Dost thou count his company more precious than the whole world? Dost thou count all things but poor, lifeless, empty, vain things without communion with him? Doth his company sweeten all things? and his absence embitter all things? Soul, I beseech thee be serious, and lay it to heart, and do not take things of such weighty concernment as the salvation or damnation of thy soul without good ground.

2. Art thou unladen of the things of this world, as pride, pleasures, profits, lusts, vanities? What, dost thou think to run fast enough with the world, thy sins, and lusts, in thy heart? I tell thee, soul, they that have laid all aside, every weight, every sin, and are got into the nimblest posture, they find work enough to run; so to run as to hold out. To run through all that opposition, all the jostles, all these rubs, over all the stumbling-blocks, over all the snares, from all the entanglements that the devil, sin, the world, and their own hearts lay before them; I tell thee, if thou art going heavenward, thou wilt find it no small or easy matter. Art thou therefore discharged and unladen of these things? Never talk of going to heaven if thou art not. It is to be feared thou wilt be found among the many that "will seek to enter in, and shall not be able." (Luke xiii. 24.)

The Second Use.

If so, then, in the next place, what will become of them that are grown weary before they are got half way thither? Why, man, it is he that holdeth out to the end that must be saved; it is he that overcometh that shall inherit all things; it is not every one that begins. Agrippa gave a fair step for a sudden; he steps almost into the bosom of Christ in less than half an hour. Thou, saith he to Paul, hast "almost persuaded me to be a Christian." (Acts xxvi. 26.) Ah! but it was but *almost;* and so he had as good have been never a whit; he stepped fair indeed, but yet he stopped short; he was hot while he was at it, but he was quickly out of wind. O this *but almost!* I tell you, this *but almost,* it lost his soul. Methinks I have seen sometimes how these poor wretches that get but almost to heaven, how fearfully their *almost,* and their *but almost,* will torment them in hell. When they shall cry out in the bitterness of their souls, saying, *almost a Christian;* I was *almost* got into the kingdom, *almost* out of the hands of the devil, *almost* out of my sins, *almost* from under the curse of God. *Almost,* and that was all; *almost,* but not altogether. O that I should be *almost* at heaven, and should not go quite through! Friend, it is a sad thing to sit down before we are in heaven, and to grow weary before we come to the place of rest; and if it should be thy case, I am sure thou dost not so run as to obtain. But again,

The Third Use.

In the next place, what then will become of them that some time since were running *post-haste* to heaven, insomuch that they seemed to outstrip many, but now are running as fast back again? Do you think those will ever come thither? What! to run back again, back again to sin, to the world, to the devil, back again to the lusts of the flesh. Oh! "it had been better for them not to have known the way of righteousness, than after they have known it, to turn," to turn back again, "from the holy commandment." (2 Pet. ii. 22.) Those men shall not only be damned for sin, but for professing to all the world that sin is better than Christ: for the man that runs back again, he doth as good as say, "I have tried Christ, and I have tried sin, and I do not find so much profit in Christ as in sin." I say, this man declareth this, even by his running back again. O sad! what a doom will they have, who were almost at heaven gates, and then run back again. "If any man draw back," saith Christ, "my soul shall have no pleasure in him." (Heb. x. 38.) Again, "No man having put his hand to the plough"—that is, set forward in the ways of God—"and looking back"—turning back again—"is fit for the kingdom of God." (Luke ix. 62.) And if not fit for the kingdom of heaven, then for certain he must needs be fit for the fire of hell. "And therefore," saith the apostle, those that "bring forth" these apostatizing fruits, as "briars and thorns, are rejected, and nigh unto cursing, whose end is to be burned." (Heb. vi. 8.) O there is never another Christ to save them by bleeding and dying for them! And "if they shall not escape that neglect," then how shall they escape, that reject and turn their backs upon "so great a salvation?" And if the righteous—that is, they that run for it—will find work enough to get to heaven, "then where will the ungodly," backsliding "sinner appear?" Or if Judas the traitor, or Francis Spira the backslider, were but now alive in the world to whisper these men in the ear a little, and tell them what it hath cost their souls for backsliding, surely it would stick by them, and make them afraid of running back again, so long as they had one day to live in this world.

The Fourth Use.

So again, fourthly, how like to these men's sufferings will those be that have all this while sat still, and have not so much as set one foot forward to the kingdom of heaven. Surely he that backslideth, and he that sitteth still in sin, they are both of one mind; the one he will not stir, because he loveth his sins, and the things of this world; the other he runs back again, because he loveth his sins, and the things of this world. Is it not one and the same thing? They are all one here, and

shall not one and the same hell hold them hereafter? He is an ungodly one that never looked after Christ, and he is an ungodly one that did once look after him, and then ran quite back again; and therefore that word must certainly drop out of the mouth of Christ against them both, "Depart from me, ye cursed, into everlasting fire, prepared for the devil and his angels." (Matt. xxv. 41.)

The Fifth Use.

Again, here you may see in the next place, that is, they that will have heaven must *run* for it; then this calls aloud to those who began but a while since to run, I say, for them to mend their pace if they intend to win; you know that they which come hindmost had need run fastest. Friend, I tell thee, there be those that have run ten years to thy one, nay, twenty to five, and yet if thou talk with them, sometimes they will say, they doubt they shall come late enough. How then will it be with thee? Look to it, therefore, that thou delay no time, not an hour's time, but part speedily with all, with everything that is an hindrance to thee in thy journey, and *run*; yea, and so *run* that thou mayest obtain.

The Sixth Use.

Again, sixthly, you that are old professors, take you heed that the young striplings of Jesus, that began to strip but the other day, do not outrun you, so as to have that scripture fulfilled on you, "The first shall be last, and the last first," which will be a shame to you, and a credit for them. What, for a young soldier to be more courageous than he that hath been used to wars! To you that are hindermost, I say, strive to outrun them that are before you; and you that are foremost, I say, hold your ground, and keep before them in faith and love, if possible: for indeed that is the right running, for one to strive to outrun another; even for the hindermost to endeavour to overtake the foremost, and he that is before should be sure to lay out himself to keep his ground, even to the very utmost. But then,

The Seventh Use.

Again, how basely do they behave themselves; how unlike are they to win, that think it enough to keep company with the hindmost? There are some men that profess themselves such as run for heaven as well as any, yet if there be but any lazy, slothful, cold, half-hearted professors in the country, they will be sure to take example by them: they think if they can but keep pace with them, they shall do fair; but these do not consider that the hindmost lose the prize. You may know it if you will, that it cost the foolish virgins dear for their coming too late: "They that were ready went in with him, and the door was shut. Afterward"—mark, afterward—"came the other" (the foolish) "virgins, saying, Lord, Lord, open to ns. But he answered and said," depart, "I know you not." (Matt. xxv. 10—12.) Depart, lazy professors, cold professors, slothful professors. Oh, methinks, the word of God is so plain for the overthrow of your lazy professors, that it is to be wondered men do take no more notice of it. How was Lot's wife served for running lazily, and for giving but one look behind her after the things she left in Sodom? How was Esau served for staying too long before he came for the blessing? And how were they served that are mentioned in the 13th of Luke, for staying till the door was shut? Also the foolish virgins; a heavy after-groan will they give that have thus stayed too long. It turned Lot's wife into a pillar of salt, (Gen. xix. 26;) it made Esau weep with an exceeding loud and bitter cry; it made Judas hang himself; yea, and it will make thee curse the day in which thou wast born, if thou miss of the kingdom, as thou wilt certainly do, if this be thy course. But,

The Eighth Use.

Again: how and if thou, by thy lazy running, shouldest not only destroy thyself, but also thereby be the cause of the damnation of some others; for thou, being a professor, thou must think that others will take notice of thee; and because thou art but a poor, cold, lazy runner, and one that seeks to drive the world and pleasure along with thee: why, thereby others will think of doing so too. Nay, say they, why may not we as well as he? He is a professor, and yet he seeks for pleasures, riches, profits; he loveth vain company, and he is so and so, and professeth that he is going for heaven; yea, and he saith also he doth not fear but he shall have entertainment; let us, therefore, keep pace with him: we shall fare no worse than he. Oh, how fearful a thing will it be, if that thou shalt be instrumental to the ruin of others by thy halting in the way of righteousness! Look to it, thou wilt have strength little enough to appear before God, to give an account of the loss of thy own soul; thou needest not have to give an account for others; why, thou didst stop them from entering in. How wilt thou answer that saying, You would not enter in yourselves, and them that would you hinder; for that saying will be eminently fulfilled on them that through their own idleness do keep themselves out of heaven, and by giving of others the same example, hinder them also.

The Ninth Use.

Therefore, now to speak a word to both of you, and so I shall conclude.

First. I beseech you in the name of our Lord Jesus Christ, that none of you do run so lazily in the way to heaven as to hinder either yourselves or others. I know that even he which runs laziest, if he should see a man running for a temporal life, if he should so much neglect his own well-being in this world as to venture, when he is a running for his life, to pick up here and there a lock of wool that hangeth by the wayside, or to step now and then aside out of the way for to gather up a straw or two, or any rotten stick, I say, if he should do this when he is a running for his life, thou wouldest condemn him: and dost thou not condemn thyself that dost the very same in effect, nay, worse, that loiterest in thy race, notwithstanding thy soul, heaven, glory, and all is at stake. Have a care, have a care, poor wretched sinner, have a care.

Second. If yet there shall be any that, notwithstanding this advice, will still be flagging and loitering in the way to the kingdom of glory, be thou so wise as not to take example by them. Learn of no man further than he followeth Christ. But look unto Jesus, who is not only the author and finisher of faith, but who did, for the joy that was set before him, endure the cross, despise the shame, and is now set down at the right hand of God. I say, look to no man to learn of him no further than he followeth Christ. "Be ye followers of me," saith Paul, "even as I also am of Christ." (1 Cor. xi. 1.) Though he was an eminent man, yet his exhortation was, that none should follow him any further than he followed Christ.

VII. Provocation.

Now, that you may be provoked to run with the foremost, take notice of this. When Lot and his wife were running from cursed Sodom to the mountains to save their lives, it is said that his wife looked back from behind him, and she became a pillar of salt; and yet you see that neither her practice nor the judgment of God that fell upon her for the same, would cause Lot to look behind him. I have sometimes wondered at Lot in this particular; his wife looked behind her, and died immediately, but let what would become of her, Lot would not so much as look behind him to see her. We do not read that he did so much as once look where she was, or what was become of her; his heart was indeed upon his journey, and well it might: there was the mountain before him, and the fire and brimstone behind him; his life lay at stake, and he had lost it if he had but looked behind him. Do thou so run: and in thy race remember Lot's wife, and remember her doom; and remember for what that doom did overtake her; and remember that God made her an example for all lazy runners to the end of the world; and take heed thou fall not after the same example. But if this will not provoke thee, consider thus—

1. Thy soul is thy own soul, that is either to be saved or lost; thou shalt not lose my soul by thy laziness: it is thy own soul, thy own ease, thy own peace, thy own advantage or disadvantage. If it were my own that thou art desired to be good unto, methinks reason should move thee some-

what to pity it.   But, alas, it is thy own, thy own soul! "What shall it profit a man if he shall gain the whole world, and lose his own soul." (Mark viii. 36.) God's people wish well to the souls of others, and wilt not thou wish well to thy own? And if this will not provoke thee, then think again—

2. If thou lose thy soul, it is thou also that must bear the blame. It made Cain stark mad to consider that he had not looked to his brother Abel's soul. How much more will it perplex thee to think that thou hadst not a care of thy own? And if this will not provoke thee to bestir thyself, think again—

3. That if thou wilt not run, the people of God are resolved to deal with thee even as Lot dealt with his wife, that is, leave thee behind them. It may be thou hast a father, mother, brother, &c., going post-haste to heaven, wouldest thou be willing to be left behind them? Surely no! Again—

4. Will it not be a dishonour to thee to see the very boys and girls in the country to have more wit than thyself? It may be the servants of some men, as the horsekeeper, ploughman, scullion, &c., is more looking after heaven than their masters. I am apt to think, sometimes, that more servants than masters, that more tenants than landlords will inherit the kingdom of heaven. But is not this a shame for them that are such? I am persuaded you scorn that your servants should say that they are wiser than you in the things of this world; and yet, I am bold to say, that many of them are wiser than you in the things of the world to come, which are of greater concernment.

VIII. Expostulation.

Well, then, sinner, what sayest thou? Where is thy heart? Wilt thou run? Art thou resolved to strip? or art thou not? Think quickly, man; it is no dallying in this matter. Confer not with flesh and blood; look up to heaven, and see how thou likest it; also to hell—of which thou mayest understand something in my book, called, *A few Sighs from Hell; or, the Groans of a damned Soul,* which I wish thee to read seriously over—and accordingly devote thyself. If thou dost not know the way, inquire at the word of God. If thou wantest company, cry for God's Spirit. If thou wantest encouragement, entertain the promises. But be sure thou begin betimes; get into the way; run apace, and hold out to the end, and the Lord give thee a prosperous journey.

FAREWELL.

PREFATORY REMARKS

ON

THE SEVENTH-DAY SABBATH.

Bunyan allowed none of the controversies of his day to pass unstudied. He was in this, as in other respects, eminently practical. The spiritual dangers which assailed all men, and belonged to all times, he viewed with the comprehensive glance of a genuine Christian theologian. In treating of these he went to the fountain-head of divine knowledge, and generally expounded the doctrines concerned with a no less tranquil and sedate than enlightened spirit. But a party question roused him as quickly as if he had only lived for controversy. He employed both the art and the language of a disputant; and grappled with the adversary like a deadly foe, to every opinion but his own.

The Sabbatarian controversy of Bunyan's time was but the revival of an old and often repeated dispute; it agitated many a pious mind in the second century. The Christian convert, who had unquestioningly adopted the practice of his first teachers, and had never thought of any other Sabbath than that which they observed, might happily continue to the end fully satisfied with this course. But if circumstances, or his own inquiring disposition turned his attention to the Old Testament, it is not unreasonable to suppose, that he might feel somewhat surprised and alarmed at this apparent disagreement of his Sabbath observance with the injunctions of the fourth commandment. His anxiety would be in proportion to the tenderness of his conscience; the continuance of his doubts would rather be measured by his capacity for argument.

Nor was it the early Christian convert only, whose mind might be deeply affected by the importance of this question. Almost every reflecting man, confined in the early stages of his religious life to an unconsidered routine of observances, feels himself, on awakening to a deeper sense of their meaning, in similar perplexity. That a sufficient answer may be given to his doubts is not then evident to him; and it is easy to see that if, instead of meeting with persons of sound information, he communicate his anxiety to others in his own state of mind, a sect may be readily formed, and grow into sufficient importance to give the controversy a permanent place in history.

A large amount of learning and ingenuity have been employed on this subject. With some scholars the sanctity of the Sabbath, and the authority for observing it, have no stronger foundation than that which may be derived from the mention of it at the beginning of Genesis. These are met by geologists who, though not absolutely repudiating the argument, render it obscure and vague. Other divines are contented with the direct language of the fourth commandment; while these again have to encounter the objection that, as a legal enactment, the Sabbath has become subject to the same change as all other observances belonging to the law. Were this not the case, it is argued, the seventh day must still be as sacred as ever, and the obligation to keep it holy, as binding upon the Christian as upon the Jew.

Questions of this kind may be viewed in such a variety of lights, according to men's habits of thinking, that when revived, after long lapses of time, they are debated with as much interest as if never before disputed. It is evident that, in the case of the fourth commandment, no agreement can be effected between those who insist upon its verbal authority and observance, and those who declare only for its general and spiritual application. To the former, "The Seventh Day" and "A Seventh Day" sound as totally different expressions. Before they could be rendered identical in their opinion, a long process of argument must be instituted, and should end in showing that a seventh part of time is sabbatical rather than the seventh day; that the church of Christ had a right to take the first day for this consecrated gift to God and devotion instead of the seventh; and that there is sufficient historical proof that the church really did assume to itself the authority to make this change. These several divisions of argument have themselves, in the course of the controversy, separated into minor branches; and hence the subject, viewed at large, is one of vast extent, and equally adapted to excite learned speculation, and perplex a simple and anxious conscience.

It seems difficult, even for the laborious student of ecclesiastical antiquity, to find any primitive record of the transfer of the Sabbath from the seventh to the first day of the week. The practice of Christians does not prove that any such change had formally taken place in the earliest age of the church.   To meet together, and celebrate the resurrection of Jesus, by prayer and communion, on the first day of the week, was not necessarily to make it their Sabbath instead of the seventh day.   This could not be the case in respect to Jewish converts, as far as they retained any of their old domestic relations.   For them the seventh day must unavoidably have still been the Sabbath, a day of actual rest : the first day, however dear and sacred to them, can only have been a day of extra thought and devotion.   With the breaking up of former connections, by removal into distant lands, and a gradual deepening of purely evangelical impressions, even the convert from Judaism would feel the instinctive necessity for a strict observance of the seventh-day Sabbath less and less imperative.   Neither the change of place, nor the separation from friends, would of itself have been sufficient to produce this effect.   But as the original Sabbath became divested of all the outward garb of solemn ordinances, and visible claims to strict devotion, the new day of worship and communion acquired more of the Sabbatical character.   In proportion to the increase of services on that day, there was an increased demand for time and leisure.   At first the earliest hour of the day, or some portion of the night, might suffice for the devout commemoration of the Lord's victory over the grave.   Blessed and content with the enjoyment of the solemn but brief services, the Christian might still be able to fulfil all the labours required of him, however humble or servile his position.   The addition of such a day of worship to the seventh day would be no tax too large for the poorest to pay.   But when to the earlier or later assemblies there were joined the meetings, which could only be attended at the expense of the entire day, the generality of Christians must have found themselves compelled to consider afresh how the calls upon their religious affections could best be met.   A title had been given to the new Sabbath, full of noble meaning, and involving a character of authority.   It was called " The Lord's Day."   No one could hear it so designated, and refuse to hallow it.   The services performed on such a day must have the foremost claim to attention.   To devote any portion of it to mean cares or worldly pursuits could not be consistent with due honour to the Redeemer, whose own it was ; and thus, however truly and reverentially the seventh day might still be confessed the Sabbath, the first day would, by change of circumstances, practically take its place.   What the heads of the Christian church did, by authority, in this matter, only followed what had already been done by necessity.   Their acts and decrees were simply intended to give stability to arrangements which had grown with time and circumstance, and could not now be altered.   Had they neglected to settle the Christian Sabbath, the want of any definite rule on the subject might have been fatal to both Sabbaths.   For those who acknowledge the power of the Christian church, taking the term in its most undisputed sense, to establish ordinances, and determine all questions concerning them, this subject has been happily settled by common consent, and on the surest basis.   To the few who hesitate to decide by this rule, the subject presents a field of inquiry of very formidable extent.   Bunyan's tract is ingenious and useful.

H. S.

QUESTIONS ABOUT THE NATURE AND PERPETUITY

OF

THE SEVENTH-DAY SABBATH,

AND PROOF THAT THE FIRST DAY OF THE WEEK IS THE CHRISTIAN SABBATH.

" The Son of Man is Lord also of the Sabbath day."

TO THE READER.

SOME may think it strange, since God's church has already been so well furnished with sound grounds and reasons by so many wise and godly men, for proof that the first day of the week is our true Christian sabbath, that I should *now* offer this small treatise upon the same account. But when the scales are even by what already is put in, a little more you know makes the weight the better.

Or grant we had down weight before, yet something over and above may make his work the harder, that shall by hanging fictions on the other end, endeavour to make things seem too light.

Besides, this book being little, may best suit such as have but shallow purses, short memories, and but little time to spare, which usually is the lot of the mean and poorest sort of men.

I have also written upon this subject, for that I would, as in other gospel-truths, be a fellow witness with good men that the day in which our Lord rose from the dead should be much set by of Christians.

I have observed that some, otherwise sound in faith, are apt to be entangled with a Jewish sabbath, &c.; and that some also that are far off from the observation of that, have but little to say for their own practice, though good; and might I help them I should be glad.

A Jewish seventh-day sabbath has no promise of grace belonging to it, if that be true, as to be sure it is, where Paul says, The command to honour parents is the first commandment with promise. (Eph. vi. 1—3.)

Also it follows from hence, that the sabbath that has a promise annexed to the keeping of it, is rather that which the Lord Jesus shall give to the churches of the Gentiles. (Isa. lvi.)

Perhaps my method here may not in all things keep the common path of argumentation with them that have gone before me : but I trust the godly wise will find a taste of scripture truth in what I present them with as to the sanction of our Christian sabbath.

I have here, by handling four questions, proved, that the seventh-day sabbath was not moral. For that must of necessity be done, before it can be made appear that the first day of the week is that which is the sabbath day for Christians. But withal it follows, that if the seventh-day sabbath was not moral, the first day is not so. What is it then ? Why, a sabbath for holy worship is moral ; but *this* or *that* day appointed for such service, is sanctified by precept or by approved example. The timing then of a sabbath for us lies in God, not man ; in grace, not nature ; nor in the ministration of death, written and engraven in stones : God always reserving to himself a power to alter and change both *time* and *modes* of worship according to his own will.

A sabbath then, or day of rest from worldly affairs to solemnize worship to God in, all good men do by nature conclude is meet ; yea, necessary : yet *that*, not nature, but God reveals.

Nor is that day or time by God so fixed on, in its own nature, better than any other : the holiness then of a sabbath lies, not in the nature or place of a day, but in the ordinance of God.

Nor doth our sanctifying of it, to the ends for which it is ordained, lie in a bare confession that it is such ; but in a holy performance of the duty of the day to God by Christ, according to his word.

But I will not enlarge to detain the reader longer from the following sheets ; but shall commit both him and them to the wise dispose of God, and rest,

Thine to serve thee,

JOHN BUNYAN.

NATURE AND PERPETUITY OF THE SEVENTH-DAY SABBATH.

QUESTION I.

Whether the seventh-day sabbath is of, or made known to, man by the law and light of nature.

SOMETHING must be here premised before I show the grounds of this question. First, then, by the law or light of nature, I mean that law which was concreate with man; that which is natural to him, being original with, and essential to, himself; consequently, that which is invariable and unalterable, as is that nature.

Secondly. I grant that by this law of nature, man understands that there is one eternal God; that this God is to be worshipped according to his own will; consequently, that *time* must be allowed to do it in: but whether the law or light of nature teacheth, and that of itself, without the help of revelation, that the seventh day of the week is *that* time sanctified of God and set apart for his worship, that is the question; and the grounds of it are these:

First. Because the law of nature is antecedent to this day, yea, completed as a law before it was known or revealed to man, that God either did or would sanctify the seventh day of the week at all.

Now this law, as was said, being natural to a man, for man is a law unto himself, (Rom. ii.,) could only teach the things of a man, and there the apostle stints it. (1 Cor. ii. 11.) But to be able to determine, and that about things that were yet without being, either in nature or by revelation, is that which belongs not to a man as a man; and the seventh-day sabbath, as yet, was such. For Adam was completely made the day before; and God did not sanctify the seventh day before it was, none otherwise than by his secret decree. Therefore, by the law of nature, Adam understood it not; it was not made known to him thereby.

Secondly. To affirm the contrary, is to make the law of nature supernatural, which is an impossibility. Yea, they that do so make it a predictor, a prophet; a prophet about divine things to come; yea, a prophet able to foretell what shall be, and that without a revelation; which is a strain that never yet prophet pretended to.

Besides, to grant this, is to run into a grievous error; for this doth not only make the law of nature the first of prophets, contrary to Gen. iii. 10, compared with John i. 1, but it seems to make the will of God, made known by revelation, a needless thing. For if the law of nature, as such, can predict, or foretell God's secrets, and that before he reveals them, and this law of nature is universal in every individual man in the world, what need is there of particular prophets, or of their holy writings? And indeed here the Quakers and others split themselves. For if the law of nature can of itself reveal unto me one thing pertaining to instituted worship, for that we are treating of now, and the exact time which God has not yet sanctified and set apart for the performance thereof, why may it not reveal unto me more, and so still more; and at last all that is requisite for me to know, both as to my salvation, and how God is to be worshipped in the church on earth?

Thirdly. If it be of the law of nature, then all men by nature are convinced of the necessity of keeping it, and that though they never read or heard of the revealed will of God about it; but this we find not in the world.

For though it is true that the law of nature is common to all, and that all men are to this day under the power and command thereof, yet we find not that they are by nature under the conviction of the necessity of keeping of a seventh-day sabbath. Yea, the Gentiles, though we read not that they ever despised the law of nature, yet never had, as such, a reverence of a seventh-day sabbath, but rather the contrary.

Fourthly. If therefore the seventh-day sabbath is not of the law of nature, then it should seem not to be obligatory to all. For instituted worship, and the necessary circumstances thereunto belonging, is obligatory but to some. The tree that Adam was forbid to eat of, we read not but that his children might have eat the fruit thereof: and circumcision, the passover, and other parts of instituted worship, was enjoined but to some.

Fifthly. I doubt the seventh-day sabbath is not of the law of nature, and so not moral; because though we read that the law of nature, and that before Moses, was charged upon the world, yet I find not till then that the profanation of a seventh-day sabbath was charged upon the world: and indeed to me this very thing makes a great scruple in the case.

A law, as I said, we read of, and that from Adam to Moses. (Rom. v. 13, 14.) The transgressions also of *that* law, we read of them, and that particularly, as in Gen. iv. 8; vi. 5; ix. 21, 22; xii. 13; xiii. 13; xviii. 12—15; xix. 5. Ezek. xvi. 49, 50. Gen. xxxi. 30; xxxv. 2; xl. 15; xliv. 8—10. Deut. viii. 19, 20; xii. 2. Ps. cvi. 35—37, and Romans the first and second chapters.

But in all the scriptures we do not read, that the breach of a seventh-day sabbath was charged upon men as men all that time. Whence I gather, that either a seventh-day sabbath was not discerned by the light of nature, and so not by that law imposed; or else, that men by the help and assistance of that, for we speak of men as men, in old time kept it better, than in after ages did the church of God with better assistance by far. For they are there yet found fault with as breakers of the sabbath. (Ezek. xx. 13.)

It follows therefore, that, if the law of nature doth not of itself reveal to us, as men, that the seventh day is the holy sabbath of God, that day, as to the sanction of it, is not moral, but rather arbitrary, to wit, imposed by the will of God upon his people, until the time he thought fit to change it for another day.

And if so, it is hence to be concluded, that though by the light of nature men might see that time must be allowed and set apart for the performance of that worship that God would set up in his house, yet, as such, it could not see what time the Lord would to that end choose. Nature therefore saw *that* by a positive precept, or a word revealing it, and by no other means.

Nor doth this at all take away a whit of that sanction which God once put upon the seventh-day sabbath; unless any will say, and by sufficient argument prove, that an ordinance for divine worship receiveth greater sanction from the law of nature than from a divine precept; or standeth stronger when it is established by a law humane, for such is the law of nature, than when imposed by revelation of God.

But the text will put this controversy to an end. The sanction of the seventh-day sabbath, even as it was the rest of God, was not till after the law of nature was completed; God rested the seventh day and sanctified it. (Gen. ii. 3.) Sanctified it: that is, set it apart to the end there mentioned, to wit, to rest thereon.

Other grounds of this question I might produce, but at present I will stop here and conclude, That if a seventh-day sabbath was an essential necessary to the instituted worship of God, then itself also as to its sanction for that work, was not founded but by a positive precept; consequently not known of man at first, but by revelation of God.

QUESTION II.

Whether the seventh-day sabbath, as to man's keeping of it holy, was ever made known to, or imposed by a positive precept upon him, until the time of Moses, which from Adam was about two thousand years.

Something must also be here premised, in order to my propounding of my grounds for this question; and that is, That the seventh day was sanctified so soon as it had being in the world, unto the rest of God, as it is Gen. ii. 2, 3, and he did rest, from all his works which he had made therein. But the question is, Whether when God did thus sanctify this day to his *own rest*, he did also by the space of time above-mentioned, impose it as an holy sabbath of rest upon men; to the end they might solemnize worship to him in special manner thereon? And I question this,

First, Because we read not that it was. And reading, I mean, of the divine testimony, is ordained of God, for us to find out the mind of God, both as to faith and our performance of acceptable service to him.

In reading, also, we are to have regard to two things.

I. To see if we can find a precept: or,

II. A countenanced practice for what we do. For both these ways we are to search, that we may find out what is that good, that acceptable will of God.

For the first of these we have Gen. ii. 16, 17, and for the second, Gen. viii. 20, 21.

Now as to the imposing of a seventh-day sabbath upon men from Adam to Moses, of that we find nothing in holy writ either from precept or example. True, we find that solemn worship was performed by the saints that then lived; for both Abel, Noah, Abraham, Isaac, Jacob, sacrificed unto God, (Gen. iv. 4; viii. 20, 21; xii. 7; xiii. 4; xxxv. 1;) but we read not that the seventh day was the time prefixed of God for their so worshipping, or that they took any notice of it. Some say, that Adam in eating the forbidden fruit, brake also the seventh-day sabbath, because he fell on that day; but we read not that the breach of a sabbath was charged upon him. That which we read is this: "Hast thou eaten of the tree, whereof I commanded thee that thou shouldest not eat?" (Gen. iii. 11.) Some say also that Cain killed Abel on a sabbath day; but we read not that, in his charge, God laid any such thing at his door. This was it of which he stood guilty before God; namely, That his brother's blood cried unto God against him from the ground. (Gen. iv. 10.)

I therefore take little notice of what a man saith, though he flourisheth his matter with many brave words, if he bring not with him, "Thus saith the Lord." For that, and that only, ought to be my ground of faith as to how my God would be worshipped by me. For in the matters material to the worship of God, it is safest that thus I be guided in my judgment: for here only I perceive "the footsteps of the flock." (Ezek. iii. 11. Sol. Song i. 8.) They say further, that for God to sanctify a thing, is to set it apart. This being true, then it follows, that the seventh-day sabbath was sanctified, that is, set apart for Adam in paradise; and so, that it was ordained a sabbath of rest to the saints from the beginning.

But I answer, as I hinted before, that God did sanctify it to his own rest. "The Lord also hath set apart him that is godly for himself." But again, it is one thing for God to sanctify this or that thing to an use, and another thing to command that that thing be forthwith in being to us. As for instance: the land of Canaan was set apart many years for the children of Israel before they possessed that land. Christ Jesus was long sanctified; that is, set apart to be our Redeemer before he sent him into the world. (Deut. xxxii. John x. 36.)

If, then, by God's sanctifying of the seventh day for a sabbath, you understand it for a sabbath for man, (but the text saith not so,) yet it might be so set apart for man, long before it should be, as such, made known unto him. And that the seventh-day sabbath was not as yet made known to men, consider,

Secondly. Moses himself seems to have the knowledge of it at first, not by tradition, but by revelation; as it is Exod. xvi. 23: "This is that (saith he) which the Lord hath said, (namely, to me; for we read not, as yet, that he said it to anybody else,) *To-morrow is the sabbath of the holy rest unto the Lord.*"

Also holy Nehemiah suggesteth this, when he saith of Israel to God, Thou "madest known unto them thy holy sabbath." (Neh. ix. 14.) The first of these texts shows us, that tidings of a seventh-day sabbath for men, came *first* to Moses from heaven: and the second, that it was to Israel before unknown.

But how could be either the one or the other, if the seventh-day sabbath was taught to men by the light of nature, which is the moral law? Or if from the beginning it was given to men by a positive precept for to be kept.

This therefore strengtheneth my doubt about the affirmative of the first question, and also prepareth an argument for what I plead as to this we have now under consideration.

Thirdly. This yet seems to me more scrupulous, because that the punishment due to the breach of the seventh-day sabbath was hid from men to the time of Moses; as is clear, for that it is said of the breaker of the sabbath, "They put him in ward, because it was not as yet declared what should be done to him." (Numb. xv. 32—36.)

But methinks, had this seventh-day sabbath been imposed upon men from the beginning, the penalty or punishment due to the breach thereof had certainly been known before now.

When Adam was forbidden to eat of the tree of the knowledge of good and evil, the penalty was then, if he disobeyed, annexed to the prohibition. So also it was as to circumcision, the passover, and other ordinances for worship. How then can it be thought, that the seventh-day sabbath should be imposed upon men from the beginning; and that the punishment for the breach thereof should be hid with God for the space of two thousand years! (Gen. ii. 16, 17; xvii. 13, 14. Exod. xii. 43—48, and the same chapter, verse 19.)

Fourthly. God's giving of the seventh-day sabbath was with respect to *stated* and *stinted* worship in his church; the which, until the time of Moses, was not set up among his people. Things till then were adding or growing: *now* a sacrifice,

then circumcision, then again long after that the passover, &c. But when Israel was come into the wilderness, there to receive as God's congregation, a stated, stinted, limited way of worship, then he appoints them a time, and times, to perform this worship in; but as I said afore, before that it was not so, as the whole five books of Moses plainly show: wherefore the seventh-day sabbath, as such a limited day, cannot be moral, or of the law of nature, nor imposed till then.

And methinks Christ Jesus and his apostles do plainly enough declare this very thing. For that when they repeat unto the people, or expound before them the moral law, they quite exclude the seventh-day sabbath. Yea, Paul makes that law to us complete without it.

We will first touch upon what Christ doth in this case.

As in his sermon upon the mount, (Matt. v.—vii.) In all that large and heavenly discourse upon this law, you have not one syllable about the seventh-day sabbath.

So when the young man came running, and kneeling, and asking what good thing he should do to inherit eternal life, Christ bids him keep the commandments; but when the young man asked which, Christ quite leaves out the seventh day, and puts him upon the other. As in Matt. xix. 16—19. As in Mark x. 17—20. As in Luke xviii. 18—20.

You will say, he left out the first, and second, and third likewise. To which I say, that was because the young man by his question did presuppose that he had been a doer of them: for he professed in his supplication, that he was a lover of that which is naturally good, which is God, in that his petition was so universal for every thing which he had commanded.

Paul also when he makes mention of the moral law, quite leaves out of that the very name of the seventh-day sabbath, and professeth, that to us Christians the law of nature is complete without it. As in Rom. iii. 7—19. As in Rom. xiii. 7—10. As in 1 Tim. i. 8—11.

"He that loveth another, saith he, hath fulfilled the law. For this, Thou shalt not commit adultery, Thou shalt not kill, Thou shalt not steal, Thou shalt not covet; and if there be any other commandment, it is briefly comprehended in this saying, Thou shalt love thy neighbour as thyself. Love worketh no ill to his neighbour: therefore love is the fulfilling of the law."

I make not an argument of this, but take an occasion to mention it as I go. But certainly, had the seventh-day sabbath been moral, or of the law of nature, as some would fain persuade themselves, it would not so slenderly have been passed over in all these repetitions of this law, but would by Christ or his apostles have been pressed upon the people, when so fair an opportunity as at these times offered itself unto them. But they knew what they did, and wherefore they were so silent as to the mention of a seventh-day sabbath when they so well talked of the law as moral.

Fifthly. Moses and the prophet Ezekiel both, do fully confirm what has been insinuated by us; to wit, that the seventh day, as a sabbath, was not imposed upon men until Israel was brought into the wilderness.

1. Moses saith to Israel, " Remember that thou wast a servant in the land of Egypt, and that the Lord thy God brought thee out thence through a mighty hand and by a stretched out arm: *therefore* the Lord thy God commanded thee to keep the sabbath day." Yea, he tells us, that the covenant which God made with them in Horeb, that written in stones, was not made with their forefathers, to wit, Abraham, Isaac, and Jacob, but with them. (Deut. v. 1—15.)

2. Ezekiel also is punctual as to this: I caused them, saith God by that prophet, " to go forth out of the land of Egypt, and brought them into the wilderness. And I gave them my statutes, and showed them my judgments, which if a man do, he shall even live in them. Moreover also I gave them my sabbaths, to be a sign between me and them, that they might know that I am the Lord that sanctify them." (Ezek. xx. 10—12. Exod. xx. 8; xxxi. 13; xxxv. 2.)

What can be more plain? And these to be sure, are two notable witnesses of God, who, as you see, do jointly concur in this; to wit, That it was not from paradise, nor from the fathers, but from the wilderness, and from Sinai, that men received the seventh-day sabbath to keep it holy.

True, it was God's sabbath before: for on the first seventh day we read, that God rested thereon, and sanctified it. Hence he calls it in the first place, My sabbath. I gave them my sabbath: but it seems it was not given to the church till he had brought them into the wilderness.

But I say, if it had been *moral*, it had been natural to man; and by the light of nature men would have understood it, even both before it was, and otherwise. But of this you see we read nothing, either by positive law, or countenanced example, or any other way, but rather the flat contrary; to wit, that Moses had the knowledge of it first from heaven, not by tradition. That Israel had it, not of, or from their fathers, but in the wilderness, from him, to wit, Moses, after he had brought them out of the land of Egypt. And that that whole law in which the seventh-day sabbath is placed, was given for the bounding and better ordering of them in their church state for their time, till the Messias should come and put, by a better ministration, this out of his church, as we shall further show anon.

The seventh-day sabbath therefore was not from paradise, nor from nature, nor from the fathers, but from the wilderness, and from Sinai.

QUESTION III.

Whether when the seventh-day sabbath was given to Israel in the wilderness, the Gentiles, as such, were concerned therein.

Before I show my ground for this question, I must also first premise, That the Gentiles, as such, were then without the church of God, and pale thereof; consequently had nothing to do with the essentials or necessary circumstances of that worship which God had set up for himself now among the children of Israel.

Now then for the ground of the question.

First. We read not that God gave it to any but to the seed of Jacob. Hence it is said to Israel, and to Israel only, " The Lord hath given YOU the sabbath." (Exod. xvi. 29.) And again, " Also I gave THEM my sabbaths." (Ezek. xx. 12.)

Now, if the gift of the seventh-day sabbath was only to Israel, as these texts do more than seem to say, then to the Gentiles, as such, it was not given. Unless any shall conclude, that God by thus doing preferred the Jew to a state of Gentileism; or that he bestowed on them, by thus doing, some high Gentile privilege. But this would be very fictions. For, to lay aside reason, the text always, as to preference, did set the Jew in the first of places. (Rom. ii. 10.) Nor was his giving the seventh-day sabbath to them but a sign and token thereof.

But the great objection is, because the seventh-day sabbath is found amongst the rest of those precepts which is so commonly called the moral law; for thence it is concluded to be of a perpetual duration.

But I answer, That neither that as given on Sinai is moral: I mean, as to the manner and ends of its ministration; of which, God permitting, we shall say more in our answer to the fourth question, whither I direct you for satisfaction. But,

Secondly. The Gentiles could not be concerned, as such, with God's giving of a seventh-day sabbath to Israel, because, as I have showed before, it was given to Israel, considered as a church of God. (Acts vii. 32.) Nor was it given to them, as such, but with rites and ceremonies thereto belonging, so Lev. xxiv. 5—9. Numb. xxviii. 9, 10. Neh. xiii. 22. Ezek. xlvi. 4.

Now, I say, if this sabbath hath ceremonies thereto belonging, and if these ceremonies were essential to the right keeping of the sabbath: and again, if these ceremonies were given to Israel only, excluding all but such as were their proselytes, then this sabbath was given to them as excluding the Gentiles as such. But if it had been moral, the Gentiles could have soon as been deprived of their nature as of a seventh-day sabbath, though the Jews should have appropriated it unto themselves only.

Again, to say that God gave this seventh-day sabbath to the Gentiles, as such, (and yet so he must, if it be of the moral law,) is as much as to say, that God hath ordained that *that* sabbath should be kept by the Gentiles *without;* but by the Jews, *not* without her ceremonies. And what conclusion will follow from hence, but that God did at *one* and the *same* time set up two sorts of acceptable worships in the world: one among the Jews, another among the Gentiles! But how ridiculous such a thought would be, and how repugnant to the wisdom of God, you may easily perceive.

Yea, what a diminution would this be to God's church that then was, for one to say, the Gentiles were to serve God with more liberty than the Jew! For the law was a yoke, and yet the Gentile is called the dog, and said to be without God in the world. (Deut. vii. 7. Ps. cxlvii. 19, 20, Matt. xv. 26. Eph. ii. 11, 12.)

Thirdly. When the Gentiles, at the Jews' return from Babylon, came and offered their wares to sell to the children of Israel at Jerusalem on this sabbath; yea, and sold them to them too: yet *not they,* but the *Jews* were rebuked as the only breakers of that sabbath. Nay, there dwelt then at Jerusalem men of Tyre, that on *this* sabbath sold their commodities to the Jews, and men of Judah: yet not they, but the men of Judah, were contended with, as the breakers of this sabbath.

True, good Nehemiah did threaten the Gentiles that were merchants, for lying then about the walls of the city, for that by that means they were a temptation to the Jews to break *their* sabbaths; but still he charged the breach thereof *only* upon his own people. (Neh. xiii. 15—20.)

But can it be imagined, had the Gentiles now been concerned with this sabbath by law divine, that so holy a man as Nehemiah would have let them escape without a rebuke for so notorious a transgression thereof; especially considering, that now also they were upon God's ground, to wit, within and without the walls of Jerusalem.

Fourthly. Wherefore he saith to Israel again, " Verily my sabbaths YE shall keep." And again, " YE shall keep my sabbaths." And again, "The children of Israel shall keep my sabbaths, to observe my sabbaths, throughout THEIR generations." (Exod. xxxi. 14—16; xvi. 29.)

What can be more plain, these things thus standing in the testament of God, than that the seventh-day sabbath, as such, was given to Israel, to Israel ONLY; and that the Gentiles, as such, were not concerned therein.

Fifthly. The very reason also of God's giving of the seventh-day sabbath to the Jews, doth exclude the Gentiles, as such, from having any concern therein. For it was given to the Jews, as was said before, as they were considered God's church, and for a sign and token by which they should know that he had chosen and sanctified them to himself for a peculiar people. (Exod. xxxi. 13—17. Ezek. xx. 12, 13.) And a great token and sign it was that he had so chosen them: for

in that he had given to them this sabbath, he had given to them (his own rest) a figure and pledge of his sending his Son into the world to redeem them from the bondage and slavery of the devil: of whom indeed this sabbath was a shadow or type. (Col. ii. 16, 17.)

Thus have I concluded my ground for this third question. I shall therefore now propound another.

QUESTION IV.

Whether the seventh-day sabbath did not fall, as such, with the rest of the Jewish rites and ceremonies. Or whether that day, as a sabbath, was afterwards by the apostles imposed upon the churches of the Gentiles.

I would now also, before I show the grounds of my proposing this question, premise what is necessary thereunto; to wit, that *time* and *day* were both fixed upon by law, for the solemn performance of divine worship among the Jews; and that *time* and *day* is also by law fixed, for the solemnizing of divine worship to God in the churches of the Gentiles. But that the seventh-day sabbath, as such, is *that* time, *that* day, that still I question.

Now before I show the grounds of my questioning of it, I shall inquire into the nature of that ministration in the bowels of which this seventh-day sabbath is placed. And,

First. I say, as to that, the *nature* of that law is moral, but the ministration, and circumstances thereunto belonging, are shadowish and figurative.

By the nature of it, I mean the matter thereof: by the ministration and circumstances thereto belonging, I do mean the giving of it by such hands, at such a place and time, in such a mode, as when it was given to Israel in the wilderness.

The matter therefore, to wit, " Thou shalt love the Lord thy God with all thy heart, and with all thy soul, and with all thy mind, and with all thy strength:" and "thy neighbour as thyself," is everlasting, (Mark xii. 30, 31,) and is not from Sinai, nor from the two tables of stone, but in nature; for this law commenced and took being and place that day in which man was created. Yea, it was concreate with him, and without it he cannot be a rational creature, as he was in the day in which God created him. But for the ministration of it from Sinai, with the circumstances belonging to that ministration, they are not moral, nor everlasting, but shadowish and figurative only.

That ministration cannot be moral for three reasons.

1. It commenced not when morality commenced, but two thousand years after. 2. It was not universal as the law, as moral, is; it was given only to the church of the Jews in those tables. 3. Its end is past as such a ministration, though the same law as to the morality thereof abides. Where are the tables of stone and this law as therein

contained? We only, as to that, have the notice of such a ministration, and a rehearsal of the law, with that mode of giving of it, in the testament of God.

But to come to particulars.

1. The very preface to that ministration carrieth in it a type of our deliverance from the bondage of sin, the devil, and hell. Pharaoh, and Egypt; and Israel's bondage there, being a type of these.

2. The very stones in which this law was engraven, was a figure of the tables of the heart. The first two were a figure of the heart carnal, by which the law was broken: the last two, of the heart spiritual, in which the new law, the law of grace, is written and preserved. (Exod. xxxiv. 1. 2 Cor. iii. 3.)

3. The very mount on which this ministration was given, was typical of Mount Zion. See Heb. xii., where they are compared, verses 18—22.

4. Yea, the very church to whom that ministration was given, was a figure of the church of the gospel that is on Mount Zion. See the same scripture, and compare it with Acts vii. 38. Rev. xiv. 1—5.

5. That ministration was given in the hand and by the disposition of angels, to prefigure how the new law or ministration of the Spirit was to be given afterwards to the churches under the New Testament by the hands of the angel of God's everlasting covenant of grace, who is his only begotten Son. (Isa. lxiii. 9. Mal. iii. 1. Acts iii. 22, 23.)

6. It was given to Israel also in the hand of Moses, as mediator, to show, or typify out, that the law of grace was in after times to come to the church of Christ by the hand and mediation of Jesus our Lord. (Gal. iii. 19. Deut. v. 5. Heb. viii. 6. 1 Tim. ii. 5. Heb. ix. 15; xii. 24.)

7. As to this ministration, it was to continue but "till the seed should come;" and then must, as such, give place to a better ministration. (Gal. iii. 19.) "A better covenant, established upon better promises." (Heb. viii. 6.)

From all this therefore I conclude that there is a difference to be put between the morality of the law, and the ministration of it upon Sinai. The law, as to its morality was before; but as to *this* ministration, it was not till the church was with Moses, and he with the angels on Mount Sinai in the wilderness.

Now in the law, as moral, we conclude a time propounded, but no seventh-day sabbath enjoined. But in that law, as thus ministered, which ministration is already out of doors, we find a seventh day, that seventh day on which God rested, on which God rested from all his works, enjoined. What is it then? Why the whole ministration as written and engraven in stones being removed, the seventh-day sabbath must also be removed; for that the *time*, nor yet the *day*, was as to our holy sabbath, or rest, moral; but imposed with that whole ministration, as such, upon the church, until the time of reformation: which time being come, this ministration, as I said, as such, ceaseth; and the whole law, as to the morality of it, is delivered into the hand of Christ, who imposes it now also; but not as a law of works, nor as that ministration written and engraven in stones, but as a rule of life to those that have believed in him. (1 Cor. ix. 21.)

So then, that law is still moral, and still supposes, since it teaches that there is a God, that time must be set apart for his church to worship him in, according to that will of his that he had revealed in his word. But though by that law *time* is required; yet by that, as moral, the time never was prefixed.

The time then of old was appointed by such a ministration of that law as we have been now discoursing of; and when that ministration ceaseth, that time did also vanish with it. And now by our new law-giver, the Son of God, he being "lord also of the sabbath day," we have a time prefixed, as the law of nature requireth, a *new* day, by him who is the lord of it; I say, appointed, wherein we may worship, not in the oldness of that letter written and engraven in stones, but according to, and most agreeing with, his new and holy testament. And this I confirm further by those reasons that now shall follow.

First. Because we find not from the resurrection of Christ to the end of the Bible, anything written by which is imposed that seventh-day sabbath upon the churches. *Time*, as I said, the law as moral requires; but *that* time we find no longer imposed. And in all duties pertaining to God and his true worship in his churches, we must be guided by his laws and testaments. By his old laws, when his old worship was in force; and by his new laws, when his new worship is in force. And he hath verily now said, "Behold, I make all things new." (Rev. xxi. 5.)

Secondly. I find, as I have showed, that this seventh-day sabbath is confined, not to the law of nature as such, but to that ministration of it which was given on Sinai: which ministration as it is come to an end as such, so it is rejected by Paul as a ministration no ways capable of abiding in the church now, since the ministration of the Spirit also hath taken its place. (2 Cor. iii.) Wherefore, instead of propounding it to the churches with arguments tending to its reception, he seeks by degrading it of its old lustre and glory, to wean the churches from any likement thereof:

1. By calling of it the ministration of death, of the letter, and of condemnation, a term most frightful, but no ways alluring to the godly.

2. By calling it a ministration that *now* has *no* glory, by reason of the exceeding glory of that ministration under which by the Holy Spirit the New Testament churches are. And these are weaning considerations. (2 Cor. iii.)

3. By telling of them it is a ministration that tendeth to blind the mind, and to veil the heart

as to the knowledge of their Christ: so that they cannot, while under that, behold his beauteous face, but as their heart shall turn from it to him. (2 Cor. iii.)

4. And that they might not be left in the dark, but perfectly know what ministration it is that he means, he saith expressly, it is that " written *and* engraven in stones." (See again 2 Cor. iii. 7.) And in that ministration it is that this seventh-day sabbath is found.

But, *thirdly,* shall we think that the apostle speaks anything of all here said, to wean saints off from the law of nature, as such! No verily, that he retains in the church, as being managed there by Christ: but *this ministration* is dangerous *now,* because it cannot be maintained in the church, but in a way of contempt to the ministration of the Spirit, and is derogatory to the glory of that.

Now these, as I said, are weaning considerations. No man, I do think, that knows himself, or the glory of a gospel ministration, can, if he understands what Paul says here, desire that such a ministration should be retained in the churches.

Fourthly. This seventh-day sabbath has lost its ceremonies, (those unto which before you are cited by the texts,) which was with it imposed upon the old church for her due performance of worship to God thereon. How then can *this* sabbath *now* be kept? Kept, I say, according to law. For if the church on which it was first imposed, was not to keep it, yea, could not keep it legally without the practising of those ceremonies; and if those ceremonies are long ago dead and gone, how will those that pretend to a belief of a continuation of the sanction thereof, keep it, I say, according as it is written?

If they say, they retain the day, but change their manner of observation thereof, I ask, who has commanded them so to do? This is one of the laws of *this* sabbath. " Thou shalt take fine flour, and bake twelve cakes thereof: two tenth deals shall be in one cake. And thou shalt set them in two rows, six on a row, upon the pure table before the Lord. And thou shalt put pure frankincense upon each row, that it may be on the bread for a memorial, even an offering made by fire unto the Lord. Every sabbath he shall set it in order before the Lord continually, being taken from the children of Israel by an everlasting covenant." (Lev. xxiv. 5—8.) You may see also other places, as Numb. xxviii. 9.

Now if these be the laws of the sabbath, this seventh-day sabbath; and if God did never command that *this* sabbath should by his church be sanctified without them; and, as was said before, if these ceremonies have been long since dead and buried, how must *this* sabbath be kept?

Let men take heed, lest, while they plead for law, and pretend themselves to be the only doers of God's will, they be not found the biggest transgressors thereof. And why can they not as well keep the other sabbaths? As the sabbaths

of months, of years, and the jubilee? For this, as I have showed, is no moral precept; it is only a branch of the ministration of death and condemnation.

Fifthly. The seventh-day sabbath, as such, was a sign and shadow of things to come; and a sign cannot be the thing signified and substance too. Wherefore when the thing signified, or substance, is come, the sign or thing shadowing ceaseth. And, I say, the seventh-day sabbath being so, as a seventh-day sabbath it ceaseth also. (See again, Exod. xxxi. 13, 14. Ezek. xx. 12, 21. Col. ii. 14.)

Nor do I find that our Protestant writers, notwithstanding their reverence for the sabbath, do conclude otherwise, but that, though time as to worshipping God, must needs be contained in the bowels of the moral law, as moral, yet they, for good reasons, forbear to affix the seventh day as *that* time there too.

They do it, I say, for good reasons; reasons drawn from the Scripture, or rather for that the Scripture draws them so to conclude: yet they cast not away the morality of a sabbath of rest to the church. It is to be granted, then, that time for God's worship abideth for ever, but the seventh day vanishes as a shadow and sign; because such, indeed, it was, as the scripture above cited declares, as to the sanction thereof as a sabbath.

The Law of Nature then calls for time; but the God of nature assigns it, and has given power to his Son to continue such time as himself shall, by his eternal wisdom, judge most meet for the churches of the Gentiles to solemnize worship to God by him in. Hence he is said to be " Lord even of the sabbath-day." (Matt. xii. 8.)

Sixthly. I find, by reading God's word, that Paul—by authority apostolical—takes away the sanctions of all the Jews' festivals and sabbaths.

This is manifest, for that he leaves the observation or non-observation of them, as things indifferent, to the mind and discretion of the believers. " One man esteemeth one day above another: another esteemeth every day alike. Let every man be fully persuaded in his own mind." (Rom. xiv. 5.)

By this last clause of the verse, " Let every man be fully persuaded in his own mind," he doth plainly declare, that *such* days are now stript of their sanction. For none of God's laws, while they retain their sanction, are left to the will and mind of the believers, as to whether they will observe them or no. Men, I say, are not left to their liberty in such a case; for when a stamp of divine authority is upon a law, and abides, so long we are bound, not to *our* mind, but to that law: but when a thing, once sacred, has lost its sanction, then it falls, as to faith and conscience, among other *common* or indifferent things. And so the seventh-day sabbath did. Again—

Seventhly. Thus Paul writes to the church of Coloss: " Let no man, therefore, judge you in meat, or in drink, or in respect of an holyday, or of the new moon, or of the sabbath: which are a shadow of things to come; but the body *is* of Christ." (Col. ii. 16, 17.) Here also, as he serveth other holy days, he serveth the sabbath. He gives a liberty to believers to refuse the observation of it, and commands that no man should judge against them for their so doing. And, as you read, the reason of his so doing, is because the body, the substance, is come. Christ, saith he, is the body, or that which these things were a shadow or figure of. "The body *is* of Christ."

Nor hath the apostle, since he saith, "or of the sabbath," one would think, left any hole, out at which men's inventions could get: but man has sought out many; and, so, many he will use.

But again, that the apostle, by this word, "sabbath," intends the seventh-day sabbath, is clear; for that it is by Moses himself counted for a sign, as we have showed: and for that none of the other sabbaths were a more clear shadow of the Lord Jesus Christ than this. For that, and that alone, is called "*the* rest of God:" in it God rested from all his works. Hence he calls it, by way of eminency, "My sabbath, and my holy day." (Isa. lvi. 4; lviii. 13.)

Yet could that rest be nothing else but typical; for God, never since the world began, really rested, but in his Son. "This is he," saith God, "in whom I am well pleased." This sabbath, then, was God's rest typically, and was given to Israel as a sign of his grace towards them in Christ. Wherefore when Christ was risen, it ceased, and was no longer of obligation to bind the conscience to the observation thereof. [Or of the sabbath.] He distinctly singleth out *this* seventh day, as that which was a most noble shadow, a most exact shadow. And then puts that with the other together, saying, they are a shadow of things to come, and that Christ has answered them all. "The body *is* Christ."

Eighthly. No man will, I think, deny but that Heb. iv. 4 intends the seventh-day sabbath, on which God rested from all his works; for the text doth plainly say so: yet may the observing reader easily perceive that both it, and the *rest* of Canaan also, made mention of ver. 5, were typical, as to a day made mention of verses 7, 8, which day he calls *another*. He would not afterwards have made mention of *another* day—if Joshua had given them rest, he would not. Now if they had not that rest in Joshua's days, be sure they had it not by Moses; for he was still before.

All the rests, therefore, that Moses gave them, and that Joshua gave them too, were but typical of *another* day, in which God would give them rest. (Heb. iv. 9, 10.) And whether the day *to come* was Christ, or Heaven, it makes no matter: it is enough that they before did fail, as always shadows do, and that, therefore, mention by David is, and that afterward, made of another day. "There remains, therefore, a rest to the people of God:"

a rest to come, of which the seventh day in which God rested, and the land of Canaan, was a type; which rest begins in Christ *now*, and shall be consummated in glory.

And in that he saith, "There remains a rest," referring to that of David, what is it, if it signifies not that the other rests remain not? There remains, therefore, a rest, a rest prefigured by the seventh day, and by the rest of Canaan, though they are fled and gone.

"There remains a rest;" a rest which stands not now in signs and shadows, in the seventh day, or Canaan, but in the Son of God, and his kingdom, to whom, and to which the weary are invited to come for rest. (Isa. xxviii. 12. Matt. xi. 20. Heb. iv. 11.)

Yet this casts not out the Christians' holiday or sabbath: for that was not ordained to be a type or shadow of things to come, but to sanctify the name of their God in, and to perform that worship to him which was also in a shadow signified by the ceremonies of the law, as the epistle to the Hebrews doth plentifully declare.

And I say again, the seventh-day sabbath cannot be it, for the reasons showed afore.

Ninthly. Especially if you add to all this, that nothing of the ministration of death written and engraven in stones, is brought by Jesus, or by his apostles, into the kingdom of Christ, as a part of his instituted worship. Hence it is said of that ministration in, the bowels of which this seventh-day sabbath is found, that it has now no glory; that its glory is done away, in or by Christ, and so is laid aside; the ministration of the Spirit, that excels in glory, being come in the room thereof.

I will read the text to you. "But if the ministration of death, written and engraven in stones, was glorious, so that the children of Israel could not steadfastly behold the face of Moses for the glory of his countenance; which glory was to be done away," (it was given at first with this proviso, that it should not always retain its glory, that sanction, as a ministration): "how shall not the ministration of the Spirit be rather glorious? For if the ministration of condemnation *be* glory, much more doth the ministration of righteousness exceed in glory. For even that which was made glorious had no glory in this respect, by reason of the glory that excelleth. For if that which is done away was glorious, much more that which remaineth is glorious." (2 Cor. iii. 7—11.)

What can be more plain? The text says expressly, that this ministration doth NOT remain; yea, and insinuates, that in its first institution it was ordained with this proviso, "It was to be done away." Now, if, in its first institution upon Sinai, it was thus ordained; and if, by the coming in of the ministration of the Spirit, this ordination is now executed; that is, if by it, and the apostle saith it, it is done away by a ministration that remains: then where is that seventh-day sabbath?

Thus, therefore, I have discoursed upon this fourth question. And having showed by this discourse that the old seventh-day sabbath is abolished and done away, and that it has nothing to do with the churches of the Gentiles, I am next to show what day it is that must abide as holy to the Christians, and for them to perform their New Testament church service in.

Take the question thus.

QUESTION V.

Since it is denied that the seventh-day sabbath is moral, and is found that it is not to abide as a sabbath for ever in the church, What time is to be fixed on for New Testament saints to perform together divine worship to God by Christ in?

Upon this question hangs the stress of all, as to the subject now under consideration; but before I can speak distinctly to it, I must premise, as I have in order to my speaking to the questions before, something for the better clearing of our way—

First, then, we are not now speaking of *all* manner of worshipping God, nor of *all* times in which *all* manner of worship is to be performed; but of that worship, which is *Church-worship*, or worship that is to be performed by the assembly of saints, when by the will of God they in all parts of his dominion assemble together to worship him; which worship hath a prefixed time allotted to, or for its performance, and without which it cannot, according to the mind of God, be done. This is the time, I say, that we are to discourse of, and not of ALL time appointed for all manner of worship.

I do not question but that worship by the godly is performed to God every day of the week; yea, and every night too, and that time is appointed or allowed of God for the performance of such worship But this time is not fixed to the same moment or hour universally, but is left to the discretion of the believers, as to their frame of spirit, or occasions, or exigencies, or temptations, or duty shall require.

We meddle then only with that time that the worship aforesaid is to be performed in; which time the law of nature as such supposes, but the God of nature chooses. And this time as to the churches of the Gentiles, we have proved is not that time which was assigned to the Jews, to wit, THAT seventh day which was imposed upon them by the ministration of death; for, as we have showed already, that ministration indeed is done away by a better and more glorious ministration, the ministration of the Spirit; which ministration surely would be much more inferior than that which has now no glory, was it defective as to this. That is, if it imposed a gospel service, but

appointed not time to perform that worship in: or if, notwithstanding all its commendation, it should be forced to borrow of a ministration inferior to itself; that, to wit, the time without which by no means its most solemn worship can be performed.

This, then, is the conclusion—that TIME to worship God in is required by the law of nature, but that the law of nature doth, as such, fix it on the seventh day from the creation of the world, that I utterly deny, by what I have said already, and have yet to say on that behalf. Yea, I hope to make it manifest, as I have, that this seventh day is removed; that God, by the ministration of the Spirit, has changed the time to another day, to wit, the first day of the week. Therefore we conclude the time is fixed for the worship of the New Testament Christians, or churches of the Gentiles, unto that day.

Now in my discourse upon the subject, I shall—

I. Touch upon those texts that are more close, yet have a divine intimation of this thing in them.

II. And then I shall come to texts more express.

FIRST. For those texts that are more close, yet have a divine intimation of this thing in them.

First. The comparison that the Holy Ghost makes between the rest of God from his works, and the rest of Christ from his, doth intimate such a thing. "He that is entered into his rest, he also hath ceased from his own works, as God *did* from his." (Heb. iv. 10.)

Now God rested from his works, and sanctified a day of rest to himself, as a signal of that rest, which day he also gave to his church as a day of holy rest likewise. And if Christ thus rested from his own works, and the Holy Ghost says he did thus rest, he also hath sanctified a day to himself, as that in which he hath finished his work, and given it also to his church to be an everlasting memento of his so doing, and that they should keep it holy for his sake.

And see, as the Father's work was first, so his day went before; and as the Son's work came after, so his day accordingly succeeded. The Father's day was on the seventh day from the creation, the Son's the first day following.

Nor may this be slighted, because the text says, as God finished his work, so Christ finished his. He also hath ceased from his own works as God did from his. He rested, I say, as God did; but God rested on his resting-day, and therefore so did Christ. Not that he rested on the Father's resting-day; for it is evident, that then he had great part of his work to do; for he had not as then got his conquest over death, but the next day he also entered into his rest, having by his rising again, finished his work, viz., made a conquest over the powers of darkness, and brought life and immortality to light through his so doing.

So then, that being the day of the rest of the Son of God, it must needs be the day of the rest of his churches also. For God gave his resting-day to his church to be a sabbath; and Christ rested from his own works as God did from his, therefore he also gave the day in which he rested from his works, a sabbath to the churches, as did the Father. Not that there are TWO sabbaths at once: the Father's was imposed for a time, even until the Son's should come; yea, as I have showed you, even in the very time of its imposing it was also ordained to be done away. Hence he saith, that ministration "was to be done away." (2 Cor. iii. 7.) Therefore we plead not for two sabbaths to be at one time, but that a succession of time was ordained to the New Testament saints, or churches of the Gentiles, to worship God in; which time is that in which the Son rested from his own works as God did from his.

Secondly. Hence he calls himself, the "Lord even of the sabbath day," as Luke v., Matt. xii. 8, shows. Now to be a LORD, is to have dominion, dominion over a thing, and so power to alter or change it according to that power; and where is he that dares say Christ has not this absolutely! We will therefore conclude that it is granted on all hands he hath. The question then is, Whether he hath exercised that power to the demolishing or removing of the Jews' seventh day, and establishing another in its room? The which I think is easily answered, in that he did not rest from his own works therein, but chose, for his own rest, to himself another day.

Surely, had the Lord Jesus intended to have established the seventh day to the churches of the Gentiles, he would himself in the first place have rested from his own works therein; but since he passed by that day, and took no notice of it, as to the finishing of his own works, as God took notice of it when he had finished his, it remains that he fixed upon another day, even the first of the week, on which, by his rising again, and showing himself to his disciples after his passion, he made it manifest that he had chosen, "as Lord of the sabbath," that day for his own rest: consequently, and for the rest of his churches, and for his worship to be solemnized in.

Thirdly. And on THIS day some of the saints that slept arose, and began their eternal sabbath. (Matt. xxvii. 52, 53.) See how the Lord Jesus hath glorified *this* day! Never was such a stamp of divine honour put upon any other day, no not since the world begun. "And the graves were opened; and many bodies of the saints which slept arose, and came out of the graves after his resurrection," &c. That is, they rose as soon as he was risen. But why was not all this done on the seventh day? No, that day was set apart that saints might adore God for the works of creation, and that saints through that might look for redemption by Christ. But now a work more glorious than that is to be done, and therefore another day is assigned for the doing of it in. A work, I say, of redemption completed, a day therefore by itself must be assigned for this; and some

of the saints to begin their eternal sabbath with God in heaven, therefore a day by itself must be appointed for this. Yea, and that this day might not want that glory that might attract the most dim-sighted Christian to a desire after the sanction of it, the resurrection of Christ, and also of those saints met together on it: yea, they both did begin their eternal rest thereon.

Fourthly. The psalmist speaks of a day that the Lord Jehovah, the Son of God, has made; and saith, "we will rejoice and be glad in it." But what day is this? Why the day in which Christ was made the "head of the corner," which must be applied to the day in which he was raised from the dead, which is the first of the week.

Hence Peter saith to the Jews, when he treateth of Christ before them, and particularly of his resurrection: "This is the stone which WAS set at nought of you builders, which is become the head of the corner." He *was* set at nought by them, the whole course of his ministry unto his death, and was made the head of the corner by God, on *that* day he rose from the dead. This day, therefore, is the day that the Lord Jehovah has made a day of rejoicing to the church of Christ, and we will rejoice and be glad in it. (Ps. cxviii. 24.)

For can it be imagined, that the Spirit by the prophet should thus signalize this day for nothing; saying, "This is the day *which* the Lord hath made:" to no purpose? Yes, you may say, for the resurrection of his Son.

But I add, that that is not all, it is a day that the Lord has made both for that, and that we might "rejoice and be glad in it." Rejoice, that is, before the Lord while solemn divine worship is performed on it, by all the people that shall partake of the redemption accomplished then.

Fifthly. God *the Father* again leaves such another stamp of divine note and honour upon this day as he never before did leave upon any; where he saith to our Lord, "Thou art my Son, this day have I begotten thee." (Acts xiii. 33.) Still, I say, having respect to the first day of the week; for that, and no other, is the day here intended by the apostle. This day, saith God, is the day: "And as concerning that he raised him up from the dead, *now* no more to return to corruption, he said on this wise, I will give thee the sure mercies of David. Wherefore he saith also in another *Psalm*, Thou shalt not suffer thine Holy One to see corruption." Wherefore the day in which God did this work, is greater than that in which he finished the work of creation; for his making of the creation saved it not from corruption, but now he hath done a work which corruption cannot touch, wherefore the day on which he did this, has this note from his own mouth, THIS day, as a day that doth transcend.

And, as I said, this day is the first of the week; for it was on that day that God begat his beloved Son from the dead. This first day of the week therefore, on it God found that pleasure which he found not in the seventh day from the world's creation, for that in it his Son did live again to him.

Now shall not Christians, when they do read that God saith, "This day," and that too with reference to a work done on it by him, so full of delight to him, and so full of life and heaven to them, set also a remark upon it, saying, This was the day of God's pleasure, for that his Son did rise thereon, and shall it not be the day of my delight in him!

This is the day on which his Son was both begotten and born, and became the first fruits to God of them that sleep; yea, and in which also he was made by him the chief, and head of the corner; and shall not we rejoice in it? (Acts xiii. 33. Heb. i. 5. Col. i. 18. Rev. i. 5.)

Shall kings, and princes, and great men set a remark upon the day of their birth and coronation, and expect that both subjects and servants should do them high honour on that day, and shall the day in which Christ was both begotten and born, be a day contemned by Christians! And his name not be but of a common regard on that day?

I say again, shall God, as with his finger, point, and that in the face of the world, at this day, saying, "Thou art my Son, this day," &c., and shall not Christians fear, and awake from their employments, to worship the Lord on this day!

If God remembers it, well may I! If God says, and that with all gladness of heart, "Thou art my Son, this day have I begotten thee!" may not, ought not, I also to set this day apart to sing the songs of my redemption in?

This day my redemption was finished.

This day my dear Jesus revived.

This day he was declared to be the Son of God with power.

Yea, this is the day in which the Lord Jesus finished a greater work than ever yet was done in the world; yea, a work in which the Father himself was more delighted than he was in making of heaven and earth. And shall darkness and the shadow of death stain this day! Or shall a cloud dwell on this day! Shall God regard this day from above! And shall not his light shine upon this day! What shall be done to them that curse this day, and would not that the stars should give their light thereon. This day! After this day was come, God never, that we read of, made mention with delight, of the old seventh-day sabbath more.

Sixthly. Nor is that altogether to be slighted, when he saith, "When he bringeth in the first-begotten into the world, Let all the angels of God worship him." To wit, at that very time and day. (Heb. i. 6.)

I know not what our expositors say of this text, but to me it seems to be meant of his resurrection from the dead; both because the apostle is speaking of that, (ver. 5,) and closes that argument with this text, "Thou art my Son, this day have

I begotten thee? And again, I will be to him a Father, and he shall be to me a Son? And again, when he bringeth in the first-begotten into the world, he saith, And let all the angels of God worship him."

So then, for God's bringing of his first-begotten now into the world, was by his raising him again from the dead after they by crucifying of him had turned him out of the same.

Thus then God brought him into the world, never by them to be hurried out of it again. For Christ being now raised from the dead, dies no more; death hath no more dominion over him.

Now, saith the text, when he bringeth him thus into the world, he requireth that worship be done unto HIM. When? That very day, and that by all the angels of God. And if by *all*, then ministers are not excluded; and if not ministers, then not churches; for what is said to the angels, is said to the church itself. (Rev. ii. 1—7, 8, 11, 12, 17, 18, 29; iii. 1, 6, 7, 13, 14, and 22.)

So then, if the question be asked, when they must worship him, the answer is, when he brought him into the world, which was on the first day of the week, for then he bringeth him again from the dead, and gave the whole world and the government thereof into his holy hand. This text therefore is of weight as to what we have now under consideration, to wit, that the first day of the week, the day in which God brought his first-begotten into the world, should be the day of worshipping him by all the angels of God.

Seventhly. Hence this day is called "the Lord's day," as John saith, "I was in the Spirit on the Lord's day," the day in which He rose from the dead. (Rev. i. 10.)

"The Lord's day." Every day, say some, is the Lord's day. Indeed this for discourse sake may be granted; but strictly, no day can so properly be called *the* Lord's day, as this first day of the week; for that no day of the week or of the year has those badges of the Lord's glory upon it, nor such divine grace put upon it as has the first day of the week.

This we have already made appear in part, and shall make appear much more before we have done therewith.

There is nothing, as I know of, that bears this title but the Lord's supper, and this day. (1 Cor. xi. 20. Rev. i. 10.) And since Christians count it an abuse to allegorize the first, let them also be ashamed to fantasticalize the last. The Lord's day is doubtless the day in which he rose from the dead. To be sure it is not the old seventh day; for from the day that he arose, to the end of the Bible, we find not that he did hang so much as one twist of glory upon that; but this day is beautified with glory upon glory, and that both by the Father and the Son; by the prophets and those that were raised from the dead thereon; therefore this day must be more than the rest.

But we are as yet but upon divine intimations,

drawn from such texts which, if candidly considered, do very much smile upon this great truth; namely, that the first day of the week is to be accounted the Christian sabbath, or holy day for divine worship in the churches of the saints. And now I come to the texts that are more express. SECONDLY, then,

First. This was the day in the which he did use to show himself to his people, and to congregate with them after he rose from the dead. On the first first-day, even on the day on which he rose from the dead, he visited his people, both when together and apart, over, and over, and over, as both Luke and John do testify. (Luke xxiv. John xx.) And preached such sermons of his resurrection, and gave unto them, yea, and gave them such demonstration of the truth of all, as was never given them from the foundation of the world. Showing, he showed them his risen body; opening, he opened their understandings; and dissipating, he so scattered their unbelief on THIS day, as he never had done before. And this continued one way or another even from before day until the evening.

Secondly. On the next first-day following the church was within again; that is, congregated to wait upon their Lord. And John so relates the matter, as to give us to understand that they were not so assembled together again till then. "After eight days," saith he, "again the disciples were within," clearly concluding, that they were not so on the days that were between, no not on the old seventh day.

Now why should the Holy Ghost thus precisely speak of their assembling together upon the first day, if not to confirm us in this, that the Lord had chosen that day for the *new* sabbath of his church? Surely the apostles knew what they did in their meeting together upon that day; yea, and the Lord Jesus also; for that he used *so* to visit them when *so* assembled, made his practice a law unto them. For practice is enough for us New Testament saints, specially when the Lord Jesus himself is in the head of that practice, and that after he rose from the dead.

Perhaps some may stumble at the word "after," after eight days; but the meaning is, at the conclusion of the eighth day, or when they had spent in a manner the whole of their sabbath in waiting upon their Lord, then in comes their Lord, and finisheth that their day's service to him with confirming of Thomas's faith, and by letting drop other most heavenly treasure among them. Christ said, he must lie three days and three nights in the heart of the earth, yet it is evident that he rose the third day. (1 Cor. xv. 4.)

We must take then a part for the whole, and conclude, that from the time that the Lord Jesus rose from the dead, to the time that he showed his hands and his side to Thomas, eight days were almost expired; that is, he had sanctified unto them two first days, and had accepted that service they had performed to him therein, as he testified by giving of them so blessed a farewell at the conclusion of both those days.

Hence now we conclude, that this was the custom of the church at this day, to wit, upon the first day of the week to meet together, and to wait upon their Lord therein. For the Holy Ghost counts it needless to make a continued repetition of things; it is enough therefore if we have now and then mention made thereof.

Obj. But Christ showed himself alive to them at other times also, as in John xxi., &c.

Ans. The names of all those days in which he so did are obliterated and blotted out, that they might not be idolized, for Christ did not set them apart for worship; but *this* day, the first day of the week, by its name is kept alive in the church, the Holy Ghost surely signifying thus much, that how hidden soever other days were, Christ would have *his* day, the *first day*, had in everlasting remembrance among saints.

Churches also meet together now on the week days, and have the presence of Christ with them too in their employments; but that takes not off from them the sanction of the first day of the week, no more than it would take away the sanction of the old seventh day, had it still continued holy to them: wherefore this is no let or objection to hinder our sanctifying of the first day of the week to our God. But,

Thirdly. Add to this, that upon Pentecost, which was the first day of the week, mention is made of their being together again: for Pentecost was always the morrow after the sabbath, the old seventh-day sabbath. Upon *this* day, I say, the Holy Ghost saith, they were again "with one accord together in one place."

But oh! the glory that then attended them, by the presence of the Holy Ghost among them: never was such a thing done as was done on that first day until then. We will read the text, "And when the day of Pentecost was fully come, they were all with one accord in one place. And suddenly there came a sound from heaven as of a rushing mighty wind, and it filled all the house where they were sitting. And there appeared unto them cloven tongues like as of fire, and it sat upon each of them. And they were all filled with the Holy Ghost." (Acts ii. 1—4.)

Here's a first day glorified! Here's a countenance given to the day of their Christian assembling. But we will note a few things upon it.

1. The church was now, as on other first days, all with one accord in one place. We read not that they came together by virtue of any precedent revelation, nor by accident, but contrariwise by agreement, they were together "with one accord," or by appointment, in pursuance of their duty, setting apart *that* day, as they had done the first days afore, to the holy service of their blessed Lord and Saviour Jesus Christ.

2. We read that this meeting of theirs was not

begun on the old sabbath, but when Pentecost was *fully* come: the Holy Ghost intimating that they had left now, and begun to leave, the seventh-day sabbath to the unbelieving Jews.

3. Nor did the Holy Ghost come down upon them till every moment of the old sabbath was past, Pentecost, as was said, was FULLY come first. "And when the day of Pentecost was fully come, they were all with one accord in one place." And then, &c.

And why was not this done on the seventh-day sabbath? But, possibly, to show, that the ministration of death and condemnation was not that, by or through which Christ the Lord would communicate so good a gift unto his churches. (Gal. iii. 1—5.)

This gift must be referred to the Lord's day, the first day of the week, to fulfil the scripture, and to sanctify yet farther this holy day unto the use of all New Testament churches of the saints. For since on the first day of the week our Lord did rise from the dead, and by his special presence, I mean his personal, did accompany his church therein, and so preach as he did, his holy truths unto them, it was most meet that they on the same day also should receive the first fruits of their eternal life most gloriously.

And, I say again, since from the resurrection of Christ to this day, the church then did receive upon the first day, (but as we read, upon no other,) such glorious things as we have mentioned, it is enough to beget in the hearts of them that love the Son of God, a high esteem of the first day of the week. But how much more, when there shall be joined to these, proof that it was the custom of the first gospel church, the church of Christ at Jerusalem, after our Lord was risen, to assemble together to wait upon God on the first day of the week with their Lord as leader.

To say little more to this head, but only to repeat what is written of this day of old, to wit, that it should be proclaimed the selfsame day, to wit, the morrow after the sabbath, which is the first day of the week, " that it may be an holy convocation unto you; ye shall do no servile work therein : it shall be a statute for ever in all your dwellings." (Lev. xxiii. 21.)

This ceremony was about the sheaf that was to be waved, and bread of first fruits, which was a type of Christ; for he is unto God " the first fruits of them that slept." (1 Cor. xv. 20.)

This sheaf, or bread, must not be waved on the old seventh day, but on the morrow after, which in the first day of the week, the day in which Christ rose from the dead, and waved himself as the first fruits of the elect unto God. Now from this day they were to count seven sabbaths complete, and on the morrow after the seventh sabbath, which was the first day of the week again; and this Pentecost upon which we now are, then they were to have a new meat offering, with meat offerings and drink offerings, &c.

And on the selfsame day they were to proclaim that that first day should be a holy convocation unto them. The which the apostles did, and grounded that their proclamation so on the resurrection of Jesus Christ, not on ceremonies, that at the same day they brought three thousand souls to God. (Acts ii. 41.)

Now what another signal was here put upon the first day of the week! The day in which our Lord rose from the dead, assembled with his disciples, poured out so abundantly of the Spirit, and gathered even by the first draught that his fishermen made by the gospel, such a number of souls to God.

Thus then they proclaimed, and thus they gathered sinners on the first first-day that they preached : for though they had assembled together over and over with their Lord before therein, yet they began not jointly to preach until this first-day Pentecost.

Now, after this the apostles to the churches did never make mention of a seventh-day sabbath. For as the wave-sheaf and the bread of first fruits were a figure of the Lord Jesus, and the waving, of his life from the dead—so that morrow after the sabbath on which the Jews waved their sheaf, was a figure of *that* on which our Lord did rise : consequently, when their morrow after the sabbath ceased, *our* morrow after that began, and so has continued a blessed morrow after their sabbath, as a holy sabbath to Christians from that time ever since.

Fourthly. We come yet more close to the custom of churches; I mean, to the custom of the churches of the Gentiles; for as yet we have spoken but of the practice of the church of God which was at Jerusalem; only we will add, that the customs that were laudable and binding with the church at Jerusalem, were with reverence to be imitated by the churches of the Gentiles; for there was but one law of Christ for them both to worship by.

Now then, to come to the point, to wit, that it was the custom of the churches of the Gentiles, on the first day of the week, but upon no other that we read of, to come together to perform divine worship to their Lord.

Hence it is said, " And upon the first *day* of the week, when the disciples came together to break bread," &c. (Acts xx. 7.) This is a text, that as to matter of fact cannot be contradicted by any, for the text saith plainly they did so, the disciples then came together to break bread, the disciples among the Gentiles, did so.

Thus you see that the solemnizing of a first day to holy uses was not limited to, though first preached by the church that was at Jerusalem. The church at Jerusalem was the mother church, and not that at Rome, as some falsely imagine; for from this church went out the law and the holy word of God to the Gentiles. Wherefore it must be supposed that this meeting of the Gentiles on the first day of the week to break bread, came to them by holy tradition from the church at Jerusalem, since they were the first that kept the first day as holy unto the Lord their God.

And indeed, they had the best advantage to do it; for they had their Lord in the head of them to back them to it by his presence and preaching thereon.

But we will a little comment upon the text. " Upon the *first day* of the week." Thus you see the day is nominated, and so is kept alive among the churches. For in that the day is nominated on which this religious exercise was performed, it is to be supposed that the Holy Ghost would have it live, and be taken notice of by the churches that succeed.

It also may be nominated to show, that both the church at Jerusalem, and those of the Gentiles did harmonize in their sabbath, jointly concluding to solemnize worship on a day. And then again to show, that they all had left the old sabbath to the unbelievers, and jointly chose to sanctify the day of the rising of their Lord, to this work.

They " came together to break bread," to partake of the supper of the Lord. And what day so fit as the Lord's day for this? This was to be the work of that day, to wit, to solemnize that ordinance among themselves, adjoining other solemn worship thereto, to fill up the day, as the following part of the verse shows. This day therefore was designed for this work, the *whole* day, for the text declares it. The first day of the week was set by them apart for this work.

" Upon THE first day;" not upon A first day, or upon *one* first day, or upon *such* a first day; for had he said so, we had had from thence not so strong an argument for our purpose : but when he saith, " upon the first *day* of the week" they did it, he insinuates *it was their custom.* Also upon one of these, Paul being among them, preached unto them, ready to depart on the morrow. Upon the first day : what, or which first day of this, or that, of the third or fourth week of the month? No, but upon the first day, every first day ; for so the text admits us to judge.

" Upon the first *day* of the week, WHEN the disciples came together," supposes a custom *when,* or as they were wont to come together to perform such service among themselves to God : *then* Paul preached to them, &c.

It is a text also that supposes an agreement among themselves as to this thing. They came together then *to* break bread ; they had appointed to do it then, for that then was the day of their Lord's resurrection, and that in which he himself congregated after he revived, with the first Gospel-church, the church at Jerusalem.

Thus you see, breaking of bread, was the work, the work that by general consent was agreed to be by the churches of the Gentiles performed upon the first day of the week. I say, by the *Churches :* for I doubt not but that the practice here was also the practice of the rest of the Gentile churches,

even as it had been before the practice of the church at Jerusalem.

For this practice now did become universal, and so this text implies : for he speaks here universally of the practice of all disciples as such, though he limits Paul preaching to that church with whom he at present personally was. Upon the first day of the week, " when the disciples came together to break bread," Paul being at that time at Troas preached to them on that day.

Thus then you see how the Gentile churches did use to break bread, not on the old sabbath, but on the first day of the week. And, I say, they had it from the church of Jerusalem ; where the apostles were first seated, and beheld the way of their Lord with their eyes.

Now, I say, since we have so ample an example, not only of the church at Jerusalem, but also of the churches of the Gentiles, for the keeping of the first day to the Lord, and that as countenanced by Christ and his apostles, we should not be afraid to tread in their steps, for their practice is the same with law and commandment. But,

Fifthly. We will add to this another text. " Now (saith Paul) concerning the collection for the saints, as I have given order to the churches of Galatia, even so do ye. Upon the first *day* of the week let every one of you lay by him in store, as *God* hath prospered him, that there be no gatherings when I come." (1 Cor. xvi. 1, 2.)

This text some have greatly sought to evade, counting the duty here, on this day to be done, a duty too inferior for the sanction of an old seventh-day sabbath ; when yet to show mercy to an ass on the old sabbath, was a work which our Lord no ways condemns. (Luke xiii. 15 ; xiv. 5.)

But to pursue our design, we have a duty enjoined, and that of no inferior sort. If charity be indeed as it is, the very bond of perfectness, and if without it all our doings, yea, and sufferings too, are not worth so much as a rush, (1 Cor. xiii. Col. iii. 14,) we have here a duty, I say, that a seventh-day sabbath, when in force, was not too big for it to be performed in.

The work now to be done, was, as you see, to bestow their charity upon the poor ; yea, to provide for time to come. And I say, it must be collected upon the first day of the week. Upon THE first day ; not A first day, as signifying one or two, but upon THE first day, even *every* first day ; for so your ancient Bibles have it ; also our later must be so understood, or else Paul had left them to whom he did write utterly at a loss. For if he intended not every first day, and yet did not specify a particular one, it could hardly even have been understood which first day he meant. But we need not stand upon this. This work was a work for A first-day, for EVERY first day of the week.

Note again that we have this duty here commanded and enforced by an apostolical order : " I have given order," saith Paul, for this ; and his orders, as he saith in another place, " are the commandments of the Lord." You have it in the same epistle. (1 Cor. xiv. 37.)

Whence it follows, that there was given even by the apostles themselves, a holy respect to the first day of the week above all the days of the week; yea, or of the year besides.

Further, I find also by this text, that this order is universal. I have, saith he, given this order not only to you, but to the churches of Galatia. Consequently to all other that were concerned in this collection. (2 Cor. viii.; ix., &c.)

Now this, whatever others may think, puts yet more glory upon the first day of the week. For in that all the churches are commanded, as to make their collections, so to make them on *this* day, what is it, but that this day, by reason of the sanction that Christ put upon it, was of virtue to sanctify the offering through and by Christ Jesus, as the altar and temple afore did sanctify the gift and gold that was, and was afforded on them. The proverb is, " The better day, the better deed." And I believe that things done on the Lord's day, are better done than on other days of the week, in his worship.

Obj. But yet, say some, here are no orders to keep this first day holy to the Lord.

Ans. 1. That is supplied; for that by this very text this day is appointed, above all the days of the week, to do this holy duty in.

2. You must understand that this order is but additional, and now enjoined to fill up that which was begun as to holy exercise of religious worship by the churches long before.

3. The universality of the duty being enjoined to this day, supposes that this day was universally kept by the churches as holy already.

4. And let him that scrupleth this, show me, if he can, that God by the mouth of his apostles did ever command that all the churches should be confined to this or that duty on such a day, and yet put no sanction upon that day; or that he has commanded that this work should be done on the first day of the week, and yet has reserved other church ordinances as a public solemnization of worship to him, to be done of another day, as of a day more fit, more holy.

5. If charity, if a general collection for the saints in the churches is commanded on this day, and on no other day but this day—for church collection is commanded on no other—there must be a reason for it : and if that reason had not respect to the sanction of the day, I know not why the duty should be so strictly confined to it.

6. But for the apostle now to give with this a particular command to the churches to sanctify that day as holy unto the Lord, had been utterly superfluous; for that they already, and that by the countenance of their Lord, and his church at Jerusalem, had done.

Before now, I say, it was become a custom, as by what hath been said already is manifest : where-fore what need that their so solemn a practice be imposed again upon the brethren ? An intimation now of a continued respect thereto, by the very naming of the day, is enough to keep the sanctity thereof on foot in the churches. How much more then, when the Lord is still adding holy duty to holy duty, to be performed upon that day ? So then, in that the apostle writes to the churches to do this holy duty on the first day of the week, he puts them in mind of the sanction of the day, and insinuates, that he would still have them have a due respect thereto.

Quest. But is there yet another reason why this holy duty should, in special as it is, be commanded to be performed on the first day of the week ?

Ans. 1. Yes : for that now the churches were come together in their respective places, the better to agree about collections, and to gather them. You know church worship is a duty so long as we are in the world, and so long also is this of making collections for the saints. And for as much as the apostle speaks here, as I have hinted afore, of a church collection, when is it more fit to be done, than when the church is come together upon the first day of the week to worship God ?

2. This part of worship is most comely to be done upon the first day of the week, and that at the close of that day's work. For thereby the church shows, not only her thankfulness to God for a sabbath day's mercy, but also returneth him, by giving to the poor, that sacrifice for their benefit that is most behoveful to make manifest their professed subjection to Christ. (Prov. xix. 17. 2 Cor. ix. 12—16. It is therefore necessary that this work be done on the first day of the week, for a comely close of the worship that we perform to the Lord our God on that day.

3. On the first day of the week, when the church is performing of holy worship unto God, then that of collection for the saints is most meet to be performed; because then, in all likelihood, our hearts will be most warm with the divine presence; consequently most open and free to contribute to the necessity of the saints. You know that a man when his heart is open, is taken with some excellent thing; then, if at all, it is most free to do something for the promoting thereof.

Why, waiting upon God in the way of his appointments, opens, and makes free, the heart to the poor : and because the first day of the week was it in which now such solemn service to him was done, therefore also the apostle commanded, that upon the same day also, as on a day most fit, this duty of collecting for the poor should be done. " For God loveth a cheerful giver." (2 Cor. ix. 6, 7.)

Wherefore the apostle by this, takes the churches as it were at the advantage, and as we say, while the iron is hot, to the intent he might, what in him lay, make their collections, not sparing nor of a grudging mind, but to flow from cheerfulness. And the first day of the week, though its institution was set aside, doth most naturally tend to this;

because it is the day, the only day, on which we received such blessings from God. (Acts iii. 26.)

This is the day on which, at first, it rained manna all day long from heaven upon the new testament church, and so continues to do this day.

Oh! the resurrection of Christ, which was on this day, and the riches that we receive thereby. Though it should be, and is, I hope thought on every day, yet when the first of the week is *fully* come! Then *to*-day! This day! This is the day to be warmed; this day he was begotten from the dead.

The thought of this will do much with an honest mind : this is the day, I say, that the first saints did find, and that after saints do find the blessings of God come down upon them ; and therefore this is the day here commanded to be set apart for holy duties.

And although what I have said may be but little set by of some, yet, for a closing word as to this, I do think, could but half so much be produced from the day Christ rose from the dead quite down, for the sanction of a seventh-day sabbath in the churches of the Gentiles, it would much sway with me. But the truth is, neither doth the Apostle Paul, nor any of his fellows, so much as once speak one word to the churches that shows the least regard, as to conscience to God, of a seventh-day sabbath more. No, the first day, the first day, the first day, is now all the cry in the churches by the apostles, for the performing church worship in to God. Christ began it on THAT day : then the Holy Ghost seconded it on *that* day : then the churches practised it on *that* day. And to conclude ; the apostle by the command now under consideration, continues the sanction of *that* day to the churches to the end of the world.

But as to the old seventh-day sabbath, as hath been said afore in this treatise, Paul, who is the apostle of the Gentiles, has so taken away that whole ministration in the bowels of which it is ; yea, and has so stript it of its old testament grandeur, both by terms and arguments, that it is strange to me it should by any be still kept up in the churches ; specially, since the same apostle, and that at the same time, has put a better ministration in its place. (2 Cor. iii.)

But when the consciences of good men are captivated with an error, none can stop them from a prosecution thereof, as if were itself of the best of truths.

Obj. But Paul preached frequently on the old sabbath, and that after the resurrection of Christ.

Ans. To the unbelieving Jews and their proselytes, I grant he did. But we read not that he did it to any new testament church on that day : nor did he celebrate the instituted worship of Christ in the churches on that day. For Paul, who had before cast out the ministration of death, as that which had no glory, would not now take thereof any part for new testament instituted worship ; for he knew that that would veil the heart, and blind the mind from that, which yet instituted worship was ordained to discover.

He preached then on the seventh-day sabbath, of a divine and crafty love to the salvation of the unbelieving Jews.

I say, he preached now on that day to them and their proselytes, because that day was theirs by their estimation. He did it, I say, of great love to their souls, that, if possible, he might save some of them.

Wherefore, if you observe, you shall still find, that where it is said that he preached on that day, it was to that people, not to the churches of Christ. (See Acts ix. 20 ; xiii. 14—16 ; xvi. 13 ; xvii. 1—3 ; xviii. 4.)

Thus, though he had put away the sanction of that day as to himself, and had left the Christians that were weak to their liberty as to conscience to it, yet he takes occasion upon it to preach to the Jews that still were wedded to it, the faith, that they might be saved by grace.

Paul did also many other things that were Jewish and ceremonial, for which he had, as then, no conscience at all, as to any sanction that he believed was in them.

As his circumcising of Timothy. (Acts xvi. 1—3.)

His shaving of his head. (Acts xviii. 18.)

His submitting to Jewish purifications. (Acts xxi. 24—26.)

His acknowledging of himself a Pharisee. (Acts xxiii. 6.)

His implicit owning of Ananias for high priest after Christ was risen from the dead. (Acts xxiii. 1—5.)

He tells us also that, "unto the Jews he became as a Jew" that he might save the Jew. And without law to them that were without law, that also he might gain them. Yea, he became, as he saith, all things to all *men*, that he might gain the more, as it is 1 Cor. ix. 19—23.

But these things, as I said, he did not of conscience to the things ; for he knew that their sanction was gone. Nor would he suffer them to be imposed upon the churches directly or indirectly ; no, not by Peter himself. (Gal. ii. 11.)

Were I in Turkey with a church of Jesus Christ, I would keep the first day of the week to God, and for the edification of his people ; and would also preach the word to the infidels on their sabbath day, which is our Friday ; and be glad, too, if I might have such opportunity to try to persuade them to a love of their own salvation.

Obj. But if the seventh-day sabbath is, as you say, to be laid aside by the churches of the Gentiles, why doth Christ say to his, "Pray ye that your flight be not in the winter, neither on the sabbath-day ?" For, say some, by this saying it appears that the old seventh-day sabbath, as you have called it, will, as to the sanction of it, abide in force after Christ is ascended into heaven.

Ans. I say first, these words were spoken to the

Jewish Christians, not to the Gentile churches. And the reason of this first hint, you will see clearer afterwards.

The Jews had several sabbaths ; as, their seventh-day sabbath, their monthly sabbaths, their sabbath of years, and their jubilee. (Lev. xxv.)

Now if he means their ordinary sabbaths, or that called the seventh-day sabbath, why doth he join the winter thereto? for in that he joineth the winter with *that* sabbath, that he exhorteth them to pray their flight might not be in, it should seem that he meaneth rather their sabbath of years, or their jubilee, which did better answer one to another than one day and a winter could.

And I say again, that Christ should suppose that their flight should, or might last some considerable part of a winter, and yet that then they should have their rest on those seventh-day sabbaths, is a little beside my reason, if it be considered again, that the Gentiles before whom they were then to fly, were enemies to their sabbath, and consequently would take opportunity at their sabbaths to afflict them so much the more. Wherefore, I would that they who plead for a continuation of the seventh-day sabbath from this text, would both better consider it, and the incoherence that seems to be betwixt such a sabbath and a winter.

But again, were it granted that it is the seventh-day sabbath that Christ here intendeth, yet since, as we have proved, the sanction before this was taken away, I mean before this flight should be, he did not press them to pray thus because by any law of heaven they should then be commanded to keep it holy ; but because some would, through their weakness, have conscience of it till then. And such would, if their flight should happen thereon, be as much grieved and perplexed as if it yet stood obligatory to them by a law.

This seems to have some truth in it, because among the Jews that believed, there continued a long time many that were wedded yet to the law, to the ceremonial part thereof, and were not so clearly evangelized as the churches of the Gentiles were. " Thou seest brother," said James to Paul, " how many thousands of Jews there are which believe ; and they are all zealous of the law." (Acts xxi. 20 ; xv. 5.)

Of these, and such weak unbelieving Jews, perhaps Christ speaks, when he gives this exhortation to them to pray thus ; whose consciences he knew would be weak, and being so, would bind when they were entangled with an error, as fast as if it bound by a law indeed.

Again, though the seventh-day sabbath and ceremonies lost their sanction at the resurrection of Christ, yet they retained some kind of being in the church of the Jews, until the desolation spoken of by Daniel should be.

Hence it is said, that then the oblation and sacrifices shall cease. (Dan. ix. 27.) And hence it is, that Jerusalem and the temple are still called the holy place, even until this flight should be. (Matt. xxiv. 15.)

Now if Jerusalem and the temple are still called holy, even after the body and substance, of which they were shadows, were come ; then no marvel though some to that day that believed were entangled therewith, &c. For it may very well be supposed that all conscience of them would not be quite taken away, until all reason for that conscience should be taken away also. But when Jerusalem, and the temple, and the Jews' worship, by the Gentiles was quite extinct by ruins, then in reason that conscience did cease. And it seems by some texts, that all conscience to them was not taken away till then.

Quest. But what kind of being had the seventh-day sabbath, and other Jewish rites and ceremonies, that by Christ's resurrection was taken away.

Ans. These things had a virtual and a nominal being. As to their virtual being, that died that day Christ did rise from the dead, they being crucified with him on the cross. (Col. ii.)

But now, when the virtual being was gone, they still with the weak retained their name, among many of the Jews that believed, until the abomination that maketh desolate stood in the holy place : for in Paul's time they were, as to that, but ready to vanish away.

Now, I say, they still retaining their nominal grandeur, though not by virtue of a law, they could not, till time and dispensation came, be swept out of the way. We will make what hath been said, as to this, out by a familiar similitude.

There is a lord or great man dies ; now being dead, he has lost his virtual life. He has now no relation to a wife, to children, virtually ; yet his name still abides, and that in that family to which otherwise he is dead. Wherefore they embalm him, and also keep him above ground for many days. Yea, he is still reverenced by those of the family, and that in several respects. Nor doth anything but time and dispensation wear this name away.

Thus, then, the Old Testament signs and shadows went off the stage in the Church of Christ among the Jews. They lost their virtue and signification when Christ nailed them to his cross. (Col. ii.) But as to their name, and the grandeur that attended that, it continued with many that were weak, and vanished not, but when the abomination that made them desolate came.

The sum, then, and conclusion of the matter is this—the seventh-day sabbath lost its glory when that ministration in which it was, lost its. But yet the name thereof might abide a long time with the Jewish legal Christians, and so might become obligatory still, though not by the law, to their conscience, even as circumcision and other ceremonies did : and to them it would be as grievous to fly on that day, as if by law it was still in force.

For I say, to a weak conscience, that law which

has lost its life, may yet, through their ignorance, be as binding as if it stood still upon the authority of God.

Things then become obligatory these two ways. (1) By an institution of God. (2.) By the over-ruling power of a man's misinformed conscience. And although by virtue of an institution divine worship is acceptable to God by Christ, yet con‑science will make that a man shall have but little ease if such rules and dictates as it imposes be not observed by him.

This is my answer, upon a supposition that the seventh-day sabbath is in this text intended: and the answer, I think, stands firm and good.

Also, there remains, notwithstanding this objec‑tion, no divine sanction in or upon the old seventh-day sabbath.

Some indeed will urge, that Christ here meant the first day of the week, which here he puts under the term sabbath. But this is foreign to me, so I waive it till I receive more satisfaction in the thing.

Quest. But if indeed the first day of the week be the new Christian sabbath, why is there no more spoken of its institution in the testament of Christ?

Ans. No more! What need is there of more than enough! Yea, there is a great deal found in the testament of the Lord Jesus to prove its authority divine.

(1.) For we have showed from sundry scriptures, that from the very day our Lord did rise from the dead, the church at Jerusalem, in which the twelve apostles were, did meet together on that day, and had the Lord himself for their preacher, while they were auditors; and thus the day began.

(2.) We have showed that the Holy Ghost, the third person in the Trinity, did second this of Christ, in coming down from heaven upon this day, to manage the apostles in their preaching; and in that very day so managed them in that work, that by his help they then did bring three thousand souls to God.

(3.) We have showed also, that after this the Gentile churches did solemnize this day for holy worship, and that they had from Paul both coun‑tenance and order so to do.

And now I will add, that more need not be spoken: for the practice of the first church, with their Lord in the head of them to manage them in that practice, is as good as many commands. What then shall we say, when we see a first practice turned into holy custom?

I say, moreover, that though a seventh-day sabbath is not natural to man as man, yet our Christian holy day is natural to us as saints, if our consciences are not clogged before with some old fables, or Jewish customs.

But if an old religion shall get footing and root‑ing in us, though the grounds thereof be vanished away, yet the man concerned will be hard put to t, should he be saved, to get clear of his clouds,

and devote himself to that service of God which is of his own prescribing.

Luther himself, though he saw many things were without ground which he had received for truth, had yet work hard enough, as himself intimates, to get his conscience clear from all those roots and strings of inbred error.

But, I say, to an untainted and well-bred Chris‑tian, we have good measure, shaken together, and running over, for our Christian Lord's day. And I say again, that the first day of the week, and the spirit of such a Christian, suit one another as nature suiteth nature; for there is as it were a natural instinct in Christians, as such, when they understand what in a first day was brought forth, to fall in therewith to keep it holy to their Lord.

1. The first day of the week! Why it was the day of our life. "After two days he will revive us," and in the third day "we shall live in his sight." "After two days" there is the Jews' preparation, and seventh-day sabbath, quite passed over; and in the third day, that is the first day of the week, which is the day our Lord did rise from the dead, we began to live by him in the sight of God. (Hos. vi. 2. John xx. 1. 1 Cor. xv. 4.)

2. The first day of the week! That is the day in which, as I hinted before, our Lord was wont to preach to his disciples after he rose from the dead; in which also he did use to show them his hands and his feet, (Luke xxiv. 38, 39. John xx. 25,) to the end they might be confirmed in the truth of his victory over death and the grave for them. The day in which he made himself known to them in breaking bread. The day in which he so plentifully poured out the Holy Ghost upon them. The day in which the church, both at Jerusalem and those of the Gentiles, did use to perform to God divine worship: all which has before been sufficiently proved. And shall we not imitate our Lord, nor the church that was immediately acted by him in this, and the churches their fellows? Shall, I say, the Lord Jesus do all this in his church, and they together with him! Shall the churches of the Gentiles also fall in with their Lord and with their mother at Jerusalem herein! And again, shall all this be so punctually committed to sacred story, with the day in which these things were done, under denomination, over and over, saying, these things were done on the *first* day, on the *first* day, on the *first* day of the week, while all other days are, as to name, buried in everlasting oblivion! And shall we not take that notice thereof as to follow the Lord Jesus and the churches herein? Oh stupidity!

3. This day of the week! They that make but observation of what the Lord did of old, to a many sinners, and with his churches on this day, must needs conclude, that in this day the treasures of heaven were broken up, and the richest things therein communicated to his church. Shall the children of this world be, as to this also, wiser in

their generations than the children of light, and former saints, upon whose shoulders we pretend to stand, go beyond us here also?

Jacob could by observation gather that the place where he lay down to sleep was no other but the house of God, and the very gate of heaven. (Gen. xxviii. 17.)

Laban could gather by observation, that the Lord blessed him for Jacob's sake. (Gen. xxx. 27.)

David could gather by what he met with upon Mount Moriah, that that was the place where God would have the temple builded, therefore he sacrificed there. (1 Chron. xxi. 26—28; xxii. 1, 2. 2 Chron. iii. 1.)

Ruth was to mark the place where Boaz lay down to sleep, and shall not Christians also mark the day in which our Lord rose from the dead? (Ruth iii. 4.)

I say, shall we not mark it, when so many memorable things were done on it, *for* and *to* and *in* the churches of God! Let saints be ashamed to think that such a day should be looked over, or counted common, (when tempted to it by Satan,) when kept to religious service of old, and when beautified with so many divine characters of sanctity, as we have proved, by Christ, his church, the Holy Ghost, and the command of apostolical authority it was.

But why, I say, is this day, on which our Lord rose from the dead, nominated as it is? Why was it not sufficient to say "he rose again," or, he rose again the third day? without a specification of the very name of the day. For, as was said afore, Christ appeared to his disciples, after his resurrection, on other days also, yea, and thereon did miracles too. Why then did not these days live? Why was their name, for all that, blotted out, and this day only kept alive in the churches?

The day on which Christ was born of a virgin; the day of his circumcision, the day of his baptism, and of his transfiguration, are not by their names committed by the Holy Ghost to holy writ to be kept alive in the world, nor yet such days in which he did many great and wonderful things. But THIS day, this day is still nominated; the first day of the week is the day. I say, why are things thus left with us? But because we, as saints of old, should gather, and separate, what is of divine authority from the rest. For in that this day is so often nominated while all other days lie dead in their graves, it is as much as if God should say, Remember the first day of the week to keep it holy to the Lord your God.

And set this aside, and I know not what reason can be rendered, or what prophecy should be fulfilled by the bare naming of the day.

When God, of old, did sanctify for the use of his church a day, as he did many, he always called them either by the name of the day of the month, or of the week, or by some other signal by which they might be certainly known, why should it not then be concluded, that for this very reason the first day of the week is thus often nominated by the Holy Ghost in the testament of Christ?

Moreover, he that takes away the first day, as to this service, leaves us now no day, as sanctified of God, for his solemn worship to be by his churches performed in. As for the seventh-day sabbath, that, as we have seen, is gone to its grave with the signs and shadows of the Old Testament. Yea, and has such a dash left upon it by apostolical authority, that it is enough to make a Christian fly from it for ever. (2 Cor. iii.)

Now, I say, since that is removed by God: if we should suffer the first day also to be taken away by man, what day that has a divine stamp upon it, would be left for us to worship God in?

Alas! the first day of the week is the Christian's market day, that which they so solemnly trade in for sole provision for all the week following. This is the day that they gather manna in. To be sure the seventh-day sabbath is not that. For of old the people of God could never find manna on that day. "On the seventh day, (said Moses,) which is the sabbath, in it there shall be none." (Exod. xvi. 26.)

Any day of the week manna could be found, but on that day it was not to be found upon the face of the ground. But now our first day is the manna day; the only day that the churches of the New Testament, even of old, did gather manna in. But more of this anon.

Nor will it out of my mind but that it is a very high piece of ingratitude, and of uncomely behaviour, to deny the Son of God his day, the Lord's day, the day that he has made. And as we have showed already, this first day of the week is it; yea, and a great piece of unmannerliness is it too, for any, notwithstanding the old seventh day is so degraded as it is, to attempt to impose it on the Son of God. To impose a day upon him which yet Paul denies to be a branch of the ministration of the Spirit, and of righteousness. Yea, to impose a part of that ministration which he says plainly "which was to be done away," for that a better ministration stript it of his glory, is a high attempt indeed. (2 Cor. iii. 7.)

Yet again, the apostle smites the teachers of the law upon the mouth, saying, "understanding neither what they say, nor whereof they affirm." (1 Tim. i. 7.)

The seventh-day sabbath, was indeed God's rest from the works of creation; but yet the rest that he found in what the first day of the week did produce, for Christ was born from the dead in it, more pleased him than did all the seventh days that ever the world brought forth: wherefore, as I said before, it cannot be but that the well-bred Christian must set apart this day for solemn worship to God, and to sanctify his name therein.

Must the church of old be bound to remember that night in which they did come out of Egypt! must Jephtha's daughter have four days for the virgins of Israel yearly to lament her hard case in!

Yea, must two days be kept by the church of old, yearly, for their being delivered from Haman's fury! And must not one to the world's end be kept by the saints for the Son of God their Redeemer, for all he has delivered them from a worse than Pharaoh or Haman, even from the devil, and death, and sin, and hell! Oh stupidity! (Exod. xii. 24. Judges xi. 39, 40. Esther ix. 26—32.)

A day! say some, God forbid but he should have a day. But what day? Oh! the old day comprised within the bounds and bowels of the ministration of death.

And is this the love that thou hast to thy Redeemer, to keep that day to him for all the service that he hath done for thee, which has a natural tendency in it to draw thee off from the consideration of the works of thy redemption, to the creation of the world! Oh stupidity!

But why must he be imposed upon? Has he chosen that day? Did he finish *his* work thereon? Is there in all the New Testament of our Lord, from the day he rose from the dead, to the end of his holy book, one syllable that signifies in the least the tenth part of such a thing? Where is the scripture that saith that this Lord of the sabbath commanded his church, from that time, to do any part of church service thereon? Where do we find the churches to gather together thereon?

But why the seventh day? What is it? Take but the shadow thereof away. Or what shadow now is left in it, since its institution, as to divine service, is taken long since from it.

Is there anything in the works that were done in that day, more than shadow, or that in the least tends otherwise to put us in mind of Christ; and he being come, what need have we of that shadow? And I say again, since that day was to be observed by a ceremonial method, and no way else, as we find; and since ceremonies are ceased, what way by divine appointment is there left to keep that old sabbath by Christians in?

If they say, ceremonies have ceased. By the same argument, so is the sanction of the day in which they were to be performed. I would gladly see the place, if it is to be found, where it is said, *That day retains its sanction, which yet has lost that method of service which was of God appointed for the performance of worship to him thereon.*

When Cannaan worship fell, the sanction of Canaan fell. When temple worship, and altar worship, and the sacrifices of the Levitical priesthood fell, down also came the things themselves. Likewise so, when the service, or shadow and ceremonies of the seventh-day sabbath fell, the seventh-day sabbath fell likewise.

On the seventh-day sabbath, as I told you, manna was not to be found. But why? For that *that* day was of Moses and of the ministration of death. But manna was not of him. Moses, saith Christ, "gave you not that bread from heaven." (John vi. 32.) Moses, as was said, gave that sabbath in tables of stone, and God gave that

manna from heaven. Christ, nor his Father, gives grace by the law: no not by that law in which is contained the old seventh-day sabbath itself.

The law is not of faith, why then should grace be by Christians expected by observation of the law? The law, even the law written and engraven in stones, enjoins perfect obedience thereto on pain of the curse of God. Nor can that part of it now under consideration, according as is required, be fulfilled by any man, was the ceremony thereto belonging, allowed to be laid aside. (Isa. lviii. 13.) Never man yet did keep it perfectly, except he whose name is Jesus Christ: in him, therefore, we have kept it, and by him are set free from that law, and brought under the ministration of the Spirit.

But why should we be bound to seek manna on that day, on which God says, none shall be found?

Perhaps, it will be said, that the sanction of *that* day would not admit that manna should be gathered on it.

But that was not all, for on that day there was none to be found. And might I choose, I had rather sanctify that day to God on which I might gather this bread of God all day long, than set my mind at all upon that in which no such bread was to be had.

The Lord's day, as was said, is to the Christians the principal manna-day.

On this day, even on it, manna in the morning very early gathered was by the disciples of our Lord, as newly springing out of the ground. The true bread of God; the sheaf of first fruits, which is Christ from the dead, was ordained to be waved before the Lord on the morrow after the sabbath, the day on which our Lord ceased from his *own* work, as God did from *his*. (Lev. xxiii.)

Now therefore the disciples found their green ears of corn indeed! Now they read life, both *in* and out of the sepulchre in which the Lord was laid. Now they could not come together nor speak one to another, but either their Lord was with them, or they had heart-inflaming tidings from him. *Now* cries one and says, The Lord is risen: And then another, and says, He hath appeared to such and such.

Now comes tidings to the eleven that their women were early at the sepulchre, where they had a vision of angels that told them their Lord was risen: then comes another, and says, The Lord is risen indeed. Two also come from Emmaus and cry, We have seen the Lord: and by and by, while they yet were speaking, their Lord shows himself in the midst of them.

Now he calls to their mind some of the eminent passages of his life, and eats and drinks in their presence, and opens the scriptures to them: yea, and opens their understanding too, that their hearing might not be unprofitable to them; all which continued from early in the morning till late at night. Oh! what a manna-day was this to the church. And more than all this you will find, if you read but the four evangelists upon this subject.

Thus began the day after the sabbath, and *thus* it has continued through all ages to this very day. Never did the seventh-day sabbath yield manna to Christians. A new world was now begun with the poor church of God, for so said the Lord of the sabbath, " Behold, I make all things new." A new covenant, and why not then a new resting-day to the church ? Or why must the old sabbath be joined to this new ministration ? let him that can, show a reason for it.

Christians, if I have not been so large upon things as some might expect, know, that my brevity on this subject is from consideration that must not needs be spoken thereto, and because I may have occasion to write a second part.

Christians, beware of being entangled with old testament ministrations, lest by one you be brought into many inconveniences.

I have observed, that though the Jewish rites have lost their sanction, yet some that are weak in judgment, do bring themselves into bondage by them. Yea, so high have some been carried as to a pretended conscience to these, that they have at last proceeded to circumcision, to many wives, and the observation of many bad things besides.

Yea, I have talked with some pretending to Christianity, who have said, and affirmed, as well as they could, that the Jewish sacrifices must up again.

But do you give no heed to these Jewish fables, " That turn from the truth." (Tit. i. 14.) Do you, I say, that love the Lord Jesus, keep close to his testament, his word, his gospel, and observe HIS holy day.

And this caution in conclusion I would give, to put stop to this Jewish ceremony, to wit, That a seventh-day sabbath pursued according to its imposition by law, (and I know not that it is imposed by the apostles,) leads to blood and stoning to death those that do but gather sticks thereon. (Numb. xv. 32—36.) A thing which no way becomes the gospel, that ministration of the Spirit and of righteousness, (2 Cor. iii. ;) nor yet the professors thereof. (Luke ix. 54—56.)

Nor can it with fairness be said that *that* sabbath day remains, although the law thereof is repealed. For confident I am, that there is no more ground to make such a conclusion, than there is to say that circumcision is still of force, though the law for cutting of the uncircumcised is by the gospel made null and void.

I told you also in the epistle, that if the fifth commandment was the first that was with promise, then it follows that the fourth, or that seventh-day sabbath, had no promise entailed to it. Whence it follows that where you read in the prophet of a promise annexed to a sabbath, it is best to understand it of our Gospel-sabbath. (Isa. lvi.)

Now if it be asked, What promise is entailed to our first-day sabbath ? I answer, the biggest of promises. For,

First. The resurrection of Christ was tied by promise to this day, and to none other. He rose the third day after his death, and that was the first day of the week, *according* to what was fore-promised in the scriptures. (Hos. vi. 1, 2. 1 Cor. xv. 3—6.)

Second. That we should live before God by him, is a promise to be fulfilled on this day : " After two days will he revive us : in the third day we shall live in his sight." (Hos. vi. 2.) See also Isa. xxvi. 19, and compare them again with 1 Cor. xv. 4.

Third. The great promise of the new testament, to wit, the pouring out of the Spirit, fixeth upon these days : and so he began in the most wonderful effusion of it upon Pentecost, which was the first day of the week, that the scriptures might be fulfilled. (Acts ii. 16—19.)

Nor could these three promises be fulfilled upon any other days, for that the scripture had fixed them to the first day of the week.

I am of opinion that these things, though but briefly touched upon, cannot be fairly objected against, however they may be disrelished by some.

Nor can I believe that any part of our religion, as we are Christians, stands in not kindling of fires, and not seething of victuals, or in binding of men not to stir out of those places on the seventh day, in which at the dawning thereof they were found. And yet these are ordinances belonging to that seventh-day sabbath. (Exod. xvi. 23—29.)

Certainly it must needs be an error to impose these things by divine authority upon new testament believers, our worship standing now in things more weighty, spiritual, and heavenly.

Nor can it be proved, as I have hinted before, that this day was, or is to be imposed without those ordinances, with others in other places mentioned and adjoined, for the sanction of that day, they being made necessary parts of that worship that was to be performed thereon.

I have charity for those that abuse themselves and their Lord, by their preposterous zeal and affection for the continuing of this day in the churches. For I conclude, that if they did either believe, or think of the incoherence that this day, with its rites and ceremonies, has with the ministration of the Spirit, our new testament ministration, they would not so stand in their own light as they do, nor so stiffly plead for a place for it in the churches of the Gentiles. But as Paul insinuates in other cases, there is an aptness in men to be under the law because they do not hear it. (Gal. iv.)

Nor will it out of my mind, but if the seventh-day sabbath was by divine authority, and to be kept holy by the churches of the Gentiles, it should not have so remained among the Jews, Christ's deadliest enemies, and have been kept so much hid from the believers, his best friends. For who has retained the pretended sanction of that day from Christ's time, quite down in the world, but the Jews, and a few Jewish Gentiles, I will except some. But, I say, since a sabbath is that without which the great worship of God under the gospel cannot be well performed, how can it be thought that it should, as to the knowledge of it, be confined to so blasphemous a generation of the Jews, with whom that worship is not ?

I will rather conclude that those Gentile professors that adhere thereto are Jewified, legalized, and so far gone back from the authority of God, who from such bondages has set his churches free.

I do at this time but hint upon things, reserving a fuller argument upon them for a time and place more fit; where, and when, I may perhaps also show some other wild notions of those that so stiffly cleave to this.

Meantime, I entreat those who are captivated with this opinion, not to take it ill at my hand that I thus freely speak my mind. I entreat them also to peruse my book without prejudice to my person. The truth is, one thing that has moved me to this work, is the shame that has covered the face of my soul, when I have thought of the fictions and fancies that are growing among professors. And while I see each fiction turn itself to a faction, to the loss of that good spirit of love, and that oneness that formerly was with good men.

I doubt not but some unto whom this book may come, have had seal from God, that the first day of the week is to be sanctified by the church to Jesus Christ. Not only from *his* testimony, which is, and should be, the ground of our practice ; but also, for that the first conviction that the Holy Ghost made upon their consciences, to make them know that they were sinners, began with them for breaking this sabbath day; which day, by that same spirit was told them, was that now called the first day, and not the day before, and the Holy Ghost doth not use to begin this work with a lie, which first conviction the Spirit has followed so close, with other things tending to complete the same work, that the soul from so good a beginning could not rest until it found rest in Christ. Let this then to such be a second token that the Lord's day is by them to be kept in commemoration of their Lord and his resurrection, and of what he did on this day for their salvation. Amen.

DOCTRINE OF JUSTIFICATION BY FAITH IN JESUS CHRIST.

THAT doctrine, prior to any other consideration, is most likely to be true which, with reference to man's salvation, tends most to humble him in respect both to his weakness and demerits. Such a doctrine cannot involve the notion of his self-justification. The being who can justify himself before God must either have a capacity and endowments far beyond the reach of our ordinary state, or he must have allowed his understanding to be darkened by the most dangerous of any kind of vanity. Justification is an assertion or acknowledgment of right, either in the way of actually fulfilled duty, or of duty fulfilled, when originally violated, by way of compensation. In the former respect, a being retaining his original nature unweakened, or unperverted, and acting according to its laws and relations, is necessarily in a state of justification. It is impossible that more should be required of a being for his justification than the entire fulfilment of the law of his nature. Justice can only be perfect in the Creator, or as a rule originating with him; and he will, evidently, never require of his creatures that which he has not given them capacity to perform. It matters not, in this respect, what may be the rank of the being in the scale of creation. A law is given, or implanted, in every case: fulfilment of that law is the justification of the creature to whom it is the rule.

But while this conclusion is derivable from the very nature of the relation of the creature to the Creator, the subject is altogether changed, and becomes complicated with numerous difficulties, as soon as the being spoken of has lost by sin all pretensions to original righteousness, and stands charged with treachery and rebellion. The question, can a creature, thus circumstanced, justify himself? would be readily answered, and answered aright, even by men of the world, were it not a matter of religion. They would at once confess that no being, having incurred guilt, can recover his original righteousness. Generous deeds, heroic acts of self-devotion and denial, patient virtue, and perseverance in efforts to do good, can never fail among men of deserving admiration; but the honour or love which they elicit can pronounce no sentence of justification. They declare a present merit, a claim to sympathy and regard, but they enter into no judicial inquiry or estimate. The law and the legal responsibilities remain precisely what they were. Could affection, or the feelings of respect or tenderness excited by the appearance of any species of excellence, justify, justification would be almost as readily attained as sin can be committed. Suppose even that a sovereign, admiring the virtuous conduct of some late criminal, penitent and changed, should, out of regard to his present qualities, receive him into favour, this would not be a judicial act : to justify the penitent culprit, the sovereign must pronounce an acquittal by his supreme, legal authority; and this he would do, if wise and righteous, not for reasons derived from his sympathies or tenderness merely, but only as such reasons are in harmony with truth and equity.

Of human guilt in respect to God it is impossible to doubt. Justification is a subject of universal concern. If one man could be justified by his return to virtue, all might be so justified. In this case, the main difficulty would be to determine what degree of contrition, what amount of merit, would secure so vast a benefit. On such a point, it would seem the height of presumption for man himself to speak with confidence; and without confidence, in a matter of life and death, there can be no peace. Thus, were justification depending on claims involved in repentance, awfully anxious must the penitent ever be to find out some measure by which to determine their sufficiency. The Almighty alone could give him satisfaction on this momentous point. To expect that He would, would be to look for an especial revelation, virtues and merits varying in infinite degrees, and the hope, therefore, allowed to one man being no sufficient assurance of pardon to another.

But the notion of a compromise can in no wise be made agreeable to the idea of perfect justice. When forgiveness is exercised by one creature towards another, justice may either have made no claim to heavy penalties, or it may have received sufficient satisfaction in the voluntary sacrifices of the offender. But in the case of divine justice, it is emphatically declared, " The soul which sinneth, it shall die." Here the penalty, if paid, involves the absolute destruction of the guilty. The demand is made, and it seems inconsistent with the majesty of divine justice that, having insisted upon the death of the sinner, it should be ready to grant him pardon, and even pronounce him righteous, for the sake of a subsequent obedience, still, at best, but imperfect.

How much more agreeable to the soberest view of God's counsels, how much more consolatory to the penitent, is the doctrine of justification, as represented in the Epistle to the Romans? There divine, eternal justice appears in its unchangeable glory. It reverses none of its decrees, it makes no compromise, it lowers none of its demands. The debt incurred by the human race is not denied. Its huge amount is exactly known. Not an item more or less in the terrible columns of the book of reckoning has ever been omitted, or set down in error. The whole was clearly displayed in the eyes of the wonderful Being who undertook to discharge it. He paid the debt. He asked no favour of justice, because he knew it is not consistent with the nature of justice to grant favours. The debt could not be lessened. No part of its payment could be remitted. He met the necessity, and justice was satisfied. Mercy had now an open field—it knew what to do with the sinner. Though no species of repentance would of itself avail, it might lead the penitent to embrace the method of salvation which God had appointed. Righteousness existing in a representative Saviour might become the righteousness of a man who had none in himself, or of his own. God, who had created this atoning righteousness for the penitent, might also in equal mercy and wisdom appoint an intelligible and ready way for its application. He did so, and said, " Believe, and thou shalt be saved." How happy are they who thus seek peace and life! How sad the case of those who obscure the light of such a system by blending it with any human claim!

A DEFENCE OF THE DOCTRINE

OF

JUSTIFICATION BY FAITH IN JESUS CHRIST;

SHOWING

TRUE GOSPEL HOLINESS FLOWS FROM THENCE:

OR, MR. FOWLER'S PRETENDED DESIGN OF CHRISTIANITY PROVED TO BE NOTHING MORE THAN TO
TRAMPLE UNDER FOOT THE BLOOD OF THE SON OF GOD; AND THE IDOLIZING OF
MAN'S OWN RIGHTEOUSNESS.

AS ALSO,

How while he pretends to be a Minister of the Church of England, he overthroweth the wholesome Doctrine contained in the
10th, 11th, and 13th of the Thirty-nine Articles of the same, and that he falleth in with the Quaker and Romanist against
them.

" Disallowed indeed of men, but chosen of God, and precious."—1 PET. ii. 4.

A PREMONITION TO THE READER.

GENTLE READER,—That thou mayest not be tired with longing to know what errors and doctrines destructive to Christianity Mr. Fowler, in his feigned design of Christianity, hath presented the world withal,—and that thou mayest even in the entry see that which more fully is shown in the house, namely, of the contradiction that is in his book, to the wholesome doctrine of the Church of England, while he stands a minister of the same,—I have thought convenient, instead of an epistle, to present thee with those doctrines contained in his; and that are refuted by the book that thou hast in thy hand. The which also, I hope, will be a sufficient apology for this my undertaking.

His Doctrines are these :

1. That the first principles of morals, those first written in men's hearts, are the essentials, the indispensable and fundamental points or doctrines of the gospel (pp. 8, 281, 282).

2. That these first principles are to be followed, principally, as they are made known to us, by the dictates of human nature : and that this obedience is the first and best sort of obedience we Christians can perform (pp. 8—10).

3. That there is such a thing as a soundness of soul ; and the purity of human nature in the world (p. 6).

4. That the law, in the first principles of it, is far beyond, and more obliging on the hearts of Christians than is that of coming to God by Christ (pp. 7—10).

5. That the precept of coming to God by Christ, &c., is in its own nature a thing different, and, absolutely considered, neither good nor evil (pp. 7—9).

6. That Christ's great errand in coming into the world, was to put us again in possession of the holiness we had lost (p. 12).

7. That John the Baptist, the angel that was sent to Zacharias, and Mary, preached this doctrine, and so also did Malachi the prophet (p. 13).

8. That Christ by saving us from sin is meant, not first, his saving us from the punishment, but from the filth, and from the punishment as a consequence of that (pp. 14, 15).

9. That Christ's work, when he was come, was to establish ONLY an inward real righteousness (p. 16).

10. That Christ's fulfilling the law FOR US, was by giving more perfect and lighter instances of moral duties than were before expressly given (p. 17).

11. That Christ's doctrine, life, actions, miracles, death, resurrection, ascension, and coming again to judgment, is also preached to establish us in this righteousness (chap. 2—8).

12. That it is not possible a wicked man should have God's pardon (p. 119).

13. That it is impossible Christ's righteousness should be imputed to an unrighteous man (p. 120).

14. And that if it were, he boldly affirms, it would signify as little to his happiness, while he continueth so, as would a gorgeous and splendid garment to one that is almost starved (p. 120).

15. For God to justify a wicked man, &c.,

would far more disparage his justice and holiness, than advance his grace and kindness (p. 130).

16. He saith, men are not capable of God's pardoning grace till they have truly repented them of all their sins (p. 130).

17. The devils, saith he, have a large measure of these attributes of God; as his power, knowledge, &c. (p. 124).

18. That Christ did himself perform, as our example, whatever he required of us to do ; yea, that he trod himself EVERY step of our way to heaven (p. 148).

19. The salvation of Christ, first, consists in curing our wounds, (our filth,) and secondarily, in freeing us from the smart (p. 216).

20. That pardon doth not so much consist in remission, as in healing ; to wit, our filth (p. 216).

21. Faith justifieth, as it includeth true holiness in the nature of it ; it justifieth AS it doth so (p. 221).

22. That faith, which entitles a sinner to so high a privilege as that of justification, must needs be such as complieth with *all* the purposes of Christ's coming into the world, &c. And it is no less necessary that it should justify AS it doth *this* (p. 222).

23. He wonders that any worldly man should be so difficultly persuaded to embrace THIS account of justifying faith (p. 222).

24. There can be no pretence for a man to think that faith should be the condition or instrument of justification, as it complieth with only the precept of relying on Christ's merits for the obtaining of it (p. 223).

25. It is, saith he, as clear as the sun at noonday that obedience to the other precepts must go before obedience to this (p. 223).

26. He shall be his Apollo that can give him a sufficient reason why justifying faith should consist in recumbence and reliance on Christ's merits for the pardon of sin (p. 224),

27. He will take the boldness to tell those who are displeased with this account of justifying faith, that in his opinion it is impossible they should *once* think of any other (p. 225).

28. The imputation of Christ's righteousness, consisteth in dealing with sincerely righteous persons, as if they were perfectly so, &c. (p. 225).

29. The grand intent of the gospel is to make us partakers of inward real righteousness, and it is but secondary that we should be accepted as before (p. 226).

30. It is not possible, he saith, that any other notion of this doctrine should have truth in it (p. 226).

31. Whatsoever is commanded by the customs of the place we live in, or commanded by superiors, or made by ANY circumstances convenient to be done, our Christian liberty consists in this—that we have leave to do them (p. 242).

32. For our refusing to comply with these can hardly proceed from anything than a proud affectation of singularity, or at best from superstitious scrupulosity (p. 242).

33. Those ministers hinder the design of Christianity that preach up free grace, and Christian privileges, OTHERWAYS than as motives to obedience, and that scarce ever insist upon any other duties than those of believing, laying hold of Christ's righteousness, applying the promises, &c. (p. 262).

34. But to make the Christian duties to consist either wholly or mostly in these, &c., is the way effectually to harden hypocrites (p. 262).

35. Those ministers do nothing less than promote the design of Christianity that are never in their element but when they are talking of the irrespectiveness of God's decrees, and his absolute promises, the utter disability, and perfect impotency, of natural men to do anything towards their own conversion (p. 262).

36. He is the only child of Abraham who, in the purity of his heart, obeyeth those substantial laws that are by God imposed upon him (p. 283).

37. There is no duty more affectionately commanded in the gospel than that of almsgiving (p. 284).

38. It is impossible we should not have the design of Christianity accomplished in us, &c., if we make our Saviour's most excellent life the pattern of our lives (p. 296).

39. To do well is better than believing (p. 299).

40. To be imitators of Christ's righteousness, even of the righteousness we should rely on, is counted, by Mr. Fowler, more noble than to rely thereon, or trust thereto (p. 300).

Reader, I have given thee here but a taste of these things ; and by my book but a brief reply to the errors that he by his hath divulged to the world : ay, though many more are by me reflected than the forty thou art here presented with.

God give thee eyes to see, and a heart to shun and escape all these things that may yet come to pass, for hurt, and to stand before the Son of Man.

Thus hoping that this short taste may make Mr. Fowler ashamed, and thee receive satisfaction, touching the truth and state of this man's spirit and principles, I rest,

Thine to serve thee in the gospel of Christ,

JOHN BUNYAN.

From Prison, the 27th of the 12th month, 1671.

A DEFENCE OF THE

DOCTRINE OF JUSTIFICATION BY FAITH IN JESUS CHRIST.

Sir,—Having heard of your book, entitled, *The Design of Christianity*, and in that was contained such principles as gave just offence to Christian ears, I was desirous of a view thereof, that from my sight of things I might be the better able to judge; but I could not obtain it till the thirteenth of this eleventh month, which was too soon for you, Sir, a pretended minister of the word, so vilely to expose to public view the rottenness of your heart in principles diametrically opposite to the simplicity of the gospel of Christ. And had it not been for this consideration, that it is not too late to oppose open blasphemy (such as endangereth the souls of thousands), I had cast by this answer, as a thing out of season.

Two things are the design of your book—

1. To assert and justify a thing which you call inward, real righteousness and holiness.

2. To prove that the whole, the grand, the only, and ultimate design of the gospel of Christ, is to begin and perfect this righteousness.

Into the truth or untruth of both these, as briefly as I may, I shall at this time inquire.

First. Therefore, a little to examine the nature of your holiness and righteousness, as yourself hath described the same.

"It is," say you, "so sound a complexion of soul, as maintains in life and vigour whatsoever is essential to it, and suffereth not anything unnatural to mix with that which is so; by the force and power whereof a man is enabled to behave himself as a creature endued with a principle of reason, keeps his supreme faculty in its throne, brings into due subjection all his inferior ones, his sensual imagination, his passions and brutish affections."

You add further, "It is the purity of the human nature, engaging those in whom it resides, to demean themselves suitably in that state in which God hath placed them, and not to act disbecomingly in any condition, circumstance, or relation."

You say, moreover, "It is a divine, or God-like nature, causing an hearty approbation of, and an affectionate compliance with the eternal laws of righteousness; and a behaviour agreeable to the essential and immutable differences of good and evil" (p. 6).

Further, you call it "a principle or habit of soul, originally dictates of human nature" (p. 8).

"A disposition and temper of the inward man, as powerfully incline it to regard and attend to, affectionately to embrace and adhere to, to be actuated by, and under the government of, all those practical principles, that are made known either by revelation, nature, or the use of reason" (p. 11). Which, in conclusion, you call *that* holiness which already we have lost (p. 12).

Thus, Sir, is your holiness, by you described, which holiness you aver is that which is the great and only design of Christ to promote both by his life and glorious gospel.

To take, therefore, your description in pieces, if happily, there may be found aught, but naught, therein.

1. "It is," say you, "an healthful complexion of soul, the purity of the human nature," &c.

Ans. These are but words; there is no such thing as the purity of our nature, abstract and distinct from the sinful pollution that dwelleth in us. (Rom. vii. 24.) It is true, a man may talk of, and by argument distinguish between nature and sin; but that there is such a principle in man (since Adam's fall), a principle by which he may act, or that Christ's whole gospel-design is the helping forward such a principle, is altogether without Scripture or reason. There is no man by nature, that hath any soundness in him, (Isa. i. 6;) no, neither in soul nor body: his understanding is darkened, his mind and conscience is defiled, (Tit. i. 15,) his wills perverted and obstinate, (Eph. iv. 18:) "There is no judgment in his goings." (Isa. lix. 6—10.) Where, now, is the sound and healthful complexion of soul? Let the best come to the best, when we have mustered up all the excellences of the soul of man, as man, shall naught we find there, but the lame, the blind, the defiled, the obstinate, and misled faculties thereof. And never think to evade me by saying, the graces of the Spirit of God are pure: for with them you have nothing to do; your doctrine is of the sound complexion of soul, the purity of the human nature, a habit of soul, and the holiness we lost in Adam, things a great way off from the Spirit of grace, or the gracious workings of the Spirit. You talk, indeed, of a divine or godlike nature, but this is still the same with your pure human nature, or with your sound complexion, or habit of soul; and so must either respect man, as he was created in the image or likeness of God, or else you have palpable contradiction in this your description. But it must be concluded that the divine nature you talk of is that and no other than the dictates of the human nature, or your feigned purity thereof; because you make it by your words the selfsame; it is the purity of the human nature, it is a divine or godlike nature.

2. But you proceed to tell us of a degree, it is so sound and healthful a complexion or temperature of the faculties, qualities, or virtues of soul, "as maintains in life and vigour whatsoever is essential to it, and suffereth not anything unnatural to mix with that which is so " (p. 6).

Ans. If, as was said before, there is no soundness

of soul in man, as man, and no such thing as a purity of our nature, abstract from that which is sin, then where shall we find so healthful a complexion, or temperature of soul, as to maintain in life and vigour whatsoever is essential to it, and that suffereth not anything unnatural to mix with that which is so ?

But let us take Paul's definition of a man: " There is none righteous, no, not one; there is none that understandeth, there is none that seeketh after God.   They are all gone out of the way, they are together become unprofitable; there is none that doeth good, no not one.   Their throat is an open sepulchre, with their tongues they have used deceit, the poison of asps is under their lips, whose mouth is full of cursing and bitterness; their feet are swift to shed blood, destruction and misery are in their ways, and the way of peace have they not known; there is no fear of God before their eyes." (Rom. iii. 10—18.)   I the rather give you this of Paul than any of my own, because it is the *soundest* complexion of soul that the Holy Ghost himself *could* draw.   Here is now no purity of the human nature, nor such sound complexion of soul as can keep itself from mixing with that which is contrary to itself.   And note, that this is the state of all men, and that as they stand in themselves before God : wherefore together, even altogether, all the men in the world, take them in their most pure naturals, or with all the purity of humanity which they can make, and together, they still will be unprofitable, and so must come short of doing good, " that every mouth might be stopped, and all the world become guilty before God." (Rom. iii. 19.)

3. But proceeding, you say that this complexion is so forcible as to " keep his supreme faculty (I suppose you mean the conscience) in its throne (and that), brings into due subjection all his inferior ones (as namely), his sensual imagination, brutish passions and affections" (p. 6).

Ans. These words suppose that it is within the power of a man's own soul always to keep sin out of itself, and so guilt out of the conscience; albeit the scripture saith that both the mind and it are defiled with the filth of sin in all whoever do not believe the gospel, with which belief this description meddleth not. (Tit. i. 15.)

They suppose that this conscience is perfectly clear and light when the Scriptures say they have the understanding darkened; yea, and further, in despite of these your sayings of the sound complexion of soul, of the purity of human nature, and of this supreme faculty, the Scriptures teach that man in his best estate is altogether vanity, that they are darkness and night, &c. (Eph. iv. 18, 19. 1 Thess. v.   Ps. xxxix. 5.)

" Yea," say you, " this sound complexion brings into due subjection all his inferior ones " (p. 6).

Ans. Here seems to be a contradiction to the former part of this description, yea, to the nature of the soul itself; for you say, before it suffereth

not anything unnatural to mix itself therewith, when yet here you seem to suggest that part, I say, even part of itself is disobedient and rebellious, " it brings into subjection all his inferior ones."

" It brings into due subjection."

Ans. Due subjection is such as is everlasting, universal, perfect in nature, kind, and manner, such as the most righteous, perfect, comprehensive law, or commandment cannot object against, or find fault therewith.   Here's a soul! here's a pure human nature! here are pure dictates of a brutish beastly man, that neither knows himself nor one tittle of the word of God.   But " there is a generation that are pure in their own eyes, yet are not washed from their filthiness." (Prov. xxx. 12.)

" It is the purity of the human nature engaging those in whom it resides," &c. (p. 6).

Ans. That is, *verily*, in none at all; for there is no such thing in any man in this world as a purity of human nature ; " we are all as an unclean thing," (Isa. lxiv. 6 ;) and " who can bring a clean thing out of an unclean ? not one." (Job xiv. 4.) Again, " What is man that he should be clean ? or he which is born of a woman that he should be righteous ?" (Job xv. 14.)   These are therefore expressions without the testimony of the word, arising from your own phantasy.

" It is a divine, or godlike nature " (p. 6).

Ans. This you seem also to fetch from the similitude or likeness of God that was in us at our first creation, before we sinned ; but that similitude being at best but created, and since most unspeakably defiled, defaced, and polluted with sin, there is now, no not in the best of men, as men, any sinless likeness and similitude of God to be found, no such *petty* divine, or godlike nature to be found, as you imagine.

But having thus stated your holiness in its nature and essence, you come in the next place to tell us, under what considerations it moveth a person to act, also by what rules and laws it squareth its acts and doings.

FIRST. By or under what considerations it acts, and these you scatter here and there in your description of holiness, under these heads—

I. To act, " as becomes a creature endued with a principle of reason," eyeing the state or place in which God hath set him ; approving of, affecting, and complying with the eternal laws of righteousness (p. 6), which eternal laws, in p. 8, you call " divine moral laws," those that were first written in the hearts of men, and originally dictates of human nature, &c.

II. To do these from truly generous motives and principles (p. 7), such as these—

1. " Because it is most highly becoming all reasonable creatures (you might also have added, and those unreasonable) to obey God in everything, (within their spheres ;) and as much disbecoming them to disobey him " (p. 8).

2. " Because it is a base thing to do unjustly " (p. 11).

Now a little to touch upon all these, and then to proceed to what is behind.

I. To act and do the things of the moral law, but as " creatures endued with a principle of reason," is but to do things in our sphere as men, as the beast, the hog or horse doth things in his, as a beast—which is at best, if it could be attained, to act but as pure naturals, which state of man is of at infinite distance from that, in which it is by God expected the man must act, that doth aught that is pleasing in his sight.   For—

1. The qualification and consideration by you propounded is that which is in all men, in men simply as men, they being reasonable creatures, and somewhat, though but somewhat, capable of acting as such.

2. This qualification is not only in, but of men; reason is of the man himself, even that which is as essential to him, as is that of his being created or made.

3. The law also which you call divine, moral, and eternal, is that which is naturally seated in the heart, and, as you yourself express it, is originally the dictates of human nature, or that which mankind doth naturally assent to (p. 11).

Now I say that a man cannot by these principles, and these qualifications, please the God of heaven, is apparent.

(1.) Because none of these are faith, " but without faith it is impossible to please him." (Heb. xi. 6.)

(2.) Because none of these are of the Holy Ghost, but there is nothing accepted of God, under a New Testament consideration, but those which are the fruits of the Spirit. (Gal. v. 22—24.)

(3.) The man and principles, you have stated, may be such as are utterly ignorant of Jesus Christ, and of all his New Testament things, as such : " But the natural man receiveth not the things of the Spirit of God," (the things of his New Testament,) " for they are foolishness to him, neither can he know them, because they are spiritually discerned." (1 Cor. ii. 14.)

(4.) Your qualifications and considerations know nothing at all of the adoption of sons, and of our acting and doing our duty as such.   You only content yourself to rest within the confines of the human nature, acts of reason, as men or creatures only, or in their supposed pure, natural principles.

And, Sir, a little by way of digression : I will tell you also of our truly Christian righteousness, both as to its original or first principle, and also how, or under what capacity, it puts the person that is acted by it.

First. The principle which is laid within us, it is not the purity of the human nature, but of the Holy Ghost itself, (1 Cor. vi. 19,) which we have of God received, by believing in the Son of God, a principle as far above yours of humanity as is the heavens above the earth ; yours being but like those of the first Adam, but ours truly those of the second.   " As is the earthy, such are those that

are earthy ; and as is the heavenly, such are they also that are heavenly." (1 Cor. xv. 48.)

Now, whosoever hath not this principle, although he be a creature, and also have the dictates of the human nature, yea, and also follows them, yet he is not Christ's : " If any man have not the Spirit of Christ, he is none of his." (Rom. viii. 9.)   Thus, therefore, is the Christian principle another from, and far above, your heathenish pagan one.   By this Spirit is the Christian qualified with principles, not natural, but spiritual, such as faith, hope, joy, peace, &c., all which are the fruits of the revelation of the forgiveness of sins, freely by grace, (Gal. v. 25,) " through the redemption that is in Jesus Christ." (Rom. iii. 24.)   In this spirit and faith we walk, by this spirit we are led, (Rom. viii. 14,) even into the joy and peace of the New Testament of our Lord; wherefore our holy actions are the fruits of righteousness, that is by Jesus Christ, not by our human nature, or the purity of it in us; yea, they are the fruits of the Spirit of God, the qualifications that attend the new covenant, and those that by the work of regeneration are brought within the bounds and privileges thereof.   Wherefore—

Second. The capacity that we are in, who act and do from the heavenly principle ; it is that of sons, the sons of God by adoption, as the apostle said, " Because ye are sons, God hath sent forth the Spirit of his Son into your hearts, crying, Abba, Father." (Gal. iv. 14.)   And again, " As many as are led by the Spirit of God, they are the sons of God." (Rom. vii. 14.)   This is a far other than is your human description of acting as a creature endued with a principle of reason ; for here is a man acts as a son, endued with the holy Spirit of God, who hath, before the world was, predestinated him to this estate, by Jesus Christ, to himself. (Eph. i. 4 ; iv. 6.)   As a son, therefore, the Christian acts and does, because he is endued with that high and heavenly principle mentioned before ; by which principle this man hath received a new heart, a new spirit, a new understanding, a good conscience, so made by " faith in the blood of the Lord Jesus." (Heb. x.)   Thus being made again anew and another man, he acts from a new and another principle than yours ; a principle as far beyond and above you as a man above a brute, and as is grace above nature. (2 Cor. v. 14—16.)

Third. As the Christian acts and does from a better principle, and under a better capacity or consideration than that you have described, so (to allude to your own notion) the first principles by which they receive this spirit and adoption, are not those principles of morals, or those originally dictates of human nature ; but it is through the hearing of faith, (Gal. iii. 1—3,) by which we understand that the Son of God became a man, died for our sins, hath saved us from the curse of God, and accounted us to be the righteousness of God in him : this being heard with the gospel, and a New Testament hearing, the Holy Ghost forthwith possesseth us, by the glorious working whereof we are helped, through the Son, to call the God of heaven our Father.

Now thus being made free from sin, by the only faith of Jesus Christ, "we have our fruit unto holiness, and the end everlasting life." (Rom. vi. 22, 23.)

And here come in those reasonable conclusions, which you would make the very radicals of Christianity, they being only remote and after conclusions, drawn from the fore-mentioned mercy of God, viz., from predestination, calling, adoption, and justification by Christ's blood, while we in ourselves are sinners. I say these are the things which Paul endeavoured to provoke the Romans, Philippians, and Colossians, to an holy conversation by.

1. To the Romans, "I beseech you, therefore," saith he, " by the mercies of God," (what mercies? why, those of election, redemption, calling, justification, and adoption, mentioned in the foregoing chapters,) "that you present your bodies a living sacrifice, holy, acceptable to God, which is your reasonable service." (Rom. xii. 1.)

2. To the Philippians, "If there be therefore any consolation in Christ, if any comfort of love, if any fellowship of the Spirit, if any bowels and mercies, fulfil ye my joy, that ye be like minded." (Phil. ii. 1.)

3. To the Colossians, "If ye be risen with Christ, seek those things that are above, where Christ sitteth on the right hand of God. Set your affection on things above, not on things of the earth ; for ye are dead, and your life is hid with Christ in God. When Christ, who is our life, shall appear, then shall ye also appear with him in glory." (Col. iii. 1—4.) Now mark, mortify therefore, therefore! wherefore ? why, because they were risen with Christ ; because they should appear at the end of this world with Christ himself in glory ; therefore mortify the deeds of the body, or our members that are upon the earth.

These, Sir, are the motives by which we Christians act ; because we are forgiven, because we are sons, and if sons, then heirs, and so we act. But to speak to this more anon.

Perhaps you will say I deal not fairly with you, because you treat, as of moral, so of gospel or New Testament laws.

But to that I will answer at present, that in this description of your holy principle, which is the foundation of your book, whether the laws be natural or spiritual, moral or of grace, the principle by which you do them is no other than the principle of nature, the dictates of human nature ; and so such as can by no means reach the doctrines of the gospel any farther than to make a judgment of them, by that wisdom which is " enmity with God," as will farther be seen in my progress through your book.

Indeed, you make mention of divine laws, and that under two heads.

1. Such as are of an indispensable and eternal obligation, as those purely moral (pp. 7, 8).

2. Such which you call positive precepts, in themselves of an indifferent nature, and absolutely considered, are neither good nor evil. Of those of this kind that we have under the gospel, you say you know but three, viz., that of coming to God by Christ, and the institutions of baptism, and the Lord's supper (p. 9).

So then, although you talk of gospel positive laws, and particularly that of coming to God by Christ, yet those which you call first principles of morals, are of higher concern with you, and more indispensable by far than this, this being a thing of an indifferent nature, and in itself absolutely considered, is neither good nor evil ; but the other is the life of the matter. But a little to gather you up.

The morals, say you, are indispensable, and good in themselves ; but that of coming to God by Christ a thing indifferent, and in itself neither good nor evil. Wherefore though in this your description, you talk of confirming to all those good and practical principles, that are made known either by revelation, nature, or the use of reason, yet in this your obedience you reckon coming to God by Christ but an act of a very indifferent nature, a thing if done not good in itself, neither evil in itself, should a man leave it undone ; and so consequently a man may have in him the ground and essentials of Christianity without it—may be saved, and go to heaven without it : for this I say, whatsoever is of an indifferent nature in itself, is not essential to the Christian religion, but may or may not be done without the hazard of eternal salvation ; but say you, this of coming to God by Christ is one of the positive precepts (p. 9), which are in themselves things indifferent, and neither good nor evil, therefore not of the substance of Christianity.

But, Sir, where learned you this new doctrine, as to reckon coming to God by Christ a thing of so indifferent a nature, a thing not good in itself, but with respect to certain circumstances (p. 7). Had you said this of baptism and the supper of the Lord, I could with some allowance have borne your words, but to count coming to God by Christ a thing indifferent in itself, is a blasphemy that may not be borne by Christians, it being too high a contempt of the blood, and too great a disgrace to the person of the Lord, the King of Glory, of which more hereafter ; but to return.

II. The intent of this your description is to set before us these two things.

(1.) What are the essentials of the rule of that holiness, which by the gospel we are immediately obliged to, if we would be justified in the sight of God.

(2.) What are the principles by which we act, when we do these works aright.

1. For the first you tell us, " they are the first principles of morals, such as are self-evident, and therefore not capable of being properly demon-

strated; as being no less knowable, and easily assented to, than any proposition that may be brought for the proof of them" (p. 8). Such as are self-evident, or evident of themselves: to what? to us as men that know the principles of reason, and that are as easily assented to as any proposition. Why said you not such as may be as easily known, , as we know there is a day or night, winter and summer, or any other thing that may be brought for the proof of them. This law therefore is none other than that mentioned in Rom. ii. 14, 15, which is the law of our nature, or that which was implanted in us in the day of our creation, and therefore is said to be ourselves, even nature itself. (1 Cor. xi. 14.)

2. The principle, say you, by which we act, and in the strength of which we do this law, it is the principle of reason, or a reasonable compliance with this law written in our hearts, and originally dictates of human nature, &c.; which certain principle, say you, is this, to count it most highly becoming all reasonable creatures to obey God in everything, and as much disbecoming them in anything to disobey him (p. 8).

The sum is, this your holiness both in root and act is no other than what is common to all the men on earth; I mean so common as that for the first is in their nature, as the second is also part of themselves, they being creatures whose prime or principal distinction from other, consisteth in that they are reasonable, and such as have reason as a thing essential to them. Wherefore the excellency that you have discoursed of, is none other than the excellency and goodness that is of this world, such as in the first principles of it is common to heathens, pagans, Turks, infidels: and that as evidently dictates to those that have not heard the gospel, (I mean as to the nature the good and evil,) as it doth in them that sit under the sound thereof; and is the selfsame which our late ungodly heretics the Quakers have made such a stir to promote and exalt, only in the description thereof you seem more ingenious than they: for whereas they erroneously call it Christ, the light of Christ, faith, grace, hope, the Spirit, the word that is nigh, &c., you give it the names due thereto, viz., a complexion or complication and combination of all the virtue of the soul, the human nature, the dictates of it, the principles of reason, such as are self-evident, than which there is nothing mankind doth more naturally assent to, (pp. 6—11.) Only here, as I have said, you glorify your errors also with names and titles that are not to be found, but in your own deluded brains: as that the virtues of the souls can keep themselves incommixed, that there is yet in us the purity of the human nature, or such a disposition that can both by light and power give a man to see, and powerfully incline him to and bring him under the government of all those good and practical principles that are made known either by revelation, nature, or the use of reason.

But I say, these principles thus stated by you,

being the principles and the goodness of this world, and such as have not faith, but the law, not the Holy Ghost, but human nature in them, they cannot be those which you affirm, was or is the design, the great, the only, and ultimate design of Christ, or his gospel to promote, and propagate in the world: neither with respect to our justification before God from the curse; neither with respect to the workings of his Spirit, and the faith of Jesus in our hearts, the true gospel or evangelical holiness.

First. It is not the righteousness that justifieth us before God from the curse; because it is that which is properly our own, and acted and managed by principles of our own, arising originally in the roots of it, from our own. There is the righteousness of men, and the righteousness of God: that which is the righteousness of men, is that which we do work from matter and principles of our own; but that which is the righteousness of God, is that which is wrought from matter and principles purely divine, and of the nature of God. Again, that which is our own righteousness, is that which is wrought in and by our own persons as men; but that which is the righteousness of God, is that which is wrought in and by the second person in the Trinity, as God and man in one person; and that resideth only in that person of the Son. I speak now of the righteousness by which we stand just before God, from the curse of the law. Now this righteousness of ours, our own righteousness, the apostle always opposeth to the righteousness of God, saying, They, going about to establish their own righteousness, have not submitted themselves to the righteousness of God, (Rom. xix. 3.) Farther, this righteousness of our own, Paul counts loss and dog's meat, in comparison of that other far more glorious righteousness, which he calleth, as it is in truth, the righteousness of God, (Phil. iii, 7—9;) which as I said but now, resideth in the person of the Son. Therefore, saith Paul, I cast away my own righteousness, and do count it loss, and "but dung, that I may win Christ, and be found in him, not having mine own righteousness, which is of the law, but that which is through the faith of Christ, the righteousness which is of God by faith." The righteousness, therefore, that is our own, that ariseth from matter and principles of our own (such as that which you have described) justifieth us not before God from the curse.

Second. The righteousness that you have described, justifieth us not, as before, because it is the righteousness which is of the moral law, that is, it is wrought by us, as walking in the law. Now it mattereth not whether you respect the law in its first principles, or as it is revealed in the table of the ten commandments; they are in nature but one and the same, and their substance and matter is written in our hearts, as we are men. Now this righteousness the apostle casteth away, as was showed before; "not having mine own righteousness," saith he, "which is of the law."

Why? Because the righteousness that saveth us from the wrath of God, is the righteousness of God; and so a righteousness that is without the law. "But now the righteousness of God without the law is manifested, being witnessed by the law and the prophets, even the righteousness of God, which is by faith of Jesus Christ, unto all, and upon all them that believe." (Rom. iii. 21, 22.) The righteousness of God without the law, the righteousness of Christ who is naturally God; wherefore such a righteousness as was accomplished by him that was Lord, and the very God of the law; whose nature was infinite, and not that which the law could command or condemn. Neither was the command of the law the great and principal argument with him, no, not in its first and highest principles, to do or continue to do it; but even that which the law commanded of us, that he did, not by the law, but by that Spirit of life, that eternal Spirit, and Godhead, which was essential to his very being. He did naturally and infinitely that which the law required of us, from higher and more mighty principles than the law could require of him: for I should reckon it a piece of prodigious blasphemy to say that the law could command his God, the creature, his Lord and Creator. But this Lord God, Jesus Christ, even he hath accomplished righteousness, even righteousness that is without, that is above, higher and better than that of the law: and that is the righteousness that is given to, and put upon all them that believe. Wherefore the Lord Jesus Christ, in his most blessed life, was neither prompted to actions of holiness, nor managed in them, by the purity of human nature, or those you call first principles of morals, or as he was simply a reasonable creature; but, being the natural Son of God, truly and essentially eternal as the Father, by the eternal Spirit, his Godhead, was his manhood governed, and acted, and spirited to do and suffer. "He through the eternal Spirit offered himself without spot to God," (Heb. ix. 14;) which offering respects not only his act of dying, but also that by which he was capacitated to die without spot in his sight; which was the infinite dignity, and sinlessness of his person, and the perfect justice of his actions. Now this person, thus acting, is approved of, or justified by the law to be good; for if the righteousness of the law be good—which law is but a creature—the righteousness of the Lord, the God of this law, must needs be much more good: wherefore here is the law, and its perfection swallowed up, even as the light of a candle or star is swallowed up by the light of the sun. Thus then is the believer made, not the righteousness of the law, but "the righteousness of God in Christ," (2 Cor. v. 21;) because Christ Jesus, who is the righteousness of the Christian, did walk in this world in and under the law, not by legal and human principles, which are the excellences of men, but in and by those that are divine, even such as were and are of his own nature, and the

essence of his eternal Godhead. This is the righteousness *without* the law, accomplished by a person and principles far otherwise than is he or those you make description of; and therefore yours cannot be that by which we stand just before the justice of God without the law. Now if it be a righteousness without the law, then it is a righteousness without men, a righteousness that cannot be found in the world; for take away the law, the rule, and you take away not only the righteousness, but that by which men, as men, work righteousness in the world: "mine own righteousness which is of the law." The righteousness then by which a man must stand just in the sight of God from the curse, is not to be found in men, nor in the law, but in him, and him only, who is greater, and also, without the law; for albeit for our sakes he became under the law, even to the curse and displeasures of God, yet the principles by which he walked in the world to Godward, they were neither human, nor legal, but heavenly, and done in the Spirit of the Son. Wherefore it is not the righteousness you have described, by which we stand just before God.

Third. The righteousness you have described cannot be that which justifieth us before God, because of its imperfections, and that both with respect to the principle and the power with which it is managed: for though you have talked of a sound complexion of soul, the purity of the human nature, and that with this addition of power, as to be able to keep itself incommixed with that which is not of itself, yet we Christians know, and that by the words of God, that there is in man, as man, now no soundness at all, but from the crown of the head to the sole of the foot, botches and boils, putrefactions and sores. (Isa. i. 6.) We are ALL an unclean thing, and our righteousness as filthy ulcerous rags. (Isa. lxiv. 6.) "If there had been a law given that could have given life, verily righteousness should have been by the law." (Gal. iii. 21.) Could a man perform the law to the liking of the justice of the eternal Majesty, then would the law give life to that man; but because of the perfection of an infinite justice, and the weakness and unprofitableness of the law through our flesh, therefore, though you speak yet further of the excellency of your sound complexion, and of the purity of the human nature, you must fly from yourself, to another righteousness for life, or at the last stick in the jaws of death and everlasting desperation. "For by the works of the law shall no flesh be justified." (Gal. ii. 16.)

It is therefore no better than error, thus to ascribe to poor man, "that hath drank iniquity like water," a soundness of soul, a purity of human nature. Wherefore Jude saith of you, and of all such naturalists, that "even in the things that you know naturally, as the brute, in them you corrupt yourselves," (Jude 10,) even in the very principles, the first or original dictates of your nature or humanity. There is none that understandeth or is good, therefore there is none that doth good, no not one : that is, none as continuing in a natural state ; none by the power or principles of nature ; for he meaneth here, in your own sense, as men by natural principles have to do with the justice of the law.

Fourth. The righteousness which you have described cannot be that which justifieth us before God, because it is that which is not of faith. " The law is not of faith, but the man that doeth them shall live in them." (Gal. iii, 12.) The apostle also in the tenth chapter of the Romans tells us, that the righteousness that is completed by doing the law is one, and another besides the righteousness of faith. For faith in the justification of a sinner from the curse and wrath of God, respecteth only the mercy of God, and forgiveness of sins for the sake of Christ. " God for Christ's sake hath forgiven him that is enabled to believe, that is, trust to, and venture the eternal concern of his soul upon the righteousness that is nowhere to be found, but in the person of the Son of God." For there is justice more than answerable to all the demands of the law, and the requirements of the eternal justice of God, and he is our justice ; he is made unto us of God, righteousness, or justice ; that is, the righteousness or justice that is in him, is by God, accounted the man's that shall accept thereof by faith, that he might be made the justice or righteousness of God in him. For the righteousness that saveth a sinner from damnation must be equal to that in the eternal Deity. But where can that be found but in him that is naturally God, as is indeed the Son of the Father ? in him, therefore, and not in the law, there is a righteousness fit for faith to apply to. Besides the law is not, neither can be, the object of faith to men ; for that which is the object of faith, (I speak now as to justifying righteousness,) it must be a righteousness already completed, and as I said, a righteousness to be received and accepted, being now perfected and offered, and given to us by the kindness and mercy of God ; but a man may believe long enough in the law, before that performs for him a perfect righteousness. The law can work nothing unless it be wrath. " No, thou must work by, and not believe in, the law." (Rom. iv.) Besides, all that cometh out of the mouth of the law is, " Cursed is every one that continueth not in all things which are written in the book of the law to do them," (Gal. iii. 10,) which no man is capable of doing, so as to escape the curse by doing, that hath once or first transgressed the same. Wherefore it is a vain thing, yea, an horrible wickedness in you, thus to abuse the law, and the weakness of man, by suggesting that the only, the ultimate, or grand design of Christ Jesus was, or is, the promoting of a righteousness by the law, that is performed by human principles in us.

I could double, yea ten times double, the number of these arguments against you, but I will pass from this to the second thing. " The righteous-

ness you have described, is not the true gospel inward holiness,"

I told you before, that the principles which you have described are not evangelical principles ; and now I will add, that as they are not such in themselves, so neither do they fetch in, or obtain by our adhering to them, those things which alone can make, or work in the soul, those truly gospel inward acts of holiness.

There are three things which are essential to the inward gospel holiness ; of which as your description is utterly destitute, so neither can they by that be obtained, or come into the heart.
1. *The Holy Ghost.*
2. *Faith in Christ.*
3. *A new heart, and a new spirit.*

Without these three there is no such thing as gospel holiness in man, as before I have also hinted at. But now as there is none of these three found in your description of inward holiness, so neither can you, or others, by all your inclinations, either to those you call first principles of natural reason, or the dictates of human nature, obtain or fetch into the soul the least dram of that which is essential, to that which is indeed according to the gospel description of inward gospel holiness, as will further be manifest in this that followeth.

1. *The Holy Ghost* is not obtained by your description, that consisting only in principles of nature, and in putting forth itself in acts of civility and morality. When the apostle would convince the bewitched Galatians that your doctrine, which was also the doctrine of the false apostles, was that, which instead of helping forward, did hinder, and pervert the gospel of Christ, he applieth himself to them in this manner : " This only would I learn of you, Received ye the Spirit by the works of the law, or by the hearing of faith ?" (Gal. iii. 2.) By the works of the law, that is, by putting of your principles into practice. Nay, may I not add, by putting of your principles into practice, by a more bright and clear rule than, in the beginning of your description, is inserted by you ; for the law as written and engraven in stones, with the addition of all the Mosaical precepts, was a more ample and full discovery of the mind of God, than can be obtained by your virtues of soul, your purity of human nature, or the first principles of morality as they are writtten in the heart of man ; and originally dictates of human nature. Yet by these, by following these, by labouring to live up to the light of these, their own experience told them, that they neither could nor did obtain the enjoyment of the Holy Ghost ; but that rather their now declining the word of faith, by which indeed they receive it at first (whatever pretences of holiness and godliness were the arguments to prevail with them so to do,) was in truth none other but the very witchcraft and enchantments of the devil.

Farther, the apostle sets this your spirit and principles, and that which indeed is the Spirit of God, in a line diametrically opposite one against another; yea the receiving of the one, opposeth the receiving of the other. "Now we have received," saith he, "not the spirit of the world," (that is, your spirit, and principles of humanity,) "to walk by it, or live in it; but the Spirit which is of God, that we may know the things that are freely given to us of God." (1 Cor. ii. 12.) But what is the spirit of the world? He tells us in the verse before, it is the spirit of a man; which Solomon calls, "the candle of the Lord; that which searcheth all the inward parts of the belly," (Prov. xx. 27,) by human principles, good motions to moral duties, workings of reason, dictates of nature to obey God as Creator. These things flow from the spirit of a man, which is the spirit of all the world. They that preach, or speak by this spirit, they preach or speak of the world, of the virtues of the world; and the world, "the whole world heareth them," (1 John iv. 5,) or know in themselves what they say.

Now when this spirit is received, embraced, and followed, as the Spirit that is of God, then it must be branded with the mark of the spirit of error, and of Antichrist; because the act in so doing is most wicked; yea, and Christ himself is made head against by it.

But I say, the Holy Ghost is not obtained by these principles, nor by the pursuit of them.

2. *Faith* is not obtained by the pursuit of your principles, but by hearing of another doctrine. He that presseth men to look to, and live by the purity of human nature, principles of natural reason, or by the law, as written in the heart, or Bible, he sets the word of faith out of the world; for these doctrines are as opposite as the spirits I spake of before, "for Moses describeth the righteousness that is of the law, That the man which doeth those things shall live by them." Now he that receiveth this law, to do and live by, he hath set up, and is in pursuit of a doctrine of another nature than that which is called the righteousness of faith; that being such, as for justification, and deliverance from the curse, maketh no mention at all of hearing the law, or of doing good works, but of hearing of the mercy of God, as extended to sinners, and of its coming to us through the death and resurrection of Christ Jesus. "The righteousness which is of faith, speaketh on this wise, Say not in thine heart, Who shall ascend into heaven? (that is, to bring Christ down from above,) or, Who shall descend into the deep? (that is, to bring up Christ again from the dead.) But what saith it? The word is nigh thee, even in thy mouth, and in thy heart; that is the word of faith which we preach: that if thou shalt confess with thy mouth the Lord Jesus, and shall believe in thine heart that God hath raised him from the dead, thou shalt be saved." (Rom. x. 5, 9.) This then is the doctrine of faith, or the righteousness with which faith hath to do. Now as old covenant-works, are begotten in men by the doctrine of works; so faith is begotten by the doctrine of faith. Therefore after

he had said, "faith cometh by hearing," he insinuates it to be the hearing the preaching of the gospel of peace, (peace by the blood of the cross,) and the glad tidings of good things, (Rom. x. 14—17,) of good things promised for the sake of the Lord Jesus; not for the sake of good deeds done of us, by human principles, or the dictates of our nature.

Faith, then, the second essential, comes into the heart, not by the preaching, or the practice of your principles; but by another, a higher, and far more heavenly doctrine. And hence the apostle completely puts the difference betwixt the worker of good works in the spirit of the law, and the believer that taketh hold of grace by Christ, that he may be saved thereby. The one he calls "them that are of the works of the law;" the other, "they which are of faith." (Gal. iii.) This being done, he tells us, that as they differ in the principles, to wit, of faith and words, so they shall differ in conclusion: "For the law is not of faith, the promise is only made to faith; therefore, they only that are of faith are blessed with faithful Abraham."

3. The third essential is *a new heart, and a new spirit* or mind; and this also comes not by your principle, that being but the old covenant that gendereth to bondage, and that holds its Ishmaels under the curse for ever: there comes no new heart by the law, nor new spirit. It is by the new covenant, even the gospel, that all things are made new. (Jer. xxxi. 33. Ezek. xxxvi. Heb. viii. 8. 2 Cor. v. 17—19.)

The apostle, after a large discourse of the two ministrations, and their excellences, (2 Cor. iii.,) tells us that the heart is nothing changed, so long as it abideth in the works of the law, but remaineth blind and ignorant: "Nevertheless," saith he, "when it shall turn (from the law) to the Lord, the veil shall be taken away." But what is it to turn from the law to the Lord? Why, even to leave and forsake your spirit and principles, and works from those principles, and fly to the grace and merits, "the glory of the Lord Jesus Christ." Now when the heart is turned to Christ, then the veil of Moses is taken off; wherefore then the soul "with open face, beholding, as in a glass, the glory of the Lord, is changed from glory to glory, even as by the Spirit of the Lord." (2 Cor. iii. 14, 18.)

Obj. But it seems a paradox to many, that a man should live to the law, that is devote himself to the works of the ten commandments, the most perfect rule of life, and yet not be counted one changed, or new.

Ans. Though it seemeth an untruth, yet it is most true, that by the works of the law no heart is made new, no man made new. A man from principle of nature and reason, (which principles are of himself, and as old,) may give up himself to the goodness of the law: yet these principles are so far off from being new, that they are as old as Adam in Paradise; and come into the world with all the children of men. To which principles the law, or the first principles of morals, so equally suit, that, as you have said (p. 8), "they are self-evident, than which there is nothing mankind doth more naturally assent to" (p. 11). Now nature is no new principle, but an old: even our own, and of ourselves. The law is no new principle, but old, and one with ourselves (as also you well have called it) "first written in men's hearts and originally dictates of human nature." Let a man, then, be as devout as is possible for the law, and the holiness of the law; yet if the principles from which he acts be but the habit of soul, the purity (as he feigns) of his own nature—principles of natural reason, or the dictates of human nature—all this is nothing else but the old gentleman in his holiday clothes: the old heart, the old spirit, the spirit of the man, not the Spirit of Christ, is here.

And hence the apostle, when he would show us a man alive, or made a new man indeed, as he talketh of the Holy Ghost, and faith, so he tells us such are dead to the law—to the law as a law of works, to the law as to principles of nature. "Wherefore, my brethren, you are also become dead to the law (the moral law, and the ceremonial law) by the body of Christ, that you should be married to another (another than the law) even to him, who is raised from the dead, that we should bring forth fruit unto God." (Rom. vii. 4.)

Ye are become dead to the law. Dead to the law! Why? That you should be married to another. Married to another! Why? "That you should bring forth fruit unto God." But doth not a man bring forth fruit unto God that walketh orderly according to the ten commandments? No, if he do it before faith, in the spirit of a man, by the dictates of human nature, respecting the law, as that, by the obeying of which, he must obtain acceptance with God. This is bringing forth fruit unto himself; for all that he doth, he doth it as a man, as a creature, from principles natural, and of himself, his own, and for none other than himself; and therefore he serveth in an old spirit—the oldness of the letter, and for himself. But now (that is, ye being dead to the law, and married to Christ) that (the law) being dead by which (while in ourselves) we were held, now we are delivered from that law, both as to its curse and impositions, as it stands a law of works in the heart of the world; we serve in newness of the spirit, "and not in the oldness of the letter." (Rom. vii. 6.) A man must first then be dead to your principles, both of nature and the law, if he will serve in a new spirit, if he would bring forth fruit unto God. Wherefore your description of the principle of holiness in man, and also the principles by which this holiness is put forth by him into righteous acts, they are such as are altogether void of the true essentials of inward gospel-holiness and righteousness.

But there is one thing more in this description, or rather effect thereof, which I shall also inquire into; and that is, your saying, "As it was the errand of Christ to effect our deliverance out of that sinful state we had brought ourselves into; so to put us again into possession of that holiness which we had lost" (p. 12). The proof of this position is now your next business; that is, if I understand your learning, the remaining part of your book, which consisteth of well nigh three hundred pages, is spent for proof thereof: which I doubt not but effectually to confute with less than *three hundred lines*. Only first, by the way, I would have my reader to take notice that in this last clause (to put us again into possession of that holiness which we had lost) is the sum of all this large description of his holiness in the foregoing pages; that is, the holiness and righteousness that Mr. Fowler hath been describing; and adds, that Christ's whole business when he came into the world was, as to effect our deliverance from sin, "so to put us again in possession of that holiness which we had lost." The holiness, therefore, that here he contendeth for, is that, and only that, which was in Adam before the fall, which he lost by transgression; and we by transgressing in him. A little, therefore, to inquire into this, if perhaps his reader and mine may come to a right understanding of things.

First then, Adam before the fall, even in his best and most sinless state, was but a pure natural man, consisting of body and soul; these (to use your own terms) were his pure essentials (p. 11); in this man's heart God also did write the law: that is, (as you term them,) the first principles of morals (p. 8). This, then, was the state of Adam, he was a pure natural man, made by God sinless; all the faculties of his soul and members of his body were clean. "God made man upright." (Eccles. vii.) But he made him not then a spiritual man; "the first Adam was made a living soul," "howbeit that was not first which is spiritual; but that which is natural, and afterward that which is spiritual. The first man is of the earth, earthy." (1 Cor. xv. 45—47.) A living soul he was; yet but a natural man, even in his first and best estate—but earthly when compared to Christ, or with them that believe in Christ. So then, the holiness of Adam in his best estate, even that which he lost, and we in him, it was none other than that which was natural, even the sinless state of a natural man. This holiness, then, was not of the nature of that which hath for its root the Holy Ghost; for of that we read not at all in him, he only was endued with a living soul, his holiness then could not be gospel, nor that which is a branch of the second covenant; his acts of righteousness were not by the operations of the Spirit of grace, but the dictates of the law in his own natural heart. But the apostle, when he treateth of the Christian inherent holiness, first excluding that in Adam as earthly, he tells us it is such as is in Christ: "As is the earthy, such are they that are earthy; and as is the heavenly, such are they that are heavenly."

Let, then, those that are the sons of Adam, in the state of nature as he, though not so pure and spotless as he, be reckoned to bear his image and similitude : but let them that are the children of Christ, though not so pure as he, bear the image and similitude of Christ ; "for they are conformable to the image of the Son of God." (Rom. viii. 29.) The holiness, therefore, that was in Adam, being but that which was natural, earthly, and not of the Holy Ghost, cannot be that which Christ came into the world to give us possession of.

Second. Adam in his best, and most sinless state, was but a type or figure—"the figure of him that was to come." (Rom. v. 14.) A type in what ? A type or figure doubtless, in his sinless and holy estate, a type and figure of the holiness of Christ ; but if Christ should come from heaven to put us in possession of this sinless holiness that was in Adam, or that we lost in him, to what more would his work amount than to put us into the possession of a natural, figurative, shadowish righteousness or holiness. But this he never intended ; therefore it is not the possessing of his people with that holiness that was the great errand Christ came into the world upon.

Third. The holiness and righteousness that was in (and that we lost by) Adam before the fall, was such as stood in, and was to be managed by his natural perfect compliance with a covenant of works. For " do this sin and die," were the terms that was from God to Adam. But Christ at his coming brings in another, a better, a blessed covenant of grace, and likewise possesseth his children with the holiness and privileges of that covenant ; not with Adam's heart nor Adam's mind, but a new heart, a new spirit, a new principle to act by, and walk in a new covenant. Therefore the holiness that was in Adam before, or that we lost in him by the fall, could not but be the holiness that Christ at his coming made it his great or only business to put us in possession of.

Fourth. The holiness that was in Adam before, and that we lost in him by the fall, was such as might stand with perfect ignorance of the mediation of Jesus Christ ; for Christ was not made known to Adam as a Saviour, before that Adam was a sinner ; neither needed he at all to know him to be his Mediator, before he knew he had offended. (Gen. iii.) But Christ did not come into the world to establish us in, or give us possession of such holiness as might stand with perfect ignorance of his mediatorship. No ; the holiness that we believers have, and the righteous acts that we fulfil, they come to us, and are done by us, through the knowledge of the Lord Jesus, and of his being the Messiah promised. (Eph. iv. 21, 22. 2 Pet. i. 3.)

Fifth. The holiness that was in Adam, was neither given him through the promise, neither encouraged by the promise. Adam had no promise to possess him with a principle of holiness ; it came to him by creation : neither had he any promise to strengthen or encourage him in holiness. All he had was instructions concerning his duty, and death threatened if he did it not. (Gen. ii. 15—17.) But Christ came not to give us possession of an holiness or righteousness that came to us by our creation, without a promise, and that hath no promise to encourage us to continue therein, but of an holiness that comes to us by the best of promises, and that we are encouraged to by the best of promises. Therefore it was not his great errand when he came from heaven to earth, to put us in possession of that promiseless holiness that Adam had before, and that was lost in him by the fall.

Lastly. In a word ; the holiness that Adam had before and that we lost in him by the fall, it was a natural shadowish old covenant, promiseless holiness ; such as stood and might be walked in, while he stood perfectly ignorant of the Mediator Christ. Wherefore it is rather the design of your Apollo the devil, whom in p. 101 you bring forth to applaud your righteousness,—I say, it is rather his design than Christ's, to put men upon an endeavour after a possession of that ; for that which is truly evangelical is the spiritual, substantial, new covenant promised holiness ; that which cometh to us by, and standeth in the Spirit, faith and knowledge of the Son of God, not that which we lost in Adam. Wherefore the song which there you learnt of the devil, is true, in the sense he made it, and in the sense for which you bring it, which is, to beget in men the highest esteem of their own human nature, and to set up this natural, shadowish, promiseless, ignorant holiness, in opposition to that which is truly Christ's.

To dwell in heaven doth not more please him, than
Within the souls of pious mortal men.

This is the song ; but you find it not in Matthew, Mark, Luke, or John, but among the heathens who were his disciples, and who were wont to inquire at his mouth, and learn of him.

Thus have I razed the foundation of your book, even by overthrowing the holiness and righteousness which by you is set up as that which is the only true gospel, and evangelical. Wherefore it remaineth, that the rest of your book, viz., whatever therein is brought and urged for the proof of this your description of holiness, &c., it is but the abuse of Christ, of Scripture, and reason ; it is but a wresting and corrupting the word of God, both to your own destruction, and them that believe you.

But to pass this, and to come to some other passages in your book ; and first to that in p. 5, where you say—

" The holiness, which is the design of the religion of Christ Jesus, is not such as is subjected in anything without us, or is made ours by a mere external (or outward) application," &c.

Ans. 1. These words secretly smite at the justification that comes by the imputation of that most glorious righteousness that alone resideth in the person of the Lord Jesus; and that is made ours by an act of eternal grace, we resting upon it by the faith of Jesus.

2. But if the holiness of which you speak, be not subjected in anything without us, then it is not of all that fulness which it pleased the Father should dwell in Christ: for the holiness and righteousness, even the inward holiness that is in saints, it is none other than that which dwelleth in the person of the Son of God in heaven: neither doth any man partake of, or enjoy the least measure thereof, but as he is united by faith to this Son of God, the thing is true in him and in us; in him as the head, and without measure, (1 John ii. 8;) and is originally seated in him, not in us. "Of his fulness have all we (saints) received, and grace for grace." (John i. 16.) Wherefore the holiness that hath its original from us, from the purity of the human nature, (which is the thing you aim at,) and that originally, as you term it, is the dictates thereof, is the religion of the Socinians, Quakers, &c., and not the religion of Jesus Christ.

And now I will come to your indifferent things, viz., those which you call "positive precepts;" things, say you, "of an indifferent nature; and, absolutely considered, are neither good nor evil; but are capable of becoming so; only by reason of certain circumstances:" of these positive indifferent precepts, you say, you know but three in the gospel; but three, that are purely so, viz., "That of going to God by Christ, the institutions of baptism, and the Lord's supper." This we have in pp. 7 and 9.

Ans. These words, as I hinted before, are highly derogatory to the Lord, the King of glory; and trample as much upon the blood of the Son of God, as words can likely do. For,

. 1. If going to God by Christ, be in itself but an indifferent thing, then, as I also hinted before, it is not of the substance of Christianity; but a man may be truly a Christian without it; may be saved, and go to heaven without it; this is in truth the consequence of your words: for things purely of an indifferent nature, do not in themselves either make or mar the righteousness that justifieth us from the curse before God. Wherefore, by your argument, if a man remain ignorant of that positive precept, of "coming to God by Christ," he remaineth ignorant but of an indifferent thing, a thing that in itself is neither good nor evil, and therefore not essentially material to his faith or justifying righteousness.

2. An indifferent thing in itself is next to nothing, neither good nor evil, then but a thing betwixt them both.

Then is the blood of the Lord Jesus, in itself, of no value at all; nor faith in him, of itself, any more than a thing of nought: their virtue and goodness only dependeth upon certain circumstances that make them so. For the indifferency of the thing lieth not simply in coming to God, but in coming to him by Christ: coming otherwise to God, even in this man's eyes, being the all in all; but in *this* coming, in coming to him by Christ, there lieth the indifferency. I marvel what injury the Lord Jesus hath done this man, that he should have such indifferent thoughts of coming to God by him?

But hath he no better thoughts of his own good deeds, which are by the law? Yes, doubtless, for those, saith he, "are of an indispensable, and eternal obligation, which were first written in men's hearts, and originally dictates of human nature" (p. 8). Mark, not a dictate of human nature, or necessary conclusion or deduction from it, is of an indifferent, but of an indispensable, not of a transient, but of an eternal obligation. It is only going to God by Christ, and two other things that he findeth in the gospel, that of themselves are of an indifferent nature.

But how indifferent? Even as indifferent in itself as the blood of a silly sheep, or the ashes of an heifer; for these are his very words. "Seen (that is, such ordinances as in themselves are of an indifferent nature) were all the injunctions and prohibitions of the ceremonial law; and some few such we have under the gospel" (p. 7). Then, in p. 9, he tells you what these positive precepts under the gospel, or things indifferent, are: "That of going to God by Christ, is one; and the other two, are institutions of baptism, and the Lord's supper." Such therefore as were the ceremonies of the law, such, even such, (saith he,) is that of going to God by Christ, &c.

Wherefore, he that shall lay no more stress upon the Lord Jesus to come to God by, than this man doth, would lay as much (were the old ceremonies in force) upon a silly sheep, as upon the Christ of God. For these are all alike positive precepts, such as were the ceremonies of the law, things in themselves neither good nor evil, but absolutely considered of an indifferent nature.

So that to come to God by Christ, is reckoned, of itself, by him, a thing of a very indifferent nature, and therefore this man cannot do it, but with a very *indifferent* heart; his great and most substantial coming to God, must needs be by some other way. (John x. 1.) But why should this thief love thus to clamber, and seek to go to God by other means; such which he reckoneth of a more indispensable nature, and eternal; seeing Christ only (as indifferent as he is) is the *only* way to the Father. "I am the way, (saith he,) the truth, and the life; no man cometh to the Father but by me." If he be the only way, then there is none other; if he be thus the truth, then is all other the lie; and if he be here the life, then is all other the death; let him call them indispensable and eternal never so often.

So then, how far off this man's doctrine is, of sinning against the Holy Ghost, let him that is wise consider it. For if coming to God by Christ, be in itself but a thing indifferent, and only made a duty upon the account of certain circumstances, then, to come to God by Christ, is a duty incumbent upon us only by reason of certain circumstances; not that the thing in itself is good, or that the nature of sin, and the justice of God, layeth a necessity on us so to do. But what be these certain circumstances? For it is because of these (if you will believe him) that God the Father, yea, the whole Trinity, did consult in eternity, and consent that Christ should be the way to life. Now, I say, it is partly because by him was the greatest safety, he being naturally the justice, wisdom, and power of God; and partly, because it would, we having sinned, be utterly impossible we should come to God by other means and live. He that will call *these* circumstances—that is, things over and above besides the substantials of the gospel—will but discover his unbelief and ignorance, &c.

As for your saying that Calvin, Peter Martyr, Musculus, Zanchy, and others did not question but that God could have pardoned sin without any other satisfaction than the repentance of the sinner (p. 84), it matters nothing to me; I have neither made my creed out of them nor other than the holy Scriptures of God.

But if Christ was from before all worlds ordained to be the Saviour, then was he from all eternity so appointed and prepared to be. And if God be, as you say, infinitely (p. 136), and, I will add, eternally just, how can he pardon without he be presented with that satisfaction for sin that to all points of the highest perfection doth answer the demands of this infinite and eternal justice? Unless you will say that the repentance of a sinner is sufficient to answer whatever could be justly demanded as a satisfaction thereto, which, if you should, you would in consequence say, that man is, or may be in himself, just, that is, equal with God; or that the sin of man was not a transgression of the law that was given, and a procurer of the punishment that is threatened by that eternal God that gave it. (But let me give you a caution, take heed that you belie not these men.) Christ cries, "If it be possible, let this cup pass from me." (Matt. xxvi. 39.) If what be possible? Why, that sinners should be saved without his blood. (Heb. ix. 22. Luke xxiv. 26. Acts xvii. 3.) " Ought not Christ to have suffered?" " Christ must needs have suffered," not because of some certain circumstances, but because the eternal justice of God could not consent to the salvation of the sinner without a satisfaction for the sin committed. Of which more in the next, if you shall think good to reply.

Now, that my reader may see I have not abused you in this reply to your sayings, I will repeat your words at large, and leave them upon you to answer it.

You say, " Actions may become duties or sins these two ways :—First, as they are compliances with, or transgressions of, divine positive precepts: these are the declarations of the *arbitrary* will of God, whereby he restraineth our liberty, for great and wise reasons, in things that are of an indifferent nature, and, absolutely considered, are neither good nor evil; and so makes things not good in themselves (and capable of becoming so only by reason of certain circumstances) *duties,* and things not evil in themselves, *sins.* Such were all the injunctions and prohibitions of the ceremonial law, and some few such we have under the gospel" (p. 7). Then (p. 9) you tell us, that " the reason of the positive laws (that is, concerning things in themselves indifferent) in the gospel are declared; of which (say you) I know but three that are purely so—viz., that of coming to God by Christ, the institutions of baptism, and the Lord's supper."

Here now let the reader note, that the positive precepts, declarations of the arbitrary will of God, in things of an indifferent nature, being such as, absolutely considered, are neither good nor evil, some few such, say you, we have under the gospel —namely, that of coming to God by Christ, &c. I am the more punctual in this thing because you have confounded your weak reader with a crooked parenthesis in the midst of the paragraph, and also by deferring to spit your intended venom at Christ, till again you had puzzled him, with your mathematics and metaphysics, &c., putting in another page betwixt the beginning and the end of your blasphemy.

Indeed, in the seventh chapter of your book you make a great noise of the effects and consequences of the death of Christ, as that it was a sacrifice for sin, an expiatory and propitiatory sacrifice (p. 83). Yet he that well shall weigh you and compare you with yourself, shall find that words and sense with you are two things; and also that you have learned of your brethren of old to dissemble with words, that thereby your heart-errors, and the snake that lieth in your bosom, may yet there abide the more undiscovered. For in the conclusion of that very chapter, even in and by a word or two, you take away that glory that of right belongeth to the death and blood of Christ, and lay it upon other things. For you say, "The Scriptures that frequently affirm that the end of Christ's death was the forgiveness of our sins, and the reconciling of us to the Father, we are not so to understand as if the blessings were absolutely thereby procured for us any otherwise than upon condition of our effectual believing" (p. 91). I answer, by the death of Christ was the forgiveness of sins effectually obtained for all that shall be saved, and they, even while yet enemies, by that were reconciled unto God. So 'that, as to forgiveness from God, it is purely upon the account of grace in Christ; " We are justified by his blood, we are reconciled to God by the death of his Son." (Rom. v. 9, 10.) Yea, peace is made by the blood of his cross, (Col. i. 20,) and God, for Christ's sake, hath forgiven us. (Eph. iv. 32.) So, then, our effectual believing is not a procuring cause in the sight of God, or a condition of ours foreseen by God, and the motive that prevaileth with him to forgive us our manifold transgressions : believing being rather that which makes application of that forgiveness, and that possesseth the soul with that peace that already is made for us with God, by the blood of his Son Christ Jesus; "being justified by faith, we have peace with God through our Lord Jesus Christ." (Rom. v. 1.) The peace and comfort of it cometh not to the soul but by believing. Yet the work is finished, pardon procured, justice being satisfied already, or before, by the precious blood of Christ.

Observe, I am commanded to believe, but what should I believe? or what should be the object of my faith in the matter of my justification with God? Why, I am to believe in Christ, I am to have faith in his blood. But what is it to believe in Christ? and what to have faith in his blood? Verily, to believe that while we were yet sinners Christ died for us, that even then, when we were enemies, we were reconciled to God by the death of his Son: to believe that there is a righteousness *already* for us completed.

I had as good give you the apostle's argument and conclusion in his own language: "But God commended his love toward us, in that while we were yet sinners, Christ died for us. Much more then, being now justified by his blood, we shall be saved from wrath through him." (Rom. v. 6—8.) And note that this word now respects the same time with yet that went before. "For if when we were enemies we were reconciled to God by the death of his Son, much more being reconciled we shall be saved by his life, or intercession." (Rom. v. 10.)

Believing then, as to the business of my deliverance from the curse before God, is an accepting of, (1 Tim. i. 15,) a trusting to, (Eph. i. 12, 13,) or a receiving (John i. 12) the benefit that Christ hath already obtained for me; by which act of faith, I see my interest in that peace that is made before with God by the blood of his cross: for if peace be made already by his blood, then is the curse taken away from his sight; if the curse be taken away from his sight, then there is no sin with the curse of it to be charged from God by the law, for so long as sin is charged by the law, with the curse thereto belonging, the curse, and so the wrath of God, remaineth.

"But (say you) Christ died to put us into a capacity of pardon" (p. 91).

Ans. True; but that is not all, he died to put us into the personal possession of pardon: yea, to put us into a personal possession of it, and that before we know it.

"But (say you) the actual removing of our guilt is not the necessary and immediate result of his death" (p. 91).

Ans. Yea, but it is from before the face of God, and from the judgment and curse of the law; for before God the guilt is taken away, by the death and blood of his Son, immediately for all them that shall be saved; else how can it be said we are justified by his blood; he hath made peace by his blood; "He loved us, and washed us from our

sins in his own blood," (Rev. i. 5;) and that we are reconciled to God by the death of his Son? which can by no means be, if, notwithstanding his death and blood, sin in the guilt, and consequently the curse that is due thereto, should yet remain in the sight of God. But what saith the apostle? "God was in Christ, reconciling the world to himself, not imputing their trespasses unto them." (2 Cor. v. 19.) Those that are but reconciling, are not yet reconciled: I mean, as Paul, not yet come aright over in their own souls by faith; yet to these he imputeth not their trespasses. Wherefore? because they have none, or because he forgiveth them as they believe and work? Neither of both, but because he hath first made his Son to be sin for them, and laid all the guilt and curse of their sin upon him, that they might be made the righteousness of God in him. Therefore even because by him their sin and curse is taken off, from before the law of God, therefore God, for the sake of Christ, seeketh for and beseecheth the sinner to be reconciled, that is, to believe in and embrace his majesty.

"No (say you) the actual removing of guilt is not the necessary and immediate result of his death, but suspended until such time as the forementioned conditions, by the help of his grace, are performed by us" (p. 92).

Ans. 1. Then may a man have the grace of God within him—yea, the grace and mercy of the new covenant, viz., faith, and the like—that yet remaineth under the curse of the law, and so hath yet his sins untaken away from before the face of God; for where the curse is only suspended, it may stand there notwithstanding, in force against the soul. Now, let the soul stand accursed, and his duties must stand accursed: for first the person, and then the offering must be accepted of God. God accepted not the works of Cain, because he had not accepted his person, (Gen. iv. 5;) but having first accepted Abel's person, he therefore did accept his offering. (Heb. xi. 4.) And here it is said that Abel offered by faith: he believed that his person was accepted of God, for the sake of the promised Messiah, and therefore he believed also that his offering should be accepted.

2. Faith, as it respecteth justification in the sight of God, must know nothing to rest upon but the mercy of God, through Christ's blood. But if the curse be not taken away, mercy also hangeth in suspense; yea, lieth as drowned, and hid in the bottom of the sea. This doctrine then of yours overthroweth faith, and rusheth the soul into the works of the law, the moral law, and so quite involveth it in the fear of the wrath of God, maketh the soul forget Christ, taketh from it the object of faith, and, if a miracle of mercy prevent not, the soul must die in everlasting desperation.

"But (say you) it is suspended till such time as the forementioned conditions, by the help of his grace, be performed by us" (p. 92).

Ans. Had you said the manifestation of it is

kept from us, it might, with some allowance, have been admitted; but yet the revelation of it in the word, which in some sense may be called a manifestation thereof, is first discovered to us by the word; yea, is seen by us, and also believed as a truth recorded, before the enjoyment thereof be with comfort in our own souls. (1 John v. 11.)

But you proceed and say, "Therefore was the death of Christ designed to procure our justification from all sins past, that we might be by this means provoked to become new creatures" (p. 92).

Ans. That the death of Christ is a mighty argument to persuade with the believer, to devote himself to God in Christ, in all things, as becometh one that hath received grace and redemption by his blood, is true; but that it is in our power, as is here insinuated, to become new creatures, is as untrue. The new creature is of God, yea, immediately of God; man being as incapable to make himself anew, as a child to beget himself. (2 Cor. v. 17, 18.) Neither is our conformity to the revealed will of God anything else (if it be right) than the fruit and effect of that. All things are already, or before, become new in the Christian man. But to return:

After all the flourish you have made about the death of Christ, even as he is an expiatory, and propitiatory sacrifice, in conclusion, you terminate the business far short of that for which it was intended of God; for you almost make the effects thereof but a bare suspension of present justice and death for sin; or that which hath delivered us at present from a necessity of dying, that we might live unto God; that is, according as you have stated it, "That we might from principles of humanity and reason, act towards the first principles of morals, &c., till we put ourselves into a capacity of personal and actual pardon."

Ans. The sum of your doctrine therefore is, that Christ by his death only holds the point of the sword of justice, *not that he received it into his own soul;* that he suspends the curse from us, not that himself was made a curse for us; that the guilt might be remitted by our virtues, not that sin was made to be our sin : but Paul and the New Testament giveth us account far otherwise, viz., "that Christ was made our sin, our curse, and death, that we by him (not by the principle of pure humanity, or our obedience to your first principles of morals, &c.,) should be set free from the law of sin and death." (2 Cor. v. 21. Gal. iii. 13.)

If any object that Christ hath designed the purifying our hearts and natures, I answer, but he hath not designed to promote, or to perfect that righteousness that is founded on, and floweth from, the purity of our human nature; for then he must design the setting up man's righteousness, that which is of the law; and then he must design also the setting up that which is directly in opposition, both to the righteousness that of God is designed to justify us, and that by which we are inwardly made holy. As I have showed before.

You have therefore, Sir, in all that you have yet asserted, showed no other wisdom than a heathen, or of one that is short, even of a novice in the gospel.

In the next place, I might trace you chapter by chapter, and at large refute, not only the whole design of your book by a particular replication to them, but also sundry and damnable errors, that like venom drop from your pen.

But as before I told you in general, so here I tell you again, that neither the Scriptures of God, the promise or threatenings, the life or death, resurrection, ascension, or coming again of Christ to judgment, hath the least syllable or tendency in them to set up your heathenish and pagan holiness or righteousness, wherefore your whole discourse is but a mere abuse of, and corrupting the holy Scriptures, for the fastening, if it must have been, your errors upon the godly. I conclude then, upon the whole, that the gospel hath cast out man's righteousness to the dogs, and conclude that there is no such thing as a purity of human nature, as a principle in us, thereby to work righteousness withal. Farther, it never thought of returning us again to the holiness we lost in Adam, or to make our perfection to consist in the possession of so natural and ignorant a principle as that is, in all the things of the holy gospel; but hath declared another and far better way, which you can by no means understand by all the dictates of your humanity.

I will, therefore, content myself at present with gathering up some few errors, out of those abundance which are in your book, and so leave you to God, who can either pardon those grievous errors, or damn you for your pride and blasphemies.

You pretend in the beginning of your second chapter to prove your assertion, viz., "That the great errand that Christ came upon was to put us again into possession of that holiness which we had lost" (p. 12). For proof whereof you bring John the Baptist's doctrine, (Matt. iii. 1, 2,) and the angel's saying to Zacharias, (Luke i. 16, 17,) and the prophet Malachi, (Mal. iii. 1—3,) in which texts there is as much for your purpose, and no more, than there is in a perfect blank; for which of them speak a word of the righteousness or holiness which we have lost? or where is it said, either by these mentioned or by the whole Scriptures, that we are to be restored *to,* and put again into possession of, *that* holiness? These are but the dictates of your human nature.

John's ministry was, "to make ready a people prepared for the Lord Jesus;" not to possess them with themselves, and their own, but now lost, holiness. And so the angel told his father, saying, "Many of the children of Israel shall he turn to the Lord their God:" not to Adam's innocency, or to the holiness that we lost by him. Neither did the prophet Malachi prophesy that Christ at his coming should put men again in possession of the holiness we had lost. And I say again, as you here fall short of your purpose, so I challenge you to produce but one piece of a text, that in the least looketh to such a thing. The whole tenor of the scripture, that speaks of the errand of Christ Jesus, tells us another lesson, to wit, that he himself came to save us, and that by his *own* righteousness—not *that* in Adam, or which we have lost in him, unless you can say and prove that we had once, even before we were converted, the holiness of Christ within us, or the righteousness of Christ upon us.

But you yet get on, and tell us, " That this was also the prophesy of the angel to Joseph (p. 14), in these words, HE (Jesus) shall save his people from their sins." " Not (say you) from the punishment of them, although that be a true sense too ; but not the primary, but secondary, and implied only, and the consequence of the former salvation" (p. 15).

Ans. 1. Thus Penn the Quaker and you run in this in one and the selfsame spirit—he affirming that sanctification is antecedent to justification, but not the consequence thereof.

2. But what salvation ? Why salvation ? say you. First from the filth : for that is the primary and first sense ; justification from the guilt being the never-failing consequence of this. But how then must Jesus Christ first save us from the filth ? You add in p. 16, " that he shall bring in, instead of the ceremonial observations, a far more noble, viz., an inward substantial righteousness : and by abrogating that (namely, of the ceremonies) he shall establish only this inward righteousness." This is that holiness or righteousness you tell us of in the end of the chapter going before, that you acknowledge we had lost ; so that the sum of all that you have said is, that the way that Christ will take to save his people from their sins is, first, to restore unto them, and give them possession of the righteousness that they had lost in Adam : and having established this in them, he would acquit them also of guilt. But that this is a shameless error and blasphemy is apparent from what hath already been asserted of the nature of the holiness or righteousness that we have lost, viz., that it was only natural of the old covenant, typical : and such as might stand with perfect ignorance of the mediation of Jesus Christ : and now I add, that for Christ to come to establish this righteousness, is alone as if he should be sent from heaven to overthrow and abrogate the eternal purpose of grace, which the Father had purposed should be manifested to the world by Christ : for Christ came not to restore, or to give us possession of that which was once our own holiness, but to make us partakers of that which is in him, " that we might be made partakers of HIS holiness." Neither (were it granted that you speak the truth) is it possible for a man to be filled with inward gospel holiness and righteousness that yet abideth, as before the face of God, under the curse of the law, or the guilt of his own transgressions. (Heb. xii.) The guilt must therefore first be taken off, and we set free by faith in that blood that did it, before we can act upon pure Christian principles.

Pray tell me the meaning of this one text, which, speaking of Christ, saith, " Who, when he had by himself purged our sins, sat down on the right hand of the Majesty on high." (Heb. i. 3.) Tell me, I say, by this text, whether is here intended the sins of all that shall be saved ? If so, what kind of a purging is here meant, seeing thousands, and thousands of thousands, of the persons intended by this act of purging were not then in being, nor their personal sins in act ? And note, he saith, he purged them before he sat down at the right hand of God : purging them in this place cannot first, and primarily, respect the purging of the conscience : but the taking, the complete taking of the guilt, and so the curse from before the face of God, according to other scriptures : " He hath made him to be sin, and accursed of God for us." Now he being made the sin which we committed, and the curse which we deserved, there is no more sin nor curse—I mean, to be charged by the law—to damn, them that shall believe ; not that their believing takes away the curse, but puts the soul upon trusting to him, that before purged this guilt and curse : I say, before he sat down on the right hand of God, not to suspend, (as you would have it,) but to take away the sin of the world. " The Lord hath laid upon him the iniquities of us all," (Isa. liii. 6 ;) and he bare them in his own body on the tree. (1 Pet. ii. 24.) Nor yet that he should often offer himself, for then must he often have suffered since the foundation of the world : but now, (and that at once,) in the end of the world hath he appeared, to put away sin, by the sacrifice of himself. (Heb. ix. 24—26.) Mark, he did put it away by the sacrifice of his body and soul, when he died on the cross ; but he would not then put away the inward filth of those that then remained unconverted, or those that as yet wanted being in the world. The putting away of sin, therefore, that the Holy Ghost here intendeth, is, *such* a putting of it away as respecteth the guilt, curse, and condemnation thereof, as it stood by the accusations of the law, against all flesh before the face of God ; which guilt, curse, and condemnation Christ himself was made in that day when he died the death for us. And this is the first and principal intendment of the angel, in that blessed saying to godly Joseph, concerning Christ —" he shall save his people from their sins ;" from the guilt and curse due to them, first, and afterwards from the filth thereof. This is yet manifest, further, because the heart is purified by faith and hope. (Acts xv. 9. 1 John iii. 3.) Now it is not the nature of faith—I mean, of justifying faith—to have anything for an object, from which it fetcheth peace with God, and holiness before, or besides the Christ of God himself, for he is the way to the Father ; and no man can come to the Father but by him. Come ; that is, so as to find acceptance, and peace with him : the reason is, because without his blood, guilt remains. (Heb. ix. 22.) He hath made peace by the blood of his cross : so then, faith in the first place seeketh peace. But why peace first? Because till peace is fetched into the soul, by faith's laying hold on the blood of Christ, sin remains in the guilt and curse, though not in the sight of God, yet upon the conscience, through the power of unbelief: " He that believeth not, stands yet condemned." (John iii. 18, 19.) Now, so long as guilt and the curse in power remains, there is not purity, but unbelief; not joy, but doubting; not peace, but peevishness; not content, but murmuring, and anger, against the Lord himself. " The law worketh wrath." (Rom. iv. 15.) Wherefore, as yet there can be no purity of heart, because that faith yet wants his object: but having once found peace with God by believing what the blood of Christ hath done, joy followeth, so doth peace, quietness, content, and love; which is also the fulfilling of the law: yet not from such dungish principles as yours,—for so the apostle calls them (Phil. iii.),—but from the Holy Ghost itself; which God, by faith, hath granted to be received by them that believe in the blood of his Jesus.

But you add, that Christ giveth, first repentance, and then forgiveness of sins (p. 17).

Ans. 1. This makes nothing for the holiness which we lost in Adam : for the proof of which you bring that text, Acts v. 31.

2. But for Christ to take away guilt and the curse from before the face of God is one thing, and to make that discovery is another.

3. Again, Christ doth not give forgiveness for the sake of that repentance which hath its rise originally from the dictates of our own nature, which is the thing you are to prove; for that repentance is called the sorrow of this world, and must be again repented of : but the repentance mentioned in the text is that which comes from Christ.

4. But it cannot be for the sake of gospel-repentance that the forgiveness of sins is manifested, because both are his peculiar gift.

5. Therefore, both faith, and repentance, and forgiveness of sins, are given by Christ; and come to us, for the sake of that blessed offering of his body, once for all : for after he rose from the dead, having led captivity captive, and taken the curse from before the face of God, therefore his Father gave him gifts for men, even all the things that are necessary and effectual for our conversion and preservation in this world, &c. (Eph. iv. 8.)

This text therefore, with all the rest you bring, falleth short of the least show of proof, " That the great errand for which Christ came into the world was—to put us in possession of the holiness that we had lost."

Your third chapter is as empty of the proof of your design, as that through which we have passed, there being not one scripture therein cited that giveth the least intimation that ever it entered into the heart of Christ to put us again into possession of that holiness which we had before we were converted : for such was that we lost in Adam.

You tell us the sum of all is, " that we are com-manded to add to our faith, virtue," &c. (p. 25). I suppose you intend a gospel faith, which if you can prove Adam had before the fall, and that we lost this faith in him, and also that this gospel faith is none other but that which originally ariseth from or is the dictates of human nature, I will confess you have scripture and knowledge beyond me. In the meantime you must suffer me to tell you, you are as far in this from the mind of the Holy Ghost, as if you had yet never in all your days heard whether there be a Holy Ghost or no.

" Add to your faith :" the apostle here lays a gospel principle, viz., faith in the Son of God : which faith layeth hold of the forgiveness of sins alone for the sake of Christ; therefore he is a great way off of laying the purity of the human nature, the law, as written in the heart of natural man, as the principle of holiness ; from whence is produced good works in the soul of the godly.

In your fourth chapter also, (p. 28,) even in the beginning thereof, even with one text, you have overthrown your whole book,

This chapter is to prove, that the only design of the promises and threatenings of the gospel is to promote, and put us again in possession of, the holiness we had lost; for that the reader must still remember, is the only design of your book (p. 12). Whereas the first text you speak of, (2 Pet. i. 4,) maketh mention of the Divine nature, or of the Spirit of the living God, which is also received by the precious faith of Christ, and the revelation of the knowledge of him ; this blessed Spirit, and therefore not the dictates of human nature, is the principle that is laid in the godly : but Adam's holiness had neither the knowledge, or faith, or Spirit of the Lord Jesus, as its foundation or principle : yea, nature was his foundation, even his own nature was the original, from whence his righteousness and good works arose.

The next scriptures also, viz., 2 Cor. vii. 1. Rom. xii. 1, overthrow you; for they urge the promises as motives to stir us up to holiness. But Adam had neither the Spirit of Jesus, or faith in him, as a principle, nor any promises to him as motives; wherefore this was not that to which he, or which we Christians are exhorted to seek the possession of; but that which is operated by that Spirit which we receive by the faith of Jesus, and that which is encouraged by those promises, that God hath since given to them that have closed by faith with Jesus.

The rest also, (in p. 29,) not one of them doth promise us the possession of the holiness we have lost, or any mercy to them that have it.

You add, " And whereas the promises of pardon and of eternal life, are frequently made to *believing ;* there is nothing more evidently declared, than that this faith is such as purifieth the heart, and is productive of good works " (p. 30).

Ans. 1. If the promise be made at all to believing, it is not made to us upon the account of the holiness we had lost; for I tell you yet again, that holiness is not of faith, neither was faith the object thereof. But,

2. The promises of pardon, though they may be made to such a faith as is fruitful in good works, yet not to it, as it is fruitful in doing, but in receiving good. Sir, the quality of justifying faith is this—*not to work, but to believe*, as to the business of pardon of sin: and that not only because of the sufficiency that this faith sees in Christ to justify, but also for that it knows those whom God thus pardoneth, he justifieth as ungodly. "But to him that worketh not, but believeth," (mark, here faith and works are opposed)—"But to him that worketh not, but believeth on him that justifieth the ungodly, his faith is counted for righteousness." (Rom. iv. 5.)

You add farther, "That the promises may be reduced to these three heads—that of the Holy Spirit, of remission of sins, and eternal happiness, in the enjoyment of God" (p. 30).

Ans. If you can prove that any of these promises were made to the holiness that we had lost, or that by these promises we are to be possessed with that holiness again, I will even now lay down the bucklers. For albeit, the time will come when the saints shall be absolutely and perfectly sinless; yet then shall they be also spiritual, immortal, and incorruptible; which you cannot prove Adam was in the best of his holiness, even that which we lost in him.

The threatenings you speak of (p. 35) are every one made against sin, but not one of them to drive us into a possession of that holiness that we had lost; nay, contrariwise, he that looks to, or seeks after that, is as sure to be damned, and go to hell, as he that transgresseth the law; because that is not the righteousness of God, the righteousness of Christ, the righteousness of faith, nor that to which the promise is made.

And this was manifested to the world betimes, even in that day when God drove the man and his wife out of Eden, and placed cherubims and a flaming sword in the way by which they came out, to the end, that by going back by *that* way, they might rather be killed and die, than lay hold of the "tree of life." (Gen. iii.)

Which the apostle also respects, when he calleth the way of the gospel, the NEW and LIVING way, even that which is made by the blood of Christ, (Heb. x. 20,) concluding by this description of the way that is by blood, that the other is old, and the way of death, even that which is by the moral law, or the dictates of our nature, or by that fond conceit of the goodly holiness of Adam.

Your fifth chapter tells us, "that the promoting of holiness was the design of our Saviour's whole life and conversation among men" (p. 36).

Ans. 1. Were this granted, it reacheth nothing at all the design for which you in your way present us with it.

2. For that which you have asserted is, that the errand about which Christ came was, as the effecting our deliverance out of that sinful state we had

brought ourselves into, so to put us again into possession of that holiness which we had lost; for that, you say, is the business of your book (p. 12). Wherefore you should have told us in the head of this chapter, not so much that our Saviour designed the promoting of holiness in general by his life, but that the whole design of our Saviour's life and conversation was to put us again into possession of *that* holiness which we had lost—into a possession of that natural, old covenant, figurative, ignorant holiness. But it seems you count that there is no other than that now lost, but never again to be obtained holiness, that was in Adam.

3. Farther, you also falter here, as to the stating of the proposition; for in the beginning of your book, you state it thus: that the enduing men with inward real righteousness, or true holiness, was the ultimate end of our Saviour's coming into the world, still meaning the holiness we lost in Adam. You should therefore in this place also have minded your reader of this your proposition, and made it manifest, if you could, "that the ultimate end of our Saviour's whole life and conversation was the enduing men with this Adamitish holiness." But *holiness*, and *that* holiness, is alone with you; and to make it his end, and whole end—his business, and the whole business of his life—is but the same with you.

But you must know, that the whole life and conversation of our Saviour was intended for another purpose than to drive us back to, or to endue us with, such an holiness and righteousness as I have proved this to be.

You have therefore, in this your discourse, put an insufferable affront upon the Son of God, in making all his life and conversation to centre and terminate in the holiness we had lost: as if the Lord Jesus were sent down from heaven, and the word of God made flesh, that by a perfect life and conversation, he might show us how holy Adam was before he fell; or what an holiness that *our* holiness was, which we had before we were converted.

Your discourse, therefore, of the life and conversation of the Lord Jesus is none other than heathenish; for you neither treat of the principle, his Godhead, by which he did his works; neither do you in the least, in one syllable, aver the first, the main and prime reason of this his conversation—only you treat of it so far as a mean man might have considered it. And indeed it stood not with your design to treat aright with these things; for had you mentioned the first, though but once, your Babel had tumbled about your ears; for if in the holy Jesus did "dwell the word," one of the three in heaven, or if the Lord and Saviour Jesus Christ was truly, essentially, and naturally God, then must the principle from whence his works did proceed be better than the principle from whence proceeded the goodness in Adam; otherwise Adam must be God and man. Also you do, or may know, that the self-same act may be done from several principles; and again, that it is the principle from whence the act is done, and not the bare doing of the act, that makes it better or worse accepted, or not, in the eyes either of God or men.

Now then, *to show you the main*, or *chief design of the life and conversation of the Lord Jesus.*

First. It was not to show us what an excellent holiness we once had in Adam, but that thereby God, the eternal Majesty, according to his promise, might be seen by, and dwell with, mortal men: for the Godhead being altogether in its own nature invisible, and yet desirous to be seen by, and dwell with, the children of men, therefore was the Son, who is the self-same substance with the Father, closed with, or tabernacled in our flesh, that in that flesh, the nature and glory of the Godhead might be seen by, and dwell with us : "The word was made flesh, and dwelt among us, (and we beheld his glory, [what glory? the glory,] as of the only-begotten of the Father,) full of grace and truth." (John i. 14.) Again, "The life (that is, the life of God, in the works and conversation of Christ) was manifest, and we have seen it, and bear witness, and show unto you that eternal life which was with the Father, and was manifested unto us." (1 John i. 2.) And hence he is called the image of the invisible God, (Col. i. 15 ;) or he by whom the invisible God is most perfectly presented to the sons of men. Did I say before, that the God of glory is desirous to be seen of us ? Even so, also, have the pure in heart a desire that it should be so : "Lord, say they, show us the Father, and it sufficeth us." (John xiv. 8.) And therefore the promise is for their comfort, that "they shall see God." (Matt. v. 8.) But how then must they see him ? Why, in the person, and by the life and works of Jesus. When Philip, under a mistake, thought of seeing God some other way than in and by this Lord Jesus Christ, what is the answer? "Have I been so long time with you," saith Christ, "and hast thou not known me, Philip ? He that hath seen me, hath seen the Father ; and how sayest thou then, Show us the Father? Believest thou not that I am in the Father, and the Father in me ? The words that I speak unto you, I speak not of myself, but the Father, that dwelleth in me, he doth the works. Believe me, that I am in the Father, and the Father in me ; or else believe me for the very work's sake." (John xiv. 9—11.) See here, that both the words and works of the Lord Jesus were not to show you, and so to call you back to, the holiness that we had lost, but to give us visions of the perfections that are in the Father. He hath given us "the knowledge of the glory of God in the face of Jesus Christ." (2 Cor. iv. 6.) And hence it is that the apostle, in that brief collection of the wonderful mystery of godliness, placeth this in the front thereof: "God was manifest in the flesh." (1 Tim. iii. 16.) Was manifest, viz., in and by the person of Christ, when in the flesh he lived among us ; manifest, I say, for this, as one reason, that the pure in heart, who long after nothing more, might see him. "I

beseech thee," said Moses, "show me thy glory." "And will God indeed dwell with men on the earth ?" saith Solomon.

Now to fulfil the desires of them that fear him, hath he showed himself in flesh unto them ; which discovery principally is made by the word and works of Christ. But,

Second. Christ by his words and works of righteousness, in the days of his flesh, neither showed us which was, nor called us back to the possession of, the holiness that we had lost ; but did perfect, in and by himself, the law for us, that we had broken. Man being involved in sin and misery, by reason of transgression committed against the law, or ministration of death, and being utterly unable to recover himself therefrom, the Son of God himself assumeth the flesh of man, and for sin condemned sin in that flesh ; and that first, by walking, through the power of his eternal Spirit, in the highest perfection to every point of the whole law, in its most exact and full requirements ; which was to be done, not only without commixing sin in his doing, but by one that was perfectly without the least being of it in his nature ; yea, by one that now was God-man, because it was God whose law was broken, and whose justice was offended : for, were it now possible to give a man possession of that holiness that he hath lost in Adam, that holiness could neither in the principle nor act deliver from the sin by him before committed. This is evident by many reasons, first, because it is not a righteousness able to answer the demands of the law for sin ; *that* requiring not only a perfect abiding in the thing commanded, but a satisfaction by death, for the transgression committed against the law. "The wages of sin is death." (Rom. vi. 23.) Wherefore he that would undertake the salvation of the world, must be one who can do both these things ; one that can perfectly do the demands of the law in thought, word, and deed, without the least commixture of the least sinful thought in the whole course of his life : he must be also able to give by death, even by the death that hath the curse of God in it, a complete satisfaction to the law for the breach thereof. Now this could none but Christ accomplish ; none else having power to do it. "I have power (said he) to lay down my life, and I have power to take it again : and this commandment have I received of my Father." (John x. 18.) This work then must be done, not by another earthly Adam, but by the Lord from heaven ; by one that can abolish sin, destroy the devil, kill death, and rule as Lord in heaven and earth. Now the words and works of the Lord Jesus declared him to be such a one. He was first without sin ; then he did no sin ; neither could either the devil, the whole world, or the law, find any deceit in his mouth : but by being under the law, and walking in the law, by that Spirit which was the Lord God of the law, he not only did always the things that pleased the Father, but by that means in man's flesh, he did perfectly accomplish and fulfil that law which all flesh stood condemned by. It is a foolish and an heathenish thing, nay worse, to think that the Son of God should only, or specially fulfil, or perfect the law, " and the prophets, by giving more and higher instances of moral duties than were before expressly given" (p. 17). This would have been but the lading of men with heavy burthens. But know then, whoever thou art that readest, that Christ's exposition of the law was more to show thee the perfection of his own obedience, than to drive thee back to the holiness thou hadst lost; for God sent him to fulfil it, by doing it, and dying to the most sore sentence it could pronounce: not as he stood a single person, but common, as Mediator between God and man ; making up in himself the breach that was made by sin betwixt God and the world. For,

Third. He was to die as a lamb, as a lamb without blemish, and without spot, according to the type : " Your Lamb shall be without blemish." (Exod. xii. 5.) But because there was none such to be found BY and AMONG all the children of men, therefore God sent HIS from heaven. Hence John calls him the Lamb of God, (John i. 29,) and Peter him that was without spot, who washed us by his blood. (1 Pet. i. 18, 19.) Now, wherein doth it appear that he was without spot and blemish but as he walked in the law ? These words, therefore, " without spot," are the sentence of the law, who, searching him, could find nothing in him why he should be slain, yet he died because there was sin. Sin ! where ? Not in him, but in his people : " For the transgression of my people was he stricken." (Isa. liii. 8.) He died, then, for our sins, and qualified himself so to do, by coming sinless into the world, and by going sinless through it; for had he not done both these, he must have died for himself. But being God, even in despite of all that stumble at him, he conquered death, the devil, sin, and the curse, by himself, and then sat down at the right hand of God.

Fourth. And because he hath a second part of his priestly office to do in heaven, therefore it was thus requisite that he should thus manifest himself to be holy and harmless, undefiled, and separate from sinners on the earth, (Heb. vii. 26,) as Aaron first put on the holy garments, and then went into the holiest of all. The life, therefore, and conversation of our Lord Jesus, was to show us with what a curious robe and girdle he went into the holy place, and not to show us with what an Adamitish holiness he would possess his own. " Such an high priest became us, who is holy, harmless, and undefiled, separate from sinners, and made higher than the heavens," that he might always be accepted, both in person and offering, when he presenteth his blood to God, the atonement for sin. Indeed, in some things he was an example to us to follow him ; but mark, it was not as he was Mediator, not as he was under the law to God, not as he died for sin, nor as he maketh

reconciliation for iniquity. But in these things consist the life of our soul, and the beginning of our happiness. He was then exemplary to us, as he carried it meekly and patiently, and self-denyingly towards the world : but yet not so neither to any but such to whom he first offered justification by the means of his own righteousness ; for before he saith " learn of me," he saith " I will give you rest," rest from the guilt of sin, and fear of everlasting burnings. (Matt. xi.) And so Peter first tells us he died for our sins, and next, that he left us an example. (1 Pet. ii. 21.) But should it be granted that the whole of Christ's life and conversation among men was for our example, and for no other end at all but that we should learn to live by his example, yet it would not follow, but be as far from truth as the ends of the earth are asunder, that by this means he sought to possess us with the holiness we had lost, for that he had not in himself. It is true he was born without sin, yet born God and man; he lived in the world without sin, but he lived as God-man ; he walked in and up to the law, but it was as God-man. Neither did his manhood, even in those acts of goodness, which as to action, most properly respected it, do aught without, but by and in conjunction with his Godhead : wherefore all and every whit of the righteousness and good that he did was that of God-man, the righteousness of God. But this was not Adam's principle, nor any holiness that we had lost.

Your fifth chapter, therefore, consisteth of words spoken to the air.

Your sixth chapter tells us, " That to make men truly virtuous and holy was the design of Christ's inimitable actions, or mighty works and miracles; and these did only tend to promote it" (p. 68).

He neither did nor needed so much as one small piece of a miracle to persuade men to seek for the holiness which they had lost, or to give them again possession of that; for that, as I have showed— though you would feign have it otherwise—is not at all the Christian, or gospel-righteousness. Wherefore, in one word, you are as short by this chapter to prove your natural old covenant, promiseless, figurative holiness, to be here designed, as if you had said so much as amounts to nothing. Further, Christ needed not to work a miracle to persuade men to fall in love with themselves, and their own natural dictates; to persuade them that they have a purity of the human nature in them, or that the holiness which they have lost is the only, true, real, and substantial holiness. These things, both corrupted nature and the devil, have of a long time fastened, and fixed in their minds.

His miracles, therefore, tend rather to take men off of the pursuit after the righteousness or holiness that we had lost, and to confirm unto us the truth of a far more excellent and blessed thing; to wit, the righteousness of God, of Christ, of faith, of the Spirit, which that you speak of never knew; neither is it possible that he should know it who is hunting for your sound complexion, your purity of human nature, or its dictates, as the only true, real, and substantial righteousness. "They are ignorant of God's righteousness, that go about to establish their own righteousness;" and neither have, nor can, without a miracle, submit themselves unto the righteousness of God. They cannot submit *themselves* thereto; talk thereof they may, notion it they may, profess it too they may; but for a man to submit *himself* thereto is by the mighty power of God.

Miracles and signs are for them that believe not. (1 Cor. xiv. 22.) Why for them? That they might believe; therefore their state is reckoned fearful that have not yet believed for all his wondrous works. And though he did so many miracles among them, yet they believed him not. (John xii. 37—40.) But what should they believe? That Jesus is the true Messiah, the Christ that should come into the world. Do you say that I blaspheme, (saith Christ,) because I said I am the Son of God? "if I do not the works of my Father, believe me not; but if I do, though you believe not me, believe the works, that ye may know and believe that the Father is in me, and I in him." (John x. 37, 38.) But what is it to believe that he is Messiah, or Christ? Even to believe that this man Jesus was ordained, and appointed of God (and that before all worlds) to be the Saviour of men, by accomplishing in himself an everlasting righteousness for them, and by bearing their sins in his body on the tree; that it was he that was to reconcile us to God, by the body of his flesh, when he hanged on the cross. This is the doctrine that at the beginning Christ preached to that learned ignorant Nicodemus. "As Moses," said he, "lifted up the serpent in the wilderness, so must the Son of man be lifted up, that whosoever believeth in him should not perish, but have eternal life." (John iii. 14, 15.) The serpent was lifted up upon a pole, (Numb. xxi. 1, 10:) "Christ was hanged on a tree." The serpent was lifted up for murmurers: "Christ was hanged up for sinners." The serpent was lifted up for them that were bitten with fiery serpents, the fruits of their wicked murmuring: Christ was hanged up for them that are bitten with guilt, the rage of the devil, and the fear of death and wrath. The serpent was hanged up to be looked on: Christ was hanged up that we might believe in him, that we might have faith in his blood. They that looked upon the serpent of brass lived: they that believe in Christ shall be saved, and shall never perish. Was the serpent, then, lifted up for them that were good and godly? No, but for the sinners: "So God commended his love to us, in that, while we were yet sinners, Christ died for us." But what if they that were stung could not, because of the swelling of their face, look up to the brazen serpent? then without remedy they die. So he that believeth not in Christ shall be damned. But might they not be healed by humbling themselves? one would think that better than to live by looking up only. No, only looking up did it, when death swallowed up them that looked not. This, then, is the doctrine: "Christ came into the world to save sinners:" according to the proclamation of Paul, "Be it known unto you, therefore, men and brethren, that through this man is preached unto you the forgiveness of sins; and by him all that believe are justified from all things, from which ye could not be justified by the law of Moses." The forgiveness of sins; but what is meant by forgiveness? Forgiveness doth strictly respect the debt or punishment that by sin we have brought upon ourselves. But how are we by this man forgiven this? because by his blood he hath answered the justice of the law, and so made amends to an offended Majesty. Besides, this man's righteousness is made over to him that looks up to him for life; yea, that man is made the righteousness of God in him. This is the doctrine that the miracles were wrought to confirm, and that both by Christ and his apostles, and not that holiness and righteousness that is the fruit of a feigned purity of our nature.

Take two or three instances for all.

First. "Then came the Jews round about him, and said unto him, How long dost thou make us to doubt? If thou be the Christ, tell us plainly. Jesus answered them, I told you, and ye believed not: the works that I do in my Father's name, they bear witness of me. But ye believe not, because ye are not of my sheep." (John x. 24—26.)

By this scripture the Lord Jesus testifies what was the end of his words and wondrous works, viz., that men might know that he was the Christ; that he was sent of God to be the Saviour of the world; and that these miracles required of them, first of all, that they accept of him by believing; a thing little set by, by our author, for in p. 299, he preferreth his doing righteousness far before it, and above all things else: his words are verbatim thus, "Let us exercise ourselves unto real and substantial godliness, (such as he hath described in the first part of his book, viz., that which is the dictates of his human nature, &c.,) and in keeping our consciences void of offence, both towards God and towards men, and in studying the gospel to enable us, not to discourse, or only to believe, but also, and above all things, to do well." But believing, though not with this man, yet by Christ and his wondrous miracles, is expected first, and above ALL things, from men; and to do well, in the best sense, (though his sense is the worst,) is that which by the gospel is to come after.

Second. "Go into all the world, and preach the gospel unto every creature. He that believeth and is baptized shall be saved; but he that believeth not shall be damned. And these signs shall follow them that believe: in my name shall they cast out devils; they shall speak with new tongues; they shall take up serpents; and if they drink any deadly thing, it shall not hurt them," &c. (Mark xvi. 15—18.)

Mark you here, it is believing, *believing;* it is, I say, believing that is here required by Christ.

Believing what? The gospel; even good tidings to sinners by Jesus Christ; good tidings of good, glad tidings of good things. Mark how the apostle hath it; the glad tidings is, "That through this man [Jesus] is preached unto you the forgiveness of sins; and by him all that believe are justified from all things, from which ye could not be justified by the law of Moses." (Acts xiii. 38, 39.)

These signs shall follow them that believe. Mark, signs before, and signs after, and all to excite to and confirm the weight of believing. "And they went forth and preached everywhere; the Lord working with them, and confirming the word with signs following. Amen." (Mark xvi. 20.)

Third. "Therefore we ought to give the more earnest heed to the things that we have heard, lest at any time we should let them slip. For if the word spoken by angels was steadfast, and every transgression and disobedience received a just recompence of reward, how shall we escape if we neglect so great salvation; which at the first began to be spoken by the Lord, and was confirmed unto us by them that heard him; God also bearing them witness with signs and wonders, and with divers miracles and gifts of the Holy Ghost, according to his own will." (Heb. ii. 1—4.)

Here we are excited to the faith of the Lord Jesus, under these words, "so great salvation." As if he had said, give earnest heed, the most earnest heed, to the doctrine of the Lord Jesus, because it is "so great salvation." What this salvation is he tells us; it is that which was preached by the Lord himself: "For God so loved the world, that he gave his only-begotten Son, that whosoever believeth in him should not perish, but have everlasting life." (John iii. 16.) God *so* loved, that he gave his Son to be "so great salvation." Now, as is expressed in the text, to be the better for this salvation, is, to give heed to hear it; for "faith cometh by hearing." (Rom. x. 17.)

He saith not give heed to doing, but to the word you have *heard;* faith, I say, cometh by hearing, and hearing by the word of God. (Rom. x.) But that this hearing is the hearing of faith, is further evident.

1. Because he speaketh of a great salvation, accomplished by the love of God in Christ, accomplished by his blood. "By his own blood he entered in once into the holy place, having obtained eternal redemption for us." (Heb. ix. 12.)

2. This salvation is set in opposition to that which was propounded before, by the ministration of angels, which consisted in a law of works; that which Moses received to give to the children of Israel. "For the law"—a command to works and duties—was given by Moses; but "grace and truth came by Jesus Christ." (John i. 17.) To live by doing works is the doctrine of the law and Moses; but to live by faith and grace is the doctrine of Christ, and the gospel.

Besides, the threatening being pressed with an "How shall we escape?" respects still a better, a freer, a more gracious way of life, than either the moral or ceremonial law; for both these were long before: but here comes in another way, not that propounded by Moses, or the angels, but since by the Lord himself. "How shall we escape, if we neglect so great salvation; which at the first began to be spoken by the Lord, and was confirmed unto us by them that heard him." (Heb. ii. 3.)

Now mark, it is this salvation, this so great and eternal salvation, that was obtained by the blood of the Lord himself; it was this, even to confirm faith in this, that the God of heaven himself came down, to confirm by signs and wonders: "God bearing them witness, both with signs and wonders, and with divers miracles, and gifts of the Holy Ghost, according to his own will." (Heb. xx. 4.)

Thus we see, that to establish a holiness that came from the first principles of morals in us, or that ariseth from the dictates of our human nature, or to drive us back to that figurative holiness that we had once, but lost in Adam, is little thought on by Jesus Christ, and as little intended by any of the gospel miracles.

A word or two more. The tribute money you mention, p. 72, was not as you would clawingly insinuate, for no other purpose than to show Christ's loyalty to the magistrate: but first, and above all, to show his Godhead, to confirm his gospel, and then to show his loyalty, the which, Sir, the persons you secretly smite at, have respect for, as much as you.

Again, also the curse of the barren fig-tree, mentioned p. 73, was not (if the Lord himself may be believed) to give us an emblem of a person void of good works; but to show his disciples the power of faith, and what a wonder-working thing that blessed grace is. Wherefore, when the disciples wondered at that sudden blast that was upon the tree, Jesus answered not, Behold an emblem of one void of moral virtues; but, "Verily, I say unto you, if ye have faith, and doubt not, ye shall not only do this which is done to the fig-tree, but also if ye shall say unto this mountain, Be thou removed, and be thou cast into the sea, it shall be done; and all things whatsoever ye shall ask in prayer, believing, ye shall receive." (Matt. xxi. 21, 22.) Again, Mark saith, when Peter saw the fig-tree that the Lord had cursed dried up from the roots, he said to his master, "Behold, the fig-tree which thou cursedst is withered away." (Mark xi. 21.) Christ now doth not say as you, This tree was an emblem of a professor void of good works: but, "Have faith in, or the faith of God; for, verily I say unto you, that whosoever shall say unto this mountain, Be thou removed, and be thou cast into the sea, and shall not doubt in his heart, but shall believe that those things which he saith shall come to pass, he shall have whatsoever he saith: therefore I say unto you, What things soever ye desire, when ye pray, believe that ye receive them, and ye shall have them." Christ Jesus therefore had a higher, and a better end, than that which you propound, in his cursing the barren fig-tree, even to show, as himself expounds it, the mighty power of faith; and how it lays hold of things in heaven, and tumbleth before it things on earth. Wherefore your scriptureless exposition doth but lay you even Solomon's proverb, "The legs of the lame are not equal," &c. (Prov. xxvi. 7.)

I might enlarge; but enough of this: only here I add, that the wonders and miracles that attend the gospel were wrought, and are recorded, to persuade to faith in Christ. By faith in Christ men are justified from the curse and judgment of the law. This faith worketh by love, by the love of God it brings up the heart to God, and goodness; but not by your covenant, (Ezek. xvi. 61;) not by principles of human nature, but of the Spirit of God; not in a poor, legal, old covenant, promiseless, ignorant, shadowish natural holiness, but by the Holy Ghost.

I come now to your seventh chapter; but to that I have spoken briefly already, and therefore here shall be the shorter.

In this chapter you say, "that to make men holy was the design of Christ's death" (p. 78).

Ans. 1. But not with your described principles of humanity, and dictates of human nature. He designed not, as I have fully proved, neither by his death nor life, to put us into a possession of the holiness which we had lost, though the proof of that be the business of your book.

2. To make men holy, was doubtless designed by the death and blood of Christ; but the way and manner of the proceeding of the Holy Ghost therein, you write not of, although the first text you mention (pp. 78, 79) doth fairly present you with it. For the way to make men inwardly holy by the death and blood of Christ, is, first, to possess them with the knowledge of this—that their sins were crucified with him, or that he did bear them in his body on the tree. "Knowing this, that our old man is crucified with him, that the body of sin might be destroyed, that henceforth we should not serve sin." (Rom. vi. 6.) So he died for all, that they that live should not henceforth live unto themselves, (as you would have them,) nor to the law or dictates of their own nature, as your doctrine would persuade them; "but to him that died for them, and rose again." (2 Cor. v. 14.)

There are two things, in the right stating of the doctrine of the effects of the death and blood of Christ, that do naturally effect in us an holy principle, and also a life becoming such a mercy.

First. For that by it we are set at liberty, by faith therein, from the guilt and curse that is due to guilt, from death, the devil, and the wrath to come. No encouragement to holiness like this, like the persuasion and belief of this; because this carrieth in it the greatest expression of love that we are capable of hearing or believing, and there is nothing that worketh on us so powerfully as love. "Herein is love, not that we loved God, but that he loved us, and sent his Son to be the

propitiation for our sins." (1 John iv. 10.) He then that by faith can see that the body of his sin did hang upon the cross, by the body of Christ, and that can see by that action, death and sin, the devil and hell, destroyed for him, it is he that will say, "Bless the Lord, O my soul, and all that is within me bless his holy name," &c. (Ps. ciii. 1—4.)

Second. Moreover, the knowledge of this giveth a man to understand this mystery, that Christ and himself are united in one: for faith saith, if our old man was crucified with Christ, then were we also reckoned in him, when he hanged on the cross: "I am crucified with Christ." (Gal. ii. 20.) All the elect did mystically hang upon the cross in Christ. "We then are dead to the law, and sin, first, by the body of Christ." (Rom. vii. 4.) Now he that is dead is free from sin; now if we be dead with Christ, we believe that we shall live with him, knowing that Christ being raised from the dead, dieth no more, death hath no more dominion over him; for in that he died, he died unto sin once; but in that he liveth, he liveth unto God; likewise reckon yourselves also dead unto sin, but alive unto God, through Jesus Christ our Lord. (Rom. vi.) This also Peter doth lively discourse of: "Forasmuch then," saith he, "as Christ hath suffered for us in the flesh, arm yourselves likewise with the same mind; for he that hath suffered in the flesh hath ceased from sin." (1 Pet. iv. 1, 2.) By which words he insinuateth the mystical union that is between Christ the head, and the elect his body; arguing from the suffering of a part, there should be a sympathy in the whole. If Christ then suffered for us, we were (even our sins, bodies and soul) reckoned in him when he so suffered. Wherefore, by his sufferings, the wrath of God for us is appeased, the curse is taken from us: for as Adam, by his acts of rebellion, made all that were in him guilty of his wickedness, so Christ, by his acts and doings of goodness and justice, made all that were reckoned in him good and just also. But as Adam's transgression did first and immediately reside with and remain in the person of Adam only, and the imputation of that transgression to them that sprang from him, so the goodness and justice that was accomplished by the second Adam, first and immediately resideth in him, and is made over to his also, by the imputation of God. But again, as they that were in Adam, stood not only guilty of sin, by imputation, but polluted by the filth that possessed him at his fall, so the children of the second Adam do not only (though first) stand just by virtue of the imputation of the personal acts of justice and goodness done by Christ, but they also receive of that inward quality, the grace and holiness that was in him at the day of his rising from the dead.

Thus therefore come we to be holy—by the death and blood of the Lord; this also is the contents of those other scriptures, which abusively you cite to justify your assertion, to wit, "that the great errand of Christ in coming into the world was—to put us again into possession of the holiness which we had lost: and that only designed the establishing such a holiness, as is sealed originally in our natures, and originally dictates of the human nature." The rest of the chapter being spoken to already, I pass it, and proceed to the next.

Your eighth chapter tells us, "that it is only the promoting of the design of making men holy that is aimed at by the apostles' insisting on the doctrines of Christ's resurrection, ascension, and coming again to judgment."

Though this should be granted, as indeed it ought not, yet there is not one syllable in all their doctrines that tendeth in the least to drive men back to the possession of the holiness we had lost; which is still the thing asserted by you, and that for the proof of which you make this noise and ado. Neither did Christ at all design the promoting of holiness by such principles as you have asserted in your book; neither doth the holy Spirit of God either help us in or excite us to our duty SIMPLY from such natural principles.

But the apostles in these doctrines you mention had far other glorious designs; such as were truly gospel, and tended to strengthen our faith yet further: as,

First. For the resurrection of Christ; they urged that, as an undeniable argument, of his doing away sin by his sacrificing and death: "he was delivered for our offences," because he put himself into the room and state of the wicked, as undertaking their deliverance from death, and the everlasting wrath of God. Now putting himself into their condition, he bears their sins and dies their death; but how shall we know that by undertaking this work he did accomplish the thing he intended? The answer is, "He was raised again for our justification," (Rom. iv. 25;) even to make it manifest that by the offering of himself he had purged our sins from before the face of God. For in that he was raised again, and that by him, for the appeasing of whose wrath he was delivered up to death, it is evident that the work for us, was by him effectually done: for God raised him up again. And hence it is that Paul calls the resurrection of Christ, "the sure mercies of David. And as concerning that he raised him up from the dead, now no more to return to corruption, he saith on this wise, I will give you the sure mercies of David." (Acts xiii. 34.) For Christ having conquered and overcome death, sin, the devil, and the curse, by himself, as it is manifest he did, by his rising from the dead, what now remains for him, for whom he did this, but mercy and goodness for ever?

Wherefore the resurrection of Christ is that which sealeth the truth of our being delivered from the wrath by his blood.

Second. As to his ascension they [the apostles] urge, and make use of that, for divers weighty reasons also.

1. As a further testimony yet, of the sufficiency of his righteousness to justify sinners withal: for if he that undertaketh the work is yet entertained by him, whose wrath he was to appease thereby, what is it, but that he hath so completed that work? Wherefore he saith that the Holy Ghost shall convince the world, that he hath a sufficient righteousness, and that because he went to the Father, and they saw him no more, (John xvi.,) because he, when he ascended up to the Father, was there entertained, accepted, and embraced of God. That is an excellent word. " He is chosen of God, and precious:" chosen of God to be the righteousness, that his Divine Majesty is pleased with and takes complacency in. God hath chosen, exalted, and set down Christ at his own right hand; for the sweet savour that he smelled in his blood, when he died for the sins of the world.

2. By his ascension he showeth how he returned conqueror and victor over our enemies. His ascension was his going home, from whence he came to deliver us from death: now it is said that when he returned home, or ascended, " he led captivity captive," (Eph. iv. ;) that is, carried them prisoners whose prisoners we were: he rode to heaven in triumph, having in chains the foes of believers.

3. In that he ascended, it was that he might perform for us the second part of his priestly office, or mediatorship. He is gone into heaven itself, there, " now to appear in the presence of God for us." (Heb. ix. 24.) "Wherefore, he is able also to save them to the uttermost, that come to God by him, (as indifferent a thing as you make it to be,) seeing he ever liveth (viz., in heaven, whither he is ascended) to make intercession for them." (Heb. vii. 25.)

4. He ascended that he might be exalted not only above, but be made head over all things to the church. "Wherefore now in heaven, as the Lord in whose hand is all power, he ruleth over both men and devils, sin and death, hell and all calamities, for the good and profit of his body, the church." (Eph. i. 19—23.)

5. He ascended to prepare a place for us, who shall live and die in the faith of Jesus. (John xiv. 1—3.)

6. He ascended because there he was to receive the Holy Ghost, the great promise of the New Testament; that he might communicate of that unto his chosen ones, to give them light to see his wonderful salvation, and to be as a principle of holiness in their souls: "for the Holy Ghost was not yet given, because that Jesus was not yet glorified." (John vii. 39.) But when he ascended on high, even as he led captivity captive, so he received gifts for men; by which gifts he meaneth the Holy Ghost, and the blessed and saving operations thereof. (Luke xxiv. Acts i. 2.)

Third. As to his coming again to judgment, that doctrine is urged to show the benefit that the godly will have at that day, when he shall gather together his elect and chosen from one end of heaven unto the other. As also to show you what an end he will make with those who have not obeyed his gospel. (Matt. xxv. 2 Thess. i. 8. 1 Pet. iii. 7—11.)

Now it is true, all these doctrines do forcibly produce an holy and heavenly life, but neither from your principles, nor to the end you propound; to wit, that we should be put into possession of our first, old covenant righteousness, and act from human and natural principles.

Your ninth chapter is spent, as you suppose, to show us the nature and evil of sin; but because you do it more like a heathen philosopher than a minister of the gospel, I shall not much trouble myself therewith.

Your tenth chapter consisteth in a commendation of virtue, but still of that, and no other, though counterfeited for another, than at first you have described, (chap. i.,) even such, which is as much in the heathens you make mention of, as in any other man, being the same both in root and branches, which is naturally to be found in all men, even as is sin and wickedness itself. And hence you call it here, a living up to your feigned "highest principle, like a creature possessed of a mind and reason." Again, "While we do thus, we act most agreeably to the right frame and temper of our souls, and consequently most naturally; and all the actions of nature are confessedly very sweet and pleasant;" of which very thing you say, "the heathens had a very great sense " (pp. 113, 114).

Ans. No marvel, for it was their work, not to search the deep things of God, but those which be the things of a man, and to discourse of that righteousness and principle of holiness which was naturally founded, and found within themselves, as men; or, as you say, " as creatures possessed with a mind and reason." But as I have already showed, all this may be where the Holy Ghost and faith is absent, even by the dictates, as you call them, of human nature; a principle, and actions, when trusted to that, as much please the devil as any wickedness that is committed by the sons of men. I should not have thus boldly inserted it, but that yourself did tell me of it, (p. 101 :) but I believe it was only extorted from you; your judgment and your Apollo suit not here, though indeed the devil is in the right,—for this righteousness and holiness which is our own, and of ourselves, is the greatest enemy to Jesus Christ: the post against his post, and the wall against his wall. "I came not to call the righteous, (puts you quit of the world,) but sinners to repentance."

Your eleventh chapter is to show what a miserable creature that man is that is destitute of your holiness.

Ans. And I add, as miserable is he that hath or knoweth no better. For such an one is under the curse of God, because he abideth in the law of works, or in the principles of his own nature, which neither can cover his sins from the sight of God, nor possesss him with faith or the Holy Ghost.

There are two things in this chapter, that proclaim you to be ignorant of Jesus Christ.

First. You say, it is not possible a wicked man should have God's pardon (pp. 119, 130).

Second. You suppose it to be impossible for Christ's righteousness to be imputed to an unrighteous man (p. 120).

Ans. To both which, a little briefly; God doth not use to pardon *painted* sinners, but such as are really so. Christ died for sinners, (1 Tim. i. 15;) and God justifieth the ungodly, (Rom. v. 6—9;) even him that worketh not, (Rom. iv. 3, 5;) nor hath no works to make him godly. (Rom. ix. 18. Isa. xxxiii. 11.) Besides, pardon supposeth sin; now he that is a sinner is a wicked man, by nature a child of wrath, and, as such, an object of the curse of God, because he hath broken the law of God. But such God pardoneth, not because they have made themselves holy, or have given up themselves to the law of nature, or to the dictates of their human principles, but because he will be gracious, and because he will give to his beloved Son Jesus Christ, the benefit of his blood.

As to the second head, what need is there that the righteousness of Christ should be imputed where men are righteous first? God useth not thus to do; his righteousness is for the "stout-hearted, that are far from righteousness." (Isa. xlvi. 12.)

The believing of Abraham was while yet he was uncircumcised; and circumcision was added, not to save him by, but as a seal of the righteousness of that faith which he had, being yet uncircumcised. Now we know that circumcision in the flesh was a type of circumcision in the heart, (Rom. ii.;) wherefore the faith that Abraham had before his outward circumcision, was to show us that faith, if it be right, layeth hold upon the righteousness of Christ, before we be circumcised inwardly: and this must needs be so; for if faith doth purify the heart, then it must be there *before* the heart is perished. Now this inward circumcision is a seal, or sign of this: that that is the only saving faith, that layeth hold upon Christ before we be circumcised. But he that believeth before he be inwardly circumcised, must believe in another, in a righteousness without him, and that, as he standeth at present in himself ungodly, for he is not circumcised; which faith, if it be right, approveth itself also so to be, by an after work of circumcising inwardly. But, I say, the soul that thus layeth hold on Christ, taketh the only way to please his God, because this is that also which himself hath determined shall be accomplished upon us. "Now to him that worketh, is the reward, not reckoned of grace, but of debt; but to him that worketh not, but believeth in him that justifieth the ungodly, his faith is counted for righteousness." (Rom. iv.) He that is ungodly, hath a want of righteousness, even of the inward righteousness of works: but what must become of him? Let him believe in him that justifieth the ungodly, because, for that purpose, there is in him a righteousness. We will now return to Paul himself; he had righteousness before he was justified by Christ, yet he chose to be justified rather as an unrighteous man, than as one endued with so brave a qualification. That I may "be found in him, not having mine own righteousness;" away with mine own righteousness; I choose rather to be justified as ungodly, by the righteousness of Christ, than by mine own, and his together. (Phil. iii.)

You argue therefore, like him that desireth to be a teacher of the law, nay, worse, that neither knoweth what he saith, nor whereof he affirmeth. But you say—"Were it possible that Christ's righteousness could be imputed to an unrighteous man, I dare boldly affirm that it would signify as little to his happiness, while he continueth so, as would a gorgeous, and splendid garment, to one that is almost starved," &c. (p. 120).

Ans. 1.—That Christ's righteousness is imputed to men, while sinners, is sufficiently testified by the word of God. (Ezek. xvi. 1—8. Zech. iii. 1—5. Rom. iii. 24, 25; iv. 1—5; v. 6—9. 2 Cor. v. 18 —21. Phil. iii. 6—8. 1 Tim. i. 15, 16. Rev. i. 5.)

2. And that the sinner, or unrighteous man, is happy in this imputation, is also as abundantly evident. For,

(1.) The wrath of God, and the curse of the law, are both taken off by this imputation.

(2.) The graces and comforts of the Holy Ghost are all entailed to, and followers of, this imputation. "Blessed is he to whom the Lord will not impute sin." It saith not, that he is blessed that hath not sin *to* be imputed, but he to whom God will not impute them; he saith, therefore, the non-imputation of sin, doth not argue a non-being thereof in the soul, but a glorious act of grace, imputing the sufficiency of Christ's righteousness to justify him that is yet ungodly.

But what blessedness doth follow the imputation of the righteousness of Christ, to one that is yet ungodly?

Ans. Even the blessing of Abraham, to wit, "Grace and eternal life: for Christ was made the curse and death that was due to us as sinners; that the blessing of Abraham might come upon the Gentiles, through faith in Jesus Christ; that we might receive the promise of the Spirit through faith." (Gal. iii. 13, 14.) Now faith hath its eye upon two things, with respect to its act of justifying. First, it acknowledgeth that the soul is a sinner, and then, that there is a sufficiency in the righteousness of Christ, to justify it in the sight of God, though a sinner.

We have believed in Jesus Christ, that we might be justified by the faith of Christ, and not by the works of the law; therefore, they that believe aright, receive righteousness, even the righteousness of another, to justify them, while yet in themselves they are sinners.

Why do they believe in Christ? The answer is:

that they *might* be justified, not because in their own eyes they are. They therefore at present stand condemned in themselves, and *therefore* they believe in Jesus Christ, that they *might* be set free from present condemnation. Now being justified by his blood, as ungodly, they shall be saved by his life, that is, by his intercession: for whom he justifieth by his blood, he saveth by his intercession; for by that is given the spirit, faith, and all grace that preserveth the elect unto eternal life and glory.

I conclude, therefore, that you argue not gospelly, in that you so *boldly affirm* that it would signify as little to the happiness of one, to be justified by Christ's righteousness, while a sinner, as would a gorgeous and splendid garment to one that is ready to perish. For farther, thus to be justified, is meat and drink to the sinner; and so the beginning of eternal life in him. "My flesh is meat indeed," said Christ, "and my blood is drink indeed; and he that eateth my flesh and drinketh my blood, hath eternal, or everlasting life." He affirmeth it once again: "As the living Father hath sent me, and I live by the Father, so he that eateth me, even he shall live by me." (John vi. 57.) Here now is a man an hungered, what must he feed upon? Not his pure humanity, not upon the sound complexion of his soul, nor yet on the dictates of his human nature, nor those neither which you call truly generous principles; but upon the flesh and blood of the Son of God, which was once given for the sin of the world. Let those then, that would be saved from the devil and hell, and that would find a fountain of grace in themselves, first receive, and feed upon Christ, as sinners and ungodly; let them believe that both his body, and blood, and soul, was offered for them, as they were sinners. The believing of this, is the eating of Christ: this eating of Christ is the beginning of eternal life, to wit, of all grace and health in the soul; and of glory to be enjoyed most perfectly in the next world.

Your twelfth chapter is to show, "that holiness being perfected, is blessedness itself; and that the glory of heaven consists chiefly in it."

Ans. But none of your holiness, none of that inward holiness, which we have lost before conversion, shall ever come to heaven: that being, as I have showed, a holiness of another nature, and arising from another root, than that we shall in heaven enjoy.

But further, your description of the glory that we shall possess in heaven, is questionable as to your notion of it; your notion is, that the substance of it consists in a perfect resemblance to the divine nature (pp. 123, 124).

Ans. Therefore not in the enjoyment of the divine nature itself: for that which in substance is but a bare resemblance, though it be a most perfect one, is not the thing itself of which it is a resemblance. But the blessedness that we shall enjoy in heaven, in the very substance of it, consisteth not wholly nor principally in a resemblance of, but in the enjoyment of God himself, "heirs of God." Wherefore there shall not be in us a likeness only to, but the very nature of God: "heirs of God, and joint heirs with Christ." (Rom. viii. 17.) Hence the apostle tells us, that he "rejoiced in hope of the glory of God." (Rom. v. 2.) Not only in hope of a resemblance of it. "The Lord is my portion, saith my soul." But this is like the rest of your discourse. You are so in love with your Adamitish holiness, that with you it must be God —in earth and heaven.

Who they are that hold that our happiness in heaven shall come by a mere fixing our eyes upon the divine perfections, I know not: but thus I read, "we shall be like him." Why? or how? "For we shall see him as he is." Our likeness then to God, even in the very heavens, will in great part come by the visions of him. And to speak the truth, our very entrance into eternal life, or the beginnings of it here, they come to us thus, "But we all, (every one of us that shall be saved, come by it only thus,) with open face beholding as in a glass the glory of the Lord, are changed from glory to glory, even as by the Spirit of the Lord." (2 Cor. iii. 18).

And whereas you tell us, (p. 124,) that the devils themselves have a large measure of some of the attributes of God, as knowledge, power, &c., though themselves are unlike unto him.

In this you most prodigiously blaspheme.

Your thirteenth chapter is to show, "that our Saviour's preferring the business of making men holy, before any other, witnesseth, that this is to do the best service to God."

But still respecting the holiness you have in your first chapter described, which still the reader must have his eye upon, it is false, and a slander of the Son of God. He never intended to promote or prefer your natural old covenant holiness, viz., that which we had lost in Adam, or that which yet from him, in the dregs thereof, remaineth in human nature; but that which is of the Holy Ghost, of faith, of the new covenant.

I shall not here again take notice of your 130th page, nor with the error contained therein, about justification by imputed righteousness.

But one thing I observe, that in all this chapter you have nothing fortified what you say, by any word of God; no, though you insinuate (p. 129 and p. 131) that some dissent from your opinion. But instead of the holy words of God, being, as you feign, conscious to yourself, you cannot do it so well as by another method, viz., the words of Mr. John Smith, therefore you proceed with his, as he with Plato's, and so wrap you up the business.

You come next to an improvement upon the whole, where you make a comparison between the heathens and the gospel; showing how far the gospel helpeth the light the heathens had in their pursuit after your holiness. But still the excellency of the gospel, as you have vainly dreamt, is to make improvement first of the heathen principles; such good principles, say you, "as were by the light of nature dictated to them" (p. 133). As,

1. "That there is but one God; that he is infinitely perfect," &c.

2. "That we owe our lives, and all the comforts of them, to him."

3. "That he is our sovereign Lord."

4. "That he is to be loved above all things" (p. 136).

Ans. 1. Seeing all these are, and may be known, as you yourself confess, by them that have not the gospel,—and I add, nor yet the Holy Ghost, nor any saving knowledge of God, or eternal life,—therefore it cannot be the design of Jesus Christ by the gospel to promote or help forward this knowledge, simply from this principle, viz., natural light, and the dictates of it. My reason is, because when nature is strained to the highest pin, it is but nature still; and so all the improvement of its light and knowledge is but an increase of that which is but natural. "But," saith Paul, "the natural man receiveth not the things of the Spirit of God: for they are foolishness unto him: neither can he know them, because they are spiritually discerned." (1 Cor. ii. 14.)

But the gospel is the ministration of the Spirit; a revelation of another thing than is found in, or can be acquired by, heathenish principles of nature: I say, a revelation of another thing; or rather, another discovery of the same. As,

1. Concerning the Godhead; the gospel giveth us another discovery of it, than is possible to be obtained by the dictates of natural light, even a discovery of a trinity of persons, and yet unity of essence, in the same Deity. (1 John v. 1, 5, 8.)

2. The light of nature will not show us that God was in Christ, reconciling the world to himself.

3. The light of nature will not show us that we owe what we are, and have, to God, because we are the price of the blood of his Son.

4. The light of nature will not show that there is such a thing as election in Christ.

5. Or that there is such a thing as the adoption of children to God, through him.

6. Nor that we are to be saved by faith in his blood.

7. Or, that the *man* Christ shall come from heaven to judgment.

These things, I say, the light of nature teacheth not; but these things are the great and mighty things of the gospel, and those about which it chiefly bendeth itself, touching upon other things, still as those that are knowable, by a spirit inferior to this of the gospel.

Besides, as these things are not known by the light of nature, so the gospel, when it comes,—as I also told you before,—doth implant in the soul another principle, by which they may be received, and from which the soul should act and do, both towards God and towards men, as namely the Holy Ghost, faith, hope, the joy of the Spirit, &c.

The other things you mention, viz.,

1. "The immortality of the soul" (p. 138).

2. "The doctrine of rewards and punishments in the life to come" (p. 140).

3. "Of the forgiveness of sin upon true repentance," &c. (p. 142).

4. "The doctrine of God's readiness to assist men by his special grace in their endeavours after virtue" (p. 143).

Ans. All these things may be assented to, where yet the grace of the gospel is not, but yet the apprehension must be such as is the light by which they are discovered; but the light of nature cannot discover them, according to the light and nature of the gospel, because the gospel knowledge of them ariseth also from another principle: so then, these doctrines are not confirmed by the gospel, as the light of nature teacheth them: wherefore, Paul, speaking of the things of the gospel, and so consequently of these, he saith, "Which things also we speak, NOT in the WORDS which MAN's wisdom teacheth, but which the HOLY GHOST teacheth; comparing spiritual things with spiritual." (1 Cor. ii. 13.) As if he should say, we speak of God, of the soul, of the life to come, of repentance, of forgiveness of sins, &c. Not as philosophers do, nor yet in their light; but as saints, Christians, and sons of God, as such who have received, not the spirit of the world, but the spirit which is of God; that we may know the things that are freely given to us of God.

But you add, (for the glory of the gospel,) that we have other things which no man could, without divine revelation, once have dreamed of. As,

1. That God hath made miserable sinners the objects of such transcendent love as to give them his only-begotten Son.

Ans. I must confess, if this one head had by you been handled well, you would have written like a worthy gospel minister. But you add (p. 146),

1. That when Christ was sent, it was to show us upon what terms God was reconcileable to us, viz., "by laying before us all the parts of holiness, which are necessary to restore our nature to his own likeness; and most pathetically, moreover, to entreat us to do what lieth on our parts to put them in practice, that so it may be to eternity well with us."

What these things are, you mention not here; therefore I shall leave them to be spoken to under the third head.

2. A second thing you mention is, "that this Son of God conversed upon equal terms with men, becoming the Son of man, born of a woman (a great demonstration that God hath a liking to the human nature)." But little to the purpose as you have handled it.

3. "That the Son of God taught men their duty, by his own example, and did himself perform what he required of them; and that himself did tread before us every step of that which he hath told us leadeth to eternal life."

Ans. Now we are come to the point, viz., "That the way to eternal life is, first of all to take Christ for our example, treading his step." And the reason, if it be true, is weighty: "for he hath trod every step before us, which he hath told us leadeth to eternal life."

1. *Every step.* Therefore he went to heaven by virtue of an imputative righteousness: for this is one of our steps thither.

2. *Every step.* Then he must go thither by faith in his own blood for pardon of sin; for this is another of our steps thither.

3. *Every step.* Then he must go thither by virtue of his own intercession at the right hand of God, before he came thither: for this is one of our steps thither.

4. *Every step.* Then he must come to God, and ask mercy for some great wickedness which he had committed: for this is also one of our steps thither.

But again, we will consider it the other way.

1. *Every step.* Then we cannot come to heaven before we first be made accursed of God: for so was he before he came thither.

2. *Every step.* Then we must first make our body and soul an offering for the sin of others: for this did he before he came thither.

3. *Every step.* Then we must go to heaven for the sake of our own righteousness: for that was one of his steps thither.

O, Sir! what will thy gallant, generous mind do here? Indeed you talk of his being an expiatory sacrifice for us, but you put no more trust to that, than to baptism, or the Lord's supper; counting that, with the other two, but things indifferent in themselves (pp. 6—9).

You add again, "That this Son of God being raised from the dead, and ascended to heaven, is our high priest there." But you talk not at all of his sprinkling the mercy-seat with his blood, but clap upon him the heathen's demons, negotiating the affairs of men with the supreme God, and so wrap up, with a testification that it is needless to enlarge on the point (p. 30).

But to be plain, and in one word to tell you about all these things you are heathenishly dark, there hath not in these one hundred and fifty pages one gospel truth been Christianly handled by you, but rather a darkening of truth by words without knowledge. What man that ever had read, or assented to the gospel, but would have spoken (yet kept within the bounds of truth) more honourably of Christ, than you have done? His sacrifice must be stept over, as the spider straddleth over the wasp; his intercession is needless to be enlarged upon. But when it falleth in your way to talk of your human nature, of the dictates, of the first principles of morals within you, and of your generous mind to follow it, oh, what need is there now of amplifying, enlarging, and pressing it on men's consciences! As if that poor heathenish pagan principle was the very Spirit of God within us: and as if righteousness done by that, was that, and that only, that would or could fling heaven gates off the hinges.

Yea, a little after you tell us, that " the doctrine of sending the Holy Ghost, was to move and excite us to our duty, and to assist, cheer, and comfort us in the performance of it:" still meaning our close adhering, by the purity of our human nature, to the dictates of the law, as written in our hearts as men. Which is as false as God is true. For the Holy Ghost is sent into our hearts, not to excite us to a compliance with our old and wind-shaken excellences, that came into the world with us, but to write new laws in our hearts; even the law of faith, the word of faith and of grace, and the doctrine of remission of sins, through the blood of the Lamb of God, that holiness might flow from thence.

Your fifteenth chapter is to show, that the gospel giveth far greater helps to an holy life than the Jewish ceremonies did of old. I answer,

But the reader must here well weigh, that in the gospel you find also some positive precepts that are of the same nature with the ceremonies under the law; of which, that of coming to God by Christ, you call one, and baptism, and the Lord's supper, the other two. So then by your doctrine, the excellency of the gospel doth not lie in that we have a Christ to come to God by, but in things as you feign more substantial. What are they? "Inward principles of holiness," (p. 159,) spiritual precepts, (p. 162,) that height of virtue, and true goodness, that the gospel designeth to raise us to: all which are general words, falling from a staggering conscience, leaving the world, that are ignorant of his mind, in a muse; but tickling his brethren with the delights of their moral principles, with the dictates of their human nature, and their gallant generous minds. Thus making a very stalking-horse of the Lord Jesus Christ, and of the words of truth and holiness, thereby to slay the silly one; making the Lord of life and glory, instead of a Saviour, by his blood, the instructor, and schoolmaster only of human nature, a chaser away of evil affections, and an extinguisher of burning lusts; and that not so neither, but by giving perfect explications of moral precepts, (p. 17,) and setting himself an example before them to follow him (p. 297).

Your sixteenth chapter containeth an answer to those that object against the power of the Christian religion to make men holy.

Ans. And to speak truth, what you at first render as the cause of the unholiness of the professors thereof (p. 171) is to the purpose, had it been Christianly managed by you, as, namely, men's gross unbelief of the truth of it; for it "effectually worketh in them that believe," (1 Thess. ii. 13:) but that you only touch and away, neither showing what is the object of faith, nor the cause of its being so effectual to that purpose; neither do you at all treat of the power of unbelief, and how all men by nature are shut up therein. (Rom.

xi. 32.) But presently, according to your old and natural course, you fall first upon a supposed power in men to embrace the gospel, both by closing with the promise, and shunning the threatening, (p. 172,) further adding, that " mankind is endued with a principle of freedom, and that this principle is as essential as any other to the human nature," (p. 173;) by all which it is manifest, that however you may make mention of unbelief, because the gospel hath laid the same in your way, yet your old doctrine of the purity of the human nature—now broken out into a freedom of will, and that, as an essential of the human nature—is your great principle of faith, and your following of that, as it dictateth to you obedience to the first principles of morals, the practice of faith by which you think to be saved. That this is so, must unavoidably be gathered from the good opinion you have yourself of coming to God by Christ; viz., that in the command thereof, it is one of these positive precepts, and a thing in itself absolutely considered indifferent, and neither good nor evil. Now he that looketh upon coming to God by Christ with such an eye as this, cannot lay the stress of his salvation upon the faith, or belief thereof. Indifferent faith will serve for indifferent things; yea, a man must look beyond that which he believeth is but one with the ceremonial laws, but not the same with baptism, or the Lord's supper; for with those you compare that of coming to God by Christ. Wherefore faith with you must be turned into a cheerful and generous complying with the dictates of the human nature; and unbelief, into that which opposeth this, or that makes the heart backward and sluggish therein. This is also gathered from what you aver of the divine moral laws, that they be of an indispensable and eternal obligation, (p. 8,) things that are good in themselves, (p. 9,) considered in an abstracted notion, (p. 10,) wherefore, things that are good in themselves, must needs be better than those that are in themselves but indifferent; neither can a positive precept make that, which of itself is neither good nor evil, better than that which in its own nature remaineth the essentials of goodness.

I conclude then, by comparing you with yourself, by bringing your book to your book, that you understand neither faith nor unbelief any further than by obeying or disobeying the human nature, and its dictates in chief; and that of coming to God by Christ as one of the things that is indifferent in itself.

But a little to touch upon your principle of freedom, which in p. 9 you call an understanding and liberty of will.

Ans. First, that there is no such thing in man by nature as liberty of will, or a principle of freedom, in the saving things of the kingdom of Christ, is apparent by several scriptures. Indeed there is in men, as men, a willingness to be saved their own way, even by following (as you) their own natural principles, as is seen by the Quakers as well as yourself; but that there is a freedom of will in men, as men, to be saved by the way which God hath prescribed, is neither asserted in the Scriptures of God, neither standeth with the nature of the principles of the gospel.

The apostle saith, " the natural man receiveth not the things that be of the Spirit of God." And the reason is, not because, not principally because, he layeth aside a liberty of will, but because " they are foolishness to him." (1 Cor. ii. 14.) Because in his judgment they are things of no moment, but things (as you have imagined of them) that in themselves are but indifferent. And that this judgment that is passed by the natural man concerning the things of the Spirit of God, (of which that of coming to God by Christ is the chief,) is that which he cannot but do as a man, is evident from that which followeth : " Neither can he know them, because they are spiritually discerned." Neither can he know them as a man, because they are spiritually discerned. Now, if he cannot know them, from what principle should he will them ? For judgment, or knowledge, must be before the will can act. I say again, a man must know them to be things in chief, that are absolutely and indispensably necessary, and those in which resteth the greatest glory, or else his will will not comply with them, nor centre and terminate in them as such ; but still count themselves (as you, though somewhat convinced that he ought to adhere unto them) things that in themselves are only indifferent, and, absolutely considered, neither good nor evil.

A further enlargement upon this subject will be time enough, if you shall contradict.

" Another reason, or cause, which you call an immediate one, of the unsuccessfulness of the gospel, is men's strange and unaccountable mistaking the design of it (not to say worse) as to conceive no better of it than as a science, and a matter of speculation," &c. (p. 173).

Ans. If this be true, you have showed us the reason why yourself have so base and unworthy thoughts thereof; for although coming to God by Christ be the very chief, first, the substance and most essential part of obedience thereto, yet you have reckoned this but like one of the ceremonies of the law, or as baptism with water, and the Lord's supper (pp. 7—9) : falling more directly upon the body of the moral law as written in the heart of men, and inclining more to the teaching, or dictates of human nature, (which were neither of them both ever any essential part of the gospel,) than upon that which indeed is the gospel of Christ.

And here I may, if God will, timely advertise my reader that the gospel, and its attendants, are to be accounted things distinct ; the gospel, properly taken, being " glad tidings of good things ;" or the doctrine of the forgiveness of sins freely by grace, through the redemption that is in Christ Jesus. For, to speak strictly, neither is the grace of faith, hope, repentance, or newness of life the

gospel; but rather things that are wrought by the preaching thereof, things that are the effects of it, or its inseparable companions to all them that shall be saved. Wherefore the gospel is said to be preached in all nations for the obedience of faith. (Rom. xvi. 26.) Hope also is called the hope of the gospel, not the gospel itself. So, again, the gospel is preached that men should repent, but it is not preached that men should gospel.

But your gospel, which principally or chiefly centres in the dictates of human nature ; and your faith, which is chiefly a subjecting to those dictates, are so far off from being at all any near attendants of the gospel, that they never are urged in the New Testament, but in order to show men they have forgotten to act as men. (Rom. i. 19— 21 ; ii. 14, 15. 1 Cor. xi. 14.)

Your last reason is, because of " several untoward opinions," the gospel is very unsuccessful (p. 174).

Ans. But what these opinions are, we hear not; nor how to shun them, you tell us here nothing at all. This I am sure, there are no men in this day have more opposed the light, glory, and lustre of the gospel of Christ than those, as the Quakers and others, that have set up themselves, and their own humanity, as the essential parts of it.

You, in answer to other things, add many other reasons to prove they are mistaken that count the gospel a thing of but mean operation to work holiness in the heart : at which you ought yourself to tremble, seeing the Son himself, who is the Lord of the gospel, is of so little esteem with you, as to make coming to God by him so trivial a business as you have done.

Your large transcript of other men's sayings, to prove the good success of the gospel of old, did better become that people and age than you and yours ; they being a people that lived in the power thereof, but you such bats as cannot see it. That saying you mention of Rigaltias, doth better become you and yours : " Those now-a-days do retain the name, and the society of Christians, which live altogether antichristian lives. Take away publicans, and a wretched rabble, &c., and your Christian churches will be lamentably weak, small, and insignificant things" (p 181).

I shall add to yours another reason of the unsuccessfulness of the gospel in our days, and that is, because so many ignorant Sir John's, on the one hand, and so many that have done violence to their former light, and that have damned themselves in their former anathematizing of others, have now for a long time, as a judgment of God, been permitted to be, and made the mouth to the people: persons whose lives are debauched, and who in the face of the world, after seeming serious detestings of wickedness, have for the love of filthy lucre, and the pampering their idle carcasses, made shipwreck of their former faith, and that feigned good conscience they had. From which number if you, Sir, have kept yourself clear, the less blood of the damned will fall upon your head. I know you not by face, much less your personal practice; yet I have heard as if blood might pursue you, for your unstable weathercock spirit, which doubtless could not but stumble the weak, and give advantage to the adversary to speak vilifyingly of religion.

As to your seventeenth and eighteenth chapters, I shall say little, only I wish that your eighteenth had been more express in discovering how far a man may go, with a notion of the truth of the gospel, and yet perish because he hath it not in power.

Only in your inveighing so much against the pardon of sin, while you seem so much to cry up healing, you must know that pardon of sin is the beginning of health to the soul. "He pardoneth our iniquities, and healeth all our diseases." (Ps. ciii. 3.) And where he saith, by the stripes of Christ we are healed, it is evident that healing beginneth at pardon, and not pardon after healing, as you would rather have it. (1 Pet. ii. 24; compare Isa. liii.) As for your comparison of the plaister and the physician's portion, (p. 217,) I say, you do but abuse your reader, and muddy the way of the gospel. For the first thing of which the soul is sick, and by which the conscience receiveth wounding, it is the guilt of sin, and fear of the curse of God for it. For which is provided the wounds and precious blood of Christ, which flesh and blood, if the soul eat thereof by faith, giveth deliverance therefrom. Upon this the filth of sin appears most odious, for that it hath not only at present defiled the soul, but because it keeps it from doing those duties of love, which by the love of Christ it is constrained to endeavour the perfecting of. For filth appears filth; that is irksome, and odious to a contrary principle now implanted in the soul; which principle had its conveyance thither by faith in the sacrifice and death of Christ going before. "The love of Christ constraineth us, because we thus judge, that if one died for all, then were all dead; and that he died for all, that they which live should not henceforth live unto themselves, but to him which died for them, and rose again." (2 Cor. v. 14.) The man that hath received Christ, desireth to be holy, because the nature of the faith that layeth hold on Christ (although I will not say as you, it is of a generous mind) worketh by love, and longeth, yea, greatly longeth that the soul may be brought, not only into an universal conformity to his will, but into his very likeness; and because that state standeth not with what we are now, but with what we shall be hereafter: "therefore in this we groan, being burdened (with that which is of a contrary nature) to be clothed upon with our house which is from heaven," (2 Cor. v. 1—8,) which state is not that of Adam's innocency; but that which is spiritual, and heavenly, even that which is now in the Lord in heaven.

But I will descend to your nineteenth chapter— it may be more may be discovered there.

Your nineteenth chapter is to show, "that a right understanding of the design of Christianity (viz., as you have laid it down) will give satisfaction concerning the true notion."

First. " Of justifying faith."

Second. " Of the imputation of Christ's righteousness" (p. 221).

First. Of justifying faith. " It is (say you) such a belief of the truth of the gospel, as includes a sincere resolution of obedience to all its precepts."

Ans. To this I shall answer, first, that the faith which we call justifying faith, " is like precious faith " with all the elect, (2 Pet. i. 1,) and that which is most holy, (Jude 20 ;) but those acts of it which respect our justification with God from the curse of the law that is due for sin, are such, as respect not any good work done by us, but the righteousness that resideth in the person of Christ; and is made ours by the imputation of grace. This faith, I say, accounteth him in whom it is now a sinner, and without works; yea, if he have any that in his own eyes are such, this faith rejects them, and throweth them away; for it seeth a righteousness in the person of Christ sufficient, even such as is verily the righteousness of God. " Now to him that worketh not, but believeth." Works and faith are put here in opposition, faith being considered as justifying, in the sight of God, from the curse. The reason is, because the righteousness by which the soul must thus stand justified is a righteousness of God's appointing, not of his prescribing us; a righteousness that entirely is included in the person of Christ. The apostle also, when he speaks of God's saving the election, which hangeth upon the same hinge as this of justification doth, to wit, on the grace of God, he opposeth it to works; and that, not to this or that sort only, but even to work, in the nature of work. " If by grace, then is it no more of works; otherwise grace is no more grace; but if it be of works, then it is no more of grace: otherwise work is no more work." (Rom. xi. 6.) By this text, I say, the apostle doth so thoroughly distinguish between grace and works, as that which soever standeth in the case, the other must be annihilated: if it be by grace, then must works be no more, " then it is no more of works;" but if it be of works, then is grace no more, " then it is no more of grace."

But this, notwithstanding, you urge farther; " that faith justifieth, as it includes a sincere resolution," &c.

Ans. Although, as I have said before, the faith which is the justifying faith, is that of the holiest nature, yet in the act, by which it layeth hold of justifying righteousness, it respects it, simply, as a righteousness offered by grace, or given unto the person that by faith layeth hold thereon as he stands yet ungodly and a sinner.

Faith justifieth not separate from the righteousness of Christ as it is a grace in us, nor as it subjecteth the soul to the obedience of the moral law, but as it receiveth a righteousness offered to that sinner, that as such will lay hold on, and accept thereof. Christ Jesus came into the world to save sinners, by being their redemption, and righteousness himself. (1 Cor. i. 30.)

But you add, "The faith which entitles the sinner to so high a privilege as that of justification, must needs be such as complieth with *all* the purposes of Christ's coming into the world," &c. (p. 222).

Ans. By this supposition, faith justifieth not by receiving of the righteousness that Christ by himself accomplished for sinners; but by falling in with *all* good works, which because they cannot be known, much less done, by the soul at first, his faith being then as to the perfection of knowledge of duties, weak, he standeth still before God unjustified, and so must stand until he doth comply with all those purposes of Christ's coming into the world.

But yet again you recall yourself, and distinguish *one* purpose from the rest, as a grand one (p. 222). And that is to receive Christ as Lord, as well as a Saviour.

Ans. 1. Although the soul that in truth receiveth Christ, receiveth him wholly, and entirely as Christ, and not as chopped, and pulled in pieces, yet I distinguish between the act of faith, which layeth hold of Christ for my justification from the curse before God, and the consequences of that act, which are to engage me to newness of life. And indeed, as it is impossible for a man to be a new man, before he be justified in the sight of God, so it is also as impossible, but that when faith hath once laid hold on Christ for life, it should also follow Christ by love. But,

2. Christ may be received at first as Lord, and that in our justification, and yet not at all be considered as a lawgiver, for so he is not the object of faith for our justification with God, but a requirer of obedience to laws and statutes, of them that already are justified by the faith that receiveth him as righteousness. But Christ is as well a Lord for us, as to, or over us; and it highly concerneth the soul, when it believeth in, or trusteth to the righteousness of Christ, for justification with God, to see that this righteousness lords it over death and sin, and the devil, and hell for us: the name wherewith he shall be called, is, "the Lord our righteousness." (Jer. xxiii. 6.) Our righteousness, then, is Lord and conqueror over all; and we more than conquerors through this Lord that loved us. (Rom. viii.) The author, to the Hebrews, calls him "King of righteousness," (Heb. vii.,) because by his righteousness he ruleth as Lord and King, and can reign and lord it, at all times, over all those that seek to separate us from the presence and glory of God.

Now, how you will brook this doctrine I know not; I am sure he stands in need thereof, that is lorded over by the curse of the law, the guilt of sin, the rage of the devil, and the fear of death and hell; he, I say, would be glad to know that in Christ there is a righteousness that LORDS IT, or that Christ, as he is righteousness, is LORD.

Wherefore, reader, when thou shalt read or hear that Jesus Christ is Lord, if thou art at the same time under guilt of sin, and fear of hell, then do thou remember that Christ is Lord more ways than one: he is Lord as he is righteousness; he is Lord as he is imputative righteousness; he is "the Lord *our* righteousness." (Jer. xxiii. 6.) Of the same import is that also, "he is a Prince, and a Saviour," he is a Prince, as he is a Saviour; because the righteousness by which he saveth, beareth rule in heaven and earth. And hence we read again, that even when he was in the combat with our sins, the devils, the curse, and death, upon the cross, "he even in that place made a show of them openly, and triumphed over them." (Col. ii. 15, 16.) Now in these things he is Lord *for us*, and the Captain of our salvation; as also in that "he led captivity captive," (Eph. iv. 8, 9;) all which places, with many more, being testimonies to us, of the sufficiency of that righteousness which saveth us from the justice of the law and wrath of God. But you respect not this his manner of lording; but will have him be a Saviour, as he giveth laws, especially those you call indispensable and eternal, the moral law. You would have him a Saviour, as he bringeth us back to the holiness we had lost. But this is none other than barbarous Quakerism, the stress of their writing also tending to no other purpose.

But you tell us, "That you scarcely admired at anything more in all your life, than that any, worthy men especially, should be so difficultly persuaded to receive or embrace this account of justifying faith, and should perplex and make intricate so plain a doctrine" (p. 222).

Ans. And doubtless they far more groundedly stand amazed at such as you, who, while you pretend to show the design of the gospel, make the very essential of it a thing in itself indifferent, and, absolutely considered, neither good nor evil, (p. 7;) that makes obedience to the moral laws (p. 8) more essential to salvation than that of going to God by Christ, (p. 9;) that maketh it the great design of Christ, to put us into a possession of that promiseless, natural, old covenant holiness which we had lost long since in Adam, that maketh as if Christ, rejecting all other righteousness, or holiness, hath established only this (pp. 10—16). Yea, that maketh the very principle of this holiness to consist in "a sound complexion of soul, the purity of human nature in us, a habit of soul, truly generous motives and principles, divine moral laws, which were first written in men's hearts, and originally dictates of human nature." All this villany against the Son of God, with much more as bad, is comprised within less than the first sixteen pages of your book.

But, say you, "What pretence can there be for thinking that faith is the condition, or instrument of justification, as it complieth with only the precept of relying upon Christ's merits for the obtaining of it? especially when it is no less manifest than the sun at noon-day, that obedience to the *other precepts* must go before obedience to this; and that a man may not rely upon the merits of Christ for the forgiveness of his sins, and he is most presumptuous in so doing, and puts an affront upon his Saviour too, till he be sincerely willing to be reformed from them" (p. 223).

Ans. That the merits of Christ, for justification, are made over to that faith that receiveth them, while the person that believeth it stands in his own account by the law a sinner, hath already been showed; and that they are not by God appointed for another purpose, is manifest through all the Bible.

1. In the type, when the bloody sacrifices were to be offered, and an atonement made for the soul, the people were only to confess their sins over the head of the bullock, or goat, or lamb, by laying their hands thereon, and so the sacrifice was to be slain. They were only to acknowledge their sins. And observe it, in the day that these offerings were made, they were "not to work at all; for he that did any work therein, was to be cut off from his people." (Lev. iv.; xvi.; xxiii.)

2. In the antitype thus it runs: "Christ died for our sins; Christ gave himself for our sins; he was made to be sin for us; Christ was made a curse for us."

"Yea, but (say you) what pretence can there be, that faith is the condition, or instrument of justification, as it complieth with only the precepts of relying upon Christ's merits?" that is, first, or before the soul doth other things.

Ans. I say, avoiding your own ambiguous terms, that it is the duty—the indispensable duty—of all that would be saved, first, immediately, now to close in by faith with that work of redemption, which Christ by his blood hath purchased for them, as they are sinners.

1. Because God doth hold it forth—yea, hath set it forth to be received by us—as such. (Rom. iii. 23—27.)

2. Because God hath commanded us by faith to receive it as such. (Acts xvi.)

And I add, if the jailer was altogether ignorant of what he must do to be saved, and Paul yet bids him then, before he knew anything else, believe in the Lord Jesus Christ, and he should be saved, that then believing—even believing on Christ for a righteousness to justify, and save him—must go first, and may, nay, ought to be pressed, even then, when the soul stands ignorant of what else he ought to do. (Acts xvi. 30—32.)

"But (you say) it is evident as the sun at noon-day, that obedience to the other precepts must go before obedience to this, that is, before faith in Christ."

Ans. This you say; but Paul said to the ignorant jailer, that knew nothing of the mind of God in the doctrine of justification, that he should first believe on the Lord Jesus Christ, and so should be saved. Again, when Paul preached to the Corin-

thians, the first doctrine that he delivered unto them was, "That Christ died for their sins, according to the scriptures," &c. (1 Cor. xv. 1—3.)

But what be these other precepts? Not baptism, nor the supper of the Lord; for these you say are (as poor and inconsiderable) as that of coming to God by Christ, even all three things in themselves neither good nor evil, but of an indifferent nature; they must be therefore some more weighty things of the gospel, than these positive precepts. But what things are they? It is good that you tell us, seeing you tacitly forbid all men, upon pain of presumption, and of doing affront to Jesus Christ, that they rely not on the merits of Christ for forgiveness, till they be sincerely willing to perform them first; yet I find not here one particular precept instanced by you. But perhaps we shall hear of them hereafter, therefore now I shall let them pass. You tell us farther, "That such a reliance (as that of acting faith, first, on the merits of Christ for justification) is ordinarily to be found amongst unregenerate, and even the worst of men" (p. 223).

Ans. This is but a falsehood and a slander, for the unregenerate know him not; how then can they believe on him? (1 John iii. 1.) Besides, the worst of men, so far as they pretend religion, set up your idol in their hearts, viz., their own good meanings, their own good nature, the notions and dictates of their nature; living that little which they do live upon the snuff of their own light, the sparks of their own fire, and therefore woe unto them.

But you add, "How can it be otherwise, than that that act of faith must needs have a hand in justifying, and the special hand too, which distinguisheth it from that which is found in such persons?"

Ans. 1. There is no act of faith doth more distinguish true faith from false, and the Christian from the painted hypocrite, than that which first lays hold on Christ, while the person that hath it stands in his own esteem ungodly; all other, like yourself, being fearful and unbelieving (Rev. xxi. 8) despisers, who wonder, and perish. (Acts xiii. 40, 41.)

2. And this faith, by thus acting, doth more subdue sin (though it doth not justify as subduing, but as applying Christ's righteousness) than all the wisdom and purity of human nature, or the dictates of that nature, that is found in the whole world.

But you add farther, "What good ground can men have for this fancy, when as our Saviour hath merited the pardon of sin for this end, that it might be an effectual motive to turn from it?"

Ans. Although you speak this in great derision to faith when it worketh right, yet know that therefore (seeing you would hear it) I say, therefore hath our Saviour merited pardon, and bestowed it on men freely, and bid them believe or receive it, and have it; that thereby they might be encouraged to live to him, and love him, and comply with his commandments. "For scarcely for a righteous man will one die, yet peradventure for a good man some would even dare to die: but God commendeth his love to us, in that while we were yet sinners, Christ died for us. Much more then, being now justified by his blood, we shall be saved from wrath through him." (Rom. v.) Now, as here we are said to be justified by his blood, that is, as his blood appeaseth the justice of God, so again, it is said that this blood is set forth by God for us to have faith in it, by the term of a propitiation. "Whom God hath set forth to be a propitiation (or a sacrifice to appease the displeasure of God) through faith in his blood. To declare at this time his righteousness, that he might be just, and the justifier of him that believeth in Jesus." (Rom. iii. 25, 26.)

Again, as we are thus justified by blood in the sight of God, by faith in it, so also it is testified of his blood, that it sprinkleth the conscience of the faithful, but still only as it is received by faith. But from what is the conscience sprinkled, but from those dead works that remain in all that have not yet been justified by faith in this blood. Now if faith in this blood doth sprinkle the conscience, and so doth purge it from all dead works, then must faith go first to the blood of Christ for justification, and must bring this home to the defiled conscience, before it be delivered from those dead works that are in it, and made capable of serving the living God. (Rom. v. 7—10; iii. 24, 25. Heb. ix. 14; x. 19—22.)

But you say, "You will never trust your discursive faculty so long as you live, if you are mistaken here" (p. 224).

Tell me not of your discursive faculty: the word of God is plain. And never challenge man; for he that condemneth your way to heaven, to the pit of hell, as Paul doth, can yet set forth a very better.

Second. I come now to the second thing, viz., *the doctrine of the imputation of Christ's righteousness,* which you thus expound.

"It consists in dealing with sincerely righteous persons, as if they were perfectly so, for the sake, and upon the account of Christ's righteousness" (pp. 225, 226).

Ans. 1. Anything but truth; but I would know how sincerely righteous they were that were justified without works? or how sincerely righteous they were whom God justified as ungodly? (Rom. iv. 3—5.)

2. Your explication of the imputation of Christ's righteousness makes it respect our works rather than our persons: "It consists," say you, "in dealing with sincerely righteous persons, as if they were perfectly so:" that is, it justifieth their imperfect righteousness first, and so secondarily their persons for the sake of that.

But observe a few things from this explication.

1. This concludeth that a man may be sincerely righteous in God's account, WITHOUT the righteousness of Christ; for that is to be imputed to such, and none but such.

2. This concludeth that men may be sincerely righteous, before Christ's righteousness is imputed: for this sincere righteousness is precedent to the imputation of Christ's.

3. This concludeth that a man may have true, yea, saving grace, in great and mighty action in him, before he hath faith in the righteousness of Christ. For if a man must be sincerely righteous first, then he must not only have that we call the habit, but the powerful acts of grace.

Besides, if the righteousness of Christ is not to be looked to first, but secondarily, not before, but after we be made sincerely righteous, then may not faith be thus acted if a man should have it, until he be first a sincerely righteous person?

4. This concludeth that a man may be brought from under the curse of the law in God's sight before he have faith in the righteousness of Christ, yea, before it be imputed to him; for he that in God's account is reckoned sincerely righteous, is beloved of his God.

5. This concludeth that a man may be from under the curse of God, without the imputation of the righteousness of Christ; for if a man must be sincerely righteous in God's account without it, then he is from under the curse of God without it.

6. This doctrine teacheth farther, that Christ came to call and justify the righteous, contrary to his express word. In short, by this account of things, first we must be healed, and then the plaister comes.

Yea, so confident is this man in this his assertion, that he saith, "It is not possible any other notion of this doctrine should have truth in it" (p. 226). O this Jesus! this rock of offence! But he that believeth on him shall not be confounded.

But blessed be God for Jesus Christ, and for that he took our nature, and sin, and curse, and death upon him; and for that he did also by himself, by one *offering,* purge our sins. We that have believed have found rest, even there where God and his Father hath smelled a sweet savour of rest; because we are presented to God, even now complete in the righteousness of him, and stand discharged of guilt, even by the faith of him; yea, as sins past, so sins to come, were taken up and satisfied for, by that offering of the body of Jesus. We who have had a due sense of sins, and of the nature of the justice of God, we know that no remission of the guilt of any one can be, but by atonement made by blood. (Heb. ix. 22.) We also know that where faith in Jesus Christ is wanting, there can be neither good principle nor good endeavour, for faith is the first of all graces, and without it there is nothing but sin. (Rom. xiv. 23.) We know also, that faith as a grace in us, severed from the righteousness of Christ, is only a beholder of things, but not a justifier of persons; and that if it lay not hold of, and applieth not that righteousness which is in Christ, it carrieth us no farther than to the devil's. We know that this doctrine killeth sin, and curseth it at the very roots; I say, we know it, "who have mourned over him whom WE have pierced," (Zech. xii. 10;) and who have been confounded to see that God, by his blood, should be pacified towards us for all the wickedness we have done. (Ezek. xvi. 63.) Yea, we have a double motive to be holy and humble before him; one because he died for us on earth, and another because he now appears for us in heaven, there sprinkling for us the mercy-seat with his blood, there ever-living to make intercession for them that come unto God by him. "If any man sin, we have an advocate with the Father, Jesus Christ the righteous, and he is the propitiation for our sins." (1 John ii. 1, 2.) Yet this worketh in us no looseness, nor favour to sin, but so much the more an abhorrence of it: "She loveth much, for much was forgiven her." (Luke vii. 47.) Yea, she weeps, she washeth his feet, and wipeth them with the hairs of her head, to the confounding of Simon the Pharisee, and all such ignorant hypocrites.

But I pass this, and come to the twentieth chapter, which is to learn us by what measure and standard we are to judge of doctrines; and that is by the design of Christianity as stated, you must know, by Mr. Fowler. Wherefore it will be requisite here again, that a collection of principles and doctrines be gathered out of this book, that the man that hath a short memory may be helped the better to bear them in mind, and to make them, if he shall be so bewitched by them, instead of the Bible, a standard for truth, and a rule for him to obtain salvation by.

First. Then he must know that the principle by which he must walk must be the purity of the human nature, a divine or God-like nature, which yet is but an habit of soul, or more plainly, the moral law, as written in the heart, and originally the dictates of human nature; a generous principle, such an one as although it respects law, yet acts in a sphere above it; above it as a written law, that acts even in the first principles of it (pp. 7—10).

Second. He must know that the holiness Christ designed to possess his people with, is that which we had lost in Adam, that which he had before he fell—that natural, old covenant, Christless holiness (p. 12).

Third. He must put a difference between those laws of the gospel that are essential to holiness, and those positive precepts that in themselves are indifferent, and, absolutely considered, neither good nor evil; but must know also that of these positive precepts he alloweth but three in the gospel, but three that are purely such; to wit, that of coming to God by Christ, the institutions of baptism, and the Lord's supper (pp. 7—9).

Fourth. He must hold for certain, that the faith which entitleth a sinner to so high a privilege as that of justification, must needs be such as complieth with all the purposes of Christ's coming into the

world, (whether at present it understands them or not,) and it is no less necessary it should justify as it doth so (p. 222).

Fifth. He must know that a man may not rely upon the merits of Christ for the forgiveness of his sins, before he has done other good works first (p. 223).

Sixth. And that the right explication of the imputation of Christ's righteousness is this, that it consisteth in having to do with persons that are sincerely righteous (p. 225). For it is not possible for Christ's righteousness to be imputed to an unrighteous man (p. 120).

These things, with many like to them, being the main points by this man handled, and by him asserted to be the design of Christianity, by these we must, as by a rule and standard, understand how to judge of the truth of doctrines. "And," saith he, "seeing the design of Christianity is to make men holy, (still meaning from principles of humanity, and by possessing us again, with the often-repeated holiness which we had lost,) whatsoever opinions do either directly, or in their evident consequences, obstruct the promoting of it, are perfectly false" (pp. 227, 228).

Ans. Thus with one word, as if he were Lord and Judge himself, he sendeth to the pit of hell all things that sanctify or make holy the hearts of men, if they oppose the design of his Christianity. But what if the Holy Ghost will become a principle in the hearts of the converted, and will not now suffer them to act simply and alone upon the principles of pure humanity? or what now if faith will become a principle to act by, instead of these that are originally dictates of human nature? or what if a man should act now as a son, rather than simply as a creature endued with a principle of reason? I question here whether these things thus doing do not obstruct, put by, yea, and take the way of his pure humanity, dictates of human nature, and instead thereof, act and govern the soul by and with their own principles. For albeit, there be the dictates of human nature in the sons of men, yet neither is this nature, nor yet the dictates of it, laid by Jesus Christ as the truly Christian principles in his. But you add:

"Those doctrines which in their own nature do evidently tend to the serving of THIS design of Christianity, we may conclude are most true and genuine" (p. 229).

Ans. The holiness which you so often call the design of Christianity, being by yourself said to be that which we had lost, for this one sentence is it on which your whole book is built (p. 12), whatsoever doctrine or doctor it be that asserts it, both that doctrine is of the devil, and that doctor an angel of darkness, or rather a minister of Satan, become as a minister of righteousness: for where is it said, in all the whole book of God, that ever the Lord designed, yea, made it his errand from heaven, to put us again in possession of the holiness which we had lost? Yet this you affirm, and tell us the business of your book is to prove it. But, blessed be God, your shifts are discovered, and your fig-leaves rent from off you, and the righteousness or holiness so much cried up by you, proved to be none of the holiness of the gospel, but that which stood with perfect ignorance thereof. I might speak to what yet remains of falsehood, in the other part of this chapter; but having overthrown the foundation, and broken the head of your leviathan, what remains falleth of itself, and dieth of its own accord.

What you say of modes or forms, and sticklers for little trifles, such as place their religion in mere externals, you may fasten them where of due they belong : yet I tell you the least of the commandments of Christ is better than your Adamitish holiness.

Your twenty-first chapter tells us, if we will believe you, how we shall judge of the necessity of doctrine, to be embraced or rejected; also you say, it giveth us a brief discourse of the nature of fundamentals : but because your discourse of them is general, and not any one particularized, I might leave you in your generals till you dealt more candidly, both with the word of God and your abused reader.

First. Indeed you tell us of *primary fundamentals,* " Such as without the knowledge and belief of which it is impossible to acquire that inward righteousness and holiness which the Christian religion aimeth at; but the particulars of these," say you, " I shall not enumerate, because (as will appear from what will be said anon) it is not needful to have a just table of them" (p. 234).

Ans. Deep divinity !

1. They are such as without the knowledge and belief of them it is not possible we should acquire your true holiness, and yet for all that, it is not needful that we be told what they are, or that we should have a just table of them !

2. But if they be things necessary—things without the knowledge of which it is impossible we should be truly holy, then is it needful that we understand what they are : yea, then is it needful that they be written, and presented one by one unto us, that our knowledge of them being distinct and full, we may the better be able to obtain or acquire your glorious (so pretended) holiness.

But I know your primary fundamentals; they are your first principles of morals, not faith in the righteousness of Christ, for that is comprehended in your positive, and in themselves indifferent things : your morals are the things in themselves absolutely necessary, of an indispensable and eternal obligation (pp. 8, 9).

Second. But you tell us of points of faith that are *secondarily fundamental;* the disbelief of which cannot consist with true holiness, in those to whom the gospel is sufficiently made known.

Ans. The secondary fundamentals also, are all kept close and hid, and not otherwise to be understood, but by implication ; however, the disbelief of these is not of so sad a consequence as is that of the former, because, say you, " they are not in their own nature, holiness," (p. 235 ;) yea, he insinuateth that the disbelief of them may stand with true holiness in those to whom the gospel is not sufficiently made known.

Of these secondary fundamentals, therefore, whatever is their number, this is one, even coming to God by Christ ; for, as in pp. 7 and 9, he calleth it a positive precept, a thing that in itself is neither good nor evil, so here he speaks of such as are not in their own nature holy; not such, as that holiness is not in some degree or other attainable without the belief of them.

That one of these secondary fundamentals is intended by Mr. Fowler, that of coming to God by Christ, I farther gather because he saith, that " in the number of these, are all such doctrines as are with indisputable clearness revealed to us," that is, by the holy scriptures of the New Testament (p. 235). For therein is this revealed to be a fundamental ; but he saith, not a primary one, because that in itself, it is but indifferent, and not in its own nature good. " Now, the belief of these," saith he, " though it is not in itself any more, than in higher or lower degrees, profitable, (confusion ! darkness ! confusion !) yet it is absolutely necessary from an external cause :" that is, with such abundant clearness, as that nothing can cause men to refuse to admit them, but that which argueth them to be stark naught.

Ans. 1. Then, hence it seems that the reason why you admit these secondary sort of fundamentals, is not from any internal power, but an external declaration only.

2. Nay, and you do but admit them neither, and that too, for some external cause ; not because of the worthiness of the nature of the points themselves.

3. And were it not, but that you are loth to be counted stark naught in the eyes of men, so far as I can discern, you would not at all make profession of them, with pretence as unto God; for, say you, " We must take notice here, that all such points as these (viz., these fundamentals) are not of equal necessity to be received by all Christians ; because that in regard of the diversity of their capacities, education, and other means and advantages, some of them may be most plainly perceived by some, to be delivered in the scriptures, which cannot be so by others, with the like ease."

Ans. From these words I take notice of four things.

1. That by this universal (all Christians) is comprehended the heathen and pagan people, that give heed to, and mind to, follow that light that originally and naturally stirreth them to moral duties. These be they that want the education and advantages of others, and are not in such a capacity as they to whom these things are delivered by the scriptures.

2. That this people, notwithstanding they want a scripture revelation of these secondary fundamentals, yet have the more necessary, the first sort of fundamentals; for the secondary sort, say you, are not in their own nature such, as that holiness is not in some degree or other attainable without the belief of them.

3. That, therefore, these secondary sort of fundamentals are only necessary to be believed by them that have the indisputable (the scripture) revelation of them; and that, in truth, the others may be saved without them.

4. But yet, even those that are made capable, by education and other advantages, to obtain the belief of them, ought, notwithstanding, not to have the same respect for them, as for those of the first sort of fundamentals, because they are not in their own nature such.

But will this man know, that Christ is not only a fundamental, but the very foundation of all other fundamental truths, revealed both in the Old Testament and the New; and that his pure human nature, with the dictates of it, with his feigned Adamitish holiness, is no fundamental at all; I mean no fundamental of faith, no gospel fundamental. (1 Cor. iii. 14. Eph. ii. 19, 20.) Yea, will he know, that from heaven there is none other name given, than the name of Jesus Christ, whereby we must be saved, none other name given under the whole heavens. (Acts iv. 12.)

Oh the witchcrafts by which some men's spirits are intoxicated! and the strength of delusion by which some are infatuated, and turned aside from the simplicity that is in Jesus Christ! But I proceed.

Your great question, or rather your Urim and Thummim, by which you would have all men make judgment of their saveable or damnable state (p. 236), is, according to your description of things, most devilish and destructive. For to obey God and Christ in all things, with you, is to do it from principles purely human in the faith of this: that Christ hath designed to possess us again with that holiness we had lost. Again, to obey God and Christ, with you, is, so to obey all their laws, as respecting the first principles of morals; and our obedience to them, far more indispensable than that of coming to God by Christ. Farther, he that obeys them in all things, with your directions, must not look upon faith in the blood of Christ, and justification by his righteousness, as the main and first, but the second part of our duty; other commands, or precepts, more naturally holy and good, first being embraced, and lived in the practice of, by us.

This, I say, being the doctrine you have asserted, and the foundation on which your Urim and Thummim stands, the foundation, with your trial, are both from the devil and hell, as hath at large been proved, and discovered in this book.

And I now will add, and bid you take your advantage, that should a man with all his might,

strive to obey all the moral laws, either as they are contained in the first principles of morals, or in the express decalogue, or ten commandments, without faith, first, in the blood, and death, and resurrection of Christ, &c., for his justification with God, his thus doing would be counted wickedness, and he in the end, accounted a rebel against the gospel, and shall be damned for want of faith in the blood of the Lord Jesus.

Your twenty-second chapter, saith, "That the design of Christianity teacheth us what doctrines and practices we ought, as Christians, to be most zealous for, or against" (p. 237).

Ans. But there is not by that, it being rightly stated, one syllable that tendeth to encourage any man, to have lower thoughts of coming to God by Christ, than of keeping the moral law. For even the first text you bring doth utterly overthrow it. "Contend," say you, "earnestly for the faith;" I answer then, not for the law of works, for the law is not of faith; but the man that doth these things, shall live in them, by them. "Contend earnestly for the faith, for there are certain men crept in unawares, which were before of old, ordained unto this condemnation;" even the condemnation that is to come upon them that contend against the faith; for these ungodly men turn the grace of God into lasciviousness, and deny the only Lord God, and our Lord Jesus Christ. Now these creeping, ungodly men, may be divided in three ranks.

1. Such as by principle, and practice both, say, "Let us do evil, that good may come; whose damnation is just." (Rom. iii. 8.)

2. Such as by practice only appear to be such, denying to profess the principle thereof; such are they that made excuse and delay, when invited to come to the wedding. (Matt. xxii. 1—5. Luke xiv.)

3. There is yet another sort; and they are such as seem to deny it, both in principle and practice also; only they do it covertly, PRIVILY bringing in damnable heresies, even denying the Lord that bought them. These "bring upon themselves swift destruction." (2 Pet. ii. 1.)

This third sort make of the doctrine of grace, and of the forgiveness of sins through the faith of the righteousness of Christ, a loose and licentious doctrine, or a doctrine that giveth liberty to the flesh: by reason of these the way of truth is evil spoken of, and the hearts of innocent ones alienated therefrom. These will not stick to charge it upon the very chief of the brethren, if they shall say, "as sin abounded, grace hath much more abounded; that they press men to do evil, that good may come of it." (Rom. iii. 8, 9.) But, as I said, these vilify Christ, not with open words, but covertly; privily they bring in their blasphemy under a cloak, crying, the law, holiness, strictness, good works, &c. Besides, these clothe their doctrines with names and notions that belong not at all unto them; as of Christ, grace, the Spirit, the gospel, when there is only there the devil and his angels and errors; as angels of light and ministers of unrighteousness. Of this last sort are you, and the subject matter of your book; for you bring into the world an anti-gospel holiness, anti-gospel principles, and anti-gospel fundamentals; and that these things might be worshipped by your disciples, you give them the name of holiness, the design of Christ and of Christianity; by which means you remove the Christ of God from before, and set him behind, forbidding men to believe on him, till they have practised your things first: nay, after they have practised yours, they then must come to God by him: still respecting the principles and dictates of humanity, as things of the greatest weight, things that are good in themselves; still considering that "coming to God by Christ is not good in itself, but so only upon the account of certain circumstances; a thing in itself of an indifferent nature, and, absolutely considered, neither good nor evil."

Wherefore, Sir, laying aside all fear of men, not regarding what you may procure to be inflicted upon me for this my plain dealing with you, I tell you again, that yourself is one of them, that have closely, privily, and devilishly, by your book, turned the grace of our God into a lascivious doctrine, bespattering it with giving liberty to looseness, and the hardening of the ungodly in wickedness; against whom, shall you persist in your wickedness, I shall not fail (may I live, and know it, and be helped of God to do it) to discover yet farther the rottenness of your docrine, with the accursed tendencies thereof.

What you say about "doubtful opinion, alterable modes, rites, and circumstances in religion" (p. 239), I know none so wedded thereto as yourselves, even the whole gang of your rabbling, counterfeit clergy; who generally, like the ape you speak of, lie blowing up the applause and glory of your trumpery, and, like the tail, with your foolish and sophistical arguings you cover the filthy parts thereof, as you sweetly argue in the next chapter (p. 242), saying, "*Whatsoever of such are commended by the custom of the place we live in, or commanded by superiors, or made by any circumstance convenient to be done, our Christian liberty consists in this, that we have leave to do them.*" So that do but call them things indifferent, things that are the customs of the place we live in, or made by ANY circumstance convenient, and a man may not doubt but he hath leave to do them, let him live at Rome or Constantinople, or amidst the greatest corruption of worship and government! These are, therefore, doubtless a third sort of fundamentals, by which you can wrestle with conviction of conscience, and stifle it; by which you can suit yourself for every fashion, mode, and way of religion. Here you may hop from Presbyterianism to a prelatical mode; and, if time and chance should serve you, backward and forward again: yea, here you can make use of several consciences, one for this way now, another for that anon; now putting out the light of this by a sophistical, delusive argument, then putting out the other, by an argument that best suits the time. Yea, how oft is the candle of the wicked put out, by such glorious learning as this. Nay, I doubt not, but a man of your principles, were he put upon it, would not stick to count those you call gospel-positive precepts, of no value at all in the Christian religion; for now, even now, you do not stick to say that, that even *that* of going to God by Christ, is one of these, and that such an one, as if absolutely considered in itself, is neither good nor evil. How then, if God should cast you into Turkey, where Mahomet reigns as lord? It is but reckoning that it is the religion and custom of the country, and that which is authorized by the power that is there; wherefore it is but sticking to your dictates of human nature, and remembering that coming to God by Christ is a thing of an indifferent nature in itself, and then for peace' sake, and to sleep in a whole skin, you may comply, and do as your superior commands. Why? Because in Turkey are your first sort of fundamentals found: there are men that have human nature, and the law of morals written in their hearts; they have also the dictates thereof written within them, which teach them those you call the eternal laws of righteousness; wherefore you both would agree in your essential and immutable differences of good and evil (p. 6), and differ only about these positive laws, indifferent things. Yea, and Mahomet also *for the time*, because by a custom made convenient, might be now accounted worshipful, and the circumstances that attend his worship, especially those of them that clash not with the dictates of your human nature, might also be swallowed down.

Behold you here, then, good reader, a glorious Latitudinarian, that can, as to religion, turn and twist like an eel on the angle, or rather like the weathercock that stands on the steeple.

"For," saith he, "our refusing to comply with these can hardly proceed from anything better than a proud affectation of singularity, or at best, from superstitious scrupulosity" (p. 242).

Do but believe him therefore in what he saith, and you cannot choose but be ready with him to comply with all modes that may serve for advantage.

Besides, he saith, "that the word superstition, in the Greek, implieth a rightful and over-timorous apprehension of the divine nature; and consequently a base and undervaluing conception of it."

So that to be tender of conscience, especially in things of divine worship, binding up the soul to the words of the everlasting testament, in such things especially as a fool can call little and insignificant trivial matters, rendereth a man such an one as hath a very erroneous conscience.

But he would not be understood (p. 244) as if he here intended to vilify things that are plainly commanded, or to tolerate that which is plainly forbidden, only he would have all things that may fall within the reach of these two general heads, be examined by this general rule, " his description of the design of Christianity."

Ans. But I could tell him, that whatsoever is imposed as a part of God's worship, is judged by a better rule than his, both as to its goodness and badness; neither can we account anything indifferent that is a part thereof. Besides, whatsoever is reputed a part of God's worship, layeth hold on the conscience of the godly: although a ranting Latitudinarian may say, " If the devil should preach, I would hear him, before I would suffer persecution ;" as a brave fellow which I could name, in his zeal, was pleased to declare.

But what trust should any man put to the rule to which you direct him for help and relief therein ? seeing that from the beginning to the end, from the top to the bottom, it is a cursed, blasphemous book—a book that more vilifieth Jesus Christ than many of the Quakers themselves; for which of them said worse of him, and make coming to God by him a more insignificant thing, than you by your pretended design of Christianity have done ?

We have, therefore, a more sure word of the prophets, to the which " we do well to take heed," (2 Pet. i. 19 ;) by which, both your doctrine and practice is already judged to be naught, as will be farther discovered time enough, when you shall justify or condemn particulars.

Your twenty-fourth chapter I shall now pass by, until I can better compare you and popery, against which you there so stoutly diggle together.

Your twenty-fifth chapter carrieth in it an hideous outcry against many of *your* ministers and guides, complaining and confessing " that nothing hath so conduced to the prejudice of your Church of England, and done the separating parties so much service, as the scandalous lives of some that exercise your ministerial function " (p. 258).

Ans. I will grant it, if you respect these poor carnal people, who yet have been shamed from your assemblies by such vicious persons you mention : but the truly godly, and spiritually judicious, have left you from other arguments, of which I shall not here dilate.

But from page 261 to the end of the chapter, you take upon you to particularize other of your ministers that are an offence to you, and to the design of your Christianity.

1. " Such as affect to make people stare at their high-flown, bombastic language, or to please their fantasies with foolish jugglings, and pedantic or boyish wit; or to be admired for their ability in dividing of an hair, their metaphysical acuteness and scholastic subtlety, or for their doughty dexterity in controversial squabbles." And, I add, had you joined herewith, such as vilify and trample upon the blood of the Lord Jesus, preferring the snivel of their own brains before him, you had herein but drawn your own picture, and given your reader an emblem of yourself.

2. The second sort you blame, are "such as

seek to approve themselves to their auditories to be men of mysteries, and endeavour to make the plain and easy doctrines of the gospel as intricate and obscure as ever they are able."   I will add to these, such as take away the doctrine of faith, and that set themselves and their works in the room thereof : such as have sought to overturn the foundation, Jesus Christ, and have made coming to God by him, in itself of a far more indifferent nature than the dictates of our humanity.

3. Another sort (you say) are " such as preach upon free grace, and Christian privileges, otherwise than as motives to cite to obedience, and never scarce insist upon any duties but those of believing, laying hold on Christ's righteousness, applying the promises, and renouncing our own righteousness," which they that have none at all to renounce have a mighty kindness for.

Ans. (1.) Who they are that preach free grace in your church, to excite men to uncleanness, you may know better than I. But if these words (otherwise than to cite men to obedience) be thus thrust in, of purpose thereby to speak evil of the preachers of free grace, and the exalters of the imputed righteousness of Christ, then look to it; for such venom language as this doth but involve you within the bowels of that most dreadful prophecy, concerning the false prophets of the last days, that shall privily bring in damnable heresies, even denying the Lord that bought them.

(2.) The preaching of free grace, pressing to believing, and laying hold on Christ's righteousness, is the most available means under heaven to make men holy and righteous : first before God, and then before men.

(3.) The preaching of these are first, and principally, to beget faith, to beget life, to beget souls to God; yea, to beget in men such a principle, whereby they may serve God acceptably, with reverence and godly fear.

(4.) But to preach free grace doth much condemn your free will; to preach Christ's righteousness doth utterly curse and condemn yours ; and to preach the promise of grace doth quite shut out a covenant of works : therefore no marvel if you, who are so wedded to these things, be such an enemy to free grace, the righteousness of Christ, and the gospel-promises, that you make even these things a characteristical note (first abusing the consequences of them) of a church-troubling preacher.

(5.) You tauntingly proceed, saying, " Such preachers also press us to renounce our own righteousness, which they that have none at all to renounce have a mighty kindness for."

Ans. Indeed those that have a righteousness of their own, as the Pharisees and hypocrites of old, had never much kindness for the doctrine of grace, and the ministers of Christ; but the publicans and harlots had : and therefore these, while they that had righteousness stumbled and fell, entered into the kingdom of heaven.   " The publicans and the harlots go into the kingdom of heaven before you." But what righteousness have you of your own, to which you so dearly are wedded, that it may not be let go for the sake of Christ? seeing also so long as you go about to establish it, you submit not yourself " to the righteousness of God." (Rom. x. 3.) Yea, why do you taunt those ministers that persuade us to renounce our own righteousness, and those also that follow their doctrine? seeing this was both the doctrine and practice of Paul and all others, save only those that had Moses' veil over their hearts.

Another sort of ministers that you say are enemies to the promoting of holiness, are "such as are never in their element but when they are talking of the irrespectiveness of God's decrees, the absoluteness of his promises, the utter disability and perfect impotency of natural men to do anything towards their own conversion, and that insist with great emphasis and vehemency upon such like false and dangerous opinions" (p. 262).

Ans. The men that preach these things, being rightly stated, preach the truth of God, if the Scriptures may bear sway, they having all been proved the truth of the gospel, both by the prophets and apostles; and when you shall think meet by argument to contradict them, either I, or some other, may show you the folly of your undertaking. In the meantime, let the reader take notice that here you have judged not by Scripture, nor by reason, but upon a bare presumption, arising from your pride or ignorance. Wherefore I pray you, in your next, show us,

(1.) What is in man that the decree of election should respect as a thing foreseen of God, to prevail with him to predestinate him to eternal life by Jesus Christ our Lord.

(2.) Make it manifest that in the word of God there neither is, nor can be, any absolute promise contained.

(3.) Show us what ability there is in a natural man, as such, to do things towards his own conversion; I mean things immediately tending to, and that must infallibly consummate therein, and let us see what things they are. And know that when you have well done all this, according to the scriptures of truth, that then it will be time enough to condemn the contrary for false and dangerous opinions.

But shall I speak the truth for you? The reason of this your presumptuous exclamation and condemnation of these things, is because they stand in the way of promoting your ignorant, tottering, promiseless, and gospelless holiness; they stand in the way of old Adam; they stand in the way of your dunghill, rebellious righteousness; they stand in the way of your freedom of will; and a great rabble more of such-like pretended virtues. Yea, they do, and must, and shall stand there, when you and the rest of the Socinians and Quakers have said their all against them.

There is yet another sort of preachers whom you condemn, and so do I as well as you, though not in your spirit, nor to advance your pestiferous principles; and they are "such as make it their great business to advance the petty interest of any party whatsoever, and concern themselves more about doing this, than about promoting and carrying on that wherein consists the chief good of all mankind; and are more zealous to make proselytes to their particular sects, than converts (I will add first, to Jesus Christ, and then) to a holy life; and press more exact and rigid conformity to their modes and forms than to the laws of God, and the essential duties of the Christian religion" (p. 263).

Lastly, the caution which you give to ministers, because there wanteth for it among *you* a foundation, is to be esteemed but an error and an abuse of the words and practices of the apostle. And as for your subtle and close incensing the power to persecute Nonconformists, know that we are willing, God assisting, to overcome you with truth and patience, not sticking to sacrifice our lives and dearest concerns in a faithful witness-bearing against your filthy errors, compiled and foisted into the world by your devilish design to promote paganism against Christianity (pp. 265, 266).

I come now to your twenty-sixth chapter, which is spent to prove, "that an obedient temper of mind is a necessary and excellent qualification to prepare men for a firm belief, and a right understanding of the gospel of Christ" (p. 267).

Ans. 1. Forasmuch as the obedient temper you mention is precedent to, or before faith, and the right understanding of the gospel, it must needs be also that which stands with unbelief, and ignorant of the same. Now, that this should be an excellent and necessary qualification to a firm belief and right understanding of the gospel, is altogether without proof and truth. But this is affirmed, for the further promoting of your human nature, and the things that originally are dictates thereof. But,

2. The obedience, or inclination to obedience, that is before faith, or the understanding of the gospel, is so far off from being an excellent preparative, or good qualification for faith and the knowledge of the gospel, that in its nature (which is more than in its consequences) it is a great obstruction thereto.

For, while a man remains faithless and ignorant of the gospel, to what doth his obedient temper of mind incline? Not to faith, nor the gospel of Christ, for with these, as yet, you suppose he hath not to do; therefore he inclineth to the law of morals, either as it was delivered in tables of stone from Sinai, or as written in the hearts of all the children of men, to it, under the last consideration, (which is, in truth, the most heathen and pagan,) to it, as so you intend your obedient temper of mind should incline (pp. 7—10).

Now, this doctrine being in itself of quite another nature than the doctrine of faith, and also, as such, a covenant by itself, it requireth the mind by virtue of its commands, to stand to THAT, and to rest in that; for of necessity the heart and mind of a man can go no further than it seeth, and hath learnt, but by this moral doctrine; the heart and mind is bound and limited to itself by the power of the dictate to obedience, and the promise of obtaining the blessing when the preceptive part of it is fulfilled. Hence Paul tells us, 2 Cor. iii., that though that ministration that was written and en-graven in stones (which in nature is the same with this) is glorious, yet these imperfections attended the man that was in it.

1. He was but within the bounds of the minis-tration of death.

2. In this estate he was blind and could not see how to be delivered therefrom; "the veil is over their heart," so that they could not heretofore, neither can they now, see to the end of that which was commanded, neither to the perfection of the command, nor their own insufficiency to do it, nor to the death and curse of God that attended him, that in everything continued not in all that was written in the book of the law to do them.

3. Every lecture, or reading of this old law, is as a fresh hood-winking of its disciples, and a doubling of the hindrance of their coming to Christ for life. "But their minds were blinded: for until this day the same vail remaineth untaken away in reading of the Old Testament; which vail is done away in Christ. But even unto this day, when Moses is read, the vail is over their heart." (2 Cor. iii. 14, 15.)

And let the reader note, that all these things attend the doctrine of morals; the ceremonies being in themselves more apt to instruct men in the knowledge of Christ, they being by God's ordination, figures, shadows, representations, and emblems of him; but the morals are not so, neither as written in our natures, nor as written and en-graven in stones. (Gal. iii. 24.) Wherefore, your so highly commended obedient temper of mind (you intending thereby an hearty compliance before faith, with morals for righteousness) is so far off from being an excellent temper, and a necessary qualification, to help a man to a firm belief, and a right understanding of the gospel, that it is the most ready way of all ways in the world, to keep a man perpetually blind and ignorant thereof. Wherefore the apostle saith, that the vail, the ignorance, cannot be taken away, but when the heart shall turn to the Lord, that is, from the doc-trine of morals, as a law and covenant in our na-tures, or, as it was written and engraven in stones, to Christ for mercy to pardon our transgressions against it, and for imputative righteousness to justify us from it. While Moses is read, the vail is over the heart; that is, while men with their minds stand bending also to do it: but mark, when it (the heart) shall turn to the Lord, or to the word of the gospel, which is the revelation of him, then the vail shall be taken away.

And hence it will not be amiss, if again we consider how the Holy Ghost compareth, or setteth one against another, these two administrations.

The law he calls the letter, even the law of morals, that law that was written and engraven in stones. The other ministration he calls the minis-tration of the Spirit, even that which Christ offered to the world upon believing.

Again, he denieth himself to be a minister of the law of morals. He hath made us able ministers of the New Testament, not of the letter, or law, but of the Spirit, or gospel. The reason is, for the letter, or law, can do nothing but kill, curse, or condemn; but the Spirit, or the gospel, giveth life. Farther, in comparing, he calls the law, the ministration of death, or that which layeth death at the doors of all flesh; but the gospel, the minis-tration of righteousness, because, by this ministry, there is a revelation of that righteousness, that is fulfilled by the person of Christ; and to be imputed for righteousness to them that believe, that they might be delivered from the ministration of death. How then—hath the ministration of God no glory? Yes, forasmuch as it is a revelation of the justice of God against sin. But yet again, its glory is turned into no glory, when it is compared with that which excelleth. For if the ministration of death, written and graven in the stones, was glorious, so that the children of Israel could not steadfastly behold the face of Moses, for the glory of his countenance,—which glory was to be done away,—how shall not the ministration of the Spirit be rather glorious? for if the ministration of con-demnation be glory, much more doth the ministra-tion of righteousness exceed in glory; for even that which was made glorious hath no glory in this respect, by reason of the glory that excelleth. (2 Cor. iii. 7—10.)

So then, your obedient temper of mind, foras-much as it respecteth the law of morals, and that too, before faith, or a right understanding of the gospel, is nothing else but an obedience to the law, a living to death, and the ministration of condemnation; and is a persuading the world, that to be obedient to that ministration—that is, not the ministration of the gospel, but holdeth its disciples in blindness and ignorance, in which it is impossible Christ should be revealed—is an excellent, yea, a necessary qualification to prepare men for a firm belief, and a right understanding of the gospel of Christ, which yet even blindeth, and holdeth all blind that are the followers of that ministration. I come now to your proof, which indeed is no proof of this anti-gospel assertion, but texts abused, and wrestled out of their place, to serve to underprop your erroneous doctrine. The first is, "If any man will do his will, he shall know of the doctrine, whether it be of God, or whether I speak of myself." (John vii. 17; p. 268.)

Ans. This scripture respecteth not at all the moral law, or obedience to the dictates of human nature, as an acceptable qualification precedent to faith, or that for the sake of which God will give men faith in, and a right understanding of the gospel, but is itself an immediate exhortation to believing, with a promise of what shall follow; as who shall say, The Father hath sent me into the world to be salvation to it, through faith in my blood : my Father's will therefore is, "that men believe in me;" and if any will do his will, he shall know of the doctrine, he shall feel the power thereof, by the peace and comfort that will presently possess the soul, and by the holy effects that follow.

That this is the true exposition of this place will be verified if you consider, that to do the will of God, in a New Testament sense, is to be taken under a double consideration. 1. As it respecteth Christ. 2. Man.

1. As it respecteth *Christ*, so it concerns his completing the redemption of man by himself, by his own personal performances. (John vi. 38, 39. Heb. x. 5—10.)

2. As it respecteth *man*, it doth first and immediately respect our believing on him for remission of sins and eternal life. "And this is the will of the Father which sent me, (saith Christ :) that every one that seeth the Son, and believeth on him, may have everlasting life : and I will raise him up at the last day." (John vi. 40.) This then is the will of God—that men do believe in Jesus Christ.

Again, when the Jews asked Jesus Christ what they should do, that they might work the works of God, he did not send them first to the moral precept, or to its first principles in the hearts of men, by obeying that to fit themselves for faith, but immediately he tells them, "This is the work of God, that ye believe on him whom he hath sent." (John vi. 29.) This is the work of God; that is, "This is his commandment, That we should believe on the name of his Son Jesus Christ, &c., and love one another, as he gave us commandment." (1 John iii. 23.) If any man will do his will, he shall know of the doctrine, that is, (as I have said,) he shall feel, and have the authority of this faith in his heart, both to give peace and joy in his heart, and assurance, and the sealing of his soul to glory. For all these things come in upon believing first in Christ.

1. "By faith we have peace with God." (Rom. v. 1.)

2. "We have joy and peace through believing." (Rom. xv. 13.)

3. "Assurance comes also through believing." (John vi. 69. Heb. x. 22.)

4. Yea, and the sealings up to eternal life. "In whom also after that ye believed, ye were sealed with that holy spirit of promise." (Eph. i. 13.)

5. Sanctification, and a right obedient temper, is not to be found in men before, but after they have believed. "He purified their hearts by faith." Yea, heaven and eternal happiness is promised to them who are sanctified by faith, which is in Christ. (Acts xv. 9; xxvi. 18.)

The first text, therefore, hath been by you abused, in that you have ungodly strained it, but in vain, to make it warrant your heathenish preparations to faith.

The second scripture, "He that is of God heareth God's words; ye therefore hear them not, because ye are not of God." (John viii. 47.)

Ans. This scripture supposeth men must first be of God, before they can hear God's word; before they can hear it with the hearing of faith; and therefore nothing respecteth those that before they have faith live in the law of works, and least of all those that become obedient thereto, that thereby they may obtain everlasting life. For these are not of God, not of him in a New Testament sense; not sons, because they are born of men, of the will of men, of the law, and according to the wisdom of flesh and blood. (John i. 12, 13.)

Your third scripture is, "And as many as were ordained to eternal life believed." (Acts xiii. 48.) Which text you thus expound, "That as many of the Gentiles as were disposed, or in a ready preparedness for eternal life, believed; that is, those which were proselytes of the gate, who were admitted by the Jews to the hope of eternal life, and to have a portion in the age to come, without submitting to the whole law, or any more than owning the God of Israel, and observing the seven precepts of Noah."

Ans. 1. That obedience to the moral law is not a preparative to faith, or an excellent and necessary qualification to the right understanding of the gospel, I have proved.

2. That to be a Jewish proselyte was to live in the faith of Messias to come, is the strain of all the scriptures that have to deal with them.

3. But that ordaining men to eternal life respects an act of the Jews, or that the Jews did dispense with the Gentile proselytes, in their casting off all their laws, but the seven precepts of Noah;

4. Or that God counted this a fit, or forerunning qualification to faith in Jesus Christ, neither stands with the word of God, nor the zeal of that people.

5. Besides, the words presently following seem to me to insinuate more, viz., that the Jews and religious proselytes that adhered to Paul at his first sermon, (ver. 43,) did contradict and blaspheme at his second, (ver. 45;) and moreover, that it was they that raised persecution upon him, and expelled him out of their coasts, (ver. 50.) When the Gentiles, even those that were more barbarously ignorant at his coming, when they heard that by Christ there was offered to them the forgiveness of sins, they believed, (ver. 48,) and glorified the word of the Lord: the wisdom of heaven so disposing such of their hearts, that were before by HIM, not by Jews, ordained to life. "And as many as were ordained to eternal life believed."

But you come again, in p. 269, to the scripture first urged by you, "If any man will do his will," &c., and you tell us, that this must also needs be implied, he shall rightly understand the doctrine too; which word, understand, you so carry as may best help you in case you should meet with an adversary. As if any should thus object that here you have granted that the words make promise of an understanding of the gospel, yea, require in it the very first act of the will, then you readily shift it by saying, That this is implied only; suggesting that obedience to morals is expressed, and therefore must first be thought on and done. But, if one of your brotherhood stop here, and make the objection, then you add, " It is knowledge, at least, in all the necessary points thereof, absolutely necessary and essential parts," from among which you long since did cast out, " Coming to God by Jesus Christ." Yea, you add, " That by (that which you call) the design of the gospel, it may be presumed, that whosoever considereth it with a design of being so, (that is, of living up to human principles, and that desireth to be possessed again of the holiness he hath lost, for that is it for the proof of which you have written above 300 pages,) he must needs believe the gospel to have come from God, and also be enlightened in the true knowledge of at least the necessary points of it," viz., all moral duties contained therein, which are never a one of them as such an essential of the gospel, but are such duties as are consequential to the belief thereof.

Wherefore (although you feign it) this honest temper, as you call it, will not help you, 1. To judge of the gospel without prejudice; nor 2. To evidence it with satisfaction; nor 3. Secure those in whom it is from error and delusion : no man being more brutish or heathenish, nor so void of satisfaction about it, nor more involved in error concerning it, than yourself; being truly what you charge upon others : 1. Grossly ignorant; 2. Too highly opinionate; 3. Proud in affectation; 4. Liquorish; 5. A self-lover; 6. And for your blasphemy under the just judgment of God. " If our gospel be hid, it is hid to them that are lost : in whom the God of this world hath blinded the minds of them that believe not, lest the light of the glorious gospel of Christ, who is the image of God, should shine unto them." (2 Cor. iv. 3, 4.)

I am come now to your last chapter, (p. 281,) which tells us wherein the essence and life of Christianity consisteth, viz., in a good state and habit of mind, in a holy frame and temper of soul.

Ans. 1. It consisteth in a life of faith, when I live in the belief of this, that Christ loved me, and gave himself for me. " The life that I now live in the flesh," saith Paul, " it is by the faith of the Son of God, who loved me, and gave himself for me."

2. And besides a good state and habit of mind, or an holy frame and temper of soul, in your notion of them, which respecteth purely obedience to morals, from natural impulses, or dictates of our humanity, they are rather heathenish than Christian, and being alone, end in death rather than life. " As many as are of the works of the law, are under the curse;" he saith not they that sin against it, but they that are of the works of it, such as do justice, righteousness, charity, goodness, mercy, patience, and all kind of moral duties, from principles human,

natural, or, as men, they are under the curse, because they have sinned first, and also are infirm and weak in their pursuit after the perfections they desire. These follow after righteousness, but that flies from them; wherefore they do not obtain it, because they seek it not by faith in Christ, but as it were by the works, the righteous, good, and holy works of the law. (Rom. ix. 30—32.) But you add,

" It is such a habit of mind, such a frame and temper of soul, as esteemeth God as the chiefest good, and preferreth him and his Son Jesus Christ before all the world, and that prizeth above all things an interest in the divine perfections," &c.

Ans. God must needs be esteemed the chiefest good, by all that have but, and are ruled by, the light of nature, because they see him by his works to be almighty, merciful, and eternal. (Rom. i. 20.) But this may be where the knowledge of the man, the Mediator, is not; therefore this, in this and in your sense, cannot be of the essence of Christianity, for that it is common to all the world. That estimation of God which is common to natural men cannot be of the essence of Christianity, because they want that knowledge of him that comes by Jesus Christ, and so are not capable to esteem of him under a Christian consideration.

But you say, " It is that good habit and temper of mind that preferreth God, and his Son Jesus Christ, before all the world."

Ans. He that esteemeth God above all, must needs, at least in his judgment, so prefer him; but whereas you add, and his Son Jesus Christ, you put in them words but as a cloak, for yourself have not preferred his Son Jesus Christ, no not before a moral law, no not before your obedience to it, although but by human principles; yea, you have accounted the command of God, by which we are enjoined by him to come to God, a thing in itself but like levitical ceremonies, or as baptism and the Lord's supper—a thing in itself indifferent, and, absolutely considered, neither good nor evil (pp. 7—9).

You add, " It is such a temper as prizeth above all things an interest in the divine perfections, such as justice and righteousness, universal charity, goodness, mercy, patience, and all kind of purity."

Ans. 1. Seeing by these expressions you only intend moral virtues, and those that are inherent in you, and originally operations of humanity, it is evident that you have but impiously and idolatrously attributed to your own goodness so high and blessed a title. For whatsoever is in your nature, and originally the dictates thereof, and whatsoever proficiency you make therein by human principles, and helps of natural endowments, these things are but of yourself, your own justice, your own righteousness, your own charity, goodness, mercy, patience, kindness, &c. Now to call these the divine perfections, when they are only your own human virtues, bespeaks you, I say, fond, impious, and idolatrous, and shows you, in the midst of all your pretended design to glorify God, such an one who have set up your own goodness with him, yea, and given it the title of his blessed grace and favour.

That scripture you mention, Rom. xiv. 17, although by the word righteousness, there is intended obedience to the moral law, yet to it by persons already justified by Christ's righteousness; hence they are said to do it in the joy and peace of the Holy Ghost, or by the joy and peace which they had by faith in Christ's righteousness, as revealed to them by the Spirit of God. Hence again, they are said in it to serve Christ, or to receive the law at his hand, which he giveth to them to walk after, having first justified them from the curse thereof by his blood.

2. The law was given twice on Sinai; the last time with a proclamation of mercy going before, and he that receiveth it thus, receiveth it after a gospel manner; for they as justified persons are dead to the law as a covenant of works by the body of Christ, that they might live to another, even to him that is raised from the dead. (Rom. vii. Gal. ii. 19.) But you by this scripture intend not this doctrine, for you make justification by Christ come after, not before, obedience to the law; yea, you make obedience thereto the essential, and coming to God by Christ but a thing of a more remote nature from true and substantial gospel-righteousness.

In p. 283, you speak again of the old principle, and thus you comment: "A principle of holiness that respecteth duty, as with respect to the nature of the command, so not with respect to the duty as occasioned by certain external inducements and motives, but from a good temper and disposition of soul."

Ans. This I say, still respecting your old principle of humanity, and the purity of your nature, the most amounts but to this: Your principle is confined to a liberty of will and affections, with respect to doing of the law of works, which many have professed to have, and do before you, and yet have come short of the glory of God. For as I told you before, I tell you now again, that the gospel principles are the Holy Ghost and faith, which help that soul in whom they dwell to count believing in Jesus Christ the great and essential part of our Christianity, and our reckoning ourselves pardoned for the sake of him: "And thus being set free from sin, we become the servants of God, and have our fruit unto holiness, and the end everlasting life." (Rom. vi. 22.)

Your description of a child of Abraham, you meaning in a New Testament sense, is quite beside the truth. For albeit the sons of Abraham will live holy lives, and become obedient to the substantial laws, yet it is not their subjection to morals, but faith in Jesus, that giveth them the denomination of children of Abraham. "Know ye, therefore, that they that are of faith are the children of Abraham: they that are of faith the same are

the children of Abraham: yea, they that are of faith are blessed with faithful Abraham." (Gal. iii. 7, 9.) In p. 284, you say, "That there is not one duty more affectionately recommended to us in the gospel than is almsgiving."

Ans. Yes, that there is, and that which more immediately respecteth our justification with God, than ten thousand such commandments; and that is, faith in Christ. Almsdeeds is also a blessed command; yet but one of the second table, such as must flow from faith going before. Faith, I mean, that layeth hold on Christ's righteousness, if it be accepted of God: for before the heart be good, the action must be naught; now the heart is good by faith, because faith, by applying Christ's righteousness, makes over whole Christ to the soul, of whose fulness it receiveth, and grace for grace. (John i. 16.) Many things in this last chapter are worthy reprehension, but because you tell us, in the last two pages thereof, is the sum of all that need to be said, I will immediately apply myself to what is there contained.

You say (p. 296), "It is not possible we should not have the design of Christianity accomplished in us, and therefore that we should be destitute of the power of it, if we make our Saviour's most excellent life the pattern of our lives." By our Saviour's life (as by a parenthesis you also express), you mean, as yourself hath, in short, described it (chap. v.,) viz., "The greatest freedom, affability, courtesy, candour, ingenuity, gentleness, meekness, humility, contempt of the world, contentation, charity, tenderness, compassion, patience, submission to the divine will, love of God, devoutest temper of mind towards him, mighty confidence and trust in God," &c.

Ans. Our Saviour's life, in not only these, but all other duties that respected morals, was not principally or first to be imitated by us, but that the law, even in the preceptive part thereof, might be fully and perfectly fulfilled for us. "Christ is the end of the law for righteousness;" the end, not only of the ceremonial law, but the ten commandments too; for if the word, righteousness respecteth in special them, "Jesus increased in favour with God." (Luke ii. 52. Matt. iii. 17.) This respecteth him as made under the law, and his pleasing of God in that capacity. So also doth that, "In him I am well pleased." Now, I say, as Jesus stood in this capacity, he dealt with the law in its greatest force and severity, as it immediately came from God, without the advantage of a Mediator, and stood by his perfect complying with and fulfilling every tittle thereof. Besides, as Jesus Christ had thus to do with the law, he did it in order to his " finishing transgression, and putting an end to sin," (Dan. ix. 24,) and so, consequently, as Mediator, and undertaker for the world. For his perfect complying withal, and fulfilling every tittle of the law, respected nothing his own private person, that he for himself might be righteous thereby; for in himself he was eternally just and holy, even as the Father, but it respected us, even us : for us he was made under the law, that we, by his fulfilling the law, might by him be redeemed from under the law, and also receive the adoption of sons. (Gal. iv. 4, 5.) For we having sinned and transgressed the law, and the justice of God, yet requiring obedience thereto, and the law being too weak through our flesh to do it, God therefore sent his own Son in the likeness of sinful flesh, who himself for us did first of all walk in the law, and then for sin suffered also in his flesh, the sentence and curse pronounced against us by the law. For it was nothing less necessary, when the Son of God became undertaker for the sin of the world, that he should walk in obedience to the whole of the precepts of the law, to deliver us from the judgment of the law; I say it was no less necessary he should do so, than that he should bear our curse and death. For it would have been impossible for him to have overcome the last, if he had not been spotless touching the first : for therefore it was impossible he should be holden of death, because he did nothing worthy of death, no, not in the judgment of the law, to which he immediately stood. Now, as Christ Jesus stood thus to, and walked in the law, it is blasphemy for any to presume to imitate him, because thus to do so is to turn mediator and undertaker for the sin of the world. Besides, whoso doth attempt it undertakes an impossibility, for no man can stand by the moral law, as it immediately comes from the Divine Majesty, he having sinned first, even before he goeth about to fulfil it. And in this sense is that to be understood, " As many as are of the works of the law are under the curse," (Gal. iii. 10,) held accursed, because they have sinned first; accursed in their performances because of imperfection, and therefore assuredly accursed at last, because they come short of the righteousness thereof.

1. Christ Jesus did never set himself forth for an example, that we by imitating his steps in morals should obtain justification with God from the curse of that law; for this would be to overthrow and utterly abolish the work which himself came into the world to accomplish, which was not to be our example, that we by treading his steps might have remission of sins, but that through the faith of him, through faith in his blood, we might be reconciled to God.

2. Besides, thus to imitate Christ is to make of him a Saviour, not by sacrifice, but by example : nay, to speak the whole, this would be to make his mediatorship wholly to centre, rather in prescribing of rules, and exacting obedience to morals, than in giving himself a ransom for men. Yea, I will add, to imitate Christ as you have prescribed, may be done by him that yet may be ignorant of the excellency of his person, and the chief end of his being made flesh. For in all these things which you have discoursed in that fifth chapter of him, you have only spoken of that something of which is ap-

prehended by the light of nature; yea, nature itself will teach that men should trust in God, which is the most excellent particular that there you mention. Wherefore our Lord Jesus himself foreseeing that in men there will be a proudness to content themselves with that confidence, he intimateth that it would be in us insignificant if it stand without faith in himself. " Ye believe naturally in God, (saith he,) believe also in me." (John xiv. 1.) Faith in Jesus is as absolutely necessary as to believe immediately in the Divine Being : yea, without faith in Jesus, whosoever believeth in God is sure to perish and burn in hell. " If you believe not that I am he, ye shall die in your sins." (John viii. 24.) And to take Jesus in morals for example, is nowhere called believing in him, neither is there one promise of eternal life annexed to such a practice. But you say, " If we tread in his blessed steps, and be such, according to our measure and capacity, as we have understood he was in this world."

Ans. I say, for a man to confine himself only to the life of the Lord Jesus for an example, or to think it enough to make him, in his life, a pattern for us to follow, leaveth us, through our shortness in the end, with the devil and his angels, for want of faith in the doctrine of remission of sins; for Christ did nowhere make another mediator between God and him, nor did he ever trust to another man's righteousness to be thereby justified from the curse of the law; neither did he at all stand in need thereof, without which we must be damned and perish. Now, I say, these things being nowhere practised by him, he cannot therein be an example to us. And I say again, seeing that in these things, by faith in them, is immediately wrapped up our reconciliation with God, it followeth, that though a man take the Lord Jesus Christ in his whole life for an example in the end, that, notwithstanding, he abideth unreconciled to God. Neither will that clause " and be such" help such a person at all : for justification with God comes not by imitating Christ as exemplary in morals, but through faith in his precious blood. In the law I read, that the paschal lamb was neither to be eaten sodden nor raw, but roast with fire must it be eaten. (Exod. xii.) Now, to make salvation principally to depend upon imitating Christ's life, it is to feed upon him raw, or at most, as sodden, not sanctified and holy ; but the precept is, " eat it roast with fire ;" is the antitype, as accursed of God for sin, and enduring the punishment for it. (Exod. xix. Deut. xxxiii. 2. Mal. iv. 1.) The law is compared to fire, and its curse to a burning oven. Now, under the curse of this fiery law, was the Lord Jesus afflicted for the sins of the world : wherefore, as so considered, our faith must lay hold upon him for justification with God. " This is the law of the burnt offering, (which was the offering for sin :) it is the burnt offering, because of the burning upon the altar all night unto the morning, and the fire of the altar shall be burning in it." (Lev. vi. 9.) But now I would inquire, had Israel done the commandment, if they had eaten the passover raw, or boiled in water? or if they had offered that offering, that was to be burnt as a sin-offering, otherwise than it was commanded? Even so, to feed upon Christ, as he is holy, and of good life only; and also, as taking him therein for an example to us, to follow his steps for justification with God; this is, to eat the passover raw, and not as roast with fire; this is, to feed upon Jesus, without respecting him as accursed of God for our sin, and so consequently to miss of that eternal life; that by his blood he hath obtained for every one that believeth on him. I have been pleased with this observation: "That none of the signs and wonders in Egypt could deliver the children of Israel thence, till the Lamb was slain, and roast with fire." (Exod. xii.) And I have been also pleased with this: "That the Father, not Moses, gave the manna from heaven, which was a type of the flesh and blood of Christ, that whoso feedeth on, shall live for ever." (John vi. 32.) Yea, circumcision also, which was a type of inward, and heart-holiness, was not of Moses, but of the Fathers, and principally a consequence of the faith of Abraham. (John vii. 22.) Whence I gather, that no wonder, but the blood of Christ can save; that no kindness, but the mercy of God, can give this to us; and that no law, but the law of faith, can make us truly holy in heart. But you add, "Those that sincerely, and industriously, endeavour to imitate the holy Jesus in his Spirit and actions, can never be ignorant what it is to be truly Christians." Those that follow Jesus in his Spirit, must first receive that Spirit from heaven, which Spirit is received, as I have often said, by applying first, by faith, the merits of Christ to the soul, for life and justification with God. The Spirit is not received by the works of the law, but by the hearing of faith: neither comes it in the ministry, or doctrine of morals, but in and by the ministry of faith; and the law is not of faith. Wherefore, seeing you have, in p. 223, of your book, forbidden sinners to come first to Jesus for justification with God, the spirit you talk of, however you call it the Spirit of Jesus, can be no other than the spirit of a man; which you also yourself (in pp. 7, 8, 9) call "the purity of human nature, a principle of reason, the first principles of morals, or those that are originally dictates of human nature." Wherefore by these words (in his Spirit) you do but blaspheme the Holy Ghost, and abuse your ignorant reader; calling now (Quaker-like) the dictates of your humanity, and your Socinian compliances therewith, the Spirit of Holy Jesus. I conclude therefore, that the way of salvation, or the design of Christianity as prescribed by you, is none other than the errors of your own brain, the way of death, the sum and heart of Papistical Quakerism, and is quite denied by the Lord Jesus, and by his blessed Testament. And now go your ways, and imitate the Lord Jesus, and take the whole history of his life for your example, and walk in his steps, and be such as much as you can, yet without faith in his blood first; yea, and if you stand not just before God through the imputation of his righteousness, your imitating will be found no better than rebellion, because by that, instead of faith in his blood, you hope to obtain remission of sins, thrusting him thereby from his office and work, and setting your dunghill righteousness up in his stead.

I come now to your conclusion. First, in p. 298, you press men to betake themselves to find (that which you call) the design of Christianity, accomplished in their hearts and lives.

Ans. Seeing that the holiness, that your erroneous book hath exalted, is none other but that which we have lost; yea, and again, seeing you have set this in the head of, and before the righteousness of Christ, I admonish my reader to tremble at the blasphemy of your book, and account the whole design therein to be none other but that of an enemy to the Son of God, and salvation of the world. For that holiness as I have showed, is none other but a shadowish, Christless, graceless holiness; and your so exalting of it, very blasphemy. You proceed, saying, "Let us exercise ourselves unto real and substantial godliness, (still meaning your Adamitish holiness;) let us study the gospel not to discourse, or only to believe, but also, and above all things, to do well."

Ans. Herein still you manifest, either ignorance of, or malice against, the doctrine of faith; that doctrine which, above all doctrines, is the quintessence of the New Testament, because therein (and not principally, as you feign, by doing well) is the righteousness of God revealed, and that from faith to faith; not from faith to works, nor yet from works to faith. Besides, the gospel is preached in all nations, for the obedience of faith. (Rom. xvi. 26.) Neither works, the law, the dictates of humanity, nor the first principles of morals, knowing what to do with the righteousness of the gospel, which is a righteousness imputed by God, not wrought by us; a righteousness given, not earned; a righteousness received by believing, not that which floweth from our obedience to laws; a righteousness which comes from God to us, not one that goeth from us to God. Besides, as I also have hinted before, the apostle and you are directly opposite. You cry, "Above all things do well;" that is, work and do the law: but he, "Above all, take the shield of faith, wherewith are quenched all the fiery darts of the wicked." (Eph. vi.)

But you add (p. 300), "Let us do what lieth in us to convince our atheist, that the religion of the blessed Jesus is no trick or device; and our wanton and loose Christians, that it is no notional business, or speculative science."

Ans. This you cannot do by your moral natural principles of humanity: for even some of your brave philosophers, whose godliness you have so much applauded, were even then in the midst of their, and your virtues, atheistically ignorant of the religion of Jesus. And as to the loose Christian, Christ neither hath need of, nor will he bless your blasphemous opinions, nor feigned godliness, but real ungodliness, to make them converts to his faith and grace; neither can it be expected it should, seeing you have not only dirty thoughts, but vilifying words, and sayings of his person, work, and righteousness. You have set your works before his (p. 223), calling them substantial, indispensable, and real, but coming to God by him a thing in itself indifferent (p. 7—9). You go on, and say, " Let us declare, that we are not barely reliers on Christ's righteousness, by being imitators of it" (p. 300). You cannot leave off to contemn and blaspheme the Son of God. Do you not yet know that the righteousness of Christ, on which the sinner ought to rely for life, is such, as consisted in his standing to, and doing of the law, without a Mediator? And would you be doing this? What, know you not that an essential of the righteousness he accomplished for sinners when he was in the world is, "That he was conceived by the Holy Ghost, born without sin, did all things in the power of, and union with, his own eternal Godhead?" And are you able thus to imitate him? Again, the righteousness on which we ought to rely for life, is that which hath in it the merit of blood: "We are justified by his blood through faith in his blood." (Rom. v. 9.) Is this the righteousness you would imitate? Farther, the righteousness on which poor sinners should rely is that for the sake of which God forgiveth the sins of him that resteth by faith thereupon. But would you be imitating of, or accomplishing such a righteousness?

Your book, Sir, is begun in ignorance, managed with error, and ended in blasphemy.

Now the God of glory, if it may stand with his glory, give you a sight of your sins against the Son of God, that you may, as Saul, lie trembling, and being astonished, cry out to be justified with the righteousness of God, without the law, even that which is by faith of Jesus Christ, unto all, and upon all them that believe.

Many other gross absurdities, which I have omitted in your whole book, may perhaps be more thoroughly gathered up, when you shall have taken the opportunity to reply. In the meantime I shall content myself with this.

" Behold the Lamb of God, which taketh away the sin of the world." (John i. 29.)

" Even Jesus, who delivered us from the wrath to come." (1 Thess. i. 10.)

" Who when he had by himself purged our sins, sat down on the right hand of the Majesty on high." (Heb. i. 3.)

" Christ died for our sins." (1 Cor. xv. 3.)

" God hath made him to be sin for us." (2 Cor. v. 21.)

" Christ was made a curse for us." (Gal. iii. 13.)

" He bare our sins in his own body on the tree." (1 Pet. ii. 24.)

" He loved us, and washed us from our sins in his own blood." (Rev. i. 5.)

" God for Christ's sake hath forgiven you." (Eph. iv. 32.)

" We have redemption through his blood, the forgiveness of sins, according to the riches of his grace." (Eph. i. 7.)

Now unto the King, eternal, immortal invisible, the only wise God, be honour, and glory, for ever and ever. Amen.

THE CONCLUSION.

That my reader may farther perceive that Mr. Fowler, even by the chief of the articles of the Church of England, is adjudged erroneous, and besides the very fundamentals of the doctrine of Jesus Christ, and that in those very principles that are in the main, I say, and that most immediately concern Christ, faith, and salvation, will be evident to them that compare his design of Christianity with these articles hereunder recited.

The Article concerning Free will.

" The condition of man after the fall of Adam, is such, that he cannot turn and prepare himself, by his own natural strength and good works, to faith, and calling upon God: wherefore we have no power to do good works, pleasant and acceptable to God, without the grace of God by Christ preventing us, that they may have a good will and working with us, when we have that good will."

The Article concerning Justification.

" We are accounted righteous before God, ONLY for the merit of our Lord and Saviour Jesus Christ, by faith; and not for our own works, or deservings. Wherefore that we are justified by faith ONLY, is a most wholesome doctrine, and full of comfort," &c.

The Article of Works before Justification.

" Works done before the grace of Christ, and the inspiration of his Spirit, are not pleasant to God, for as much as they spring not of faith in Jesus Christ, or deserve grace of congruity: yea, rather for that they are not done as God hath willed and commanded them to be done, we doubt. not but they have the nature of sin."

These articles, because they respect the points in controversy betwixt Mr. Fowler, and myself; and because they be also fundamental truths of the Christian religion, as I do heartily believe, let all men know that I quarrel not with him, about things wherein I dissent from the Church of England, but do contend for the truth contained, even in these very articles of theirs, from which he hath so deeply revolted, that he clasheth with every one of them, as may farther be shown when he shall take heart to reply.

But to wind up this unpleasant scribble, I shall have done when I have farther showed how he joineth with Papist and Quaker, against these wholesome and fundamental articles.

Mr. Fowler's Doctrine compared with Campian the Jesuit, upon that question whether Faith only justifieth : saith Campian—

1. *Campian.* "We (Papists) say, that as grace is put into us in justification, so also our righteousness is enlarged through good works, and is inherent in us; therefore it is not true that God doth justify by faith ONLY."

Fowler. "Justifying faith is such a belief of the truth of the gospel as includes a sincere resolution of obedience unto all its precepts; and that it justifieth *as* it doth so. . . . . In short, is it possible that faith in Christ's blood, for the forgiveness of sins, should be the only act which justifieth a sinner ? " (pp. 221, 224.)

2. *Campian.* "So that faith is urged, but not faith ONLY. Again, by faith is meant all Christianity, and the whole religion of Christians."

Fowler. "For surely the faith which entitles the sinner to so high a privilege as that of justification must needs be such as complieth with all the purposes of Christ's coming into the world, especially with his grand purpose, ... as Lord, and that it is no less necessary that it should justify as it doth this " (p. 222).

3. *Campian.* "Though works void of Christ are nothing, yet through grace they serve to justification."

Fowler. "Of the imputation of Christ's righteousness, ... this is the true explication : it consists in dealing with sincerely righteous persons, as if they were perfectly so, for the sake and upon the account of Christ's righteousness. The grand intent of the gospel being to make us partakers of an inward and real righteousness ; and it being but a secondary one, that we should be accepted, and rewarded, as if we were completely righteous" (pp. 225, 226).

4. *Campian.* "Speaking of faith, hope, and charity, he confesseth, that faith in nature is before them, but it doth not justify before they come."

Fowler. "What pretence can there be for think-,ing, that faith is the condition, or instrument, of justification, as it complieth with only the precept of relying on Christ's merits, for the obtaining of it : especially when it is no less manifest than the sun at noon-day, that obedience to the other precepts must go before obedience to this " (pp. 223, 284).

5. *Campian.* "I deny that faith ONLY doth justify, for you have not in all the word of God that faith only doth justify."

Fowler. "And, for my part, I must confess that I would not willingly be he that should undertake to encounter one of the champions of that foul cause, with the admission of this principle, that faith jus-

tifieth, only as it apprehendeth the merits and righteousness of Jesus Christ. I must certainly have great luck, or my adversary but little cunning, if I were not forced to repent me of such an engagement" (p. 225).

6. *Campian.* "Abraham being a just man, was made more just by a living faith."

Fowler. "He only is a true child of Abraham, who, in the purity of the heart, obeyeth those substantial laws that are imposed by God upon him" (p. 283).

7. *Campian.* "I say that charity and good works are not excluded (in the causes of our justification)."

Fowler. "For we have shown, not only that reformation of life from the practice, and purification of heart from the liking of sin, are as plainly as can be asserted in the gospel to be absolutely necessary to give men a right to the promises of it, but also that its great salvation doth even consist in it" (pp. 214, 215).

Mr. Fowler's Doctrine compared with William Penn the Quaker.

1. *Penn.* "Life and salvation is to them that follow Christ, the light, in all his righteousness, which every man comes only to experiment, as he walks in a holy subjection to that measure of light and grace, wherewith the fulness hath enlightened him " (*Sandy Foundation*, p. 19).

Fowler. "That is, those which are of an indispensable, and eternal obligation, which were first written in men's hearts, and originally dictates of human nature " (p. 8).

2. *Penn.* "I really confess that Jesus Christ fulfilled the Father's will, and offered up a most satisfactory sacrifice, but not to pay God, or help him to save men " (p. 32).

Fowler. "Christ was set forth to be a propitiatory sacrifice for sin; I will not say that his Father (who is perfectly *sui juris*) might be put by this means into a capacity of forgiving it " (p. 85).

3. *Penn.* "God's remission is grounded on man's repentance, not that it is impossible for God to pardon without a plenary satisfaction " (p. 16).

Fowler. "There are many that do not question but that God could have pardoned sin, without any other satisfaction than the repentance of the sinner," &c. (p. 84.)

4. *Penn.* "Justification doth not go before, but is subsequential to the mortification of lusts " (p. 27).

Fowler. "This blessing of making men holy was so much the design of Christ's coming, that he had his very name from it :" observe the words are, " He shall save his people from their sins;" not from the punishment of them. And that is the primary sense of them, which is most plainly expressed in them : " That he shall save his people from the punishment of sin, is a true sense too; but it is secondary and implied only, as this latter is the never-failing and necessary consequent of the former salvation " (pp. 14, 15).

5. *Penn.* " Since, therefore, there can be no admittance had, without performing that righteous will, and doing those holy, and perfect sayings, alas! to what value will an imputative righteousness amount?" &c. (p. 25.)

Fowler. " Christ shall bring in an inward, substantial, and everlasting righteousness, and, by abrogating the outward, and establishing ONLY this righteousness, he should enlarge the Jewish church, an accession of the Gentiles being by that means made unto it " (p. 16).

6. *Penn.* " Since God has prescribed an inoffensive life as that which only can give acceptance with him, and on the contrary hath determined never to justify the wicked, &c. . . , . Will not the abomination appear greatest of all where God shall be found condemning the just on purpose to justify the wicked? and that he is thereto compelled, or else no salvation, which is the tendency of their doctrine, who imagine the righteous and merciful God to condemn and punish his righteous Son, that he having satisfied for our sins, we might be justified (while unsanctified) by the imputation of his perfect righteousness.   Oh, why should this horrible thing be contended for by Christians?" (pp. 24, 25.)

Fowler. " If it were possible (as it hath been proved it is not) that a wicked man should have God's pardon, it would not make him cease to be miserable " (p. 119).

Penn. " Were it possible that Christ's righteousness could be imputed to an unrighteous man, I dare boldly affirm it would signify as little to his happiness, as would a gorgeous and splendid garment, to one that is almost starved with hunger, or that lieth racked by the torturing diseases of the stone, or colic " (p. 120).

Fowler. " To justify a wicked man, while he continueth so, if it were possible for God to do it, would far more disparage his justice and holiness than advance his grace and kindness " (p. 130).

7. *Penn.* " Unless we be doers of that law, which Christ came not to destroy, but as our example to fulfil, we can never be justified before God" (p. 26).

Fowler. " It is impossible we should not have the design of Christianity accomplished in us, and therefore that we should be destitute of the power of it, if we make our Saviour's most excellent life, the patron of our lives.   Those that sincerely and industriously endeavour to imitate the holy Jesus in his spirit and actions, can never be ignorant what it is to be truly Christians, nor can they fail to be so " (p. 296).

8. *Penn.* " Nor let any fancy that Christ hath so fulfilled it for them, as to exclude their obedience from being requisite to their acceptance, but only as their pattern " (p. 26).

Fowler. " This Son of God taught men their duty, by his own example, and did himself perform among them, what he required of them. Now that he should tread before us EVERY step of that way, which he hath told us leadeth to eternal happiness, and commend those duties which are most ungrateful to our corrupt inclinations, by his own practice, our having so brave an example is no small encouragement to a cheerful performance of all that is commanded " (p. 148).

Understandest thou what thou readest?

PREFATORY REMARKS

ON

THE SAINTS' PRIVILEGE AND PROFIT.

THE enthronement of grace,—the elevation of mercy to supreme power and dominion,—presents an image to the mind on which it may well meditate with delight. But, beautiful as such figurative representations of the truth might be made, the truth itself, in the simplest mode in which it can be conveyed to the soul, is far more deeply and permanently affecting. Did mercy exist by itself, or had grace a life and substance of its own, and could we see it on its high path of glory till it was crowned, and became invested with regal authority, the triumph of such a power, so essential to our hopes of safety, would be a joyful event. But it is a far greater cause for joy to know that God himself is the minister of grace and mercy: that it is to his throne we are to go in the time of need; and that, instead of having to personify some quality or attribute, we have only the Lord to think of, and of him alone to ask the help we require. It is of great importance, both to the correctness of our views, and to the support of our hopes, that we should thus strip all essential doctrines, all primary truths, of metaphorical dress. The severer the simplicity of our ideas, on all subjects connected with God's treatment of sinners, the less likely we are to indulge in error. It is with a deeper sense of the force of truth that a doctrine is received when it comes to us in its own shape, unmasked and uncoloured by the touch of imagination. The only absolutely safe method of explaining divine mysteries by comparisons or metaphors, or any other such resources of human language, is by collecting them into groups from Scripture itself, and showing, without forcing their meaning, in what degree they bear upon the subject in hand. This, generally speaking, is Bunyan's method. His vast command of Biblical illustration enabled him to throw the pure light of heavenly wisdom upon every topic which he discussed. But, even in his case, there was a tendency to clothe the main truth, or central fact, in too great an abundance of analogous matter. Strong convictions are attended with a feeling of repose. This feeling is disturbed, or weakened, rather than increased, by an excess of illustration.

A mine of precious evangelical thought is opened in the following discourse. It can hardly be read with attention and not leave a powerful impression on the mind. Great would have been the loss had the early editors and publishers of Bunyan's works neglected to preserve it. But, valuable as it is in so many important respects, it affords a striking example of the effect of redundancy in lessening the direct force of a noble and sublime truth. The "throne of grace" is an expression to which only a very vague meaning will be attached by minds uninstructed in divine things. To the Christian, who ascribes whatever degree of peace and hope which he enjoys to the pure mercy of God, it has a full, rich significance. He knows that for the purpose of his salvation nothing but omnipotent grace could have availed; and, whenever it is spoken of, he looks at it as existing in the will of God only, and, therefore, as enthroned amid all the other glories of his nature. In neither case will the idea intended by the expression, be rendered more intelligible or effective by the suggestion that God has many thrones. To suppose, even in the way of imagery, that he has one throne for judgment, another for grace or mercy,—that he changes from seat to seat when he condemns or pardons, is a dangerous tampering with that exactness of thought which should be strictly cultivated, and never sacrificed for any consideration in the mention of God. It is not sufficient for us, in a matter of such extreme importance, to know what is true. The feelings, or affections, have a far greater influence over us in religion than knowledge, however exact. Thus, though a bold figure of speech may leave our faith, as founded in knowledge only, altogether unharmed, it may so effect our general state of feeling as to throw a thick shade over practical views of truth; and perplex us just at those very periods of anxiety when we most need immediate consolation. "God hath more thrones than one" is Bunyan's strong statement. When fully understood, according to the writer's own meaning, it may be adopted as only representing the various execution of God's counsels. But an inexperienced or incautious reader will suffer no little harm from accepting it, if he find it leading his thoughts in the train of literal interpretation. The first step in such a process would take him far away from the line of sober meditation. He would lose sight of the fact, that as God is "without variableness or shadow of turning," "the same yesterday, to-day, and for ever," the perfections of his nature cannot act separately, or be exalted the one above the other. A throne of grace, or a throne of holiness, is not the same expression, strictly considered, as the throne of God. The language of metaphor, even when proper to his attributes or operations, cannot always, with safety, be applied to God himself.

In the account given of the " throne of grace " Bunyan's own spirituality and holy affections connect the expression with many comforting truths. But in some cases the interpretation is far too complicated with notions not necessary to the meaning of the phrase; and tending, therefore, to render it less intelligible and impressive. When ordinary readers are told that the throne of grace is the " heart and soul of Jesus Christ," one, that is, of the thrones of God " in which he sits and resteth for ever," they are startled by the boldness of the language, and feel how much easier it is to understand the fact that God exercises mercy through Jesus, and accepts all who come to him in his name, than the statement that he sits on the heart and soul of Jesus.

If we except these occasional excesses of devout ingenuity, the following discourse may be regarded as a treasury of spiritual reflections. Bunyan himself would, probably, have been little sparing of criticism on what Catholic writers say about the holy heart of Jesus. But the language of religious metaphor retains its character in all ages, and by whomever used : the truth or error which it may convey is only to be discovered by patient thought. It should evidently, therefore, be a serious question, with writers on subjects of great interest, to what degree they may indulge themselves in such a style. There are vital principles, facts of sublimest grandeur, sentiments of deepest pathos, which impress some minds with increasing force the more remote the provinces of thought through which they can be traced. In this case none of the countless analogies, combinations, and suggestions which pious erudition may command, will be without its use. The discovery that truth exists under a vast multiplicity of forms is, with speculative inquirers, a source of genuine delight. For them it is a benefit to set the holy and the learned on the path before them. They are thereby, at least, kept safe from sinful, presumptuous error. Even fancy will not often fall into any injurious mysticism when under the government of experienced piety.

H. S.

THE SAINTS' PRIVILEGE AND PROFIT.

" Let us therefore come boldly unto the throne of grace, that we may obtain mercy, and find grace to help in time of need."—
HEB. iv. 16.

THIS epistle is indicted and left to the church by the Holy Ghost, to show particularly, and more distinctly, the high priesthood of Jesus Christ, and the excellent benefits that his people have thereby. In which both the excellency of his person, and transcendent glory of his office, beyond either priest or priesthood of the law, is largely set forth before us in chap. i. and ii., &c.

Wherefore in order to our beneficial reading of this epistle, the Spirit of God calls upon us, first most seriously to consider what an one this excellent person is. " Wherefore, holy brethren," said he, " you that are partakers of the heavenly calling :" consequently you that are related to, and that are concerned in the undertaking of this holy one, " consider the apostle and high priest of our profession, Christ Jesus." (Heb. iii. 1.) Consider how great and how fit this man is for so holy and glorious a calling. He being so high, as to be far above all heavens ; so great, as to be the Son of, and God equal with the Father. Consider him also as to his humanity, how that he is really flesh of our flesh ; sinlessly so, sympathisingly so, so in all the compassions of a man ; he is touched with, compassioneth, pitieth, loveth, succoureth us, and feeleth our infirmities, and maketh our case his own. Nay, he again from the consideration of his greatness and love, puts us upon a confident reliance on his undertaking, and also presseth us to a bold approach of that throne of grace, where he continually abideth in the execution of his office : " Seeing then," saith he, " that we have a great high priest that is passed into the heavens, Jesus the Son of God, let us hold fast our profession. For we have not an high priest which cannot be touched with the feeling of our infirmities, but was in all points tempted like as we are, yet without sin. Let us therefore come boldly unto the throne of grace." (Heb. iii. 14—16.)

In the words we have,

1. An exhortation. 2. An implication, that we shall reap a worthy benefit if we truly put the exhortation into practice. The exhortation is, That we shall come bodly to the throne of grace, " Let us therefore come boldly unto the throne of grace." In all we have an intimation of five things.

I. That God hath more thrones than one. Else the throne of grace need not to be specified by name. " Let us come unto the throne of grace."

II. That the godly can distinguish one throne from another. For the throne here is not set forth, by where or what signs it should be known; it is only propounded to us by its name, and so left for saints to make their approach unto it. " Let us come unto the throne of grace."

III. The third thing is, The persons intended by this exhortation, " Let us therefore come." Us ?—what us ? or who are they that by this exhortation are called upon to come ? " Let us."

IV. The manner of the coming of these persons to this throne of grace ; and that is through the veil, boldly, confidently. " Let us come boldly unto the throne of grace."

V. The motive to this exhortation, and that is twofold. 1. Because we have so great an high priest, that cannot but be touched with the feeling of our infirmities. " Let us therefore come boldly unto the throne of grace." 2. And because we are sure to speed ; " That we may obtain mercy, and find grace," &c.

I shall, as God shall help me, handle these things in order.

I. *That God hath more Thrones than one.*

For the first, that God hath more thrones than one. He hath a throne in heaven, and a throne on earth. " The Lord's throne is in heaven," and " they shall call Jerusalem the throne of the Lord." (Ps. xi. 4. Jer. iii. 17.) He ruleth over the angels, He ruleth in his church. " He ruleth in Jacob unto the ends of the earth," (Ps. lix. 13 :) yea, he has a throne and seat of majesty among the princes and great ones of the world. He ruleth or " judgeth among the gods." (Ps. lxxxii.1.) There is a throne for him as a Father, and a throne for Christ as a giver of reward to all faithful and overcoming Christians ; " To him that overcometh, will I grant to sit with me on my throne, even as I also overcame, and am set down with my Father in his throne." (Rev. iii. 21.)

There is also to be a throne of judgment, on which God by Christ, at the great and notable day shall sit to give to the whole world their last or final sentence: from which, no, not by any means, they shall never be released. This throne is made mention of in the New Testament; and is called by Christ, " the throne of his glory," and " a great white throne." (Matt. xxv. 31. Rev. xx. 11.) And his presence, when he sits upon this throne, will be so terrible, that nothing shall be able to abide it, that is not reconciled to God by him before.

Wherefore it is not amiss that I give you this hint, because it may tend to inform unwary Christians, when they go to God, that they address not themselves to him at rovers, or at random; but that when they come to him for benefits, they direct their prayer to the throne of grace, or to God as considered on a throne of grace. For he is not to be found a God merciful and gracious, but as he is on the throne of grace. This is his holy place, out of which he is terrible to the sons of men, and cannot be gracious unto them. For as when he shall sit at the last day upon his throne of judgment, he will neither be moved with the tears or misery of the world to do anything for them, that in the least will have a tendency to a relaxation of the least part of their sorrow; so now let men take him where they will, or consider him as they list, he gives no grace, no special grace, but as considered on the throne of grace: wherefore they that will pray, and speed, they must come to a throne of grace; to a God that sitteth on a throne of grace. "Let us therefore come boldly unto the throne of grace, that we may obtain," &c.

The unbeliever, the erroneous and superstitious consider not this; wherefore they speak to God as their fancies lead them, not as the word directs them, and therefore obtain nothing. Ask the carnal man to whom he prays; he will say to God. Ask him where this God is; he will say in heaven. But ask him how, or under what notion he is to be considered there; and he will give a few generals, but cannot direct his soul unto him as he is upon a throne of grace, as the apostle here biddeth him, saying, "Let us come boldly unto the throne of grace." Wherefore they come and go, or rather go and come to no advantage at all; they find nothing but their labour or words for their pains. For the right considering of God when I go unto him, and how or where I may find him gracious and merciful, is all in all; and mercy and grace is then obtained when we come to him as sitting upon a throne of grace.

II. *That the Godly can distinguish one Throne from another.*

We will therefore come to the second thing, to wit, that the godly can distinguish one throne from another. And the reason why I so conclude is, as I said, because the throne here is not set forth unto us here, by where or what signs it should be known; it is only propounded to us by its name, a throne of grace, and so left for saints to make their approach thereto. "Let us therefore come boldly unto the throne of grace."

We will therefore take this conclusion into two parts, and consider it under this double position.

FIRST. That there is a throne of grace.

SECOND. That it is the privilege of the godly to distinguish from all other thrones whatever, this throne of grace.

FIRST. *There is a throne of grace.* This must be true, because the text saith it; also it is that of which the mercy-seat so often made mention of in the Old Testament was a type, shadow, or figure; nor is the terms of seat, and throne, of any strength to make this supposition void. For it is common for the antitype to be put forth in words unto us more glorious than is the figure or shadow of that thing. And the reason is, for that the heavenly things themselves are far more excellent than the shadow by which they are represented. What is a sheep, a bull, an ox, or calf, to Christ; or their blood, to the blood of Christ? What is Jerusalem, that stood in Canaan, to that new Jerusalem that shall come down from heaven? or the tabernacle made with corruptible things, to the body of Christ, or heaven itself? No marvel then if they be set forth unto us by words of an inferior rank; the most full and aptest being reserved to set out the highest things withal.

Before I proceed to give you a more particular description of this throne of grace, as also how it may be known, I will a little touch upon the terms themselves, and show briefly what must be implied by them.

First. By this word, grace, we are to understand God's free sovereign good pleasure, whereby he acteth in Christ towards his people. Grace and mercy, therefore, are terms that have their distinct significations; mercy signifies pitifulness, or a running over of infinite bowels to objects in a miserable and helpless condition; but grace signifies that God still acts in this as a free agent, not being wrought upon by the misery of the creature as a procuring cause, but of his own princely mind.

Was there no objects of pity among those that in the old world perished by the flood, or that in Sodom were burned with fire from heaven? doubtless according to our apprehension there were many; but Noah, and he only, found grace in God's eyes, not because that of himself he was better than the rest, but God acted as a gracious prince towards him, and let him share in mercy of his own sovereign will and pleasure. But this, at first, was not so fully made manifest as it was afterwards. Wherefore the propitiatory was not called as here, a throne of grace, but, a mercy-seat, albeit there was great glory in them terms also; for, by mercy-seat was showed, not only that God had compassion for men, but that also to be good, was as his continual resting-place, whither he would at length retire, and where he would sit down and abide, whatever terrible or troublesome work for his church was on the wheel at present. For a seat is a place of rest, yea, is prepared for that end; and in that here mercy is called that seat, it is to show, as I said, that whatever work is on the wheel in the world, let it be never so dreadful and amazing, yet to God's church it shall end in mercy, for that is God's resting-place. Wherefore after God had so severely threatened and punished his church, under the name of a whorish woman, as you may read in the prophet Ezekiel, he saith, "So will I make my fury toward thee to rest, and my jealousy shall depart from thee, and I will be quiet, and will be no more angry." And again, speaking of the same people, and of the same punishments, he saith, " Nevertheless I will remember my covenant with thee in the days of thy youth, and I will establish unto thee an everlasting covenant." And again, " I will establish my covenant with thee, and thou shalt know that I am the Lord. That thou mayest remember, and be confounded, and never open thy mouth any more, because of thy shame, when I am pacified towards thee for all that thou hast done, saith the Lord God." (Ezek. xvi. 42, 60—63.) These, with many more places, show that mercy is God's place of rest, and thither he will retire at last, and from thence will bless his church, his people.

But yet these terms, a throne, the throne of grace, doth more exceed in glory, not only because the word, grace, shows that God, by all that he doth towards us in saving and forgiving, acts freely as the highest Lord, and of his own good will and pleasure, but also for that he now saith, that his grace is become a king, a throne of grace. A throne is not only a seat for rest, but a place of dignity and authority. This is known to all. Wherefore by this word, a throne, or the throne of grace, is intimated, that God ruleth, and governeth by his grace. And this he can justly do. " Grace reigns through righteousness unto eternal life through Jesus Christ our Lord." (Rom. v. 21.) So then, in that here is mention made of a throne of grace, it showeth that sin, and Satan, and death, and hell must needs be subdued. For these last mentioned are but weakness and destruction ; but grace is life, and the absolute sovereign over all these to the ruling of them utterly down. A throne of grace !

By this, then, God plainly declareth that he is resolved this way to rule, and that he pointeth at sin as his deadly foe : and if so, then, " where sin abounded, grace did much more abound." (Rom. v. 20.) For it is the wisdom and discretion of all that rule, to fortify themselves against them that rebel against them what they can. Wherefore he saith again, " Sin shall not have dominion over you ; for ye are not under the law, but under grace." (Rom. vi. 14.) Sin seeks for the dominion, and grace seeks for the dominion ; but sin shall not rule, because it has no throne in the church among the godly. Grace is king, grace has the throne, and the people of God are not under the dominion of sin, but of the grace of God, the which they are here implicitly bid to acknowledge, in that they are bid to come boldly to it for help. " That we may obtain mercy, and find grace to help ; to help in time of need." For as from the hand and power of the king comes help and succour to the subject, when assaulted by an enemy, so from the throne of grace, or from grace, as it reigns, comes the help and health of God's people. Hence it is said again, " A glorious high throne from the beginning is the place of our sanctuary." (Jer. xvii. 12.)

Here then the saints take shelter from the roaring of the devil, from the raging of their lusts, and from the fury of the wicked. That also is a very notable place, " He will subdue our iniquities, and thou wilt cast all their sins into the depths of the sea." (Micah vii. 19.) He speaks here of God as solacing himself in mercy, and as delighting of himself in the salvation of his people, and that without comparison. " Who is a God like unto thee, that pardoneth iniquity, and passeth by the transgression of the remnant of his heritage ? he retaineth not his anger for ever, because he delighteth in mercy." (Micah vii. 18.) Thus is mercy and grace got into the throne, reigns, and will assuredly conquer all ; yea, will conquer, and that with a shout ; " Mercy rejoiceth against judgment," (James ii. 13 :) yea, glorieth when it getteth the victory of sin, and subdueth the sinner unto God and to its own salvation, as is yet more fully showed in the parable of the Prodigal Son. (Luke xv.) But this briefly, to show you something of the nature of the terms, and what must necessarily be implied thereby.

Second. We will in the next place show what is to be inferred from hence. And,

1. To be sure this is inferred, that converted men are not every way, or in every sense, free from the being of sin : for, were they, they need not betake themselves to a throne of grace for help. When it saith there is grace in God, it inferreth that there is sin in the godly ; and when it saith, grace reigns, as upon a throne, &c., it implies that sin would ascend the throne, would reign, and would have the dominion over the children of God. This also is manifest, when he saith, " Let not sin therefore reign in your mortal body, that ye should obey it in the lusts thereof." (Rom. vi. 12.) And the only way to prevent it is to apply ourselves as by the text we are directed, to the throne of grace for help against it.

2. The text implies that at certain times, the most godly man in the world may be hard put to it, by the sin that dwelleth in him ; yea, so hard put to it, as that there can be no ways to save himself from a fall, but by imploring heaven and the throne of grace for help. This is called the needy time, the time when the wayfaring man that knocked at David's door shall knock at ours, (2 Sam. xiii. ;) or when we are got into the sieve into which Satan did get Peter, (Luke xxii. 31;) or when those fists are about our ears that were about Paul's ; and when that thorn pricks us that Paul said was in his flesh. (2 Cor. xii. 7, 8.) But why or how comes it to pass that the godly are so hard put to it at these times, but because there is in them, that is, in their flesh, no good thing, but consequently all aptness to close in with the devil and his suggestions to the overthrow of the soul?

But now here we are presented with a throne of grace, unto which, as David says, we must continually resort, and that is the way to obtain relief, and to find help in time of need. (Ps. lxxi. 3.)

3. As Christians are sometimes in imminent dangers of falling, so sometimes it is so that they are fallen, are down, down dreadfully, and can by no means lift up themselves. And this happeneth unto them because they have been remiss as to the conscionable performance of what by this exhortation they are enjoined to. They have not been constant supplicants at this throne for preserving grace; for had they, they should, as the text suggests, most certainly have kept from such a fall; help should have been granted them in their needful time. But that is it, of which such are guilty, which is written in the prophet Isaiah, " But thou hast not called upon me, O Jacob; but thou hast been weary of me, O Israel." (Isa. xliii. 22.) Therefore thou art profaned, therefore thou art given to reproaches. (Isa. xliii. 28.)

Now, as they which are falling are kept from coming down by coming to this throne of grace, so those that are fallen must rise by the sceptre of love extended to them from thence. Men may fall by sin, but cannot raise up themselves without the help of grace. Wherefore it is worthy of our inquiry after a more thorough knowledge of this throne of grace, whence, as we may well perceive, our help comes, and by what comes from thence we are made to stand.

I therefore come now to a more particular description of this throne of grace, and to show how the godly know, or may know it, from other thrones of God.

First, then, this throne of grace is the humanity or heart and soul of Jesus Christ, in which God sits and resteth for ever, in love towards them that believe in him : forasmuch as Christ did, by the body of his flesh when here, reconcile them unto the Father. " The key of the house of David," saith God, " will I lay upon his shoulder; so he shall open, and none shall shut; and he shall shut, and none shall open. And I will fasten him as a nail in a sure place; and he shall be for a glorious throne to his father's house." (Isa. xxii. 22, 23.) For a glorious throne to his father's house, that is, for his father's house to come to their Father by; for that they shall always find him thereon; or, as another scripture saith, in Christ, reconciling them unto him, not imputing to them their trespasses and sins. (2 Cor. v. 19.)

Nor is it possible that we lay aside the human nature of Christ, for us to find any such thing as a throne of grace either in earth or heaven; for that then nothing can be found to be the rest of God. " This is my beloved Son, in whom I am well-pleased," (Matt. iii. 17,) is God's own language, but there is none other of whom he hath so said. Wherefore he resteth in him towards us, and in him only. Besides, grace cannot be extended towards us but in a way of justice; for that the law, and our sin obstructeth another way. But lay the human nature of Christ aside, and where will you find *that* that shall become such a sacrifice to justice for the sin of men, as that God, for the sake

of that, shall both forgive, and cause that grace for ever should reign towards us in such a way? It reigns through righteousness, or justice, by Jesus Christ, and no way else. Christ Jesus, therefore, is this throne of grace, or him, or that by which grace reigns towards the children of God.

That scripture also gives us a little light herein. '' And I beheld, and, lo, in the midst of the throne," &c., " stood a Lamb as it had been slain." (Rev. v. 6.) This is to show the cause why grace is so freely let out to us, even for that there stands there in the midst of the throne and in the midst of the elders, a lamb as it had been slain, or as it was made a sacrifice for our sin; for as a slain lamb he now lives in the midst of the throne, and is the meritorious cause of all the grace that we enjoy. And though it seems by this text, that the throne is one thing, and the Lamb another, yet the Lamb of God is the throne, though not as a lamb or sacrifice, but as one that by his sacrifice has made way for grace to run like a river into the world. The Son of God, Jesus Christ, is ALL : he is the throne, the altar, the priest, the sacrifice, and all; but he is the throne, the priest, the altar, and the sacrifice under divers considerations. He is not the throne, as he is the priest; he is not the priest, as he is the sacrifice; he is not the sacrifice, as he is the altar; yet is truly all these : yea, there is no throne of grace, no high priest, no propitiatory sacrifice, &c., but he; of all which we may yet speak further before we conclude this treatise.

I conclude, then, that Christ Jesus, in his human nature, is this throne of grace : in his human nature, I say, he has by that completely accomplished all things necessary for the making way for grace to be extended to men; and that that is not only God's place of rest, but that by, and from which, as upon a glorious throne, his grace shall reign over devil, death, sin, hell, and the grave for ever.

This human nature of Christ is also called the tabernacle of God, for the fulness of the Godhead dwells in it bodily. It is God's habitation, his dwelling-place, his chair and throne of state. He doth all in and by it, and without it he doth not anything. But to pass this, let us come to the next thing.

Second. We will now come to discourse of the placing of this throne of grace, or to discover where it is erected. And for this we must repair to the type which, as was said before, is called the mercy-seat. The which we find, not in the outward court, nor yet within the first veil, (Heb. ix. 3—5,) which signifies, not in the world, nor in the church on earth; but in the holy of the holies, or after the second veil, the flesh of Christ. (Heb. x. 20.) There then is the throne of God, this throne of grace, and no where here below. And forasmuch as it is called the throne of God, of grace, and is there, it signifieth that it is the highest, and most honourable. Hence he is said to be far above all heavens, and to have a name above every name.

Wherefore he that will come to this throne of grace, must know what manner of coming it is by which he must approach it, and that is, not personally, but by runnings out of heart; not by himself, but by his Priest, his High priest; for so it was in the type. (Heb. ix. 7.) Into the second, where the mercy-seat was, went the high-priest alone, that is, personally, and the people by him, as he made intercession for them. This then must be done by those that will approach this throne of grace: they must go to God as he is enthroned in Christ, by Christ as he is the High priest of his church; and they must go to him in the holiest, by him.

But again, as this throne of grace is in the holiest, not in the world, not in the church on earth, so it is in this holiest set up above the ark of the testimony; for so was the mercy-seat; it was set up in the most holy place, above the ark of the testimony. (Deut. x. 1—5. 1 Kings viii. 9. 2 Chron. v. 10.) The ark of the testimony; what was that? Why it was the place of the law, the ark in which it was kept: the testimony was the law, the ark was prepared to put that in. This ark, in which was put this law, was set up in the holiest, and the ·mercy-seat was set above it; for so was Moses commanded to place them. Thou shalt make an ark, saith God, " and thou shalt make a mercy-seat:" the ark shall be called the ark of the testimony, and there "thou shalt put the testimony I shall give thee," that is, the law, " and thou shalt put the mercy-seat above upon the ark, and there I will meet with thee, from above the mercy-seat between the two cherubims which are upon," that is, above, "the ark of the testimony," " shadowing the mercy-seat." (Exod. xxv. 16—22. Heb. ix. 5.)

Thus, then, were things of old ordained in the type by which we gather what is now to be minded in our worshipping of God. There was an ark made, and the two tables of stone, in which the law was writ, was put therein. (Deut. x. 2—5.) This ark, with these two tables, were put into the holiest, and this mercy-seat was set above it. The Holy Ghost, in my mind, thus signifying that grace sits upon a throne that is higher than the law, above the law; and that grace therefore is to rule before the law, and notwithstanding all the sentence of the law; for it sitteth, I say, upon a throne, but the law sits on none; a throne, I say, which the law, instead of accusing, justifieth and approveth. For although it condemneth all men, yet it excepteth Christ, who in his manhood is this throne of grace. Him, I say, it condemneth not, but approveth, and liketh well of all his doings; yea, it granteth him, as here we see, as a throne of grace, to be exalted above itself; yea, it cannot but so do, because by wisdom and holiness itself, which is also the Lord of the law, it is appointed so to do. Here then is the throne of God, the throne of grace, namely, above the ark of the testimony: on this God and his grace, sits, reigns,

and gives leave to sinners to approach his presence for grace and mercy. He gives, I say, for those sinners so to do, that have washed before in the brazen laver that is prepared to wash in first, of which we may speak more anon.

Now behold the wisdom of God in his thus ordaining of things; in his placing, in the first place the law, and Christ the ark of the testimony, and the mercy-seat, or throne of grace, so nigh together; for doubtless it was wisdom that thus ordained them, and it might so ordain for these reasons.

1. That we that approach the throne of grace might, when we come there, be made still to remember that we are sinners,—" for by the law is the knowledge of sin," (Rom. iii. 20,)—and behold just before us is this ark in which are the two tables that condemn all flesh. Yea, we must look that way, if we look at all; for just above it is the mercy-seat, or throne of grace. So then here is a memento for them that come to God, and to his throne of grace for mercy, to wit, the law, by which they are afresh put in remembrance of themselves, their sins, and what need they have of fresh supplies of grace. I read that the laver of brass, and the foot of it, was made of the looking-glasses of the women that assembled at the door of the tabernacle, (Exod. xxxviii. 8,) methinks to signify, that men might see their smyrches (smudges) when they came to wash; so here you see, the law is placed even with the mercy-seat, only that stood above, whereby those that come to the throne of grace for mercy, might also yet more be put in mind that they are sinners.

2. This also tendeth to set an edge upon prayer, and to make us more fervent in spirit when we come to the throne of grace. Should a king ordain that the axe and halter should be before all those that supplicate him for mercy, it would put yet an edge upon all their petitions for his grace, and make them yet the more humbly and fervently implore his majesty for favour. But behold, the mercy-seat stands above, is set up above the ark and testimony that is in it. Here, therefore, we have encouragement to look for good. For observe, though here is the law, and that too in the holiest of all, whither we go, yet above it is the mercy-seat and throne of grace triumphant, unto which we should look, and to which we should direct our prayers. Let us, therefore, come boldly to the throne of grace, notwithstanding the ark and testimony is by; for the law cannot hurt us when grace is so nigh; besides, God is now not in the law, but upon the throne of grace that is above it, to give forth pardons, and grace, and helps, at a time of need.

This then may serve to inform some whereabout they are, when they are in their closets, and at prayer. Art thou most dejected when thou art at prayer? Hear me, thou art not far from the throne of grace; for thy dejection proceedeth from thy looking into the ark, into which God hath ordained, that whosoever looks shall die. (1 Sam. vi. 19.) Now if thou art indeed so near as to see thy sins, by thy reading of thyself by the tables in the ark, cast but up thine eyes a little higher, and behold, there is the mercy-seat and throne of grace to which thou wouldst come, and by which thou must be saved. When David came to pray to God, he said, he would direct his prayer to God, and would look up. (Ps. v. 3.)

As who should say, When I pray, I will say to my prayers, O my prayers, mount up, stay not at the ark of the testimony, for there is the law and the condemnation; but soar aloft to the throne that stands above, for there is God, and there is grace displayed, and there thou mayest obtain what is necessary to help in time of need.

Some indeed there be that know not what these things mean: they never read their sin nor condemnation for it when they are upon their knees at their devotion, and so are neither dejected at the sight of what they are, nor driven with sense of things to look higher for help at need; for need, indeed, they see none. Of such I shall say, they are not concerned in our text, nor can they come hither before they have been prepared so to do, as may appear before we come to an end.

Second. And thus have I showed you what this throne of grace is, and where it stands. And now I shall come to show you how you shall find it, and know when you are come to it, by several other things.

First, then, *about the throne of grace, there is a "rainbow, in sight like unto an emerald."* (Rev. iv. 1.) This was the first sight that John saw after he had received his epistles for the seven churches. Before he received them, he had the great vision of his Lord, and heard him say to him, I am he that was dead and am alive, or "that liveth, and was dead; and, behold, I am alive for evermore, and have the keys of hell and of death." (Rev. i. 18.) And a good preparation it was for a work of that nature that now he was called unto; to wit, that he might the more warmly, and affectionately, and confidently attest the truth which his Lord had now for him to testify to them.

So here, before he entereth upon his prophecy of things to come, he hears a first voice, and sees a first sight. The first voice that he heard was, "Come up hither;" and the first sight that he saw, was a throne with a rainbow round about it: "And immediately," saith he, "I was in the spirit; and, behold, a throne was set in heaven, and one sat on the throne. And he that sat was to look upon like a jasper, and a sardine stone; and there was a rainbow round about the throne." (Rev. iv. 1—3.)

The first time that we find in God's word mention made of a rainbow, we read also of its spiritual signification, to wit, that it was a token of the firmness of the covenant that God made with Noah, as touching his not drowning the earth any more with the waters of a flood. "I do set," saith he, "my bow in the cloud, and it shall be a token of a covenant between me and the earth. And it shall come to pass, when I bring a cloud over the earth, that the bow shall be seen in the cloud. And I will remember my covenant, which is between me and you, and every living creature of all flesh; and the waters shall no more become a flood to destroy all flesh." (Gen. ix. 13—15.)

The first use, therefore, of the rainbow, it was to be a token of a covenant of mercy and kindness to the world; but that was not the utmost end thereof. For that covenant was but a shadow of the covenant of grace which God hath made with his elect in Christ, and that bow but a shadow of the token of the permanency and lastingness of that covenant. Wherefore the next time we read of the rainbow, is in the first of Ezekiel, and there we read of it only with reference to the excellences of its colour: for that it is there said to be exactly like the colour of the glory of the man that the prophet there saw, as sitting upon a throne. (Ezek. i. 28.) The glory, that is the priestly robes, for he is a priest upon the throne, and his robes become his glory and beauty. (Zech. vi. 13.) His *robes*, what is, or are they, but his blessed righteousness, with the skirts of which he covereth the sinful nakedness of his people, and with the perfection of which he decketh and adorneth them "as a bride adorneth herself with jewels." (Isa. lxi. 10.)

Now here again, in the third place, we find a rainbow; a rainbow round about the throne, round about the throne of grace. A rainbow, that is, a token of the covenant, a token of the covenant of grace in its lastingness, and that token is the appearance of the man Christ. The appearance, that is, his robes, his righteousness, "from the appearance of his loins even upwards, and from the appearance of his loins even downward," (Ezek. i. 27,) even down to the foot, as you have it in the book of the Revelations. (Rev. i. 13.) "As the appearance of the bow that is in the cloud in the day of rain, so was the appearance of the brightness round about. This was the appearance of the likeness of the glory of the Lord," &c. (Ezek. i. 28.)

The sum then is, that by the rainbow round about the throne of grace, upon which God sitteth to hear and answer the petitions of his people, we are to understand the obediential righteousness of Jesus Christ, which in the days of his flesh he wrought out and accomplished for his people; by which God's justice is satisfied and their persons justified, and they so made acceptable to him. This righteousness, that shines in God's eyes, more glorious than the rainbow in the cloud doth in ours, saith John, is round about the throne. But for what purpose? Why, to be looked upon. But who must look upon it? Why God and his people; the people when they come to pray, and God when he is about to hear and give. "And the bow shall be in the cloud," says God, "and I will look upon it, that I may remember the everlasting covenant between God and every living creature of all flesh that is upon the earth." (Gen. ix. 16.)

And I say, as the bow is for God to look on, so it is also for our sight to behold. A rainbow round about the throne, in sight; in whose sight? in John's, and his companions, like unto an emerald.

We read of Solomon's great throne of ivory, that though there was not its like in any kingdom, yet he was not willing that the bow of it should stand before him. It was round behind. (1 Kings x. 19.) Oh, but, God's throne has the bow before, even round about, to view, to look upon in sight. Solomon's was but a shadow, and therefore fit to be put behind: but this is the sum and substance, and therefore fit to be before, in view, in sight, for God and his people to behold.

Thus you see that a rainbow is round about the throne of grace, and what this rainbow is. Look then when thou goest to prayer for the throne, and that thou mayest not be deceived with a fancy, look for the rainbow too. The rainbow, that is, as I have said, the personal performances of Christ thy Saviour for thee. Look, I say, for that, it is his righteousness; the token of the everlastingness of the covenant of grace; the object of God's delight, and must be the matter of the justification of thy person and performances before God. God looks at it, look thou at it, and at it only. For in heaven or earth, if that be cast away, there is nothing to be found that can please God or justify thee. If it be said, faith pleases God, I answer, faith is a relative grace; take then the relative away, which, as to justification, is this spangling robe, this rainbow, this righteousness of Christ, and faith dies and becomes as to what we now treat of, extinct and quenched as tow.

And a very fit emblem the rainbow is of the righteousness of Christ, and that in these particulars.

1. The rainbow is an effect of the sun that shines in the firmament; and the righteousness by which this throne of grace is encompassed is the work of the Son of God.

2. The rainbow was a token that the wrath of God in sending the flood was appeased; this righteousness of Christ is that for the sake of which God forgiveth us all trespasses.

3. The rainbow was set in the cloud that the sinful man might look thereon and wax confident in common mercy; this righteousness is showed us in the word, that we may by it believe unto special mercy.

4. The bow is seen but now and then in the cloud; Christ's righteousness is but here and there revealed in the word.

5. The bow is seen commonly upon, or after rain; Christ's righteousness is apprehended by faith upon, or soon after the apprehensions of wrath.

6. The bow is seen sometimes more, sometimes less; and so is this righteousness, even according to the degree or clearness of the sight of faith.

7. The bow is of that nature as to make whatever you shall look upon through it, to be of the same colour of itself, whether that thing be bush, or man, or beast; and the righteousness of Christ is that that makes sinners, when God looks upon them through it, to look beautiful, and acceptable in his sight, for we are made comely through his comeliness and made accepted in the beloved. (Ezek. xvi. 14. Eph. i. 6.)

One word more of the rainbow, and then to some other things. As here you read that the rainbow is round about the throne, so, if you read on even in the same place, you shall find the glorious effects thereof to be far more than all that I have said. But,

Second. As the throne of grace is known by the rainbow that is round about it, so also thou shalt know it by this: *the high priest is continually ministering before it;* the high priest, or Christ as priest, is there before God in his high priest's robes, making continual intercession for thy acceptance there.

Now, as I said before, Christ is priest and throne and all: throne in one sense, priest in another; even as he was priest, and sacrifice, and altar too, when he became our reconciler to God.

As a priest here, he is put under the notion of an angel that came and stood at the altar to offer incense for the church, all the time that the seven angels were to sound out with trumpets the alarum of God's wrath against the antichristian world, lest that wrath should swallow them up also. " And," saith John, " another angel came and stood at the altar, having a golden censer; and there was given unto him much incense, that he should offer it with the prayers of all saints upon the golden altar which was before the throne. And the smoke of the incense, which came with the prayers of the saints, ascended up before God out of the angel's hand." (Rev. viii. 3, 4.)

Here, then, you have before the throne, that is, the throne or mercy-seat, the high priest, for there it was that God appointed that the altar of incense, or that to burn incense on, should be placed. This incense-altar, in the type, was to be over-laid with gold; but here the Holy Ghost implies that it is all of gold. This throne, then, is the mercy-seat, or throne of grace, to which we are bid to come: and as you see, here is the angel, the high priest with his golden censer, and his incense, ready to wait upon us. For so the text implies; for he is there to offer his incense with the prayers of all saints that are waiting without at his time of offering incense within. (Luke i. 10.) So then at the throne of grace, or before it, stands the high priest of our propitiation, Christ Jesus, with his golden censer in his hand, full of incense, therewith to perfume the prayers of saints that come thither for grace and mercy to help in time of need. And he stands there, as you see, under the name of an angel; for he is the angel of God's presence, and messenger of his covenant.

But now it is worth our considering, to take notice how, or in what method, the high priest under the law was to approach the incense-altar. When he came to make intercession for the saints before the throne, he was to go in thither to do this work in his robes and ornaments; not without them, lest he died. The principal of these ornaments were, " a breastplate, an ephod, a robe, an embroidered coat, a mitre, and a girdle." (Exod. xxviii. 4.) These are briefly called *his garments*, in Revelations the first; and in the general they show us that he is clothed with righteousness, girded with truth and faithfulness, for that is the girdle of his reins to strengthen him, (Isa. xi. 5,) and that he beareth upon his heart the names of the children of Israel that are Israelites indeed: for as on Aaron's breastplate was fixed the names of the twelve tribes of Israel, and he was to bear the weight of them by the strength of his shoulders, so are we on the heart of Christ.

Thus, therefore, is our high priest within the holiest to offer incense upon the golden altar of incense that is before the throne. Wherefore, when thou goest thither, even to the throne of grace, look for him, and be not content though thou shouldest find God there; if thou findest there not him, (I suppose now an impossibility, for edification's sake,) for without him nothing can be done; I say, without him as a priest. He is the throne, and without him as a throne, God has no resting-place as to us; he is a priest, and without him as such, we can make no acceptable approach to God: for by him as priest, our spiritual sacrifices are accepted. (1 Pet. ii. 5.) " By him, therefore, let us offer the sacrifice of praise to God continually, giving thanks," and confessing to and " in his name." (Heb. xiii. 15.) And for our further edification herein, let us consider that as God has chosen and made him his throne of grace, so he as sworn that he shall be accepted as a priest for ever there. For his natural qualifications we may speak something to them afterwards; in the meantime know that there is no coming to God, upon pain of death, without him.

Nor will it out of my mind, but that his wearing the rainbow upon his head doth somewhat belong to him as priest, his priestly vestments being for glory and beauty, as afore was said, compared to the colour of it. (Rev. x. 1. Ezek. i. 28.) But why doth he wear the rainbow upon his head? but to show that the sign, that the everlastingness of the covenant of grace, is only to be found in him; that he wears it as a mitre or frontlet of gold, and can always plead it with acceptance to God, and for the subduing of the world and good of his people. But,

Third. The throne of grace is to be known *by the sacrifice that is presented there.* The high priest was not to go into the holiest, nor come near the mercy-seat, the which, as I have showed you, was a type of our throne of grace, " without blood." " But into the second went the high

priest alone once every year, not without blood, which he offered for himself, and for the errors of the people." (Heb. ix. 7.) Yea, the priest was to take of the blood of his sacrifice, and sprinkle it seven times before the Lord, that is, before the mercy-seat, or throne of grace; and was to put some of the blood upon the horns of the altar of incense before the Lord. (Lev. iv. 5—7.) So, then, the throne of grace is known by the blood that is sprinkled thereon, and by the atonement that by it is made there. I told you before, that before the throne of grace there is our high priest, and now I tell you, there is his sacrifice too; his sacrifice which he there presenteth as amends for the sins of all such as have a right to come with boldness to the throne of grace. Hence, as I mentioned before, there is said to be in the midst of the throne, (the same throne of which we have spoken before,) " a Lamb as it had been slain." (Rev. v. 6.) The words are to the purpose, and signify that in the midst of the throne is our sacrifice, with the very marks of his death upon him, showing to God, that sitteth upon the throne, the holes of the thorns, of the nails, of the spear, and how he was disfigured with blows and blood when at his command he gave himself a ransom for his people; for it cannot be imagined that either the exaltation or glorification of the body of Jesus Christ should make him forget the day in which he died the death for our sins, especially since that which puts worth into his whole intercession is the death he died, and blood he shed upon the cross for our trespasses.

Besides, there is no sight more taketh the heart of God than to see of the travail of the soul, and the bruisings of the body of his Son for our transgressions. Hence it is said, he " is in the midst of the throne " as he died, or as he had been slain. It is said again, " The Lamb which is in the midst of the throne shall feed them." (Rev. vii. 17.) The Lamb, that is, the Son of God, as a sacrifice, shall be always in the midst of the throne to feed and comfort his people. He is the throne, he is the priest, he is the sacrifice. But then, how as a Lamb is he in the midst of the throne? Why, the meaning in mine opinion is, that Christ, as a dying and bleeding sacrifice, shall be chief in the reconciling of us to God; or that his being offered for our sins shall be of great virtue when pleaded by him as priest, to the obtaining of grace, mercy, and glory for us. (Heb. ix. 12.) By his blood he entereth into the holy place; by his blood he hath made an atonement for us before the mercy-seat. His blood it is that speaketh better for us than the blood of Abel did for Cain. (Heb. xii. 24.) Also it is by his blood that we have bold admittance into the holiest, (Heb. x. 19:) wherefore no marvel if you find him here a Lamb, as it had been slain, and that in the midst of the throne of grace.

While thou art, therefore, thinking on him as he is in the throne of grace, forget him not as he is priest and sacrifice; for as a priest he makes atonement, but there is no atonement made for sin without a sacrifice. Now, as Christ is a sacrifice, so he is to be considered as passive, or a sufferer; as he is a priest, so he is active, or one that hath offered up himself; as he is an altar, so he is to be considered as God; for in and upon the power of his Godhead he offered up himself. The altar, then, was not the cross, as some have foolishly imagined: but as a throne, a throne of grace; so he is to be considered as distinct from these three things, as I also have hinted before.

Wouldest thou then know this throne of grace, where God sits to hear prayers and give grace? then cast the eyes of thy soul about, and look till thou findest the Lamb there, a Lamb there " as it had been slain," for by this thou shalt know thou art right. A slain Lamb, or a Lamb as it had been slain, when it is seen by a supplicant in the midst of the throne, whither he is come for grace, is a blessed sight. A blessed sight indeed! and it informs him he is where he should be.

And thou must look for this the rather, because without blood is no remission. He that thinks to find grace at God's hand, and yet enters not into the holiest by the blood of Jesus, will find himself mistaken, and will find a dead, instead of " a living way." (Heb. x. 20.) For if not anything below, or besides blood, can yield remission on God's part, how should remission be received by us without our acting faith therein? We are justified by his blood, through faith in his blood. (Rom. v.) Wherefore, I say, look when thou approachest the throne of grace, that thou give diligence to see for the Lamb, that is " as it had been slain," in the midst of the throne of grace: and then thou wilt have, not only a sign that thou presentest thy supplications to God, where, and as thou shouldest, but there also wilt thou meet with matter to break, to soften, to bend, to bow, and to make thy heart as thou wouldest have it: for if the blood of a goat will, as some say, dissolve an adamant, a stone that is harder than flint, shall not the sight of " a Lamb as it had been slain," much more dissolve and melt down the spirit of that man that is upon his knees before the throne of grace for mercy; especially when he shall see, that not his prayers, nor his tears, nor his wants, but the blood of the Lamb, has prevailed with a God of grace, to give mercy and grace to an undeserving man? This, then, is the third sign by which thou shalt know when thou art at the throne of grace: that throne is sprinkled with blood; yea, in the midst of that throne, there is to be seen to this day a Lamb as it had been slain; and he is in the midst of it, to feed those that come to that throne, and to lead them by and to " living fountains of waters." (Rev. vii. 17.) Wherefore,

Fourth. The throne of grace is to be known *by the streams of grace that continually proceed therefrom*, and that like a river run themselves out into the world. And, saith John, " He showed me a pure river of water of life, clear as crystal

proceeding out of the throne of God and of the Lamb." (Rev. xxii. 1.) Mark you, here is again a throne, the throne of God, which, as we have showed, is the human nature of his Son; out of which, as you read, proceeds a river, a river of water of life, clear as crystal. And the joining of the Lamb also here with God, is to show that it comes, I say, from God, by the Lamb; by Christ, who as a lamb, or sacrifice for sin, is the procuring cause of the running of this river; it proceedeth out of the throne of God and of the Lamb. Behold, therefore, how carefully here the Lamb is brought in, as one from or through whom proceeds the water of life to us. God is the spring-head; Christ the golden pipe of conveyance; the elect the receivers of this water of life. He saith not here, " the throne of the Lamb," but " and of the Lamb," to show, I say, that he it is out of or through whom this river of grace should come. But if it should be understood that it proceedeth from the throne of the Lamb, it may be to show that Christ also has power as a mediator, to send grace like a river into the church. And then it amounts to this, that God, for Christ's sake, gives this river of grace, and that Christ, for his merit's sake, has power to do so too. And hence is that good wish, so often mentioned in the epistles, " Grace to you, and peace from God our Father, and the Lord Jesus Christ." And again, " Grace, mercy, and peace, from God the Father, and from the Lord Jesus Christ." For Christ has power with the Father to give grace and forgiveness of sins to men. But let us come to the terms in this text. Here we have a throne, a throne of grace; and to show that this throne is it indeed, therefore there proceeds therefrom a river of this grace, put here under the term of " water of life," a term fit to express both the nature of grace, and the condition of him that comes for it to the throne of grace.

It is called by the name of water of life, to show what a reviving cordial the grace of God in Christ is, shall be, and will be found to be, of all those that by him shall drink thereof. It " shall be in him," even in him that drinks it, " a well of water springing up into everlasting life." (John iv. 14.) It will therefore beget life, and maintain it; yea, will itself be a spring of life, in the very heart of him that drinks it. Ah, it will be such a preservative also to spiritual health, as that by its virtue the soul shall for ever be kept, I say, the soul that drinks it, from total and final decay; it shall be in them a well of living water, " springing up into everlasting life."

But there is also by this phrase or term briefly touched the present state of them that shall come hither to drink; they are not the healthful, but the sick. It is with the throne of grace, as it is with the bath, and other places of sovereign and healing waters, they are most coveted of them that are diseased, and do also show their virtues on those that have their health and limbs; so, I say, is the throne of grace; its waters are for healing, for soul-healing, that is their virtue. Wherefore, as at those waters above-mentioned, the lame leave their crutches, and the sick have such signs of their recovery as may be a sign of their receiving health and cure there, so at the throne of grace it is where true penitents, and those that are sick for mercy, do leave their sighs and tears. " And the Lamb that is in the midst of the throne shall feed them, and shall lead them unto living fountains of waters, and God shall (there) wipe away all tears from their eyes." (Rev. vii. 17.) Wherefore as Joseph washed his face and dried his tears away when he saw his brother Benjamin, so all God's saints shall here, even at the throne of grace, where God's Benjamin, or the Son of his right hand is, wash their souls from sorrow, and have their tears wiped from their eyes. Wherefore, O thou that art diseased, afflicted, and that wouldst live, come by Jesus to God as merciful and gracious; yea, look for this river when thou art upon thy knees before him, for by that thou shalt find whereabout is the throne of grace, and so where thou mayest find mercy.

But again, as that which proceeds out of this throne of grace is called " water of life," so it is said to be a river, a river of water of life. This, in the first place, shows that with God is plenty of grace, even as in a river there is plenty of water; a pond, a pool, a cistern, will hold much, but a river will hold more; from this throne come rivers and streams of water of life, to satisfy those that come for life to the throne of God.

Further, as by a river is showed what abundance of grace proceeds from God through Christ, so it shows the unsatiable thirst and desire of one that comes indeed aright to the throne of grace for mercy. Nothing but rivers will satisfy such a soul; ponds, pools, and cisterns will do nothing; such an one is like him of whom it is said, " Behold he drinketh up a river, and hasteth not; he trusteth that he can draw up Jordan into his mouth." (Job xl. 23.) This David testifies when he saith, " As the hart panteth after the water-brooks, so panteth my soul after thee, O God." (Ps. xliii. 1.) Hence the invitation is proportionable, "Drink abundantly," (Sol. Song v. 1;) and that they that are saved, are said to receive abundance of grace : " they which receive abundance of grace, and of the gift of righteousness, shall reign in life by one, Jesus Christ." (Rom. v. 17.) And hence it is said again, " When the poor and needy seek water, and there is none, and their tongue faileth for thirst, I the Lord will hear them, I the God of Israel will not forsake them." But, Lord, how wilt thou quench their boundless thirst ? " I will open rivers in high places, and fountains in the midst of the valleys : I will make the wilderness a pool of water, and the dry land springs of water." (Isa. xli. 17, 18.) Behold, here is a pool of water as big as a wilderness, enough one would think to satisfy any thirsty soul. Oh, but that will not do ! wherefore he will open rivers, fountains, and springs, and all this is to quench the drought of one that thirsteth for the grace of God, that they may have enough. " They shall be abundantly satisfied with the fatness of thy house; and thou shalt make them drink of the river of thy pleasures; for with thee is the fountain of life," &c. (Ps. xxxvi. 8, 9.)

This abundance the throne of grace yieldeth for the help and health of such as would have the water of life to drink; and to cure their diseases withal, it yields a river of water of life. Moreover, since grace is said here to proceed as a river from the throne of God and of the Lamb, it is to show the commonness of it; rivers you know are common in the stream, however they are at the head. And to show the commonness of it, the apostle calls it " the common salvation;" and it is said in Ezekiel and Zechariah, to go forth to the desert, and into the sea, the world, to heal the beasts and fish of all kinds that are there. This, therefore, is a text that shows us what it is to come to a throne where the token of the covenant of grace is, where the high priest ministereth, and in the midst of which there is a Lamb, " as it had been slain :" for from thence there cometh not drops, nor showers, but rivers of the grace of God, a river of water of life.

Again, as the grace that we here read of is said, as it comes from this throne, to come as a river of water of life, so it is said to be pure and clear as crystal. *Pure* is set in opposition to *muddy* and *dirty waters;* and *clear* is set in opposition to those waters that are *black,* by reason of the cold and icyish nature of them; therefore there is conjoined to this phrase, the word crystal, which all know is a clear and shining stone. Indeed, the life and spirit that is in this water will keep it from looking black and dull; and the throne from whence it comes, will keep it from being muddy, so much as in the streams thereof. "The blessing of the Lord, it maketh rich, and he addeth no sorrow with it." (Prov. x. 22.) Indeed, all the sorrow that is mixed with our Christianity it proceedeth as the procuring cause, from ourselves, not from the throne of grace; for that is the place where our tears, as was showed you, are wiped away; and also where we hang up our crutches. The streams thereof are pure and clear, not muddy nor frozen, but warm and delightful, and that " make glad the city of God." (Ps. xlvi. 4.)

These words also show us, that this water of itself can do without a mixture of anything of ours. What comes from this throne of grace is pure grace, and nothing else; clear grace, free grace, grace that is not mixed, nor need be mixed with works of righteousness which we have done; it is of itself sufficient to answer all our wants, to heal all our diseases, and to help us at a time of need. It is grace that chooses, it is grace that calleth, it is grace that preserveth, and it is grace that brings to glory : even the grace that like a river of water of life proceedeth from this throne. And hence it is, that from first to last, we must cry "Grace, grace unto it."

Thus you see what a throne the Christian is invited to; it is a throne of grace whereon doth sit the God of all grace; it is a throne of grace before which the Lord Jesus ministereth continually for us; it is a throne of grace sprinkled with the blood, and in the midst of which is a lamb as it had been slain; it is a throne with a rainbow round about it, which is the token of the everlasting covenant, and out of which proceeds, as here you read, a river, a pure river of water of life, clear as crystal.

Look then for these signs of the throne of grace, all you that would come to it, and rest not until by some of them you know that you are even come to it; they are all to be seen, have you but eyes; and the sight of them is very delectable, and has a natural tendency in them, when seen, to revive and quicken the soul. But,

Fifth. As the throne of grace is known and distinguished by the things above-named, *so it is by the effects which these things have wrought.* There is about that throne "four and twenty seats; and upon the seats four and twenty elders sitting, clothed in white raiment; and they have on their heads crowns of gold." (Rev. iv. 4.) There is no throne that has these signs and effects belonging to it but this; wherefore, as by these signs, so by the effects of them also, one may know which is, and so when he is indeed come to, the throne of grace. And a little as we commented upon what went before, we will also touch upon this.

1. By seats, I understand places of rest and dignity; places of rest, for that they that sit on them do rest from their labours; and places of dignity, for that they are about the throne. (Rev. xiv. 13.) "And the four and twenty elders which sat before God on their seats, fell upon their faces and worshipped God." (Rev. xi. 16.) And forasmuch as the seats are mentioned before they are mentioned that sat thereon, it is to show that the places were prepared before they were converted.

2. The elders, I take to be the twelve patriarchs and the twelve apostles, or the first fathers of the churches; for they are the elders of both the churches, that is, both of the Jewish and Gentile church of God; they are the ancients, as also they are called in the prophet Isaiah, which are in some sense the fathers of both these churches. These elders are well set forth by that four and twenty that you read of in the book of Chronicles, who had every one of them for sons twelve in number. There, therefore, the four and twenty are. (1 Chron. xxv.)

3. Their sitting denoteth also their abiding in the presence of God. "Sit thou at my right hand," was the Father's word to the Son, and also signifieth the same. (Ps. cx. 1.) It is then the throne of grace where the four and twenty seats are, and before which the four and twenty elders sit.

4. Their white robes are Christ's righteousness,

their own good works and glory; not that their works brought them thither, for they were of themselves polluted, and were washed white in the blood of the Lamb: but yet God will have all that his people have done in love to him be rewarded. Yea, and they shall wear their own labours, being washed, as afore is hinted, as a badge of their honour, before the throne of grace, and this is grace indeed. "They have washed their robes, and made them white in the blood of the Lamb; therefore are they before the throne of God." (Rev. vii. 14, 15.) They have washed as others did do before them.

5. "And they had on their heads crowns of gold." (Rev. iv. 4.) This denotes their victory, and also that they are kings, and as kings shall reign with him for ever and ever.

6. But what! were they silent? did they say, did they do nothing while they sat before the throne? Yes, they were appointed to be singers there. This was signified by the four and twenty that we made mention of before, who, with their sons, were instructed in the songs of the Lord, and all that were cunning to do so then, were two hundred fourscore and eight. (1 Chron. xxv. 7.) These were the figure of that hundred forty and four thousand redeemed from the earth. For as the first four and twenty, and their sons, are said to sing and to play upon cymbals, psalteries, and harps, and as they are there said to be instructed and cunning in the songs of the Lord: so these that sit before the throne are said also to sing with harps in their hands their song before the throne: and such song it was, and so cunningly did they sing it, that "no man could learn it, but the hundred and forty and four thousand, which were redeemed from the earth." (Rev. xiv. 3.)

Now, as I said, as he at first began with four and twenty, in David, and ended with four and twenty times twelve, so here, in John, he begins with the same number, but ends with such a company that no man could number. For, he saith, "After this I beheld, and, lo, a great multitude, which no man could number, of all nations, and kindreds, and people, and tongues, stood before the throne, and before the Lamb, clothed with white robes, and palms in their hands. And cried with a loud voice, saying, Salvation to our God, which sitteth upon the throne, and unto the Lamb. And all the angels stood round about the throne, and about the elders, and the four beasts, and fell before the throne on their faces, and worshipped God." (Rev. vii. 9—11.) This numberless number seems to have got the song by the end; for they cry aloud, "Salvation, salvation to our God, and to the Lamb;" which to be sure is such a song that none can learn but them that are redeemed from the earth.

But I say, what a brave encouragement is it for one that is come for grace to the throne of grace to see so great a number already there, on their seats, in their robes, with their palms in their hands, and their crowns upon their heads, singing of salvation to God, and to the Lamb! And I say again, and speak now to the dejected, methinks it would be strange, O thou that art so afraid that the greatness of thy sins will be a bar unto thee, if amongst all this great number of pipers and harpers that are got to glory thou canst not espy one that, when here, was as vile a sinner as thyself. Look man, they are there for thee to view them, and for thee to take encouragement to hope when thou shalt consider what grace and mercy has done for them. Look again, I say, now thou art upon thy knees, and see if some that are among them have not done worse than thou hast done. And yet behold, they are set down; and yet behold, they have their crowns on their heads, their harps in their hands, and sing aloud of salvation to their God, and to the Lamb.

This, then, is a fifth note, or sign that doth distinguish the throne of grace from other thrones. There are before that to be seen for our encouragement, a numberless number of people sitting and singing round about it; singing, I say, to God for his grace, and to the Lamb for his blood, by which they are secured from the wrath to come. "And the four and twenty elders fell down before the Lamb, having every one of them harps, and golden vials full of odours, which are the prayers of saints; and they sung a new song, saying, Thou art worthy to take the book, and to open the seals thereof; for thou wast slain, and hast redeemed us to God by thy blood, out of every kindred, and tongue, and people, and nation; and hast made us unto our God kings and priests: and we shall reign on the earth." (Rev. v. 8—10.)

Behold, tempted soul, dost thou not yet see what a throne of grace here is, and what multitudes are already arrived thither to give thanks unto his name that sits thereon, and to the Lamb for ever and ever? And wilt thou hang thy harp upon the willows, and go drooping up and down the world, as if there was no God, no grace, no throne of grace to apply thyself unto, for mercy and grace to help in time of need. Hark! dost thou not hear them what they say. "Worthy," say they, "is the Lamb that was slain to receive power, and riches, and wisdom, and strength, and honour, and glory, and blessing. And every creature which is in heaven," where they are, "and on the earth," where thou art, "and under the earth, and such as are in the sea, and all that are in them, heard I, saying, Blessing, honour, glory, and power, be unto him that sitteth upon the throne, and unto the Lamb, for ever and ever." (Rev. v. 12, 13.)

All this is written for our learning, that we through patience and comfort of the Scriptures might have hope; and that the drooping ones might come boldly to the throne of grace, to obtain grace and find mercy to help in time of need. They bless, they all bless; they thank, they all thank; and wilt thou hold thy tongue? "They have all received of his fulness, and grace for grace;" and will he shut thee out? Or is his grace

so far gone, and so near spent, that now he has not enough to pardon and secure, and save one sinner more? For shame! leave off this unbelief. Wherefore, dost thou think, art thou told all this, but to encourage thee to come to the throne of grace? And wilt thou hang back or be sullen, because thou art none of the first? since he hath said, "The first shall be last, and the last first." Behold, the legions, the thousands, the untold and numberless number that stand before the throne, and be bold to hope in his mercy.

Sixth. As the throne of grace is distinguished from other thrones by these, so "out of this throne proceed lightnings, and thunderings, and voices." Also, before this throne are "seven lamps of fire burning, which are the seven Spirits of God." (Rex. iv. 5.) This, then, is another thing by which the throne of grace may be known as an effect of what is before. So again it is said, that from the altar of incense that stood before the throne, "there were voices, and thunderings, and lightnings, and an earthquake." (Rev. viii. 5.) All these, then, come out of the holiest, where the throne is, and are inflamed by this throne, and by him that sits thereon.

1. Lightnings here are to be taken for the illuminations of the Spirit in the gospel; as it is said in the book of Psalms, "They looked unto him," on the throne, "and were lightened," (Ps. xxxiv. 5;) or, as it is said in other places, "The voice of thy thunder was in the heaven, the lightnings lightened the world," (Ps. lxxvii. 18;) and again, "His lightnings enlightened the world: the earth saw, and trembled." (Ps. xcvii. 4.)

This lightning, therefore, communicates light to them that sit in darkness: "God," saith the apostle, "who commanded the light to shine out of darkness, hath shined in our hearts, to give the light of the knowledge of the glory of God in the face of Jesus Christ." (2 Cor. iv. 6.) It was from this throne that the light came that struck Paul off his horse, when he went to destroy it, and the people that professed it. (Acts ix. 3.) These are those lightnings by which sinners are made to see their sad condition, and by which they are made to see the way out of it. Art thou then made to see thy condition how bad it is, and that the way out of it is by Jesus Christ? for, as I said, he is the throne of grace. Why, then, come orderly in the light of these convictions to the throne from whence thy light did come, and cry there, as Samuel did to Eli, "Here am I, for thou hast called me." (1 Sam. iii. 8.) Thus did Saul by the light that made him see; by it he came to Christ, and cried, "Who art thou, Lord;" and, "What wouldest thou have me to do?" (Acts ix. 5, 6.) And is it not an encouragement to thee to come to him, when he lights thy candle, that thou mayest see the way; yea, when he doth it on purpose, that thou mightest come to him? "He gives light to them that sit in darkness, and in the shadow of death," what to do? "to guide our feet in the way of peace." (Luke i. 79.)

This interpretation of this place seems to me most to cohere with what went before; for first you have here a throne, and one sitting on it; then you have the elders, and in them presented to you the whole church, sitting round about the throne; then you have in the words last read unto you a discourse how they came thither, and that is, by the lightnings, thunderings, and voices that proceed out of the throne.

2. As you have here lightnings, so thereto is adjoined thunders. There proceeded out of this throne lightnings and thunders. By thunders, I understand that powerful discovery of the majesty of God by the word of truth, which seizeth the heart with a reverential dread and awe of him; hence it is said, "The voice of the Lord is full of majesty; the voice of the Lord breaketh the cedars," (Ps. xxix. 4, 5;) the voice, that is, his thundering voice. "Canst thou thunder with a voice like him?" (Job xl. 9.) And "the thunder of his power who can understand?" (Job xxvi. 14.) It was upon this account that Peter, and James, and John were called "the sons of thunder," because, in the word which they were to preach there was to be not only lightnings, but thunders; not only illuminations, but a great seizing of the heart with the dread and majesty of God, to the effectual turning of the sinner to him.

Lightnings without thunder are in this case dangerous, because they that receive the one without the other are subject to miscarry. They were "once enlightened," but you read of no thunder they had; and they were subject to fall into an irrecoverable state. (Heb. vi. 4—6.) Saul had thunder with his lightnings, to the shaking of his soul; so had the three thousand; so had the jailer. They that receive light without thunder, are subject to turn the grace of God into wantonness; but they that know the terror of God will persuade men. So then, when he decrees to give the rain of his grace to a man, he makes a way for the lightning and thunder; not the one without the other, but the one following the other. (Job xxviii. 26.) Lightning and thunder is made a cause of rain, but lightning alone is not: "Who hath divided a water-course for the overflowing of waters, or a way for the lightning of thunder, to cause it to rain on the earth, where no man is; on the wilderness, wherein there is no man?" (Job xxxviii. 25, 26.)

Thus, therefore, you may see how in the darkest sayings of the Holy Ghost there is as great an harmony with truth as in the most plain and easy: there must be thunder with light, if thy heart be well poised, and balanced with the fear of God. We have had great lightnings in this land of late years, but little thunders; and that is one reason why so little grace is found where light is, and why so many professors run on their heads in such a day as this is, notwithstanding all they have seen.

Well, then, this also should be an help to a soul to come to the throne of grace; the God of glory has thundered, has thundered to awaken thee, as well as sent lightnings to give thee light; to awaken thee to a coming to him, as well as to the enabling of thee to see his things. This, then, has come from the throne of grace, to make thee come hither: wherefore observe where it is by these signs made mention of before, and by these effects; and go, and come to the throne of grace.

3. As there proceeds from this throne lightnings and thunders, so from hence it is said voices proceed also: now these voices may be taken for such as are sent with this lightning and thunder to instruct, or for such as this lightning and thunder begets in our hearts.

(1.) It may be taken in the first sense for light and dread, when it falleth from God into the soul, is attended with a voice or voices of instruction to the soul, to know what to do. Thus it was in Paul's case: he had light and dread, and voices for his instruction; he had lightnings, and thunderings, and voices. "Good and upright is the Lord; therefore will he teach sinners in the way. The meek will he guide in judgment; and the meek will he teach his way." (Ps. xxv. 8, 9.)

(2.) Or by voices you may understand, such as the lightning and thunder begets in our hearts; for though man is as mute as a fish to Godward, before this thunder and lightning comes to him, yet after that he is full of voices. And how much more numerous are the voices that in the whole church on earth are begot by these lightnings and thunders that proceed from the throne of grace; their faith has a voice, their repentance has a voice, their subjection to God's word has a voice in it; yea, there is a voice in their prayers, a voice in their cry, a voice in their tears, a voice in their groans, in their roarings, in their bemoaning of themselves, and in their triumphs.

This, then, is an effect of the throne of grace; hence it is said that they proceed from it, even the lightning, and the thunder, and the voices; that is, effectual conversion to God. It follows, then, that if all these are with thy soul, the operations of the throne of grace have been upon thee to bring thee to the throne of grace; first in thy prayers, and then in thy person. And this leads me to the next thing propounded to be spoken to, which is to show who are the persons invited here to come to the throne of grace. "Let us therefore come."

III. *The Persons intended by this Exhortation.*

Now the persons here called upon to come to the throne of grace are not all, or every sort of men, but the men that may properly be comprehended under this word Us and We; "let Us therefore come boldly, that We may obtain." And they that are here put under these particular terms are expressed, both before and after, by those that have explication in them.

They are called in the epistle to the Hebrews—
1. Such as give the most earnest heed to the word

which they have heard. (Heb. ii. 1.) 2. They are such as see Jesus crowned with glory and honour. (Heb. ii. 9.) 3. They are called the children. (Heb. ii. 14.) 4. They are called the seed of Abraham. (Heb. ii. 16.) 5. They are called Christ's brethren. (Heb. ii. 17.)

So, chapter the third, they are called holy brethren, and said to be partakers of the heavenly calling, and the people of whom it is said, that Christ Jesus is the apostle and high priest of their profession. (Heb. iii. 1.) They are called Christ's own house, and are said to be partakers of Christ. (Heb. iii. 14.)

They are said to be the believers, those that do enter in into rest, those that have Christ for a high priest, and with the feeling of whose infirmities he is touched and sympathiseth. (Heb. iv. 3, 14, 15.)

So, in chapter the sixth, they are called beloved, and the heirs of promise; they that have fled for refuge to lay hold on the hope set before them; they are called those that hope as an anchor, and those for whom Christ as a forerunner hath entered and taken possession of heaven. (Heb. vi. 9, 17—20.)

So, chapter the seventh, they are said to be such as draw nigh unto God. (Heb. vii. 19.)

And, chapter the eighth, they are said to be such with whom the new covenant is made Christ.

Chapter the ninth, they are such for whom Christ has obtained eternal redemption, and such for whom he has entered the holy place. (Heb. ix. 12, 22.)

Chapter the tenth, they are such as are said to be sanctified by the will of God, such as have boldness to enter into the holiest by the blood of Jesus, such as draw near with a true heart, in full assurance of faith, (or that have liberty to do so,) having their hearts sprinkled from an evil conscience, and their bodies washed with pure water; they were those that had suffered much for Christ in the world, and that became companions of them that so were used. (Heb. x. 10, 19, 22—25.)

Yea, he tells them, in the eleventh chapter, that they and their patriarchs must be made perfect together. (Heb. xi. 40.)

He also tells them, in the twelfth chapter, that already they are come to Mount Sion, to the city of the living God, the heavenly Jerusalem, and to an innumerable company of angels; to the general assembly and church of the first-born which are written in heaven, and to God the Judge of all; and to the spirits of just men made perfect, and to Jesus the mediator of the New Testament, and to the blood of sprinkling, that speaketh better things than that of Abel.

Thus you see what terms, characters, titles, and privileges, they are invested with, that are here exhorted to come to the throne of grace: from whence we may conclude that every one is not capable of coming thither; no, not every one that is under convictions, and that hath a sense of the need of, and a desire after, the mercy of God in Christ.

Wherefore we will come, in the next place, to show the orderly coming of a soul to the throne of grace for mercy: and for this we must first apply ourselves to the Old Testament, where we have the shadow of what we now are about to enter upon the discourse of, and then we will come to the antitype, where yet the thing is far more explained.

First, then, the mercy-seat was for the church, not for the world; for a Gentile could not go immediately from his natural state to the mercy-seat, by the high priest, but must first orderly join himself, or be joined, to the church, which then consisted of the body of the Jews. (Exod. xii. 43—49.) The stranger, then, must first be circumcised, and consequently profess faith in the Messias to come, which was signified by his going from his circumcision directly to the passover, and so orderly to other privileges, specially to this of the mercy-seat, which the high priest was to go but once a year into. (Ezek. xliv. 6—9.)

Second. The church is again set forth unto us by Aaron and his sons. Aaron as the head, his sons as the members; but the sons of Aaron were not to meddle with any of the things of the holiest until they had washed in a laver. "And the Lord spake unto Moses, saying, Thou shalt also make a laver of brass, and his foot also of brass, to wash withal: and thou shalt put it between the tabernacle of the congregation and the altar, and thou shalt put water therein. And Aaron and his sons shall wash their hands and their feet thereat: when they go into the tabernacle of the congregation, they shall wash with water, that they die not; or when they come near to the altar to minister, to burn offerings made by fire unto the Lord: so they shall wash their hands and their feet, that they die not: and it shall be a statute for ever to them, even to him and to his seed throughout their generations." (Exod. xxx. 17—21.)

Third. Nay, so strict was this law, that if any of Israel, as well as the stranger, were defiled by any dead thing, they were to wash before they partook of the holy things, or else still to abstain: but if they did not, their sin should remain upon them. (Lev. xvii. 15, 16.) So again, "The soul that hath touched any such" uncleanness "shall be unclean until even, and shall not eat of the holy things," much less come within the inner veil, "unless he wash his flesh with water." (Lev. xxii. 4—6.)

Now, I would ask, what all this should signify, if a sinner, as a sinner, before he washes, or is washed, may immediately go unto the throne of grace? Yea, I ask again, why the apostle supposes washing as a preparation to the Hebrews entering into the holiest, if men may go immediately from under convictions to a throne of grace? For thus he says, "let us draw near" "the holiest," (Heb. x. 19,) "with a true heart, in full assurance of faith, having our hearts sprinkled from an evil conscience, and our bodies washed with pure water." (Heb. x. 22.) Let us draw near: he saith not that we may have; but having first been washed and sprinkled.

The laver then must first be washed in, and he that washed not first there, has not right to come to the throne of grace ; wherefore you have here also a sea of glass standing before the throne, to signify this thing. (Rev. iv. 6.) It stands before the throne, for them to wash in, that would indeed approach the throne of grace. For this sea of glass is the same that is shadowed forth by the laver made mention of before, and with the brazen sea that stood in Solomon's temple, whereat they were to wash before they went into the holiest. But you may ask me, what the laver or molten sea should signify to us in the New Testament ? I answer, it signifieth the word of the New Testament, which containeth the cleansing doctrine of remission of sins, by the precious blood of Jesus Christ. Wherefore we are said to be clean through the word, through the washing of water by the word. The meaning then is, a man must first come to Christ, as set forth in the word, which is the sea of glass, before he can come to Christ in heaven, as he is the throne of grace. For the word, I say, is this sea of glass that stands before the throne, for the sinner to wash in first. Know, therefore, whoever thou art, that are minded to be saved, thou must first begin with Christ crucified, and with the promise of remission of sins through his blood : which crucified Christ thou shalt not find in heaven as such, for there he is alive ; but thou shalt find him in the word, for there he is to this day set forth in all the circumstances of his death, as crucified before our eyes. There thou shalt find that he died ; when he died ; what death he died ; why he died ; and the word open to thee to come and wash in his blood. The word, therefore, of Christ's Testament is the laver for all New Testament priests—and every Christian is a priest to God—to wash in.

Here, therefore, thou must receive thy justification, and that before thou goest one step further ; for if thou art not justified by his blood, thou wilt not be saved by his life. And the justifying efficacy of his blood is left behind, and is here contained in the molten sea, or laver, or word of grace, for thee to wash in. Indeed, there is an interceding voice in his blood for us before the throne of grace, or mercy-seat ; but that is still to bring us to wash, or for them that have washed therein, as it was shed upon the cross. We have boldness, therefore, to enter into the holiest by the blood of Jesus, that is, by faith in his blood as shed without the gate ; for as his blood was shed without the gate, so it sanctifies the believer, and makes him capable to approach the holy of holies. Wherefore, after he had said, " that he might sanctify the people with his own blood," " he suffered without the gate." (Heb. xiii. 12.) Let us by him, therefore, that is, because we are first sanctified by faith in his blood, offer to God the sacrifice of praise continually, that is, the fruits of our lips, giving thanks in his name. Wherefore the laver of regeneration, or Christ set forth by the word, as

crucified, is for all coming sinners to wash in unto justification ; and the throne of grace is to be approached by saints, or as sinners justified by faith in a crucified Christ ; and so, as washed from sin in the sea of his blood, to come to the mercy-seat.

And it is yet far more evident ; for that those that approach this throne of grace, they must do it through believing ; for, saith the apostle, " How shall they call on him in whom they have not believed ?" of whom they have not heard, and in whom they have not believed ? for to that purpose runs the text. (Rom. x. 14.) " How then shall they call on him in whom they have not believed ?" antecedent to their calling on him ; " and how shall they believe in him of whom they have not heard " first ? So then hearing goes before believing, and believing before calling upon God, as he sits on the throne of grace. Now, believing is to be according to the sound of the beginning of the gospel, which presenteth us, not first with Christ as ascended, but as Christ dying, buried, and risen. " For I delivered unto you first of all, that which I also received ; how that Christ died for our sins according to the scriptures ; and that he was buried, and that he rose again the third day, according to the scriptures." (1 Cor. xv. 3, 4.)

I conclude then, as to this, that the order of heaven is that men wash in the laver of regeneration, to wit, in the blood of Christ, as held forth in the word of the truth of the gospel, which is the ordinance of God ; for there sinners, as sinners, or men as unclean, may wash, in order to their approach to God, as he sits upon the throne of grace.

And besides, is it possible that a man that passeth by the doctrine of Christ as dead, should be admitted with acceptance to a just and holy God for life ? or that he that slighteth and trampleth under foot the blood of Christ, as shed on the cross, should be admitted to an interest in Christ, as he is the throne of grace ? It cannot be. He must then wash there first, or die ; let his profession, or pretended faith, or holiness be what it will. For God sees iniquity in all men ; nor can all the nitre or soap in the world cause that our iniquity should not be marked before God. (Jer. ii. 22.) " For without shedding of blood is no remission." (Heb. ix. 22.)

Nothing that polluteth, that defileth, or that is unclean, must enter into God's sanctuary, much less into the most holy part thereof ; but by their sacrifice, by which they are purged, and for the sake of the perfection thereof, they, believing, are accepted. We have " therefore, brethren, boldness to enter into the holiest by the blood of Jesus," and no way else. (Heb. x. 19.)

IV. *How we are to approach the Throne of Grace.*

But this will yet be further manifest by what we have yet to say of the manner of our approach unto the throne of grace.

First, then, we must approach the throne of

grace *by the second veil;* for the throne of grace is after the second veil. So, then, though a man cometh into the tabernacle, or temple, which was a figure of the church, yet if he entered but within the first veil, he only came where there was no mercy-seat, or throne of grace. And what is this second veil, in, at, or through which, as the phrase is, we must, by blood, enter into the holiest? Why, as to the law, the second veil did hang up between the holy and the most holy place, and it did hide what was within the holiest from the eyes or sight of those that went no further than into the first tabernacle. Now this second veil in the tabernacle, or temple, was a figure of the second veil that all those must go through that will approach the throne of grace. And that veil is the flesh of Christ.

This is that which the holy apostle testifies in his exhortation, where he saith, we have " boldness to enter into the holiest by the blood of Jesus, by a new and living way, which he hath consecrated for us, through the veil, that is to say, his flesh." (Heb. x. 19, 20.) The second veil then is the flesh of Christ, the which, until a man can enter or go through by his faith, it is impossible that he should come to the holiest, where the throne of grace is, that is, to the heart and soul of Jesus, which is the throne.

The body of Christ is the tabernacle of God, and so that in which God dwells; for the fulness of the Godhead dwells in him bodily. (Col. ii. 9.) Therefore, as also has been hinted before, Christ Jesus is the throne of grace. Now, since his flesh is called the veil, it is evident that the glory that dwells within him, to wit, God resting in him, cannot be understood but by them that by faith can look through, or enter through, his flesh to that glory. For the glory is within the veil; there is the mercy-seat, or throne of grace; there sitteth God as delighted, as at rest, in and with sinners, that come to him by and through that flesh, and the offering of it for sin without the gate. " I am the way," saith Christ; but to what? and how? (John xiv. 6.) Why, to the Father, through my flesh. "And, having made peace through the blood of his cross, by him to reconcile all things to himself; by him, I say, whether they be things on earth, or things in heaven. And you that were some time alienated, and enemies in your mind by wicked works, yet now hath he reconciled;" but how? "in the body of his flesh," that then must be first: to what? "to present you holy and un-blameable, and unreprovable in his sight," (Col. i. 20—22:) that is, when you enter into his presence, or approach by this flesh, the mercy-seat, or the throne of grace.

This, therefore, is the manner of our coming, (if we come aright to the throne of grace for mercy,) we must come by blood through his flesh, as through the veil; by which, until you have entered through it, the glory of God, and that he is resolved that grace shall reign, will be utterly hid from your eyes. I will not say, but by the notion of these things, men may have their whirling fancies, and may create to themselves wild notions, and flattering imaginations of Christ, the throne of grace, and of glory; but the gospel knowledge of this, is of absolute necessity to my right coming to the throne of grace for mercy. I must come by his blood, through his flesh, or I cannot come at all; for here is no back door. This then is the sum—Christ's body is the tabernacle, the holiest; "thy law," saith he, " is within my heart," or in the midst of my bowels. (Ps. xl. 7, 8.) In this tabernacle then God sitteth, to wit, on the heart of Christ, for that is the throne of grace. Through this tabernacle men must enter, that is, by a godly understanding of what by this tabernacle, or flesh of Christ, has been done to reconcile us to God that dwells in him. This is the way, all the way; for there is no way but this to come to the throne of grace. This is the new way into the heavenly paradise, for the old way is hedged and ditched up by the flaming sword of cherubims. (Gen. iii. 24.) The new and living way, for to go the other, is present death; so then, this " new and living way, which he has consecrated for us through the veil, that is to say, his flesh," is the only way into the holiest, where the throne of grace is. (Heb. x. 20.)

Second. We must approach this throne of grace, as having our hearts, first, *sprinkled from an evil conscience.* The priest that was the representator of all Israel, when he went into the holiest, was not to go in, but as sprinkled with blood first. (Exod. xxix.) Thus it is written in the law, "not with-out blood;" thus it is written in the gospel. (Heb. ix. 7.) And now since by the gospel we have all admittance to enter in through the veil, by faith, we must take heed that we enter not in without blood; for if the blood, virtually, be not seen upon us, we die, instead of obtaining mercy, and finding the help of grace. This I press the oftener, be-cause there is nothing to which we are more naturally inclined, than to forget this. Who, that understands himself, is not sensible how apt he is to forget to act faith in the blood of Jesus, and to get his conscience sprinkled with the virtue of that, that attempteth to approach the throne of grace? Yet the scripture calls upon us to take heed that we neglect not thus to prepare ourselves. " Let us draw near with a true heart, in full assurance of faith, having our heart sprinkled from an evil con-science," to wit, with the blood of Christ, lest we die. (Heb. x. 22.) In the law all the people were to be sprinkled with blood, and it was necessary that the patterns of things in the heavens should be purified with these, that is, with the blood of bulls; but the heavenly things themselves, with better sacrifices than these, that is, with the offering of the body, and shedding of the blood of Christ. By this then must thou be purified and sprinkled, who by Christ wouldest approach the throne of grace.

Third. Therefore it is added, "*And our bodies washed with pure water.*" This the apostle taketh also out of the law, where it was appointed, as was showed before. Christ, also, just before he went to the Father, gave his disciples a signification of this, saying to Peter, and by him to all the rest, "If I wash thee not, thou hast no part with me." (John xiii. 8.) This pure water is nothing but the wholesome doctrine of the word mixed with Spirit, by which, as the conscience was before sprinkled with blood, the body and outward conversation is now sanctified and made clean. "Now ye are clean through the word," saith Christ, "which I have spoken unto you." (John xv. 3.) Hence, washing, and sanctifying, and justifying, are put together, and are said to come by the name of our Lord Jesus Christ, and by the Spirit of our God. (1 Cor. vi. 11.) Thou must then be washed with water and sprinkled with blood, if thou wouldest orderly approach the throne of grace; if thou wouldest orderly approach it with a true heart, in full assurance of faith; or if thou wouldest, as the text biddeth thee here, to wit, "Come boldly unto the throne-of-grace, to obtain mercy, and find grace to help in time of need."

To tell you what it is to come boldly, is one thing; and to tell you how you should come boldly, is another. Here you are bid to come boldly, and are also showed how that may be done. It may be done through the blood of sprinkling, and through the sanctifying operations of the Spirit, which are here by faith to be received. And when what can be said, shall be said to the utmost, there is no boldness, godly boldness, but by blood. The more the conscience is a stranger to the sprinkling of blood, the further off it is of being rightly bold with God, at the throne of grace; for it is the blood that makes the atonement, and that gives boldness to the soul. (Lev. xvii. 11. Heb. x. 19.) It is the blood, the power of it by faith upon the conscience, that drives away guilt, and so fear, and, consequently, that begetteth boldness. Wherefore, he that will be bold with God at the throne of grace, must first be well acquainted with the doctrine of the blood of Christ; namely, that it was shed, and why; and that it has made peace with God, and for whom. Yea, thou must be able by faith to bring thyself within the number of those that are made partakers of this reconciliation, before thou canst come boldly to the throne of grace. But,

First. There is a coming to the throne of grace before or without this boldness; but that is not the coming to which by these texts we are exhorted; yet that coming, be it never so deficient, if it is right, it is through some measure an inlet into the death and blood of Christ, and through some management, though but very little, or perhaps scarce at all discerned of the soul, to hope for grace from the throne; I say, it must arise, the encouragement must, from the cross, and from Christ as dying there. Christ himself went that way to God, and it is not possible but we must go the same way too. So, then, the encouragement, be it little, be it much, (and it is little or much,

even as the faith is in strength or weakness, which apprehendeth Christ,) it is according to the proportion of faith; strong faith gives great boldness, weak faith doth not so, nor can it.

Second. There is a sincere coming to the throne of grace without this boldness, even a coming in the uprightness of one's heart without it. Hence a true heart and full assurance are distinguished. "Let us draw near with a true heart, in full assurance of faith." (Heb. x. 22.) Sincerity may be attended with a great deal of weakness, even as boldness may be attended with pride; but be it what kind of coming to the throne of grace it will, either a coming with boldness, or with that doubting which is incident to saints, still the cause of that coming, or ground thereof, is some knowledge of redemption by blood, redemption which the soul seeth it has faith in, or would see it has faith in: for Christ is precious, sometimes in the sight of the worth, sometimes in the sight of the want, and sometimes in the sight of the enjoyment of him.

Third. There is an earnest coming to the throne of grace, even with all the desire of one soul. When David had guilt and trouble, and that so heavy that he knew not what to do, yet he could say, "Lord, all my desire is before thee, and my groaning is not hid from thee." (Ps. xxxviii. 9.) He could come earnestly to the throne of grace, he could come hither with all the desire of his soul; but still this must be from that knowledge that he had of the way of remission of sins by the blood of the Son of God.

Fourth. There is also a constant coming to the throne of grace. "Lord," said Heman, "I have cried day and night before thee; let my prayer come before thee: incline thine ear unto my cry; for my soul is full of troubles: and my life draweth nigh unto the grave." (Ps. lxxxviii. 1—3.) Here you see his constant crying before the throne of grace, crying night and day; and yet the man that cries, seems to be in a very black cloud, and to find hard work to bear up in his soul: yet this he had, namely, the knowledge of how God was the God of salvation; yea, he called him his God as such, though with pretty much difficulty of spirit, to be sure. Wherefore it must not be concluded, that they come not at all to the throne of grace, that come not with a full assurance: or that men must forbear to come, till they come with assurance: but this I say, they come not at all aright, that take not the ground of their coming from the death and blood of Christ; and that they that come to the throne of grace with but little knowledge of redemption by blood, will come with but little hope of obtaining grace and mercy to help in time of need.

I conclude, then, that it is the privilege, the duty and glory of a man, to approach the throne of grace as a prince, as Job said, could he but find it, he would be sure to do. "O that I knew where I might find him!" saith he, "that I might come even to his seat. I would order my cause before him, and fill my mouth with arguments. I would know the words which he would answer me, and understand what he would say unto me. Will he plead against me with his great power? No; but he would put strength in me. There the righteous might dispute with him; so should I be delivered for ever from my judge." (Job xxiii. 3—7.) Indeed, God sometimes tries us. "He holdeth back," sometimes, "the face of his throne, and spreadeth his cloud upon it." (Job xxvi. 9.) And this seems to be Job's case here, which made him to confess he was at a loss, and to cry out, "O that I knew where I might find him!" And this he doth for trial, and to prove our honesty and constancy; for the hypocrite will not pray always. Will he always call upon God? No, verily; especially not when thou bindest them, afflictest them, and makest praying hard work to them. (Job xxxvi. 13.)

But difficulty as to finding of God's presence, and the sweet shining of the face of his throne, doth not always lie in the weakness of faith. Strong faith may be in this perplexity, and may be hard put to it to stand at times. It is said here, that God did hold back the face of his throne, and did spread a cloud upon it; not to weaken Job's faith, but to try Job's strength, and to show to men of after ages how valiant a man Job was. Faith, if it be strong, will play the man in the dark; will, like a mettled horse, flounce in a bad way; will not be discouraged at trials, at many or strong trials: "Though he slay me, yet will I trust in him," is the language of that invincible grace of God. (Job xiii. 15.)

There is also an aptness in those that come to the throne of grace, to cast all degrees of faith away, that carries not in its bowels self-evidence of its own being and nature; thinking that if it be faith, it must be known to the soul; yea, if it be faith, it will do so and so, even so as the highest degrees of faith will do. When, alas! faith is sometimes in a calm, sometimes up, and sometimes down, and sometimes at it with sin, death, and the devil, as we say, blood up to the ears. Faith now has but little time to speak peace to the conscience; it is now struggling for life, it is now fighting with angels, with infernals; all it can do now is to cry, groan, sweat, fear, fight, and gasp for life.

Indeed, the soul should now run to the cross, for there is the water, or rather the blood and water that is provided for faith, as to the maintaining of the comfort of justification; but the soul whose faith is thus attacked, will find hard work to do this, though much of the well-managing of faith, in the good fight of faith, will lie in the soul's hearty and constant adhering to the death and blood of Christ; but a man must do as he can.

Thus now have I showed you the manner of right coming to the throne of grace, for mercy and grace to help in time of need.

The next thing that I am to handle is, first, To show you, that it is the privilege of the godly to distinguish from all thrones whatsoever this throne of grace. This, as I told you, I gathered from the apostle in the text, for that he only maketh mention thereof, but gives no sign to distinguish it by; no sign, I say, though he knew that there were more thrones than it, "Let us come boldly," saith he, "to the throne of grace;" and so leaves it, knowing full well that they had a good understanding of his meaning, being Hebrews. They being now also enlightened from what they were taught by the placing of the ark of the testimony and the mercy-seat in the most holy place; of which particular the apostle did then count it not of absolute necessity distinctly to discourse. Indeed, the Gentiles, as I have showed, have this throne of grace described and set forth before them by those tokens which I have touched upon in the sheets that go before, for with the book of Revelations the Gentiles are particularly concerned, for that it was writ to churches of the Gentiles; also the great things prophesied of there relate unto Gentile believers, and to the downfall of Antichrist, as he standeth among them.

But yet, I think, that John's discourse of the things attending the throne of grace were not by him so much propounded, because the Gentiles were incapable of finding of it without such description, as to show the answerableness of the antitype with the type; and also to strengthen their faith, and illustrate the thing: for they that know, may know more, and better of what they know; yea, may be greatly comforted with another's dilating on what they know.

Besides, the Holy Ghost by the word doth always give the most perfect description of things; wherefore to that we should have recourse for the completing of our knowledge. I mean not by what I say, in the least to intimate, as if this throne of grace was to be known without the text, for it is that that giveth revelation of Jesus Christ; but my meaning is, that a saint as such, has such a working of things upon his heart, as makes him able, by the word, to find out this throne of grace, and to distinguish it to himself from others. For,

First. The saint has strong guilt of sin upon his conscience, especially at first; and this makes him better judge what grace in the nature of grace is, than others can that are not sensible of what guilt is. What it was to be saved was better relished by the jailer when he was afraid of, and trembled at, the apprehensions of the wrath of God, than ever it was with him all his life before. (Acts xvi.) Peter then also saw what saving was, when he began to sink into the sea, "Lord, save me!" said he; "I perish!" (Matt. xiv. 30.) Sin is that without a sense of which a man is not apprehensive what grace is: sin and grace, favour and wrath, death and life, hell and heaven, are opposites, and are set off, or out, in their evil or good, shame or glory, one by another. What makes grace so good to us as sin in its guilt and filth? What makes sin so horrible and damnable a thing in our eyes, as when we see there is nothing can save us from it but the infinite grace of God? Further, there seems, if I may so term it, to be a kind of natural instinct in the new creature to seek after the grace of God; for so saith the word, "They that are after the flesh, do mind the things of the flesh; but they that are after the Spirit, the things of the Spirit." (Rom. viii. 5.) The child by nature nuzzles in its mother's bosom for the breast; the child by grace does by grace seek to live by the grace of God. All creatures, the calf, the lamb, &c., so soon as they are fallen from their mother's belly, will by nature look for, and turn themselves towards the teat, and the new creature doth so too. For guilt makes it hunger and thirst, as the hunted hart does pant after the water brooks. Hunger directs to bread, thirst directs to water; yea, it calls bread and water to mind. Let a man be doing other business, hunger will put him in mind of his cupboard, and thirst of his cruse of water; yea, it will call him, make him, force him, command him, to bethink what nourishing victuals is, and will also drive him to a search out after where he may find it, to the satisfying of himself. All right talk also to such an one sets the stomach and appetite a craving; yea, into a kind of a running out of the body after this bread and water, that it might be fed, nourished, and filled therewith. Thus it is by nature, and thus it is by grace; thus it is for the bread that perisheth, and for that which endureth to everlasting life. But,

Second. As nature, the new nature, teaches this by a kind of heavenly natural instinct, so experience also herein helpeth the godly much: for they have found all other places, the throne of grace excepted, empty, and places or things that hold no water. They have been at Mount Sinai for help but could find nothing there but fire and darkness, but thunder and lightning, but earthquake and trembling, and a voice of killing words, which words they that heard them once, could never endure to hear them again; and as for the sight of vengeance there revealed against sin, it was so terrible that Moses, even Moses said, "I exceedingly fear and quake." (Heb. xii. 18—21.)

They have sought for grace by their own performances; but, alas! they have yielded them nothing but wind and confusion: not a performance, not a duty, not an act in any part of religious worship, but they, looking upon it in the glass of the Lord, do find it specked and defective. They have sought for grace by their resolutions, their vows, their purposes, and the like; but, alas! they all do as the other, discover that they have been very imperfectly managed, and so such as can by no means help them to grace. They have gone to their tears, their sorrow, and repentance, if perhaps they might have found some help there; but all has either fled away like the early dew, or if they have stood, they have stunk even in the nostrils of those whose they were: how much more, then, in the nostrils of a holy God! They

have gone to God as the great Creator, and have beheld how wonderful his works have been; they have looked to the heavens above, to the earth beneath, and to all their ornaments; but neither have these, nor what is of them, yielded grace to those that had sensible want thereof.

Thus have they gone, as I said, with these pitchers to their fountains, and have returned empty and ashamed; they found no water, no river of water of life; they have been as the woman with her bloody issue, spending, and spending, till they have spent all, and been nothing better, but rather grew worse. (Mark v. 25—34.) Had they searched into nothing but the law, it had been sufficient to convince them that there was no grace, nor throne of grace, in the world. For since the law, being the most excellent of all the things of the earth, is found to be such as yieldeth no grace, (for grace and truth comes by Jesus Christ, not by Moses, John i. 17,) how can it be imagined that it should be found in anything inferior? Paul, therefore, not finding it in the law, despairs to find it in anything else below; but presently betakes himself to look for it there, where he had not yet sought it, (for he sometimes sought it not by faith, but as it were by the works of the law;) he looked for it, I say, by Jesus Christ, who is the throne of grace, where he found it, and rejoiced in hope of the glory of God. But.

Third. Saints come to know and distinguish the throne of grace from other thrones, by the very direction of God himself: as it is said of the well that the nobles digged in the wilderness, they digged it by the direction of the lawgiver, so saints find out the throne of grace by the direction of the grace-giver. Hence, Paul prays, that the Lord would direct the hearts of the people into the love of God. (2 Thess. iii. 5.) Man, as man, cannot aim directly at this throne, but will drop his prayers short, besides, or the like, if he be not helped by the Spirit. Hence the Son saith of himself, "No man can come to me, except the Father which has sent me draw him." (John vi. 44.) Which text doth not only justify what is now said, but insinuates that there is an unwillingness in man of himself to come to this throne of grace; he must be drawn thereto. He setteth us in the way of his steps, that is, in that way to the throne by which grace and mercy is conveyed unto us.

Fourth. We know the throne of grace from other thrones, by the glory that it always appears in when revealed to us of God; its glory outbids all: there is no such glory to be seen anywhere else, either in heaven or earth. But I say this comes by the sight that God gives, not by any excellency that there is in my natural understanding as such; my understanding and apprehension, simply as natural, is blind and foolish: wherefore, when I set to work in mine own spirit, and in the power of mine own abilities, to reach to this throne of grace, and to perceive somewhat of the glory thereof, then am I dark, rude, foolish, see nothing; and my heart grows flat, dull, savourless, lifeless, and has no warmth in the duty. But it mounts up with wings like an eagle, when the throne is truly apprehended.

Therefore that is another thing by which the Christian knows the throne of grace from all others; it meets with that good there, that it can meet with nowhere else. But at present, let these things suffice for this.

V. *Motives for coming boldly to the Throne of Grace.*

I come now to the motives by which the apostle stirreth up the Hebrews, and encourageth them to come boldly to the throne of grace.

First. The first is, because we have there such an high priest so and so qualified.

Second. Because we that come thither for grace are sure there to speed, or find grace and obtain it.

First. For the first of these, to wit, we have encouragement to move us to come with boldness to the throne of grace, because we have an high priest there; because we have such an high priest there. "For we have not an high priest which cannot be touched with the feeling of our infirmities; but was in all points tempted like as we are, yet without sin. Let us therefore come boldly unto the throne of grace."

Of this high priest I have already made mention before, to wit, so far as to show you that Christ Jesus is he, as well as he is the altar and sacrifice and throne of grace, before which he also himself makes intercession. But forasmuch as by the apostle here, he is not only presented unto us as a throne of grace, but as an high priest ministering before it, it will not be amiss if I do somewhat particularly treat of his priesthood also: but the main or chief of my discourse will be to treat of his qualifications to his office, which I find to be in general of two sorts. *First.* Legal. *Second.* Natural.

First. When I say *legal,* I mean, as the apostle's expression is, not by "the law of a carnal commandment," but by an eternal covenant, and "the power of an endless life" thereby; of which the priesthood of old was but a type, and the law of their priesthood but a shadow. (Heb. vii. 16.) But because their law, and their entrance into their priesthood thereby, was, as I said, a shadow of good things to come, therefore where it will help to illustrate, we will make use thereof so to do; and where not, there we will let it pass. (Heb. x. 1.)

The thing to be now spoken to is, that the consideration of Jesus Christ being an high priest before the throne of grace, is a motive and encouragement to us to come boldly thither for grace: "Seeing then that we have a great high priest, that is passed into the heavens, Jesus the Son of God, let us hold fast our profession," and "come boldly unto the throne of grace." (Heb. iv. 14, 16.) Now, he was made an high priest, for so is the expression, "made an high priest for ever after the order of Melchisedec." (Heb. vi. 20.) •

First. He took not his honour upon himself without a lawful call thereto; thus the priests under the law were put into office; and thus the Son of God. "No man taketh this honour unto himself, but he that is called of God, as was Aaron. So also Christ glorified not himself to be made an high priest; but he that said unto him, Thou art my Son, to-day have I begotten thee." Wherefore he "was called of God an high priest after the order of Melchisedec." (Heb. v. 4—6, 10.) Thus far, therefore, the law of his priesthood answereth to the law of the priesthood of old; they both were made priests by a legal call to their work or office.

But yet the law by which this Son was made high priest excelleth, and that in these particulars:—

1. He was made a priest after the similitude of Melchisedec, "For he testifieth, Thou art a priest for ever after the order of Melchisedec." (Heb. vii. 17.) Thus they under the law were not made priests, but after the order of Aaron, that is, by a carnal commandment, not by an everlasting covenant of God.

2. "And," saith he, "inasmuch as not without an oath he was made priest; for those priests were made without an oath; but this with an oath, by him that said unto him, The Lord sware, and will not repent, Thou art a priest for ever after the order of Melchisedec." (Heb. vii. 20, 21.)

3. The priesthood under the law, with their law and sacrifices, were fading, and were not suffered to continue, by reason of the death of the priest, and ineffectualness of his offering. (Heb. vii. 23.) "But this man, because he continueth ever, hath an unchangeable priesthood." (Heb. vii. 24.) "For the law maketh men high priests which have infirmity; but the word of the oath, which was since the law, maketh the Son, who is consecrated for evermore." (Heb. vii. 28.)

From what hath already been said, we gather:

1. What kind of person it is that is our high priest.

2. The manner of his being called to and stated in that office.

1. What manner of person he is. He is the Son, the Son of God, Jesus the Son of God. Hence the apostle saith, "We have a great high priest," such an high priest, "that is passed into the heavens." (Heb. iv. 14.) Such an high priest as is "made higher than the heavens." (Heb. vii. 26.) And why doth he thus dilate upon the dignity of his person, but because thereby is insinuated the excellency of his sacrifice, and the prevalency of his intercession, by that, to God for us. Therefore he saith again, "Every," Aaronical, "priest standeth daily ministering and offering oftentimes the same sacrifices, which can never take away sins: but this man," this great man,

this Jesus, this Son of God, "after he had offered one," one only, one once, but one, "sacrifice for sin for ever, sat down on the right hand of God; from henceforth expecting till his enemies be made his footstool. For by one offering he hath perfected for ever them that are sanctified." (Heb. x. 11—14.) Thus, I say, the apostle toucheth upon the greatness of his person, thereby to set forth the excellency of his sacrifice, and prevalency of his intercession. "Wherefore, holy brethren, partakers of the heavenly calling, consider the Apostle and High Priest of our profession, Christ Jesus." (Heb. iii. 1.) Or, as he saith again, making mention of Melchisedec, "consider how great this man was," (Heb. vii. 4 :) we have such a high priest, so great a high priest; one that is entered into the heavens, Jesus the Son of God.

2. The manner also of his being called to and stated in his office, is not to be overlooked. He is made a priest after the power of an endless life, or is to be such an one as long as he lives, and as long as we have need of his mediation. Now Christ being raised from the dead, dies no more; death hath no more dominion over him. He is himself the Prince of life. Wherefore it follows, "he hath an unchangeable priesthood." And what then ? Why, then "he is able to save them to the uttermost that come unto God by him, seeing he ever liveth to make intercession for them." (Heb. vii. 24, 25.)

But again, he is made a priest with an oath, "The Lord sware, and will not repent, thou art a priest for ever." Hence I gather,

(1.) That before God there is no high priest but Jesus, nor ever shall be.

(2.) That God is to the full pleased with his high priesthood; and so with all those for whom he maketh intercession. For this priest, though he is not accepted for the sake of another, yet he is upon the account of another. "For every high priest taken from among men is ordained for men in things pertaining to God," to make reconciliation for the sins of the people. (Heb. v. 1.) And again, he is entered "into heaven itself, now to appear in the presence of God for us." (Heb. ix. 24.)

God therefore, in that he hath made him a priest with an oath, and also determined that he will never repent of his so doing, declareth that he is, and for ever will be, satisfied with his offering. And this is a great encouragement to those that come to God by him; they have by this oath a firm ground to go upon, and the oath is, "Thou art a priest for ever," shalt be accepted for ever, for every one for whom thou makest intercession; nor will I ever reject anybody that comes to me by thee. Therefore here is ground for faith, for hope, and rejoicing; for this consideration a man has ground to come boldly to the throne of grace.

Second. But again, as Christ is made a priest by call with an oath, and so, so far legally, so he, being thus called, has other preparatory legal qualifications. The high priest under the law was not by law to come into the holiest, but in those robes that were ordained for him to minister in, before God; which robes were not to be made according to the fancy of the people, but according to the commandment of Moses. (Exod. xxviii.) Christ, our high priest in heaven, has also his holy garment, with which he covereth the nakedness of them that are his, which robe was not made of corruptible things, as silver and gold, &c., but by a patient continuance in a holy life, according to the law of Moses, both moral and ceremonial. Not that either of these were that eternal testament by which he was made a priest; but the moral law was to be satisfied, and the types of the ceremonial law to be, as to this, eminently fulfilled; and he was bound by that eternal covenant by which he is made a mediator to do so. Wherefore, before he could enter the holiest of all, he must have these holy garments made; neither did he trust others, as in the case of Aaron, to make these garments for him, but he wrought them all himself, according to all that Moses commanded.

This garment Christ was a great while a making. What time, you may ask, was required? And I answer, All the days of his life; for all things that were written concerning him, as to this, were not completed till the day that he hanged upon the cross. For then it was that he said, "It is finished; and he bowed his head, and gave up the Ghost." (John xix. 30.) This robe is for glory and for beauty. This is it that afore I said was of the colour of the rainbow, and that compasseth even round about this throne of grace, unto which we are bid to come. This is that garment that reaches down to his feet, and that is girt to him with a golden girdle. (Rev. i. 13.) This is that garment that covereth all his body mystical, and that hideth the blemishes of such members from the eye of God, and of the law. And it is made up of his obedience to the law, by his complete perfect obedience thereto. This Christ wears always; he never puts it off, as the high priest puts off his, by a ceremonial command. He ever lives to make intercession, consequently he ever wears this priestly robe. He might not go into the holy place without it, upon danger of death, or at least of being sent back again; but he died not, but lives ever; is not sent back, but is set down at God's right hand; and there shall sit till his foes are made his footstool.

This is that for the sake of which all are made welcome, and embraced and kissed, forgiven and saved, that come unto God by him. This is that righteousness, that mantle spotless, that Paul so much desired to be found wrapped in; for he knew that being found in that, he must be presented thereby to God a glorious man, not having spot, or wrinkle, or any such thing. This, therefore, is another of the Lord Jesus's legal qualifications, as preparatory to the executing of his high priest's office in heaven. But of this something has been spoken before, and therefore I shall not enlarge upon it here.

Third. When the high priest under the law was thus accomplished by a legal call, and a garment suitable to his office, then again there was another thing that must be done, in order to his regular execution of his office ; and that was, he must be consecrated, and solemnly ushered thereunto by certain offerings, first presented to God for himself.

This you have mention made of in the Levitical law ; you have there first commanded that in order to the high priest's approaching the holiest for the people, there must first be an offering of consecration for himself, and this is to succeed his call, and the finishing of his holy garments. (Exod. xxix.) For this ceremony was not to be observed until his garments were made and put upon him. Also the blood of the ram of consecration was to be sprinkled upon him, his garments, &c., that he might be hallowed, and rightly set apart for the high priest's office. The Holy Ghost, I think, thus signifying that Jesus the Son of God, our great high priest, was not only to sanctify the people with his blood, but first, by blood, must to that work be sanctified himself : " For their sakes," saith he, " I sanctify myself, that they also might be sanctified through the truth." (John xvii. 19.)

But it may be asked, When was this done to Christ, or what sacrifice of consecration had he precedent to the offering up of himself for our sins ? I answer, It was done in the garden when he was washed in his own blood, when his sweat was as great drops of blood, falling down to the ground. For there it was that he was sprinkled with his blood, not only the tip of his ear, his thumb, and toe, but there he was washed all over ; there, therefore, was his most solemn consecration to his office ; at least, so I think. And this, as Aaron's was, was done by Moses ; it was Moses that sprinkled Aaron ; it was Moses that sprinkled Christ's garments. It was by virtue of an agony also that his bloody sweat was produced ; and what was the cause of that agony, but the apprehension of the justice and curse of Moses's law, which now he was to undergo for the sins of the people ?

With this sacrifice he then subjoined another, which was also preparatory to the great acts of his high priest's office, which he was afterwards to perform for us. And that was his drink offering, his tears, which were offered to God with strong cries. (Exod. xxix.) For this was the place and time that in a special manner he caused his strong wine to be poured out, and that he drank his tears as water. This is called his offering, his offering for his own acceptance with God. After " he had offered up prayers and supplications, with strong crying and tears, unto him that was able to save him," he " was heard " for his piety, for his acceptance as to this office, for he

merited his office, as well as his people. (Heb. v. 7.) Wherefore it follows, " and being made perfect," that is, by a complete performance of all that was necessary for the orderly attaining of his office as high priest, " he became the author of eternal salvation, unto all them that obey him." (Heb. v. 9.)

For your better understanding of me as to this, mind that I speak of a twofold perfection in Christ ; one as to his person, the other as to his performances. In the perfection of his person, two things are to be considered : first, the perfection of his humanity, as to the nature of it ; it was at first appearing wholly without pollution of sin, and so completely perfect : but yet this humanity was to have joined to this another perfection, and that was a perfection of stature and age. Hence it is said, that as to his humanity he increased, that is, grew more perfect. For this his increasing was in order to a perfection, not of nature, simply as nature, but of stature : " Jesus increased in wisdom and stature." (Luke ii. 52.) The paschal lamb was a lamb the first day it was weaned ; but it was not to be sacrificed until it attained such a perfection of age as by the law of God was appointed to it. (Exod. xii. 5, 6.) It was necessary, therefore, that Christ as to his person should be perfect in both these senses. And indeed, " in due time Christ died for the ungodly." (Rom. v. 6.)

Again, as there was a perfection of person, or of nature and personage in Christ, so there was to be a perfection of performances in him also. Hence it is said, that Jesus increased in favour with God ; that is, by perfecting of his obedience to him for us. Now, his performances were such as had a respect to his bringing in of righteousness for us in the general ; or such as respected preparations for his sacrifice as an high priest. But let them be applied to both, or to this and that in particular ; it cannot be, that while the most part of his performances were wanting, he should be as perfect as when he said, " The things concerning me have an end." (Luke xxii. 37.)

Not but that every act of his obedience was perfect, and carried in it a length and breadth proportionable to that law by which it was demanded ; nor was there at any time in his obedience, that which made to interfere one commandment with another. He did all things well, and so stood in the favour of God. But yet one act was not actually all, though virtually any one of his actions might carry in it a merit sufficient to satisfy and quiet the law. Hence, as I said, it is told us, not only that he is the Son of God's love, but that he increased in favour with God ; that is, by a going on in doing, by a continuing to do that always, that pleased the God of heaven.

A man that pays money at the day appointed, beginning first at one shilling, or one pound, and so ceaseth not until he hath in current coin told over the whole sum to the creditor, does well at the beginning; but the first shilling, or first pound, not being the full debt, cannot be counted, or reckoned the whole, but a part; yet is it not an imperfect part, nor doth the creditor find fault at all, because there is but so much now told; but concludes that all is at hand, and accepteth of this first, as a first fruits: so Christ, when he came into the world, began to pay, and so continued to do, even until he had paid the whole debt, and so increased in favour with God. There was, then, a gradual performance of duties, as to the number of them, by our Lord when he was in the world, and consequently a time wherein it might be said that Christ had not, as to act, done all, as was appointed him to do, to do as preparatory to that great thing which he was to do for us. Wherefore, in conclusion, he is said to be made perfect, "and being made perfect, he became the author of eternal salvation unto all them that obey him." (Heb. v. 9.)

It will be objected, then, that at some time it might be said of Christ, that he was imperfect in his obedience.

Ans. There was a time wherein it might have been said, Christ had not done all that he was to do for us on earth. But it doth not follow thereupon, that he therefore was imperfect in his obedience; for that all his acts of obedience were done in their proper time, and when they should, according to the will of God. The timing of performances adds or diminishes as to the perfection of obedience, or the imperfection of it. Had the Jews killed the passover three days sooner than the time appointed, they had transgressed. (Exod. xii. 6.) Had the Jews done that on the fourth day to Jericho, which was to have been done on the seventh day, they had sinned. (Josh. vi.) Duty is beautiful in its time, and the Son of God observed the time. " I must," saith he, " work the works of him that sent me, while it is day," that is, in their seasons. You must keep in mind that I speak all this while of that part of Christ's perfection, as to duties, which stood in the number of performances, and not in the nature or quality of acts. And I say, as to the thing in hand, Christ had duty to do, with respect to his office as high priest for us, which immediately concerned himself; such duties as gave him a legal admittance unto the execution thereof; such duties, the which, had they not orderly been done, the want of them would have made him an undue approacher of the presence of God, as to that. Wherefore, as I said afore, by what he did thereabout, he consecrated, or sanctified himself for that work, according to God, and was accepted for his piety, or in that he feared, and did orderly do what he should do.

Fourth. The next thing preparatory to the execution of this office of high priest was the sacrifice itself. The sacrifice, you know, must, as to the being of it, needs precede the offering of it: it must be, before it can be offered. Nor could Christ have been a high priest, had he not had a sacrifice to offer. " For every high priest is ordained to offer gifts and sacrifices: wherefore it is of necessity that this man have somewhat also to offer." (Heb. viii. 3.)

And I bring in the sacrifice as the last thing preparatory, not that it was last, as to being, for it was before he could be capable of doing any of the aforenamed duties, being his body, in and by which he did them; but it was the last as to fitness: it was not to be a sacrifice before the time, the time appointed of the Father. For since he had prepared it to that end, it was fit as to the time of its being offered, that that should be when God thought best also. (Heb. x. 5.)

Behold, then, here is the high priest with his sacrifice; and behold, again, how he comes to offer it. He comes to offer his burnt-offering at the call of God; he comes to do it in his priestly garments, consecrated, and sanctified in his own blood; he comes with blood and tears, or by water and blood, and offereth his sacrifice, himself a sacrifice unto God for the sin of the world; and that too at a time when God began to be weary of the service and sacrifices of all the world. " Wherefore when he cometh into the world, he saith, Sacrifice and offerings thou wouldest not, but a body hast thou prepared me," thou hast fitted me : " in burnt offerings and sacrifices for sin thou hast had no pleasure. Then said I, Lo, I come (in the volume of the book it is written of me) to do thy will, O God." (Heb. x. 5—7.)

Thus you see how our high priest proceeded to the execution of his priestly office : and now we are come to his sacrifice, we will consider a little of the parts thereof, and how he offered, and pleads the same. The burnt-offering for sin hath two parts, the flesh and the fat, which fat is called the fat of the inwards, of the kidneys, and the like. (Lev. iii.) Answerable to this, the sacrifice of Christ hath two parts, the body and the soul. The body is the flesh, and his soul the fat—that inward part that must not by any means be kept from the fire. For without the burning of the fat, the burnt-offering and sin offering, both which was a figure of the sacrifice of our high priest, was counted imperfect, and so not acceptable.

And it is observable that in these kind of offerings, when they were to be burned, the fat and the head must be laid and be burned together. And the priest "shall cut it into his pieces, with his head and his fat; and the priest shall lay them in order on the wood that is on the fire which is upon the altar," (Lev. i. 12:) to signify, methinks, the feeling sense that this sacrifice of his body and soul should have of the curse of God due to sin, all the while that it suffered for sin. And therefore it is from this that this sacrifice has the name of burnt-offering, it is the burnt-offering for the burning, because of the burning upon the altar all night, until the morning ; and the fire of the altar shall be burning in it.

The fat made the flame to increase, and to ascend ; wherefore God speaks affectionately of the fat, saying, the fat of mine offerings. And again, "He shall see of the travail of his soul, and shall be satisfied." (Isa. liii. 11.) The soul-groans, the soul-cries, the soul-conflicts that the Son of God had, together with his soul-submission to his Father's will, when he was made a sacrifice for sin, did doubtless flame bright, ascend high, and cast out a sweet savour unto the nostrils of God, whose justice was now appeasing for the sin of men.

His flesh also was part of this sacrifice, and was made to feel that judgment of God for sin that it was capable of. And it was capable of feeling much, so long as natural life, and so bodily sense, remained. It also began to feel, with the soul, by reason of the union that was betwixt them both; the soul felt, and the body bled; the soul was in an agony, and the body sweat blood; the soul wrestled with the judgment and curse of the law, and the body, to show its sense and sympathy, sent out dolorous cries, and poured out rivers of tears before God. We will not here at large speak of the lashes, of the crown of thorns, of how his face was bluft with blows and blood; also how he was wounded, pierced, and what pains he felt while life lasted, as he suffered for our sins; though these things are also prefigured in the old law, by the nipping or wringing of the head, the cutting of the sacrifice in pieces, and burning it in the fire. (Lev. i.)

Now, you must know, that as the high priest was to offer his sacrifice, so he was to bring the blood thereof to the mercy-seat or throne of grace, where now our Jesus is; he was to offer it at the door of the tabernacle, and to carry the blood within the veil: of both which a little.

1. He was to offer it, and how? Not grudgingly, nor as by compulsion, but of a voluntary will and cheerful mind: "If his offering be a burnt sacrifice of the herd, let him offer a male without blemish: he shall offer it of his own voluntary will." (Lev. i. 3.) Thus did Christ when he offered up himself, as is manifest by that which follows:—(1.) He offered a male, "himself," without blemish. (Heb. vii. 27.) (2.) He gave himself a ransom: he "gave his life a ransom." (Matt. xx. 28.) (3.) He laid down his life of himself. (John x. 18.) (4.) He longed for the day of his death, that he might die to redeem his people. (5.) Nor was he ever so joyful in all his life, that we read of, as when his sufferings drew near; then he takes the sacrament of his body and blood into his own hands, and with thanksgiving bestows it among his disciples; then he sings an hymn, then he rejoices, then he comes with a "Lo, I come." Oh the heart, the great heart, that Jesus Christ had for us to do us good! He did it with all the desire of his soul.

2. He did it, not only voluntary, and of a free will, but of love and affection to the life of his enemies. Had he done thus for the life of his friends, it had been much; but since he did it out of love to the life of his enemies, that is much more. "Scarcely for a righteous man will one die; yet peradventure for a good man some would even dare to die. But God commended his love toward us, in that, while we were yet sinners, Christ died for us." (Rom. v. 7, 8.)

3. He did it without relinquishment of mind, when he was in: no discouragement disheartened him; cry and bleed he did, yea, roar by reason of the troubles of his soul, but his mind was fixed: his Father sware, and did not repent, that he should be his priest; and he vowed, and said he would not repent, that he had threatened to be the plague and death of death. (Hos. xiii. 14.)

4. He did it effectually, and to purpose; he hath stopped the mouth of the law with blood; he hath so pacified justice, that it now can forgive; he hath carried sin away from before the face of God, and set up quit in his sight; he hath destroyed the devil, abolished death, and brought life and immortality to light through the gospel; he hath wrought such a change in the world by what he has done for them that believe, that all things work together for their good, from thenceforward and for ever.

I should now come to the second part of the office of this high priest, and speak to that; as also to those things that were preparatory unto his executing it; but first, I think convenient a little to treat of the altar also, upon which this sacrifice was offered to God.

Some, I conceive, have thought the altar to be the cross on which the body of Christ was crucified, when he gave himself an offering for sin; but they are greatly deceived, for he also himself was the altar, through which he offered himself; and this is one of the treasures of wisdom which are hid in him, and of which the world and Antichrist are utterly ignorant. I touched this in one hint before, but now a little more express.

The altar is always greater than the gift; and since the gift was the body and soul of Christ, (for so saith the scripture, "He gave himself for our sins,") the altar must be something else than a sorry bit of wood, or than a cursed tree. Wherefore I will say to such, as one wiser than Solomon said to the Jews, when they superstitiated the gift, in counting it more honourable than the altar: "Ye fools, and blind: for whether is greater, the gift, or the altar that sanctifieth the gift?" (Matt. xxiii. 18, 19.)

If the altar be greater than the gift, and yet the gift so great a thing as the very humanity of Christ, can it,—I will now direct my speech to the greatest fool,—can that greater thing be the cross? Is, was the cross, the wooden cross, the cursed tree, that some worship, greater than the gift, to wit, than the sacrifice which Christ offered, when he gave himself for our sins? O idolatry! O blasphemy!

Quest. But what then was the altar?

Ans. The divine nature of Christ, that eternal Spirit, by and in the assistance of which "he offered himself without spot to God;" he, through the eternal Spirit, "offered himself." (Heb. ix. 14.)

1. And it must be THAT, because, as was said, the altar was greater than the gift; but there is nothing but Christ's divine nature, greater than his human; to be sure a sorry bit of wood, a tree, the stock of a tree, is not.

2. It must be this, because the scripture says plainly, "the altar sanctifies the gift," that is, puts worth and virtue into it. But was it the tree, or the Godhead of Christ, that put virtue and efficacy into this sacrifice that he offered to God for us? If thou canst but tell thy fingers, judge.

3. The altar was it of old, that was to bear up the sacrifice until it was consumed; and with reference to the sacrifice under consideration, the tree could not bear up that; for our sacrifice being a man consisting of soul and body, that which could bear him up in his suffering condition, must be that that could apply itself to his reasonable and sensible part for relief and succour, and that was of power to keep him even in his spirit, and in a complete submissiveness to God, in the present condition in which he was; and could the tree do this, think you? Had the tree that command and government of the soul and sense of Christ, of the reason and feeling of the Lord Jesus, as to keep him in this bitter suffering, in that evenness and spotlessness in his torment, as to cause that he should come off this great work, without the least smell or tang of imperfection? No, no: it was through the eternal Spirit, that "he offered himself without spot to God."

Quest. Wherefore then served the cross?

Ans. I ask, and wherefore then served the wood by which the sacrifices were burned? The sacrifices were burned with wood upon the altar, the wood then was not the altar, the wood was that instrument by which the sacrifice was consumed, and the cross that by which Christ suffered his torment and affliction. The altar then was it that did bear both the wood and sacrifice, that did uphold the wood to burn, and the sacrifice to abide the burning. And with reference to the matter in hand, the tree on which Christ was hanged, and the sacrifice of his body, were both upheld by his divine power; yet the tree was no more a sacrifice, nor an altar, than was the wood upon the altar; nor was the wood, but the fire, holy, by which the sacrifice was consumed. Let the tree then be the tree, the sacrifice the sacrifice, and the altar the altar; and let men have a care how in their worship, they make altars upon which, as they pretend, they offer the body of Christ; and let them leave off foolishly to dote upon wood, and the works of their hands. The altar is greater than the gift or sacrifice that was, or is, upon it.

We come now to the second part of the office of this high priest, and to show how he performeth that. In order to which I must, as I did with reference to the first, show you what things, as preparatory, were to precede the execution of it.

We have here, as you see, "our passover sacrificed for us," for our encouragement to come to the throne of grace; and now let us look to it, as it is presented in the holiest of all, and to the order of its being so presented.

1. First, then, before there was anything further done, I mean by this high priest, as to a further application of his offering, the judgment of God was waited for by him, with respect to his estimation of what was already done, to wit, how that was resented by him; the which he declared to the full by raising him from the dead. For in that he was raised from the dead, when yet he died for our sins, it is evident that his offering was accepted, or esteemed of value sufficient to effect that for the which it was made a sacrifice, which was for our sins: this, therefore, was in order to his being admitted into heaven. God, by raising him from the dead, justified his death, and counted it sufficient for the saving of the world. And this Christ knew would be the effect of his death, long before he gave himself a ransom; where he saith, " This also shall please the Lord better than an ox or bullock that hath horns and hoofs." (Ps. lxix. 31.) And again, " For the Lord God will help me; and therefore shall I not be confounded; therefore I have set my face like a flint, and I know I shall not be ashamed. He is near that justifieth me; who will contend with me? Let us stand together; who is mine adversary? let him come near to me. Behold, the Lord God will help me; who is he that shall condemn me? Lo, they all shall wax old as a garment; the moth shall eat them up." (Isa. l. 7—9.) All this is the work of the Lord God, his Father, and he had faith therein, as I said before. And since it was God who was to be appeased, it was requisite that he should be heard in the matter, to wit, whether he was pacified or no; the which he has declared, I say, in raising him up from the dead. And this the apostles, both Paul and Peter, insinuate, when they ascribe his resurrection to the power of another, rather than to his raising of himself, saying, " this Jesus hath God raised up," (Acts ii. 32;) " God hath raised" him up " from the dead," (Acts iii. 15;) " whom God raised from the dead," (Acts iv. 10;) and the like. I say, therefore, that God by raising up Christ from the dead, hath said, that thus far his offering pleased him, and that he was content.

2. But lest the world, being besotted by sin, should not rightly interpret actions, therefore God added to his raising him up from the dead, a solemn exposing of him to view, not to all men, but to such as were faithful, and that might be trusted with the communicating of it to others. " Him," saith Peter, " God raised" from the dead, " and showed him openly; not to all the people, but unto witnesses chosen before of God, even to us, who did eat and drink with him after he rose from the dead." (Acts x. 40, 41.) And this was requisite, not for that it added anything to the value and worth of his sacrifice, but for the help of the faith of them that were to have eternal salva-

tion by him. And it is for this cause that Paul so enlargeth upon this very thing, to wit, that there were them that could testify that God had raised him up from the dead, namely, that men might see that God was well pleased, and that they had encouragement to come boldly by him to the throne of grace for mercy. And this exposing of him to view was not for the length of a surprising or dazzling moment, but days and nights, to the number of no less than forty; and that to the self-same persons, to wit, "the apostles whom he had chosen: to whom also," says the text, "he showed himself alive after his passion by many infallible proofs, being seen of them forty days, and speaking of the things pertaining to the kingdom of God." (Acts i. 2, 3.) Thus God, therefore, being willing more abundantly to show him unto the world, ordered this great season betwixt his resurrection and ascension, that the world might see that they had ground to believe an atonement was made for sin.

3. But again, a third thing that was to precede the execution of the second part of this his priestly office, was, the manner and order of his going into the holiest; I say, the manner and order of his going. He was to go thither in that *robe*, of which mention was made before, to wit, in the virtue of his obedience, for it was that which was to make his way for him, as now sprinkled with his blood. He was to go thither with a noise which the Holy Ghost calls a shout, saying, "God is gone up with a shout, the Lord with the sound of a trumpet." (Ps. xlvii. 5.) This was prefigured by the bells, as I said, which did hang on the border of Aaron's garments. This shout seems to signify the voice of men and angels; and this trumpet, the voice and joy of God; for so it says he shall descend: "For the Lord himself shall descend from heaven with a shout, with the voice of the archangel, and with the trump of God." (1 Thess. iv. 16.) Even as he ascended and went up: for Aaron's bells were to be heard when he went into, and when he came out of, the holy place. (Exod. xxviii.) But what men were to ascend with him but, as was said afore, the men that "came out of the graves after his resurrection?" (Matt. xxvii. 53.) And what angels, but those that ministered to him here in the day of his humiliation? As for the evil ones, he then rode in triumph over their heads, and crushed them, as captives, with his chariot wheels. He is ascended on high, he has led captivity captive, he has received gifts for men. (Eph. iv. 8.)

Thus then he ascended unto, into the holy paradise, where he was waited for of a multitude of the heavenly host, and of thousands of millions of the spirits of just men made perfect. So, approaching the highest heavens, the place of the special presence of God, he was bid sit down at his right hand, in token that for his sufferings' sake, God had made him the highest of every creature, and given him a name above every name,

and commanded that at the name of Jesus now all things in heaven should bow, and promised that at the day of judgment, all on earth, and under it, should do so too, to the glory of God the Father. (Phil. ii.)

Thus he presented himself on our behalf unto God, a sacrifice of a sweet-smelling savour, in which God resteth for ever, for that the blood of this sacrifice has always with him a pleasing and prevailing voice. It cannot be denied, it cannot be out-weighed by the heaviness, circumstances, or aggravations of any sin whatsoever, of them that come unto God by him. He is always, as I said before, in the midst of the throne, and before the throne, " a Lamb as it had been slain," now appearing in the presence of God for us. Of the manner of his intercession, whether it is vocal or virtual, whether by voice of mouth, or merit of deed, or both, I will not determine; we know but little while here how things are done in heaven, and we may soon be too carnal or fantastical in our apprehensions. Intercession he makes, that is, he manages the efficacy and worth of his suffering with God for us; and is always prevalent in his thus managing of his merits on our behalf. And as to the manner, though it may be in itself infinitely beyond what we can conceive while here, yet God hath stooped to our weakness, and so expressed himself in this matter, that we might somewhat, though but childishly, apprehend him. And we do not amiss if we conceive as the word of God hath revealed; for the Scriptures are the green poplar, hazel, and chestnut-rods that lie in the gutters where we should come to drink; all the difficulty is, in seeing the white strakes, the very mind of God there, that we may conceive by it.

But the text says, he prayeth in heaven, he makes intercession there. Again, it saith, his blood speaks, and, consequently, why may not his groans, his tears, his sighs, and strong cries, which he uttered here in the days of his flesh? I believe they do, and have a strong voice with God for the salvation of his people. He may then intercede both vocally and virtually; virtually to be sure he does, and we are allowed so to apprehend, because the text suggesteth such a manner of intercession to us. And because our weakness will not admit us to understand fully the thing as it is, our belief that he maketh intercession for us has also the advantage of being purged from its faultiness by his intercession, and we shall be saved thereby, because we have relied upon his blood shed, and the prevalency of the worthiness of it with God for us; though as to this circumstance, the manner of his interceding, we should be something at a loss.

The word says, that we have yet but the image of heavenly things, or of things in the heavens. I do not at all doubt but that many of those that were saved before Christ came in the flesh,—though they were as to the main right, and relied upon him to the saving of their souls,—yet came far short of the knowledge of many of the circumstances of his suffering for them. Did they all know that he was to be betrayed of Judas? that he was to be scourged of the soldiers? that he was to be crowned with thorns? that he was to be crucified between two thieves, and to be pierced till blood and water came out of his side? or that he was to be buried in Joseph's sepulchre? I say, did all that were saved by faith that he was to come and die for them understand these, with many more circumstances that were attendants of him to death? It would be rude to think so; because for it we have neither Scripture nor reason.

Even so, we now that believe that "he ever lived to make intercession for us," are also very short of understanding of the manner or mode of his so interceding. Yet we believe that he died, and that his merits have a voice with God for us; yea, that he manages his own merits before God in way of intercession for us, far beyond what we, while here, are able to conceive.

The Scripture saith that "all the fulness of the Godhead" dwells in him "bodily." (Col. ii. 9.) It saith also that he is the throne of God, and yet again, that he sits "on the right hand of the throne." (Heb. xii. 2.)

These things are so far from being comprehended by the weakest, that they strain the wits and parts of the strongest, yet there is a heavenly truth in all. Heavenly things are not easily believed, no, not of believers themselves, while here on earth, and when they are, they are so but weakly and infirmly. I believe that the very appearing of Christ before God is an intercession as a priest, as well as a plea of an advocate; and I believe again, that his very life there is an intercession there, a continual intercession.

But there is yet something further to be said. Christ, the humanity of Christ, if in it dwells all the fulness of the Godhead bodily, how then appears he before him to make intercession? or if Christ is the throne of grace and mercy-seat, how doth he appear before God as sitting there, to sprinkle that now with his blood? Again, if Christ be the altar of incense, how stands he as a priest by that altar to offer the prayers of all saints thereon before the throne?

That all this is written is true, and that it is all truth is as true; but that it is all understood by every one that is saved, I do not believe is true. I mean, so understood as that they could all reconcile the seeming contradictions that are in the Scripture. There are therefore three lessons that God has set us to the perfecting of our understanding in the mysteries of God. 1. Letters. 2. Words. 3. Meanings.

1. *Letters:* I call the ceremonial law so; for there all is set forth distinctly, everything by itself, as letters are to children. There you have a priest, a sacrifice, an altar, a holy place, a mercy-seat; and all distinct.

2. Now in the gospel these letters are put all into *a word*, and Christ is that word, that word of God's mind; and therefore the gospel makes Christ that priest, Christ that sacrifice, Christ that altar, Christ that holy place, Christ that throne of grace, and all; for Christ is all: all these meet in him, as several letters meet in one word.

3. Next to the word you have *the meaning*, and the meaning is more difficult to be learned than either the letters or the word: and, therefore, the perfect understanding of that is reserved till we arrive to a higher form, till we arrive to a perfect man: and "when that which is perfect is come, that" knowledge "which is in part shall be done away." (1 Cor. xiii. 10.) Meantime our business is to learn to bring the letters into a word; to bring the ceremonies to Christ; and to make them terminate in him: I mean, to find the priesthood in Christ, the sacrifice in Christ, the altar in Christ, the throne of grace in Christ, and also God in Christ, reconciling the world unto himself by him. And if we can learn this well, while here, we shall not at all be blamed; for this is the utmost lesson set us, to wit, to learn Christ, as we find him revealed in the gospel. "I determined," saith Paul, "not to know anything among you, save Jesus Christ, and him crucified." (1 Cor. ii. 2.) And Christians, after some time, I mean those that pray, and pry into the word well, do attain to some good measure of knowledge of him. It is life eternal to know him, as he is to be known here, as he is to be known by the holy Scriptures. (John xxii. 3.) Keep then close to the Scriptures, and let thy faith obey the authority of them, and thou wilt be sure to increase in faith; "for therein is the righteousness of God revealed from faith to faith: as it is written, the just shall live by faith." (Rom. i. 17.)

Believe then that Christ died, was buried, rose again, ascended, and ever liveth to make intercession for thee; and take heed of prying too far, for in mysteries men soon lose their way. It is good therefore that thou rest in this, to wit, that he doth so, though thou canst not tell how he doth it. A man at court gets by his intercession a pardon for a man in the country; and the party concerned, after he hath intelligence of it, knows that such an one hath obtained his pardon, and that by his interceding; but for all that he may be ignorant of his methods of intercession: and so are we, at least in part, of Christ.

The meaning then is, that I should believe that for Christ's sake God will save me, since he has justified me with his blood; "being justified by his blood, we shall be saved from wrath through him." (Rom. v. 9.) Through his intercession, or through his coming between the God whom I have offended, and me a poor sinner; through his coming between with the voice of his blood and merits, which speaketh on my behalf to God, because that blood was shed for me, and because those merits, in the benefit of them, are made over to me by an act of the grace of God, according to his eternal covenant made with Christ. This is what I know of his intercession; I mean, with reference to the act itself, to wit, how he makes intercession. And since ALL the fulness of the Godhead dwells in him bodily; and since he also, as to his humanity, is the throne of grace; yea, and since he also is the holiest of all, and the rest of God for ever, it has been some scruple to me, whether it be not too carnal to imagine as if Christ stood distinct in his humanity, distinct I say as to space, from the Father as sitting upon a throne, and as so presenting his merits, and making vocal prayers for the life and salvation of his people. The more true meaning in my apprehension is, that the presence and worth of the human nature, being with the divine, yea, taken into union with God for ever, for the service that was done for God, by it, in the world, in reconciling his elect unto him, is still, and ever will be, so deserving in his sight as to prevail, (I know not how to express it,) with the divine nature, in whom alone is a power to subdue all impossibilities to itself, to preserve those so reconciled to eternal life.

When I speak of the human nature, I mean the man Christ, not bereft of sense and reason, nor of the power of willing and effecting; but thus I mean, that the human nature so terminates in the will of the divine; and again, the will of the divine so terminates, as to saving of sinners, in the merit and will of the human, that what the Father would, the Son wills; and what the Son wills, the Father acquiesces in for ever. And this the Son wills, and his will is backed with infinite merit, in which also the Father rests, that those, all those whom the Father hath given him, be with him where he is, that they may behold his glory. (John xvii. 24.) And now I come to the will and affections of the high priest.

Second. This leads me to the second head, namely, to the *natural* qualifications of him. And,

First. This is one thing that I would urge, he is not of a nature foreign to that of man; the angels love us well, but they are not so capable of sympathizing with us in our distresses, because they are not partakers of our nature. Nature has a peculiar sympathy in it; now he is naturally one with us, sin only excepted, and that is our advantage too. He is man as we are, flesh and blood as we are; born of a woman, and in all points made like unto us, that excepted which the Holy Ghost excepteth. "Forasmuch then as the children are partakers of flesh and blood, he also himself likewise took part of the same. For verily he took not on him the nature of angels; but he took on him the seed of Abraham." (Heb. ii. 14, 16.) This doth qualify him much; for, as I said before, there is a sympathy in nature. A man will not be so affected with the hurt that comes to a beast, as he naturally will with the hurt that comes to a man; a beast will be more affected with those attempts that are made upon its own kind to hurt it, than it will be with those that are made upon man: wherefore? why, there is a sympathy in nature. Now that Christ, the high priest of the house of God, is naturally one with

us, you see the Scriptures plainly affirm: "God sent forth his Son, made of a woman," (Gal. iv. 4;) he was "made of the seed of David, according to the flesh," (Rom. i. 3;) from the fathers of whom, "as concerning the flesh, Christ came," &c. (Rom. ix. 5.) And this must needs tend to make him a well-qualified high priest. We will not now speak of the necessity of his taking upon him the human nature, to wit, that he might destroy him that had the power of death, that is the devil, and deliver his people; for that would be here too much beside our matter, and be a diversion to the reader. We are now upon his high priest's office, and of those natural qualifications that attend him, as to that; and I say, nature is a great qualification, because in nature there is sympathy; and where there is sympathy, there will be a provocation to help, a provocation to help with jealousy and indignation against those that afflict. A bear robbed of her whelps is not more provoked than is the Lord Jesus, when there is means used to make them miss of life eternal, for whom he hath died, and for whom he ever lives to make intercession. But,

Second. As there is natural sympathy in Christ to those for whom he is an high priest, so there is relative sympathy; he has not only taken to or upon him our nature, but he is become one brotherhood with us. Now you know brotherhood will carry a man further than nature: so then, when nature and relation meet, there is a double obligation. "For both he that sanctifieth," which is Christ, "and they who are sanctified," his saints, "are all of one," which is God; they are all of God, as children of a Father; "for which cause he is not ashamed to call them brethren, saying, I will declare thy name unto my brethren, in the midst of the church will I sing praise unto thee." (Heb. ii. 11, 12.) Now a relation is much, and a natural relation most of all. Why, here is a natural relation betwixt Christ the high priest, and those for whom "he ever liveth to make intercession;" a natural relation, I say, and that with respect to the humanity, which is the nature subject to affliction and distress: "Forasmuch then as the children are partakers of flesh and blood, he also himself likewise took part of the same." (Heb. ii. 14.) So then it is for a brother that he is engaged, for a brother that he doth make intercession.

When Gideon knew by the confession of Zebah and Zalmunna, that the men that they slew at Tabor were his brethren, his fury came into his face, and he sware they should therefore die. (Judges viii.) Relation is a great matter. And therefore it is said again, "In all things it behoved him to be made like unto his brethren, that he might be a merciful high priest." (Heb. ii. 17.) A brother is born for adversity; and a brother will go far.

This, therefore, is a second thing, or another qualification, with which Christ Jesus is furnished to be an high priest,—he is a brother, there is a brotherly relation betwixt him and us; therefore, by virtue of this relation, he maketh intercession for us more affectionately.

Third. There are other things in Christ Jesus that make him naturally of an excellent qualification with reference to his priesthood for us; and they are the temptations and infirmities wherewith he was exercised in the days of his humiliation. It is true, temptations and infirmities, strictly considered, are none of our nature, no more are they of his; but yet, if it be proper to say temptations and afflictions have a nature, his and ours were naturally the same, and that in all points too, for so says the scripture, " He was tempted in all points, like as we are, yet without sin." (Heb. iv. 15.) Are we tempted to distrust God? so was he: are we tempted to murder ourselves? so was he: are we tempted with the bewitching vanities of this world? so was he: are we tempted to commit idolatry, and to worship the devil? so was he. (Matt. iv. Luke iv.) So that herein we also were alike; yea, from his cradle to his cross he was a man of sorrows and acquainted with griefs, a man of affliction throughout the whole course of his life. (Isa. liii. 3.)

And observe it, he was made so, or subjected thereto, by the ordinance of God; nay, further, it behoved him to be made so, that is, to be made like unto us in all things, the better to capacitate him to the work of his priesthood, with the more bowels and compassion. We will read to you the text: " Wherefore in all things it behoved him to be made like unto his brethren, that he might be," qualified to be, " a merciful and faithful high priest in things pertaining to God, to make reconciliation for the sins of the people. For in that he himself hath suffered, being tempted, he is able to succour them that are tempted." (Heb. ii. 17, 18.)

See here how he is qualified, and to what end: he was tempted as we are, suffered by temptations as we do, in all points and things as we are, that he might be bowels, that he might be a merciful and faithful high priest, in things pertaining to God, to make up the difference that is made by sin between God and his people, to make reconciliation for the sins of the people. Yea, he by being tempted, and by suffering as he did, he is prepared and enabled so to do; " for in that he himself hath suffered, being tempted, he is able to succour them that are tempted."

Wherefore, I also call this qualification both natural and necessary: natural, because in kind the same with ours; that is, his temptations were the same with ours; the same in nature, the same in design, the same as to their own natural tendency; for their natural tendency was to have ruined both him and us, but God prevented. They also were necessary, though not of themselves, yet made so by him that can bring good out of evil, and light out of darkness; made so, I say, to us, for whose sakes they were suffered to assault and

afflict him, namely, that he might be able to be merciful, faithful, and succouring to us.

Fourth. Another qualification with which our high priest is furnished, for the better fitting of him to make intercession for us, is, that we are his members; to be a member is more than to be of the same nature, or the nearest of relations, that excepted. So, then, now he makes intercession for his own self, for his own body, and for the several members of his body. The high priest under the law did use to offer up sacrifice for himself; first " for himself," for his own sins, and then " for the errors of the people." I will not say that Christ had any sin that was personally, or by his act, his own, for that would be to blaspheme the name of that Holy One; but yet I will say, he made the sins of the people his own: yea, God the Father made them his. Those also for whom he ever liveth to make intercession are united to him, made members of his body, of his flesh, and of his bones; and so are any part of himself. (2 Cor. v. 21.)

But we are now about his natural qualifications, and this is one, that they for whom he ever liveth to make intercession are his members, the members of his body: " we are the members of his body, of his flesh, and of his bones," so saith the word. (Eph. v. 30.) Wherefore here is a near concern, for that his church is part of himself; it is his own concern, it is for our own flesh. " No man ever yet hated his own flesh; but nourisheth and cherisheth it." (Eph. v. 29.) Things are thus spoken, because of the infirmity of our flesh. So that had Christ no love to us as we are sinners, yet because we are part of himself, he cannot but care for us, nature puts him upon it; yea, and the more infirm and weak we are, the more he is touched with the feeling of our infirmities, the more he is afflicted for us: " For we have not an high priest which cannot be touched with the feeling of our infirmities." (Heb. iv. 15.) He at no time loseth this his fellow-feeling, because he always is our head, and we the members of his. I will add, the infirm member is most cared for, most pitied, most watched over to be kept from harms, and most consulted for.

I love to play the child with little children, and have learnt something by so doing. I have met with a child that has had a sore finger, yea, so sore as to be altogether at present useless; and not only so, but by reason of its infirmity, has been a let or hindrance to the use of all the fingers that have been upon that hand: then have I began to bemoan the child, and said, Alas! my poor boy, or girl, hast got a sore finger? Ah! quoth the child, with water in its eyes, and hath come to me to be bemoaned. Then I have begun to offer to touch the sore finger. Oh! saith the child, pray do not hurt me. I then have replied, Canst thou do nothing with this finger? No, saith the child; nor with this hand neither. Then have I said, Shall we cut off this finger, and buy my child a better, a brave golden finger? At this the child has started, stared in my face, gone back from me, and entertained a kind of indignation against me, and has no more cared to be intimate with me. Then have I begun to make some use of that good sermon which this little child had preached unto me; and thus have I gone on. If membership be so dear, if this child has such tenderness to the most infirm, the most useless of its members; if it counts me his friend no longer than while I have a mouth to bemoan, and carriages that show tenderness to this useless finger; what an interest doth membership give one in the body, and what compassions hath the soul for such a useless thing, because it is a member! And turning all this over to Jesus Christ, then instead of matter and corruption, there presently comes honey to me out of this child's sore finger. I take leave to tell you now how I use to play. And though I have told you this tale upon so grave a truth as is the membership of Christians with their head, yet bear with me; no child can be so tender of its sore finger as is the Son of God of his afflicted members; he cannot but be touched with the feeling of our infirmities.

Ah! who would not make many supplications, prayers, and intercessions, for a leg, for an eye, for a foot, for a hand, for a finger, rather than they will lose it? And can it be imagined that Christ alone shall be like the foolish ostrich, hardened against his young, yea, against his members? It cannot be.

Should he lose a member he would be disfigured, maimed, dismembered, imperfect, next to monstrous. For his body is called his fulness, yea, the fulness of him that fills all in all. This, therefore shows you that Christ as high priest has naturally a respect for those for whom he ever liveth to make intercession; yea, an unfathomable respect for them, because they are his members.

Fifth. But again, when nature, relation, and membership is urged to show the fit qualifications wherewith Christ is endued, I intend not to intimate, as if the bottom of all lay here; for then it might be urged that one imperfect has all these: for who knows not that sinful man has all these qualifications in him towards his nature, relations, and members? I have therefore, as I said, thus discoursed, only for demonstration's sake, and to suit myself with the infirmity of your flesh. I might come, also, in the next place to tell you that Jesus Christ our high priest is thus, with reference to other designs. We are his purchase, and he counts us so; his jewels, and he counts us so; his estate real, and he counts us so. And, you know, a man will do much, speak much, intercede much and long, for that which he thus is interested in. But we will come to speak more particularly of the exceeding excellency of his natural qualifications, and show you that he hath such as are peculiar to himself alone, and that we are concerned in them.

1. He is holy, and so a suitable high priest. There is a holiness that sets further from, and a holiness that brings one nearer to, and to be concerned the more with, the condition of those in affliction; and that holiness is that which is entailed unto office. When a man is put into an office, the more unholy he is, the worse he performs his office; and the more holy, the better he performs his office. For his holiness obliges him to be faithful unto men, wherein he is concerned by his office. Hence you read, that he is "a faithful high priest," because he is a holy one, and "such an high priest became us, who is holy," &c. (Heb. ii. 17; vii. 26;) "Good and upright is the Lord" Jehovah, Christ Jesus, "therefore he will teach sinners in the way," (Ps. xxv. 8;) "He that ruleth over men must be just, ruling in the fear of God." (2 Sam. xxiii. 3.) I mention these texts to show you, that holiness, when entailed to office, makes a man do that office the better. Now then, Christ is holy, and he is made, called, and made of God an high priest, after the order of Melchisedec, and is to manage that his office for thee with God; that is to say, to continue to make reconciliation for iniquity, for that iniquity that cleaveth unto thee, and that spuriously breaketh or issueth from thy flesh after thou art called and converted. For we are now upon the second part of the execution of the priesthood of Christ: that which he executeth, I say, and by executing takes away the iniquity of our holy things, and of our life, after our turning to God by him. Now he that is to do this is holy, and so one that will make conscience of performing that office for us, with which he is entrusted of God. Hence he is set in opposition to those high priests that had infirmities, that were not holy, upon this very account preferred above them. "For the law maketh men high priests which have infirmity; but the word of the oath, which was since the law, maketh the Son, who is consecrated," perfected, or holy "for evermore." (Heb. vii. 28.)

This, therefore, is a great thing, to wit, that we have an high priest that is holy, and so one that will not fail to perform to the utmost the trust committed to him on our behalf, to wit, "to offer both gifts and sacrifices for sins." This is one thing. (Heb. v. 1.)

2. There is added to this of his holiness another, and that is, harmless: "For such an high priest became us, who is holy, harmless." (Heb. vii. 26.) A harmful man, when he is in office, oh how much mischief may he do! Such an one is partial in doing his office; such an one will put the poor by his right; such an one will buy and sell a cause, a man, an interest; will do, or not do, as his harmfulness prompts him to it. "So is a wicked ruler over the poor people." (Prov. xxviii. 15.) But now our Jesus, our high priest, is holy, harmless; he will wrong no man, he will deprive no man, he will contemn no man, he will deny to no man that comes to God by him, the benefit and advantage of his blessed intercession; he respecteth not persons, nor taketh reward. A harmful man will stomach, and hate, and prejudice a man; will wait for an

opportunity to do him a mischief, will take the advantage, if he can, to deny him his right, and keep from him his due, when yet it is in the power of his hand to help him. Oh! but Christ is harmless, harmless as a dove, he thinks no ill, intends no ill, doth no ill; but graciously, innocently, harmlessly, makes intercession for thee; nor will he be prevailed with to prejudice thy person, or to forbear to take up thy name into his lips, be thy infirmities, and weaknesses, and provocations never so many, if thou indeed comest to God by him. He is holy, and harmless, and so the more fit to become our high priest, and to make intercession for us.

3. But again, this is not all; he also is undefiled: "For such an high priest became us, who is holy, harmless, undefiled." This term is put in to show that he neither is, nor can be found, neither now, nor at any time, faulty in his office. A man that is holy may yet be defiled; a man that is harmless may yet be defiled. We are bid to be holy and harmless; and in a gospel sense so every Christian is. Oh! but Christ is so in a legal sense, in the eye of the law perfectly so. This is a great matter, for it shows, that as nothing done by us can tempt him to be hurtful to us, so there is nothing in himself that can tempt him so to be. A man that is defiled has that within him that will put him upon using of his office unfaithfully, though he should have no provocation from those for whose good he is to execute his office; but he that is undefiled,—undefiled in a law-sense, as our Lord Jesus is,—is such an one that doth not only not do hurt, and not act falsely in his office, but one that cannot, one that knoweth not how to be unfaithful to his trust. He is holy, harmless, undefiled; this, therefore, is a great thing. He has not the original of hurtfulness in him, there is no such root there; there is a root of bitterness springing up in us, by which, not only ourselves, but ofttimes others are defiled. (Heb. xii. 15.) Oh! but our high priest is undefiled; he is not corrupt, nor corrupteth; he doth his office fairly, faithfully, holily, justly, according to, or answering, our necessities, and the trust reposed in him, and committed to him. But,

4. This is not all: as he is holy, harmless, and undefiled, so he is separate from sinners, both in his conception, in his composition, and the place ordained for him to execute this part of his high priest's office in. He was not conceived in the womb by carnal generation; he was not made up of polluted and defiled nature; he officiateth not with those materials that are corrupt, stained, or imperfect; but with those that are unspotted; even with the spotless sacrifice of his own unblemished offering. He, nor his offering, has any such tang as had the priests, and their sacrifices under the law, to wit, sin and imperfection; he is separate from them in this respect, further than is an angel from a beast. He has none of the qualities, actions, or inclinations of sinners; his ways are only his own; he never saw them, nor learnt them, but of the Father: there is none upright among men, wherefore he is separated from them to be a priest. Again,

5. As he is thus, so again, he is said to be "higher than the heavens." "For such an high priest became us, who is holy, harmless, undefiled;" separate from sinners, and made higher than the heavens. The text saith that neither saint, nor heavens, are clean in God's sight. "Behold, he put no trust in his servants," he chargeth his angels with folly; and again, "Behold, he putteth no trust in his saints; yea, the heavens are not clean in his sight." (Job iv. 18; xv. 15.) Wherefore, by this expression, he shows us, that our high priest is more noble than either heaven or angel; yea, more clean and perfect than any. It shows us also that all the heavenly host are at his command, to do as his intercession shall prevail with the Father for us. All angels worship him, and at his word they become, they all become, ministering spirits for them who shall be heirs of salvation.

Besides, by this word he shows, that it is impossible that our high priest should degenerate or decay; for that he is made "higher than the heavens." The spirits, sometimes, in the heavens have decayed, (2 Pet. ii. 4;) the heavens themselves decay and wax old, (Heb. i. 10—12;) and that is the furthest that by the word we are admitted to go: but as for him that is above the heavens, that is made higher than the heavens, that is ascended up far above all heavens, he is the same, and "his years fail not," (Heb. i. 12;) "the same yesterday, to-day, and for ever." (Heb. xiii. 8.)

This, therefore, is added, to show that Christ is neither as the angels, nor heavens, subject to decay, or degenerate, or to flag and grow cold in the execution of his office; but that he will be found, even at the last, when he is come to the end of this work, and is about to come out of the holy place, as affectionate, as full of love, as willing and desirous after our salvation, as he was the first moment that he was made high priest, and took upon him to execute that his blessed office for us.

Wherefore our high priest is no such one as you read of in the law. (Lev. xxi. 18.) He is no dwarf, hath no blemish, nor any imperfection; therefore is not subject to flag or fail in the due execution of his office; but is able to save to the uttermost them that come unto God by him, "seeing he ever liveth to make intercession for them."

And it is well worth our consideration, that it is said he is made thus; that is, appointed, instituted, called, and qualified thus of God; this shows the Father's heart as well as the Son's to usward, to wit, that this priesthood was of him, and the glorious effects thereof by him. "Let us therefore come boldly unto the throne of grace, that we may obtain mercy, and find grace to help in time of need."

SECOND. I come now to the second motive, to

wit, that we may find grace and mercy to help in time of need; or we shall find grace and mercy to help, if we come, as we should, to the throne of grace.

In this motive we have these three things.

First. That saints are like to meet with needy times while they are in this world.

Second. That nothing can carry us through our needy times but more, or a continual supply, of mercy and grace.

Third. That mercy and grace is to be had at the throne of grace, and we must fetch it from thence by prayer, if we would, as we should, go through these needy times.

First. For the first of these, *that saints are like to meet with needy times;* or with such times as will show them that they need a continual assistance of the grace of God, that they may go rightly through this world. This is, therefore, a motive that weareth a spur in the heel of it, a spur to prick us forward to supplicate at the throne of grace. This needy time is in other places called the perilous time, the evil day, the hour and power of darkness, the day of temptation, the cloudy and dark day. (Ezek. xxxiv. 12. Luke xxii. 53. Eph. vi. 13. 2 Tim. iii. 1.)

And indeed, in the general, all the days of our pilgrimage here are evil; yea, every day has a sufficiency of evil in it to destroy the best saint that breatheth, were it not for the grace of God. But there are also, as I have hinted, particular, specious times, times more eminently dangerous and hazardous unto saints. As,

1. There are their young days, the days of their youth and childhood in grace. This day is usually attended with much evil towards him, or them, that are asking the way to Zion, with their faces thitherward. Now the devil has lost a sinner; there is a captive has broke prison, and one run away from his master; now hell seems to be awakened from sleep, the devils are come out, they roar, and roaring they seek to recover their runaway. Now tempt him, threaten him, flatter him, stigmatize him, throw dust in his eyes, poison him with errors, spoil him while he is upon the potter's wheel; anything to keep him from coming to Jesus Christ. And is not this a needy time? doth not such an one want abundance of grace? is it not of absolute necessity that thou, if thou art the man thus beset, shouldest ply it at the throne of grace for mercy and grace to help thee in such a time of need as this? To want a spirit of prayer now, is as much as thy life is worth. Oh, therefore, you that know what I say, you that are broke loose from hell, that are fled for refuge to lay hold on the hope set before you, and that do hear the lion roar after you, and that are kept awake with the continual voice of his chinking chain, cry as you fly; yea, the promise is, that they that come to God with weeping, with supplication, he will lead them.

Well, this is one needy time, now thy hedge is low, now thy branch is tender, now thou art but in the bud. Pray that thou beest not marred in the potter's hand.

2. The time of prosperity is also a time of need, I mean, of thy spiritual prosperity. For as Satan can tell how to suit temptations for thee in the day of thy want, so he has those that can entangle thee in the day of thy fulness. He has his spiritual wickednesses in the high and heavenly places. (Eph. vi. 12.) He can tell how to lay a snare for thee in the land of Canaan, as well as in the wilderness; in thy time of receiving good things, as well as in thy hungry and empty hours. Nay, such times seem to be the most dangerous, not in themselves, but through the deceits of our heart. Hence Moses gives this caution to the children of Israel, that when God had given them the promised land, and vineyards, and wells, and olive-trees, and when they had eaten and were full, "Then," says he, " beware lest thou forget the Lord, which brought thee forth out of the land of Egypt, from the house of bondage." (Deut. vi. 10—13.) And, again, he doubleth this caution, saying, "When thou hast eaten and art full, then thou shalt bless the Lord thy God for the good land which he has given thee. Beware that thou forget not the Lord thy God, in not keeping his commandments, and his judgments, and his statutes, which I command thee this day; lest when thou hast eaten and art full," and thou in all good things art increased, "then thine heart be lifted up, and thou forget the Lord thy God, which brought thee forth out of the land of Egypt, from the house of bondage." (Deut. viii. 10—14.) All this may be applied spiritually: for there are, as I said, snares laid for us in our best things; and he that has great enjoyments, and forgets to pray for grace to keep him humble then, shall quickly be where Peter was, after his knowledge of the Lord Jesus by the revelation of the Father.

3. Another needy time, is a time when men are low and empty, as to worldly good; this time is full of temptations and snares. At this time men will, if they look not well to their doings and goings, be tempted to strain courtesies both with conscience and with God's word, and adventure to do things that are dangerous, and that have a tendency to make all their religion and profession vain. This holy Agur was aware of, so he prayed, Let me not be rich and full, lest I deny thee; let me not be poor, lest I steal, and take the name of my God in vain. (Prov. xxx. 7—9.) There are many inconveniences that attend him that is fallen into decay in this world. It is an evil day with him; and the devil will be as busy with him, as the flies are with a lean and scabbed sheep. It shall go hard but such a man shall be full of maggots: full of silly, foolish, idle inventions, to get up, and to abound with fulness again. It is not a time now, will Satan say, to retain a tender conscience, to regard thy word or promise, to pay for what thou buyest, or to stick at pilfering, and filch from thy neighbour. This Agur was afraid of;

therefore he prayed that God would keep him from that which would be to him a temptation to do it. How many in our day have, on these very accounts, brought religion to a very ill savour, and themselves into the snare of the devil! and all because they have not addicted themselves to pray to God for grace to help in this time of need, but rather have left off the thing that is good, and given up themselves to the temptations of the devil, and the subtle and ensnaring motions of the flesh.

4. Another needy time is the day of persecution; this is called, as was hinted before, "the hour of darkness," "the cloudy and dark day." This day, therefore, is full of snares and of evils of every kind. Here is the fear of man, the terrors of a prison, of loss of goods and life. Now all things look black, now the fiery trial is come. He that cannot now pray, he that now applieth not himself to God on the throne of grace, by the priesthood of Jesus Christ, is like to take a fall before all men upon the stage; a foul fall, a fall that will not only break his own bones, but also the hearts of those that fear God and behold it. "Come therefore boldly unto the throne of grace, that ye may obtain mercy, and find grace to help in time of need."

5. Another time of need is that time wherein thou changest thy condition, and enterest into a new relation. For here also the snares and traps lie waiting for thee. There is a hopeful child goes to service, or to be an apprentice; there is a young man and a young maid entered into a married condition; and though they pray before, yet they leave off to pray then. Why these people are oftentimes ruined and undone, the reason is, this change is attended with new snares, with new cares, and with new temptations; of the which, because through unwatchfulness they are not aware, they are taken, drawn to perdition and destruction by them. Many in my short day have gone, I doubt, down to the pit this way, that have sometimes been to appearance the very foremost and hopefulest in the place where they have lived. Oh! how soon has their fire gone out, has their lamps forborn to burn! How quickly have they lost their love to their ministers, by whom they were illuminated, and to the warmest Christians, through communion with whom they used to be kept awake and savoury! How quickly have they found them out new friends, new companions, new ways and methods of life, and new delights to feed their foolish minds withal! Wherefore, oh thou that art in this fifth head concerned, "Come boldly unto the throne of grace, to obtain mercy, and find grace to help in time of need."

6. Another time of need is when the generality of professors are decayed; when the custom of fancies and fooleries have taken away all gravity and modesty from among the children of men. Now pray, or thou diest; yea, pray against those decays, those vain customs, those foolish fancies, those light and vain carriages that have overtaken

others; else they will assuredly knock at thy door, and obtain favour at thy hand; the which if they do, they will quickly bring thee down into the dirt with others, and put thee in peril of damnation as well as they.

7. Another time of need is, the time of guilt contracted, and of the hiding of God's face. This is a dangerous time. If thou now shalt forbear to pray, thou art undone; for the natural tendency of guilt is to drive a man from God. So it served our first father; and ofttimes when God hides his face, men run into desperation, and so throw up all duties, and say as he of old, "What should I wait for the Lord any longer?" (2 Kings vi. 33.) Now thy great help against this is prayer, continuing in prayer. Prayer wrestleth with the devil, and will overthrow him; prayer wrestleth with God, and will overcome him; prayer wrestleth with all temptations, and makes them fly. Great things have been done by prayer, even by the prayer of those that have contracted guilt, and that have by their sins lost the smiles, and sense of the favour of God. Wherefore, when this needy, this evil time has overtaken thee, pray. "Come boldly unto the throne of grace, to obtain mercy, and find grace to help in time of need."

8. The day of reproach and slander is another time of need, or a day in which thou wilt want supplies of grace. Sometimes we meet with such days wherein we are loaden with reproaches, slanders, scandals, and lies. Christ found the day of reproach a burdensome day unto him; and there is many a professor driven quite away from all conscience towards God, and open profession of his name, by such things as these. Reproach is, when cast at a man, as if he was stoning to death with stones. Now ply it hard at the throne of grace, for mercy and grace to bear thee up, or thou wilt either miscarry, or sink underground by the weight of reproach that may fall upon thee.

9. Another time of need is that wherein a man's friends desert and forsake him, because of his gospel principles, or of those temptations that attend his profession. This is a time that often happeneth to those that are good. Thus it was with Christ, with Paul, with Job, with Heman, and so has been with many other of God's servants in the day of their temptations in this world; and a sore time it is. Job complained under it, so did Heman, Paul, and Christ. (John vi. 66. 2 Tim. i. 15. Job xix. 13—19.) Now a man is as forlorn as a pelican in the wilderness, as an owl in the desert, or as a sparrow upon the housetop. If a man cannot now go to the throne of grace by prayer, through Christ, and so fetch grace for his support from thence, what can he do? He cannot live of himself. Wherefore this is a sore evil.

10. Another time of need is the day of death, when I am to pack up all to be gone from hence, the way of all the earth. Now the greatest trial is come, excepting that of the day of judgment. Now a man is to be stript of all, but that which

cannot be shaken. Now a man grows near the borders of eternity. Now he begins to see into the skirts of the next world. Now death is death, and the grave the grave indeed. Now he begins to see what it is for body and soul to part, and what to go and appear before God. Now the dark entry, and the thoughts of what is in the way from a death-bed to the gate of the holy heaven, comes nearer the heart than when health and prosperity do compass a man about. Wherefore this is like to be a trying time, a time of need indeed. A prudent man will make it one of the great concerns of his whole life to get, and lay up, a stock of grace for this day, though the fool will rage and be confident; for he knows all will be little enough to keep him warm in his soul, while cold death strokes his hand over his face, and over his heart, and is turning his blood into jelly; while strong death is loosing his silver cord, and breaking his golden bowl. (Eccles. xii. 6.) Wherefore, I say, this motive weareth a spur on his heel, a spur to prick us on to the throne of grace for mercy, and grace to help us in time of need.

Second. I come now to the next thing, which is to show that nothing can carry us through our needy times, but *more, or a continual supply, of mercy and grace.* This the scripture fully implies, because it directeth us to the throne of grace for mercy and grace for that very end. And had there been any thing else that could have done it, the apostle would have made mention of it, and would also have directed the saints unto it. But forasmuch as he here makes mention of the needy time, and directs them to the throne of grace for mercy and grace to help, it followeth that mercy and grace, and that only, can help us in the evil time.

Now mercy and grace are to be distinctly considered.

1. Mercy, for that by it we have through Christ the continuation and multiplication of forgivenesses, without which there is no salvation.

2. Grace, for that by it we are upheld, supported, and enabled to go through our needy times, as Christians, without which there is no salvation neither. The first all will grant, the second is clear. "If any man draw back, my soul shall have no pleasure in him. But we are not of them who draw back unto perdition; but of them that believe to the saving of the soul." (Heb. x. 38, 39.)

1. Mercy is that by which we are pardoned even all the falls, faults, failings, and weaknesses that attend us, and that we are incident to, in this our day of temptation; and for THIS mercy we should pray, and say, "Our Father, forgive us our trespasses." (Matt. vi. 9—12.) For though mercy is free in the exercise of it to usward, yet God will have us ask, that we may have; as he also saith in the scripture, "Let us come boldly unto the throne of grace, that we may obtain mercy." Here then we have one help, and that is, the mercy of God is to be extended to us from his

throne through Jesus Christ, for our pardon and forgiveness in all those weaknesses that we are attended with in the needy or evil times; and we should come to God for this very thing. This is that which David means, when he says, " Surely goodness and mercy shall follow me all the days of my life: and I will dwell in the house of the Lord for ever." (Ps. xxiii. 6.) And again, " When I said, My foot slippeth; thy mercy, O Lord, held me up." (Ps. xciv. 18.) Set me clear and free from guilt, and from the imputation of sin unto death, by Christ.

Nor can anything help where this is wanting: for our parts, our knowledge, our attainments, nor our graces, cannot so carry us through this world, but that we shall be guilty of that that will sink us down to hell, without God's pardoning mercy. It is not the grace that we have received can do it, nor the grace that is to be received that can do it: nothing can do it but the pardoning mercy of God; for because all our graces are here imperfect, they cannot produce a spotless obedience. But where there is not a spotless obedience, there must of necessity follow a continuation of pardon and forgiveness by mercy, or I know what will become of the soul.

Here, therefore, the apostle lays an obligation upon thee to the throne of grace, to wit, that thou mayest obtain mercy, a continuation of mercy; mercy as long as thou art like to live this vain life on the earth; mercy that will reach through all thy days: for there is not a day, nor a duty, not a day that thou livest, nor a duty that thou doest, but will need that mercy should come after to take away thy iniquity. Nay, thou canst not receive mercy so clearly as not to stand in need of another act of mercy, to pardon weakness in thy no better receiving the last. We receive not our mercies so humbly, so readily, so gladly, and with that thankfulness as we should; and, therefore, for the want of these, have the need of another and another act of God's sin-pardoning mercy; and need shall have thereof, as long as evil time shall last with us.

But is not this great grace, that we should thus be called upon to come to God for mercy? Yea, is not God unspeakably good, in providing such a throne of grace, such a sacrifice, such an high priest, and so much mercy for us, and then to invite us to come with boldness to him for it? Nay, doth not his kindness yet further appear, by giving of us items and intimations of needy times, and evil days, on purpose to provoke us to come to him for mercy?

This then shows us, as also we have hinted before, that the throne of grace, and Christ Jesus our high priest, are both provided upon the account of our imperfections, namely, that we who are called might not be, by remaining weaknesses, hindered of, but obtain, eternal inheritance. Weaknesses, such weaknesses, remain in the justified: and such slips and failings are found in and upon them, that call for a course of mercy and forgiveness to attend them.

Farther, this also intimates that God's people should not be dejected at the apprehensions of their imperfections; I say, not so dejected, as therefore to cast off faith, and hope, and prayer; for a throne of grace is provided for them, to the which they may, they must, they ought, continually to resort for mercy, sin-pardoning mercy.

2. As we are here to obtain mercy, so we are here to find grace. They that obtain mercy, shall find grace, therefore they are put together. That they may obtain mercy, and find grace, (only they must obtain mercy first; for as forgiveness at first goes before sanctification, in the general, so forgiveness afterwards goes before particular acts of grace for further sanctification,) God giveth not the spirit of grace to those that he has not first forgiven by mercy, for the sake of Christ. Also, so long as he, as a Father, forbears to forgive us, his adopted, so long we go without those further additions of grace that are suggested in the scripture. But when we have obtained mercy to forgive, then we also find grace to our renewing. Therefore he saith, First obtain mercy, and then find grace.

Grace here I take to be that grace which God has appointed for us, to dwell in us; and that by and through the continual supply of which we are to be enabled to do and suffer, and to manage ourselves in doing and suffering, according to the will of God. "Let us have grace, whereby we may serve God acceptably with reverence and godly fear." (Heb. xii. 28.) So again, "He giveth more grace; wherefore, he saith, God resisteth the proud, but giveth grace unto the humble." (James iv. 6.) The grace, therefore, that is meant is, grace given or to be given; grace received or to be received; grace, a root, a principle of grace, with its continual supplies for the perfecting of that salvation that God has designed for us.

This was that which comforted Paul, when the messenger of Satan was sent to buffet him: it was said unto him by Christ, "My grace is sufficient for thee," (2 Cor. xii. 9:) as who should say, Paul, be not utterly cast down, I have wherewithal to make thee stand, and overcome; and that is my grace, by which thou shalt be supported, strengthened, comforted, and made to live a triumphant life, notwithstanding all that oppress thee. But this came to him upon his praying; for this I prayed to God thrice, said he. So again, "God is able to make all grace abound towards you; that ye, always having all sufficiency in all things, may abound to every good work." (2 Cor. ix. 8.) Thus you see that by grace in these places is meant that spirit, and those principles of grace, by the increase and continual supply of which we are inwardly strengthened, and made to abound to every good work.

This then is the conclusion: That as there is mercy to be obtained by us, at the throne of grace, for the pardon of all our weaknesses, so there is also grace there to be found, that will yet strengthen us more, to all good walking and living before him. He giveth more grace, and they receive one time or another abundance of grace that shall reign in life by one Jesus Christ.

This then teaches us several things, some of which I will mention. As,

1. That nature, as nature, is not capable of serving of God: no, nor nature where grace dwells, as considered abstract from that grace that dwells in it. Nothing can be done aright without grace, I mean, no part or piece of gospel duty. "Let us have grace, whereby we may serve God acceptably." Nature managed by grace, seasoned with grace, and held up with grace, can serve God acceptably. Let us have grace, seek for and find grace to do so; for we cannot do so but by grace: "By the grace of God I am what I am: and his grace which was bestowed on me, was not in vain; but I laboured more abundantly than they all; yet not I, but the grace of God which was with me." (1 Cor. xv. 10.) What can be more plain than this beautiful text? For the apostle doth here quite shut out nature, sanctified nature, (for he indeed was a sanctified man,) and concludes that even he, as of himself, did nothing of all the great works that he did; but they were done, he did them by the grace of God that was in him. Wherefore nature, sanctified nature, as nature, can of itself do nothing to the pleasing of God the Father.

Is not this the experience of all the godly? Can they do that at all times, which they can do at some times? Can they pray, believe, love, fear, repent, and bow before God always alike? No. Why so? they are the same men, the same human nature, the same saints. Ay, but the same grace, in the same degree, operation, and life of grace, doth not so now work on that man, that nature, that saint; therefore, notwithstanding he is what he is, he cannot do at all times alike.

Thus, therefore, it is manifest that nature, simply as such, is a great way off doing that which is acceptable with God. Refined, purified, sanctified nature, cannot do but by the immediate supplies, lifts, and helps of that spirit and principle of grace by the which it is so sanctified.

2. As nature, even where grace is, cannot without the assistance of that grace do anything acceptably before God, so grace received, if it be not also supplied with more grace, cannot cause that we continue to do acceptable service to God. This also is clear by the text. For he speaketh there to them that had received grace; yea, puts himself into the number, saying, "Let us come boldly unto the throne of grace, that we may find grace to help in time of need." If grace received would do, what need of more? What need we pray for more? What need we go to the throne of grace for more? This very exhortation saith it will not: present supplies of grace are proportioned to our present need, and to help us to do a present work or duty. But is our present need all the need that we are

like to have, and the present work all the work that we have to do in the world? Even so the grace that we have received at present, though it can help us to do a present work, it cannot, without a further supply, help us to do what is to be done hereafter. Wherefore, the apostle saith, that his continuing to do was through his obtaining help, continual help of God. "Having, therefore," saith he, " obtained help of God, I continue to this day, witnessing both to small and great," &c. (Acts xxvi. 22.) There must be a daily imploring of God for daily supplies from him, if we will do our daily business as we should.

A present dispensation of grace is like a good meal, a seasonable shower, or a penny in one's pocket, all which will serve for the present necessity. But will that good meal that I eat last week enable me, without supply, to do a good day's work in this? or will that seasonable shower that fell last year be, without supplies, a seasonable help to the grain and grass that is growing now? or will that penny that supplied my want the other day, I say, will the same penny also, without a supply, supply my wants to-day? The same may, I say, be said of grace received; it is like the oil in the lamp, it must be fed, it must be added to. And there shall be a supply, " wherefore he giveth more grace." Grace is the sap, which from the root maintaineth the branches: stop the sap, and the branch will wither. Not that the sap shall be stopped where there is union, not stopped for altogether; for as from the root the branch is supplied, so from Christ is every member furnished with a continual supply of grace, if it doth as it should. " Of his fulness have all we received, and grace for grace." (John i. 16.)

The day of grace is the day of expense; this is our spending time. Hence we are called pilgrims and strangers in the earth, that is, travellers from place to place, from state to state, from trial to trial. (Heb. xi. 13.) Now, as the traveller at a fresh inn is made to spend fresh money, so Christians, at a fresh temptation, at a new temptation, are made to spend a fresh and a new supply of grace. Great men, when and while their sons are travellers, appoint that their bags of money be lodged ready, or conveniently paid in at such and such a place, for the suitable relief of them; and so they meet with supplies. Why, so are the sons of the Great One, and he has allotted that we should travel beyond sea, or at a great distance from our Father's house; wherefore he has appointed that grace shall be provided for us, to supply at such a time, such a state or temptation, as need requires. But withal, as my lord expecteth his son should acquaint him with the present emptiness of his purse, and with the difficulty he hath now to grapple with, so God our Father expects that we should plead by Christ our need at the throne of grace, in order to a supply of grace. " Let us therefore come boldly unto the throne of grace, that we may obtain mercy, and find grace to help in time of need."

Now, then, this shows the reason why many Christians, that are indeed possessed with the grace of God, do yet walk so oddly, act so poorly, and live such orderly lives in the world. They are like to those gentlemen's sons that are of the more extravagant sort, that walk in their lousy hue, when they might be maintained better. Such young men care not, perhaps scorn, to acquaint their fathers with their wants; and therefore walk in their threadbare jackets, with hose and shoes out at heels, a right emblem of the uncircumspect child of God.

This also shows the reason of all those dreadful falls and miscarriages that many of the saints sustain; they make it not their business to watch to see what is coming, and to pray for a supply of grace to uphold them. They, with David, are too careless, or with Peter too confident, or with the disciples too sleepy; and so the temptation comes upon them, and their want like an armed man.

This also shows the reason why some that, to one's thinking, would fall every day,—for that their want of parts, their small experience, their little knowledge of God's matters, do seem to bespeak it,—yet stand, walk better, and keep their garments more white than those that have, when compared with them, twice as much as they. They are praying saints, they are often at the throne of grace, they are sensible of their weakness, keep a sight of their danger before their faces, and will not be contented without more grace.

Third. And this leads me, in the third place, to show you that were we wise, and did we ply it at the throne of grace, for grace as we should, oh what spotless lives might we live! We should then have always help in time of need; for so the text insinuates, " That we may obtain mercy, and find grace to help in time of need." This is that which Peter means, when he says, " And besides this," that is, besides your faith in Christ, and besides your happy state of justification, " giving all diligence, add to your faith virtue; and to virtue, knowledge; and to knowledge, temperance; and to temperance, patience; and to patience, godliness; and to godliness brotherly kindness, and to brotherly kindness, charity. For if these things be in you and abound," and be continually supplied with a supply from the throne of grace, " they make you that ye shall neither be barren nor unfruitful in the knowledge of our Lord Jesus Christ. But he that lacketh these things is blind, and cannot see afar off, and hath forgotten that he was purged from his old sins. Wherefore the rather, brethren, give diligence to make your calling and election sure; for if you do these things, ye shall never fall: for so an entrance shall be ministered unto you abundantly into the everlasting kingdom of our Lord and Saviour Jesus Christ." (2 Pet. i.)

The greatest part of professors now-a-days take up their time in contracting of guilt, and asking for pardon, and yet are not much the better. Whereas, if they had but the grace to add to their faith, virtue, &c., they might have more peace, live better lives, and not have their heads so often in a bag as they have. "To him that ordereth his conversation aright, will I show the salvation of God." (Ps. l. 23.) To him that disposeth his way aright; now this cannot be done without a constant supplicating at the throne of grace for more grace. This then is the reason why every new temptation that comes upon thee so foils, so overcomes thee, that thou wilt need a new conversion to be recovered from under the power and guilt that cleaves to thee by its overshadowing of thee. A new temptation, a sudden temptation, an unexpected temptation, usually foils those that are not upon their watch, and that have not been before with God, to be inlaid with grace proportionable to what may come upon them.

"That ye may find grace to help in time of need." There is grace to be found at the throne of grace, that will help us under the greatest straits. "Seek, and ye shall find;" it is there, and it is to be found there; it is to be found there of the seeking soul, of the soul that seeketh him. Wherefore I will conclude as I did begin: "Let us therefore come boldly unto the throne of grace, that we may obtain mercy, and find grace to help in time of need."

Conclusion.

We will now speak something by way of conclusion, and so wind up the whole.

First. You must remember that we have been hitherto speaking of the throne of grace, and showing what it is. That we have also been speaking of Christ's sacrifice, and how he manages his high priest's office before the throne of grace. We have also here, as you see, been speaking of the mercy and grace that is to be obtained and found at this throne of grace; and of what advantage it is to us in this our pilgrimage. Now, from all this, it follows, that sin is a fearful thing; for all this ado is, that men might be saved from sin. What a devil then is sin; it is the worst of devils; it is worse than all devils: those that are devils sin hath made them so; nor could anything else have made them devils but sin. Now, I pray, what is it to be a devil, but to be under, for ever, the power and dominion of sin, an implacable spirit against God? Such an one, from which implacableness all the power in heaven and earth cannot release them, because God of his justice has bound them over to judgment. These spirits are by sin carried quite away from themselves, as well as from God that made them; they cannot design their own good; they cannot leave that which yet they know will be everlastingly mischievous to themselves. Sin has bound them to itself so fast, that there can be no deliverance for them, but by the Son of God, who also has refused them, and left them to themselves, and to the judgment which they have deserved. Sin also has got a victory over man, has made him an enemy to God, and to his own salva-

tion; has caught him, and captivated him, carried away his mind, and will, and heart from God; and made him choose to be vain, and to run the hazard of eternal damnation with rejoicing and delight. But God left not man where he left those wicked spirits, to wit, under the everlasting chains of darkness, reserved unto judgment; but devised means for their ransom and reconciliation to himself: which is the thing that has been discoursed of in the foregoing part of this book. But, I say, what a thing is sin—what a devil, and master of devils is it, that it should, where it takes hold, so hang, that nothing can unclinch its hold, but the mercy of God, and the heart-blood of his dear Son! Oh the fretting, eating, infecting, defiling, and poisonous nature of sin, that it should so eat into our flesh and spirit, body and soul, and so stain us with its vile and stinking nature! yea, it has almost turned man into the nature of itself; insomuch as that sometimes, when nature is mentioned, sin is meant, and when sin is mentioned, nature is meant.

Wherefore sin is a fearful thing; a thing to be lamented, a thing to be abhorred, a thing to be fled from with more astonishment and trembling than one would fly from any devil; because it is the worst of things, and that without which nothing can be bad; and because where it takes hold, it so fasteneth, that nothing, as I have said, can release whom it has made a captive, but the mercy of God and the heart-blood of his dear Son. Oh what a thing is sin!

Second. As by what hath been said, sin appears to be exceeding sinful, so from hence it also follows that the soul is a precious thing. For you must know all this is for the redemption of the soul. The redemption of the soul is precious. (Ps. xlix. 8.) I say, it is for the redemption of the soul; it was for this that Christ was made a priest, a sacrifice, an altar, a throne of grace; yea sin, a curse, and what not, that was necessary for our deliverance from sin, and death, and everlasting damnation.

He that would know what a soul is, let him read in letters of blood the price and purchase of the soul. It was not for a light, a little, and inconsiderable thing, that Christ Jesus underwent what he suffered when he was in the world, and gave himself a ransom for souls. No, no! The soul is a great, a vast great thing, notwithstanding it is so little set by of some. Some prefer anything that they fancy above the soul; a slut, a lie, a pot, an act of fraudulency, the swing of a prevailing passion, anything shall be preferred when the occasion offereth itself. If Christ had set as little by souls as some men do, he had never left his Father's bosom and the glory that he had with him; he had never so humbled himself, so gave himself to punishment, affliction, and sorrow; and made himself so the object of scorn, and contempt, and reproach, as he did; and all that the souls of sinners might live a life in glory with him.

But methinks this is the mystery of all as to

this, that the soul should take that pains, contrive such ways, and take such advantages against itself! for it is the soul that sins, that the soul might die. Oh sin, what art thou? What hast thou done? and what still wilt thou further do? if mercy, and blood, and grace doth not prevent thee! Oh silly soul! what a fool has sin made of thee! what an ass art thou become to sin! That ever an immortal soul, at first made in the image of God, for God, and for his delight, should so degenerate from its first station, and so abase itself that it might serve sin, as to become the devil's ape, and to play like Jack Pudding for him upon any stage or theatre in the world!

But I recall myself; for if sin can make one, who was sometimes a glorious angel in heaven, now so to abuse himself as to become, to appearance, as a filthy frog, a toad, a rat, a cat, a fly, a mouse, a dog, or bitch's whelp, to serve its ends upon a poor mortal, that it might gull them of everlasting life, no marvel if the soul is so beguiled as to sell itself from God and all good, for so poor a nothing as a momentary pleasure is. But,

Third. If sin and the soul are such great things, then behold the love and care of God; the love to souls, the care he hath taken to deliver them from sin. Sin, as I have said, is such a thing as from which no man can deliver himself; the soul is such a thing, so rich and valuable in the nature of it, that scarce one in twenty thousand counts of it as they should. But God, the lover of mankind, and the greatest enemy to sin, has provided means effectually to overthrow the one, and to save and secure the other. Behold, therefore, the love of God, the care of God for us; for when we neither loved nor cared for ourselves, God both loved us and cared for us. God commended his love towards us in sending his Son to be the propitiation for our sins.

Let it be then concluded, that "God is love," and that the love that God hath to us is such as we never had for ourselves. We have been often tried about our own love to ourselves, and it has been proved over and over, that sometimes, even we that are Christians, could and would, had it been possible, have pawned ourselves, our souls, and our interest in Christ, for a foul and beastly lust. But God, who is rich in mercy, for his great love wherewith he loved us, would not suffer it so to be. Now, if we are so fickle and uncertain in our love to ourselves, as to value our salvation at so low and so base a rate, can it be imagined that ever we should, had it been left to our choice, have given the best of what we have for the salvation of our souls? Yet God gave his Son to be the Saviour of the world. I say again, if our love is so slender to our own souls, can any think that it should be more full to the souls of others? And yet God had such love to us, as to give his only-begotten Son for our sins. Yet again, how should it be that we, who are usually so affected with the conceit of our own happiness, since we care no more for our own souls, do our best to secure the souls of others? And yet God, who is infinitely above all creatures, has so condescended, as to concern himself, and to give the best of his flock, even his only beloved Son, for very dust and ashes. Wherefore, "Herein is love, not that we loved God," or our neighbour, "but that God loved us, and sent his Son to be the propitiation for our sins." (1 John iv. 10.)

Fourth. Is sin so vile a thing; is the soul so precious a thing; and is God's love and care of the salvation of the souls of sinners infinitely greater than is their own care for their own souls? Then this should teach those concerned to blush, to blush, I say, and to cover their faces with shame. There is nothing, as I know of, that more becomes a sinner, than blushing and shame doth. For he is the harbourer, the nurse, and the nourisher of that vile thing called sin; that so great an enemy of God, and that so great an enemy to the soul. It becomes him also, if he considers what a creature God has made him, and how little he hath set by his own creation, and by the matter of which God has made his soul. Let him also consider unto what base things he has stooped, and prostrated himself, while things infinitely better have stood by and offered themselves unto him freely; yea, how he has cast that God that made him, and his Son that came to redeem him, quite behind his back, and before their faces embraced, loved, and devoted himself unto him that seeks nothing more than the damnation of his soul.

Ah, Lord! when will foolish man be wise, and come to God with his hands upon his head, and with his face covered with shame, to ask him forgiveness for that wickedness which he has committed? which is wickedness committed not only against holiness and justice, against which also men by nature have an antipathy, but against mercy and love, without which man cannot tell what to do.

Blush, sinner, blush! Ah, that thou hadst grace to blush! But this is God's complaint: "Were they ashamed when they had committed abomination? Nay, they were not at all ashamed; neither could they blush." (Jer. viii. 12.) It is a sad thing that men should be thus void of consideration, and yet they are so. They are at a continual jest with God and his word, with the devil and sin, with hell and judgment. But they will be in earnest one day; but that one day will be too late!

Fifth. Is it so that God, though sin is so fearful a thing, has prepared an effectual remedy against it, and purposed to save us from the evil and damning effects thereof?

1. Then this should beget thankfulness in the hearts of the godly, for they are made partakers of this grace; I say, it should beget thankfulness in thy heart. "Thanks be unto God for his unspeakable gift," said the apostle, when he seriously thought of that which was much inferior to what we have been a discoursing of. (2 Cor. ix. 15.)

That was about man's willingness to do good; this is about God's. That was about men's willingness to give money to poor saints; this about God's willingness to give Christ Jesus his Son to the world. It was the thoughts of this redemption and salvation that made David say, " Bless the Lord, O my soul; and all that is within me, bless his holy name." (Ps. ciii. 1.) Oh! they that are partakers of redeeming grace, and that have a throne of grace, a covenant of grace, and a Christ, that is, the Son of God's love, to come to, and to live by, should be a thankful people. " By him, therefore, let us offer the sacrifice of praise to God continually, giving thanks to his name." (Heb. xiii. 15.) How many obligations has God laid upon his people, to give thanks to him at every remembrance of his holiness!

2. Study the priesthood, the high priesthood of Jesus Christ, both the first and second part thereof. The first part was that when he offered up himself without the gate, when he bare our sins in his own body on the tree. The second part is that which he executeth there whither he is now gone, even in heaven itself, where the throne of grace is. I say, study what Christ has done, and is doing. Oh! what is he doing now? he is sprinkling his blood, with his priestly robes on, before the throne of grace; that is too little thought on by the saints of God: " We have such an high priest, who is set on the right hand of the throne of the Majesty in the heavens; a minister of the sanctuary, and of the true tabernacle, which the Lord pitched, and not man." (Heb. viii. 1, 2.) Busy thyself, fellow-Christian, about this blessed office of Christ. It is full of good, it is full of sweet, it is full of heaven, it is full of relief and succour for the tempted and dejected; wherefore, I say again, study these things, give thyself wholly to them.

Sixth. Since God has prepared himself a lamb, a sacrifice, a priest, a throne of grace, and has bid thee come to him, come to him as there sitting; come, come boldly, as he bids thee. What better warrant canst thou have to come, than to be bid to come of God? When the goodman himself bids the beggar come to his house, then he may come, then he may come boldly; the consideration of the invitation doth encourage. That we have our friend at court, should also make us come boldly. Jesus, as has been showed, as sacrifice and high priest, is there, " in whom we have boldness, and access with confidence by the faith of him." (Eph. iii. 12.) Again, " By whom also we have access by faith into this grace, wherein we stand, and rejoice in hope of the glory of God." (Rom. v. 2.) Again, " We have boldness, brethren, to enter into the holiest by the blood of Jesus." (Heb. x. 19.) What can be more plain, more encouraging, more comfortable to them that would obtain mercy, " and find grace to help in time of need." It is a dishonour to God, disadvantage to thee, and an encouragement to Satan, when thou hangest back, and seemest afraid to " come boldly unto the throne of grace." " Let us," therefore, " draw near with a true heart, in full assurance of faith, having our hearts sprinkled from an evil conscience, and our bodies washed with pure water. Let us hold fast the profession of our faith without wavering, (for he is faithful that promised;) and let us consider one another to provoke unto love and to good works." (Heb. x. 23, 24.) Farewell.

PREFATORY REMARKS

THE WORK OF JESUS CHRIST AS AN ADVOCATE.

THE character of Jesus Christ opens a field for wide and various observation. It may be studied profitably first in its combination of personal qualities, and then in the exhibition of those qualities through the medium of his several offices. Dignity and meekness, the severity of unerring judgment, and the tenderness of pure charity, have never been so united in any other instance as in that of Jesus. These qualities form an essential portion of his character; they are the light and the fire of which the earnest reader of his gospel becomes more and more sensible, the more devoutly he ponders the meaning of his words and actions. Let one only of these virtues of his sublime character be forgotten, and perplexity attends every attempt to fathom the meaning of his sayings, or the reason of his works. Had he been either less meek, less dignified, less charitable, or less just, he could not have spoken or acted as he did. His words and actions are, therefore, only thoroughly explicable, when there is a clear and general apprehension of his character. Reversely, his character, to be understood, must be studied through the mediums by which its graces were exercised and developed. Of these, the most obvious are his offices. It is as Redeemer, as Teacher, and Advocate, that we see him bringing forth the mighty host of his virtues into action. Without such dispositions as those virtues indicate, he would either never have undertaken the offices, or, undertaking them, would have stopped short of executing the designs contemplated in his call.

An advocate is endowed with a measure of respect and honour by his very title. Supposing he be not a mere pretender to the office, self-chosen and unauthorised, he is entrusted by one party with some dear and important interest, and is accounted by another party, powerful to determine the appeal, worthy of favour and credit. In any case of importance, the selected and acknowledged advocate is exalted to a station of dignity, and qualities of a very high character are required to fulfil its obligations.

The advocateship of Jesus Christ has necessarily many things in common with that of any other intercessor. He stands between two parties—trusted by the one, acknowledged by the other. Like any other advocate, he has undertaken to plead for those whom he represents, he urges claims of a personal nature to be patiently heard, and deeply sympathises with those whose cause he has devoted himself to uphold. But no sooner do we understand the objects of Christ's advocateship, than we also see that the qualities necessary in this case must be of the highest order. The party whom he represents is properly the entire human race; in reality, it consists of men whose understandings have been awakened to a terrible sense of danger—to a new feeling of the value of the soul, and a solemn apprehension of God's power and righteousness. Aroused by these emotions, they not only discover the necessity of an advocate with God, but plainly perceive that, to be entrusted with their cause, he must have merits, a wisdom and holiness, to which no one who ever shared in their sins and follies can pretend. Even supposing a person thus richly endowed to be aware of their necessity, it is not certain that he would care to involve himself with their concerns; his vast superiority in wisdom and virtue might rather dispose him to turn from them with disdain:—to advocate their pardon might seem like a soil on the exceeding brightness of his splendid purity.

To the qualities, therefore, of wisdom and holiness, the advocate of sinners must add the virtues of tenderness, benignity, and love. Without these, he could never be persuaded to look patiently into their state, and then to go before God, and ask for the pardon of all their numberless offences, and for the means of completely re-establishing them in peace and hope. But let this also be assumed. The wise and holy person, surpassing all others in the grandeur of his virtues and endowments, is ready, we will suppose, to undertake the office of an advocate. Crowds of suppliants surround him; they burden his very soul with their remorse. He approaches the throne of God. His prayers are the fruit of fervent charity. He weeps for his fellow-men. His heart is full of anguish; and he pleads their cause with devout and patient affection. But he stands before the judgment-seat trembling and appalled. It has been decreed that atonement must precede intercession; and the best and wisest of men can bring no sacrifice for sin, existing in themselves or others. Their virtues, however great, have no redeeming power; they might be willing to die a thousand deaths, and yet, by dying, could not even save themselves. The advocate would still have to be sought, though a host of the noblest and devoutest men came forward in behalf of the world. They could do nothing effectual for it, unless they could propitiate as well as intercede.

To the infinite benefit of mankind, Jesus, their willing advocate, has not only the virtues essential to the office of an intercessor, but a fund of atoning merits, so that, in every case in which his aid is sought, he prefaces his prayer for the sinner with an offering for his redemption.

The character and work of such an advocate engage our interest the more we become aware of our weaknesses and dangers. It is a strange fact, that most men feel the want of an advocate in some circumstances of their lives, but that the rarest cases are those which arise from a conviction of sin, and the imminent peril which attends it. In the instances, however, where this danger is properly apprehended, the knowledge of Jesus Christ as an advocate affords inexpressible consolation. The tenderness with which he speaks to the afflicted assures them of his pity; the wisdom apparent in his precepts and doctrines gives them confidence in his counsels; his holiness and power show them that he can save to the uttermost. As the mind opens to a more perfect understanding of these qualities of his character, so there is an increasing disposition to seek his aid. But Jesus could no more be an effectual advocate than any other virtuous and holy person, were there not superadded to his personal qualities the merits which belong to him as Redeemer. Hence the conscience-stricken sinner, who should be attracted to him simply by the contemplation of his wisdom and benignity, would commit an error little short of that of which he would be guilty, did he depend upon any other advocate remarkable for saintly virtues. It was the union of charity and wisdom, exalted to divine perfection, with the worth inherent in his nature, which qualified Jesus to become the advocate of a lost world. But he did not take the office upon him till he had atoned for sin. His willing suffering on our behalf is the act in which all his virtues appear concentrated with intensest force; and it is from the contemplation of his suffering that we best learn both his readiness and his fitness to be the one Mediator between man and God. Had he not been inspired by the most perfect charity, he would not have been willing to suffer for us; had he not possessed an infinite worth, he could not have redeemed us by his death. Did not his charity, and holiness, and the merit of his atoning suffering, still retain all their force and efficacy, it could not be said that "He ever liveth to make intercession for us."

H. S.

THE WORK OF JESUS CHRIST AS AN ADVOCATE,

CLEARLY EXPLAINED, AND LARGELY IMPROVED,

FOR THE BENEFIT OF ALL BELIEVERS.

"And if any man sin, we have an advocate with the Father, Jesus Christ the righteous."—1 JOHN ii. 1.

THE EPISTLE TO THE READER.

COURTEOUS READER,—Of all the excellent offices which God the Father has conferred upon Jesus Christ our Lord, this of his being an advocate with him for us is not the least, though, to the shame of saints it may be spoken, the blessed benefits thereof have not with that diligence and fervent desire been inquired after as they ought.

Christ, as sacrifice, priest, and king, with the glories in and that flow from him as such, has, God be thanked, in this our day, been much discovered by our seers, and as much rejoiced in by those who have believed their words; but as he is an advocate with the Father, an advocate for us, I fear the excellency of that doth still too much lie hid; though I am verily of opinion that the people of God in this age have as much need of the knowledge thereof, if not more need, than had their brethren that are gone before them.

These words, "if not more need," perhaps may seem to some to be somewhat out of joint; but let the godly wise consider the decays that are among us as to the power of godliness, and what abundance of foul miscarriages the generality of professors now stand guilty of, as also how diligent their great enemy is to accuse them at the bar of God for them, and I think they will conclude that, in so saying, I indeed have said some truth. Wherefore, when I thought on this, and had somewhat considered also the transcendent excellency of the advocateship of this our Lord; and again, that but little of the glory thereof has by writing been, in our day, communicated to the church, I adventured to write what I have seen thereof, and do, by what doth follow, present it unto her for good.

I count not myself sufficient for this, or for any other truth as it is in Jesus; but yet, I say, I have told you somewhat of it, according to the proportion of faith. And I believe that some will thank God for what I here have said about it; but it will be chiefly those whose right and title to the kingdom of heaven and glory doth seem to themselves to be called in question by their enemy, at the bar of the Judge of all.

These, I say, will read, and be glad to hear, that they have an advocate at court that will stand up to plead for them, and that will yet secure to them a right to the heavenly kingdom. Wherefore, it is more particularly for those that at present, or that hereafter, may be in this dreadful plight, that this my book is now made public; because it is, as I have showed, for such that Jesus Christ is advocate with the Father.

Of the many and singular advantages, therefore, that such have by this their advocate in his advocating for them, this book gives some account; as, where he pleads, how he pleads, what he pleads, when he pleads, with whom he pleads, for whom he pleads, and how the enemy is put to shame and silence before their God and all the holy angels.

Here is also showed to those herein concerned, how they indeed may know that Jesus is their advocate; yea, and how their matters go before their God, the Judge; and particularly that they shall well come off at last, yea, though their cause, as it is theirs, is such, in justification of which, themselves do not dare to show their heads.

Nor have I left the dejected souls without directions how to entertain this advocate to plead their cause; yea, I have also shown that he will be with ease prevailed with, to stand up to plead for such, as one would think, the very heavens would blush to hear them named by him. Their comfort also is, that he never lost a cause, nor a soul, for whom he undertook to be an advocate with God.

But, reader, I will no longer detain thee from the perusal of the discourse. Read and think; read, and compare what thou readest with the word of God. If thou findest any benefit by what thou readest, give the Father and his Son the glory; and also pray for me. If thou findest me short in this, or to exceed in that, impute all such things to my weakness, of which I am always full. Farewell. I am thine to serve thee what I may,

JOHN BUNYAN.

THE WORK OF JESUS CHRIST AS AN ADVOCATE.

1 John ii. 1.

"And if any man sin, we have an advocate with the Father, Jesus Christ the righteous."

THAT the apostle might obtain due regard from those to whom he wrote, touching the things about which he wrote, he tells them that he received not his message to them at second or third hand, but was himself an eye and ear witness thereof—"That which was from the beginning, which we have heard, which we have seen with our eyes, which we have looked upon, and our hands have handled, of the Word of life, (for the life was manifested, and we have seen it, and bear witness and show unto you that eternal life, which was with the Father, and was manifested unto us;) that which we have seen and heard, declare we unto you." Having thus told them of his ground for what he said, he proceeds to tell them also the matter contained in his errand, to wit, that he brought them news of eternal life, as freely offered in the word of the gospel to them; or rather, that that gospel which they had received would certainly usher them in at the gates of the kingdom of heaven, were their reception of it sincere and in truth—for, saith he, then "the blood of Jesus Christ the Son of God cleanseth you from all sin."

Having thus far told them what was his errand, he sets upon an explication of what he had said, specially touching our being cleansed from all sin —Not, saith he, *from a Being of Sin;* for should we say so, we should deceive ourselves, and should prove that we have no truth of God in us; but by cleansing, I mean a being delivered from all sin, so as that none at all shall have the dominion over you, to bring you down to hell: for that, for the sake of the blood of Christ, all trespasses are forgiven you.

This done, he exhorts them to shun or fly sin, and not to consent to the motions, workings, enticings, or allurements thereof, saying, "I write unto you, that ye sin not." Let not forgiveness have so bad an effect upon you as to cause you to be remiss in Christian duties, or as to tempt you to give way to evil. Shall we sin because we are forgiven? or shall we not much matter what manner of lives we live, because we are set free from the law of sin and death? God forbid. Let grace teach us another lesson, and lay other obligations upon our spirits. "My little children," saith he, "these things write I unto you, that ye sin not." What things? Why, tidings of pardon and salvation, and of that nearness to God, to which you are brought by the precious blood of Christ. Now, lest also by this last exhortation he should yet be misunderstood, he adds, "And if any man sin, we have an advocate with the Father, Jesus Christ the righteous." I say, he addeth this to prevent desponding in those weak and sensible Christians that are so quick of feeling and of discerning the corruptions of their natures; for these cry out continually, that there is nothing that they do but it is attended with sinful weaknesses. Wherefore, in the words we are presented with two great truths.

I. With a supposition that men in Christ, while in this world, *may sin*—"If any man sin;" any man; none are excluded; for all, or any one of the all of them that Christ hath redeemed and forgiven, are incident to sin. By "may" I mean, not a toleration, but a possibility: "For there is not a man, not a just man upon earth, that doeth good, and sinneth not." (Eccles. vii. 20. 1 Kings viii. 46.)

II. The other thing with which we are presented is, an advocate—"If any man sin, we have an advocate with the Father, Jesus Christ the righteous."

Now there lieth in these two truths two things to be inquired into, as—First. What the apostle should here mean by sin. Second. And also, what he here doth mean by an advocate—"If any man sin, we have an advocate." There is ground to inquire after the first of these, because, though here he saith, they that sin have an advocate, yet in the very next chapter he saith, "Such are of the devil, have not seen God, neither know him, nor are of him." There is ground also to inquire after the second, because an advocate is supposed in the text to be of use to them that sin—"If any man sin, we have an advocate."

First. For the first of these, to wit, what the apostle should here mean by sin—"If any man sin."

I answer, since there is a difference in the persons, there must be a difference in the sin. That there is a difference in the persons is showed before; one is called a child of God, the other is said to be of the wicked one. Their sins differ also, in their degree at least; for no child of God sins to that degree as to make himself incapable of forgiveness; for "he that is born of God keepeth himself, and that wicked one toucheth him not." (1 John v. 18.) Hence, the apostle says, "There is a sin unto death," (ver. 16; see also Matt. xii. 32,) which is the sin from which he that is born of God is kept.

The sins, therefore, are thus distinguished: The sins of the people of God are said to be sins that men commit, the others are counted those which are the sins of devils.

1. The sins of God's people are said to be sins which men commit, and for which they have an advocate, though they who sin after the example of the wicked one have none. "When a man or

woman," saith Moses, " shall commit any sin that men commit, they shall confess their sin, and an atonement shall be made for him." (Numb. v. 5—7.) Mark, it is when they commit a sin which men commit; or, as Hosea has it, When they transgress the commandment like Adam. (Hos. vi. 7.) Now, these are the sins under consideration by the apostle, and to deliver us from which, " we have an advocate with the Father." 2. But for the sins mentioned in the third chapter, since the persons sinning go here under another character, they also must be of another stamp—to wit, a making head against the person, merits, and grace of Jesus Christ. These are the sins of devils in the world, and for these there is no remission. These, they also that are of the wicked one commit, and therefore sin after the similitude of Satan, and so fall into the condemnation of the devil.

Second. But what is it for Jesus to be an advocate for these ? " If any man sin, we have an advocate."

An advocate is one who pleadeth for another at any bar, or before any court of judicature ; but of this more in its place. So, then, we have in the text a Christian, as supposed, committing sin, and a declaration of an advocate prepared to plead for him—" If any man sin, we have an advocate with the Father."

And this leads me first to inquire into what, by these words the apostle must, of necessity, presuppose ? For making use here of the similitude or office of an advocate, thereby to show the preservation of the sinning Christian, he must,

1. Suppose that God, as judge, is now upon the throne of his judgment; for an advocate is to plead at a bar, before a court of judicature. Thus it is among men ; and forasmuch as our Lord Jesus is said to be an " advocate with the Father," it is clear that there is a throne of judgment also. This the prophet Micaiah affirms, saying, " I saw the Lord sitting on his throne, and all the host of heaven standing by him on the right hand and on the left." (1 Kings xxii. 19.) Sitting upon a throne for judgment; for from the Lord, as then sitting upon that throne, proceeded that sentence against king Ahab, that he should go and fall at Ramothgilead ; and he did go, and did fall there, as the award or fruit of that judgment. This is the first.

2. The text also supposeth that the saints as well as sinners are concerned at that bar ; for the apostle saith plainly that there "we have an advocate." And the saints are concerned at that bar ; because they transgress as well as others, and because the law is against the sin of saints as well as against the sins of other men. If the saints were not capable of committing of sin, what need would they have of an advocate ? (1 Chron. xxi. 3—6. 1 Sam. xii. 13, 14.) Yea, though they did sin, yet if they were by Christ so set free from the law as that it could by no means take cognizance of their sins, what need would they have of an advocate ? None at all. If there be twenty places where there are assizes kept in this land, yet if I have offended no law, what need have I of an advocate ? specially if the judge be just, and knows me altogether, as the God of heaven does. But here's a Judge that is just ; and here's an advocate also, an advocate for the children, an advocate to plead ; for an advocate as such is not of use but before a bar to plead ; therefore, here is an offence, and so a law broken by the saints as well as others. That's the second thing.

3. As the text supposeth that there is a judge, and crimes of saints, so it supposeth that there is an accuser, one that will carefully gather up the faults of good men, and that will plead them at this bar against them. Hence we read of " the accuser of the brethren, that accuseth them before God day and night." (Rev. xii. 10—12.) For Satan doth not only tempt the godly man to sin, but, having prevailed with him, and made him guilty, he packs away to the court to God the judge of all ; and there addresses himself to accuse that man, and to lay to his charge the heinousness of his offence, pleading against him the law that he has broken, the light against which he did it, and the like. But now, for the relief and support of such poor people, the apostle, by the text, presents them with an advocate ; that is, with one to plead for them, while Satan pleads against them ; with one that pleads for pardon, while Satan, by accusing, seeks to pull judgment and vengeance upon our heads. " If any man sin, we have an advocate with the Father, Jesus Christ the righteous." That's the third thing.

4. As the apostle supposeth a judge, crimes, and an accuser, so he also supposeth that those herein concerned, to wit, the sinning children, neither can nor dare attempt to appear at this bar themselves to plead their own cause before this Judge and against this accuser. For if they could or durst do this, what need they have an advocate? for an advocate is of use to them whose cause themselves neither can nor dare appear to plead. Thus Job prayed for an advocate to plead his cause with God, (Job xvi. 21 ;) and David cries out, " Enter not into judgment with thy servant, O God, for in thy sight shall no man living be justified." (Ps. cxliii. 2.) Wherefore it is evident that saints neither can nor dare adventure to plead their cause. Alas ! the Judge is the almighty and eternal God ; the law broken is the holy and perfect rule of God, in itself a consuming fire. The sin is so odious, and a thing so abominable, that it is enough to make all the angels blush to hear it but so much as once mentioned in so holy a place as that is, where this great God doth sit to judge. This sin now hangs about the neck of him that hath committed it ; yea, it covereth him as doth a mantle. The adversary is bold, cunning, and audacious, and can word a thousand of us into an utter silence in less than half a quarter of an hour. What, then, should the sinner, if he could come there, do at this bar to plead ? Nothing : nothing

for his own advantage. But now comes in his mercy; he has an advocate to plead his cause. "If any man sin, we have an advocate with the Father, Jesus Christ the righteous." That's the fourth thing. But again,

5. The apostle also supposeth by the text that there is an aptness in Christians when they have sinned, to forget that they "have an advocate with the Father;" wherefore this is written to put them in remembrance, "If any man sin," (*let him remember*,) "we have an advocate." We can think of all other things well enough, namely, that God is a just judge, that the law is perfectly holy, that my sin is a horrible and an abominable thing, and that I am certainly thereof accused before God by Satan.

These things, I say, we readily think of, and forget them not. Our conscience puts us in mind of these, our guilt puts us in mind of these, the devil puts us in mind of these, and our reason and sense hold the knowledge and remembrance of these close to us. All that we forget is, that we have an advocate, "an advocate with the Father,"—that is, one that is appointed to take in hand in open court, before all the angels of heaven, my cause, and to plead it by such law and arguments as will certainly fetch me off, though I am clothed with filthy garments. But this, I say, we are apt to forget, as Job, when he said, "Oh, that one might plead for a man with God, as one pleads for his neighbour!" (Job xvi. 21.) Such an one Job had, but he had almost at this time forgot it; as he seems to intimate also where he wisheth for a days-man that might lay his hand upon them both. (Job ix. 33.) But our mercy is, we have one to plead our cause, "an advocate with the Father, Jesus Christ the righteous," who will not suffer our soul to be spilt and spoiled before the throne, but will surely plead our cause.

6. Another thing that the apostle would have us learn from the words is this, that to remember and to believe that Jesus Christ is an advocate for us when we have sinned, is the next way to support and strengthen our faith and hope. Faith and hope are very apt to faint when our sins in their guilt do return upon us; nor is there any more proper way to relieve our souls than to understand that the Son of God is our advocate in heaven. True, Christ died for our sins as a sacrifice, and as a priest he sprinkleth with his blood the mercy-seat; ay, but here is one that has sinned after profession of faith, that has sinned grievously, so grievously, that his sins are come up before God; yea, are at his bar pleaded against him by the accuser of the brethren, by the enemy of the godly. What shall he do now? Why, let him believe in Christ. Believe, that's true. But how now must he conceive in his mind of Christ for the encouraging of him so to do? Why, let him call to mind that Jesus Christ is an advocate with the Father, and as such he meeteth the accuser at the bar of God, pleads for this man that has sinned against this accuser, and prevaileth for ever against him. Here, now, though Satan be turned lawyer, though he accuseth, yea, though his charge against us is true, (for suppose that we have sinned,) yet our advocate is with the Father, Jesus Christ the righteous.

Thus is faith encouraged, thus is hope strengthened, thus is the spirit of the sinking Christian revived, and made to wait for a good deliverance from a bad cause and a cunning adversary; specially if you consider—

7. That the apostle doth also further suppose by the text that Jesus Christ, as advocate, if he will but plead our cause, let that be never so black, is able to bring us off, even before God's judgment-seat, to our joy, and the confounding of our adversary. For when he saith, "We have an advocate," he speaks nothing if he means not thus. But he doth mean thus, he must mean thus, because he seeketh here to comfort and support the fallen. Has any man sinned? We have an advocate. But what of that, if yet he be unable to fetch us off when charged for sin at the bar, and before the face of a righteous judge?

But he is able to do this. The apostle says so, in that he supposes a man has sinned, as any man among the godly ever did: for so we may understand it; and if he giveth us not leave to understand it so, he saith nothing to the purpose neither, for it will be objected by some. But can he fetch me off, though I have done as David, as Solomon, as Peter, or the like? It must be answered, Yes. The openness of the terms "any man," the indefiniteness of the word "sin," doth naturally allow us to take him in the largest sense; besides, he brings in this saying as the chief, most apt, and fittest to relieve one crushed down to death and hell by the guilt of sin and a wounded conscience.

Further, methinks by these words the apostle seems to triumph in his Christ, saying, My brethren, I would have you study to be holy; but if your adversary the devil should get the advantage of you, and besmear you with the filth of sin, you have yet, besides all that you have heard already, an advocate with the Father, Jesus Christ the righteous, who is as to his person, interest with God, his wisdom and worth, able to bring you off, to the comforting of your souls.

Let me, therefore, for a conclusion as to this, give you an exhortation to believe, to hope, and expect, that though you have sinned, (for now I speak to the fallen saint,) that Jesus Christ will make a good end with thee: "Trust," I say, in him, and he shall bring it to pass. I know I put thee upon a hard and difficult task for believing and expecting good, when thy guilty conscience doth nothing but clog, burden, and terrify thee with the justice of God, the greatness of thy sins, and the burning torments is hard and sweating work. But it must be; the text calls for it, thy case calls for it, and thou must do it, if thou wouldst glorify Christ. And this is the way to hasten the issue of thy cause in hand; for believing daunts the devil, pleaseth Christ, and will help thee beforehand to sing that song of the church, saying, " O Lord, thou hast pleaded the causes of my soul, thou hast redeemed my life." (Lam. iii. 28.) Yea, believe, and hear thy pleading Lord say to thee, " Thus saith thy Lord the Lord, and thy God that pleadeth the cause of his people, Behold, I have taken out of thine hand the cup of trembling, even the dregs of the cup of my fury; thou shalt no more drink it again." (Isa. li. 22.) I am not here discoursing of the sweetness of Christ's nature, but of the excellency of his offices, and of his office of advocateship in particular, which, as a lawyer for his client, he is to execute in the presence of God for us. Love may be where there is no office, and so where no power is to do us good; but now, when love and office shall meet, they will surely both combine in Christ to do the fallen Christian good. But of his love we have treated elsewhere; we will here discourse of the office of this loving one. And for thy further information, let me tell thee that God thy Father counteth that thou wilt be, when compared with his law, but a poor one all thy days; yea, the apostle tells thee so, in that he saith there is an advocate provided for thee. When a father provides crutches for his child, he doth as good as say, I count that my child will be yet infirm; and when God shall provide an advocate, he doth as good as say, My people are subject to infirmities. Do not, therefore, think of thyself above what, by plain texts, and fair inferences drawn from Christ's offices, thou art bound to think. What doth it bespeak concerning thee that Christ is always a priest in heaven, and there ever lives to make intercession for thee, (Heb. vii. 24,) but this, that thou art at the best in thyself, yea, and in thy best exercising of all thy graces too, but a poor, pitiful, sorry, sinful man; a man that would, when yet most holy, be certainly cast away, did not thy high priest take away for thee the iniquity of thy holy things. The age we live in is a wanton age; the godly are not so humble, and low, and base in their own eyes as they should, though their daily experience calls for it, and the priesthood of Jesus Christ too.

But, above all, the advocateship of Jesus Christ declares us to be sorry creatures; for that office does, as it were, predict that some time or other we shall basely fall, and by falling be undone, if the Lord Jesus stand not up to plead. And as it shows this concerning us, so it shows concerning God that he will not lightly or easily lose his people. He has provided well for us: blood to wash us in; a priest to pray for us, that we may be made to persevere; and, in case we foully fall, an advocate to plead our cause, and to recover us from under, and out of all that danger, that by sin and Satan we at any time may be brought into.

But having thus briefly passed through that in the text which I think the apostle must necessarily presuppose, I shall now endeavour to enter into the bowels of it, and see what, in a more particular manner, shall be found therein.

And, for my more profitable doing of this work, I shall choose to observe this method in my discourse :—

FIRST. I shall show you more particularly of this advocate's office, or what and wherein Christ's office as advocate doth lie.

SECONDLY. After that, I shall also show you how Jesus Christ doth manage this office of an advocate.

THIRDLY. I shall also then show you who they are that have Jesus Christ for their advocate.

FOURTHLY. I shall also show you what excellent privileges they have, who have Jesus Christ for their advocate.

FIFTHLY. And to silence cavillers, I shall also show the necessity of this office of Jesus Christ.

SIXTHLY. I shall come to answer some objections; and,

LASTLY. To the use and application.

FIRST. To begin with the first of these; namely, *to show you more particularly of Christ's office as an advocate, and wherein it lieth;* the which I shall do these three ways :—First. Touch again upon the nature of this office; and then, Secondly. Treat of the order and place that it hath among the rest of his offices; and, Thirdly. Treat of the occasion of the execution of this office.

First. To touch upon the nature of this office. It is that which empowereth a man to plead for a man, or one man to plead for another; not in common discourses, and upon common occasions, as any man may do, but at a bar, or before a court of judicature, where a man is accused or impleaded by his enemy: I say, this advocate's office is such, both here, and in the kingdom of heaven. An advocate is as one of our attorneys, at least in the general, who pleads according to law and justice for one or other that is in trouble by reason of some miscarriage, or of the naughty temper of some that are about him, who trouble and vex, and labour to bring him into danger of the law. This is the nature of this office, as I said, on earth; and this is the office that Christ executeth in heaven. Wherefore he saith, " If any man sin, we have an advocate;" one to stand up for him, and to plead for his deliverance before the bar of God. (Joel iii. 2. Isa. lxvi. 16. Ezek. xxxviii. 22. Jer. ii.)

For though in some places of Scripture Christ is said to plead for his with men, and that by terrible arguments, as by fire, and sword, and famine, and pestilence, yet this is not that which is intended by this text; for the apostle here saith, he is an advocate with the Father, or before the Father, to plead for those that there, or that to the Father's face, shall be accused for their transgressions: " If any man sin, we have an advocate with the Father, Jesus Christ the righteous." So, then, this is the employ of Jesus Christ as he is for us, an advocate. He has undertaken to stand up for his people at God's bar, and before that great court, there to plead, by the law and justice of heaven, for their deliverance; when, for their faults, they are accused, indicted, or impleaded by their adversary.

And now to treat of the order or place that this office of Christ hath among the rest of his offices, which he doth execute for us while we are here in a state of imperfection. And I think it is an office that is to come behind as a reserve, or for a help at last, when all other means shall seem to fail. Men do not use to go to law upon every occasion; or if they do, the wisdom of the judge, the jury, and the court, will not admit that every brangle, and foolish quarrel shall come before them; but an advocate doth then come into place, and then to the exercise of his office, when a cause is counted worthy to be taken notice of by the judge and by the court. Wherefore he, I say, comes in the last place, as a reserve, or help at last, to plead; and, by pleading, to set that right by law which would otherwise have caused an increase to more doubts, and to further dangers.

Christ, as priest, doth always works of service for us, because in our most spiritual things there may faults and spots be found, and these he taketh away, of course, by the exercise of that office; for he always wears that plate of gold upon his forehead before the Father, whereon is written, "Holiness to the Lord." But now, besides these common infirmities, there are faults that are highly gross and foul, that oft are found in the skirts of the children of God. Now, these are they that Satan taketh hold on; these are they that Satan draweth up a charge against us for; and to save us from these it is that the Lord Jesus is made an advocate. When Joshua was clothed with filthy garments, then Satan stood at his right hand to resist him; and then the angel of the covenant, the Lord Jesus, pleaded for his help. (Zech. iii.) By all which it appears, that this office comes behind, is provided as a reserve, that we may have help at a pinch, and then be lifted out, when we sink in mire, where there is no standing.

This is yet further hinted at by the several postures that Christ is said to be in, as he exerciseth his priestly and advocate's office. As a priest, he sits; as an advocate, he stands. (Isa. iii. 13.) The Lord stands up when he pleads; his sitting is more constant and of course, Sit thou, (Ps. cx. 1, 4;) but his standing is occasional, when Joshua is indicted, or when hell and earth are broken loose against his servant Stephen. For as Joshua was accused by the devil, and as then the angel of the Lord stood by, so when Stephen was accused by men on earth, and that charge seconded by the fallen angels before the face of God, it is said, the Lord Jesus stood on the right hand of God, (Acts vii. 55,) to wit, to plead; for so I take it, because standing is his posture as an advocate, not as a priest; for, as a priest, he must sit down; but he standeth as an advocate, as has been showed afore. (Heb. x. 12.) Wherefore,

Secondly. The occasion of his exercising of this office of advocate is, as hath been hinted already, when a child of God shall be found guilty before God of some heinous sin, of some grievous thing in his life and conversation. For as for those infirmities that attend the best, in their most spiritual sacrifices, if a child of God were guilty of ten thousand of them, they are of course purged, through the much incense that is always mixed with those sacrifices in the golden censer that is in the hand of Christ; and so he kept clean, and counted upright, notwithstanding those infirmities. And, therefore, you shall find that, notwithstanding those common faults, the children of God are counted good and upright in conversation, and not charged as offenders. "David," saith the text, "did that which was right in the eyes of the Lord, and turned not aside from any thing that he commanded him, all the days of his life, save only in the matter of Uriah the Hittite." (1 Kings xv. 5.) But was David, in a strict sense, without fault in all things else? No, verily; but that was foul in a higher degree than the rest, and therefore there God sets a blot; ay, and doubtless for that he was accused by Satan before the throne of God; for here is adultery, and murder, and hypocrisy, in David's doings; here is notorious matter, a great sin, and so a great ground for Satan to draw up an indictment against the king; and a thundering one, to be sure, shall be preferred against him. This is the time, then, for Christ to stand up to plead; for now there is room for such a question—Can David's sin stand with grace? or, Is it possible that a man that has done as he has, should yet be found a saint, and so in a saved state? or, Can God repute him so, and yet be holy and just? or, Can the merits of the Lord Jesus reach, according to the law of heaven, a man in this condition? Here is a case dubious; here is a man whose salvation, by his foul offences, is made doubtful; now we must to law and judgment, wherefore now let Christ stand up to plead. I say, now was David's case dubious; he was afraid that God would cast him away, and the devil hoped he would, and to that end charged him before God's face, if, perhaps, he might get sentence of damnation to pass upon his soul. (Ps. li.) But this was David's mercy: he had an advocate to plead his cause, by whose wisdom and skill in matters of law and judgment he was brought off of those heavy charges, from those gross sins, and delivered from that eternal condemnation, that, by the law of sin and death, was due thereto.

This is then the occasion that Christ taketh to plead, as advocate, for the salvation of his people—to wit, the cause: He "pleadeth the cause of his people." (Isa. li. 22.) Not every cause, but such and such a cause; the cause that is very bad, and by the which they are involved, not only in guilt and shame, but also in danger of death and hell. I say, the cause is bad, if the text be true, if sin can make it bad, yea, if sin itself be bad—"If any man sin, we have an advocate," an advocate to plead for him; for him as considered guilty, and so, consequently, as considered in a bad condition. It is true, we must distinguish between the person and the sin ; and Christ pleads for the person, not the sin: but yet he cannot be concerned with the person, but he must be with the sin ; for though the person and the sin may be distinguished, yet they cannot be separated. He must plead, then, not for a person only, but for a guilty person, for a person under the worst of circumstances—If any man sin, we have an advocate for him, as so considered.

When a man's cause is good, it will sufficiently plead for itself, yea, and for its master too, specially when it is made appear so to be, before a just and righteous judge. Here, therefore, needs no advocate ; the judge himself will pronounce him righteous. This is evidently seen in Job, "Thou movedst me against him (this said God to Satan) to destroy him without a cause." (Job ii. 3.) Thus far Job's cause was good, wherefore he did not need an advocate ; his cause pleaded for itself, and for its owner also. But if it was to plead good causes for which Christ is appointed advocate, then the apostle should have written thus : If any man be righteous, we have an advocate with the Father. Indeed, I never heard but one in all my life preach from this text, and he, when he came to handle the cause for which he was to plead, pretended it must be good, and therefore said to the people, See that your cause be good, else Christ will not undertake it. But when I heard it, Lord, thought I, if this be true, what shall I do, and what will become of all this people, yea, and of this preacher too ? Besides, I saw by the text, the apostle supposeth another cause, a cause bad, exceeding bad, if sin can make it so. And this was one cause why I undertook this work.

When we speak of a cause, we speak not of a person simply as so considered ; for, as I said before, person and cause must be distinguished. Nor can the person make the cause good but as he regulates his action by the word of God. If, then, a good, a righteous man doth what the law condemns, that thing is bad ; and if he be indicted for so doing, he is indicted for a bad cause ; and he that will be his advocate, must be concerned in and about a bad matter ; and how he will bring his client off, therein doth lie the mystery.

I know that a bad man may have a good cause depending before the judge, and so also good men have. (Job xxxi.) But then they are bold in their own cause, and fear not to make mention of it, and in Christ to plead their innocency before the God of heaven, as well as before men. (Ps. lxxi. 3—5. 2 Cor. i. 23. Gal. i. 10. Phil. i. 8.) But we have in the text a cause that all men are afraid of, a cause that the apostle concludes so bad that none but Jesus Christ himself can save a Christian from it. It is not only sinful, but sin itself, "If any man sin, we have an advocate with the Father."

· Wherefore there is in this place handled by the apostle, one of the greatest mysteries under heaven, to wit, that an innocent and holy Jesus should take in hand to plead for one before a just and righteous God, that has defiled himself with sin ; yea, that he should take in hand to plead for such an one against the fallen angels ; and that he should also by his plea effectually rescue, and bring them off from the crimes and curse whereof they were verily guilty, by the verdict of the law, and approbation of the Judge.

This, I say, is a great mystery, and deserves to be pried into by all the godly, both because much of the wisdom of heaven is discovered in it, and because the best saint is, or may be, concerned with it.

Nor must we by any means let this truth be lost, because it is the truth ; the text has declared it so, and to say otherwise is to belie the word of God, to thwart the apostle, to soothe up hypocrites, to rob Christians of their privilege, and to take the glory from the head of Jesus Christ. (Luke xviii. 11, 12.)

The best saints are most sensible of their sins, and most apt to make mountains of their mole-hills. Satan also, as has been already hinted, doth labour greatly to prevail with them to sin, and to provoke their God against them, (Job ii. 9,) by pleading what is true, or by surmising evilly of them, to the end they may be left with him to be tried, that they may be accused by him. Great is his malice towards them, great is his diligence in seeking their destruction ; wherefore greatly doth he desire to sift, to try, and winnow them, if perhaps he may work in their flesh to answer his design ; that is, to break out in sinful acts, that he may have by law to accuse them to their God and Father. Wherefore, for their sakes this text abides, that they may see that, when they have sinned, "they have an advocate with the Father, Jesus Christ the righteous." And thus have I showed you the nature, the order, and occasion of this office of our blessed Lord Jesus.

SECONDLY. I come now *to show you how Jesus Christ doth manage this his office of an advocate for us.* And that I may do this to your edification, I shall choose this method for the opening of it— First. Show you how he manages this office with his Father. Secondly. I shall show you how he manages it before him against our adversary.

First. How he manages this his office of advocate with his Father.

1. He doth it by himself, by no other as deputy under him. No angel, no saint ; no work has place here but Jesus, and Jesus only. This the text implies : " We have an advocate ;" speaking of one, but one, one alone ; without an equal or an inferior. We have but one, and he is Jesus Christ. Nor is it for Christ's honour, nor for the honour of the law, or of the justice of God, that any but Jesus Christ should be an advocate for a sinning saint. Besides, to assert the contrary, what doth it but lessen sin, and make the advocateship

of Jesus Christ superfluous? It would lessen sin should it be removed by a saint or angel; it would make the advocateship of Jesus Christ superfluous, yea, needless, should it be possible that sin could be removed from us by either saint or angel.

Again, if God should admit of more advocates than one, and yet make mention of never an one but Jesus Christ; or if John should allow another, and yet speak nothing but of Jesus only; yea, that an advocate under that title should be mentioned but once, but once only in all the book of God, and yet that divers should be admitted, stands neither with the wisdom or love of God, nor with the faithfulness of the apostle. But saints have but one advocate, if they will use him, or improve their faith in that office for their help, so; if not, they must take what follows. This I thought good to hint at, because the times are corrupt, and because ignorance and superstition always wait for a countenance with us, and these things have a natural tendency as to darken all truth, so especially this, which bringeth to Jesus Christ so much glory, and yieldeth to the godly so much help and relief.

2. As Jesus Christ alone is advocate, so God's bar, and that alone, is that before which he pleads, for God is judge himself. (Deut. xxxii. 36. Heb. xii. 23.) Nor can the cause which now he is to plead be removed into any other court, either by appeals, or otherwise.

Could Satan remove us from heaven, to another court, he would certainly be too hard for us, because there we should want our Jesus, our advocate, to plead our cause. Indeed, sometimes he impleads us before men, and they are glad of the occasion, for they and he are often one; but then we have leave to remove our cause, and to pray for a trial in the highest court, saying, " Let my sentence come forth from thy presence; let thine eyes behold the things that are equal." (Ps. xvii. 2.) This wicked world doth sentence us for our good deeds, but how, then, would they sentence us for our bad ones? But we will never appeal from heaven to earth for right, for here we have no advocate; " our advocate is with the Father, Jesus Christ the righteous."

3. As he pleadeth by himself alone, and nowhere else but in the court of heaven with the Father, so as he pleadeth with the Father for us, he observeth this rule—

(1.) He granteth and confesseth whatever can rightly be charged upon us; yet so as that he taketh the whole charge upon himself, acknowledging the crimes to be his own. O God, says he, " thou knowest my foolishness, and my sins; my guiltiness is not hid from thee." (Ps. lxix. 5.) And this he must do, or else he can do nothing. If he hides the sin, or lesseneth it, he is faulty; if he leaves it still upon us, we die. He must, then, take our iniquity to himself, make it his own, and so deliver us. For having thus taken the sin upon himself, as lawfully he may, and lovingly doth, " for we are members of his body," (so 'tis his hand,

'tis his foot, 'tis his ear that hath sinned,) it followeth that we live if he lives; and who can desire more? This, then, must be thoroughly considered, if ever we will have comfort in a day of trouble and distress for sin.

And thus far there is, in some kind, a harmony betwixt his being a sacrifice, a priest, and an advocate. As a sacrifice, our sins were laid upon him. (Isa. liii.) As a priest, he beareth them. (Exod. xxviii. 38.) And as an advocate, he acknowledgeth them to be his own. (Ps. lxix. 5.) Now, having acknowledged them to be his own, the quarrel is no more betwixt us and Satan, for the Lord Jesus has espoused our quarrel, and made it his. All, then, that we in this matter have to do, is to stand at the bar by faith among the angels, and see how the business goes. Oh, blessed God, what a lover of mankind art thou! and how gracious is our Lord Jesus, in his thus managing matters for us!

(2.) The Lord Jesus having thus taken our sins upon himself, next pleads his own goodness to God on our behalf, saying, " Let not them that wait on thee, O Lord God of hosts, be ashamed for my sake: let not those that seek thee be confounded for my sake, O God of Israel: because for thy sake I have borne reproach; shame hath covered my face." (Ps. lxix. 6, 7.) Mark, let them not be ashamed for my sake; let them not be confounded for my sake. Shame and confusion are the fruits of guilt, or of a charge for sin, (Jer. iii. 25.) and are but an entrance into condemnation. (Dan. xii. 2. John v. 29.) But behold how Christ pleads, saying, Let not that be for my sake, for the merit of my blood, for the perfection of my righteousness, for the prevalency of my intercession. Let them not be ashamed for my sake, O Lord God of hosts. And let no man object, because this text is in the Psalms, as if it were not spoken by the prophet, of Christ; for both John and Paul, yea, and Christ himself, do make this psalm a prophecy of him. (Compare ver. 9 with John ii. 17, and with Rom. xv. 3; and ver. 21 with Matt. xxvii. 48, and Mark xv. 25.)

But is not this a wonderful thing, that Christ should first take our sins, and account them his own, and then plead the value and worth of his whole self for our deliverance? For by these words, " for my sake," he pleadeth his own self, his whole self, and all that he is and has; and thus he put us in good estate again, though our cause was very bad.

To bring this down to weak capacities. Suppose a man should be indebted twenty thousand pounds, but has not twenty thousand farthings wherewith to pay; and suppose also that this man be arrested for this debt, and that the law also, by which he is sued, will not admit of a penny bate: this man may yet come well enough off, if his advocate or attorney will make the debt his own, and will, in the presence of the judges, out with his bags, and pay down every farthing. Why, this is the way of our advocate.

Our sins are called debts. (Matt. vi. 12.) We are sued for them at the law. (Luke xii. 59.) And the devil is our accuser; but behold the Lord Jesus comes out with his worthiness, pleads it at the bar, making the debt his own. (Mark x. 45. 2 Cor. iii. 5.) And saith, Now let them not be ashamed, for my sake, O Lord God of hosts: let them not be confounded, for my sake, O God of Israel. And hence, as he is said to be an advocate, so he is said to be a propitiation, or amends-maker, or one that appeaseth the justice of God for our sins, " If any man sin, we have an advocate with the Father, Jesus Christ the righteous; and he is the propitiation for our sins."

And who can now object against the deliverance of the child of God? God cannot: for he, for Christ's sake, according as he pleaded, hath forgiven us all trespasses. (Col. ii. 13. Eph. iv. 32.) The devil cannot; his mouth is stopped, as is plain in the case of Joshua. (Zech. iii.) The law cannot; for that approveth of what Christ has done. This, then, is the way of Christ's pleading. You must know, that when Christ pleads with God, he pleads with a just and righteous God, and, therefore, he must plead law, and nothing but law; and this he pleaded in both these pleas, first, in confessing of the sin he justified the sentence of the law in pronouncing of it evil; and then in his laying of himself, his whole self, before God for that sin, he vindicated the sanction and perfection of the law. Thus, therefore, he magnifies the law, and makes it honourable, and yet brings off his client safe and sound in the view of all the angels of God.

(3.) The Lord Jesus having thus taken our sins upon himself, and presented God with all the worthiness that is in his whole self for them, in the next place he calleth for justice, or a just verdict upon the satisfaction he hath made to God and to his law. Then proclamation is made in open court, saying, Take away the filthy garments from him, from him that hath offended, and clothe him with change of raiment. (Zech. iii.)

Thus the soul is preserved that hath sinned; thus the God of heaven is content that he should be saved; thus Satan is put to confusion, and Jesus applauded and cried up by the angels of heaven, and by the saints on earth.

Thus have I showed you how Christ doth advocate it with God and his Father for us; and I have been the more particular in this, because the glory of Christ, and the comfort of the dejected, are greatly concerned and wrapt up in it. Look, then, to Jesus, if thou hast sinned; to Jesus, as an advocate pleading with the Father for thee. Look to nothing else; for he can tell how, and that by himself, to deliver thee; yea, and will do it in a way of justice, which is a wonder; and to the shame of Satan, which will be his glory; and also to thy complete deliverance, which will be thy comfort and salvation.

Secondly. But to pass this and come to the second thing, which is, to show you how the Lord Jesus

manages this his office of an advocate before his Father against the adversary; for he pleadeth with the Father, but pleadeth against the devil; he pleadeth with the Father law and justice, but against the adversary he letteth out himself.

I say, as he pleads against the adversary, so he enlargeth himself with arguments over and besides those which he pleadeth with God his Father.

Nor is it meet or needful that our advocate, when he pleads against Satan, should so limit himself to matter of law, as when he pleadeth with his Father. The saint, by sinning, oweth Satan nothing; no law of his is broken thereby; why, then, should he plead for the saving of his people, justifying righteousness to him?

Christ, when he died, died not to satisfy Satan, but his Father; not to appease the devil, but to answer the demands of the justice of God; nor did he design, when he hanged on the tree, to triumph over his Father, but over Satan. "He redeemed us," therefore, "from the curse of the law," by his blood, (Gal. iii. 13;) and from the power of Satan, by his resurrection. (Heb. ii. 14.) He delivered us from righteous judgment by price and purchase; but from the rage of hell by fight and conquest.

And as he acted thus diversely in the work of our redemption, even so he also doth in the execution of his advocate's office. When he pleadeth with God, he pleadeth so; and when he pleadeth against Satan, he pleadeth so; and how he pleadeth with God when he dealeth with law and justice I have showed you. And now I will show you how he pleadeth before him against the accuser of the brethren.

1. He pleads against him the well-pleasedness that his Father has in his merits, saying, This shall please the Lord; or this doth or will please the Lord, better than anything that can be propounded. (Ps. lxix. 31.) Now this plea being true, as it is, being established upon the liking of God Almighty; whatever Satan can say to obtain our everlasting destruction is without ground, and so unreasonable. "I am well pleased," saith God, (Matt. iii. 17;) and again, "The Lord is well pleased for his," Christ's, "righteousness' sake." (Isa. xlii. 21.) All that enter actions against others, pretend that wrong is done, either against themselves or against the king. Now Satan will never enter an action against us in the court above, for that wrong by us has been done to himself; he must pretend, then, that he sues us, for that wrong has, by us, been done to our king. But, behold, "We have an advocate with the Father," and he has made compensation for our offences; he gave himself for our offences. But still Satan maintains his suit; and our God, saith Jesus, is well pleased with us for this compensation's sake, yet he will not leave off his clamour. Come, then, says the Lord Jesus, the contention is not now against my people, but myself, and about the sufficiency of the amends that I have made for the transgressions of my people. But he is near that justifieth me, that

approveth and accepteth of my doings, therefore shall I not be confounded. Who is mine adversary? let him come near me. Behold, the Lord God will help me. (Isa. l. 7—9.) Who is he that condemneth me? Lo, they all shall, were there ten thousand times as many more of them, wax old as a garment; the moth shall eat them up. Wherefore, if the Father saith Amen to all this, as I have showed already that he hath and doth, the which also further appeareth, because the Lord God has called him the Saviour, the Deliverer, and the Amen; what follows, but that a rebuke should proceed from the throne against him? And this, indeed, our advocate calls for from the hand of his Father, saying, Oh, enemy, "the Lord rebuke thee;" yea, he doubles this request to the judge, to intimate his earnestness for such a conclusion, or to show that the enemy shall surely have it, both from our advocate, and from him before whom Satan has so grievously accused us. (Zech. iii.)

For what can be expected to follow from such an issue in law as this is, but sound and severe snibs from the judge upon him that hath thus troubled his neighbour, and that hath, in the face of the country, cast contempt upon the highest act of mercy, justice, and righteousness, that ever the heavens beheld? And all this is true with reference to the case in hand, wherefore, "the Lord rebuke thee," is that which, in conclusion, Satan must have for the reward of his works of malice against the children, and for his contemning of the works of the Son of God.

Now, our advocate having thus established, by the law of heaven, his plea with God for us against our accuser, there is way made for him to proceed upon a foundation that cannot be shaken; wherefore, he proceedeth in his plea, and further urges against this accuser of the brethren—

2. God's interest in this people; and prayeth that God would remember that: "The Lord rebuke thee, O Satan; the Lord that hath chosen Jerusalem, rebuke thee." True, the church, the saints, are despicable in the world: wherefore men do think to tread them down. The saints are also weak in grace, but have corruptions that are strong, and, therefore, Satan, the god of this world, doth think to tread them down; but the saints have a God, the living, the eternal God, and therefore, they shall not be trodden down; yea, they "shall be holden up, for God is able to make them stand." (Rom. xiv. 4.)

It was Haman's mishap to be engaged against the queen, and the kindred of the queen; it was that that made him he could not prosper: that brought him to contempt and the gallows. Had he sought to ruin another people, probably he might have brought his design to a desired conclusion; but his compassing the death of the queen spoiled all. Satan, also, when he fighteth against the church, must be sure to come to the worst, for God has a concern in that; therefore, it is said, "The gates of hell shall not prevail against it;"

but this hindereth not but that he is permitted to make almost what spoils he will of those that belong not to God. Oh, how many doth he accuse, and soon get out from God, against them, a license to destroy them, as he served Ahab, and many more. But this, I say, is a very great block in his way when he meddleth with the children; God has an interest in them—"Hath God cast away his people? God forbid!" (Rom. xi. 1, 2.)

The text intimates that they for sin had deserved it, and that Satan would fain have had it been so. But God's interest in them preserved them—"God hath not cast away his people, which he foreknew." Wherefore, when Satan accuseth them before God, Christ, as he pleadeth his own worth and merit, pleadeth also against him, that interest that God has in them.

And though this, to some, may seem but an indifferent plea; for what engagement lieth, may they say, upon God to be so much concerned with them, for they sin against him, and often provoke him most bitterly? Besides, in their best state, they are altogether vanity, and a very thing of nought—"What is man (sorry man), that thou art mindful of him," or that thou shouldest be so?

I answer, Though there lieth no engagement upon God for any worthiness that is in man, yet there lieth a great deal upon God for the worthiness that is in himself. God has engaged himself with his having chosen them to be a people to himself: and by this means they are so secured from all that all can do against them, that the apostle is bold, upon this very account, to challenge all despite to do its worst against them, saying, "Who shall lay anything to the charge of God's elect?" (Rom. viii. 33.) Who? saith Satan; why, that will I. Ay, saith he, but who can do it, and prevail? "It is God that justifieth, who is he that condemneth?" (ver. 34.) By which words the apostle clearly declareth that charges against the elect, though they may be brought against them, must needs prove ineffectual as to their condemnation; because their Lord God still will justify, for that Christ has died for them.

Besides, a little to enlarge, the elect are bound to God by a sevenfold cord, and a threefold one is not quickly broken.

(1.) Election is eternal as God himself, and so without variableness or shadow of change, and hence it is called an eternal purpose, and a purpose of God that must stand. (Eph. iii. 11. Rom. ix. 11.)

(2.) Election is absolute, not conditional; and, therefore, cannot be overthrown by the sin of the man that is wrapt up therein. No works foreseen to be in us was the cause of God's choosing of us; no sin in us shall frustrate or make election void. Who shall lay anything to the charge of God's elect? It is God that justifieth. (Rom. viii. 33; ix. 11.)

(3.) By the act of election the children are involved, wrapped up, and covered in Christ, (he hath chosen us in him;) not in ourselves, not in our virtues, no, not for or because of anything, but of his own will. (Eph. i. 4—11.)

(4.) Election includeth in it a permanent resolution of God to glorify his mercy on the vessels of mercy, thus foreordained unto glory. (Rom. ix. 15, 18, 23.)

(5.) By the act of electing love, it is concluded that all things whatsoever shall work together for the good of them whose call to God is the fruit of this purpose, this eternal purpose of God. (Rom. viii. 28—30.)

(6.) The eternal inheritance is by a covenant of free and unchangeable grace made over to those thus chosen. And to secure them from the fruits of sin, and from the malice of Satan, it is sealed by this our advocate's blood, as he is Mediator of this covenant, who also is become surety to God for them; to wit, to see them forthcoming at the great day, and to set them then safe and sound before his Father's face after the judgment is over. (Rom. ix. 23. Heb. vii. 22; ix. 15, 17—24; xiii. 20. John x. 28, 29.)

(7.) By this choice, purpose, and decree, the elect, the concerned therein, have allotted them by God, and laid up for them, in Christ, a sufficiency of grace to bring them through all difficulties to glory; yea, and they, every one of them, after the first act of faith, the which also they shall certainly attain, (because wrapt up in the promise for them,) are to receive the earnest and first fruits thereof into their souls. (2 Tim. i. 9. Acts xiv. 22. Eph. i. 4, 5, 13, 14.)

Now, put all these things together, and then feel if there be not weight in this plea of Christ against the devil. He pleads God's choice and interest in his saints against him, an interest that is secured by the wisdom of heaven, by the grace of heaven, by the power, will, and mercy of God, in Christ; an interest in which all the three Persons in the Godhead have engaged themselves, by mutual agreement and operation, to make good when Satan has done his all. I know there are some that object against this doctrine as false; but such, perhaps, are ignorant of some things else as well as of this. However, they object against the wisdom of God, whose truth it is, and against Christ our advocate, whose argument, as he is such, it is; yea, they labour, what in them lieth, to wrest that weapon out of his hand, with which he so cudgelleth the enemy when, as advocate, he pleadeth so effectually against him for the rescuing of us from the danger of judgment, saying, "The Lord rebuke thee, O Satan, even the Lord that hath chosen Jerusalem, rebuke thee."

Thirdly. As Christ, as advocate, pleads against Satan the interest that his Father hath in his chosen, so also he pleads against him by no less authority, his own interest in them. Holy Father, saith he, keep through thine own name those whom thou hast given me. (John xvii. 11.) Keep them while in the world from the evil, the soul-damning evil of it. These words are directed to the Father, but they are levelled against the accusations of the enemy, and were spoken here to show what Christ will do for his, against our foe, when he is above. How, I say, he will urge before his Father his own interest in us against Satan, and against all his accusations, when he brings them to the bar of God's tribunal, with design to work our utter ruin. And is there not a great deal in it? As if Christ should say, Father, my people have an adversary who will accuse them for their faults before thee; but I will be their advocate, and as I have bought them of thee, I will plead my right against him. (John x. 28.) Our English proverb is, Interest will not lie; interest will make a man do that which otherwise he would not. How many thousands are there for whom Christ doth not so much as once open his mouth, but leaves them to the accusations of Satan, and to Ahab's judgment, nay, a worse, because there is none to plead their cause? And why doth not he concern himself with them? but because he is not interested in them—"I pray not for the world, but for them which thou hast given me, for they are thine; and all mine are thine, and I am glorified in them." (John xvii. 9, 10.)

Suppose so many cattle in such a pound, and one goes by whose they are not, doth he concern himself? No; he beholds them, and goes his way. But suppose that at his return he should find his own cattle in that pound, would he now carry it toward them as he did unto the other? No, no; he has interest here, they are his that are in the pound; now he is concerned, now he must know who put them there, and for what cause too they are served as they are; and if he finds them rightfully there, he will fetch them thence by ransom; but if wrongfully, he will replevy them, and stand a trial at law with him that has thus illegally pounded his cattle. And thus it is betwixt Jesus Christ and his. He is interested in them; the cattle are his own, "his own sheep," (John x. 3, 4;) but pounded by some other, by the law, or by the devil. If pounded by the law, he delivereth them by ransom; if pounded by the devil, he will replevy them, stand a trial at law for them, and will be, against their accuser, their advocate himself. Nor can Satan withstand his plea, though he should against them join argument with the law; forasmuch, as has been proved before, he can and will, by what he has to produce and plead of his own, save his from all trespasses, charges, and accusations. Besides, all men know that a man's proper goods are not therefore forfeited, because they commit many, and them too great transgressions—"And if any man sin, we have an advocate with the Father, Jesus Christ the righteous." Now, the strength of this plea thus grounded upon Christ's interest in his people is great, and hath many weighty reasons on its side; as,

1. They are mine; therefore in reason at my dispose, not at the dispose of an adversary; for

while a thing can properly be called mine, no man has therewith to do but myself; nor doth (a man, nor) Christ lose his right to what he has by the weakness of that thing which is his proper right. He, therefore, as an advocate, pleadeth interest, his own interest, in his people, and right must, with the Judge of all the earth, take place—"Shall not the Judge of all the earth do right?" (Gen. xviii. 25.)

2. They cost him dear; and that which is dear bought is not easily parted with. (1 Cor. vi. 20.) They were bought with his blood. (Eph. i. 7. 1 Pet. 18, 19.) They were given him for his blood, and therefore are dear children, (Eph. v. 1;) for they are his by the highest price; and this price he, as advocate, pleadeth against the enemy of our salvation; yea, I will add, they are his, because he gave his all for them. (2 Cor. viii. 9.) When a man shall give his all for this or that, then that which he so hath purchased is become his all. Now Christ has given his all for us; he made himself poor for us, wherefore we are become his all, his fulness; and so the church is called. (Eph. i. 23.) Nay, further, Christ likes well enough of his purchase, though it hath cost him his all—"The lines," says he, "are fallen to me in pleasant places; I have a goodly heritage." (Ps. xvi.) Now, put all these things together, and there is a strong plea in them. Interest, such an interest, will not be easily parted with. But this is not all; for,

3. As they cost him dear, so he hath made them near to himself, near by way of relation. Now that which did not only cost dear, but that by way of relation is made so, that a man will plead heartily for. Said David to Abner, "Thou shalt not see my face except thou first bring Michal, Saul's daughter, when thou comest to see my face." (2 Sam. iii. 13, 14.) Saul's daughter cost me dear; I bought her with the jeopardy of my life; Saul's daughter is near to me; she is my beloved wife. He pleaded hard for her, because she was dear and near to him. Now, I say, the same is true in Christ; his people cost him dear, and he hath made them near unto him; wherefore, to plead interest in them, is to hold by an argument that is strong.

(1.) They are his spouse, and he hath made them so; they are his love, his dove, his darling, and he accounts them so. Now, should a wretch attempt in open court, to take a man's wife away from him, how would this cause the man to plead! Yea, and what judge that is just, and knows that the man has this interest in the woman pleaded for, would yield to, or give a verdict for the wretch, against the man whose wife the woman is? Thus Christ, in pleading interest—in pleading "thou gavest them me"—pleads by a strong argument, an argument that the enemy cannot invalidate. True, were Christ to plead this before a Saul, (1 Sam. xxv. 44,) or before Samson's wife's father, the Philistine, (Judges xiv. 20,) perhaps such treach-

erous judges would give it against all right. But, I have told you, the court in which Christ pleads is the highest and the justest, and that from which there can be no appeal; wherefore Christ's cause, and so the cause of the children of God, must be tried before their Father, from whose face, to be sure, just judgment shall proceed. But,

(2.) As they are called his spouse, so they are called his flesh, and members of his body. Now said Paul to the church, Ye are the body of Christ, and members in particular. (1 Cor. xii. 27. Eph. v. 30.) This relation also makes a man plead hard. Were a man to plead for a limb, or a member of his own, how would he plead? what arguments would he use! and what sympathy and feeling would his arguments flow from! I cannot lose a hand, I cannot lose a foot, cannot lose a finger: why, saints are Christ's members, his members are of himself. With what strength of argument would a man plead the necessariness of his members to him, and the unnaturalness of his adversary in seeking the destruction of his members, and the deformity of his body? Yea, a man would shuck and cringe, and weep, and entreat, and make demurs, and halts, and delays, to a thousand years, if possible, before he would lose his members, or any one of them.

But, I say, how would he plead and advocate it for his members, if judge, and law, and reason, and equity, were all on his side, and if, by the adversary, there could be nothing urged, but that against which the advocate had long before made provision for the effectual overthrow thereof? And all this is true as to the case that lies before us. Thus we see what strength there lieth in this second argument, that our advocate bringeth for us against the enemy. They are his flesh and bones, his members; he cannot spare them; he cannot spare this, because, nor that, because, nor *any*, because they are his members. As such, they are lovely to him; as such, they are useful to him; as such, they are an ornament to him; yea, though in themselves they are feeble, and through infirmity weak, much disabled from doing as they should. Thus, "If any man sin, we have an advocate with the Father, Jesus Christ the righteous." But,

4. As Christ, as advocate, pleads for us, against Satan, his Father's interest in us and his own; so he pleadeth against him that right and property that he hath in heaven, to give it to whom he will. He has a right to heaven as Priest and King; it is his also by inheritance; and since he will be so good a benefactor as to bestow this house on somebody, but not for their deserts, but not for their goodness, and since, again, he has to that end spilt his blood for, and taken a generation into covenant relation to him, that it might be bestowed on them; it shall be bestowed on them; and he will plead this, if there be need, if his people sin, and if their accuser seeks, by their sin, their ruin and destruction: Father, saith he, I will that they also, whom thou hast given me, be

with me where I am; that they may behold my glory, which thou hast given me. (John xvii. 24.) Christ's will is the will of heaven, the will of God Shall not Christ, then, prevail?

I will, saith Christ; I will, saith Satan; but whose will shall stand? It is true, Christ in the text speaks more like an arbitrator than an advocate; more like a judge than one pleading at a bar. I will have it so; I judge that so it ought to be, and must. But there is also something of plea in the words both before his Father, and against our enemy; and therefore he speaketh like one that can plead and determine also; yea, like one that has power so to do. But shall the will of heaven stoop to the will of hell? Or the will of Christ to the will of Satan? Or the will of righteousness to the will of sin? Shall Satan, who is God's enemy, and whose charge wherewith he chargeth us for sin, and which is grounded, not upon love to righteousness, but upon malice against God's designs of mercy, against the blood of Christ, and the salvation of his people,—I say, shall this enemy and this charge prevail with God against the well-grounded plea of Christ, and against the salvation of God's elect! and so keep us out of heaven? No, no; Christ will have it otherwise, he is the great donator, and his eye is good. True, Satan was turned out of heaven for that he sinned there, and we must be taken into heaven, though we have sinned here; this is the will of Christ, and, as advocate, he pleads it against the face and accusation of our adversary. Thus, "If any man sin, we have an advocate with the Father, Jesus Christ the righteous." But,

5. As Christ, as advocate, pleadeth for us, against Satan, his Father's interest in us, and his own, and pleadeth also what right he has to dispose of the kingdom of heaven; so he pleadeth against this enemy, that malice and enmity that is in him, and upon which chiefly his charge against us is grounded, to the confusion of his face. This is evident from the title that our advocate bestows upon him, while he pleads for us against him: "The Lord rebuke thee, O Satan," O enemy, saith he; for Satan is an enemy, and this name given him signifies so much. And lawyers, in their pleas, can make a great matter of such a circumstance as this; saying, My lord, we can prove that what is now pleaded against the prisoner at the bar is of mere malice and hatred, that has also a long time lain burning and raging in his enemy's breast against him. This, I say, will greatly weaken the plea and accusation of an enemy. But, says Jesus Christ, Father, here is a plea brought in against my Joshua, that clothes him with filthy garments, but it is brought in against him by an enemy, by an enemy in the superlative or highest degree. One that hates goodness worse than he, and that loveth wickedness more than the man against whom at this time he has brought such a heinous charge. Then leaving with the Father the value of his blood for the accused, he turneth him to the accuser, and pleads against him as an enemy: O Satan, thou that accusest my spouse, my love, my members, art SATAN, an enemy. But it will be objected, that the things charged are true. Grant it; yet what law takes notice of the law of one who doth professedly act as an enemy, because it is not done of love to truth, and justice, and righteousness, nor intended for the honour of the king, nor for the good of the prosecuted; but to gratify malice and rage, and merely to kill and destroy. There is, therefore, a great deal of force and strength in an advocate's pleading of such a circumstance against an accuser; especially when the crimes now charged are those, and only those for which the law, in the due execution of it, has been satisfied before; wherefore now a lawyer has double and treble ground or matter to plead for his client against his enemy. And this advantage against him has Jesus Christ.

Besides, it is well known that Satan, as to us, is the original cause of those very crimes for which he accuses us at the bar of God's tribunal. Not to say anything of how he cometh to us, solicits us, tempts us, flatters us, and always, in a manner, lies at us to do those wicked things for which he so hotly pursues us to the bar of the judgment of God. For though it is not meet for us thus to plead, to wit, laying that fault upon Satan, but rather upon ourselves; yet our advocate will do it, and make work of it too, before God. "Simon, Simon, behold, Satan hath desired to have you, that he might sift you as wheat; but I have prayed for thee, that thy faith fail not." (Luke xxii. 31, 32.) He maketh here mention of Satan's desires, by way of advantage against him; and, doubtless, so he did in his prayer with God for Peter's preservation. And what he did here, while on earth, as a Saviour, in general, that he doth now in heaven as a priest and an advocate in special.

I will further suppose that which may be supposed, and that which is suitable to our purpose. Suppose, therefore, that a father that has a child whom he loveth, but the child has not half that wit that some of the family hath, (and I am sure that we have less wit than angels;) and suppose, also, that some bad-minded neighbour, by tampering with, tempting of, and by unwearied solicitations, should prevail with this child to steal something out of his father's house or grounds, and give it unto him; and this he doth on purpose to set the father against the child. And suppose, again, that it comes to the father's knowledge that the child, through the allurements of such an one, has done so and so against his father; will he therefore disinherit this child? Yea, suppose, again, that he that did tempt this child to steal, should be the first that should come to accuse this child to its father for so doing, would the father take notice of the accusation of such an one? No, verily, we that are evil can do better than so. How then should we think that the God of heaven should do such a thing, since also we have a brother that is wise, and that will and can plead the very malice of our enemy that doth to us all these things against him for our advantage? I say, this is the sum of this fifth plea of Christ our advocate, against Satan. O Satan, says he, thou art an enemy to my people; thou pleadest not out of love to righteousness, nor to reform, but to destroy my beloved and inheritance. The charge wherewith thou chargest my people is thine own. (Job viii. 4—6.) Not only as to a matter of charge, but the things that thou accusest them of are thine, thine in the nature of them. Also, thou hast tempted, allured, flattered, and daily laboured with them, to do that for which now thou so willingly wouldest have them destroyed. Yea, all this hast thou done of envy to my Father, and to godliness; of hatred to me and my people; and that thou mightest destroy others besides. (1 Chron. xxi. 1.) And now, what can this accuser say? Can he excuse himself? Can he contradict our advocate? He cannot; he knows that he is a Satan, an enemy, and as an adversary has he sown his tares among the wheat, that it might be rooted up: but he shall not have his end; his malice has prevented him, and so has the care and grace of our advocate. The tares, therefore, he shall have returned to him again; but the wheat, for all this, shall be gathered into God's barn. (Matt. xiii. 25—30.)

Thus, therefore, our advocate makes use, in his plea against Satan, of the rage and malice that is the occasion of the enemy's charge wherewith he accuseth the children of God. Wherefore, when thou readest these words, "O Satan," say with thyself, Thus Christ our advocate accuseth our adversary of malice and envy against God and goodness, while he accuseth us of the sins which we commit, for the which we are sorry, and Christ has paid a price of redemption—"And" (thus) "if any man sin, we have an advocate with the Father, Jesus Christ the righteous." But—

6. Christ, when he pleads as an advocate for his people, in the presence of God against Satan, he can plead those very weaknesses of his people for which Satan would have them damned, for their relief and advantage. "Is not this a brand plucked out of the fire?" This is part of the plea of our advocate against Satan for his servant Joshua, when he said, "The Lord rebuke thee, O Satan." (Zech. iii. 2.) Now, to be a brand plucked out of the fire is to be a saint, impaired, weakened, defiled, and made imperfect by sin; for so also the apostle means when he saith, "And others save with fear, pulling them out of the fire; hating even the garment spotted by the flesh." (Jude 23.) By fire, in both these places, we are to understand sin; for that it burns and consumes as fire. (Rom. i. 27.) Wherefore a man is said to burn when his lusts are strong upon him, and to burn in lusts to others, when his wicked heart runs wickedly after them. (1 Cor. vii. 9.)

Also, when Abraham said, "I am but dust and ashes," (Gen. xviii. 27,) he means, he was but what sin had left; yea, he had something of the smutch and besmearings of sin yet upon him. Wherefore it was a custom with Israel, in days of old, when they set days apart for confession of sin, and humiliation for the same, to sprinkle themselves with, or to wallow in dust and ashes, as a token that they did confess they were but what sin had left, and that they also were defiled, weakened, and polluted by it. (Esther iv. 1, 3. Jer. vi. 26. Job xxx. 19; xlii. 6.)

This, then, is the next plea of our goodly advocate for us: O Satan, this is "a brand plucked out of the fire." As who should say, Thou objectest against my servant Joshua that he is black like a coal, or that the fire of sin at times is still burning in him. And what then? The reason why he is not totally extinct, as tow, is not thy pity, but my Father's mercy to him; I have plucked him out of the fire, yet not so out but that the smell thereof is yet upon him; and my Father and I, we consider his weakness, and pity him; for since he is as a brand pulled out, can it be expected by my Father or me that he should appear before us as clear, and do our biddings as well, as if he had never been there? This is "a brand plucked out of the fire," and must be considered as such, and must be borne with as such. Thus, as Mephibosheth pleaded for his excuse, his lameness, (2 Sam. xix. 24—26,) so Christ pleads the infirm and indigent condition of his people, against Satan, for their advantage.

Wherefore Christ, by such pleas as these for his people, doth yet further show the malice of Satan, (for all this burning comes through him,) yea, and by it he moveth the heart of God to pity us, and yet to be gentle, and long-suffering, and merciful to us; for pity and compassion are the fruits of the yearning of God's bowels towards us, while he considereth us as infirm and weak, and subject to slips, and stumbles, and falls, because of weakness.

And that Christ our advocate, by this pleading, doth turn things to our advantage, consider—

(1.) That God is careful, that through our weakness, our spirits do not fail before him when he chides. (Isa. lvii. 16—18.)

(2.) "He stayeth his rough wind in the day of the east wind," and debates about the measure of affliction, when, for sin, we should be chastened, lest we should sink thereunder. (Isa. xxvii. 7—9.)

(3.) He will not strictly mark what is done amiss, because if he should, we cannot stand. (Ps. cxxx. 3.)

(4.) When he threateneth to strike, his bowels are troubled, and his repentings are kindled together. (Hosea xi. 8, 9.)

(5.) He will spin out his patience to the utmost length, because he knows we are such bunglers at doing. (Jer. ix. 24.)

(6.) He will accept of the will for the deed, because he knows that sin will make our best performances imperfect. (2 Cor. viii. 12.)

(7.) He will count our little a very great deal, for

that he knows we are so unable to do anything at all. (Job i. 21.)

(8.) He will excuse the souls of his people, and lay the fault upon their flesh, which has greatest affinity with Satan, if through weakness and infirmity we do not do as we should. (Matt. xxvi. 41. Rom. vii.)

Now, as I said, all these things happen unto us, both infirmities and pity, because and for that we were once in the fire, and for that the weakness of sin abides upon us to this day. But none of this favour could come to us, nor could we, by any means, cause that our infirmities should work for us thus advantageously; but that Christ our advocate stands our friend, and pleads for us as he doth.

But again, before I pass this over, I will, for the clearing of this, present you with a few more considerations, which are of another rank: to wit, that Christ our advocate, as such, makes mention of our weaknesses so, against Satan, and before his Father, as to turn all to our advantage.

(1.) We are, therefore, to be saved by grace, because by reason of sin we are disabled from keeping of the law. (Deut. ix. 5. Isa. lxiv. 6.)

(2.) We have given unto us the Spirit of grace to help, because we can do nothing that is good without it. (Eph. ii. 5. Rom. viii. 26.)

(3.) God has put Christ's righteousness upon us to cover our nakedness therewith, because we have none of our own to do it withal. (Phil. iii. 7, 8. Ezek. xvi. 8.)

(4.) God alloweth us to ride in the bosom of Christ to the grave, and from thence in the bosom of angels to heaven, because our own legs are not able to carry us thither. (Isa. xl. 11; xlvi. 4. Ps. xlviii. 14. Luke xvi. 22.)

(5.) God has made his Son our head, our priest, our advocate, our Saviour, our captain, that we may be delivered from all the infirmities and all the fiends that attend us, and that plot to do us hurt. (Eph. i. 22. Col. i. 18. Heb. vii. 21.)

(6.) God has put the fallen angels into chains, (2 Pet. ii. 4. Rev. xx. 1, 2,) that they might not follow us too fast, and has enlarged us, (Ps. iv. 1,) and directed our feet in the way of his steps, that we may haste us to the strong tower and city of refuge for succour and safety, and has given good angels a charge to look to us. (Heb. i. 14. Ps. xxxiv. 7.)

(7.) God has promised that we, at our counting days, shall be spared, " as a man spareth his own son that serveth him." (Mal. iii. 17.)

Now, from all these things, it appears that we have indulgence at God's hand, and that our weaknesses, as our Christ manages the matter for us, are so far off from laying a block or bar in the way to the enjoyment of favour, that they also work for our good; yea, and God's foresight of them has so kindled his bowels and compassions to us, as to put him upon devising of such things for our relief, which by no means could have been, had not sin been with us in the world, and had not the best of the saints been as a brand plucked out of the burning.

I have seen men (and yet they are worse than God) take most care of, and, also, best provide for, those of their children that have been most infirm and helpless; and our advocate shall gather his lambs with his arms, and carry them in his bosom; yea, and I know that there is such an art in showing and making mention of weaknesses as shall make the tears stand in a parent's eyes, and as shall make him search to the bottom of his purse to find out what may do his weakling good. Christ, also, has that excellent art, as he is an advocate with the Father for us: he can so make mention of us and of our infirmities, while he pleads before God, against the devil, for us, that he can make the bowels of the Almighty yearn towards us, and to wrap us up in their compassions. You read much of the pity, compassion, and of the yearning of the bowels of the mighty God towards his people; all which, I think, is kindled and made burn towards us, by the pleading of our advocate.

I have seen fathers offended with their children; but when a brother had turned a skilful advocate, the anger has been appeased, and the means have been concealed. We read but little of this advocate's office of Jesus Christ, yet much of the fruit of it is extended to the churches. But as the cause of smiles, after offences committed, is made manifest afterwards, so at the day when God will open all things, we shall see how many times our Lord, as an advocate, pleaded for us, and redeemed us by his so pleading, into the enjoyment of smiles and embraces, who, for sin, but a while before, were under frowns and chastisements.

And thus much for the making out how Christ doth manage his office of being an advocate for us with the Father. "If any man sin, we have an advocate with the Father, Jesus Christ the righteous."

THIRDLY. And I shall come now to the third head; to wit, *to show you more particularly who they are that have Jesus Christ for their advocate.*

In my handling of this head, I shall show, First. That this office of an advocate differeth from that of a priest, and how. Secondly. I shall show you how far Christ extendeth this his office of advocateship, I mean, in matters concerning the people of God. And then, Thirdly. I shall come more directly to show who they are that have Christ for their advocate.

First. For the first of these, That this office of Christ, as an advocate, differeth from that of a priest. That he is a priest, a priest for ever, I heartily acknowledge; but that his priesthood and advocateship should be one and the self-same office, I cannot believe.

1. Because they differ in name. We may as well say a father, as such, is a son, or that father and son is the self-same relation, as say a priest and an advocate, as to office, are but one and the same thing. They differ in name as much as

priest and sacrifice do : a priest is one, and a sacrifice is another ; and though Christ is priest and sacrifice too, yet as a priest he is not a sacrifice ; nor, as a sacrifice, a priest.

2. As they differ in name, so they differ in the nature of office. A priest is to slay a sacrifice ; an advocate is to plead a cause ; a priest is to offer his sacrifice, to the end that, by the merit thereof, he may appease ; an advocate is to plead, to plead according to law. A priest is to make intercession, by virtue of his sacrifice ; an advocate is to plead law, because amends is made.

3. As they differ in name and nature, so they also differ as to their extent. The priesthood of Christ extendeth itself to the whole of God's elect, whether called or in their sins ; but Christ, as advocate, pleadeth only for the children.

4. As they differ in name, in nature, and extent, so they differ as to the persons with whom they have to do. We read not anywhere that Christ, as priest, has to do with the devil as an antagonist ; but, as an advocate, he hath.

5. As they differ in these, so they differ as to the matters about which they are employed. Christ, as priest, concerns himself with every wry thought, and, also, with the least imperfection or infirmity that attends our most holy things ; but Christ, as advocate, doth not so, as I have already showed.

6. So that Christ, as priest, goes before, and Christ, as an advocate, comes after ; Christ, as priest, continually intercedes ; Christ, as advocate, in case of great transgressions, pleads : Christ, as priest, has need to act always, but Christ, as advocate, sometimes only. Christ, as priest, acts in times of peace ; but Christ, as advocate, in times of broils, turmoils, and sharp contentions : wherefore, Christ, as advocate, is, as I may call him, a reserve ; and his time is then to arise, to stand up and plead, when HIS are clothed with some filthy sin that of late they have fallen into, as David, Joshua, or Peter. When some such thing is committed by them, as ministereth to the enemy a show of ground to question the truth of their grace ; or when it is a question, and to be debated, whether it can stand with the laws of heaven, with the merits of Christ, and the honour of God, that such an one should be saved ? Now let an advocate come forth, now let him have time to plead, for this is a fit occasion for the saints' advocate to stand up to plead for the salvation of his people. But,

Secondly. I come next to show you how far this office of an advocate is extended. I hinted at this before, so now shall be the more brief.

1. By this office he offereth no sacrifice ; he only, as to matters of justice, pleads the sacrifice offered.

2. By this office he obtains the conversion of none : he only thereby secureth the converted from the damnation which their adversary, for sins after light and profession, endeavoureth to bring them to.

3. By this office he prevents not temporal punishment, but by it he chiefly preserveth the soul from hell.

4. By this office he brings in no justifying righteousness for us, he only thereby prevaileth to have the dispose of that brought in by himself, as priest, for the justifying of those, by a new and fresh act, who had made their justification doubtful by new falls into sin. And this is plain in the history of our Joshua, so often mentioned before. (Zech. iii.)

5. As priest, he hath obtained eternal redemption for us ; and as advocate, he by law, maintaineth our right thereto, against the devil and all his angels.

Thirdly. I come now to show you who they are that have Jesus Christ for their advocate. And this I shall do first, more generally, and then shall be more particular and distinct about it.

1. More generally. *They are all the truly gracious ; those that are the children by adoption ;* this the text affirmeth—" Little children, I write unto you, that ye sin not." And " If any man sin, we have an advocate with the Father, Jesus Christ the righteous." They are, then, the children, the children by adoption, that are the persons concerned in the advocateship of Jesus Christ. The priesthood of Christ extendeth itself to the whole body of the elect, but the advocateship of Christ doth not so. This is further cleared by this apostle ; and in this very text, if you consider what immediately follows—" We have an Advocate," says he, and he is also the propitiation for our sins. He is our advocate, and also our priest. As an advocate, ours only ; but as a propitiation not ours only, but also for the sins of the whole world : to be sure, for the elect throughout the world,— and they that will extend it further, let them.

And I say again, had he not intended that there should have been a straiter limit put to the advocateship of Christ than he would have us put to his priestly office, what needed he, when he speaketh of the propitiation which relates to Christ as priest, have added, " And not for ours only ?" As an advocate, then, he engageth for us that are children ; and as a priest, too, he hath appeased God's wrath for our sins ; but as an advocate his offices are confined to the children only, but as a priest he is not so. He is the propitiation for our sins, and not for ours only. The sense, therefore, of the apostle should, I think, be this : That Christ, as a priest, hath offered a propitiatory sacrifice for all ; but as an advocate he pleadeth only for the children. Children, we have an advocate to ourselves, and he is also our priest ; but as he is a priest, he is not ours only, but maketh, as such, amends for all that shall be saved. The elect, therefore, have the Lord Jesus for their advocate then, and then only, when they are by calling put among the children ; because, as advocate, he is peculiarly the children's, " My little children, we have an advocate."

Objection. But he also saith, " If any man sin,

we have an advocate;" any man that sinneth seems, by the text, notwithstanding what you say, "to have an advocate with the Father."

Answer. By *any man,* must not be meant any of the world, nor any of the elect, but any man in faith and grace; for he still limits this general term, "any man," with this restriction, "we"— Children, "if any man sin, we have an advocate." WE, any man of us. And this is yet further made appear, since he saith that it is to them he writes, not only here, but further in this chapter—"I write unto YOU, little children; I write unto you, fathers; I write unto you, young men." (ver. 12, 13.) These are the persons intended in the text, for under these three heads are comprehended all men; for they are either children, and so men in nature; or young men, and so men in strength; or else they are fathers, and so aged, and of experience. Add to this, by "any man," that the apostle intendeth not to enlarge himself beyond the persons that are in grace; but to supply what was wanting by that term "little children;" for since the strongest saint may have need of an advocate, as well as the most feeble of the flock, why should the apostle leave it to be so understood as if the children, and the children only, had an interest in that office? Wherefore, after he had said, "My little children, I write unto you, that ye sin not;" he then adds, with enlargement, "If any man sin, we have an advocate with the Father." Yet the little children may well be mentioned first, since they most want the knowledge of it, are most feeble, and so by sin may be forced most frequently to act faith on Christ, as advocate. Besides, they are most ready, through temptation, to question whether they have so good a right to Christ in all his offices as have better and more well-grown saints; and, therefore, they, in this apostle's salutation, are first set down in the catalogue of names—"My little children, I write unto you, that ye sin not, and if any man sin, we have an advocate with the Father, Jesus Christ the righteous." So, then, the children of God are they who have the Lord Jesus, an advocate for them with the Father. The least and biggest, the oldest and youngest, the feeblest and the strongest; ALL the children have an advocate with the Father, Jesus Christ the righteous.

(1.) Since, then, the children have Christ for their advocate, art thou a child? Art thou begotten of God by his word? (James i. 18.) Hast thou in thee the spirit of adoption? (Gal. iv. 6.) Canst thou in faith say, Father, Father, to God? Then is Christ thy advocate! thine advocate, "now to appear in the presence of God for thee." (Heb. ix. 24.) To appear there, and to plead there, in the face of the court of heaven, for thee; to plead there against thine adversary, whose accusations are dreadful, whose subtilty is great, whose malice is inconceivable, and whose rage intolerable: to plead there before a just God, a righteous God, a sin-revenging God: before whose face thou

wouldst die if thou wast to show thyself, and at his bar to plead thine own cause. But,

(2.) There is a difference in children; some are bigger than some; there are children and little children—"My little children, I write unto you." Little children; some of the little children can neither say Father, nor so much as know that they themselves are children.

This is true in nature, and so it is in grace; wherefore, notwithstanding what was said under the first head, it doth not follow, that if I be a child I must certainly know it, and also be able to call God Father. Let the first, then, serve to poise and balance the confident ones, and let this be for the relief of those more feeble; for they that are children, whether they know it or no, have Jesus Christ for their advocate, for Christ is assigned to be our advocate by the Judge, by the King, by our God and Father, although we have not known it. True, at present, there can come from hence, to them that are thus concerned in the advocateship of Christ, but little comfort; but yet it yields them great security; they have "an advocate with the Father, Jesus Christ the righteous." God knows this, the devil feels this, and the children shall have the comfort of it afterwards. I say, the time is coming when they shall know that even then, when they knew it not, they had an advocate with the Father; an advocate who was neither loath, nor afraid, nor ashamed, to plead for their defence against their proudest foe.

And will not this, when they know it, yield them comfort? Doubtless it will; yea, more, and of a better kind, than that which flows from the knowledge that one is born to crowns and kingdoms.

Again; as he is an advocate for the children, so he is also, as before was hinted, for the strong and experienced; for no strength in this world secureth from the rage of hell; nor can any experience, while we are here, fortify us against his assaults. There is also an incidency in the best to sin; and the bigger man, the bigger fall; for the more hurt, and the greater damage. Wherefore it is of absolute necessity that an advocate be provided for the strong as for the weak. "Any man;" he that is most holy, most reformed, most refined, and most purified, may as soon be in the dirt as the weakest Christian; and, so far as I can see, Satan's design is against them most. I am sure the greatest sins have been committed by the biggest saints. This wayfaring man came to David's house, and when he stood up against Israel, he provoked David to number the people. (2 Sam. xii. 4, 7. 1 Chron. xxi. 1.) Wherefore they have as much need of an advocate as have the youngest and most feeble of the flock. What a mind had he to try a fall with Peter! and how quickly did he break the neck of Judas! The like, without doubt, he had done to Peter, had not Jesus, by stepping in, prevented. As long as sin is in our flesh, there is danger. Indeed, he saith of the young men that they are strong, and that they have overcome the wicked one; but he doth not say they have killed him. As long as the devil is alive there is danger; and though a strong Christian may be too hard for, and may overcome him in one thing, he may be too hard for, yea, and may overcome him two for one afterwards. Thus he served David, and thus he served Peter, and thus he, in our day, has served many more. The strongest are weak, the wisest are fools, when suffered to be sifted as wheat in Satan's sieve; yea, and have often been so proved, to the wounding of their great hearts, and the dishonour of religion. To conclude this: God of his mercy hath sufficiently declared the truth of what I say, by preparing for the best, the strongest, and most sanctified, as well as for the least, weakest, and most feeble saint, an advocate—"My little children, I write unto you, that ye sin not. And if any man sin, we have an advocate with the Father, Jesus Christ the righteous."

2. *Object.* But some may object, that what has been said as to discovering for whom Christ is an advocate has been too general, and, therefore, would have me come more to particulars, else they can get no comfort.

Ans. Well, inquiring soul, so I will; and, therefore, hearken to what I say.

(1.) Wouldest thou know whether Christ is thine advocate or no? I ask, *Hast thou entertained him* so to be? When men have suits of law depending in any of the King's courts above, they entertain their attorney or advocate to plead their cause, and so he pleads for them. I say, hast thou entertained Jesus Christ for thy lawyer to plead thy cause? "Plead my cause, O Lord," said David, (Ps. xxxv. 1;) and again, "Judge me, O God, and plead my cause." (Ps. xliii. 1.) This, therefore, is the first thing that I would propound to thee: Hast thou, with David, entertained him for thy lawyer, or, with good Hezekiah, cried out, "O Lord, I am oppressed; undertake for me." (Isa. xxxviii. 14.) What sayest thou, soul? Hast thou been with him, and prayed him to plead thy cause, and cried unto him to undertake for thee? This I call entertaining of him to be thy advocate, and I choose to follow the similitude, both because the Scripture seems to smile upon such a way of discourse, and because thy question doth naturally lead me to it. Wherefore, I ask again, hast thou been with him? Hast thou entertained him? Hast thou desired him to plead thy cause?

Quest. Thou wilt say unto me, How should I know that I have done so?

Ans. I answer, Art thou sensible that thou hast an action commenced against thee in that high court of justice that is above? I say, Art thou sensible of this? For the defendants (and all God's people are defendants) do not use to entertain their lawyers, but from knowledge, that an action either is, or may be, commenced against them before the God of heaven. If thou sayest yea, then I ask, Who told thee that thou standest accused for transgression before the judgment-seat of God?

I say, Who told thee so? Hath the Holy Ghost, hath the world, or hath thy conscience? For nothing else, as I know of, can bring such tidings to thy soul.

Again: Hast thou found a failure in all others that might have been entertained to plead thy cause? Some make their sighs, their tears, their prayers, and their reformations, their advocates—Hast thou tried these, and found them wanting: Hast thou seen thy state to be desperate, if the Lord Jesus doth not undertake to plead thy cause? for Jesus is not entertained so long as men can make shift without him. But when it comes to this point, I perish for ever, notwithstanding the help of all, if the Lord Jesus steps not in. Then Lord Jesus, Lord Jesus, good Lord Jesus! undertake for me. Hast thou therefore been with Jesus Christ as concerned in thy soul, as heartily concerned about the action that thou perceivest to be commenced against thee?

Quest. You will say, How should I know that?

Ans. I answer, Hast thou well considered the nature of the crime wherewith thou standest charged at the bar of God? Hast thou also considered the justness of the Judge?

Again I ask, Hast thou considered what truth, as to matter of fact, there is in the things whereof thou standest accused? Also, Hast thou considered the cunning, the malice, and diligence of thy adversary, with the greatness of the loss thou art like to sustain, shouldst thou with Ahab, in the book of Kings, (1 Kings xxii. 17—23,) or with the hypocrites in the sixth of Isaiah, (vi. 5—10.) have the verdict of the Lord God go out from the throne against thee?

I ask thee these questions, because if thou art in the knowledge of these things to seek, or if thou art not deeply concerned about the greatness of the damage that will certainly overtake thee, and that for ever, shouldest thou be indeed accused before God, and have none to plead thy cause, thou hast not, nor canst not, let what will come upon thee, have been with Jesus Christ to plead thy cause; and so, let thy case be never so desperate, thou standest alone, and hast no helper, (Job xxx. 13; ix. 13.) Or if thou hast, they, not being the advocate of God's appointing, must needs fall with thee, and with thy burden. Wherefore, consider of this seriously, and return thy answer to God, who can tell if truth shall be found in thy answers, better by far than any; for it is he that tries the reins and the heart, and therefore to him I refer thee. But.

(2.) Wouldst thou know whether Jesus Christ is thine advocate? Then I ask again, *Hast thou revealed thy cause unto him?*—I say, Hast thou revealed thy cause unto him? For he that goeth to law for his right, must not only go to a lawyer, and say, Sir, I am in trouble, and am to have a trial at law with mine enemy, pray undertake my cause; but he must also reveal to his lawyer his cause. He must go to him and tell him what is the matter, how things stand, where the shoe pinches, and so. Thus did the church of old, and thus doth every true Christian now. For though nothing can be hid from him, yet he will have things out of thine own mouth; he will have thee to reveal thy matters unto him. (Matt. xx. 32.) "O Lord of hosts," said Jeremiah, "that judgest righteously, that triest the reins and the heart, let me see thy vengeance on them: for unto thee have I revealed my cause." (Jer. xi. 20.) And again; "But, O Lord of hosts, that triest the righteous, and seest the reins and the heart, let me see thy vengeance on them; for unto thee have I opened my cause." (Jer. xx. 12.) Seest thou here, how saints of old were wont to do? how they did, not only in a general way, entreat Christ to plead their cause, but in a particular way, go to him and reveal, or open their cause unto him?

O! it is excellent to behold how some sinners will do this when they get Christ and themselves in a closet alone; when they, upon their bare knees, are pouring out of their souls before him; or, like the woman in the gospel, telling of him all the truth. (Mark v.) O! saith the soul, Lord, I am come to thee upon an earnest business; I am arrested by Satan: the bailiff was mine own conscience, and I am like to be accused before the judgment-seat of God. My salvation lies at stake; I am questioned for my interest in heaven; I am afraid of the Judge; my heart condemns me. (1 John iii. 20.) Mine enemy is subtle, and wanteth not malice to prosecute me to death, and then to hell. Also, Lord, I am sensible that the law is against me, for indeed I have horribly sinned, and thus and thus have I done. Here I lie open to law, and there I lie open to law; here I have given the adversary advantage, and there he will surely have a hank against me. Lord, I am distressed, undertake for me! And there are some things that thou must be acquainted with about thine advocate, before thou wilt venture to go thus far with him. As,

1. Thou must know him to be a friend, and not an enemy, unto whom thou openest thy heart: and until thou comest to know that Christ is a friend to thee, or to souls in thy condition, thou wilt never reveal thy cause unto him, not thy whole cause unto him. And it is from this that so many that have soul-causes hourly depending before the throne of God, and that are in danger every day of eternal damnation, forbear to entertain Jesus Christ for their advocate, and so wickedly conceal their matters from him; but "he that hideth his sins shall not prosper." (Prov. xxviii. 13.) This, therefore, must first be believed by thee before thou wilt reveal thy cause unto him.

2. A man, when his estate is called in question, I mean his right and title thereto, will be very cautious, especially if he also questions his title to it himself, unto whom he reveals that affair; he must know him to be one that is not only friendly, but faithful, to whom he reveals such a secret as this. Why, thus it is with Christ and the soul. If the soul is not somewhat persuaded of the faithfulness of Christ—to wit, that if he can do him no good, he will do him no harm, he will never reveal his cause unto him, but will seek to hide his counsel from the Lord.

This, therefore, is another thing by which thou mayest know that thou hast Christ for thine advocate, if thou hast heartily and in very deed revealed thy cause unto him.

Now, they that do honestly reveal their cause to their lawyer, will endeavour to possess him, as I hinted before, with the worst; they will, with words, make it as bad as they may; for, think they, by that means I shall prepare him for the worst that mine enemy can do. And thus souls deal with Jesus Christ; see Ps. li., also xxxviii., with several others that might be named, and see if God's people have not done so. "I said," saith David, "that I would confess my transgressions, against myself, Lord; and thou forgavest the iniquity of my sin." But,

(3.) Hast thou Jesus Christ for thine advocate? or wouldst thou know if thou hast? Then I ask again, *Hast thou committed thy cause to him?* When a man entertains his lawyer to stand for him and to plead his cause, he doth not only reveal, but commit his cause unto him. "I would seek unto God," said Eliphaz to Job, "and unto him would I commit my cause." (Job v. 8.) Now there is a difference betwixt revealing my cause and committing of it to a man. To reveal my cause is to open it to one; and to commit it to him is to trust it in his hand. Many a man will reveal his cause to him unto whom he will yet be afraid to commit it; but now, he that entertains a lawyer to plead his cause, doth not only reveal but commit his cause unto him. As, suppose right to his estate be called in question; why, then, he not only reveals his cause to his lawyer, but puts into his hands his evidences, deeds, leases, mortgages, bonds, or what else he hath, to show a title to his estate by. And thus do Christians deal with Christ; they deliver up all unto him, to wit, all their signs, evidences, promises, and assurances, which they have thought they had for heaven and the salvation of their souls, and have desired him to peruse, to search, and try them every one. "And see if there be any wicked way in me, and lead me in the way everlasting." (Ps. cxxxix. 23, 24.) This is committing of thy cause to Christ. and this is the hardest task of all, for the man that doth thus, he trusteth Christ with all; and it implieth, that he will live and die, stand and fall, lose and win, according as Christ will manage his business. Thus did Paul, (2 Tim. i. 12,) and thus Peter admonisheth us to do. Now he that doth this must be convinced,

1. Of the ability of Jesus Christ to defend him; for a man will not commit so great a concern as his all is to his friend; no, not to his friend, be he never so faithful, if he perceives not in him ability to save him, and to preserve what he hath, against

all the cavils of an enemy. And hence it is that the ability of Jesus Christ, as to the saving of his people, is so much insisted on in the Scripture; as, "I have laid help upon one that is mighty." (Ps. lxxxix. 19.) "I that speak in righteousness, mighty to save." (Isa. lxiii. 1.) And again, "I will send them a Saviour, and a great one." (Isa. xix. 20.)

2. As they must be convinced of his ability to help them, so they must of his courage. A man that has parts sufficient may yet fail his friend for want of courage; wherefore, the courage and greatness of Christ's Spirit, as to his undertaking of the cause of his people, is also amply set out in Scripture. "He shall not fail nor be discouraged, till he have set judgment in the earth," "till he send forth judgment unto victory." (Isa. xlii. 4. Matt. xii. 20.)

3. They must also be convinced of his willingness to do this for them; for though one be able and of courage sufficient, yet if he is not willing to undertake one's cause, what is it the better? Wherefore, he declareth his willingness also, and how ready he is to stand up to plead the cause of the poor and of them that are in want. "The Lord will plead their cause, and spoil the soul of those that spoiled them." (Prov. xxii. 23.)

4. They must also be convinced of this, that Christ is tender, and will not be offended at the dulness of his client. Some men can reveal their cause to their lawyers better than some, and are more serviceable and handy in that affair than others. But, saith the Christian, I am dull and sorry that way, will not Christ be shuff and shy with me because of this? Honest heart! He hath a supply of thy defects in himself, and knoweth what thou wantest, and where the shoe pinches, though thou art not able distinctly to open matters to him. The child is pricked with a pin, and lies crying in the mother's lap, but cannot show to its mother where the pin is; but there is pity enough in the mother to supply this defect of the child; wherefore she undresses it, opens it, searches every clout from head to the foot of the child, and so finds where the pin is. Thus will thy lawyer do; he will search and find out thy difficulties, and where Satan seeketh an advantage of thee, accordingly will provide his remedy.

5. O, but will he not be weary? The prophet complains of some, "that they weary God." (Isa. vii. 13.) And mine is a very cross and intricate cause; I have wearied many a good man while I have been telling my tale unto him, and I am afraid that I shall also weary Jesus Christ.

Ans. Soul, he suffered and did bear with the manners of Israel forty years in the wilderness; and hast thou tried him half so long? (Acts xiii. 18.) The good souls that have gone before thee have found him "a tried stone," a sure one to be trusted to as to this. (Isa. xxviii. 16.) And the prophet saith positively that "he fainteth not, neither is weary;" and that "there is no searching of his understanding." (Isa. xl. 28.) Let all these

things prevail with thee to believe, that if thou hast committed thy cause unto him, he will bring it to pass, to a good pass, to so good a pass as will glorify God, honour Christ, save thee, and shame the devil. But,

(4.) Wouldst thou know whether Jesus Christ is thine advocate, whether he has taken in hand to plead thy cause? Then, I ask, *dost thou,* together with what has been mentioned before, *wait upon him according to his counsel, until things shall come to a legal issue?* Thus must clients do. There is a great many turnings and windings about suits and trials at law; the enemy, also, with his supersedeas, cavils, and motions, often defers a speedy issue. Wherefore, the man, whose is the concern must wait; as the prophet said, "I will look," said he, "unto the Lord; I will wait for the god of my salvation." But how long, prophet, wilt thou wait? Why, says he, "until he plead my cause, and execute judgment for me." (Micah vii. 7—10.)

Perhaps when thy cause is tried, things for the present are upon this issue; thy adversary, indeed, is cast, but whether thou shalt have an absolute discharge, as Peter had, or a conditional one, as David, and as the Corinthians had, that is the question. (2 Sam. xii. 10—14.) True, thou shalt be completely saved at last; but yet whether it is not best to leave to thee a memento of God's displeasure against thy sin, by awarding that the sword shall never depart from thy house, or that some sore sickness or other distresses shall haunt thee as long as thou livest, or perhaps, that thou shalt walk without the light of God's countenance for several years, and a day. Now, if any of these three things happen unto thee, thou must exercise patience, and wait. Thus did David—"I waited patiently;" and again he exercises his soul in this virtue, saying, "My soul, wait thou only upon him; for my expectation is from him." (Ps. lxii. 5.) For now we are judged of the Lord, *that we may not be condemned with the world.* And by this judgment, though it sets us free from their damnation, yet we are involved in many troubles, and, perhaps, must wait many a day before we can know that, as to the main, the verdict hath gone on our side. Thus, therefore, in order to thy waiting upon him without fainting, it is meet that thou shouldest know the methods of him that manages thy cause for thee in heaven; and suffer not mistrust to break in and bear sway in thy soul, for "he will" at length "bring thee forth to the light, and thou shalt behold his righteousness. She, also, that is thine enemy shall see it, and shame shall cover her which said unto thee, Where is thy God?" (Micah vii. 10.)

Quest. But what is it to wait upon him according to his counsel?

Ans. 1. To wait is to be of good courage, to live in expectation, and to look for deliverance, though thou hast sinned against thy God. "Wait on the Lord, be of good courage, and he shall strengthen thine heart; wait, I say, on the Lord." (Ps. xxvii. 14.)

2. To wait upon him is to keep his way, to walk humbly in his appointments. "Wait on the Lord, and keep his way, and he shall exalt thee to inherit the land." (Ps. xxxvii. 34.)

3. To wait upon him is to observe and keep those directions which he giveth thee; to observe even while he stands up to plead thy cause; for without this, or not doing this, a man may mar his cause in the hand of him that is to plead it: wherefore, keep thee far from an evil matter, have no correspondence with thine enemy, walk humbly for the wickedness that thou hast committed, and loathe and abhor thyself for it, in dust and ashes. To these things doth the Scripture everywhere direct us.

4. To wait, is also to incline, to hearken to those further directions which thou mayest receive from the mouth of thine advocate, as to any fresh matters that may forward and expedite a good issue of thine affair in the court of heaven. The want of this was the reason that the deliverance of Israel did linger so long in former times. "O," says he, "that my people had hearkened unto me, and Israel had walked in my ways! I should soon have subdued their enemies, and turned my hand against their adversaries. The haters of the Lord should have submitted themselves unto him; but their time should have endured for ever." (Ps. lxxxi. 13—15.)

5. Also, if it tarry long, wait for it. Do not conclude that thy cause is lost because at present thou dost not hear from court. Cry, if thou wilt, O, when wilt thou come unto me? But never let such a wicked thought pass through thy heart, saying, "This evil is of the Lord; what should I wait for the Lord any longer?" (2 Kings vi. 33.)

6. But take heed that thou turnest not thy waiting into sleeping. Wait thou must, and wait patiently too; but yet wait with much longing and earnestness of spirit, to see or hear how matters go above. You may observe, that when a man that dwells far down in the country, and has some business at the term, in this or another of the king's courts, though he will wait his lawyer's time and conveniency, yet he will so wait as still to inquire at the post-house, or at the carrier's; or if a neighbour comes down from term, at his mouth, for letters, or any other intelligence, if possibly he may arrive to know how his cause speeds, and whether his adversary or he has the day. Thus, I say, thou must wait upon thine advocate. His ordinances are his post-house, his ministers are his carriers, where tidings from heaven are to be had, and where those that are sued in that court by the devil may, at one time or another, hear from their lawyer, their advocate, how things are like to go. Wherefore, I say, wait at the posts of wisdom's house; go to ordinances with expectation to hear from thy advocate there; for he will send in due time; "though it tarry, wait for it; because it will surely come, and will not tarry."

(Hab. ii. 1—3.) And now, soul, I have answered thy request, and let me hear what thou sayest unto me.

Soul.—Truly, says the soul, methinks that by what you have said, I may have this blessed Jesus to be mine advocate; for I think, verily, I have entertained him to be mine advocate. I have also revealed my cause unto him, yea, committed both it and myself unto him; and, as you say, I wait; oh! I wait! and my eyes fail with looking upwards. Fain would I hear how my soul standeth in the sight of God, and whether my sins, which I have committed since light and grace were given unto me be, by mine advocate, taken out of the hand of the devil, and by mine advocate removed as far from me as the ends of the earth are asunder; whether the verdict has gone on my side, and what a shout there was among the angels when they saw it went well with me! But, alas! I have waited, and that a long time, and have, as you advise, ran from ordinance to minister, and from minister to ordinance, or, as you phrase it, from the post to the carrier, and from the carrier to the post-house, to see if I could hear aught from heaven how matters went about my soul there. I have also asked those that pass by the way, "if they saw him whom my soul loveth," and if they had anything to communicate to me? But nothing can I get or find but generals; as, that I have an advocate there, and that he pleadeth the cause of his people, and that he will thoroughly plead their cause. But what he has done for ME, of that as yet I am ignorant. I doubt if my soul shall by him be effectually secured, that yet a conditional verdict will be awarded concerning me, and that much bitter will be mixed with my sweet, and that I must drink gall and wormwood for my folly: for if David, and Asa, and Hezekiah, and such good men, were so served for their sins, (2 Chron. xvi. 7, 12,) why should I look for other dealing at the hand of God? But as to this, I will endeavour to "bear the indignation of the Lord, because I have sinned against him," (Mic. vii. 9,) and shall count it an infinite mercy if this judgment comes to me from him, that I may "not be condemned with the world." (1 Cor. xi. 32.) I know it is dreadful walking in darkness; but if that also shall be the Lord's lot upon me, I pray God I may have faith enough to stay upon him till death, and then will the clouds blow over, and I shall see him in the light of the living.

Mine enemy, the devil, as you say, is of an inveigling temper; and though he has accused me before the judgment-seat of God, yet when he comes to me at any time, he glavers and flatters as if he never did mean me harm; but I think it is that he might get further advantage against me. But I carry it now at a further distance than formerly; and O that I was at the remotest distance not only from him, but also from that self of mine, that laboureth with him for my undoing!

But although I say these things now, and to

you, yet I have my solitary hours, and in them I have other strange thoughts; for thus I think, my cause is bad, I have sinned, and I have been vile. I am ashamed myself of mine own doings, and have given mine enemy the best end of the staff. The law, and reason, and my conscience, plead for him against me; and all is true he puts into his charge against me, that I have sinned more times than there be hairs on my head. I know not of anything that ever I did in my life but it had flaw, or wrinkle, or spot, or some such thing in it. Mine eyes have seen vileness in the best of my doings; what, then, think you, must God needs see in them? Nor can I do anything yet, for all I know that I am accused by my enemy before the judgment-seat of God, better than what already is imperfect. "I lie down in my shame, and my confusion covers my face." "I have sinned: what shall I do unto thee, O thou preserver of men?" (Jer. iii. 25. Job vii. 20.)

Reply. Well, soul, I have heard what thou hast said, and if all be true which thou hast said, it is good, and gives me ground of hope that Jesus Christ is become thine advocate; and if that be so, no doubt but thy trial will come to a good conclusion. And be not afraid because of the holiness of God; for thine advocate has this for his advantage, that he pleads before a judge that is just, and against an enemy that is unholy and rejected. Nor let the thoughts of the badness of thy cause terrify thee overmuch. Cause thou hast, indeed, to be humble, and thou dost well to cover thy face with shame; and it is no matter how base and vile thou art in thine own eyes, provided that it comes not by renewed acts of rebellion, but through a spiritual sight of thine imperfections. Only let me advise thee here to stop. Let not thy shame, nor thy self-abasing apprehension of thyself, drive thee from the firm and permanent ground of hope, which is the promise and the doctrine of an advocate with the Father. No; let not the apprehension of the badness of thy cause do it, forasmuch as he did never yet take cause in hand that was good, perfectly good of itself; and his excellency is, to make a man stand that has a bad cause; yea, he can make a bad cause good, in a way of justice and righteousness.

FOURTHLY. And, for thy further encouragement in this matter, I will here bring in the fourth chief head, to wit, *to show what excellent privilege* (I mean over and above what has already been spoken of) *they have that are made partakers of the benefit of this office*:—"If any man sin, we have an advocate with the Father, Jesus Christ the righteous."

Privilege 1. Thy advocate pleads to a price paid, to a propitiation made; and this is a great advantage. Yea, he pleads to a satisfaction made for all wrongs done, or to be done, by his elect: "For by one offering he hath perfected for ever them that are sanctified." (Heb. x. 10, 14; ix. 26.) "By one offering," that is, by the offering of himself, by one offering once offered, once

offered in the end of the world. This, I say, thine advocate pleads. When Satan brings in fresh accusations for more transgressions against the law of God, he forces not Christ to shift his first plea. I say, he puts him not to his shifts at all; for the price once paid hath in it sufficient value (would God impute it to that end) to take away the sin of the whole world. There is a man that hath brethren; he is rich, and they are poor (and this is the case betwixt Christ and us), and the rich brother goeth to his Father, and saith, Thou art related to my brethren with me, and out of my store, I pray thee, let them have sufficient, and for thy satisfaction I will put into thy hand the whole of what I have, which perhaps is worth an hundred thousand pounds by the year; and this other sum I also give, that they be not disinherited. Now, will not this last his poor brethren to spend upon a great while? But Christ's worth can never be drawn dry.

Now, set the case again, that some ill-conditioned man should take notice that these poor men live all upon the spend (and saints do so), and should come to the good man's house, and complain to him of the spending of his sons, and that while their elder brother stands by. What do you think the elder brother would reply, if he was as good-natured as Christ? Why, he would say, I have yet with my Father in store for my brethren, wherefore then seekest thou to stop his hand? As he is just, he must give them for their conveniency; yea, and as for their extravagancies, I have satisfied for them so well, that, however he afflicteth them, he will not disinherit them. I hope you will read and hear this, not like them that say, "Let us do evil that good may come," but like those whom the love of Christ constrains to be better. However, this is the children's bread, that which they have need of, and without which they cannot live; and they must have it, though Satan should put pins into it, therewith to choke the dogs. And, for the further clearing of this, I will present you with these few considerations:

1. Those that are most sanctified have yet a body of sin and death in them, and so also it will be, while they continue in this world. (Rom. vii. 24.) 2. This body of sin strives to break out, and will break out, to the polluting of the conversation, if saints be not the more watchful. (vi. 12.) Yea, it has broke out in a most sad manner, and that in the strongest saints. (Gal. v. 17.) 3. Christ offereth no new sacrifice for the salvation of these his people. "For, being raised from the dead, he dieth no more." (Rom. vi. 9.) So then, if saints sin, they must be saved, if saved at all, by virtue of the offering already offered; and if so, then all Christ's pleas as an advocate are grounded upon that one offering which before, as a priest, he presented God with for the taking away of sin. So then, Christians live upon this old stock; their transgressions are forgiven for the sake of the worth, that yet God finds in the offering that

Christ hath offered. And all Christ's pleadings as an advocate are grounded upon the sufficiency and worth of that one sacrifice; I mean, all his pleadings with his Father, as to the charge which the accuser brings in against them. For though thou art a man of infirmity, and so incident to nothing as to stumble and fall, if grace doth not prevent—and it doth not always prevent—yet the value and worth of the price that was once paid for thee is not yet worn out; and Christ, as an advocate, still pleadeth, as occasion is given, that, with success to thy salvation. And this privilege they have, who indeed have Christ for their advocate; and I put it here, in the first place, because all other do depend upon it.

Privilege 2. Thine advocate, as he pleadeth a price already paid, so, and therefore, he pleads for himself as for thee. We are all concerned in one bottom: if he sinks, we sink; if we sink, he sinks. Give me leave to make out my meaning.

1. Christ pleads the value and virtue of the price of his blood and sacrifice for us. And admit of this horrible supposition a little, for argument's sake, that though Christ pleads the worth of what, as priest, he offereth, yet the soul for whom he so pleads perishes eternally. Now, where lieth the fault? In sin, you say: true; but it is because there was more virtue in sin to damn, than there was in the blood pleaded by Christ to save; for he pleaded his merit, he put it into the balance against sin; but sin hath weighed down the soul of the sinner to hell, notwithstanding the weight of merit that he did put in against it. Now, what is the result, but that the advocate goes down, as well as we: we to hell, and he in esteem? Wherefore, I say, he is concerned with us; his credit, his honour, his glory, and renown, flies all away, if those for whom he pleads as an advocate perish for want of worth in his sacrifice pleaded. But shall this ever be said of Christ? or will it be found that any, for whom Christ as advocate pleads, yet perish for want of worth in the price, or of neglect in the advocate to plead it? No, no; himself is concerned, and that as to his own reputation and honour, and as to the value and virtue of his blood; nor will he lose these for want of pleading for them concerned in this office.

2. I argue again; Christ, as advocate, must needs be concerned in his plea; for that every one, for whose salvation he advocates, is his own; so, then, if he loses, he loses his own, his substance, and inheritance. Thus, if he lose the whole, and if he lose a part, one, any one of his own, he loseth part of his all, and of his fulness; wherefore we may well think that Christ, as advocate, is concerned, even concerned with his people, and therefore will thoroughly plead their cause.

Suppose a man should have a horse, though lame, and a piece of ground, though somewhat barren, yet if any should attempt to take these away, he would not sit still, and so lose his own; no, saith he, "since they are mine own, they shall cost me five times more than they are worth, but I will maintain my right." I have seen men sometimes strongly engaged in law for that which, when considered by itself, one would think was not worth regarding; but when I have asked them, why so concerned for a thing of so little esteem? they have answered, Oh, it is some of that by which I hold a title of honour, or my right to a greater income, and, therefore, I will not lose it. Why, thus is Christ engaged; what he pleads for is his own, his all, his fulness; yea, it is that by which he holds his royalty, for he is "King of saints." (Rev. xv. 3. John vi. 37—39. Ps. xvi. 5, 6.) It is part of his estate, and that by which he holds some of his titles of honour. (Eph. v. 23. Jer. l. 34. Rom. xi. 26. Heb. ii. 10.) Saviour, Redeemer, Deliverer, and Captain, are some of his titles of honour; but if he loseth any of those, upon whose account he weareth those titles of honour, for want of virtue in his plea, or for want of worth in his blood, he loseth his own, and not only so, but also part of his royalty, and does also diminish and lay a blot upon his glorious titles of honour; and he is jealous of his honour; his honour he will not give to another.

Wherefore he will not, be not afraid, he never will leave nor forsake those who have given themselves unto him, and for whom he is become an advocate with the Father, to plead their cause; even because thou art one, one of his own, one by whom he holdeth his glorious titles of honour.

Obj. Oh, but I am but one, and a very sorry one, too; and what is one, specially such an one as I am? Can there be a miss of the loss of such an one?

Ans. One and one makes two, and so *ad infinitum.* Christ cannot lose one, but as he may lose more, and so, in conclusion, lose all: but of all that God has given him, he will lose nothing. (John vi. 38, 39.) Besides, to lose one would encourage Satan, disparage his own wisdom, make him incapable of giving in at the day of account, the whole tale to God of those that he has given him. Further, this would dishearten sinners, and make them afraid of venturing their cause and their souls in his hand; and would, as I said before, either prove his propitiation in some sense ineffectual, or else himself defective in his pleading of it; but none of these things must be supposed. He will thoroughly plead the cause of his people, execute judgment for them, bring them out to the light, and cause them to behold his righteousness. (Micah vii. 9.)

Privilege 3. The plea of Satan is groundless, and that is another privilege: for albeit thou hast sinned, yet since Christ before has paid thy debt, and also paid for more; since thou hast not yet run beyond the price of thy redemption, it must be concluded that Satan wants a good bottom to ground his plea upon, and, therefore, must, in conclusion, fail of his design. True, there is sin committed, there is a law transgressed, but there is also a satisfaction for this transgression, and that which superabounds; so, though there be sin, yet there wants a foundation for a plea. Joshua was clothed with filthy garments, but Christ had other garments provided for him, change of raiment; wherefore iniquity, as to the charge of Satan, vanishes. "And the angel answered and said, Take away the filthy garments from him," [this intimates that there was no ground, no sufficient ground, for Satan's charge;] " and unto him he said, Behold I have caused thine iniquity to pass from thee, and I will clothe thee with change of raiment." (Zech. iii. 4.) Now, if there be no ground, no sound and sufficient ground, to build a charge against the child upon—I mean, as to eternal condemnation; for that is the thing contended for—then, as I said, Satan must fall "like lightning to the ground," and be cast over the bar, as a corrupt and illegal pleader. But this is so, as in part is proved already, and will be further made out by that which follows. They that have indeed Christ to be their advocate, are themselves, by virtue of another law than that against which they have sinned, secured from the charge that Satan brings in against them. I granted before, that the child of God has sinned, and that there is a law that condemneth for this sin; but here is the thing, this child is removed by an act of grace into and under another law : " For we are not under the law," and so, consequently, " there is now no condemnation for them." (Rom. vi. 14; viii. 1.) Wherefore, when God speaketh of his dealing with his, he saith, It shall " not be by their covenant," that is, not by that of the law, they then being not under the law. (Ezek. xvi. 61.) What if a plea be commenced against them, a plea for sin, and they have committed sin; a plea grounded upon the law, and the law takes cognizance of their sin ? Yet, I say, the plea wants a good bottom, for that the person thus accused is put under another law. Hence, he says, " sin shall not have dominion over you, for ye are not under the law." If the child was under the law, Satan's charge would be good, because it would have a substantial ground of support; but since the child is dead to the law, (Gal. ii. 19,) and that also dead to him, for both are true as to condemnation, (Rom. vii. 6,) how can it be that Satan should have a sufficient ground for his charge, though he should have matter of fact, sufficient matter of fact, that is sin ? For by his change of relation, he is put out of the reach of that law. There is a woman, a widow, that oweth a sum of money, and she is threatened to be sued for the debt; now, what doth she, but marrieth; so, when the action is commenced against her as a widow, the law finds her a married woman; what now can be done ? Nothing to her; she is not who she was; she is delivered from that state by her marriage; if anything be done, it must be done to her husband. But if Satan will sue Christ for my debt, he oweth him nothing; and as for what the law can claim of me while I was under it, Christ has delivered me by redemption from that curse, " being made a curse for me." (Gal. iii. 13.)

Now the covenant into which I am brought by grace, by which also I am secured from the law, is not a law of sin and death, as that is from under which I am brought, (Rom. viii. 2,) but a law of grace and life; so that Satan cannot come at me by that law; and by grace, I am by that secured also from the hand, and mouth, and sting of all other; I mean still, as to an eternal concern. Wherefore God saith, " If we break his law, the law of works, he will visit our sin with a rod, and our iniquity with stripes; but his covenant, his new covenant, will he not break," but will still keep close to that, and so secure us from eternal condemnation. (Ps. lxxxix. 30—37.)

Christ also is made the mediator of that covenant, and therefore an advocate by that; for his priestly office and advocateship are included by his mediation; wherefore when Satan pleads by the old, Christ pleads by the new covenant, for the sake of which the old one is removed. "In that he saith, A new covenant, he hath made the first old. Now that which decayeth and waxeth old is ready to vanish away." (Heb. viii. 13.) So, then, the ground of plea is with Jesus Christ, and not with our accuser. Now, what doth Christ plead, and what is the ground of his plea ? Why, he pleads for exemption and freedom from condemnation, though by the law of works his children have deserved it; and the ground for this his plea, as to law, is the matter of the covenant itself, for thus it runs : " For I will be merciful to their unrighteousness, and their sins and their iniquities will I remember no more." (Heb. viii. 12.) Now here is a foundation—a foundation in law, for our advocate to build his plea upon; a foundation in a law not to be moved, or removed, or made to give place, as that is forced to do, upon which Satan grounds his plea against us.

Men, when they plead before a judge, use to plead matter of law. Now, suppose there is an old law in the realm, by which men deserve to be condemned to death, and there is a *new* law in this realm that secureth men from that condemnation which belongs to them by the old; and suppose also, that I am completely comprehended by all the provisoes of the new law, and not by any tittle thereof excluded from a share therein; and suppose, again, that I have a brangling adversary that pursues me by the *old* law, which yet cannot in right touch me, because I am interested in the new; my advocate also is one that pleads by the new law, where only there is a ground of plea; shall not now mine adversary feel the power of his plea to the delivering of me, and the putting of him to shame ? Yes, verily; specially since the plea is good, the judge just; nor can the enemy find any ground for a demur to be put in against my present discharge in open court, and that by proclamation; specially since my advocate has also, by his blood, fully satisfied the Old law, that he might establish the New (Heb. x. 9—12.)

Privilege 4. Since that which goeth before is true, it follows, that he that entereth his plea against the children must needs be overthrown; for always before just judges it is the right that taketh place. Judge the right, O Lord, said David; or, "let my sentence come forth from thee," according to the law of grace. And he that knows what strong ground, or bottom, our advocate has for his pleadings, and how Satan's accusations are without sound foundation, will not be afraid, he speaking in Christ, to say, I appeal to God Almighty, since Christ is my advocate by the new law, whether I ought to be condemned to death and hell for what Satan pleads against me by the old. Satan urgeth that we have sinned, but Christ pleads to his propitiatory sacrifice; and so Satan is overthrown. Satan pleads the law of works, but Christ pleads the law of grace. Further, Satan pleads the justice and holiness of God against us; and there the accuser is overthrown again. And to them Christ appeals, and his appeal is good, since the law testifies to the sufficiency of the satisfaction that Christ has made thereto by his obedience. (Rom. iii. 22, 23.) And also, since by another covenant, God himself has given us to Jesus Christ, and so delivered us from the old. Wherefore you read nothing as an effect of Satan's pleading against us, but that his mouth is stopped, as appears by the third of Zechariah; and that he is cast; yea, cast down, as you have it in the twelfth of Revelations.

Indeed, when God admits not, when Christ wills not to be an advocate, and when Satan is bid stand at the right hand of one accused, to enforce, by pleading against him, the things charged on him by the law, then he can prevail; prevail for ever against such a wretched one. (Ps. cix. 6, 7.) But when Christ stands up to plead, when Christ espouses this or that man's cause, then Satan must retreat, then he must go down. And this necessarily flows from the text, "We have an advocate," a prevailing one, one that never lost cause, one that always put the children's enemy to the rout before the judgment-seat of God. This, therefore, is another privilege that they have, who have Jesus Christ for their advocate; their enemy must needs be overthrown, because both law and justice are on their side.

Privilege 5. Thine advocate has pity for thee, and great indignation against thine accuser: and these are two excellent things. When a lawyer hath pity for a man whose cause he pleadeth, it will engage him much; but when he has indignation also against the man's accuser, this will yet engage him more. Now, Christ has both these, and that not of humour, but by grace and justice; grace to us, and justice to our accuser. He came down from heaven that he might be a priest, and returned thither again to be a priest and advocate for his: and in both these offices he levelleth his whole force and power against thine accuser: "For this purpose the Son of God was manifested, that he might destroy the works of the devil." (1 John iii. 8.)

Cunning men will, if they can, retain such an one to be their advocate, who has a particular quarrel against their adversary; for thus, think they, he that is such, will not only plead for me, but for himself, and to right his own wrongs also; and since, if it be so, (and it is so here,) my concerns and my advocate's are interwoven, I am like to fare much the better for the anger that is conceived in his heart against him. And this, I say, is the children's case; their advocate counteth their accuser his greatest enemy, and waiteth for a time to take vengeance, and he usually then takes the opportunity when he has aught to do for his people against him. Hence he says, "The day of vengeance is in mine heart, and the year of my redeemed is come." (Isa. lxiii. 3, 4.)

I do not say that this revenge of Christ is, as ofttimes is a man's, of spite, prejudice, or other irregular lettings out of passions; but it ariseth from righteousness and truth; nor can it be but that Jesus must have a desire to take vengeance on his enemy and ours, since holiness is in him, to the utmost bounds of perfection. And I say again, that in all his pleading as an advocate, as well as in his offering as a priest, he has a hot and flaming desire and design to right himself upon his foe and ours; hence he triumphed over him when he died for us upon the cross, and designed the spoiling of his principality, while he poured out his blood for us before the face of God. We then have this advantage more, in that Christ is our advocate, our enemy is also his, and the Lord Jesus counts him so. (Col. ii. 14, 15.)

Privilege 6. As thine advocate, so thy judge holdeth thine accuser for his enemy also; for it is not of love to righteousness and justice that Satan accuseth us to God, but that he may destroy the workmanship of God. Wherefore he also fighteth against God when he accuseth the children; and this thy Father knows right well. He must therefore needs distinguish between the charge and the mind that brings it; specially when what is charged upon us is under the gracious promise of a pardon, as I have showed it is. Shall not the Judge then hear his Son (for our advocate is his Son,) in the cause of one that he favours, and that he justly can, against an enemy who seeks his dishonour, and the destruction of his eternal designs of grace?

A mention of the judge's *son* goes far with countrymen; and great striving there is with them who have great enemies and bad causes to get the judge's son to plead, promising themselves that the judge is as like to hear him, and to yield a verdict to his plea, as to any other lawyer. But what now shall we say concerning our Judge's Son, who takes part, not only with his children, but with him, and with law and justice, in pleading against our accuser? Yea, what shall we say when both Judge, and advocate, and law, are all bent to make our persons stand and escape, whatever, and how truly soever, the charge and accusation is by which we are assaulted of the devil. And yet all this is true ; wherefore, here is another privilege of them that have Jesus for their advocate.

Privilege 7. Another privilege that they have who have Jesus Christ for their advocate is, that he is undaunted, and of a good courage, as to the cause that he undertakes ; for that is a requisite qualification for a lawyer, to be bold and undaunted in a man's cause. Such an one is coveted, especially by him that knows he has a brazen-faced antagonist. Wherefore, he saith that " he will set his face like a flint," when he stands up to plead the cause of his people. (Isa. l. 5—7.) Lawyers, of all men, need this courage, and to be above others, men of hard foreheads, because of the affronts that sometimes they meet with, be their cause never so good, in the face, sometimes, of the chief of a kingdom. Now Christ is our lawyer, and stands up to plead, not only sometimes, but always, for his people, before the God of gods, and that not in a corner, but while all the host of heaven stands by, both on the right hand and on the left. Nor is it to be doubted but that our accuser brings many a sore charge against us into the court ; but, however, we have an advocate that is valiant and courageous, one that will not fail, nor be discouraged till he has brought judgment unto victory. Hence John inserts his name, saying, " If any man sin, we have an advocate with the Father, Jesus Christ."

Men love to understand a man before they commit their cause unto him—to wit, whether he be fitly qualified for their business. Well, here is an advocate propounded, an advocate to plead our cause against our foe. But what is he ? What is his name ? Is he qualified for my business ? The answer is, It is Jesus Christ. How ? Jesus Christ, what ! that old friend of publicans and sinners ? Jesus Christ ! he used never to fail, he used to set his face like a flint against Satan when he pleaded the cause of his people. Is it Jesus Christ ? says the knowing soul ; then he shall be mine advocate.

For my part, I have often wondered, when I have considered what and causes Jesus Christ sometimes takes in hand, and for what sad souls he sometimes pleads with God his Father. He had need of a face as hard as flint, else how could he bear up in that work in which for us sometimes he is employed ; a work enough to make angels blush. Some, indeed, will lightly put off this, and say, " It is his office ;" but, I say, his office notwithstanding, the work in itself is hard, exceeding hard. When he went to die, had he not despised the shame, he had turned his back upon the cross, and left us in our blood. And now it is his turn to plead, the case would be the same, only he can make argument upon that which to us seems to yield no argument at all, to take courage to plead for a Joshua, for a Joshua clothed, clothed with filthy garments. He, saith he, that " is ashamed of me and of my words

in this adulterous and sinful generation ; of him will I be ashamed," &c. (Mark viii. 38.) Hence it follows that Christ will be ashamed of some ; but why not ashamed of others ? It is not because their cause is good, but because they are kept from denying of him professedly ; wherefore, for such he will force himself, and will set his face like a flint, and will, without shame, own, plead, and improve his interest with God for them, even for them whose cause is so horribly bad and gross that themselves do blush while they think thereof. But what will not love do ? what will not love bear with ? and what will not love suffer ? Of all the offices of Jesus Christ, I think this trieth him as much as any. True, his offering himself in sacrifice tried him greatly, but that was but for awhile ; his grappling, as a captain, with the Curse, and Death, and Hell, tried him much, but that also was but for a while. But this office of being an advocate, though it meeteth not with such sudden depths of trouble, yet what it wants in shortness it may meet with in length of time. I know Christ, being raised from the dead, dies no more ; yet he has not left off, though in heaven, to do some works of service for his saints on earth ; for there he pleads as an advocate or lawyer for his people. (Heb. viii. 1, 2.) And let it be that he has no cause of shame when he standeth thus up to plead for so vile a wretch as I, who have so vilely sinned, yet I have cause to think that well he may, and to hold my hands before my face for shame, and to be confounded with shame, while he, to fetch me off from condemnation for my transgressions, sets his face like a flint to plead for me with God, and against my accuser. But thus much for the seventh privilege that they have by Christ, who have him for their advocate.

Privilege 8. Another privilege that they have who have Jesus Christ to be their advocate is this, He is always ready, always in court, always with the judge, then and there to oppose, if our accuser comes, and to plead against him what is pleadable for his children. And this the text implies where it saith, " We have an advocate with the Father," always with the Father. Some lawyers, though they are otherwise able and shrewd, yet not being always in court and ready, do suffer their poor clients to be baffled and nonsuited by their adversary ; yea, it so comes to pass because of this neglect, that a judgment is got out against them for whom they have undertaken to plead, to their great perplexity and damage. But no such opportunity can Satan have of our advocate, for he is with the Father, always with the Father ; as to be a priest, so to be an advocate, " We have an advocate with the Father." It is said of the priests, they wait at the altar, and that they give attendance there, (1 Cor. ix. 13 ;) also of the magistrate, that as to his office, he should attend " continually on this very thing." (Rom. xiii. 6.) And as these, so Christ, as to his office of an advocate, attends continually upon that office with his Father. " We have an advocate with the Father," always with the Father. And truly such an advocate becomes the children of God, because of the vigilancy of their enemy; for it is said of him, that "he accuseth us day and night," so unweariedly doth he both seek and pursue our destruction. (Rev. xii. 10.) But behold how we are provided for him, "We have an advocate with the Father." If he comes a-days, our advocate is with the Father; if he comes a-nights, our advocate is with the Father. Thus, then, is our advocate ready to put check to Satan. come he when he will or can, to accuse us to the Father. Wherefore these two texts are greatly to be minded,—one of them, for that it shows us the restlessness of our enemy; the other, for that it shows us the diligence of our advocate.

That, also, in the Hebrews shows us the carefulness of our advocate, where it saith, He is gone "into heaven itself, now to appear in the presence of God for us." (Heb. ix. 24.) *Now*, just the time present; *now*, the time always present; *now*, let Satan come when he will! Nor is it to be omitted that this word that thus specifies the time, the present time, doth also conclude it to be that time in which we are imperfect in grace, in which we have many failings, in which we are tempted and accused of the devil to God : this is the time, .and in it, and every whit of it, he *now* appeareth in the presence of God for us. Oh, the diligence of our enemy; oh, the diligence of our friend! the one against us, the other for us, and that continually. " If any man sin, we have an advocate with the Father, Jesus Christ the righteous." This, then, that Jesus Christ is always an advocate with the Father for us, and so continually ready to put a check to every accusation that Satan brings into the presence of God against us, is another of the privileges that they have, who have Jesus Christ for their advocate.

Privilege 9. Another privilege that they have who have Jesus Christ to be their advocate is this, he is such an one that will not, by bribes, by flattery, nor fair pretences, be turned aside from pursuing of his client's business. This was the fault of lawyers in old time, that they would wrest judgment for a bribe. Hence the Holy One complained, that a bribe did use to blind the eyes of the wise, and pervert the judgment of the righteous. (1 Sam. xii. 3. Amos v. 12. Deut. xvi. 19.)

There are three things in judgment that a lawyer must take heed of—one is the nature of the offence, the other is the meaning and intendment of the law-makers, and a third is to plead for them in danger, without respect to affection or reward. And this is the excellency of our advocate, he will not, cannot be biased to turn aside from doing judgment. And this the apostle intendeth when he calleth our advocate " Jesus Christ the righteous." " We have an advocate with the Father, Jesus Christ the righteous ;" or, as another prophet calls him, to wit, " The just Lord, one that

will do no iniquity ;" that is, no unrighteousness in judgment. (Zeph. iii. 5.) He will not be provoked to do it, neither by the continual solicitations of thine enemy; nor by thy continual provocations wherewith, by reason of thy infirm condition, thou dost often tempt him to do it. And remember that thy advocate pleads by the new covenant, and thine adversary accuses by the old; and again, remember that the new covenant is better and more richly provided with grounds of pleading for our pardon and salvation, than the old can be with grounds for a charge to be brought in by the devil against us, suppose our sin be never so heinous. It is a better covenant, established upon better promises.

Now, put these two together; namely, that Jesus Christ is righteous, and will not swerve in judgment ; also, that he pleads for us by the new law, with which Satan hath nothing to do, nor, had he, can he by it bring in a plea against us, because that law, in the very body of it, consists in free promises of giving grace unto us, and of an everlasting forgiveness of our sin. (Jer. xxxi. 31—34. Ezek. xxxvi. 25—30. Heb. viii. 8—13,) Oh, children, your advocate will stick to the law, to the new law, to the new and everlasting covenant, and will not admit that anything should be pleaded by our foe that is inconsistent with the promise of the gift of grace, and of the remission of all sin. This, therefore, is another privilege that they are made partakers of who have Jesus Christ to be their advocate. He is just, he is righteous, he is " Jesus Christ the righteous ;" he will not be turned aside to judge awry, either of the crime or the law, or for favour or affection. Nor is there any sin but what is pardonable committed by those that have chosen Jesus Christ to be their advocate.

Privilege 10. Another privilege that they have who have Jesus Christ to be their advocate is this, the Father has made him, even him that is thine advocate, the umpire and judge in all matters that have, do, or shall fall out betwixt him and us. Mark this well; for when the judge himself, before whom I am accused, shall make mine advocate the judge of the nature of the crime for which I am accused, and of matter of law by which I am accused, to wit, whether it is in force against me to condemnation, or whether by the law of grace I am set free, (especially since before my advocate has espoused my cause, promised me deliverance, and pleaded my right to the state of eternal life,) must it not go well with me ? Yes, verily. The judge, then, making thine advocate the judge, for he " hath committed all judgment unto the Son," hath done it also for thy sake who hast chosen him to be thine advocate. (John v. 22.) It was a great thing that happened to Israel when Joseph was become their advocate, and when Pharaoh had made him a judge. " Thou," says he, " shalt be over my house, and according unto thy word shall all my people be ruled. See, I have set thee over all the land of Egypt, and without thee shall no man lift up his hand or foot in all the land of Egypt, only in the throne will I be greater than thou." (Gen. xli. 40, 44.) Joseph in this was a type of Christ, and his government here of the government of Christ for his church. Kings seldom make a man's judge his advocate; they seldom leave the issue of the whole affair to the arbitration of the poor man's lawyer; but when they do, methinks it should even go to the heart's desire of the client whose the advocate is, especially when, as I said before, the cause of the client is become the concern of the advocate, and that they are both wrapt up in the self-same interest; yea, when the judge himself also is therein concerned; and yet thus it is with that soul who has Jesus Christ for his advocate. What sayest thou, poor heart, to this? The judge, to wit, the God of heaven, has made thy advocate, arbitrator in thy business; he is to judge; God has referred the matter to him, and he has a concern in thy concern, an interest in thy good speed. Christian man, dost thou hear? Thou hast put thy cause into the hand of Jesus Christ, and hast chosen him to be thine advocate to plead for thee before God and against thy adversary; and God has referred the judgment of that matter to thy advocate, so that he has power to determine the matter. I know Satan is not pleased with this. He had rather things should have been referred to himself, and then woe had been to the child of God: but, I say, God has referred the business to Jesus Christ, has made him umpire and judge in thine affair. Art thou also willing that he should decide the matter? Canst thou say unto him as David, " Judge me, O God, and plead my cause ?" (Ps. xliii. 1.) Oh, the care of God towards his people, and the desire of their welfare! He has provided them an advocate, and he has referred all causes and things that may by Satan be objected and brought in against us, to the judgment and sentence of Christ our advocate. But to come to a conclusion for this; and, therefore—

Privilege 11. The advantage that he has that has the Lord Jesus for his advocate, therefore, is very great. Thy advocate has the cause, has the law, has the judge, has the purse, and so, consequently, has all that is requisite for an advocate to have, since, together with these, he has heart, he has wisdom, he has courage, and loves to make the best improvement of his advantages for the benefit of his client. And that which adds to all is, he can prove the debt paid, about which Satan makes such ado; a price given for the ransom of my soul and for the pardon of my sins. Lawyers do use to make a great matter of it, when they can prove that that very debt is paid for which their client is sued at law. Now this Christ Jesus himself is witness to; yea, he himself has paid it, and that out of his own purse, for us, with his own hands, before and upon the mercy-seat, according as the law requireth. (Lev. xvi. 13—15. Heb. ix. 11—

24.) What, then, can accrue to our enemy? or what advantage can he get by his thus vexing and troubling the children of the Most High? Certainly nothing, but, as has been said already, to be cast down; for the kingdom of our God, which is a kingdom of grace, and the power of his Christ will prevail. Samson's power lay in his hair, but Christ's power, his power to deliver us from the accusation and charge of Satan, lieth in the worth of his undertakings. And hence it is said again, "And they overcame him by the blood of the Lamb," and he was cast out and down. (Rev. xii. 10—12.) And thus much for the privileges that those are made partakers of, who have Jesus Christ to be their advocate.

FIFTHLY. I come now to the fifth and last thing, which is, *to show you what necessity there is that Christ should be our advocate.*

That Christ should be a priest to offer sacrifice, a king to rule, and a prophet to teach, all seeing men acknowledge is of necessity: but that he should be an advocate, a pleader for his people, few see the reason of it. But he is an advocate, and as an advocate has a work and employ distinct from his priestly, kingly, or prophetical office. John says, "He is our advocate," and signifieth also the nature of his work as such, in that very place where he asserteth his office; as also I have showed you in that which goes before. But having already showed you the nature, I will now show you the necessity of this office.

First. It is necessary for the more full and ample vindication of the justice of God against all the cavils of the infernal spirits. Christ died on earth to declare the justice of God to men in his justifying the ungodly. God standeth upon the vindication of his justice, as well as upon the act thereof. Hence the Holy Ghost, by the prophets and apostles, so largely disputeth for the vindication thereof, while it asserteth the reality of the pardon of sin, the justification of the unworthy, and their glorification with God. (Rom. iii. 24. Isa. Jer. Mal. Rom. iii.; iv.; viii. Gal. iii.; iv.) I say, while it disputeth the justness of this high act of God against the cavils of implacable sinners. Now the prophets and apostles, in those disputes by which they seek to vindicate the justice of God in the salvation of sinners, are not only ministers of God to us, but advocates for him; since, as Elihu has it, they " speak on God's behalf," or, as the margin has it, " I will show thee that there are yet words for God," words to be spoken and pleaded against his enemies for the justification of his actions. (Job xxxvi. 2.) Now, as it is necessary that there should be advocates for God on earth to plead for his justice and holiness, while he saveth sinners, against the cavils of an ungodly people, so it is necessary that there should be an advocate also in heaven, that may there vindicate the same justice and holiness of God from all those charges that the fallen angels are apt to charge it with, while it consenteth that we, though ungodly, should be saved.

That the fallen angels are bold enough to charge God to his face with unjustness of language, is evident in the 1st and 2nd of Job; and that they should not be as bold to charge him with unjustness of actions, nothing can be showed to the contrary. Further, that God seeks to clear himself of this unjust charge of Satan is as manifest; for all the troubles of his servant Job were chiefly for that purpose. And why he should have one also in heaven to plead for the justness of his doing in the forgiveness and salvation of sinners appears also as necessary, even because there is one, even an advocate with the Father, or on the Father's side, seeking to vindicate his justice, while he pleadeth with him for us against the devil and his objections. God is wonderfully pleased with his design in the saving of sinners; it pleases him at the heart. And since he also is infinitely just, there is need that an advocate should be appointed to show how, in a way of justice as well as mercy, a sinner may be saved.

The good angels did not at first see so far into the mysteries of the gospel of the grace of God, but that they needed further light therein for the vindication of their Lord as servants. Wherefore they yet did pry and look narrowly into it further, and also bowed their heads and hearts to learn yet more, by the church, of "the manifold wisdom of God." (1 Pet. i. 12. Eph. iii. 9, 10.) And if the standing angels were not yet to the utmost perfect in the knowledge of this mystery, (and yet surely they must know more thereof than those that fell could do,) no wonder if those devils, whose enmity could not but animate their ignorance, made, and do make, their cavils against justice, insinuating that it is not impartial and exact, because it, as it is just, justifieth the ungodly.

That Satan will quarrel with God I have showed you, and that he will also dispute against his works with the holy angels, is more than intimated by the apostle Jude (ver. 9), and why not quarrel with, and accuse the justice of God as unrighteous, for consenting to the salvation of sinners? since his best qualifications are most profound and prodigious attempts to dethrone the Lord God of his power and glory.

Nay, all this is evident, since "we have an advocate with the Father, Jesus Christ the righteous." And again, I say, it is evident that one part of his work as an advocate is to vindicate the justice of God while he pleadeth for our salvation, because he pleadeth a propitiation; for a propitiation respecteth God as well as us; the appeasing of his wrath, and the reconciling of his justice to us, as well as the redeeming of us from death and hell; yea, it therefore doth the one, because it doth the other. Now, if Christ, as an advocate, pleadeth a propitiation with God, for whose conviction doth he plead it? Not for God's; for he has ordained it, allows it, and gloriously acquiesces therein, because he knows the whole virtue thereof. It is therefore for the conviction of the fallen angels, and for the confounding of all those cavils that can be invented and objected against our salvation by those most subtle and envious ones. But,

Secondly. There is matter of law to be objected, and that both against God and us; at least, there seems to be so, because of the sanction that God has put upon the law, and also because we have sinned against it.

God has said, "In the day thou eatest thereof thou shalt surely die;" and, "the soul that sinneth, it shall die." God also standeth still upon the vindication of his justice: he also saveth sinners. Now, in comes our accuser and chargeth us of sin, of being guilty of sin, because we have transgressed the law. God also will not be put out of his way, or steps of grace, to save us; also he will say, he is just and righteous still. Aye, but these are but say-so's. How shall this be proved? Why, now, here is room for an advocate that can plead to matter of law, that can preserve the sanction of the law in the salvation of the sinner. "He will magnify the law and make it honourable." (Isa. xlii. 21.) The margin saith, "and make him honourable;" that is, he shall save the sinner, and preserve the holiness of the law, and the honour of his God. But who is this that can do this? "It is the servant of God," saith the prophet, (ver. 1, 13,) "the Lord, a man of war." But how can this be done by him? The answer is, It shall be done, "for God is well pleased for his righteousness' sake;" for it is by that he magnifies the law, and makes his Father honourable: that is, he, as a public person, comes into the world under the law, fulfils it, and having so done, he gives that righteousness away, for he, as to his own person, never had need thereof; I say, he gives that righteousness to those that have need, to those that have none of their own, that righteousness might be imputed to them. This righteousness, then, he presenteth to God for us, and God, for this righteousness' sake, is well pleased that we should be saved, and for it can save us, and secure his honour, and preserve the law in its sanction. And this Christ pleadeth against Satan as an advocate with the Father for us; by which he vindicates his Father's justice, holdeth the child of God, notwithstanding his sins, in a state of justification, and utterly overthroweth and confoundeth the devil.

For Christ, in pleading thus, appeals to the law itself, if he has not done it justice, saying, "Most mighty law, what command of thine have I not fulfilled? what demand of thine have I not fully answered? where is that jot or tittle of the law that is able to object against my doings for want of satisfaction?" Here the law is mute; it speaketh not one word by way of the least complaint, but rather testifies of this righteousness that it is good and holy. (Rom. iii. 22, 23; v. 15—19.) Now, then, since Christ did this as a public person, it follows that others must be justified thereby; for that was the end and reason of Christ's taking on him to do the righteousness of the law. Nor can the law object against the equity of this dispensation of heaven. For why might not that God, who gave the law his being and his sanction, dispose as he pleases of the righteousness which it commendeth? Besides, if men be made righteous, they are so; and if by a righteousness which the law commendeth, how can fault be found with them by the law? Nay, it is "witnessed to by the law and the prophets," who consent that it should be unto all, and upon all them that believe, for their justification. (Rom. iii. 20, 21.)

And that the mighty God suffereth the prince of the devils to do with the law what he can against this most wholesome and godly doctrine, it is to show the truth, goodness, and permanency thereof; for this is as who should say, Devil, do thy worst! When the law is in the hand of an easy pleader, though the cause that he pleadeth be good, a crafty opposer may overthrow the right; but here is the salvation of the children in debate, whether it can stand with law and justice: the opposer of this is the devil, his argument against it is the law; he that defends the doctrine is Christ the advocate, who, in his plea, must justify the justice of God, defend the holiness of the law, and save the sinner from all the arguments, pleas, stops, and demurs that Satan is able to put in against it. And this he must do fairly, righteously, simply, pleading the voice of the self-same law for the justification of what he standeth for, which Satan pleads against it; for though it is by the new law that our salvation comes, yet by the old law is the new law approved of, and the way of salvation thereby by it consented to.

This shows, therefore, that Christ is not ashamed to own the way of our justification and salvation, no, not before men and devils. It shows also that he is resolved to dispute and plead for the same, though the devil himself shall oppose it. And since our adversary pretends a plea in law against it, it is meet that there should be an open hearing before the Judge of all about it; but, forasmuch as we neither can nor dare appear to plead for ourselves, our good God has thought fit we should do it by an advocate: "We have an advocate with the Father, Jesus Christ the righteous."

This, therefore, is the second thing that shows the need that we have of an advocate; to wit, our adversary pretends that he has a plea in law against us, and that by law we should be otherwise disposed of than to be made possessors of the heavenly kingdom. But,

Thirdly. There are many things relating to the promise, to our life, and to the threatenings, that minister matter of question and doubt, and give the advantage of objections unto him that so eagerly desireth to be putting in cavils against our salvation, all which it hath pleased God to repel by Jesus Christ our advocate.

1. There are many things relating to the promises, as to the largeness and straitness of words, as to the freeness and conditionality of them, which we are not able so well to understand; and, therefore, when Satan dealeth with us about them, we quickly fall to the ground before him; we often conclude that the words of the promise are too narrow and strait to comprehend us; we also think, verily, that the conditions of some promises do utterly shut us out from hope of justification and life. But our advocate, who is for us with the Father, he is better acquainted with, and learned in this law than to be baffled out with a bold word or two, or with a subtle piece of hellish sophistication. (Isa. l. 4.) He knows the true purport, intent, meaning, and sense of every promise, and piece of promise, that is in the whole Bible, and can tell how to plead it for advantage against our accuser, and doth so. And I gather it not only from his contest with Satan for Joshua, (Zech. iii.,) and from his conflict with him in the wilderness, (Matt. iv.,) and in heaven, (Rev. xiv.,) but also from the practice of Satan's emissaries here; for what his angels do, that doth he. Now, there is here nothing more apparent than that the instruments of Satan do plead against the church, from the pretended intricacy, ambiguity, and difficulty of the promise; whence I gather, so doth Satan before the tribunal of God; but there we have one to match him; "we have an advocate with the Father," that knows law and judgment better than Satan, and statute and commandment better than all his angels; and by the verdict of our advocate, all the words, and limits, and extensions of words, with all conditions of the promises, are expounded and applied. And hence it is that it sometimes so falleth out that the very promise we have thought could not reach us, to comfort us by any means, has at another time swallowed us up with joy unspeakable. Christ, the true prophet, has the right understanding of the word as an advocate, has pleaded it before God against Satan, and having overcome him at the common law, he hath sent to let us know it by his good Spirit, to our comfort, and the confusion of our enemy. Again,

2. There are many things relating to our lives that minister to our accuser occasions of many objections against our salvation; for, besides our daily infirmities, there are in our lives gross sins, many horrible backslidings; also we ofttimes suck and drink in many abominable errors and deceitful opinions, of all which Satan accuseth us before the judgment-seat of God, and pleadeth hard that we may be damned for ever for them. Besides, some of these things are done after light received, against present convictions and dissuasions to the contrary, against solemn engagements to amendment, when the bonds of love were upon us. (Jer. ii. 20.) These are crying sins; they have a loud voice in themselves against us, and give to Satan great advantage and boldness to sue for our destruction before the bar of God. Nor doth he want skill to aggravate and to comment profoundly upon all occasions and circumstances that did attend us in these our

miscarriages, to wit, that we did it without a cause; also, when we had, had we grace to have used them, many things to have helped us against such sins, and to have kept us clean and upright. "There is also a sin unto death," (1 John v. 16,) and he can tell how to labour, by argument and sleight of speech, to make out transgressions, not only to border upon, but to appear in the hue, shape, and figure of that, and thereto make his objection against our salvation. He often argueth thus with us, and fasteneth the weight of his reasons upon our consciences, to the almost utter destruction of us, and the bringing of us down to the gates of despair and utter destruction. The same sins, with their aggravating circumstances, as I said, he pleadeth against us at the bar of God. But there he meeteth with Jesus Christ, our Lord and advocate, who entereth his plea against him, unravels all his reasons and arguments against us, and shows the guile and falsehood of them. He also pleadeth as to the nature of sin, as also to all those high aggravations, and proveth that neither the sin in itself, nor yet as joined with all its advantageous circumstances, can be the sin unto death, (Col. ii. 19,) because we hold the head, and have not "made shipwreck of faith," (1 Tim. i. 19,) but still, as David and Solomon, we confess, and are sorry for our sins. Thus, though we seem, through our falls, to come short of the promise, with Peter, (Heb. iv. 3,) and leave our transgressions as stumbling-blocks to the world, with Solomon, and minister occasion of a question of our salvation among the godly, yet our advocate fetches us off before God, and we shall be found safe and in heaven at last, by them in the next world, who were afraid they had lost us in this.

But all these points must be managed by Christ for us, against Satan, as a lawyer, an advocate, who to that end now appears in the presence of God for us, and wisely handleth the very crisis of the word, and of the failings of his people, together with all those nice and critical juggles by which our adversary laboureth to bring us down, to the confusion of his face.

3. There are also the threatenings that are annexed to the gospel, and they fall now under our consideration. They are of two sorts: such as respect those who altogether neglect and reject the gospel, or those that profess it, yet fall in, or from the profession thereof.

The first sort of threatening cannot be pleaded against the professors of the gospel as against those that never professed it; wherefore he betaketh himself to manage those threatenings against us that belong to those that have professed, and that have fallen in, or from that profession. (Ps. cix. 6.) Joshua fell in it. (Zech. iii. 1, 2.) Judas fell from it, and the accuser stands at the right hand of them both, before the judgment of God, to resist them, by pleading the threatenings against them, to wit, that God's soul should have no pleasure in them. "If any man draw back, my soul shall have no pleasure in him." Here is a plea for Satan, both against the one and the other; they are both apostatized, both drawn back, and he is subtle enough to manage it.

Ay, but Satan, here is also matter sufficient for a plea for our advocate against thee, forasmuch as the next words distinguish betwixt drawing back, and drawing back "unto perdition;" every one that draws back, doth not draw back unto perdition. (Heb. x. 38, 39.) Some of them draw back *from*, and some *in* the profession of the gospel. Judas drew back *from*, and Peter *in* the profession of his faith; wherefore Judas perishes, but Peter turns again, because Judas drew back unto perdition, but Peter yet believed in the saving of the soul. Nor doth Jesus Christ, when he sees it is to no boot, at any time step in to endeavour to save the soul. Wherefore, as for Judas, for his backsliding from the faith, Christ turns him up to Satan, and leaveth him in his hand, saying, "When he shall be judged, let him be condemned: and let his prayer become sin." (Ps. cix. 7.) But he will not serve Peter so—"The Lord will not leave him in his hand, nor condemn him when he is judged." (Ps. xxxvii. 33.) He will pray for him before, and plead for him after, he hath been in the temptation, and so secure him, by virtue of his advocation, from the sting and lash of the threatening that is made against final apostacy. But,

Fourthly. The necessity of the advocate's office of Jesus Christ appears plainly in this; to plead about the judgments, distresses, afflictions, and troubles that we meet withal in this life for our sins. For though, by virtue of this office, Christ fully takes us off from the condemnation that the unbelievers go down to for their sins, yet he doth not thereby exempt us from temporal punishments, for we see and feel that they daily overtake us; but for the proportioning of the punishment, or affliction for transgression, seeing that comes under the sentence of the law, it is fit that we should have an advocate that understands both law and judgment, to plead for equal distribution of chastisement, according, I say, to the law of grace; and this the Lord Jesus doth.

Suppose a man for transgression be indicted at the assizes; his adversary is full of malice, and would have him punished sorely, beyond what by the law is provided for such offence; and he pleads that the judge will so afflict and punish as he in his malicious mind desireth. But the man has an advocate there, and he enters his plea against the cruelty of his client's accuser, saying, My lord, it cannot be as our enemy would have it. The punishment for these transgressions is prescribed by that law that we here ground our plea upon; nor may it be declined to satisfy his envy. We stand here upon matters of law, and appeal to the law. And this is the work of our advocate in heaven. Punishments for the sin of the children come not headlong, not without measure, as our accuser would have them, nor yet as they fall upon those who have none to plead their cause. Hath he smote the children according to the stroke wherewith he hath smitten others? No; "in measure when it shooteth forth," or seeks to exceed due bounds, "thou wilt debate with it: he stayeth his rough wind in the day of the east wind." (Isa. xxvii. 8.) "Thou wilt debate with it," inquiring and reasoning by the law, whether the shootings forth of the affliction (now going out for the offence committed) be not too strong, too heavy, too hot, and of too long a time admitted to distress and break the spirit of this Christian. And if it be, he applies himself to the rule to measure it by, he fetches forth his plumb-line, and sets it in the midst of his people, (Amos vii. 8. Isa. xxviii. 7,) and lays righteousness to that, and will not suffer it to go further; but according to the quality of the transgression, and according to the terms, bounds, limits, and measures which the law of grace admits, so shall the punishment be. Satan often saith of us when we have sinned, as Abishai said of Shimei after he had cursed David, Shall not this man die for this? (2 Sam. xix. 21.) But Jesus, our advocate, answers as David, What have I to do with thee, O Satan? Thou this day art an enemy to me; thou seekest for a punishment for the transgressions of my people above what is allotted to them by the law of grace, under which they are, and beyond what their relation that they stand in to my Father and myself will admit. Wherefore, as advocate, he pleadeth against Satan when he brings in against us a charge for sins committed, for the regulating of punishments, both as to the nature, degree, and continuation of punishment. And this is the reason why, when we are judged, we are not condemned, but chastened, "that we should not be condemned with the world." (1 Cor. xi. 32.) Hence King David says, the Lord hath not given him over to the will of his enemy. (Ps. xxvii. 12.) And again, "The Lord hath chastened me sore; but he hath not given me over unto death." (Ps. cxviii. 18.) Satan's plea was, that the Lord would give David over to his will, and to the tyranny of death. No, says our advocate, that must not be; to do so would be an affront to the covenant under which grace has put them; that would be to deal with them by a covenant of works, under which they are not. There is a rod for children; and stripes for those of them that transgress. This rod is in the hand of a Father, and must be used according to the law of that relation, not for the destruction, but correction of the children; not to satisfy the rage of Satan, but to vindicate the holiness of my Father; not to drive them further from, but to bring them nearer to their God. But,

Fifthly. The necessity of the advocateship of Jesus Christ is also manifest in this, for that there is need of one to plead the efficacy of old titles to our eternal inheritance, when our interest thereunto seems questionable by reason of new trans-gressions. That God's people may, by their new and repeated sins, as to reason at least, endanger their interest in the eternal inheritance, is manifest by such groanings of theirs as these: "Why dost thou cast me off?" (Ps. xliii. 2.) "Cast me not away from thy presence." (Ps. li. 11.) And, "O God, why hast thou cast us off for ever?" (Ps. lxxiv. 1.) Yet I find in the book of Leviticus, that though any of the children of Israel should have sold, mortgaged, or made away with their inheritance, they did not thereby utterly make void their title to an interest therein, but it should again return to them, and they again enjoy the possession of it, in the year of jubilee. In the year of jubilee, saith God, you shall return every man to his possession; "the land shall not be sold for ever," nor be quite cut off, "for the land is mine; for ye are strangers and sojourners with me. And in all the land of your possession, ye shall grant a redemption for the land." (Lev. xxv. 23, 24.)

The man in Israel that, by waxing poor, did sell his land in Canaan, was surely a type of the Christian who, by sin and decays in grace, has forfeited his place and inheritance in heaven; but as the ceremonial law provided that the poor man in Canaan should not, by his poverty, lose his portion in Canaan for ever, but that it should return to him in the year of jubilee; so the law of grace has provided that the children shall not, for their sin, lose their inheritance in heaven for ever, but that it shall return to them in the world to come; the last *jubilee*, or day of judgment: for then, they are not to be condemned with the world. (1 Cor. xi. 32.) All therefore that happeneth in this case is, they may live without the comfort of it here, as he that had sold his house in Canaan might live without the enjoyment of it till the jubilee. They may also seem to come short of it when they die, as he in Canaan did that deceased before the year of jubilee; but as certainly as he that died in Canaan before the jubilee did yet receive again his inheritance by the hand of his relative survivor when the jubilee came, so certainly shall he that dieth, and that seemeth in his dying to come short of the celestial inheritance now, be yet admitted, at his rising again, to the repossession of his old inheritance at the day of judgment. But here is now room for a caviller to object, and to plead against the children, saying, They have forfeited their part of paradise by their sin; what right, then, shall they have to the kingdom of heaven? Now let the Lord stand up to plead, for he is advocate for the children; yea, let them plead the sufficiency of their first title to the kingdom, and that it is not their doings that can sell the land for ever. The reason why the children of Israel could not sell the land for ever was, because the Lord, their head, reserved to himself a right therein—"The land shall not be sold for ever, for the land is mine." Suppose two or three children have a lawful title to such an estate, but they are all profuse and prodigal; but there is a brother also that has by law a chief right to the same estate: this brother, he may hinder the estate from being sold for ever, because it is also his inheritance, and he may, when the limited time that his brethren had sold their share therein is out, if he will, restore it to them again. And in the meantime, if any that are unjust should go about utterly and for ever to deprive his brethren, he may stand up and plead for them, that in law the land cannot be sold for ever, for that it is his as well as theirs, he being resolved not to part with his right. O my brethren! Christ will not part with his right of the inheritance unto which you are also born. Your profuseness and prodigality shall not make him let go his hold that he hath for you of heaven; nor can you, according to law, sell the land for ever, since it is his, and he hath the principal and chief title thereto. This also gives him ground to stand up to plead for you against all those that would hold the kingdom from you for ever; for let Satan say what he can against you, yet Christ can say, The land is mine, and consequently that his brethren could not sell it.

Yes, says Satan, if the inheritance be divided.

O but, says Christ, the land is undivided; no man has his part set out, and turned over to himself; besides, my brethren yet are under age, and I am their guardian; they have not power to sell the land for ever; the land is mine; also my Father has made me feoffee in trust for my brethren, that they may have what is allotted them when they are all come to a perfect man, "unto the measure of the stature of the fulness of Christ," (Eph. iv. 13,) and not before, and I will reserve it for them till then; and thus to do is the will of my Father, the law of the Judge, and also my unchangeable resolution. And what can Satan say against this plea? Can he prove that Christ has no interest in the saints' inheritance? Can he prove that we are at age, or that our several parts of the heavenly house are already delivered into our own power? And if he goes about to do this, is not the law of the land against him? Doth it not say that our advocate is "Lord of all," (Acts x. 36,) that the kingdom is Christ's, that it is laid up in heaven for us, (Eph. v. 5. Col. i. 5;) yea, that the "inheritance which is incorruptible, undefiled, and that fadeth not away, is reserved in heaven for us, who are kept by the power of God, through faith unto salvation." (1 Pet. i. 4, 5.) Thus therefore is our heavenly inheritance made good by our advocate against the thwartings and branglings of the devil; nor can our new sins make it invalid, but it abideth safe to us at last, notwithstanding our weaknesses; though, if we sin, we may have but little comfort of it, or but little of its present profits, while we live in this world. A spendthrift, though he loses not his title, may yet lose the present benefit, but the principal will come again at last; for "we have an advocate with the Father, Jesus Christ the righteous."

Sixthly. The necessity of the advocateship of Jesus Christ for us further appears in this—to wit, for that our evidences, which declare that we have a right to the eternal inheritance, are often out of our own hand, yea, and also sometimes kept long from us, the which we come not at the sight or comfort of again but by our advocate, specially when our evidences are taken from us, because of a present forfeiture of this inheritance to God by this or that most foul offence. Evidences, when they are thus taken away, as in David's case they were, (Ps. li. 12,) why then they are in our God's hand, laid up, I say, from the sight of them to whom they belong, till they even forget the contents thereof. (2 Pet. i. 5—9.)

Now when writings and evidences are out of the hand of the owners, and laid up in the court, where in justice they ought to be kept, they are not ordinarily got thence again but by the help of a lawyer, an advocate. Thus it is with the children of God. We do often forfeit our interest in eternal life, but the mercy is, the forfeit falls into the hand of God, not of the law nor of Satan, wherefore he taketh away also our evidences, if not all, yet some of them, as he saith, "I have taken away my peace from this people, even loving-kindness and mercies." (Jer. xvi. 5.) This he took from David, (yet not as he took it from him that went before him,) and he entreats for the restoration of it, saying, "Restore unto me the joy of thy salvation, and uphold me with thy free Spirit," (1 Chron. xvii. 13. Ps. li. 12;) and, "Lord, turn us again, cause thy face to shine, and we shall be saved." (Ps. lxxx. 3, 7, 19.)

Satan now also hath an opportunity to plead against us, and to help forward the affliction, as his servants did of old, when God was but a little angry, (Zech. i. 15;) but Jesus Christ our advocate is ready to appear against him, and to send us from heaven our old evidences again, or to signify to us that they are yet good and authentic, and cannot be gainsaid. "Gabriel," saith he, "make this man to understand the vision." (Dan. viii. 16.) And again, saith he to another, "Run, speak to this young man, saying, Jerusalem shall be inhabited as towns without walls." (Zech. ii. 4.) Jerusalem had been in captivity, had lost many evidences of God's favour and love by reason of her sin, and her enemy stepped in to augment her sin and sorrow. But there was a man "among the myrtle trees" that were in the bottom, that did prevail with God to say, I am returned to Jerusalem with mercies; and then commands it to be proclaimed that his "cities through prosperity shall yet be spread abroad." (Zech. i. 11—17.) Thus, by virtue of our advocate, we are either made to receive our old evidences for heaven again, or else are made to understand that they yet are good, and stand valid in the court of heaven; nor can they be made ineffectual, but shall abide the test at last, because our advocate is also concerned in the inheritance of the saints in light.

Christians know what it is to lose their evidences for heaven, and to receive them again, or to hear that they hold their title by them: but perhaps they know not how they come at this privilege; therefore the apostle tells them "they have an advocate;" and that by him, as advocate, they enjoy all these advantages is manifest, because his advocate's office is appointed for our help when we sin—that is, commit sins that are great and heinous —"If any man sin, we have an advocate."

By him the justice of God is vindicated, the law answered, the threatenings taken off, the measure of affliction that for sin we undergo determined, our titles to eternal life preserved, and our comfort of them restored, notwithstanding the wit, and rage, and envy of hell. So, then, Christ gave himself for us as a priest, died for us as a sacrifice, but pleadeth justice and righteousness in a way of justice and righteousness; for such is his sacrifice, for our salvation from the death that is due to our foul or high transgressions, as an advocate. Thus have I given you, thus far, an account of the nature, end, and necessity of the advocateship of Jesus Christ, and should now come to the use and application, only I must first remove an objection or two.

Sixthly. *Objection* 1. But what need all these offices of Jesus Christ? or, what need you trouble us with these nice distinctions? It is enough for us to believe in Christ, in the general, without considering him under this and that office.

Answer. The wisdom of God is not to be charged with needless doing when it giveth to Jesus Christ such variety of offices, and calleth him to so many sundry employments for us. They are all thought necessary by heaven, and therefore should not be counted superfluous by earth. And to put a question upon thy objection: What is a sacrifice without a priest, and what is a priest without a sacrifice? And the same I say of his advocate's office: What is an advocate without the exercise of his office? and what need of an advocate's office to be exercised, if Christ, as sacrifice and priest, by God was thought sufficient? Each of these offices is sufficient for the perfecting of the work for which it is designed; but they are not all designed for the self-same particular thing. Christ as sacrifice offereth not himself; it is Christ as priest does that. Christ as priest dieth not for our sins; it is Christ as sacrifice does so. Again, Christ as a sacrifice and a priest limits himself to those two employs, but as an advocate he launches out into a third. And since these are not confounded in heaven, nor by the Scriptures, they should not be confounded in our apprehension, nor accounted useless.

It is not, therefore, enough for us that we exercise our thoughts upon Christ in an indistinct and general way, but we must learn to know him in all his offices, and to know the nature of his offices also; our condition requires this, it requireth it, I say, as we are guilty of sin, as we have to do with

God, and with our enemy the devil. As we are guilty of sin, so we need a sacrifice; and because we are also sinners, we need one perfect to present our sacrifice for us to God. We have need also of him as priest to present our persons and services to God. And since God is just, and upon the judgment-seat, and since also we are subject to sin grievously; and again, since we have an accuser who will by law plead at this bar of God our sins against us, to the end we might be condemned, we have need of, and also "have an advocate with the Father, Jesus Christ the righteous."

Alas! how many of God's precious people, for the want of a distinct knowledge of Christ in all his offices, are at this day sadly baffled with the sophistications of the devil? To instance no more than this one thing: when they have committed some heinous sin after light received, how are they, I say, tossed and tumbled and distressed with many perplexities! They cannot come to any anchor in this their troubled sea; they go from promise to promise, from providence to providence, from this to that office of Jesus Christ, but forget that he is (or else understand not what it is for this Lord Jesus to be) an advocate for them. Hence they so oft sink under the fears that their sin is unpardonable, and that therefore their condition is desperate; whereas, if they could but consider that Christ is their advocate, and that he is therefore made an advocate to save them from those high transgressions that are committed by them, and that he waits upon this office continually before the judgment-seat of God, they would conceive relief, and be made to hold up their head, and would more strongly twist themselves from under that guilt and burden, those ropes and cords wherewith by their folly they have so strongly bound themselves, than commonly they have done, or do.

Obj. 2. But notwithstanding what you have said, this sin is a deadly stick in my way; it will not out of my mind, my cause being bad, but Christ will desert me.

Ans. It is true, sin is, and will be, a deadly stick and stop to faith, attempt to exercise it on Christ as considered under which of his offices or relations you will; and, above all, the sin of unbelief is "the sin that doth so," or most "easily beset us." (Heb. xii. 1, 2.) And no marvel, for it never acteth alone, but is backed, not only with guilt and ignorance, but also with carnal sense and reason. He that is ignorant of this knows but little of himself, or of what believing is. He that undertakes to believe, acts upon the hardest task that ever was proposed to man; not because the things imposed upon us are unreasonable or unaccountable, but because the heart of man, the more true anything is, the more it sticks and stumbles thereat; and, says Christ, "Because I tell you the truth, ye believe me not." (John viii. 45.) Hence believing is called labouring (Heb. iv. 11;) and it is the sorest labour, at times, that any man can take in hand, because assaulted with the greatest oppositions; but believe thou must, be the labour never so hard, and that not only in Christ in a general way, but in him as to his several offices, and as to this of his being an advocate in particular, else some sins and some temptations will not, in their guilt or vexatious trouble, easily depart from thy conscience; no, not by promise, nor by thy attempts to apply the same by faith. And this the text insinuateth by its setting forth of Christ as advocate, as the only or best and most speedy way of relief to the soul, in certain cases.

There is, then, an order that thou must observe in the exercise of thy soul in a way of believing.

1. Thou must believe unto justification in general; and for this thou must direct thy soul to the Lord Christ as he is a sacrifice for sin, and as a priest offering that sacrifice; so as a sacrifice thou shalt see him appeasing divine displeasure for thy sin, and as a priest spreading the skirt of his garment over thee, for the covering of thy nakedness; thus being clothed, thou shalt not be found naked.

2. This, when thou hast done as well as thou canst, thou must, in the next place, keep thine eye upon the Lord Christ as improving, as priest in heaven, the sacrifice which he offered on earth for the continuing of thee in a state of justification thy lifetime, notwithstanding those common infirmities that attend thee, and to which thou art incident in all thy holy services, or best of thy performances. (Rom. v. 10. Exod. xxviii. 31—38.) For therefore is he a priest in heaven, and by his sacrifices interceding for thee.

3. But if thy foot slippeth, if it slippeth greatly, then know thou it will not be long before a bill be in heaven preferred against thee by the accuser of the brethren: wherefore then thou must have recourse to Christ as advocate, to plead before God, thy judge, against the devil, thine adversary, for thee.

4. And as to the badness of thy cause, let that nothing move thee, save to humility and self-abasement, for Christ is glorified by being concerned for thee; yea, the angels will shout aloud to see him bring thee off. For what greater glory can we conceive Christ to obtain as advocate, than to bring off his people when they have sinned, notwithstanding Satan so charging of them for it as he doth?

He gloried when he was going to the cross to die; he went up with a shout and the sound of a trumpet, to make intercession for us; and shall we think that by his being an advocate he receives no additional glory? It is glory to him, doubtless, to bear the title of an advocate, and much more to plead and prosper for us against our adversary, as he doth.

5. And, I say again, for thee to think that Christ will reject thee for that thy cause is bad, is a kind of thinking blasphemy against this his office and his word; for what doth such a man but side with Satan, while Christ is pleading against him? I say,

it is as the devil would have it, for it puts strength into his plea against us, by increasing our sin and wickedness. But shall Christ take our cause in hand, and shall we doubt of good success? This is to count Satan stronger than Christ; and that he can longer abide to oppose, than Christ can to plead for us. Wherefore, away with it, not only as to the notion, but also as to the heart and root thereof. Oh! when shall Jesus Christ our Lord be honoured by us as he ought? This dastardly heart of ours, when shall it be more subdued and trodden under foot of faith? When shall Christ ride Lord, and King, and advocate, upon the faith of his people, as he should? He is exalted before God, before angels, and above all the power of the enemy: there is nothing comes behind but the faith of his people.

Obj. 3. But since you follow the metaphor so close, I will suppose, if an advocate be entertained, some recompence must be given him. His fee, who shall pay him his fee? I have nothing. Could I do anything to make this advocate part of amends, I could think I might have benefit from him; but I have nothing. What say you to this?

Ans. Similitudes must not be strained too far; but yet I have an answer for this objection. There is, in some cases, law for them that have no money; ay, law and lawyers too; and this is called a suing *in forma pauperis;* and such lawyers are appointed by authority for that purpose. Indeed, I know not that it is thus in every nation, but it is sometimes so with us in England; and this is the way altogether in the kingdom of heaven before the bar of God. All is done there for us *in forma pauperis,* on free cost; for our advocate or lawyer is thereto designed and appointed of his Father.

Hence Christ is said to plead the cause, not of the rich and wealthy, but of the poor and needy; not of those that have many friends, but of the fatherless and widow; not of them that are fat and strong, but of those under sore afflictions. (Prov. xxii. 22, 23; xxiii. 10, 11; xxxi. 9.) "He shall stand at the right hand of the poor, to save him from those that condemn his soul," or, as it is in the margin, "from the judges of his soul." (Ps. cix. 31.) This, then, is the manner of Jesus Christ with men; he doth freely what he doth, not for price nor reward. "I have raised him up," says God, "and I will direct all his ways; he shall build my city, and he shall let go my captives, not for a price nor reward." (Isa. xlv. 13.)

This, I say, is the manner of Jesus Christ with men; he pleads, he sues *in forma pauperis,* gratis, and of mere compassion: and hence it is that you have his clients give him thanks; for that is all the poor can give. "I will greatly praise the Lord with my mouth; yea, I will praise him among the multitude. For he shall stand at the right hand of the poor, to save him from those that condemn his soul." (Ps. cix. 30, 31.)

They know but little that talk of giving to

Christ, except they mean they would give him blessing and praise. He bids us come freely, take freely, and tells us that he will give and do freely. (Rev. xxi. 6; xxii. 17.) Let him have that which is his own, to wit, thyself; for thou art the price of his blood. David speaks very strangely of giving to God for mercy bestowed on him; I call it strangely, because indeed it is so to reason. What, says he, shall I render unto the Lord for all his benefits? I will take this cup, and call for more. (Ps. cxvi. 12, 13.) God has no need of thy gift, nor Christ of thy bribe, to plead thy cause. Take thankfully what is offered, and call for more; that is the best giving to God. God is rich enough; talk not then of giving, but of receiving, for thou art poor. Be not too high, nor think thyself too good to live by the alms of heaven: and since the Lord Jesus is willing to serve thee freely, and to maintain thy right to heaven against thy foe, to the saving of thy soul, without price or reward, "let the peace of God rule in your hearts, to the which, also ye are called," as is the rest of the body, "and be ye thankful." (Col. iii. 15.) This, then, is the privilege of a Christian, "We have an advocate with the Father, Jesus Christ the righteous:" one that pleadeth the cause of his people against those that rise up against them, of his love, pity, and mere good-will. Lord, open the eyes of dark readers, of disconsolate saints, that they may see who is for them, and on what terms!

Obj. 4. But if Christ doth once begin to plead for me, and shall become mine advocate, he will always be troubled with me, unless I should, of myself, forsake him; for I am ever in broils and suits of law, action after action is laid upon me, and I am sometimes ten times in a day summoned to answer my doings before God.

Ans. Christ is not an advocate to plead a cause or two; nor to deliver the godly from an accusation or two. "He delivereth Israel out of all his troubles," (Ps. xxv. 22. 2 Sam. xxii. 28;) and chooses to be an advocate for such; therefore, the godly of old did use to make, from the greatness of their troubles, and the abundance of their troublers, an argument to the Lord Christ to send and lend them help: "Have mercy upon me," saith David; "consider my trouble, which I suffer of them that hate me." (Ps. ix. 13.) And again, "Many are they that rise up against me; many there be which say of my soul, There is no help for him in God." (Ps. iii. 1, 2.) Yea, the troubles of this man were so many and great, that his enemies began to triumph over him, saying, "There is no help for him in God." But could he not deliver him, or did the Lord forsake him? No, no; "Thou hast smitten," saith he, "all mine enemies upon the cheek bone; thou hast broken the teeth of the ungodly." And as he delivereth them from their troublers, so also he pleadeth all their causes: "O Lord," saith the church, "thou hast pleaded the causes of my soul; thou hast re-

deemed my life." (Lam. iii. 58.) Mark, troubled Christian, thou sayest thou hast been arrested ofttimes in a day, and as often summoned to appear at God's bar, there to answer to what shall be laid to thy charge. And here, for thy encouragement, thou readest that the church hath an advocate that pleadeth the causes of her soul; that is, all her causes, to deliver her. He knows that, so long as we are in this world, we are subject to temptation and weakness, and through them made guilty of many bad things; wherefore he hath prepared himself to our service, and to abide with the Father, an advocate for us. As Solomon saith of a man of great wrath, so it may be said of a man of great weakness, (and the best of saints are such,) he must be delivered again and again, (Prov. xix. 19); yea, "many a time," saith David, "did he deliver them," (Ps. cvi. 43;) to wit, more than once or twice; and he will do so for thee, if thou entertain him to be thine advocate. Thou talkest of leaving him, but then whither wilt thou go? all else are vain things, things that cannot profit; and he will not forsake his people, (1 Sam. xii. 20—23,) "though their land be filled with sin against the Holy One of Israel." (Jer. li. 5.) I know the modest saint is apt to be abashed to think what a troublesome one he is, and what a make-work he has been in God's house all his days: and let him be filled with holy blushing, but let him not forsake his advocate.

SEVENTHLY. Having thus spoken to these objections, let us now come to make some use of the whole. And,

Use First. I would exhort the children to consider the dignity that God hath put upon Jesus Christ their Saviour; for by how much God hath called his Son to offices and places of trust, by so much he hath heaped dignities upon him. It is said of Mordecai, that he was next to the king Ahasuerus. And what then? Why, then the greatness of Mordecai, and his high advance, must be written in the book of the Chronicles of the kings of Media and Persia, to the end his fame might not be buried or forgotten, but remembered and talked of in generations to come. (Esther x.) Why, my brethren, God hath exalted Jesus of Nazareth, hath made him the *only* great one, having given him a name above every name. A name, did I say? a name and glory beyond all names, and above all names, as doth witness both his being set above all, and the many offices which he executeth for God on behalf of his people. It is counted no little addition to honour when men are not only made near to the king, but also entrusted with most, if not almost with all the most weighty affairs of the kingdom. Why, this is the dignity of Christ. He is, it is true, the natural Son of God, and so high, and one that abounds with honour. But this is not all; God has conferred upon him, as man, all the high and most mighty honours of heaven. He hath made him lord mediator betwixt him and the world. This is general. And particularly, he hath called him to be his high priest for ever, and hath sworn he shall not be changed for another. (Heb. vii. 21—24.) He hath accepted of his offering once for ever, counting that there is wholly enough in what he did once "to perfect for ever them that are sanctified;" to wit, set apart to glory. (Heb. x. 11—14.)

He is captain-general of all the forces that God hath in heaven and earth, the king and commander of his people. (2 Chron. ix. 25—28.) He is Lord of all, and made "head over all things to the church," and is our advocate with the Father. (Eph. i. 22.) O the exaltation of Jesus Christ! Let Christians, therefore, in the first place, consider this. Nor can it be but profitable to them, if withal they consider that all this trust and honour is put and conferred upon him in relation to the advantage and advancement of Christians. If Christians do but consider the nearness that is betwixt Christ and them, and, withal, consider how he is exalted, it must needs be matter of comfort to them. He is my flesh and my bone that is exalted: it is my friend and brother that is thus set up and preferred. It was something to the Jews when Mordecai was exalted to honour; they had thereby ground to rejoice and be glad, for that one of themselves was made lord-chief by the king, and the great governor of the land, for the good of his kindred. True, when a man thinks of Christ as severed from him, he sees but little to his comfort in Christ's exaltation; but when he looks upon Christ, and can say, My Saviour, my priest, or the chief bishop of my soul, then he will see much in his being thus promoted to honour. Consider, then, of the glories to which God has exalted our Saviour, in that he hath made him so high. It is comely, also, when thou speakest of him, that thou name his name with some additional title, thereby to call thy mind to the remembrance, and so to the greater reverence of the person of thy Jesus; as, our Lord Jesus, our Lord and Saviour Jesus Christ, "the apostle and high priest of our profession, Christ Jesus." (2 Pet. ii. 20. Heb. iii. 1, &c.) Men write themselves by their titles; as, John, earl of such a place, Anthony, earl of such a place, Thomas, lord, &c. It is common, also, to call men in great places by their titles rather than by their names; yea, it also pleaseth such great ones well; as, my lord high chancellor of England, my lord privy seal, my lord high admiral, &c. And thus should Christians make mention of Jesus Christ our Lord, adding to his name some of his titles of honour; specially since all places of trust and titles of honour conferred on him are of special favour to us. I did use to be much taken with one sect of Christians, for that it was usually their way, when they made mention of the name of Jesus, to call him "The blessed King of Glory." Christians should do thus; it would do them good: for why doth the Holy Ghost, think you, give him all these titles but that we should call him by them, and so

make mention of him one to another; for the very calling of him by this or that title, or name, belonging to this or that office of his, giveth us occasion, not only to think of him as exercising that office, but to inquire, by the word, by meditation, and one of another, what there is in that office, and what, by his exercising of that, the Lord Jesus profiteth his church.

How will men stand for that honour that by superiors is given to them, expecting and using all things; to wit, actions and carriages, so as that thereby their grandeur may be maintained. And saith Christ, "Ye call me Master and Lord: and ye say well; for so I am." (John xiii. 13.) Christ Jesus our Lord would have us exercise ourselves in the knowledge of his glorious offices and relative titles, because of the advantage that we get by the knowledge of them, and the reverence of, and love to, him that they beget in our hearts. "That disciple," saith the text, "whom Jesus loved, saith unto Peter, It is the Lord. Now, when Simon Peter heard that it was the Lord, he girt his fisher's coat unto him (for he was naked), and did cast himself into the sea. And the other disciples came in a little ship:" to wit, to shore, to wait upon their Lord. (John xxi.) The very naming of him under the title of Lord, bowed their hearts forthwith to come with joint readiness to wait upon him. Let this also learn us to distinguish Christ's offices and titles, not to confound them, for he exerciseth those offices, and beareth those titles, for great reason, and to our commodity.

Every circumstance relating both to Christ's humiliation and exaltation ought to be duly weighed by us, because of that mystery of God, and of man's redemption that is wrapped up therein. For as there was not a pin, nor a loop, nor a tack in the tabernacle but had in it an use of instruction to the children of Israel, so there is not any part, whether more near or more remote to Christ's suffering and exaltation, but is, could we get into it, full of spiritual advantage to us.

To instance; the water that came out of Christ's side, a thing little taken notice of either by preachers or hearers, and yet John makes it one of the witnesses of the truth of our redemption, and a confirmation of the certainty of that record that God to the world hath given of the sufficiency that is in his Son to save. (John xix. 34. 1 John iii. 5—9. Rom. iv. 9—12.)

When I have considered that the very timing of Scripture expressions, and the season of administering ordinances, have been argumentative to the promoting of the faith and way of justification by Christ, it has made me think that both myself, and most of the people of God, look over the Scriptures too slightly, and take too little notice of that, or of those many honours that God, for our good, has conferred upon Christ. Shall he be called a King, a Priest, a Prophet, a Sacrifice, an Altar, a Captain, a Head, a Husband, a Father, a Fountain, a Door, a Rock, a Lion, a Saviour, &c., and shall we not consider these things? And shall God to all these add, moreover, that he is an advocate, and shall we take no notice thereof, or jumble things so together, that we lose some of his titles and offices, or so be concerned with one as not to think we have need of the benefit of the rest? Let us be ashamed thus to do or think, and let us give to him that is thus exalted the glory due unto his name.

Use Second. As we should consider the titles and offices of Christ in general, so we should consider this of his being an advocate in particular; for this is one of the reasons which induced the apostle to present him here under that very notion to us, namely, that we should have faith about it, and consider of it to our comfort; " If any man sin, we have an advocate with the Father, Jesus Christ the righteous." " An advocate:" an advocate, as I said, is one that hath power to plead for another in this, or that, or any court of judicature. Be much, therefore, in the meditation of Christ, as executing of this his office for thee, for many advantages will come to thee thereby. As,

1. This will give thee to see that thou art not forsaken when thou hast sinned; and this has not in it a little relief only, but yieldeth consolation in time of need. There is nothing that we are more prone unto than to think we are forsaken when we have sinned, when for this very thing, to wit, to keep us from thinking so, is the Lord Jesus become our advocate, " If any man sin, we have an advocate." Christian, thou that hast sinned, and that with the guilt of thy sin art driven to the brink of hell, I bring thee news from God; thou shalt not die, but live, for thou hast " an advocate with the Father." Let this therefore be considered by thee, because it yieldeth this fruit.

2. The study of this truth will give thee ground to take courage to contend with the devil concerning the largeness of grace by faith, since thy advocate is contending for thee against him at the bar of God. It is a great encouragement for a man to hold up his head in the country, when he knows he has a special friend at court. Why, our advocate is a friend at court, a friend there ready to give the onset to Satan, come he when he will. " We have an advocate with the Father;" an advocate, or one to plead against Satan for us.

3. This consideration will yield relief, when, by Satan's abuse of some other of the offices of Christ, thy faith is discouraged and made afraid. Christ as a prophet pronounces many a dreadful sentence against sin; and Christ as a king is of power to execute them; and Satan as an enemy has subtilty enough to abuse both these, to the almost utter overthrow of the faith of the children of God. But what will he do with him as he is an advocate? Will he urge that he will plead against us? He cannot; he has no such office. " Will he plead against me with his great power? no, but he would put strength in me." (Job xxiii. 6.) Where-

fore Satan doth all he may to keep thee ignorant of this office; for he knows that as advocate, when he is so apprehended, the saints are greatly relieved by him, even by a believing thought of that office.

4. This consideration, or the consideration of Christ as exercising of this office, will help thee to put by that vizor wherewith Christ by Satan is misrepresented to thee, to the weakening and affrighting of thee. There is nothing more common among saints than thus to be wronged by Satan; for as he will labour to fetch fire out of the offices of Christ to burn us, so to present him to us with so dreadful and so ireful a countenance, that a man in temptation, and under guilt, shall hardly be able to lift up his face to God. But now, to think really that he is my advocate, this heals all! Put a vizor upon the face of a father, and it may perhaps for a while fright the child; but let the father speak, let him speak in his own fatherly dialect to the child, and the vizor is gone, if not from the father's face, yet from the child's mind; yea, the child, notwithstanding that vizor, will adventure to creep into its father's bosom. Why, thus it is with the saints when Satan deludes and abuses them by disfiguring of the countenance of Christ to their view. Let them but hear their Lord speak in his own natural dialect, (and then he doth so indeed when we hear him speak as an advocate,) and their minds are calmed, their thoughts settled, their guilt made to vanish, and their faith to revive.

Indeed, the advocateship of Jesus Christ is not much mentioned in the word, and because it is no oftener made mention of, therefore perhaps it is that some Christians do so lightly pass it over; when, on the contrary, the rarity of the thing should make it the more admirable: and perhaps it is therefore so little made mention of in the Bible, because it should not by the common sort be abused, but is as it were privately dropped in a corner, to be found by them that are for finding relief for their soul by a diligent search of the Scriptures; for Christ in this office of advocateship is only designed for the child of God, the world hath nothing therewith to do. Methinks that which alone is proper to saints, and that which by God is peculiarly designed for them, they should be mightily taken withal: the peculiar treasure of kings, the peculiar privilege of saints, oh, this should be affecting to us! why, Christ, as an advocate, is such. " Remember me, O Lord," said the Psalmist, " with the favour that thou bearest unto thy people: O visit me with thy salvation; that I may see the good of thy chosen, that I may rejoice in the gladness of thy nation, that I may glory with thine inheritance." (Ps. cvi. 4, 5.) The Psalmist, you see here, is crying out for a share in, and the knowledge of, the peculiar treasure of saints: and this of Christ as advocate is such; wherefore study it, and prize it so much the more, this advocate is ours.

(1.) Study it with reference to its peculiarity.

It is for the children, and nobody else : for the children, little and great. This is children's bread; this is a mess for Benjamin ; this is to be eaten in the holy place. Children use to make much of that which, by way of speciality, is by their relations bestowed on them, "And Naboth said to Ahab, The Lord forbid it me, that I should give the inheritance of my fathers to thee." (1 Kings xxi. 3.) No, truly will I not. Why so? Because it was my father's gift, not in common to all, but to me in special.

(2.) Study this office in the nature of it; for therein lies the excellency of anything, even in the nature of it. Wrong thoughts of this or that abuses it, and takes its natural glory from it. Take heed, therefore, of misapprehending, while thou art seeking to apprehend Christ as thy advocate. Men judge of Christ's offices while they are at too great a distance from them; but "let them come near," says God, "then let them speak," (Isa. xli. 1 ;) or as Elihu said to his friends, when he had seen them judge amiss, "Let us choose to us judgment, let us know among ourselves what is good." (Job xxxiv. 4.) So say I; study to know, rightly to know, the advocate-office of Jesus Christ. It is one of the easiest things in the world to miss of the nature, while we speak of the name and offices of Jesus Christ. Wherefore look to it, that thou study the nature of the office of his advocateship, of his advocateship for, for so you ought to consider it. There is an advocate for, not against, the children of God, "Jesus Christ the righteous."

(3.) Study this office with reference to its efficacy and prevalency. Job says, "After my words, they spake not again." (Job xxix. 22.) And when Christ stands up to plead, all must keep silence before him. True, Satan had the first word, but Christ the last, in the business of Joshua, and such a last as brought the poor man off well, though "clothed with filthy garments." (Zech. iii.) Satan must be speechless after a plea of our advocate, how rampant soever he is afore; or as Elihu has it, "They were amazed ; they answered no more; they left off speaking." Shall he that speaks in righteousness give place, and he who has nothing but envy and deceit be admitted to stand his ground ? Behold, the angels cover their faces when they speak of his glory, how then shall not Satan bend before him ? In the days of his humiliation, he made him cringe and creep; how much more then now he is exalted to glory, to glory to be an advocate, an advocate for his people! "If any man sin, we have an advocate with the Father, Jesus Christ the righteous."

(4.) Study the faithfulness of Christ in his execution of this office, for he will not fail nor forsake them that have entertained him for their advocate : "He will thoroughly plead their cause." (Jer. l. 34.) Faithful and true, is one of his titles; and you shall be faithfully served by him. You may boldly commit your cause unto him, nor shall the badness of it make him fail, or discourage him in his work ;

for it is not the badness of a cause that can hinder him from prevailing, because he hath wherewith to answer for all thy sins, and a new law to plead by, through which he will make thee a conqueror. He is also for sticking to a man to the end, if he once engages for him. (John xiii. 1, 2.) He will threaten and love, he will chastise and love, he will kill and love; and thou shalt find it so. And he will make this appear at the last; and Satan knows it is so now, for he finds the power of his repulses while he pleadeth for us at the bar against him. And all this is in very faithfulness.

(5.) Study also the need that thou hast of a share in the execution of the advocateship of Jesus Christ. Christians find that they have need of washing in the blood of Christ, and that they have need of being clothed with the righteousness of Christ; they also find that they have need that Christ should make intercession for them, and that by him, of necessity, they must approach God, and present their prayers and services to him : but they do not so well see that they need that Christ should also be their advocate. And the reason thereof is this : they forget that their adversary makes it his business to accuse them before the throne of God ; they consider not the long scrolls and many crimes wherewith he chargeth them in the presence of the angels of God. I say, this is the cause that the advocateship of Christ is so little considered in the churches : yea, many that have been relieved by that office of his, have not understood what thereby he has done for them.

But perhaps this is to be kept from many till they come to behold his face, and till all things shall be revealed, that Christ might have glory given him in the next world for doing of that for them which they so little thought of in this. But do not thou be content with this ignorance, because the knowledge of his advocating of it for thee will yield thee present relief. Study, therefore, thine own weakness, the holiness of the judge, the badness of thy cause, the subtilty, malice, and rage, of thine enemy ; and be assured that, whenever thou sinnest, by and by thou art for it accused before God at his judgment-seat. These things will, as it were, by way of necessity, instil into thy heart the need that thou hast of an advocate, and will make thee look, as to the blood and righteousness of Jesus Christ to justify thee, so to Christ as an advocate to plead thy cause, as did holy Job in his distresses. (Job xvi. 21.)

Use Third. Is Christ Jesus not only a priest of, and a King over, but an advocate for his people ? Let this make us stand and wonder, and be amazed at his humiliation and condescension. We read of his humiliation on earth when he put himself into our flesh, took upon him our sins, and made them as his own unto condemnation and death. And to be an advocate is an office reproachful to the malicious, if any man be such an one, for those that are base and unworthy. Yea, and the higher and more honourable the person is that pleads for such, the more he humbles himself. The word doth often in effect account him, now in heaven, as a servant for us, and acts of service are acts of condescension; and I am sure some acts of service have more of that in them than some; and I think, when all things are considered, that Christ neither doth nor can do anything for us there, of a more condescending nature, than to become our advocate. True, he glories in it; but that doth not show that the work is excellent in itself. It is also one of his titles of honour; but that is to show how highly God esteems of, and dignifies all his acts; and though this shall tend at last to the greatening of his honour and glory in his kingdom, yet the work itself is amazingly mean.

I speak after the manner of men. It is accounted so in this world. How ignoble and unrespectful doth a man make himself, especially to his enemy, when he undertakes to plead a bad cause, if it happeneth to be the cause of the base and unworthy? And I am sure we are, every one, so in ourselves, for whom he is become an advocate with the Father. True, we are made worthy in him, but that is no thanks to us; as to ourselves and our cause, both are yet bad enough. And let us now leave off disputing, and stand amazed at his condescension; "Who humbleth himself to behold the things that are in heaven." (Ps. cxiii. 6.) And men of old did use to wonder to think that God should so much stoop, as to open his eyes to look upon man, or once so much as to mind him. (Job vii. 17; xiv. 1—3. Ps. viii. 4; cxliv. 3, 4.) And if these be acts that speak a condescension, what will you count of Christ's standing up as an advocate to plead the cause of his people? Must not that be much more so accounted? Oh, the condescension of Christ in heaven! While cavillers quarrel at such kind of language, let the saints stay themselves and wonder at it, and be so much the more affected with his grace. The persons are base, the crimes are base, with which the persons are charged; wherefore one would think that has but the reason to think, that it is a great condescension of Christ, now in heaven, to take upon him to be an advocate for such a people, specially if you consider the openness of this work of Christ; for this thing is not done in a corner. This is done in open court.

1. With a holy and just God: for he is the judge of all, and his eyes are purer than to behold iniquity; yea, his very essence and presence is a consuming fire; yet, before and with this God, and that for such a people, Jesus Christ, the King, will be an advocate. For one mean man to be an advocate for the base, with one that is not considerable, is not so much; but for Christ to be an advocate for the base, and for the base, too, under the basest consideration, this is to be wondered at. When Bathsheba, the queen, became an advocate for Adonijah unto king Solomon, you see how he flounced at her, for that his cause was bad. "And why," saith he, "dost thou ask Abishag for Ado-

nijah? ask for him the kingdom also." (1 Kings ii. 16—23.) I told you before, that to be an advocate did run one upon hazards of reproach; and it may easily be thought that the queen did blush, when, from the king, her son, she received such a repulse; nor do we hear any more of her being an advocate; I believe she had enough of this. But oh, this Christ of God, who himself is greater than Solomon, he is become an advocate, " an advocate with the Father," who is the eternally just, and holy, and righteous God; and that for a people, with respect to him, far worse than could be Adonijah in the eyes of his brother Solomon. Majesty and justice are dreadful in themselves, and much more so when approached by any, specially when the cause, as to matter of fact, is bad that the man is guilty of, who is concerned in the advocateship of his friend, and yet Jesus Christ is still an advocate for us, " an advocate with the Father."

2. Consider, also, before whom Jesus Christ doth plead as an advocate, and that is before, or in the presence and observation of, all the heavenly host; for whilst Christ pleadeth with God for his people, all the host of heaven stand by on the right hand and on the left. (Matt. x. 32.) And though as yet there may seem to be but little in this consideration, yet Christ would have us know, and account it an infinite kindness of his to us, that he will confess and not be ashamed of us before the angels of his Father. (Mark viii. 38.) Angels are holy and glorious creatures, and, in some respect, may have a greater knowledge of the nature and baseness of sin than we, while here, are capable of; and so may be made to stand and wonder while the advocate pleads with God for a people, from head to foot clothed therewith. But Christ will not be ashamed to stand up for us before them, though they know how bad we are, and what vile things we have done. Let this, therefore, make us wonder.

3. Add to these, how unconcerned ofttimes those are with themselves, and their own desolate condition, for whom Christ, as an advocate, laboureth in heaven with God. Alas! the soul is as far off of knowing what the devil is doing against it at God's bar as David was when Saul was threatening to have his blood, while he was hid in the field. (1 Sam. xx. 26—34.) But, O true Jonathan! how didst thou plead for David! Only here thou hadst the advantage of our advocate, thou hadst a good cause to plead; for when Saul, thy father, said, "David shall surely die," thy reply was, "Wherefore shall he be slain? What evil hath he done?" But Christ cannot say thus when he pleadeth for us at God's bar; nor is our present senselessness and unconcernedness about his pleading but an aggravation to our sin. Perhaps David was praying while Jonathan was playing the advocate for him before the king his father, but perhaps the saint is sleeping, yea, sinning more, whilst Christ is pleading for him in heaven. Oh, this should

greatly affect us; this should make us wonder; this should be so considered by us, as to heighten our souls to admiration of the grace and kindness of Christ.

4. Join to these the greatness and gravity, the highness and glorious majesty of the man that is become our advocate. Says the text, it is Jesus Christ, " We have an advocate with the Father, Jesus Christ." Now, that he should become an advocate, that he should embrace such an employ as this of his advocateship, let this be a wonderment, and so be accounted. But let us come to the fourth use.

Use Fourth. Is it so? Is Jesus Christ the Saviour also become our advocate? Then let us labour to make that improvement of this doctrine as tendeth to strengthen our graces and us in the management of them. Indeed, this should be the use that we should make of all the offices of Christ; but let us, at this time, concern ourselves about this; let, I say, the poor Christian thus expostulate with himself—

1. Is Christ Jesus the Lord mine advocate with the Father? Then awake, my faith, and shake thyself like a giant; stir up thyself, and be not faint; Christ is the advocate of his people, and pleadeth the cause of the poor and needy. And as for sin, which is one great stumble to thy actings, O my faith, Christ has not only died for that as a sacrifice, nor only carried his sacrifice unto the Father, into the holiest of all, but is there to manage that offering as an advocate pleading the efficacy and worth thereof before God, against the devil, for us. Thus, I say, we should strengthen our faith; for faith has to do not only with the word, but also with the offices of Christ. Besides, considering how many the assaults are that are made upon our faith, we find all little enough to support it against all the wiles of the devil.

Christians too little concern themselves, as I have said, with the offices of Jesus Christ; and therefore their knowledge of him is so little, and their faith in him so weak. We are bid to have our conversation in heaven, and then a man so hath, when he is there, in his spirit, by faith, observing how the Lord Jesus doth exercise his offices there for him. Let us often by faith go to the bar of God, there to hear our advocate plead our cause; we should often have our faith to God's judgment-seat, because we are concerned there; there we are accused of the devil, there we have our crimes laid open, and there we have our advocate to plead. And this is suggested in the text, for it saith, " We have an advocate with the Father;" therefore thither our faith should go for help and relief in the day of our straits. I say we should have our faith to God's judgment-seat, and show it there, by the glass of our text, what Satan is doing against, and the Lord Jesus for, our souls. We should also show it how the Lord Jesus carries away every cause from the devil, and from before the judgment-seat, to the comfort of the

children, the joy of angels, and the shame of the enemy. This would strengthen and support our faith indeed, and would make us more able than, for the most part, we are to apply the grace of God to ourselves, and hereafter to give more strong repulses to Satan. It is easy with a man, when he knows that his advocate has overthrown his enemy, at the King's Bench bar or Court of Common Pleas, less to fear him the next time he sees him, and more boldly to answer him when he reneweth his threats upon him. Let faith, then, be strengthened, from its being exercised about the advocateship of Jesus Christ.

2. As we should make use of Christ's advocateship for the strengthening of our faith, so we should also make use thereof to the encouraging of us to prayer. As our faith is, so is our prayer; to wit, cold, weak, and doubtful, if our faith be so. When faith cannot apprehend that we have access to the Father by Christ, or that we have an advocate, when charged before God for our sins by the devil, then we flag and faint in our prayer; but when we begin to take courage to believe, (and then we do so when most clearly we apprehend Christ,) then we get up in prayer. And according as a man apprehends Christ in his undertakings and offices, so he will wrestle with and supplicate God. As, suppose a man believes that Christ died for his sins; why, then, he will plead that in prayer with God. Suppose, also, that a man understands that Christ rose again for his justification; why, then, he will also plead that in prayer; but if he knows no further, no further will he go. But when he shall know that there is also for him an advocate with the Father, and that that advocate is Jesus Christ; and when the glory of this office of Christ shall shine in the face of this man's soul; oh, then, he takes courage to pray with that courage he had not before; yea, then is his faith so supported and made strong, that his prayer is more fervent, and importuning abundance. So that, I say, the knowledge of the advocateship of Christ is very useful to strengthen our graces; and, as of graces in general, so of faith and prayer in particular. Wherefore our wisdom is so to improve this doctrine that prayer may be strengthened thereby.

3. As we should make use of this doctrine to strengthen faith and prayer, so we should make use of it to keep us humble; for the more offices Christ executeth for us with the Father, the greater sign that we are bad; and the more we see our badness, the more humble should we be. Christ gave for us the price of blood; but that is not all: Christ, as a captain, has conquered death and the grave for us; but that is not all: Christ, as a priest, intercedes for us in heaven; but that is not all. Sin is still in us, and with us, and mixes itself with whatever we do, whether what we do be religious or civil: for not only our prayers and our sermons, our hearings and preaching, and so; but our houses, our shops, our trades, and our beds, are all polluted

with sin. Nor doth the devil, our night and day adversary, forbear to tell our bad deeds to our Father, urging that we might for ever be disinherited for this. But what should we now do, if we had not an advocate; yea, if we had not one who would plead *in forma pauperis;* yea, if we had not one that could prevail, and that would faithfully execute that office for us? Why, we must die. But since we are rescued by him, let us, as to ourselves, lay our hand upon our mouth, and be silent, and say, "Not unto us, O Lord, not unto us, but unto thy name give glory." And I say again, since the Lord Jesus is fain to run through so many offices for us before he can bring us to glory, oh, how low, how little, how vile and base in our own eyes should we be!

It is a shame for a Christian to think highly of himself, since Christ is fain to do so much for him, and he again not at all able to make him amends; but some, whose riches consist in nothing but scabs and lice, will yet have lofty looks. But are not they much to blame who sit lifting up of lofty eyes in the house, and yet know not how to turn their hand to do anything so, but that another, their betters, must come and mend their work? I say, is it not more meet that those that are such, should look and speak, and act as such that declare their sense of their unhandiness, and their shame, and the like, for their unprofitableness? yea, is it not meet that to every one they should confess what sorry ones they are? I am sure it should be thus with Christians, and God is angry when it is otherwise. Nor doth it become these helpless ones to lift up themselves on high. Let Christ's advocateship therefore teach us to be humble.

4. As we should improve this doctrine to strengthen faith, to encourage prayer, and keep us humble, so we should make use of it to encourage perseverance, that is, to hold on, to hold out to the end: for, for all those causes the apostle setteth Christ before us as an advocate. There is nothing more discourages the truly godly than the sense of their own infirmities, as has been hinted at all along; consequently, nothing can more encourage them to go on than to think that Christ is an advocate for them. The services, also, that Christ has for us to do in this world are full of difficulty, and so apt to discourage: but when a Christian shall come to understand that, if we do what we can, it is not a failing either in matter or manner that shall render it wholly unserviceable, or give the devil that advantage as to plead thereby to prevail for our condemnation and rejection; but that Christ, by being our advocate, saves us from falling short, as also from the rage of hell; this will encourage us to hold on, though we do but hobble in all our goings, and fumble in all our doings; for we have Christ for an advocate in case we sin in the management of any duty: "If any man sin, we have an advocate with the Father, Jesus Christ the righteous." Let us, therefore, go on in all God's ways as well as we can for our

hearts; and when our foot slips, let us tell God of it, and his mercy in Christ shall hold us up. (Ps. lxxxiv. 9—12.)

Darkness, and to be shut up in prison, is also a great discouragement to us; but our advocate is for giving us light, and for fetching us out of our prison. True, he that Joseph chose to be his advocate with Pharaoh remembered not Joseph, but forgat him, (Gen. xl. 14, 23;) but he that has Jesus Christ to be his advocate shall be remembered before God. (Micah vii. 8—10.) "He remembered us in our low estate; for his mercy endureth for ever." (Ps. cxxxvi. 23.) Yea, he will say to the prisoners, Show yourselves; and to them that are in the prison-house, Go forth. Satan sometimes gets the saints into the prison when he has taken them captive by their lusts. (Rom. vii. 23.) But they shall not be always there; and this should encourage us to go on in godly ways; for "we must through much tribulation enter into the kingdom of God."

Obj. But I cannot pray, says one, therefore how should I persevere? When I go to prayer, instead of praying, my mouth is stopped. What would you have me do?

Ans. Well, soul, though Satan may baffle thee, he cannot so serve thine advocate; if thou must not speak for thyself, Christ thine advocate can speak for thee. Lemuel was to open his mouth, for the dumb, to wit, for the sons of destruction, and to plead the cause of the poor and needy. (Prov. xxxi. 8, 9.) If we knew the grace of our Lord Jesus Christ, so as the word reveals it, we would believe, we would hope, and would, notwithstanding all discouragements, wait for the salvation of the Lord. But there are many things that hinder, wherefore faith, and prayer, and perseverance, are made difficult things unto us, "But if any man sin, we have an advocate with the Father, Jesus Christ the righteous;" and "God shall fight for you, and you shall hold your peace," was once a good word to me when I could not pray.

5. As we should improve this doctrine for the improvement and encouragement of these graces, so we should improve it to the driving of difficulties down before us, to the getting of ground upon the enemy. "Resist the devil," drive him back; this is it for which thy Lord Jesus is an advocate with God in heaven; and this is it for the sake of which thou art made a believer on earth. (1 Pet. v. 9. Heb. xii. 4.) Wherefore has God put this sword, WE HAVE AN ADVOCATE, into thy hand, but to fight thy way through the world? "Fight the good fight of faith, lay hold on eternal life," and say, "I will go in the strength of the Lord God." And since I have an advocate with the Father, Jesus Christ the righteous, I will not despair, though "the iniquity of my heels shall compass me about." (Ps. xlix. 5.)

Use Fifth. Doth Jesus Christ stand up to plead for us with God, to plead with him for us against the devil?   Let this teach us to stand up to plead for him before men, to plead for him against the enemies of his person and gospel.   This is but reasonable; for if Christ stands up to plead for us, why should we not stand up to plead for him?

He also expects this at our hands, saying, "Who will rise up for me against the evil doers? Who will stand up for me against the workers of iniquity?" (Ps. xciv. 16.)   The apostle did it, and counted himself engaged to do it, where he saith, he preached "the gospel of God with much contention." (1 Thess. ii. 2.)   Nor is this the duty of apostles or preachers only, but every child of God should "earnestly contend for the faith which was once delivered unto the saints." (Jude 3.)

And, as I said, there is reason why we should do this; he standeth for us.   And if we (1.) Consider the disparity of persons to plead, it will seem far more reasonable.   He stands up to plead with God, we stand up to plead with men.   The dread of God is great, yea, greater than the dread of men. (2.) If we consider the persons pleaded for.   He pleads for sinners, for the inconsiderable, vile, and base; we plead for Jesus, for the great, holy, and honourable.   It is an honour for the poor to stand up for the great and mighty; but what honour is it for the great to plead for the base?   Reason, therefore, requireth that we stand up to plead for him, though there can be but little rendered why he should stand up to plead for us. (3.) He standeth up to plead for us in the most holy place, though we are vile; and why should we not stand up for him in this vile world, since he is holy? (4.) He pleads for us, though our cause is bad; why should not we plead for him, since his cause is good? (5.) He pleads for us, against fallen angels; why should we not plead for him against sinful vanities? (6.) He pleads for us to save our souls; why should not we plead for him to sanctify his name? (7.) He pleads for us before the holy angels; why should not we plead for him before princes? (8.) He is not ashamed of us, though now in heaven; why should we be ashamed of him before this adulterous and sinful generation? (9.) He is unwearied in his pleading for us; why should we faint and be dismayed while we plead for him?

My brethren, is it not reasonable that we should stand up for him in this world? yea, is it not reason that in all things we should study his exaltation here, since he in all things contrives our honour and glory in heaven?   A child of God should study in every of his relations to serve the Lord Christ in this world, because Christ, by the execution of every one of his offices, seeks our promotion hereafter.

If these be not sufficient arguments to bow us to yield up our members, ourselves, our whole selves to God, that we may be servants of righteousness unto him; yea, if by these and such like we are not made willing to stand up for him before men, it is a sign that there is but little, if any, of the grace of God in our hearts.

Yea, further, that we should have now at last in reserve Christ as authorized to be our advocate to plead for us; for this is the last of his offices for us while we are here, and is to be put in practice for us when there are more than ordinary occasions. This is to help, as we say, at a dead lift, even then when a Christian is taken for a captive, or when he sinks in the mire where is no standing, or when he is clothed with filthy garments, or when the devil doth desperately plead against us our evil deeds, or when by our lives we have made our salvation questionable, and have forfeited our evidences for heaven.   And why then should not we have also in *reserve* for Christ?   And when profession and confession will not do, when loss of goods and a prison will not do, when loss of country and of friends will not do, then to bring it in, then to bring it in as the reserve, and as that which will do, to wit, willingly to lay down our lives for his name; and since he doth his part without grudging for us, let us do ours with rejoicing for him. (Isa. xxiv. 15.   John xxi. 19.)

Use Sixth.   Doth Jesus Christ stand up to plead for us, and that of his mere grace and love?   Then this should teach Christians to be watchful and wary how they sin against God.   This inference seems to run retrograde; but whoso duly considers it, will find it fairly fetched from the premises. Christianity teaches ingenuity, and aptness to be sensible of kindnesses, and doth instruct us to a loathness to be overhard upon him from whom we have all at free cost.   "Shall we sin that grace may abound?   God forbid.   Shall we do evil that good may come?   God forbid.   Shall we sin because we are not under the law, but under grace? God forbid." (Rom. vi. 1, 2, 15.)

It is the most disingenuous thing in the world not to care how chargeable we are to that friend that bestows all upon us gratis.   When Mephibosheth had an opportunity to be yet more chargeable to David, he would not, because he had his life and his all from the mere grace of the king. (2 Sam. xix. 24—28.)   Also David thought it too much for all his household to go to Absalom's feast, because it was made of free cost.   Why, Christ is our advocate of free cost, we pay him neither fee nor income for what he doth; nor doth he desire aught of us, but to accept of his free doing for us thankfully.   Wherefore let us put him upon this work as little as may be, and by so doing we shall show ourselves Christians of the right make and stamp.   We count him but a fellow of a very gross spirit that will therefore be lavishing of what is his friend's, because it is prepared of mere kindness for him.   Esau himself was loath to do this; and shall Christians be disingenuous?

I dare say, if Christians were sober, watchful, and of a more self-denying temper, they need not put the Lord Jesus to that to which, for the want of these things, they do so often put him.   I know he is not unwilling to serve us, but I know also that the love of Christ should constrain us to live not to ourselves, but to him that loved us, that died for us, and rose again. (2 Cor. v. 14, 15.) We shall do that which is naught too much, even then when we watch and take care what we can to prevent it. Our flesh, when we do our utmost diligence to resist it, will defile both us and our best performances. We need not lay the reins on its neck and say, What care we? the more sin the more grace, and the more we shall see the kindness of Christ, and what virtue there is in his advocate's office to save us. And should there be any such here, I would present them with a scripture or two; the first is this, "Do ye thus requite the Lord, O foolish people and unwise?" (Deut. xxxii. 6.) And if this gentle check will not do, then read the other, Shall we say, Let us do evil, that good may come? their damnation is just. (Rom. iii. 8.) Besides, as nothing so swayeth with us as love, so there is nothing so well pleasing to God as it. Let a man love, though he has opportunity to do nothing, it is accepted of the God of heaven. But where there is no love, let a man do what he will, it is not at all regarded. (1 Cor. xiii. 1—3.) Now to be careless and negligent, and that from a supposed understanding of the grace of Christ in the exercise of his advocateship for us in heaven, is as clear sign as can be, that in thy heart there is no love to Christ, and that consequently thou art just a nothing, instead of being a Christian. Talk, then, what thou wilt, and profess never so largely, Christ is no advocate of *thine*, nor shalt thou, thou so continuing, be ever the better for any of those pleas that Christ, at God's bar, puts in against the devil, for his people.

Christians, Christ Jesus is not unwilling to lay out himself for you in heaven, nor to be an advocate for you in the presence of his Father; but yet he is unwilling that you should render him evil for good: I say, that you should do so by your remissness and carelessness for want of such a thinking of things as may affect your hearts therewith. It would be more comely in you, would please him better, would better agree with your profession, and also better would prove you gracious, to be sound in the power and nature of these conclusions. " How shall we that are dead to sin, live any longer therein?" (Rom. vi. 2.) " If ye be risen with Christ, seek those things which are above, where Christ sitteth on the right hand of God: for ye are dead, and your life is hid with Christ in God. Mortify, therefore, your members which are upon the earth, fornication, uncleanness, inordinate affection, evil concupiscence, and covetousness, which is idolatry; for which things' sake the wrath of God cometh on the children of disobedience." (Col. iii. 1—6.)

I say, it would be more comely for Christians to say, We will not sin because God will pardon; we will not commit iniquity because Christ will advocate for us. " I write unto you that ye sin not; though if any man sin, we have an advocate with the Father." Why, the brute would conclude, I will not do so, because my master will beat me; I will do thus, for then my master will love me. And Christians should be above men, brutish men.

And for a conclusion as to this, let me present you with three considerations :—(1.) Know that it is the nature of grace to draw holy arguments to move to goodness of life from the love and goodness of God, but not thence to be remiss. (2 Cor. v. 14.) (2.) Know therefore that they have no grace that find not these effects of the discoveries of the love and goodness of God. (3.) Know also that among all the swarms of professors that from age to age make mention of the name of Christ, they only must dwell with him in heaven that do part from iniquity, and are zealous of good works. (2 Tim. ii. 19.) He gave himself for these. (Tit. ii. 11—14.) Not that they were so antecedent to this gift. But those that he hath redeemed to himself are thus sanctified by the faith of him. (Acts xxvi. 18.)

Use Seventh. Is it so? Is Jesus Christ an advocate with the Father for us? Then this should encourage strong Christians to tell the weak ones where, when they are in their temptations and fears through sin, they may have one to plead their cause. Thus the apostle doth by the text; and thus we should do one to another. Mark, he telleth the weak of an advocate: " My little children, I write unto you," &c.

Christians, when they would comfort their dejected brethren, talk too much at rovers, or in generals: they should be more at the mark: "A word spoken in season, how good is it?" I say, Christians should observe and inquire, that they may observe the cause or ground of their brother's trouble; and having first taken notice of that, in the next place consider under which of the offices of Jesus Christ this sin or trouble has cast this man; and so labour to apply Christ in the word of the gospel to him. Sometimes we are bid to consider him as an apostle and high-priest, and sometimes as a forerunner and an advocate. And he has, as was said afore, these divers offices, with others, that we by the consideration of him might be relieved under our manifold temptations. This, as I said, as I perceive John teaches us here, as he doth a little before of his being a sacrifice for us; for he presenteth them that after conversion shall sin with Christ as an advocate with the Father. As who should say, My brethren, are you tempted, are you accused, have you sinned, has Satan prevailed against you? " We have an advocate with the Father, Jesus Christ the righteous."

Thus we should do, and deliver our brother from death. There is nothing that Satan more desires than to get good men into his sieve to sift them as wheat, that if possible he may leave them nothing but bran; no grace, but the very husk and shell of religion. And when a Christian comes to know this, should Christ as priest or advocate be hid from him, what could bear him up? But let him now remember and believe that " we have an advocate with the Father, Jesus Christ the righteous," and he forthwith conceiveth comfort; for an advocate is to plead for me according as has been showed afore, that I may be delivered from the wrath and accusation of my adversary, and still be kept safe under grace.

Further, by telling of my brother that he hath an advocate, I put things into his mind that he has not known, or do bring them to remembrance which he has forgotten, to wit, that though he hath sinned, he shall be saved in a way of justice. For an advocate is to plead justice and law, and Christ is to plead these for a saint that has sinned; yea, so to plead them that he may be saved. This being so, he is made to perceive that by law he must have his sins forgiven him; that by justice he must be justified. For Christ, as an advocate, pleadeth for justice, justice to himself; and this saint is of himself,—a member of his body, of his flesh, and of his bones.

Nor has Satan so good a right to plead justice against us, though we have sinned, that we might be damned, as Christ has to plead it, though we have sinned, that we might be saved. For sin cannot cry so loud to justice as can the blood of Christ; and he pleads his blood as advocate, by which he has answered the law; wherefore the law having nothing to object, must needs acquit the man for whom the Lord Jesus pleads. I conclude this with that of the Psalmist, "Surely his salvation is nigh them that fear him; that glory may dwell in our land. Mercy and truth are met together; righteousness and peace have kissed each other. Truth shall spring out of the earth; and righteousness shall look down from heaven. Yea, the Lord shall give that which is good; and our land shall yield her increase. Righteousness shall go before him; and shall set us in the way of his steps." (Ps. lxxxv. 9—13.)

Use Eighth. But what is all this to you that are not concerned in this privilege? The children, indeed, have the advantage of an advocate; but what is this to them that have none to plead their cause? (Jer. xxx. 12, 13); they are, as we say, left to the wide world, or to be ground to powder between the justice of God and the sins which they have committed. This is the man that none but the devil seeks after; that is pursued by the law, and sin, and death, and has none to plead his cause. It is sad to consider the plight that such an one is in. His accuser is appointed, yea, ordered to bring in a charge against him, "Let Satan stand at his right hand," in the place where accusers stand. "And when he shall be judged, let him be condemned," let there be none to plead for his deliverance. If he cries, or offereth to cry out for mercy or forgiveness, "let his prayer become sin." (Ps. cix. 6.) This is the portion of a wicked man: "Terrors take hold on him as waters, a tempest stealeth him away in the night, the east wind carrieth him away, and he departeth, and as a storm hurleth him out of his place; for God shall cast

upon him, and not spare; he would fain flee out of his hand. Men shall clap their hands at him, and shall hiss him out of his place." (Job xxvii. 20—23.) And what shall this man do? Can he overstand the charge, the accusation, the sentence, and condemnation? No, he has none to plead his cause. I remember that somewhere I have read, as I think, concerning one who, when he was carrying upon men's shoulders to the grave, cried out as he lay upon the bier, "I am accused before the just judgment of God;" and a while after "I am condemned before the just judgment of God." Nor was this man but strict as to the religion that was then on foot in the world; but all the religion of the world amounts to no more than nothing, I mean as to eternal salvation, if men be denied an advocate to plead their cause with God. Nor can any advocate, save Jesus Christ the righteous, avail anything at all, because there is none appointed but him to that work, and therefore not to be admitted to enter a plea for their client at the bar of God.

Objection. But some may say, There is God's grace, the promise, Christ's blood, and his second part of priesthood now in heaven. Can none of these severally, nor all of them jointly, save a man from hell, unless Christ also become our advocate?

Ans. All these, his advocate's office not excluded, are few enough, and little enough, to save the saints from hell; for the righteous shall scarcely be saved. (1 Pet. iv. 18.) There must then be the promise, God's grace, Christ's blood, and him to advocate too, or we cannot be saved. What is the promise without God's grace, and what is that grace, without a promise to bestow it on us? I say, what benefit have we thereby? Besides, if the promise and God's grace, without Christ's blood, would have saved us, wherefore then did Christ die? Yea, and again I say, if all these, without his being an advocate for us, would have delivered us from all those disadvantages that our sins and infirmities would bring us to, and into; surely in vain and to no purpose was Jesus made an advocate. But, soul, there is need of all, and therefore be not thou offended that the Lord Jesus is of the Father made so much to his, but rather admire and wonder that the Father and the Son should be so concerned with so sorry a lump of dust and ashes as thou art. And I say again, be confounded to think that sin should be a thing so horrible, of power to pollute, to captivate and detain us from God, that without all this ado (I would speak with reverence of God and his wisdom) we cannot be delivered from the everlasting destruction that it hath brought upon the children of men.

But I say, what is this to them that are admitted to a privilege in the advocate-office of Christ? Whether he is an advocate or no, the case to them is the same. True, Christ as a Saviour is not divided. He that hath him not in all, shall have him in none at all of his offices in a saving manner. Therefore he for whom he is not an advocate, he is nothing, as to eternal life.

Indeed Christ, by some of his offices, is concerned for the elect, before by some of them he is. But such shall have the blessing of them all before they come to glory. Nor hath a man ground to say, Christ is here or there mine, before he has ground to say, he also is mine advocate; though that office of his, as has been already showed, stands in the last place, and comes in as a reserve. But can any imagine that Christ will pray for them as priest, for whom he will not plead as advocate? Or that he will speak for them to God, for whom he will not plead against the devil? No, no, they are his own that he loveth to the end, (John xiii. 1,) to the end of their lives, to the end of their sins, to the end of their temptations, to the end of their fears, and of the exercise of the rage and malice of Satan against them. " To the end " may also be understood, even until he had given them the profit and benefit of all his offices in their due exercise and administration. But, I say, what is all this to them that have him not for their advocate?

You may remember that I have already told you that there are several who have not the Lord Jesus for their advocate, to wit, those that are still in their sins pursuing of their lusts, those that are ashamed of him before men, and those that are never otherwise but lukewarm in their profession. And let us now, for a conclusion, make further inquiry into this matter.

Is it likely that those should have the Lord Jesus for their advocate to plead their cause, who despise and reject his person, his word, and ways? Or those either who are so far off from sense of and shame for sin, that it is the only thing they hug and embrace? True, he pleadeth the cause of his people, both with the Father and against the devil, and all the world besides; but open profaneness, shame of good, and without heart or warmth in religion, are no characters of his people.

It is irrational to think that Christ is an advocate for, or that he pleadeth the cause of such, who in the self-same hour, and before his enemies, are throwing dirt in his face, by their profane mouths and unsanctified lives and conversations.

If he pleads as an advocate for any, he must plead against Satan for them, and so consequently must have some special bottom to ground his plea upon,—I say, a bottom better than that upon which the carnal man stands; which bottom is either some special relation that this man stands in to God, or some special law he hath privilege by, that he may have some ground for an appeal, if need be, to the justice and righteousness of God. But none of these things belong to them that are dead in trespasses and sins. They stand in no special relation to God; they are not privileged by the law of grace.

Obj. But doth not Christ as advocate plead for his elect, though not called as yet?

Ans. He died for all his elect, he prayeth for all his elect as a priest; but as an advocate he pleadeth only for the children, the CALLED only. Satan objecteth not against God's election, for he knows it not: but he objecteth against the called, to wit, Whether he be truly godly or no, (Job i. 9, 10. Zech. iii.,) or, Whether they ought not to die for their transgressions. And for these things he has some colour to frame an accusation against us, (and now it is time enough for Christ to stand up to plead,) I say, for these things he has some colour to frame a plea against us, for there is sin and a law of works, and a judge, too, that has not respect of persons. Now, to overthrow this plea of Satan is Jesus Christ our advocate; yea, to overthrow it by pleading law and justice; and this must be done with respect to the children only. " My little children, I write unto you, that ye sin not. And if any man sin, we have an advocate with the Father, Jesus Christ the righteous."

HEART'S EASE IN HEART TROUBLE.

IT is the happy privilege of some minds to discover in affliction motives for their healthiest exercise. They are confident that the burden which lies so heavy upon them conceals, amidst a heap of cares and pains, an abundant reward for patient suffering. It is pleasant to think of this, as they toil along their rough path, or are compelled for a time to lie down in darkness. In some cases, the consolation hence enjoyed seems to spring spontaneously from a faith instinctive to the heart. In others, it is the fruit of careful thought, of inquiry, and meditation. The former cases have the brighter look; but the latter are the more instructive and encouraging. It is not for the generality of sufferers to hope that, in time of trouble, some good emotion will spring up of itself, and restore their elasticity of spirit. The probability is, that they will feel themselves growing sadder, and more desolate every day, and that any constitutional cheerfulness of nature will only serve to render their sorrow more intense. Thus, a prudent man, when he considers what may be the likelihood of his bearing adversity with fortitude, and of finding consolation when cut off from ordinary comforts and supports, will place little trust in his buoyancy of heart, or in the possibility that he may be one of the very few whose strength increases with the necessity of its exercise. He will rather prepare for the trials which the circumstances of the present teach him to look for in the future, by the consideration of his weakness, and his manifold want of support. He will then discover a source of unfailing encouragement in the example and counsels of those who have encountered corresponding distresses. In so far as they sustained their burdens by some force peculiar to themselves, neither their narratives nor their precepts can afford him any direct comfort. But if they assert that their only availing support, their only abiding supply of consolation, was derived from means open to all sufferers, then the lesson which they teach is one of the first to be studied.

The ills to which we are exposed in this life are almost as various as numerous. Did every distress need its own special antidote, the wretchedness of mankind would be far greater than it is. But, happily, there are some few grand and sovereign remedies for multitudes of griefs, distinct in themselves, but gathered into one class, and overcome by the irresistible mercy which has provided for their cure. Thus men's affections may be wounded in countless ways, but the one grace of divine love is an all-sufficient balm, however deep the wound, or however inflicted. So too, numberless as are the agitations to which the mind is subject, truth, speaking by God's Word and Spirit, surmounts them all; leaves not one beyond the circle of its benign influence.

Once assured of this all-important fact, a man may prepare himself for any possible change of condition—for any trial of fortitude and patience. He has good and reasonable cause to believe, that, with a mind open to conviction, he may imbibe new strength from a closer attention to the designs of his being. No less assured may he become that nothing will happen sufficient to turn him from his course, unless by the consent or unfaithfulness of his own will. To suppose the contrary is to cast a doubt upon the only principles which give security to hope, or even to morality. It is inconsistent with the knowledge which we possess of God's ways and works, to believe that on any of the paths opened for us by his providence, either enemies can arise, or events occur without his permission. But that which he permits can only be allowed in furtherance of his ultimate purposes; and they who meekly look to these as the end of their own course, can never reasonably doubt of their final triumph.

Whatever tends to establish the mind in the conviction of these truths, prepares it for a calm and happy future. The records left us of men who have thus preserved a serene, and even joyous temper in the stormiest passages of life, are proofs of the value of their principles. But here, too, caution is necessary. The effect produced on our feelings by examples, or instances, must not be mistaken for the operation of the grace from which they sprung. By contemplating the triumphs of martyrs and confessors, we may learn how possible it is to be " sorrowful, yet always rejoicing;" but the profoundest admiration of such characters, the most confident belief that they were made sufficient for their labours and sufferings by heavenly gifts, can afford us no support of itself in the day of adversity. By shifting the ground of our hope from truth to human sympathy and affection, we become dependent upon feelings instead of knowledge. Hence, while we cheer ourselves with the books which record the successful labours and patient endurance of God's children, it is not the biographical element in such reading which, fascinating as it is, can inspire strength, but a hearty reception of the very same truths and principles by which the characters admired were moulded. For direct, practical purposes, therefore, it can matter little from whose pen a work on religious consolation has proceeded. The question for the reader is, the soundness of the advice,—the ready applicability of its counsels. It may be soothing, and in some respects useful, for him to know that the author had himself proved the worth of his belief; but to imitate him will prove, under any circumstances, a much more difficult, and certainly a much less effective process than a direct pursuit of the faith itself. A want of this consideration has led to some serious failures in the ardent hopes inspired by religious sympathies. The ordinary differences of character existing among the best of men must always render any imitation of an example, merely as such, equally doubtful and laborious. But the power of divine grace overcomes differences and inequalities of every kind; and the person who might utterly fail in an attempt to imitate another's excellence because he admired and loved him—who might struggle in vain, all his life long, to mould the features of his character after those of his friend, may, notwithstanding the invincible obstacles to any conformity of this kind, succeed in becoming like him as one child of God is like another, by the direct operation of the same Spirit.

The following treatise was printed with Bunyan's name on the title-page about four years after his death. There are reasons for doubting its authenticity; but it is probably one of those productions which, as before suggested, Bunyan may have committed to the care of publishers to be printed on any fitting occasion.

The author, whoever he was, had suffered much; but he wisely leads the reader to meditate rather on the helps which came to him,—on the methods of God's sustaining mercy,—than on any peculiarities of his own character or understanding.

H. S.

HEART'S EASE IN HEART TROUBLE.

" Let not your heart be troubled ; ye believe in God, believe also in me."—JOHN xiv. 1.

THESE words are a part of our blessed Saviour's last sermon upon earth just before his passion, which begins, as is probable, at the 13th verse of the 13th chapter of this gospel, and ends at the last verse of the 16th chapter ; in which verse our Lord tells his disciples, (how dear soever they were to him, yet) in the world they should have persecution, tribulation : of which he had often told them before, in effect, that they should not expect their heaven here, but his cross they must bear, if they would wear his crown ; tribulations of all kinds, outward and inward, you must endure—it is your portion here, you are thereunto appointed. Man is naturally born to trouble, as the sparks naturally fly upwards, and new-born to trouble also, and commonly to new and more troubles. "All that will live godly in Christ Jesus, shall suffer persecution," (Acts xiv. 22. 2 Tim. iii. 18,) of hand, or tongue, one way or other. Indeed, such as can be content with a profession of a godliness that may suit with the times—that can please themselves with any kind of godliness, or with a form, any form of godliness, and that can change their forms when they please—such may avoid persecution ; but all that will live godly in Christ Jesus, in the power and spirit of Christ Jesus, and resolve to live up to the example and rule of Christ Jesus, they shall have persecution—no avoiding it. No entering into the kingdom of God but by tribulation. But, notwithstanding this, our Lord lays this positive command on his disciples, "Let not your heart be troubled."

These poor disciples were like shortly to sustain an heavy loss of their dearest Lord ; he was now going away from them—a greater loss they could not have ; and yet saith Christ, "Let not your hearts be troubled ;" which command is repeated and explained in the 27th verse, "Let not your heart be troubled, nor let it be afraid."

What! might they say, must we not be troubled at all? must nothing trouble us ? No, we must not be troubled for any outward loss ; for any outward tribulation, for parting with the nearest and dearest relation, we must not be troubled ; yet we are not forbidden to be troubled for Zion. It is a grievous sin not to be grieved for the afflictions of Joseph ; surely, we must be troubled for God's dishonour, because men break God's commandments. Trouble of heart, except for sin, is sinful trouble. Where sin lies heavy, affliction lies light. They shall not say, I am sick ; for their iniquities shall be forgiven them. (Isa. xxxiii. 24.) Sense of pardon to those souls that have felt the burden of sin, much alleviates and lightens the burden of affliction. " Strike, Lord," said Luther, " now I am absolved from my sin."

We are always too prone to fall into extremes, to sin either in excess or in defect ; too much, or too little : we are faulty both ways. As for sin, which is the worst of evils, we are apt to be troubled too little. How few fail here in the excess, though it is possible so to do ; and some have, that refuse to be comforted by all the sweet promises of Christ in the gospel ; but there are but few of those : most of us fail in the defect. We are not troubled for sin so much as we should ; our sins do not lie so hard and heavy upon us as they should ; our hearts do seldom feel the weight of sin pressing us down ; many sins lie light on us : our vain thoughts, our omissions, careless performance of holy duties, mis-spending precious time, idle talk, &c., and such-like evils, which should trouble us most, they trouble us least.

But, our afflictions, which, comparatively, are but light, lie too heavy upon us, and press us down, even to the dust. So, in respect of afflictions themselves, we are apt to run into extremes, against which the Holy Ghost gives caution as to both extremes. " My son, despise not the chastening of the Lord ; neither be weary of his correction," (Prov. iii. 11 :) the apostle explains it, "nor faint when thou art rebuked of him." (Heb. xii. 5.) Adding a most powerful argument against those extremes : " For whom the Lord loveth he chasteneth," (Heb. xii. 6,) even as a father the son in whom he delighteth ; and therefore despise not his chastisements and fatherly corrections, slight them not, for they come from a loving father, a wise father, and should not be despised by his children : they are the fruits of his love. Also you must not be weary of them, nor faint under them, for the same reason, viz. because they shall not hurt you ; they flow from your Father's love, from a Father they come who delighteth in you, and therefore ye ought not to faint under them, or, as it is in the text, whatever affliction befalls you, "Let not your heart be troubled."

It is *heart trouble* you see that is here forbidden ; not a filial sense of God's hand, nor a child-like acknowledgment of God's rod ; God's rod hath a voice, and its voice must be heard. When his hand is lifted up to strike, to lay on any blows on us, or on any of our relations, or earthly comforts, we must observe it, and him, and acknowledge the same; but not to acknowledge and observe the hand of God, not to consider in the day of adversity, not to humble ourselves under his mighty hand, not to stoop and yield to God, but to think or say of our affliction that it cannot be helped, there is no remedy, it is common and ordinary, and the like—this is to despise the chastening of the Lord: take heed of this. But yet, we must take heed, too, that under the pretence of being sensible of the hand of God, and of his strokes upon us, that we do not fall into the other extreme, of being weary of his chastisements, and of despondency, and fainting under his corrections; we must be careful that we do not let our hearts be troubled.

Quest. But is it possible that we should be afflicted, deprived of liberty, of estate, of loving relations, of the desire of our eyes, and of the delight of our hearts, (for such in a most eminent manner was Jesus Christ to his disciples, he was "the desire of all nations,") and not be troubled at our very hearts? Can we behold our Benjamins, our Sarahs, our Rebekahs, our Josephs, &c., taken away, our dear husbands, our loving, faithful, tender wives, snatched away from us with a stroke, with a sudden stroke, to be in a moment deprived of such comforts, and in such a time too, in an evil time, in a sad and suffering time, when such helpers would sweeten our sufferings, and help to bear our burdens, would give us sweet counsel, and uphold us in the way of God;—what! is it possible such knots should be untied, and so suddenly, such flowers cropt off, cut down, such sweet friends removed from us, as lay once in our bosoms, and sent to the chambers of darkness, sealed up in the dust, made silent in the grave, to see their sweet faces no more, till the heavens be no more;—is it possible, I say, in such cases, not to be troubled? or if it be possible, is it necessary, or is it attainable? May we arrive to such a temper, may we get such a calm, quiet, tranquil, and submissive frame of spirit? It is admirable, but is it attainable?

I answer, we must not despise the chastenings of the Lord, as was noted before; we must not be as stocks or stones, altogether insensible of the hand of God upon us; no, we must be sensible, we must lay those things to our hearts, and consider the work of God. Such losses, and of such, are to be lamented; they will be found wanting, their relations will find them wanting, their families will find them wanting, the poor will find them wanting, and the church also. David lamented the loss of Jonathan, and the disciples the loss of Lazarus: lawful it is, then, to be affected with the deaths and departures of our dear relations and friends, and moderately to mourn for them; but our care must be, that we suffer not nature to work alone without grace, for then it will soon go beyond its bounds;

nature must be restrained and bounded. It is moderate mourning that is lawful. Mourn we may, "but not as those that have no hope," (1 Thess. iv. 13, 14,) for those that sleep in Jesus, they being safe and happy; for "if we believe that Jesus died and rose again, even so they that sleep in Jesus will God bring with him." Troubled we cannot choose but be in such cases, and under such strokes, but we must "not let our hearts be troubled," saith our Lord. And what this imports you shall see by and by. It is trouble of heart that is here forbidden; but what is it that will prevent or cure this heart trouble? Our Saviour answers in the next words: "Ye believe in God, believe also in me: in my father's house are many mansions," &c. In which we may observe these parts, viz.:—

1. An evil disease, or spiritual distemper, intimated and prohibited, to which the disciples of Christ are incident and prone in time of affliction; and that is trouble of heart: this may seize you, but take heed of it, labour against it. As if the Lord had said, I know it will be a cutting, a killing thing to you to part with me, your dear and loving Lord and master; but part with me you must, and take heed of this indecent distemper of heart trouble; "let not your hearts be troubled," saith our Lord Jesus.

2. The best preventative of, or remedy for, this spiritual distemper proposed and enjoined: "ye believe in God, believe also in me." As if our Lord had said, Surely you believe in God, why then are your hearts troubled? Cannot your faith in God support you, if you act it upon him? But if that cannot, then act your faith also on me; believe also in me. Set your faith to work on me. Believe that I love you, that when I leave you, I will not leave you comfortless: "I will send the Comforter unto you, and he shall abide with you for ever." (John xiv. 16, 17.) Therefore, let not your hearts be troubled. "Believe in me." I must leave you, and I and you must part: but believe where I am going, and let the consideration of that quiet you, and comfort you: "in my Father's house are many mansions;" there is a better, a far better condition for you above, than that you are in here; for here you are tossed up and down from place to place, and are exposed to many straits. I myself here, on earth, have not a house where to lay my head; but in my Father's house are many mansions. There is an house above, "not made with hands, eternal in the heavens." (2 Cor. v. 1.) When once you come thither, you shall remove no more; there are many mansions, room enough for you all, and for all the innumerable company of angels and saints; therefore, "believe in me," for, these things are most true that I tell you. And believe also, "that I go to prepare a place for you;" I go to take possession of those celestial mansions, of those everlasting habitations for you, in your name and stead. While you are here on earth, I shall prepare you for those mansions; and when I go from you, I will prepare them for you. There-

fore, to prevent those heart troubles which you are subject to, because of my departure from you, and to fortify you against them, (for I am solicitous for you,) this is the remedy that I purpose and enjoin you to practise: that seeing "you believe in God, believe also in me," act your faith on me. From which words thus explained, I commend to your Christian consideration this gospel doctrine, viz. :—

Doct. That the lively acting of true faith upon God and Christ, or upon God in Christ, is the best preventative of, and remedy against, heart trouble, under the greatest loss whatever. Or, Faith acted on God in Christ is the sovereign cure of heart trouble.

Our Lord Jesus is very tender over his poor disciples, and having foretold them of the hard usage, and bad entertainment they should meet with in the world, losses and crosses, tribulations and persecutions, he now leaves with them some antidotes against distempers of mind, some cordials against those faintings of spirit, and troubles of heart, to which he knew, they being flesh and blood, were subject. And this in the text is chief and principal: "Let not your hearts be troubled ; ye believe in God, believe also in me." This your faith will be your best cure, your best remedy.

Poor believers are but princes in disguise here in this world: princes they are, Christ hath made them all so ; but while here below they are in a foreign land, under a veil. "It doth not now appear what they shall be." (1 John iii. 2.) They have a large patrimony, but it lies, indeed, in a land unknown to the world; it is in Terra Incognita, if the expression can be borne. The holy, the great God himself is their portion, their heritage ; God is their sure, their full, their lasting, their everlasting portion. They are heirs of a kingdom. (James ii. 5.) Heirs of salvation. (Heb. i. 14.) Heirs of God, co-heirs with Christ. (Rom. viii. 17.) Yea, all things of this world are theirs. (1 Cor. iii. 21.) All things are blessed and sanctified to them, and shall conduce to their spiritual and eternal welfare. (Rom. viii. 28.) Yet notwithstanding all this, and although heaven and earth lies at the feet (as it were) of godliness, and of those who profess it, in the power of it,—godliness having the promise of this life, and of that which is to come, (1 Tim. iv. 8,)—and, notwithstanding believers have a true title to all the good of both worlds, yet may those poor but blessed saints be exposed to manifold temptations and tribulations in this world : they may have a dark, and sad, and stormy way of it to their Father's house ; they may be stripped of all their earthly comforts, may be deprived of their liberty, estate, nearest friends and relations, as we read in Scripture, that such hath been the portion of the best saints. And upon this the people of God have been dejected and disquieted ; they have desponded, their hearts have been troubled, and have thereby displeased their heavenly Father, who would have

them believe that all things shall work together for their good.

Now, our Lord, in this text, forbids this distemper of mind, and would not have his disciples, who had God for their Father, and himself for their Redeemer, and who had title to such happiness in the other world, to despond, and to be disquieted ; therefore he lays this charge on them, "let not your hearts be troubled :" adding the proper means to prevent this sinful malady of heart trouble, that it might not seize on them ; or, if it had, to cure them of it, viz. "ye believe in God, believe also in me."

"The lively acting of true faith upon God in Christ, it is the best preventative of, and remedy against, heart trouble," under the greatest loss whatsoever. Which proposition I shall prosecute, in the assistance of God's Spirit, and according to the measure of light and grace I have received, after this manner and method following :

First, by way of demonstration. Secondly, of confirmation ; and then to apply and make improvement of it for our use.

First, by way of demonstration ; endeavouring to show—

FIRST. That God's choicest saints are in this world subject to all kinds of troubles, losses, and afflictions ; and whence it is, and why so.

SECOND. That under those losses and afflictions, they are subject to despond, to be dejected, and to be troubled in their hearts.

THIRD. What this heart trouble is that Christ forbids here.

FOURTH. How, that believing in God and Christ, is the best means to prevent and cure this heart trouble.

FIRST. That God's choicest saints are liable to all kinds of troubles, losses, and afflictions, even in the greatest, heaviest, and sorest ; as we read of Job, David, Heman, and others.

God had but one Son without sin, but no son without suffering. His only-begotten Son was a man of sorrows ; and the Holy Ghost assures us that, "If ye be without chastening, whereof all are partakers, then are ye bastards, and not sons." (Heb. viii. 12.)

God's children are liable to sufferings, whether we consider them as men or as Christians ; as men, "Man that is born of a woman is full of trouble." (Job xiv. 1.) As our relations and comforts increase, so do the occasions of trouble. God never appointed this world to be the place of man's rest, but of our exercise, and only a passage to another world : and in this our passage we must look for storms and tempests ; if we can through mercy obtain a tolerable passage through this world, and a comfortable passage out of it into that better above, we shall have cause to bless the Lord to all eternity.

And much more, as Christians, must we expect troubles ; for man is no sooner brought home to God, but he must expect to be hated by the world, assaulted by Satan, chastened by the Lord; our own corrupt hearts will be always vexing; the old man, the flesh, thwarting all the motions of the new nature, lusting against the spirit. The lusts of the flesh will be as pricks in our eyes, and as thorns in our sides; we shall have enemies in our own houses.

But this truth is so manifest in all the Scriptures, that I shall insist no longer on it, only shall add this by way of use: let all Christians prepare for affliction by getting an interest in God through Christ, by getting sin pardoned and purged, by getting peace with God and conscience, by getting hearts crucified to the world; and then when troubles come, let us bear them as Christians, not murmur nor repine, but in patience possess our souls; not desponding nor fainting; remembering that our troubles are no more, but infinitely less than we have deserved. "He will not lay upon man more than right." (Job xxxiv. 23.) God perfectly understands our need, and knows our strength. "If need be, ye are in heaviness," (1 Pet. i. 6;) "he is faithful, who will not suffer you to be tempted above that ye are able." (1 Cor. x. 13.) It is the wise, just, and gracious God, and our Father, that tempers our cup for us. Many earthly parents do not correct their children in measure, being ignorant of their nature and disposition; and therefore their correction doth them no good. Many physicians mistake the constitutions of their patients, and therefore may do them more hurt than good; but God knows our need, and our strength, and so suits all his remedies accordingly; therefore let us be patient, bearing our troubles with an equal mind, not suffering as per force, but willingly. It is said that they "yielded their bodies," that is, cheerfully, to the fire. (Dan. iii. 28.) In our affliction, let us search our hearts, and try our ways; let us fly to God by prayer, and resign up ourselves to him, and trust in him, casting our cares and burdens on him. (Ps. lv. 22. 1 Pet. v. 7.)

Moreover, it is our wisdom, that while we are at ease, have our comforts about us, let us look for troubles; afflictions from God, as well as for God, are part of our cross which we must take up daily. Sickness, death of friends, loss of estate, &c., we must look for them, that we may not be surprised.

He that buildeth an house, or a ship, doth not make this his work and care, that it should not rain upon it, or that it should have no storms or tempests, for this cannot be prevented by any care of ours; but that the house or ship may be made able to endure all without prejudice. So must it be our care to provide for afflictions; for to prevent them altogether we cannot; but prepare for them we may, and must, as was hinted before; to treasure up God's promises, and store our souls with graces, and spiritual comforts, and firm resolutions in God's strength, to bear up and hold on, we had need be well "shod with the preparation of the gospel of peace." (Eph. vi. 15.)

Most Christians are not mortified and crucified to the world, not acquainted with God and the promises, as they ought to be, nor so resolved to follow God fully, as they ought, and therefore are so dejected and discontented when affliction comes. Oh that we did count the cost, when we first begin to make profession of Christ; and that we had had such full persuasions of the incomparable worth and excellencies of the Lord Jesus, as that we could willingly part with all things for his sake! Oh that we had such believing apprehensions of the wisdom, faithfulness, righteousness and mercy of God, such sights of his reconciled face, and such tastes of his fatherly love to us in Christ, as that we could quietly submit to his holy will, and be well satisfied with all his dispensations towards us! So much of this first particular.

SECOND. The disciples of Christ, under the afflictions which they meet with in this world, are apt to be troubled in their hearts, to be disquieted in their minds, to be dejected and discouraged. It was so with holy David, "Why art thou cast down, O my soul? and why art thou disquieted in me?" (Ps. xlii. 5.) He was sensible of his afflictions, and that disquieted him, and cast him down. God's people are subject to such disquietments, because they are flesh and blood, subject to the same passions, made of the same mould, subject to the same impressions without as other men; and their natures are upheld with the same supports and refreshments as others, the withdrawings and want of which affecteth them as well as others. And besides those troubles they suffer in common with others, by reason of their being called out of the world, the world hates them, and they are therefore more exposed to tribulation than others, and so are apt to be cast down and discouraged: this our Lord foresaw would befall his disciples after his departure from them; and therefore he counsels them against the same: "Let not your hearts be troubled."

Quest. But it may be demanded, "Whence ariseth this heart trouble and disquietment of mind under affliction?"

Ans. There are many causes of it, which is necessary for us to know, that so, knowing the causes, we may the better find the cure; there are outward and inward causes.

First. *Outward causes.*—1. And the first may be God himself. He sometimes withdraws the beams of his countenance, withholds the sense of his love, hideth his face from his children, which the saints in Scripture so bitterly complain of, and so earnestly pray against: whereupon the souls even of the strongest Christians are disquieted. This caused trouble to the soul of Jesus Christ himself. (John vii. 27.) When a poor child of God, together with his affliction, apprehends God to be his enemy, and that his troubles are mixed with God's displeasure, (and it may be his conscience tells him that God hath a just quarrel against him, because he hath not walked so holily, so humbly, so evenly, and so strictly with God as he might, had he been more watchful, careful, and circumspect, and that he hath not renewed and kept his peace with God as he should, and might have done,) this sense of God's displeasure puts a sting into all his afflictions, and this causeth trouble of heart and disquietment of mind. And justly may such a soul be troubled that has ever felt the joys of God's salvation, the sweet influences of his love,—that has tasted that the Lord is gracious, seeing, that in his favour is life, and his loving-kindness is better than life. (Ps. xxx. 5; lxiii. 3.)

2. The devil is the cause sometimes of the heart trouble of God's children. For he being a cursed spirit cast out of heaven, full of disquietment and discontent himself, labours all he can to trouble and disquiet others, to bring others (as much as in him lies) into the same cursed condition with himself. He being cast out of Paradise himself, envies us the paradise of a good and quiet conscience, for that is our paradise until we come to heaven : and this paradise a poor child of God may possess in a prison, in a dungeon, on a dunghill.

Two main designs the devil hath upon men : the one is, if possible, by all imaginable slights, temptations, and enticements, he may keep men in a course of ungodliness, to hinder them from coming to Christ by faith and repentance, to deter them from his holy ways. And when he is not able to do this, but that unsearchable rich and free grace takes hold of some poor souls, and they are snatched out of his hands, their captivity led captive by that mighty Redeemer, then all the devil's labour is to hinder their comfort, and to interrupt their peace, and to make their way to heaven as hard and uncomfortable to them as possible, pursuing them with all dejecting and heart-troubling temptations.

3. Wicked men are also active in the troubling of God's people ; they are indeed the true troublers of God's Israel. They load God's people with reproaches, and there is nothing that the nature of man is more impatient of than reproaches, for there is no man so mean but thinks himself worthy of some respect ; now a reproachful scorn shows an utter disrespect of a man, which flows from the very superfluity of malice. "Reproach hath broken my heart," saith David, (Ps. lxix. 20,) and nothing more doth he complain of than reproach, and nothing more are God's people liable to than this. These are the causes from without.

Second. There are *inward causes* also of heart trouble and despondency : when God's people are in affliction, most time that black cloud of melancholy also surrounds them, and darkness makes men fearful and dejected.

There are many causes within ourselves : as ignorance of God, and of Christ, of the covenant of grace, of the name of God. They that know God's name, will trust in him and not be dejected. Also, forgetfulness of God, and of what he hath done for us. We forget God, when we are afraid of man. Our overlooking and passing by the many comforts we enjoy, even while we are under affliction, taking little notice of our mercies, but let them be all swallowed up in our miseries : as Abraham, because he had no heir; and Rachel, who said, "Give me children, or I die ;" though she had all other earthly comforts, yet the want of this one so troubled her, that all the rest seemed nothing.

It is an evil thing for us to be wedded to our own wills. None more subject to discontent than those who would have all things after their own way, and are mere strangers to self-denial. Likewise, false apprehension of things cause heart trouble : to think God hates us because he corrects us, and when he takes from us, that it is all in wrath. Another common cause is our own watchlessness and carelessness, our neglect of keeping our hearts and consciences pure and clean; and in time of affliction, these former neglects of duty come to our minds, then conscience awakes, and tells our former faults, and this brings trouble of heart. (1 Kings xvii. 18.)

Moreover, unnecessary scruples cause disquietness, solitariness, idleness : when persons will not do what is needful, they are troubled with that which is needless ; and idleness tempts the devil to tempt us and trouble us : if we cannot find work for ourselves, the devil will make work for us.

Also, when we are guilty of neglecting doing good to others, as to our relations : not reproving, admonishing, or encouraging them as we ought ; or have neglected to receive that good from them that we might ; but now they are dead and gone, and we can no more do any good to them, nor receive any from them, this hath troubled men on their sick and death-beds.

Inconstantly wavering in the ways of God will also breed disquiet. And our inordinate love of creature-comforts, our setting of our hearts on friends, estates, and the like, letting out our hearts on husbands, wives, children, &c., this is to build castles in the air, expecting contentment in and from those things that cannot yield it. Also multitude of worldly business, and too much poring on our afflictions, and forecasting the events of things. You see what a crowd of causes here be within ourselves of disquiet and heart trouble.

THIRD. The third particular proposed is, What is this heart trouble which Christ here forbids his people, and that he would fortify them against?

Ans. This heart trouble is such a sense of evils felt or feared as creates to us heart disquietment, dejection, despondency, depriving us of that tranquillity, peace, and comfort which we had in ourselves, or otherwise might have : it is such a disturbance of our passions, such a storm and tempest in our spirits, as causeth inward motions, emotions, and commotions of mind, putting all things in the soul out of order ; and it carries in it several evil things, as follow :—

First. Sinful sorrow, worldly sorrow. When

Christ had told his disciples that he would leave them, and that after he was gone, they should be exposed to hard and heavy things from the world, bitter persecution for his name's sake; then sorrow filled their hearts. (John xvi. 1—6.)

God's own servants, Christ's own disciples, may have their hearts filled with sorrow; against this our Lord commands many preservatives in this sermon. The ground of this sorrow is from ourselves, from our own hearts, though Satan will have a hand in it: and it comes not from *humility*, but from pride, because we cannot have our wills, therefore we are discontented. We may thank ourselves, not only for our troubles, but for our overmuch troubling ourselves in our troubles. If we ward and guard against this worldly sorrow, our troubles would not lie so heavy on us as they do; for, as the joy of the Lord doth raise and strengthen the soul, so doth sorrow deject and weaken it. Sorrow and grief doth lie like lead to the heart, cold and heavy, and sinks it downward still; sorrow contracteth and draweth the soul into itself from that communion and comfort it might have with God and man; and it weakeneth the execution of the offices of it, because it drinketh up the spirits, it melteth the soul, it causeth it to drop away. Yea, in this kind of heart trouble, God's own people are many times more excessive than others.

1. Because many times their burdens are greater, their temptations, desertions, troubles for sin greater; as their joys are unspeakable and glorious, so their sorrows are sometimes above expression. Common and natural courage will carry a man through other single afflictions; but sin is a heavier burden than affliction, and the wrath of God than the wrath of man.

2. They have a greater sense than others, their hearts being made tender by religion; they have also a clearer judgment than others, and see more into the nature of things than others, they see a greater evil in sin, and in the displeasure of God, than others. They value God's favour more than others, therefore when he hides his face, they cannot but be troubled. They observe more of the displeasure of God in afflictive providences than others do, and therefore they have more sorrow.

3. They have more tender affections than others; the new heart is a soft heart. A stamp is sooner set upon the wax than upon a stone. A wicked man hath more cause to be troubled than a godly man; but he is not a man of that tenderness and sense, and therefore is not so affected either with God's dealings with him, or with his dealings with God.

Thus we find often in Scripture good souls depressed with sorrow. David said he was like a skin-bottle in the smoke, all wrinkled and dried up. Read Ps. xxxviii. and Ps. xxxix. 11. "When thou with rebukes dost correct man for sin, (that is, by sickness, death of relations, and other losses,) thou makest his beauty (that is of his outward man) to consume away like a moth." Whereas the beauty of the soul grows fair by affliction, but that of the body is blasted. Age, sickness, losses, will make the beauty of the body to fade, but of the soul to shine. "Though our outward man perish, yet the inward man is renewed day by day." (2 Cor. iv. 16.) But for worldly sorrow; that, too often, not only weakeneth the body, but also causeth heart trouble. "A merry heart doth good like a medicine, but a broken spirit drieth the bones." (Prov. xvii. 22.)

Quest. But is this worldly sorrow lawful and commendable?

Ans. No, surely, for there are many evils in it, which we should avoid. As—

1. Impatience and murmuring against God, that is an effect of immoderate sorrow; when our wills are crossed, we cannot bear it, for want of self-denial.

2. Quarrelling at instruments.

3. Using indirect means for our relief. It is better to pine away in our afflictions, than to be freed from them by sinning.

4. Desponding and distrustful thoughts of God. "Is his mercy clean gone? will he be favourable no more?" (Ps. lxxvii. 7, 8.)

5. Questioning our interest in God, merely because of the afflictions upon us. "If God be with us, why has all this befallen us?" (Judges vi. 13.) Not considering how hard soever God dealeth with his people, yet he loveth them. (Heb. xii. 6.)

6. Sometimes atheistical thoughts do arise, as if there were no God, no Providence, (Ps. lxviii. 13,) as if it were in vain to serve the Lord.

7. This worldly sorrow indisposeth to all good duties; it makes a man like an instrument out of tune, or a bone out of joint: which makes the body move both uncomely and painfully; it unfits for duty to God and man.

8. It makes a man forget former mercies, and overlook present mercies; all is nothing under present sufferings. "Give me children, or I die."

9. It makes us unfit to receive mercies, and to embrace the best counsels; such plaisters will not stick; they refuse to be comforted. (Ps. lxxvii. 2.)

10. It disposeth us to receive any temptation: Satan hath never more advantage than upon discontent.

11. It hinders beginners from coming unto the ways of God.

12. It rejoiceth and hardeneth the wicked, and it grieves and damps the spirits of our friends. All these, and many more evils, are in worldly sorrow.

Therefore, this evil temper we must labour against, and not suffer ourselves to be dejected in sickness, contempt in the world, loss of friends and relations, loss of honour, and earthly interest. May we only think to be exempted from chastisements, whereof all God's children are partakers? (Heb. xii. 8.) And must God make a new way to heaven for us? Or, do we think it best for us to live here for ever, in ease, in plenty, and honour, and never see a change? No, surely it is in vain to think so. It becometh us betimes to prepare for crosses. None so strong, lively, and brisk now, but they shall shortly wither and decay. None hold their heads so high now, but they must shortly lay them down in the dust. We and our dearest relations must part.

It would be our wisdom, to turn the stream of our sorrow for losses and crosses, into godly sorrow for sin, then it will run in its right channel. Let our sins lie heavy upon us, and then our afflictions will be light. Let us grow weary of our sins, not of our sufferings. "God doth not afflict willingly, nor grieve the children of men." (Lam. iii. 33.) Let us consider, also, the real spiritual benefit of affliction. God aims at our profit; and in good time, in the best time, he will send deliverance. And be sure, those that are not unmindful of their duty, God will not be unmindful of their safety.

But that which should mostly affect us, and make us take heed of immoderate worldly sorrow, is to consider, that this kind of sorrow of heart is God's curse, imprecated on God's enemies, "Give them sorrow of heart, they curse." (Lam. iii. 65.) As godly sorrow is God's blessing, a grace of God's Spirit, a fruit of the covenant of grace, and a fruit of faith, (Zech. xii. 10,) so worldly sorrow is God's curse, and a bitter fruit of unbelief. They that sorrow for sin shall be comforted, (Matt. v. 4;) but they that mourn immoderately for outward losses, there shall be none to comfort them. This is the first piece of heart trouble which Jesus Christ hath forbidden : "Let not your heart be troubled;" that is, not filled and overcome with worldly sorrow; whatever your losses and crosses be, let not your sorrow go beyond its lawful bounds; take heed, "let not your heart be troubled."

Second. Another piece of heart trouble is sinful fear. And against this distemper also Christ counselleth his disciples, "Let not your heart be troubled, nor let it be afraid." (John xiv. 27.) As if he had said, let not that distemper of base, slavish fear seize your hearts.

This fear is a passion, or rather a perturbation of mind, whereby upon the sense of approaching evils, the mind is discomposed and disordered, and the heart troubled and dejected.

This fear is a tyrant where it comes, and it tyrannizeth where it prevails, as Job iv. 14, 15. We read how it prevailed over that famous believer, the father of believers, Abraham, to his prejudice, and to the discredit of his religion, who for fear denied his wife once and again. (Gen. xii. 13.) And good Isaac was taken in the same fault. (Gen. xxvi.) This fear troubles men's peace, and disquiets their minds, that they are said sometimes to be like the leaves of the forest; and this fear is often forbidden to Abraham, (Gen. xv. 1 ;) and to Isaac. (Gen. xxvi. 24.) And when Israel was in the greatest dangers that ever men were, they were forbid to fear. (Exod. xiv. 13. Isa. viii. 12.) And in the New Testament, our Lord strongly cautions against this fear. (Luke xii. 4. 32.) "Fear none of those things which thou shalt suffer." (Rev. ii. 10.) Slavish fear troubles the heart more than anything.

Objection. But may we not fear God's judgments ? Did not good Josiah tremble at them ? and did not holy David say, " I am afraid of thy judgments." (Ps. cxix. 120.)

Ans. Doubtless it is our duties so to do. When we see the same sins abound, for which God hath executed his judgments in former times, we ought to lay them to heart, and to be affected. (Jer. vii. 12. Luke xvii. 26, &c.) Remember Lot's wife, said our Lord. So, 1 Cor. x. 2. Pet. ii. 6. Rom. ii. 18. Zeph. iii. 6, 7, a remarkable scripture.

Although it went well with Nehemiah himself, yet had he a sad resentment of the state of Jerusalem. (Neh. i.)

God's people have tender hearts, wicked men have hearts of stone ; when God smites them they are not grieved. (Jer. v. 3.)

But we must distinguish of fear.

1. There is a natural lawful fear, when evils are approaching to our bodies, or names, or friends, or the like dangers are apparent, it is natural to fear. This was in the best men in the world ; it was in Christ himself. (Mark xii. 14, 15.) Also it is said, he feared, and was sore amazed, (Mark xiv. 33,) yet without sin.

2. There is a lawful, filial fear of God's judgments, which ariseth from the consideration of the evil of sin, and of God's righteousness, of his hatred of sin and his wrath against it ; which fear produceth repentance, self-examination, a turning to God with our whole hearts, through reformation, and an endeavour to secure ourselves in God's covenant, and to hide ourselves. "A prudent man foreseeth the evil, and hideth himself." (Prov. xxii. 3.) A striving to get into Christ, and to get clear evidence of God's love to us in Christ; I say, such a fear that worketh these effects is a great duty.

3. There is a base, slavish fear of approaching evils, arising from our misapprehensions of God, producing in us unworthy thoughts, sinking into despondency, and inciting to murmuring and impatience, and putting us upon sinful shifts, the use of unlawful means to prevent or escape dangers ; a fear of despondency, a vexatious, distracting fear, that drives from God, and unfits for service. A tormenting, disquieting fear, that unsettles and discomposeth our minds, disturbs our peace, suspends our acts of faith, and disposeth us to diffidence, distrust, and impatience; this is the fear that Christ would not have his people's hearts troubled with.

Third. Another piece of heart trouble is care, vexatious, distracting care, which our Lord would not have his disciples trouble themselves with, and therefore he useth so many powerful arguments to dissuade them from it, Matt. vi. from verse 25, onward. 1. He assures us, it is God that takes care for our bodily life, we trust him with that, how much more should we for food and raiment.

2. Saith he, your Father takes care for the fowls, and provides for them, "are ye not much better than they?" 3. He clotheth the lilies, "And will he not clothe you?" 4. You cannot by all your care make your condition better than God hath appointed it shall be. (Matt. vi. 27.) 5. Your heavenly Father knows you want all these things. 6. They that are ignorant of God, and of his fatherly care and good providence, that have no God to care for them, they trouble themselves with those cares; therefore you should not do so who have an heavenly Father, that dearly loves you, and looks after you. 7. You have the promise of the faithful God, to have all necessaries provided for you, while you make it your care to serve, and please, and trust him: "All these things shall be added unto you." (Matt. vi. 33.) 8. We have no cause to be thoughtful for time to come, because every day brings evil enough with it: and therefore it is no wisdom to perplex ourselves with cares. (Matt. vi. 34.) So again, Luke xxi. 34. Phil. iv. 6: "Be careful in nothing." Our Lord also shows us how prejudicial such cares are to our profiting by the word. (Matt. xiii. 22.) And expressly commands us, "To cast our cares upon him, for he careth for us." (1 Pet. v. 7.)

Fourth. Despondency of spirit, dejectedness, distrust, discouragement, are other pieces of heart trouble. Such as was in David, Ps. xlii. 5; cxlii. 3; cxliii. 4. Casting down breeds disquietness, because it springs from pride, which is a turbulent passion; and everything that crosseth and disappoints it, causeth a combustion in the mind. When a man cannot come down, and stoop to that condition that God casts him into, then is he discontented; and this comes from his pride.

A Christian should be very careful to keep up his spirits, when his condition in the world falls down. Could we but bring our minds to our conditions, to like and be pleased with our conditions, as being certainly persuaded that our present condition is best for us, it would be all as good, all as well, all as comfortable to us, as if we could bring our conditions to our minds; for one of these must be done, or else we shall never be free from heart trouble while we live: either our minds must be brought just even to, and suited and compliant to our conditions, be it sickness, poverty, shame, prison, &c., or, our conditions must be suited just even to our minds. We have a mind to health, to liberty, &c., we must have them, or we are troubled. Now this latter is wholly and altogether out of our power, we cannot add a cubit to our stature. (Matt. vi. 27.) It is the Lord that appoints all our conditions for us; we cannot make our conditions happy, honourable, &c., of ourselves, and without God; but the former is in our power, by the help of God's spirit and grace, we may bring our minds to our conditions: it is an holy art, attainable in the use of God's means. Contentment in, and with, our condition, is the bringing of our minds to our conditions, to lie

even, and suitable, and square one with the other; and this is, as I said, an holy art, attainable by Christians. (Phil. iv. 11.) St. Paul had learned it, and so may other Christians. It is suitableness between our minds, and our conditions, that breeds quiet and content; and if we have not quiet in our own minds, all outward comforts will do no more good than a silken stocking to a scabbed leg; or a golden slipper to a gouty foot.

Now, it is only God that can, but never will, (except in wrath,) bring any man's condition to his mind, for then his condition should be changed almost every moment—so mutable is man's mind: God will not bring the condition of the wicked to their mind, (except in wrath, as was said.) For, as their outward prosperity doth increase, so do their desires after more: *crescit amor nummi, &c.* And the wise man tells us, "The eye is never satisfied with seeing." And the more they have, the more they crave. They can never have enough. And for the godly themselves, they are not so free from covetousness as they should be, but still need to learn this lesson of contentment, and to be learning of it all their days. And most commonly, if not always, God by his grace brings their minds to their conditions, and not their conditions to their minds. And for this, wise Agur prays. (Prov. xxx. 9.) Two dangerous extremes he prays against: the one is poverty, that would breed discontent, in that his mind would be below his condition, debased to vile and sinful practices, as stealing, &c.; the other is riches, that would breed discontent, in that his mind would be above his condition, and that would lift him up to base pride and forgetfulness of God; therefore he begs a suitableness and conveniency between his mind and his condition: "Feed me with food convenient." (Prov. xxx. 8.)

Certainly we shall never be free from heart trouble till our minds be brought suitable to our conditions, and such a frame would prevent casting down in time of affliction. To like our condition, to be pleased and satisfied with it, and with the holy will of God in it,—that is, to be content, content with sickness, poverty, shame, prison, loss of relations and friends, &c.,—in a word, when our wills lie even with God's will, (as in reason they should,) and our minds lie even with our conditions, then have we inward peace, and tranquillity, quietness, and contentment, and never till then: and then sickness is as good as health, and poverty is as good as riches; and a prison, &c. And this is that blessed frame of spirit we must labour for, and we ourselves shall have the sweetness of it: otherwise, it is in a man's mind, as it is with the body when bones are out of joint, there is nothing but pain and trouble; but this bringing of our minds to our conditions, is as the setting of the bone again. Casting down ourselves, despondency, discouragement, which arise from discontent, are great pieces of heart trouble.

This distrust of God's providence is a grand evil; when we think we cannot live, unless we have a greater portion of earthly things, and this sets us upon carking cares: we know not how we and ours shall be provided for, &c. Now this we may cure, by casting ourselves upon God's promises. (1 Pet. v. 7. Ps. xxxiv. 10; lxxiv. 11. Heb. xiii. 5.) Let us cast ourselves on God's providence. Will he provide for ravens, lilies, and neglect his own children? It cannot be imagined.

Earthly things are but a vain show, they can give us no joy of heart, nor peace of conscience: they cannot add one cubit to our stature, nor one moment to our lives.

Moreover, this happy state of mind is attainable; Eli had it, (1 Sam. iii. 18,) and David. (2 Sam. xv. 25, 26.) "It is the Lord, let him do what seemeth him good." Therefore let us labour for such a spirit: such a contented frame of mind is worth a kingdom; without it, godliness itself is not great gain. It must be laboured for; Paul said, he had learned it: it was a hard lesson, but sweet when learnt.

Fifth. Persecution may cause heart trouble, when men are offended, (Matt. xiii. 21;) when Peter was an offence to Christ, he was a trouble to him. Our Lord did on purpose foretell his disciples what persecutions they should undergo, that they might not be offended, (John xvi. 1;) forewarned, forearmed. It is a blessed thing not to be offended at persecution for Christ. He foretold his disciples the night before his passion, that "all of them should be offended at him that night," (Matt. xvi. 31, 56;) which came to pass, for one of them openly denied him, and the rest forsook him and fled. To be troubled at persecution for Christ's sake, is to be offended at the cross of Christ; and that he would not have his disciples to be by any means. (Mark viii. 38.)

Object. But is it not said, "Great peace have they that love thy law, and nothing shall offend them?" (Ps. cxix. 165.) How then come the people of God to be offended?

I answer, they that truly love God's law, because they love God, such shall have peace with God, and with their own consciences, and that is great peace, and nothing shall offend them; that is, much trouble them, since they have peace with God, and with their own consciences. Outward losses and crosses are easily borne, they shall make no breach upon their inward peace. They that have this character of God's children, will not be stumbled at God's dispensations, let them be never so cross to their desires, because they have a God to fly unto in all their troubles, and a sure covenant to rest upon. Therefore the reproaches cast on them, and on the ways of God, do not scandalize them, for they have found God in that very way which others speak evil of; they are not so offended by anything that attends the way of God, as to dislike or forsake that way. Nevertheless we must take heed that we be not offended.

Sixth. Temptations from Satan may cause heart trouble and vexation. Satan's suggestions, his fiery darts, those tormenting thoughts which he casts into the minds of Christ's disciples, create to them much disturbance and heart trouble. So soon as any man is plucked out of the devil's hands by the mighty power of Christ's spirit, he falls upon him speedily with all his force, to trouble such a soul and vex it, so that he shall enjoy little peace if Satan can hinder it. So long as the devil keeps possession in the soul, he keeps all in peace —a sad peace! But when a stronger than he comes, and casteth out this strong man armed, then Satan rageth, to recover his lost captive soul, and vexeth that soul with all his temptations. But let not this break your peace, nor cause heart trouble. As Christ hath overcome the world, and therefore bids his disciples be of good cheer, (Job xvi. 20,) so hath he also overcome the devil, he hath trodden this serpent under his feet already, and this prince of peace will tread him under your feet also shortly. Therefore, "let not your hearts be troubled."

Seventh. Desertion, another (and not the least) piece of heart trouble; this may be the case of Christ's disciples. We read of the saints complaining that God hath forsaken them, and when he hideth his face they cannot but be troubled.

Sometimes God doth but seem to hide his face. (Isa. xlix. 14, 15.) When God takes away their earthly comforts from them, and suffereth sharp and bitter afflictions to befall them, and though they cry unto him he doth not remove them, then they think that God hath forsaken them.

Sometimes God doth really forsake his people, as to the sense of his favour: "For a small moment have I forsaken thee. In a little wrath I hid my face from thee for a moment," (Isa. liv. 7, 8;) and this is, either by withholding comfort from them which they cry for, or by withdrawing that comfort from them which they had. (Ps. li. 11; lxxvii. 1.) Yet here God supported and sustained his servant's soul with grace many times. When God's people have least comfort, they have most grace, most humility, patience, self-denial, thirsting after God, heavenly-mindedness, &c. God's people may lose the sense of his love, but never lose his love, for that is everlasting; but to lose the sense of his love is a grievous trouble to a gracious soul that hath tasted and felt the love of God and his favour, for their great happiness is to have the favour of God: "In his favour is life, and his loving-kindness is better than life." This is the joy of their lives, which David so earnestly prayed for. (Ps. cxix. 135.) No, such as have found this, must needs be troubled when they lose it.

Two things chiefly cause God to hide his face from his people.

1. When their hearts are too much set upon, and carried out after, earthly comforts. (Ps. xxx. 6, 7.) Fleshly delight, and confidence in earthly things, provokes God to hide his face: when a

man smiles so much on the world, and gives it so much room in his heart, God frowns, and is offended that the gift should be so much loved, and the giver so neglected.

2. When their hearts are let out too little after God, and there grows a strangeness between God and them, and they begin to grow cold, dull, and dead in duty, then God withdraws and hides himself; but no affliction like this, this disquieteth and dejecteth the people of God indeed. And as all the candles in the world cannot make it day when the sun is set, so all the comforts in the world cannot rejoice such a soul, nor can there be any day in such a soul, " Until the Sun of righteousness arise with healing in his wings." (Mal. iv. 2.)

So much for this third particular, showing what this heart trouble is which our Lord here forbids his disciples, namely, worldly sorrow, sinful slavish fear, distracting care, despondency, dejectedness of spirit, distrust, offence at persecution for Christ's sake, Satan's temptations and spiritual desertions; all which may either be the causes, or the parts and pieces, of heart trouble, which must be avoided.

Fourth. The fourth particular to be opened, is to show how that believing in God, and in Christ, is the best antidote against this sinful heart trouble: Christ proposeth it as a special remedy.

Quest. But how is it so ?

Ans. To answer this, I shall endeavour to show these three things :

I. What this believing in God is, which our Saviour here grants that they had : " Ye believe in God."

II. What is it to believe in Christ : " Believe also in me."

III. That this faith acted on God and Christ is the best remedy to prevent and cure heart trouble, in all those several parts of it I have mentioned.

I. What this faith in God is: briefly, the apostle tells us, (Heb. xi. 6,) it is to believe that God is, that there is a God, an infinite first and best being: to believe that God is that, all that, which he hath revealed himself in his word to be, viz. that he is an all-sufficient, almighty, only-wise God : a righteous, gracious, merciful God ; an holy God, a loving God. He proclaims his name himself : " The Lord, the Lord God, merciful and gracious, long-suffering, and abundant in goodness and truth," &c. (Exod. xxxiv. 6.) To believe that he is " wonderful in counsel, and excellent in working." (Isa. xxviii. 29.) That he is the Father of mercies, the true and faithful God, the God of all grace, and of all consolation ; with many more admirable attributes of God doth the Scripture furnish us, that we may build our faith, and place our trust in him, to prevent heart trouble, and to cure it when it hath seized on us. Whatsoever is revealed of God in his word, that true faith believes.

Also this faith in God is, to believe that " he is a rewarder of them that diligently seek him."

That he being God all-sufficient, he is able to support, to supply, to deliver his people out of all their troubles, and that he is willing so to do, as well as able, for he hath promised ; and he is a rewarder, a God that will abundantly, plentifully reward all his suffering ones : great shall be their reward in heaven. (Matt. v. 12.) And to believe God to be a rewarder, is to lay hold on his covenant, wherein he promiseth so to be : I will be thy God, " Thy shield, and thy exceeding great reward." (Gen. xv. 1.) The sum of the covenant is, " I will be thy God :" what is that but this, I will be that all to thee, and I will do that all for thee which a God can be to thee, and do for thee. I will be a " sun and shield to thee." (Ps. lxxxiv. 11.) I will give thee grace and glory, and will withhold no good thing from thee. I that am the infinite first and best being of all things, the living fountain of all mercy, the original of all power and goodness, I will be a God to thee, thy God, thy Father, if thou wilt take me for thy God, and place all thy happiness in me, and wilt become my servant, and give up thyself sincerely to me, to serve and obey, to love and fear, and trust me only. This is to believe in God : to accept of God for our God, and to yield up ourselves to him ; to be his people, to choose the things that please him, (Isa. lvi. 4,) to give him our hearts, and become his servants, (Deut. xxvi. 17, 18.) And so God proposed himself to Abraham, when he called him, (Gen. xii. 1—3,) as a rewarder, and more fully in Gen. xv. 1, " I am thy shield, and thy exceeding great reward :" and so Abraham's faith was to act on God so manifested : and, Gen. xvii. 1 : I am God all-sufficient ; all-sufficient to support thee in thy way, and work, and all-sufficient to reward thee in the end ; therefore be thou upright and faithful ; let not thy heart be troubled, whatever dangers and difficulties thou meetest with in my way and work, and what losses soever thou sustainest for my sake, believe I am God all-sufficient ; I will sufficiently reward thee ; thou shalt be no loser by following and serving me. Also Moses his faith had an eye to " the recompence of the reward." (Heb. xi. 26.) And that you may see that this is not legal and mercenary, our Lord Jesus proposeth this as an encouragement to his people, " Great is your reward in heaven." (Matt. v. 12.) And he himself took encouragement from it, as in Heb. xii. 1, 2 : " for the joy that was set before him," &c.

So that this is to believe in God, to believe that God is really and truly, he is all that which he hath revealed himself to be, and to believe that he is a rewarder, &c. This faith in God, Christ took for granted that his disciples had : Ye believe in God, ye believe that God is, and that he is a rewarder of them that diligently seek him ; and if ye believe this, let not your hearts be troubled ; be not afraid nor dejected, but act your faith in God, and seriously consider what God that is in whom you believe ; and believing also your interest in that God, that he is your God, this God all-sufficient is your God, you will have no cause to be troubled. Your acting of faith on God, your God, will prevent and cure your heart trouble, and that these several ways.

First, more generally.

He that believes in God as his God, believes God is always present with him, according to his promises. In the worst times God is present with his people. And can there be any cause of heart trouble to such souls as have always the presence of God with them, whose presence makes heaven, and in whose presence is fulness of joy, and at whose right hand are pleasures for evermore? (Ps. xvi. 11.) Surely, beloved, this will prevent heart trouble, when a soul can act this faith and firmly believe it. God is always present with his people, and that for gracious purposes, (and not as a bare spectator,) as to proportion and measure out their afflictions to them, that they may not be above their strength, nor more than need. (1 Cor. x. 13. 1 Pet. i. 6.) All the afflictions of God's people are measured by the hand of the most wise, most merciful and gracious God: all the malice of men and devils cannot add a drachm to the weight, nor a drop to the measure, beyond God's appointment. He is present to order and fix the time of our sufferings: it is an hour of temptation. (Rev. ii. 10.) It is our loving Father that sets up the glass of the time of our troubles; he appoints their beginning, their duration, their end; he holds the glass in his own hand. All the powers on earth cannot bring trouble on us, till the hour come, till the appointed time, nor continue our troubles longer than his time: "The rod of the wicked shall not rest upon the lot of the righteous." (Ps. cxxv. 3.) God is present to mix some comforts with the cross, thereby to allay the bitterness of it, present to support the soul with inward strength, "Thou strengthenedst me with strength in my soul," (Ps. cxxxviii. 3 :) present to sanctify afflictions for good, and at length in his good time, which is the best time, when he hath perfected his own work in his people, he is present for their full deliverance.

A true believer in God hath always a God to go unto: oh what a comfort, what a happiness is that! He dwells in the love of God, as well in affliction as out of it; he may be cast out of his happy condition in the world, but never out of the favour of his God: this, believed by us, will cure heart sorrow, heart fear, heart care, all despondency, dejectedness, disquietments and distractions whatever. Faith acted on God, the almighty, all-sufficient God, and our God, always present with us, is the sovereign antidote against, and the best cure of, all heart trouble. In Ps. cxlii. 1—4, there are the Psalmist's troubles; and, ver. 5, there is his cure—"I cried unto thee, O Lord, thou art my refuge and my portion in the land of the living." So, Ps. cxliii. 4, 6, 8, his spirit was overwhelmed with trouble; but he cried to God, and trusted in him, and that was his relief: his trusting in God was an high exercise of his faith. This kept David from sinking under his great distress; he "encouraged himself in the Lord his God." (1 Sam. xxx. 6.) Thus in general.

More particularly I shall endeavour to show what there is in God that a believer's faith fetcheth virtue from to cure his heart trouble in his great distress, even under the loss of the personal presence of his best and dearest friends on earth; for such was like to be the case of the disciples in the text.

First. That in God which faith looks unto, and fetcheth comfort from, is his *sweet and gracious nature.* "God is love," (1 John iv. 16,) the very element of love, and his gracious name, which discovers his nature, "The Lord, merciful and gracious." (Exod. xxxiv. 6.) When he gives to his people, he gives in love; when he takes, he takes in love. Now when a soul believes that all is from love, and all in love, he is supported. When a man can believe that all his troubles come to him from the Father of mercies, and his Father in Christ, he cannot but bear them patiently. Ye believe in God, said Christ, ye believe that God loves you, therefore let not your hearts be troubled.

Quest. But how shall I know that God loves me when he afflicts me?

I answer, when we can discern that we have received any spiritual benefit by any affliction, we may certainly conclude that the love of God was in that affliction. Fury is not in God towards his people. (Isa. xxvii. 4.) And he intends nothing but our profit; all his ends are for our good: to purge away our sins, to wean us from the world, to draw us nearer to himself, to humble us, to try us, to conform us to Christ, to prepare us for glory, &c. Now seeing God's ends are so much for our good, we must conclude that all our afflictions proceed from his love; and when we find any of those ends accomplished in us, and on us, and that we have received real spiritual good by them, we ought to be strengthened in our belief that God hath corrected us in love; so that faith acted on the love of God in our affliction, will prevent or cure our heart trouble. Our Lord told his disciples, " that the Father had loved them." (John xvi. 27.)

Secondly. Faith acted upon God's glorious *attributes,* will fortify against heart trouble.

1. Upon his all-sufficiency. Ye believe that God is all-sufficient in and of himself alone : every way able to supply all wants, to make up and repair all losses, to satisfy all desires, to sustain under all burdens, and that without all earthly comforts : for how else are the saints in heaven happy, who have none of these earthly enjoyments? Ye believe this, act your faith on it. He must needs be all-sufficient who made the world, and all things in it, and upholds it to this day; he that owns all things, and is possessor of heaven and earth, he it is that is your God, your Father: act your faith on him and be comforted.

2. He is all-mighty; you believe this. So Christ hath told his disciples: "All things are

possible to God." He can break the hardest heart, and can bind up the most broken spirit : he can make up the greatest loss. "We are kept by the mighty power of God." (1 Pet. i. 5.) Oh, how safe is that man that is in the love and covenant, and that lies in the arms and bosom of the almighty God! (Deut. xxxiii. 27.) He can bring light out of darkness, and make the greatest loss to prove the greatest gain. He hath the keys of the grave, to him belongs the issues from death. All power belongeth to him; nothing is too hard for him.

3. His absolute sovereignty and supremacy: all souls are his. (Ezek. xviii. 4.) He gives, he takes, who can hinder him? May he not do with his own what pleaseth him? Ye believe this. Hath he not a right in all the works of his hands, and may he not dispose of all as he will?

4. His unchangeableness. God is "in one mind." (Job xxiii. 13.) The thoughts of his heart stand to all generations. He sets bounds to the sea, to the life of man, and to all the comforts of life : the number of his months is with God. (Job xiv. 5.) Believe this.

5. His wisdom. God is only wise, the fountain of wisdom ; he doth all he doth in infinite wisdom. He is wise in heart, and worketh all things according to the counsel of his will. He knows what is best for us ; when to give, when to take, and what will do us most good. Believe this, and "let not your hearts be troubled."

6. His righteousness. All his ways are just and equal; yea, when clouds and darkness are round about him, (his providences towards us dark,) yet then "righteousness and judgment are the habitation of his throne." God, the judge of the world, can do no wrong : believe this of God, and it will quiet your minds.

Lastly. His faithfulness. "In faithfulness thou hast afflicted me," saith holy David. (Ps. cxix. 75.) He hath promised, he will withhold no good thing from his people. Now he sees and knows that afflictions are good for them, good for their souls ; his daily rod as good for their souls as his daily bread is for their bodies. Therefore he brings afflictions on them, and so makes good his promise to them. Oh believe this, and "let not your hearts be troubled." Certainly, faith acted on God's attributes will support under the greatest strokes and most grievous losses.

Third. Faith acted on the *covenant of grace.* God's everlasting covenant will help to support under trouble. Ye believe in God, that God hath made a covenant with you, to become your God : I will be your God, and ye shall be my people. (Jer. xxxi. 33.) This is infinitely more, for God to become our God, to give himself to us, than if he had said, I will give you crowns and kingdoms, sons and daughters ; when God saith, I will be your God, he saith, I will be all that to you, and I will do all that for you, and bestow all that upon you, which a God can be, or do, and which shall make you most happy for ever. I will pardon your sins; I will give new hearts, give you my spirit; I will give you grace here, and glory hereafter. This acting of faith in God's covenant supported David in his greatest troubles, (2 Sam. xxiii. 5, a notable text;) when the Lord had made breach upon breach in his family, this comforted him, "That God had made with him an everlasting covenant." That he was in covenant with God, that God was his God in covenant, this balanced all his losses, and repaired all the breaches made in his relations ; though his family was wasted and blasted, this answered all, that "he was in covenant with God."

This is the language of faith : If God be my God, if I be his child, born of him, reconciled to him, pardoned, justified, sanctified, in covenant with him, why am I troubled, though he give me neither health, nor wealth, nor friends, nor relations? Have I not enough, in having God to be my God? Is not God more than all? But if God be not my God, I have cause enough to be troubled then, considering the danger I am in: and my trouble for this should swallow up all other trouble. For surely, either God is mine in covenant, or he is not: if he be mine in covenant, then, though he break my family, make breaches upon all my earthly comforts, yet he will not break his covenant, (Ps. lxxxix. 34,) and so long I am well enough. If he leave me neither son nor daughter, if he strip me of friends, estate, liberty, health, &c., yet he remains my God still; and so long it is well enough; it cannot be ill with a man so long as God is his : ye believe this.

Fourth. Faith acted upon the *word of God* will support the soul ; ye believe God's word, the word of truth. "This is my comfort in my affliction : for thy word hath quickened me;" (Ps. cxix. 50 ;) and had not thy law been my delight, I had perished in my affliction. (Ps. cxix. 92.)

1. Consider the word of precept : as in the text, it is Christ's command, "Let not your hearts be troubled." Many such commands we have in Scripture, as "not to fear," "not to be cast down," "sorrow not as those that have no hope," and such like. Now faith applies such commands to the soul: I must not be troubled in my heart, God forbids it. Why must we not profane the Sabbath, nor swear, nor lie, &c., but because God hath forbidden these evils? So here, God hath forbidden us to be troubled, and commanded us to be quiet, patient, contented, submissive to his will in all his dealings. Thus we should urge God's command on our souls; yea, we are commanded to be so far from troubling ourselves when afflictions befall us, as that we must "count it all joy when we fall into divers temptations" (James i. 2 ;) and to rejoice in sufferings ; for "blessed is the man that endureth temptation." (James i. 12.)

2. Consider the word of promise. Many exceeding great and precious promises are in the word of God, which are as a full feast for faith to feed upon. God promiseth to be our God, to be

with us in the fire, and in the water; and to support us and sustain us, (Isa. xli. 10; xliii. 2,) to lay no more upon us than he will enable us to bear, (1 Cor. x. 13 ;) that all things shall work together for our good. (Rom. viii. 28.) And what can we desire more? There is no trouble that can befall us, but we may find a promise suitable to it : and "faithful is he that hath promised, who also will do it." (1 Thess. v. 25.) And why the great God so wonderfully condescended to poor creatures, as to make so many sweet promises which are recorded in the Holy Scriptures, but for this, that the heirs of promise might have strong consolation, (Heb. vi. 17;) and that their hearts might not be troubled?

3. The word of threatening. "He that loveth father or mother, son or daughter, (so husband or wife,) more than me, is not worthy of me," saith Christ. (Matt. x. 37.) Now by our immoderate sorrow for the loss of these, we manifest our immoderate love of these ; we should consider, that when these are removed, that Christ remains ours still, and with us still ; our relation to him is not broken : and Christ will be instead of all, and better than all to us, and this should keep us from heart trouble.

4. The examples of God's saints in the word. We should consider also, what a famous example is Abraham, who was content to part with his Isaac, at the command of God, his only son, the son of his old age, the son of the promise, in whom all the nations of the earth were to be blessed; yea, content to lay his own hands upon him, to slay him, and burn him : but when he was tried, God spared him. (Gen. xxii. 12.) The way to keep our earthly comforts, is to be willing to part with them, when God calls for them. So Eli, when very sad tidings were told him, "It is the Lord," said he, "let him do what seemeth him good." (1 Sam. iii. 18.) So Aaron, when that heavy stroke fell upon him, that both his sons were struck dead upon the place for their sin, and it may be in their sin too, it is said, "Aaron held his peace." (Lev. x. 3.) So Job, stript of all his friends at once, "The breath of his wife was strange to him." And David complained, that "lover and friend was put far from him." Now, we should consider these examples, and set faith a-work on them, and know that it is our duty to "be followers of them who through faith and patience inherit the promises." (Heb. vi. 12.)

5. The word of experience. David tells us his experience, and saith, "It was good for him that he had been afflicted." And many Christians living can, and do bless God for their afflictions, and that God, by taking away of their relations from them, he made more room in their hearts for himself, and communicated more of himself to their souls : thus by acting of faith upon the word of God, we may again support, and be preserved from heart trouble.

Fifth. Faith acted upon the *work of God* will support under heart trouble. "Consider the work of God." (Eccles. vii. 13.) Faith looks to the work of God; who it is that killeth, who it is that taketh away : who can stop, or mend, or hinder his work? This disquieted David's heart, when the stroke of God was heavy upon him, "I opened not my mouth, because thou didst it." (Ps. xxxix. 9.) It is the Lord, he hath done it. It is he that doeth whatsoever he pleaseth.

Sixth. Faith acted on the *will of God.* Faith resigns up all to the good and holy will of God; so did our Lord himself: " not my will, but thine, be done," (Luke xxii. 42 ;) and so we pray continually, " Thy will be done :" and therefore when it is done, our hearts must not be troubled.

Lastly. Faith acted on the *gracious ends and designs* of God in afflicting us, and removing our earthly comforts from us, will prevent heart trouble. God hath holy and good ends which faith looks unto ; God aims at our profit. (Heb. xii. 10.) Such ends as these—

1. God's end is to discover and purge away our sins. " By this shall the iniquity of Jacob be purged; this is all the fruit to take away his sin." (Isa. xxvii. 9.)

2. To try and exercise our graces. (Job xxiii. 10. 1 Pet. i. 6, 7.)

3. To crucify our hearts unto, and to estrange our affections from, the things of this world.

4. To draw our hearts nearer to himself. Therefore many times God takes away our earthly comforts from us, because they had too much of our hearts, and because they lay between God and our hearts, and kept us at a distance from him.

5. To bestow greater, and better mercies upon us. God never takes away any darling comfort from his people, but his design is, to give a better in the room of it ; as in the text, Christ leaves his disciples, in regard of his bodily presence, because he would send the Comforter to them, which would abide with them for ever. (John xiv. 16.)

6. To make them partakers of his holiness. (Heb. xii. 10.)

7. To fit and prepare them for that far more exceeding and eternal weight of glory. (2 Cor. iv. 17.) These are God's holy and good ends in afflicting his people, unto which faith looks, and so supports the heart.

Thus you see how faith, acted on God in these particulars, will prevent or cure all our heart trouble : faith acted on the sweet and gracious nature of God—he is love, all love ; on his glorious attributes, his all-sufficiency, his omnipotency, his absolute sovereignty, his unchangeableness, his wisdom, his righteousness, his faithfulness ; faith acted on God's gracious everlasting covenant ; on the word of God, on the word of precept, of promise, of threatening, of example, of experience ; and faith acted on the work of God, on the will of God, and on his holy ends in all his chastisements. I say, faith thus acted on God, will exceedingly support under all trouble. " Let not your heart be troubled: ye believe in God." So much of this first particular. And before I enter upon the second, I shall make some short application of this.

First. It follows hence, that heart trouble under the afflicting hand of God argues the weakness, if not the want of faith. All those sorts of heart trouble, and the parts of it which I have mentioned, as heart sorrow, worldly sorrow, immoderate mourning, sinful fear, vexatious care, despondency of spirit, being offended, disturbance of mind, distraction, dejection, discouragement, and the like, all these flow from the want of faith, or, at least, from the weakness of faith in God. We do not believe in God; we see the causes of our troubles, they are mostly in ourselves, even our unbelief. Whatever we profess, we do not believe in God; if we could but believe in God, our hearts would not be troubled. Oh our want of faith! let us heartily lament it, and cry to God for pardon through the blood of Christ. If our hearts be troubled, where is our faith in God? What doth God, and all that is in God, signify to us? What are we the better for all that infinite all-sufficiency and goodness that is in God, if we do not act faith upon it? our heart troubles would be cured could we act faith on God as we ought to do.

Immoderate sorrow then is very unbecoming in believers in God. If we will prove ourselves believers in God, let us discharge ourselves from heart trouble, and let us draw our consolation for our hearts by faith, from all those comfortable considerations of God, and from all those abundant excellencies that are in God. Oh let us labour for faith, and act it; let us live in the exercise of it, and then surely we shall find comfort.

Second. Let us all labour to get an interest in God, by faith in Jesus Christ, that so we may be able to look upon God as our God, and then we may claim an interest in all that God is, and in all that God hath, and so shall we have no cause of heart trouble in any condition. For if God be ours all his attributes are ours, his gracious covenant is ours, his word and promises are ours: all is ours; therefore should we labour in this above all things, spending all our thoughts, affections, and spirits upon this. Oh let us lay hold on God and his covenant; let us choose him for our portion, and resign up our whole selves unfeignedly to him, terminating and centring all our desires, hope, love, delight, in him alone, placing all our happiness in him, and then commit all to him. " Whom have I in heaven but thee? and there is none upon earth that I desire beside thee." (Ps. lxxiii. 25.)

II. What is it to believe in Christ? For, saith he in the text, " Believe also in me." It is God in Christ that we must believe in; not in God without Christ, not in God out of Christ; but believe in God in Christ.

Now what this believing in Christ is, I shall endeavour to show; looking up to the Father of lights, and to the author and finisher of our faith, for light and assistance.

In general, it is to believe all that which is revealed in the Holy Scriptures concerning Christ, to believe the record that God hath given of him in his word, (1 John v. 10—13.) To believe that Jesus Christ is the eternal Son of God. That he came out from the Father, (John i. 18 ;) was made flesh ; took upon him our nature ; was born of a virgin ; lived on earth in the form of a servant, a poor despicable life, preached the gospel, working miracles, &c. That he suffered upon the cross, with all the sins of his people upon his soul and body ; that he bore the cross of the law, the wrath of God, which was due to man for sin. That he died a most painful, shameful, and cruel death, dying as a sacrifice to satisfy God's justice, to atone and pacify his wrath, to make our peace, and to reconcile us to God ; that he rose again from the dead, ascended into heaven, to prepare a place there for his people ; that he sitteth at the right hand of God everlasting, to make continual intercession for us ; and that he shall come to judge the world at the last day : and while he is absent from us in person here on earth, he promised to send his Spirit the Comforter into the world, to convince and convert all those which his Father hath given him, to call them by his word, to quicken, strengthen, establish, comfort, and confirm them, until he come again, to take them to himself, that where he is, they may be also. (John xiv. 3.) This is the record that God hath given of his Son : " that whosoever believeth in him should not perish, but have everlasting life." (John iii. 16, 36.) Now, to believe in Christ, is to believe all this testimony of him. And also, out of a deep sense of our sin and misery, and sight of Christ's infinite excellency, all-sufficiency, and willingness to save sinners, and upon his call to us in the gospel, to come unto him weary and heavy laden with our sins, heartily willing to accept of the Lord Jesus upon his own terms, to take him for our only Lord, to give up our whole selves, souls and bodies, to his blessed government by his word and spirit in all things, and unfeignedly and unreservedly to enter into covenant with him, to become his, and his alone, and his for ever; and to rely upon him for life, for grace and salvation : this is to believe in Christ. Thus believe in Christ, and let not your hearts be troubled. The acting of this faith on blessed Jesus, is a singular means to prevent and cure all heart trouble, all heart sorrows, cares, fears, vexations, despondencies, dejections, and distractions whatsoever, that may arise in our hearts, by reason of any loss, cross, disappointment, distress, or affliction that may befall us. If we can but thus believe in Christ, and rest and rely upon him, and trust in him, our hearts shall not be troubled.

Quest. But what is that in Christ which faith must act upon, to effect this cure of heart trouble when afflictions come upon us?

Ans. Such like things (as I showed before) as are in God for faith to act upon, which are these that follow.

First. Faith must be acted upon the *loving, gracious, sweet nature* of Jesus Christ. Our Lord Jesus is of a most loving and sweet nature; he is love indeed, son of his Father's love, and altogether lovely. His thoughts of us who believe in him, were thoughts of love from everlasting. All his words are sweet, his mouth is most sweet. Oh what sweet language doth he give his church! My dove, my love, my fair one, my sister, my spouse, &c. (Sol. Song v. 5, 16.) He loved us, and gave himself for us; loved us and washed us in his blood. (Rev. i. 6.) He is one of our nature, our kinsman, our husband, our father, our elder brother, &c. So that, if there be any love in the head to the members, if any in the father to the child, if any in the husband to the wife, or in any near and dear relation, then sure there is love, strong love, in Jesus Christ to all believers; for in him is the love of all relations, and therefore he expresseth it under all these relations. He calls us his friends. He is of a most tender, a most merciful nature, full of bowels of compassion, and of tender mercies. It would be endless to express the loving nature of Jesus Christ to poor believers; which when a believer duly considers, ponders upon, and acteth faith upon, it cannot but support him under all heart trouble.

Act your faith on Christ as yours, your Jesus, he that died for you, he that sweated great drops of blood for you in the garden, wrestling and grappling with his Father's wrath for you, in your name and stead there, and upon the cross. Consider, that this your dearest Jesus now in glory, knows your souls in adversity; he seeth all the trouble of your hearts, he sympathizeth with you in all your afflictions, his heart, now in heaven, is touched with the feeling of your infirmities on earth. (Heb. iv. 15.) He hath human nature still, though glorified. He feels our losses, crosses, griefs, pains, and sorrows; his heart, his most tender heart, is affected. Oh that we could but believe this! and thus consider with ourselves: here I sit solitary as a widow, or a widower, or childless, or fatherless, or motherless, or friendless; my family is broken; I feel pains and sicknesses; I am deprived of my liberty; my sweet relations and comfortable friends are laid in the dust; I have none about me to counsel or comfort me; I am brought low in the world, my estate is diminished, my honour and reputation lost, my pleasure gone, my flesh faileth me, my strength faileth, lovers and friends fail me, &c. Such complaints we are apt enough to make, and it may be worse than these: my God hath forsaken me, he hides his face from me; I am compassed about with temptation, sad, dejecting, and distracting thoughts; I am persecuted, banished from house and home, all my outward and inward comforts fail me. These have been the cases and conditions of God's dearest servants—as Job, David, Heman, and others; but yet let not your hearts be troubled for all this; ye believe in God, act your faith in God, yea, and act it on Christ also: believe in Jesus, look up by faith unto Jesus your dear Lord; whatsoever, whomsoever you have lost, you have not lost your Jesus, your best friend, your heavenly husband: you have his heart, his bowels towards you still; you have his eye, his tender, watchful, provident eye, upon you still; you have his ear open to your cries still; yea, you have his everlasting arms underneath you to sustain you still, for else you would sink. Oh then, act faith upon the sweet nature of Christ as your head and husband. "Can a woman forget her sucking child, that she should not have compassion on the son of her womb?" (Isa. xlix. 15;) possibly she may: but can Jesus forget those whom he died for, and travailed for? No, no, he will not hide his face for ever, he will never forget his people. Your Maker is your husband; and he is the Father of mercies.

If we read these things, or hear them read, and do not apply them to our own souls by faith; if we do not meditate on them, and let them sink down into our hearts, if we do not pray earnestly that the holy Spirit would bring them home, and lay them close to and fix them on our hearts, they will do us no good, yield us no comfort; therefore meditate on them, apply them, and act faith upon them.

Second. We must act faith upon the many precious *attributes* of Jesus Christ; all which afford to faith much matter of support under all our heart troubles whatever. And these are exceeding many; I shall mention only some.

1. Jesus Christ is our advocate with the Father. (1 John ii. 1, 2.) One that undertaketh for us to plead our cause in that highest court of heaven. If a man be sued in law, or be accused of any crime in any court, it is a great privilege to have a solicitor there for him, that is skilful and faithful, and powerful with the judge in that court. Jesus Christ is such an advocate, or solicitor, for us, in heaven he will plead our cause: and he is wise, he is the wisdom of the Father; he is a great counsellor, and the only counsellor, none else can plead in that high court; and he is most faithful, he is a "merciful and faithful high-priest in things pertaining to God." (Heb. ii. 17.) He appears for us in heaven. (Heb. ix. 24.) When a man is indicted in a court, and hath none to appear for him there, he is in a bad case; but all poor believers are in a better case: they have a blessed advocate to appear in the presence of God for them; he continually presents his blood, his sacrifice to the Father for them. (Heb. x. 10.) And it is his will, to have that sacrifice accepted for our justification and sanctification. Christ prevails so with his Father, that he always heareth him, (John xi. 42:) now if we can act faith on this blessed advocate in heaven, who is there always pleading for us, ever

living to make continual intercession for us, (Rom. iii. 25,) presenting himself before God as our sacrifice and propitiation;—when men accuse us, and our own consciences too; when we are deprived of our near and dear relations, distressed with pains and sicknesses, pinched with wants and necessities;—I say, then for us to act our faith on this precious advocate at the right hand of God for us, interceding there for us, one who knows and feels all our misery, it must needs be a great support and relief to us, and the best remedy against our heart troubles. Oh that we could act faith strongly on this our advocate!

To have a friend in heaven, and such a friend, so wise, so powerful, so faithful, so merciful, so sensibly affected with all our misery, so tender, so able, and so willing to hear and help us; I say, this is infinitely better than all the friends that ever we had, or could have on earth: and this friend ever liveth, and maketh continual intercession for us. And as this is matter of comfort in case of suffering, so in case of sin too. "If any man sin, we have an advocate with the Father, Jesus Christ the righteous; and he is the propitiation for our sins." (1 John ii. 1, 2.) Faith acted on this blessed advocate, is the best remedy against heart trouble, in case both of sin and suffering.

2. Jesus Christ is bread from heaven; the true bread for souls, the bread of life, the water of life. (John vi. 35, 48, 51.) Now when poor saints are fed with the bread of affliction, and with the water of adversity, let them look up to Christ, and act faith upon him, he will be living bread, life-giving bread, living water to their souls, to revive their drooping, and to refresh their fainting spirits. By acting faith on this blessed Jesus, the fountain of living water, their souls shall be so satisfied, as that they shall never hunger more, never thirst more (that is, inordinately) after the things of this world. When your souls want strength to bear your burdens, want comfort in your distresses, act faith on this Jesus, this bread of life, this water of life, and you shall be refreshed, you shall "have joy and peace in believing." (Rom. xv. 13.)

3. Jesus Christ is called "the Sun of righteousness," (Mal. iv. 2,) and "the bright and morning star." (Rev. xxii. 16.) He is the fountain of righteousness and life, as the sun is of light; he hath healings in his wings. "He was wounded for our transgressions, that by his stripes we might be healed." (Isa. liii. 5.) He was appointed to heal the broken hearted. (Luke iv. 18. Isa. lxi. 1.) He will heal our backslidings. (Hos. xiv. 4.) He is the great physician, he can heal all our spiritual and corporeal diseases. His blood is an healing blood; his spirit, an healing spirit; his word, an healing word; his promises, healing promises. He hath all healing virtue in him; he is the true brazen serpent; could we but act faith on this Jesus, we should be healed of all our diseases. He is the bright morning star. We are in darkness, clouds and darkness upon our spirits; many dark

providences befall us, we see not our way many times, know not what to do: now, let us act faith on Jesus, he will bring light out of darkness. We are under black fears and sorrows, and all dark night sometimes with us; but if we can look up to this bright morning star, he will enlighten our darkness, he will shine in upon our hearts, and scatter all the clouds, and give us a joyful morning.

4. Jesus Christ is called the captain of the Lord's hosts, and the captain of our salvation. (Josh. v. 14, 15. Heb. ii. 10.) He hath the command of all the creatures, for he is "head over all things," (Eph. i. 22,) over men and devils; all power in heaven and earth is his. (Matt. xxviii. 18.) Oh, if we could act faith on this almighty Jesus, our hearts would not be troubled for anything! What can hurt us? What should we fear? Our blessed Jesus, our Saviour, our husband, commands all things; he rules and over-rules all things; no creature, no man, no devil, can act anything against us without our Lord's leave. Believe in this captain, and let not your hearts be troubled, he will bruise Satan under your feet shortly. (Rom. xvi. 20.) He will make all his and our enemies his footstool. Let us look by faith unto our captain, and keep our eye on him, and follow him whithersoever he goeth. Let us make him our leader, and by faith in him we shall be more than conquerors. He hath overcome the devil and the world for us, and he will overcome all our corruptions, fears, and sorrows in us, and will shortly set his crown upon our heads. Christ is the captain of our salvation; and in bringing of many sons to glory, he was made perfect through suffering. (Heb. ii. 10.) Act faith in him who hath perfected our salvation for us; that work is done, and it was through suffering, to teach us to be willing to suffer also, to walk in his steps; for in the way of suffering he entered into his glory: and the very same way will he bring all his sons and daughters unto glory; so that, while we are suffering for him, or from him, if we be his children, (which we may know if we have his spirit,) we are in the right and ready way to glory. And then have we any cause to let our hearts be troubled with sinful fears, cares, and sorrows? Have we any cause to be cast down and discouraged while we are following our captain, are walking conformable to him, travelling the same way to heaven that he went thither—the same way to glory, the way of reproach, shame, grief, sorrow, fear, poverty, persecution, tribulation, desertion, the same steps that our Lord went to glory? Oh that we could but still keep our eye on Jesus, and often consider what way he went to heaven; and being our captain, we should show ourselves his good soldiers, and be content to go the same way.

5. Jesus Christ is called the "consolation of Israel," (Luke ii. 25;) a sweet name indeed. He is the only person that brings true comfort, being the fountain of the spring of all consolation; that one of a thousand who gave himself a ransom for

us. He it is that comforteth his people in all their tribulations. (2 Cor. i. 3, 4.) He it is that speaketh and giveth his peace to his people : and when he giveth peace, none can cause trouble. And it is his promise, that when he hath brought his people into the wilderness of fears and troubles, that they know not which way to turn, that then he will speak comfortably to them; will speak to their hearts, as the word in the original signifies. (Hos. ii. 14.)

I might largely show here that Jesus Christ is the consolation of his people many ways; as by his coming from his Father into the world to become our surety, to undertake for us, to take our sins upon him, and to make his soul an offering for our sins, and by his blood to purchase our remission. (Eph. i. 7.) Oh how comfortable is a surety to one that is arrested, indicted, and arraigned! How comfortable is a redeemer to a poor miserable captive! How comfortable is a pardon to a condemned malefactor! All this is Jesus to his people, and infinitely more. He is gold to make us rich, white raiment to cover our nakedness, eye-salve to make us see. He is light, the light of life, the fountain of life, of spiritual and eternal life; no life but by him. And he hath assured us, that, whosoever cometh to him, and believeth in him, shall have everlasting life, and shall not come into condemnation. (John iii. 16, 36.) He is afflicted in all our afflictions. (Isa. lxiii. 9.) And is not this a comfortable consideration ? All his promises are so many breasts of consolation, all his ordinances means of consolation; his word a word of consolation ; yea, his rod of affliction, as well as his staff, is blessed for the comfort of his people. (Ps. xxiii.) He hath also promised to send his Spirit, the Comforter, to his people, to abide with them for ever. (John xvi. 7.) Yea, Christ himself makes this his own special work also, to "comfort all that mourn," (Isa. lxi. 2 ;) and hath blessed those that mourn, that is, with godly sorrow; for, saith he, "They shall be comforted." (Matt. v. 4.)

How greatly, then, doth it concern us to believe in this Jesus, the consolation of Israel ; to look by faith to this fountain of comfort ; look to his office, look to his word and promises ; beg him earnestly to send the Spirit, the Comforter, into your hearts; look to Jesus alone for all comfort, and draw from this spring, by prayer, faith, and meditation, all supplies and comfort : and, " Let not your hearts be troubled."

6. Jesus Christ is called a counsellor. (Isa. ix. 6.) He is most wise: he is the wisdom of the Father : in him " are hid all the treasures of wisdom and knowledge." (Col. ii. 3.) Yea, he is made of God our wisdom. (1 Cor. i. 30.) So that when we are in doubts and darkness, perplexed with temptations, and know not what to do ; when we are under sad and dark providences, and know not how to interpret them ; when we are under various exercises, and know not how to answer God's ends in them, not how to improve them ; when we are in the dark, and know not the meaning of God's dispensations, nor the design of God in them ; now are our hearts troubled in all such cases. But here is our remedy ; this is the course we must take : act faith now upon Jesus, he is wisdom ; he is a most wise and faithful counsellor; we may freely open all our cases and conditions to him ; he will not betray us nor bewray us ; we may safely trust him with all the secrets of our hearts : and let us labour by faith to trust him for counsel in all cases; let us wait for his counsel, trust to it, and " let not your hearts be troubled."

7. Jesus is a redeemer, that is his name : he came into the world on this very business, to redeem his people, to redeem them from all iniquity, (Tit. ii. 14 ;) from this present evil world ; from our vain conversations. He hath shed his precious blood to purchase us, we are " bought with a price." (1 Cor. vi. 20.) We are none of our own, we are his, the purchase of his blood ; and we may be confident that he dearly love us, for he dearly bought us ; and if he had not dearly loved us, he would never have given himself for us. (Gal. ii. 20.) That was the highest testimony of his love ; he " loved us, and washed us from our sins in his own blood." (Rev. i. 5.) He will redeem us from the wrath to come. Oh then let us act faith on our sweet Redeemer, as Job did in the midst of all his troubles : " I know," saith he, " that my Redeemer liveth," &c. So may every believer say, although my friends and dearest relations die, my credit and estate dies ; though my outward comforts all die, this supports me, that " my Redeemer liveth ; " and this our Redeemer is mighty, mighty to save, able to save to the uttermost. (Heb. vii. 25.)

Therefore, let us act faith on our Redeemer, and upon his redemption ; and let us believe that shortly, the day of our full redemption will come, when we shall be delivered fully and for ever from sin, Satan, and the world ; from all our burdens, fears, and sorrows, temptations, and tribulations.

I might mention many other sweet names and titles of Jesus Christ, which would be food for faith to feed upon : as, that he is the everlasting Father, (Isa. ix. 6,) he hath pity and compassion for all his poor children, and power to help them, being the Father almighty, and hath a portion for them too ; he is their portion, and hath provided for them an " inheritance incorruptible, and undefiled, and that fadeth not away." (1 Pet. i. 4.) He is the Prince of peace : he giveth his peace to his people, even that peace that the world can never give to them, nor take from them. When he speaks peace, none can cause trouble. He is our peace, and hath made our peace with God ; and it is he alone that speaketh peace, and creates the fruit of the lips, peace. (Isa. lvii. 19.) He is also our shepherd, therefore (said David) I shall want nothing. (Ps. xxiii. 1.) He is a fountain opened, a fountain of light, life, love, grace, and truth. He is the head of his body the church. The husband, the bridegroom, his people are his members, his spouse. He is the "heir of all things." (Heb. i. 2.) In him dwelleth all fulness. He is the "King of saints, the rock of ages." Yea, he is all and in all. Oh beloved, had we but faith to act on this blessed Jesus, and on these his most sweet names and gracious attributes, our hearts would not be troubled, into what condition soever we were brought. Could we act faith on Jesus as our head, husband, and father, who is all fulness, all in all, could we doubt of having all seasonable supplies from him? Let our faith but apprehend, apply, and appropriate Jesus as our blessed head, our most dear husband, and then consider in earnest who he is, and what he is; how mighty, how full, loving, pitiful, compassionate, tender-hearted, and kind; how ready to help, how engaged to us by many promises; and can we then take up such unworthy thoughts of him, as to think he hath forgotten us? Will he not timely support and supply us? Hath he shed his blood for us, and will he forget us? Are not all his people as dear to him as "the apple of his eye?" (Zech. ii. 8.) Surely it is our want, or the weakness of our faith, that causeth all our heart trouble. Oh my poor soul, how comfortably mightest thou live, if thou couldest live by faith! Lord, I believe; help, strengthen my faith. Could we but apply and appropriate Christ to our souls, and act faith upon those precious names of Christ, which are not as so many empty titles which are sometimes given to men, but they are real representations of that most dear love and tender affection, of that special care, mercy, and loving-kindness that is in Jesus towards all his poor children, that they might draw out the same for their strong consolation; and that they might trust in him, and not despond nor be dejected. Thus if we can believe in Jesus, our hearts shall not be troubled.

Third. Faith acted on the *covenant of grace*, whereof Christ is the mediator, and upon all his exceeding great and precious promises, will prevent and cure all heart trouble. Believe in the blessed mediator of the new covenant, who hath undertaken, not only on God's part, to see that his part be performed to us, but also is become our surety; undertaking for us, and by himself, to fulfil the whole law of God both actively and passively; "to fulfil all righteousness" for us, and by his Spirit to enable us to fulfil the conditions of the covenant, working in us faith, love, obedience, and all grace.

In this sense God hath given Christ to be a covenant to us, (Isa. xlii. 6,) and his blood is the blood of the covenant, by which he rescueth poor souls, that were prisoners to sin and Satan, out of the pit of destruction. (Zech. ix. 11.) By this covenant, upon Christ's shedding of his blood as a sacrifice for sin, and his performing all the work of mediation, and upon our receiving of him, and believing in him as he is offered to us in the gospel, God is pleased to promise to become our

God, our reconciled Father, to pardon all our sins, to give us his Spirit, and all grace here, and glory hereafter. Now Christ, our blessed Mediator, hath perfectly fulfilled all that God required for us, and in our room and stead; that is most certain, for he finished the work that his Father gave him to do: and he hath made many sweet promises to us, that he will send the Spirit into our hearts, to work faith in us, to receive him, and to apply the merit of his blood to us, to sanctify and renew us thereby; and hath promised, that whosoever comes unto him, he will in no wise cast out. (John vi. 37.) And all that come unto him, shall find rest to their souls. That whosoever believeth in him shall be saved; that he will keep them, and none shall pluck them out of his hand. (John x. 28.) That he will raise them up at the last day. Assuring us, that he is gone to heaven, as our forerunner, to prepare a place for us there, and that he will come again and take us to himself, that where he is, we may be also. Now, if we can but act faith on this Jesus, and on the covenant, whereof he is the mediator, and on his promises, applying them, and relying on them, our hearts shall not be troubled.

Besides, let us consider, there is not a passage of providence from God to us, but it comes through the hand of this Mediator, "By whom are all things." (1 Cor. viii. 6.) Put what you will in the hand of a mediator, and in his power, it must needs turn to the good of him for whom he is a mediator. Now to support and comfort us in all our troubles, let us consider two things.

1. This mediator steps in between God's wrath and us, in all our afflictions; that no fury, or effects of it, may break forth from God on his people, for whom he is the Mediator; that nothing but fatherly love may be in the chastisement; and if love send the affliction, whatever it be, to try and purge, &c., there can be no hurt in that affliction. Again, our mediator interposeth, either to hold off the smart, or to allay and mitigate it, that it shall not distract, (Dan. iii. 25,) no, nor hurt.

2. He steps in to uphold us, and to strengthen our weakness, enabling us to endure. (Phil. iv. 4, 12, 13.) It was the Mediator that did strengthen Paul: "The Lord stood by me and strengthened me," said he: faith acted on this blessed Mediator, eyeing him, and believing that our afflictions come through his hands, even his who loved us, and died for us, our dearest friend, and who hath all power in heaven and earth, must be a mighty support to us in all our troubles.

Fourth. Let faith be acted on the *word of Christ* also; ye believe the word of God, believe the word of Christ also; his mouth is most sweet, none but gracious words proceed out of his mouth. "Grace is poured into his lips," (Ps. xlv. 2,) and he pours out grace in all his words; his whole gospel is a gospel of grace, words of peace and salvation. Hear him speaking most sweetly, "Come unto me all ye that labour and are heavy laden, and I will give you rest." (Matt. xi. 28.) Oh what sweet words are these!

Ho, every one that thirsteth, come ye to the waters and drink, without money and without price. (Isa. lv. 1, 2.) "I am the way, the truth, and the life." (John xiv. 6.) "Behold, I stand at the door, and knock: if any man hear my voice, and open the door, I will come in to him, and will sup with him, and he with me." (Rev. iii. 20.) This is but a taste of those sweet clusters of most refreshing grapes which hang upon the boughs of the gospel; let us take frequent views of what lies upon record in the evangelists, and often read over the manifold promises of grace that fell from the sweet mouth of our blessed Lord, and meditate, and ponder, and consider of them, and act our faith upon them, and we shall find comfort in them; his words drop as an honey-comb; his words are spirit and life. More particularly,

1. Our faith must be acted upon Christ's word of precept, his word of command in time of trouble: fear not him that can kill the body, but him that can cast both soul and body into hell. (Luke xii. 4, 5, 32.) Fear none of those things which thou shalt suffer. Let not your heart be troubled, nor let it be afraid. Rejoice when men shall persecute you, &c. In patience possess ye your souls; with many such. (Luke xxi. 19.) Now Christians must yield up the obedience of faith to such commands, and urge them upon their hearts, charging themselves to obey them, saying, O my soul, my Lord hath forbidden me to fear, to be troubled, to be thoughtful, to be dejected, &c.; he hath commanded me to be patient, yea, to rejoice in my suffering; he is my Lord, and I must obey him; I must keep his commandments, else I cannot love him; I must keep his sayings, or else I cannot be his disciple. If I keep his commandments, he will manifest himself to my soul, his Father will love me, and he will love me, and they both will make their abode with me: for it is his promise. (John xiv. 21, 23.) Say thus, O my soul, Jesus Christ is my "king and law-giver," I must obey him; he is my *prophet* also, "and I must hear him in all things whatsoever he shall say unto me." I have taken him for my Lord as well as for my Saviour; my king to rule me, as well as for my Jesus to save me; for my prophet to teach me, as well as for my priest to satisfy for me. O my soul, consider, "he is the author of eternal salvation only to those that obey him." Thus applying the commands of Christ to ourselves, and urging his authority upon our hearts, it will help us to bear up under our troubles.

2. Act faith upon the promises of Christ, of which somewhat was said before. He hath promised to be always with us, to send the Comforter, to manifest himself unto us; that he will not break the bruised reed, nor quench the smoking flax, (Matt. xii. 20. Isa. xlii. 3;) that he will give us an hundredfold for all our losses for his sake; that he will gather us with his arm, carry us in his bosom; that he will hear our prayers; that he will give us a crown, a kingdom, everlasting life, with many more. Oh could we act our faith upon these precious promises, and lie sucking by faith on those full breasts of consolation, and draw by faith, prayer, and meditation, from these wells of salvation, we should find sweet support under all our troubles.

3. Faith acted on the word of threatening, may put a stop to heart trouble. Jesus Christ hath dreadfully threatened those that love father or mother, son or daughter, more than him, or their own lives; and those that are ashamed of him, or his word; and those that fall from him; and those that hear his sayings, and do them not; and those that are fruitless branches, &c. (Matt. x. 37. Luke xiv. 26. Mark viii. 38. John xv.)

4. Faith acted on the examples in the word of Christ, especially his own example; learn of me, saith he, "I am meek and lowly in heart." (Matt. xi. 29.) He was as a lamb dumb before the shearers, (Isa. liii. 7:) and we must follow his steps. We have also a cloud of witnesses, the examples of the primitive Christians, who bore all their troubles with patience, and holy courage; and we are expressly commanded to be followers of them "who through faith and patience inherit the promise." (Heb. vi. 12.) Thus faith acted on the word of Christ will help against all heart trouble.

Fifth. Faith acted on the *work of Christ* will either prevent or cure heart trouble. And that again if faith be acted upon the work he hath done for us already, and upon the work he is now doing for us in heaven, and upon the work he is now doing in us on earth, and upon the work he will do for us, and in us, and upon us, at the last day. All which works of Christ, if we act our faith on them, we shall not be much troubled in our hearts. Believe also in Christ: "Believe me (saith he) for the very works' sake." (John xiv. 11.)

1. Faith must be acted upon that great and glorious work of Christ for us when he was upon earth, that work which his Father gave him to do in the days of his flesh, as our Redeemer, and that in doing and in suffering; for he came to do the will of God by his obedience, as well as to suffer it by his satisfaction, and this is his state of humiliation. He assumed human nature, entered the Virgin's womb, was born here yet without sin. He lived on earth a time, doing good, and healing all manner of diseases; spent most of his time in preaching, praying, fasting, and revealing to men the whole will of God for their salvation, and fulfilling all righteousness. He professed he came not to do his own will, but the will of him that sent him. (John vi. 38, 39.) And saith he, This is the Father's will which sent me, that of all which he hath given me, I should lose nothing, but should raise it up at the last day. A comfortable consideration indeed, and a cure for our heart trouble: that our Lord Jesus will raise up all our dead, dear relations and friends, now rotting in their graves. "All that died in Jesus, will Jesus

bring with him." (1 Thess. iv. 14—17.) And this also is the Father's will, that every one that seeth the Son, that is, every one that by faith receiveth and believeth in the Son, shall have everlasting life. Now to accomplish and finish this will of the Father, was the whole work of Christ upon earth, even to draw poor souls unto him, to work faith in them by his word and spirit, to fulfil the whole law of God for them and in them, (Rom. viii. 4;) and to begin and finish the whole work of our redemption. Faith acted on this work of Christ upon earth for us, in the several parts of it, He being partaker of flesh and blood with us, to deliver us from him that had the power of death, that is the devil, and to free us from the fear of death, by which we were always subject to bondage, (Heb. ii.,)I say, if we can act faith on these works of Christ for us, we shall have no cause of heart trouble.

Let us consider, that our blessed Lord denied himself on earth, and was well pleased not to have his own will, nor to do his own will, but referred himself entirely to his Father's ; what reason have we poor worms to be troubled when our wills are crossed ? Let us in heart and life say as we pray, " Thy will be done on earth as it is in heaven." (Matt. vi. 10.) And when the will of God is done upon our families, and relations, let not your hearts be troubled ; but let us imitate Jesus Christ in our submission to the will of God, making it our work on earth to be doing all the good we can, and so to put him on, and walking as he walked, and not to be troubled.

2. Faith acted on Christ's suffering work on earth, will greatly contribute to our support : he was " a man of sorrows," (Isa. liii. 3;) so that if we meet with sorrows on earth, we do but drink of our Master's own cup, and that should quiet us.

Christ's sufferings on earth were of two kinds, viz. for our imitation, and for satisfaction for our sins.

(1.) For our imitation. His patient suffering of reproaches, scorns, revilings, contradiction of sinners, temptations, persecutions, bonds, poverty, shame, loss of friends, &c., suffering all with invincible patience, and meekness, without the least murmuring, repining, disquiet or discontent, without any retaliation ; for when he was reviled, he reviled not again: he prayed for his enemies, &c.; and all this as our example, that we should follow his steps. (1 Pet. ii. 21—23.) And if our Lord, the Lord of heaven and earth, suffered such things, what reason or cause have we to be troubled in our hearts when we are persecuted, reviled, forsaken of all our friends, impoverished, exposed to shame and sorrow, seeing our blessed Lord was so exposed, and so exercised upon earth ? Is it not enough for the servant to be as his master ? Shall we think to fare better than him ? His sufferings were to teach us to bear ours with Christian patience, and to sanctify ours to us ; yea, in all our sufferings he sympathized with us.

Let us then act our faith upon Christ's sufferings on earth : his whole life being a life of suffering, he knew what trouble meant ; he was acquainted with grief ; he knew what it was to lose a friend, for in his greatest trouble all his disciples (whom he calls his friends) forsook him and fled ; and being tempted, himself, he knows how to succour them that are tempted. (Heb. ii. 18 ; iv. 15.) He hath a feeling of all our infirmities. Let us labour to act faith on Jesus, and our hearts will not be troubled.

(2.) But his great suffering work for us, was his work of satisfaction. All our sins being laid on him, it pleased the Lord to bruise him, and to put him to grief, and to make his soul an offering for sin. He poured out his soul unto death ; was numbered among transgressors, (Isa. liii. 6, 10, 12;) was made sin for us—he bare our sins on his own body on the tree, (2 Cor. v. 21 ;) he was made a curse for us, (Gal. iii. 10 ;) suffered the wrath of God for us, to deliver us from the wrath to come. Oh blessed Jesus ! when our sins were upon him, he was sore amazed, groaned, was exceeding sorrowful, even unto death ; he was in a bloody sweat, in a bitter agony in the garden ; he was falsely accused, unjustly condemned, and then barbarously crucified, suffering that cursed and cruel shameful and painful death of the cross, and all as our surety, and as a sacrifice to God for our sins. " Christ our passover is sacrificed for us," (1 Cor. v. 7,) to make atonement and satisfaction to the law and justice of God for us. (Rom. iii. 25.)

This was the great work of the transcendent love of Jesus Christ when he was upon earth, when he travailed in soul, drank of the brook in the way, (Ps. cx. 7,) that black torrent of wrath and curses that lay in the way betwixt our souls and heaven, which stopped up our passage thitherward, and made it utterly impossible for us ; but Jesus made a passage by his blood, that his redeemed might pass through. So great were his sufferings in this world for us, that they made him cry out, " My God, my God, why hast thou forsaken me?" (Matt. xxvii. 46,) offering up strong cries with tears. (Heb. v. 7.)

Now then, let us act our faith on the sufferings of Christ here on earth, and believe that he suffered all those hard and heavy, those bitter and grievous things for us, and in our names ; that he bore our sins to satisfy God's justice for them, to purchase and procure our pardon. Oh that we could but believe in this Jesus ! that he sweated great drops of blood for us, and that he shed his very heart-blood upon the cross for us, and by faith apply and appropriate all this to our own souls : believing that he was wounded for our transgressions, smitten for our sins ; that the chastisement of our peace was upon him, (Isa. liii. 5:) that by the blood of his cross he hath made our peace, and hath purchased for us eternal life. Believe this, and then see what little cause you have to have your hearts troubled for any loss or cross whatsoever. The consideration, in a way of believing of what Christ hath done for us, and of what he hath suffered for us, should make us patiently do or suffer anything for him and from him. Believe also in me.

3. Our faith must be acted upon the work of Christ, which he is now doing for us in heaven. He is not idle there, although "he be set down on the right hand of the Majesty on high;" but he is at work for his people there; there he maketh continual intercession for us. (Rom. viii. 34.) He is there as our advocate to plead our cause, and manage all our business there, presenting his blood in the virtue of it to his Father for our pardon, presenting our persons and services perfumed with the incense of his own righteousness, and by his Spirit applying the virtue of all to our souls. "He is able to save them to the uttermost that come unto God by him, seeing he ever liveth to make intercession for them." (Heb. vii. 25.) Of this I have spoken before. Now, if we can act our faith upon the intercession of Christ, who knows all our wants, burdens, cares, and fears, and whose office it is to plead and intercede for us in heaven, (though we may scarce have any to plead or speak a word for us on earth, yet) we should have no cause to have our hearts troubled: we have a faithful friend to whom we may commit our cause.

4. Christ is doing a work in us on earth, while he himself is in heaven. He is humbling us, purging us, teaching us, mortifying our corruptions, crucifying our inordinate affections, sanctifying us, and so preparing us for heaven: he is making us meet for the kingdom; he is fitting us for his Father's house, by all his ordinances, and by all his providences, by every loss and cross; by all our afflictions : " Our light afflictions, which are but for a moment, work for us (that is, by the way of preparation) a far more exceeding and eternal weight of glory." (2 Cor. iv. 17.) Jesus Christ is in the word, and in the rod, he is all in all: he is still forming, squaring, fashioning, and working by his Spirit, word, and rod, upon his people, to make them more and more comfortable to himself, to square them as stones for his building, to make them habitations for himself, temples for the holy God to dwell in, and that he himself may delight to dwell in them here, and to make them fit to dwell with him for ever in glory. Now let us labour to act our faith on those blessed works of Christ in us, and believe that he is thus working in us, even in and by all our afflictions, and labour to feel and find these gracious works carrying on in us, and we shall have no cause to be troubled.

Moreover, our faith should be acted upon the work that Christ is now doing for us in heaven; besides his intercession for us there, he is preparing for us a place in heaven, as he told his disciples, to comfort them : " In my Father's house are many mansions; I go to prepare a place for you."

A place in heaven is infinitely better, and more to be desired, than the best place on earth. A place in the Father's house, in the highest heavens, in the glorious paradise above, that is the place of all places, there the great and glorious God dwells, there blessed Jesus dwells. Oh that new Jerusalem, the city of the living God, that is the place indeed, that " house not made with hands, eternal in the heavens." (2 Cor. v. 1.) Some think that Jesus went locally into hell, but we are sure he went locally into heaven; and we know for what he went there, for he hath told us, it was to prepare a place for us there. Here below all places are full of darkness, snares, temptations, fears, dangers, persecutions; but that is a place of perfect peace, perfect rest, of light, comfort, joy and consolation. Here we are pilgrims and strangers, there is our home, our Father's house. Here we have "no continuing city," (Heb. xiii. 14. 1 Cor. iv. 11,) no abiding place. Christ's people here in this world, many times, have no certain dwelling-place, but are driven from house and home, forced to fly from one city to another, from town to country, from one kingdom to another; constrained to wander from place to place; while others abide in their habitations, they must seek their quarters where they can find them, & while under one friend's roof, a while under another's; which is no small affliction to them that feel it, though others lay it not to heart. Now what should comfort us in this our pilgrimage and wilderness condition— what should support us in this our wandering and desolate state, but that it was even thus with our blessed Lord himself upon earth, who had not an house to put his head in? And so it was with his disciples, and with many choice saints. (Heb. xi. 37, 38.) What should bear up our spirits, but this comfortable consideration, that our Lord went to heaven on purpose to prepare a place for us there? If the earth cast us out, heaven will receive us. If men say to us, remove, begone hence, depart away, here is no place, no abiding for you, our dear Lord will call to us out of heaven, and say, "Come up hither." (Rev. xi. 12.) Come up to me, I have prepared a place for you here. There is room enough in our Father's house, there are many mansions, and from thence there shall be no removal for ever, no more any changing houses for ever, when once we are lodged in our Father's house. There is our forerunner for us entered. (Heb. vi. 20.) The hope we have through grace of getting into that blessed place, by that new and living way, to rest there after all our weary wanderings here, and never to remove more, is that which comforts us in these our troublesome removals here. Oh that place, and that blessed state in that place, " To see God, and to be ever with the Lord, to see our lovely Lord Jesus as he is, and to be made like unto him." Could we fix our hearts and eyes more steadfastly upon those invisible and eternal things, we should more quietly and comfortably bear our present troubles, yea, and rejoice in them. And when we can act our faith upon that place and state above, and conclude our title to it by our interest in Christ, then our hearts will not be troubled.

Also this consideration should preserve us from heart trouble and sorrow for the loss of our dear relations who died in Jesus, for that they are gone home to their Father's house, they are arrived at their labour, they are safely housed, they are where they would be; they are gone to the place that their beloved Lord went to prepare for them, to that city of God, to the general assembly of the firstborn, whose names are written in heaven, &c. (Heb. xii. 22, 23.) They would not exchange their place now for the most stately and most magnificent place in the whole world. Oh, could we but realize by faith that most happy state and place where our deceased pious friends are gone, our hearts would not be troubled for them.

And this may comfort us also under all our present sufferings and sadnesses, that ere long we also shall go to that place, to that city above, which God hath prepared for us. Our Lord assures us, that " he will come again, and take us to himself, that where he is, we may be also." Oh, could we believe this, we should say, Come, Lord Jesus, come quickly.

5. Our faith must be acted upon the work that Christ will do for us, and in us, and upon us, in heaven at the last. It is above all our understanding to conceive what glorious works Christ will do for us and in us at the last day. " It doth not yet appear what we shall be." (1 John iii. 2.) There shall be a day of the manifestation of the sons of God. The poor despised saints, all black and cloudy here, covered with shame and reproach now, shall then be manifested to be the Lord's jewels: that will be a day of their full redemption both of soul and body, their wedding and their solemn coronation day: then their blessed Redeemer shall publicly own them, and bid them welcome to his Father's house, saying, " Come, ye blessed of my Father," &c. (Matt. xxv. 34.) Then will Jesus put the crown of glory, of righteousness, and of life upon their heads. Then will Jesus present them to his Father without spot or wrinkle, or any such thing. (Eph. v. 27.) Then will he make their (own) vile bodies (subject now to vile corruptions, to vile diseases, to vile abuses, and to a dissolution at death) like unto his own glorious body; and their souls shall be like to his, to their full satisfaction. Then the poor disciples of Christ shall have a full end put to all their heart troubles, sorrows, fears, and cares. Then their hearts shall rejoice, and their joy no man (nor devil) shall take from them. Sorrow and sighing shall flee away, and they shall enter in into everlasting rest; and into that unspeakable blessed state which was purchased by the precious blood of Jesus, and by him prepared and possessed in our names and stead. All our dear relations that died in Jesus are already entered. Christ their

dearest Lord hath wrought this glorious work on their souls already; they are triumphing, singing hallelujahs in the highest heavens: while we are fighting, sighing, and sobbing here below, they are with blessed Jesus above, according to his prayers for them, seeing his glory, and participating of it. Thus much for the work of Christ, upon which our faith must act, that our hearts may not be troubled.

Sixth. Our faith must act upon the *will of Christ*, in order to the preventing and curing our heart troubles, fears, and sorrows. What is the will of Christ? It is his will that his people's hearts should not be troubled nor afraid, as in the text. It is his will that in the world they should have tribulation, but yet that they should be of good cheer. It is his will that in their patience they should possess their souls, and not faint nor be discouraged. It is his will they should be sanctified, and that all their afflictions should promote their sanctification. It is his will, that although he love them, yet to rebuke and chasten them: and when he doth so, that they shall be zealous and repent. It is his will that they should deny themselves, and take up their cross daily and follow him. That they should fear none of those things that they should suffer. That they should walk in his steps, hold fast to the end, be faithful unto death. That they should overcome. It is his will that they should not love father or mother, son or daughter, more than himself; no, nor their lives, but be willing to part with all for his sake. Yea, it is his will, his last will, that all his poor disciples, after they have suffered awhile, may be with him where he is, to behold his glory. Thus, if we act faith upon the will of Christ, and labour to yield to it, and acquiesce in it, we shall procure much freedom from heart trouble.

Lastly. Our faith must be acted upon the *ends and designs* of Christ in all his afflictive providences towards us; and these his ends are all very good and gracious. With this argument he himself used to cure the heart trouble of his disciples for his departure from them, viz. that he had good ends in his going away from them; his end was, to prepare a place for them, a better place than any to be found here; a place in heaven, in the Father's house. And his end was to send the Spirit, the Comforter unto them, which would not come if he did not go away. (John xvi. 7.) He had told them of his going away from them, upon which sorrow had filled their hearts, (and it is even so with us, when our earthly comforts leave us, sorrow fills our hearts;) but to cure this, our Lord answers them, that it was expedient for them (good and necessary for them) that he should go away, showing them his end in going away, to wit, that he might send them the Comforter; he would remove from them a great mercy, the greatest earthly mercy that ever they enjoyed—which was his personal presence; they must part with so dear and near, so sweet, so loving, so faithful a friend as himself was to them: and could there be a greater loss? for this sorrow had filled their hearts. But he tells them, it was to make way for a greater mercy, which was, to send them the Comforter, in all the saving and miraculous gifts of the Holy Ghost, by which they should be able to do greater works than he himself did, (John xiv. 12,) which was a greater mercy than his bodily presence with them; and with this he calms and quiets their minds. Now, if we can act faith upon the blessed ends of Christ in removing our earthly comforts from us,—which are, to bestow upon us better mercies, to give us more of his spirit, and of the graces and comforts of it,—our hearts would not be troubled; could we believe that Christ's end in all his chastisements is, to prepare us for that place in his Father's house, it would comfort and support us. His ends are very good, and that should quiet us. So long as the people of Christ enjoy most of the comforts of this world (I speak it by sad experience) commonly they enjoy least of God, and of his Spirit; and usually when Christ takes away their earthly comforts, then he manifests most of himself, and of his tender love to them: he brings them into the wilderness, and then speaks comfortably to them, (Hos. ii. 14;) then he speaks to their hearts, and not to the ears only, as in time of prosperity; then he gives out most of the graces and comforts of his Spirit. Christ never takes away these outward mercies from his people but with design to bestow better, if our discontent and unbelief do not hinder. When the Lord took away from his servant David the young child begotten in adultery, it was to give him a Solomon.

Thus I have endeavoured to show what it is also to believe in Christ, that thereby we may prevent and cure our heart trouble.

III. The last thing I have to do is, to show how faith acted thus on God and Christ, or, on God in Christ, is the best preventative of, and remedy to cure, all our heart troubles, which hath indeed been shown partly in the two former particulars, and will serve for the confirmation of the point also.

Two ways principally faith acted on God and Christ, doth effect this great cure of heart trouble, and procure heart's ease.

First, by way of application and appropriation.

Secondly, by way of holy confidence and reliance.

First. By applying and appropriating God and Christ to the soul, and all that God is, and all that Christ is, and all that God hath, and all that Christ hath, and all that God and Christ hath promised: faith applieth and appropriateth all this to the soul, faith gives the soul right, title, claim, propriety, and interest to and in God and Christ; faith makes all the believer's own. Believe, and all is thine. This is the language of faith—my God, my Lord, my Christ, my Saviour, my Redeemer; and this quiets and satisfies the soul fully, or nothing in heaven or earth can do it,

when it can thus act its faith on God and Christ. So was David cured of his great troubles. He encouraged himself in the Lord his God, his God in Christ. (1 Sam. xxx. 6.) His interest in God's everlasting covenant (whereby God was become his God in Christ) he acted his faith upon, and that satisfied him: so, Mic. vii. 7. Ps. xxxvii. 25, 26.

Either God is ours, or he is not; either Christ is ours, or he is not; if God and Christ be not ours, we have cause enough of heart trouble, cause enough to mind our danger, and to be troubled at our very hearts, that we are in such a woeful case; and should now above all things labour after an interest in God and in Christ: whatever our losses in the world be, this dangerous state of our souls should be most minded, and speedily looked after above all things.

But if God be ours, and if Christ be ours—if we have chosen God for our portion in Christ, and if we have rightly and truly received Jesus Christ the Lord, for our only Lord and Saviour, and have unfeignedly given up our whole selves to him—then may we act our faith upon God, as our God, and upon Jesus Christ as ours, and may claim our right in God and in Christ, and in all that God and Christ is and hath, as our own; and then, what cause of any heart trouble? If God be ours, if Christ be ours, all is ours—life ours, death ours. What if we want relations and friends, honour, wealth, and health—is not the all-sufficient God enough? Is not Jesus, in whom dwells all fulness, enough to supply the want of all? This God proposed to Abraham, I am thy God; and to Israel. (Isa. xli. 10.) Jesus Christ is all and in all; and if Christ be yours, all is yours; God is yours, and the good of both worlds are yours; and what can you desire more?

Secondly. Faith exercised in holy confidence in and reliance upon God, and Christ, and the promises, will prevent or cure all our heart trouble. David was cured both these ways, viz. by appropriating God to himself, and by trusting in him: "I trusted in thee, O Lord: I said, Thou art my God," (Ps. xxxi. 14;) for God is pleased to engage himself, to discharge those souls from heart trouble and sinful fear who trust in him. (Ps. xxxvii. 40.) Trouble doth disorder the heart, and discompose the mind: but faith in this exercise of it, trusting in the Lord, doth fix and settle the heart; so that then no evil tidings shall make such a person afraid, for "his heart is fixed, trusting in the Lord." (Ps. cxii. 7.) God hath promised to keep them in perfect peace, whose minds are stayed on him because they trust in him. (Isa. xxvi. 3.) Diffidence is the cause of all disquiet; no true rest can be had, nor quiet to our minds, but by confidence in God. Oh the blessedness of those that trust in Christ! (Ps. ii. 12.) God in Christ is the only fit object of our confidence in all our extremities. A believer hath a God to go to in all his troubles, an all-mighty and loving father in Christ; and this should be our comfort—that we are in covenant with him that rules the world, and hath committed the government of all things to his Son, our dear Redeemer, who hath bought us with his blood: and we may be sure that no hurt shall befall us that he can hinder; and what cannot he hinder? who hath all power in heaven and earth, and that hath the keys of hell and death, unto whom we are so near that he carries our names on his heart, and who will in his due time make all the world know that his people are as dear to him as the apple of his eye.

Trust, then, depend and rely upon God in Christ, and by an holy confidence, resign up your will to his will, to do what he would have us do, to be what he would have us be, to suffer what he would have us suffer; and then heart trouble will cease, and sweet peace cometh; when having trusted all with God, we can in heart say, Lord, if thou wilt have me poor, disgraced, imprisoned, diseased, deprived of all my dearest friends, I am content to be so, I trust all my concerns with thee : oh the sweet peace and quiet that will be in that soul!

There is the almightiness, the wisdom, goodness, love, mercy, and faithfulness of God in Christ for us to trust in, and rely upon, a bottom and foundation strong enough to build our confidence upon, in all storms and straits. God hath also made many exceeding great and precious promises in his word, and not a naked promise, but he hath entered into covenant with us, founded upon full satisfaction by the blood of Jesus, and confirmed it with an oath, (Heb. vi. 17,) and to this covenant, sealed by the blood of his Son, he hath added the seals of the sacraments; and all this, that the heirs of the promises, namely, all true believers, might have strong consolation, and be cured of all their heart troubles.

Upon this sure foundation then must our faith act in an holy confidence in God, and in Christ, the soul being taken off from all other objects, carried, out of self, unto God and Christ; who presently (as soon as trusted in) communicate themselves, and their love, and goodness to the soul, filling it with peace, strength, and settlement. By this trusting in God, we honour God most, and best provide for our own safety.

The way, then, whereby faith quieteth the soul, and cures it of its troubles, is, by raising it above all disquietments, and pitching it solely upon God in Christ: and thereby uniting it to God in Christ; from whence it draws virtue and strength, to subdue whatever troubleth its peace. For the soul is made for God, and never finds rest till it return unto, and settle and centre itself upon him again. And that we may thus place our confidence in God and Christ for all supplies, we must most earnestly beg, cry, and seek to God for grace and strength so to do; we must trust in God alone, for all things, and at all times; and thus by appropriating God to us, and Christ to us, and placing our confidence in them, we may be cured of all our heart troubles.

First. For information. These inferences follow :—

1. If faith acted upon God in Christ be such a remedy against heart trouble, then surely faith is a very precious, a very excellent thing,—a grace of very great worth and value, and of great use and efficacy: it is precious faith indeed, the very trial of it is more precious than gold. (1 Pet. i. 7.) Precious for its author—the Lord Jesus; for its object — precious Jesus, and all the exceeding great and precious promises, the purchased inheritance; for its offices—it unites us to Christ, gives us title to eternal life, it supports under all afflictions, prevents or cures all heart troubles; and precious for its end—which is the salvation of our souls. (Eph. iii. 17. 1 Pet. i. 9.)

This grace of faith is of a transforming, spiritual nature; and the soul of a believer, by acting it on God and Christ, and on divine, heavenly, and spiritual things, becomes divine, heavenly, and spiritual. Faith unfasteneth the heart from the creature, showing the soul the vanity of it, and carries the soul unto God and Christ, showing it God's all-sufficiency, and Christ's all-fulness; for faith believes what God in his word hath revealed of both. It is the great design of God in all the troubles he sends upon his people, effectually to teach them the exceeding vanity of the creature, to embitter the things of this world to them, to wean their hearts from them, to bring earthly things out of request with them, to make them see that there is no true contentment nor solid satisfaction for the soul to be found in them, and to make them see where true happiness and contentment is to be had even in God and in Christ alone, for whom their souls were created, redeemed, and sanctified. Now the great work of faith is, to take off the soul from the creature, and fix and settle it upon God and Christ, the true foundation. Naturally our hearts hang loose from God, and cleave to the creature, and when the creature fails, our hearts are troubled; but faith takes off the heart from the creature, and settles it upon God in Christ, where it finds rest; and this is the great service it doth us. All the great and famous things which those worthies did, and all the hard and heavy things they suffered, mentioned in Heb. xi., were all done and suffered by the power of faith. The settling of our hearts upon God in Christ, trusting all there, is the best means to cure our heart trouble; and thus faith does, and therefore it is precious.

2. It follows from the promises, that the want of faith in God, and in Christ, is the great cause of all our heart troubles, despondencies, and disquietness. Could we but act our faith strongly on God and Christ, as our God in Christ, our troubles would be prevented or cured; for by faith the soul looks up to God in Christ, through the promises, looking off from all other supports unto God for all supplies, for the removing of all evil felt or feared,

and not for the obtaining of all good promised and needed; and by this exercise of faith, the soul is raised up above all discouragements and disquietments, but where this faith is wanting, or the lively exercises of it suspended, there the soul sinks under heart trouble. But of this somewhat was said before.

3. Hence also we may clearly see the absolute necessity of getting faith in God, and in Christ; and of acting it, and living by it; there is no living quietly and comfortably without it, no standing under our burdens, no bearing with patience and cheerfulness our losses and crosses without this faith; no joy and peace but by believing; by faith we stand.

4. Then the things of the world are not to be trusted to, nor trusted in, for comfort in time of trouble. Nothing but God and Christ to be trusted in, and trusted to, and there is enough in them to support and comfort us, as hath been showed: but no confidence to put in the creature; there is a curse upon such confidence, but a blessing on them that trust in God. No trusting in friends, riches, gifts, or anything; for so to do, is idolatry, to give that to the creature, which is due to God alone.

5. Hence we see the reason why so many faint in the day of adversity, and sin under trouble; and others use unlawful means to prevent trouble, or to get out of it. It is because they want this faith in God and Christ; and for want of it, too many miscarry under affliction.

Second. The second use is, by way of exhortation to all the disciples of Christ, in the words of the text: let not your hearts be troubled, but believe in God, and believe in Christ. You must get and act faith in God and Christ, this is the only preventative, the only remedy against heart trouble. Our Lord in this text commands it and commends it. We must needs get faith above all gettings; next to Christ we must get faith, for we cannot have Christ without faith. Go to God for it. it is his work, his gift, yea, it is his operation; yea, the same power that raised up Jesus from the dead, must be put forth upon a soul to work faith, (Eph. i. 19, 20,) the exceeding great and mighty working of the power of God, to raise up the soul to God and Christ, and to enable it to lay hold on God and Christ; for such is our natural proneness to live by sense and carnal reason; and such is the most transcendent excellency of God and Christ, and of divine things, which faith looks unto; and so great an inclination we have to self-sufficiency and so much rooted in self-love, and inordinate love of the creature, and so hard to take off the soul from false bottoms; and because we are such strangers to God naturally; and because there is so much guilt of sin still remaining on us, by our renewed provocations, that we are afraid to entertain serious thoughts of God; and because of that infinite distance between God and us,—we can never come to believe in him, and rely upon him, until our hearts be renewed by the power of grace,

and this divine grace of faith infused into them. Therefore must we go to God and Christ, and put up strong cries and prayers to God to work faith in us, and never give over, until it be wrought in us.

And having got faith, we must act and exercise it upon God in Christ; upon God, I say, he only is the object of faith, and is worthy of it; for a man can be in no condition, in which God is at a loss, and cannot help him. If comforts and means of deliverance be wanting, God can create comforts, and command deliverance. (Isa. lvii. 19.) He can bring light out of darkness, to him all things are possible.

1. Then faith assents to, and is persuaded that there is a God, the infinite first, and best being of all things, and who giveth being to all things. (Heb. xi. 6.)

2. That in this blessed being are three persons, Father, Son, and Holy Ghost, and all the object of our faith.

3. Faith must always act on God in Christ, and not otherwise; for in Christ God reconciles the world. In Christ, God becomes our friend, is at peace with us; by Christ, the enmity between God and us is taken away; in Christ, God becomes our Father. (John i. 12. Gal. iii. 26.)

4. Faith is acted by meditation on, considering of, and applying, and appropriating of God in Christ to the soul, laying claim to all that God is, and to all that God hath as its own.

5. It must also act upon the promises of God in his word, and upon God and Christ in them. God hath opened all his heart to us in his word, making many sweet promises, exceeding great and precious promises, (2 Pet. i. 4;) and also he hath made a covenant of grace with us, to bestow himself and all good things upon us, upon which we must live, until promises end in performances. These promises are our spiritual treasury; promises of pardon of sin, upon repentance and faith; promises of renewing sanctifying grace; promises of the Spirit, of heaven, of eternal life and glory, of mansions in the Father's house, and of all things needful in the way to the kingdom, that we shall want no good thing, and that all things shall work together for our good, &c.

Lastly, that our hearts may not be troubled, but fully satisfied and comforted, we must by faith lay hold on God, take hold of God's strength, which is his mercy in Christ, and most solemnly, most considerately, and most sincerely take God for our God in Christ, and actually enter into covenant with him: this covenant is founded upon Jesus Christ, his satisfaction and righteousness; and therefore we must also believe in Christ, taking him for our only Lord and Saviour, receiving him by faith as he is offered to us in the gospel, to be all in all to us.

As God offers, so faith receives; God offers himself in Christ, and so faith receives him. God doth, as it were, say in the gospel, Oh, poor lost sinner, come to my Son Jesus, take him for the only Lord and Saviour; and by him come to me, and take me for thy God and Father. And by faith the poor believer echoeth back, My Lord and my God, I humbly and heartily come to thee, accept of thee, close with thee. And so by faith the believing soul becomes one with God and Christ; and hereupon the soul by faith cleaves to God and Christ, and unfeignedly and unreservedly resigns and gives up its whole self to God in Christ, taking God in Christ for his, and entirely surrenders up itself to be the Lord's. " My beloved is mine, and I am his." Now faith thus acted will certainly cure all heart troubles.

In order, then, to obtain solid comfort in all our distresses, let us carefully look whether these acts of faith have really passed upon our souls; have we thus actually, understandingly, and sincerely believed in God, and in Christ? Have we unfeignedly entered into covenant with God in Christ? Can we conclude that God is our God in Christ, by our being his? If we be entirely his, he is ours for certain. (1 John iv. 19. Sol. Song ii. 16.) If we place all our happiness in him, (Ps. lxxiii. 25;)—if we give him the throne in our hearts, subjecting our whole selves to his government, making God in Christ all our love, our trust, joy, desire, delight, fear, our all, cleaving to him alone and above all, depending upon him as our chief good, contenting ourselves with him as all-sufficient for us, resigning up ourselves to his goodwill, to be, to do, and suffer what he will;—if we can and do engage ourselves to sincere obedience, that none of his commandments be grievous to us;—if in all things we give Christ the pre-eminence;—if we have received the spirit of Christ, (Rom. viii. 9. Gal. iv. 6,) which joins us to him, and makes us one spirit with him, and which is a spirit of adoption, whereby the soul, seeing his interests in God as his Father, can freely go to God in all his straits;—if we have the graces of the Spirit, as " love, meekness, patience, humility," &c.;—if we have a resemblance of our Father in us, a likeness of disposition to God and Christ, the image of God, the life of Christ manifest in us;—if we do side with God, and his cause, in evil times, so that we are willing to part with all things for Christ's sake, and at his call;—if it be thus with us in the main bent and constant frame of our hearts, and in the sincerity and integrity of our souls, our consciences in the sight of God bearing us witness that thus it is with us, then may we upon good grounds conclude, that God, the all-sufficient God, is ours, and Christ Jesus, who is all fulness, is ours; and then our hearts should not be troubled. And to prevent and cure all our heart trouble, we must act faith on all these things, in God and in Christ, which I mentioned before, and which would be too long to repeat again here; therefore I earnestly desire you to look back and view over those several particular things considerable in God and in Christ, applying and appropriating them to ourselves, and we shall see we have no cause of heart trouble. If the great God be ours, and the Lord Jesus be ours; if we have no husband, nor wives, nor sons, daughters, nor health, nor wealth, we have enough to content and satisfy our souls for ever.

But to draw to a conclusion, that there may be an effectual cure of all our heart trouble, whatever our distress may be, let us labour to act faith on Christ, in considering and believing—

First. What he is. Second. Where he is. Third. What he hath declared. Fourth. What he hath promised; and all within the confines of this text. (John xiv. 2, 3.)

First. Let Christ's disciples labour to believe what Christ is, and who he is. He himself asked his disciples this question, " Whom say ye that I am?" (Matt. xvi. 15.) Peter answered, " Thou art Christ, the son of the living God. I know in whom I have believed," saith the apostle; and that supported him; and for this knowledge of Jesus Christ his Lord, he counted all things but dung and dross. (Phil. iii. 8.) To believe all things that are written of Christ is not enough; but to believe in him, is by faith to receive him for our only Lord and Saviour; (John i. 12. Col. ii. 6;) and actually, unreservedly, unfeignedly and heartily to give up our whole selves unto him, taking him for our absolute Lord, our head, our treasure, and our all; and believing he is all that to us that he is. That he was made sin for us, made wisdom, righteousness, sanctification, and redemption to us. That he is indeed our husband, our head, our high-priest, our safety, our ransom, our Redeemer. That he hath loved us, and washed us in his blood. That he was delivered up to death for our offences, and rose again for our justification. That he hath made " our peace with God by the blood of his cross; and purchased our pardon, and an inheritance for us with the saints in light; and that by believing in him we shall have everlasting life." (John iii. 16, 36.) I say, this is to believe in Christ; and such as thus believe in him have no cause of heart trouble. And thus we must believe in him, and it is the great commandment of God to believe in him, (1 John iii. 23,) and the positive command of Christ himself in the text, " Believe also in me." (John xiv. 1.) And he that hath this faith hath Christ, and hath life, eternal life. (1 John v. 11.) " Verily, verily, I say unto you," saith Christ, the eternal truth himself, " He that believeth on me hath everlasting life." (John vi. 47.) He hath it *in pretio,* in the price of it, that was punctually paid down upon the cross, therefore called the purchased possession; he hath eternal life in promises, in the promises of it; it is promised to every one that believe; God, that cannot lie, hath promised it, (Tit. i. 2;) and he hath it *in primitiis,* in the first-fruits of it, the saving graces of the Spirit, which in some measure every true believer hath. (2 Cor. v. 5. Eph. i. 13, 14.)

Now, he that thus believes in Christ, Christ is his; and all that Christ hath done, and suffered, and merited, is his, he hath right and title to it; for by faith he is become the child of God. We are all the children of God by faith in Jesus Christ. (Gal. iii. 26.) And if we be Christ's, then are we the heirs of the promise, (Gal iii. 29 ;) yea, "heirs of God, and joint heirs with Christ." (Rom. viii. 17.) Yea, then all things are ours. All is ours, if we be Christ's, whether Paul, or Apollos, or Cephas. (1 Cor. iii. 21—23.) All the gifts, graces, labours, prayers of all gospel ministers, all gospel ordinances, are ordained and designed for our good, (Eph. iv. 11—13,) for the gathering of us in, and for the perfecting and building of us up in Christ Jesus, until we all come to heaven. The world is ours; the good and evil of it, the bitter and the sweet of it, the comforts and the crosses of it, the gains and the losses of it, the love and the hate of it, the smiles and the frowns, the friends and foes in it; all is designed for, and shall further promote our spiritual and eternal welfare. Life is ours. All the troubles, sicknesses, pains, evil tidings, persecutions, disappointments, losses of relations, shame, reproach, or whatever attends this mortal life, shall be sanctified and blessed to us for our good. Yea, death is ours, that shall be our advantage, our gain, that shall put a full end and period to all our sin and suffering, and be a door of entrance for us into glory in our Father's house. Our things present, our present tears, sorrows, miseries, infirmities, &c., shall be so ordered and overruled by the wisdom and love of our Father, that they shall all help us onward to heaven. And things to come are ours, all that glory to be revealed, that saints' everlasting rest that is prepared for the people of God, that crown of righteousness, of glory, and of life; that kingdom of glory, that unspeakable, that inconceivable state of happiness and blessedness which Christ our Lord hath purchased by his blood—all this is ours also. But how come we to have a right and title to all this? Why, saith the apostle, thus "ye are Christ's, and Christ is God's." As sure as Christ is God's, so sure, if you be Christ's, all is yours : and, as I have proved, if we be true believers in Christ, then we are Christ's, we are his members, his spouse, his children ; and then, what cause have we to be troubled at anything, or in any condition? What cause hath such a soul to be dejected, whatever crosses or losses do befall him? Is there not enough in Christ, in the promises, in the purchase of Christ? Is there not enough in heaven, in all that glory, to quiet, content, and fully to satisfy our souls? Oh my beloved, (and oh my base and faithless heart,) it is our base unbelief that doth us all the mischief, that spoils our peace, that hinders our comfort, and makes us walk so heavily. Oh let us bewail this God-dishonouring sin, this peace-destroying sin; and let us, who have received Jesus for our Lord and Saviour, believe that he is ours indeed, and that we are his indeed, and then act our faith upon him, and our hearts shall not be troubled.

Quest. But may some say, It's true, if Christ be ours, all is ours, we believe that; but how shall we know that Christ is ours?

Ans. Briefly thus. If we be Christ's entirely, and sincerely Christ's, then Christ is ours ; " I am my beloved's, and my beloved is mine." (Sol. Song ii. 16 ; vi. 3.) Her being Christ's, was a sure evidence to her that Christ was hers. Now it is not very hard to know whose we are, whether we be Christ's or our own, Christ's or the world's, Christ's or the devil's. Let us take a little pains in trying and searching ourselves, the matter requires it: whose are we? Put this question seriously to our hearts, in the sight of God; whose am I? whose image do I bear? by whose spirit am I acted? who hath my heart, my chief love and delight? Have we unfeignedly given up ourselves to Christ? Have we actually entered into covenant with him, taken him for our head and husband? have we passed over and surrendered up our whole selves to Christ, our souls, bodies, all our concerns? have we given up our hearts, heads, tongues, time, talents, estates, liberties, relations, and all to Christ? have we done sincerely?—then we have received Christ upon his terms. If we be Christ's and not our own, and live unto Christ, and not to ourselves, (Rom. xiv. 8. 1 Cor. vi. 20, Gal. ii. 20,) and are content that Christ should dispose of us and ours as he pleaseth, and are always labouring to be more and more like him, and still longing for more and more communion with him, &c., then may we, upon good grounds conclude that Christ is ours. If we be his, he is ours.

Again, if we truly believe in Christ, then he is ours, for it is by faith that we receive him, and are united to him, and made one with him, (John i. 12, 13,) and are by his Spirit and word regenerated, and made new creatures, and are enabled to walk after the Spirit, and not after the flesh. (2 Cor. v. 17. Rom. viii. 1, 2.) He that believeth hath the witness in himself, (1 John v. 10,) he need not go far to seek. Make sure thy believing in Christ, and thou hast the witness in thyself that he is thine, and that thou art his.

Quest. But how shall we know that we have true faith, and that we do truly believe in Christ?

Ans. Briefly, thus: if we have been made sensible of our lost condition by nature, of our misery by sin, of our unbelief;—if we have found it an hard work to believe;—if we have been made weary and heavy laden with sin, so as to be truly willing to part with all sin ;—if we have been convinced of our absolute need of Christ, and of his incomparable excellency, of his all-sufficiency and willingness to save us ;—if Christ be most precious to us ;—if these convictions have been powerful in us, to drive us from ourselves, and the creature, and sin ;—if we have hereupon been persuaded and enabled sincerely to come unto Christ upon his call in the gospel, to accept of him upon his terms, and to receive him, as he is offered to us in the gospel;—if our whole hearts have opened to him, and closed with him, and we have given up our whole selves entirely to him, and taken him for our only Lord and Saviour, as the only way to God, and do most sincerely resign up ourselves to his government, trusting in him alone, and relying upon him for life and righteousness, for grace and glory :—then we do believe in him, then have we this true faith; which is further to be known thus, that it worketh in us true sincere love to him, and to all that is his, his word, his people ; your hearts will run out after him, all your affections will centre in him. This true faith draws virtue from Christ to purify the heart, and works sanctification and holiness ; it doth crucify your affections to the world, it works true repentance, and enables you to overcome the world, and to realize the glory of heaven, and to bear us up under all the troubles in our way thither, (Heb. xi.,) enabling us to trust and betrust ourselves, our souls and bodies, and all our concernments with Christ : by this faith we shall stand, by it we walk, by it we live, and hold on, and hold out in following the Lamb to the end of our life. (Heb. x. 38, 39.)

Now certainly he that thus believes in Christ, hath no cause of heart trouble, but quietly submits to the goodwill of his God and Christ under all the dispensations of his providence, while he is here in this vale of tears, until he come home to his Father's house in peace, where he shall meet his dearest Lord, and an hearty welcome. Oh this faith, this precious faith in Christ will conquer all our base fears, moderate all our worldly sorrows ; ease our minds perplexed with earthly cares, and quiet our disturbed and distracted thoughts about our outward losses and troubles. By this faith we shall find all our losses made up in God and in Christ. Oh then labour for it, cry mightily to God for this great gift ; cry to Jesus for it, he is the author and finisher of it, and labour to act it upon him continually, and your hearts shall not be troubled.

I dare affirm, that if anything bring heart's ease, in heart trouble, this will do it. So long as our faith holds up in act and exercise upon Christ, we shall be free from heart trouble ; but when our faith fails, our heart troubles prevail; as when Moses lifted up his hands, (and his heart too by faith,) Israel prevailed ; but when his hands were down, Amalek prevailed. Faith and heart trouble are like a pair of balances, when one goes up the other goes down ; faith is the counterpoise of trouble of heart. Believe then in Jesus, act faith on him, and that will prevent or cure heart trouble. Continue in the faith, and your heart troubles will cease ; believe what Christ is, and what he is to us.

Secondly. Let us believe in Christ and believe where he is. As to his essential presence, he is in heaven, at the Father's right hand, (Heb. xii. 2,) making continual intercession for us to the Father.

(Heb. vii. 25.) He is our advocate with the Father, (1 John ii. 1, 2,) pleading our cause, presenting all our services, perfumed with his own righteousness, and resenting and feeling our infirmities, sorrows, and sufferings, sympathizing with us ; in all our afflictions he is afflicted. (Isa. lxiii. 9.) He knows all our troubles, trials, temptations, sickness, losses, and miseries. Jesus himself knew, when he was on earth, what it was to lose a friend; he wept when his friend Lazarus was dead. He is a most tender-hearted Saviour, a most merciful high priest, he sees and feels now in heaven all the miseries of his people upon earth, and pleads for them there ; believe this, and let not your hearts be troubled.

And as to his spiritual and providential presence, he is always with his people on earth ; he is in his people, Christ in you the hope of glory. (Col. i. 27.) He is in his word and ordinances by his Spirit, to bless them to his people. "Christ is all, and in all." (Col. iii. 11.) He is all, that is, instead of all, of father, mother, husband, wife ; of son and daughter ; instead of health, wealth, liberty, and all to his people ; in him dwelleth all fulness. (Eph. iii. 19.) And he is also in all, he filleth all in all. (Eph. i. 23.) In all his people, he dwells in their hearts by faith. All our flesh-springs are in him ; all the strength, support, and comfort we have, comes from him ; he is in all providences, be they never so bitter, so afflicting, never so smarting, so destructive to our earthly comforts, Christ is in them all ; his love, his wisdom, his mercy, his pity and compassion is in them all, every cup is of his preparing ; it is Jesus, your best friend, (oh ye poor, poor believers!), who most dearly loves you ; it is he that died for you, that appoints all providences, orders them all, overrules, moderates, and sanctifies them all, and will sweeten them all ; and in his due time will make them all profitable unto you, that you shall have cause one day to praise and bless his name for them all. Oh that we could but believe all this, and could by faith look unto our Jesus in all dark providences, and by faith behold this Jesus managing of them, and believe his love, wisdom, tenderness, and faithfulness in all ; in our sicknesses, losses, prisons, restraints, &c., then surely our hearts should not be troubled.

Thirdly. Believe in Christ, believe what he hath told us : " In my Father's house are many mansions ; if it were not so, I would have told you. I go to prepare a place for you." (John xiv. 2.) Let us act faith upon these true, sweet sayings of our dear Lord, who is truth itself : " In my Father's house are many mansions." In my Father's house ; my Father's, and your Father's house, one house must hold us all. " I ascend unto my Father, and your Father ; and to my God, and your God," (John xx. 17;) and it is in that house which is far above all heavens, all visible elementary heavens, the third heaven ; that is, the Father's house, that house not made with hands, whose builder and maker is God, and is eternal, (2 Cor. v. 1;) this city of the living God, this new Jerusalem ; there, saith Christ, are many mansions, many dwellings ; many fixed, abiding, lasting, everlasting habitations. Not tents and tabernacles, such as we live in here on earth, but mansions, abiding places. Is not this a most comfortable consideration to such poor saints as have here on earth no certain dwelling-place ? not an house of their own wherein to lay their heads, but are forced to remove from place to place, still seeking an habitation, banished from family and friends, from relations and acquaintance ; some cast into prisons, (while others dwell safely in their own houses, and none to make them afraid,) and others exposed to much hardship and danger ; I say this is good news to them, that in their Father's house are many mansions ; there are everlasting habitations ready to receive them, made ready for them ; from which, when once they are entered, they shall never be cast out more, from whence there shall be no more any remove for ever. When once their earthly house of this tabernacle is broken down, they shall possess that house not made with hands, eternal in the heavens. Let us then by faith often look into the Father's house, and view, and review, those many mansions that are there ; and let us act and hope also, that shortly we shall possess that place, and enjoy that blessed state. The believing, frequent prospects of that place, will prevent our heart trouble, or cure it.

" If it were not so, I would have told you," saith our Lord : if there were not such a blessed state, and glorious place for you, my disciples, in the other world, after all your sufferings in this, I would have told you so. For I have told of the many troubles you must endure in this world ; and for your support and comfort, I am now telling you what good things you shall shortly enjoy above in my Father's house, where is all joy, peace, rest, and consolation. There are many mansions, no prisons, chains, nor fetters, but glorious dwellings, enough to hold all the saints that ever were, and that ever shall be in the world, where they shall enjoy full and free communion with the blessed Trinity, and with one another ; perfect liberty, without any restraint or remove for ever. Believe this, and let not your hearts be troubled.

" I go to prepare a place for you ;" I have purchased this most glorious place for you by my blood ; I have promised it to you ; now I go away to take possession of it for you, in your name and stead : oh, what an heart-comforting and heart-easing consideration should this be to us poor believers, that our Lord went from earth to heaven on purpose to prepare a place in heaven for us, to possess it in our name and stead : and in the meantime, he is preparing us by his word and Spirit, by afflictions and deliverances, for that glorious place ! Hence he is called the " forerunner," who is for us entered into that within the

veil. (Heb. vi. 20.) So that, as sure as Christ himself ascended, and went into the highest heavens, so sure shall all his disciples, all true believers ascend, and enter into heaven also : because he went thither himself, to prepare heaven for them, by taking possession of it in his human nature for us, as our head and Saviour: "God hath prepared for them a city." (Heb. xi. 16.) Heaven and heavenly glory is said to be prepared : " A kingdom prepared from the foundation of the world." (Matt. xxv. 34.) If we could believe that Christ hath prepared a place in heaven for us, and that heaven will make amends for all our sufferings in the way thither ; and if we could keep the eye of our faith upon that " recompence of reward," (Heb. ii. 2,) that " far more exceeding and eternal weight of glory," (1 Cor. iv. 17,) we should bear up bravely under our sufferings, and not have our hearts troubled.

Let us then look more heaven-ward, more to our Father's house ; let us have our conversations more in heaven, and set our affections more upon things above, upon that blessed state and place above ; and know that when Christ, who is our life, shall appear, we shall appear with him in glory. (Col. iii. 1—4.) Believe this, and be comforted.

Certainly we are too much taken up with, and too solicitous about our earthly tabernacles, these houses of clay, whose foundation is in the dust, crushed before the moth. We are always minding the diseases, distempers, and dangers of our bodies, those old crazy, tottering houses, the prisons of our souls : we mind earthly places too much, but too little those " heavenly places in Christ Jesus," (Eph. ii. 6,) where we shall shortly sit with him. Were we more heavenly-minded, we should be more free from heart trouble and disquietness of mind.

Fourth. To prevent and cure all our heart trouble, let us labour to believe what Christ hath promised here in the text, " I will come again, and receive you unto myself ; that where I am, there ye may be also." (John xiv. 3.) Most sweet and comfortable promises !

1. " I will come again." So ver. 18 : I will come again ; " I will not leave you comfortless." For when I am absent from you, in respect of my bodily presence, " I will send the Comforter to you, that shall abide with you for ever." And I myself will come again unto you : you shall not long be without my company. Though Christ seems to withdraw and hide his face from his people, it shall be but for a little moment. (Isa. liv. 7, 8.) He will return again and have mercy ; yea, with everlasting kindness will he return. " I will come again ;" I will not stay long from you ; my heart is still towards you while I am absent, therefore I will come quickly. (Rev. iii. 11.) I will come to you with my messenger death ; though it be the king of terrors in itself, and a grim porter, yet, by my coming with it, it shall be

to you the king of comforts: I will come with it, by my Spirit, to strengthen you, to look it in the face, to apply to you the virtue of my death, and thereby to take out the sting of it; and I will come to you by my angels, to secure your souls through the regions of devils, into my Father's house. If death did come alone to us, it would be terrible to us indeed, its ghastly countenance would affright us; but here is the comfort, that Christ, our dearest Lord, will come with death, to sweeten it to us, and support us under it. This prevented David's fear. (Ps. xxiii. 4.) "Though I walk through the valley of the shadow of death, I will fear no evil, for thou art with me." Oh welcome death, when Christ comes with it! This bitter cup, of which we must all drink, is brought to us by the hand of our dearest Lord; this last stroke is given by the hand of love; it is a taking us home to our Father's house. This last enemy hath Christ conquered for us, because his children are "partakers of flesh and blood, he likewise took part of the same, that through death (that is, his own death) he might destroy him that had the power of death, that is, the devil; and deliver them who, through fear of death, were all their lifetime subject to bondage." (Heb. ii. 14, 15.) Jesus knew what death was, he himself had the pangs of death upon him; sin, the sting of death, was laid on him; and the law, which is the strength of sin, the curse of the law was upon him; but now for us, who believe in Jesus, the sting and strength of death is taken out, and when we die, we shall die in the Lord, sleep in Jesus, in union and communion with Jesus; we shall fall asleep in the blessed arms of our dear Redeemer. He will come then to keep us company through that dark entry (death) into the Father's house; his angels shall carry our souls into Abraham's bosom, yea, into the Father's bosom. Oh that we would make sure of our union with Christ! And then let us believe, that he will come with death, to translate our souls out of these earthly tabernacles, these prison-houses, these houses of bondage, (wherein our poor souls have been fettered and chained, cloyed and clogged with corruptions and temptations, kept at a distance, and absent from the Lord, and in which they have been groaning for deliverance,) into the glorious liberty of the sons of God, in their Father's house, and shall ever be with the Lord. (1 Thess. iv. 17.)

2. I will receive you to myself: oh sweet promise! This is all the hope, all the desire, all the longing, thirsting, breathing, of poor believers, viz., that Christ would take them to himself. This is the sum of all their prayers and labours, that they may be fitted for Christ, and then that Christ would take them to himself. Well, saith Christ, work and wait a little longer; do, and suffer a little more; act your faith and patience a little longer, and I will come to you, and take you home to myself, where your soul shall be at rest for ever. The saints, while they are here, at home in the body,

they are absent from the Lord; they see but in part darkly, and know but in part very imperfectly, and enjoy but a little, a very little, of God and Christ. Oh how sweet are a few drops, a few glimpses and glances of divine love now to a poor soul! the least cast of Christ's eye, the least beam of his loving kindness, the least intimation of his favour, the least hint of his goodness, how refreshing to a poor believer! But when Christ shall receive them to himself, they shall then see him as he is, shall be like him, and shall be satisfied with his likeness. (1 John iii. 2. Ps. xvii. 15.) Then shall they see him whom their souls love, face to face; and then will Jesus open to them all the treasures of his love and grace, to their everlasting consolation. They shall then be admitted into the glorious presence of the great God, and our Saviour Jesus Christ, in whose presence is fulness of joy; and at whose right hand are pleasures for evermore. (Ps. xvi. 11.) When the world shall cast them out, and their habitations shall cast them out, and shall know them no more, yea, when their houses of clay shall be broken down and dissolved, and can hold them no longer, then will Jesus, blessed Jesus, receive them to himself; then shall they be solemnly married to their glorious bridegroom, the King of heaven's Son, the Prince of the kings of the earth; he will receive them to himself, he will take them for his bride, embrace them in his everlasting arms, and lay them in his blessed bosom for ever and ever. "I will receive you to myself:" into the nearest union and communion with myself; and therefore be not unwilling to part with your dear relations; be not afraid to be separated from your bodies, your old friends; for when these earthly tabernacles are dissolved, immediately I will receive you to myself, which is best of all. You shall then enjoy the fruits of all my sufferings—death, resurrection, ascension, and intercession; and the fruits of all your own labours, prayers, tears, and sufferings; and shall find that I am faithful in making good all my promises, and that your labour was not in vain in the Lord; then shall there be no more any distance between you and me for ever. Comfort yourselves, and comfort one another with these words. Believe this, and "let not your hearts be troubled."

3. "That where I am, ye may be also;" and what more can be desired? Where is Christ, but at the right hand of the Majesty on high, far above all principalities and powers, far above all heavens? (Heb. xii. 2.) There shall you be also. Oh admirable, astonishing dignity, that blessed Jesus will advance his poor saints unto at that day! This high and wonderful honour shall all his saints have: they shall now receive the kingdom prepared for them, and that crown of glory, of righteousness, and of life, which Christ hath purchased for them, perfectly freed now from all sin and sorrow, and stated in an unchangeable state of happiness and blessedness. What cause have we then to grieve for our dear relations, whom Christ hath taken to

himself, and placed in the Father's house, who are now sitting at his right hand in glory, and singing hallelujahs? And could we but firmly believe these promises of our Lord, and act our faith in meditating fixedly on them, and in Jesus in them, applying and appropriating them, and Christ in them, to our own souls, considering and pondering on them, until our hearts be warmed, and our affections stirred and kindled with them, acting also hope, love, joy, desire, delight, hunger, thirst, panting, breathing; pouring out our hearts in prayer to God for his Spirit to bring home these promises to our souls in power; fixing them upon our hearts, and helping us to lay hold on them and upon Christ in them, and resigning up our whole souls to Christ in them, steadfastly relying on his goodness and faithfulness, and trusting in him: I say, could we but do so, and in the strength of God betrust our whole selves, and all our concerns, thus with Christ, and live in the lively exercises of faith thus on God, and on Christ, we should find this to be heart's ease to us in all our heart trouble. "Behold, I lay in Sion a chief corner stone, elect, precious; and he that believeth in him shall not be confounded." (1 Pet. ii. 6.)

> Let all heart trouble cease,
> Let nought disturb your peace,
> Who faith in God profess,
> And in his Son no less:
> For in his Father's house
> Are many mansions sweet,
> Christ hath prepared for us,
> When we're for them made meet.

APPENDIX.

QUESTION. *It may be demanded, that having heard the excellency and usefulness of this sovereign medicine to cure heart trouble, namely, faith in God and in Christ, can you tell us how we may get this faith? and what means we shall use to obtain it?*

Answer. I shall endeavour, by the help of God's Spirit, and scripture light, to direct you herein, and as briefly as I may.

Direction I.

First, You must be convinced of your unbelief, of the greatness of the sin of unbelief, and of your absolute need of faith. Of these three things you must be fully convinced.

1. Of your unbelief; for most people think they have faith, and that they never were without it, and therefore labour not for it. Pray earnestly therefore that the Holy Spirit may be sent into your hearts to work this conviction in you, for it is his proper work (John xvi. 8) to convince the world of sin, because they believe not on me, saith our Lord; this is the great sin, the damned sin of the world, their not believing on Christ. Now that we may be convinced, that by nature we have no faith, let us consider these scriptures, Eph. ii. 1, 2, 12; and that until we are regenerate and born again we have no faith, is evident from John i. 12, 13—there, believing in Christ, and regeneration, are inseparably joined together; Acts xv. 9; xx. 21; xxv. 18. From which scriptures it is most evident, that such as are strangers to the heart-purifying, the heart-sanctifying work of faith, have no faith—if we have not truly repented, nor know any saving change wrought in us and upon us, by the Spirit of God; for certain, whatever we think, we have no true saving faith, it is but a fancy: of this then we must be fully convinced, and must most heartily beg the help of the Spirit to convince us.

2. Of the greatness of the sin of unbelief: it binds the guilt of all other sins upon us; it is disobedience and rebellion against the great God: for he commands us to believe, 1 John iii. 23, and by our unbelief we make God a liar, (1 John v. 10:) oh horrible wickedness!

3. We must be convinced also of our absolute need of faith; we must needs have it, or we must perish. Without faith it is impossible to please God, (Heb. xi. 6;) without it we cannot be the children of God, (John i. 12. Gal. iii. 26;) without it we can have no pardon of sin. (Acts x. 43. Rom. iii. 25. John viii. 24.) And in what a dangerous case are we, so long as we lie under the guilt of all our sins? Without faith we are not reconciled to God, nor justified. (Rom. v. 1,) Nor can we be sanctified. (Acts xxvi. 18. 2 Thess. ii. 13.) No access to God but by faith. (Rom. v. 2. Eph. ii. 18.) No living the life of religion, nor bearing up under affliction, nor holding out to the end without faith. (Heb. xi.) No salvation, nor eternal life without it. (John iii. 16, 36. Heb. x. 39.) Of all these things we must be convinced, if ever we will have faith.

Direction II.

Secondly, If we would have faith, we must diligently search the Scriptures, read the gospel, attend on the reading and preaching of the gospel for this very end, that we may get faith by it; I say for this very end, certainly, that should be our end, in reading and in hearing the word, which was God's end in publishing of it; now this was his end in publishing of it: John xx. 21. Rom. x. 17; xvi. 25, 26. Acts xiii. 48. Eph. i. 13. This is the ordinary means appointed by God, to work faith in the souls of men, as appears by Acts ii. 42; iv. 4; xi. 20, 21, and many more. There are few that read, and hear the word for this end, and therefore get no faith by it.

Now that the word read and heard may be effectual to work this precious, this most necessary grace of faith in us, there are some things antecedent, some concomitant, and some consequent upon our attendance on the word, and our use of it.

First. Some things antecedent are necessary.

1. Preparation : for want of this the word most times proves ineffectual. It is the empty, hungry soul that relisheth and taketh in this food, (James i. 21. 1 Pet. ii. 1. Matt. xiii. 22 ;) usually our success is according to our preparation ; as in prayer. (Ps. x. 17. 2 Chron. xii. 14 ; xix. 3.) Make conscience then of preparation.

2. Prayer : pour out your hearts to God in prayer, for a blessing on the word that you read or hear. Oh lift up a cry to God, and say, Lord, make this word effectual to work faith in my soul, &c.

3. Earnest desire and expectation of meeting God in the word, and of his blessing on it : if we expect nothing from it, no wonder if we receive nothing ; there is a fulness of blessing in the gospel. (Rom. xv. 29.) We should bring hungry and thirsty souls after God, the living God, as Ps. lxiii. 1—3 ; lxxxiv. 1, 2. God " filleth the hungry with good things." (Luke i. 53.)

Second. Some things are concomitant. As,

1. We must read and hear it as the word of God, and not as the word of man, (1 Thess. ii. 13. Acts x. 33 ;) and we must acknowledge God's authority in it.

2. Receive it with meekness, opening our hearts to it, and give it the most tender entertainment. (James i. 21.)

3. With love, readiness of mind, and gladness of heart. (2 Thess. ii. 10. Acts ii. 41.)

4. With faith, giving credit to it, believing it to be the word of God. (Heb. iv. 2.)

5. We must be careful to remember it. See what great stress is laid upon our remembering. (1 Cor. xv. 2.) Our salvation lies upon it. (Ps. cxix. 11.) Love the word, for love is the act of memory.

6. Prayer must be added again for a blessing.

Third. Some things must be done afterward also. As,

1. Meditation upon what you have heard and read ; for want of this usually all is lost. I am persuaded, this is one great reason why most profit so little by the word, because they make no conscience of meditation ; they hear and read, but never think more on it afterwards ; so preaching, hearing, reading, and all lost : and souls, and heaven, and all lost. For God's sake then—whose word you read and hear, and for your own souls' sake, if you are not willing they should perish for want of faith—make conscience of meditation on the word, (Ps. i. 2 ; cxix. 97 ;) if ever you get good by the word, meditate upon it.

2. Application of it : take it home to yourselves. (Job v. 27.) Let it sink down into your hearts, saith Christ ; it must be an engrafted word, you must receive it into your hearts, and not into your heads only, (2 Cor. iv. 6 ;) your hearts must be joined to it, and mixed with it.

3. Practice : yielding up ourselves to the government of it, making it the standard and rule of your whole conversation. We must be " doers of the word, and not hearers only," lest we deceive our own souls. (James i. 22. 1 Pet. i. 22. Matt. vii. 22, 24.) And in observing these scripture rules here laid down, in the careful and conscientious use of God's word after this manner, you may not doubt but the Holy Spirit of God will work with the word of God, to make is effectual to work this most precious grace of faith in us, whereby to believe in God and in Christ, to the consolation and eternal salvation of our souls. But if we neglect the means that God hath ordained to get faith, and for want of it die in our sins and perish eternally, our destruction will be of ourselves.

Direction III.

Thirdly, Would we have faith ? Let us engage our whole souls in the deep and serious consideration of the infinite, unspeakable, inconceivable love of God the Father, in this, the highest and fullest demonstration of it, in giving his Son, his only-begotten Son, to be a sin-offering, a sacrifice, a ransom for poor sinners ; and that for this very end and purpose, that we poor sinners might believe in him, and by believing, might not perish, but might have eternal life. I pray read and ponder upon the following texts, and let your most serious thoughts fix on them, and meditate on them, Isa. liii. John iii. 16, 17. Rom. iii. 25 ; v. 8—10; viii. 3, 32. Col. i. 12, 13. 2 Cor. v. 19—21 ; with many other which for brevity sake I cannot transcribe. If we can but believe this wonderful love of God the Father, in giving his dear Son to be a surety, a sin-offering, to lay all our iniquities on him ; that he was pleased to bruise him, and put him to grief for us ; and consider and meditate upon the height and depth, the breadth and length of this immense, incomprehensible love of God in giving his Son, and that on purpose that we might believe in him, and by believing might have eternal life ; I say, it will greatly help us to believe in his Son, to accept of this his unspeakable gift, and to receive him as he is offered to us in the gospel.

Moreover, let us also consider of, and deeply meditate upon, the transcendent love of the Son of God himself ; who, though he were the delight of his Father, and lay in the bosom of his Father, even then his delights were with the sons of men, then was his heart full of love to poor sinners ; and his love brought him down from heaven to earth, to assume human nature, to take upon him all the sins of his people, to bear them on his soul and body in the garden, there sweating great drops of blood, and on the cross there pouring out his heart blood, made a curse, endured the full measure of the wrath of God due for sin, and become the ransom of souls. (Phil. ii. 6—8. Luke xxii. 44. Gal. ii. 20.) He loved us, and gave himself for us : " Loved us, and washed us from our sins in his own blood." (Rev. i. 6. Pet. i. 18, 19; ii. 24. Gal. iii. 13. Tit. ii. 14.)

But while I am writing these things, I cannot but conceive an indignation against myself, and heartily wish I were filled with shame, sorrow, and grief of spirit, that having read and heard so often of the surpassing love of God the Father, in giving his Son, and so often of the unspeakable love of Jesus, and to be no more affected with it, no more sensible of it; to have my affections no more stirred and moved, no more quickened and warmed: alas! my dead heart! my adamantine heart! Lord, sprinkle it with the blood; Lord, shed abroad that love of thine upon my heart abundantly by the Holy Ghost; Lord Jesus, manifest thy love to me, that I may love thee! I am ashamed and pained for want of love to God, to Jesus; oh that I could believe thy love to my soul, then I should not choose but love thee! " Lord, I believe; help thou mine unbelief." (Mark ix. 24.) The consideration of this love of God, and of Christ, is a means to work faith; try it, I pray you, and you will find it so.

Direction IV.

Fourthly, Improve and act the historical faith you have, on the doctrines, promises, and threatening in the gospel, which you profess you do believe. Act the faith you have on the doctrines of the gospel, the promises of rest for your souls, pardon for your sins, life and righteousness, grace and glory, made to those who believe in Christ, and to none else. Believe and think what heaven is, that state of infinite blessedness, in the seeing and enjoying the blessed God to all eternity. Believe what eternal life is, eternal glory; and believe also what hell is, separation from God; " Depart from me, ye cursed, into everlasting fire," (Matt. xxv. 41;) lakes of fire and brimstone, into everlasting death, the wrath of God, damnation. And seeing you profess that you believe all this, then believe also and consider it well, that neither is heaven's infinite happiness to be attained, nor hell's unspeakable misery to be avoided, but only by believing in the Lord Jesus Christ. (John iii. 16, 17, 36; viii. 24.)

Direction V.

Fifthly, Would you have faith? then seek it diligently; pray, oh pray for it as for your lives; cry mightily to God for it; pour out your hearts to God in prayer for it; pray continually for faith, pray without ceasing, be importunate with God for it, go all day and night panting and breathing after it. Oh that God would give me faith! Go to Jesus also for it, cry to him, for he is the author as well as the object of it. (Heb. xii. 1, 2.) It is the gift of God, oh pray for it!

Direction VI.

Lastly, Consider seriously, and often, how wonderful willing God is that you should believe in Christ, as you have heard; and how much he is displeased with those that will not believe in him; and how dreadfully he has threatened them. (Rev. xxi. 8.) Also consider how exceeding willing Jesus Christ himself is, that poor sinners should come to him, and believe in him; how sweetly he calls them; how freely he offers himself, and all he is, to them, be they never so bad, never so vile and wicked; " Ho, every one that thirsteth," (Isa. lv. 1 :) they that have no worthiness in them, nothing but sin and misery. (John vi. 37; vii. 37. Rev. iii. 18.) Oh set your hearts to the consideration of the incomparable, unparalleled love of Jesus, in dying that cursed death of the cross for sinners. Consider and meditate, hold your hearts to it, until your hearts be affected with his love, his love that passeth the love of women, love passing understanding; and consider how well he deserves, and how much he challengeth your love. Consider once again, what a most lovely person Jesus is, who is altogether lovely, the brightness of his Father's glory, in whom dwells all fulness, (Heb. i. 3,) and in whom is all power in heaven and earth, (Matt. xxviii. 18,) and labour to affect your hearts with his most admirable excellencies, and then come unto him weary and heavy laden with your sins, willing to part with them all; give up your whole selves to him, give him your whole hearts, and take him for your head and husband, for your only Lord and Saviour: enter actually into covenant with him, to become his, and his alone, and his for ever. Thus work out your salvation and your consolation, by believing in Jesus, in blessed, all-sufficient Jesus, trusting to him, be trusting all with him, and God will work in you, "both to will and to do." (Phil. ii. 13.) Use these means in the strength of God, and doubt not but in the use of them, you shall obtain this precious faith; which having, and acting, you shall find it to be your *heart's ease* in all your *heart trouble.*

AN EXHORTATION TO PEACE AND UNITY.

PREFATORY NOTE.

THE authenticity of this discourse is very reasonably suspected; but the arguments against it can hardly overbalance the fact that it was published as early as the year 1688, that of Bunyan's death; and we know of no protest uttered by any of his friends, tending to deny that it proceeded from his pen. The learning which it is supposed to display is far too slight and accidental to be properly urged as a proof that he did not write it. He speaks, even in some of his verses, of Machiavel, and alludes throughout his writings to various points of erudition, easily collected by a man of good understanding and memory. The very nature of the subject would lead him to employ expressions less strictly expressive of peculiar views than those which he may have used in more controversial treatises. His broad and tolerant language, therefore, ought not to be a plea for robbing him of any credit due to this discourse. None, indeed, of the common objections urged against its authenticity seem of much weight; and we should gladly give Bunyan the praise to which the kindly, charitable writer, whoever he may be, is richly entitled.

H. S.

AN EXHORTATION TO PEACE AND UNITY.

EPH. iv. 3.

" Endeavouring to keep the unity of the spirit in the bond of peace."

BELOVED, religion is the great bond of human society; and it were well if itself were kept within the bond of unity; and that it may so be, let us, according to the text, use our utmost endeavours to keep the unity of the spirit in the bond of peace.

These words contain a counsel and a caution: the counsel is, that we endeavour [to keep] the unity of the spirit; the caution is, that we do it in the bond of peace. As if I should say, I would have you live in unity, but yet I would have you to be careful, that you do not purchase unity with the breach of charity.

Let us therefore be cautioned that we do not so press after unity in practice and opinion, as to break the bond of peace and affection.

In the handling of these words I shall observe this method :—

First. I shall open the sense of the text.

Second. I shall show wherein this unity and peace consists.

Third. I shall show you the fruits and benefits of it, together with nine inconveniences and mischiefs that attend those churches where unity and peace is wanting.

Fourth. And lastly, I shall give you twelve directions and motives for the obtaining of it.

First. As touching the sense of the text. When we are counselled to keep the unity of the spirit, we are not to understand the Spirit of God, as personally so considered; because the Spirit of God in that sense is not capable of being divided, and so there would be no need for us to endeavour to keep the unity of it.

By the unity of the spirit, then, we are to understand that unity of mind which the Spirit of God calls for, and requires Christians to endeavour after; hence it is that we are exhorted by one spirit, with one mind, to strive together for the faith of the gospel. (Phil. i. 27.)

But farther; the apostle in these words alludes to the state and composition of a natural body, and doth thereby inform us that the mystical body of Christ holds an analogy with the natural body of man: as,

1. In the natural body there must be a spirit to animate it; for " the body without the spirit is dead." (James ii. 26.) So it is in the mystical body of Christ; the apostle no sooner tells of that one body, but he minds us of that one spirit. (Eph. iv. 4.)

2. The body hath joints and bands to unite all the parts; so hath the mystical body of Christ. (Col. ii. 19.) This is that bond of peace men-

tioned in the text, as also in the 16th verse of the same chapter, (Eph. iv.,) where "the whole body" is said to be "fitly joined together, and compacted by that which every joint supplieth."

3. The natural body receives counsel and nourishment from the head; so doth the mystical body of Christ. He is their counsellor, and him they must hear; he is their head, and him they must hold. Hence it is that the apostle complaineth, (Col. ii. 19,) of some that did "not hold the head, from which all the body by joints and bands hath nourishment."

4. The natural body cannot well subsist, if either the spirit be wounded, or the joints broken or dislocated; the body cannot bear a wounded or broken spirit. "A broken spirit drieth the bones," (Prov. xvii. 22,) and "a wounded spirit who can bear?" (Prov. xviii. 14.) And on the other hand, how often have the disjointing of the body, and the breakings thereof, occasioned the expiration of the spirit? In like manner it fares with the mystical body of Christ: how do divided spirits break the bonds of peace, which are the joints of this body! And how doth the breakings of the body and church of Christ wound the spirit of Christians, and oftentimes occasion the spirit and life of Christianity to languish, if not to expire! How needful is it, then, that we endeavour [to keep] the unity of the spirit in the bond of peace?

Second. I now come to show you *wherein this unity and peace consists;* and this I shall demonstrate in five particulars.

1. This unity and peace may consist in the ignorance of many truths, and in the holding of some errors; or else this duty of peace and unity could not be practicable by any on this side perfection; but we must now endeavour the unity of the spirit, "till we all come in the unity of the faith, and of the knowledge of the Son of God." (Eph. iv. 13.) Because now, as the apostle saith, "we know in part, and we prophesy in part," and "now we see through a glass darkly." (1 Cor. xiii. 12.) And as this is true in general, so we may find it true if we descend to particular instances. The disciples seemed to be ignorant of that great truth which they had often, and in much plainness, been taught by their Master once and again, viz.—that his kingdom was not of this world, and that in the world they should suffer and be persecuted; yet in the first chapter of the Acts, ver. 6, we read, that they asked of him if he would "at this time restore again the kingdom to Israel?" thereby discovering that Christ's kingdom, as they thought, should consist in his temporal jurisdiction over Israel, which they expected should now commence and take place amongst them. Again, our Lord tells them, that he had many things to say (and these many were important truths) which they could not now bear. (John xvi. 12.) And that these were important truths, appears by the tenth and eleventh verses, where he is discoursing of righteousness and judgment; and then adds, that he had yet many things to say, which they could not bear; and thereupon promises the Comforter to lead them into ALL TRUTH; which implies, that they were yet ignorant of many truths, and consequently held divers errors; and yet for all this he prays for, and presses them to their great duty of peace and unity. (John xiv. 27; xvii. 21.) To this may be added that of Heb. v. 11, where the author saith, he had many things to say of the priestly office of Christ, which, by reason of their dulness, they were not capable to receive; as also that in the tenth chapter of the Acts, where Peter seems to be ignorant of that truth, viz., that the gospel was to be preached to all nations; and, contrary hereunto, he erred in thinking it unlawful to preach amongst the Gentiles. I shall add two texts more, one in Acts xix., where we read, that those disciples which had been discipled and baptized by John, were yet ignorant of the Holy Ghost, and knew not (as the text tells us) whether there were any Holy Ghost or no; though John did teach constantly, that he that should come after him, should baptize with the Holy Ghost and fire. From hence we may easily and plainly infer, that Christians may be ignorant of many truths, by reason of weak and dull capacities, and other such-like impediments, even while those truths are with much plainness delivered to them. Again, we read (Heb. v. 13) of some that were unskilful in the word of righteousness, who nevertheless are called babes in Christ, and with whom unity and peace is to be inviolably kept and maintained.

2. As this unity and peace may consist in the ignorance of many truths, and in the holding some errors, so it must consist with (and it cannot consist without) the believing and practising those things which are necessary to salvation and church communion; and they are,

(1.) Believing that Christ the Son of God died for the sins of men.

(2.) That whoever believeth, ought to be baptized.

(3.) The third thing essential to this communion is a holy and a blameless conversation.

(1). That believing that the Son of God died for the sins of men is necessary to salvation, I prove by these texts, which tells us, that he that doth not believe, shall be damned. (Mark xvi. 16. John iii. 18. Rom. x. 10.)

That it is also necessary to church communion, appears from Matt. xvi. 16—18. Peter having confessed that Christ was the Son of the living God, Christ thereupon assures Peter, that upon this rock, viz., this profession of faith, or this Christ which Peter had confessed, he would build his church, and the gates of hell should not prevail against it. And (1 Cor. iii. 11) the apostle having told the Corinthians they were God's building, presently adds, that they could not be built upon any foundation but upon that which was laid, which was Jesus Christ. All which proves that

Christian society is founded upon the profession of Christ; and not only Scripture, but the laws of right reason dictate this, that some rules and orders must be observed for the founding all society, which must be consented to by all that will be of it. Hence it comes to pass, that to own Christ as the Lord and head of Christians, is essential to the founding Christian society.

(2.) The Scriptures have declared that this faith gives the professors of it a right to baptism, as in the case of the eunuch, (Acts viii.,) when he demanded why he might not be baptized? Philip answereth, that if he believed with all his heart, he might; the eunuch thereupon confessing Christ, was baptized.

Now that baptism is essential to church communion, I prove from 1 Cor. xii., where we shall find the apostle labouring to prevent an evil use that might be made of spiritual gifts, as thereby to be puffed up; and to think that such as wanted them, were not of the body, or to be esteemed members; he thereupon resolves, that whoever did confess Christ, and own him for his head, did it by the Spirit, (1 Cor. xii. 3,) though they might not have such a visible manifestation of it as others had, and therefore they ought to be owned as members, as appears, ver. 23. And not only because they have called him Lord by the Spirit, but because they have by the guidance and direction of the same Spirit been baptized, ver. 13, " For by one Spirit we are all baptized into one body," &c. I need not go about to confute that notion that some of late have had of this text, viz., that the baptism here spoken of is the baptism of the Spirit, because you have not owned and declared that notion as your judgment; but, on the contrary, all of you that I have ever conversed with have declared it to be understood of baptism with water, by the direction of the Spirit. If so, then it follows, that men and women are declared members of Christ's body by baptism, and cannot be by Scripture reputed and esteemed so without it; which farther appears from Rom. vi. 5, where men by baptism are said to be planted into " the likeness of his death ;" and in Col. ii. 12 we are said to be buried with him by baptism : all which, together with the consent of all Christians, (some few in these latter times excepted,) do prove that baptism is necessary to the initiating persons into the church of Christ.

(3.) Holiness of life is essential to church communion, because it seems to be the reason why Christ founded a church in the world, viz., that men might thereby be watched over, and kept from falling; and that if any be overtaken with a fault, he that is spiritual might restore him.

That by this means men and women might be preserved without blame to the coming of Christ, and " the grace of God teacheth us to deny ungodliness and worldly lusts, and to live soberly and uprightly in this present evil world." (Tit. ii. 11, 12.) " And let every one that nameth the name of the Lord depart from iniquity." (2 Tim. ii. 19.) And James tells us, speaking of the Christian religion, that " pure religion, and undefiled, before God, is to visit the fatherless and widows in their affliction, and to keep himself unspotted from the world." (James i. 27.) From all which, together with many more texts that might be produced, it appears that an unholy and profane life is inconsistent with Christian religion and society, and that holiness is essential to salvation and church communion ; so that these three things — faith, baptism, and a holy life — as I said before, all churches must agree and unite in, as those things which, when wanting, will destroy their being. And let not any think, that when I say believing the Son of God died for the sins of men is essential to salvation and church communion, that I hereby would exclude all other articles of the Christian creed as not necessary—as the belief of the resurrection of the dead, and eternal judgment, &c., which for want of time I omit to speak particularly to ; and the rather, because I understand this great article of believing the Son of God died for the sins of men, is comprehensive of all others, and is that from whence all other articles may easily be inferred.

And here I would not be mistaken, as though I held there were nothing else for Christians to practise, when I say this is all that is requisite to church communion ; for I very well know that Christ requires many other things of us, after we are members of his body, which if we knowingly or maliciously refuse, may be the cause, not only of excommunication, but damnation. But yet these are such things as relate to the well-being, and not to the being of churches : as laying on of hands in the primitive times upon believers, by which they did receive the gifts of the Spirit ; this, I say, was for the increase and edifying of the body, and not that thereby they might become of the body of Christ, for that they were before. And do not think that I believe laying on of hands was no apostolical institution, because I say men are not thereby made members of Christ's body, or because I say that it is not essential to church communion. Why should I be thought to be against a fire in the chimney, because I say it must not be in the thatch of the house ? Consider then how pernicious a thing it is to make every doctrine, though true, the bound of communion ; this is that which destroys unity, and by this rule all men must be perfect before they can be in peace. For do we not see daily, that as soon as men come to a clearer understanding of the mind of God, to say the best of what they hold, that presently all men are excommunicable, if not damnable, that do not agree with them. Do not some believe and see that to be pride and covetousness which others do not, because, it may be, they have more narrowly and diligently searched into their duty of these things than others have ? What then ! Must all men that have not so large acquaintance of their duty herein be excommunicated? Indeed it were to be wished that more moderation in apparel and secular concernments were found among churches; but God forbid, that if they should come short herein, that we should say, as one lately said, that he could not communicate with such a people, because they were proud and superfluous in their apparel.

Let me appeal to such, and demand of them, if there was not a time, since they believed and were baptized, wherein they did not believe laying on of hands a duty? and did they not then believe, and do they not still believe, they were members of the body of Christ? And was not there a time when you did not so well understand the nature and extent of pride and covetousness as now you do? And did you not then believe, and do you not still believe, that you were true members of Christ, though less perfect? Why then should you not judge of those that differ from you herein, as you judged of yourselves when you were as they now are? How needful then is it for Christians to distinguish, if ever they would be at peace and unity, between those truths which are essential to church communion and those that are not!

3. Unity and peace consists in our making one shoulder to practise and put in execution the things we do know. "Nevertheless whereto we have attained, let us walk by the same rule, and mind the same thing." (Phil. iii. 16.) How sad is it to see our zeal consume us and our precious time in things doubtful and disputable, while we are not concerned nor affected with the practice of those indisputable things we all agree in! We all know charity to be the great command, and yet how few agree to practise it! We all know they that labour in the word and doctrine are worthy of double honour, and that God hath ordained that they which preach the gospel should live of the gospel: these duties, however others have cavilled at them, I know you agree in them, and are persuaded of your duty herein; but where is your zeal to practise? Oh how well would it be with churches if they were but half as zealous for the great, and plain, and indisputable things, and the more chargeable and costly things of religion, as they are for things doubtful or less necessary, or for things that are no charge to them, and cost them nothing but the breath of contention, though that may be too great a price for the small things they purchase with it.

But further: do we not all agree that men that preach the gospel should do it like workmen that need not be ashamed? And yet how little is this considered by many preachers who never consider before they speak of what they say, or whereof they affirm? How few give themselves to study that they may be approved? How few meditate and give themselves to these things, that their profiting may appear to all?

For the Lord's sake let us unite to practise those things we know; and if we would have more talents, let us all agree to improve those we have.

See the spirit that was among the primitive professors, that knowing and believing how much it concerned them in the propagating of Christianity, to show forth love to one another, that so all might know them to be Christ's disciples, rather than there should be any complainings among them, they sold all they had. Oh how zealous were these to practise, and with one shoulder to do that that was upon their hearts for God! I might further add, how often have we agreed in our judgment? and hath it not been upon our hearts that this and the other thing is good to be done to enlighten the dark world, and to repair the breaches of churches, and to raise up those churches that now lie gasping, and among whom the soul of religion is expiring? But what do we more than talk of them? Do not most decline these things when they either call for their purses, or their persons, to help in this and such-like works as these? Let us, then, in what we know, unite, that we may put it in practice, remembering, that if we know these things, we shall be happy if we do them.

4. This unity and peace consists in our joining and agreeing to pray for, and to press after, those truths we do not know. The disciples in the primitive times were conscious of their imperfections, and therefore they with one accord continued in prayer and supplications. If we were more in the sense of our ignorances and imperfections, we should carry it better towards those that differ from us; then we should abound more in the spirit of meekness and forbearance, that thereby we might bring others, or be brought by others, to the knowledge of the truth. This would make us go to God, and say with Elihu, That which we know not, teach thou us. (Job xxxiv. 32.) Brethren, did we but all agree that we were erring in many things, we should soon agree to go to God, and pray for more wisdom and revelation of his mind and will concerning us.

But here is our misery, that we no sooner receive anything for truth but we presently ascend the chair of infallibility with it, as though in this we could not err. Hence it is we are impatient of contradiction, and become uncharitable to those that are not of the same mind; but now a consciousness that we may mistake, or that if my brother err in one thing, I may err in another, this will unite us in affection, and engage us to press after perfection, according to that of the apostle, "Brethren, I count not myself to have apprehended: but this one thing I do, forgetting those things which are behind, and reaching forth to those things which are before, I press toward the mark, for the prize of the high calling of God in Christ Jesus. And if in any thing ye be otherwise minded, God shall reveal even this unto you." (Phil. iii. 13—15.) Oh then, that we could but unite and agree to go to God for one another, in confidence that he will teach us ; and that, if any one of us want wisdom—as who of us does not—we might agree to ask of God, who giveth to all men liberally, and upbraideth no man. Let us, like those people spoken of in the second of Isaiah, say one to another, Come, let us go to the Lord, for he will teach us of his ways, and we will walk in his paths.

5. This unity and peace mainly consists in unity of love and affection. This is the great and indispensable duty of all Christians. By this they are declared Christ's disciples. And hence it is that love is called the great commandment, the old commandment, and the new commandment—that which was commanded in the beginning, and will remain to the end, yea, and after the end. "Charity never faileth ; but whether there be tongues, they shall cease ; or whether there be knowledge, it shall vanish away." (1 Cor. xiii. 8.) And ver. 13 : " And now abideth faith, hope, and charity ; but the greatest of these is charity." And Col. iii. 14 : " Above all these things put on charity, which is the bond of perfectness." Because charity is " the end of the commandment." (1 Tim. i. 5.) Charity is therefore called the royal law ; and though it had a superintendency over other laws, and doubtless is a law to which other laws must give place, when they come in competition with it. " Above all things, therefore, have fervent charity among yourselves, for charity shall cover the multitude of sins." (1 Pet. iv. 8.) Let us therefore live in unity and peace, and the God of love and peace will be with us.

That you may so do, let me remember you, in the words of a learned man, that the unity of the church is a unity of love and affection, and not a bare uniformity of practice and opinion.

Third. Having shown you wherein this unity consists, I now come to the third general thing propounded ; and that is, *to show you the fruits and benefits of unity and peace ; together with the mischiefs and inconveniences that attend those churches where unity and peace are wanting.*

1. Unity and peace is a duty well-pleasing to God, who is styled the author of peace, and not of confusion, in all the churches. God's Spirit rejoiceth in the unity of our spirits : but on the other hand, where strife and divisions are, there the Spirit of God is grieved. Hence is it that the apostle no sooner calls upon the Ephesians not to grieve the Spirit of God, but he presently subjoins us a remedy against that evil, that they put away bitterness and evil-speaking, " And be kind one to another, and tender-hearted, forgiving one another, even as God for Christ's sake hath forgiven you." (Eph. iv. 30, 32.)

2. As unity and peace is pleasing to God, and rejoiceth his Spirit, so it rejoiceth the hearts and spirits of God's people—unity and peace brings heaven down upon earth among us. Hence it is that the apostle tells us, (Rom. xiv. 17,) that " the kingdom of God is not meat and drink, but right-

eousness and peace, and joy in the Holy Ghost." Where unity and peace is, there is heaven upon earth ; by this we taste the first fruits of that blessed estate we shall one day live in the fruition of ; when we shall come to the general assembly and church of the first-born, " Whose names are written in heaven, and to God the judge of all, and to the spirits of just men made perfect." (Heb. xii. 23.)

This outward peace of the church, as a learned man observes, distils into peace of conscience, and turns writings and readings of controversy into treatises of mortification and devotion.

And the Psalmist tells us, that it is not only good, but pleasant "for brethren to dwell together in unity." (Ps. cxxxiii.) But where unity and peace is wanting, there are storms and troubles ; " Where envy and strife is, there is confusion, and every evil work." (James iii. 16.) It is the outward peace of the church that increaseth our inward joy ; and the peace of God's house gives us occasion to eat our meat with gladness in our own houses. (Acts ii. 46.)

3. The unity and peace of the church makes communion of saints desirable. What is it that embitters church communion, and makes it burdensome, but divisions ? Have you not heard many complain that they are weary of church communion, because of church contention ? but now, where unity and peace is, there Christians long for communion.

David saith, that he was glad when they said unto him, " Let us go into the house of the Lord." (Ps. cxxii. 1.) Why was this, but because, as the third verse tells us, Jerusalem was a city compact together, where the tribes went up—the tribes of the Lord—to give thanks to his name ? And David, speaking of the man that was once his friend, doth thereby let us know the benefit of peace and unity : " We," saith he, " took sweet counsel together, and walked unto the house of God in company." (Ps. lv. 14.) Where unity is strongest, communion is sweetest and most desirable. You see, then, that peace and union fill the people of God with desires after communion. But, on the other hand, hear how David complains. " Woe is me that I sojourn in Mesech, that I dwell in the tents of Kedar !" (Ps. cxx.) The psalmist here is thought to allude to a sort of men that dwelt in the deserts of Arabia, that got their livings by contention ; and therefore he adds, ver. 6, that his soul had long dwelt with them that hated peace. This was that which made him long for the courts of God, and esteem one day in his house better than a thousand. This made his soul even faint for the house of God, because of the peace of it. " Blessed are they," saith he, " that dwell in thy house : they will be still praising thee." (Ps. lxxxiv. 4.) There is a certain note of concord, as appears, Acts ii., where we read of primitive Christians meeting with one accord praising God.

4. Where unity and peace is, there many mischiefs and inconveniences are prevented, which attend those people where peace and unity are wanting. And of those many that might be mentioned, I shall briefly insist upon these nine.

(1.) Where unity and peace are wanting, there is much precious time spent to no purpose. How many days are spent, and how many fruitless journeys made to no profit, where the people are not in peace! How often have many redeemed time—even in seed-time and harvest—when they could scarce afford it, to go to church, and, by reason of their divisions, come home worse than they went, repenting they have spent so much precious time to so little benefit! How sad it is to see men spend their precious time, in which they should work out their salvation, by labouring, as in the fire, to prove an uncertain and doubtful proposition; and to trifle away their time, in which they should make their calling and election sure, to make sure of an opinion which, when they have done all, they are not infallibly sure whether it be true or no, because all things necessary to salvation and church communion are plainly laid down in Scripture, in which we may be infallibly sure of the truth of them; but for other things that we have no plain texts for, but the truth of them depends upon our interpretations, here we must be cautioned that we do not spend much time in imposing those upon others, or venting those among others, unless we can assume infallibility, otherwise we spend time upon uncertainty. And whoever cast their eyes abroad, and doth open their ears to intelligence, shall both see, and, to their sorrow, hear, that many churches spend most of their time in jangling and contending about those things which are neither essential to salvation or church communion; and that which is worse, about such doubtful questions which they are never able to give an infallible solution of. But now where unity and peace is, there our time is spent in praising God; and in those great questions—what we should do to be saved? and how we may be more holy and more humble towards God, and more charitable and more serviceable to one another?

(2.) Where unity and peace is wanting, there is evil surmising and evil speaking, to the damage and disgrace, if not to the ruining of one another. (Gal. v. 14, 15.) The whole law is fulfilled in one word, "Thou shalt love thy neighbour as thyself; but if ye bite and devour one another, take heed that ye be not consumed one of another." No sooner the bond of charity is broken, which is as a wall about Christians, but soon they begin to make havoc and spoil of one another; then there is raising evil reports, and taking up evil reports against each other. Hence it is that whispering and backbiting proceeds, and going from house to house to blazon the faults and infirmities of others. Hence it is that we watch for the haltings of one another, and do inwardly rejoice at the mis-carriages of others, saying, in our hearts, "Ah, ah, so we would have it!" But now, where unity and peace is, there is charity; and where charity is, there we are willing to hide the faults, and cover the nakedness of our brethren. "Charity thinketh no evil," (1 Cor. xiii. 5,) and therefore it cannot surmise, neither will it speak, evil.

(3.) Where unity and peace is wanting, there can be no great matters enterprised; we cannot do much for God, nor much for one another. When the devil would hinder the bringing to pass of good in nations and churches, he divides their councils, and, as one well observes, he divides their heads, that he may divide their hands. When Jacob had prophesied of the cruelty of Simeon and Levi, who were brethren, he threatens them with the consequences of it. (Gen. xlix. 7.) "I will divide them in Jacob, and scatter them in Israel." The devil is not to learn that maxim he hath taught the Machiavellians of the world, *divide et impera*—divide and rule; it is an united force that is formidable. Hence the spouse in the Canticles is said to be " but one, and the only one of her mother." (Sol. Song vi. 9.) Hereupon it is said of her, ver. 10, that she is " terrible as an army with banners." What can a divided army do, or a disordered army, that have lost their banners, or for fear or shame thrown them away? In like manner, what can Christians do for Christ, and the enlarging his dominions in the world, in bringing men from darkness to light, while themselves are divided and disordered? Peace is to Christians, as great rivers are to some cities, which, besides other benefits and commodities, are natural fortifications, by reason whereof those places are made impregnable; but when, by the subtlety of an adversary, or the folly of the citizens, these waters come to be divided into little petty rivulets, how soon are they assailed and taken! Thus it fares with churches; when once the devil or their own folly divides them, they will be so far from resisting of him, that they will be soon subjected by him.

Peace is to churches as walls to cities; nay, unity hath defended cities that had no walls. It was once demanded of Agesilaus why Lacedemon had no walls; he answers, pointing back to the city, that the concord of the citizens was the strength of the city. In like manner, Christians are strong when united; then they are more capable to resist temptation, and to succour such as are tempted. When unity and peace is among the churches, then are they like a walled town; and when peace is the church's walls, salvation will be her bulwarks.

Plutarch tells us of one Silurus that had eighty sons, whom he calls to him as he lay upon his death-bed, and gave them a sheaf of arrows; thereby to signify, that if they lived in unity, they might do much; but if they divided, they would come to nothing. If Christians were all of one piece, if they were all but one lump, or but one sheaf or bundle, how great are the things they might do for Christ and his people in the world, whereas otherwise they can do little but dishonour him, and offend his.

It is reported of the leviathan, that his strength is in his scales. (Job xli. 15—17.) "His scales are his pride, shut up together, as with a close seal. One is so near to another, that no air can come between them. They join together, they stick together, they cannot be sundered." If the church of God were united like the scales of leviathan, it would not be every brain-sick notion, nor angry speculation, that would cause their separation.

Solomon saith, two are better than one, because if one fail the other may raise him; then surely twenty are better than two, and an hundred are better than twenty, for the same reason—because they are more capable to help one another. If ever Christians would do anything to raise up the fallen tabernacles of Jacob, and to strengthen the weak, and comfort the feeble, and to fetch back those that have gone astray, it must be by unity.

We read of the men of Babel, (Gen. xi. 6,) "the Lord said, Behold the people is one. And now nothing will be restrained from them which they have imagined to do."

We learn by reason what great things may be done in worldly achievements where unity is. And shall not reason, assisted with the motives of religion, teach us, that unity among Christians may enable them to enterprise greater things for Christ? Would not this make Satan fall from heaven like lightning? For as unity built literal Babel, it is unity that must pull down mystical Babel. And, on the other hand, where divisions are, there is confusion. By this means a Babel hath been built in every age. It hath been observed by a learned man, and I wish I could not say truly observed, that there is most of Babel and confusion among those that cry out most against it.

Would we have a hand to destroy Babylon, let us have a heart to unite one among another.

Our English histories tell us, that after Austin the monk had been some time in England, that he heard of some of the remains of the British Christians, which he convened to a place, which Camden in his *Britannica* calls "Austin's Oak." Here they met to consult about matters of religion; but such was their division, by reason of Austin's imposing spirit, that our stories tell us that synod was only famous for this, that they only met, and did nothing. This is the mischief of divisions, they hinder the doing of much good; and if Christians that are divided be ever famous for anything, it will be that they have often met together, and talked of this and the other thing, but they did nothing.

(4.) Where unity and peace is wanting, there the weak are wounded, and the wicked are hardened. Unity may well be compared to precious oil. (Ps. cxxxiii. 2.) It is the nature of oil to heal that which is wounded, and to soften that which is hard.

Those men that have hardened themselves against God and his people, when they shall behold unity and peace among them, will say, God is in them indeed. And, on the other hand, are they not ready to say, when they see you divided, that the devil is in you that you cannot agree?

(5.) Divisions, and want of peace, keep those out of the church that would come in; and cause many to go out that are in.

"The divisions of Christians," as a learned man observes, "are a scandal to the Jews, an opprobrium to the Gentiles, and an inlet to atheism and infidelity." Insomuch that our controversies about religion, especially as they have been of late managed, have made religion itself become a controversy. Oh, then, how good and pleasant a thing is it for brethren to dwell together in unity! The peace and unity that was among the primitive Christians, drew others to them. What hinders the conversion of the Jews, but the divisions of Christians? Must I be a Christian, says the Jew; what Christian must I be, of what sect must I be of? The Jews, as one observes, glossing upon that text in Isa. xi. 6, where it is prophesied that the lion and the lamb shall lie down together, and that there shall be none left to hurt nor destroy in all God's holy mountain; they interpreting these sayings to signify the concord and peace that shall be among the people that shall own the Messiah, do from hence conclude that the Messiah is not yet come, because of the contentions and divisions that are among those that profess him. And the apostle saith, (1 Cor. xiv. 23,) that if an unbeliever should see their disorders, he would say they were mad; but where unity and peace is, there the churches are multiplied. We read, Acts ix. 31, that when the churches had rest they multiplied; and Acts ii. 46, 47, when the church was serving God with one accord, the Lord added to them daily such as should be saved.

It is unity brings men into the church, and divisions keep them out. It is reported of an Indian passing by the house of a Christian, and hearing them contending, being desired to turn in, he refused, saying, Habamach dwells there, meaning that the devil dwelt there: but where unity and peace is, there God is; and he that dwells in love, dwells in God. The apostle tells the Corinthians that if they walked orderly, even the unbelievers would hereby be enforced to come and worship, and say God was in them indeed. And we read, Zech. viii. 23, of a time when ten men shall take hold of a Jew, and say, "We will go with you, for we have heard that God is with you."

And hence it is that Christ prays, (John xvii. 21,) that his disciples might be one, as the Father and he were one, that the world might believe the Father sent him. As if he should say, you may preach me as long as you will, and to little purpose, if you are not at peace and unity among yourselves. Such was the unity of Christians in former days, that the intelligent heathen would say of them, that though they had many bodies, yet they had but one soul. And we read the same of them, Acts iv. 32, that "the multitude of them that believed were of one heart and one soul."

And as the learned Stillingfleet observes in his *Irenicum*, "The unity and peace that was then among Christians, made religion amiable in the judgment of impartial heathens. Christians were then known by the benignity and sweetness of their dispositions, by the candour and ingenuity of their spirits, by their mutual love, forbearance, and condescension to one another; but either this is not the practice of Christianity"—viz., a duty that Christians are now bound to observe—" or else it is not calculated for our meridian, where the spirits of men are of too high an elevation for it: for if pride and uncharitableness, if divisions and strifes, if wrath and envy, if animosities and contentions were but the marks of true Christians, Diogenes need never light his lamp at noon to find out such among us; but if a spirit of meekness, gentleness, and condescension—if a stooping to the weaknesses and infirmities of one another—if pursuit after peace, when it flies from us, be the indispensable duties, and characteristical notes of Christians, it may possibly prove a difficult inquest to find out such, among the crowds of those that shelter themselves under that glorious name."

It is the unity and peace of churches that brings others to them, and makes Christianity amiable. What is prophesied of the church of the Jews, may in this case be applied to the Gentile church, (Isa. lxvi. 12:) that when once God extends peace to her like a river, the Gentiles shall come in like a flowing stream; then—and not till then—the glory of the Lord shall arise upon his churches, and his glory shall be seen among them; then shall their hearts fear and be enlarged, because the abundance of the nations shall be converted to them.

(6.) As want of unity and peace keeps those out of the church that would come in, so it hinders the growth of those that are in. Jars and divisions, wranglings and prejudices, eat out the growth, if not the life, of religion. These are those waters of Marah that embitter our spirits, and quench the Spirit of God. Unity and peace is said to be like the dew of Hermon, and as a dew that descended upon Zion, where the Lord commanded his blessing. (Ps. cxxxiii. 3.)

Divisions run religion into briers and thorns, contentions and parties. Divisions are to churches like wars in countries. Where war is, the ground lieth waste and untilled; none takes care of it. It is love that edifieth, but division pulleth down. Divisions are as the north-east wind to the fruits, which causeth them to dwindle away to nothing; but when the storms are over, everything begins to grow. When men are divided, they seldom speak the truth in love; and then no marvel they

grow not up to him in all things, which is the head.

It is a sad presage of an approaching famine, as one well observes, not of bread nor water, but of hearing the word of God, when the thin ears of corn devour the plump full ones; when the lean kine devour the fat ones; when our controversies about doubtful things, and things of less moment, eat up our zeal for the more indisputable and practical things in religion; which may give us cause to fear, that this will be the character by which our age will be known to posterity, that it was the age that talked of religion most, and loved it least.

Look upon those churches where peace is, and there you shall find prosperity. When the churches had rest, they were not only multiplied, but, walking in the fear of the Lord, and the comforts of the Holy Ghost, they were edified; it is when the whole body is knit together, as with joints and bands, that they increase with the increase of God.

We are at a stand sometimes, why there is so little growth among churches, why men have been so long in learning, and are yet so far from attaining the knowledge of the truth; some have given one reason, and some another; some say pride is the cause, and others say covetousness is the cause. I wish I could say these were no causes. But I observe, that when God entered his controversy with his people of old, he mainly insisted upon some one sin, as idolatry, and shedding innocent blood, &c. as comprehensive of the rest; not but that they were guilty of other sins, but those that were the most capital are particularly insisted on: in like manner, whoever would but take a review of churches that live in contentions and divisions, may easily find that breach of unity and charity is their capital sin, and the occasion of all other sins. No marvel then, that the Scripture saith, the whole law is fulfilled in love; and if so, then where love is wanting, it needs must follow, the whole law is broken. It is where love grows cold, that sin abounds; and therefore the want of unity and peace is the cause of that leanness and barrenness that is among us; it is true in spirituals as well as temporals, that peace brings plenty.

(7.) Where unity and peace is wanting, our prayers are hindered. The promise is, that what we shall agree to ask, shall be given us of our heavenly Father. No marvel we pray and pray, and yet are not answered; it is because we are not agreed what to have.

It is reported that the people in Lacedemonia, coming to make supplications to their idol god, some of them asked for rain, and others of them asked for fair weather. The oracle returns them this answer, that they should go first and agree among themselves. Would a heathen god refuse to answer such prayers, in which the supplicants were not agreed, and shall we think the true God will answer them?

We see, then, that divisions hinder our prayers, and lay a prohibition on our sacrifice. "If thou bring thy gift to the altar," saith Christ, "and there rememberest that thy brother hath ought against thee, leave there thy gift, and go, and first be reconciled to thy brother, and then come and offer it." (Matt. v. 24.) So that want of unity and charity hinders even our particular prayers and devotions.

This hindered the prayers and fastings of the people of old from finding acceptance, (Isa. lviii. 3;) the people ask the reason wherefore they fasted, and God did not see nor take notice of them? He gives this reason, because they fasted for strife and debate, and hid their face from their own flesh. Again, (Isa. lix.,) the Lord saith, his hand was not shortened, that he could not save; nor his ear heavy, that he could not hear: but their sins had separated between their God and them. And among those many sins they stood chargeable with, this was none of the least, viz., that the way of peace they had not known. You see where peace was wanting, prayers were hindered, both under the Old and New Testament.

The sacrifice of the people in the 65th of Isaiah, that said, Stand farther off, I am holier than thou, was as smoke in the nostrils of the Lord. On the other hand, we read how acceptable those prayers were that were made " with one accord." (Acts iv. 24, compared with ver. 31.) They prayed with one accord, and they were all of one heart, and of one soul. And see the benefit of it : "They were all filled with the Holy Ghost, and they spake the word with boldness ;" which was the very thing they prayed for, as appears, ver. 29. And the apostle exhorts the husband to dwell with his wife, that their prayers might not be hindered. (1 Pet. iii. 7.) We see, then, want of unity and peace, either in families or churches, is a hindrance of prayers.

(8.) It is a dishonour and disparagement to Christ that his family should be divided. When an army falls into mutiny and division, it reflects disparagement on him that hath the conduct of it. In like manner the divisions of families are a dishonour to the heads, and those that govern them. And if so, then how greatly do we dishonour our Lord and Governor, who gave his body to be broken, to keep his church from breaking, who prayed for their peace and unity, and left peace at his departing from them for a legacy, even a peace which the world could not bestow upon them.

(9.) Where there is peace and unity, there is a sympathy with each other; that which is the want of one, will be the want of all. Who is afflicted, saith the apostle, and I burn not? We should then remember them that are in bonds, as bound with them; and them which suffer adversity, as being ourselves also of the body. (Heb. xiii. 3.) But where the body is broken, or men are not reckoned or esteemed of the body, no marvel we are so little affected with such as are afflicted.

Where divisions are, that which is the joy of the one, is the grief of another; but where unity, and peace, and charity abounds, there we shall find Christians in mourning with them that mourn, and rejoicing with them that rejoice; then they will not envy the prosperity of others, nor secretly rejoice at the miseries or miscarriages of any.

Fourth. Last of all; I now come to give you *twelve directions and motives for the obtaining peace and unity.*

1. If ever we would live in peace and unity we must pray for it. We are required to seek peace: of whom, then, can we seek it with expectation to find it but of him who is a God of peace, and hath promised to bless his people with peace ? It is God that hath promised to give his people one heart, and one way; yet, for all these things, he will be sought unto. Oh, then, let us seek peace, and pray for peace, because God shall prosper them that love it.

The peace of churches is that which the apostle prays for in all his epistles; in which his desire is, that grace and peace may be multiplied and increased among them.

2. They that would endeavour the peace of the churches, must be careful who they commit the care and oversight of the churches to; as, first, over and besides those qualifications that should be in all Christians, they that rule the church of God, should be men of counsel and understanding; where there is an ignorant ministry, there is commonly an ignorant people,—according as it was of old, Like priest, like people.

How sad is it to see the church of God committed to the care of such that pretend to be teachers of others, that understand not what they say, or whereof they affirm. No marvel the peace of churches is broken when their watchmen want skill to preserve their unity, which of all other things is as the church's walls; when they are divided, no wonder they crumble to atoms if there is no skilful physician to heal them. It is sad when there is no balm in Gilead, and when there is no physician there. Hence it is that the wounds of churches become incurable, like the wounds of God's people of old, either not healed at all, or else slightly healed, and to no purpose. May it not be said of many churches at this day, as God said of the church of Israel, that he sought for a man among them that should stand in the gap, and make up the breach, but he found none ?

Remember what was said of old, (Mal. ii. 7,) the priest's lips should preserve knowledge ; and the people "should seek the law at his mouth:" but when this is wanting, the people will be stumbling and departing from God and one another ; therefore God complains, (Hos. iv. 6,) that his people were destroyed for want of knowledge—that is, for want of knowing guides; for if the light that is in them that teach be darkness, how great is that darkness ; and if the blind lead the blind, no marvel both fall into the ditch.

How many are there that take upon them to teach others, that had need be taught in the beginning of religion; that instead of multiplying knowledge, multiply words without knowledge; and instead of making known God's counsel, darken counsel by words without knowledge? The apostle speaks of some that did more than darken counsel, for they wrested the counsel of God. (2 Pet. iii. 16.) In Paul's epistles, saith he, are "some things hard to be understood, which they that are unlearned and unstable wrest, as they do also the other scriptures unto their own destruction." Some things in the Scripture are hard to be known, and they are made harder by such unlearned teachers, as utter their own notions by words without knowledge.

None are more bold and adventurous to take upon them to expound the dark mysteries and sayings of the prophets and revelations, and the 9th of the Romans,—which I believe contains some of those many things which in Paul's epistles Peter saith were hard to be understood,—I say, none are more forward to dig in these mines than those that can hardly give a sound reason for the first principles of religion; and such as are ignorant of many more weighty things that are easily to be seen in the face and superficies of the Scripture. Nothing will serve these but swimming in the deeps, when they have not yet learned to wade through the shallows of the Scriptures. Like the Gnostics of old, who thought they knew all things, though they knew nothing as they ought to know. And as those Gnostics did of old, so do such teachers of late break the unity and peace of churches. How needful then is it that, if we desire the peace of churches, that we choose out men of knowledge, who may be able to keep them from being shattered and scattered with every wind of doctrine, and who may be able to convince and stop the mouths of gainsayers!

3. You must not only choose men of counsel, but if you would design the unity and peace of the churches, you must choose men of courage to govern them : for as there must be wisdom to bear with some, so there must be courage to correct others; as some must be instructed meekly, so others must be rebuked sharply, that they may be sound in the faith ; there must be wisdom to rebuke some with long-suffering, and there must be courage to suppress and stop the mouths of others. The apostle tells Titus of some whose mouths must be stopped, or else they would subvert whole houses. (Tit. i. 11.) Where this courage hath been wanting, not only whole houses, but whole churches, have been subverted. And Paul tells the Galatians, that when he saw some endeavour to bring the churches into bondage, that he did not give place to them. " No, not for an hour," &c. (Gal. ii. 5.) If this course had been taken by the rulers of churches, their peace had not been so often invaded by unruly and vain talkers.

4. In choosing men to rule, if you would en-deavour to keep the unity of the Spirit, and the bond of peace thereby, be careful you choose men of peaceable dispositions. That which hath much annoyed the peace of churches, hath been the froward and perverse spirits of the rulers thereof. Solomon therefore adviseth, that, " With a furious man we should not go, lest we learn his ways, and get a snare to our souls," (Prov. xxii. 24, 25,) and with the froward we learn frowardness. How do some men's words eat like a canker ; who, instead of lifting up their voices like a trumpet, to sound a parley for peace, have rather sounded an alarum to war and contention. If ever we would live in peace, let us reverence the feet of them that bring the glad tidings of it.

Oh how have some men made it their business to preach contentions, and upon their entertainment of every novel opinion, to preach separation! How hath God's word been stretched and torn to furnish these men with arguments to tear churches! Have not our ears heard those texts, that saith, " Come out from among them, and be separate," &c., and " withdraw from every brother that walks disorderly ?" I say, have we not heard these texts, that were written to prevent disorder, brought to countenance the greatest disorder that ever was in the church of God, even schism and division ? whereas one of these exhortations was written to the church of Corinth, to separate themselves from the idol's temple, and the idol's table—in which many of them lived in the participation of, not-withstanding their profession of the true God, (as appears, 2 Cor. vi. 16, 17, compared with 1 Cor. viii. 7, and 1 Cor. x. 14, 20, 22, recites,)—and not for some few or more members, who shall make themselves both judges and parties, to make separation, when and as often as they please, from the whole congregation and church of God where they stood related ; for, by the same rule, and upon the same ground, may others start some new question among these new separatists, and become their own judges of the communicableness of them, and thereupon make another separation from these, till at last two be not left to walk together. And for that other text mentioned, (2 Thess. iii. 9,) where Paul exhorts the church of Thessalonica to withdraw themselves from every brother that walks disorderly ; I cannot but wonder that any should bring this to justify their separation, or withdraw from the communion of a true, though a disorderly church. For,

(1.) Consider that this was not writ for a few members to withdraw from the church, but for the church to withdraw from disorderly members.

(2.) Consider, that if any offended members, upon pretence of error, either in doctrine or practice, should by this text become judges, as well as parties, of the grounds and lawfulness of their separation ; then it will follow, that half a score notorious heretics, or scandalous livers, when they have walked so that they foresee the church are ready to deal with them, and withdraw from them, shall anticipate the church, and pretend somewhat against them, of which themselves must be judges, and so withdraw from the church, pretending either heresy or disorder; and so condemn the church, to prevent the disgrace of being condemned by the church. How needful then is it, that men of peaceable dispositions, and not of froward and factitious, and dividing spirits, be chose to rule the church of God, for fear lest the whole church be leavened and soured by them.

5. As there must be care used in choosing men to rule the church of God, so there must be a consideration had, that there are many things darkly laid down in Scripture; this will temper our spirits, and make us live in peace and unity the more firmly in things in which we agree; this will help us to bear one another's burden, and so fulfil the law of Christ, inasmuch as all things necessary to salvation and church communion are plainly laid down in Scripture. And where things are more darkly laid down, we should consider that God intended hereby to stir up our diligence, that thereby we might increase our knowledge, and not our divisions; for it may be said of all discoveries of truth we have made in the Scriptures, as it is said of the globe of the earth, that though men have made great searches, and thereupon great discoveries, yet there is still a *terra incognita*—an unknown land: so there is in the Scriptures, for after men have travelled over them, one age after another, yet still there is, as it were, a *terra incognita*, an unknown tract to put us upon farther search and inquiry, and to keep us from censuring and falling out with those who have not yet made the same discoveries; that so we may say with the Psalmist, when we reflect upon our short apprehensions of the mind of God, that we have seen an end of all perfections, but God's commands are exceeding broad; and as one observes, speaking of the Scriptures, that there is a path in them leading to the mind of God, which lieth a great distance from the thoughts and apprehensions of men. And on the other hand, in many other places, God sits, as it were, on the superficies, and the face of the letter, where he that runs may discern him speaking plainly, and no parable at all. How should the consideration of this induce us to a peaceable deportment towards those that differ.

6. If we would endeavour peace and unity, we must consider how God hath tempered the body, that so the comely parts should not separate from the uncomely, as having no need of them. (1 Cor. xii. 22—25.) There is in Christ's body and house some members and vessels less honourable. (2 Tim. ii. 20.) And therefore we should not, as some now-a-days do, pour the more abundant disgrace, instead of putting the more abundant honour upon them. Did we but consider this, we should be covering the weakness, and hiding the miscarriages of one another, because we are all members one of another, and the most useless member in his place is useful.

7. If we would live in peace, let us remember our relations to God—as children to a father, and to each other as brethren. Will not the thoughts that we have one Father quiet us; and the thoughts that we are brethren, unite us? It was this that made Abraham propose terms of peace to Lot, (Gen. xiii.,) "Let there be no strife," saith he, "between us, for we are brethren." And we read of Moses, in Acts vii. 26, using this argument to reconcile those that strove together, and to set them at one again: "Sirs," saith he, "ye are brethren, why do ye wrong one to another?" A deep sense of this relation, that we are brethren, would keep us from dividing.

8. If we would preserve peace, let us mind the gifts, and graces, and virtues that are in each other; let these be more in our eye than their failings and imperfections. When the apostle exhorted the Philippians to peace, as a means hereunto, that so the peace of God might rule in their hearts, he tells them, chap. iv. 8, that if there were any virtue, or any praise, they should think of these things. While we are always talking and blazoning the faults of one another, and spreading their infirmities, no marvel we are so little in peace and charity; for as charity covereth a multitude of sins, so malice covereth a multitude of virtues, and makes us deal by one another as the heathen persecutors dealt with Christians, viz., put them in bears' skins, that they might the more readily become a prey to those dogs that were designed to devour them.

9. If we would keep unity and peace, let us lay aside provoking and dividing language, and forgive those that use them. Remember that old saying, "Evil words corrupt good manners." When men think to carry all afore them, with speaking uncharitably and disgracefully of their brethren, or their opinions, may not such be answered as Job answered his unfriendly visitants? (Job vi. 25.) How forcible are right words! But what does your arguing reprove? How healing are words fitly spoken! A word in season, how good is it! If we would seek peace, let us clothe all our treaties for peace with acceptable words; and where one word may better accommodate than another, let that be used to express persons or things by; and let us not, as some do, call the different practices of our brethren, will-worship, and their different opinions, doctrines of devils, and the doctrine of Balaam, who taught fornication, &c., unless we can plainly, and in expressness of terms, prove it so; such language as this hath strangely divided our spirits, and hardened our hearts one towards another.

10. If we would live in peace, let us make the best constructions of one another's words and actions. Charity judgeth the best, and it thinks no evil; if words and actions may be construed to a good sense, let us never put a bad construction upon them. How much hath the peace of Christians been broken by an uncharitable interpreta-

tion of words and actions! As some lay to the charge of others that which they never said, so, by straining men's words, others lay to their charge that they never thought.

11. Be willing to hear, and learn, and obey those that God by his providence hath set over you; this is a great means to preserve the unity and peace of churches. But when men—yea, and sometimes women—shall usurp authority, and think themselves wiser than their teachers, no wonder if these people run into contentions and parties, when any shall say they are not free to hear those whom the church thinks fit to speak to them. This is the first step to schism, and is usually attended, if not timely prevented, with a sinful separation.

12. If you would keep the unity of the Spirit in the bond of peace, be mindful that the God whom you serve is a God of peace, and your Saviour is a Prince of peace, and that his ways are ways of pleasantness, and all his paths are peace, and that Christ was sent into the world to give light to them that sit in darkness, and in the shadow of death, and to guide our feet in the way of peace.

13. Consider the oneness of spirit that is among the enemies of religion; though they differ about other things, yet to persecute religion, and extirpate religion out of the earth, here they will agree; the devils in the air, and the devils in the earth, all the devils in hell, and in the world, make one at this turn. Shall the devil's kingdom be united, and shall Christ's be divided? Shall the devils make one shoulder to drive on the design of damning men, and shall not Christians unite to carry the great design of saving of them? Shall the papists agree and unite to carry on their interest, notwithstanding the multitudes of orders, degrees, and differences that are among them, and shall not those that call themselves reformed churches unite to carry on the common interest of Christ in the world, notwithstanding some petty and disputable differences that are among them? Quarrels about religion, as one observes, were

sins not named among the Gentiles. What a shame is it, then, for Christians to abound in them, especially considering the nature of the Christian religion, and what large provisions the Author of it hath made, to keep the professors of it in peace! Insomuch, as one well observes, it is next to a miracle that ever any, especially the professors of it, should fall out about it.

14. Consider and remember, that the Judge stands at the door. Let this moderate our spirits, that the Lord is at hand. What a sad account will they have to make when he comes, that shall be found to smite their fellow-servants, and to make the way to his kingdom more narrow than ever he made it? Let me close all in the words of that great apostle, " Finally, brethren, farewell; be perfect, be of good comfort, be of one mind, live in peace, and the God of love and peace shall be with you." (2 Cor. xiii. 11.)

POSTSCRIPT.

Reader, I thought good to advertise thee, that I have delivered this to thy hand, in the same order and method, in which it was preached, and almost in the same words, without any diminishings, or considerable enlargings, unless it be in the fourteen last particulars, upon some of which I have made some enlargements, which I could not then do for want of time, but the substance of every one of them was then laid down in the same particular order as here thou hast them. And now I have done, I make no other account—to use the words of a moderate man upon the like occasion—but it will fall out with me, as doth commonly with him that parts a fray, both parties may perhaps drive at me for wishing them no worse than peace. My ambition of the public tranquillity of the church of God, I hope, will carry me through these hazards. Let both beat me; so their quarrels may cease, I shall rejoice in those blows and scars I shall take for the church's safety.

VALE.

A CASE OF CONSCIENCE RESOLVED;

VIZ.,

WHETHER, WHERE A CHURCH OF CHRIST IS SITUATE, IT IS THE DUTY OF THE WOMEN OF THAT CONGREGATION, ORDINARILY, AND BY APPOINTMENT, TO SEPARATE THEMSELVES FROM THEIR BRETHREN, AND SO TO ASSEMBLE TOGETHER, TO PERFORM SOME PARTS OF DIVINE WORSHIP, AS PRAYER, ETC., WITHOUT THEIR MEN?

AND THE ARGUMENTS MADE USE OF FOR THAT PRACTICE, EXAMINED.

PREFATORY NOTE.

It is somewhat remarkable that the following paper was never again printed, after its first appearance in 1683. The questions which it is intended to answer, had lost none of their interest after Bunyan's death. A respectable religious body insisted, with the patience which knows no defeat, on the equal rights of women in all spiritual assemblies and exercises. The opinion thus asserted by a particular class of Christians was never likely to become popular. It could receive no indulgence from church-men. Every principle upon which the discipline and dignities of the church rested, stood opposed to the Quaker notion of female equality. The Presbyterians and Independents of Bunyan's time were even, in this respect, of a sterner spirit than churchmen. Neither Calvin, nor Knox, nor Goodwin would have been content to sit quietly while a woman preached to him, or prayed for his congregation. It was only in cases where extreme notions of spiritual freedom prevailed, that the rights of women were, in this respect, proclaimed. The usual discipline of a sect, or of a single congregation, was as repugnant to the idea of a female ministry as the severest traditions of Catholicism. In the Society of Friends alone it was contended that a divine call to minister in the congregation might be looked for no less by women than by men. Some of the most fanatical among the Anabaptists advocated notions easily confounded with the more reasonably adopted opinions of the Quakers. Here and there also there might be found respectable individuals who, without departing from the general rule of church discipline, were disposed to believe that women ought to be allowed a much greater latitude than is commonly granted them in the employment of their spiritual knowledge and experience. Such was the case in the neighbourhood of Bedford, where some pious women had. been encouraged by a Mr. Keach to assemble, in a little society of their own, to pray and read the Scriptures. An alarm was excited, and Bunyan, it is said, wrote the following paper in answer to an urgent request for his judgment on the question.

H. S.

THE EPISTLE DEDICATORY

TO THOSE GODLY WOMEN CONCERNED IN THE FOLLOWING TREATISE.

Honoured Sisters,—It is far from me to despise you, or to do anything to your reproach. I know you are beloved of God for the sake of Christ, and that you stand fixed for ever by faith upon the same foundation with *us*. I also know that the Lord doth put no difference betwixt male and female, as to the communications of his saving graces, but hath often made many of your sex eminent for piety; yea, there hath been of you, I speak now of ordinary Christians, that for holiness of life have outgone many of the brethren. Nor can their virtuous lives but be renown and glory to *you*, and conviction to those of *us* that have come behind you in faith and holiness. The love of women in spirituals, as well as naturals, ofttimes outgoes that of men.

When Christ was upon earth, we read not that any man did to, and for him, as did the woman that was a sinner, Joanna, Susanna, and many others. (Luke vii. 36—38; viii. 1—3.) And as they have showed themselves eminent for piety, so for Christian valour and fortitude of mind, when called of God to bear witness to, and for his name in the world: as all histories of that nature doth sufficiently testify. They were women, as I take it as well as men, that were tortured, and that would not accept of deliverance, that they might obtain a better resurrection. (Heb

xi. 35.) Wherefore I honour and praise your eminency in virtue; and desire to be provoked by the exceeding piety of any of you, in all holy conversation and godliness.

And although, as you will find, I have not without a cause, made a question of the lawfulness of your assembling together, by yourselves, to perform, without your men, solemn worship to God; yet I dare not make you yourselves the authors of your own miscarriage in this. I do therefore rather impute it to your leaders, who whether of a fond respect to some seeming abilities they think is in you for this, or from a persuasion that you have been better than themselves in other things; or whether from a preposterous zeal, they have put you upon a work so much too heavy for you; I shall not at this time concern myself to inquire into. But this is certain, at least it is so in my apprehension, that in this matter you are tempted by them to take too much upon you.

I am not insensible but that for my thus writing, though I thereby have designed your honour and good order, I am like enough to run the gauntlet among you, and to partake most smartly of the scourge of the tongues of some, and to be soundly brow-beaten for it by others: specially by our author, who will find himself immediately concerned, for that I have blamed him for what he hath irregularly done, both with the word, to you,

and me. I look also to be sufficiently scandalized, and counted a man not for prayer, and meetings for prayer, and the like; but I will labour to bear them with patience, and seek their good that shall be tempted to abuse me

I had not, indeed I had not, spoke a word to this question in this manner, had not Mr. K. sent his paper abroad, and amongst us, for the encouraging this practice with us, in opposition to our peace. I do not say he designed our breach, but his arguments tended thereto; and had not our people been of a wise and quiet temper, his paper might have set us into a flame. But thanks be to God, we are at quiet, and walk in love, notwithstanding the *lifts* that have been to make us do otherwise. There are also the mouths of some opened against me for this, who lie at wait for occasions, and show that they are glad to take them before they are given by me: to whom I now show by this ensuing discourse, that I had a reason to do what I did.

I commend you to God, and to the word of his grace, which is able to build you up, and to give you an inheritance among them that are sanctified by faith in Jesus Christ: to whom be honour and glory for ever. And remain, your faithful friend and brother to pray for you, to love you in the gospel, and to do you what Christian service I can,

JOHN BUNYAN.

A CASE OF CONSCIENCE RESOLVED.

THE occasion of my meddling in this manner with this controversy, is this. After I had, for reasons best known to myself, by searching found, that those called the women's meetings wanted for their support, a bottom in the word, I called them in our fellowship into question. Now having so done, my reasons for so doing, as was but reason, were demanded; and I gave them, to the causing of that practice with us to cease. So subject to the word were our women, and so willing to let go what by that could not be proved a duty for them to be found in the practice of. But when I had so done, by what means I know not, Mr. K., hearing of my proceeding in this matter, though I think he knew little of question or answer, sets pen to paper, and draws up four arguments for the justification of these meetings. The which, when done, were sent down into our parts; not to me, but to some of his own persuasion, who kept them, or sent them, or lent them whither they thought good; and so about two years after, with this note immediately following, they were conveyed to my hand:—

"Brother Bunyan,—This enclosed, was sent to me from godly women, whose custom for a long

time hath been to meet together to pray; who hearing of your contrary opinion, sent this. It came from Mr. K., who would desire to know what objections you have against it; and he is ready to give his further advice. Pray be pleased to give your answer in writing, for Mr. K. expects it.

"Your friends in the Lord,

"S. B.   S. F.

"Pray be pleased to leave your answer with S. F. in Bedford."

Now, having received the papers, and considering the contents thereof, I was at first at a question with myself whether the thing was feigned or true, and, to that purpose, writ to these women again; but calling to mind that I had heard something of this before, I concluded there was ground to believe as I do: and so resolved to answer his demand and expectation. But to say nothing more as to this, I will next present you with the arguments he sent, and then with my manner of handling of them.

He begins with this question, Whether women fearing God may meet to pray together, and whether it be lawful for them so to do? Which done, he falls to a wonderment, saying, It seems very strange to me, that any who profess the fear of God, can make any question touching the lawfulness thereof—the rule for praying being so general to all, and there being so many instances for the practice thereof, upon several occasions in the word of God, for their encouragement therein.

He next presents us with his arguments, which are in number *four*, but in verity not one, to prove that thing for the which he urgeth them : as I hope to make appear that I have done.

First, saith he, if women may praise God together for mercies received for the church of God, or for themselves, then they may pray together—the proof whereof is plain. (Exod. xv. 20, 21.) If it be objected the case was extraordinary, and that Miriam was a prophetess : to which I answer, that the danger of ruin and destruction, and our deliverance from it, if the Lord grant it, cannot be looked at but as extraordinary—the designs of ruin to the church, and servants of God, being as great as at that time when God delivered his people from the land of Pharaoh ; and will call for praises, if the Lord please to send it, as then. And whereas it is further objected, that Miriam was an extraordinary person. To which I answer, that the duty itself of praising God for the mercy, was incumbent upon all, inasmuch as they were partakers of the mercy. And the same spirit of Christ that was in her, is also in all his servants ; given for the same end, both to pray for mercies we stand in need of, and to praise God for them.

Second. If women have in imminent danger to themselves and the church of God, prayed jointly together for deliverance, and God hath answered and approved of the same, then may women jointly pray together. The instance we have is famous. (Ezra iv. 16.) We there see she and her maidens did pray and fast together, and the Lord gave a gracious answer and deliverance.

Third. If God hath in gospel times promised the pouring out of his Spirit to women, to that very end that they may pray together apart from men, then it is not only their liberty, but duty to meet and pray together. But God hath promised his Spirit to that end. (Zech. xii. 10—13.) Which scripture it is plain is a promise of gospel times. And it is to be noted that the text doth not in the singular number say, He shall pray apart, and his wife apart ; but *they* shall pray apart, and *their* wives apart. And (Mal. iii. 16) God takes notice of all them that speak often together, and call upon his name.

Fourth. If God hath so approved of women's meeting together to pray in gospel times, as then, and at that time to take an advantage to make known to them his mind and will concerning Jesus Christ, then it is lawful for women to pray together. But God hath so approved of their meeting to pray together. (Acts xvi. 13.) By which text it appeareth it was a frequent practice for women to meet and pray together.

These are Mr. K.'s arguments ; the conclusion of his paper follows. And besides all these particular instances, says he, what means those general rules to build up one another in our most holy faith, and pray in the Holy Ghost ? (Jude 20.) But it extends to all that believe, both men and women ; unless any will say women are not to be built up in their most holy faith. Therefore let not any hinder you from a duty so incumbent upon you in a special manner, in such a day as this is. Cannot many women that have used this practice, by experience, say they have met with the Lord in it, and have found many blessed returns of prayer from God, both to themselves and the church, wherein God hath owned them ? Therefore what God hath borne witness to, and approved of, let no man deter you from. Pray turn to the scriptures quoted, which I hope will give you full satisfaction.

These are his arguments, and this his conclusion, in which I cannot but say, there is not only boldness, but flattery. Boldness, in fathering of his misunderstanding upon the authority of the word of God ; and flattery, in soothing up persons in a way of their own, by making of them the judges in their own cause : the which I hope to make farther appear anon.

For since his women in their letter told me that Mr. K. expects my answer, I count myself called to show the unsoundness of his opinion. Indeed he would, as they insinuate, confine me to answer by writing. But his papers have been I know not where, and how to put check to his extravagances, that also, I know not, but by scattering [my reply] abroad. And as I will not be confined to an answer in writing, so neither to his methods of argumentation. What scholar he is, I know not ; for my part, I am not ashamed to confess, that I neither know the mode nor figure of a syllogism, nor scarce which is major nor minor. Methinks I perceive but little sense, and far less truth in his arguments ; also I hold that he has stretched and strained the holy word out of place, to make it, if it might have been, to shore up his fond conceits. I shall, therefore, first take these texts from the errors to which he hath joined them, and then fall to picking the bones of his syllogisms.

But as I shall not confine myself to his mode and way of arguing, so neither shall I take notice of his question upon which he stateth the matter in controversy. But shall propound the same question here, which, for the substance of it, was handled among us, when the thing itself was in doubt among us, namely—

Whether, where a church of Christ is situate, it is the duty of the women of that congregation, ordinarily, and by appointment, to separate themselves from their brethren, and so to assemble together, to perform some parts of divine worship, as prayer, &c. without their men ?

This was our question, this we debated, and this Mr. K. might have sent for, and have spoken to, since he will needs be a confuter. And, courteous reader, since I have here presented thee with the question, I will also present thee with the method which I took when I handled it among my brethren.

First. I opened the terms of the question.

Second. Then showed what assemblies they were that used to perform divine worship to God.

Third. And so showed whose prayers in such worship was used, or by Paul and others desired.

First. By church of Christ, I mean, one gathered or constituted by, and walking after, the rule of the word of God. By situate, I mean, where such church shall happen to be, in whole, or in the parts thereof. By separating, I mean, their meetings together by appointment of their own, and as so met, to attempt to perform divine worship [and] prayer without their men. Having thus explained the question, I, as a preparatory to a solution thereof, come,

Second. To show what manner of assemblies they were that used to perform divine worship to God of old. Now I find that there have been three sorts of assemblies in which divine worship has been performed. 1. It has been performed in mixed assemblies—in assemblies made up of saints and sinners. I say divine worship has been performed in such assemblies, for that there the saints have been edified, sinners convinced and converted, and made to confess their sins, to the glory of God. Of these assemblies we read, Matt. v. 1; xiii. 1; xxiii. 1. Mark iv. 1; ii. 1; vi. 2; x. 1, Luke v. 1; viii.; xii. 1; xiii 1; xv. 1; xx. 1. 1 Cor. xiv. 23; and in many other scriptures. 2. I also find that the church, by herself, or as distinct from the world, have met together to perform it by themselves. (Mark iv. 34. Acts ii. 1—4; xiii. 1, 2; xv. 4; xx. 7; John xx. 19—26.) 3. I find also that assemblies for divine worship have been made up of the elders, and principal brethren of the church, none of the rest of the congregation being present. (Mat. x. 1. Luke ix. 1. Acts i. 3; ii. 17, 18. Gal. ii. 1, 2, with several other scriptures beside.) But in all the Scripture, I find not that the women of the churches of Christ did use to separate themselves from their brethren, and as so separate, perform worship together among themselves, or in that *their* congregation : or that they made, by allowance of the word, appointment so to do. Thus far therefore this must stand for a human invention, and Mr. K. for the promoter thereof.

Third. This done, in the third place, I come to show you whose prayers, or by whose mouth prayer in such assemblies, as are above proved lawful, used to be made, or by Paul or others were desired. 1. Whose prayers were used, or who was the mouth ? and I find them called the prayers of the church in general, or of the principal men thereof in particular. (Judges ii. 4, 5; xx. 8, 26. Joel i. 14; ii. 15—17. Acts xii. 5; xiii. 1—3.)

2. Also when Paul, or others, desired that prayers should be made of others for them, they either desired the prayers of the church in general, or of the brethren in particular (but never desireth, or biddeth a woman's meeting, that prayers might there be made for them.) (1.) He desireth the prayers of the church in general, Col. iv. 2. Phil. i. 19; iv. 6. 1 Thess. v. 17. Heb. xiii. 18. (2.) Or if he desireth prayers of certain persons, he only calls upon the men and brethren in particular ; but never upon a woman by name nor sex to do it. (1 Thess. v. 25. 2 Thess. iii. 1. Rom. xv. 30. 1 Tim. ii. 8.) Nor was, as I said, the apostle alone in this thing. Christ speaks a parable to this end, that *men* ought always to pray. (Luke xviii. 1.) James saith, the effectual fervent prayer of a righteous *man.* (v. 16.) Moses sent the young men to sacrifice. (Exod. xxiv. 5.) And the people in the time of Zacharias, sent their *men* to pray before the Lord. (Zech. vii. 2.) I do not believe that by any of these the prayers of women are despised, but by these we are taught, who, as the mouth in assemblies to pray, is commended unto us.

One word more : The women in the time of Jeremiah the prophet, when they had made their cakes to the queen of heaven, (though the thing which they did was as right in their own eyes, as if they had done true worship indeed,) and were questioned by the prophet for what they had done, could not justify what they had done, as to the act, but by pleading, They did it not "without their men." (Jer. xliv. 17—19.)

Thus having premised these few things, I shall now come more directly to discourse of the question itself, *to wit,* Whether, where a church of Christ is situate, it is the duty of the women of that congregation, ordinarily, and by appointment, to separate themselves from their brethren, and as so separate, to assemble together to perform divine worship, [and] prayer, without their men?

This was our question, and this I will now give a negative answer unto. For I find not in Christ's testament any command so to do; no nor yet example: and where there is none of these, it cannot be a duty upon them ; no, nor yet liberty, but presumption to attempt it.

The command, says Mr. K., is general to all. But I answer, yet limited, and confined to order and manner of performance. Women may, yea ought to pray ; what then ? Is it their duty to help to carry on prayer in public assemblies with men, as they ? Are they to be the audible mouth there, before all, to God ? No verily, and yet the command is general to all to pray. Women of the respective churches of Christ, have no command to separate themselves from the men of their congregations, to perform prayer in their own company without them, and yet the command is general to all to pray. We must therefore distinguish of persons and performances, though we may not exclude either. The manner also, and order in which such and such duties must be done, Mr. K. knows is as essential, in some cases, as the very matter of worship. But we will come to my reasons for my dissenting from Mr. K. in this. After which I will consider his arguments, and the scriptures that he would under-prop them with. As for my reasons for my dissenting from him, they are these :—

First. To appoint meetings for divine worship, either in the whole church or in the parts of it, is an act of power: which power resideth in the elders in particular, or in the church in general. But never in the women as considered by themselves. Mr. K. indeed doth insinuate that this power also resided in them; for he saith, God hath in gospel times promised the Spirit to women to that very end, that they may pray together, apart from men. Now, if the Spirit is given them to *this* very end, that they may do it apart from men, then they have a power residing in themselves to call their own sex together to do it. And what brave doings will such a conclusion make, even the blind himself will perceive. But further of this anon : meanwhile we will attend to our own assertion ; namely, " That to call the church, or parts thereof together, to perform divine worship to God, is an *act* of *power*, which power resideth in the church in general, or in the elders in particular." We will treat of the last first.

1. For the eldership, Moses and Aaron of old were they, with the priests, that were to call the church together to perform divine worship to God, and that both as to the whole, or as to the parts of it. (Numb. x. 7, 8. Deut. iv. 14 ; xxxi. 11, 12. Exod. iv. 29 ; xii. 21 ; xvii. 5.) Also, in after times, they were the elders and chief of the church that did it. (Josh. xxiv. 1. Ezra x. 5—9. Acts xiv. 27 ; xv. 3.) Or, 2. If their calling together to perform divine worship, was not by the elders alone, yet it was by the power that resided in the church for that thing, who jointly ordered the same. (Judges xx. 8, 18. Ezra iii. 1. Zeph. ii. 1—3. Acts xii. 12. 1 Cor. v. 4 ; xi. 20.) All these are plain cases. But never, as I ever did read of in the Bible, did women, ordinary believing ones, assume this power of the elders, or of the church, to themselves.

If it be asked, Who did appoint that meeting made mention of in Acts xii. 12 ?

I answer, It was appointed by the power of the church, who, for her own conveniency, if she cannot come all into one place at once to perform the duty, as it is not likely four or five thousand should, in times of persecution, which was their case, may meet some here, some there, for their edification and comfort. (Compare ver. 5 with 12 and 17.) Nor do I question the lawfulness of this or that part of the church's assembling together for prayer, though the elders, and greatest part of the brethren, be absent; if, first, such *men* that call such assemblies are countenanced by the elders, or church, to do it. (1 Tim. ii. 8. 2 Tim. ii. 22.) But that the sisters of this or that church,

may call their own sex together to perform such worship by themselves to God, (for this is the thing in debate,) I find no warrant for.

Second. Because this kind of worship, when done in and by a company, is *ministerial* to that company, as well as petitionary to God. That is, they that, as the mouth in assemblies pray to God, teach that assembly, as well as beg mercies of him. And I find not that women may assemble to do thus. That such prayer is a kind of ministering in the word to standers-by, consider well 1 Cor. xiv. 15—19. Wherefore let them keep silence in the church, and in the parts thereof, when assembled to worship God.

In all public worship by prayer, teaching is set on foot two ways : 1. By propounding to that assembly the things that must, by agreement, be prayed for. 2. And by proving them to suit with the will of God, that prayer may be made in faith. (1 John v. 14.)

1. For all such prayer must be made for the things agreed upon first ; and consequently for things that by the word are proved good, and suitable for the seasons, persons, or things, for or about which such prayers are made. For they that have meetings for prayer, without this, pray at random, and not by rule.

" If two of you shall agree on earth, as touching anything that they shall ask, (according to God's will,) it shall be done for them," saith Christ, " of my Father which is in heaven." (Matt. xviii. 19.) Now, I say, if things prayed for in assemblies must first be jointly agreed upon, then must such things, by some one, or more of that assembly, be first propounded, expounded, and proved to be good by the word — good for such persons, seasons, or things, for which such prayer is made. And, besides, the gifts required to do this, if this is not teaching, I am out. And yet this must first be done to instruct all present, to help their faith, and to quicken their spirits *to*, and *in* that worship, that they may as one man have their eyes unto the Lord. (Zech. ix. 1.) But that this power is given to women, to ordinary believing ones that are in the highest account in churches, I do not believe. I do not believe they should minister to God in prayer before the whole church, for then I should be a Ranter or a Quaker ; nor do I believe they should do it in their own womanish assembly, for the reason urged before. And I will add, if brethren not heretofore called by the church to open scriptures, or to speak in the church to God in prayer, are not at first to be admitted to do this, but before the elders or principal brethren, that they may hear and judge, (1 Cor. xiv. 26—29,) how can it be thought to be meet or lawful for women, of whom it must be supposed, that they have received no such gifts, that they should use this power ?—I say, how can it be imagined that the women should be bound of God to do this in such sort as doth utterly exclude the elders and all the men in the congregation from a possibility of understanding and of judging of what they do? And yet this is the doctrine of Mr. K.; for he saith, "That the Spirit of God is promised to women to this very end, that they may pray together apart from men." But God is not the author of this confusion in the churches.

2. But secondly. As teaching by prayer in assemblies is thus set on foot, so every one also that shall in such meetings be the mouth of the whole, to God, ministereth so, doctrine to that assembly, as well as presenteth petitions to God. Else how can that assembly say *Amen* at their prayer or giving of thanks? For to say *Amen* is an effect of conviction, or of edification received of the stander-by, from him that now is so ministering in that assembly before God. (1 Cor. xiv. 15—17.) Yea, I believe that they that pray in assemblies, or that shall give thanks for mercies received there, ought to labour to speak, not only with fervency of words, but with such soundness of doctrine while they mention, urge, or plead the promise with God, that that whole assembly may be enlightened, taught, taken, and carried away in their spirits, on the wing of that prayer, and of faith, to God, whose face they are come to seek, and whose grace they are gathered together to beg. Now this is called praying and praising, to the teaching and edifying of others, as by the scripture afore named is made appear. (1 Cor. xiv. 14—19.) But by what word of God the sisters of the respective churches may set up this way of teaching of one another in their assemblies, I am ignorant of. For,

Third. The Holy Ghost doth particularly insist upon the inability of women, as to their well managing of the worship *now* under consideration, and therefore it ought not to be presumed upon by them. They are forbidden to teach, yea to speak in the church of God. And why forbidden, but because of their inability. They cannot orderly manage that worship to God, that in assemblies is to be performed before him; I speak now of our ordinary believing ones, and I know none extraordinary among the churches. They are not builded to manage such worship, "they are not the image and glory of God, as the men are." (1 Cor. xi. 7.) They are placed beneath, and are called the glory of the man. Wherefore they are weak, and not permitted to perform public worship to God. When our first mother, who was not attended with those weaknesses, either sinful or natural, as our women now are, stept out of her place but to speak a good word for worship, you see how she was baffled and befooled therein; she utterly failed in the performance, though she briskly attempted the thing. Yea she so failed thereabout, that at one clap she overthrew, not only, as to that, the reputation of women for ever, but her soul, her husband, and the whole world besides. (Gen. iii. 1—7.) The fallen angel knew what he did when he made his assault upon the woman. His subtilty told him that the woman was the weaker vessel. He knew also that the man was made the head in worship, and the keeper of the garden of God. The Lord God *took* the man, *said* unto the man, *commanded* the man, and made him keeper of the garden. (Gen. ii. 15—17.) Wherefore the management of worship belonged to him. This, the serpent, as I said, was aware of. And therefore he comes to the woman, says to the woman, and deals with the woman about it, and so overcomes the world. Wherefore it is from this consideration that Paul tells Timothy that he permitted not a woman to teach, nor to usurp authority over the man, but to be in silence. But to call the church or parts thereof together, to perform solemn worship, and in such a call to exclude or shut out the men, is an usurping of that authority over them to a high degree. And he renders the reason of this his prohibition thus, "For Adam was first formed, then Eve, (and therefore had the headship in worship.) And Adam was not deceived, but the woman being deceived, was in the transgression." (1 Tim. ii. 13, 14.) But again, it should seem, methinks, if women must needs be managers of worship in assemblies, they should do it, as Eve, before Adam, in presence of the men: but that I think none will allow, though that would be the way best to correct miscarriages; how then should it be thought convenient for them to do it alone? If children are not thought fit to help to guide the ship with the mariners, shall they be trusted so much as with a boat at sea alone? The thing in hand is a parallel case. For,

Fourth. If the weightiness of *this* worship be, as indeed it is, so great, that the strongest and best able to perform it do usually come off with blushing, and with repentance for their shortness, as to the well performance thereof; though they engage therein by good and lawful authority; what will they do who are much weaker here, and when, as Eve, they set to it in a way of usurping of authority, and of their own head and will? To offer strange fire with incense, which was a type of prayer, you know what it cost Nadab and Abihu, though men, and the sons of Aaron; but Mr. K. cries the sisters, the women, the women's meetings, and the like, and how they have prevailed with heaven. Poor man, I am sorry for his weakness, and that he should show that himself is so *nunnish* in such a day as this.

But to return, as all worship in assemblies ought to be performed with the most exact order and solemnity, so this of prayer with that, if possible, that is more than all the rest; and therefore this makes it more heavy still. When men preach they have to do with men, but when they pray in assemblies they have to do both with men and with God at once. And I say, if it be so great a matter to speak to men *before* God, *how* great a matter is it to speak to men and God at once; to God by way of petition, and to men by way of instruction. But I am persuaded if those most fond of the women's meetings for prayer were to petition the king for their lives, they would not set women to be their advocates to him; specially if the king should declare beforehand by law, that he permitted not a woman in an open auditory to speak before him.

There are also many temptations that attend the duty of praying in assemblies, especially those that are immediately employed therein. These temptations, they awake are aware of, are forced to wrestle with, and greatly to groan under. Wherefore we put not the weak upon this service; not the weak, though they be men; not they in the presence of the strong. How then should the weakest of all be put upon it, and that when together by themselves? Men, though strong, and though acting by lawful authority in this, are not able, but with unutterable groans, to do it. How then shall all those that attempt it without that authority, perform it as acceptable worship to God? This work, therefore, is as much too heavy for our women now, as that about which Eve engaged in at first, was too heavy for her. But,

Fifth. If this worship may be managed by the sisterhood of the churches, being congregated together in the absence of their men, of what signification is it that man is made head of the woman as well in worship as in nature? (1 Cor. xi. 3, 7.) Yea more, why are the elders of the churches called watchmen, overseers, guides, teachers, rulers, and the like, if this kind of worship may be performed, without their conduct and government? (Ezek. iii. 17; xxxiii. 7. Acts xx. 28. Eph. iv. 11. Ps. xxviii. 72. Heb. xiii. 17.)

1. Why is man made the head of the woman in worship, in the worship now under debate, in that worship that is to be performed in assemblies? And why are the women commanded silence there, if they may congregate by themselves, and set up and manage worship there? Worship was ordained before the woman was made, wherefore the word of God at the first did not immediately come to her, but to him that was first formed, and made the head in worship. (Gen. ii. 16—18. 1 Cor. xiv. 35, 36.) And hence it is that women are so strictly tied up to this headship; that if they will learn, they must ask their husbands at home, (ver. 35,) not appoint meetings of their own sex to teach one another. "But what must they do that have unbelieving ones? and what must they do that have none?" Answer, Let them attend upon those ordinances that God has appointed for the building up and perfecting of the body of Christ, (Eph. iv. 11—13,) and learn as the angels do. (Eph. iii. 10. 1 Pet. i. 12.)

2. But I say, if they must do as Mr. K. says they are in duty bound, to wit, meet by themselves apart from their men, and as so met, perform this most solemn worship to God, how shall the elders and overseers, the watchmen, rulers, and guides in worship, perform their duty to God, and to the church of God, in this, since from this kind of worship they are quite excluded, and

utterly shut out of doors? unless it be said, that to watch, to oversee, and to guide in the matter and manner of performance of this worship in assemblies, is no part of the watchman or overseer's work; or, in their lawful absence, the work of the principal men of the church. Nor will the faithful and dutiful overseer leave worship, no, not in the best part of the congregation assembled to worship, to be performed by every weak brother, though I believe it might with more warrant be left to them, than to the strongest among our ordinary ones of the other sex.

Also our elders and watchmen covet, if we have unbelievers to behold, that our worship be performed by the most able. How then shall it be thought that they should be so silly, to turn a company of weak women loose to be abused by the fallen angels? Can it be thought that their congregation, since they have it without a command, shall fare better among those envious spirits than those that are lawfully called shall fare before the world? Watchman, watchman, see to thy duty, look well to the manner of worship that is to be performed according to thy commission. Trust not Eve, as Adam did, with worship, and with its defence. Look that all things be done in worship as becomes thee—a head, both in nature and by office—and leave not so solemn a part of worship as prayer in company is, and ought to be accounted, to be done thou canst by no means tell how. Watch in and over all such worship thyself. Be diligent to know the state of thy flocks, whether they be flocks of men, or women; and look well to thy herds, and thou shalt have milk enough, not only for men and babes, but also for the maintenance and life of thy maidens, so that they need not go with their pitchers to seek water there where their God has not sent them. (Prov. xxvii. 23—27.) Besides, the shepherds' tents is provision sufficient for them. (Sol. Song i. 8.) But, for a conclusion of this, I will ask this man, If he doth not, by pleading for these women's meetings, declare, that the women, without their men, are better able by themselves to maintain divine worship, than the men are without their elders? forasmuch as he himself will not allow that the men should always perform worship without his oversight and inspection, and yet will plead for the women to have such worship in their congregation, among themselves, excluding for ever the men therefrom. For, saith he, the Spirit is promised to be given to them to that very end, that they may meet together to pray apart without their men. And now for Mr. K.'s arguments, which, as I said, are in number four. 1. We will take the scriptures from them; and, 2. Then pick the bones of their carcases.

Yet in my taking of the scriptures from his arguments, I will do it in a way that is most to his advantage, making of each of them as formidable an objection as I can against myself.

I. *Object.* Miriam took a timbrel in her hand, and went out, and all the women went out after her, praising God with timbrels and dances for their deliverance. Therefore the women of the churches of Christ may appoint meetings of their own, as separate from their brethren, and then and there perform divine worship [and] prayer, in that, their congregation, without their men. (Exod. xv. 20, 21.)

Ans. 1. Miriam was a prophetess; and, I suppose, that none of our women will pretend to be such. And though Mr. K. labours to get over this, by saying that the work of praising was incumbent upon all, yet, by his leave, judgment and discretion, and a spirit of conduct suitable to the duty, as we read of, was found among the women in none but she. Why is it else said, Miriam led them forth; Miriam the prophetess did it? Another, by Mr. K.'s argument, might have done it as well. Thus degrades he the prophetess, that he may get favour with the ordinary women, and prompt them on to a work that he has a superstitious affection for.

2. But his assertion is of no weight. The women were not left in that extraordinary service to the spirit of ordinary believers. Nor can I count it but crooked dealing to bring in extraordinary persons, in their extraordinary acts, to prove it lawful for ordinary persons to do that which is not commanded them.

3. But though Miriam did go forth, or come out with the women, yet not from the men, into some remote place in the wilderness to worship by themselves. She rather went or came out, and the women followed her from the place by the sea, where now they were, after Moses, to sing as her sex became her; for she, though an extraordinary woman, might not make herself an equal with Moses and Aaron, therefore she came behind in worship, yet with the body of the people, as it is said, " So Moses brought Israel from the Red Sea." (Exod. xv. 22.) Women, though prophetesses, must wear some badge or other of inferiority to those that are prophets indeed. (1 Cor. xi. 3—9.) And I choose to understand that Miriam did this. (1.) Because the text last mentioned says so. (2.) Because Miriam, and all the women, did sing with the words of the men—ver. 1 compared with 21. (3.) For that they did sing them after the men, as taking them from their mouth. For, saith the text, Miriam answered them, and so handed it down to them of her sex, saying, " Sing ye to the Lord, for he hath triumphed gloriously," (verses 1 and 21.) (4.) For that she commanded the women that they should sing the same song, hence it is called the song of Moses, not of Miriam. (Rev. xv. 3.) (5.) From all which I conclude, that Miriam did not draw the women away into some such place where neither Moses, nor Aaron, nor the elders of Israel 'could see, behold, and observe their manner of worship; but that she, as her modesty became her, did lead them out from that place where they were, to sing, and to dance, and to praise God, after the men. (6.) This scrip-

ture, therefore, favoureth not this man's opinion, to wit, " That it is the duty of the women of the churches of Christ to separate themselves from their brethren, and as so separate to perform divine worship by themselves."

II. *Object.* Esther, the queen, performed, with her maidens, this duty of prayer, without their men: therefore the women of gospel churches may separate themselves from their brethren, and perform it among themselves. (Esther iv. 16.)

Ans. 1. Esther was in the house of the king's chamberlain, and could not at this time come to her brethren; no, not to her uncle, Mordecai, to consult how to prevent an approaching judgment. Yea, Mordecai and she were fain to speak one to another by Hatach, whom the king had appointed to attend upon the queen, (verses 5—9.) So she could by no means, at that time, have communion with the church. No marvel, therefore, if she fasted with her maidens alone : for so she must now do, or not do it at all. But I will here ask this, our argumentator, whether Esther did count it a burden or a privilege thus now to be separated from her brethren, and so forced to perform this work as she did? If a privilege, let him prove it. If a burden, he has little cause to make use of it to urge that, her practice then, for a ground to women that are at liberty, to separate from their brethren to perform such worship by themselves in *their* company, without their men. 2. We do not read that she desired that any of the women that were at liberty should come from the men to be with her; whence we may gather, that she preferred their liberty to worship with men, far beyond a woman's meeting. She counted that too many, by herself and her maidens, were in such bondage already. 3. Neither did she attempt to take that unavoidable work upon herself, but as begging of the men that she might, by their faith and prayers, be borne up therein; clearly concluding that she did count such work too hard for women to perform by themselves, without the help of their men, (verses 15, 16.) 4. Besides this woman's meeting, as Mr. K. would have it, was made up of none but the queen and her household maids, and with but few of them; nor will we complain of our honest women when the case is so that they cannot go out to the church to do this, if they pray with their maids at home. 5. But what if Esther did pray with her maids in her closet, because she could not come out to her brethren. Is it fair to make the necessity of a woman in bondage a law to women at liberty? This argument, therefore, is erroneous, and must not have this text to show it up; we therefore take it away from his words and proceed to a sight of his next.

III. *Object.* But it is said by the prophet Zecharias, that the Spirit is promised to be given, in New Testament times, to women, that they may pray together apart from men. (Zech. xii. 11—13.)

Ans. The text says nothing so, but is greatly abused by this man. Indeed, it says their wives shall mourn apart, but it saith not, they shall do so together. Yea, that they shall separate themselves by the dictate of God, from their brethren, to do so, is that which this text knows nothing of. Sometimes many may be together, apart from others; but why Mr. K., to serve his purpose, should rack and strain this text to justify his woman's meeting, I see no reason at all. My reason against him is, for that the *look here* upon him whom we have pierced, which is to be the cause of this mourning, is to be by an immediate revelation of the Holy Ghost, who doth not use to tell beforehand when he will so come down upon us. But such a meeting as Mr. K. intends, must be the product of consultation and time. "I will pour," saith God, "upon the house of David, the spirit of grace and of supplications: and then they shall look;" that is, when that spirit so worketh with them as to enable them so to do. Now, I say, I would know, since this mourning is to be the effect of this look, and so before one is aware, (Sol. Song vi. 12,) whether Mr. K. can prove that these women were to have an item beforehand, when they should have this look. But as it would be ridiculous thus to conclude, so as ridiculous is it to think to prove his women's meetings from hence.

Nor doth the conclusion that he hath made hereupon prove more but that he is ignorant of the work of the Spirit in this matter, or that his fondness for the women's meetings hath made him forget his own experience. For how can one that never had but one such look upon Jesus Christ, draw such a conclusion from hence. And that all those women should have this look at the same time, even all the women of the house of David and of the inhabitants of Jerusalem, that they might, all of them, by the direction of the Holy Ghost, separate themselves from their men to hold a woman's meeting or meetings by themselves for this, is more fictitious than one would imagine a man should dream. If he says that the women have a promise to have this look when they please, or that they are sure to have it because it is entailed to *their* meeting—for this seems to come nearest his conclusion—yet what unavoidable inconveniences will flow therefrom, I leave to any to judge. But I take this mourning to be according as another of the prophets says, "They shall be on the mountains like doves of the valleys, all of them mourning, every one for his iniquity." (Ezek. vii. 16.) All those souls, therefore, that shall be counted worthy to have *this look* shall mourn apart, or by themselves, when they have it. For though a man cannot appoint to himself when he will repent of his sins, or when the Holy Ghost will work, yet he shall repent indeed; he shall do it, I say, when HE doth so work, not staying till another can do so too. And since our own iniquity will then make us best consider our own case, mourning apart, or every one for their own iniquity, is most naturally proper thereto. And this is the mourning that shall be in the house of David,

Jerusalem, the church, both with men and women, at all times when the Holy Ghost shall help us to look upon him whom we have pierced. Pray God give Mr. K. and myself more of these looks upon a crucified Christ, for then we shall understand this and other such like scriptures otherwise than to draw such incoherent inferences from them as he doth.

IV. *Object.* "Women were wont in gospel times to meet together to pray. Therefore the women in gospel churches may separate themselves from their brethren to perform divine worship by themselves without their men." (Acts xvi. 13.) This is another of his scriptures, brought to uphold this fancy. But,

Ans. 1. It is not said that the women of churches met together alone to pray. But that Paul went down to a river-side where prayer was wont to be made, and spake unto the women that resorted thither. It looks therefore most agreeable to the word, to think that there the law was read by the Jewish priests to the proselyted women of that city, and that prayer, as was their custom in all such service, was intermixed therewith. But this is but conjectural. And yet, for all that, it is better grounded, and hath more reason on its side, than hath any of this man's arguments for his opinion of his women's meetings. But,

2. There was there at that time no gospel church of Christ, nor before that any gospel ministry, consequently no church obedience. Should it then be granted, that there were none but women at that meeting, and that their custom was to meet at that river-side to pray, it doth not therefore follow, that their practice was to be a pattern, a rule, a law to women in churches, to separate from their brethren, to perform divine worship, in their own woman's congregation without their men.

3. There was there no gospel believer. Lydia herself, before Paul came thither, had her heart shut up against the faith of Jesus Christ; and how a company of strangers to gospel faith, should in that their doing, be a pattern to the women in churches, a pattern of Christian worship, I do not understand.

4. If Paul's call to Philippi had been by the vision of a woman, or woman's meeting, what an argument would this man have drawn from thence to have justified his women's meetings? But since it was by a man, he hath lost an argument thereby. Though he, notwithstanding, doth adventure to say, that God so approved of that meeting, as then, and at that time, to take advantage to make known his mind and will to them concerning Jesus Christ.

5. And now I am in, since Mr. K. will needs have this scripture to justify such a practice, I wonder that he so lightly overlooked Paul's going to that meeting, for thither he went to be sure. (Acts xvi. 13—16.) Yea how fairly, to his thinking, might he have pleaded, that Paul by this act of his, was a great lover, countenancer, and commender of those he calls the women's *meetings*

Paul went to the women's meeting at Philippi, therefore it is lawful for the women of gospel churches to separate from their brethren, and to congregate by themselves for the performance of some parts of divine worship. I say how easily might he have said this, and then have popt in those two verses above quoted, and so have killed the old one? For the word lies liable to be abused by the ignorance of men, and it had been better than it is, if this had been the first time that this man had served it so, for the justification of his rigid principles; but when men, out of a fond conceit of their own abilities, or of prejudice to them that contradict their errors, are tempted to show their folly, they will not want an opportunity from false glosses put upon the text, to do it.

6. But Paul went to that company to preach Christ's gospel to them, not for that they merited his coming, but of the grace of God, as also did Peter and John, when at the hour of prayer they went up into the temple, and Paul into the synagogue at Antioch. (Acts iii. 1—3; xiii. 14—16.) But as fairly might this man have urged, that the healing of the lame man that lay at that time at the gate of the temple, and the conversion of them by Paul at Antioch, was by the procurement of the prayers of the sisters and by their reading of the law in that synagogue at Antioch, as to argue as he has done, that God was so well pleased, or so well approved of that woman's meeting as he feigns it at Philippi, as to send, &c. to them his minister.

7. But again, that this woman's meeting should be so deserving, and that while they were without the faith of Christ, as to procure a gospel minister to be sent unto them, that Christ might to them be made known, and yet that so few of them should be converted to the faith, seems a greater paradox to me. For we read not that one of the women then, or of them of the town, that did use to go to that meeting, (for Lydia was of Thyatira,) was ever converted to Christ; brethren we read of several, but we hear not of any one more of those women, (ver. 40.) But Lydia worshipped God, therefore her practice might prevail. Although it is said she worshipped God, yet she was but a proselyte, as those (Acts xiii.) were, and knew no more of Christ than the eunuch did. (Acts viii.) But hold, she had faith, will that make all practice acceptable; yea, law and commandment to others, and the work of those that have none, meritorious? But we must touch upon these things anon.

V. *Object.* "But (saith Mr. K.) Mal. iii. 16 doth countenance these meetings."

Ans. Not at all; though Mr. K. has pleased to change a term in the text, to make it speak his mind, for he has put out *thought*, and put in *call:* but all will not do his work, for when he has done what he can, it will be difficult to make that scripture say, "It is the duty of women in gospel churches to separate from their brethren, to perform divine worship among themselves."

VI. *Object.* "But Jude 20 doth justify these meetings, except," saith he, "any will say, women are not to be built up in their most holy faith."

Ans. How fain would the man lay hold on something, only he wants divine help, that is, the word of God, to bottom his things upon. But doth the apostle here at all treat of the women and their meetings, or are they only the beloved; and to be built up, &c., speaks he not there to the church, which consisteth of men and women? and are not men the more noble part in all the churches of Christ? But can women no other way be built up in their most holy faith, but by meetings of their own without their men? But, building up *yourselves*, I suppose is the thing he holds by. But cannot the church, and every woman in it, build up themselves without their woman's meetings? wherefore have they the word, their closet, and the grace of meditation, but to build up themselves withal? He saith not, "Build up one another," but if he had, it might well have been done without a woman's meeting. But anything to save a drowning man. This text then is written to the church of Christ, by which it is exhorted to faith and prayer; but it speaks not a word of a woman's meeting, and therefore it is fooling with the word to suggest it. I cannot therefore, while I see this impertinent dealing, but think our argumentator dotes, or takes upon him to be a head of those he thinks to rule over. The woman's letter to me also seems to import the same, when they say, "Mr. K. would desire to know what objections you have against it, (his arguments,) and he is ready to give his further advice."

Thus having taken from his arguments those holy words of God which he has abused, to make them stand, I come next to the arguments themselves, and intend to pick their bones for the crows.

1stly. He saith, "That the same spirit that was in Miriam is also in all God's servants for the same end, both to pray for mercies we stand in need of, and to praise God for mercies received."

Ans. 1. But the question is, whether Miriam did, as she led out the women to dance, act only as an ordinary saint. And if you evade this, you choose the tongue of the crafty, and use the words of deceit; for she managed that work as she was "Miriam the prophetess;" and in your next, pray tell your women so. 2. But as Miriam the prophetess, she did not lead the women from their men, to worship in some place remote by themselves, as we have showed before.

2ndly. He saith, "That God hath promised to pour out his Spirit in gospel times to that very end, that women might pray together apart from men."

Ans. 1. Not mentioning again what was said before, I add, if by *men*, he means the brethren, the prophet will not be his voucher, for he neither saith nor intimates such a thing. 2. And how far short this saying is, of making of God and his holy prophet the author of schism in worship, and an encouragement unto schism therein, it is best in time that he looks to it. For if they may withdraw to do thus at one time, they may withdraw to do thus at another. And if the Spirit is given to them to this very end, that they may go by themselves from the church, to perform this divine worship at one time, they may, for what bounds this man has set them, go by themselves to do thus always. But, as I said, the whole of this proposition being false, the error is still the greater.

3rdly. "God," saith he, "hath so well approved of women meeting together to pray in gospel times, as then, and at that time, to take occasion to make known his mind and will to them concerning Jesus Christ." (Acts xvi. 13.)

Ans. Let the reader consider what was said before, and now it follows, if this assertion be true, then the popish doctrine of merit is good, yea, the worst sort of it, which is, works done before faith. For that we read of none of these women save Lydia feared or worshipped God; and yet, saith he, God so approved of that meeting as then, and at that time, to send them his gospel, which is one of the richest blessings; nor will it help to lay Cornelius, now in my way, for the deservings here were, for aught we read, of women that feared not God. Here Lydia only bare that character; it is said *she* worshipped God; but she was not *all* the women. But Mr. K. saith thus of them all. I know also there was faith in some in Messias to come, though when he came they knew not his person: but this is not the case neither; these women, who held up as he feigned, this meeting, were not as we read of, of this people.

4thly. He said, "That Esther and her maids fasted and prayed, and the Lord gave a gracious return, or answer and deliverance." That is, to the church, that then was under the rage of Haman.

Ans. Let the reader remember what was said before, and now I ask this man, 1. Whether Mordecai and the good men then did not pray and fast as well as she? And if so, Whether they might not obtain at least, some little of the mercy, as well as those women? If so, 2. Whether Mr. K., in applying the deliverance of this people to the prayer of the queen and her maids—for he lays it only there—be not deceitfully arguing, and do not tend to puff up that sex to their hurt and damage? Yea, whether it doth not tend to make them unruly and headstrong? But if they be more gently inclined to obedience, no thanks to Mr. K. 3. And if I should ask Mr. K. who gave him authority to attribute *thus* the deliverance of this people, to who and what prayers he please, I suppose it would not be easy for him to answer. The text saith not that the prayers of these women procured the blessing. But Mr. K. hath here a woman's meeting to vindicate, and therefore it is that he is thus out in his mind. Prayers were heard and the church was delivered. And I doubt not but that these good women had hand and heart in the work. But should all be admitted that Mr. K. hath said as to this also, yet this scripture, as hath already been proved, will not justify his woman's meeting.

5thly. "He makes his appeal to the women, if they have not obtained, by their prayers in these their meetings, many blessed returns of prayer from God, both to themselves and the church of God."

Ans. I count this no whit better than the very worst of his paper, for besides the silliness of his appeal, by which he makes these good women to be judges in their own cause, his words have a direct tendency in them to puff them up to their destruction. I have wondered sometimes, to see when something extraordinary hath happened to the church of God for good, that a few women meeting together to pray, should be possessed with a conceit, that they fetched the benefit down from heaven, when perhaps ten thousand men in the land prayed for the mercy as hard as they. Yea I have observed, that though the things bestowed were not so much as thought of by them, yet they have been apt to conclude that their meeting together has done it. But poor women, you are to be pitied; your tempter is to bear the blame, to wit, this man and his fellows.

I come now to some objections that may yet be thought on; and will speak a word to them.

Object. 1. It is said, "Where two or three are gathered together in my name, there am I in the midst of them." (Matt. xviii. 20.)

Ans. To gather together in Christ's name, is to gather by his authority; that is, by his law and commandment. (Acts iv. 17, 18, 30; v. 28, 40. Col. iii. 17.) But we have no law of Christ, nor commandment, that the women of *this* or *that* church should separate themselves from their brethren, to maintain meetings among themselves, for the performing of divine worship; and therefore such meetings cannot be in his name; that is, by his authority, law, and commandment; and so ought not to be at all.

Object. 2. "But women may, if sent for by them of their own sex, come to see them when they are sick, and when so come together, pray in that assembly before they part."

Ans. The law of Christ is, "Is any sick among you? let him (and the woman is included in the man) call for the elders of the church; and let them pray over him," &c. And to this injunction there is a threefold promise made. (1.) "And the prayer of faith shall save the sick." (2.) "And the Lord shall raise him up." (3.) "And if he have committed sins, they shall be forgiven him." (James v. 14, 15.) And considering that this advice is seconded with so much grace, I think it best in all such cases, as in all other, to make the word of God our rule.

Object. 3. "But women have sometimes cases

which modesty will not admit should be made known to men; what must they do then?"

Ans. Their husbands and they are one flesh, and are no more to be accounted two. Let them tell their grief to them. Thus Rachel asked children of her husband, and went not to a nest of women to make her complaint to them. (Gen. xx. 1.) Or let them betake themselves to their closets, with Rebecca. (Gen. xxv. 20—23.) Or if they be in the assembly of the saints, let them pray in their hearts, with Hannah; and if their petition be lawful, I doubt not but they may be heard. (1 Sam. i. 13.)

Our author, perhaps, will say I have not spoken to his question; which was, "Whether women, fearing God, may meet to pray together? And whether it be lawful for them so to do?"

But I answer, I have, with respect to all such godly women as are in the churches of the saints. (1 Cor. xiv. 33—35, compared with ver. 15—17.) And when he has told us that his question respected only those out of churches, then will I confess that I did mistake him. Yet he will get nothing thereby, forasmuch as his question, to be sure, intends those in special, also his arguments are for the justifying of that their practice. Now the reason why I waved the form of his question was, because it was both scanty and lean of words, as to the matter of the controversy in hand; also I thought it best to make it more ample and distinct, for the edification of our reader. And if, after all, Mr. K. is not pleased at what I have done, let him take up the question and answer it better. The man perhaps may fly to the case of utter necessity, and so bring forth another question, to wit, whether, if the men of a church should all die, be murdered, or cast into prison, the women of that church may not meet together to pray? and whether it be not lawful for them so to do? But when he produceth a necessity for the putting of such a question, and then shall put it to me, I will, as God shall help me, give him an answer thereto.

But, may some say, Our women in this do not what they do of their own heads, they are allowed to do what they do by the church.

I answer, No church allowance is a foundation sufficient to justify that which is neither commanded nor allowed by the word. Besides, who knows not, that have their eyes in their heads, what already has, and what further may, come into the churches, at such a gap as this. And now to give the reader a cautionary conclusion.

Caution 1. Take heed of letting the name, or good show of a thing, beget in thy heart a religious reverence of that thing; but look to the word for thy bottom, for it is the word that authorizeth whatever may be done with warrant in worship to God; without the word things are of human invention, of what splendour or beauty soever they may appear to be. Without doubt the friars and nuns, and their religious orders, were of a good intent at first, as also compulsive vows of chastity, single life, and the like. But they were all without the word, and therefore, as their bottom wanted divine authority, so the practice wanted sanctity by the Holy Ghost. The word prayer is, of itself, in appearance so holy, that he forthwith seems to be a devil that forbids it. And yet we find that prayers have been out of joint, and disorderly used; and therefore may by one, without incurring the danger of damnation, be called into question; and if found without order by him, he may labour to set them in joint again. (Matt. vi. 5—8; xxiii. 14. James iv. 3.)

I am not of the number of them that say, "What profit should we have if we pray unto God?" (Job xxi. 15.) But finding no good footing in the word for that kind of service we have treated about above, and knowing that error and human inventions in religion will not offer themselves, but with wiped lips, and a countenance as demure as may be, and also being persuaded that this opinion of Mr. K. is vagrant, yea a mere alien as to the Scriptures, I being an officer, have apprehended it, and put it in the stocks, and there will keep it, till I see by what authority it has leave to pass and repass as it lists, among the godly in this land.

Caution 2. Yet by all that I have said, I never meant to intimate in the least, but that believing women are saints as well as men: and members of the body of Christ. And I will add, that as *they*, and *we*, are united to Christ, and made members of his mystical body, the fulness of him that fills all in all, so there is no superiority, as I know of, but we are all one in Christ. For the man is not without the woman, nor "the woman without the man, in the Lord," (1 Cor. xi. 11,) nor are we counted "as male or female" in him. (Gal. iii. 28. Eph. i. 23.) Only we must observe that *this* is spoken of that church which is his true mystical body, and not of every particular congregation of professing Christians. The churches of Christ *here* and *there* are also called his body. But no church *here*, though never so famous, must be taken for that of which mention was made afore.

As Christ then has a body mystical, which is called his members, his flesh, and his bones, (Eph. v. 30,) so he has a body politic, congregations modelled by the skill that his ministers have in his word, for the bearing up of his name, and the preserving of his glory in the world against Antichrist. In *this* church, order and discipline, for the nourishing up of the true mystical body of Christ, has been placed from the foundation of the world. Wherefore in *this*, laws, and statutes, and government is to be looked after, and given heed unto, for the edification of *that* which is to arrive at last to a perfect man: to the measure of the stature of the fulness of Christ. (1 Cor. xii. 27—30. Eph. iv. 11—13.)

Now, where there is order and government by laws and statutes, there must, of necessity, be also a distinction of sex. degrees, and age. Yea, offices and officers must also be there, for our furtherance and joy of faith. From which government and rule our ordinary women are excluded by Paul; nor should it, since it is done by the wisdom of God, be any offence unto them.

In this church there are ofttimes many hypocrites, and formal professors, and heresies, "That they which are approved may be made manifest." (1 Cor. xi. 19.) These therefore being there, and being suffered to act as they many times do, provoke the truly godly to contend with them by the word; for that these hypocrites, and formal professors, naturally incline to a denial of the power of godliness, and to set up forms of their own in the stead thereof. (Mark vii. 6—9. 2 Tim. iii. 5.)

And this is done for the sake and for the good of those that are the true members of the body of Christ, and that are to arrive at his haven of rest: from whom those others at last shall be purged, and with them, all their things that offend. "Then shall the righteous shine forth as the sun in the kingdom of their Father. Who hath ears to hear let him hear." (Matt. xiii. 43.)

This church, that thus consisteth of all righteous, that are so in God's account: they are to have a house in heaven, and to be for God's habitation there. Who, then, shall be governed by their head without those officers and laws that are necessary here? And both at last shall be subject to him, that some time did put all things under Christ, that God may be all in all. (John xiv. 1—3. Eph. ii. 21. 1 Cor. xv. 23—27.) Wherefore, my beloved sisters, this inferiority of yours will last but a little while. When the day of God's salvation is come, to wit, when our Lord shall descend from heaven, with a shout, with the voice of the archangel, and the trump of God, these distinctions of sexes shall be laid aside, and every pot shall be filled to the brim. For with a *notwithstanding* you shall be saved, and be gathered up to that state of felicity, if you continue in faith, and charity, and holiness, with sobriety. (1 Tim. ii. 15.)

Caution 3. I doubt not at all of the lawfulness of women's praying, and that, both in private and public: only when they pray publicly, they should not separate from, but join with the church in that work. They should also not be the mouth of the assembly, but in heart, desires, groans, and tears, they should go along with the men. In their closets they are at liberty to *speak* unto their God, who can bear with, and pity them with us; and pardon all our weakness for the sake of Jesus Christ.

And here I will take an occasion to say there may be a twofold miscarriage in prayer, one in doctrine, the other in the frame of the heart. All are too much subject to the last, women [more easily] to the first. And for this cause it is, at least so I think, that women are not permitted to teach, nor speak in assemblies, for divine worship, but to *be* and *learn* in silence. (1 Cor. xiv. 33—35; xv. 33.) For he that faileth as to the frame of his spirit,

hurteth only himself: but he that faileth in doctrine corrupteth them that stand by. Let the women be alone with Rebecca in the closet; or, if in company, let her, with Hannah, speak to herself and to God; and not doubt, but if she be humble, and keep within compass, she shall be a sharer with her brethren in the mercy.

Caution 4. Nor are women, by what I have said, debarred from any work or employ, unto which they are enjoined by the word. They have often been called forth to be God's witnesses, and have borne famous testimony for him against the sons of the sorceress and the whore. I remember many of them with comfort, even of these eminent daughters of Sarah, whose daughters you also are, so long as you do well, and are not afraid with any amazement. (1 Pet. iii. 1—6.) What by the word of God you are called unto, what by the word is enjoined you, do; and the Lord be with you.

But this of the women's meetings—since indeed there is nothing for its countenance in the word, and since the calling together of assemblies for worship is an act of power, and belongeth to the church, elders, or chief men of the same—let me entreat you to be content to be under subjection and obedience, as also saith the law. We hold that it is God's word that we are to look to, as to all things pertaining to worship, because it is the word that authorizeth and sanctifieth what we do.

Caution 5. *Women!* They are an ornament in the church of God on earth, as the *Angels* are in the church in heaven. Betwixt whom also there is some comparison, for they cover their faces in acts of worship. (Isa. vi. 2. 1 Cor. xi. 10.) But as the angels in heaven are not Christ, and so not admitted to the mercy-seat to speak to God, so neither are women on earth, but man; who is to worship with open face before him, and to be the mouth in prayer for the rest. As the angels then cry, Holy, Holy, Holy, with faces covered in heaven, so let the women cry, Holy, Holy, Holy, with their faces covered on earth: yea, thus they should do, because of the angels. "For this cause ought the woman to have power," that is a covering, "on *her* head, because of the angels." (1 Cor. xi. 10.) Not only because the angels are present, but because women and angels, as to their worship, in their respective places, have a semblance. For the angels are inferior to the great man Christ, who is in heaven; and the woman is inferior to the man, that truly worships God in the church on earth.

Methinks, holy and beloved sisters, you should be content to wear this power, or badge of your inferiority, since the cause thereof arose at first from yourselves. It was the woman that at first the serpent made use of, and by whom he then overthrew the world: wherefore the woman, to the world's end, must wear tokens of her underlingship in all matters of worship. To say nothing of that which she cannot shake off, to wit, her pains and sorrows in child-bearing, which God has riveted to her nature, there is her silence, and shame, and a covering for her face, in token of it, which she ought to be exercised with whenever the church comes together to worship. (Gen. iii. 16. 1 Tim. ii. 15. 1 Cor. xi. 13. 1 Tim. ii. 9.)

Do you think that God gave the woman her hair that she might deck herself, and set off her fleshly beauty therewith? It was given her to cover her face with, in token of shame and silence, for that by the woman sin came into the world. (1 Tim. ii. 9.) And perhaps the reason why the angels cover their faces when they cry, Holy, Holy, Holy, in heaven, is to show that they still bear in mind, with a kind of abhorrence, the remembrance of their fellows falling from thence. Modesty and shamefacedness becomes women at all times, especially in times of public worship, and the more of this is mixed with their grace and personage, the more beautiful they are both to God and men. But why must the women have shamefacedness, since they live honestly as the men? I answer, in remembrance of the fall of Eve, and to that the apostle applies it. For a woman—necessity has no law—to shave her head, and to look with open face in worship, as if she could be a leader there, is so far from doing that which becomes her, that it declares her to have forgot what God would have her for ever with shame remember.

Caution 6. In what I have said about the women's meetings, I have not at all concerned myself about those women that have been extraordinary ones, such as Miriam, Deborah, Huldah, Anna, or the rest, as the daughters of Philip the Evangelist, Priscilla, the women that Paul said laboured with him in the gospel, or such like: for they might teach, prophecy, and had power to call the people together so to do. Though this I must say concerning them, they ought to and did, notwithstanding so high a calling, still bear about with them the badge of their inferiority to them that were prophets indeed. And hence it is said, under pain of being guilty of disorder, that if they prayed in the church, or prophesied there, with their head uncovered, they then dishonoured their head. (1 Cor. xi. 5.)

The prophetesses were below the prophets, and their covering for their head was to be worn in token thereof; and, perhaps, it was for want of regard to this order, that when Miriam began to perk it before Moses, that God covered her face with a leprous scab. (Numb. xii. 10.) Hence these women, when prophets were present, did use to lie still as to acts of power, and leave that to be put forth by them that were higher than they.

And even Miriam herself, though she was one indeed, yet she came always behind, not only in name but worship, unless when she was in her own disorders. (Numb. xii. 1.)

And it is worth your farther noting, that when God tells Israel that they should take heed in the plague of leprosy, that they diligently observed to do what the priests and Levites taught them, that he conjoins with that exhortation, that they should "remember what God did unto Miriam by the way," (Deut. xxiv. 8, 9;) intimating surely that they should not give heed to women that would be perking up in matters of worshipping God. Much less should we invest them with power to call congregations of their own, there to perform worship without their men.

Yet, will I say, notwithstanding all this, that if any of these high women had, but we never read that they did, separate themselves, and others of their own sex with them, apart to worship by themselves; or if they had given out commandment so to do, and had joined God's name to that commandment, I should have freely consented that our women should do so too, when led out and conducted in worship by so extraordinary a one. Yea, more; if any of these high women had given it out for law, that the women of the churches in New Testament times ought to separate themselves from their men, and as so separate, perform divine worship among themselves, I should have subscribed thereto. But finding nothing like this in the word of God for the sanctifying of such a practice, and seeing so many scriptures wrested out of their place to justify so fond a conceit, and all this done by a man of conceit, and of one that, as his sisters say, expects my answer, I found myself engaged to say something for the suppressing of this his opinion.

But to return to the good women in the churches, and to make up my discourse with them.

First. These meetings of yours, honourable women, wherein you attempt to perform divine worship by yourselves, without your men, not having the authority of the word to sanctify them, will be found will-worship in the day when you, as to that, shall be measured with that golden reed, the law of God. And "who hath required this at your hand?" may put you to your shifts for an answer, notwithstanding all Mr. K. has said to uphold you. (Isa. i. 12. Rev. xi. 1.)

Second. These meetings of yours need not be; there are elders or brethren in all churches, to call to, and manage this worship of God in the world, if you abide in your subjection and worship as you are commanded.

Third. These meetings of yours, instead of being an ornament to the church in which you are, are a shame and blemish to those churches. For they manifest the unruliness of such women, or that the church wants skill to govern them. (1 Cor. xiv. 23.) Have you not "in your flock a male?" (Mal. i. 14.)

Fourth. Suppose your meetings in some cases were lawful, yet since by the brethren they may be managed better, you and your meetings ought to give place. That the church together, and the brethren, as the mouth to God, are capable of managing this solemn worship best, consider—
1. The gifts for all such service are most to be

found in the elders and leading men in the church, and not in the women thereof. 2. The spirit for conduct and government in that worship, is not in the women but in the men. 3. The men are admitted in such worship, to stand with open face before God, a token of much admittance to liberty and boldness with God, a thing denied to the women. (1 Cor. xi. 4, 5.) 4. For that when meetings for prayers are commanded, the men, to be the mouth to God, are mentioned, but not in ordinary women, in all the Scriptures. Where the women and children, and them that suck the breasts are called, with the bride and bridegroom, and the whole land, to mourn, yet the ministers and elders, and chiefest of the brethren, are they, and they only, that are bid to say, " Spare thy people, O Lord! and give not thine heritage to reproach." (Joel i. 13, 14; ii. 15—17.) 5. The word for encouragement to pray believingly in assemblies is given to men. And it is the word that makes, and that sanctifies an ordinance of God; men, therefore, in all assemblies for worship should be they that should manage it, and let others join in their places.

Object. But the woman is included in the man, for the same word signifies both.

Ans. 1. If the woman is included here, let her not exclude the man. But the man is excluded—the man is excluded by this woman's meeting from worship; from worship, though he be the head in worship over the woman, and by God's ordinance appointed to manage it, and this is an excluding of the worst complexion. (1 Cor. xi. 3.) 2. Though the woman is included when the man sometimes is named, yet the man is not excluded when himself as chief is named. But to cut him off from being the chief in all assemblies for worship, is to exclude him, and that when he for that in chief is named. 3. The woman is included when the man is named, yet but in her place; and if she worships in assemblies, her part is to hold her tongue, to learn in silence; and if she speaks, she must do it, I mean as to worship, in her heart to God. 4. Nor do I think that any woman that is holy and humble, will take offence at what I have said; for I have not in anything sought to degrade them, or to take from them what either nature or grace, or an appointment of God hath invested them with: but have laboured to keep them in their place. And doubtless to abide where God has put us, is that which not only highly concerns us, but that which becomes us best. Sisters, I have said what I have said to set you right, and to prevent your attempting to do things in such sort unto which you are not appointed. Remember what God did to Miriam, and be afraid.

Be as often in your closets as you will; the oftener there the better. This is your duty, this is your privilege: this place is sanctified to you for service by the holy word of God. Here you may be, and not make ordinances interfere, and not presume upon the power of your superiors, and not thrust out your brethren, nor put them behind your backs in worship.

Be also as often as possibly you can, in worship, when the church, or parts thereof, are assembled for that end, according to God's appointment. And when you are there, join with heart and soul with your brethren in all holy petitions to God. Let the men in prayer be the mouth to God, and the women list after with groans and desires. Let the men stand with open face in this worship, for that they are the image and glory of God, and let the women be clothed in modest apparel, with shamefacedness, in token of the remembrance of what has been touched afore.

When women keep their places, and men manage their worshipping of God as they should, we shall have better days for the church of God, in the world. (Jer. xxix. 10—14.) Women are not to be blamed for that they are forward to pray to God, only let them know their bounds; and I wish that idleness in men be not the cause of their putting their good women upon this work. Surely they that can scarce tie their shoes, and their garters, before they arrive at the tavern, or get to the coffee-house door in a morning, can scarce spare time to be a while in their closets with God. Morning closet-prayers are now, by most London professors, thrown away; and what kind of ones they make at night, God doth know, and their conscience, when awake, will know; however I have cause, as to this, to look at home: and God mend me and all his servants about it, and wherein we else are out.

I have done, after I have said that there are some other things concerning women touching which, when I have an opportunity, I may also give my judgment. But at present, I entreat that these lines be taken in good part, for I seek edification, not contention.

NESS OF LIFE.
2 Pet. 2. 20. 21.
BLASTS THE SOUL
Rom. 11. 8.
OF SLUMBER
LIKE THE
HIS
DOG TO
VOMIT
LIES TO
ETERNITY.
INTO EVERLASTING FIRE
PREPARED FOR THE DEVIL AND
HIS ANGELS
COME SINNER COME
THOU ART MY RIGHT
I AM THY HOME
GRACE THOU DIDST SLIGHT
Pilgrim's Progress.

INTRODUCTORY REMARKS

TO

BUNYAN'S POETICAL WORKS.

Nothing is more difficult in the province of criticism, than to adjudge rightly the merit of a great prose writer in his experimental or occasional character as a poet. Most readers have in their minds some popular illustration of this subject. They remember Cicero, can cite Burke, and even refer to Archdeacon Paley, as instances of striking failures where the mind, tempered and accustomed to prose, as its proper medium, ventured to change it for verse. The power of genius, or a very active talent, to use both with equal skill, has not been unfrequently proved. No one will dispute this who is acquainted with the prose as well as the poetry of Milton and Dryden, or who has read the letters of Pope and Cowper. All these writers, and others of corresponding fame, could use at will that form and measure of expression which best suited their immediate purpose. Even habit in the long employment of one, did not render them strange to the peculiarities of the other. That great prose writers have not so often adopted verse to convey some novel idea, as poets have availed themselves of prose, when engaged in history or argument, creates no surprise. The tendency of the vigorous and eloquent prose writer is not so likely to be interrupted by caprices of feeling and imagination, requiring a new medium for their expression, as the poet is likely to meet with occasions when prose must be resorted to as fitter for the business of the day. But when we find such men as Baxter and Bunyan resorting to verse, the subject excites a greater interest. Neither of these excellent writers pretended to the name of poet; nor is it probable that they would have attained the end contemplated in all their labours, had they supposed themselves invested with that character. It is obvious that their readers would then have been numbered by tens, instead of by hundreds and thousands; and that their appeals to the unconverted, and their full, rich expositions of heavenly truth, must have been confined within the strict enclosure of the most epigrammatic expressions.

Much, however, as there would have been to lament had either Baxter or Bunyan preferred verse to prose, there is something pleasing in the fact, that both could find amusement and comfort in slight trials of poetic power. The very nature of their compositions in metre shows that no vain conceit or ambition was connected with the attempt. Their verses are of the most homely character. The subjects which they selected for the experiment are such as lay on the surface of their minds,—thoughts not to be searched for, and readily assuming the light dress which rhymes, not very exact or musical, might help to furnish.

We must not, however, go further in thus mentioning Baxter and Bunyan together as poets. They both took pleasure in seeing ideas familiar to their souls rise before them in novel forms, with some degree of unusual colour about them, and speaking with a new kind of utterance. But Baxter's efforts were of a much higher character than Bunyan's. His more strictly cultivated intellect, and larger stores of general learning, gave him an unquestionable superiority in the art of composition. The genius which shows itself in numberless passages of the *Saint's Rest*, and other works of his, appears so creative of imagery, that Baxter might easily have become one of the most respectable poets of his age.

Bunyan's compositions in verse are both few and unimportant, in comparison with those of Baxter; but they are not unworthy of study. The productions of a mind like his, under whatever form they are presented, help us to new views of the man himself. Hence, even if insignificant in themselves, they are valuable and interesting, considered in relation to the author. Bunyan's first rhymes were like the steps of an infant, tentative of a strength which it was delightful to exercise, however feebly. He soon found that it was not in the leading-strings of verse he could put forth the vigour of his rapid growth. To run freely, to plunge at once into the midst of the enemies of God and man, and tell them all that was passing in his awakened soul, this was his earliest impulse, and he could not obey it as a poet.

Thus the very urgency and abundance of his thoughts would have kept him from becoming a poet, even had other things been more favourable to the development of his genius in this direction. Many readers of the *Pilgrim's Progress* feel, no doubt, that it would have made an admirable

poem; and so, probably, it would have become, had its author been trained under different circumstances, and called to the office of a teacher under less severe auspices. But it would have required
a very careful art to enable him to put into effective verse all the varied scenes, and the characters,
still more difficult of such representation, which now charm us in that work. No doubt it might have
been done; and in a poem, that which at present betrays somewhat of harshness, or want of propriety,
might have been softened; and all that which is bright and powerful might have shone out, under the
intense illumination peculiar to poetry, still clearer and more impressive. This would have been
a gain for some readers; but whether for the myriads, with whom Bunyan's own simple state of mind
so eminently fitted him to sympathise, it is hard to say.

Though ceasing, at a very early period of his course, from any serious attempt to write in verse,
he never wholly lost the youthful feeling of pleasure which the effort awakened,—the happy and
innocent accompaniment of the humblest talent for poetry. The age in which he lived was favourable
to this indulgence. Poetry had not become so strict and refined in form as at a later period. Rhyme
was a common medium for children's stories, for proverbs, and all sorts of religious maxims. In these
cases no one thought of criticism; and where some short lesson was to be taught, which the instructor
wished to render acceptable to untutored or inattentive listeners, the ringing echo of simple verse
became a very useful auxiliary. Several of Bunyan's compositions in rhyme may readily be traced to
these causes. They formed a resource in occasional hours of lassitude. He loved the exercise, and it
became far more pleasant and exciting to him when, as was often the case, he could believe that his
verses would be useful teachers.

It will be generally understood from these remarks, that poetry, as such, is not to be looked for
from the pen of Bunyan. In the few instances in which it occurs, it pleases the more from being
unexpected. Some lines, indeed, there are, and even here and there a stanza, which he must have
written at times of unusual felicity. They are precious, not only because of their rarity, but for
intrinsic beauty. It is a not unfrequent phenomenon, that occasional writers in verse, exhibiting, for
the most part, little ability or originality, will sometimes suddenly present an idea noble in itself, and
clothed in the fittest language. That Bunyan should not have been oftener the subject of these
felicitous accidents of poetic thought, may be matter of surprise; but humble as are the pretensions of
the following pieces, they are not wholly void of such scattered lights. The observant reader will be
rewarded for his patience as he meets from time to time with these evidences of Bunyan's happy
feeling; traces of some sudden, festive emotion in his mind prompting it to immediate utterance.
But still better repaid will he be, if the perusal of the verses impress upon him a deeper idea of the
spirit of the writer; and, as in the case of the commentaries, of that love and zeal which prompted
him to search every corner of his thinking nature for some offering to God,—for some means or faculty
whereby he might make his fellow men more willing to receive, and more anxious to obey truth. In
none of his writings is this sublime characteristic wanting; and where it exists, it invests the simplest
composition with a species of grandeur.

H. S.

ONE THING IS NEEDFUL;

OR,

SERIOUS MEDITATIONS UPON THE FOUR LAST THINGS:

DEATH, JUDGMENT, HEAVEN, AND HELL.

PREFATORY NOTE.

BUNYAN had a quick ear, and he had long familiarized it to the old English ballad rhymes before he wrote these poems. It is supposed that they were the fruit of his compulsory leisure during the early times of his imprisonment. The date and manner of their first publication are uncertain. They probably obtained considerable popularity, a third edition having been published in the life-time of the author. For readers who can be satisfied with great truths, however expressed, style is a matter of indifference. With many it is a subject for consideration merely because, if wanting in simplicity, it may interfere with strength and clearness of thought. But there is a large class of persons to whom it is a help as well as a delight, to receive instruction by easy, flowing verse. They are conscious that they shall retain it better when thus conveyed to them. Their memory feels it as a sort of indulgence and luxury to be aided by words put into measure for it. Thus, if the advantage of metre be not counterbalanced by perplexed phrases, unusual words, or awkward inversions, many benefits may attend its employment even in the most serious compositions. The humble, and sometimes the unwilling reader, is found yielding himself with increasing attention to a subject, otherwise remote from his mind, when the ear is first entertained. Hence the people of Elstow and Bedford might well account Bunyan's poetry no unfitting accompaniment to his labours as a preacher. The *One Thing Needful*, and *The Four last Things*, were better themes than most of those familiar to their early memories. Thus they took the place of many a rude ballad and idle song, the rhyme in both these latter cases affording the only claim to popularity. Few men can remain wholly insensible to solemn facts fairly deposited in their minds ; and Bunyan has here heaped together a mass of such truths and awful suggestions, that the verse which floated them, as it were, into the midst of crowds, ought to be valued as any other medium for the ready conveyance of a benefit.

H. S.

ONE THING IS NEEDFUL.

AN INTRODUCTION TO THE ENSUING DISCOURSE.

1. THESE lines I at this time present
   To all that will them heed,
   Wherein I show to what intent
   God saith, *Convert with speed.*

2. For these four things come on apace,
   Which we should know full well,
   Both death and judgment, and, in place
   Next to them, *heaven and hell.*

3. For doubtless man was never born
   For this life and no moe :
   No, in the resurrection morn
   They must have weal or woe.

4. Can any think that God should take
   That pains, to form a man
   So like himself, only to make
   Him here a moment stand ?

5. Or that he should make such ado,
   By justice and by grace,
   By prophets and apostles too,
   That men might see his face ?

6. Or that the promise he hath made,
   Also the threatenings great,
   Should in a moment end and fade ?
   Oh no ! this is a cheat.

7. Besides, who is so mad, or worse,
   To think that Christ should come
   From glory, to be made a curse,
   And that in sinners' room,

8. If nothing should by us be had,
    When we are gone from hence,
   But vanities, while here, oh mad
    And foolish confidence!

9. Again, shall God, who is the truth,
    Say there is heaven and hell,
   And shall men play that trick of youth
    To say, *But who can tell?*

10. Shall he that keeps his promise sure
     In things both low and small,
    Yet break it, like a man impure,
     In matters great'st of all?

11. Oh, let all tremble at that thought,
     That puts on God the lie,
    That saith men shall turn into nought,
     When they be sick and die!

12. Alas! death is but as the door
     Through which all men do pass,
    To that which they for evermore
     Shall have by wrath or grace.

13. Let all, therefore, that read my lines,
     Apply them to the heart;
    Yea, let them read, and turn betimes,
     And get the better part.

14. Mind, therefore, what I treat on here—
     Yea, mind and weigh it well;
    'Tis death and judgment, and a clear
     Discourse of *Heaven and Hell.*

OF DEATH.

1. DEATH, as a king, rampant and stout,
    The world he dare engage;
   He conquers all, yea, and doth rout
    The great, strong, wise, and sage.

2. No king so great, nor prince so strong,
    But death can make to yield;
   Yea, bind and lay them all along,
    And make them quit the field.

3. Where are the victors of the world,
    With all their men of might?
   Those that together kingdoms hurl'd,
    By death are put to flight.

4. How feeble is the strongest hand,
    When death begins to gripe?
   The giant now leaves off to stand,
    Much less withstand and fight.

5. The man that hath a lion's face
    Must here give place, and bend;
   Yea, though his bones were bars of brass,
    'Tis vain here to contend.

6. Submit he must to feeble ones,
    To worms who will enclose
   His skin and flesh, sinews and bones,
    And will thereof dispose

7. Among themselves, as merchants do,
    The prizes they have got;
   Or as the soldiers give unto
    Each man the share and lot,

8. Which they by dint of sword have won,
    From their most daring foe;
   While he lies by as still as stone,
    Not knowing what they do.

9. Beauty death turns to rottenness,
    And youth to wrinkled face;
   The witty he brings to distress,
    And wantons to disgrace.

10. The wild he tames, and spoils the mirth
     Of all that wanton are,
    He takes the worldling from his worth,
     And poor man from his care.

11. Death favours none, he lays at all,
     Of all sorts and degree;
    Both old and young, both great and small,
     Rich, poor, and bound, and free.

12. No fawning words will flatter him,
     Nor threat'nings make him start;
    He favours none for worth or kin,
     All must taste of his dart.

13. What shall I say? the graves declare
     That death shall conquer all;
    There lie the skulls, dust, bones, and there
     The mighty daily fall.

14. The very looks of death are grim,
     And ghastly to behold;
    Yea, though but in a dead man's skin,
     When he is gone and cold.

15. How 'fraid are some of dead men's beds,
     And others of their bones!
    They neither care to see their heads,
     Nor yet to hear their groans.

16. Now all these things are but the shade
     And badges of his coat;
    The glass that runs, the scythe and spade,
     Though weapons more remote:

17. Yet such as make poor mortals shrink
     And fear, when they are told,
    These things are signs that they must drink,
     With death; oh then how cold!

18. It strikes them to the heart! how do
     They study it to shun!
    Indeed who can bear up, and who
     Can from these shakings run?

19. But how much more then when he comes
     To grapple with thy heart;
    To bind with thread thy toes and thumbs,[*]
     And fetch thee in his cart?

* A common custom when death takes place. The two
great toes are tied together, to make the body look *decent;*
and formerly the hands were placed with the palms together, as if in the attitude of prayer, and were kept in that
posture by tying the thumbs together.—(*Offor.*)

20. Then will he cut thy silver cord,
    And break thy golden bowl;
Yea, break that pitcher which the Lord
    Made cabin for thy soul.

21. Thine eyes, that now are quick of sight,
    Shall then no way espy
How to escape this doleful plight,
    For death will make thee die.

22. Those legs that now can nimbly run,
    Shall then with faintness fail
To take one step, death's dart to shun,
    When he doth thee assail.

23. That tongue, that now can boast and brag,
    Shall then by death be tied,
So fast, as not to speak or wag,
    Though death lies by thy side.

24. Thou that didst once incline thine ear
    Unto the song and tale,
Shall only now death's message hear,
    While he, with face most pale,

25. Doth reason with thee how thy days
    Hath hitherto been spent;
And what have been thy deeds and ways,
    Since God thee time hath lent.

26. Then will he so begin to tear
    Thy body from thy soul,
And both from life, if now thy care
    Be not on grace, to roll.

27. Death puts on things another face
    Than we in health do see:
Sin, Satan, hell, death, life, and grace
    Now great and weighty be.

28. Yea, now the sick man's eye is set
    Upon a world to come:
He also knows too, without let,
    That there must be his home.

29. Either in joy, in bliss and light,
    Or sorrow, woe, and grief;
Either with Christ and saints in white,
    Or fiends, without relief.

30. But, oh, the sad estate that then
    They will be in that die
Both void of grace and life! poor men!
    How will they fear and cry,

31. Ha! live I may not, though I would
    For life give more than all;
And die I dare not, though I should
    The world gain by my fall.

32. No, here he must no longer stay,
    He feels his life run out,
His night is come, also the day
    That makes him fear and doubt.

33. He feels his very vitals die,
    All waxeth pale and wan;
Nay, worse, he fears to misery
    He shortly must be gone.

34. Death doth already strike his heart
    With his most fearful sting
Of guilt, which makes his conscience start,
    And quake at every thing.

35. Yea, as his body doth decay
    By a contagious grief,
So his poor soul doth faint away
    Without hope or relief.

36. Thus while the man is in this scare,
    Death doth still at him lay;
Live, die, sink, swim, fall foul or fair,
    Death still holds on his way.

37. Still pulling of him from his place,
    Full sore against his mind;
Death like a sprite stares in his face,
    And doth with links him bind.

38. And carries him into his den,
    In darkness there to lie,
Among the swarms of wicked men
    In grief eternally.

39. For only he that God doth fear
    Will now be counted wise:
Yea, he that feareth him while here,
    He only wins the prize.

40. 'Tis he that shall by angels be
    Attended to that bliss
That angels have; for he, oh, he,
    Of glory shall not miss.

41. Those weapons and those instruments
    Of death, that others fright
Those dreadful fears and discontents
    That brings on some that night,

42. That never more shall have a day,
    Brings this man to that rest,
Which none can win but only they
    Whom God hath called and blest,

43. With the first fruits of saving grace,
    With faith, hope, love, and fear,
Him to offend; this man his face,
    In visions high and clear,

44. Shall in that light which no eye can
    Approach unto, behold
The rays and beams of glory, and
    Find there his name enroll'd,

45. Among those glittering stars of light
    That Christ still holdeth fast
In his right hand with all his might,
    Until that danger's past,

46. That shakes the world, and most hath dropt,
    Into grief and distress,
Oh blessed then is he that's wrapt
    In Christ his righteousness.

47. This is the man death cannot kill,
    For he hath put on arms;
Him sin nor Satan hath not skill
    To hurt with all their charms.

48. A helmet on his head doth stand,
    A breastplate on his heart;
    A shield also is in his hand,
    That blunteth every dart.

49. Truth girds him round the reins, also
    His sword is on his thigh;
    His feet in shoes of peace do go
    The ways of purity.

50. His heart it groaneth to the Lord,
    Who hears him at his call,
    And doth him help and strength afford,
    Wherewith he conquers all.

51. Thus fortified, he keeps the field
    While death is gone and fled;
    And then lies down upon his shield,
    Till Christ doth raise the dead.

OF JUDGMENT.

1. As 'tis appointed men should die,
    So judgment is the next
    That meets them most assuredly;
    For so saith holy text.

2. Wherefore of judgment I shall now
    Inform you what I may,
    That you may see what 'tis, and how
    'Twill be with men that day.

3. This world it hath a time to stand,
    Which time when ended, then
    Will issue judgment out of hand
    Upon all sorts of men.

4. The Judge we find, in God's record,
    The Son of man, for he
    By God's appointment is made Lord
    And Judge of all that be.

5. Wherefore this Son of man shall come
    At last to count with all,
    And unto them shall give just doom,
    Whether they stand or fall.

6. Behold ye now the majesty
    And state that shall attend
    This Lord, this Judge, and Justice high
    When he doth now descend.

7. He comes with head as white as snow,
    With eyes like flames of fire;
    In justice clad from top to toe,
    Most glorious in attire.

8. His face is filled with gravity;
    His tongue is like a sword;
    His presence awes both stout and high,
    The world shakes at his word.

9. He comes in flaming fire, and
    With angels clear and bright,
    Each with a trumpet in his hand,
    Clothed in shining white.

10. The trump of God sounds in the air,
    The dead do hear his voice;
    The living too run here and there,
    Who made not him their choice

11. Thus to his place he doth repair,
    (Appointed for his throne,)
    Where he will sit to judge, and where
    He'll count with every one.

12. Angels attending on his hand
    By thousands on a row;
    Yea, thousand thousands by him stand,
    And at his beck do go.

13. Thus being set, the books do ope
    In which all crimes are writ.
    All virtues, too, of faith and hope,
    Of love; and every whit

14. Of all that man hath done or said,
    Or did intend to do;
    Whether they sinn'd, or were afraid
    Evil to come into.

15. Before this bar each sinner now
    In person must appear;
    Under his judgment there to bow
    With trembling and with fear:

16. Within whose breast a witness then
    Will certainly arise,
    That to each charge will say *Amen*,
    While they seek and devise

17. To shun the sentence which the Lord
    Against them then will read,
    Out of the books of God's record,
    With majesty and dread.

18. But every heart shall opened be
    Before this Judge most high;
    Yea, every thought to judgment he
    Will bring assuredly.

19. And every word and action too
    He there will manifest;
    Yea, all that ever thou didst do,
    Or keep within thy breast,

20. Shall then be seen and laid before
    The world, that then will stand
    To see thy Judge open ev'ry sore,
    And all thy evils scann'd;

21. Weighing each sin and wickedness
    With so much equity,
    Proportioning of thy distress
    And woful misery;

22. With so much justice, doing right,
    That thou thyself shalt say,
    My sins have brought me to this plight,
    I threw myself away;

23. Into that gulph my sins have brought
    Me justly to possess,
    For which I blame not Christ, I wrought
    It out by wickedness.

24. But oh! how willingly would these
    That thus in judgment be,
  If that they might have help or ease,
    Unto the mountains flee.

25. They would rejoice if that they might
    But underneath them creep,
  To hide them from revenging right,
    For fear of which they weep.

26. But all in vain, the mountains then
    Will all be fled and gone;
  No shelter will be found for men
    That now are left alone.

27. For succour they did not regard
    When Christ by grace did call
  To them, therefore they are not heard,
    No mountains on them fall.

28. Before this Judge no one shall shroud
    Himself, under pretence
  Of knowledge, which hath made him proud,
    Nor seeming penitence.

29. No high profession here can stand,
    Unless sincerity
  Hath been therewith commixed, and
    Brought forth simplicity.

30. No mask nor vizor here can hide
    The heart that rotten is;
  All cloaks now must be laid aside,
    No sinner must have bliss.

31. Though most approve of thee, and count
    Thee upright in thy heart;
  Yea, though preferred and made surmount
    Most men to act thy part,

32. In treading where the godly trod,
    As to an outward show;
  Yet this holds still, the grace of God
    Takes hold on but a few,

33. So as to make them truly such
    As then shall stand before
  This Judge with gladness; this is much,
    Yet true for evermore.

34. The tree of life this paradise
    Doth always beautify,
  'Cause of our health it is the rise
    And perpetuity.

35. Here stands the golden throne of grace
    From out of which do run
  Those crystal streams that make this place
    Far brighter than the sun.

36. Here stands Mount Zion with her king,
    Jerusalem above,
  That holy and delightful thing,
    So beautified with love.

37. That, as a mother succours those
    Which of her body be,
  So she far more, all such as close
    In with her Lord; and she

38. Her grace, her everlasting doors
    Will open wide unto
  Them all, with welcome, welcome, poor,
    Rich, bond, free, high and low,

39. Unto the kingdom which our Lord
    Appointed hath for all
  That hath his name and word ador'd;
    Because he did them call

40. Unto that work, which also they
    Sincerely did fulfil,
  Not shunning always to obey
    His gracious holy will.

41. Besides, this much doth beautify
    This goodly paradise,
  That from all quarters, constantly,
    Whole thousands as the price

42. Of precious blood, do here arrive;
    As safe escaping all,
  Sin, hell, and Satan did contrive
    To bring them into thrall.

43. Each telling his deliverance
    I' th' open face of heaven;
  Still calling to remembrance
    How fiercely they were driven

44. By deadly foe, who did pursue
    As swift as eagles fly;
  Which if thou have not, down thou must
  With those that then shall die
  The second death, and be accurs'd
    Of God. For certainly,

45. The truth of grace shall only here
    Without a blush be bold
  To stand, whilst others quake and fear,
    And dare not once behold.

46. That heart that here was right for God
    Shall there be comforted;
  But those that evil ways have trod,
    Shall then hang down their head,

47. As sore confounded with the guilt
    That now upon them lies,
  Because they did delight in filth
    And beastly vanities.

48. Or else because they did deceive
    With hypocritical
  Disguises their own souls, and leave
    Or shun that best of all

49. Approved word of righteousness,
    They were invited to
  Embrace, therefore they no access
    Now to him have, but woe.

50. For every one must now receive
    According to their ways,
  They that unto the Lord did cleave,
    The everlasting joys.

51. Those that did die in wickedness,
    To execution sent,
There still to grapple with distress,
    Which nothing can prevent.

52. Of which two states I next shall write,
    Wherefore I pray give ear,
And to them bend with all your might
    Your heart with filial fear.

OF HEAVEN.

1. HEAVEN is a place, also a state,
    It doth all things excel,
No man can fully it relate,
    Nor of its glory tell.

2. God made it for his residence,
    To sit on as a throne,
Which shows to us the excellence
    Whereby it may be known.

3. Doubtless the fabric that was built
    For this so great a king,
Must needs surprise thee, if thou wilt
    But duly mind the thing.

4. If all that build do build to suit
    The glory of their state,
What orator, though most acute,
    Can fully heaven relate?

5. If palaces that princes build,
    Which yet are made of clay,
Do so amaze when much beheld,
    Of heaven what shall we say?

6. It is the high and holy place;
    No moth can there annoy,
Nor make to fade that goodly grace
    That saints shall there enjoy.

7. Mansions for glory and for rest
    Do there prepared stand;
Buildings eternal for the blest
    Are there provided, and

8. The glory and the comeliness
    By deepest thought none may
With heart or mouth fully express,
    Nor can before that day.

9. These heav'ns we see, be as a scroll,
    Or garment folded up,
Before they do together roll,
    And we call'd in to sup

10. There with the king, the bridegroom, and
    By him are led into
His palace chambers, there to stand
    With his prospect to view,

11. And taste and smell, and be inflam'd,
    And ravished to see
The buildings he hath for us fram'd,
    How full of heaven they be.

12. Its state also is marvellous,
    For beauty to behold;

All goodness there is plenteous,
    And better far than gold.

13. Adorn'd with grace and righteousness,
    While fragrant scents of love
O'erflow with everlasting bliss,
    All that do dwell above.

14. The heavenly majesty, whose face
    Doth far exceed the sun,
Will there cast forth its rays of grace
    After this world is done.

15. Which rays and beams will so possess
    All things that there shall dwell,
With so much glory, light, and bliss,
    That none can think or tell.

16. That wisdom which doth order all
    Shall there be fully shown;
That strength that bears the world, there
    shall
    By every one be known.

17. That holiness and sanctity
    Which doth all thought surpass,
Shall there in present purity
    Outshine the crystal glass.

18. The beauty and the comeliness
    Of this Almighty shall
Make amiable with lasting bliss
    Those he thereto shall call.

19. The presence of this God will be
    Eternal life in all,
And health and gladness, while we see
    Thy face, O immortal!

20. Here will the Lord make clear and plain
    How sweetly did agree
His attributes, when Christ was slain
    Our Saviour to be.

21. How wisdom did find out the way,
    How strength did make him stand,
How holiness did bear the sway,
    And answer just demand.

22. How all these attributes did bend
    Themselves to work our life,
Thorow the Christ whom God did send
    To save us by his might.

23. All this will sparkle in our eye
    Within the holy place,
And greatly raise our melody,
    And flow our hearts with grace.

24. The largest thought that can arise
    Within the widest heart,
Shall then be filled with surprise,
    And pleas'd in every part.

25. All mysteries shall here be seen,
    And every knot untied;
Electing love, that hid hath been,
    Shall shine on every side

26. The God of glory here will be
 The life of every one;
 Whose goodly attributes shall we
 Possess them as our own.

27. By wisdom we all things shall know,
 By light all things shall see,
 By strength, too, all things we shall do,
 When we in glory be.

28. The Holy Lamb of God, also,
 Who for our sakes did die,
 The holy ones of God shall know,
 And that most perfectly.

 Those small and short discoveries
 That we have of him here,
 Will there be seen with open eyes,
 In visions full and clear.

30. Those many thousand acts of grace
 That here we feel and find,
 Shall there be read with open face
 Upon his heart most kind.

31. There he will show us how he was
 Our prophet, priest, and king;
 And how he did maintain our cause,
 And us to glory bring.

32. There we shall see how he was touch'd
 With all our grief and pain
 (As in his word he hath avouch'd),
 When we with him shall reign;

33. He'll show us, also, how he did
 Maintain our faith and love,
 And why his face sometimes he hid
 From us, who are his dove;

34. These tempting times that here we have,
 We there shall see were good;
 Also that hidden strength he gave,
 The purchase of his blood.

35. That he should stand for us before
 His Father, thus we read,
 But then shall see, and shall adore
 Him for his gracious deed.

36. Though we are vile, he without shame
 Before the angels all,
 Lays out his strength, his worth, and name,
 For us, who are in thrall.

37. This is He who was mock'd and beat,
 Spit on, and crown'd with thorns;
 Who for us had a bloody sweat,
 Whose heart was broke with scorns.

38. 'Tis he who stands so much our friend,
 As shortly we shall see,
 With open face, world without end,
 And in his presence be.

39. That head that once was crown'd with thorns,
 Shall now with glory shine:
 That heart that broken was with scorns,
 Shall flow with life divine;

40. That man that here met with disgrace,
 We there shall see so bright,
 That angels can't behold his face
 For its exceeding light.

41. What gladness will possess our heart
 When we shall see these things!
 What light and life, in every part,
 Will rise like lasting springs!

42. Oh blessed face, and holy grace,
 When shall we see this day?
 Lord, fetch us to this goodly place,
 We humbly do thee pray.

43. Next to this Lamb we shall behold
 All saints, both more and less,
 With whit'ned robes in glory roll'd,
 'Cause him they did confess.

44. Each walking in his righteousness
 With shining crowns of gold,
 Triumphing still in heav'nly bliss,
 Amazing to behold.

45. Each person for his majesty
 Doth represent a king;
 Yea, angel-like for dignity,
 And seraphims that sing.

46. Each motion of their mind, and so
 Each twinkling of their eye;
 Each word they speak, and step they go,
 It is in purity.

47. Immortal are they every one,
 Wrapt up in health and light,
 Mortality from them is gone,
 Weakness is turn'd to might.

48. The stars are not so clear as they,
 They equalize the sun;
 Their glory shines to perfect day,
 Which day will ne'er be done.

49. No sorrow can them now annoy,
 Nor weakness, grief or pain;
 No faintness can abate their joy,
 They now in life do reign.

50. They shall not there, as here, be vex'd
 With Satan, men, or sin;
 Nor with their wicked hearts perplex'd,
 The heavens have cop'd them in.

51. Thus as they shine in their estate,
 So too in their degree;
 Which is most goodly to relate,
 And ravishing to see.

52. The majesty whom they adore,
 Doth them in wisdom place
 Upon the thrones, and that before
 The angels, to their grace.

53. The saints of the Old Testament,
 Full right to their degree;
 Likewise the New, in excellent
 Magnificency be.

54. Each one his badge of glory wears,
    According to his place;
    According as was his affairs
    Here, in the time of grace.

55. Some on the right hand of the Lamb,
    Likewise some on the left,
    With robes and golden chains do stand
    Most grave, most sage, and deft.

56. The martyr here is known from him
    Who peaceably did die,
    Both by the place he sitteth in,
    And by his dignity.

57. Each father, saint, and prophet shall,
    According to his worth,
    Enjoy the honour of his call,
    And plainly hold it forth.

58. Those bodies which sometimes were torn,
    And bones that broken were
    For God's word, he doth now adorn
    With health and glory fair.

59. Thus, when in heav'nly harmony
    These blessed saints appear,
    Adorn'd with grace and majesty,
    What gladness will be there?

60. The light, and grace, and countenance,
    The least of these shall have,
    Will so with terror them advance,
    And make their face so grave,

61. That at them all the world will shake,
    When they lift up their head;
    Princes and kings will at them quake,
    And fall before them dead.

62. This shall we see, thus shall we be,
    Oh would the day were come!
    Lord Jesus, take us up to thee,
    To this desired home.

63. Angels also we shall behold,
    When we on high ascend,
    Each shining like to men of gold,
    And on the Lord attend.

64. These goodly creatures, full of grace,
    Shall stand about the throne,
    Each one with lightning in his face,
    And shall to us be known.

65. These cherubims with one accord
    Shall cry continually,
    Ah! holy, holy, holy, Lord,
    And heavenly majesty!

66. These will us in their arms embrace,
    And welcome us to rest,
    And joy to see us clad with grace,
    And of the heavens possess'd.

67. This we shall hear, this we shall see,
    While raptures take us up,
    When we with blessed Jesus be,
    And at his table sup.

68. O shining angels! what, must we
    With you lift up our voice?
    We must, and with you ever be,
    And with you must rejoice.

69. Our friends that lived godly here,
    Shall there be found again;
    The wife, the child, and father dear,
    With others of our train.

70. Each one down to the foot in white,
    Fill'd to the brim with grace,
    Walking among the saints in light,
    With glad and joyful face.

71. Those God did use us to convert,
    We there with joy shall meet,
    And jointly shall, with all our heart,
    In life each other greet.

72. A crown to them we then shall be,
    A glory and a joy;
    And that before the Lord, when he
    The world comes to destroy.

73. This is the place, this is the state,
    Of all that fear the Lord;
    Which men nor angels may relate
    With tongue, or pen, or word.

74. No night is here, for to eclipse
    Its spangling rays so bright,
    Nor doubt, nor fear to shut the lips
    Of those within this light.

75. The strings of music here are tun'd
    For heavenly harmony,
    And every spirit here perfum'd
    With perfect sanctity.

76. Here run the crystal streams of life,
    Quite thorow all our veins;
    And here by love we do unite
    With glory's golden chains.

77. Now that which sweet'neth all will be
    The lasting of this state;
    This heightens all we hear or see
    To a transcendent rate.

78. For should the saints enjoy all this
    But for a certain time,
    Oh, how would they their mark then miss,
    And at this thing repine!

79. Yea, 'tis not possible that they
    Who then shall dwell on high,
    Should be content, unless they may
    Dwell there eternally.

80. A thought of parting with this place
    Would bitter all their sweet,
    And darkness put upon the face
    Of all they there do meet.

81. But far from this the saints shall be,
    Their portion is the Lord,
    Whose face for ever they shall see,
    As saith the *Holy Word*.

82. And that with everlasting peace,
    Joy, and felicity,
From this time forth they shall increase
    Unto eternity.

OF HELL, AND THE ESTATE OF THOSE THAT
PERISH.

1. Thus, having show'd you what I see
    Of heaven, I now will tell
You also, after search, what be
    The damned wights of hell.

2. And oh! that they who read my lines
    Would ponder soberly,
And lay to heart such things betimes
    As touch eternity.

3. The sleepy sinner little thinks
    What sorrows will abound
Within him, when upon the brinks
    Of Tophet he is found.

4. Hell is beyond all thought a state
    So doubtful and forlorn,
So fearful, that none can relate
    The pangs that there are borne.

5. God will exclude them utterly
    From his most blessed face,
And them involve in misery,
    In shame, and in disgrace.

6. God is the fountain of all bliss,
    Of life, of light, and peace;
They then must needs be comfortless
    Who are depriv'd of these.

7. Instead of life, a living death
    Will there in all be found;
Dyings will be in every breath,
    Thus sorrow will abound.

8. No light, but darkness here doth dwell;
    No peace, but horror strange:
The fearful damning wights of hell
    In all will make this change.

9. To many things the damned's woe
    Is liked in the Word,
And that because no one can show
    The vengeance of the Lord.

10. Unto a dreadful burning lake,
    All on a fiery flame,
Hell is compared, for to make
    All understand the same.

11. A burning lake, a furnace hot,
    A burning oven too
Must be the portion, share, and lot,
    Of those which evil sow.

12. This plainly shows the burning heat
    With which it will oppress
All hearts, and will like burnings eat
    Their souls with sore distress.

13. This burning lake, it is God's wrath
    Incensed by the sin
Of those who do reject his path,
    And wicked ways walk in.

14. Which wrath will so perplex all parts
    Of body and of soul,
As if up to the very hearts
    In burnings they did roll.

15. Again, to show the stinking state
    Of this so sad a case,
Like burning brimstone God doth make
    The hidings of his face.

16. And truly as the steam and smoke,
    And flames of brimstone smell,
To blind the eyes, and stomach choke,
    So are the pangs of hell.

17. To see a sea of brimstone burn,
    Who would it not affright?
But they whom God to hell doth turn
    Are in most woful plight.

18. This burning cannot quenched be,
    No, not with tears of blood,
No mournful groans in misery
    Will here do any good.

19. Oh damned men! this is your fate,
    The day of grace is done;
Repentance now doth come too late,
    Mercy is fled and gone.

20. Your groans and cries they sooner should
    Have sounded in mine ears,
If grace you would have had, or would
    Have me regard your tears.

21. Me you offended with your sin,
    Instructions you did slight,
Your sins against my law hath been,
    Justice shall have his right.

22. I gave my Son to do you good,
    I gave you space and time
With him to close, which you withstood,
    And did with hell combine.

23. Justice against you now is set,
    Which you cannot appease;
Eternal justice doth you let
    From either life or ease.

24. Thus he that to this place doth come
    May groan, and sigh, and weep;
But sin hath made that place his home,
    And there it will him keep.

25. Wherefore hell in another place
    Is call'd a prison too,
And all to show the evil case
    Of all sin doth undo,

26. Which prison, with its locks and bars
    Of God's lasting decree,
Will hold them fast; oh how this mars
    All thought of being free!

27. Out at these brazen bars they may
    The saints in glory see;
But this will not their grief allay,
    But to them torment be.

28. Thus they in this infernal cave
    Will now be holden fast
From heavenly freedom, though they crave,
    Of it they may not taste.

29. The chains that darkness on them hangs
    Still ratt'ling in their ears,
Create within them heavy pangs,
    And still augment their fears.

30. Thus hopeless of all remedy,
    They dyingly do sink
Into the jaws of misery,
    And seas of sorrow drink.

31. For being cop'd on every side
    With helplessness and grief,
Headlong into despair they slide
    Bereft of all relief.

32. Therefore this *Hell* is called a pit,
    Prepared for those that die
The second death, a term most fit
    To show their misery.

33. A pit that's bottomless is this,
    A gulf of grief and woe,
A dungeon which they cannot miss,
    That will themselves undo.

34. Thus without stay they always sink,
    Thus fainting still they fail,
Despair they up like water drink,
    These prisoners have no bail.

35. Here meets them now that worm that gnaws,
    And plucks their bowels out,
The pit too on them shuts her jaws;
    This dreadful is, no doubt.

36. This ghastly worm is guilt for sin,
    Which on the conscience feeds,
With vipers' teeth, both sharp and keen,
    Whereat it sorely bleeds.

37. This worm is fed by memory,
    Which strictly brings to mind
All things done in prosperity,
    As we in Scripture find.

38. No word, nor thought, nor act they did,
    But now is set in sight,
Not one of them can now be hid,
    Memory gives them light.

39. On which the understanding still
    Will judge, and sentence pass;
This kills the mind, and wounds the will,
    Alas, alas, alas!

40. Oh! conscience is the slaughter-shop,
    There hangs the axe and knife,
'Tis there the worm makes all things hot,
    And wearies out the life.

41. Here then is execution done
    On body and on soul:
For conscience will be brib'd of none,
    But gives to all their dole.

42. This worm, 'tis said, shall never die,
    But in the belly be
Of all that in the flames shall lie,—
    Oh, dreadful sight to see!

43. This worm now needs must in them live,
    For sin will still be there,
And guilt, for God will not forgive,
    Nor Christ their burden bear;

44. But take from them all help and stay,
    And leave them to despair,
Which feeds upon them night and day,—
    This is the damned's share.

45. Now will confusion so possess
    These monuments of ire,
And so confound them with distress.
    And trouble their desire.

46. That what to think, or what to do,
    Or where to lay their head,
They know not; 'tis the damned's woe
    To live and yet be dead.

47. These cast-aways would fain have life,
    But no, they never shall;
They would forget their dreadful plight,
    But that sticks fast'st of all.

48. God, Christ, and heaven, they know are best,
    Yet dare not on them think;
The saints they know in joys do rest,
    While they their tears do drink.

49. They cry alas, but all in vain,
    They stick fast in the mire;
They would be rid of present pain,
    Yet set themselves on fire.

50. Darkness is their perplexity,
    Yet do they hate the light;
They always see their misery,
    Yet are themselves all night.

51. They are all dead, yet live they do,
    Yet neither live nor die;
They die to weal, and live to woe.
    This is their misery.

52. Amidst all this so great a scare
    That here I do relate,
Another falleth to their share
    In this their sad estate.

53. The legions of infernal fiends
    Then with them needs must be,
A just reward for all their pains,
    This they shall feel and see.

54. With yellings, howlings, shrieks, and cries,
    And other doleful noise,
With trembling hearts and failing eyes,
    These are their hellish joys.

55. These angels black they would obey,
    And serve with greedy mind,
And take delight to go astray,
    That pleasure they might find.

56. Which pleasure now like poison turns
    Their joy to heaviness;
Yea, like the gall of asps it burns,
    And doth them sore oppress.

57. Now is the joy they lived in
    All turned to brinish tears,
And resolute attempts to sin
    Turn'd into hellish fears.

58. The floods run trickling down their face,
    Their hearts do prick and ache;
While they lament their woful case,
    Their loins totter and shake.

59. O wetted cheeks, with bleared eyes,
    How fully do you show
The pang that in their bosom lies
    And grief they undergo!

60. Their dolour in their bitterness
    So greatly they bemoan,
That hell itself this to express
    Doth echo with their groan.

61. Thus broiling on the burning grates,
    They now to wailing go,
And say of those unhappy fates
    That did them thus undo,

62. Alas, my grief! hard hap had I
    Those dolours here to find,
A living death, in hell I lie,
    Involv'd with grief of mind.

63. I once was fair for light and grace,
    My days were long and good;
I lived in a blessed place
    Where was most heav'nly food.

64. But wretch I am, I slighted life,
    I chose in death to live;
Oh! for these days now if I might
    Ten thousand worlds would give.

65. What time had I to pray and read,
    What time to hear the word!
What means to help me at my need,
    Did God to me afford!

66. Examples too of piety
    I every day did see,
But they abuse and slight did I,
    Oh! woe be unto me.

67. I now remember how my friend
    Reproved me of vice,
And bid me mind my latter end,
    Both once, and twice, and thrice.

68. But, oh! deluded man, I did
    My back upon him turn;
Eternal life I did not heed,
    For which I now do mourn.

69. Ah, golden time, I did thee spend
    In sin and idleness;
Ah, health and wealth, I did you lend
    To bring me to distress.

70. My feet to evil I let run,
    And tongue of folly talk;
My eyes to vanity hath gone,
    Thus did I vainly walk.

71. I did as greatly toil and strain
    Myself with sin to please,
As if that everlasting gain
    Could have been found in these.

72. But nothing, nothing have I found
    But weeping, and alas!
And sorrow, which doth now surround
    Me, and augment my cross.

73. Ah, bleeding conscience, how did I
    Thee check when thou didst tell
Me of my faults, for which I lie
    Dead while I live in hell.

74. I took thee for some peevish foe,
    When thou didst me accuse,
Therefore I did thee buffet so,
    And counsel did refuse.

75. Thou often didst me tidings bring,
    How God did me dislike,
Because I took delight in sin:
    But I thy news did slight.

76. Ah, *Mind*, why didst thou do those things
    That now do work my woe?
Ah, *Will*, why wast thou thus inclin'd
    Me ever to undo?

77. My *Senses*, how were you beguil'd
    When you said sin was good!
It hath in all parts me defil'd,
    And drown'd me like a flood.

78. Ah, that I now a being have,
    In sorrow and in pain;
Mother, would you had been my grave,
    But this I wish in vain.

79. Had I been made a cockatrice,
    A toad, or such-like thing;
Yea, had I been made snow or ice,
    Then had I had no sin;

80. A block, a stock, a stone, or clot,
    Is happier than I;
For they know neither cold nor hot,
    To live, nor yet to die.

81. I envy now the happiness
    Of those that are in light,
I hate the very name of bliss,
    'Cause I have there no right.

82. I grieve to see that others are
    In glory, life, and well,
Without all fear, or dread, or care,
    While I am wreck'd in hell.

83. Thus will these souls with watery eyes,
    And hacking of their teeth,
    With wringing hands, and fearful cries,
    Expostulate their grief.

84. O set their teeth they will, and gnash,
    And gnaw for very pain,
    While as with scorpions God doth lash
    Them for their life so vain.

85. Again, still as they in this muse,
    Are feeding on the fire,
    To mind there comes yet other news,
    To screw their torments higher.

86. Which is the length of this estate,
    Where they at present lie,
    Which in a word I thus relate,
    'Tis to eternity.

87. This thought now is so firmly fix'd
    In all that comes to mind,
    And also is so strongly mix'd
    With wrath of every kind;

88. So that whatever they do know,
    Or see, or think, or feel,
    For ever still doth strike them through
    As with a bar of steel.

89. For EVER shineth in the fire,
    EVER is on the chains;
    'Tis also in the pit of ire,
    And tastes in all their pains.

90. For ever separate from God,
    From peace, and life, and rest;
    For ever underneath the rod
    That vengeance liketh best.

91. O *ever, ever*, this will drown'd
    Them quite, and make them cry,
    We never shall get o'er thy bound,
    Oh, great eternity!

92. They sooner now the stars may count
    Than loose these dismal bands;
    Or see to what the motes amount,
    Or number up the sands,

93. Than see an end of this their woe,
    Which now for sin they have:
    O wantons, take heed what ye do,
    Sin will you never save.

94. They sooner may drink up the sea,
    Than shake off these their fears;
    Or make another in one day
    As big with brinish tears,

95. Than put an end to misery,
    In which they now do roar,
    Or help themselves; no, they must cry,
    Alas, for evermore.

96. When years by thousands on a heap
    Are passed o'er their head;
    Yet still the fruits of sin they reap
    Among the ghostly dead.

97. Yea, when they have time out of mind
    Been in this case so ill,
    For *ever, ever* is behind *
    Yet for them to fulfil.

* How does this remind us of the awfully impressive cries
of the man in the iron cage—" O, eternity, eternity ! how
shall I grapple with the misery that I must meet with in
eternity !" " A thousand deaths live in him, he not dead."
— *Offor.*

Mount Gerizim and the Vale of Nablous.

EBAL AND GERIZIM;

OR,

THE BLESSING AND THE CURSE:

BEING A SHORT EXHORTATION TO SINNERS, BY THE MERCY AND SEVERITY OF GOD.

PREFATORY NOTE.

ACCORDING to the first line of the following poem, the author intended it to form a species of supplement to that on the *One Thing Needful*. It is full of solemn thoughts, often expressed, though not poetically, with admirable vigour. If we may judge from the kind of verse employed, and the general style of the language, Bunyan aimed at a somewhat higher class of readers when he wrote this poem, than those whom he hoped to instruct by the preceding "Meditations." The long heroic line was itself a bold experiment for a writer so little acquainted, as he is said to have been, with poetry as an art. On comparing, however, some of his couplets with those of his great contemporary, Dryden, we find that he could not have depended for his versification on a wholly untaught ear. To readers who are acquainted only with the writers of heroic verse since the reign of Queen Anne, Bunyan's lines must often appear painfully rugged; but to those who are familiar with the looser and more varied construction of this measure, as employed by earlier poets, there will be no great difficulty in extracting music from our author's versification. It would be unfair to judge him by any modern standard: when estimated according to that of his own times, his rough, heavy lines appear little inferior to much that was then accounted very tolerable poetry. To this consideration, we may add, that he skilfully compressed into the following verses the substance of the most powerful arguments to faith and holiness, and that frequently the nobler and clearer the truth, the better the versification.

The little poem, entitled *A Caution to stir up to watch against Sin*, reads like a good imitation of George Herbert. It would scarcely be to Bunyan's credit to suppose that he was not a student of that admirable writer, accessible as his poems were to the humblest class of readers.

H. S.

EBAL AND GERIZIM.

FROM MOUNT GERIZIM.

BESIDES what I said of the *Four Last Things*,
And of the weal and woe that from them springs;
An after-word still runneth in my mind,
Which I shall here expose unto that wind
That may it blow into that very hand
That needs it. Also that it may be scann'd
With greatest soberness, shall be my prayer,
As well as diligence and godly care;
So to present it unto public view,
That only truth and peace may thence ensue.
  My talk shall be of that amazing love
Of God we read of; which, that it may prove,
By its engaging arguments to save
Thee, I shall lay out that poor help I have

Thee to entice; that thou wouldst dearly fall
In love with thy salvation, and with all
That doth thereto concur, that thou mayst be
As blessed as the Blessed can make thee,
Not only here but in the world to come,
In bliss, which, I pray God, may be thy home.
  But first, I would advise thee to bethink
Thyself, how sin hath laid thee at the brink
Of hell, where thou art lulled fast asleep
In Satan's arms, who also will thee keep
As senseless and secure as e'er he may,
Lest thou shouldst wake, and see't, and run away
Unto that Jesus, whom the Father sent
Into the world, for this cause and intent,
That such as thou from such a thrall as this
Might'st be released, and made heir of bliss.

E E 2

Now that thou may'st awake, the danger fly,
And so escape the death that others die,
Come, let me set my trumpet to thine ear,
Be willing all my message for to hear :
'Tis for thy life, O do it not refuse;
Wo unto them good counsel do abuse.
Thou art at present in that very case,
Which argues thou art destitute of grace :
For he that lies where sin hath laid him, lies
Under the curse, graceless, and so he dies
In body and in soul, within that range,
If God his heart in mercy doth not change
Before he goes the way of all the earth,
Before he lose his spirit and his breath.
Repentance there is none within the grave,
Nor Christ, nor grace, nor mercies for to save
Thee from the vengeance due unto thy sin,
If now thou dost not truly close with him.

Thou art like him that sleepeth in the sea
On broken boards, which, without guide or stay,
Are driven whither winds and water will;
While greedy beasts do wait to have their fill
By feeding on his carcass, when he shall
Turn overboard, and without mercy fall
Into the jaws of such as make a prey
Of those whom justice drowneth in the sea.

Thou art like him that snoring still doth lie
Upon the bed of vain security,
Whilst all about him into burning flame
By fire is turned; yea, and while the frame
Aud building where he lies consuming is,
And while himself these burnings cannot miss.

Thou art like one that hangeth by a thread
Over the mouth of hell, as one half-dead;
And oh, how soon this thread may broken be
Or cut by death, is yet unknown to thee !
But sure it is, if all the weight of sin,
And all that Satan too hath doing been,
Or yet can do, can break this crazy thread,
'Twill not be long before, among the dead,
Thou tumble do, as linked fast in chains,
With them to wait in fear for future pains.

What shall I say ?   Wilt thou not yet awake ?
Nor yet of thy poor soul some pity take ?
Among the lions it hood-winked lies ;
Oh, that the Lord would open once thine eyes
That thou might'st see it, then I dare say thou,
As half-bereft of wits, wouldst cry out, how
Shall I escape ?   Lord help, oh ! help with speed,
Reach down thy hand from heav'n, for help I need,
To save me from the lions, for I fear
This soul of mine they will in pieces tear.

Come, then, and let us both expostulate
The case betwixt us, till we animate
And kindle in our hearts that burning love
To Christ, to grace, to life, that we may move
Swifter than eagles to this blessed prey,
Then shall it be well with us in that day
The trump shall sound, the dead made rise, and stand,
Then to receive, for breach of God's command,
Such thunder-claps as these, *Depart from me
Into hell-fire, you that the wicked be,*

Prepared for the devil, and for those
That with him and his angels rather chose
To live in filthy sin and wickedness,
Whose fruit is everlasting bitterness.

We both are yet on this side of the grave,
We also gospel-privileges have ;
The Word, and time to pray ; God give us hearts,
That, like the wise man, we may act our parts,
To get the pearl of price ; then we shall be
Like godly Mary, Peter, Paul, and we
Like Jacob, too, the blessing shall obtain ;
While Esau rides a-hunting for the gain
Of worldly pelf, which will him not avail
When death or judgment shall him sore assail.

Now, to encourage us for to begin,
Let us believe the kingdom we may win,
And be possess'd thereof, if we the way
Shall hit into, and then let nothing stay
Or hinder us ; the crown is at the end,
Let's run and strive, and fly, and let's contend
With greatest courage it for to obtain ;
'Tis life, and peace, and everlasting gain.
The gate of life, the new and living way,
The promise holdeth open all the day,
Which thou by Jacob's ladder must ascend,
Where angels always wait, and do attend
As ministers, to minister for those
That do with God, and Christ, and glory close.

If guilt of sin still lieth at our door,
Us to discourage, let us set before
Our eyes a bleeding Jesus, who did die
The death, and let's believe the reason why
He did it, was that we might ever be
From death and sin, from hell and wrath set free.
Yea, let's remember for that very end
It was his blessed Father did him send ;
That he the law of God might here fulfil,
That so the mystery of his blessed will
Might be revealed in the blessedness
Of those that fly to Christ for righteousness.

Now let us argue with ourselves, then, thus
That Jesus Christ our Lord came to save us,
By bearing of our sins upon his back,
By hanging on the cross as on a rack,
While justice cut him off on every side,
While smiles divine themselves from him did hide,
While earth did quake, and rocks in pieces rent,
And while the sun, as veiled, did lament
To see the innocent and harmless die
So sore a death, so full of misery.

Yea, let us turn again, and say, All this
He did and suffered for love of his.
He brought in everlasting righteousness,
That he might cover all our nakedness ;
He wept and wash'd his face with brinish tears
That we might saved be from hellish fears :
Blood was his sweat, too, in his agony,
That we might live in joyful ecstasy ;
He apprehended was and led away,
That grace to us-ward never might decay.
With swords, and bills, and outrage in the night,
That to the peace of heav'n we might have right.

Condemn'd he was between two thieves to die,
That we might ever in his bosom lie ;
Scourged with whips his precious body were,
That we lashes of conscience might not fear ;
His head was crowned with thorns, that we might be
Crowned with glory and felicity ;
He hanged was upon a cursed tree
That we delivered from death might be :
His Father from him hides his smiles and face,
That we might have them in the heavenly place ;
He cried, *My God, why hast forsaken me?*
That we forsaken of him might not be.
Into his side was thrust a bloody spear,
That we the sting of death might never fear :
He went into the grave after all this,
That we might up to heav'n go, and have bliss.
Yea, rise again he did out of the earth,
And shook off from him all the chains of death,
Then at his chariot wheels he captive led
His foes, and trod upon the serpent's head ;
Riding in triumph to his Father's throne,
There to possess the kingdom as his own.
What say'st thou, wilt not yet unto him come ?
His arms are open, in his heart is room
To lay thee ; be not then discouraged,
Although thy sins be many, great, and red,
Unto thee righteousness he will impute,
And with the kisses of his mouth salute
Thy drooping soul, and will it so uphold,
As that thy shaking conscience shall be bold
To come to mercy's seat with great access,
There to expostulate with that justice
That burns like fiery flames against all those
That do not with this blessed Jesus close ;
Which unto thee will do no harm, but good,
Because thou hast reliance on that blood
That justice saith hath given him content,
For all that do unfeignedly repent
Their ill-spent life, and roll upon free grace,
That they within that bosom might have place,
That open is to such, where they shall lie
In ease, and gladness, and felicity,
World without end, according to that state
I have, nay, better than I, can relate.
  If thou shalt still object, thou yet art vile,
And hast a heart that will not reconcile
Unto the holy law, but will rebel,
Hark yet to what I shall thee farther tell.
Two things are yet behind that help thee will,
If God should put into thy mind that skill,
So to improve them as becometh those
That would with mercy and forgiveness close.
  First, then, let this sink down into thy heart,
That Christ is not a Saviour in part,
But every way so fully he is made
That all of those that underneath his shade
And wing would sit, and shroud their weary soul,
That even Moses dare it not control,
But justify it, approve of it, and conclude
No man nor angel must himself intrude
With such doctrine that may oppose the same,
On pain of blaspheming that holy name,

Which God himself hath given unto men,
To stay, to trust, to lean themselves on, when
They feel themselves assaulted, and made fear
Their sin will not let them in life appear.
  For as God made him perfect righteousness,
That he his love might to the height express,
And us present complete before the throne ;
Sanctification, too, of his own
He hath prepared, in which do we stand,
Complete in holiness, at his right hand.
Now this sanctification is not
That holiness which is in us, but that
Which in the person of this Jesus is,
And can inherently be only his,
But is imputed to us for our good,
As is his active righteousness and blood ;
Which is the cause, though we infirm are found,
That mercy and forgiveness doth abound
To us-ward, and that why we are not shent
And empty, and away rebuked sent,
Because that all we do imperfect is.
Bless God, then, for this holiness of his,
And learn to look by faith on that alone,
When thou seest thou hast nothing of thy own ;
Yea, when thy heart most willing is to do
What God by his good word doth call thee to ;
And when thou find'st most holiness within,
And greatest power over every sin,
Yet then to Jesus look, and thou shalt see
In him sanctification for thee,
Far more complete than all that thou canst find
In the most upright heart and willing mind,
That ever men or angels did possess,
When most fill'd with inherent righteousness.
Besides, if thou forgettest here to live,
And Satan get thee once into his sieve,
He will so hide thy wheat, and show thy bran,
That thou wilt quickly cry, I am undone.
Alas, thy godliest attainments here,
Though like the fairest blossoms they appear,
How quickly will they lour and decay,
And be as if they all were fled away,
When once the east-wind of temptations beat
Upon thee, with their dry and blasting heat,
Rich men will not account their treasure lies
In crack'd groats and four-pence half-pennies,
But in those bags they have within their chests,
In staple goods, which shall within their breasts
Have place accordingly, because they see
Their substance lieth here.   But if that be
But shaken, then they quickly fear, and cry,
Alas ! 'tis not this small and odd money,
We carry in our pockets for to spend,
Will make us rich, or much will stand our friend ;
If famine or if want do us assail,
How quickly will these little pieces fail !
  If thou be wise, consider what I say,
And look for all in Christ. where no decay
Is like to be ; then though thy present frame
Be much in up-and-down, yet he the same
Abideth, yea, and still at God's right hand,
As thy most perfect holiness will stand.

It is, I say, not like to that in thee,
Now high, then low, now out, then in, but he
Most perfect is, when thou art at the worst,
The same, the very same, I said at first.
This helpeth much when thou art buffeted,
And when thy graces lie in thee as dead,
Then to believe they are all perfect still
In Christ thy head, who hath that blessed skill,
Yet to present thee by what is in him
Unto his Father, one that hath no sin.
Yea, this will fill thy mouth with argument
Against the tempter, when he shall present
Before thee all thy weakness, and shall hide
From thee thy graces, that thou mayst abide
Under the fretting fumes of unbelief,
Which never yielded Christian man relief.
Now help thyself thou mayst against him thus:
O Satan, though my heart indeed be worse
Than 'twas awhile ago, yet I perceive
Thou shalt me not of happiness bereave,
Nor yet of holiness; for by the Word
I find that Jesus Christ, our blessed Lord,
Is made sanctification for me
In his own person, where all graces be,
As water in the fountain; and that I,
By means of that, have yet a sanctity,
Both personal and perfect every way;
And that is Christ himself, as Paul doth say.
Now, though my crazy pitcher oft doth leak,
By means of which my graces are so weak,
And so much spent, that one I cannot find
Able to stay or help my feeble mind,
Yet then I look to Jesus, and see all
In him that wanting is in me, aud shall
Again take courage, and believe he will
Present me upright in his person, till
He humble me for all my foolishness,
And then again fill me with holiness.
Now, if thou lovest inward sanctity,
As all the saints do most unfeignedly,
Then add, to what I have already said,
Faith in the promise; and be not afraid
To urge it often at the throne of grace,
And to expect it in its time and place.
Then he that true is, and that cannot lie,
Will give it unto thee, that thou thereby,
Mayst serve with faith, with fear, in truth and love,
That God that did at first thy spirit move
To ask it to his praise, that he might be
Thy God, and that he might delight in thee.
  If I should here particulars relate,
Methinks it could not but much animate
Thy heart, though very listless to inquire
How thou mayst that enjoy, which all desire
That love themselves, and future happiness;
But oh! I cannot fully it express:
The promise is so open and so free,
In all respects, to those that humble be,
That want they cannot what for them is good;
But there 'tis, and confirmed is with blood,
A certain sign, all those enjoy it may,
That see they want it, and sincerely pray

To God the Father, in that Jesus' name
Who bled on purpose to confirm the same.
Now wouldst thou have a heart that tender is,
A heart that forward is to close with bliss;
A heart that will impressions freely take
Of the new covenant, and that will make
The best improvement of the word of grace,
And that to wickedness will not give place;
All this is in the promise, and it may
Obtained be of them that humbly pray.
Wouldst thou enjoy that spirit that is free,
And looseth those that in their spirits be
Oppress'd with guilt, or filth, or unbelief;
That spirit that will, where it dwells, be chief;
Which breaketh Samson's cord as rotten thread,
And raiseth up the spirit that is dead;
That sets the will at liberty to choose
Those things that God hath promised to infuse
Into the humble heart?   All this, I say,
The promise holdeth out to them that pray.
Wouldst thou have that good, that blessed mind,
That is so much to heavenly things inclined
That it aloft will soar and always be
Contemplating on blest eternity,—
That mind that never thinks itself at rest
But when it knows it is for ever blest;
That mind that can be here no more content,
Than he that in the prison doth lament;
That blessed mind that counts itself then free,
When it can on the throne with Jesus be,
There to behold the mansions he prepares
For such as be with him and his co-heirs.
This mind is in the covenant of grace,
And shall be theirs that truly seek his face.
Is godly fear delightful unto thee,
That fear that God himself delights to see
Bear sway in them that love him? then he will
Thy godly mind in this request fulfil.
By giving thee a fear that tremble shall,
At every trip thou takest, lest thou fall,
And him offend, or hurt thyself by sin,
Or cause poor souls that always blind have been
To stumble at thy falls, and harder be
Against their own salvation and thee.
  That fear that of itself would rather choose
The rod, than to offend or to abuse
In anything that blessed worthy name,
That hath thee saved from that death and shame;
That sin would soon have brought thee to, if he
Had not imputed righteousness to thee.
I will love them, saith God, and not depart
From them, but put my fear within their heart,
That I to them may always lovely be,
And that they never may depart from me.
Wouldst thou be very upright and sincere?
Wouldst thou be that within thou dost appear,
Or seem to be in outward exercise
Before the most devout, godly, and wise?
Yea, art thou thus when no eye doth thee see
But that which is invisible? and be
The words of God in truth thy prop and stay?
And do they in thy conscience bear more sway

To govern thee in faith and holiness,
Than thou canst with thy heart and mouth ex-
    press?
And do the things that truly are divine,
Before thee more than gold and rubies shine?
And if, as unto Solomon, God should
Propound to thee, *What wouldst thou have?* how
    would
Thy heart and pulse beat after heav'nly things,
After the upper and the nether springs?

    Couldst, with unfeigned heart and upright lip,
Cry, Hold me fast, Lord, never let me slip,
Nor step aside from faith and holiness,
Nor from the blessed hope of future bliss?
Lord, rather cross me anywhere than here;
Lord, fill me always with thy holy fear,
And godly jealousy of mine own heart,
Lest I, Lord, should at any time depart
From thy most blessed covenant of grace,
Where Jesus rules as King, and where thy face,
Is only to be seen with comfort, and
Where sinners justified before thee stand.

    If these thy groanings be sincere and true,
If God doth count thee one that dost pursue
The things thou cryest after with thy heart,
No doubt but in them thou shalt have a part.
The next word that I would unto thee say,
Is how thou mayst attain, without delay,
Those blessed graces, and that holiness
Thou dost with so much godly zeal express
Thy love to, and thy longing to enjoy,
That sins and weakness might thee less annoy.
Know then, as I have hinted heretofore,
And shall now speak unto a little more,
All graces in the person of the Son
Are by the Father hid, and therefore none
Can them obtain but they who with him close;
All others graceless are but only those;
For of his fulness 'tis that we receive,
And grace for grace. Let no man then deceive
Himself or others with a feigned show
Of holiness, if Jesus they eschew.
When he ascended to his Father, then
It was that he received gifts for men;
Faith, hope, and love, true zeal, an upright heart,
Right humbleness of mind, and every part
Of what the word of life counts holiness,
God then laid up in him, that we redress
And help might have, who do unto him fly
For righteousness and gospel sanctity.
Now, if thou wouldst inherit righteousness,
And so sanctification possess
In body, soul, and spirit, then thou must
To Jesus fly, as one ungodly first;
And so by him crave pardon for thy sin
Which thou hast loved, and hast lived in;
For this cannot all forgiven be,
For any righteousness that is in thee;
Because the best thou hast is filthy rags,
Profane, presumptuous, and most beastly brags
Of flesh and blood, which always cross doth lie
To God, to grace, and thy felicity.

    Then righteousness imputed thou must have,
Thee from that guilt and punishment to save
Thou liest under as a sinful man,
Throughout polluted, and that never can
By any other means acquitted be,
Or ever have true holiness in thee.
The reason is, because all graces are
Only in Christ, and be infused where,
Or into those whom he doth justify,
By what himself hath done, that he thereby
Might be the whole of all that happiness
The sinner shall enjoy here, and in bliss.
Besides, if holiness should first be found
In those whom God doth pardon, then the ground
Why we forgiven are would seem to be,
He first found holiness in thee and me;
But this the holy Scriptures will refute,
And prove that righteousness he doth impute
Without respect to goodness first in man;
For, to speak truth indeed, no goodness can
Be found in those that underneath the law
Do stand; for if God goodness in them saw,
Why doth he once and twice say, *There is none
That righteous be; no, not so much as one:*
None understandeth, none seek after God,
His ways they have not known, but have abode
In wickedness, unprofitably they
Must needs appear to be then every way.
Their throats an open sepulchre, also
Their mouths are full of filthy cursings too;
And bitterness, yea, underneath their lips
The asp hath poison. Oh, how many slips
And falls in sin must such poor people have!
Now where's the holiness that should them save,
Or, as a preparation, go before,
To move God to do for them less or more?
No, grace must on thee righteousness bestow,
Or else sin will for ever thee undo.
Sweet Paul this doctrine also doth express,
Where he saith, *Some may have righteousness,
Though works they have not;* and it thus may stand,
Grace by the promise gives what the command
Requireth us to, and so are we
Quitted from doing, and by grace made free.
Now, then, if holiness thou wouldst obtain,
And wouldst a tender Christian man remain,
Keep faith in action, let that righteousness
That Christ fulfilled always have express
And clear distinction in thy heart, from all
That men by Scripture, or besides it, call
Inherent gospel holiness, or what
Terms else they please to give it: for 'tis that,
And that alone, by which all graces come
Into the heart; for else there is no room
For aught but pride, presumption, or despair,
No love or other graces can be there.
*Received you the Spirit, saith St. Paul,
By hearing, faith, or works? not works, and shall
No ways retain the same, except you do
Hear faith, embrace the same, and stick thereto.*
The word of faith unto me pardon brings,
Shows me the ground and reason whence it springs;

To wit, free grace, which moved God to give
His Son to die and bleed, that I might live.
This word doth also loudly preach to me,
Though I a miserable sinner be,
Yet in this Son of God I stand complete,
Whose righteousness is without all deceit;
'Tis that which God himself delighteth in,
And that by which all his have saved been.
When I do this begin to apprehend,
My heart, my soul, and mind, begins to bend
To God-ward, and sincerely for to love
His Son, his ways, his people, and to move
With brokenness of spirit after him
Who broken was, and killed for my sin.
Now is mine heart grown holy, now it cleaves
To Jesus Christ my Lord, and now it leaves
Those ways that wicked be; it mourns because
It can conform no more unto the laws
Of God, who loved me when I was vile,
And of sweet Jesus, who did reconcile
Me unto justice by his precious blood,
When no way else was left to do me good.
If you would know how this can operate
Thus on the soul, I shall to you relate
A little farther what my soul hath seen
Since I have with the Lord acquainted been.
The word of grace, when it doth rightly seize
The spirit of a man, and so at ease
Doth set the soul, the Spirit of the Lord
Doth then with might accompany the word;
In which it sets forth Christ as crucified,
And by that means the Father pacified
With such a wretch as thou, and by this sight,
Thy guilt is in the first place put to flight,
For thus the Spirit doth expostulate:
Behold how God doth now communicate
(By changing of the person) grace to thee
A sinner, but to Christ great misery,
Though he the just one was, and so could not
Deserve this punishment: behold, then, what
The love of God is! how 'tis manifest,
And where the reason lies that thou art blest.
This doctrine being spoken to the heart,
Which also is made yield to every part
Thereof, it doth the same with sweetness fill,
And so doth sins and wickednesses kill;
For when the love of God is thus reveal'd,
And thy poor drooping spirit thereby seal'd,
And when thy heart as dry ground drinks this in
Unto the roots thereof, which nourish sin,
It smites them, as the worm did Jonah's gourd,
And makes them dwindle of their own accord,
And die away; instead of which there springs
Up life and love, and other holy things.
Besides, the Holy Spirit now is come,
And takes possession of thee as its home;
By which a war maintained always is
Against the old man and the deeds of his.
　When God at first upon Mount Sinai spake,
He made his very servant Moses quake;
But when he heard the law the second time,
His heart was comforted, his face did shine.

What was the reason of this difference,
Seeing no change was in the ordinance,
Although a change was in the manner, when
The second time he gave it unto men?
At first 'twas given in severity,
In thunder, blackness, darkness, tempest high,
In fiery flames it was delivered.
This struck both Moses and the host as dead.
But Moses, when he went into the mount
The second time, upon the same account,
No fear, nor dread, nor shaking of his mind,
Do we in all the holy Scripture find;
But rather in his spirit he had rest,
And look'd upon himself as greatly blest.
He was put in the rock, he heard the name,
Which on the mount the Lord doth thus proclaim:
The Lord, merciful, gracious, and more,
Long-suffering, and keeping up in store
Mercy for thousands, pardoning these things,
Iniquity, transgressions, and sins,
And holding guilty none but such as still
Refuse forgiveness, of rebellious will.
　This proclamation better pleased him
Than all the thunder and the lightning
Which shook the mount, this rid him of his fear,
This made him bend, make haste, and worship there.
　Jehoshaphat, when he was sore opprest
By Amnon and by Moab, and the rest
Of them that sought his life, no rest he found,
Until a word of faith became a ground
To stay himself upon; oh, then they fell,
His very song became their passing-bell.
Then holiness of heart a consequence
Of faith in Christ is, for it flows from thence;
The love of Christ in truth constraineth us,
Of love sincerely to make judgment thus:
He for us died that for ever we
Might die to sin, and Christ's own servants be.
Oh! nothing's like to the remembrance
Of what it is to have deliverance
From death and hell, which is of due our right,—
Nothing's, I say, like this to work delight
In holy things; this like live honey runs,
And needs no pressing out of honeycombs.
Then understand my meaning by my words,
How sense of mercy unto faith affords
Both grace to sanctify, and holy make
That soul that of forgiveness doth partake.
Thus having briefly showed you what is　.
The way of life, of sanctity, of bliss,
I would not in conclusion have you think,
By what I say, that Christian men should drink
In these my words with lightness, or that they
Are now exempted from what every day
Their duty is.　No, God doth still expect,
Yea, doth command, that they do not neglect
To pray, to read, to hear, and not dissent
From being sober, grave, and diligent
In watching, self-denial, and with fear
To serve him all the time thou livest here.
Indeed I have endeavoured to lay
Before your eyes the right and only way

Pardon to get, and also holiness,
Without which never think that God will bless
Thee with the kingdom he will give to those
That Christ embrace, and holy lives do choose
To live, while here all others go astray,
And shall in time to come be cast away

FROM MOUNT EBAL.

Thus having heard from Gerizim, I shall
Next come to Ebal, and you thither call,
Not there to curse you, but to let you hear
How God doth curse that soul that shall appear
An unbelieving man, a graceless wretch;
Because he doth continue in the breach
Of Moses' law, and also doth neglect
To close with Jesus; him will God reject
And cast behind him; for of right his due
Is that from whence all miseries ensue.
Cursed, saith he, are they that do transgress
The least of my commandments, more or less.
Nothing that written is must broken be,
But always must be kept unto by thee,
And must fulfilled be; for here no man
Can look God in the face, or ever stand
Before the judgment-seat; for if he be
Convict, condemned too assuredly.
Now keep this law no mortal creature can,
For they already do as guilty stand
Before the God that gave it; so that they
Obnoxious to the curse lie every day,
Which also they must feel for certainty,
If unto Jesus Christ they do not fly.
Hence, then, as they for ever shall be blest,
That do by faith upon the promise rest,
So peace unto the wicked there is none;
'Tis wrath and death that they must feed upon.
 That what I say may some impression make
On carnal hearts, that they in time may take
That course that best will prove when time is done,
These lines I add to what I have begun.
 First, thou must know that God, as he is love
So he is justice, therefore cannot move,
Or in the least be brought to favour those
His holiness and justice doth oppose.
 For though thou mayst imagine in thy heart
That God is this or that, yet if thou art
At all besides the truth of what He is,
And so doth build thy hope of life amiss,
Still he the same abideth, and will be
The same, the same for ever unto thee.
 As God is true unto his promise, so
Unto his threat'ning he is faithful too.
Cease to be God he must, if he should break
One tittle that his blessed mouth did speak.
 Now, then, none can be saved but the men
With whom the Godhead is contented when
It them beholds with the severest eye
Of justice, holiness, and yet can spy
No fault nor blemish in them; these be they
That must be saved, as the Scriptures say.

If this be true, as 'tis assuredly,
Woe be to them that wicked live and die;
Those that as far from holiness have been
All their life long as if no eye had seen
Their doings here, or as if God did not
At all regard, or in the least mind what,
Wherein, or how they did his law transgress,
Either by this or other wickedness;
But how deceived these poor creatures are,
They then shall know when they their burthen bear.
 Alas, our God is a consuming fire;
So is his law, by which he doth require
That thou submit to him, and if thou be
Not in that justice found that can save thee
From all and every sentence which he spake
Upon Mount Sinai, then as one that brake
It, thou the flames thereof shalt quickly find
As scourges thee to lash, while sins do bind
Thee hand and foot, thee ever to endure
The strokes of vengeance for thy life impure.
 What I have said will yet evinced be,
And manifest abundantly to thee,
If what I have already spoken to
Be joined with these lines that do ensue.
Justice discovers its antipathy
Against profaneness and malignity.
Not only by the law it gave to men
And threatenings thereunto annexed then,
But inasmuch as long before that day,
He did prepare for such as go astray,
That dreadful, that so much amazing place,
Hell, with its torments, for those men that grace
And holiness of life slight and disdain,
There to bemoan themselves with hellish pain.
 his place, also, the pains so dismal be,
Both as to name and nature, that in me
It is not to express the damning wights,
The hellish torture, and the fearful plights
Thereof; for as intolerable they
Must needs be found, by those that disobey
The Lord, so can no word or thought express
Unto the full the height of that distress;
Such miserable caitiffs, that shall there
Rebukes of vengeance, for transgressions bear.
 Indeed the holy Scriptures do make use
Of many metaphors, that do conduce
Much to the symbolizing of the place,
Unto our apprehension; but the case,
The sad, the woful case, of those that lie
As wracked there in endless misery,
By all similitudes no mortals may
Set forth in its own nature; for I say
Similitudes are but a shade, and show
Of those or that they signify to you.
The fire that doth within thine oven burn,
The prison where poor people sit and mourn,
Chains, racks, and darkness, and such others, be
As painting on the wall, to let thee see
By word and figures the extremity
Of such as shall within these burnings lie.
 But certainly, if wickedness and sin
Had only foolish toys and trifles been,

And if God had not greatly hated it,
Yea, could he any ways thereof admit,
And let it pass, he would not thus have done.
He doth not use to punish any one
With any place or punishment that is
Above or sharper than the sin of his
Hath merited, and justice seeth due.
Read sin, then, by the death that doth ensue.
Most men do judge of sin, not by the fruits
It bears and bringeth forth, but as it suits
Their carnal and deluded hearts, that be
With sensual pleasures eaten up; but he
That now so judgeth, shortly shall perceive
That God will judge thereof himself, and leave
Such men no longer to their carnal lusts,
To judge of wickedness, and of the just
And righteous punishment that doth of right
Belong thereto; and will, too, in despite
Of all their carnal reason, justify
Himself, in their eternal misery.
Then Hell will be no fancy, neither will
Men's sins be pleasant to them; but so ill
And bitter, yea, so bitter, that none can
Fully express the same, or ever stand
Under the burden it will on them lay,
When they from life and bliss are sent away.
When I have thought how often God doth speak
Of their destruction, who his law do break,
And when the nature of the punishment
I find so dreadful, and that God's intent,
Yea, resolution is, it to inflict
On every sinner that shall stand convict,
I have amazed been, yet to behold,
To see poor sinners yet with sin so bold,
That like the horse that to the battle runs,
Without all fear, and that no danger shuns,
Till down he falls. Oh, resolute attempts!
Oh, sad, amazing, damnable events!
The end of such proceedings needs must be,
From which, O Lord, save and deliver me.
But if thou think that God thy noble race
Will more respect, than into such a place
To put thee; hold, though thou his offspring be,
And art so lovely, yet sin hath made thee
Another kind of creature than when thou
Didst from his fingers drop, and therefore now
Thy first creation stands thee in no stead.
Thou hast transgressed, and in very deed
Set God against thee, who is infinite,
And that for certain never will forget
Thy sins, nor favour thee if thou shalt die
A graceless man : this is thy misery.

When angels sinned, though of higher race
Than thou, and also put in higher place,
Yet them he spared not, but cast them down
From heaven to hell; where also they lie bound
In everlasting chains, and no release
Shall ever have, but wrath, that shall increase
Upon them, to their everlasting woe.
As for the state they were exalted to,
That will by no means mitigate their fear,
But aggravate their hellish torment here.
For he that highest stands, if he shall fall,
His danger needs must be the great'st of all.
Now if God noble angels did not spare
Because they did transgress, will he forbear
Poor dust and ashes? Will he suffer them
To break his law, and sin, and not condemn
Them for so doing? Let not man deceive
Himself or others : they that do bereave
Themselves by sin of happiness, shall be
Cut off by justice, and have misery.
Witness his great severity upon
The world that first was planted, wherein none
But only eight the deluge did escape,
All others of that vengeance did partake.
The reason was, that world ungodly stood
Before him, therefore he did send the flood,
Which swept them all away. A just reward
For their most wicked ways against the Lord,
Who could no longer bear them and their
    ways,
Therefore into their bosom vengeance pays.
We read of Sodom, and Gomorrah too,
What judgments they for sin did undergo;
How God from heaven did fire upon them rain,
Because they would not wicked ways refrain;
Condemning of them with an overthrow,
And turned them to ashes. Who can know
The miseries that these poor people felt
While they did underneath those burnings
    melt?
Now these, and many more that I could name,
That have been made partakers of the flame
And sword of justice, God did then cut off,
And make examples unto all that scoff
At holiness, or do the gospel slight.
And long it will not be before the night
And judgment, painted out by what he did
To Sodom and Gomorrah, fulfilled
Upon such sinners be, that they may know
That God doth hate the sin, and persons too
Of such as still rebellious shall abide,
Although they now at judgment may deride.

A CAUTION TO STIR UP TO WATCH AGAINST SIN.

The first eight lines one did commend to me,
The rest I thought good to commend to thee :
Reader, in reading be thou ruled by me,
With rhymes nor lines, but truths, affected be.

I.

Sin will, at first, just like a beggar, crave
One penny, or one halfpenny to have;
But if you grant its first suit, 'twill aspire,
From pence to pounds, and still will mount up
    higher
To the whole soul : but if it makes its moan,
Then say, here is not for you, get you gone.
    For if you give it entrance at the door,
    It will come in, and may go out no more.

II.

Sin, rather than 'twill out of action be,
Will pray to stay, though a short space with thee,
One night, one hour, one moment, will it cry,
Embrace me in thy bosom or I die :
Time to repent, saith it, I will allow,
And help, if to repent thou know'st not how.
    But if you give it entrance at the door,
    It will come in, and may go out no more.

III.

If begging doth not do, Sin promise will
Rewards to those that shall its lusts fulfil :
Some pence in hand, yea pounds 'twill offer thee,
If at its motion, and its beck thou'lt be.
'Twill heaven seem to outbid, and all to gain
Thy love, and win thee it to entertain.
    But give it not admittance at thy door,
    Lest it comes in, and so goes out no more.

IV.

If promising and begging will not do,
'Twill by its wiles attempt to flatter you.
I'm harmless, mean no ill, be not so shy,
Will ev'ry soul-destroying motion cry.
Its sting 'twill hide, 'twill change its native hue,
Vile 'twill not, but a beauty seem to you.
    But if you give it entrance at the door,
    Its sting will in, and may come out no more.

V.

Rather than fail, Sin will itself divide,
Bid thee do this and lay the rest aside.
Take little ones, 'twill say, throw great ones by,
(As if for little sins men should not die.)
Yea, Sin with itself a quarrel will maintain,
On purpose that by it thou might'st be slain.
    Beware the cheat, then, keep it out of door ;
    It would come in, and would go out no more.

VI.

Sin, if you will believe it, will accuse,
What is not hurtful, and itself excuse :

'Twill make a vice of virtue, and 'twill say,
Good is destructive, doth men's souls betray ;
'Twill make a law, where God has made man free,
And break those laws by which men bounded be.
    Look to thyself, then, keep it out of door ;
    Thee 'twould entangle, and enlarge thy score.

VII.

Sin is that beastly thing that will defile
Soul, body, name, and fame in little while :
'Twill make him, who some time God's image was,
Look like the devil, love, and plead his cause ;
Like to the plague, poison, or leprosy.
Defile 'twill, and infect contagiously.
    Wherefore beware, against it shut the door ;
    If not, it will defile thee more and more.

VIII.

Sin, once possessed of the heart, will play
The tyrant, force its vassal to obey :
'Twill make thee thine own happiness oppose,
And offer open violence to those
That love thee best ; yea, make thee to defy
The law and counsel of the Deity.
    Beware then, keep this tyrant out of door,
    Lest thou be his, and so thy own no more.

IX.

Sin harden can thy heart against thy God,
Make thou abuse his grace, despise his rod ;
'Twill make you run upon the very pikes,
Judgments foreseen bring such to no dislikes
Of sinful hazards ; no, they venture shall
For one base lust, their soul, and heaven, and all.
    Take heed, then, hold it, crush it at the door ;
    It comes to rob thee, and to make thee poor.

X.

Sin is a prison, hath its bolts, its chains,
Brings into bondage who it entertains ;
Hangs shackles on them, bends them to its will,
Holds them, as Samson's grinding at the mill,
'Twill blind them, make them deaf ; yea, 'twill
    them gag,
And ride them, as the devil rides his hag.
    Wherefore look to it, keep it out of door.
    If once its slave, thou mayst be free no more.

XI.

Though Sin at first its rage dissemble may,
'Twill soon upon thee as a lion prey ;
'Twill roar, 'twill rend, 'twill tear, 'twill kill out-
    right,
Its living death will gnaw thee day and night.
Thy pleasures now to paws and teeth it turns,
In thee its tickling lusts, like brimstone, burns.
    Wherefore beware and keep it out of door,
    Lest it should on thee as a lion roar.

XII.

Sin will accuse, will stare thee in the face,
Will for its witness quote both time and place
Where thou it didst commit, and so appeal
To conscience, who thy facts dare not conceal,
But on thee as a judge such sentence pass,
As will to thy sweet meats prove bitter sauce.
 Wherefore beware against it, shut thy door,
 Repent what's past, believe, and sin no more.

XIII.

Sin is the living worm, the lasting fire,
Hell would soon lose its heat, could Sin expire;
Better sinless, in hell, than to be where
Heaven is, and to be found a sinner there.
One sinless with infernals might do well,
But Sin would make a very heav'n a hell.
 Look to thyself, then, to keep it out of door,
 Lest it gets in, and never leaves thee more.

XIV.

No match has Sin but God in all the world,
Men, angels, it has from their stations hurl'd:
Holds them in chains, as captives in despite,
Of all that here below is called might.

Release, help, freedom from it none can give,
But even he by whom we breathe and live.
 Watch, therefore, keep this giant out of door,
 Lest, if once in, thou get him out no more.

XV.

Fools make a mock at Sin, will not believe
It carries such a dagger in its sleeve;
How can it be, say they, that such a thing,
So full of sweetness, should e'er wear a sting:
They know not that it is the very spell
Of Sin, to make men laugh themselves to hell.
 Look to thyself, then, deal with Sin no more,
 Lest he that saves, against thee shuts the door.

XVI.

Now let the God that is above,
That hath for sinners so much love:
These lines so help thee to improve,
That he to him thy heart may move.
 Keep thee from outward enemies,
 Help the infernal to despise,
 Deliver thee from them infernal,
 And bring thee safe to life eternal. Amen.

DIVINE EMBLEMS;

OR,

TEMPORAL THINGS SPIRITUALIZED:

FITTED FOR THE USE OF BOYS AND GIRLS.

PREFATORY NOTE.

A BOOK entitled *Meditations on Seventy-four Things* is named in the catalogue of Bunyan's works given by *The Struggler*. This is said to be identical with the volume first published in 1688, as *Country Rhymes for Children upon Seventy-four Things*, or as *A Book for Boys and Girls; or, Country Rhymes for Children*. At length it became known as *Divine Emblems; or, Temporal Things Spiritualized*. It may be fairly questioned whether the following poems be really identical with the *Meditations on Seventy-four Things*. A great effort of ingenuity is required to force the *Book for Boys and Girls* into a shape corresponding with *Meditations on Seventy-four Things*. Even if that number of topics be made out, it must appear very doubtful whether the author intended them to be so arranged or divided. There is no mark to guide us to the exact seventy-four things designed by the title. It is, therefore, very probable that the original *Meditations* were only in part reprinted, and that they became incorporated with the book of *Emblems*, which changed its title according to the notions of the publisher. As in all works of this kind, both the pleasure and the profit will be measured to the reader according to his own temper. A very little pride of intellect will shut the heart against all the humble but faithful teaching of the following verses. The mind which is more disposed to look for traces of heavenly wisdom than for signs of misapprehension or bad taste, in a work like this, will have its reward. Much may be learnt from the emblems selected by the author. Rustic as they are, they tell truths as valuable as they are plain. The anxious, honest self-instructor will ask his conscience, " Did I ever think of them before ?"

H. S.

TO THE READER.

COURTEOUS READER,
THE title-page will show, if thou wilt look,
Who are the proper subjects of this book,
They 're boys and girls, of all sorts and degrees,
From those of age to children on the knees,
Thus comprehensive am I in my notions,
They tempt me to it by their childish motions.
We now have boys with beards, and girls that be
Huge as old women, wanting gravity.
Then do not blame me, since I thus describe 'em,
Flatter I may not, lest thereby I bribe them
To have a better judgment of themselves,
Than wise men have of babies on the shelves.
Their antic tricks, fantastic modes, and way,
Show they like very boys and girls do play
With all the frantic fooleries of the age,
And that in open view, as on a stage ;
Our bearded men do act like beardless boys,
Our women please themselves with childish toys.

Our ministers long time, by word and pen,
Dealt with them, counting them not boys but men :
They shot their thunders at them, and their toys,
But hit them not, 'cause they were girls and boys.
The better charg'd, the wider still they shot,
Or else so high, these dwarfs they touched not.
Instead of men, they found them girls and boys,
To nought addicted but to childish toys,
Wherefore, dear reader, that I save them may,
I now with them the very dotterel play.
And since at gravity they make a tush,
My very beard I cast behind a bush.
And, like a fool, stand fingering of their toys,
And all to show they are but girls and boys.

  Nor do I blush, although I think some may
Call me a child, because I with them play :
I aim to show them how each single fangle
On which they dote does but their souls entangle,

As with a web, a trap, a gin, a snare;
And will destroy them, have they not a care.
　Paul seem'd to play the fool, that he might gain
Those that were fools indeed, if not in grain;
He did it by such things to let them see
Their emptiness, their sin, and vanity:
A noble act, and full of honesty!
　Nor he, nor I, would like them be in vice,
But by their playthings I would them entice,
That they might raise their thoughts from childish
　　　toys,
To heaven, for that's prepared for girls and boys.
Nor would I so confine myself to these,
As to shun graver things, but seek to please
Those more composed with better things than toys,
Tho' I would thus be catching girls and boys.
　Wherefore if men inclined are to look,
Perhaps their graver fancies may be took
With what is here, tho' but in homely rhymes:
But he who pleases all must rise betimes.
Some, I persuade me, will be finding fault,
Concluding, here I trip, and there I halt:
No doubt some could those grovelling notions raise
By fine spun terms, that challenge might the bays.
Should all be forced their brains to lay aside
That cannot regulate the flowing tide;
By this or that man's fancy, we should have
The wise unto the fool become a slave,
What tho' my text seems mean, my morals be
Grave, as if fetch'd from a sublimer tree.

And if some better handle can a fly,
Than some a text, wherefore should we deny
Their making proof, or good experiment,
Of smallest things great mischiefs to prevent?
Wise Solomon did fools to pismires send,
To learn true wisdom, and their lives to mend.
Yea, God by swallows, cuckoos, and the ass,
Shows they are fools who let that season pass,
Which he put in their hand, that to obtain
Which is both present and eternal gain.
　I think the wiser sort my rhyme may slight,
While I peruse them, fools will take delight.
Then what care I? the foolish, God has chose;
And doth by foolish things their minds compose,
And settle upon that which is divine;
Great things by little ones are made to shine.
I could, were I so pleased, use higher strains;
And for applause on tenters stretch my brains.
But what needs that? the arrow, out of sight,
Does not the sleeper nor the watchman fright;
To shoot too high doth make but children gaze,
'Tis that which hits the man doth him amaze.
　As for the inconsiderableness
Of things by which I do my mind express:
May I by them bring some good things to pass,
As Samson with the jaw-bone of an ass;
Or as brave Shamgar, with his ox's goad
(Both things unmanly, not for war in mode),
I have my end, though I myself expose—
For God will have the glory at the close.
　　　　　　　　　　　　　　JOHN BUNYAN.

DIVINE EMBLEMS.

I.
UPON THE BARREN FIG-TREE IN GOD'S VINEYARD.

WHAT barren here! in this so good a soil?
The sight of this doth make God's heart recoil
From giving thee his blessing; barren tree,
Bear fruit, or else thine end will cursed be!
Art thou not planted by the water side?
Know'st not thy Lord by fruit is glorified?
The sentence is, Cut down the barren tree:
Bear fruit, or else thine end will cursed be!
Thou hast been digg'd about and dunged too,
Will neither patience nor yet dressing do?
The executioner is come, oh tree,
Bear fruit, or else thine end will cursed be!
He that about thy roots takes pains to dig,
Would, if on thee were found but one good fig,
Preserve thee from the axe: but barren tree,
Bear fruit, or else thy end will cursed be!
The utmost end of patience is at hand,
'Tis much if thou much longer here doth stand.
Oh, cumber-ground, thou art a barren tree;
Bear fruit, or else thy end will cursed be!

Thy standing nor thy name will help at all;
When fruitful trees are spared, thou must fall.
The axe is laid unto thy roots, oh tree!
Bear fruit, or else thy end will cursed be.

II.
UPON THE LARK AND THE FOWLER.

THOU simple bird, what makes thee here to play?
Look, there's the fowler, prythee come away.
Dost not behold the net? look, there 'tis spread;
Venture a little further, thou art dead.
Is there not room enough in all the field
For thee to play in, but thou needs must yield
To the deceitful glitt'ring of a glass,
Between nets placed to bring thy death to pass?
Bird, if thou art so much for dazzling light,
Look there's the sun above thee; dart upright:
Thy nature is to soar up to the sky,
Why wilt thou come down to the nets and die?
Heed not the fowler's tempting flattering call;
This whistle he enchanteth birds withal.
Or if thou seest a live bird in his net,
She's there, because from thence she cannot get

Look how he tempteth thee with his decoy;
That he may rob thee of thy life, thy joy.
Come, prythee, bird, I prythee come away,
Why shouldst thou to this net become a prey?
Hadst thou not wings, or were thy feathers pull'd,
Or wast thou blind, or fast asleep wer't lull'd,
The case would somewhat alter: but for thee
Thy eyes are ope, and thou hast wings to flee.
Remember that thy song is in thy rise,
Not in thy fall; earth's not thy paradise.
Keep up aloft then, let thy circuits be
Above, where birds from fowlers' nets are free.

COMPARISON.

This fowler is an emblem of the devil,
His nets and whistle, figures of all evil.
His glass an emblem is of sinful pleasure,
Decoying such who reckon sin a treasure.
This simple lark's a shadow of a saint,
Under allurings, ready now to faint.
What you have read, a needful warning is,
Design'd to show the soul its share and bliss,
And how it may this fowler's net escape,
And not commit upon itself this rape.

III.
UPON THE VINE-TREE.

WHAT is the vine, more than another tree?
Nay most, than it, more tall, more comely be.
What workman thence will take a beam or pin,
To make out which may be delighted in?
Its excellency in its fruit doth lie:
A fruitless vine it is not worth a fly.

COMPARISON.

What are professors more than other men?
Nothing at all. Nay, there's not one in ten,
Either for wealth, or wit, that may compare,
In many things, with some that carnal are.
Good then they are, when mortified their sin;
But without that, they are not worth a pin.

IV.
MEDITATIONS UPON AN EGG.

THE egg's no chick by falling from the hen;
Nor man a Christian till he's born again.
The egg's at first contained in the shell:
Men afore grace, in sins and darkness dwell.
The egg, when laid, by warmth is made a chicken,
And Christ by grace the dead in sin does quicken.
The chick at first is in the cell confined;
So heav'n-born souls are in the flesh detain'd.
The shell doth crack, the chick doth chirp and peep,
The flesh decays, and men then pray and weep.
The shell doth break, the chick's at liberty,
The flesh falls off, the soul mounts up on high.
But both do not enjoy the self-same plight;
The soul is safe, the chick now fears the kite.
But chicks from rotten eggs do not proceed;
Nor is a hypocrite a saint indeed.

The rotten egg, though underneath the hen,
If crack'd, stinks, and is loathsome unto men.
Nor doth her warmth make what is rotten sound;
What's rotten, rotten will at last be found.
The hypocrite, sin has him in possession,
He is a rotten egg under profession.
Some eggs bring cockatrices; and some men,
Some hatched and brooded in the viper's den.
Some eggs bring wild-fowls; and some men there be,
As wild as are the wildest fowls that flee.
Some eggs bring spiders; and some men appear
More venomed than the worst of spiders are.
Some eggs bring pismires; and some seem to me
As much for trifles as the pismires be.
And thus do divers eggs form diff'rent shapes,
As like some men as monkeys are like apes.
But this is but an egg, were it a chick,
Here had been legs, and wings, and bones to pick.

V.
OF FOWLS FLYING IN THE AIR.

METHINKS I see a sight most excellent,
All sorts of birds fly in the firmament:
Some great, some small, all of a divers kind,
Mine eye affecting, pleasant to my mind.
Look how they wing along the wholesome air,
Above the world of worldlings, and their care.
And as they divers are in bulk and hue,
So are they in their way of flying too.
So many birds, so many various things,
Swim in the element upon their wings.

COMPARISON.

These birds are emblems of those men, that shall
Ere long possess the heavens, their all in all.
They each are of a diff'rent shape and kind;
To teach, we of all nations there shall find.
They are some great, some little, as we see,
To show some great, some small in glory be.
Their flying diversely, as we behold,
Do show saints' joys will there be manifold.
Some glide, some mount, some flutter, and some do,
In a mixed way of flying, glory too,
To show that each shall to his full content,
Be happy in that heavenly firmament.

VI.
UPON THE LORD'S PRAYER.

OUR Father which in heaven art,
  Thy name be always hallowed;
Thy kingdom come, thy will be done;
  Thy heavenly path be followed:
By us on earth, as 'tis with thee,
  We humbly pray;
And let our bread us given be
  From day to day.
Forgive our debts, as we forgive
  Those that to us indebted are:
Into temptation lead us not;
  But save us from the wicked snare.

The kingdom's thine, the power too,
We thee adore;
The glory also shall be thine
For evermore.

VII.

MEDITATIONS UPON THE PEEP OF DAY.

At peep of day I often cannot know
Whether 'tis night, whether 'tis day or no.
I fancy that I see a little light,
But cannot yet distinguish day from night;
I hope, I doubt, but certain yet I be not,
I am not at a point, the sun I see not.
Thus such, who are but just of grace possess'd,
They know not yet if they be cursed or blest.

VIII.

UPON THE FLINT IN THE WATER.

This flint time out of mind has there abode,
Where crystal streams make their continual road,
Yet it abides a flint as much as 'twere,
Before it touch'd the water, or came there.
It's hardness is not in the least abated,
'Tis not at all by water penetrated;
Though water hath a soft'ning virtue in't,
It can't dissolve the stone, for 'tis a flint.
Yea, though in the water it doth still remain,
Its fiery nature still it does retain.
If you oppose it with its opposite,
Then in your very face its fire 'twill spit.

COMPARISON.

This flint an emblem is of those that lie,
Under the word like stones, until they die.
Its crystal streams have not their natures changed,
They are not from their lusts by grace estranged.

IX.

UPON THE FISH IN THE WATER.

The water is the fish's element;
Take her from thence, none can her death prevent:
And some have said, who have transgressors been,
As good not be, as to be kept from sin.
The water is the fish's element;
Leave her but there, and she is well content.
So's he who in the path of life doth plod,
Take all, says he, let me but have my God.
The water is the fish's element;
Her sportings there to her are excellent:
So is God's service unto holy men,
They are not in their element till then.

X.

UPON THE SWALLOW.

This pretty bird, oh! how she flies and sings!
But could she do so if she had not wings?
Her wings bespeak my faith, her songs my peace;
When I believe and sing, my doubtings cease.

XI.

UPON THE BEE.

The bee goes out, and honey home doth bring;
And some who seek that honey find a sting.
Now wouldst thou have the honey, and be free
From stinging; in the first place kill the bee.

COMPARISON.

This bee an emblem truly is of sin,
Whose sweet unto a many death has been.
Wouldst thou have sweet from sin, and yet not die,
Sin in the first place thou must mortify.

XII.

UPON A LOURING MORNING.

Well, with the day I see the clouds appear,
And mix the light with darkness everywhere;
This threatens those who on long journeys go,
That they shall meet with slabby rain or snow.
Else while I gaze, the sun doth with his beams
Belace the clouds, as 'twere with bloody streams;
Then suddenly those clouds do wat'ry grow,
And weep, and pour their tears out where they go.

COMPARISON.

Thus 'tis when gospel light doth usher in
To us, both sense of grace, and sense of sin;
Yea, when it makes sin red with Jesus' blood,
Then we can weep, till weeping does us good.

XIII.

UPON OVERMUCH NICENESS.

'Tis strange to see how over-nice are some
About their clothes, their bodies, and their home;
While what's of worth, they slightly pass it by,
Not doing it at all, or slovenly.
Their houses must well furnish'd be in print;
While their immortal soul has no good in't
Its outside also they must beautify,
While there is in't scarce common honesty.
Their bodies they must have trick'd up and trim:
Their inside full of filth up to the brim.
Upon their clothes there must not be a spot,
Whereas their lives are but one common blot.
How nice, how coy, are some about their diet,
That can their crying souls with hog's-meat quiet.
All must be dressed t' a hair, or else 'tis nought,
While of the living bread they have no thought.
Thus for their outside they are clean and nice,
While their poor inside stinks with sin and vice.

XIV.

MEDITATIONS UPON A CANDLE.

Man's like a candle in a candlestick,
Made up of tallow, and a little wick;
For what the candle is before 'tis lighted,
Just such be they who are in sin benighted.
Nor can a man his soul with grace inspire,
More than the candles set themselves fire.

Candles receive their light from what they are not:
Men grace from him, for whom at first they care
　　not.
We manage candles when they take the fire;
God men, when he with grace doth them inspire.
And biggest candles give the better light,
As grace on biggest sinners shines most bright,
The candle shines to make another see,
A saint unto his neighbour light should be.
The blinking candle we do much despise,
Saints dim of light are high in no man's eyes.
Again, though it may seem to some a riddle,
We use to light our candle at the middle:
True light doth at the candle's end appear,
And grace the heart first reaches by the ear.
But 'tis the wick the fire doth kindle on,
As 'tis the heart that grace first works upon;
Thus both do fasten upon what's the main,
And so their life and vigour do maintain.
The tallow makes the wick yield to the fire,
And sinful flesh doth make the soul desire
That grace may kindle on it, in it burn;
So evil makes the soul from evil turn.
But candles in the wind are apt to flare;
And Christians in a tempest, to despair.
We see the flame with smoke attended is;
And in our holy lives there's much amiss.
Sometimes a thief will candlelight annoy:
And lusts do seek our graces to destroy.
What brackish is will make a candle sputter;
'Twixt sin and grace there's oft a heavy clutter.
Sometimes the light burns dim, 'cause of the snuff,
And sometimes 'tis blown quite out with a puff;
But watchfulness preventeth both these evils,
Keeps candles light, and grace in spite of devils.
But let not snuffs nor puffs make us to doubt;
Our candles may be lighted, though puff'd out.
The candle in the night doth all excel,
Nor sun, nor moon, nor stars, then shine so well:
So is the Christian in our hemisphere,
Whose light shows others how their course to
　　steer.
When candles are put out, all's in confusion;
Where Christians are not, devils make intrusion.
They then are happy who such candles have,
All others dwell in darkness and the grave.
But candles that do blink within the socket,
And saints whose eyes are always in their pocket,
Are much alike; such candles make us fumble,
And at such saints good men and bad do stumble.
Good candles don't offend, except sore eyes,
Nor hurt, unless it be the silly flies:
Thus none like burning candles in the night,
Nor aught to holy living for delight.
But let us draw towards the candle's end:
The fire, you see, doth wick and tallow spend;
As grace man's life, until his glass is run,
And so the candle and the man is done.
The man now lays him down upon his bed;
The wick yield up its fire, and so is dead.
The candle now extinct is, but the man,
By grace mounts up to glory, there to stand.

XV.

UPON THE SACRAMENTS.

Two sacraments I do believe there be,
　　Baptism and the Supper of the Lord;
Both mysteries divine, which do to me,
　　By God's appointment, benefit afford:
But shall they be my God, or shall I have
　　Of them so foul and impious a thought,
To think that from the curse they can me save?
　　Bread, wine, nor water, me no ransom bought.

XVI.

UPON THE SUN'S REFLECTION UPON THE CLOUDS IN A FAIR MORNING.

Look yonder, ah! methinks mine eyes do see
Clouds edged with silver, as fine garments be!
They look as if they saw the golden face
That makes black clouds most beautiful with grace.
　　Unto the saints' sweet incense of their prayer
These smoky curled clouds I do compare.
For as these clouds seem edged or laced with gold,
Their prayers return with blessings manifold.

XVII.

UPON APPAREL.

God gave us clothes to hide our nakedness,
　　And we by them do it expose to view.
Our pride and unclean minds, to an excess,
　　By our apparel we to others show.

XVIII.

THE SINNER AND SPIDER.

Sinner.

What black, what ugly crawling thing art thou?

Spider.

I am a spider——

Sinner.

A spider, aye; truly a filthy creature.

Spider.

Not filthy as thyself in name or feature
My name entailed is to my creation;
My features, from the God of thy salvation.

Sinner.

I am a man, and in God's image made;
I have a soul shall neither die nor fade:
God has possessed me with human reason,
Speak not against me, lest thou speakest treason.
For if I am the image of my Maker,
Of slanders laid on me he is partaker.

Spider.

I know thou art a creature far above me,
Therefore I shun, I fear, and also love thee;

G G

But though thy God hath made thee such a
 creature,
Thou hast against him often played the traitor.
Thy sin has fetched thee down: leave off to boast;
Nature thou hast defiled, God's image lost,
Yea, thou thyself a very beast hath made,
And art become like grass, which soon doth fade.
Thy soul, thy reason, yea, thy spotless state,
Sin has subjected to th' most dreadful fate.
But I retain my primitive condition,
I've all but what I lost by thy ambition.

Sinner.

Thou venom'd thing, I know not what to call
 thee;
The dregs of nature surely did befall thee!
Thou wast composed o' th' dross and scum of all.
Men hate thee, and, in scorn, thee spider call.

Spider.

My venom's good for something, since God
 made it;
Thy nature sin hath spoil'd, and doth degrade it.
Thou art despoil'd of good; and though I fear
 thee,
I will not, though I might, despise and jeer
 thee.
Thou sayst I am the very dregs of nature;
Thy sin's the spawn of devils, 'tis no creature.
Thou sayst man hates me, 'cause I am a spider;
Poor man, thou at thy God art a derider.
My venom tendeth to my preservation;
Thy pleasing follies work out thy damnation.
Poor man, I keep the rules of my creation,
Thy sin hast cast thee headlong from thy station.
I hurt nobody willingly, but thou
Art a self-murderer : thou knowest not how
To do what's good; no, for thou lovest evil :
Thou fly'st God's law, adherest to the devil.

Sinner.

Thou ill-shaped thing, there's an antipathy
'Twixt man and spiders, 'tis in vain to lie.
Stand off, I hate thee ; if thou dost come nigh
 me
I'll crush thee with my foot ; I do defy thee.

Spider.

They are ill-shaped who warped are by sin,
Hatred in thee to God hath long time been ;
No marvel then, indeed, if me his creature
Thou dost defy, pretending name and feature.
But why stand off ? My presence shall not throng
 thee ;
'Tis not my venom, but thy sin doth wrong thee.
Come, I will teach thee wisdom, do but hear
 me,
I was made for thy profit, do not fear me.
But if thy God thou wilt not hearken to,
What can the swallow, ant, and spider do ?
Yet I will speak, I can but be rejected—
Sometimes great things by small means are effected.

Hark then, though man is noble by creation,
He's lapsed now to such degeneration
As not to grieve, so careless is he grown ;
Though he himself has sadly overthrown
And brought to bondage every earthly thing,
Ev'n from the very spider to the king :
This we poor sensitives do feel and see,
For subject to the curse you made us be.
Tread not upon me, neither from me go ;
'Tis man which has brought all the world to
 woe.
The law of my creation bids me teach thee ;
I will not for thy pride to God impeach thee.
I spin, I weave, and all to let thee see
Thy best performances but cobwebs be.
Thy glory now is brought to such an ebb,
It doth not much excel the spider's web.
My webs, becoming snares and traps for flies,
Do set the wiles of hell before thine eyes ;
Their tangling nature is to let thee see,
Thy sins, too, of a tangling nature be.
My den, or hole, for that 'tis bottomless,
Doth of damnation show the lastingness.
My lying quiet till the fly is catch'd,
Shows secretly hell hath thy ruin hatch'd.
In that I on her seize, when she is taken,
I show who gathers whom God hath forsaken.
The fly lies buzzing in my web to tell
How sinners always roar and howl in hell.
Now since I show thee all these mysteries,
How canst thou hate me, or me scandalize ?

Sinner.

Well, well ; I will no more be a derider,
I did not look for such things from a spider.

Spider.

Come, hold thy peace, what I have yet to say,
If heeded, may help thee another day.
Since I an ugly ven'mous creature be,
There's some resemblance 'twixt vile man and
 me.
My wild and heedless runnings are like those
Whose ways to ruin do their souls expose.
Daylight is not my time, I work i' th' night,
To show they are like me who hate the light.
The maid sweeps one web down, I make another,
To show how heedless ones convictions smother.
My web is no defence at all to me,
Nor will false hopes at judgment be to thee.

Sinner.

O, spider, I have heard thee, and do wonder,
A spider should thus lighten and thus thunder ?

Spider.

Do but hold still, and I will let thee see,·
Yet in my ways more mysteries there be,
Shall not I do thee good, if I thee tell,
I show to thee a four-fold way to hell.
For since I set my web in sundry places,
I show men go to hell in divers traces.

One I set in the window, that I might
Show some go down to hell with gospel-light.
One I set in a corner, as you see,
To show how some in secret snared be.
Gross webs, great store, I set in darksome places,
To show how many sin with brazen faces.
Another web I set aloft on high,
To show there's some professing men must die.
Thus in my ways, God wisdom doth conceal;
And by my ways that wisdom doth reveal.

I hide myself when I for flies do wait,
So doth the devil when he lays his bait;
If I do fear the losing of my prey,
I stir me, and more snares upon her lay.
This way, and that, her wings and legs I tie,
That sure as she is catch'd, so she must die;
But if I see she's like to get away,
Then with my venom I her journey stay.
All which, my ways, the devil imitates
To catch men, 'cause he their salvation hates.

Sinner.

O, spider, thou delight'st me with thy skill,
I prythee spit this venom at me still.

Spider.

I am a spider, yet I can possess
The palace of a king, where happiness
So much abounds.   Nor when I do go thither,
Do they ask what, or whence I come, or whither
I make my hasty travels; no, not they:
They let me pass, and I go on my way.
I seize the palace, do with hands take hold
Of doors, of locks, or bolts; yet I am bold,
When in, to clamber up unto the throne,
And to possess it, as if 'twere my own.
Nor is there any law forbidding me
Here to abide, or in this palace be.
At pleasure I ascend the highest stories,
And then I sit, and so behold the glories
Myself is compassed with, as if I were
One of the chiefest courtiers that be there.
Here lords and ladies do come round about me
With grave demeanour, nor do any flout me
For this, my brave adventure, no, not they;
They come, they go, but leave me there to stay.

Now, my reproacher, I do by all this
Show how thou mayst possess thyself of bliss:
Thou art worse than a spider, but take hold
On Christ the door, thou shalt not be controll'd:
By him do thou the heavenly palace enter;
None e'er will chide thee for thy brave adventure.
Approach thou then unto the very throne,
There speak thy mind; fear not; the day's thine own.
Nor saint, nor angel will thee stop or stay,
But rather tumble blocks out of the way.
My venom stops not me; let not thy vice
Stop thee: possess thyself of paradise.
Go on, I say, although thou be a sinner,
Learn to be bold in faith, of me a spinner.
This is the way true glories to possess,
And to enjoy what no man can express.

Sometimes I find the palace-door up-lock'd,
And so my entrance thither has up-block'd.
But am I daunted?   No, I here and there
Do feel, and search; and so if anywhere,
At any chink or crevice find my way,
I crowd, I press for passage, make no stay:
And so through difficulty I attain
The palace, yea, the throne where princes reign.
I crowd sometimes, as if I'd burst in sunder;
And art thou crush'd with striving, do not wonder.
Some scarce get in, and yet indeed they enter:
Knock, for they nothing have, that nothing venture.
Nor will the king himself throw dirt on thee,
As thou hast cast reproaches upon me.
He will not hate thee, O thou foul backslider!
As thou didst me, because I am a spider.
Now, to conclude: since I much doctrine bring,
Slight me no more, call me not ugly thing.
God wisdom hath unto the pismire given,
And spiders may teach men the way to heaven.

Sinner.

Well, my good spider, I my errors see,
I was a fool for railing so at thee.
Thy nature, venom, and thy fearful hue,
But show what sinners are, and what they do.
   Thy way and works do also darkly tell
How some men go to heaven, and some to hell
Thou art my monitor, I am a fool;
They may learn, that to spiders go to school.

XIX.

MEDITATIONS UPON THE DAY, BEFORE THE SUN-RISING.

But all this while, where's he whose golden rays
Drives night away, and beautifies our days?
Where's he whose goodly face doth warm and heal,
And show us what the darksome nights conceal?
Where's he that thaws our ice, drives cold away?
Let's have him, or we care not for the day.
   Thus 'tis with those who are possess'd of grace,
There's nought to them like their Redeemer's face.

XX.

OF THE MOLE IN THE GROUND.

The mole's a creature very smooth and slick,
She digs i' th' dirt, but 't will not on her stick.
So 's he who counts this world his greatest gains,
Yet nothing gets but labour for his pains.
Earth's the mole's element, she can't abide
To be above ground, dirt-heaps are her pride;
And he is like her, who the worldling plays,
He imitates her in her works and ways.
   Poor silly mole, that thou shouldst love to be
Where thou nor sun, nor moon, nor stars canst see!
But oh! how silly 's he, who doth not care,
So he gets earth, to have of heaven a share!

XXI.

OF THE CUCKOO.

Thou booby, sayst thou nothing but Cuckoo?
The Robin and the Wren can thee outdo.
They to us play thorough their little throats,
Not one, but sundry pretty tuneful notes.
But thou hast fellows, some like thee can do
Little but suck our eggs, and sing Cuckoo.

Thy notes do not first welcome in our spring,
Nor dost thou its first tokens to us bring.
Birds less than thee by far, like prophets, do
Tell us 'tis coming, though not by Cuckoo.

Nor dost thou summer have away with thee,
Though thou a yawling, bawling cuckoo be.
When thou dost cease among us to appear,
Then doth our harvest bravely crown our year.

But thou hast fellows, some like thee can do
Little but suck our eggs, and sing Cuckoo.
Since cuckoos forward not our early spring,
Nor help with notes to bring our harvest in;
And since, while here, she only makes a noise,
So pleasing unto none as girls and boys,
The Formalist we may compare her to,
For he doth suck our eggs, and sing Cuckoo.

XXII.

OF THE BOY AND BUTTERFLY.

Behold how eager this our little boy
Is for this butterfly; as if all joy,
All profits, honours, yea, and lasting pleasures,
Were wrapt up in her, or the richest treasures,
Found in her, would be bundled up together,
When all her all is lighter than a feather.
He holloas, runs, and cries out, here boys here,
Nor doth he brambles or the nettles fear:
He stumbles at the molehills, up he gets,
And runs again, as one bereft of wits.
And all his labour and his large outcry,
Is only for a silly butterfly.

This little boy an emblem is of those,
Whose hearts are wholly at the world's dispose;
The butterfly doth represent to me,
The world's best things at best but fading be.
All are but painted nothings and false joys,
Like this poor butterfly to these our boys.
His running through nettles, thorns, and briars,
To gratify his boyish fond desires;
His tumbling over molehills to attain
His end, namely, his butterfly to gain;
Doth plainly show what hazards some men run,
To get what will be lost as soon as won.
Men seem in choice, than children far more wise,
Because they run not after butterflies:
When yet, alas! for what are empty toys,
They follow children, like to beardless boys.

XXIII.

OF THE FLY AT THE CANDLE.

What ails this fly thus desperately to enter
A combat with the candle? Will she venture
To clash at light? Away, thou silly fly;
Thus doing thou wilt burn thy wings and die.
But 'tis a folly her advice to give,
She'll kill the candle, or she will not live.
Slap, says she at it; then she makes retreat,
So wheels about, and doth her blows repeat.
Nor doth the candle let her quite escape,
But gives some little check upon the ape:
Throws up her nimble heels, and down she falls,
Where she lies sprawling, and for succour calls.
When she recovers, up she gets again,
And at the candle comes with might and main
But now behold the candle takes the fly,
And holds her, till she doth by burning die.

This candle is an emblem of that light
Our gospel gives in this our darksome night.
The fly a lively picture is of those
That hate, and do this gospel-light oppose.
At last the gospel doth become their snare,
Doth them with burning hands in pieces tear.

XXIV.

ON THE RISING OF THE SUN.

Look, look, brave Sol doth peep up from beneath,
Shows us his golden face, doth on us breathe;
Yea, he doth compass us around with glories,
Whilst he ascends up to his highest stories.
Where he his banner over us displays,
And gives us light to see our works and ways.
Nor are we now, as at the peep of light,
To question, is it day, or is it night?
The night is gone, the shadow's fled away,
And now we are most certain that 'tis day,
And thus it is when Jesus shows his face,
And doth assure us of his love and grace.

XXV.

UPON THE PROMISING FRUITFULNESS OF A TREE.

A comely sight indeed it is to see
A world of blossoms on an apple-tree:
Yet far more comely would this tree appear,
If all its dainty blooms young apples were.
But how much more might one upon it see,
If all would hang there till they ripe should be.
But most of all in beauty 'twould abound,
If every one should truly then be found.
But we, alas! do commonly behold
Blooms fall apace, if mornings be but cold.
They, too, which hang till they young apples are,
By blasting winds, and vermin take despair

Store that do hang, while almost ripe we see
By blust'ring winds are shaken from the tree.
So that of many, only some there be,
That grow and thrive to full maturity.

COMPARISON.

This tree a perfect emblem is of those
Which do the garden of the Lord compose.
Its blasted blooms are motions unto good,
Which chill affections do nip in the bud.
Those little apples which yet blasted are,
Show some good purposes no good fruits bear.
Those spoil'd by vermin are to let us see
How good attempts by bad thoughts ruin'd be.
Those which the wind blows down, while they are
   green,
Show good works have by trials spoiled been.
Those that abide, while ripe upon the tree,
Show in a good man some ripe fruit will be.
Behold then how abortive some fruits are,
Which at the first most promising appear;
The frost, the wind, the worm, with time doth show,
There flow from much appearance, works but few.

XXVI.
UPON THE THIEF.

The thief when he doth steal, thinks he doth gain;
Yet then the greatest loss he doth sustain.
Come thief, tell me thy gains, but do not falter,
When summ'd, what comes it to more than the
   halter?
Perhaps thou'lt say, the halter I defy;
So thou mayst say, yet by the halter die.
Thou'lt say, then there's an end; no, prythee hold,
He was no friend of thine that thee so told.
Hear thou the word of God, that will thee tell,
Without repentance thieves must go to hell.
But should it be as thy false prophet says,
Yet nought but loss doth come by thievish ways;
All honest men will flee thy company,
Thou liv'st a rogue, and so a rogue will die.
Innocent boldness thou hast none at all,
Thy inward thoughts do thee a villain call.
Sometimes when thou liest warmly on thy bed,
Thou art like one unto the gallows led.
Fear as a constable breaks in upon thee,
Thou art as if the town was up to stone thee.
If hogs do grunt, or silly rats do rustle,
Thou art in consternation, think'st a bustle
By men about the door is made to take thee:
And all because good conscience doth forsake thee.
Thy case is so deplorable and bad;
Thou shunn'st to think on't, lest thou shouldst be
   mad.
Thou art beset with mischiefs every way,
The gallows groaneth for thee every day.
Wherefore, I prythee, thief, thy theft forbear,
Consult thy safety, prythee have a care.
If once thy head be got within the noose,
 Twill be too late a longer life to choose.

As to the penitent thou readest of,
What's that to them who at repentance scoff?
Nor is that grace at thy command or pow'r,
That thou shouldst put it off till the last hour.
I prythee thief, think on't, and turn betime:
Few go to life, who do the gallows climb.

XXVII.
OF THE CHILD WITH THE BIRD ON THE BUSH.

My little bird, how canst thou sit,
   And sing amidst so many thorns?
Let me but hold upon thee get,
   My love with honour thee adorns.
Thou art at present little worth;
   Five farthings none will give for thee.
But prythee little bird come forth,
   Thou of more value art to me.
'Tis true it is sunshine to day,
   To-morrow birds will have a storm;
My pretty one, come thou away,
   My bosom then shall keep thee warm.
Thou subject art to cold o' nights,
   When darkness is thy covering;
At day thy danger's great by kites,
   How canst thou then sit there and sing?
Thy food is scarce and scanty too,
   'Tis worms and trash which thou dost eat;
Thy present state I pity do,
   Come, I'll provide thee better meat.
I'll feed thee with white bread and milk,
   And sugar-plums, if thou them crave;
I'll cover thee with finest silk,
   That from the cold I may thee save.
My father's palace shall be thine,
   Yea, in it thou shalt sit and sing;
My little bird, if thou'lt be mine,
   The whole year round shall be thy spring.
I'll teach the all the notes at court;
   Unthought-of music thou shalt play:
And all that hither do resort.
   Shall praise thee for it every day.
I'll keep thee safe from cat and cur,
   No manner o' harm shall come to thee:
Yea, I will be thy succourer,
   My bosom shall thy cabin be.
But lo, behold, the bird is gone;
   These charmings would not make her yield:
The child's left at the bush alone,
   The bird flies yonder o'er the field.

COMPARISON.

This little child of Christ an emblem is;
   The bird to sinners I compare:
The thorns are like those sins of his,
   Which do surround him ev'rywhere.
Her songs, her food, and sunshine day,
   Are emblems of those foolish toys,
Which to destruction lead the way,
   The fruit of worldly, empty joys.

The arguments this child doth choose,
　To draw to him a bird thus wild,
Shows Christ familiar speech doth use,
　To make to him be reconciled.
The bird in that she takes her wing,
　To speed her from him after all;
Shows us, vain man loves anything,
　Much better than the heav'nly call.

XXVIII.

OF MOSES AND HIS WIFE.

This Moses was a fair and comely man;
His wife a swarthy Æthiopian:
Nor did his milk-white bosom change her skin,
She came out thence as black as she went in.
Now Moses was a type of Moses' law,
His wife likewise of one that never saw
Another way unto eternal life;
There's myst'ry then, in Moses and his wife.
The law is very holy, just, and good,
And to it is espoused all flesh and blood;
But yet the law its goodness can't bestow
On any that are wedded thereunto.
Therefore as Moses' wife came swarthy in,
And went out from him without change of skin,
So he that doth the law for life adore,
Shall yet by it be left a black-a-moor.

XXIX.

OF THE ROSE-BUSH.

This homely bush doth to mine eyes expose
A very fair, yea comely, ruddy rose.
This rose doth always bow its head to me,
Saying, Come pluck me, I thy rose will be;
Yet offer I to gather rose or bud,
Ten to one but the bush will have my blood.
This looks like a trepan, or a decoy,
To offer, and yet snap, who would enjoy;
Yea, the more eager on't, the more in danger,
Be he the master of it or a stranger.
Bush, why dost bear a rose, if none must have it?
Why dost expose it, yet claw those that crave it!
Art become freakish? Dost the wanton play,
Or doth thy testy humour tend this way?

COMPARISON.

This rose God's Son is, with his ruddy looks:
But what's the bush, whose pricks, like tenter-
　　hooks,
Do scratch and claw the finest lady's hands,
Or rend her clothes, if she too near it stands.
This bush an emblem is of Adam's race,
Of which Christ came, when he his Father's grace
Commended to us in his crimson blood,
While he in sinners' stead and nature stood.
Thus Adam's race did bear this dainty rose,
And doth the same to Adam's race expose:
But those of Adam's race which at it catch,
Them will the race of Adam claw and scratch.

XXX.

OF THE GOING DOWN OF THE SUN.

What, hast thou run thy race, art going down?
Why, as one angry, dost thou on us frown?
Why wrap thy head with clouds, and hide thy face,
As threatening to withdraw from us thy grace?
Oh, leave us not! When once thou hid'st thy head,
Our horizon with darkness will be spread,
Tell, who hath thee offended, turn again;
Alas! too late, entreaties are in vain!

COMPARISON.

The gospel here has had a summer's day,
But in its sunshine we, like fools, did play,
Or else fall out, and with each other wrangle,
And did, instead of work, not much but jangle.
And if our sun seems angry, hides his face,
Shall it go down, shall night possess this place?
Let not the voice of night-birds us afflict,
And of our mis-spent summer us convict.

XXXI.

UPON THE FROG.

The frog by nature is both damp and cold,
Her mouth is large, her belly much will hold;
She sits somewhat ascending, loves to be
Croaking in gardens, though unpleasantly.

COMPARISON.

The hypocrite is like unto this frog,
As like as is the puppy to the dog.
He is of nature cold, his mouth is wide,
To prate, and at true goodness to deride.
And though the world is that which has his love,
He mounts his head, as if he lived above.
And though he seeks in churches for to croak,
He neither loveth Jesus nor his yoke.

XXXII.

UPON THE WHIPPING OF A TOP.

'Tis with the whip the boy sets up the top,
The whip doth make it whirl upon its toe;
Hither and thither makes it skip and hop:
'Tis with the whip the top is made to go.

COMPARISON.

Our Legalist is like this nimble top,
Without a whip he will not duty do.
Let Moses whip him he will skip and hop;
Forbear to whip, he'll neither stand nor go.

XXXIII.

UPON THE PISMIRE.

Must we upon the pismire go to school,
To learn of her in summer to provide,
For winter next ensuing? man's a fool,
Or silly ants would not be made his guide.

But, sluggard, is it not a shame for thee
To be outdone by pismires?   Pr'ythee, hear:
Their works, too, will thy condemnation be,
When at the judgment-seat thou shalt appear.
But since thy God doth bid thee to her go,
Obey, her ways consider, and be wise:
The pismires will inform thee what to do,
And set the way to life before thine eyes.

XXXIV.

UPON THE BEGGAR.

He wants, he asks, he pleads his poverty;
They within doors do him an alms deny.
He doth repeat and aggravate his grief;
But they repulse him, give him no relief.
He begs, they say, begone; he will not hear,
He coughs and sighs, to show he still is there;
They disregard him, he repeats his groans;
They still say nay, and he himself bemoans,
They call him vagrant, and more rugged grow;
He cries the shriller—trumpets out his woe.
At last, when they perceive he'll take no nay,
An alms they give him without more delay.

COMPARISON.

This beggar doth resemble them that pray
To God for mercy, and will take no nay;
But wait, and count that all his hard gainsays
Are nothing else but fatherly delays.
Then imitate him, praying souls, and cry ·
There's nothing like to importunity.

XXXV.

UPON THE HORSE AND HIS RIDER.

There's one rides very sagely on the road,
Showing that he affects the gravest mode;
Another rides tantivy, or full trot,
To show such gravity he matters not.
Lo! here comes one amain, he rides full speed,
Hedge, ditch, or miry bog, he doth not heed.
One claws it up-hill, without stop or check,
Another down, as if he'd break his neck.
Now every horse has his especial guider:
Then, by his going, you may know the rider.

COMPARISON.

Now let us turn our horse into a man,
The rider to a spirit, if we can;
Then let us, by the methods of the guider,
Tell ev'ry horse how he should know his rider.
Some go as men direct, in a right way,
Nor are they suffered e'er to go astray:
As with a bridle they are govern'd well,
And so are kept from paths that lead to hell.
  Now this good man hath his especial guider:
  Then, by his going, let him know his rider.

Another goes as if he did not care
Whether of heaven or hell he should be heir.
The rein, it seems, is laid upon his neck,
And he pursues his way without a check.
  Now this man, too, has his especial guider,
  And by his going he may know his rider.
Again, some run, as if resolv'd to die,
Body and soul to all eternity.
Good counsel they by no means can abide;
They'll have their course, whatever them betide,
  Now these poor men have their especial
    guider;
  Were they not fools, they soon might know
    their rider.
There's one makes head against all godliness,
Those, too, that do profess it he'll distress.
He'll taunt and flout if goodness doth appear;
And those that love it he will flout and jeer.
  Now this man, too, has his especial guider,
  And by his going he may know his rider.

XXXVI.

UPON THE SIGHT OF A POUND OF CANDLES FALLING TO THE GROUND.

But are the candles down, and scatter'd too,
Some lying here, some there?   What shall
  we do?
Hold! light the candle there that stands on high,
The other candles you may find thereby.
Light that, I say, and so take up the pound,
Which you let fall and scatter'd on the ground.

COMPARISON.

The fallen candles to us intimate
The bulk of God's elect in their lapsed state,
Their lying scatter'd in the dark may be,
To show by man's lapsed state his misery.
The candle that was taken down and lighted,
Thereby to find them fallen and benighted,
Is Jesus Christ: God by his light doth gather
Whom he will save, and be to them a Father.

XXXVII.

UPON A PENNY LOAF.

Thy price one penny is, in time of plenty;
In famine doubled, 'tis from one to twenty.
Yea, no man knows what price on thee to set,
When there is but one penny loaf to get.

COMPARISON.

This loaf's an emblem of the word of God,
A thing of low esteem before the rod
Of famine smites the soul with fear of death;
But then it is our all, our life, our breath.

XXXVIII.

THE BOY AND THE WATCHMAKER.

This watch my father did on me bestow,
A golden one it is, but 'twill not go,
Unless it be at an uncertainty;
But as good none, as one to tell a lie.
When 'tis high day, my hand will stand at nine;
I think there's no man's watch so bad as mine.
Sometimes 'tis sullen, 'twill not go at all,
And yet 'twas never broke, nor had a fall.

Watchmaker.

Your watch, though it be good, through want of
    skill
May fail to do according to your will.
Suppose the balance, wheels, and spring be good,
And all things else, unless you understood
To manage it, as watches ought to be,
Your watch will still be at uncertainty.
Come, tell me, do you keep it from the dust,
And wind it duly, that it may not rust?
Take heed too that you do not strain the spring;
You must be circumspect in everything,
Or else your watch will not exactly go,
'Twill stand, or run too fast, or move too slow.

COMPARISON.

This boy resembles one that's turn'd from sin;
His watch the curious work of grace within.
The watchmaker is Jesus Christ our Lord,
His counsel, the directions of his word.
Then, convert, if thy heart be out of frame,
Of this watchmaker learn to mend the frame.
Do not lay ope thy heart to worldly dust,
Nor let thy graces overgrow with rust;
Be oft renewed in th' spirit of thy mind,
Or else uncertain thou thy watch wilt find.

XXXIX.

UPON A LOOKING-GLASS.

In this, see thou thy beauty, hast thou any,
Or thy defects, should they be few or many;
Thou mayst, too, here thy spots and freckles see,
Hast thou but eyes, and what their numbers be.
But art thou blind? There is no looking-glass
Can show thee thy defects, thy spots, or face.

COMPARISON.

Unto this glass we may compare the word,
For that to man assistance doth afford,
Has he a mind to know himself and state;
To see what will be his eternal fate.
But without eyes, alas! how can he see?
Many that seem to look here, blind men be.
This is the reason, they so often read
Their judgment there, and do it nothing dread.

XL.

OF THE LOVE OF CHRIST.

The love of Christ, poor I may touch upon;
But 'tis unsearchable. Oh, there is none
Its large dimensions can comprehend,
Should they dilate thereon world without end.
When we had sinned, he in his zeal did swear
That he upon his back our sins would bear,
And since to sin there is entailed death,
He vow'd that for our sins he'd lose his breath.
He did not only say, vow, or resolve,
But to astonishment did so involve
Himself in man's distress and misery,
As for, and with him both to live and die.
To his eternal fame in sacred story,
We find that he did lay aside his glory,
Stepp'd from the throne of highest dignity,
Became poor man, did in a manger lie ·
Yea, was beholden upon his for bread,
Had, of his own, not where to lay his head:
Though rich, he did, for us, become thus poor
That he might make us rich for evermore.
Yet this was but the least of what he did;
But the outside of what he suffered.
God made his blessed Son under the law,
Under the curse, which like the lion's paw,
Did rend and tear his soul, for mankind's sin,
More than if we for it in hell had been.
His cries, his tears, and bloody agony,
The nature of his death doth testify.
Nor did he of constraint himself thus give,
For sin to death, that man might with him live.
He did do what he did most willingly,
He sung, and gave God thanks that he must die.
Did ever king die for a captive slave?
Yet such were we whom Jesus died to save.
Yea, when he made himself a sacrifice,
It was that he might save his enemies.
And, though he was provoked to retract
His blest resolves to do so kind an act
By the abusive carriages of those
That did both him, his love, and grace oppose,
Yet he, as unconcern'd about such things,
Goes on, determines to make captives kings;
Yea, many of his murderers he takes
Into his favour, and them princes makes.

XLI.

ON THE CACKLING OF A HEN.

The hen so soon as she an egg doth lay,
Spreads the fame of her doing what she may.
About the yard a cackling she doth go,
To tell what 'twas she at her nest did do.
Just thus it is with some professing men;
If they do aught that's good, they, like our hen,
Cannot but cackle on't where'er they go,
And what their right hand doth, their left must
    know.

XLII.

UPON AN HOUR-GLASS.

This glass when made, was by the workman's skill,
The sum of sixty minutes to fulfil.
Time more, nor less, by it will out be spun,
But just an hour, and then the glass is run.
Man's life, we will compare unto this glass,
The number of his months he cannot pass;
But when he has accomplished his day,
He, like a vapour, vanisheth away.

XLIII.

UPON A SNAIL.

She goes but softly, but she goeth sure,
She stumbles not, as stronger creatures do
Her journey's shorter, so she may endure
Better than they which do much further go.
She makes no noise, but stilly seizeth on
The flow'r or herb appointed for her food;
The which she quietly doth feed upon,
While others range and glare, but find no good.
And though she doth but very softly go,
However slow her pace be, yet 'tis sure;
And certainly they that do travel so,
The prize which they do aim at they procure.
Although they seem not much to stir or go,
Who thirst for Christ, and who from wrath do flee;
Yet what they seek for, quickly they come to,
Though it doth seem the farthest off to be.
One act of faith doth bring them to that flow'r
They so long for, that they may eat and live;
Which to attain is not in others' power,
Though for it a king's ransom they would give.
Then let none faint, nor be at all dismay'd,
That life by Christ do seek, they shall not fail
To have it; let them nothing be afraid:
The herb and flow'r are eaten by the snail.

XLIV.

OF THE SPOUSE OF CHRIST.

Who's this that cometh from the wilderness,
Like smoky pillars thus perfumed with myrrh,
Leaning upon her dearest in distress,
Placed in his bosom by the Comforter?
She's clothed with the sun, crowned with twelve
 stars,
The spotted moon her footstool she hath made.
The dragon her assaults, fills her with jars;
Yet rests she under her beloved's shade.
But whence was she? What is her pedigree?
Was not her father a poor Amorite?
What was her mother but as others be,
A Hittite sinful, poor, and helpless quite.
Yea, as for her, the day that she was born,
As loathsome, out of doors they did her cast,
Naked and filthy, stinking and forlorn;
This was her pedigree from first to last.

Nor was she pitied in this estate,
All let her lie polluted in her blood;
None her condition did commiserate,
There was no heart that sought to do her good.
Yet she unto these ornaments is come,
Her breasts are fashioned, and her hair is grown;
She is made heiress of a heavenly home,
All her indignities away are blown.
Cast out she was, but now she home is taken,
Once she was naked, now you see she's clad;
Now made the darling, though before forsaken,
Barefoot, but now as prince's daughters shod.
Instead of filth, she now has her perfumes,
Instead of ignominy, chains of gold:
Instead of what the beauty most consumes,
Her beauty's perfect, lovely to behold.
Those that attend and wait upon her be
Princes of honour clothed in white array;
Upon her head's a crown of gold, and she
Eats honey, wheat, and oil, from day to day.
For her beloved, he's the high'st of all,
The only Potentate, the King of kings:
Angels and men do him Jehovah call,
And from him life and glory always springs.
He's white and ruddy, and of all the chief;
His head, his locks, his eyes, his hands, and feet,
Do for completeness out-do all belief,
His cheeks like flowers are, his mouth most sweet.
As for his wealth, he's made heir of all;
What is in heav'n, what is in earth is his:
And he this lady his joint-heir doth call,
Of all that shall be, or at present is.
Well, lady, well, God has been good to thee,
Thou of an outcast now art made a queen.
Few or none may with thee compared be,
A beggar made thus high is seldom seen.
Take heed of pride, remember what thou art
By nature, though thou hast in grace a share,
Thou in thyself doth yet retain a part
Of thine own filthiness; wherefore beware.

XLV.

UPON A SKILFUL PLAYER ON AN INSTRUMENT.

He that can play well on an instrument,
Will take the ear, and captivate the mind
With mirth or sadness, when it is intent;
And music into it a way doth find.
But if one hears that hath therein no skill,
(As often music lights of such a chance),
Of its brave notes they soon be weary will:
And there are some can neither sing nor dance.

COMPARISON.

To him that thus most skilfully doth play,
God doth compare a gospel-minister,
That doth with life and vigour preach and pray,
Applying right, what he doth there infer.
Whether this man of wrath or grace doth preach,
So skilfully he handles every word,
And by his saying, doth the heart so reach,
That it doth joy or sigh before the Lord.

But some there be, which, as the brute doth lie
Under the word without the least advance.
Such do despise the gospel-ministry—
They weep not at it, neither to it dance.

XLVI.

OF MAN BY NATURE.

From God he's a backslider,
Of ways he loves the wider;
With wickedness a sider,
More venom than a spider.
In sin he's a confider,
A make-bate and divider;
Blind reason is his guider,
The devil is his rider.

XLVII.

UPON THE DISOBEDIENT CHILD.

Children, when little, how do they delight us;
When they grow bigger, they begin to fright us.
Their sinful nature prompts them to rebel,
And to delight in paths that lead to hell.
Their parents' love and care they overlook,
As if relation had them quite forsook.
They take the counsels of the wanton, rather
Than the most grave instructions of a father.
They reckon parents ought to do for them,
Though they the fifth commandment do contemn.
They snap, and snarl, if parents them control,
Although in things most hurtful to the soul,
They reckon they are masters, and that we
Who parents are, should to them subjects be!
If parents fain would have a hand in choosing,
The children have a heart still in refusing.
They by wrong doings, from their parents gather,
And say it is no sin to rob a father.
They'll jostle parents out of place and power,
They'll make themselves the head, and them
    devour.
How many children by becoming head
Have brought their parents to a piece of bread!
Thus they who at the first were parents' joy,
Turn that to bitterness, themselves destroy.
But wretched child, how canst thou thus requite
Thy aged parents, for that great delight
They took in thee, when thou, as helpless lay,
In their indulgent bosoms day by day?
Thy mother long before she brought thee forth,
Took care thou shouldst want neither food nor
    cloth.

Thy father glad was at his very heart,
Had he, to thee, a portion to impart.
Comfort they promised themselves in thee,
But thou, it seems, to them a grief will be.
How oft, how willingly, brake they their sleep,
If thou, their bantling, didst but winch or weep.
Their love to thee was such, they could have giv'n,
That thou mightst live, all but their part of heav'n.
But now, behold, how they rewarded are
For their indulgent love and tender care!
All is forgot, this love they do despise,
They brought this bird up to pick out their eyes.

XLVIII.

UPON A SHEET OF WHITE PAPER.

This paper's handled by the sons of men,
Both with the fairest and the foulest pen.
'Twill also show what is upon it writ,
Whether 'tis wisely done, or void of wit;
Each blot and blur it also will expose
To the next readers, be they friends or foes.

COMPARISON.

Some souls are like unto this blank or sheet,
(Though not in whiteness:) the next man they
    meet,
Be what he will, a good man or deluder,
A knave or fool, the dangerous intruder
May write thereon, to cause that man to err
In doctrine or in life, with blot and blur.
Nor will that soul conceal wherein it swerves,
But show itself to each one that observes.
A reading man may know who was the writer,
And, by the hellish nonsense, the inditer.

XLIX.

UPON THE FIRE.

Who falls into the fire shall burn with heat,
While those remote scorn from it to retreat.
Yea, while those in it, cry out, Oh! I burn,
Some farther off those cries to laughter turn.

COMPARISON.

While some tormented are in hell for sin;
On earth some greatly do delight therein.
Yea, while some make it echo with their cry,
Others count it a fable and a lie.

A DISCOURSE OF THE

BUILDING, NATURE, EXCELLENCY, AND GOVERNMENT

OF

THE HOUSE OF GOD;

WITH

COUNSELS AND DIRECTIONS TO THE INHABITANTS THEREOF.

" Lord, I have loved the habitation of thy house, and the place where thine honour dwelleth."—Ps. xxvi. 8.

PREFATORY NOTE.

HOMELY as is the style of this versified " discourse " it may be regarded as the best entitled of any of Bunyan's writings in rhyme to the appellation of a poem. There are traces of inventiveness in its plan ; and advantage is taken of some beautiful scriptural images to enliven the general sobriety of the descriptions. A reader must be very fond of controversy who cannot find more to admire in this account of *The House of God* than to question or assail. Had the author not been known, it would have seemed very questionable to what party he belonged, or whether his views of church government were not those of Cyprian or Ambrose.

> " The man that worthily rejected is,
> And cast out of this house, his part in bliss
> Is lost for ever."

It is very apparent that a sentiment like this admits of an interpretation conformable to the broadest or the narrowest meaning given to the word " church," or " house of God." Bunyan's honest intention was to delineate from Scripture a perfect transcript of what he understood to be the divine plan. With this desire he lost sight of nice distinctions, and cold, unbrotherly limitations, and drew his outline on such a large scale, that while an earnest spiritually-minded man, of any party, must be soothed by its agreement with Scripture, the churchman can scarcely object to it for any defect in the tests applicable to his purposes.

The reader who wishes to discover instances of the writer's want of taste will not be disappointed, however rapid his perusal of this discourse. Thus in the description of our Lord, as " the Chief of all," the features of his person and character are so heaped together that it is impossible to shape from them any form or likeness whatsoever. A very questionable feeling is excited by a line like this—

> " His legs, like marble, stand in boots of gold."

But notwithstanding these blemishes the whole is worthy of attentive reading. It may afford many persons a much more edifying idea of the church than they would otherwise have possessed ; nor, as a poem, is it wanting in couplets which, taken of themselves, might be quoted as examples of great rythmical learning.

H. S.

A DISCOURSE OF THE HOUSE OF GOD, &c.

I.

BY WHOM THIS HOUSE IS BUILT.

THE builder's God, the materials his elect ;
His Son's the rock on which it is erect ;
The Scripture is his rule, plummet, or line,
Which gives proportion to this house divine ;
His working-tools his ordinances are,
By them he doth his stones and timber square ;
Affections knit in love, the couplings are.
Good doctrine, like to mortar, doth cement
The whole together, schism to prevent :
His compass, his decree ; his hand's the Spirit
By which he frames what he means to inherit—
A holy temple, which shall far excel
That very place where now the angels dwell.

Call this a temple or a house of prayer,
A palace, oracle, or spouse most fair ;
Or what you will : God's love is here display'd,
And here his treasure safely up is laid ;
For his own darling none can find a place,
Where he, as here, is wont to show his face.

What though some slight it, it a cottage call,
Give't the reproachful name of beggar's hall ;
Yea, what though to some it an eyesore is,
What though they count it base, and at it hiss,
Call it an almshouse, builded for the poor ;
Yet kings of old have begged at the door.

II.

OF THE BEAUTY OF THE CHURCH.

Lo ! her foundations laid with sapphires are ;
Her goodly windows made of agates fair ;
Her gates are carbuncles, or pearls ; nor one
Of all her borders but's a precious stone ;
None common, nor o' th' baser sort are here,
Nor rough, but squared and polished everywhere ;
Her beams are cedars, firs her rafters be ;
Her terraces are of the algum-tree ;
The thorn or crab-tree here are not of use :
Who thinks them here utensils, puts abuse
Upon the place, yea, on the builder too ;
Would they be thus controll'd in what they do ?

With carved-work of lily, and palm-tree,
With cherubims and chains adorned be
The doors, the walls, and pillars of this place ;
Forbidden beasts here must not show their face.
With grace like gold, as with fine painting, he
Will have this house within enriched be ;
Fig-leaves nor rags, must here keep out no cold,
This builder covers all with cloth of gold,
Of needlework, prick'd more than once or twice
(The oft'ner prick'd, still of the higher price),
Wrought by his Son, put on her by his merit,
Applied by faith, revealed by the Spirit.

III.

OF THE CONVENIENCES OF THIS HOUSE.

Within these walls the builder did devise
That there the householders might sacrifice ;
Here is an altar, and a laver too,
And priests abundance, temple work to do.
Nor want they living offerings, nor yet fire,
Nor holy garments ; what divine desire
Commands, it has bestowed upon this place ;
Here be the censers, here's the throne of grace :
None of the householders need go elsewhere
To offer incense, or good news to hear.

A throne for judgment he did here erect,
Virtue to cherish, folly to detect ;
Statutes and laws unto this house he gave,
To teach who to condemn, and who to save :
By things thus wholesome taught is every brother
To fear his God, and to love one another.

And now for pleasure, solace, recreation,
Here's such as helpeth forward man's salvation
Equal to these none can be found elsewhere,
All else turn to profuseness, sin, and care.
So situate it is, so roomy, fair,
So warm, so blessed, with such wholesome air,
That 'tis enticing : whoso wishes well
To his soul's health, should covet here to dwell.
Here's necessaries, and what will delight
The godly ear, the palate, with the sight
Of each degree and sex ; here's everything
To please a beggar, and delight a king.
Chambers and galleries he did invent,
Both for a prospect and a retirement.
For such as unto music do incline,
Here are both harps and psalteries divine :
Her cellars aud banqueting-house have been,
In former days, a palace for a queen.
O house ! what title to thee can be given,
So fit as that which men do give to heaven !

IV.

OF THE STRENGTH AND DEFENCE OF THIS HOUSE.

This house, you may be sure, will always stand—
She's builded on a rock, not on the sand ;
Storms, rain, yea, floods, have oft upon her beat,
Yet stands she : here's a proof she is no cheat.
Fear not therefore in her for to abide,
She keeps her ground, come weather, wind, or tide :
Her corner-stone has many times been tried,
But never could the scorn, or rage, or pride
Of all her foes, by what force they could make,
Destroy her battlements, or ground-work shake.
Here's God the Lord encamping round about
His dwelling place ; nor ought we once to doubt
But that he as a watchman succour will
Those that do dwell upon his holy hill.
A wall of fire about her I will be,
And glory in the midst of her, and she
Shall be the place where I my name record ;
Here I will come and bless you, saith the Lord.

The holy watchers at her gates do stand,
With their destroying weapons in their hand,
Those to defend, that in this house do dwell,
From all her enemies in earth and hell ;
Safety ! where is it, if it is not here ?
God dwelleth in her, doth for her appear,
To help her early, and her foes confound,
And unto her will make his grace abound ;
Safety is here, and also that advance,
Will make a beggar sing, a cripple dance.

V.

THE DELICATENESS OF THE SITUATION OF THIS HOUSE.

As her foundation and her beauty's much ;
Conveniences, and her defences such
As none can parallel, so doth the field
About her, richest, rarest, danties yield.

Moriah, where Isaac was offered,
Where David from his sin was ransomed;
Where Solomon the temple did erect,
Compared with this is worthy no respect.
Under the very threshold of this place
Arise those goodly springs of lasting grace,
Whose crystal streams minister life to those
That here of love to her make their repose.
Sweet is her air (as one may well infer),
'Cause 'tis the breathings of the comforter.
The pomegranates at all her gates do grow,
Mandrakes and vines, with other dainties mo;
Her gardens yield the chief, the richest spice,
Surpassing them of Adam's paradise.
Here be sweet ointments, and the best of gums;
Here runs the milk, here drops the honeycombs.
Here are perfumes most pleasant to the sense,
Here grows the goodly trees of frankincense;
Her arbours, walks, fountains, and pleasant springs,
Delightful formerly have been to kings.

Such mountains round about this house do stand
As one from thence may see the holy land.
Her fields are fertile, do abound with corn;
The lilies fair, her valleys do adorn.
The birds that do come thither every spring,
For birds, they are the very best that sing.
Her friends, her neighbours too, do call her blest;
Angels do here go by, turn in and rest.
The road to paradise lies by her gate,
Here pilgrims do themselves accommodate
With bed and board, and do such stories tell
As do for truth and profit all excel.
Nor doth the porter here say any nay
That hither would turn in, that here would stay.
This house is rent-free; here the man may dwell
That loves his landlord, rules his passions well.

VI.

And wouldst thou know the customs of this place,
How men are here admitted to this grace;
And, consequently, whether thou mayst be
Made one of this most blest fraternity:
Come hither then, unto me lend an ear,
And what is doubtful to thee, I will clear.

This place, as mercy's arms, stands ope to those
That their own happiness used to oppose;
Those under hedges, highwaymen, or they
That would not God, nor yet good men obey;
Those that among the bushes used to browse,
Or under hedges used themselves to louze—
The vilest men, of sinners who are chief,
A fornicator, liar, or a thief,
May turn in thither, here take up and dwell
With those who ransom'd are from death and hell.

This place, as hospitals, will entertain,
Those which the lofty of this world disdain:

The poor, the lame, the maimed, halt, and blind,
The leprous, and possessed too, may find
Free welcome here, as also such relief
As ease them will of trouble, pain, and grief.
This place, as David's heart, with free consent
Opens to th' distressed, and the discontent;
Who is in debt, that has not wherewithal
To quit his scores, may here be free from thrall:
That man that fears the bailiff, or the jail,
May find one here that will become his bail.

Art thou bound over to the great assize,
For heark'ning to the devil and his lies;
Art thou afraid thereat to show thy head
For fear thou then be sent unto the dead;
Thou mayst come hither, here is room and place,
For such as willingly would live by grace.

This place, as father's house in former days,
Is a receptacle for runaways;
He that, like to the ox, backslidden is,
Forfeited hath for sin his share of bliss,
May yet come hither, here is room and rest;
Of old such have come hither and been blest.
Had this been false, oh woe had been to David!
Nor Peter had, nor Magdalen, been saved,
Nor Jonah, nor Manasseh, nor the rest.
No runaway from God could have been blest
With kind reception at his hands; return
Would here come too late, if nought but burn
Had been the lot of the backsliding man:
But we are told there's no rebellion can
Prevent or hinder him from being saved,
That mercy heartily of God hath craved.
She that went from her God to play the whore,
Returning may be as she was before:
He that refuses to his God to turn,
That is resolved in hell-fire to burn;
If he bethinks himself, and turns again,
May find them here that will him entertain.

But bring thou with thee a certificate,
To show thou seest thyself most desolate;
Writ by the Master, with repentance seal'd,
To show also that here thou wouldst be heal'd
By those fair leaves of that most blessed tree,
By which alone poor sinners healed be;
And that thou dost abhor thee for thy ways,
And wouldst in holiness spend all thy days,
And here be entertained: or thou wilt find
To entertain thee here are none inclined.

VII.

The governors that here in office are,
Such be as service do with love and care;
Not swerving from the rule, nor yet intrude
Upon each other's work, nor are they rude
In managing their own: but to their trust
They labour to be honest, faithful, just.

The chief is he who is the Lord of all,
The Saviour; some him physician call.

He's clothed in shining raiment to the ground,
A golden girdle doth begirt him round ;
His head and hairs are white as any snow,
His eyes are like a flame of fire also ;
His feet are like fine brass, as if they burn'd
Within a furnace, or to fire were turn'd ;
His voice doth like to many waters sound ;
In his right hand seven glittering stars are found.
Out of his mouth goes a two-edged sword,
Sharper than any ('tis his holy word).
And for his countenance, 'tis as the sun
Which shineth in its strength, till day is done.
His name is call'd holy, The Word of God ;
The wine-press of his Father's wrath he trod ;
At all the power of sin he doth deride,
The keys of hell and death hang at his side.

   This is our governor, this is the chief,
From this physician comes our soul's relief.
He is the treé of life and hidden manna ;
'Tis he to whom the children sing hosanna.
The white stone he doth give with a new name ;
In heaven and earth he is of worthy fame.
This man hath death destroyed and slain the devil,
And doth secure all his from damning evil.
He is the prince of life, the prince of peace ;
He doth us from the bonds of death release.
His work is properly his own ; nor may,
In what he doth, another say him nay.

'Tis he who pays our hospitalian scores,
He's here to search, supple, and bind up sores.
He is our plaster-maker, he applies
Them to our wounds ; he wipes our wetted eyes.
'Tis he that gives us cups of consolation,
'Tis he renews the hopes of our salvation.
He'll take our parts, ofttimes to us unknown,
And make as if our failings were his own ;
He'll plead with God his name and doings too,
And save us will, from those would us undo.

His name is as an ointment poured forth ;
'Tis sweet from east to west, from south to north.
He's white and ruddy ; yea, of all the chief :
His golden head is rich beyond belief.
His eyes are like the dove's which waters wet,
Well wash'd with milk, and also fitly set ;
His cheeks, as beds of spices and sweet flowers,
He used to water with those crystal showers,
Which often flowed from his cloudy eyes :
Better by far than what comes from the skies.
His lips like lilies, drop sweet-smelling myrrh,
Scenting as do those of the Comforter ;'
His hands are as gold rings set with the beryls,
By them we are delivered out of perils ;
His legs like marble, stand in boots of gold,
His countenance is ex'lent to behold.
His mouth it is of all a mouth most sweet,
Oh kiss me then, Lord, every time we meet !
Thy sugar'd lips, Lord, let them sweeten mine,
With the most blessed scent of things divine.

This is one Governor ; and next in place,
One call'd the Ghost, in honour and in grace

No whit inferior to him ; and He
Will also in this house our helper be.
He 'twas who did at first brood the creation ;
And he's the cause of man's regeneration.
'Tis he by whom the heavens were garnished,
With all their host they then abroad did spread
(Like spangles, pearls, diamonds, or richest gems)
Far richer than the fairest diadems.
'Twas he who with his cloven tongues of fire
Made all those wise ones of the world admire,
Who heard his breathing in unlearned men.
O blessed ruler ! now the same as then !
His work our mind is to illuminate
With things divine, and to accommodate
Us with those graces, which will us adorn,
And make us look like men indeed new-born.
For our inheritance he makes us meet ;
He makes us also in this world discreet—
Prudent and wise in what we take in hand,
To do and suffer at our Lord's command.
'Tis he that leads us to the tomb and cross,
Where Jesus crucified and buried was ;
He shows us also that he did revive,
And doth assure us that he is alive ;
And doth improve the merit of his blood,
At grace's throne for our eternal good.
Dark riddles he doth here to us unfold,
Yea, makes us things invisible behold.
He sheds abroad God's love in every heart,
Where he doth dwell, yea, to them doth impart
Such tokens of a future happiness,
That's past the tongue of angels to express.
'Tis he which helpeth us, *that* to perform,
Whether becalm'd, or whether in a storm
Which God commands : without him we do nought
That's good, either in deed, or word, or thought.

'Tis he that doth with jewels us bedeck,
'Tis he puts chains of gold about our neck ;
'Tis he that doth us with fine linen gird,
That maketh us ofttimes live as a bird.
That cureth us of all our doubts and fears,
Puts bracelets on our hands, rings in our ears.
   He sanctifies our persons ; he perfumes
Our spirits also ; he our lust consumes ;
Our stinking breath he sweetens, so that we
To God and all good men sweet-scented be.
He sets God's mark upon us, and doth seal
Us unto life, and life to us reveal.

VIII.

Another sort of officers here are,
But such as must not with these first compare ;
They're under officers, but serviceable,
Not only here to rule, but wait at table.
Those clothed are with linen, fine and white,
They glitter as the stars of darksome night.
They have St. Peter's keys, and Aaron's rod ;
They ope and shut, they bind and loose for God.

The chief of these are watchmen, they have power
To mount on high and to ascend the tower
Of this brave fabric, and from thence to see
Who keeps their ground, and who the stragglers
    be.
These have their trumpet, when they do it sound
The mountains echo, yea, it shakes the ground.
With it they also sound out an alarm,
When they perceive the least mischief or harm
Is coming, so they do this house secure
Therefrom, or else prepare it to endure
Most manfully the cross, and so attain
The crown which for the victor doth remain.

This officer is call'd a steward too,
'Cause with his master's cash he has to do,
And has authority it to disburse
To those that want, or for that treasure thirst.
The distributor of the word of grace
He is, and at his mouth, when he's in place,
They seek the law, he also bids them do it;
He shows them sin, and learns them to eschew it.
By this example, too, he shows them how
To keep their garments clean, their knees to bow
Before the king, when he comes into place;
And when they do him supplicate for grace.

Another badge this officer doth wear
Is that of overseer; because the care
Of the whole house is with him, he's to see
They nothing want, nor yet abused be
By false intruders, doctrines, or perchance
By the misplacing of an ordinance.
These also are to see they wander not
From place or duty, lest they get a blot
To their profession, or bring some disease
Upon the whole, or get a trick to lease,
Or lie unto their God, by doing what
By sacred statutes he commanded not.
Call them your cooks, they're skill'd in dressing food
To nourish weak and strong, and cleanse the blood:
They've milk for babes, strong meat for men of age,
Food fit for who are simple, who are sage;
When the great pot goes on, as oft it doth,
They put not coloquintida in broth,
As do those younglings, fondlings of their skill,
Who make not what's so apt to cure as kill.

They are your sub-physicians, and know
What sickness you are incident unto;
Let them but feel your pulse, and they will tell
You quickly whether you are sick or well.
Have you the staggers? They can help you there;
Or if the falling-sickness, or do fear
A lethargy, a fever, or the gout,
God blessing of their skill, you need not doubt
A cure, for long experience has made
Those officers the masters of their trade.
Their physic works by purge and vomit too,
Fear not, nor full nor fasting but 'twill do;
Have but a care, and see you catch no cold,
And with their physic then you may be bold.

You may them prophets call, for they can tell
Of things to come; yea, here they do excel.
They prophesy of man's future event,
Whether to weal or woe his mind is bent;
Yea, so expert are they in their predictions,
Their arguments so full are of convictions,
That none who hear them, but are forced to say,
Woe unto them who wander from the way.
Art bound for hell against all wind and weather?
Or art thou one a going backward thither?
Or dost thou wink, because thou wouldst not see?
Or dost thou sideling go, and wouldst not be
Suspected? Yet these prophets can thee tell,
Which way thou art a going down to hell.
For him that would eternal life attain,
Yet will not part with all, that life to gain,
But keepeth something close he should forsake,
Or slips the time, in which he should awake;
Or saith he lets go all, yet keepeth some
Of what will make him lose the world to come.
These prophets can tell such a man his state,
And what at last will surely be his fate.
  If thou art one who tradeth in both ways,
God's now, the devil's then; or if delays
Thou mak'st of coming to God for life;
Or if thy light and lusts are at a strife
About who should be master of thy soul,
And lovest one, the other dost control;
These prophets tell thee can, which way thou
    bendest,
On which thou frown'st, to which a hand thou
    lendest.
Art one of those whose fears do go beyond
Their faith? when thou shouldst hope, dost thou
    despond?
Dost keep thine eye upon what thou hast done,
And yet hast licence to look on the sun?
Dost thou so covet more, as not to be
Affected with the grace bestow'd on thee?
Art like to him, that needs must step a mile
At every stride, or think it not worth while
To follow Christ? These prophets, they can tell
To cure this thy disease, and make thee well.

This officer is also call'd a guide,
Nor should the people but keep by his side;
Or tread his steps in all the paths they walk,
By his example they should do and talk.
He is to be to them instead of eyes;
He must before them go in any wise;
And he must lead them by the water side,
This is the work of this our Faithful Guide.
  Since snares, and traps, and gins are for us set,
Since here's a hole, and there is spread a net,
O let nobody at my muse deride,
No man can travel here without a guide.
Here's tempting apples, here are baited hooks,
With turning, twisting, cramping, tangling crooks
Close by the way; woe then to them betide,
That dare to venture here without a guide.
Here haunt the fairies with their chanting voices;
Fiends like to angels, to bewitch our choices;

Baits for the flesh lie here on every side :
Who dares set here one foot without a guide ?
　Master delusion dwelleth by our walks,
Who with confusion, sings, and prays, and talks ;
He says the straight path's his, and ours the wide :
What then can we do here without a guide ?
　Let God then give our leaders always eyes ;
Yea, let him make them holy, bold, and wise ;
And help us fast by them for to abide,
*And suffer not the blind to be our guide.**

Here are of rulers yet another sort,
Such as direct our manners to comport
With our professed faith, that we to view,
May let beholders know that we are *new.*
These are our conversations to inspect,
And us in our employments to direct,
That we in faith and love do everything,
That reacheth from the peasant to the king.
That there may be no scandal in our ways,
Nor yet in our profession all our days.
These should after our busy-bodies look,
Tale-bearers also, they have undertook
To keep in order, also they must see
None that can work among us idle be ;
Jars, discords, frauds, with grievances and wrongs,
These they're to regulate ; to them belongs
The judgment of all matters of this kind,
And happy is the house thus disciplined.

Another sort of officers we have,
Deacons we call them 'cause their work's to save
And distribute those crumbs of charity
Unto the poor, for their subsistency,
That contributed is for their relief,
Which of their bus'ness is indeed the chief.
These must be grave, not of a double tongue,
Not given to wine, nor apt to do a wrong
Unto the poor, through love to lucre. (Just
In this, their office, faithful to their trust)
The wife must answer here, as face doth face,
The husband's fitness to his work and place,
The ground of scandal or of jealousy
Obstructs not proof that he most zealously
Performs his office well, for then shall he
Be bold in faith, and get a good degree
Of credit with the church ; yea, what is more,
He shall possess the blessings of the poor.
His wisdom teach him will, to find out who
Is poor of idleness, and who comes to

---

* " He had in his pocket A MAP of all ways leading to or
from the celestial city ; wherefore he struck a light, for he
never went without his tinder-box, and took a view of his
book or map, which bid him be careful in that place to turn
to the right hand way. And had he not here been careful
to look in his map, they had, in all probability, been smothered, in the mud ; for just before them, and that in the
cleanest way, was a pit, and none knows how deep, full of
nothing but mud, there made on purpose to destroy pilgrims
in. Then thought I with myself, who that goeth on pilgrimage but would have one of these maps about him, that
he may look when he is at a stand which is the way he must
take."—*Pilgrim's Progress, Part Second.*

A low estate by sickness, age, or 'cause
The want of limbs, or sight, or work it was
That brought them to it ; or such destiny
As sometimes maketh low who once were high.
　They must remember too that some there are
Who halt before they're lame, while others care
Not to make known their wants, they'll rather die,
Than charge the churches with their poverty.
This done, they must bestow as they see cause ;
Making the word the rule, and want the laws
By which they act, and then they need not
　pause.
　The table of the Lord, he also must
Provide, for 'tis his duty and his trust.
The teacher too should have his table spread
By him ; thus should his house be clad and fed :
Thus he serves tables with the church's stock,
And so becomes a blessing to the flock.

　I read of widows also that should be
Employed here for further decency ;
I dare not say they are in office, though
A service here they are appointed to :
They must be very aged, trusty, meek,
Such who have done much good, that do not
　seek
Themselves ; they must be humble, pitiful,
Or they will make their service void and null.
These are to teach the younger women what
Is proper to their sex and state, what not ;
To be discreet, keepers at home, and chaste ;
To love their husbands, to be good, shamefac'd :
Children to bear, to love them, and to fly
What to the gospel would be infamy.
I think these to the sick should look also ;
A work unfit for younger ones to do.
Wherefore he saith, The younger ones refuse ;
Perhaps because their weakness would abuse
Them, and subject them unto great disgrace,
When such a one as Amnon is in place.
And since the good old woman this must do,
'Tis fit she should be fed and clothed too
Out of the deacon's purse,—let it so be ;
And let this be her service constantly.

IX.

THE ORDER AND MANNER OF THE GOVERNMENT HERE.

As I have show'd you who in office are,
So I will tell you how, and with what care
Those here intrusted with the government
Keep to the statutes made to that intent.
By rules divine this house is governed ;
Not sanguinary ones, nor taught nor fed
By human precepts ; for the Scripture saith,
The word's our ghostly food—food for our faith.
Nor are all forced to the same degree
In things divine, though all exhorted be
To the most absolute proficiency
That law or duty can to them descry.

Alas! here's children, here are great with young;
Here are the sick and weak, as well as strong,
Here are the cedar, shrub, and bruised reed;
Yea, here are such who wounded are, and bleed,
As here are some who in their grammar be,
So here are others in their A, B, C.
Some apt to teach, and others hard to learn;
Some see far off, others can scarce discern
That which is set before them in the glass;
Others forgetful are, and so let pass,
Or slip out of their mind what they did hear.
But now; so great our differences appear
Wherefore our Jacobs must have special care
They drive their flocks but as their flocks can
    bear;
For if they be o'erdriven, presently
They will be sick, or cast their young, or die.
The laws therefore are more and less of force,
According as they bring us to the source,
Or head, or fountain, or are more remote
To what at first we should ourselves devote.
Be we then wise in handling of the laws,
Not making a confused noise, like daws
In chambers, yea, let us seek to excel,
To each man's profit; this is ruling well.
With fundamentals then let us begin,
For they strike at the very root of sin.
So the foundation being strongly laid,
Let us go on, as the wise builder said;
For I don't mean we should at all disdain
Those that are less, we always should maintain
That due respect to either which is meet;
This is the way to sit at Jesus' feet.

Repent I must, or I am cast away;
Believe I must, or nothing I obey;
Love God I must, or nothing I can do,
That's worth so much as loosing of my shoe.
If I do not bear after Christ my cross,
If love to holiness is at a loss,
If I my lusts seek not to mortify,
If to myself, my flesh, I do not die—
What law, should I observ't, can do me good?
In little duties life hath never stood.

One reads, he prays, he catechises too;
But doth he nothing else, what doth he do?
I read to know my duty, I do pray
To God to help me do it day by day;
If this be not my end in what I do,
I am a sot, an hypocrite also.
I am baptized, what then? unless I die
To sin, I cover folly with a lie.
At the Lord's table I do eat; what though?
There some have eat their own damnation too.

I will suppose I hear, I sing, I pray,
And that I am baptized without delay,
I will suppose I do much knowledge get,
And will also suppose that I am fit
To be a preacher, yet nought profits me,
If to the first, poor I a stranger be:

They are more weighty therefore; in compare
These unto them but mint and anise are.

Not that I would the least of duty slight,
Because the least command, of divine right,
Requires that I myself subject thereto;
Wilful resisters do themselves undo.
But let's keep order, let the first be first:
Repent, believe, and love, and then I trust
I have that right, which is divine, to all
That is enjoined, be they great or small.
Only I must as cautionary speak,
In one word more, a little to the weak;
Thou must not suffer men so to enclose
Thee in their judgments, as to discompose
Thee in that faith and peace thou hast with him:
This would be like the losing of a limb;
Or like to him who thinks he doth not well,
Unless he lose the kernel for the shell.
Thou art no captive, but a child and free;
Thou wast not made for laws, but laws for thee,
And thou must use them as thy light will bear it;
They that say otherwise do rend and tear it,
More like to wicked tyrants, who are cruel,
And add unto a little fire more fuel.
But those who are true shepherds of the sheep,
To quench such burnings would most gladly weep.

  But I am yet but upon generals;
Particulars our legislator calls
For at our hands, and that in order to
Consummate what we have begun to do:—
My brother I must love, in very deed,
I'm taught of God to do it; let me heed
This divine duty, and perform it well,
Who loves his brother, God in him doth dwell.
The argument which on me this imposes,
Smells like to ointment, or the sweetest roses.
Shall God love, shall he keep his faith to me?
And shall not I? shall I unfaithful be?
Shall God love me, a sinner? and shall I
Not love a saint? Yea, shall my Jesus die
To reconcile me to my God, and shall
I hate his child, nor hear his wants that call
For my little assisting of him? Fie
On such a spirit, on such cruelty!
Fie on the thought that would me alienate,
Or tempt me my worst enemy to hate.

He that dwells here must also be a sharer
In others' griefs; must be a burden-bearer
Among his brethren, or he cannot do
That which the blessed gospel calls him to.
In order hereunto, humility
Must be put on, it is our livery,—
We must be clothed with it, if we will
The law obey, our Master's mind fulfil.
If this be so, then what should they do here,
Who in their antic pranks of pride appear?
Let lofty men among you bear no sway,
The Lord beholds the proud man far away.
It is not fit that he inhabit there
Where humbleness of mind should have the chair.

Can pride be where a soul for mercy craves?
Shall pride be found among redeemed slaves?
Shall he who mercy from the gallows brought,
Look high, or strut, or entertain a thought
That tends to tempt him to forget that fate,
To which for sin he destin'd was of late,
And could not then at all delivered be,
But by another's death and misery?
Pride is the unbecoming'st thing of all:
Besides, 'tis the forerunner of a fall.
He that is proud soon in the dirt will lie,
But honour followeth humility.
Let each then count his brother as his better,
Let each esteem himself another's debtor.
Christ bids us learn of him humble to be,
Profession's beauty is humility.

Forgive, is here another statute law;
To be revenged is not worth a straw;
He that forgives shall also be forgiven,
Who doth not so, *must lose his part in heaven;*
Nor must thou weary of this duty be,
'Cause God's not weary of forgiving thee.

Thou livest by forgiveness; should a stop
Be put thereto *one moment,* thou wouldst drop
Into the mouth of hell.   Then let this move
Thee thy dear brother to forgive in love.

And we are bid in our forgivenesses
To do as God doth in forgiving his.
If any have a quarrel against any
(As quarrels we have oft against a many),
Why then as God, for Christ's sake, pardons
   you,
For Christ's sake, pardon thou thy brother too.
We say, What freely comes doth freely go;
Then let all our forgivenesses be so.
I'm sure God heartily forgiveth thee,
My loving brother, prithee forgive me;
But then in thy forgiveness be upright;
Do 't with thine heart, or thou 'rt an hypocrite.

As we forgive, so we must watch and pray;
For enemies we have, that night and day,
Should we not watch, would soon our graces spoil,
Should we not pray, would our poor souls defile.
Without a watch, resist a foe who can?
Who prays not is not like to play the man?
Complain that he is overcome, he may;
But who would win the field must watch and pray.
Who watches should know who and who's together:
Know we not friends from foes, how know we
   whether
Of them to fight, or which to entertain?
Some have, instead of foes, familiars slain.
Sometimes a lust will get into the place,
Or work, or office, of some worthy grace
Till it has brought our souls to great decay.
Unless we diligently watch and pray,
Our pride will our humility precede:
By th' nose, our unbelief our faith will lead.

Self-love will be where self-denial should;
And passion heat, what patience sometimes cool'd.
And thus it will be with us night and day,
Unless we diligently watch and pray.

Besides what these domestics do, there are
Abroad such foes as wait us to ensnare;
Yea, they against us stand in battle-'ray,
And will us spoil, unless we *watch and pray.*
There is the world with all its vanities,
There is the devil with a thousand lies;
There are false brethren with their fair collusions,
Also false doctrines with their strong delusions;
These will us take, yea, carry us away
From what is good, unless we *watch and pray.*
Long life to many is a fearful snare;
Of sudden death we also need beware;
The smiles and frowns of men temptations be;
And there's a bait in all we hear and see.
Let them who can, to any show a way,
How they should live, that cannot watch and
   pray.

Nor is't enough to keep all well within,
Nor yet to keep all out that would be sin
If entertained; I must myself concern
With my dear brother, as I do discern
Him tempted, or a wand'ring from the way;
Else, as I should, I do not watch and pray.
Pray then and watch, be thou no drowsy sleeper,
Grudge, nor refuse, to be thy brother's keeper.
Seest thou thy brother's graces at an ebb?
Is his heel taken in the spider's web?
Pray for thy brother; if that will not do,
To him, and warn him of the present woe
That is upon him: if he shall thee hear
Thou wilt a saviour unto him appear.

Sincerity, to that we are enjoin'd,
For I do in our blessed law-book find
That duties, how well done soe'er they seem.
With our great God are but of small esteem
If not sincerely done: then have a care,
For hypocrites are hateful everywhere.
Things we may do, yea, and may let men see
Us do them too design but honestly;
Vain-gloriously let us not seek for praise,
Vain-glory's nothing worth in gospel days.
Sincerity seeks not an open place
To do, though it does all with open face;
It loves no guises, nor disfigurations,
'Tis plain, 'tis simple, hates equivocations.
Sincerity's that grace by which we poise,
And keep our duties even: nor but toys
Are all we do, if no sincerity
Attend our works, lift it up ne'er so high.
Sincerity makes heav'n upon us smile,
Lo, here's a man in whom there is no guile!
Nathaniel, an Israelite indeed!
With duties he sincerely doth proceed;
Under the fig-tree heav'n saw him at prayer—
There is but few do their devotions there.

Sincerity!   Grace is thereto entail'd,
The man that was sincere God never fail'd.
One tear that falleth from sincerity
Is worth ten thousand from hypocrisy.

Meekness is also here imposed by law,
A froward spirit is not worth a straw.
A froward spirit is a bane to rest—
They find it so, who lodge it in their breast.
A froward spirit suits with self-denial,
With taking up the cross, and ev'ry trial,
As cats and dogs, together by the ears—
As scornful men do suit with frumps and jeers.
Meek as a lamb, mute as a fish, is brave,
When anger boils, and passions vent do crave.
The meek God will in paths of judgment guide;
Good shall the meek eat, and be satisfied;
The Lord will lift the meek to highest station;
Will beautify the meek with his salvation.
The meek are blest, the earth they shall inherit:
The meek is better than the proud in spirit.
Meekness will make you quiet, hardy, strong,
To bear a burden, and to put up wrong.
Meekness, though divers troubles you are in,
Will bridle passion, be a curb to sin.
Thus God sets forth the meek before our eyes;
A meek and quiet spirit God doth prize.

Temp'rance also, is on this house imposed,
And whoso has it not, is greatly nosed
By standers-by, for greedy, lustful men:
Nor can all we can say excuse us, when
Intemp'rance anywhere to them shall be
Apparent; though we other vices flee.
Temperance the mother is of moderation,
The beauty also of our conversation.
Temperance will our affections moderate,
And keep us from being inordinate
In our embraces, or in our salutes
Of what we have, also in our pursuits
Of more, and in a sedate settlement
Of mind will make 's in all states be content.
Nor want we here an argument to prove
That who inordinate is in his love
Of worldly things, doth better things defy,
And slight salvation for the butterfly.

What argument can any man produce,
Why we should be intemperate in the use
Of any worldly good?   Do we not see
That all these things from us a fleeting be?
What can we hold? What can we keep from flying
From us?   Is not each thing we have a dying?
My house, my wife, my child, they all grow old,
Nor am I e'er the younger for my gold?
Here's none abiding, all things fade away,
Poor I at best am but a clod of clay.

If that be true, man doth not live by bread,
He that has nothing else, must needs be dead;
Take bread for what can in this world be found,
Yet all that therein is, is but a sound,

An empty sound, there is no life at all,
It cannot save a sparrow from her fall.
Let us then use this world as we are bid,
And as in olden times the godly did.
  Who buy, should be as if they did possess
None of their purchase, or themselves did bless
In what they have; and he that doth rejoice
In what he hath should rather, out of choice,
Withdraw his mind from what he hath below,
And set his heart on whither he must go.
  For those that weep under their heavy crosses,
Or that are broken with the sense of losses,
Let them remember, all things here are fading,
And as to nature, of a self-degrading
And wasting temper, yea, both we and they
Shall waste and waste, until we waste away.
Let temperance then, with moderation be
As bounds to our affections, when we see,
Or feel, or taste, or any ways enjoy
Things pleasing to the flesh, lest we destroy
Ourselves therewith, or bring ourselves thereby
To surfeits, guilt, or Satan's slavery.

Patience, another duty, as we find
In holy writ, is on this house enjoin'd;
Her state, while here, is such that she must have
This grace abounding in her, or a slave
She'll quickly be unto their lusts and will,
That seek the mind of Satan to fulfil.
He who must bear all wrongs without resistance,
And that with gladness too, must have assistance
Continually from patience, thereunto,
Or he will find such work too hard to do.
Who meets with taunts, with mocks, with flouts
      and squibs;
With railleries, reproaches, checks, and snibs;
Yea, he who for well-doing is abused,
Robb'd, spoil'd, and gaol'd, and every way mis-
      used;
Has he not patience soon will be offended,
Yea, his profession too will soon be ended.
  A Christian for religion must not fight,
But put up wrongs, though he be in the right;
He must be merciful, loving, and meek,
When they smite one, must turn the other cheek,
He must not render railing for reviling,
Nor murmur when he sees himself a spoiling;
When they shall curse, he must be sure to bless,
And thus with patience must his soul possess.
  I doubt our framper'd Christians will not down
With what I say, yet I dare pawn my gown,
Do but compare my notes with sacred story,
And you will find patience the way to glory.
  Patience under the cross, a duty is,
Whoso possesses it, belongs to bliss;
If it its present work accomplisheth;
If it holds out, and still abideth with
The Truth; then may we look for that reward,
Promised at the coming of the Lord.

To entertain good men let's not forget
Some by so doing have had the benefit;

Yea, for to recompence this act of theirs,
Angels have lodged with them unawares.
Yea, to encourage such a work as this,
The Lord himself makes it a note of his,—
When hungry or when thirsty I have been,
Or when a stranger, you did take me in.
Strangers should not to strangers but be kind,
Specially if conferring notes, they find
Themselves, though strangers here, one brother-
    hood,
And heirs, joint heirs, of everlasting good;
These should as mother's sons, when they do meet
In a strange country, one another greet
With welcome : Come in, brother, how dost do?
Whither art wand'ring?   Prithee let me know
Thy state? Dost want or meat, or drink, or
    cloth?
Art weary?   Let me wash thy feet, I'm loth
Thou shouldst depart, abide with me all night·
Pursue thy journey with the morning light,

X.

THE WAY OF REDUCING WHAT'S AMISS, INTO ORDER
HERE.

Although this house thus honourable is,
Yet 'tis not sinless, many things amiss
Do happen here, wherefore them to redress,
We must keep to our rules of righteousness.
Nor must we think it strange, if sin shall be
Where virtue is; don't all men plainly see
That in the holy temple there was dust,
That to our very gold, there cleaveth rust?
In Abraham's family was a derider,
I' th' palace of a king will be the spider.
Who saith, we have no sin, doth also say
We have no need at all to watch and pray ;
To live by faith, the flesh to mortify,
Or of more of the spirit to sanctify
Our nature.   All this wholly needless is
With him, who as to this, has nought amiss.
  But we confess, 'cause we would nôt be liars,
That we still feel the motions and desires
Of sin within us, and should fall away,
Did not Christ intercede and for us pray.
We therefore do conclude that sin is here,
But that it may not to our shame appear,
We have our rules, thereby with it to deal,
And plaisters too, our deadly wounds to heal.
And seeing idleness gives great occasions
To th' flesh, to make its rude and bold invasions
Upon good orders, 'tis ordain'd we see,
That none dwell here, but such as workers be :
So plain's the law for this, and so complete,
It bids who will not work, forbear to eat;
Let then each one be diligent to do
What grace or nature doth oblige them to.
  Who have no need to work for meat or clothes,
Should work for those that want. Not that the
    sloth
Of idleness should be encouraged,
But that those, poor indeed, be clad and fed.

Dorcas did thus, and 'tis to sacred story
Committed for her praise and lasting glory.

This house then is no nurse to idleness ;
Fig-trees are here to keep, and vines to dress ;
Here's work for all ; yea, work that must be done;
Yet work, like that, to playing in the sun ;
The toil's a pleasure, and the labour sweet,
Like that of David's dancing in the street :
The work is short, the wages are for ever,
The work like me, the wages like the giver.

No drone must hide himself under those eaves :
Who sows not, will in harvest reap no sheaves.
The slothful man himself may plainly see
That honey's gotten by the working bee.
  But here's no work for life, that's freely given ;
Meat, drink, and clothes, and life, we have from
    heav'n ;
Work's here enjoined, 'cause it *is* a pleasure
Vice to suppress, and augment heavenly treasure.
Moreover, 'tis to show, if men profess
The faith, and yet abide in idleness,
Their faith is vain, no man can ever prove
He's right, but by the faith that works by love.

If this good counsel is by thee rejected,
If work and labour is by thee neglected—
If thou, like David, lollest on thy bed,
Or art like to a horse, pamper'd and fed
With what will fire thy lusts, and so lay snares
For thine own soul, when thou shalt be i' th' wars:
Then take what follows—*sin must be detected,*
And thou without repentance quite rejected.

This is the house of God, his dwelling-place,
'Tis here that we behold his lovely face ;
But if it should polluted be with sin,
And so abide, he quickly will begin
To leave it desolate, and then woe to it,
Sin and his absence quickly will undo it.

And since sin is of things the worst of all,
And watcheth like a serpent on a wall,
Or flyeth like an eagle in the air,
Or runs as desperate ships, void of all care,
Or (as the great Solomon hath wisely said),
Is as the way of wantons with a maid,
Who tick, and toy, and with a tempting giggle,
Provoke to lust, and by degrees, so wriggle
Them into their affections, that they go
The way to death, so do themselves undo
As it is said, this mischief to prevent,
Let all men watch, yea, and be diligent
Observers of its motions, and then fly,
This is the way to live, and not to die.
  ☞ He that would never fall, must never slip.
Who would obey the call must fear the whip.
  God would also that every stander-by
That in the grass doth see the adder lie,
Should cry as he did, death is in the pot,
That many by its poison perish not.

But if that beastly thing shall hold its hold,
And make the man possessed basely bold
In pleading for it, or shall it deny,
Or it shall seek to cover with a lie;
Then take more aid, and make a fresh assault
At it again, diminish not the fault,
But charge it home. If yet he will fear,
But still unto his wickedness adhere,
Then tell the house thereof. But if he still
Persist in his abomination will,
Then fly him, 'cause he is a leprous man,
Count him with heathens and the publican.
But if he falls before thee at the first,
Then be thou to him faithful, loving just :
Forgive his sin, tell it not to a brother,
Lest thou thyself be served so by another.

If he falls not, but in the second charge,
Spread not his wickedness abroad at large.
But, if thou think his sorrow to be sound,
Forgive his sin, and hide it under ground.
If he shall stand the first and second shot ;
If he before the church repenteth not,
Deal with him as the matter shall require,
Let not the house for him be set on fire.
If after all, he shall repent and turn
To God, and you, you must not let him burn
For ever under sense of sin and shame,
You must his sin forgive in Christ his name.

Confirm your love to him in Christ, you must,
By all such ways as honest are and just.
Shy be not of him, carry't not aloof,
But rather give him of your love such proof,
That he may gather thence, ye do believe
To mercy Christ again doth him receive.

Two things 'monish you, as to this, I would—
The first, to show the church wherein she should
In all her actions so herself behave,
As to convince the faulty, she would save
His soul ; and that 'tis for this very thing,
She doth him unto open judgment bring.
Then would I show the person they reject,
What will, without repentance, be th' effect
Of this tremendous censure, so conclude ;
Leaving my judgment to the multitude
Of those who sober and judicious be,
Begging of each of them a prayer for me.

This house, in order to this work, must be
Affected with the sin and misery
Of this poor creature, yea, must mourn and weep
To think such tares, in your neglect, or sleep,
Should spring up here, nor must they once invent
To think, till he's cast out, you're innocent.

Thus leaven the whole lump has leavened ;
Israel was guilty of what Achan did ;
And so must stand, until they purged are,
Till Achan doth, for sin, his burden bear.

The reason is, Achan a member was
Of that great body, and by nature's laws,
The hand, foot, eye, tongue, ear, or one of these,
May taint the whole with Achan's foul disease.
The church must too be sensible of this,
Some lep'rous stones make all the house amiss ;
And as the stones must thence removed be,
In order to the house's sanctity,
So it must purged be (in any wise),
Before 'tis counted clean (by sacrifice).

Next have a care lest sin, which you should purge,
Becomes not unto you a farther scourge,
The which it will, if such shall judges be,
Which from its spots and freckles are not free.
Pluck thou the beam first out of thine own eye,
Else the condemned will thee vilify,
And say, let not the pot the kettle judge ;
If otherwise, it will beget a grudge,
A great one 'twixt the church and him that
    sinn'd,
Nor by such means, can ever such be winn'd
To a renew'd embrace of holiness ;
More like be tempted further to transgress.

Again, let those who loud against it cry
See they don't entertain it inwardly ;
Sin, like to pitch, will to the fingers cleave ;
Look to it then, let none himself deceive ;
'Tis catching : make resistances afresh,
Abhor the garment spotted by the flesh.
   ☞ *Some at the dimness of the candle puff,*
Wo yet can daub their fingers with the snuff.

Beware, likewise, lest rancour should appear
Against the person, do in all things fear :
Bewail the man, while you abhor his sin ;
Pity his soul ; the flesh you still are in ;
Thyself consider thou mayst tempted be,—
Hast thou no pity, who will pity thee ?

See that the ground be good on which you go ;
Sin, but not virtue show dislike unto.
Take heed of hypocritical intentions,
And quarrel not at various apprehensions
About some smaller matter, lest it breed
Needless debates, and lest that filthy seed
Contention, should o'errun your holy ground,
And lest not love, but nettles there are found.

You must likewise allow each man his grains,
For that none perfect are, sin yet remains,
And human frailties do attend the best ;
To bear and forbear here, will tend to rest.
Vain janglings, jars, and strifes will there abound,
Where moles are mountains made, or fault is found
With every little, trivial, petty thing ;
This spirit snib, or 'twill much mischief bring
Into this house, and 'tis for want of love,
'Tis entertain'd : *it is not of the dove.*
  For those that have private opinions too
We must make room, or shall the church undo :

Provided they be such as don't impair
Faith, holiness, nor with good conscience jar:
Provided also those that hold them shall
Such faith hold to themselves, and not let fall
Their fruitless notions in their brother's way,—
Do this, and faith and love will not decay.

We must also in these our dealings show
We put a difference 'twixt those sins that do
Clash with the light of nature, and what we
Perceive against the faith of Christ to be.
Those against nature, nature will detect;
Those against faith, faith from them must direct
The judgment, conscience, understanding too,
Or there will be no cure, whate'er you do.
When men are caught in immoralities,
Nature will start, the conscience will arise
To judgment; and if impudence doth recoil,
Yet guilt and self-condemnings will embroil
The wretch concern'd, in such unquietness
Or shame, as will induce him to confess
His fault, and pardon crave of God and man:
Such men with ease therefore we conquer can.

But 'tis not thus with such as swerve in faith,
With them who, as our wise apostle saith,
Entangled are at unawares, with those
Cunning to trap, to snare, and to impose
By falsifyings, their prevarications:
No, these are slyly taken from their stations,
Unknown to nature; yea, in judgment they
Think they have well done to forsake the way
Their understanding, and their judgment too,
Doth like or well approve of what they do.
These are, poor souls, beyond their art and skill,
Ta'en captive by the devil, at his will.
Here therefore you must patience exercise,
And suffer long, ye must not tyrannize
It over such, but must all meekness show;
Still dropping of good doctrine as the dew,
Against their error: so its churlishness
You conquer will, and may their fault redress.

The reason why we must not exercise
That roughness here, as where conviction lies
In nature, is because those thus ensnared
Want nature's light and help to be repair'd.
A spirit hath them taken, they are gone,
Delusions supernat'ral they're on
The wing of; they are out o' th' reach of man,
Nothing but God and gospel reach them can.
  Now since we cannot give these people eyes,
Nor regulate their judgment, wherein lies
Our work with them, if not, as has been said,
In exercising patience. While display'd
The holy word before their faces is,
By which alone they must see what's amiss
With their poor souls, and so convert again,
To him with whom salvation doth remain.

  Obj. But they are turbulent, they would confound
The truth, and all in their perdition drown'd.

  Ans. If turbulent and mischievous they are,
Imposing their opinions without care
Who they offend, or do destroy thereby;
Then must the church deal with them presently,
Lest tainted be the whole with their delusion,
And brought into disorder and confusion.

XI.

THE PRESENT CONDITION OF THOSE THUS DEALT WITH.

The man that worthily rejected is,
And cast out of this house, his part in bliss
Is lost for ever, turns he not again,
True faith and holiness to entertain.
  Nor is it boot, for who are thus cast out,
Themselves to flatter, or to go about
To shift the censure; nothing here will do,
Except a new conversion thou come to.
  He that is bound on earth, is bound in heaven,
Nor is his loosing, but the sin forgiven;
Repentance, too, forgiveness must precede,
Or thou must still abide among the dead.

XII.

AN EXPOSTULATION WITH SUCH TO RETURN.

  ☞ O shame! is't not a shame for men to be,
For sin, spued out from good society!
For man enlightened to be so base!
To turn his back upon the God of grace!
For one who for his sins has mourn'd and cried,
To slight him who for sin hath bled and died!
What fool would sell his part in paradise,
That has a soul, and that of such a price?
What parallel can suit with such so well,
As those for sin cast down from heaven to hell?
  But let me tell thee here is aggravation;
The angels, though they did fall from their station,
Had not the caution thou hast had; they fell—
This thou hast seen, and seeing, didst rebel.
One would a thought, the noise of this their fall,
A warning; yea, a warning, and a call,
Should unto thee have been, to have a care
Of falling too: O how then didst thou dare,
Since God did not spare them, thus to presume
To tempt him in his wrath, thee to consume?
  Nor did the angels from a Jesus fall,
Redeem'd they were not from a state of thrall;
But thou! as one redeem'd, and that by blood,
Redemption hast despised; and the mud
Or mire of thine own filth again embracest:
A dying, bleeding Jesus thou disgracest!
What wilt thou do? seest not how thou hast trod
Under thy foot the very Son of God?
O fearful hand of God! And fearful will
Thy doom be, when his wrath thy soul shall kill.
  Yea, with a signal these must bear their sin,
  ☞ This dirty sow from mire has washed been,
Yet there did wallow, after wash'd she was;
So to procure a lust, obtain'd this loss.

O shame! is't not a shame for man to be
So much averse to his felicity,
That none can make him leave to play the fool,
Till to the devil he be put to school,
To learn his own salvation to prize?
O fool! must now the devil make thee wise?
O sot! that will in wickedness remain,
Unless the devil drives thee back again.

Hast quite forgot how thou wast wont to pray,
And cry out for forgiveness night and day?
Or dost thou count they were but painted fears
Which from thine eyes did squeeze so many tears?
Remember, man, thy prayers and tears will cry
Thee down to hell, for thine apostasy.
Who will not have what he has prayed for,
Must die the death, his prayers shall him abhor.
　Hast thou forgotten that most solemn vow
Thou mad'st to God, when thou didst crave he bow
His ear unto thee would, and give thee grace,
And would thee also in his arms embrace?
That vow, I say, whereby thou then didst bind
Thyself to him, that now thy roving mind
Recoil against him should, and fling away
From him, and his commandments disobey.
　What has he done? wherein has he offended?
Thou actest now as if thou wast intended
To prove him guilty of unrighteousness,
Of breach of promise, or that from distress
He could, or would not save thee, or that thou
Hast found a better good than he; but how
Thou wilt come off, or how thou wilt excuse
Thyself, 'cause thou art gone, and did refuse
To wait upon him, that consider well:
Thou art as yet alive, on this side hell.
　Is't not a shame, a stinking shame to be
Cast forth God's vineyard as a barren tree?
To be thrown o'er the pales, and there to lie,
Or be pick'd up by th' next that passeth by?

Well, thou hast turn'd away, return again;
Bethink thyself, thy foot from sin refrain;
Hark! thou art call'd upon, stop not thine ear;
Return, backsliding children, come, draw near

Unto your God; repent, and he will heal
Your base backslidings, to you will reveal
That grace and peace which with him doth remain,
For them that turn away, and turn again.

Take with thee words, come to the throne of
　　grace—
There supplicate thy God, and seek his face;
Like to the prodigal, confess thy sin,
Tell him where, and how vicious thou hast been.
　☞ Suppose he shall against thee shut the door,
Knock thou the louder, and cry out the more;
What if he makes thee there to stand awhile?
Or makes as if he would not reconcile
To thee again? Yet take thee no denial,
Count all such carriages but as a trial
Whether thou art in earnest in thy suit,
As one truly forlorn and destitute.
But hide thou nought of all that thou hast done,
Open thy bosom, make confession
Of all thy wickedness, tell every whit:
Hast thou a secret sin? don't cover it;
Confess, thyself judge, if thou wouldst not die;
Who doth himself judge, God doth justify.

To sin, and stand in't, is the highest evil;
This makes a man most like unto the devil!
This bids defiance unto God and grace;
This man resists him, spitteth in his face,
Scorns at his justice, mocketh at his power,
Tempts him, provokes him, grieves him every
　　hour:
When he ariseth, he will recompense
This sturdy rebel for his impenitence:
Be not incorrigible then, come back again,
There's hope, beg mercy while life doth remain.

　Obj. But I fear I'm lost and cast away,
Sentence is past, and who reverse it may?

　Ans. The sentence past, admitteth of reprieve;
Yea, of a pardon, canst thou but believe.
TURN AGAIN, SINNER, NEVER MAKE A DOUBT;
COME, THE LORD JESUS WILL NOT CAST THEE OUT.

PRISON MEDITATIONS,

SUFFERING SAINTS AND REIGNING SINNERS.

PREFATORY NOTE.

THE sorrows and weariness of prison life might be a sufficient apology for Bunyan's worst experiments as a poet. But the bold, defiant spirit, the earnest vigour of some of the following stanzas, though not itself poetry, awakens a feeling very like that which answers to genuine heroic verse. The man who, in spite of prison-bars, can feel himself free, has only to utter the sentiments which sustain and animate him, to effect the highest purpose of poetry. He not only teaches the love of liberty, but he shows what liberty is, and how it is to be won. The sphere of existence and hope becomes wider and wider at the voice of such a teacher; and however rude and inartificial his language, there is enough both of breath and fire in what he says to make those who listen to him greater as well as better men. It is no mere notional feeling of independence that can lighten the burden of actual distress. Imprisonment, sickness, separation from friends, extreme poverty, are evils which refuse to obey conceit. The suffering which they inflict can be soothed by no other contrivance than that of balancing against it the deep convictions and steadfast hopes of a healthy soul. Whatever tends to create these supports, or to render the mind more conscious of its own wonderful resources, is one of the most precious agents on the side of humanity against the power of evil. It is the slavish notion that man depends more upon the world without him, than upon himself, which exposes him every moment to the invasions of despair. The simplest suggestion of actual experience, intimating that trouble is conquerable by certain efforts of inward life, may put a sufferer ready to perish, in the way of safety. Once taught that all things belonging to the Spirit may live and grow in us, and bear fruit, in spite of all the withering blasts of worldly misfortune, and we cherish, more and more, the wisdom which has rendered us such help. The shape in which it comes to us, its tone and utterance, can no longer divert us from valuing it at its own intrinsic worth. In a country where men dig for gold, a bank covered with violets, a myrtle or orange grove, is far less regarded than the flowerless spot which covers any portion of treasure.

H. S.

PRISON MEDITATIONS.

1. FRIEND, I salute thee in the Lord,
   And wish thou mayst abound
   In faith, and have a good regard
   To keep on holy ground.

2. Thou dost encourage me to hold
   My head above the flood,
   Thy counsel better is than gold,
   In need thereof I stood.

3. Good counsel's good at any time,
   The wise will it receive,
   Though fools count he commits a crime
   Who doth good counsel give.

4. I take it kindly at thy hand
   Thou didst unto me write,
   My feet upon Mount Sion stand,
   In that take thou delight.

5. I am, indeed, in prison now
   In body, but my mind
   Is free to study Christ, and how
   Unto me he is kind.

6. For though men keep my outward man
   Within their locks and bars,
   Yet by the faith of Christ I can
   Mount higher than the stars.

7. Their *fetters* cannot *spirits* tame,
   Nor tie up God from me;
   My faith and hope they cannot lame,
   Above them I shall be.

8. I here am very much refresh'd
   To think when I was out,
   I preached life, and peace, and rest
   To sinners round about.

9. My business then was souls to save,
    By preaching grace and faith;
    Of which the comfort now I have,
    And have it shall till death.

10. They were no fables that I taught,
    Devised by cunning men,
    But God's own Word, by which were caught
    Some sinners now and then.

11. Whose souls by it were made to see
    The evils of their sin;
    And need of Christ to make them free
    From death, which they were in.

12. And now those very hearts that then
    Were foes unto the Lord,
    Embrace his Christ and truth, like men
    Conquered by his word.

13. I hear them sigh and groan, and cry
    For grace, to God above;
    They loathe their sin, and to it die,
    'Tis holiness they love.

14. This was the work I was about
    When hands on me they laid,
    'Twas *this* from which they pluck'd me out,
    And vilely to me said,

15. You heretic deceiver, come,
    To prison you must go;
    You preach abroad, and keep not home,
    You are the church's foe.

16. But having peace within my soul,
    And truth on every side,
    I could with comfort them control,
    And at their charge deride.

17. Wherefore to prison they me sent,
    Where to this day I lie,
    And can with very much content
    For my profession die.

18. The prison very sweet to me
    Hath been, since I came here,
    And so would also hanging be,
    If God will there appear.

19. Here dwells good conscience, also peace;
    Here be my garments white;
    Here, though in bonds, I have release
    From guilt, which else would bite.

20. When they do talk of banishment,
    Of death, or such-like things,
    Then to me God sends heart's content,
    That like a fountain springs.

21. Alas, they little think what peace
    They help me to, for by
    Their rage my comforts do increase;
    Bless God therefore do I.

22. If they do give me gall to drink,
    Then God doth sweet'ning cast
    So much thereto, that they can't think
    How bravely it doth taste.

23. For, as the devil sets before
    Me heaviness and grief,
    So God sets Christ and grace much more,
    Whereby I take relief.

24. Though they say then that we are fools
    Because we here do lie,
    I answer, gaols are Christ his schools,
    In them we learn to die.

25. 'Tis not the baseness of this state
    Doth hide us from God's face,
    He frequently, both soon and late,
    Doth visit us with grace.

26. Here come the angels, here come saints,
    Here comes the Spirit of God,
    To comfort us in our restraints
    Under the wicked's rod.

27. God sometimes visits prisons more
    Than lordly palaces,
    He often knocketh at our door,
    When he their houses miss.

28. The truth and life of heavenly things
    Lift up our hearts on high,
    And carry us on eagles' wings,
    Beyond carnality.

29. It takes away those clogs that hold
    The hearts of other men,
    And makes us lively, strong, and bold
    Thus to oppose their sin.

30. By which means God doth frustrate
    That which our foes expect;
    Namely, our turning th' apostate
    Like those of Judas' sect.

31. Here comes to our remembrance
    The troubles good men had
    Of old, and for our furtherance,
    Their joys when they were sad.

32. To them that here for evil lie
    The place is comfortless,
    But not to me, because that I
    Lie here for righteousness.

33. The *truth* and *I* were both here cast
    Together, and we do
    Lie arm in arm, and so hold fast
    Each other; this is true.

34. This gaol to us is as a hill,
    From whence we plainly see
    Beyond this world, and take our fill
    Of things that lasting be.

35. From hence we see the emptiness
    Of all this world contains;
    And here we feel the blessedness
    That for us yet remains.

36. Here we can see how all men play
    Their parts, as on a stage,
    How good men suffer for God's way,
    And bad men at them rage.

37. Here we can see who holds that ground
    Which they in Scripture find;
    Here we see also who turns round
    Like *weathercocks* with wind.

38. We can also from hence behold
    How *seeming friends* appear
    But *hypocrites*, as we are told
    In Scripture everywhere.

39. When we did walk at liberty,
    We were deceived by them,
    Who we from hence do clearly see
    Are vile deceitful men.

40. These politicians that profess'd
    For base and worldly ends,
    Do now appear to us at best
    But *Machiavilian* friends.

41. Though men do say, we do disgrace
    Ourselves by lying here
    Among the rogues, yet Christ our face
    From all such filth will clear.

42. We know there's neither flout nor frown
    That we now for him bear
    But will add to our heavenly crown,
    When he comes in the air.

43. When he our righteousness forth brings
    Bright shining as the day,
    And wipeth off those sland'rous things
    That scorners on us lay.

44. We sell our earthly happiness
    For heavenly house and home;
    We leave this world because 'tis less,
    And worse than that to come.

45. We change our drossy dust for gold,
    From death to life we fly;
    We let go shadows, and take hold
    Of immortality.

46. We trade for that which lasting is,
    And nothing for it give,
    But that which is already his
    By whom we breathe and live.

47. That liberty we lose for him,
    Sickness might take away:
    Our goods might also for our sin
    By fire or thieves decay.

48. Again, we see what glory 'tis
    Freely to bear our cross
    For him, who for us took up his,
    When he our servant was.

49. I am most free that men should see
    A hole cut through mine ear;
    If others will ascertain me,
    They'll hang a jewel there.

50. Just thus it is we suffer here
    For him a little pain,
    Who, when he doth again appear,
    Will with him let us reign.

51. If all must either die for sin
    A death that's natural;
    Or else for Christ, 'tis best with him
    Who for the *last* doth fall.

52. Who now dare say we throw away
    Our goods or liberty,
    When God's most holy Word doth say
    We gain thus much thereby?

53. Hark yet again, you carnal men,
    And here what I shall say
    In your own dialect, and then
    I'll you no longer stay.

54. You talk sometimes of valour much,
    And count such bravely mann'd,
    That will not stick to have a touch
    With any in the land.

55. If these be worth commending, then,
    That vainly show their might,
    How dare you blame those holy men
    That in God's quarrel fight?

56. Though you dare crack a coward's crown,
    Or quarrel for a pin,
    You dare not on the wicked frown,
    Nor speak against their sin.

57. For all your spirits are so stout,
    For matters that are vain;
    Yet sin besets you round about—
    You are in Satan's chain.

58. You dare not for the truth engage,
    You quake at prisonment;
    You dare not make the tree your stage
    For Christ, that King potent.

59. Know, then, true valour there doth dwell
    Where men engage for God,
    Against the devil, death, and hell,
    And bear the wicked's rod.

60. These be the men that God doth count
    Of high and noble mind;
    These be the men that do surmount
    What you in nature find.

61. First they do conquer their own hearts,
    All worldly fears, and then
    Also the devil's fiery darts,
    And persecuting men.

62. They conquer when they thus do fall.
    They kill when they do die:
    They overcome then most of all,
    And get the victory.

63. The worldling understands not this,
    'Tis clear out of his sight;
    Therefore he counts this world his bliss,
    And doth our glory slight.

64. The lubber knows not how to spring
    The nimble footman's stage;
    Neither can owls or jackdaws sing
    If they were in the cage.

65. The swine doth not the pearls regard,
    But them doth slight for grains,
  Though the wise merchant labours hard
    For them with greatest pains.

66. Consider, man, what I have said,
    And judge of things aright;
  When all men's cards are fully play'd,
    Whose will abide the light?

67. Will *those* who have us hither cast?
    Or *they* who do us scorn?
  Or *those* who do our houses waste?
    Or *us*, who this have borne?

68. And let us count those things the best
    That best will prove at last;
  And count such men the only blest,
    That do such things hold fast.

69. And what though they us dear do cost,
    Yet let us buy them so;
  We shall not count our labour lost
    When we see others' woe.

70. And let saints be no longer blamed
    By carnal policy;
  But let the wicked be ashamed
    Of their malignity.

NOTE.—A volume, under the title of *Scriptural Poems*, was published with Bunyan's name, in 1701. Nothing appears to have been heard of it for the next one hundred and fifty years; and the probability is that the publisher made a bad speculation, having vainly endeavoured to sell a worthless book by using the name of a venerable man who had no concern in its composition. In the poems really written by Bunyan there is generally some trace of his own earnest way of thinking. There is not a gleam of thought, not a spark of originality, to relieve the uniform dulness of the rhyming history of Ruth, &c. Charles Doe would not have allowed this poverty of merit to prevent his inserting the *Poems* in his Catalogue, had he believed them genuine; but he knew they were none of Bunyan's, and very properly left them unnoticed.

H. S.

MR. BUNYAN'S LAST SERMON.

PREACHED JULY, 1688.

PREFATORY NOTE.

WHEN Bunyan preached his last sermon, he bore a simple, holy testimony to the inestimable preciousness of his earliest faith. For nearly forty years had his naturally powerful, active mind been engaged in examining and applying the doctrines to which he attributed his salvation. The trials which he endured, the enlargement and growing strength of his mind, his matured knowledge of human character, his accumulating literary information had no other effect upon him but that of increasing his love to Jesus Christ and his gospel. It is evident that we have but a mere outline of his last sermon. He could not have preached so briefly on a theme the dearest of all subjects to his soul. But short as are the notes of this discourse, they indicate sufficiently its scope and purpose; and it is a circumstance of deep and affecting interest, that the beginning and the end of this great preacher's work should have been knitted together in the one same vital truth.

H. S.

MR. BUNYAN'S LAST SERMON.

JOHN i. 13.

"Which were born, not of blood, nor of the will of the flesh, nor of the will of man, but of God."

THE words have a dependence on what goes before, and therefore I must direct you to them for the right understanding of it. You have it thus: "He came unto his own, and his own received him not. But as many as received him, to them gave he power to become the sons of God, even to them that believe on his name: which were born, not of blood, nor of the will of the flesh, nor of the will of man, but of God." (John i. 11—13.) In the words before, you have two things.

First. Some of his own rejecting him when he offered himself to them.

Second. Others of his own receiving him, and making him welcome. Those that reject him, he also passes by; but those that receive him, he gives them power to become the sons of God.

Now, lest any one should look upon it as good luck or fortune, says he, they "were born, not of blood, nor of the will of the flesh, nor of the will of man, but of God." They that did not receive him, they were only born of flesh and blood: but those that receive him, they have God to their Father, they receive the doctrine of Christ with a vehement desire.

FIRST. I'll show you what he means by blood. They that believe are born to it, as an heir is to an inheritance; they are born of God, not of flesh, nor of the will of man, but of God: "not of blood," that is, not by generation, not born to the kingdom of heaven by the flesh; not because I am the son of a godly man or woman, that is meant by blood. (Acts xvii. 26.) He "hath made of one blood all nations;" but when he says here, "not of blood," he rejects all carnal privileges they did boast of. They boasted they were Abraham's seed: no, no, says he, it is not of blood: think not to say you have Abraham to your father, you must be born of God, if you go to the kingdom of heaven.

SECOND. "Nor of the will of the flesh." What must we understand by that?

It is taken for those vehement inclinations that are in man to all manner of looseness, fulfilling the desires of the flesh, that must not be understood here; men are not made the children of God by fulfilling their lustful desires, it must be understood there in the best sense. There is not only in carnal men a will to be vile, but there is in them a will to be saved also, a will to go to heaven also. But this it will not do—it will not privilege a man in the things of the kingdom of God. Natural desires after the things of another world, they are not an argument to prove a man shall go to heaven whenever he dies. I am not a free-willer, I do abhor it; yet there is not the wickedest man but he desires some time or other to be saved; he will read some time or other, or it may be pray; but this will not do: "It is not of him that willeth, nor of him that runneth, but of God that showeth mercy." here is willing and running, and yet to no purpose. (Rom. ix. 16.) Israel, which followed after the law of righteousness, have not obtained it. (Rom. ix. 30.) Here I do not understand as if the apostle had denied a virtuous course of life to be the way to heaven, but that a man without grace, though he have natural gifts, yet he shall not obtain privilege to go to heaven, and be the son of God. Though a man without grace may have a will to be saved, yet he cannot have that will God's way: nature, it cannot know anything but the things of nature; the things of God know no man, but by the Spirit of God; unless the Spirit of God be in you, it will leave you on this side the gates of heaven. "Not of blood, nor of the will of the flesh, nor of the will of man, but of God." It may be some may have a will, a desire that Ishmael may be saved; know this, it will not save thy child. If it was our will, I would have you all go to heaven. How many are there in the world that pray for their children and cry for them, and ready to die, and this will not do. God's will is the rule of all, it is only through Jesus Christ, "which were born not of flesh, nor of the will of man, but of God."

Now I come to the doctrine.

Men that believe in Jesus Christ to the effectual receiving of Jesus Christ, they are born to it. He does not say they *shall* be born to it, but they *are* born to it—born of God unto God, and the things of God, before he receives God to eternal salvation: "Except a man be born again, he cannot see the kingdom of God." Now, unless he be born of God, he cannot see it. Suppose the kingdom of God be what it will, he cannot see it before he be begotten of God. Suppose it be the gospel, he cannot see it before he be brought into a state of regeneration. Believing *is* the consequence of the new birth: "not of blood, nor of the will of man, but of God."

First. I will give you a clear description of it under one similitude or two. A child, before it be born into the world, is in the dark dungeon of its mother's womb; so a child of God, before he be born again, is in the dark dungeon of sin, sees nothing of the kingdom of God. Therefore it is called a new birth; the same soul has love one way in its carnal condition, another way when it is born again.

Second. As it is compared to a birth resembling a child in its mother's womb, so it is compared to a man being raised out of the grave; and to be born again, it is to be raised out of the grave of sin: "Awake, thou that sleepest, and arise from the dead, and Christ shall give thee light." To be raised from the grave of sin, is to be begotten and born. (Rev. i. 5.) There is a famous instance of Christ: He is "the first begotten from the dead," he is the first-born from the dead, unto which our regeneration alludeth, that is, if you be born again by seeking those things that are above, then there is a similitude betwixt Christ's resurrection and the new birth, which was born, which was restored out of this dark world, and translated out of the king-

dom of this dark world into the kingdom of his dear Son, and made us live a new life; this is to be born again. And he that is delivered from the mother's womb, it is the help of the mother; so he that is born of God, it is by the Spirit of God. I must give you a few consequences of a new birth.

1. First of all, a child, you know, is incident to cry as soon as it comes into the world; for if there be no noise, they say it is dead. You that are born of God, and Christians, if you be not criers, there is no spiritual life in you—if you be born of God, you are crying ones; as soon as he has raised you out of the dark dungeon of sin, but cannot you cry to God, "What must I do to be saved?" As soon as ever God had touched the gaoler, he cries out, "Men and brethren, what must I do to be saved?" Oh! how many prayerless professors are there in London, that never pray. Coffee-houses will not let you pray, trades will not let you pray, looking-glasses will not let you pray; but if you was born of God, you would.

2. It is not only natural for a child to cry, but it must crave the breast. It cannot live without the breast, therefore Peter makes it the true trial of a new-born babe: the new-born babe desires the sincere milk of the word, that he may grow thereby. If you be born of God, make it manifest by desiring the breast of God. Do you long for the milk of the promises? A man lives one way when he is in the world, another way when he is brought unto Jesus Christ. (Isa. lxvi.) They shall suck and be satisfied; if you be born again, there is no satisfaction till you get the milk of God's word into your souls. (Isa. lxvi. 11.) To "suck and be satisfied with the breasts of her consolation." Oh what is a promise to a carnal man. A whorehouse, it may be, is more sweet to him; but if you be born again, you cannot live without the milk of God's word. What is a woman's breast to a horse? But what is it to a child? There is its comfort night and day; there is its succour night and day. Oh how loath are they it should be taken from them: minding heavenly things, says a carnal man, is but vanity, but to a child of God, there is his comfort.

3. A child that is newly-born, if it have not other comforts to keep it warm than it had in its mother's womb, it dies; it must have something got for its succour: so Christ had swaddling clothes prepared for him; so those that are born again, they must have some promise of Christ to keep them alive. Those that are in a carnal state, they warm themselves with other things; but those that are born again, they cannot live without some promise of Christ to keep them alive; as he did to the poor infant. (Ezek. xvi. 8.) I covered thee with embroidered gold: and when women are with child, what fine things will they prepare for their child! Oh, but what fine things has Christ prepared to wrap all in that are born again! oh what wrappings of gold has Christ prepared for all that are born again! Women

will dress their children, that every one may see them how fine they are : so he in Ezek. xvi. 11—"I decked thee also with ornaments, and I put bracelets upon thine hand, and a chain on thy neck, and I put a jewel on thy forehead, and earrings in thine ears, and a beautiful crown upon thine head." And says he in the 13th verse, "Thou didst prosper to a kingdom." This is to set out nothing in the world but the righteousness of Christ and the graces of the Spirit, without which a new-born babe cannot live, unless they have the golden righteousness of Christ.

4. A child, when it is in its mother's lap, the mother takes great delight to have that which will be for its comfort; so it is with God's children, they shall be kept on his knee. (Isa. lxvi. 11.) "They shall suck and be satisfied with the breasts of her consolations" (ver. 13). "As one whom his mother comforteth, so will I comfort you." There is a similitude in these things that nobody knows of, but those that are born again.

5. There is usually some similitude betwixt the father and the child. It may be the child looks like its father; so those that are born again, they have a new similitude—they have the image of Jesus Christ. (Gal. iv.) Every one that is born of God, has something of the features of heaven upon him. Men love those children that are likest them most usually; so does God his children; therefore they are called the children of God : but others do not like him; therefore they are called Sodomites. Christ describes children of the devil by their features; the children of the devil, his works they will do—all works of unrighteousness, they are the devil's works. If you are earthly, you have borne the image of the earthly; if heavenly, you have borne the image of the heavenly.

6. When a man has a child, he trains him up to his own liking. They have learned the custom of their father's house; so are those that are born of God—they have learned the custom of the true church of God : there they learn to cry, "my Father" and "my God;" they are brought up in God's house, they learn the method and form of God's house, for regulating their lives in this world.

7. Children, it is natural for them to depend upon their father for what they want. If they want a pair of shoes, they go and tell him; if they want bread, they go and tell him : so should the children of God do. Do you want spiritual bread? Go tell God of it. Do you want strength of grace? Ask it of God. Do you want strength against Satan's temptations. Go and tell God of it. When the devil tempts you, run home and tell your heavenly Father; go pour out your complaints to God : this is natural to children, if any wrong them, they go and tell their father; so do those that are born of God, when they meet with temptations, go and tell God of them.

The first use is this—to make a strict inquiry whether you be born of God or not. Examine by those things I laid down before, of a child of nature, and a child of grace. Are you brought out of the dark dungeon of this world into Christ? Have you learned to cry, "My Father?" (Jer. iii. 4.) "And I said, Thou shalt call me My Father." All God's children are criers : cannot you be quiet without you have a bellyful of the milk of God's word? cannot you be satisfied without you have peace with God? Pray you consider it, and be serious with yourselves; if you have not these marks, you will fall short of the kingdom of God, you shall never have an interest there; there is no intruding. They will say, "Lord, Lord, open to us," and he will say, "I know you not." No child of God, no heavenly inheritance. We sometimes give something to those that are not our children, but not our lands. Oh do not flatter yourselves with a portion among the sons, unless you live like sons. When we see a king's son play with a beggar, this is unbecoming; so if you be the King's children, live like the King's children. If you be risen with Christ, set your affections on things above, and not on things below; when you come together, talk of what your Father promised you; you should all love your Father's will, and be content and pleased with the exercises you meet with in the world. If you are the children of God, live together lovingly. If the world quarrel with you, it is no matter; but it is sad if you quarrel together : if this be amongst you, it is a sign of ill-breeding—it is not according to the rules you have in the word of God. Dost thou see a soul that has the image of God in him? Love him, love him; say, This man and I must go to heaven one day. Serve one another, do good for one another; and if any wrong you, pray to God to right you, and love the brotherhood.

Lastly. If you be the children of God, learn that lesson—gird up the loins of your mind as obedient children, not fashioning yourselves according to your former conversation, but be ye holy in all manner of conversation. Consider that the holy God is your Father, and let this oblige you to live like the children of God, that you may look your Father in the face with comfort another day.

A RELATION

OF

THE IMPRISONMENT OF MR. JOHN BUNYAN,

MINISTER OF THE GOSPEL AT BEDFORD, NOVEMBER, 1660.

HIS EXAMINATION BEFORE THE JUSTICES, HIS CONFERENCE WITH THE CLERK OF THE PEACE, WHAT
PASSED BETWEEN THE JUDGES AND HIS WIFE, WHEN SHE PRESENTED A PETITION FOR
HIS DELIVERANCE, ETC. WRITTEN BY HIMSELF.

*"Blessed are they which are persecuted for righteousness' sake, for theirs is the kingdom of heaven. Blessed are ye when men shall revile you and persecute you, and shall say all manner of evil against you falsely, for my sake. Rejoice, and be exceeding glad, for great is your reward in heaven: for so persecuted they the prophets which were before you."—*MATT. v. 10—12.

PREFATORY NOTE.

HOWEVER interesting the following narrative, it ought not to be forgotten that it was not published till the year 1765, that is near eighty years after Bunyan's death, and more than a hundred since the occurrences and conversations of which it professes to be a report. No information is given by the bookseller as to the manuscript from which he printed the volume, or as to the source from which he obtained it; and it is questionable, therefore, how much, or how little of its contents can be depended upon as authentic.

A very different degree of credit is due to *The Struggler*. This really valuable and authentic paper was appended by Charles Doe, Bunyan's judicious and zealous executor, to proposals for a complete edition of his works. The catalogue mentions some which were early lost, and makes no allusion to others which have since been published with Bunyan's name. It is not impossible, as his death was sudden, that some writings of his may have been in the hands of booksellers or printers at the time of his decease, and may have remained unpublished, either through mere neglect, or a question of copyright. The late appearance of those which were really genuine would afford a favourable opportunity for the publication of other volumes under the same venerable name. Hence the difficulty of determining with certainty the exact number of works which may be accounted Bunyan's. The catalogue furnished by *The Struggler* is a safe criterion as far as it goes; if in anywise incorrect, it is only so in some trifling instances; and the writings to which it makes no reference must be acknowledged to have but a very doubtful title to be added to the list.

H. S.

A RELATION OF THE IMPRISONMENT OF MR. JOHN BUNYAN.

The relation of my imprisonment in the month of November, 1660, when, by the good hand of my God, I had for five years together, without any great interruption, freely preached the blessed gospel of our Lord Jesus Christ; and had also, through his blessed grace, some encouragement by his blessing thereupon: the devil, that old enemy of man's salvation, took his opportunity to inflame the hearts of his vassals against me, insomuch, that at the last I was laid out for, by the warrant of a justice, and was taken and committed to prison. The relation thereof is as followeth:

UPON the 12th of this instant, November, 1660, I was desired by some of the friends in the country to come to teach at Samsell, by Harlington, in Bedfordshire. To whom I made a promise, if the Lord permitted, to be with them on the time aforesaid. The justice hearing thereof, (whose name is Mr. Francis Wingate,) forthwith issued out his warrant to take me, and bring me before him, and in the mean time to keep a very strong watch about the house where the meeting should be kept, as if we that were to meet together in that place did intend to do some fearful business, to the destruction of the country; when, alas! the constable, when he came in, found us only with our Bibles in our hands, ready to speak and hear the word of God; for we were just about to begin our exercise. Nay, we had begun in prayer for the blessing of God upon our opportunity, intending to have preached the word of the Lord unto them there present; but the constable coming in prevented us. So that I was taken and forced to depart the room. But had I been minded to have played the coward, I could have escaped, and kept out of his hands: for when I was come to my friend's house, there was whispering that that day I should be taken, for there was a warrant out to take me; which when my friend heard, he being somewhat timorous, questioned whether we had best have our meeting or not; and whether it might not be better for me to depart, lest they should take me and have me before the justice, and after that send me to prison, (for he knew better than I what spirit they were of, living by them :) to whom I said, No, by no means, I will not stir, neither will I have the meeting dismissed for this. Come, be of good cheer; let us not be daunted; our cause is good; we need not be ashamed of it : to preach God's word is so good a work, that we shall be well rewarded if we suffer for that; or to this purpose. But as for my friend, I think he was more afraid of me than of himself. After this I walked into the close, where, I somewhat seriously considering the matter, this came into my mind: that I had showed myself hearty and courageous in my preaching, and had, blessed be grace, made it my business to encourage others; therefore, thought I, if I should now run and make an escape, it will be of a very ill savour in the country. For what will my weak and newly-converted brethren think of it, but that I was not so strong in deed as I was in word? Also I feared that if I should run, now there was a warrant out for me, I might by so doing make them afraid to stand, when great words only should be spoken to them. Besides, I thought, that seeing God of his mercy should choose me to go upon the forlorn hope in this country—that is, to be the first that should be opposed for the gospel—if I should fly, it might be a discouragement to the whole body that might follow after. And further, I thought the world thereby would take occasion at my cowardliness to have blasphemed the gospel, and to have had some ground to suspect worse of me and my profession than I deserve. These things, with others, considered by me, I came in again to the house, with a full resolution to keep the meeting, and not to go away, though I could have been gone about an hour before the officer apprehended me; but I would not, for I was resolved to see the utmost of what they could say or do unto me; for, blessed be the Lord, I knew of no evil that I had said or done. And so, as aforesaid, I begun the meeting; but being prevented by the constable's coming in with his warrant to take me, I could not proceed. But before I went away I spake some few words of counsel and encouragement to the people, declaring to them that they

saw we were prevented of our opportunity to speak and hear the word of God, and were like to suffer for the same; desiring them that they should not be discouraged, for it was a mercy to suffer upon so good account. For we might have been apprehended as thieves or murderers, or for other wickedness; but, blessed be God, it was not so, but we suffer as Christians for well doing : and we had better be the persecuted than the persecutors, &c. But the constable and the justice's man, waiting on us, would not be at quiet till they had me away, and that we departed the house : but because the justice was not at home that day, there was a friend of mine engaged for me to bring me to the constable on the morrow morning. Otherwise the constable must have charged a watch with me, or have secured me some other ways, my crime was so great. So on the next morning we went to the constable's, and so to the justice.* He asked the constable what we did where we were met together, and what we had with us. I trow, he meant whether we had armour or not : but when the constable told him that there were only met a few of us together to preach and hear the word, and no sign of anything else, he could not well tell what to say : yet, because he had sent for me, he did adventure to put out a few proposals to me, which were to this effect—namely, what I did there ? and why I did not content myself with following my calling ? for it was against the law that such as I should be admitted to do as I did.

John Bunyan. To which I answered, that the intent of my coming thither, and to other places, was to instruct, and counsel people to forsake their sins, and close in with Christ, lest they did miserably perish, and that I could do both these without confusion—to wit, follow my calling, and preach the word also.

At which words he† was in a chafe, as it appeared; for he said that he would break the neck of our meetings.

Bun. I said it may be so.

Then he wished me to get me sureties to be bound for me, or else he would send me to the jail.

My sureties being ready, I called them in, and when the bond for my appearance was made he told them, that they were bound to keep me from preaching; and that if I did preach, their bonds would be forfeited. To which I answered, that then I should break them; for I should not leave speaking the word of God—even to counsel, comfort, exhort, and teach the people among whom I came; and I thought this to be a work that had no hurt in it, but was rather worthy of commendation than blame.

Wingate. Whereat he told me, that if they would not be so bound, my mittimus must be made, and I sent to the jail, there to lie to the quarter-sessions.

Now while my mittimus was a making, the justice was withdrawn, and in comes an old enemy to

* Justice Wingate.   † Ibid.

the truth, Dr. Lindale, who, when he was come in, fell to taunting at me with many reviling terms.

Bun. To whom I answered, that I did not come thither to talk with him, but with the justice.

Whereat he supposed that I had nothing to say for myself, triumphed as if he had got the victory; charging and condemning me for meddling with that for which I could show no warrant, and asked me if I had taken the oaths? and if I had not, it was pity but that I should be sent to prison, &c.

I told him, that if I was minded I could answer to any sober question that he should put to me. He then urged me again, how I could prove it lawful for me to preach, with a great deal of confidence of the victory.

But at last, because he should see that I could answer him if I listed, I cited him to that in Peter, which saith, "As every man hath received the gift. even so let him minister the same," &c.

Lind. Ay, saith he, to whom is that spoken?

Bun. To whom, said I, why to every man that hath received a gift from God. Mark, saith the apostle, "As every man that hath received a gift from God," &c. And again, "You may all prophecy one by one." Whereat the man was a little stopt, and went a softlier pace. But, not being willing to lose the day, he began again, and said—

Lind. Indeed I do remember that I have read of one Alexander, a coppersmith, who did much oppose and disturb the apostles. (Aiming, it is like, at me, because I was a tinker.)

Bun. To which I answered, that I also had read of very many priests and pharisees that had their hands in the blood of our Lord Jesus Christ.

Lind. Ay, saith he, and you are one of those scribes and pharisees; for you, with a pretence, make long prayers to devour widows' houses.

Bun. I answered, that if he had got no more by preaching and praying than I had done, he would not be so rich as now he was. But that scripture coming into my mind, "Answer not a fool according to his folly," I was as sparing of my speech as I could, without prejudice to truth.

Now by this time my mittimus was made, and I committed to the constable to be sent to the jail in Bedford, &c.

But as I was going, two of my brethren met with me by the way, and desired the constable to stay, supposing that they should prevail with the justice, through the favour of a pretended friend, to let me go at liberty. So we did stay, while they went to the justice, and after much discourse with him, it came to this—that if I would come to him again, and say some certain words to him, I should be released: which when they told me, I said if the words were such that might be said with a good conscience, I should, or else I should not. So through their importunity I went back again, but not believing that I should be delivered: for I feared their spirit was too full of opposition to the truth, to let me go, unless I should in something

or other dishonour my God, and wound my conscience: wherefore, as I went, I lifted up my heart to God for light and strength, to be kept, that I might not do anything that might either dishonour him, or wrong my own soul, or be a grief or discouragement to any that was inclining after the Lord Jesus Christ.

Well, when I came to the justice again,* there was Mr. Foster of Bedford, who coming out of another room, and seeing of me by the light of the candle (for it was dark night when I went thither), he said unto me, Who is there? John Bunyan? with such seeming affection as if he would have leaped on my neck and kissed me, which made me somewhat wonder, that such a man as he, with whom I had so little acquaintance, and besides, that had ever been a close opposer of the ways of God, should carry himself so full of love to me. But, afterwards, when I saw what he did, it caused me to remember those sayings, "Their tongues are smoother than oil, but their words are drawn swords." And again, "Beware of men," &c. When I† had answered him, that blessed be God I was well, he said, What is the occasion of your being here? or to that purpose. To whom I answered, that I was at a meeting of people a little way off, intending to speak a word of exhortation to them; the justice hearing thereof, said I, was pleased to send his warrant, to fetch me before him, &c.

Foster. So, said he, I understand—but, well, if you will promise to call the people no more together, you shall have your liberty to go home; for my brother is very loath to send you to prison, if you will be but ruled.

Bun. Sir, said I, pray what do you mean by calling the people together? My business is not anything among them when they are come together, but to exhort them to look after the salvation of their souls, that they may be saved, &c.

Fost. Saith he, We must not enter into explication or dispute now; but if you will say you will call the people no more together, you may have your liberty; if not, you must be sent away to prison.

Bun. Sir, said I, I shall not force or compel any man to hear me, yet if I come into any place where there is a people met together, I should, according to the best of my skill and wisdom, exhort and counsel them to seek out after the Lord Jesus Christ, for the salvation of their souls.

Fost. He said, that was none of my work; I must follow my calling, and if I would but leave off preaching, and follow my calling, I should have the justice's favour, and be acquitted presently.

Bun. To whom, I said, that I could follow my calling and that too, namely, preaching the word; and I did look upon it as my duty to do them both, as I had an opportunity.

Fost. He said, to have any such meetings was

* A right Judas.   † Bunyan.

against the law; and therefore he would have me leave off, and say, I would call the people no more together.

Bun. To whom I said, that I durst not make any further promise, for my conscience would not suffer me to do it. And, again, I did look upon it as my duty to do as much good as I could, not only in my trade, but also in communicating to all people wheresoever I came, the best knowledge I had in the world.

Fost. He told me that I was the nearest the papists of any, and that he would convince me of immediately.

Bun. I asked him wherein?

Fost. He said, in that we understood the scriptures literally.

Bun. I told him, that those that were to be understood literally we understood them so; but for those that were to be understood otherwise, we endeavoured so to understand them.

Fost. He said, which of the scriptures do you understand literally?

Bun. I said this, "He that believeth shall be saved." This was to be understood just as it is spoken—that whosoever believeth in Christ, shall, according to the plain and simple words of the text, be saved.

Fost. He said that I was ignorant, and did not understand the scriptures; for how, said he, can you understand them, when you know not the original Greek? &c.

Bun. To whom I said, that if that was his opinion, that none could understand the scriptures but those that had the original Greek, &c., then but a very few of the poorest sort should be saved (this is harsh), yet the scripture saith, "That God hides his things from the wise and prudent (that is, from the learned of the world), and reveals them to babes and sucklings."

Fost. He said there was none that heard me but a company of foolish people.

Bun. I told him that there were the wise as well as the foolish that do hear me; and again, those that are most commonly counted foolish by the world, are the wisest before God. Also, that God had rejected the wise, and mighty, and noble, and chosen the foolish, and the base.

Fost. He told me that I made people neglect their calling; and that God had commanded people to work six days, and serve him on the seventh.

Bun. I told him that it was the duty of people, both rich and poor, to look out for their souls on those days, as well as for their bodies: and that God would have his people exhort one another daily, while it is called to-day.

Fost. He said again, that there was none but a company of poor simple ignorant people that come to hear me.

Bun. I told him that the foolish and the ignorant had most need of teaching and information; and therefore it would be profitable for me to go on in that work.

Fost. Well, said he, to conclude, but will you promise that you will not call the people together any more? and then you may be released and go home.

Bun. I told him that I durst say no more than I had said; for I durst not leave off that work which God had called me to.

So he withdrew from me, and then came several of the justice's servants to me, and told me that I stood so much upon a nicety. Their* master, they said, was willing to let me go; and if I would but say I would call the people no more together, I might have my liberty, &c.

Bun. I told them there were more ways than one in which a man might be said to call the people together. As for instance, if a man get upon the market-place, and there read a book, or the like, though he do not say to the people, Sirs, come hither and hear; yet if they come to him because he reads, he, by his very reading, may be said to call them together; because they would not have been there to hear, if he had not been there to read. And seeing this might be termed a calling the people together, I durst not say I would not call them together; for then, by the same argument, my preaching might be said to call them together.

Wingate and Foster. Then came the justice and Mr. Foster to me again, (we had a little more discourse about preaching, but because the method of it is out of my mind, I pass it,) and when they saw that I was at a point, and would not be moved nor persuaded,

Mr. Foster† told the justice that then he must send me away to prison; and that he would do well, also, if he would present all them that were the cause of my coming among them to meetings.

Thus we parted.

And verily as I was going forth of the doors, I had much ado to forbear saying to them that I carried the peace of God along with me. But I held my peace, and, blessed be the Lord, went away to prison with God's comfort in my poor soul.

After I had lain in the jail five or six days, the brethren sought means again to get me out by bondsmen, for so ran my mittimus; that I should lie there till I could find sureties. They went to a justice at Elstow, one Mr. Crumpton, to desire him to take bond for my appearing at the quarter-sessions. At the first he told them he would, but afterwards he made a demur at the business, and desired first to see my mittimus, which run to this purpose: That I went about to several conventicles in this country, to the great disparagement of the government of the church of England, &c. When he had seen it, he said that there might be something more against me than was expressed in my mittimus; and that he was but a young man, therefore he durst not do it. This my jailer told

* Justice's servants.

† This is the man that did at the first express so much love to me.

me. Whereat I was not at all daunted, but rather glad, and saw evidently that the Lord had heard me; for before I went down to the justice, I begged of God, that if I might do more good by being at liberty than in prison, that then I might be set at liberty: but if not, his will be done; for I was not altogether without hopes but that my imprisonment might be an awakening to the saints in the country, therefore I could not tell well which to choose; only I, in that manner, did commit the thing to God. And verily at my return I did meet my God sweetly in the prison again, comforting of me and satisfying of me that it was his will and mind that I should be there.

When I came back again to prison, as I was musing at the slender answer of the justice, this word dropped in upon my heart with some life, "For he knew that for envy they had delivered him."

Thus have I in short declared the manner and occasion of my being in prison, where I lie waiting the good will of God, to do with me as he pleaseth; knowing that not one hair of my head can fall to the ground without the will of my Father which is in heaven. Let the rage and malice of men be never so great, they can do no more, nor go no farther than God permits them. But when they have done their worst, we know all things shall work together for good to them that love God. Farewell.

Here is the sum of my Examination before Justice Keelin, Justice Chester, Justice Blundale, Justice Beecher, and Justice Snagg, &c.

After I had lain in prison above seven weeks, the quarter-sessions was to be kept in Bedford, for the county thereof, unto which I was to be brought; and when my jailer had set me before those justices, there was a bill of indictment preferred against me. The extent thereof was as followeth: "That John Bunyan, of the town of Bedford, labourer, being a person of such and such conditions, he hath (since such a time) devilishly and perniciously abstained from coming to church to hear divine service, and is a common upholder of several unlawful meetings and conventicles, to the great disturbance and distraction of the good subjects of this kingdom, contrary to the laws of our sovereign lord the king," &c.

The Clerk. When this was read, the clerk of the sessions said unto me, What say you to this?

Bun. I said, that as to the first part of it, I was a common frequenter of the church of God. And was also, by grace, a member with the people over whom Christ is the head.

Keelin. But, saith Justice Keelin, who was the judge in that court, do you come to church—you know what I mean, to the parish church—to hear divine service?

Bun. I answered, No, I did not.

Keel. He asked me why?

Bun. I said, Because I did not find it commanded in the word of God.

Keel. He said, We were commanded to pray.

Bun. I said, But not by the Common Prayer-book.

Keel. He said, How then?

Bun. I said, With the Spirit. As the apostle saith, "I will pray with the Spirit, and with understanding." (1 Cor. xiv. 15.)

Keel. He said, We might pray with the Spirit, with understanding, and the Common Prayer-book also.

Bun. I said that those prayers in the Common Prayer-book, were such as were made by other men, and not by the motions of the Holy Ghost, within our hearts; and as I said, the apostle saith, he will pray with the Spirit, and with understanding; not with the Spirit, and the Common Prayer-book.

Another Justice. What do you count prayer? Do you think it is to say a few words over before or among a people?

Bun. I said, No, not so; for men might have many elegant, or excellent words, and yet not pray at all; but when a man prayeth, he doth, through a sense of those things which he wants, (which sense is begotten by the Spirit,) pour out his heart before God through Christ; though his words be not so many and so excellent as others are.

Justices. They said, That was true.

Bun. I said, This might be done without the Common Prayer-book.

Another. One of them said, (I think it was Justice Blundale or Justice Snagg,) How should we know that you do not write out your prayers first, and then read them afterwards to the people? This he spake in a laughing way.

Bun. I said, It is not our use, to take a pen and paper and write a few words thereon, and then go and read it over to a company of people.

But how should we know it? said he.

Bun. Sir, it is none of our custom, said I.

Keel. But, said Justice Keelin, it is lawful to use Common Prayer, and such like forms; for Christ taught his disciples to pray, as John also taught his disciples. And further, said he, cannot one man teach another to pray? Faith comes by hearing; and one man may convince another of sin, and therefore prayers made by men, and read over, are good to teach, and help men to pray.

While he was speaking these words, God brought that word into my mind, in the eighth of the Romans, at the twenty-sixth verse. I say God brought it, for I thought not on it before; but as he was speaking, it came so fresh into my mind, and was so evidently before me, as if the scripture had said, take me, take me. So when he had done speaking,

Bun. I said, Sir, the Scripture saith, that "it is the Spirit that helpeth our infirmities;" for we know not what we should pray for as we ought; but the Spirit itself makes intercession for us, with sighs and groanings which cannot be uttered.

Mark, said I, it doth not say the Common Prayer-book teaches us how to pray, but the Spirit. "And it is the Spirit that helpeth our infirmities," saith the apostle; he doth not say it is the Common Prayer-book.

And as to the Lord's prayer, although it be an easy thing to say Our Father, &c., with the mouth, yet there are very few that can, in the Spirit, say the two first words of that prayer—that is, that can call God their Father, as knowing what it is to be born again, and as having experience that they are begotten of the Spirit of God; which if they do not, all is but babbling, &c.

Keel. Justice Keelin said that that was a truth.

Bun. And I say further, as to your saying that one man may convince another of sin, and that faith comes by hearing, and that one man may tell another how he should pray, &c., I say men may tell each other of their sins, but it is the Spirit that must convince them.*

And though it be said that faith comes by hearing; yet it is the Spirit that worketh faith in the heart through hearing, or else "they are not profited by hearing." (Heb. iv. 12.)

And that though one man may tell another how he should pray, yet, as I said before, he cannot pray, nor make his condition known to God, except the Spirit help. It is not the Common Prayer-book that can do this. It is the "Spirit that showeth us our sins," (John xvi. 16.) and the "Spirit that showeth us a Saviour," (Matt. xi. 27;) and the Spirit that stirreth up in our hearts desires to come to God, for such things as we stand in need of, even sighing out our souls unto him for them with groans which cannot be uttered. With other words to the same purpose. At this they were set.

Keel. But, says Justice Keelin, what have you against the Common Prayer-book?

Bun. I said, Sir, if you will hear me, I shall lay down my reasons against it.

Keel. He said I should have liberty; but first, said he, let me give you one caution—take heed of speaking irreverently of the Common Prayer-book; for if you do so, you will bring great damage upon yourself.

Bun. So I proceeded, and said, my first reason was, because it was not commanded in the word of God, and therefore I could not do it.

Another. One of them said, Where do you find it commanded in the Scripture that you should go to Elstow, or Bedford, and yet it is lawful to go to either of them, is it not?

Bun. I said, To go to Elstow, or Bedford, was a civil thing, and not material, though not commanded, and yet God's word allowed me to go about my calling, and therefore if it lay there, then to go thither, &c. But to pray, was a great part of the divine worship of God, and therefore it

ought to be done according to the rule of God's word.

Another. One of them said, he will do harm; let him speak no further.

Just. Keel. Justice Keelin said, No, no, never fear him, we are better established than so; he can do no harm; we know the Common Prayer-book hath been ever since the apostle's time, and is lawful to be used in the church.

Bun. I said, Show me the place in the epistles where the Common Prayer-book is written, or one text of Scripture that commands me to read it, and I will use it. But yet, notwithstanding, said I, they that have a mind to use it, they have their liberty; that is, I would not keep them from it :* but for our parts, we can pray to God without it. Blessed be his name.

With that, one of them said, Who is your God? Beelzebub? Moreover, they often said that I was possessed with the spirit of delusion, and of the devil. All which sayings I passed over; the Lord forgive them! And further, I said, blessed be the Lord for it, we are encouraged to meet together, and to pray, and exhort one another; for we have had the comfortable presence of God among us, for ever blessed be his holy name.

Keel. Justice Keelin called this pedlars' French, saying that I must leave off my canting. The Lord open his eyes!

Bun. I said that we ought to exhort one another daily, while it is called to-day, &c.

Keel. Justice Keelin said that I ought not to preach; and asked me where I had my authority? with many other such like words.

Bun. I said that I would prove that it was lawful for me, and such as I am, to preach the word of God.

Keel. He said unto me, By what scripture?

I said, By that in the first epistle to Peter, ch. iv. ver. 11, and Acts xviii., with other scriptures, which he would not suffer me to mention. But said, Hold, not so many; which is the first?

Bun. I said, this: "As every man hath received the gift, even so let him minister the same unto another, as good stewards of the manifold grace of God: if any man speak, let him speak as the oracles of God," &c.

Keel. He said, Let me a little open that scripture to you: "As every man hath received the gift;" that is, said he, as every man hath received a trade, so let him follow it. If any man hath received a gift of tinkering, as thou hast done, let him follow his tinkering. And so other men their trades. And the divine his calling, &c.

Bun. Nay, Sir, said I, but it is most clear that the apostle speaks here of preaching the word; if you do but compare both the verses together, the next verse explains this gift what it is, saying. "If any man speak, let him speak as the oracles of

* If any say now that God useth means, I answer, but not the Common Prayer-book, for that is none of his institution; it is the Spirit in the word that is God's ordinance.

* It is not the spirit of a Christian to persecute any for their religion; but to pity them, and if they will turn, to instruct them.

God:" so that it is plain that the Holy Ghost doth not so much in this place exhort to civil callings, as to the exercising of those gifts that we have received from God. I would have gone on, but he would not give me leave.

Keel. He said, We might do it in our families, but not otherwise.

Bun. I said, If it was lawful to do good to some, it was lawful to do good to more. If it was a good duty to exhort our families, it is good to exhort others : but if they held it a sin to meet together to seek the face of God, and exhort one another to follow Christ, I should sin still; for so we should do.

Keel. He said he was not so well versed in Scripture as to dispute, or words to that purpose. And said, moreover, that they could not wait upon me any longer; but said to me, Then you confess the indictment, do you not? Now, and not till now, I saw I was indicted.

Bun. I said, This I confess, we have had many meetings together, both to pray to God, and to exhort one another, and that we had the sweet comforting presence of the Lord among us for our encouragement, blessed be his name therefore. I confess myself guilty no otherwise.

Keel. Then, said he, hear your judgment. You must be had back again to prison, and there lie for three months following; and at three months' end, if you do not submit to go to church to hear divine service, and leave your preaching, you must be banished the realm : and if, after such a day as shall be appointed you to be gone, you shall be found in this realm, &c., or be found to come over again without special license from the king, &c., you must stretch by the neck for it, I tell you plainly; and so he bid my jailer have me away.

Bun. I told him, as to this matter, I was at a point with him; for if I was out of prison to-day, I would preach the gospel again to-morrow, by the help of God.

Another. To which one made me some answer : but my jailer pulling me away to be gone, I could not tell what he said.

Thus I departed from them; and I can truly say, I bless the Lord Jesus Christ for it, that my heart was sweetly refreshed in the time of my examination, and also afterwards, at my returning to the prison : so that I found Christ's words more than bare trifles, where he saith, " I will give you a mouth and wisdom, which all your adversaries shall not be able to gainsay nor resist." (Luke xxi. 15.) And that his peace no man can take from us.

Thus have I given you the substance of my examination. The Lord make these profitable to all that shall read or hear them. Farewell.

The Substance of some Discourse had between the Clerk of the Peace and myself, when he came to admonish me, according to the tenor of that Law by which I was in Prison.

When I had lain in prison other twelve weeks, and now not knowing what they intended to do with me, upon the 3rd of April, 1661, comes Mr.

Cobb unto me, as he told me, being sent by the justices to admonish me, and demanded of me submittance to the church of England, &c. The extent of our discourse was as followeth.

Cobb. When he was come into the house he sent for me out of my chamber; who, when I was come unto him, he said, Neighbour Bunyan, how do you do?

Bun. I thank you, Sir, said I, very well, blessed be the Lord.

Cobb. Saith he, I come to tell you that it is desired you would submit yourself to the laws of the land, or else at the next sessions it will go worse with you, even to be sent away out of the nation, or else worse than that.

Bun. I said that I did desire to demean myself in the world both as becometh a man and a Christian.

Cobb. But, saith he, you must submit to the laws of the land, and leave off those meetings which you was wont to have : for the statute law is directly against it; and I am sent to you by the justices to tell you that they do intend to prosecute the law against you, if you submit not.

Bun. I said, Sir, I conceive that that law by which I am in prison at this time, doth not reach or condemn either me or the meetings which I do frequent : that law was made against those, that being designed to do evil in their meetings, make the exercise of religion their pretence to cover their wickedness. It doth not forbid the private meetings of those that plainly and simply make it their only end to worship the Lord, and to exhort one another to edification. My end in meeting with others is simply to do as much good as I can, by exhortation and counsel, according to that small measure of light which God hath given me, and not to disturb the peace of the nation.

Cobb. Every one will say the same, said he. You see the late insurrection at London, under what glorious pretences they went; and yet indeed they intended no less than the ruin of the kingdom and commonwealth.

Bun. That practice of theirs I abhor, said I; yet it doth not follow that because they did so, therefore all others will do so. I look upon it as my duty to behave myself under the king's government, both as becomes a man and a Christian; and if an occasion was offered me, I should willingly manifest my loyalty to my prince, both by word and deed.

Cobb. Well, said he, I do not profess myself to be a man that can dispute; but this I say, truly, neighbour Bunyan, I would have you consider this matter seriously, and submit yourself. You may have your liberty to exhort your neighbour in private discourse, so be you do not call together an assembly of people : and truly you may do much good to the church of Christ, if you would go this way; and this you may do, and the law not abridge you of it. It is your private meetings that the law is against.

Bun. Sir, said I, if I may do good to one by my discourse, why may I not do good to two? And if to two, why not to four, and so to eight? &c.

Cobb. Ay, saith he, and to a hundred, I warrant you.

Bun. Yes, Sir, said I, I think I should not be forbid to do as much good as I can.

Cobb. But, saith he, you may but pretend to do good, and, indeed, notwithstanding, do harm by seducing the people; you are therefore denied your meeting so many together, lest you should do harm.

Bun. And yet, said I, you say the law tolerates me to discourse with my neighbour; surely there is no law tolerates me to seduce any one; therefore, if I may by the law discourse with one, surely it is to do him good: and if I by discoursing may do good to one, surely, by the same law, I may do good to many.

Cobb. The law, said he, doth expressly forbid your private meetings, therefore they are not to be tolerated.

Bun. I told him that I would not entertain so much uncharitableness of that parliament in the 35th of Elizabeth, or of the queen herself, as to think they did by that law intend the oppressing of any of God's ordinances, or the interrupting any in the way of God; but men may, in the wresting of it, turn it against the way of God. But take the law in itself, and it only fighteth against those that drive at mischief in their hearts and meetings, making religion only their cloak, colour, or pretence; for so are the words of the statute. "If any meetings, under colour or pretence of religion," &c.

Cobb. Very good; therefore the king, seeing that pretences are usually in and among people, as to make religion their pretence only—therefore he, and the law before him, doth forbid such private meetings, and tolerates, only public; you may meet in public.

Bun. Sir, said I, let me answer you in a similitude. Set the case that, at such a wood corner, there did usually come forth thieves to do mischief; must there therefore a law be made, that every one that cometh out there shall be killed? May not there come out true men as well as thieves, out from thence? Just thus is it in this case. I do think there may be many that may design the destruction of the commonwealth: but it doth not follow therefore that all private meetings are unlawful; those that transgress, let them be punished. And if at any time I myself should do any act in my conversation as doth not become a man and a Christian, let me bear the punishment. And as for your saying I may meet in public, if I may be suffered, I would gladly do it. Let me have but meeting enough in public and I shall care the less to have them in private. I do not meet in private because I am afraid to have meetings in public. I bless the Lord that my heart is at that point, that if any man can lay

anything to my charge, either in doctrine or practice, in this particular, that can be proved error or heresy, I am willing to disown it, even in the very market-place; but if it be truth, then to stand to it to the last drop of my blood. And, Sir, said I, you ought to commend me for so doing. To err, and to be a heretic, are two things; I am no heretic, because I will not stand refractorily to defend any one thing that is contrary to the word. Prove anything which I hold to be an error, and I will recant it.

Cobb. But, goodman Bunyan, said he, methinks you need not stand so strictly upon this one thing, as to have meetings of such public assemblies. Cannot you submit, and notwithstanding do as much good as you can, in a neighbourly way, without having such meetings?

Bun. Truly, Sir, said I, I do not desire to commend myself, but to think meanly of myself; yet when I do most despise myself, taking notice of that small measure of light which God hath given me, also that the people of the Lord (by their own saying) are edified thereby. Besides, when I see that the Lord, through grace, hath in some measure blessed my labour, I dare not but exercise that gift which God hath given me for the good of the people. And I said further, that I would willingly speak in public if I might.

Cobb. He said that I might come to the public assemblies and hear. What though you do not preach? you may hear. Do not think yourself so well enlightened, and that you have received a gift so far above others, but that you may hear other men preach. Or to that purpose.

Bun. I told him I was as willing to be taught as to give instruction, and I looked upon it as my duty to do both; for, said I, a man that is a teacher, he himself may learn also from another that teacheth, as the apostle saith: "We may all prophesy one by one, that all may learn." That is, every man that hath received a gift from God, he may dispense it, that others may be comforted; and when he hath done, he may hear, and learn, and be comforted himself of others.

Cobb. But, said he, what if you should forbear awhile, and sit still, till you see further how things will go?

Bun. Sir, said I, Wickliffe saith, that he which leaveth off preaching and hearing of the word of God for fear of excommunication of men, he is already excommunicated of God, and shall in the day of judgment be counted a traitor to Christ.

Cobb. Ay, saith he, they that do not hear shall be so counted indeed; do you therefore hear.

Bun. But, Sir, said I, he saith, he that shall leave off either preaching or hearing, &c. That is, if he hath received a gift for edification, it is his sin if he doth not lay it out in a way of exhortation and counsel, according to the proportion of his gift, as well as to spend his time altogether in hearing others preach.

Cobb. But, said he, how shall we know that you have received a gift?

Bun. Said I, Let any man hear and search, and prove the doctrine by the Bible.

Cobb. But will you be willing, said he, that two indifferent persons shall determine the case, and will you stand by their judgment.

Bun. I said, Are they infallible?

Cobb. He said, No.

Bun. Then, said I, it is possible my judgment may be as good as theirs: but yet I will pass by either, and in this matter be judged by the Scriptures; I am sure that is infallible, and cannot err.

Cobb. But, said he, who shall be judge between you, for you take the Scriptures one way, and they another.

Bun. I said, The Scripture should, and that by comparing one scripture with another; for that will open itself, if it be rightly compared. As, for instance, if under the different apprehensions of the word Mediator, you would know the truth of it, the Scriptures open it, and tell us that he that is a mediator must take up the business between two, and a mediator is not a mediator of one, "but God is one," and "there is one mediator between God and man, even the man Christ Jesus." So likewise the Scripture calleth Christ a complete, or perfect, or able high priest. That is opened in that he is called man, and also God. His blood also is discovered to be effectually efficacious by the same things. So the Scripture, as touching the matter of moving together, &c., doth likewise sufficiently open itself and discover its meaning.

Cobb. But are you willing, said he, to stand to the judgment of the church?

Bun. Yes, sir, said I, to the approbation of the church of God; the church's judgment is best expressed in Scripture.

We had much other discourse, which I cannot well remember, about the laws of the nation, submission to governments; to which I did tell him, that I did look upon myself as bound in conscience to walk according to all righteous laws, and that whether there was a king or no; and if I did anything that was contrary, I did hold it my duty to bear patiently the penalty of the law that was provided against such offenders, with many more words to the like effect: and said, moreover, that to cut off all occasions of suspicion from any, as touching the harmlessness of my doctrine in private, I would willingly take the pains to give any one the notes of all my sermons: for I do sincerely desire to live quietly in my country, and to submit to the present authority.

Cobb. Well, neighbour Bunyan, said he, but indeed I would wish you seriously to consider of these things between this and the quarter-sessions, and to submit yourself. You may do much good if you continue still in the land; but, alas! what benefit will it be to your friends, or what good can you do to them, if you should be sent away beyond the seas, into Spain or Constantinople, or some other remote part of the world? Pray be ruled.

Jailer. Indeed, Sir, I hope he will be ruled.

Bun. I shall desire, said I, in all godliness and honesty to behave myself in the nation, whilst I am in it. And if I must be so dealt withal as you say, I hope God will help me to bear what they shall lay upon me. I know no evil that I have done in this matter to be so used. I speak as in the presence of God.

Cobb. You know, saith he, that the Scripture saith, "The powers that are, are ordained of God."

Bun. I said, Yes, and that I was to submit to the king as supreme; also to the governors, as to them that are sent by him.

Cobb. Well then, said he, the king then commands you, that you should not have any private meetings, because it is against his law, and he is ordained of God; therefore you should not have any.

Bun. I told him that Paul did own the powers that were in his day, as to be of God; and yet he was often in prison under them for all that. And also, though Jesus Christ told Pilate that he had no power against him, but of God, yet he died under the same Pilate; and yet, said I, I hope you will not say that either Paul, or Christ, were such as did deny magistracy, and so sinned against God in slighting the ordinance. Sir, said I, the law hath provided two ways of obeying: the one to do that which I in my conscience do believe that I am bound to do actively, and where I cannot obey actively, there I am willing to lie down, and to suffer what they shall do unto me.

At this he sat still, and said no more; which, when he had done, I did thank him for his civil and meek discoursing with me; and so we parted. Oh, that we might meet in heaven!—Farewell.

JOHN BUNYAN.

Here followeth a Discourse between my Wife and the Judges, with others, touching my deliverance at the Assizes following; the which I took from her own mouth.

After that I had received this sentence of banishing, or hanging, from them, and after the former admonition, touching the determination of justices if I did not recant; just when the time drew nigh in which I should have abjured, or have done worse (as Mr. Cobb told me), came the time in which the king was to be crowned. Now at the coronation of kings, there is usually a releasement of divers prisoners, by virtue of his coronation; in which privilege also I should have had my share; but that they took me for a convicted person, and therefore, unless I sued out a pardon (as they called it) I could have no benefit thereby, notwithstanding; yet, forasmuch as the coronation proclamation did give liberty from the day the king was crowned to that day twelvemonth to sue them out; therefore, though they would not let me out of prison, as they let out thousands, yet they could not meddle with me, as touching the execution of their sentence, because of the liberty offered for the suing out of pardons. Whereupon I continued in prison till the next assizes, which are called Midsummer assizes, being then kept in August, 1661.

Now at that assizes, because I would not leave any possible means unattempted that might be lawful, I did, by my wife, present a petition to the judges three times, that I might be heard, and that they would impartially take my case into consideration.

The first time my wife went, she presented it to Judge Hales, who very mildly received it at her hand, telling her that he would do her and me the best good he could; but he feared, he said, he could do none. The next day again, lest they should, through the multitude of business, forget me, we did throw another petition into the coach to Judge Twisdon; who, when he had seen it, snapped her up, and angrily told her that I was a convicted person, and could not be released, unless I would promise to preach no more, &c.

Well, after this, she yet again presented another to Judge Hales, as he sat on the bench, who, as it seemed, was willing to give her audience. Only Justice Chester being present, stepped up and said that I was convicted in the court, and that I was a hot-spirited fellow, or words to that purpose, whereat he waived it, and did not meddle therewith. But yet my wife, being encouraged by the high-sheriff, did venture once more into their presence (as the poor widow did to the unjust judge) to try what she could do with them for my liberty, before they went forth of the town. The place where she went to them was to the Swan Chamber, where the two judges, and many justices and gentry of the country, were in company together. She then, coming into the chamber with abashed face and a trembling heart, began her errand to them in this manner :—

Woman. My lord, (directing herself to Judge Hales,) I make bold to come once again to your lordship, to know what may be done with my husband.

Judge Hales. To whom he said, Woman, I told thee before I could do thee no good, because they have taken that for a conviction which thy husband spoke at the sessions; and unless there be something done to undo that, I can do thee no good.

Wom. My lord, said she, he is kept unlawfully in prison; they clapped him up before there was any proclamation against the meetings; the indictment also is false. Besides, they never asked him whether he was guilty or no; neither did he confess the indictment.

One of the Justices. Then one of the justices that stood by, whom she knew not, said, My lord, he was lawfully convicted.

Wom. It is false, said she; for when they said to him, Do you confess the indictment? he said only this, that he had been at several meetings, both where there was preaching the word, and prayer, and that they had God's presence among them.

Judge Twisdon. Whereat Judge Twisdon answered very angrily, saying, what! you think we can do what we list; your husband is a breaker of the peace, and is convicted by the law, &c. Whereupon Judge Hales called for the statute book.

Wom. But, said she, my lord, he was not lawfully convicted.

Chester. Then Justice Chester said, my lord, he was lawfully convicted.

Wom. It is false, said she; it was but a word of discourse that they took for a conviction, as you heard before.

Chest. But it is recorded, woman, it is recorded, said Justice Chester. As if it must be of necessity true because it was recorded. With which words he often endeavoured to stop her mouth, having no other argument to convince her but—It is recorded, it is recorded.

Wom. My lord, said she, I was a while since at London, to see if I could get my husband's liberty, and there I spoke with my Lord Barkwood, one of the House of Lords, to whom I delivered a petition, who took it of me, and presented to some of the rest of the House of Lords for my husband's releasement; who, when they had seen it, they said, that they could not release him, but had committed his releasement to the judges at the next assizes. This he told me; and now I come to you to see if anything may be done in this business, and you give neither releasement nor relief. To which they gave her no answer, but made as if they heard her not.

Chest. Only Justice Chester was often up with this : He is convicted, and it is recorded.

Wom. If it be, it is false, said she.

Chest. My lord, said Justice Chester, he is a pestilent fellow; there is not such a fellow in the country again.

Twis. What, will your husband leave preaching? If he will do so, then send for him.

Wom. My lord, said she, he dares not leave preaching as long as he can speak.

Twis. See here, what should we talk any more about such a fellow? must he not do what he lists? he is a breaker of the peace.

Wom. She told him again, that he desired to live peaceably and to follow his calling, that his family might be maintained; and moreover said, my lord, I have four small children that cannot help themselves, of which one is blind, and have nothing to live upon but the charity of good people.

Hales. Hast thou four children? said Judge Hales; thou art but a young woman to have four children.

Wom. My lord, said she, I am but mother-in-law to them, having not been married to him yet full two years. Indeed, I was with child when my husband was first apprehended: but, being young and unaccustomed to such things, said she, I being smayed at the news, fell into labour, and so continued for eight days, and then was delivered, but my child died.

Hales. Whereat he, looking very soberly on the matter, said, Alas, poor woman!

Twis. But Judge Twisdon told her that she made poverty her cloak; and said, moreover, that he understood I was maintained better by running up and down a preaching than by following my calling.

Hales. What is his calling? said Judge Hales.

Answer. Then some of the company that stood by said, A tinker, my lord.

Wom. Yes, said she, and because he is a tinker, and a poor man, therefore he is despised, and cannot have justice.

Hales. Then Judge Hales answered very mildly, saying, I tell thee, woman, seeing it is so, that they have taken what thy husband spake for a conviction, thou must either apply thyself to the king, or sue out his pardon, or get a writ of error.

Chest. But when Justice Chester heard him give her this counsel; and especially, as she supposed, because he spoke of a writ of error, he chafed, and seemed to be much offended; saying, My lord, he will preach and do what he lists.

Wom. He preacheth nothing but the word of God, said she.

Twis. He preach the word of God! said Twisdon, (and withal she thought he would have struck her;) he runneth up and down and doth harm.

Wom. No, my lord, said she, it is not so; God hath owned him, and done much good by him.

Twis. God! said he, his doctrine is the doctrine of the devil.

Wom. My lord, said she, when the righteous Judge shall appear, it will be known that his doctrine is not the doctrine of the devil.

Twis. My lord, said he to Judge Hales, do not mind her, but send her away.

Hales. Then, said Judge Hales, I am sorry, woman, that I can do thee no good; thou must do one of those three things aforesaid, namely, either to apply thyself to the king, or sue out his pardon, or get a writ of error; but a writ of error will be cheapest.

Wom. At which Chester again seemed to be in a chafe, and put off his hat, and, as she thought, scratched his head for anger: but when I saw, said she, that there was no prevailing to have my husband sent for, though I often desired them that they would send for him that he might speak for himself, telling them that he could give them better satisfaction than I could, in what they demanded of him, with several other things which now I forget; only this I remember, that though I was somewhat timorous at my first entrance into the chamber, yet, before I went out, I could not but break forth into tears; not so much because they were so hard-hearted against me and my husband, but to think what a sad account such poor creatures will have to give at the coming of the Lord, when they shall there answer for all things whatsoever they have done in the body, whether it be good, or whether it be bad.

So, when I departed from them, the book of statute was brought, but what they said of it I know nothing at all, neither did I hear any more from them.

Some Carriages of the Adversaries of God's Truth with me at the next Assizes, which was on the nineteenth of the first Month, 1662.

I shall pass by what befell between these two assizes, how I had, by my jailer, some liberty granted me, more than at first, and how I followed my wonted course of preaching, taking all occasions that were put into my hand to visit the people of God, exhorting them to be steadfast in the faith of Jesus Christ, and to take heed that they touched not the Common Prayer, &c., but to mind the word of God, which giveth direction to Christians in every point, being able to make the man of God perfect in all things through faith in Jesus Christ, and thoroughly to furnish him up to all good works. Also how I having, I say, somewhat more liberty, did go to see Christians at London, which my enemies hearing of, were so angry, that they had almost cast my jailer out of his place, threatening to indict him, and to do what they could against him. They charged me also, that I went thither to plot and raise division, and make insurrection, which, God knows, was a slander; whereupon my liberty was more straitened than it was before; so that I must not look out of the door. Well, when the next sessions came, which was about the 10th of the eleventh month, I did expect to have been very roundly dealt withal; but they passed me by, and would not call me, so that I rested till the assizes, which was the 19th of the first month following; and when they came, because I had a desire to come before the judge, I desired my jailer to put my name into the calendar among the felons, and made friends of the judge and high sheriff, who promised that I should be called; so that I thought what I had done might have been effectual for the obtaining of my desire. But all was in vain; for when the assizes came, though my name was in the calendar, and also though both the judge and sheriff had promised that I should appear before them, yet the justice and the clerk of the peace, did so work it about, that I, notwithstanding, was deferred, and might not appear: and though I say, I do not know of all their carriages towards me, yet this I know, that the clerk of the peace did discover himself to be one of my greatest opposers: for, first he came to my jailer, and told him that I must not go down before the judge, and therefore must not be put into the calendar; to whom my jailer said, that my name was in already. He bid him put me out again; my jailer told him that he could not, for he had given the judge a calendar with my name in it, and also the sheriff another. At which he was very much displeased, and desired to see that calendar that was yet in my jailer's hand, who, when he had given it him, he looked on it, and said it was a false calendar; he also took the calendar and blotted out my accusation, as my jailer had writ it (which accusation I cannot tell what it was, because it was so blotted out); and he himself put in words to this purpose: that John Bunyan was committed to prison; being lawfully convicted for upholding of unlawful meetings and conventicles, &c. But yet, for all this, fearing that what he had done, unless he added thereto, it would not do, he first run to the clerk of the assizes, then to the justices, and afterwards, because he would not leave any means unattempted to hinder me, he comes again to my jailer, and tells him, that if I did go down before the judge, and was released, he would make him pay my fees, which he said was due to him; and further, told him, that he would complain of him at the next quarter sessions for making of false calendars, though my jailer himself, as I afterwards learned, had put in my accusation worse than in itself it was by far. And thus was I hindered and prevented at that time also from appearing before the judge, and left in prison. Farewell.

JOHN BUNYAN.

A CONTINUATION OF MR. BUNYAN'S LIFE,

BEGINNING WHERE HE LEFT OFF, AND CONCLUDING WITH THE TIME AND MANNER OF HIS DEATH AND BURIAL, TOGETHER WITH HIS TRUE CHARACTER.

READER, the painful and industrious author of this book * has already given you a faithful and very moving relation of the beginning and middle of the days of his pilgrimage on earth: and since there yet remains somewhat worthy of notice and regard, which occurred in the last scene of his life; the which, for want of time, or fear some over-censorious people should impute it to him, as an earnest coveting of praise from men, he has not left behind him in writing: wherefore, as a true friend and long acquaintance of Mr. Bunyan's, that his good end may be known, as his evil beginning, I have taken upon me, from my knowledge, and the best account given by other of his friends, to piece this to the thread, too soon broke off, and so lengthen it out to his entering upon eternity.

He has told you at large of his birth and education; the evil habits and corruptions of his youth; the temptations he struggled and conflicted so frequently with; the mercies, comforts, and deliverances, he found; how he came to take upon him the preaching of the gospel; the slanders, reproaches, and imprisonments that attended him, and the progress he notwithstanding made, by the assistance of God's grace, no doubt to the saving of many souls: therefore take these things, as he himself has methodically laid them down in the words of verity; and so I pass on as to what remains.

After his being freed from his twelve years' imprisonment and upwards, for nonconformity, wherein he had time to furnish the world with sundry good books, &c., and by his patience, to move Dr. Barlow, the then Bishop of Lincoln, and other churchmen, to pity his hard and unreasonable sufferings, so far as to stand very much his friends, in procuring his enlargement, or there perhaps he had died, by the noisesomness and ill

* *Grace abounding to the Chief of Sinners.*

usage of the place; being now, I say, again at liberty, and having, through mercy, shaken off his bodily fetters, for those upon his soul were broken before, by the abounding grace that filled his heart, he went to visit those that had been a comfort to him in his tribulation, with a Christian-like acknowledgment of their kindness and enlargement of charity; giving encouragement by his example, if it happened to be their hard haps to fall into affliction or trouble, then to suffer patiently for the sake of a good conscience, and for the love of God in Jesus Christ, towards their souls, and by many cordial persuasions, supported some whose spirits began to sink low, through the fear of danger that threatened their worldly concernment; so that the people found a wonderful consolation in his discourse and admonitions.

As often as opportunity would admit, he gathered them together, (though the law was then in force against meetings,) in convenient places, and fed them with the sincere milk of the word, that they might grow up in grace thereby. To such as were anywhere taken and imprisoned upon these accounts, he made it another part of his business to extend his charity, and gather relief for such of them as wanted.

He took great care to visit the sick, and strengthen them against the suggestions of the tempter, which at such times are very prevalent; so that they had cause for ever to bless God, who had put into his heart, at such a time, to rescue them from the power of the roaring lion, who sought to devour them. Nor did he spare any pains or labour in travel, though to the remote counties, where he knew, or imagined, any people might stand in need of his assistance; insomuch that some of these visitations that he made, which were two or three every year, some (though in jeering manner no doubt) gave him the epithet of *Bishop Bunyan*, whilst others envied him for his so earnestly labouring in Christ's vineyard; yet the seed of the word he all this while sowed in the hearts of his congregation, watered with the grace of God, brought forth in abundance, in bringing in disciples to the church of Christ.

Another part of his time he spent in reconciling differences, by which he hindered many mischiefs, and saved some families from ruin; and, in some fallings-out, he was uneasy till he found a means to labour a reconciliation, and become a peace-maker, ou whom a blessing is promised in holy writ: and indeed, in doing this good office, he may be said to sum up his days, it being the last undertaking of his life, as will appear in the close of this paper.

When, in the late reign, liberty of conscience was unexpectedly given and indulged to dissenters of all persuasions, his piercing wit penetrated the veil, and found that it was not for the dissenters' sake they were so suddenly freed from the prose-cutions that had long lain heavy upon them, and set in a manner on an equal foot with the church of England, which the papists were undermining, and about to subvert. He foresaw all the advan-tages that could redound to the dissenters, would have been no more than what Polyphemus, the monstrous giant of Sicily, would have allowed Ulysses, viz., that he would eat his men first, and do him the favour of being eaten last. For although Mr. Bunyan, following the examples of others, did lay hold of this liberty, as an accept-able thing in itself, knowing God is the only lord of conscience, and that it is good at all times to do according to the dictates of a good conscience, and that the preaching the glad tidings of the gospel is beautiful in the preacher; yet in all this he moved with caution and a holy fear, earnestly praying for averting the impendent judgments, which he saw, like a black tempest, hanging over our heads, for our sins, and ready to break upon us, and that the Ninevites' remedy was now highly necessary. Hereupon he gathered his congre-gation at Bedford, where he mostly lived, and had lived and spent the greatest part of his life; and there being no convenient place to be had for the entertainment of so great a confluence of people as followed him, upon the account of his teaching, he consulted with them for the building of a meeting-house; to which they made their volun-tary contributions, with all cheerfulness and alac-rity; and the first time he appeared there to edify, the place was so thronged, that many were constrained to stay without, though the house was very spacious, every one striving to partake of his instructions, that were of his persuasion, and show their good will towards him, by being present at the opening of the place. And here he lived in much peace and quiet of mind, contenting himself with that little God had bestowed upon him, and sequestering himself from all secular employments, to follow that of his call to the ministry; for, as God said to Moses, he that made the lips and heart, can give eloquence and wisdom, without extraordinary acquirements in an university.

During these things, there were regulators sent into all cities and towns-corporate to new-model the government in the magistracy, &c., by turning out some, and putting in others. Against this Mr. Bunyan expressed his zeal with some warm-ness, as foreseeing the bad consequence that would attend it, and laboured with his congregation to prevent their being imposed on in this kind: and when a great man in those days, coming to Bed-ford upon some such errand, sent for him, as it is supposed, to give him a place of public trust, he would by no means come at him, but sent his excuse.

When he was at leisure from writing and teach-ing, he often came up to London, and there went among the congregations of the nonconformists, and used his talents to the great good-liking of the hearers; and even some, to whom he had been misrepresented, upon the account of his education, were convinced of his worth and know-ledge in sacred things, as perceiving him to be a man of sound judgment, delivering himself plainly and powerfully; insomuch that many who came spectators for novelty, rather than to be edified and improved, went away well satisfied with what they heard; and wondered as the Jews did at the apostles, viz., whence this man should have these things; perhaps not considering that God more immediately assists those that make it their business industriously and cheerfully to labour in his vineyard.

Thus he spent his latter years in imitation of his great Lord and Master, the ever-blessed Jesus. He went about doing good, so that the most pry-ing critic, or even malice herself, is defied to find, even upon the narrowest search or observation, any sully or stain upon his reputation, with which he may be justly charged: and this we note, as a challenge to those that have had the least regard for him, or them of his persuasion, and have one way or other appeared in the front of those that oppressed him; and for the turning whose hearts, in obedience to the commission and command-ment given him of God, he frequently prayed, and sometimes sought a blessing for them, even with tears, the effects of which they may, peradventure, though undeservedly, have found in their persons, friends, relations, estates; for God will hear the prayers of the faithful, and answer them, even for those that vex them, as it happened in the case of Job's praying for the three persons that had been grievous in their reproach against him, even in the day of his sorrow.

But yet let me come a little nearer to particu-lars, and periods of time, for the better refreshing the memories of those that knew his labour and sufferings, and for the satisfaction of all that shall read this book.

After he was sensibly convicted of the wicked state of his life, and converted, he was baptized into the congregation, and admitted a member thereof, viz., in the year 1655, and became speedily a very zealous professor. But upon the return of King Charles to the crown, in 1660, he was, on the 12th of November, taken, as he was edifying some good people that were got together to hear the word, and confined in Bedford jail for the space of six years, till the act of indulgence to dissenters being allowed, he obtained his freedom by the intercession of some in trust and power, that took pity of his sufferings. But within six years afterwards, he was again taken up, viz., in the year 1666, and was then confined for six years more, when the jailer took such pity of his religious sufferings, that he did as the Egyptian jailer did to Joseph, put all the care and trust in his hand. When he was taken this last time, he was preaching on these words, viz., "Dost thou believe on the Son of God?" and this imprisonment continued six years; and when this was over, another short affliction, which was an imprisonment of half a year, fell to his share. During these confinements, he wrote these following books, viz., *Of Prayer by the Spirit, The Holy City's Resurrection, Grace Abounding, Pilgrim's Progress, the first part.*

In the last year of his twelve years' imprisonment the pastor of the congregation at Bedford died, and he was chosen to that care of souls, on the 12th of December, 1671. And in this charge he often had disputes with scholars that came to oppose him, as supposing him an ignorant person; and though he argued plainly, and by Scripture, without phrases and logical expressions, yet he nonplussed one who came to oppose him in his congregation, by demanding whether or no we had the true copies of the original Scriptures? And another, when he was preaching, accused him of uncharitableness for saying, "It was very hard for most to be saved;" saying, by that he went about to exclude most of his congregation. But he confuted him, and put him to silence, with the parable of the stony ground, and other texts out of the 13th of Matthew, in our Saviour's sermon out of a ship; all his methods being to keep close to the Scriptures, and what he found not warranted there, himself would not warrant nor determine, unless in such cases as were plain, wherein no doubts or scruples did arise.

But not to make any further mention of this kind, it is well known, that this person managed all his affairs with such exactness, as if he had made it his study, above all other things, not to give occasion of offence, but rather suffer many inconveniences to avoid it, being never heard to reproach or revile any, what injury soever he received, but rather to rebuke those that did. And as it was in his conversation, so it is manifested in those books he has caused to be published to the world; where, like the archangel disputing with Satan about the body of Moses, as we find it in the epistle of St. Jude, he brings no railing accusation, but leaves the rebukers, those that persecuted him, to the Lord.

In his family he kept up a very strict discipline in prayer and exhortations, being in this like Joshua, as that good man expresses it, viz., Whatsoever others did, as for me and my house we will serve the Lord. And, indeed, a blessing waited on his labours and endeavours; so that his wife, as the psalmist says, was like a pleasant vine upon the wall of his house, and his children like olive-branches round his table; for so shall it be with the man that fears the Lord: and though by reason of the many losses he sustained by imprisonment and spoil, of his chargeable sickness, &c., his earthly treasure swelled not to excess, he always had sufficient to live decently and creditably; and with that he had the greatest of all treasures, which is content: for, as the wise man says, that is a continual feast.

But where content dwells, even a poor cottage is a kingly palace; and this happiness he had all his life long, not so much minding this world, as knowing he was here as a pilgrim and stranger, and had no tarrying city, but looked for one not made with hands, eternal in the highest heavens. But at length, worn out with suffering, age, and often teaching, the day of his dissolution drew near; and death, that unlocks the prison of the soul, to enlarge it for a more glorious mansion, put a stop to his acting his part on the stage of mortality: heaven, like earthly princes, when it threatens war, being always so kind as to call home its ambassadors before it be denounced. And even the last act or undertaking of his was a labour of love and charity; for it so falling out that a young gentleman, a neighbour of Mr. Bunyan's, happening into the displeasure of his father, and being much troubled in his mind upon that account, as also for that he had heard his father purposed to disinherit him, or otherwise deprive him of what he had to leave, he pitched upon Mr. Bunyan as a fit man to make way for his submission, and prepare his father's mind to receive him; and he, as willing to do any good office as it could be requested, as readily undertook it; and so, riding to Reading, in Berkshire, he there used such pressing arguments and reasons against anger and passion, as also for love and reconciliation, that the father was mollified, and his bowels yearned towards his returning son.

But Mr. Bunyan, after he had disposed all things to the best for accommodation, returning to London, and being overtaken with excessive rains, coming to his lodging extreme wet, fell sick of a violent fever, which he bore with much constancy and patience, and expressed himself as if he desired nothing more than to be dissolved, and be with Christ, in that case esteeming death as gain, and life only a tedious delaying felicity expected. And finding his vital strength decay, having settled his mind and affairs as well as the shortness of time and the violence of his disease would admit, with a constant and Christian patience, he resigned his soul into the hands of his most merciful Redeemer, following his pilgrimage from the city of Destruction to the New Jerusalem, his better part having been all along there, in holy contemplation, pantings, and breathings after the hidden manna, and water of life; as by many holy and humble consolations expressed in his letters to several persons, in prison and out of prison, too many to be here inserted at present. He died at the house of one Mr. Straddock, a grocer, at the Star on Snow Hill, in the parish of St. Sepulchre London, on the 12th of August, 1688, and in the sixtieth year of his age, after ten days' sickness; and was buried in the new burying-place near the Artillery Ground; where he sleeps to the morning of the resurrection, in hopes of a glorious rising to an incorruptible immortality of joy and happiness, where no more trouble and sorrow shall afflict him, but all tears be wiped away; when the just shall be incorporated as members of Christ their head, and reign with him as kings and priests for ever.

A BRIEF CHARACTER OF MR. JOHN BUNYAN.

He appeared in countenance to be of a stern and rough temper; but in his conversation mild and affable, not given to loquacity, or much discourse in company, unless some urgent occasion required it; observing never to boast of himself, or his parts, but rather seem low in his own eyes, and submit himself to the judgment of others, abhorring lying and swearing, being just in all that lay in his power to his word; not seeming to revenge injuries, loving to reconcile differences, and make friendship with all. He had a sharp quick eye, accomplished with an excellent discerning of persons, being of good judgment and quick wit. As for his person, he was tall of stature, strong boned, though not corpulent, somewhat of a ruddy face, with sparkling eyes, wearing his hair on his upper lip, after the old British fashion; his hair reddish, but in his latter days time had sprinkled it with grey; his nose well set, but not declining or bending, and his mouth moderate large; his forehead something high, and his habit always plain and modest. And thus have we impartially described the internal and external parts of a person whose death hath been much regretted; a person who had tried the smiles and frowns of time; not puffed up in prosperity, nor shaken in adversity, always holding the golden mean.

> In him at once did three great worthies shine,
> Historian, poet, and a choice divine;
> Then let him rest in undisturbed dust,
> Until the resurrection of the just.

POSTSCRIPT.—In his pilgrimage God blessed him with four children, one of which, named Mary, was blind, and died some years before. His other children are Thomas, Joseph, and Sarah; and his wife Elizabeth, having lived to see him overcome his labour and sorrow, and pass from this life to receive the reward of his works, long survived him not, but in 1692 she died, to follow her faithful pilgrim from this world to the other, whither he was gone before her, while his works remain, for the edifying of the reader and praise of the author. *Vale.*

MR. JOHN BUNYAN'S DYING SAYINGS.

OF SIN.

Sin is the great block and bar to our happiness; the procurer of all miseries to man, both here and hereafter. Take away sin, and nothing can hurt us; for death, temporal, spiritual, and eternal, is the wages of it.

Sin, and man for sin, is the object of the wrath of God. How dreadful, therefore, must his case be who continues in sin! for who can bear or grapple with the wrath of God?

No sin against God can be little; because it is against the great God of heaven and earth; but if the sinner can find out a little God, it may be easy to find out little sins.

Sin turns all God's grace into wantonness; it is the dare of his justice, the rape of his mercy, the jeer of his patience, the flight of his power, and the contempt of his love.

Take heed of giving thyself liberty of committing one sin, for that will lead thee to another, till by an ill custom it become natural.

To begin a sin is to lay a foundation for a continuance: this continuance is the mother of custom, and impudence at last the issue.

The death of Christ giveth us the best discovery of ourselves, in what condition we were, in that nothing could help us but that, and the most clear discovery of the dreadful nature of our sins: for if sin be so dreadful a thing as to wring the heart o. the Son of God, how shall a poor wretched sinner be able to bear it?

OF AFFLICTION.

Nothing can render affliction so insupportable as the load of sin. Would you, therefore, be fitted for afflictions, be sure to get the burden of your sins laid aside, and then what afflictions soever you may meet with will be very easy to you.

If thou canst hear and bear the rod of affliction which God shall lay upon thee, remember this lesson, Thou art beaten that thou mayst be better.

The Lord useth his flail of tribulation to separate the chaff from the wheat.

The school of the cross is the school of light it discovers the world's vanity, baseness, and wickedness, and lets us see more of God's mind. Out of dark affliction comes a spiritual light.

In times of affliction we commonly meet with the sweetest experiences of the love of God.

Did we heartily renounce the pleasures of this world, we should be very little troubled for our afflictions; that which renders an afflicted state so insupportable to many is, because they are too much addicted to the pleasures of this life, and so cannot endure that which makes a separation between them.

OF REPENTANCE, AND COMING TO CHRIST.

The end of affliction is the discovery of sin, and of that to bring us to a Saviour. Let us, therefore, with the prodigal, return unto him, and we shall find ease and rest.

A repenting penitent, though formerly as bad as the worst of men, may by grace become as good as the best.

To be truly sensible of sin is to sorrow for displeasing of God; to be afflicted that he is displeased by us more than that he is displeased with us.

Your intentions to repentance, and the neglect of that soul-saving duty, will rise up in judgment against you.

Repentance carries with it a divine rhetoric, and persuades Christ to forgive multitudes of sins committed against him.

Say not with thyself, To-morrow I will repent; for it is thy duty to do it daily.

The gospel of grace and salvation is above all doctrines the most dangerous, if it be received in word only by graceless men; if it be not attended with a sensible need of a Saviour, and bring them to him. For such men as have only the notion of it are of all men most miserable; for by reason of their knowing more than heathens, this shall only be their final portion, that they shall have greater stripes.

OF PRAYER.

Before you enter into prayer, ask thy soul these questions:—To what end, O my soul, art thou retired into this place? Art thou not come to discourse the Lord in prayer? Is he present; will he hear thee? Is he merciful; will he help thee? Is thy business slight; is it not concerning the welfare of thy soul? What words wilt thou use to move him to compassion?

To make thy preparation complete, consider that thou art "but dust and ashes," and he the great God, Father of our Lord Jesus Christ, "that clothes himself with light, as with a garment;" that thou art a vile sinner, he a holy God; that thou art but a poor crawling worm, he the Omnipotent Creator.

In all your prayers forget not to thank the Lord for his mercies.

When thou prayest, rather let thy heart be without words, than thy words without a heart.

Prayer will make a man cease from sin, or sin will entice a man to cease from prayer.

The spirit of prayer is more precious than treasures of gold and silver.

Pray often; for prayer is the shield to the soul, a sacrifice to God, and a scourge for Satan.

OF THE LORD'S DAY, SERMONS, AND WEEK DAYS.

Have a special care to sanctify the Lord's day; for as thou keepest it, so it will be with thee all the week long.

Make the Lord's day the market for thy soul; let the whole day be spent in prayer, repetitions, or meditations; lay aside the affairs of the other part of the week; let thy sermon thou hast heard be converted into prayer. Shall God allow thee six days, and wilt not thou afford him one?

In the church, be careful to serve God; for thou art in his eyes, and not in man's.

Thou mayst hear sermons often, and do well in practising what thou hearest: but thou must not expect to be told thee in a pulpit all that thou oughtest to do, but be studious in searching the Scriptures, and reading good books. What thou hearest may be forgotten: but what thou readest may better be retained.

Forsake not the public worship of God, lest God forsake thee, not only in public, but in private.

In the week days, when thou risest in the morning, consider, 1. Thou must die. 2. Thou mayest die that minute. 3. What will become of thy soul. Pray often. At night consider, 1. What sins thou hast committed. 2. How often thou hast prayed. What hath thy mind been bent upon. 4. What hath been thy dealing. 5. What thy conversation. 6. If thou callest to mind the errors of the day, sleep not without a confession to God, and a hope of pardon. Thus, every morning and evening, make up thy accounts with Almighty God, and thy reckoning will be the less at last.

OF THE LOVE OF THE WORLD.

Nothing more hinders a soul from coming to Christ than a vain love of the world; and till a soul is freed from it, it can never have a true love for God.

What are the honours and riches of this world, when compared to the glories of a crown of life?

Love not the world; for it is a moth in a Christian's life.

To despise the world is the way to enjoy heaven; and blessed are they who delight to converse with God by prayer.

What folly can be greater than to labour for the meat that perisheth, and to neglect the food of eternal life?

God or the world must be neglected at parting time; for then is the time of trial.

To seek yourself in this world is to be lost; and to be humble is to be exalted.

The epicure that delighteth in the dainties of

this world little thinketh that those very creatures will one day witness against him.

OF SUFFERING.

It is not every suffering that makes a martyr, but suffering for the word of God after a right manner: that is, not only for righteousness but for righteousness' sake; not only for truth, but out of love to truth; not only for God's word, but according to it; to wit, in that holy, humble, meek manner, as the word of God requireth.

It is a rare thing to suffer aright, and to have my spirit in suffering bent only against God's enemy, sin—sin in doctrine, sin in worship, sin in life, and sin in conversation.

The devil, nor men of the world, can kill thy righteousness, or love to it, but by thy own hand; or separate that and thee asunder without thy own act. Nor will he that doth indeed suffer for the sake of it, or out of love he bears thereto, be tempted to exchange it for the good will of all the world.

I have often thought that the best of Christians are found in the worst of times: and I have thought again that one reason why we are no better, is because God purges us no more. Noah and Lot, who so holy as they in the time of their afflictions? and yet who so idle as they in the time of their prosperity?

OF DEATH AND JUDGMENT.

As the devil labours by all means to keep out other things that are good, so to keep out of the heart as much as in him lies, the thoughts of passing from this life into another world; for he knows, if he can but keep them from the serious thoughts of death, he shall the more easily keep them in their sins.

Nothing will make us more earnest in working out the work of our salvation, than a frequent meditation of mortality: nothing hath greater influence for the taking off our hearts from vanities, and for the begetting in us desires after holiness.

Oh, sinner, what a condition wilt thou fall into when thou departest this world, if thou depart unconverted! Thou hadst better have been smothered the first hour thou wast born; thou hadst better have been plucked one limb from another; thou hadst better have been made a dog, a toad, a serpent, than to die unconverted: and this thou wilt find true if thou repent not.

A man would be counted a fool to slight a judge before whom he is to have a trial of his whole estate. The trial we have before God is of otherguise [another kind of] importance; it concerns our eternal happiness or misery; and yet dare we affront him?

The only way for us to escape that terrible judgment, is to be often passing a sentence of condemnation upon ourselves here.

When the sound of the trumpet shall be heard, which shall summon the dead to appear before the tribunal of God, the righteous shall hasten out of their graves, with joy to meet their Redeemer in the clouds; others shall call to the hills and mountains to fall upon them, to cover them from the sight of their Judge. Let us, therefore, in time be posing ourselves which of the two we shall be.

OF THE JOYS OF HEAVEN.

There is no good in this life but what is mingled with some evil. Honours perplex, riches disquiet, and pleasures ruin health. But in heaven we shall find blessings in their purity, without any ingredient to embitter, with everything to sweeten them.

Oh, who is able to conceive the inexpressible, inconceivable joys that are there? None but they who have tasted of them. Lord, help us to put such a value upon them here, that in order to prepare ourselves for them, we may be willing to forego the loss of all those deluding pleasures here.

How will the heavens echo of joy when the Bride, the Lamb's wife, shall come to dwell with her husband for ever!

Christ is the desire of nations, the joy of angels, the delight of the Father: what solace then must that soul be filled with that hath the possession of him to all eternity!

Oh, what acclamations of joy will there be, when all the children of God shall meet together, without fear of being disturbed by the Antichristian and Cainish brood!

Is there not a time coming when the godly may ask the wicked, What profit they have in their pleasure? what comfort in their greatness? and what fruit in all their labour?

If you would be better satisfied what the beatifical vision means, my request is, that you would live holily, and go and see.

OF THE TORMENTS OF HELL.

Heaven and salvation is not surely more promised to the godly than hell and damnation is threatened to, and shall be executed on the wicked.

When once a man is damned, he may bid adieu to all pleasures.

Oh, who knows the power of God's wrath? None but damned ones.

Sinners' company are the devil and his angels, tormented in everlasting fire with a curse.

Hell would be a kind of paradise, if it were no worse than the worst of this world.

As different as grief is from joy, as torment from rest, as terror from peace, so different is the state of sinners from that of saints in the world to come.

THE STRUGGLER;

CONTAINING

THE CHRONOLOGICAL ORDER IN WHICH MR. BUNYAN'S BOOKS WERE PUBLISHED, AND THE NUMBER OF EDITIONS THEY PASSED THROUGH DURING HIS LIFE.

THIRTY REASONS WHY CHRISTIAN PEOPLE SHOULD PROMOTE THEIR CIRCULATION, AND THE STRUGGLER FOR THE PRESERVATION OF THESE LABOURS.

By CHARLES DOE,

ONE OF MR. BUNYAN'S PERSONAL FRIENDS.

A CATALOGUE-TABLE OF MR. BUNYAN'S BOOKS,

AND

THEIR SUCCESSION IN PUBLISHING, MOST ACCORDING TO HIS OWN RECKONING.

NOTE.—Those that are in Italic letter are them that compose the first folio: And the rest are intended, when time serves, for a second folio.

#	Title	Year	#	Title	Year
1	*Gospel Truths opened*	1656	31	The 2nd Part Pilgrim's Progress (3 Impress.)	
2	A Vindication of that	1657	32	Life and Death of Mr. Badman	
3	Sighs from Hell (9 Impressions)		33	Holy Life the beauty of Christianity	
4	The 2 Covenants, Law and Grace		34	The Pharisee and Publican	1685
5	*I will pray with the Spirit*	1663	35	A caution against Sin	
6	*A map of salvation, &c.*		36	Meditations on seventy-four things	
7	The four last things (3 Impressions)		37	The first-day Sabbath	1685
8	Mount Ebal and Gerizim		38	The Jerusalem Sinner Saved	1688
9	Prison Meditations		39	Jesus Christ an advocate	1688
10	*The Holy City, &c.*	1665	40	The House of God	1688
11	*The Resurrection, &c.*	1665	41	The Water of Life	1688
12	Grace Abounding (6 Impressions)		42	Solomon's Temple Spiritualized	
13	Justification by Jesus Christ	1671	43	The Excell. of a broken heart	
14	Confession of Faith, &c.	1672	44	His last Sermon at London	1688
15	Difference in Judgment, &c.	1673	45	*Exposit. on ten first chap. of Genesis*	
16	Peaceable Principles, &c.	1674	46	*Justification by Imputed Righteousness*	
17	Election and Reprobation, &c.		47	*Paul's departure and crown*	
18	*Light for them in Darkness*		48	*Of the Trinity and a Christian*	
19	*Christian Behaviour (4 Impressions)*		49	*Of the Law and a Christian*	
20	*Instructions for the Ignorant*	1675	50	*Israel's Hope encouraged*	
21	Saved by Grace		51	*Desires of the righteous granted*	
22	*The Strait-Gate*	1676	52	*The unsearchable riches of Christ*	
23	The Pilgrim's Progress (12 Impressions)		53	*Christ Compleat Saviour in's Interest*	
24	The Fear of God	1679	54	*Saint's Knowledge of Christ's love*	
25	Come and Welcome to Jesus Christ (4 Impres.)		55	*House of the Forest of Lebanon*	
26	The Holy War (3 Impressions)	1682	56	*A description of Antichrist*	
27	The Barren Fig Tree		57	A CHRISTIAN DIALOGUE	
28	The Greatness of the Soul, &c.		58	THE HEAVENLY FOOTMAN	
29	A Case of Conscience of Prayer		59	A POCKET CONCORDANCE	
30	Advice to Sufferers	1684	60	AN ACCOUNT OF HIS IMPRISONMENT	

Marginal notes (right side): items 45–56 bracketed "12 Manuscripts part of the first folio 1692." Items 57–60 bracketed "4 Manuscripts yet unprinted."

Here's sixty pieces of his labours, and he was sixty years of age.

He was born at Elstow, nigh Bedford, about 1628; and about 1652 was, by irresistible grace, converted; and in 1660 he had preached five years, and then, for that, was thrown into Bedford Jail; and in 1671 was called to the pastoral office at Bedford, being the 11th of his twelve years and a half's imprisonment; and died at London, Aug. 31, 1688.

REASONS

WHY CHRISTIAN PEOPLE SHOULD PROMOTE BY SUBSCRIPTIONS THE PRINTING IN FOLIO THE LABOURS OF MR. JOHN BUNYAN, LATE MINISTER OF THE GOSPEL, AND PASTOR OF THE CONGREGATION AT BEDFORD.

I. He was a very able and excellent minister of the gospel; viz., able to express himself, and had excellent matter known to all Christians that have heard him preach.

II. He became thus able and excellent a minister by a great degree of Gospel grace bestowed upon his own soul, more than probable for that very end; for that God wrought him from a very great profane sinner, and an illiterate poor man, to this profound understanding the true or genuine spiritual meaning of the Scriptures, whereby he could experimentally preach to souls with power, and affection, and apostolical learning, the true nature of the gospel.

III. God's bestowing such great grace, to turn so great a sinner, to make such a great gospel labourer, and thrust him into his harvest, argues there was great need, and therefore without question his labours ought to be preserved.

IV. Our Bunyan being so graciously, by the Lord of the harvest, thrust into labour, clearly shows to us, (and may by this preservation to future ages,) that God is not bound to human means of learned education, (though learning may be useful in its place,) but can, when he will, make a minister of the gospel without man's forecast of education, and in spite of all the men in the world that would oppose it, though it be above sixteen hundred years after the apostles.

V. Many thousands had the soul benefit and comfort of his ministry to astonishment, as if an angel or an apostle had touched their souls with a coal of holy fire from the altar.

VI. This excellent operation of the special grace of God in him, and the gift of utterance when he preached, confounded the wisdom of his adversaries that heard him, or heard of him, he being, as it is commonly called, unlearned, or had not school education.

VII. For all these reasons before-mentioned, of the spirituality of his preaching, his labours in writing deserve preservation by printing as much as any other famous man's that have writ since the apostles' time.

VIII. Moreover he hath been a Christian sufferer for above twelve years, by imprisonment, whereby he sealed to the truth he preached.

IX. Yet, for all that imprisonment, he preached then, and there, and afterwards abroad, as a faithful labourer for the salvation of souls.

X. And he was not a man that preached by way of bargain for money, for he hath refused a more plentiful income to keep his station.

XI. And his moderation, or desire of money, was as the apostle Paul's practice, below his privilege; so that he did not, when he died, leave much wealth to his family.

XII. And the Church that wants such a pastor may find it long before they get one, and therefore ought to respect our Bunyan's labours.

XIII. If God had not put it into the heart of some Christians or Church to preserve the Epistles of the Apostle to the Romans, Corinthians, Galatians, and others, we in this age of the world should in all probability never have known that there ever were any such Christians and doctrines; their names and doctrines might have been lost, and we might have perished, and that would have been dreadful; for God mostly works by second causes.

XIV. And why should any Christian people, that have reason to reckon themselves obliged herein, set themselves aside from communicating to other Christians and the ages to come the gospel labours of so eminent a minister as God so graciously honoured and assisted them with?

XV. And if these labours (of, as I may say, an apostle of our age, if we have any) are not preserved by printing thus in folio, most of them in all probability will be lost, for there are many of them have been out of print many years, and will never otherwise be printed again because of the charge, &c.

XVI. By the late Act for liberty of conscience, it is lawful now to print the works of dissenters, though it was not so formerly; therefore much danger cannot plead excuse.

XVII. It is a good work without controversy, and therefore there can be no scruple of conscience about its pleasing God.

XVIII. There is also to the subscribers a further benefit in this folio; for, whereas these twenty books would, if bought single, cost nigh twenty shillings, now, as printed in folio, they will have them for about twelve shillings bound together in one volume, which conveniency also prevents losing.

XIX. These ten manuscripts, which were never before printed, would, if printed in small books, and bought single, cost almost the money that these twenty in folio comes for, which is great odds.

XX. Not to preserve his labours and name, which are so great, is a disingenuous slighting or despising them, and serving them no better than a wicked man's that rots. Bunyan hath preached, and freely bestowed many a good and gospel-truth, and soul-reviving expression; for which of them doth any of his friends slight him? Nay, do not they rather owe him something for his labour he bestowed on them, as Philemon did to Paul?

XXI. The price of the first part will be an easier purchase than of the whole; and all in one volume would be somewhat too big in bulk and price.

XXII. There is need of printing these books now, because errors and superstitions, like the smoke of the bottomless pit, darken Protestants understanding the purer truths of the gospel.

XXIII. And when this first part is sold off, we shall endeavour to publish a second part, whereby he that is willing may have the whole in folio.

XXIV. This preservation will preserve the name of John Bunyan, a champion of our age to future ages; whereby it may be said in the pulpit, The great convert Bunyan said so and so.

XXV. If the labours of so eminent a minister should not be preserved, I know not whose should.

XXVI. Antichristian people are diligent to preserve the works of their eminent men; and therefore Christians should be diligent to preserve theirs.

XXVII. The chief reasons we argue from are not common rules, that therefore every good minister's endeavours ought to be printed in folio. But this case is extraordinary, as an eminent minister, made so by abundance of gospel grace, who has also writ much which hath gone off well. I say eminent, though he was, when young, profane, and had not school education to enable him, as is apparent to all that knew him.

XXVIII. By this printing in folio a man may have recourse for satisfaction in a case of conscience to any of these particular books with the rest, which otherwise are not to be bought; and that I have proved by often trying most London booksellers, and before that given them above twice the price for a book; and I know not how to get another of those sorts for any price whatsoever.

XXIX. All these things, or half of them, beside many others that might be given, being considered, I cannot see but it is an absolute duty.

XXX. And lastly, (pardon me if I speak too great a word, as it may seem to some to be borne,) all things considered; that is, his own former profaneness, poverty, unlearnedness, together with his great natural parts, the great change made by grace, and his long imprisonment, and the great maturity in grace and preaching he attained to, I say our deceased Bunyan hath not left in England, or the world, his equal behind him, as I know of. And this is the unfeigned belief of,

Your Christian brother,
CHARLES DOE.

THE STRUGGLER

(FOR THE PRECEDING PRESERVATION OF MR. JOHN BUNYAN'S LABOURS IN FOLIO) THINKS IT MAY ANSWER THE DESIRES OF MANY TO GIVE THE FOLLOWING RELATION.

CHRISTIAN READER,—I do here as a further duty presume to give you, according to my understanding, a relation in three parts concerning our eminent author, Mr. John Bunyan, and his labours.

I. The author's parentage, imprisonment, times, and manner of his life and death, &c.

II. Relations and observations upon his labours, &c.

III. Notes on printing this folio and index, &c.

First, Our excellent author, by the abundant grace of God, Mr. John Bunyan, was born at Elstow, a mile side of Bedford, about the year 1628. His father was mean, and by trade a mender of pots and kettles, vulgarly called a tinker; and of the national religion, as commonly men of that trade are; and was brought up to the tinkering trade, as also were several of his brothers, whereat he worked about that country,[1] being also very profane and poor, even when married, &c.

[1 As doth appear by his book of his conversion, intituled, *Grace Abounding*, &c.]

But it pleased God, by his irresistible grace, to work in him some convictions and fears of hell, and also desires of heaven, which drove him to reading and hearing religious matters, so, controlling grace growing abundantly, he did not take up religion upon trust, but grace in him continually struggling with himself and others, took all advantages he lit on to ripen his understanding in religion, and so he lit on the dissenting congregation of Christians at Bedford, and was, upon confession of faith, baptized about the year 1651, or '52, or '53.

And after a little time, having a gift of utterance, and love to the conviction of sinners, preached about the country the same salvation he found by experience himself stood in need of, by faith and repentance, and worked at his tinkering trade for a livelihood, whereby the reigning grace of God appeared the more sovereign and glorious in this choice, even as it shone in the choice of Peter, a fisherman, and the rest of the apostles, and others of the eminent saints of old, most of them tradesmen, and of whom most excellent things are spoken, &c.

In the year 1660, being the year king Charles returned to England, having preached about[2] five years, the rage of gospel enemies was so great that, November 12, they took him prisoner at a meeting of good people, and put him in Bedford jail, and there he continued about six years, and then was let out again, 1666, being the year of the burning of London, and, a little after his release,

[2 As in his book intituled, *Grace Abounding*, s. 319.]

they took him again at a meeting, and put him in the same jail, where he lay six years more. [3] Before they took him his intent was to preach on these words, "Dost thou believe on the Son of God?" (John ix. 35.) From whence he intended to show the absolute need of faith in Jesus Christ. And after he was released again, they took him again, and put him in prison the third time, but that proved but for about half a year.

^{3 As he says in his Epistle to his Confession of Faith.}

Whilst he was thus twelve years and a half in prison, he writ several of his published books, as by many of their epistles appears, as *Pray by the Spirit, Holy City, Resurrection, Grace Abounding,* and others, also *The Pilgrim's Progress,* as himself and many others have said.

The pastor of Bedford congregation died, and, after some years' vacancy, John Bunyan, though a prisoner, was, by the church, called to the pastoral office, December 21, 1671, and as it pleased the Lord to rule the rage of men, it proved in or about the last year of his twelve years' imprisonment. And, being out, he preached the gospel publicly at Bedford, and about the counties, and at London, with very great success, being mightily followed everywhere. And it pleased the Lord to preserve him out of the hands of his enemies in the severe persecution at the latter end of King Charles II.'s reign, though they often searched and laid wait for him, and sometimes narrowly missed him.

In 1688, he published six books, being the time of King James II.'s liberty of conscience, and was seized with a sweating distemper, which, after his some weeks' going about, proved his death, at his very loving friend's, Mr. Strudwick's, a grocer, at Holborn Bridge, London, on August 31, 1688, and in the sixtieth year of his age, and was buried in Finsbury burying-ground, where many London dissenting ministers are laid; and it proved some days above a month before our great gospel deliverance was begun by the Prince of Orange's landing, whom the Lord of his continued blessing has since made our preserving king, William III.

And as to his family, he left his widow, Elizabeth, and three sons, John, Thomas, and Joseph, and three daughters, Elizabeth, Sarah, and Mary; but his blind daughter he writes of in his *Grace Abounding* died some years before him, and his widow died 1690-91.

Secondly, Concerning his labours; God did give of his extraordinary grace of the gospel to our author, Bunyan, and it is worthy our observation, for thereby God may have due honour, his people comfort, and adversaries confuted in their several corrupt notions, especially that of only them that have school education are fitly qualified for ministers of the glorious gospel of Jesus Christ. And also hereby the superstitious man is confounded in his way of worship, as were his predecessors, the rulers of the Jews, in the case of Peter and John, saying, Whence had these men this knowledge, seeing they are unlearned? but there was and is a reason beyond their false rules of education—for they had been with Jesus.

This is also apt to convince sincere-hearted Christians that God can, when he will, make a minister of his gospel, and send him forth in the power of his Spirit, and defend him, nay, may I say, it is God's prerogative to make his gospel-ministers, and he makes them effectual to all the ends of his gospel, to preach, as the great apostle saith, in season and out of season, to abase and abound, &c. He that can make the dry bones live (as in Ezek. xxxvii.), what can he not do? Yea, they shall live, and become a great host, and antichristian arts must fall; for the Lord doth make his servants, as he did Jeremiah, as brazen walls against people and priests.

And however some subtilly and vain-gloriously pretend to be the only lawful successors of the apostles, yet certain I am, from safer reasons of faith, that our author Bunyan was really, sincerely, and effectually a lawful successor of the apostles, and as lawful as any have been above this thousand years. Nay, may I say, he was a second Paul; for that his conversion was in a great measure like that great apostle's, who, of a great enemy to godliness, was, by strong and irresistible workings of sovereign grace, made a great minister of, and sufferer for, the gospel. Thousands of Christians in country and city can testify that their comfort under his ministry has been to admiration, so that their joy hath showed itself by much weeping.

To the eye of carnal reason it may seem that the great apostle Paul's imprisonment was a contradiction to his commission of effectually preaching the gospel to many countries; especially considering his commission was strengthened by his miraculous conversion, from the glory and call of the Lord Jesus from heaven, for the making of him such a great gospel preacher. And yet God suffered it so to be, and we have reason to believe for the best; because God usually works those seeming contrary things to his own end and glory. And the effect was, the saints were strengthened thereby, and several epistles were written thereby, which hath preserved much of the gospel in writing to the ages after, and even for our very great and needful help.

And I reckon I shall not be out of the way, if I observe and say, What hath the devil or his agents gotten by putting our great gospel-minister, Bunyan, in prison? for in prison, as before mentioned, he wrote many excellent books, that have published to the world his great grace, and great truth, and great judgment, and great ingenuity; and to instance in one, the *Pilgrim's Progress,* he hath suited to the life of a traveller so exactly and pleasantly, and to the life of a Christian, that this very book, besides the rest, hath done the superstitious sort of men and their practice more harm, or rather good, as I may call it, than if he had been let alone at his meeting at Bedford, to preach the gospel to his own auditory, as it might have fallen out; for none but priest-ridden ridden people know how to cavil at it, it wins so smoothly upon their affections, and so insensibly distils the gospel into them, and hath been printed in France, Holland, New England, and in Welsh, and about a hundred thousand in England, whereby they are made some means of grace, and the author become famous; and may be the cause of spreading his other gospel-books over the European and American world, and in process of time may be so to the whole universe.

When Mr. Bunyan preached in London, if there were but one day's notice given, there would be more people come together to hear him preach than the meeting-house would hold. I have seen to hear him preach, by my computation, about twelve hundred at a morning lecture, by seven o'clock, on a working-day, in the dark winter time. I also computed about three thousand that came to hear him, one Lord's-day, at London, at a town's end meeting-house; so that half were fain to go back again for want of room, and then himself was fain, at a back door, to be pulled almost over people to get upstairs to his pulpit.

Mr. Bunyan's dispute with a scholar to this effect.

As Mr. Bunyan was upon the road near Cambridge, there overtakes him a scholar that had observed him a preacher, and said to him, How dare you preach, seeing you have not the original, being not a scholar?

Then said Mr. Bunyan, Have you the original? Yes, said the scholar.

Nay, but, said Mr. Bunyan, have you the very self-same original copies that were written by the penmen of the scriptures, prophets and apostles?

No, said the scholar, but we have the true copies of those originals.

How do you know that? said Mr. Bunyan.

How? said the scholar. Why, we believe what we have is a true copy of the original.

Then, said Mr. Bunyan, so do I believe our English Bible is a true copy of the original.

Then away rid the scholar.

Another dispute with a scholar.

As Mr. Bunyan was preaching in a barn, and showing the fewness of those that should be saved, there stood one of the learned to take advantage of his words; and having done preaching, the schoolman said to him, You are a deceiver, a person of no charity, and therefore not fit to preach; for he that in effect condemneth the greatest part of his hearers hath no charity, and therefore not fit to preach.

Then Mr. Bunyan answered, The Lord Jesus Christ preached in a ship to his hearers on the shore (Matt. xiii.); and showed that they were as four sorts of ground—the high-way, the stony, the thorny, and the good ground; whereof the good ground was the only persons to be saved. And your position is, That he that in effect condemneth the greatest part of his hearers hath no charity, and therefore not fit to preach the gospel. But here the Lord Jesus Christ did so; then your conclusion is, The Lord Jesus Christ wanted charity, and therefore not fit to preach the gospel. Horrid blasphemy; away with your hellish logic, and speak Scripture.

Then replied the learned, 'Tis blasphemy to call logic hellish, which is our reason—the gift of God; for that which distinguisheth a man from a beast is the gift of God.

But Mr. Bunyan replied, Sin doth distinguish a man from a beast; is sin therefore the gift of God? &c.

They parted.

I once asked him his opinion in a common religious point, and offered some arguments to prove my opinion for the general of it; but he answered, that where the Scripture is silent we ought to forbear our opinions; and so he forbore to affirm either for or against, the Scripture being altogether silent in this point.

Thirdly, concerning this folio, &c. I have struggled to bring about this great good work; and it had succeeded in Mr. Bunyan's lifetime, even all his labours in folio, but that an interested bookseller opposed it; and notwithstanding the many discouragements I have met with in my struggles in this so great a work, we have—and I may believe by the blessing of the Lord—gotten about four hundred subscriptions, whereof about thirty are ministers, which also shows the great esteem our author's labours are in among Christian people. And that the reasonableness and duty of the preservation of his labours in folio, by subscription, may be continued to memory, I have also added my reasons, which I distributed in my late struggles to effect this work.

His effigies was cut in copper, from an original paint done to the life, by his very good friend, a limner; and those who desire it single, to put in a frame, may have it at this bookseller's, Mr. Marshal; and also the catalogue-table. The epistle is writ by two ministers, Mr. Wilson of Hichin, in Hertfordshire, and Mr. Chandler, who succeeds Mr. Bunyan at Bedford.

And Mr. Burton, that writ the epistle to *Some Gospel-truths Opened*, being the first book Mr. Bunyan writ, was minister at Bedford.

Note.—I would not charge the following running-titles upon our author, Bunyan; because they were added in the proposals, for want of running-titles and the knowledge of them, and the copies being at Bedford when the proposals were drawn up at London; and also because, perhaps, he designed some other like running-titles :—

Notes upon the Index, &c.

I did intend to print a complete table of all the texts of Scriptures used in our author's labours, that from thence, looking into his book, his sense might be easily found upon any text; so his labours might have been also in the nature of an exposition upon the whole Bible; but I have delayed till some other opportunity, it may be of the next folio, and whenever it falls I intend to give notice.

Because I and other subscribers, especially ministers, were willing this folio should be commoded with an index, I have, as a Christian, exposed myself and made one, and that without money for my labour of writing it, though I confess it might have seemed some other men's duty; yet being ignorant of the man that had the opportunity, and would have done it, unless paid for it, I was necessitated to effect it; and if the bookseller had paid for it, he would have lessened the number of 140 sheets of Mr. Bunyan's labours in this folio at ten shillings. Excuse this fault in me, if it be one.

I could have collected abundance more of excellent matter in this table; and I have placed an Italic-lettered word in every paragraph in the table, to be the guide-word to the same word in the folio, which is a black-lettered word in the folio, latter part; that is, those books formerly printed, where the printer hath not failed to make it so, and also in the manuscript, forepart, a guide-word to the same word under which I have drawn a black line, in as many folios as opportunity and time would permit me to do, because I had not time and convenience before this folio was printed to mark the manuscripts for to be a black-lettered word, as I had time for the formerly printed books. Also note, the book, though marked, doth not always refer to the table, but the table to the book.

is the intent; and because the word in the book doth not always, though very often, fall in alphabetical order, therefore some other like word is put in its place in the table.

Also note: Sometimes many principal words are in one paragraph, and then, though the matter be not to be found in the table by the word, that some perhaps may expect, yet it may be found by another word, because several words are so united that one cannot well part them; and it would be too large a table to put them all in severally in alphabetical order—as soul, sinner, saved, salvation, justification, Christ, God, &c.

Also note: When to the table-phrase more than one number is placed, then expect not that the same black-letter word is always to be found in the book to the last number, as is to the first number, but it may be some other black or marked word of like meaning; as for antichrist the black-lettered word in some places is harlot, and for apostles the black-letter word sometimes is twelve, because the word apostle is not in that part of the folio, though intended by twelve.

Also note: The phrase in the table is not always the very same, word for word, in the book, because the design of the table is to give matter in short saying, as well as most commonly a complete sentence; and, therefore, they that would have Mr. Bunyan's entire, complete, and full sense of the matter, let them look out of the table into the book, and there take all its connection together. Also, I have to keep the table as short as I well could; and yet, to direct well to the matter in the book, placed one part of the matter under one word, in alphabetical order, and another part of the same matter in another following paragraph, under another word in the table; so that, by finding one word in the table, you may often find in the same paragraph, in the book, before or after that word, other matter thereto relating.

I had but about two years' acquaintance with our author, and, therefore, have said but little of him, because of hastening this to the press; yet if any more comes to my memory, I intend to put it at the end of the index.

Your Christian brother,   C. D.

INTRODUCTION

THIRD PART OF THE PILGRIM'S PROGRESS.

So far ought no surprise to be felt at the appearance of a Third Part of *The Pilgrim's Progress*, that we might rather expect to hear of a tenth or a twelfth. Bunyan himself, by writing a Second Part, naturally opened the way to such continuations. He plainly intimated that the subject was not one to be completed by the history of a single pilgrim, or even of a single family. His own inventive genius could have expanded his first simple plan in various directions. But he wisely contented himself with working out his original idea, leaving it to others, if they pleased, to take advantage of the suggestions common to such a subject. Had he entered upon the delineation of new characters, it is not improbable that the exquisite simplicity and pathos of his narrative would have yielded to a more artificial style, the consequence of forced inventions, and the necessity of an experience not his own. The instinctive wisdom of genius warned him against this danger. But there was no reason whatsoever why other minds should not take up the threads of the story, left so temptingly still loose. A just reproach belongs to those who applied the venerable name of Bunyan to writings not his own. But it is a very rash assumption to fasten this reproach upon the author of the Third Part of *The Pilgrim's Progress*, or indeed upon any of the writers of books falsely ascribed to his pen. The sin, in all probability, was that of the printers and publishers, who had very easy consciences in the seventeenth century on all matters of this kind. They mutually offended in the indiscriminate employment of good names. It is well known, that they could appeal to very early and venerable authority as an apology for this practice. If Bunyan's name was applied to works which he never wrote, that of St. Augustine had been still more frequently so used. Nay, Dionysius, the Areopagite, who probably was no author at all, has given a title to works far weightier, in some quarters, than either Bunyan's or Augustine's.

But the continuation of *The Pilgrim's Progress* must be judged according to its merits. Unfortunately, the anxious eulogists of Bunyan have been too much offended by the false assumption of his name to read the book with a fair observation of its design. The writer, whoever he was, possessed considerable knowledge of the world, and of human character. His own Christian experience was far advanced; and he had no ordinary measure of literary talent. "Tender-Conscience," the name of the principal personage in this narrative, is a well-drawn and striking character. He belongs to a class different from any of those most prominently set forth by Bunyan. But this is obviously a merit in the writer. The path to the heavenly Jerusalem is attempted by a numberless variety of pilgrims. He who has ability enough to describe to the life any one set of these travellers, confers a vast benefit on the world. The greater the number of such observers and writers the better. In the case of "Tender-Conscience," and his adventures, we have excellent lessons in addition to those taught us by the first two parts of *The Pilgrim's Progress*. There is no great hardihood in believing, that some readers may find their particular tempers and circumstances as well delineated in these, as in the earlier chapters of the pilgrimage. It would be considered very ridiculous if the eulogistic critic of a dramatic poet should claim for his author the exclusive privilege of holding the mirror up to nature. Much more absurd is it to suppose that any writer, though it be Bunyan himself, can have engrossed the measureless expanses opened to the students of religious experience.

The author of this Third Part makes no secret of his intention to imitate, as well as continue, the early parts of the pilgrimage. Mention is made of the same places, and of the same dangers. But the nearest of the imitations have touches of originality. The Interpreter of the Third Part reminds us, at once, of the Interpreter known of old; but he shows us some things entirely fresh. Very pleasant, and full of instruction, is the picture of the two farms. Few specimens of the descriptive writing of the latter part of the seventeenth century could be instanced as surpassing it. The same may be said of the account given of the Hill of Difficulty, with its cragged paths, its deep shades, and winding rivulets; of the scenes revealed in the Cave of Contemplation; and of the Spenserian picture of the Palace of Carnal-Security, and its inmates.

Among the characters, the fullest drawn is that of Tender-Conscience. Of those but incidentally introduced, the most striking is Weary-o'-the-World. We question whether Bunyan himself could have better sketched his brief history. Spiritual-Man, Seek-Truth, and Convert, are all good specimens of this kind of writing; nor is it easy to understand how any fair critic, honestly reading this Third Part of *The Pilgrim's Progress*, can speak disrespectfully of its merits.

Its greatest defect is that which, by its very structure, it shares with Bunyan's Second Part. It is not the delineation of a continued progress; but neither is the history of Christiana. The progress, strictly so called, ended with Christian's admission to the celestial city. To this there could be no Second or Third Part. Tender-Conscience is not a supplemental, but another pilgrim. His struggles and triumphs belong to his own individual history. It is only as exhibiting new phases of human character, under the influence of divine grace that we can have *A Pilgrim's Progress* referring to more than one individual. That of Christian himself might have been divided into three, or any number of parts, that is, as stages in his progress. But it is a very dangerous experiment of fancy, to suppose him finishing his course with certain graces at one time, and then setting out with him anew to finish it by the help of others. Instead of speaking of parts, therefore, it would have been better to call each separate narrative *A Pilgrim's Progress*, or *New Pilgrim's Progress*. Under such a title, the prominent virtues and weaknesses of every Christian might form, if well traced, the admirable ground-work of a story. There could be no reason, were the narrative skilfully conducted, for casting it aside because it proved somewhat more formal, more polished and scholarly than Bunyan's. This might lessen its charm, and lower the author's claim to originality and genius; but it might still be of deep interest and value as containing vivid portraitures of individual characters; of this or that man who, while possessing the general qualities of Christian life, had one especially of such ripe growth that it gave a peculiar colour to all the rest.

These considerations will show how valuable a portion of an appendix to Bunyan's Works may be constituted by the pilgrimage of Tender-Conscience. A few objectionable passages have been omitted.

II. S.

THE PILGRIM'S PROGRESS

FROM

THIS WORLD TO THAT WHICH IS TO COME,

DELIVERED UNDER THE SIMILITUDE OF A DREAM.

PART III.

SHOWING THE SEVERAL DANGERS AND DIFFICULTIES HE MET WITH, AND THE MANY
VICTORIES HE OBTAINED OVER THE WORLD, THE FLESH, AND THE DEVIL: TOGETHER
WITH HIS HAPPY ARRIVAL AT THE CELESTIAL CITY, AND THE GLORY AND JOY HE
FOUND, TO HIS ETERNAL COMFORT.

THE PREFACE TO THE CHRISTIAN READER.

READER,—In this book is set forth a tedious pilgrimage, through the many dangerous hazards of the wilderness of this world, to the heavenly Canaan of eternal rest and peace; in which, though in the similitude of a dream, is lively represented the state of our Christian warfare; wherein, fighting valiantly under the banner of Christ, the great Captain of our salvation, we shall assuredly overcome our spiritual enemies, and be victorious conquerors over those temptations that beset frail human nature, and would hinder us from leaving, in a good time, the city of Destruction, (which is the world, and its fruitless pleasures, cares, and incumbrances,) to journey towards the heavenly Jerusalem, which is the true centre of our endless happiness in the fruition of unspeakable and soul-ravishing joys, that know no date nor consummation.

This has been, in the former as well as present age, a way of writing that has been extremely taking, representing to the mind things that command our most serious thoughts and attention, and work more upon the minds of men than if delivered in plainer terms: however, to the discerning Christian, there is nothing in this that is obscure or difficult to be understood; nothing but what is grounded upon sacred truths, and the mercies of God in Jesus Christ, held forth to us by his assured word.

It is a piece so rare, and transcending what has hitherto been published of this kind, that I dare, without any further apology, leave it to the censure of all mankind who are not partial or biassed: and so, not doubting but it will render comfort and delight, I subscribe myself, as heretofore, your soul's hearty well-wisher and fellow-labourer in the vineyard of our Lord Jesus Christ,

JOHN BUNYAN.

To his worthy Friend the Author of the Third Part of the PILGRIM'S PROGRESS, *upon the perusal thereof, &c.*

THOUGH many things are writ to please the age,
Amongst the rest for this I dare engage,
Where virtue dwells, it will acceptance find,
And, to your Pilgrim, most that read, be kind,
But all to please would be a task as hard,
As for the winds from blowing to be barr'd.
The pious Christian, in a mirror, here
May see the promis'd land, and without fear
Of threatened danger, bravely travel on
Until his journey he has safely gone,
And does arrive upon the happy shore,
Where joys increase, and sorrow is no more.
This is a dream not fabled as of old;
In this express the sacred truths are told

That do to our eternal peace belong,
And, after mourning, changes to a song
Of glorious triumphs, that are without end,
If we but bravely for the prize contend.
No pilgrimage like this can make us blest,
Since it brings us to everlasting rest:
So well in every part the sense is laid,
That it to charm the reader may be said,
With curious fancy, and create delight,
Which to an intimation must invite.
And happy are they that through stormy seas
And dangers seek adventures like to these!
Who sell the world for this great pearl of price,
Which, once procur'd, will purchase paradise!

He who in such a bark doth spread his sails
Needs never fear at last these prosperous gales,
That will conduct him to a land where he
Shall feel no storms, but in a calm shall be,
Where, crown'd with glory, he shall sit and sing
Eternal praise to his redeeming King,
Who conquer'd death, despoil'd him of his sting.

So wishes your faithful friend,

B. D.

*These lines are humbly recommended to the Reader,
written upon the perusal of this book, &c.*

In reading of this book, I plainly find
The thoughts are suited to the author's mind:
For he who virtue loves, of virtue speaks,
And the strong chains of vice with courage breaks.
What here at first seems clouded, soon reveals
The pilgrim's joys, which he no more conceals:
But still he tries his patience and his love,
To travel tow'rds the kingdom that's above.
Some interposing fears have time to reign;
But, those by faith expell'd, his soul again

Clears up, and, like the bow that paints the skies
After a shower, (on which mankind relies
As a sure pledge the deluge shall no more
Make all one boundless sea without a shore,)
Gives certain hopes that heaven's anger's past,
And he his lot in a bless'd land has cast.
You write so plainly, that the weakest mind
Under similitudes may comfort find.
A guide you give, that by the hand doth lead
Those pilgrims that the heavenly roads do tread,
And tells them always where the danger is,
How to step over, or to wisely miss,
The stumbling-blocks that Satan dayly lays,
To overthrow them that mind not their ways;
So being bruis'd against rocks of despair,
Or doubt or fear, they know not how nor where,
They faint and languish in the middle way,
Or back to Egypt haste without delay,
Preferring darkness to the glorious day
They were approaching. This book has my voice,
And is of all in this kind the most choice.
Peruse it well, and you will find it reach
From earth to heaven, in what it well does teach:
If you'd be blest, then mind what it does preach.

L. C.

THE PILGRIM'S PROGRESS.

PART III.

After the two former dreams, concerning Christian and Christiana his wife, with their children and companions' pilgrimage from the city of Destruction to the region of glory, I fell asleep again, and the visions of my head returned upon me. I dreamed another dream, and behold there appeared unto me a great multitude of people in several distinct companies and bands, travelling from the city of Destruction, the town of Carnal-Policy, the village of Morality, and from the rest of the cities, towns, villages, and hamlets that belong to the valley of Destruction; for so was the whole country called that lay on this side of the wicket-gate, which the man Evangelist showed unto Christian, and so was also that country called that was situated wide of the gate, on the right hand and on the left, extending itself along by the walls and borders of that region, wherein lay the way to the heavenly country. This was the name of that province—even the *valley of Destruction.*

Now I saw in my dream, that all the highway-roads and lanes that led from the valley of Destruction towards the gate of the Way of Life were full of people who were travelling towards that gate; and some of them walked along very vigorously; others halted and grew weary, through the violent heat of the season, which made them even ready to faint, for it was in the hottest time of all the year, and the sun burnt up the herb of the field,

and scorched the poor travellers so that many of them were forced to sit down and rest themselves; and, in the night time, many of them returned back again to their old habitations; others, more hardy than the rest, went on till they came to the Slough of Despond, where Pliable forsook Christian, and there, falling into the filth and mire of that place, were so disheartened that they returned in whole droves to their own dwellings again; and very few there were that would venture through the slough; yet some got very dextrously over the steps, without being in the least bemired; whilst others, through ignorance or heedlessness, missing those steps, were forced to wade through the dirt, which was very deep, and made their passage exceeding painful; but at length, with much ado, they weathered the point, and mastered the difficulties of that horrid quagmire, and got safe upon dry ground.

Among the rest of these travellers that got over this slough, I saw a young man of an amiable countenance walking by himself after he got clear of the slough; but he was all over bedaubed with the filth of that place, which made him go very heavily on; for what with struggling to get through, and what with the dismal apprehension he lay under during his passage, he was extremely weakened, his joints were loosened; besides, it was the nature of the dirt of this place to cause a trembling and disorder in the limbs of those that were defiled with it, and to whatsover part of their body it stuck, there it would do them some injury. Now the young man being all overclammed with it, he went a very slow pace, his head hanging down, his hands quivering, and his feet tripping at the least unevenness and ruggedness in the way; and a speck or two of the dirt being spattered near his eyes, made him dim-sighted; so that he groped along like one that is blind, and sometimes stepped out of the path.

In this condition he was, when at length I saw in my dream that he sat down upon the ground to bemoan his sad estate, and he wept very bitterly; and behold a bright cloud hovering over his head, which gradually descending overshadowed him, and out of the cloud a hand was reached forth, which with the tears, that ran like rivers from his eyes, washed the dirt off his face and his whole body, so that in a moment, as it were, his sight and his strength were restored to him again, and a voice came out of the cloud, saying, Son of man, go on in the strength of the Lord thy God. So he was mightily comforted and refreshed after this, and began to rouse up himself, being more nimble and active, more vigorous and strong, than ever he was before; and, his eyes being healed also, he clearly saw the shining light that Evangelist showed to Christian. Then he tripped along over the plain, and made direct up to the shining light, by means of which he quickly found the wicket-gate, at which he knocked aloud, minding what was written over the gate, viz.: "Knock, and it shall be opened."

Now, I saw in my dream, that, as soon as he had knocked at the wicket-gate, a whole shower of arrows were shot at him from the castle of Beelzebub, so that he was wounded in several places, and extremely frightened at the adventure; which made him knock again and again very hard, for fear those that shot at him should come and kill him outright, before he could get in; but presently, to his great comfort, the gate opened to him; and when he that opened the gate saw the arrows stick in his flesh, he bid him haste in, for fear of more danger. So he stepped in, and made obeisance to the man that opened the gate, for he seemed to be a person worthy of reverence, by his grave countenance and composed behaviour; so he spake to the man, whose name was Good-will, and said, Sir, having heard of the fame of the heavenly country, and being informed by several travellers, that the way to it was by this gate, I, being weary of living in the valley of Destruction, and earnestly desirous to see that region of bliss, humbly made bold to knock at this gate, which you have been graciously pleased to open to me; for which high favour I return you my humble and hearty thanks; but as I stood at the gate, after I knocked the first time, I was shot with these arrows, which you now see sticking in my flesh; and I fear I am mortally wounded, for my

spirits fail me, and there is a mist before my eyes; and with that he fell at Good-will's feet, begging him to tell where he might find one that had skill to probe his wounds, and cure them, if not mortal. So Good-will, taking compassion on the young man, asked his name. My name, replied the young man, is Tender-Conscience, I was born and bred in the town of Vain Delights. Then Good-will, having registered the young man's name, he wrote a certificate, and gave it him, bidding him deliver it at the next house, which was the house of the Interpreter; withal showing him the way to it, for it was but a little way off from the gate. There, says he, you will find a remedy for your wounds, and see many glorious things.

Then I saw in my dream, that Good-will gave to Tender-Conscience a strong crutch made of *lignum vitæ*, or the *tree of life*, to rest himself upon, and ease his feet as he went along, he having nothing before in his hand but a weak twig of vain opinions, which he gathered from the tree of knowledge, growing on the banks of the waters of confusion. This weak reed was all the staff that Tender-Conscience leaned upon in his journey, till such time as Good-will, bidding him throw it away, gave him the aforesaid strong crutch, which he bid him be sure not to part with, for that it should be of singular use to him all the way, and especially now when he was wounded, for that it had a particular virtue to stay the bleeding of wounds. So Good-will having given Tender-Conscience ample directions to find the way, bade him farewell, and left him to go forward on his journey.

Then Tender-Conscience began to pluck up his spirits, being much comforted, eased, and supported by the crutch which Good-will had given him; for no sooner was he in possession of it, but his wounds abated in bleeding; and by that time it grew warm in his hand, it sent forth a certain odoriferous perfume which exceedingly refreshed his spirits, and he found himself grow stronger and stronger by the healing virtues of this wonderful crutch. Then travelled he, till at length he arrived at the house of the Interpreter, where knocking at the door, one presently opened, and asking his business, Tender-Conscience made answer, I would speak with the Interpreter, who, I understand, is the master of this house. So he called the Interpreter, who came forthwith to Tender-Conscience, and demanded what he would have.

Tender-Con. Sir, said Tender-conscience, I was recommended to you by one Good-will, who keeps yonder wicket-gate. For travelling from the town where I was born, in the valley of Destruction, towards the region of life, I came to the wicket-gate, as I was directed; and, as soon as I had knocked there, I was shot with these arrows that you see now sticking in my flesh; and, when the gate was opened, I made my condition known to Good-will, and told him, I was afraid some of my wounds were mortal, desiring him to acquaint me where I might find a physician; so he recommended me to you, giving me this certificate of his hand, and bidding me deliver it unto you, assuring me that in this place I should find a remedy for my wounds, and see many glorious things. He likewise gave me this strong crutch which you see in my hand, which has afforded me great comfort and assistance, by refreshing my fainting spirits, supporting me in the way, and putting a stop to the excessive bleeding of my wounds. But it is from you that I hope for the finishing of my cure.

Interpreter. Welcome, young man, said the Interpreter, after he had read the certificate; come in and partake of the good things of this house; and before you go away, I hope to see you whole and sound. So he conducted him into a parlour, and asked him several questions concerning his country, and the manner of his life there; to all which Tender-Conscience made particular answers, giving him an exact account of his education, and how he had spent the time of his youth till that day. After which the Interpreter narrowly searched the wounds which he had received by the arrows that day, and applied a sovereign balsam to them, whereby Tender-Conscience became straightway whole and sound; and the Interpreter caused the arrows that he had pulled out of his body to be laid up safe, as a memorial of his narrow escape from death. Then he carried him into the dining-room, and entertained him at a rich yet frugal banquet, feasting him with the best restoratives in the world; for he considered that Tender-Conscience was weak and feeble, and had a tedious journey to go, therefore he judged it necessary to treat him with diet of strong nourishment, that he might be the better enabled to undergo the hardships of travel in that tiresome road.

After the banquet was over, he carried him into the several apartments of the house, and showed him all the excellent things which Christian and Christiana his wife, with their children and companions, saw in this place. And when it grew towards the going down of the sun, he conducted Tender-Conscience into the dining-room, where they took a moderate repast together, and spent the residue of that evening in profitable discourse, the Interpreter taking that opportunity to inform him fully of the laws and customs of that country, and to instruct him in his way, with directions what company he should keep or avoid, and how he should behave himself all along the road. Then he showed him to his chamber, and left him to his repose.

The next morning, by break of day, Tender-Conscience arose, and prepared for his journey; and the Interpreter, having performed all the good offices of complete hospitality, told him, he would bear him company a little way; which kind offer Tender-Conscience gladly embraced, both because he was a stranger altogether in those parts, and because he was in love with the Interpreter's good conversation. So they walked out together, and taking their way over a large corn field, through which their lay a path into the high-road from the Interpreter's house, they came to a lane, on each side of which their stood a manor-house, with lands belonging to each of them.

Then Tender-Conscience took notice that the grounds of one farm were all in a flourishing and prosperous condition, a plentiful crop of corn, lovely fat pastures, and those well-stocked with cattle, the fences everywhere strong and close, and all things in exceeding good case; whereas, on the other side, the opposite farm lay at sixes and sevens, (as the old saying is,) some part of the ground was overgrown with nettles, briers, and thorns, and all manner of unprofitable weeds; the other part was uncultivated, and lay covered with stones, the fences down, and wild beasts browsing up and down on what they could find; all things lying at rack and manger, so that there was not the least sign of a future harvest. At which Tender-Conscience greatly marvelled, and asked the Interpreter the reason why there was so great a difference between the two farms, since lying so close together, the one was a daily reproach to the other. To which the Interpreter replied, He that owns that farm on the right hand, which you behold in so fair and flourishing a condition, is the king's tenant, as likewise is the other, for both the manors belong to the king of the country. Now, upon a time, the king taking his progress this way, and being informed that he had two fair farms in this place untenanted, and that, for want of looking after, they were both run to ruin, (for at that time they were both alike,) he put them presently into the hands of these two men who live in them now; telling them withal, for their encouragement, that they should not only live rent free, (saving some homage to be paid at his court,) but should also be removed to palaces of inestimable dignity and value, provided they would but be industrious, and cleanse the farms, and improve them with the best husbandry they could; because he loved not that any part of the crown lands should run to ruin. So these two men were put in possession of the farms; each had his house and lands apart. Now, the man on the left hand, taking a survey of his new farm, and finding it all overgrown with weeds and briers, covered with stones, the fences down, wild beasts ranging up and down in the grounds, and all things like a wilderness, he sat down and folded his arms despairing ever to cleanse his farm, or bring it into any order; so he fell to rioting and drunkenness, to gaming and wantonness, never regarding his farm, or so much as once thinking of it; so that he is run deeply in debt, and has lost his reputation among all his neighbours; and unless he speedily take up, and set himself to cleansing and manuring his farm, he will certainly fall into the king's displeasure, who will cast him into prison for neglecting his farm, (for so he threatened them at the first,) whence he cannot escape till he has made full satisfaction to the king for his heinous offence. But, on the contrary, the tenant on the right hand, having surveyed his farm in like manner as the other did, and finding it in the same condition, all run to ruin and disorder, he considered with himself the great favour he had received in being intrusted with one of the king's farms, and how heinous a crime it would be to slight such a benefit as was proposed to him, both for the present and future, if he would improve his gift. Then he considered, likewise, that though it was a great farm, and all in a manner like a wilderness, yet, by endeavouring every day to cleanse it, in time he should compass the whole. These considerations made him set about it with all speed, and he began by little and little to weed, and remove the stones off from the ground; and so, by daily labouring at it, he at length reduced it to this good order you see it in now; and he is in assured hopes of obtaining the king's promise, and of being removed to a more noble and honourable station.

In my opinion, said Tender-Conscience, the farmer on the left hand is very much to blame in neglecting so fair an opportunity of raising himself. Had he but followed the steps of his opposite neighbour, and done something every day toward the cleansing of his farm, he might by this time have reaped the benefit of it, and had the returns of plentiful crops, besides the continuance and increase of the king's favour, who would, no doubt, in time, have been as good as his word, and preferred him to some higher dignity.

Inter. Just such, said the Interpreter, is the condition of you travellers who come from the valley of Destruction, and are going to the region of life and glory: the King of that place only requires of you to husband well his gifts and graces, to improve your talents, and persevere to the end of your pilgrimage, and then you will be translated to eternal mansions. Now the way to do this is not to be discouraged with the length of your journey, nor frightened with the apprehensions you may have of the difficulties to be overcome, and the dangers to be encountered by the way; but you must arm yourself with a firm resolution to go through all, making some progress every day; for to stand still is to go back; and therefore, like the wise and industrious farmer on the right hand, who every day weeded and stoned some part of his grounds, so must you daily go on and gain ground; thus, like him, you will in due time perfect your labour and travail, and finish your course with joy. The Interpreter gave him many more good counsels and admonitions as they walked along, till they came to the highway that was fenced in on either side with the wall of salvation; and there the Interpreter gave to Tender-Conscience the King's royal pass, signifying to him that it would be of singular use to him throughout his journey to the heavenly country: so, wishing

him a prosperous journey and eternal happiness, he bid him heartily farewell.

Then I saw in my dream that Tender-Conscience wept when he was to part with the Interpreter, being ravished in spirit with inexpressible love to his company, forasmuch as he had healed his wounds, entertained him most courteously, showed him many excellent and glorious things, and giving him the King's warrant or pass, whereby he should be enabled to travel more securely and quietly to the region of life: besides, he was naturally very affectionate, and could not brook a separation from such a friend without bursting into tears. But at length, overcoming his passions, he set forward on his journey, and came to the place where the cross stood, where Christian's burden fell from off his back, and, tumbling into the sepulchre, (which was at the bottom of the rising ground whereon the cross stood,) was there buried.

Now I saw in my dream that hard by the cross were built two houses: the one was called "the house of Mourning," and the other was called "the house of Mirth," and they were situated on each side of the cross, the one on the right hand and the other on the left. Now, as Tender-Conscience kept the path up the hill, there came out of the house of Mirth some young men to meet him; and they spake to him, saying, Whence comest thou, and whither art thou going? Then Tender-Conscience made answer, I am come from the valley of Destruction, and am going to the heavenly city, the region of life and glory; but I perceive it grows late, and I am a stranger in the way, and therefore would gladly take my repose this night somewhere hereabouts, if I might find so much favour among any of the inhabitants of this place. Then the young men made answer, and said, There are none but these two houses which thou seest in all this parish that give entertainment to strangers; and if thou wilt go along with us to yonder house, (pointing to that on the left hand,) there thou wilt find good usage, merry company, and all things that your heart can wish for; and in the morning we will travel along with you, for we only lodge there to-night, and in the morning will set forward toward the heavenly city. By such enticing words and persuasions as these, they prevailed upon Tender-Conscience to go along with them; but as he drew near to the house he heard a great noise, as of them that make merry—singing, dancing, and playing upon musical instruments, with much laughter; at which Tender-Conscience was greatly astonished; but as he came up to the house, he saw written over the door these words, "This is the house of Mirth." Then he remembered the words of the wise man, "That it is better to go to the house of mourning than to go to the house of feasting:" and again, "The heart of the wise is in the house of mourning, but the heart of fools is in the house of mirth." So he asked the young men what that house was called on the other side of the cross, and they

told him it was called " the house of Mourning."
Moreover they railed and scoffed at the people
that lived in it, and told him that none but a few
dull, phlegmatic fools ever frequented it; but
Tender-Conscience weighed more the words of the
wise man than their slanderous tongues, and told
them he would go seek a lodging at the house of
Mourning. Then they laughed at him, and called
out the rest of their companions to deride him;
but he departed from them, and passed by the cross,
at the sight of which he was transported with
unspeakable love, grief, compassion, and such like
affections; the young men and their companions
all the while following him and making a mock at
his tenderness; and as he wept at the foot of the
cross, they fell a laughing, ranting, and roaring,
till at length he rose up and made haste to go to
the house of Mourning; where he was no sooner
arrived, but two grave yet comely women bid him
kindly welcome, saying to him, We saw how you
were likely to be seduced into the house of Mirth,
and were rejoiced to behold your resolution not to
enter into that seat of vanity; we also saw your
constancy in withstanding their taunting scoffs and
mockery, and how you were not ashamed of the
cross, but the sight of it pierced your heart with
divine love, and caused your eyes to pour out rivers
of tears, while those profane wretches laughed you
to scorn; all this we beheld with great satisfaction:
and now come in, thou blessed of the Lord, and
rest in this place till to-morrow, and then thou
mayest go in peace. So Tender-Conscience went
in along with the courteous matrons, who washed
his feet; and having refreshed him with a morsel
of bread and a little wine, with a few figs, raisins,
and almonds, they fell into discourse about the
person who suffered death on the cross: and the
eldest matron spake to this effect.

Eld. Mat. How vain and profane are those poor
wretches who despise the cross of Christ, and are
become bitter enemies both to him and his sufferings! They profess to believe in God and worship
him, yet at the same time give both him and
themselves the lie in their practice; they profess to
believe Christ crucified for our sins, yet at the same
time they crucify him themselves afresh, and put
him to an open shame. They lay an embargo on
their faith, and suffer it not to launch beyond the
narrow limits of their senses; and taking up their
religion on the credit of flesh and blood, their
carnal passions are made the standards of its practice, and whatsoever thwarts their lusts is banished
their conversation. Hence it comes to pass, that
what at first was esteemed dull and unpleasing,
was by degrees slighted and neglected, till at length
it is become the object of their derision and scorn,
as you see experimented in the house of Mirth this
evening.

Young Mat. And that which is the more surr-
prising is, that these very persons pretend to be
honourers of the cross and disciples of Christ Jesus;
their house is built as near the cross outwardly as

ours is, and yet at the same time they are enemies
to those who tread in the steps of him who suffered
that ignominious death for our sakes.

Tender-Con. Ay, said Tender-Conscience, the
three young men told me they were going toward
the heavenly city as well as I, and if I would
repose myself in the house of Mirth this night,
they would bear me company on the morrow; but
as soon as they perceived that I would seek a
lodging in the house of Mourning, they turned their
compliments into scoffs, their pretended civility
into real rudeness, and their feigned pious purposes
into open profaneness; railing at you and your
house, and all your guests; deriding and laughing
at me for a fool and madman!—like those Greeks
to whom the cross of Christ was foolishness, and
all who took it up, or bore any affection to it were
esteemed as the offscourings of all things. Such
was my entertainment among them; for whereas,
before they were merry in the house, singing,
dancing, and playing on instruments of music, so
soon as the three young men gave intimation to
them of my design, they forsook their melody, and
came running out of the house to mock and deride
me, ranting and roaring, and raising great laughter,
while I sat weeping by the cross.

Eld. Mat. It is worth one's observation to see
by what degrees men arrive at that ridiculous
vanity as well as notorious impiety. First, they
let loose the reins to their wanton humour in
trivial and small matters, delighting in nothing so
much as a jest or droll in common and ordinary
conversation; thus having habituated and used
themselves to a jocular vein, they can hardly forbear
to play the wags with things of more serious importance, as the affairs of justice and the public
state; then, being as it were steeled and hardened
in this wanton humour, they at last fall to mocking
and jesting at the most holy and religious things,
verifying the saying of the wise man, " He who
contemns little things shall fall by little and little."
Certainly vain mirth and excessive laughter do but
raise a dust in the eyes of the soul, and interrupt
her more serene and steady prospect of better
things, and the most innocent jests may be reckoned
like mushrooms, which well ordered and spiced
may do no harm, but can do no good. Whatsoever
habit the soul gets, it is hard to remove it; and
the habit of excessive laughter is most difficult to
be overcome, because it is a faculty essential to our
nature to laugh; and he that gives way to it, and
to common jesting, betrays his mind to an unmanly
likeness and an habitual vanity, which afterwards
he will find it difficult to root out. And, therefore,
seasonable was the advice of the holy apostle Paul,
when he counselled the Ephesians to avoid foolish
talking and jesting; and the Thessalonians to
abstain from all appearance of evil. Now what
was said to them, no doubt, was written for our
instruction; and all Christians are obliged to observe
their sage counsels in this as well as other matters,
and not to pick and choose what precepts and

counsels we please to obey, as if we could compound with God for the quarter or half performance of his will. And though this prohibition of vain jests and foolish mirth seems to be of small moment with some, yet it is good to observe every tittle of the word of God with great reverence. And you have done the part of a wise man in forsaking the house of Mirth, and coming to the house of Mourning; for they think this life to be but a pastime, or a market for gain: "They drink wine in bowls; the harp and the viol, the timbrel and pipe, are in their feasts: but they regard not the work of the Lord, neither consider they the operation of his hand. Therefore hell hath enlarged herself, and opened her mouth without measure; and their glory, and their multitude, and their pomp, and he that rejoiceth among them shall descend into it."

Young Mat. Neither is it less worthy of remark, by what artifices and misrepresentations the people belonging to the house of Mirth do endeavour to frighten travellers from coming to our house, bringing an ill name upon it, and telling them we are sad melancholy folks, nothing to be heard here but sighing, lamenting, and groaning; and that many poor travellers have been driven to despair in this place, and made away with themselves: whereas there is nothing of this true; for our sorrow is not worldly sorrow which bringeth death, but mourning and repentance unto life, which needeth not to be repented of. In our sighs we rejoice, and in our tears we smile, as it is written, "They that sow in tears shall reap in joy." And the deepest of our groans are but forerunners of the soul's triumph over sin and death; and there is so near a neighbourhood betwixt this kind of grief and the most exalted pleasure, that it is hard to distinguish between the one and the other. While our eyes rain tears, the clouds that cause them are scattered from our hearts; and that very tempest of sighs and groans, which threatens to rend our breasts in pieces, does but sweep and cleanse the air of our souls, and renders it more calm and serene than it was before: thus springeth light from darkness, peace from war, and life from death. And so far is this home from leading any unto despair, or to be the occasion of any destroying themselves, that, on the contrary, many that have come from the house of Mirth in that condition, when their means were all spent in rioting and vain mirth, have desired harbour with us, and in a little time have recovered their judgment, reason, and sense again, and have gone away full of comfort and satisfaction.

Now by this time it grew late, and they broke up company, causing one of the household to show Tender-Conscience to his lodging, having wished him a good repose. He returned them hearty thanks for their good counsel and edifying discourse, took his leave for that evening, and went to rest. In the morning he rose early, and prepared for his journey, being extremely pleased with the entertainment he found in this place; so that he burst out a singing in his chamber:—

> Blessed be God who travellers doth guide,
> And with his wings doth them from danger hide.
> My foot had well nigh slipt, when I was led
> Within the house of Mirth to take a bed:
> But better things rememb'ring, I retir'd,
> As I was by the grace of God inspir'd:
> They laugh'd, I wept; they mock'd, while I did wail;
> And at the house of Mourning they did rail.
> The house of Mourning solid joys does bring,
> Whilst that of Mirth behind it leaves a sting.

Now whilst he was singing these last words, he heard a great noise without; and looking out from the window, he saw several that belonged to the house of Mirth, who had beset the house of Mourning, and demanded to have the man delivered to them that came in there last night. This put Tender-Conscience into no small fright, so that he fell to prayer; and behold three shining ones appeared to him, and bid him be of good cheer, for they would deliver him out of his enemies' hands. Then one of them breathed on him, saying, "Be thou changed;" and he was immediately transformed, and he became a new creature; and his face, which before looked meagre and pale, now became ruddy and shining, his eyes sparkling like diamonds, so that those who had seen him before could not know him now. Then the second presented him with a change of raiment, clothing him in a white robe; whereas as before he was in a crimson coloured garment. The third also set a mark in his forehead, giving him such a roll, with a seal upon it, as Christian had given to him. So the three shining ones pronounced a blessing on him, and bid him go away in peace, for that no evil should befall him. Then Tender-Conscience acquainted the matrons with what had happened to him, and taking his leave of them, went boldly out with his crutch in his hand, and passed through the liers-in-wait, and no man knew him, or had power to say, Who art thou? but he departed from them in peace, as the shining ones had foretold him.

Then I saw in my dream, that Tender-Conscience walked a great pace, till he was out of sight of the house, and of the liers-in-wait; for he had still some dread remaining upon him, which spurred him on to hasten out of their reach. Thus he walked till he came to the foot of the hill Difficulty; and having drank nothing that day, he stooped down and drank of the spring that ran by the bottom of the hill; then he sat down awhile, and considered which way to go; for there were three paths—one right up the hill, and the other two went round by the bottom of the hill to the right and to the left. That path which went straight up the hill was very steep and cragged, and that which went round the bottom on the left hand was broad and even, curiously shaded with rows of trees on each side, and the springs winding along by the path-side, which was very pleasant and inviting; and the path on the right hand was also smooth and even, shady and pleasant, and seemed to wind about upwards; so that Tender-Conscience thinking this path would bring him to the top of the hill as well as the steep one, he made choice of it. Now the name of this path was Danger, and the name of the other on the left hand was Destruction; so he went in the path of Danger, which brought him up round by the side of the hill into a great wood, which he entered, the path leading him through the middle of the wood. Now the wood seemed very pleasant and delightful at the first entrance; the birds singing in the trees, and the wind ruffling the leaves, made a very sweet harmony, and the path was green and smooth; but as he walked further in, the trees overshadowed it, and stood so thick, that it seemed dark and dismal; moreover he heard the howlings and roarings of wild beasts—for the wood was infested with wolves, bears, leopards, dragons, and other fierce creatures of prey — which made Tender-Conscience to tremble for fear, and his heart failed within him; so that he immediately returned again by the same way by which he came in; and he ran as fast as he could till he got clear back again out of the wood, and then he slackened his pace by degrees, till at length he came to the spring at the bottom of the hill Difficulty; and there he sat down again to consider which way he should go, or what course to take. At length, with much musing, he called to mind that saying, " Narrow is the way that leadeth to life, and few there be that find it." And again, " Broad is the way that leads to death, and many there be that enter in thereat." So he viewed the path that led directly up the hill, and it was exceeding narrow; and the other two paths that went round by the bottom were very broad : upon which he presently concluded that he must take the steep and narrow path, how difficult soever it seemed to flesh and blood. So up he went, panting and gaping for breath, so tiresome was that way; and by that time he got half-way up the hill, he was very much spent, and grew so faint and giddy, by reason of the great height and steepness of the ascent, that he was ready to tumble down backwards again. At length he came up to a place where was a cave in the side of the hill, and at the mouth of the cave sat a man, whose name was Good-Resolution. Now he seeing Tender-Conscience coming up the hill, panting and gasping, and almost beat off his legs, saluted him in this manner:—

Good-Res. Brother, I see that thou art weary and faint, therefore I pray thee turn in here with me into this cave, and rest thyself awhile; and when thou hast refreshed thyself, and gathered strength, then go forward in the name of the Lord. I am placed here by the king's order, to administer relief to poor tired pilgrims.

Tender-Con. Then said Tender-Conscience, Sir, I thank you for your kind invitation, which I gladly accept of; for indeed I am quite spent, and my heart fails me.

So he went along with the man into the cave, and they sat down together on seats cut out of the solid rock. Now I saw in my dream, that the room in which they sat was pure alabaster, and did let in certain skylights at the top, which gave Tender-Conscience a view of many rare pieces of antiquity cut out of the rock. (Heb. xi. 4, 5, 7, 8.) There were the figures and representations of many famous worthies, and renowned men of old, who through faith had done many marvellous things. There was the representation of Abel offering a greater and more acceptable sacrifice than Cain; and of Enoch, who walked with God, and was translated without seeing death; and of Noah, who was an hundred and twenty years in building the ark, to the saving of his household, and the kinds of all living creatures. There was also the representation of Abraham, who, when he was called, obeyed God, to go out into a place which he should afterwards receive for an inheritance; and he went out, not knowing whither he went. There was also represented, how by faith he abode in the land of promise as in a strange country, as one that dwelt in tents, with Isaac and Jacob, heirs with him of the same promise; for " they looked for a city having a foundation, whose builder and maker is God. All these men lived in faith, believing the promises, and receiving them thankfully, confessing they were pilgrims and strangers on earth. For they that say such things, declare plainly they seek another country. For if they had been mindful of their own country from whence they came out, they had leisure to have returned; but they desired a better, that is, an heavenly; wherefore God is not ashamed to be called their God, and hath prepared for them a city."

Now Tender-Conscience was greatly pleased, and much comforted, with the sight and consideration of these things; so he looked further, and there he saw the representation of Abraham offering up Isaac, (to whom it was said, " In Isaac shall thy seed be called;") and of Isaac blessing Jacob and Esau ; and of Jacob blessing his sons, the twelve patriarchs. Then he looked on that side of the room which was opposite to the entrance of the cave, and there was represented in alabaster-work, how Moses, when he came to age, refused to be called the son of Pharaoh's daughter, choosing rather to suffer affliction with the people of God, than to enjoy the pleasures of sin for a season; and how he forsook Egypt, not fearing the king's wrath, but regarding him who is invisible; and how he led the people of Israel through the Red Sea as on dry land, which the Egyptians attempting to do, were all drowned; and how the walls of Jericho fell down at the sound of their rams' horns. Many more things were represented, as the famous acts of Joshua, Gideon, Barak, and Samson, Jephtha; also, of David, Samuel, and the prophets: " who through faith subdued kingdoms, wrought righteousness, obtained the promises, stopped the mouths of lions, quenched the violence of fire, escaped the edge of the sword, out of weakness were made strong, waxed valiant in battle, turned to flight the armies of the aliens; and of others who have been tried by mockings and scourgings, by bonds and imprisonments, who were stoned and hewn asunder, tempted and slain, wandering up and down in sheep-skins and goat-skins, being destitute, afflicted, tormented, whom the world was not worthy of; they wandered in wildernesses and mountains, in dens and caves of the earth ; and these all, through faith, obtained a good report, and received the promises."

The whole room where they sat was adorned with such kind of figures as these, which Tender-Conscience viewed with a great deal of delight, and he took courage from these glorious patterns. His spirit, which before languished, now began to revive and flourish within him, so that he burst out a singing in this manner :—

> Ah, puny soul ! faint-hearted mind !
> Weak as the chaff before the wind !
> Long have I waver'd to and fro,
> But forward now I'll boldly go:
> Since me such noble patterns move,
> I'll mount the hill on wings of love.
> Methinks my heart within me burns,
> And all inflam'd to God-ward turns.
> What though, in the seraphic fire,
> My ravish'd spirit should expire ?
> Yet, phœnix-like, it will revive,
> And in immortal glory live.

Then Good-Resolution seeing Tender-Conscience so mightily refreshed with the things he had seen, told him, that he had yet greater things than these to show him, such as would even ravish his soul with joy to behold ; so he had him out of that room, by a long entry or passage, cut out of the rock, and full of skylights, that were let in at the top, and brought him to another cave, where dwelt a man named Contemplation. The man sat still in a chair of pure diamond, musing and silent; neither said they anything to him, or he to them ; but just as he saw them enter, he drew back a curtain which hung before the farthest part of the room, and veiled half the room, so that when any one came in first, he could not see what was in the farthest part of the room ; but so soon as the man Contemplation had, with a string which he held in his hand, drawn back the curtain, what a goodly and glorious sight was there ! for that part of the room was so contrived, that by letting in a certain skylight from the roof of the cave, your eyes are immediately surprised with a thousand splendours ; and that part of the cave, though an entire rock of diamond, was so artificially polished, that, by the reflection of the sunbeams, it represented to you a most glorious city, whose streets were paved with pure gold, and the walls of precious stones, the inhabitants walking up and down in long robes, and glittering like the stars. Also it represented the king of that place sitting on a throne of glory, a fiery stream issuing from before him : thousands

of thousands ministered unto him, and ten thousand times ten thousand stood before him ; whose faces were like the lightning, and their eyes like lamps of fire ; their arms and their feet were like to polished brass ; in short, the whole appearance was full of lustre and magnificence.

Tender-Conscience was astonished above measure at the sight of these glorious things, and ravished with an inexpressible delight, insomuch that he wished to live and die in that place, for he had never yet seen such a goodly sight before all his life. He continued gazing on the lovely objects ; neither could he take his eyes off from looking, till such time as Good-Resolution drew the curtain again, and so veiled them from his sight; for he was afraid lest, by too long gazing on so much brightness, his eyes might receive some damage ; remembering that saying of the wise man, " He that gazeth upon majesty, shall be oppressed with glory." So he had him back again through the passage that led to his own cave ; and when they were come into the cave, he desired Tender-Conscience to sit down and meditate on what he had seen. So Tender-Conscience sat down to meditate, while Good-Resolution got ready a small collation of fruits, of herbs, and of wine, to refresh him, and make him more vigorous and active in going up the rest of the hill.

Oh, sir, said Tender-Conscience, trouble not yourself for me, nor take any care about meat or drink; for what I have seen since my coming into this place is both meat and drink to me. I feel myself strengthened by it, and my spirits enlivened, so that methinks I could even fly up the rest of the hill.

Then Good-Resolution made answer, If the bare sight of these glorious things has wrought such a wonderful effect upon you, how much greater influence may be expected from the mature consideration and application of them ! If the bare view of the landscape be so pleasant, how much more delightful will it be to think the city there represented is the place whither you are going, and that you shall live there for ever, and be clothed and crowned with robes and crowns of endless glory ! But I must warn you of one thing that will happen to you a little after your departure from this place, as it does usually happen to all pilgrims who have seen the glorious things of this cave ; for lest they should be exalted above measure through the abundance of revelations, there is generally given unto them a thorn in the flesh, the messenger of Satan to buffet them, because they should not be exalted above measure ; and thus it is like to befall you when you are gone from this place. Now, to the end you may not be disheartened when this thing comes to pass, I tell you of it now, that being forewarned, you may also be forearmed ; and I exhort you to have always in your mind the famous examples of these worthies which you see represented before your eyes, who stemmed the tide of worldly crosses and persecutions, stood the brunt of all manner of temptations, till having at last weathered the point, and got the start of the world, the flesh, and the devil, they entered into the joy of their Lord, and took possession of an everlasting inheritance. These things you ought always to have in remembrance as you travel along, and especially when you meet with any temptations or dangers, as you must expect in this journey. At such a time you ought to reflect on the glorious things you saw in my cave, and in the cave of Contemplation; and in so doing you will find great comfort and relief.

So he desired Tender-Conscience to refresh himself with such entertainment as his cave afforded, assuring him that though it was plain and homely diet, yet he was heartily welcomed to it, and would find the benefit of it as he went up the rest of the hill. Then Good-Resolution, after the repast was over, renewed his counsel to Tender-Conscience, and told him what houses and inns he should use thereabouts in his way, and what he should refuse and avoid, adding many wholesome instructions. At length Tender-Conscience, full of courage and joy, took his leave, giving him humble thanks for the favours he had done him.

Now I saw in my dream, that by the time Tender-Conscience was got a pretty distance upward from the cave, he was met by a man whose name was Spiritual-Pride; but Tender-Conscience knew not his name at first; so the man saluted him in this manner: Hail, thou beloved among the sons of men, thou darling of the King of heaven, who hast undertaken a great tedious pilgrimage from the valley of Destruction toward the region of life and glory; who hast escaped the temptations of the house of Mirth, and rather chosen to go into the house of Mourning; who hast escaped the paths of Danger and Destruction, and hast nobly ventured to ascend up the unpleasant and rugged path of the steep hill Difficulty; and hast entered into the cave of Good-Resolution, and seen the glorious things of his cave, and the more glorious things in the cave of Contemplation: Now I am sent to congratulate thy good success, and to tell thee thy journey is at an end; thou hast all along fought the good fight, thou hast kept the faith, and now thy course is finished, and there is laid up for thee a crown of righteousness: come, turn in with me, and I will show thee thy reward, which is secured for thee, and thou needest not travel nor toil thyself any more, but take up thy rest with me.

Then Tender-Conscience was much astonished at the man's words, and wondered how he could tell him so exactly what he had done, and where he had been; and he said within himself, Surely this man is a prophet, or greater than a prophet. So he began to be puffed up in his mind, to think how the man called him the beloved among the sons of men, and darling of the King of heaven. "Surely," saith he in his heart, "my lot is fallen in goodly places, I have a fair inheritance." So

he followed the man, who led him aside out of the path that went directly up the hill, and brought him to an exceeding high tower, whose top was higher than the top of the hill itself; but before they came to the tower, even as they were going along, Tender-Conscience cast his eye upon the back of the man, and there he saw written "Spiritual-pride;" so he remembered the counsel of Good-Resolution, how, among the rest of his wholesome instructions, he bade him beware of Spiritual-Pride, who would certainly meet him on the way, and endeavour to seduce him to the tower of Lofty-Thoughts, and when he had got him to the top, would cast him down headlong and break him to pieces. So Tender-Conscience made no more ado, but ran away as fast as he could back to the path again, and so went forward up the hill, rejoicing that he had escaped from Spiritual-Pride, who with flattering speeches and deceitful words, sought to entice him out of the way, and bring him to ruin and swift destruction.

Then I looked after Tender-Conscience, and saw that he went a great pace upward, till at length he came to the top of the hill, even to the stage that was built to punish such upon who should be afraid to go farther on pilgrimage, where Mistrust and Timorous had their tongues bored through with a hot iron, for endeavouring to hinder Christian in his journey, as was to be read on the plates that hung before the stage.

Now I saw in my dream, that as Tender-Conscience went along, an old man met him in the way, whose name was Carnal-Security, and he spoke to Tender-Conscience in this manner, Friend, whence comest thou, and whither art thou going?

Tender-Conscience replied, Sir, I am come from the valley of Destruction, and am travelling toward the heavenly country.

Carnal-Sec. Truly you have undertaken a great and hazardous journey, and the perils you have gone through are many; but now the worst of your way is past, the rest being pleasant, safe, and easy: it is convenient for you to rest yourself awhile after your toils and the wearisome steps you have trodden since you first set forth from your native country; and especially since you must needs be tired and quite out of breath through the extreme steepness of the hill Difficulty, which you last ascended. Therefore, if you please to take up your quarters with me, you shall be heartily welcome, and you will be better strengthened and enabled to go forward on your journey; my house stands not far off from this place, and if you will accept my offer, I will be your guide to my habitation.

Tender-Con. Sir, I must confess your civility is very acceptable to me, and very seasonable at this time; for, indeed, I am pretty well beat out with travel, and besides it grows towards night; therefore, if you please, I will go along with you.

So they went along together, and the old man had him through a lane on the left hand of the highroad, which brought him to a stately palace, whose gate stood wide open; and they came into the first court, which was all green and full of flowers, having several delightful arbours artificially built round it, and a crystal fountain in the middle of the court; there were also beautiful trees planted round it, on whose boughs innumerable birds of several kinds sat chirping and singing with admirable harmony. So, as they walked together cross the court, there met him an ancient lady, accompanied by two beautiful young damsels, on whom she leaned: the name of the lady was Intemperance, and she was the wife of Carnal-Security. Now it seems these two had built this palace to inveigle pilgrims, and seduce them out of their way to the heavenly country; as the palace called Beautiful was built for the relief, comfort, and direction of pilgrims in their journey. But poor Tender-Conscience knew nothing of all this. He that had so lately escaped the snare that Spiritual-Pride had laid for him, was now caught in the gins of Carnal-Security. * * * * * *

Now it came to pass, that though Tender-Conscience slept a great while, being lulled by sound of incomparable melody, yet they having not taken notice of his strong crutch which he had in his hand, not knowing its secret and wonderful virtues, did not remove it from him; by which means he at length awoke from his sleep, rousing himself up, and wondering from whence all this delicious harmony might come: for his crutch being in his hand all the while he slept, at length, as he went to turn himself iu his sleep, he hit himself a blow in the eyes with the crutch, which awaked him. Then he began to wonder (as I said) where he was, and how he came there, and what music that was; at length he called to mind how an old man had invited him into his house very kindly, and how his lady had given him of her wine to drink, but could not call to mind how he came upon this bed, but concluded that he had been drunk, and so brought into the palace: and with this thought, and the pleasant harmony of the music, he was just ready to fall asleep again; but at the same instant there came such a terrible clap of thunder as was almost enough to have awaked the very dead. At this his heart quaked within him, and the music ceased playing; so he rose from his bed, and looked out at the windows, and he saw the air extremely darkened, saving only some intervals of lightning, which, accompanied with thunder, seemed to threaten the destruction of the world. Poor Tender-Conscience wept bitterly when he perceived such a dreadful tempest hanging over his head, and he in a strange place, not half way his journey: this made him very melancholy and pensive, and he burst out into these mournful expressions by himself:—

Wretch that I am! what will become of me? where shall I hide myself from the fierce anger of the Lord; or how shall I escape his heavy displeasure? I doubt I have done amiss in coming into this place, and sleeping away my precious time, which is the reason that God is angry, and thunders in the ears of my soul. Horror and confusion flash through my conscience like lightning: I know not what to do, nor where to turn my face for comfort.

Then he looked for his crutch, and could not find it at first, which made him lament grievously; but at last he bethought himself on the bed whereon he slept; so he ran thither, and there found it, to his no small comfort and joy. Then he prepared himself to go down stairs; but just as he was about to go from the window where he stood, there came another clap of thunder, which made the very house to shake; and after the thunder he heard a voice whisper him in the ear, and saying, Get thee out of this place, and beware of the woman with the golden cup in her hand, and of all that belong to her, for her ways are ways of death: sin no more, lest a worse thing come unto thee. This made poor Tender-Conscience to tremble afresh, so that the joints of his knees smote one against another, and he hastened to go down stairs; at which the music began to play again so sweetly, that he had much ado to leave it; but remembering the thunder and lightning, and the voice he heard, he went resolutely down: and as he was going through the hall, he saw a table spread with all manner of dainties, and heard the voice of young men and maidens, as he thought, singing deliciously, which made him again stand still awhile to listen to their music. Then came one to him named Mr. Gluttony, and desired him to sit down and eat what liked him best; telling him withal that the entertainment he saw there before his eyes was prepared on purpose for pilgrims; and how that many that were travelling towards the city of Zion did call in here, and partaked of the dainties this place afforded, it being built for the ease and pleasure of pilgrims. Then the young men and maidens seconded Mr. Gluttony in their song, while several instruments of music played to them in concert; and this was their song:—

> Poor pilgrims here may eat, and drink, and sleep!
> Whilst them in safety their good Lord will keep.
> Fall to, fall to, poor man, and take your fill,
> In nature's pleasure there can be no ill.
> In vain our king's indulgent hand supplies,
> What peevish man his longing soul denies.

This was enough to have staggered a stouter man than Tender-Conscience; and he himself could not have resisted so powerful a temptation, had it not been for the remembrance of the thunder and the voice. Also he called to mind that saying of the holy Jesus, "To do the will of my Heavenly Father, is both my meat and my drink." So he turned away from Mr. Gluttony, and went apace out of the hall without giving him one word, though he followed him, and intreated him to sit down and make merry with the good cheer that was before him. Then old Carnal-Security met him at the hall door, which opened into the inner court of the palace, and took him by the hand, asking him, Whither he was going in such haste?

Tender-Con. To whom Tender-Conscience replied, I am going forward on my journey.

Carnal-Sec. Ay, but tarry and eat first, for you have a long way to walk before you will find another house; and therefore it is not convenient for you to go out fasting from hence, lest you faint by the way.

Tender-Con. It is written, "Man lives not by bread alone, but by every word that proceedeth out of the mouth of God."

Carnal-Sec. This is not applicable to your case; you must not expect to be fed by miracles. Meat and drink are appointed for the support of our frail bodies; and therefore it is a foolish preciseness to abstain from eating, when we have absolute need of it.

Tender-Con. Ay, but I have no such absolute need of either eating or drinking at this time, it being early in the morning; and I have read in a certain book thus, "Wo be to thee, O land, when thy princes eat in the morning; but blessed is the land, whose princes eat in due season, for refreshment, and not for riotousness."

Carnal-Sec. Neither is this saying applicable to you; for you are not a prince, but a poor pilgrim, and this is spoken altogether of princes.

Tender-Con. Yes, I am a prince, and am going to take possession of my crown and kingdom; for we are made kings, and princes, and priests unto God, and we shall reign with him for ever; and therefore cease to persuade me in this manner, or to retard my journey, for I will go in the strength of the Lord my God.

Carnal-Sec. Well, since you are so obstinate, that you will not hearken to my counsel in this point, pray be advised to drink before you go at yonder vine, where you see the grapes hang so thick and plump.

Tender-Con. No, neither will I drink in this place; for I remember how I drank of the juice of those fatal grapes, and they intoxicated me so that I committed folly with Mrs. Wantonness, and slept away my time, when I should have been going forward on my journey; and I believe you have a design upon me, to make me drunk again, or else you would not press so hard. Again grievously tempted, he called to mind the terrible thundering and lightning, with the voice which followed them, and ran away as fast as he could; neither did he stop till he came out of the outermost gate of the palace, and till he got into the highway again, where Carnal-Security first seduced him, and then he went on singing—

My soul, like to a bird from fowler's snare,
Escaped, while after me they stare:
Their ways are pleasant, but they sting at last;
Wo be to them that in their nets are cast.
They spread their gins on every side for men,
Seducing souls to their inchanted den.
All's fair without, but rotten is within:
Fair is the form, but black the guilt of sin.

At length he came to the place where the lions lay, who began to roar at the sight of him, which put him into a great fright, so that he stood still at first; but calling to mind what he had seen in the cave of Good-Resolution, concerning the dangers that those brave worthies had encountered and overcome, he took courage and went boldly on his way, brandishing his crutch towards the lions; at which they immediately ceased their roaring, and lay still, while he passed by, and came up to the gate of the palace called Beautiful, where the porter stood ready to receive him; but first he examined from whence he came, and whither he was going.

Tender-Con. Sir, I am come from the valley of Destruction, and am going towards the holy Zion, or heavenly Jerusalem.

Porter. Did you come in by the wicket-gate, which is at the head of the way of life?

Tender-Con. Yes, sir; and was directed by one Good-will, who kept that gate, to call at the house of the Interpreter.

Porter. Let me see your pass, that I may show it to one of the virgins, who, if she be satisfied of the truth, will receive you hospitably, and show you the civilities of this house.

So Tender-Conscience pulled out his pass, and gave it to Watchful, the porter, who immediately rung a little bell; at which the virgin Discretion came out, and the porter told her what Tender-Conscience was, and whither he was going, withal giving her the Interpreter's pass to read; which when she had perused, and marked the seal, she desired him to walk in. So she had him to the hall, and there came to him Prudence, Piety, and Charity, and welcomed him to the house, and brought him a little wine and a few figs to refresh himself at present, till dinner should be ready; for they supposed him to be weary and spent with getting up the hill Difficulty, not knowing that he had taken a long rest and sleep in the house of Carnal-Security. But he voluntarily told them how he met with an old man as soon as he was past the stage on the top of the hill, who invited him into his house, which, said he, is a stately palace on the left hand of the highroad; so he told them all that had happened to him in that place, and how he was forced at last to take to his heels and run away from Mrs. Wantonness.

Then Piety desired to know his name; and he told her, saying, My name is Tender-Conscience.

Well, says she, Tender-Conscience, you have escaped one of the greatest dangers upon the road; for the old man who enticed you into his house is called Carnal-Security, and his wife is the Lady-Intemperance, who is always to be seen with a golden cup in her hand, full of inchantments, whereby she intoxicates those that drink out of it.

Tender-Con. Ay, says Tender-Conscience, I believe that was the lady who gave me the juice of grapes to drink out of a golden cup, when we were entering the second court.

Piety. And did you not see her two daughters, Mrs. Wantonness and Mrs. Forgetfulness.

Tender-Con. I know not their names, said he; but I saw two beautiful young damsels waiting upon the Lady-Intemperance.

Piety. These are the same that I mean, and they use to bewitch men to destruction. But how could you get away from them again? for they use to have so many tricks and artifices to intangle these that come once within their doors, that not one out of ten gets out of their clutches without suffering some great damage.

Tender-Con. Oh, said he, I tarried talking and arguing the case with the old man so long, that I had almost lost the day; but I, finding myself not able to struggle or resist temptation, all on a sudden gave a spring, and ran away as hard as I could drive.

Piety. In this I commend your conduct; for though it be said, "resist the devil, and he will fly from you," yet it is to be understood of other temptations. For when any one is tempted as you were, there is no time for disputing. A resolution, and speedy flight, is the only way to secure the victory. The soul may stand the battle against adversities, persecutions, crosses, and the like; but the pleasures of the flesh must be subdued by retreating from them. He that touches pitch shall be defiled, says the wise man; and he that stands capitulating with the temptations of uncleanness, is in danger to fall. The soul, like wax, is hardened by cold and stormy weather; but in the sunshine of prosperity, and the heat of lust, she melts and becomes effeminate and yielding. Therefore well said one of old, "Flee youthful lusts, which war against the soul." He does not say, stand and face them, and resist them; but, run away from them. It is, in some degree, the same in that common vice which this age does so much and so shamefully abound in, I mean excessive drinking. Men think they may safely venture into company without being obliged to drink; and, when they are in company, they think they may drink a little without doing themselves any harm; not considering that little does but embolden them to venture on more; every glass they pour down depriving them of so much of their resolution and strength to resist. And when they come to be doubtful whether they shall let this one glass go down, they throw down the fence of their soul, their reason, and expose her to be polluted by the height of debauchery and folly, letting into their unguarded breasts a flood of vain passions, with their superfluity of drink: thus, by little and little, the poor soul suffers shipwreck. In such a case, the only remedy is to flee the first occasions and temptations, to stop the avenues of the soul, to set a guard upon the senses, and so restrain the imagination within its proper limits. A man ought not so much as to fancy that company pleasant or delightful, by keeping of which he runs the hazard of his soul's health; much less

ought he to follow them, and court them; nay, rather let him refuse when courted by them. It is much better to be thought ill-natured and uncomplaisant to others, than to be really so to one's self, and to ruin ourselves to oblige our acquaintance.

Charity. There are some souls that are naturally so affable and courteous, so soft and pliant, that they comply oftentimes with company, more through the flexibleness and sweetness of their own disposition, than out of any real inclination to debauchery; nay, while they loathe the drink, they cannot forbear obliging their unreasonable companions. This a great weakness; and though it may be capable of admitting some excuse, on the account of that sweetness of temper from whence it flows, yet it is nevertheless dangerous, and therefore must not be palliated, lest in so doing we turn advocates for vice.

Prudence. If you please, let us break off our discourse for the present, and go to dinner, which is now ready, for the bell rings. So they all arose and went into the refectory, or dining-room, where more virgins of that society were waiting for their coming, who all welcomed Tender-Conscience to the house, every one saluting him with a particular congratulation, and then they sat down in exquisite order and silence. After the divine blessing was invoked, one of the virgins, whose name was Temperance, carved out for the rest, for that was her office; while another of them, named Decency, waited at the table. Here was no loud laughter to be heard, no offensive nor unseemly jests broached, but a modest cheerfulness crowned the entertainment. They had plenty without riot, variety without extravagance, and frugality and bounty seemed to hand in the dishes together. They eat to nourish nature, not to prompt lust or cloy the appetite; and they rose from the table lightsome and well refreshed, having returned thanks to the sovereign Giver of all good gifts, the Creator and Preserver of all mankind, for refreshing them with his good creatures. Then one of the virgins, named Health, proposed to the company that it would be convenient and pleasant to take the air of the garden after dinner, to which they all readily consented; and Discretion, Prudence, Piety, Charity, and Temperance, took Tender-Conscience along with them into the mount, which gave him a lovely prospect of the country round about; and there they sat down under the shade of a broad-spreading sycamore, and fell afresh into discourse. Tender-Conscience being desirous to learn the reason of their living thus in a society together, and to know the rule and manner of their life, Piety thus replied:—

Piety. When we were young and lively at home with our friends, we were daily exposed to innumerable vanities and follies, and were carried away by the flood of custom; yet being religiously inclined from our childhood, we by degrees, as we grew up, began to grow sick of our carnal education, and to despise the vanities and fooleries of the world, and sought for a place where we might be free of them, and where we might serve the Lord both night and day in all holiness and purity of life; so, after much inquiry and diligent search, at length we were informed that a certain holy woman, named Religion, had built her house in this place; and she, being an especial favourite of the King of this country, was permitted to gather together a certain number of virgins who were willing to renounce the world, and live in this retirement with her, having a particular charter granted them, whereby they should for ever be free from certain taxes, imposts, and homages which the other subjects were obliged to pay, on condition they would make it their business to observe such and such laws and statutes as the foresaid holy woman Religion should prescribe unto them, and to live in true obedience to her commands all the days of their life. Whereupon we were presently inflamed with a fervent desire to see this woman, and if possible, to come and live with her (I speak for us all, because I have heard the rest of my companions here own the same inclinations as myself had); so we consulted no longer with flesh and blood, but immediately resolved to wait upon her, and declare our intentions, hoping to find favour in her eyes, and to be admitted into her society; which we did accordingly; and having made her a visit, and heard her heavenly voice, we were ravished more than ever, and grew impatient till we were taken into the house. At length our wishes were fulfilled, our desires granted, and here we lived ever since, and would not change our life for the whole world; for this woman is of a sweet temper, and all her laws are pleasant, her yoke is easy, and her burden is light.

Charity. Not that we condemn all those who do not live in such a state, or just according to our rules; for without doubt many do live mixed with the rest of the world, yet keep themselves unspotted from the vices of the world; but they are exposed to greater danger; they run the risk of more temptations than we. For here one spirit and soul (as it were) animates us all: holiness and purity are all that we aim at, and we mutually encourage one another, assist one another, and forward one another in the practice of it. We have no cares to imbitter us, nor vain pleasures to debauch us; we have no honours to tempt us to ambition, nor riches to make us covetous. All our ambition is to approve ourselves blameless in the sight of God, and all the riches we covet are those that never fade away—the gifts and graces of the Holy Ghost.

Tender-Con. But I suppose you have some particular laws and rulers to which you are obliged to conform yourselves, which I should be glad to know.

Piety. Yes, we have so, and I will acquaint you with them in the best manner I can.

1. We are obliged to rise every morning before the sun; and then we join all together in prayer and praises to the great God of heaven, thanking him for his past blessings, and imploring his future favour and protection over us.

2. Then every one goes to their proper business, as belongs to their office, till the time of refreshment, and so again till dinner.

3. We are obliged to entertain all pilgrims that are travelling towards the heavenly country, provided they show their pass, or give such an account of themselves as may be thought equivalent.

4. At the close of the day, we are obliged to join again all in prayer and praises, as in the morning.

5. We are obliged to keep and maintain the King's armoury, and to furnish all pilgrims with weapons and armour of proof against all dangers and disasters whatsoever.

These are the general and most important laws of our society. But, besides these, we have many particular rules, of less note though very good, and in a manner necessary to our well-being, all which it would be too tedious to rehearse.

Temperance. Only give me leave to insist upon the statute of moderation in eating and drinking, which we are strictly charged to keep under severe penalties, which I suppose you had forgot.

Piety. It is true, indeed, I had forgot to mention it, and am very glad of that forgetfulness, since I have thereby given you an opportunity of discoursing more at large upon that subject, who are best able to do it, as being appointed the particular of this statute; therefore pray inform the pilgrim about it.

Temp. This statute of moderation in eating and drinking is grounded on this consideration—that Adam fell by eating the forbidden fruit. The first sin that ever was committed in the world by mankind was in eating. Now, though it be not certain whether it proceeded from some natural contagion in the fruit which Adam eat, or from the venomous breath of the serpent that recommended it to Eve, or from any other hidden cause, yet we are sure, that whereas Adam was before in the full perfection of human nature, being the lively image of the glorious God, his soul being full of the beams of eternal light, his understanding clear and serene as the morning, his will regular, and obedient to his reason, his body in perfect vigour and health, beauty and proportion, impassible and immortal, no sooner had he tasted the fatal morsel, but a strange alteration befel him; the image of God was immediately defaced and sullied, his soul grew dark and cloudy, his understanding and reason became dull and unactive, and his will went retrograde; in short, all the faculties of his soul were dislocated and disjointed. As for his body, it became weak and unhealthy, subject to divers casualties, sicknesses, and infirmities, and at last to death itself. This was the effect of irregular eating. Nor did the mischief rest here; but he transmitted it to his posterity; conveyed all those ill qualities of body and soul to his children, whereby all the generations of men in the world are under the same misfortune, corrupt both in body and soul, conceived in sin, and brought forth in iniquity. But, as if we were not unhappy enough in this original deprivation of our nature, the greatest part of mankind endeavour to increase the misery by their own actual repetition and continual practice of the same crime, gluttony and drunkenness reigning over the greatest part of the world. This is the reason why the statute of moderation in eating and drinking is so strictly enjoined to this society, and it were well if all the world would observe it, then would people have sound minds in sound bodies.

Tender-Con. Wherein does this moderation in eating and drinking consist?

Temp. It consists in bridling and regulating the appetite, as to the quantity and quality of meats and drinks.

Tender-Con. Pray show me how it consists in bridling the appetite as to quantity.

Temp. It teaches us to eat and drink no more at a time, nor no oftener in a day, than is requisite to preserve the body in health, to suffice nature, and refresh the spirits. It is a taming of the body, and bringing it into subjection to the soul, that so the inferior faculties may be subservient to the superior.

Tender-Con. But how shall a man know how much will exactly serve to keep the body in health, to suffice nature, and refresh the spirits, since there are as many different constitutions in the world as there are faces?

Temp. The way to know this is, for every one to observe his own temper, and they will quickly find out the true measure and proper time of eating and drinking. Only take this for a general rule: That it is by all means convenient to rise up from the table with an appetite, and to have a mind, after a meal, as well disposed for labour, for exercise, or for prayer, as it was before. He that eats and drinks beyond this breaks the rule of moderation; for the end of eating and drinking is to refresh nature, and make it more vigorous and active, and not to render it dull and heavy.

Tender-Con. Pray tell me what good effects this moderation produces in the soul, and how it works them.

Temp. Great, certainly, and manifold are the benefits which redound to the soul from the constant practice of this moderation in eating and drinking. For though the soul be of itself an immortal and impassible essence, yet while it is joined with our mortal body, it partakes of all its conveniences or inconveniences: if the body be in pain, the soul suffers with it; if the body feels pleasure, the soul enjoys it likewise. Nay, rather, it is the soul that is alone sensible of everything that happens to the body; for the body of itself is but dead and inactive matter, incapable of sense or motion in itself; it is the soul that gives life, motion, and sense to it. Now, therefore, as the body is

maintained in health and vigour, so does the soul flourish and triumph within herself; on the contrary, when the body is sickly and weak, the soul languishes by sympathy. He, therefore, that eats and drinks to excess, and thereby cloys his stomach, fills his body full of contagious humours, and sows the seeds of many diseases in his own bowels; this man is no friend to his soul; for she by this time grows dull and sluggish, dark and cloudy, sad and melancholy, and void of all pleasure and comfort. Whereas, on the contrary, he that bridles his appetite, and eats and drinks no more nor no oftener than what sufficeth nature and refreshes his spirits, his soul is always lively and vigorous, sprightly as youth, and serene as the morning, full of light and comfort, and in an holy triumph she often soars aloft, and basks in the rays of eternal happiness, despising the world and all that is in it, excepting her own tabernacle, which is always kept neat and clean, and therefore she takes delight to repose herself therein, when, like the eagles, she is tired with her lofty flights. Our bodies are the temples of the Holy Ghost, and he that pollutes them with riot and uncleanness is guilty of sacrilege. And therefore well said Solomon, "Be not a companion of wine-bibbers, nor riotous eaters of flesh."

Tender-Con. I thank you for your good and wholesome talk. Now pray show me how moderation in eating and drinking consists in bridling the appetite as to the quality of meats, &c.

Temp. In order to the better clearing up of this point, it is necessary to look back to Adam, who we find had permission and leave given him to eat of all the fruits of the garden of Eden, but only he was forbidden to taste of the fruit of the tree of knowledge of good and evil. And, afterwards, to intimate that God took a special regard to the qualities of man's food, he was told by God what sort of fruits and herbs should be his diet, and which should be food for the beasts; of every herb bearing seed, and of every tree bearing fruit he was allowed to eat, and the grass of the field was appointed for the beasts. Here we may observe, that there was no mention made as yet of flesh or fish to be eaten, no not till after the flood; so that many are of opinion the fathers before the flood did eat no manner of flesh; and it is not improbable that this was one reason for their living so very long, nothing more conducing to health and long life than ascetic diet, that is, a diet of fruits, roots, and herbs, honey, oil, &c., without flesh or fish.

The first time we read that God gave to man a licence to eat flesh was after the flood, when he blessed Noah and his sons, saying unto them, "Be fruitful and multiply, and replenish the earth; and the fear of you, and the dread of you, shall be upon every beast of the earth, and upon every fowl of the air, upon all that moveth upon the earth, and upon the fishes of the sea; into your hands are they delivered. Every moving thing that liveth shall be meat for you, even as the green herb have I given you all things; but flesh with the life thereof, which is the blood thereof, shall ye not eat." So that you may see, even in this first licence to eat flesh, that man was restrained from eating it with the blood; which restraint was more particularly confirmed in the law of Moses, when the fat was also forbidden to be eaten, in these words, " Speak unto the children of Israel, saying, Ye shall eat no manner of fat of ox, of sheep, or of goat, &c.," which prohibition must needs have regard to the quality of fat. And a little afterwards (Lev. xi. 1, to the end), there is a separation made between the meats that were to be eaten and those that were not; between the clean and unclean beasts, birds, and fishes; which law was strictly observed by the children of Israel throughout their generations, and so it is to this day. Now, without doubt, it was on the account of the different good or ill qualities that resided in the flesh of these creatures that some were forbidden and others allowed: and though this law was abolished by the coming of Christ, yet we find the apostles, in their council at Jerusalem, forbid the eating of things strangled, and commanded the Christians to abstain from blood. (Acts xv. 19. 20.) And in the lives of the apostles it is recorded, that some of them abstained from all flesh during their lives. And not only the apostles, but other Christians, were abstemious, living chiefly upon herbs, or the like sustenance, as Paul witnesseth in his epistle to the Corinthians.

Upon the whole matter we may conclude, that all this caution and care about the difference of meats, from the beginning of the world to the flood, and from the flood to the giving of the Mosaic law, and from thence to the time of the apostles of Jesus Christ, would not have been, had there not been some greater reason for it than barely to try men's obedience, or to furnish them with emblems of virtue and vice, as some hold. There must be something in the natures of living creatures, some different qualities, that occasioned one sort to be forbidden, another to be allowed. And though we are not obliged now to keep the law of Moses, yet I cannot find upon what grounds many Christians take the liberty to act contrary to the ordinance of the apostles of Christ, in eating blood and things strangled.

Tender-Con. I remember I have heard this point handled before by some disputants; and to this last part of your discourse it has been answered, that Jesus said, " Not that which goeth into a man defileth him, but that which cometh out." And Paul says, " To the pure all things are pure." And he calleth the doctrine of " Touch not, taste not, handle not," a doctrine of worldly elements, and beggarly rudiments.

Disc. But then, if that saying of Christ be taken literally, one may venture on all manner of venomous living creatures without danger or hurt. Without doubt there is a discreet choice to be made in our diet as to the qualities of the things we eat and drink; and every one in this is left to his own conduct; only this general rule ought to be observed, that we forbear eating and drinking such things as we find by experience or know by common observation, to be prejudicial to health, impediments of virtue and devotion, spurs to vice and passion, by intoxicating the brain, heating the blood, disordering the spirits, or by any other ways being subservient to the works of the flesh, or the temptations of the devil. In so doing we shall do well.

Prud. As to that saying of St. Paul, " To the pure all things are pure," it may be well retorted, that the same apostle said in another place, " All things are lawful for me, but all things are not expedient; all things are lawful for me, but I will not be brought under the power of anything." To which he immediately subjoins these words, " Meats for the belly, and the belly for meats; but the Lord will destroy both it and them." Now by this coherence of the text, it is plain that he spoke in reference to the liberty that was given to Christians in eating; showing, that though they were freed from the strict and punctual observation of the Mosaical law, according to the letter, yet that nevertheless they were obliged, by the law of prudence and Christian virtue, to make such an election of meats as might neither offend charity, nor interfere with the grand design of religion, which is, to make us more holy and pure, not more licentious and profane.

Char. Your mentioning the offence which may be given to charity by a dissolute libertinism in eating, puts me in mind of another passage of the same apostle, where he says, " If meat make my brother to offend (or be scandalised), I will eat no flesh while the world standeth, lest I give scandal to my brother." Certainly charity is the very flower and quintessence of all Christian virtues, the particular glory of the Christian religion, and the fulfilling both the law and the prophets. He that pretends to Christianity, and has not charity, is an infidel in masquerade, a spy upon the faith, a religious juggler, a dead mimic of divine life: he runs with the hare, and holds with the hound; he mocks God, cheats man, and damns himself; he is the very sink of sin; for in him all the vices of the world disembogue themselves, as in a common emunctory.

But lest I be mistaken by those that hear me give this character of a man that wants charity, I will explain myself more at large, and give you a particular description of this radical virtue. I do not mean by charity only that branch of it which bears the fruit of material good works, in feeding the hungry, giving drink to the thirsty, clothing the naked, visiting and redeeming prisoners and captives, harbouring those that want a place to lay their heads in, visiting and relieving, comforting and healing the sick, and the like acts of mercy; charity is of a far larger and more spiritual extent than all those good works amount to; nay, some of them may be performed without charity, as good

Paul witnesses, when he says, "Though I bestow all my goods on the poor, and though I give my body to be burned, and have not charity, it profiteth me nothing." In which words he plainly supposes, that many outward good works may be done, and yet the doers of them may want charity. Therefore, when I speak of charity, I understand that divine accomplishment of the soul which the same apostle, in the following words, describes: "Charity suffereth long, and is kind; charity envieth not; charity vaunteth not itself, is not puffed up, doth not behave itself unseemly, seeketh not her own, is not easily provoked, thinketh no evil, rejoiceth not in iniquity, but rejoiceth in the truth; beareth all things, believeth all things, hopeth all things, endureth all things." This is the complete character of charity, and he that makes it good in his practice is a perfect Christian. A believer is a believer in his true colours, a champion of the faith, an Israelite indeed, in whom there is no guile, a living stone in the temple of God: he runs with patience the race that is set before him; he practises sobriety, righteousness, and godliness toward God, and man, and himself; his soul is the receptacle of goodness, the centre of piety, in which all virtues delight to inhabit; in all things he has a holy tenderness, and acts even to the curiosity and niceness of divine love: though his body dwells on earth, his soul lives in heaven; he couches under the shadow of the trees of paradise; he breathes immortal airs, and often tastes of the fruits of the tree of life.

Now to apply this to the subject you have been handling, I say, that a man endowed with this divine and supernatural gift of charity, as he loves God above all things, so he loves his neighbour as himself, and will in all things so comport himself, as to be void of offence both toward God and man. He will (in all things indifferent) comply with the prepossessions, prejudices, and customs of his weak brother: "To the Jews he becomes as a Jew, that he may win the Jews; to them that are under the law, as under the law; to them that are without the law, as without the law (being not without the law to God, but under the law to Christ), that he might gain them that are without the law; to the weak he will become as weak, that he may gain the weak: he is made all things to all men, that by any means he may save some." With them that eat flesh, he will eat likewise, "asking no questions for conscience' sake (for the earth is the Lord's, and the fulness thereof)." With those that abstain, he will practise abstinence. "Whether he eats or drinks, or whatever he does, he does all to the glory of God; giving none offence, neither to the Jews, nor to the Gentiles, nor to the church of God; but pleasing all men in all things, not seeking his own profit, but the profit of many that they may be saved." This is the practice of a perfect Christian; this is the ultimate end of the commandments, the *non ultra* of both the law and the gospel, and the aim of our statute of moderation in eating and drinking.

To this discourse of Charity the whole company agreed, and Tender-Conscience expressed a more than ordinary satisfaction and complacency in her grave and moderate decision of a controversy that he had raised. He had long been disturbed in his mind about this point, but was now convinced of the truth, and gave them all most hearty thanks for their edifying discourse, making a particular acknowledgement and address to Charity for her evangelical conclusion.

Then the virgin Temperance, who began this discourse of moderation in eating and drinking, and whose proper office it was to interpret and expound that statute, called for two lamps, which were immediately brought by Obedience, one of the waiters. Now one of the lamps gave but a dim light, so that you could hardly discern whether it was burning or no; on the contrary, the other shined very bright and clear. Then said Temperance, You see the difference between these lamps, how the one affords but a weak faint light, and the other sheds her beams round with great splendour: the crystals are both alike, but only one of them is sullied and furred (as it were) with smoke and vapours, and the other is transparent and clean. These are emblems of moderation and riot in eating and drinking. The soul of man is a lamp, which will burn and shine with great splendour, if the body be kept clean, and purified by temperance, abstinence, and fasting; but if a man by excessive eating and drinking, does pollute and stain his body, his spirits (which are the crystal of his soul) become clouded and thickened with vapour and smoke, so that he neither shines in good works to others, nor has much light in himself; and if the light that is in him be darkness, how great must that darkness be!

Tender-Con. Pray give me leave to trouble you with one question more about fasting, because I think you mentioned that just now as one mean to purify and cleanse the body, and render it more instrumental to the operations of the soul. I desire to be informed what examples you have of fasting in scripture, and whether it be now requisite and profitable for a Christian to fast, and what are the proper effects of it.

Temperance. It will be no trouble to me, but a delight, to satisfy you in this point, according to my ability, as it is my office.

Know then, that fasting is a practice frequently recommended in the book of God, and warranted by the examples of sundry good and holy men. We read that Moses fasted forty days and forty nights in the mountain: and though no mention be made of fasting before the flood, yet the lives of men in that infancy of the world, in all probability, was a daily fast, or at least a continual abstinence from flesh; so that what seems now so grievous and burdensome a discipline, was then, peradventure, esteemed but a natural and universal diet observed by all mankind, whereby they preserved their bodies in an inviolable health and vigour, prolonging their days almost to a thousand years. But now, in these latter ages of the world, the bodies of men are grown weaker, and men count it a heavy task to fast once a month; nay, once a year seems too much for some dainty constitutions. There were several occasions of fasting among the people of God in old time. (Lev. xxiii. 27—32.) There was a day of atonement commanded to be yearly observed by the Israelites throughout their generations for ever, in which they were to fast and afflict their souls from even to even. This was an annual day of public humiliation, injoined to the people for ever. It was customary also to fast on any mournful occasion, as David fasted when his child lay sick (2 Sam. xii. 16, 17), and the men of Jabesh-gilead fasted seven days when they buried the bones of Saul and Jonathan his son under a tree at Jabesh. (1 Sam. xxxi. 13.) And as soon as David heard the news of their death, "both he and all the men that were with him took hold of their clothes and rent them; and they mourned and wept, and fasted until even, for Saul and for Jonathan his son, and for the people of the Lord, and for the house of Israel." Moreover, the people of Israel used to fast in time of any public calamity; and not only they, but other nations also, as the inhabitants of the great city Nineveh. When the prophet Jonah foretold the destruction of that stately city would come to pass in forty days, they "proclaimed a fast, and put on sackcloth, from the greatest of them even to the least; for word came unto the King of Nineveh, and he arose from his throne, and he laid his robe from him, and covered him with sackcloth, and sat in ashes; and he caused it to be proclaimed and published through Nineveh, by the decree of the king and his nobles, saying, Let neither man nor beast, herd nor flock, taste anything, let them not feed, nor drink water."

But, besides these solemn and public fasts, we read of some private men who practised it; as the prophet Daniel, who fasted full three weeks; in which time "he eat no pleasant bread, neither came flesh or wine within his mouth." And this fast of his was so acceptable to God, that he sent one of his holy angels to him, who saluted him with the title of, "A man greatly beloved," bidding him not to fear or be troubled; for, says he, "from the first day that thou did set thine heart to understand, and to chasten thyself before thy God, thy words were heard, and I am come for thy words. Now I am come to make thee understand what shall befall thy people in the latter days." And when he had thus comforted and strengthened Daniel, he revealed many wonderful and secret things that should come to pass in the world. So that, by these great favours showed to Daniel, we may plainly see how acceptable religious fasting is to God. Many more examples of this kind might be produced out of the Old Testament; but these may suffice to show that fasting was a duty often practised by the people of God, and by holy men under the law of Moses. And the gospel recommends it, from the beginning to the end, by the examples of Christ and John the Baptist, of Peter, Paul, and the rest of the apostles, as well as by their counsel and exhortations; nothing is more frequently inculcated than this duty of fasting throughout the writings of the New Testament. And, without all doubt, it is now as requisite as ever it was, since we are liable to the same infirmities, exposed to the same temptations, and beset with the same dangers as the former Christians were; against all which evils fasting is the proper remedy. Fasting mortifies the body, and tames concupiscence; it quenches lust, and kindles devotion; it is the handmaid of prayer, and the nurse of meditation; it refines the understanding, subdues the passions, regulates the will, and sublimates the whole man to a more spiritual state of life: it is the life of angels, the enamel of the soul, the great advantage of religion, the best opportunity for retirements of devotion. Whilst the smoke of carnal appetites is suppressed and extinguished, the heart breaks forth with holy fire, till it be burning like the cherubim, and the most ecstasied order of pure and unpolluted spirits. These are the proper and genuine effects of religious and frequent fasting, as they can witness who make it their private practice.

Tender-Con. You have made me in love with fasting, by giving so fair an account of it, and discovering its consequences to the soul and body, and I am resolved to make trial of it myself hereafter; for in my opinion, as you describe it, it causes men to draw nearer unto God, while his soul being by abstinence and fasting withdrawn, as it were, from the body, and abstracted from all outward things, retires into herself, and in the secret tabernacle within she sits under the shadow of the Divinity, and enjoys a more close communion and intimate union with God.

When Tender-Conscience had made an end of these words, he began to think of his journey; and giving them all his thanks for the kind entertainment he had met with in this place, and especially for their edifying discourse, he rose up to take his leave. Then they rose up with him, and accompanied him to the armoury, which stood by the gate; and there they armed him all over with armour and weapons of proof, as was the custom to do to all pilgrims, because the rest of his journey was like to be more dangerous, the ways being infested with thieves and robbers, with sons of Belial and murderers, also with fiends and devils. Also they gave him his pass, which he had delivered to them at his first coming thither; now they had all set their hands to it, to confirm and strengthen it the more, bidding him be sure to have a great care of it. So they conducted him to the gate, and wished him a prosperous journey: he parted from them with tears in his eyes.

Now I saw in my dream, that Tender-Conscience went forward a good pace, till he came to the brow of the hill, where the way lay down into the valley of Humiliation; but because it was steep and dangerous going down, he was forced to slacken his pace, and lean hard upon his strong crutch; yet he was apt to slip, and could hardly stop himself from running, or rather tumbling, down the hill; but at length, with much ado, he got safe to the bottom, and came to the valley of Humiliation. Now all this valley was a kind of marshy, boggy ground, and was at this time all overflowed with water, so that there was but one way to pass through it with safety, and that was over certain planks fastened to stumps or posts, and joined one to another; for it was but one plank's breadth all the whole way, and that a very narrow one. This set of planks was called the Bridge of Self-Denial, and it reached quite over the valley of Humiliation. Now the waters were very high, and touched the planks; nay, in some places they covered them, so that a man could hardly discern his way. The sight of this dangerous and narrow bridge did not a little discourage Tender-Conscience; but, considering that it drew towards night, he was resolved to venture over; so on he went courageously, but with a very slow pace, because of the exceeding narrowness of the planks, which also now and then would seem to yield and bend under him,' which often put him in a fright, lest they should break, and he be drowned in the waters. And the more to increase his trouble, when he was got about half way over, the air was all hung full of nets, and traps, and gins, which were placed so low, that a man could not walk upright, but he must be caught in some of them; these were planted here by the prince of the power of the air, to catch such pilgrims in as were highminded, and walked with stretched-out necks. Therefore, when Tender-Conscience perceived the danger that was spread before him, he stooped down, and crept along upon his hands and knees, and so escaped the nets and gins; and he had this advantage moreover, that he could go faster in this manner, and more securely, without danger of tottering over on either side of the planks into the water, as he was often like to do when he walked upright. In this manner crawled he along, till he was almost got over, when he saw several boats making towards him on either side of the bridge, and in the boats there were men that rowed them, who hallooed and called after Tender-Conscience; but he regarded them not, for he was afraid lest they were some of the robbers or murderers which infest that country, and therefore he kept on his pace; but they rowed hard after him, and shot several arrows at him, some of which missed him, others he received with the shield of faith, (Eph. vi. 16,) that was given him out of the king's armoury. Now the names of these men that rowed in the boats, and shot at Tender-Conscience so fiercely, were Worldly-Honour, Arrogancy, Pride, Self-

Conceit, Vain-Glory, and Shame; which last happened to let fly an arrow that wounded Tender-Conscience slightly in the cheek, fetching up all the blood in his face, but did him no greater harm; so at length he got to the end of the bridge, and then he was past the danger of the nets and gins; so that he could now walk upright, and that upon dry ground; and he went on singing:

> Through many toils and dangers I have run,
> Much pain and hardship I have undergone;
> Yet still my God has mingled sweet with sour,
> Ofttimes he smil'd when he did seem to low'r:
> O'er hills and dales he led me by his hand,
> Through bogs and fens, by water and by land.
> He feeds and clothes, and arms his pilgrims still,
> Protecting them from danger, death, and ill.
> Though Satan spreads his nets, and lays his gins,
> To trap the soul in labyrinths of sins;
> Yet by God's grace I have escaped his wiles:
> The humble pilgrim Satan ne'er beguiles;
> Humility the soul's sure refuge is—
> The lowest step that leads to highest bliss.

Then I saw in my dream, that Tender-Conscience entered the Valley of the Shadow of Death, and night overtook him, so that his feet stumbled in the dark, and he was ready to fall into the ditch, or quag, which were on each side of the narrow way; but being in the midst of summer, the sun arose within a few hours, and so he enjoyed the daylight, which was exceeding comfortable to him, though he met with dismal and frightful objects; for the valley is of itself very dark, and there hang perpetually over it such black and thick clouds of confusion, that what for them, and what for death, who spreads his wings over this valley, the sun gives a very faint and dim light here; yet that which shined at this time served to light Tender-Conscience along the hollow, dreadful way; where he heard, as he went along, a continual howling and yelling. But at length he got clear of all, and came to the end of the valley, even to the place where Christian saw blood, bones, ashes, and mangled bodies of men lying on the ground; but now they were buried, and a pillar was erected in this place, as a standing memorial of the cruelties that were acted by the two giants that lived in the cave hard by this place. There was an inscription on the pillar also, giving an account of all the righteous blood that had been shed in the world on the score of religion, from Abel's to that day. There was also a summary of all the sanguine laws that had been enacted on that account by cruel tyrants, as by Pharaoh, Nebuchadnezzar, Darius, Antiochus, Nero, &c. There was a relation of a woman and her seven sons, that were barbarously tormented with exquisite tortures, and afterwards put to death, because they would not taste of swines' flesh, contrary to their conscience and the law of God; on the same account also a venerable old man, called Eleazar, was cruelly scourged to death by the command of the tyrant. Many more curious memorials were there engraved on this pillar, which Tender-Conscience took great delight to read. Now the name of the pillar is History; and hard by it, even over against the cave of the two giants Pagan and Pope, there is another cave, wherein Tender-Conscience saw a middle-aged man sitting, of a mild, grave, and venerable countenance, and his name was Reformation. Now it was this man's charge to look after this pillar; and to see that no injury be done it by the thieves and robbers that infest that road, nor by any of giant Pope's party; for he maintained a great army under ground, his cave being of vast extent, and his army used sometimes to issue out and commit great spoils and ravages in the neighbouring countries: but now Reformation kept as strong a party as he, and had as much room in his cave to lodge them in; and sometimes they would fall out and skirmish, sometimes come to pitched battle, and then the ground would be afresh strewed with dead bodies, and stained with blood, till they were buried out of the way. All this Tender-Conscience learned from one that came out of the cave of Reformation, and fell into discourse with him, as they stood talking by the pillar.

At length the man, having understood that Tender-Conscience came from the valley of Destruction, and was going to the heavenly Jerusalem, was very inquisitive after his country, and the place of his birth; for, said he, I have heard my father say, that I was born in that country too, and brought from thence very young; and when my father came to this place, he left me in custody of Reformation, with whom I have continued ever since; and what is become of my father I know not, or whether I shall ever see him again or no; but I remember he used to talk of going to the celestial city, which, I suppose, is the same place whither you are now travelling; and, therefore, if you will accept of my company, I will gladly travel along with you, having great hopes of seeing my father there, or hearing some tidings of him; and besides, they say it is brave living in that city, and that it is the richest place in the world; therefore I would fain go along with you, in hopes of getting into that famous city to dwell.

Tender-Con. I like your motion very well, for I have travelled alone hitherto, which made the way seem more tedious to me; and a companion in the rest of my journey would divert melancholy, and we should encourage each other in our pilgrimage. But I must acquaint you with one thing first, and that is, that your journey will prove ineffectual, I doubt, unless you came in by the wicket-gate that is at the head of the narrow way, and can produce your certificate or pass from the Interpreter; for, as I am certainly informed, the King has given strict orders that none shall be admitted into the heavenly city that are not thus qualified.

Then Seek-Truth (for so was the other man called) replied, I have a pass by me, which my father procured for me when he brought me along with him, and he told me he had it from the Interpreter, giving me a strict charge to have a care of it.

Tender-Con. What was your father's name, and from whence came he?

Seek-Truth. His name was Little-Faith; he came from the town of Sincere.

Tender-Con. Oh! I believe I have heard talk of him; if it be the same man that I mean, there goes a report, as if he were robbed in a place called Dead-man's Lane.

Seek-Truth. I hope not so; though I am sure he had store of silver and gold about him, besides some very rich jewels; nay, I may say he carried his whole estate about him, so that if he were robbed on the road, he is utterly ruined and undone. I am very much concerned at the sad news, and shall not be at rest till I have inquired further about it: therefore, if you please, let us hasten to go forward in our journey; and it is ten to one but I shall be more particularly informed of this matter by the way. I will only call two or three more friends of mine own, who are very desirous to travel towards the heavenly country, and would be glad to take the opportunity of your good company. So he ran into the cave, and called for Zealous-Mind, Weary-o'-the-World, Convert, and Yielding, who all came out to know what he would have.

Zealous-Mind. Have! says Zealous-Mind, you may be sure that it is no hurt that he would have when Seek-Truth calls us.

Seek-Truth. No, my friends, I call you for your good, I hope, and to fulfil your own wishes; for you have often told me how desirous you were to travel towards the heavenly Jerusalem; and now here is a man going that way that would be glad of your company. For my part, I am resolved to go along with him; do you as you please.

Weary-o'-the-World. And I, said Weary-o'-the-World; for here is nothing in this country but trouble and vexation, cares, grief, and all manner of evil; I would not tarry a day longer in it, if I might be a king. Come, let us be jogging.

Convert. I burn with desire to go to that glorious place, of which I have heard such renowned things. I care not what hardships I undergo, nor what torments I suffer, provided I may get thither at last.

Yielding. And, for my part, I like your company so well, that I will go with you to the end of the world with all my heart. For you talk so wisely, and tell such pretty stories, that you have won my very heart. I am ready to melt when I hear Seek-Truth discourse of such strange things as are in the heavenly country, and tell his father's travels from the valley of Destruction, and how kindly he was entertained by the way at some good houses.

Seek-Truth. Well, if you are all agreed, come, follow me, and I will bring you to the man that is now on his pilgrimage to Zion; he stands not far off from our cave's mouth, hard by the pillar of

History. So they all followed him with one consent, and went out of the cave, where they found Tender-Conscience waiting for their appearance. Then they went up to him and saluted him, one by one; and, after some questions passed on both sides, they all set forward together.

Now I saw in my dream, that as they were going up a piece of rising ground, they saw before them a man walking an even moderate pace, and they made haste to overtake him; for by his gait they guessed he was no ordinary man. As certain wise men observed:—By a man's gait you know what he is. So when they came up to him, they saluted him courteously, and he returned their salutation with an air which discovered the tranquillity and peace of his soul.

Then Tender-Conscience said to him, Sir, if a stranger may take the liberty to ask you a question, I intreat you to tell me, whether your name be not Spiritual-Man; for I think I have seen you before, and was told that you were called by that name?

Spiritual-Man. Yes, said Spiritual-Man, I am the same you take me for; and though your knowledge of me be but as yet imperfect, yet I very well know you and all your company, and am glad to see you so far in your journey towards the heavenly city, whither we are all going.

Tender-Con. I do not wonder that you know me, and my fellow-travellers here with me, for I have heard a very learned and holy man, one Paul the apostle, say, that you know all things, and judge all things, (1 Cor. ii. 15;) and therefore I am very glad that we are all so happy as to overtake you upon the road. I hope we shall have your good company to our journey's end.

Spiritual-Man. With a very good will; for it is my delight to keep company with those who set their faces Zion-ward, and are going thither, as I perceive you are at this time. But I spy a young man in your company, who, I doubt, will not be able to go through this tedious journey, but will either faint by the way, or turn aside with the flatterer, or take up his abode at Vanity-Fair. Then turning himself to Yielding, he said unto him, Young man, you are the person I mean; do you think you shall be able to hold to the heavenly Jerusalem?

Yielding. I make no doubt of it, sir; for I find myself in good health, and as able to foot it as any of the company.

Then they went on together, till they came to a great wilderness, where were several paths leading divers ways; so that had it not been for Spiritual-Man (who alone knew the right way) they had wandered, no doubt, into some dangerous part or other, and either been devoured by wild beasts or taken prisoners by some cruel giants, whose castles stood in the remote corners of this wilderness. This made them all show a great deal of respect and obedience to Spiritual-Man, and esteem him as their guide and patron. So they went along together, till they came to a place where was an altar built, and there was incense burning thereon, and the smell of the incense was very fragrant, refreshing the spirits of the pilgrims. Then Spiritual-Man spake to this effect:—

My brethren, you must know that this wilderness is much haunted with wild beasts, as also by thieves and murderers, spirits and hobgoblins, which oftentimes assault poor pilgrims in the nighttime, and sometimes by day: now, had we taken any other path, we had been in danger of falling into their clutches; but now I hope there will be no such danger, if you will follow my counsel.

Tender-Con. We will readily obey thee in all things; for we see that thou art a man of God, and hast the mind of Christ. Tell us, therefore, what we shall do to be safe from the dangers that threaten us in this place.

Spiritual-Man. You see this altar of incense here perpetually smoking, and sending up clouds of a sweet-smelling savour to heaven. Now the smoke of this incense keeps off all spirits and hobgoblins, and the fire upon the altar keeps off all wild beasts. If then you would be free from the danger of wild beasts, let every man take a coal from the altar and carry along with him; and if he would be free from the spirits and hobgoblins, let him take of the incense that is in the treasury of the altar, and carry it along with him; and as he travels through the wilderness, let him often kindle a fire with a coal from the altar, and burn incense therein, so shall he be protected from all evil. Let him awaken the spirit of prayer, and kindle true devotion in himself, by making good use of the grace of God; for the heart of a devout man, and one that fears God, is an altar of incense, always sending up holy ejaculations, which are a sweet savour or perfume before God. Such a man attracts the divine blessing and protection.

Tender-Con. But how shall a man pray? in form or without? with words or in silence?

Spiritual-Man. That you may be the better satisfied in this point, you ought to consider that prayer is the soul's discourse or conversation with God. Now, seeing that God knoweth all things, and discerneth the secret thoughts of our hearts, it is a thing indifferent in private prayer, whether we use words or no; for the soul may discourse and converse with God as well in silence as with words; nay, better sometimes, because silence preserves our attention, and prevents wandering thoughts; whereas, when the soul is occupied in verbal prayer, it often proves little better than lip-service; as God complained of old, "This people serve me with their lips, but their hearts are far from me." But, however, this silent or mental prayer is a gift which all men are not capable of. Some have not that recollection of spirit, that composedness of mind, as to pray in this manner; and it is convenient that such men should use words. But, whether they use a set form or no in private is not material; only let me give this seasonable caution, that those who use extemporary prayer be careful not to commit any indecency by uttering improper expressions, vain repetitions, or using too many words, which must needs be offensive to the Divine Majesty, who knows our necessities before we declare them, and only requires an humble and fervent application of our hearts to him for what we stand in need of. All the fine words in the world without this, all the rhetorical flourishes, the elegant cadences, the softest periods, without this, are but a sounding brass and a tinkling cymbal in the ears of God: and, therefore, good was the advice of Solomon, "When thou comest into the house of God, let thy words be few; and be more ready to hear, than to offer the sacrifice of fools:" intimating hereby that multiplicity of words in prayer is but the sacrifice of fools. And a greater man than Solomon has said, "When ye pray, use not vain repetitions, as the Heathen do; for they think that they shall be heard for their much speaking. Be ye not therefore like unto them, for your Father knoweth what things ye have need of before you ask him." And, therefore, the form of prayer which Christ here prescribed them as a pattern, was very short, but comprehensive, including in less than an hundred words all the several parts of prayer, as adoration, thanksgiving, petition, oblation, intercession, &c. And this, no doubt, he prescribed for a pattern to others, that all who call upon God may do it in reverence and godly modesty, using but few words, and those pithy and significant, comprehensive and full, proper and becoming the Majesty we address ourselves unto.

Tender-Con. You have given me great satisfaction as to this matter, which has often disturbed my mind, and kept me at too remote a distance from God, not knowing certainly how to pray acceptably: but now I am convinced that God requires chiefly the heart; for it is but reason that he who is a Spirit—and the purest of all spirits—should be served in spirit and in truth; which cannot be done where the heart goes not along with the lips: and if it does, then it matters not whether it be in a set form of words or no; the fervency and attention of the mind, the regularity of the affections, and the lawfulness of our petitions, being the chief things regarded by the sovereign Majesty of heaven.

Seek-Truth. How happy am I that light into such good company! I have been long a searching and inquiring into the nature and obligation of Christian duties, and particularly this of prayer, which puzzles a great many good well-meaning people; but I never met with so much comfort and satisfaction as I now have found in your discourse.

Weary-o'-the-World. I approve of what has been said concerning prayer; for I find so many defects in the best of my devotions, that I have no heart to venture on vocal prayer at some times; for if I should, my heart would afterwards check me with putting an affront on God, while, in the midst of passionate words and devout expressions, my thoughts were employed quite another way; while my tongue chattered like a magpie to God, and my heart was upon the devil's ramble, starting a thousand vain and foolish thoughts amidst the most serious and religious, the most fervent and pious words of the world. I know not how it fares with the other people, or what advantages they may find; but, for my own part, so long as I carry flesh and blood about me, I cannot presume to be free from distractions, alienation of mind, coldness, indifference, and impertinent suggestions, even in the calmest minutes, the most recollected seasons, and the severest applications of my mind to the duty I am engaged in. Much less can I hope for an immunity from such failings, when I give the reins to my tongue, and suffer my lips to prate over a multitude of formal words; for then I find it falls out to me, as I have heard say it does to musicians, who, by long accustoming themselves to play on any instrument, at length get such a habit that they can run over their familiar tunes without minding or giving attention to what they are doing; not that I hereby condemn the use of vocal prayer, for without doubt it is expedient for some people, and necessary in the public worship of God, where many people are to join together in offering up the same petitions, thanksgivings, intercessions, &c., which cannot be performed without a form of words which are the only proper means of conveying our conceptions and thoughts one to another, and consequently making each other sensible what we all pray for. In short, my judgment is that it is all one, in respect of God's hearing us, whether we use the words or not, in public or in private; but for the sake of human necessities words are necessary in public, and a fervent attention of mind is absolutely required both in public and private, as the only efficacious means to render our prayers acceptable to the divine Majesty.

Then I heard in my dream, that as they walked along the wilderness, the wild beasts roared, and sent forth hideous noises, which put some of them into no small disorder and consternation; but the rest, who had more courage, heartened them on. So at last they got out of the wilderness, and came in sight of the town of Vanity, where Faithful was put to death for his testimony to the truth. Now the town was very magnificent and stately to the eye, full of temples and other public structures, whose lofty towers, being adorned with gold and other costly embellishments, made a glittering show in the sunshine. Likewise it was exceeding large and populous, so that there was a perpetual noise to be heard at a distance, like the roaring of the sea, because of the multitude of people that were in it, the chariots and the horses that were always running up and down the streets, which made poor Yielding think it was the city whither they were all a-going. He was so much taken with the glorious figure this town made, that he could hardly contain himself from running thither before the rest of his company; which, when Spiritual-Man perceived, he said:—

Spiritual-Man. Young man, mistake not this place; for it is not the heavenly city, as you imagine, but a mere counterfeit; it is Babylon, the town of confusion and vanity: though our way lies through it, yet we are not to take up our rest there; we may abide a while, but we must not think of settling there for ever.

Yielding. Sir, I thought by the description that had been given me of the heavenly Jerusalem, that this had been the very place indeed; but now you have satisfied me to the contrary.

So the pilgrims went forward, and entered into the town; but they met with a great many affronts and injuries by the way, by reason of the strange dress they were in, and because they had not the mark of the beast in their foreheads, nor in their right hands, as all the inhabitants of the town had. Therefore the boys hooted and hallooed at them, and gathered a rabble about them; nay, some of the graver sort threw dirt upon them as they went by their doors; they mocked and derided them, they fastened all manner of slanders and reproaches upon them, and very few there were in all that place that showed any compassion or common civility to them. But this did not at all dishearten any of them, saving the young man to whom Spiritual-Man spoke last, whose name was Yielding. He, indeed, being discouraged by the inhospitable humour and carriage of the townsmen toward his companions, and being strongly invited by a very courteous-spoken man to leave that giddy-brained company of fools, (for so he termed the pilgrims,) and come and dwell with him, and he should find all things to his content; he accordingly complied, and forsaking his company, followed the man, who conducted him to a tavern in the market-place, and sending for some of his boon companions, they fell to carousing and making merry: also they drank confusion to the pilgrims that were going to the heavenly city. But Yielding got little by the bargain; for being surfeited with excess of wine, he died suddenly in the night-time.

In the meanwhile the rest of the pilgrims passed through the streets of the town, molested on all hands by the ruder sort of people, and unpitied of them that, according to their age and stations, ought to have shown more discretion and humanity. Thus they went on, till they came to a place called the Exchange, where the merchants used to meet and traffic; there were men of all nations and families, men of all tribes and languages, each one busy in his particular occupation or commerce. But when the pilgrims came amongst them, they all with one accord left off their business and talk, and stood gazing on these strangers, saying among themselves, What countrymen are these that appear in so strange a dress, so different from all that use to frequent this place?

Then I saw in my dream that Zealous-Mind, one of the pilgrims, stood up and spoke to the multitude, saying, Men and brethren, partakers of the same flesh and blood with us, why stand ye gazing on us, as though some new thing had happened unto you which you had never seen or known before? Have you forgot the days wherein Christian and Faithful passed through your town, whereof the one was burned for the testimony which he bore to the truth; and the other, though imprisoned, yet by the mighty power and providence of God escaped your rage and malice? Are these things out of your memory already? or, are your records silent in the matter? We are come upon the same account as they, and are going to the same country whither they bent their course. Therefore wonder not at our unusual dress; for it is necessary that all those who travel Zion-ward should be apparelled after the fashion of that city, that so their entrance thereinto may be easy, and without blame. This is the reason why we are not clothed after the manner of this town or of this world; for we have no abiding city here, but we "seek one to come, whose builder and maker is God." After Zealous-Mind had made an end of speaking, some of the merchants left their affairs, and joined themselves unto the pilgrims; others mocked and derided them. But they shook the dust off their feet, and departed from that place, and the merchants that had left their merchandise went along with them. And the people followed them out of the town, hallooing and hooting at them; but they, remembering the saying of Christ, "Cursed is he that hath set his hands to the plough of the kingdom, and looketh back," regarded not the ridiculous noise they made, but kept on their course on the King's highway, neither turning to the right hand nor to the left, but walked directly in the way of the Lord, till they came to the plain of Ease, where the merchants, hearkening to the enticing words of Demas, were persuaded to go down into the silver-mine to dig for treasure that corrupteth; but the rest of the pilgrims would not turn aside out of the way to follow after filthy lucre. Yet they had not gone far before one of them, whose name was Weary-o'-the-World, was turning about to look back toward the silver-mine, when Spiritual-Man, espying him, catched hold of his arms as he was facing about, and stopped him, saying, Brother, here is a sight just before thee, which will convince thee of the danger of looking back to this place; so he showed him the pillar of salt into which Lot's wife was turned, which stood directly before them on the way-side. Then Weary-o'-the-World thanked him for his friendly admonition and assistance, confessing that he was tempted with a thought of covetousness, which made him attempt to look back towards the silver-mine; but that he was glad he so timely prevented both his crime and his punishment, by showing him the example of Lot's wife, who, for looking back on Sodom, was turned into a pillar of salt.

Now I saw in my dream, that the pilgrims went forward till they came to the river of God; their way lay along by the river-side, where grew trees, bearing all manner of delightful fruits, which the pilgrims tasted to their wonderful refreshment: they also drank of the water of the river, whose virtue is to rejoice the heart more than wine; and there being pleasant green pastures all along the banks of the river, they lay down some time to repose themselves there, and then rose up to prosecute their journey; coming at length to the place that led down to Doubting Castle, which was demolished in the days of Christiana her pilgrimage; so they passed by the stile that Christian and Hopeful went over when they were taken prisoners by giant Despair, kept the highway, never stopping till they came to the Delectable Mountains, where they again refreshed themselves in the gardens and vineyards, eating freely of the fruits that were therein. Now as they went up these Delectable Mountains, they went at last to a mountain that was at the top of all the mountains and established above the rest of the hills, and it was called the Mountain of the House of the Lord. Now there were shepherds feeding of their flocks all over this mountain, and there were men of all nations, tribes, and languages, walking up and down on the mountain, and sometimes they walked with the shepherds, at other times they talked one unto another.

So I saw in my dream, that as the pilgrims went along the highway, there stood some shepherds by the wayside, tending of their flocks; and one of the shepherds asked the pilgrims whence they came, and whither they were going? To whom Spiritual-Man replied, Sir, we come from the valley of Destruction, and are going to the celestial country.

Shepherds. Ye are welcome thus far on your journey, for now you are on the top of the Delectable Mountains, even on the mountain of the Lord's house; and here be men of all nations, tribes, and languages that are going the same journey with you; only they tarry awhile here to take the air of these Delectable Mountains, and to partake of the fruits that grow on this holy ground, which are good to refresh and strengthen them after their wearisome travel. Moreover, we shepherds have remedies for all the diseases that pilgrims are subject to in their toilsome journey, and we minister freely unto them of such things as we have, giving advice and physic unto the sick, opening the eyes of the blind, the ears of the deaf, and loosening the tongues of the dumb, causing them to show forth the praise and glory of God. To this end are we placed here, and our tents are open to all comers; where we entertain the stranger, the fatherless, and the widow, the rich and the poor, the weak and the strong, the young and the old, at the king's cost, who prepares a table for all who will come to it, and hath made us his stewards, to portion out to every one what they need: we have milk for babes, and meat for them that are of ripe age. Our doors are not shut day nor night, neither do we cease crying

out, " Ho, every one that is thirsty, let him buy milk without money, and wine without price; for the Lord hath prepared a feast of fat things, of wine well refined;" and he inviteth all men to his table.

Then the shepherds conducted them into their pavilions, and set before them such dainties as they had not met with before in all their journey; so they eat and drank cheerfully, and were mightily refreshed; and afterwards the shepherds invited them to walk out and take the air of the mountain; which they did, and found it the wholesomest, purest, and pleasantest air in the world; for it was perfumed with the odour of oranges and lemons, pomegranates and citrons, and of all manner of spice-trees, which grew upon the mountain in abundance; so that what with the admirable diet, and what with the delicious air of this place, their strength was renewed like eagles; for they rested there with the shepherds two or three days, who showed them great hospitality, for they had all things in common among themselves, and therefore the pilgrims went freely up and down from one tent to another, and were kindly received everywhere; for this is Immanuel's land— the holy mountain of the kingdom of peace—where their spears were turned into pruning hooks, and their swords into ploughshares, every one sitting peaceably under his own vine, and under his own fig-tree, and no man did harm to another, but all lived together in unity, love, and peace.

The shepherds also showed them many wonderful things of the mountain, as the hill of Error, and the hill of Caution; and, when the time came that the pilgrims were desirous to pursue their journey, the shepherds had them to their overseer, whom the king had set over them, even one of their brethren, and a shepherd. To this man they brought the pilgrims; who, when they came before him, blessed them, saying, " Peace be unto you." And when the shepherds had told him who they were, and how far they had travelled, and whither they were going, he anointed them with a certain rich and sovereign ointment, which would exceedingly strengthen them in the rest of their journey. Then the pilgrims, bowing down their heads to the ground, took their leave of the venerable old man, giving him thanks for the kindness he had showed them. Then the shepherds went along with them, and showed them the door in the side of the hill, which is a by-way to hell, and lent them their perspective-glass to take a prospect of the celestial city through it; which, when the pilgrims had a glimpse of, they were ravished at the sight of such glorious things, and longed to be there; wherefore they desired the shepherds to give them leave to depart; which was granted them; only the shepherds first gave them a direction concerning the way, bidding them have an especial care lest they slept upon the Enchanted Ground, which they must needs pass through before they could arrive at the heavenly city, and it lies just on this side the region called Beulah.

Moreover I saw in my dream, that the pilgrims, having bid adieu to the shepherds, went down from the mountain into the plain, having a large valley before, which was called the valley of Vain-Opinions. Now as they were going through this valley, they saw a company of men before them; and, as they drew nearer, they could hear them talk very eagerly one to another, as though it were about some weighty matter. So, when they came up to them, they perceived that the men were talking about the King of the country, which made them dispute very passionately, and with a great deal of heat: one asserting that the King was of his opinion; another, that he was of his judgment; a third said that he only had the right understanding of the royal mind, will, and pleasure. And each man quoted some article or sentence of the King's statute-book in confirmation of what he had said; so that there was a great noise and hurly-burly among them, insomuch that they were ready to go together by the ears; while every one thought himself in the right, and all the rest in the wrong. Thus contended they, till Spiritual-Man spoke to them, and said, Good people, what is all this clamour for? Then they all ceased their loud talking, and gave attention to what he would he would say, who thus proceeded:—

Spiritual-Man. I hear you very vehement and earnest in controversy about the King's pleasure, one saying he knows best, and another, that he is best acquainted with it. This puts me in mind of the words of Christ, where he says, " If any man shall say unto you, Lo, here is Christ; or, Lo, he is there, believe it not: for there shall arise false Christs and false prophets, and shall show great signs and wonders, insomuch that (if it were possible) they shall deceive the very elect. Behold, I have told you before; wherefore if they shall say unto you, Behold he is in the desert, go not forth; behold he is in the secret chambers, believe it not; for as the lightning cometh out of the east, and shineth even unto the west, so shall also the coming of the Son of Man be." Therefore I have reason to judge you all deceivers and false-prophets, since you so exactly make good the character which our Lord has given them. For, whereas one boasteth that he knoweth the King's mind; another, that he is the best interpreter of his will; ye are all out of the way of truth; the King's mind is with none of you—Christ is not among you. It is the shepherds who are his privy-counsellors, who know the secrets of the kingdom; go ye therefore, and feed with the flocks, and frequent the places where they lie down at noon; so shall ye learn knowledge, and preserve your feet from stumbling into error. And having spoke those words, he turned from them with all his company: and they kept on their way over the plain.

Now they had not gone far, before a man bolted out upon them from a little cave on the side of the high-way, which was called the Cave of Natural Speculations, and the name of the man was Human-Reason. So he asked them, whence they came, and whither they were going? To whom Spiritual-Man made answer, We come from the valley of Destruction, and are going toward the heavenly Jerusalem, and shall be glad of thy company, if thou wilt go along with us.

Human-Reason. I am designed for the same place myself, and would gladly accept of any good company. But I suppose you intend to go the same way as yonder shepherds showed you, who know no more of it than the man in the moon; but only it is their livelihood to tell a parcel of strange stories to strangers and travellers, making them believe they are servants to the King, and that it is their office to entertain pilgrims, and give them directions for the way. They pretend also to give them a prospect of the heavenly Jerusalem through a perspective-glass, and to show to them one of the mouths of hell; whereas they are a pack of mere jugglers and religious cheats, amusing the credulous and unwary travellers with fiction, and romantic stories of heaven and hell, and using enchantments to delude them in their way thither, casting a mist before their eyes when they pretend to give them a glimpse of the glories of that place. For that is a deceitful glass through which you looked, and presents you not with the true appearance of things, as I can prove at large, if you will be pleased to hear me out. Nay, I can demonstrate before your eyes, without the help of any glass, the situation and beauty of the Celestial City, and show you the nearest ready road thither, as plain as that two and three make five.

Spiritual-Man. Thou art as blind as a beetle thyself, and wilt thou pretend to direct us in the way to a place which thou never sawest nor knewest? Go, get thee into thy den again, and go not about to seduce poor harmless pilgrims; for we will not hearken to thy insinuating discourse, but keep on our way, as the shepherds directed us.

Tender-Con. Nay, pray let me hear what the man can say for himself; for he seems to be a smart man, and no fool; and therefore I would fain hear his reasons.

Spiritual-Man. Your curiosity is dangerous, and may cost you dear; therefore pray be persuaded to turn away your ears from hearing of vanity and delusions. You have run well hitherto, do not halt so near your journey's end.

Tender-Con. I cannot be satisfied in my mind unless I hear this man's arguments; for he seems to have something extraordinary in his very face, and more in his words.

Zealous-Mind. To the empty are empty things. If this man be so obstinate that he will tarry and hear this fellow prate, let him tarry alone; why should we lose time for his folly? Let us hasten forward to run the race that is set before us.

Spiritual-Man. No, brother, let us rather bear one another's burden, and so fulfil the royal law of

Christ our king. Let us pity his infirmity, as Paul exhorts us in the like case : "Brethren," says he, "if a man be overtaken in a fault, ye which are spiritual restore such an one in the spirit of meekness, considering thyself lest thou also be tempted." And another apostle sayeth, "Brethren, if any of you err from truth, and one convert him, let him know that he who converteth a sinner from the error of his way shall save a soul from death, and shall hide a multitude of sins." Now, therefore, since this our brother is tempted with a vain curiosity to hear the arguments of Human-Reason, let us stay awhile, and I will undertake to confute him, which will be more to our brother's profit, than if he had never heard him speak. Go to then, said he, turning to Human-Reason, let us hear what thou hast to argue against the way that we are going.

Then Human-Reason, putting on a grave and serious countenance, spoke as follows: Gentlemen, it is not manly to fall into a passion, and abuse a stranger before you have a just cause given you, especially when you are ignorant of, or may mistake, his quality. I am sprung of a right noble and illustrious family, and as ancient as any in the world by my father's side. Understanding is my father, who is a prince and courtier, and of a near kin to the royal family of heaven. Therefore, as you are gentlemen, I hope you will use me with that respect which is due to my birth and extraction, and not run me down with reproachful names and scurrilous language.

Spiritual-Man. I cry you mercy, sir; I know your father very well, and honour his noble birth and illustrious quality : but, give me leave to tell you, your mother is but of mean and obscure quality, and a notorious strumpet, and therefore you must excuse us if we esteem no better of you than a bastard, or at best a very degenerate son— a mongrel breed—partaking more of your mother's vices than of your father's virtues. Her name was Sense, the daughter of Animal-Life, an old doting sot, that minded nothing else but eating, drinking, and sleeping, his birthplace being nothing better than a dunghill : this was your goodly grandfather by your mother's side. So that you have no such reason to glory in your high birth, but rather to be ashamed of your father's infirmity. For he was once quick-sighted as an eagle, but now his eyes are dim; in this you resemble him to the life, for you are purblind. He was active and sincere, but now dull and treacherous; in this also, you are like him, for you are heavy and slow in all your operations, and as uncertain and wavering as a weathercock. I could take notice of a great many more ill features and qualities in you, but that it would be too tedious and irksome to the company.

Zealous-Mind. Ay, ay, it is not worth while to lose so much time in talking to this impostor, when we are on a journey.

Weary-o'-the-World. No indeed, brother Spi-

ritual-Man, no more it is ; and were you but half so tired as I, you would not stand reckoning up this fellow's genealogy, nor making comparisons between him and his father. I long to be at my journey's end. Come, let us be jogging.

Spiritual-Man. Have patience, my brethren, whilst this man and I discourse the point farther, for the sake of Tender-Conscience, who seems to be staggered at his first words, and has an itching desire to hear what he can say for himself, perhaps he will have a better opinion of the man, if we should refuse to converse with him. He might think that we were ashamed or afraid to stand the brunt of his boasted demonstrations, and so would conclude the truth is on his side ; therefore, for his sake, have patience awhile, and I doubt not but I shall convince this man of his error, and make him hold his peace, if not recant his ill-grounded opinions, to the glory of God, and the edification of us all, especially of poor, wavering Tender-Conscience.

Then they agreed to tarry and hear out the dispute between them; so Spiritual-Man bid Human-Reason wave all further preambles about his birth and family, and fall upon the point in hand, making as quick a dispatch as he could of this matter.

Human-Reason. Well, then, I tell you in short, you are out of your way; and, if you'll follow my directions, I will show you a far nearer and more secure road to the heavenly country. I believe and know there is a God, as well as you, and worship him day and night; but I take not up this belief, nor practise this worship on other men's credits. I do not blindly pin my faith on other men's sleeves, nor worship God according to the traditions of men, as you do; but I lay a sure foundation of my faith. I behold and contemplate this wonderful and glorious fabric of the world, and, by a regular deduction, I trace the footsteps of an eternal Divinity ; whilst climbing up the chain of inferior and second causes, I at length fasten to the uppermost link, and clearly see the first and supreme cause, source, and spring of all things visible and invisible. Thus as common bodily objects are the first and lowermost of this chain of causes, so my senses are the first and lowermost step to my faith, whilst by a chain of rational inferences I join the first and last things together, and I make my senses, reason, and faith to be all proportionally subservient to the adoration I pay the eternal Godhead. Thus I observe a due order, in letting that which is natural first take place, and then afterwards that which is spiritual ; whereas you take a quite contrary course, and so do all that hearken to these blind guides the shepherds on yonder mountain. For they teach you to begin at the wrong end, and lay aside the service of our sense and reason, which are the essential properties of our nature, to believe, by an implicit blind faith, the doctrines and opinions of such a number of men, pretending they were divinely inspired, and not only so, but to believe doctrines that are diametrically opposite to your reason, and the common sense and experience of the whole world. As, for example, they teach, and you must believe, that one can be three, and three are but one, contrary to the first principles of natural reason; that God is man, and man is God; that a virgin could conceive a son; with many more opinions of the like nature, inconsistent in themselves, and with other fundamental principles of nature.

Tender-Con. If all be true that this man says, then, for aught I see, we are guilty of downright popery; for I have heard many wise and learned men say, that the great secret of that religion is to make its proselytes believe, by a blind implicit faith, things directly contrary to common sense and reason; and if we are guilty of the same error, wherein do we differ from the papists? For my part, I am wonderfully taken with this man's discourse; he speaks home to the purpose; and I cannot see what can be objected against it, nor how he can be answered.

Spiritual-Man. Be not carried away with every wind of false doctrine, but let your heart be established in the truth. Be not credulous, but examine well his discourse, and you shall find it all sophistry and deceit, as I shall make apparent if you will give me the hearing.

In the first place, therefore, he goes upon a wrong ground in supposing your reason to be perfect in exercising itself upon its proper objects. Before the fall of Adam indeed it was so, but now it is imperfect and frail. It was then one entire shining diamond, but now it is shattered into pieces; we only retain some fragments or sparkles of the original jewel; we can boast of nothing but some broken remnants of reason escaped from that fatal shipwreck of human nature, which still float up and down in a sea of uncertainties. We grope as in the dark, and can hardly discern the things that are familiar with us. Our notions of things natural are liable to a thousand mistakes, our inferences loose and incoherent, and all our faculties turned upside down. Our discourse commonly is rather rhetoric than reason, and has either a smatch of the serpent's subtle sophistry, or the woman's soft and insinuating eloquence; these generally supply the place of true masculine reason, while the sophist does but mimic the philosopher. and both they and the orator act the divine; as this man has done in his specious and formal accusation of the shepherds, and vindication of his own way. For—

In the second place, suppose we grant his ground to be good, and that reason is perfect in its exercising itself on its proper objects; yet his inferences from thence are but the efforts of his eloquence and sophistry, while he would endeavour to persuade us that divine and supernatural things are the objects of natural reason also. It is just the same thing as if he would go about to convince us that we may hear with our noses and see with our ears.

We may as well do this, as discern divine and supernatural things by natural and human reason. God hath endowed us with different faculties, suitable and proportionable to the different objects that engage them. We discover sensible things by our senses, rational things by our reason, things intellectual by understanding; but divine and celestial things he has reserved for the exercise of our faith, which is a kind of divine and superior sense in the soul. Our reason and understanding may at some times snatch a glimpse, but cannot take a steady and adequate prospect of things so far above their reach and sphere. Thus, by the help of natural reason, I may know there is a God, the first cause and original of all things; but his essence, attributes, and will are hid within the veil of inaccessible light, and cannot be discerned by us but through faith in his divine revelation. He that walks without this light walks in darkness, though he may strike out some faint and glimmering sparkles of his own. And he that out of the gross and wooden dictates of his natural reason carves out a religion to himself, is but a more refined idolater than those who worship stocks and stones, hammering an idol out of his fancy, and adoring the works of his own imagination. For this reason God is no where said to be jealous, but upon the account of his worship. To this end was he so particularly nice (if I may so speak with reverence) in all those strict injunctions he laid on the children of Israel as to his worship. He gave to Moses in the mount an exact pattern of the tabernacle and its vessels, instruments, and appurtenances; he prescribed the particular times and seasons, the peculiar manner, rites, and ceremonies of his worship, not a tittle of which were they to transgress under pain of death. Now, what needed all this caution and severity, if it were a matter so indifferent as this man makes it, how God is worshipped? He thinks if, by patching up half-a-dozen of natural reasons together he can prove a Deity, and pay some homage or acknowledgment to him as such, that all is well with him; nay, that he is in the readiest and nearest way to heaven; in the meanwhile concluding, that we go round about, if not a quite contrary way, who take up our religion on no less credit and authority than that of divine revelation. This he calls laying aside our senses and our reason, to believe by a blind implicit faith the doctrines and opinions of a certain number of men pretending to be divinely inspired; and not only so, but believing doctrines diametrically opposite to our reason and the common sense and experience of the whole world. But tell me, O vain man, how do we lay aside our senses and our reason, when we use both in a due subordination to our faith? Faith itself comes by hearing, which is one of our senses; we hear the glad tidings of the Gospel preached to us, and our hearts are brought into subjection to the power thereof; natural reason taught us to believe there is a God, but faith teaches how to believe in him, and how to worship him. The things which we believe of him are indeed far above our senses and reason, but not contrary to them; nay, in this our senses and reason are instrumental to our faith, that when we read or hear of any of the miracles done by Christ and his apostles, our reason tells us they could not be done but by the mighty power of God, and that God would not by such miracles give testimony to a lie: therefore, consequently, our reason teaches us to believe that Christ and his apostles were really such as they professed themselves to be—he the Son of God, they his servants, and men inspired by the Holy Ghost, and consequently that all their doctrines were true. How then can I stumble at the doctrine of the Trinity, the Incarnation of Christ, his being conceived and brought forth of a virgin? Thus far my reason is serviceable to my faith—the one leads me by the hand to the vail, the other draws it back, and discovers all the sacred mysteries. Yet still let reason keep her distance; she is but the handmaid; faith the mistress; sense and reason attend in the outer courts of the temple, but faith enters into the Holy of Holies. "Now, without faith it is impossible to please God. Faith is the evidence of things not seen, the substance of things hoped for." This is that faith which thou, O Human-Reason, hast so much contemned and vilified; this is that faith which the shepherds recommended to us; this is that perspective-glass through which we saw the glories of the celestial Jerusalem: therefore cease henceforward to speak evil of the way of the Lord; cease to pervert the souls of such as seek the Lord in sincerity and with an humble faith.

When he had made an end of these words, Tender-Conscience burst out into tears for grief and joy; for grief, that he had suffered his mind to be wrapped by the seducing eloquence of Human-Reason; and for joy that Spiritual-Man had so well answered and confuted his argument, which made him address himself thus to Spiritual-Man.

Tender-Con. I am heartily sorry that my foolishness should have hindered all the company for so much time, while we might have been a good way on our journey. Now I am fully satisfied that Human-Reason is but an *ignis fatuus* to the mind, a false light, a deceiver; and therefore let us leave him to his den of shadows, and proceed in our journey.

Then I saw in my dream that they went forward, while Tender-Conscience sang :—

Vain Human-Reason boasts himself a light,
Though but a wand'ring meteor of the night:
Bred in the bogs and fens of common earth,
A dunghill was the place of his high birth;
Yet the impostor would aspire to be
Esteem'd a son of noble pedigree;
Vaunting his father's titles and his race,
Though you see *mongrel* written in his face.
A better herald has unmask'd the sham,
And prov'd a strumpet was the juggler's dam.

In vain he seeks on pilgrims to impose,
In vain he strives to lead them by the nose.
The cheat's discover'd, and bright truth prevails,
When humble faith does hold the sacred scales.
Reason and sense are but deceitful guides;
A better convoy God for us provides.
Celestial truth dwells in th' abyss of light,
Wrapt up in clouds from Human-Reason's sight.
He that would see her, as she's thus conceal'd,
Must look by faith, believing what's reveal'd.
Reason may well at her own quarry fly,
But finite cannot grasp infinity.
Rest then, my soul, from endless anguish freed,
Nor reason is thy guide, nor sense thy creed,
Faith is the best insurer of thy bliss,
The bank above must fail before the venture miss.

Now as they went along, they came to the place where Flatterer had seduced Christian and Hopeful out of the road into a byway; which might be easily done, for though it was a byway, yet it seemed to lie as straight before them as the true way. But, however, our pilgrims had the good fortune to escape the way that led to the nets, by means of Spiritual-Man's company, who had a shrewd insight into that road.

Now I saw in my dream that they had not gone far before they all began to be very drowsy, insomuch that Weary-o'-the-World began to talk of lying down and taking a nap; at which Convert, who had not spoken a word since they parted from the cave of Reformation all this time, fetched a deep sigh and wept bitterly; but amidst his tears he called out very earnestly to Weary-o'-the-World, warning him not to sleep in that place. This sudden passion and extraordinary carriage of Convert, who had been silent all the way before, made everybody curious to learn the occasion of it, and Spiritual-Man desired him to acquaint the company with the occasion of this sudden motion. Then Convert telling them if they would escape death, or very near dánger of it, they must not offer to sleep on that ground, promised to give them an account of his life in short, and desired them to give good attention to his words, which would be a means to keep them waking. So he began :—

Convert. You may remember, the shepherds at parting, among other good and wholesome advices, bid us have an especial care not to sleep on the Enchanted Ground. Now when I saw some of the company inclined to sleep, I called to mind the shepherds' exhortation, and also my own former miscarriage in this point, which made me burst forth into tears, to think how far I have gone back from heavenward by reason of sleeping in this place, and what danger you would all have run should you but have lain down on this Enchanted Ground; for this is the place the shepherds told us of.

Spiritual-Man. Blessed art thou of the Lord, O happy young man, who hast prevented us from sleeping in this place. Pray entertain us with a relation of your past travels, for I perceive by your discourse that you have been this way before now.

Convert. It is possible that you may have heard of one Atheist, that met Christian and Hopeful a little way off from this place, as they travelled to the heavenly city. I am the man, though my name be now changed; nor was that my proper name, but was given me after my sleep on the Enchanted Ground; for my name before was Well-Meaning, but now is Convert. I was born in the valley of Destruction, and brought out from thence very young by my father; but as we came along by that man behind us, even by Human-Reason, I was so pleased with his discourse, that my father could not get me along with him, but I must needs tarry awhile to converse with Human-Reason, telling my father that, he being old and crazy, I should soon overtake him. But Human-Reason had such enticing ways with him, that I had not power to leave his company a great while; nay, and at last, when he saw that I would go, he would needs accompany me to this place, and at parting he gave me something to drink out of a vial, which he told me was an excellent cephalic, and good against all the distempers of the brain, to which travellers are liable by reason of heats and colds, and the like; and so he took his leave, and went back to his cave. But he was no sooner gone, when I fell asleep on this ground, whether through the influence of that liquor he gave me, or through the nature of the vapours which arise out of the ground, I know not, but my sleep seemed very sweet unto me; and I believe I had slept my last here, had I not been used from my childhood to walk in my sleep; for, getting up in my sleep, I walked back again the same way by which I came, till I was quite off from the Enchanted Ground, and there I met with Christian and Hopeful, who were going forward to Mount Zion. So when they had told me whither they were going, I fell a laughing heartily at them, calling them an hundred fools for taking upon them so tedious a journey, when they were like to have nothing for their pains but mere labour and travel. Now all this while my brains were so stupified with that liquor which Human-Reason had made me drink, that I was not sensible I had been asleep, but was as one in a dream, and my fancy was possessed with an imagination, that I had been as far as any pilgrims could go, but could find no such place as the heavenly Jerusalem; and therefore I believed there was none, and so I told them. But, however, they would not hearken unto my foolish words, but went forward on their journey, and I kept on my course backward, until I came to the town of Vanity, where I took up my lodging for a great while; till once upon a time, being at one of the public shows in the fair, I was struck with a thunder-bolt from heaven, which had almost cost me my life; for I was forced to keep my chamber a whole year upon it. Now, in this time of my confinement I began to think of my former life, and the miserable condition I was in, if it should please God to take me

away. This made me weep day and night by myself. I fasted also, and prayed, and humbled myself before the Lord in secret; and I vowed a vow unto God, that, if it would please him to restore me to health again, I would undertake a pilgrimage to Mount Zion on the first opportunity that I could meet with to have company. So God heard my prayer, my vows, and my tears, and restored me again in a little time, and I walked abroad, and soon left that town; and remembering that I had an acquaintance or two in the cave of Reformation, men of sober dispositions and religious lives, I resolved to go to see them, if perhaps I might prevail upon them to go along with me. So I went accordingly to the aforesaid cave, and found my two friends there, whom I often broke my mind to about this matter; but they put me off till we could get more company, telling me that it would not be long before some pilgrims would come by; which made me long for the happy hour when I might hear of any travellers that were going that way. In the meantime, while I abode in the cave, and conversed with a great many men there, and, among the rest, I prevailed on Zealous-Mind and Yielding to go along with us; for my friends' names were Seek-Truth and Weary-o'-the-World, whom we have in our company now. So when Tender-Conscience came by, and was looking on the pillar of History, Seek-Truth happened to see him, and, knowing by his habit that he was a pilgrim, he presently struck a bargain with him to bear him company, and called the rest of us out of the cave; a little way off from which we overtook Spiritual-Man, and so we all joined company, and came along together, not one of us but Yielding being lost. He must needs have followed the seducer in the town of Vanity, and so taken surfeit with excess of wine, which killed him.

Now I saw in my dream that the pilgrims by this time were got over the Enchanted Ground, and entered into the country of Beulah, whose air was sweetened with all manner of aromatic perfumes, which revived their drooping spirits, grown heavy and almost stupified with walking over the Enchanted Ground. Here were trees growing whose fruits never fade away, and whose leaves are always green. In this place there is a perpetual spring, the birds always singing, the meadows adorned with flowers, and all things abounding that are delightful; for it lies within sight of Paradise, and the shadow of the celestial city reaches to it. Here they walked, and comforted themselves with the pleasures which this goodly land afforded, reflecting back upon the toils and hardships they had undergone; they solaced themselves with the thoughts that now they were near their journey's end, and within plain view of the celestial Jerusalem, which they had so long and so fervently desired to see. The farther they walked, the plainer might the glory of that place be seen, and the more earnestly did they long to come to it. So they spurred one another forward with comfortable words, saying, "Come let us go up to the house of the Lord; our feet shall be standing in thy courts, O Jerusalem." In the sight of angels we will sing unto thee, O Lord, and will adore in thy holy temple.

And as they passed along, they came to certain vineyards which belonged to the King; and the keepers invited them in, saying, "Come in, ye blessed of the Lord, and taste ye the wine that rejoices the heart of God and man." So the pilgrims went into the vineyards, and drank of the wine thereof, which inebriated them with love and joy, with desire and hope, to see the King's face, of whom the keepers of the vineyards told them many glorious things, saying that he was the fairest among ten thousand, therefore the virgins loved him, and ran after the odour of his ointments. They said also, that he was a lover of pilgrims, and that he himself took upon him once to be a pilgrim. Many more good commendations they gave of him, which made these men impatient till they got to the city : so they left the vineyards, and went forward, and run, as it were, for their lives. Thus they continued running till they came in sight of the gate; but in a kind of a bottom they were stopped by a river, which was very deep, and had no bridge to go over it.

Moreover I saw in my dream that there sat a multitude of men, women, and children, and all nations, tribes and languages, on the banks of the river, and many were in the river. So when the pilgrims came down to the river-side, they sat down likewise on the bank of the river, and began to question one another how they should get over; also they asked of some that were sitting there before them, whether there was any other way to go into the city? and they answered them, No. Then they were greatly perplexed in mind to think how they should get over this river. But Weary-o'-the-World said unto his companions, Be not discouraged because of the river, for I will venture in first, and according as it fares with me you may act. If I get over in safety, then ye may securely follow; but if I sink and perish in these deep waters, then you have your choice before you; do what seems good in your own eyes. So he boldly rushed into the river, plunging himself over head and ears in a moment, and they never saw him rise again, which did greatly dishearten the rest of the pilgrims, and they knew not what to do, or which way to turn themselves. Whilst they were thus disconsolate and melancholy, there came flying to them a man in bright clothing, who said unto them, Peace be unto you; let not your hearts be troubled because of the man who just now entered the river, and presently sunk out of your sight. His name is Weary-o'-the-World, and his circumstances answer his name; for he has a long time lain under great discontent, because the affairs of this life went not smoothly on his side. He has met with a great many crosses and losses, vexations and troubles in the world. He has been crossed in body, soul, and estate ; in wife, children, and friends. Now all these together made him weary of the world, and resolved to go out of it. But he suffered none of those things for righteousness' sake, or for the name of Christ, but for his own ambition, covetousness, and envy, which made him odious to all people that knew him; nay, he thereby put himself out of the protection of Providence, so that nothing thrived that he took in hand. His corn was blasted in the field, his barns were burned down to the ground, when they were filled with the fruits of a plentiful harvest; his body was afflicted with many diseases, which was occasioned by his lusts ; his wife and children cursed him to his face, because of his tyranny and cruelty ; his friends and neighbours mocked and derided at his calamities, and all things went against him. So in a pet he took up a resolution to leave the world; but he did it not for the love of God, which was the reason why you saw him sink in the waters of this river and rise no more. It is not enough to be weary of the world, but to be weary of sin is that which is acceptable in the sight of God and of great price. Besides, he ought not presumptuously to have rushed into the river himself without orders, but should have waited till the King's pleasure was manifested to him, as you see many sitting along the river-side, and waiting for the King's command. And now I am sent with a message to Tender-Conscience, to tell him it is the King's pleasure he should come over next. So Tender-Conscience prepared himself to obey the King's summons; but his heart panted, and all his limbs trembled to think what was become of Weary-o'-the-World, and for fear he should sink likewise. Whom when Spiritual-Man saw in this agony he comforted him, bidding him be of good cheer, saying, You are not the first, neither will you be the last, that must pass through this river ; all that have been before you since Adam have been forced to go through this river, except Enoch and Elijah, and so must all that come after you. Death is a debt we all owe to God and nature, and it must be paid one time or other, earlier or later. There is an appointed time for all men once to die, and after death to come to judgment; therefore be not afraid of that which cannot be avoided.

Tender-Con. I am not so much afraid of death, as of what will come after. I fear I shall never see the city of God, the heavenly Jerusalem, whose glittering walls and turrets ravished my eyes when we passed through the land of Beulah; I fear I am going down into a land of darkness, where my feet will stumble on the dark mountains, a land without light or order, where there dwells nothing but sempiternal horror and confusion. This is that which makes my heart-strings ready to break, and my knees to smite one against another. Oh, that some one would hide me till the fury of his anger be overpast! Oh, that he would protect me in the secrets of his tabernacle, and shelter me under the shadow of his wings! For "yet a little while, and the eye that seeth me shall see me no more." And with that word he entered the river, and finding the waters shallow at first, he was comforted; but as he waded along, they rose up even to his mouth and nostrils, so that he could hardly fetch his breath; then he cried aloud, saying, "Save me, O God, for the waters are come into my soul: I sink in deep mire, where there is no standing; I am come into deep waters, where the floods overflow me. Make haste to deliver me, O God! make haste to help me, O Lord! My flesh and my heart faileth, but God is the strength of my heart and portion for ever." Thus cried he, and still waded on till he came to the middle of the river, where he could find no bottom; so that his head was covered with water, and he had sunk away, had not the shining one that invited him come flying to his assistance, and, catching him by the hair of the head, held his head above water, till he came over towards the opposite bank, where it grew shallower, and he began to walk with ease, till he got clear of the river; and when he stood upon the bank on the other side, he leaped for joy, finding himself so marvellously light and active that he thought he could fly; for the garments which he wore all the way were very heavy, and they fell off from him in the river, so that now he was as light as a bird.

Now I saw in my dream, that the shining one had no sooner set him on the shallow side of the river, but he went to the other side, and bid Spiritual-Man, Zealous-Mind, Seek-Truth, and Convert, follow him into the river, which they did, whilst the shining one flew over their heads to the other side, where Tender-Conscience stood encompassed by five or six men in bright clothing. So the four men waded through the river with different circumstances; for Spiritual-Man having been in deep waters before, though not altogether so deep as these, had got some skill in swimming and keeping his head above water; but poor Convert and Seek-Truth were at a great loss when they came toward the middle of the river, where the waters were at the deepest, so that they cried out for help unto him that is able to save, and their prayer was heard, and a hand was reached forth which buoyed them up till they came to the shallow ground. So they walked through the rest of the river with ease, and came to their brethren on the other side. But as for Zealous-Mind, he thought to get over safer than any of them, and therefore privately he had gathered a bundle of reeds, which grew by the river-side, and he rested himself on them; but when he came to the middle of the river, the violence of the current carried away his reeds, and he sunk to the bottom, and never was seen more.

So in my dream I asked one that stood by me what was the reason, that he who appeared so forward all along in his journey should now sink at last? and he answered me, It is not enough to be zealous and forward, but to be humble and charitable also is requisite. This man was of a fiery temper, and a zeal indeed, but it was a disorderly zeal, not tempered with charity and prudence; likewise he trusted in his own strength, as you saw by his leaning on the bundle of reeds; now this was his pride, for had he called on God for help, peradventure he might have been saved.

So I saw in my dream that the four men, even Tender-Conscience, Spiritual-Man, Seek-Truth, and Convert, welcomed each other to that side of the river, and the shining ones welcomed them likewise; and there came a bright cloud and covered them all, and they were carried up in the cloud, through untracked paths of air; and as they went up, the men in bright clothing told them, that they had watched over them all the way of their pilgrimage, and had observed all their actions, which were written down in a book; and that they had saved them from many dangers, though unseen by them. Thus the cloud was carried through the boundless orb above; and as they went through the skies, they saw the glorious stars shining like suns in the firmament. At length, when they came near to the heaven of heavens, a troop of holy ones came out of the city to meet them. Now the foundation of the city was laid on the top of the eternal hills, and all round about it were fields of endless light, wherein the saints and angels walked. Then they came to the place where the Ancient-of-days was sitting, whose garments were as white as snow, and the hair of his head like the pure wool; his throne was like the fiery flame, and his wheels as burning fire; a fiery stream issued and came out from before him; thousand thousands ministered unto him, and ten thousand times ten thousand stood before him. Then they came to the gate of the city, and the pilgrims were bid to call there; which they did accordingly, and one looked over the gate, to whom the men in bright clothing said, These men are come from the valley of Destruction, these men have gone through great tribulation for the love they bear to the king; and they spoke to the pilgrims to give in their certificates, which they did; and the certificates were presented to the King, who gave orders that the gates should be opened to the pilgrims; so they entered in; and just at the entrance, one met them and said unto them, "Come in, ye blessed of my Father, inherit the kingdom prepared for you from the foundation of the world; enter ye into the joy of your Lord." Then a multitude of the heavenly hosts, with harps in their hands, met them, and sang a song which no man understood but themselves, and such as are thought worthy to be admitted into that blessed place. So I awoke, and behold it was a dream.

APPENDIX.

BOOKS OF PILGRIMAGES.

Of the numerous works which existed on pilgrimages, both real and spiritual, scarcely any religious writer from the fourteenth to the seventeenth century could fail to take advantage. In some cases these books furnished the preacher or author with occasional metaphors, or other incidental illustrations; in others, they suggested the composition of poems, or histories on a similar design. There might not be the least approach to plagiarism in either instance; but the air was full of reports about pilgrims and pilgrimages, and a writer of imaginative powers could hardly escape being affected by the common passion for such inventions.

Literary curiosity may properly be directed to the earliest of the works thus produced. But something more than this will be served by acquaintance with the writings which are marked by intrinsic excellence.

There was printed at Antwerp, in 1572, a little volume entitled—

"LE VOYAGE DU CHEVALIER ERRANT."

Its author, Jean de Cartheny, was a Carmelite monk, who lived in the early part of the fourteenth century, and must have been a man of great good sense, piety, and large experience. The work was translated into English by a merchant of Southampton, and dedicated to Sir Francis Drake. It appeared in 1607, printed in a small cheap form, so that it, no doubt, became known to most people who had any taste for religious reading.

The Wandering Knight is a young man who had long submitted himself to the tyrannous rule of Folly. In the first part of the narrative he gives an account of his various sins, and multiplied wretchedness, while thus governed. The second part thus begins:—

" *God's-Grace draweth the Knight out of the filth of sin, wherein he stuck fast.*

"I have declared in the first part of my voyage how, being governed by Folly in contemning virtue and following voluptuousness, I entered into the Palace of False Felicity, there resting myself for a certain season, and transgressing all the commandments of God, in leading a dissolute and worldly life, thinking that by living so I might be happy: whereas, indeed, I was unhappy. And why? Because that, instead of felicity, I found vanity. For, as I thought to recreate myself in hunting, I saw the Palace of Voluptuousness sink and come to utter confusion, and myself also plunged into the pit of sin, even up to the saddle. It is an easy matter for a man of himself to fall into hell, but it is impossible for him to get out again, unless by the help of God's grace. I term him to be in hell who lives in continual wickedness, committing sin with delight."

Warned by some terror of conscience, and the stings of adversity, the Wandering Knight makes his moan to God, and is heard:—

"As I was thus praying with a willing mind, shedding tears, striking my breast, conceiving grief and sorrow for my sins, suddenly I saw a lady descending down from heaven, setting herself before me fast by the bog, where I stuck fast. This lady was of a marvellous majesty, and wonderful courteous. She appeared to me in a garment of white satin; a cloak of blue damask, embroidered with gold and pearls. Her face shined like the sun, so that, with much ado, I did behold her. I was much amazed at so sudden a vision, and knew not at the first what she was. Yet I took heart at grace, supposing some help sent me from heaven, to draw me out of the bog where I lay. In the end, with all reverence, I made my petition unto her, saying, O good and gracious lady, whatsoever thou be, I most humbly beseech thee, if thou canst, that it would please thee to help me out of this beastly bog of filthy infection. For nothing is near me but venomous serpents and noisome vermin. In the name of God, therefore, I crave thy help. To the which, my request, she answered, O fool and abused beast, thou seest now what reward Voluptuousness yieldeth thee for following her. If thou hadst believed my daughter, thou hadst not been in this misery.

"Then I asked her who was that daughter of hers. She answered, saying, The sweet gentlewoman which admonished thee eleven days past to leave Voluptuousness and to follow her. Whom, because thou believedst not, but neglectedst her counsel, thou liest in this unhappiness. By this speech I knew she was God's-Grace, and the mother of Virtue. Then fell I on my knees, and weeping, thus I said, O dear lady, my cursed counsellor, Folly, drew me from thy daughter, and I—most unhappy wretch—believed her. Which deed of mine grieves me greatly, and now I cry thee mercy, most humbly desiring thee of thy clemency to deliver me out of this filthy infection, and I promise and vow henceforth to follow thee. For although I deserve damnation for my misdeeds, yet thou, being by nature merciful, wilt spare me.

"God's-Grace hearing thus my lamentation, of her dignity, stretched forth a golden rod, and commanded me to lay my hands upon it, which, when I did, I rose from my saddle, and so was set off the bog, where I left Temerity, my horse, and Folly, my governess, to fish for frogs."

Thus delivered, and having given humble thanks for the aid afforded him, the Wandering Knight readily obeys the commands of God's-Grace to follow her, " For, doubtless, our free-will guideth not God's-Grace, but God's-Grace guideth our free-will."

"Then I followed her, all bedaggled, until we came where I had seen the Palace of Worldly-Felicity, in greatest glory, turned into a dungeon of darkness, boiling with consuming fire, from whence came a wild vapour and stinking smoke of burning brimstone, over the which we must pass by a little long plank, whereat I was so afraid that the hair of my head stood an end. Then, with sorrowful sighs, I besought God's-Grace to tell me what was the sight which we saw. Quoth she, This is the place of thy Voluptuous Palace, with all thy allies, amongst whom thou wast maintained. Mark well : if I had not been thy help, and showed thee mercy, thou hadst been plagued with them. Think with thyself if the place be pleasant or no. Thou seest how the devil handleth those that be here with torments. This is the great King Lucifer, whom thou supposedst to have seen accompanied with so many nobles and peers, in the Palace of Counterfeit-Felicity. These be they that fry in the furnace : here is the reward of such as serve him."

Having allowed the Knight to contemplate for a time the terrible agonies of his former companions, God's-Grace told him that they must pass over the plank, narrow and long as it was :—

"Then I, though I was afraid, followed her, she going before me for my safety. But I had not gone three steps before I saw Cerberus, the dog of hell, with his three heads, yelping and gaping to devour me. At which sight, all amazed, my feet slipped, and straight he had me by the heels to tear me. Then I cried to God's-Grace for help, who, looking back, espied me in danger, and hearing me cry, Succour, succour, she took me up, and in a moment delivered me out of the dungeon. Then I remembered what David said, When I said my feet slipped, thy mercy, O Lord, did help me up. Now when God's-Grace carried me in her arms, I feared my filthiness would hurt her

rich array. But I found it contrary. For her precious apparel was nothing spotted, and mine, being foul, became fair, which made me much to marvel. Then said God's-Grace, My son, like as the sun shineth into the dyer's dye-fat, and yet returneth forth unspotted, even so do I, without blotting myself, enter into thy sinful soul, and in a moment do make it clean.

"Then, over the monstrous mountains and ragged rocks, alway we walked, till we came to a cross way, where Virtue wished me to follow her, whose sayings when I called to mind, it made me weep bitterly for my sins and follies past. But when God's-Grace perceived me to be weary, and noyed with the smells that I found in the loathsome lake, for pity she took me in her arms, and at the last she showed me the School of Repentance whither I must go, before I could enter into True-Felicity."

The School of Repentance was built upon a high hill, surrounded by a moat, named Humility. On being received by Repentance, a lady in plain apparel, accompanied by two waiting-maids, Sorrow-for-Sin and Confession-of-Sin, the Knight was stripped of all his old garments, as, his hat of haughtiness, his girdle of intemperance, and coat of vain-glory. After this, Repentance pointed to a very narrow passage, the only way into her school. At first he hesitated to obey, but as he stood wondering at the narrow hole, he saw " an old serpent enter in, who for lack of room left his skin behind him, and presently returned all renewed and young." This sight encouraged him, but still he delayed, when God's-Grace entered the passage, saying, " I will draw thee in, for it is none but I that showeth sinners the way of repentance. With that she plucked me in, and forthwith I became an enemy to sin."

After having been carefully disciplined and instructed, especially by a venerable hermit named Good-Understanding, the gates of the palace, in which he had now dwelt some time, were opened to the Knight, and he found awaiting him an ivory chariot, having golden wheels, and two white winged horses.

"God's-Grace got up first, and with her hand helped me up. Then followed the good hermit Understanding, then Memory, Conscience, and Repentance ; but God's-Grace governed all, who, touching the horses with her rod, they mounted up over the mountains which are above the earth. So we passed through the region of the air, where inhabiteth all the wicked spirits which watch to annoy such as would mount up to heaven. And though I was greatly aghast hereat, yet my trust was in God's-Grace, under whose wings I hid myself. I trusted not in my Conscience, for all it was at peace, nor to Repentance, nor to Understanding, but to God's-Grace only, who safely shrouded me under her wings, as the hen doth her chickens, against the coming of the night. Then she commanded the wicked enemies to get them hence, and they forthwith fled away, crying aloud, Now have we lost our Knight: lo! he is mounted up to the Palace of Virtue in despite of us all. How is he escaped? quoth one. Under the wings of God's-Grace, quoth another, from whence all we cannot fetch him.

"Being past this brunt, I heartily thanked God's-Grace for her goodness, and on the sudden I saw upon the top of a mountain a goodly palace. Now, for that love engendereth familiarity, I asked God's-Grace what place it was, and she told me it was the Palace of Virtue. It was so high that it reached even to heaven, and about it were seven fair towers of alabaster. In the first dwelt Faith, in the second Hope, in the third Charity, in the fourth Wisdom, in the fifth Justice, in the sixth Fortitude, and in the seventh Temperance.

"In the first tower God's-Grace showed me Faith, which waited for our coming, near adjoining unto whom I might perceive the Palace of True-Felicity. With that I desired Lady Memory to put me in mind in the morning to go and see that gallant city. Whiles we were thus devising, our chariot arrived at the court, where Lady Virtue, with her daughters, Faith, Hope, Charity, Wisdom, Justice, Fortitude, and Temperance dwelt. At the first sight I knew it was the same Lady Virtue which aforetime had so well admonished me and I gave no ear unto her. Then reverently, upon my knees lamenting, I cried her mercy for contemning her counsel and following Voluptuousness. Wherewith she made me arise, and in token that she took in good part my recantation, she sweetly kissed me and bade me welcome. So, with great joy, accompanied by God's-Grace, true Understanding, quiet Conscience, and unfeigned Repentance, I entered into the Palace of Lady Virtue."

It is very difficult to suppose that Bunyan was not well acquainted with this excellent little book, or that it had no influence on his thoughts while engaged on his own work. The effect which it exercised on other minds may be readily traced in the production of an author who wrote contemporaneously with Bunyan. Bunyan and Patrick were unknown to each other, and had little communion in literary tastes; but to neither could such a book as that of the good Carmelite, Jean de Cartheny, be without interest or value.

NOTICE OF PATRICK'S PILGRIM.

"The Parable of the Pilgrim," by Symon Patrick, B.D. This valuable contribution to practical divinity was first published in 1668. It describes the pilgrimage of one who called himself Philotheus, but by others was called Theophilus, that is, a lover of God, or loved by God. He had grown weary of the country where he dwelt; nothing pleased, nothing soothed him. To escape the wretchedness which he thus felt, he visited many distant lands, traversed deserts, exposed himself to the stormiest seas: but he found no relief to his melancholy. At last, as if admonished by an angel, "he felt a thought stir in his soul, remembering him of a place called Jerusalem, which he had totally forgot in all his travels, and never so much as dreamed of directing his course unto."

From henceforth his mind became wholly occupied with the idea of this sacred city. Many were the difficulties and obstacles which seemed to oppose his wish to reach it. But even his worst anxieties had a measure of hope in them. He resolved to encounter every kind of danger, and bear any burden, rather than not accomplish his purpose. Little was the encouragement to be looked for from friends and neighbours, or from outward circumstances. "That which makes the story of this person the more remarkable is, that it was toward the latter end of the year, and in the decay of all things, when these good thoughts began to spring up in his soul. When the earth had removed itself a great way from the sun; when all the gallantry of the fields had resigned its place to ice and snow; when charity grew cold, and Christian virtue seemed to be gone back to its root; when the ways were untrod, and few or no travellers upon the road, then did these zealous desires begin to bud in the heart of this honest countryman."

A fresh stimulant was given to his desire of immediately setting out on his pilgrimage. Jerusalem, he learnt, was, by interpretation, the vision of peace. How often had he yearned, amid the various scenes of his worldly life, for this vision of peace: how vain had been his efforts to win, either by toil or pleasure, the happiness which it signified.

More than ever resolved upon his journey, he began to inquire respecting the road, and the means of travelling. Deep was the perplexity which attended this inquiry. One set of people told him one thing; another, another. The chiefs of the different parties whom he thus consulted were very determined in their opinions, "and spake of the affairs of heaven as if they were counsellors of state in that kingdom;" opening "the secrets of Jesus Christ as if they were his confidants."

Distressed beyond measure at the conflicting sentiments with which he was thus assailed, he was almost on the point of despair, when a strange, venerable old man offered to lead him to a guide on whom he might safely depend for the information needed. The proposal was very gladly accepted, and the pilgrim hastened to the house of his new teacher, whom he found at home, and without " one creature in his company." A few words sufficed to explain the object of the visit. The guide viewed the inquirer with attention, and, discovering in his countenance signs of humility and earnestness, began to discourse with him on the subject of Jerusalem: " I must needs grant," he said, " that I am furnished with some knowledge of the way to that city; yet perhaps I may spare my pains of giving you any directions in it, because there is some reason to think you will not be at the pains to follow them. For if you will give any credit to my words, I must let you know that the way is both long and, also, full of many and great difficulties; and that there are many ways also which will seem to you to lead straight to it, and which many men will point you unto as the next road, which, if you should take, will lead you into great danger, and not only carry you a great deal about, but perchance conduct you to the quite contrary place, and end in your utter undoing. I would wish you, therefore, to consider awhile, whether it be an advisable thing to undertake such a journey, wherein there are so many hardships, and so many cross-paths. A journey which is so tedious also, and wherein I cannot promise you security from frights, thieves, beatings, and such ill usages as have made many men possessed with such intentions as you seem now to have, quite to lay aside all thoughts of it, and to sit down contented at their own homes. And after all this, I know not whether you will yield your belief to all that I shall tell you of the way; if you have heard some of the reports which are spread of me, and have received any prejudice at all against me, which I am sure will be increased by some of the precepts that I must give you." .

There was a sternness in this language which might have turned a less honest inquirer than the pilgrim from his purpose. But he listened with a reverent spirit, and was comforted by the feeling that he had, at length, found a wise and prudent counsellor. After remaining sufficiently long at his house to be fully instructed in the knowledge which he sought, he set forth on his pilgrimage, taking with him, as his companions, Humility and Charity. The guide further instructs him in the mystery of salvation; and he exclaims, in the fulness of his gratitude, " I feel already that I am nought; and I have nought, and desire nought, but Jesus and Jerusalem."

A description of Jerusalem is then given :—

" It is advanced far above the highest part of this heavy earth and foggy air; where the sun never withdraws his rays, and where there is not the least shadow of mist or vapour, either to obscure its light or to offend the most delicate sense. There are nothing but pure and fragrant odours which perfume that happy climate; perpetual calm and quiet reign in that noble region, and there is no noise but that which infinitely delights and charms the soul into still and quiet meditations. Here all the world presents itself before one's eyes; and makes them the centre in which the beauty and glory of it conspires to meet." Then it is added, " It will be infinitely contenting to see the beauty and fair proportions of every part of this vast frame; the fitness, usefulness, and correspondence of it to all the rest of its neighbouring parts, together with the exact and admirable order of the whole. And can you imagine into what transports it will cast your soul to hear the praises of the Creator sung by all his works of wonder ? And yet that is another privilege of this blessed place, by the advantage of whose holy silence you will receive the cheerful hymns, wherewith every creature you behold, doth celebrate the wisdom, power, and goodness of Him that made it."

Thus glorious is Jerusalem itself; " But the place is nothing so considerable as the persons that inhabit it. Enquire not, therefore, of the vastness of this place, the stateliness of its buildings, the riches of their furniture, and such like things; but know that it is the city of the Great King, the seat of the Imperial Majesty of heaven and earth, the place where the Lord and Governor of the whole world, whose dominion is an everlasting dominion, keeps his court. . . . . It will strangely transport you to see the beauty of his holiness, the splendour and brightness of his understanding, the largeness of his love; his uncorrupted justice, his unexhausted goodness, his immoveable truth, his uncontrollable power, his vast dominions, which yet he fills with his presence, and administers their affairs with ease, and is magnified and praised in them by the throng of all his creatures."

Then follows an account of the King's Son, mightiest of conquerors, but at the same time so tender and loving that " he hath rendered himself redoubtable to his greatest enemies by nothing more than this, that he hath won so many hearts, and triumphed over so many brave souls, who were vanquished by nothing else but the power of his mighty love. . . . . . For you must know that he is such a lord of love, that the hatred and malignity of men could not extinguish the fervours of his passion. All the discourtesies they could do him, were not able to prevail with him to lay aside his thoughts of kindness toward them. The innumerable affronts which he received could not make him go back to heaven, and forsake this ill-natured world, till he had expressed all the love conceived unto it. And, therefore, I cannot but think you would have a mind to take a journey to Jerusalem, and judge your pains and travel well bestowed, if it were for nothing else but to see this illustrious person; especially to behold him in all his glory, and his highest exaltation, who is the patron of all good souls, the great protector of all pilgrims; the guide, and rest too, of all noble travellers; and who bears a particular affection to yourself, who hath suffered so much for you; and who hath sent you so many messages of his love; who hath endeared himself to you by a thousand favours, and was never contented till he brought you to himself, that you might be there where he is, and behold the glory which his Father hath given him."

This account is followed by some reflections, eminently profitable in practical application. It is too commonly the habit of devout minds to represent heaven as ministering only to the thirst for contemplation. This will, doubtless, be one of the purest sources and means of joy hereafter, but it will be only one among many; and hence it is wisely observed by the instructor of the pilgrim: "You are not to suppose that the pleasure of Jerusalem is to sit whole ages, and merely gaze upon the Divinity; or that they who enjoy the repose of that happy place do nothing else but feed their eyes with the beauties of the Saviour's face. . . . . . They do not spend their time only in looking upon God, but they receive him into their hearts, and he enters into their souls. He doth not merely gild them with his beams, but they themselves become light in the Lord. They are so ravished with his goodness, that they are made good. They are so affected with his wisdom that they become wise."

After receiving various other lessons and counsels, the pilgrim, at length, sets forth on his journey.

"A fine sunshine morning it was when he first went out of his doors; the air was perfumed with the sweet odours which the sun exhaled from the flowers, the birds whistled and sung their hymns to him that made that glorious light; and there was no hedge that he passed by, but it welcomed him with some new songs and pleasures, nor any traveller he met but wished him good speed. He was so much pleased in everything that he saw and heard, in all the works of God, in his word which he bare in his mind, in the smoothness of the way, in the remembrance of the father he left, in the assurance he had of his prayers, and such like things, that he never thought himself at home, till now that he had no home at all, but was seeking one. He could do nothing but compose praises to God; nothing but laud the name of Jesus that had brought him into so happy a condition; and by his good will he would have made this the business of all the day—to sing a certain ditty, the beginning and the end of which, I remember, was nothing but this, 'Bless the Lord, O my soul.' Whether it was the novelty of those objects that presented themselves, or the greatness and beauty of them, or the good society he met withal, or an immediate touch from that Spirit which the good man prayed might be his companion, or all these, or

any other thing, that made him so merry, I had not leisure to examine; but he was never known in all his life to have expressed so much contentment in any condition, as in this pilgrimage wherein he was engaged to Jerusalem.

"Yet he had not passed many weeks in these rapturous joys (for they were little less) before he found them so much abated, that he thought himself less happy than he imagined. The ways were grown a little more rugged, the heaven began to be overcast, and the country through which he went was more barren, and yielded not those fruits which he had before tasted; which together with other things cast him into a damp, and procured to his soul more sadness than he used to be acquainted withal. At the first indeed he was only moved to some wonderment to find such an alteration, and thought that in half a day's travel, or such a space, he should recover more pleasant paths. But when he found, contrary to his expectation, that they still continued uneasy, and likewise chanced to see some of his old companions, who called to him at some distance, and persuaded him to go back again, he was much affrighted, and began to feel wild imaginations roving about his soul, and strange desires of quitting a course which was like to prove so ungrateful to that part of him which was most concerned in the things of this world. For it was represented to his thoughts, that the ensuing part of the road was very dangerous, beset with thieves and many difficulties, tedious, and of a strange length; and, besides that he might be in a wrong way, it was very doubtful whether there was such a place or no as he fancied, seeing nobody had been there. From all which, and many other considerations they told him it was most advisable, if he consulted his own peace, to return with them to his former habitation, and his ancient neighbours: who were all very sorry to hear that he had quit his present possessions, in they knew not what hopes of getting better at a place, which neither he nor any of his friends had seen.

"But though this push, by the unexpectedness of it, made him reel and stagger a little, yet he soon recollected himself; and calling to mind what he had been taught, and repeating that charm, as I may call it, which he always had about him, 'I am nought, I have nought,' &c., he found himself as firm in his resolution as if he had not been at all assaulted. Shall I forsake my Lord (said he to himself) so soon as ever I have begun his service? Is it handsome for me to recoil, merely from the noise and report of dangers? What a coward shall I for ever hold myself, if I run away before my enemies be in view, upon a rumour of their strength and power? I will march up towards them, and at least look them in the face. I will not trust this fame, which all the world hath branded for a liar; since common observation also tells us, that the lion is not so terrible as he is painted. Much more he spake to this effect, which moved him to a kind of indignation against himself, that he should so much as shrink back thus early, before sufficient trial, and upon such slight information.

" And yet it was not all to his disadvantage that he had felt this shock, but it rather had many happy effects upon him—like a fit or two of an ague, which is thought rather wholesome than to deserve the name of a disease. For as it gave him more understanding in the nature of his way (of the smoothness of which, notwithstanding all that had been said, he too much presumed), and made him watchful because he saw he could not pass without some enemies, so it gave him some degree of courage, because he perceived they might be overcome, and confirmed his belief of the wisdom of his director, who foretold these troubles; and gave a proof withal of the efficacy of that remedy which he had prescribed, and, above all, revived that joy and gladness in his heart which he thought began to languish and faint away. Full of joy he was, even to an excess, and he suffered by it a kind of transportation; partly from the brightness of the truths he had received, which yet were fresh in his mind, partly from the increase of his understanding by the experiment which he had made; but chiefly I think from the victory which he had obtained over those enemies that attacked his soul. For in truth there is no greater triumph than that which the soul feels when it comes off a conqueror, and applauds itself for the valour and courage which it hath expressed in its conflicts. There was another thing indeed which added something, though not much to his joy, viz., that his enemies he hoped had received such a foil, that he had sent them away discouraged, if not disabled, from making any further attempts upon him.

" But so mutable is our condition here, and so many are our enemies, that he had not travelled many days after this triumph, before he was arrested with a new trouble to exercise his wisdom and patience. His soul, which just now was ready to leap out of his body, he felt to sink so low, that it was as if he had no soul at all. His spirits not only began to flag and hang down their heads, but were grown quite faint and weary, as if they meant to swoon away—which was partly occasioned by his going too fast, and taking over-long journeys; and partly by a very hot day, when the sun beat very strongly upon his head; and partly by the very violence of his joys, which stirred his spirits so much, that in the agitation they flew away; and partly by letting slip two or three of those instructions which had been left with him, which should have been a cordial to him, but were as impossible, he found, to be by any means recalled, as it was to bring back his tired spirits which were flown from him. Very melancholy and sad he now began to be, and the more because he had been so joyful. Oh how desolate, said he within himself, is this place into which I have fallen! I am forsaken sure of God, or else I that

was so high yesterday, should never have sunk into this pit, which is next door to the dwelling of damned spirits. Was ever any man in such a deplorable estate? Was there ever any bereaved thus of all his comforts which should sweeten his way when he had no other company? Oh! who will restore unto me the days that are past? Who can call back but the joys of yesterday into my bosom? What are those sins that have cast me into the displeasure of my Lord? Or, what shall I do to regain his favour, which I would purchase at any rate, though I died the next moment? Thus he lay many days, sometimes bewailing his former affrightment, which he suspected might deserve this desertion (as he was apt to call it); sometimes complaining that he could not find the cause, and so could not be cured; sometimes reflecting on the times of joy which were gone; and sometimes taking a view of his misery, which made him but the more deeply miserable. And, which was worst of all, he kept his bed all this time, and stirred not a foot in his journey; being indeed so ill, that he despaired of life.

" But see how the providence of God watches for an opportune season to do us a kindness. When he was in the greatest torture that he had felt all the time of this agony, there came an unexpected letter to his hands from his beloved father, which was to this effect:—

" ' My friend (for so I cannot but call you, since you express such love to me),—These are to let you know, that though I am absent from you, yet I follow you with my thoughts and good wishes, which attend you in all your motions. I am so far from being forgetful of my promise, that I am much better, I assure you, than my word. You desire me to pray for you, and so I do. But I cannot content myself with that, unless you, as well as God, know that I have a remembrance of you. That is the very reason of my sending this paper after you; that it may be a token how regardful I am of your concerns, and solicitous about your welfare. So solicitous, that having enjoyed some good thoughts this morning, I could not but impart them unto you, because I fancied they would prove upon some occasion or other very useful to you. They are a meditation upon one of the Psalms of David, where he bids his soul not to be disquieted, but to hope in God, as the help of his countenance and his God: and they are enfolded in a distinct paper, within the bosom of this letter, because they were too long to be inserted in the body of it.—Farewell.'

"Upon the very first receipt of this letter, before he had broke it up, his pale cheeks began to be streaked with a little blood, as a prognostic of his recovery to health again. But when he opened it, and read the kind expressions of the love of his friend, one might see how the spirits crept up as he went along, out of the centre whither they were retired: insomuch that the light danced in his eyes, yea, leaped out, as if it meant to kiss those lines which now saluted them. But then, as soon as he arrived at the meditation itself, and had carefully perused all the parts of it, his face shined like an angel, and one would have thought he had not been the man that was so lately dejected. For it was so pat to his present condition, and so exactly suited to the necessities under which he laboured, that it seemed as if it had been indited by God, and not by his friend. There he found a discourse of the nature of the joy, of the causes of its decay, of the interest that our animal spirits have in it, of the way to recover it, and the means to be content without it; and above all, of the resignation of ourselves to the will of God, to serve him cheerfully without those sensible pleasures, as well as in their company. And not to name other things which were more fully debated between them afterward, these now rehearsed were so fully opened that he was partly amazed, and partly elevated to the height of his joys again, when he thought that God had put it into the heart of the father to send at this time a letter of such comfortable import unto him. I see, said the pilgrim, that not my friend only, but Jesus also is mindful of me. I see both that He prays for me, and that heaven likewise hears those prayers. It would be an insufferable wrong to my Blessed Saviour, should I hereafter think my soul forsaken of him. Nay, it will be an ill requital of the favour he hath now done me, should I not resume my ancient joyfulness again. And, therefore, be no longer disquieted, oh my soul, be not cast down within me. It is not in vain to hope in God, but in that very hope thou mayest be joyful; and, therefore, in the fruition of thy expectations, Oh how greatly oughtest thou to rejoice! 'Light is sown for the righteous, and joy for the upright in heart.' 'They that know thy name will put their trust in thee, for thou, Lord, hast not forsaken them that seek thee.' And, therefore, I cannot but say, 'Wait on the Lord; be of courage, and he shall strengthen thy heart: wait, I say, on the Lord.' 'I will sing unto the Lord, because he hath dealt bountifully with me. Yea, I will hope continually, and will yet praise him more and more.'

" Many other the like effusions of his heart, one might then have heard, and they lasted so many days, that they became instrumental to the redeeming much of that time which had been lost in fruitless complaints upon his bed. He did not go so fast as he was wont; but he went much further than before in the same number of hours. His joys were not so violent; but they became more sweet, and they grew more equal. He could not recover yet the memory of some things he had received; but this he better understood, that he must desire nought but Jesus. He was not so full of heat; but his light was more resplendent. He did not expect now to be always in the same temper; yet he was confident he should never more suspect the love of his Saviour. He perceived that he could not ever

retain the same joys; yet he learnt withal, that the way to have them sooner restored, was not to fret for want of them.

" But though in this condition he made a great progress in his way towards the Holy City of God; yet the light which was in his mind, did not cast such a splendour about his soul but that one day he suffered some obscurity. The occasion of it was a cloudy thought which came over his understanding, suggesting to him, 'That he did not serve God purely enough, because his eye was too much upon Jerusalem.' For it had been commonly received for a truth among some persons whom he had formerly conversed withal, that we must obey God out of mere love to him, without any hope of rewards at all. This, you will say, was a strange conceit, and it had as strange a cure. For it pleased God that he opening a book which he carried along with him, the next morning after these thoughts troubled him, the first thing that he cast his eye upon was this passage in a certain chapter of it, 'That Moses had respect to the recompense of reward.' You cannot think how much it surprised him that he should light upon these words rather than any other, without his choice, or so much as a design to receive satisfaction in this particular. And yet that which I am next to relate, was more wonderful in his eyes, and made him stand in a greater astonishment at the goodness of God towards him. For it being suggested to him from the memory of some fragments of certain sermons which he once heard, 'That Moses, and those under the law who were but bondmen, might have respect to rewards; but that it did not become those who had the spirit of adoption to be so mercenary;' and he being a little perplexed with this trifling objection, it happened, that looking down upon the same page of his book again, his eye fell directly upon the second verse of the next chapter, which told him that 'Jesus endured the cross for the joy that was set before him.' The first glance which he had of this place was like a beam of the sun in his eye, which immediately dispelled all his darkness, and made his soul flash out in such expressions as these. Who are these men that are wiser than Jesus? What mean these dreamers to fancy themselves above that which was not below our Saviour? Or how came they to be so proud as to despise the promises of God, and think they stand in no need at all of them? On, my soul, go on, and be not stopped a minute longer by this scruple! Fix thine eyes upon Jerusalem, and let thine heart be ravished with it; for the Mediator of the second covenant, as well as of the first, had a respect unto it.

" After he had hit so luckily on these two passages which lay so near together, a great many more of the same kind presented themselves instantly to his mind; not much unlike the beams of the sun, which having once torn a cloud in sunder, break forth more and more, till the whole body of that great light appear to us. And this likewise raised his spirits unto some further degree of cheerfulness, when he thought how our Lord still provided for his relief, and took the pains to pull the smallest thorn that troubled him out of his feet. And yet this could not hinder but that they were too much dejected a little after by a company of other petty thoughts, which, like so many importune flies, were always buzzing this new fancy in his ears, 'That he did not directly intend the glory and honour of Jesus in all his actions.' He considered indeed with himself, that he endeavoured to do well, and that he loved to do so, and that he looked upon it as the very life of God; but yet he thought he did not so actually respect him in every particular motion as his duty required. Now here it fell out very happily, and not without a divine Providence, as he thought, that one night being in a dream, he imagined he saw one coming to him, and whisper this sentence in his ear, which of a long time he had not read, 'They repented not, to give him glory.' Whereupon, starting suddenly out of his sleep, as if some good genius had awakened him, and given him a new mind, he presently began to tell himself, that when he first repented, and undertook this new life, he gave glory to God; and that by every step he took in this course of repentance, (*i. e.* amending of himself,) he did actually honour him, and more materially than any other way glorify his name. For this is a constant acknowledgment of him; a minutely confession that we are fools, and he is wise; that our will is nought, and his is good; that he is our Lord, and we his subjects; and that after all our search, we find our happiness to lie in him alone; and in separation from him, the best condition in the world will leave us miserable. And he had not long pondered upon these things with much satisfaction before those words of the Psalmist came into his mind, 'He that offereth praise, glorifieth me; and to him that ordereth his conversation aright, will I show the salvation of God,' which made him fall into the praises of God, and to resolve that he would do so every day, and early design all the employments of it to his service; concluding, that whilst he held this course, and ordered his ways aright, he exalted God in the world; by lifting up his will into a preeminence and command over his own, and subjecting himself unto it both as most supreme, and also wise and good. And after a great many thoughts of this nature, at last he made a short reflection upon the person who had made him this visit in the night. And when he remembered that he fancied it was his friend who came to his bedside, he had a new pleasure to think of the benefits of sleep, the praises of which he could not upon this occasion forbear, though at certain times he wished his thoughts might never be intermitted by it. What a heavenly power, said he, is this! for so I am ready to call it. How much am I beholden to it for its silent refreshments! That which useth to part the dearest friends, hath now brought them together. That which separateth those who touch each other, hath made those near who are far

asunder. Oh divine gift! Oh beloved rest which God bestows upon us! How great are these charms which lock our doors to all the world, and now have opened them to my friend! How much better are these dreams than many of my waking thoughts! How much rather had I be in the arms of the brother of death, than in the feeble enjoyments of many parts of my life! I am content just now to be restored to his embraces, if my friend will but meet me there again in this manner. At least I hope I may conclude that when we are dead indeed, he will not fail to meet me, whose image finds me out when I am in the images of death."

This account of the pilgrim's state of mind may be wanting in the quiet pathos of Bunyan's style, but it is a truthful and valuable lesson in the great science of religious experience. Equally so is the following chapter.

"In such thoughts, or rather dreams, as these he spent a little portion of his time with great delight. And now having vanquished so many enemies and impediments in his way of divers sorts, he was willing to believe that he should be molested no more, but pass in perfect peace to the Vision of Peace. A great many days he remained in these pleasant expectations, and went a good way onwards to his resting-place, without the least weariness of any part about him. He seldom departed from meditation, but either with his mind illuminated with new light from heaven, or his will inflamed with a new ardour, or his whole heart steeped in new sweetness. And though sundry new enemies also attempted him, yet such a profound peace seemed to have taken possession of his heart, that they could not move the least disturbance there. The joys that he felt made him despise all baits of pleasure which lay in his way. The conquests which he had got made him think himself above the scorn and laughter of the world. And though he was sometimes bitterly reproached, yet he comforted himself with this, that they did but prepare him matter for new triumphs. But he could never be drawn to any other contests wherein the generality of men were then very zealously engaged: nor did he affect any victories among the disputers of the world. He lived in love and peaceableness with all his fellow-travellers. He thought himself so rich also in these graces, that it was no trouble to him to be poor. And he had such a sense from whence he received them, that they were no temptation neither to be proud. But yet for all this, it chanced that some exercises of devotion to which he had bound himself being one day omitted, either through indisposition or by reason of some lawful, if not necessary, occasions which diverted him, he was cast into such a pensiveness of mind as proved at last a great affliction to him, for he indulged to himself those thoughts, because they pleased him at first, but, by too frequent reflections, they grew to a melancholy mood, and from thence proceeded to a dull and listless temper of spirit. In this condition you must needs think his joys were again abated, which added very much to the trouble of his mind : and, indeed, they fell in time to so low an ebb, that he feared they would never rise again, but leave him at last quite dry, and without one drop of comfort. And so truly, in the issue of things, it proved ; for, as they forsook him, so he was tempted again to forsake his way, which was now become but irksome to him without those refreshments. The pleasure and relish that he was wont to feel in holy duties was quite gone. Instead of clearness there succeeded darkness ; dryness of spirit took the place of affection, and in the room of joy and gladness he was loaded with nothing but groans and heaviness. He often professed that he could feel nothing at all, but remained as a man that had lost the use of his soul. And therefore, though he continued for a while to pray and perform his duty in other things as well as he could, yet, finding that he was but like a man that drinks very much when the liquor hath no taste, and gives him no pleasure in the going down, he was tempted to throw it all away, and thought he had as good not do those things at all as do them with no delight. And accordingly he gave up himself wholly to be tortured by his own thoughts, which employed themselves in nothing else but making sad representations of the misery of this state, which you must needs think was so grievous that it was not possible to draw a picture of it. For since the soul is of far greater force than the body, the pains and anguish which arise in it must needs be far more pungent and afflictive than those which touch the outward man. He suffered a kind of martyrdom every day : or rather, he was continually crucified, and had nothing but gall and vinegar given him to drink. He thought he had reason when he complained of greater pains than the martyrs endured. For they being inwardly illuminated and touched from heaven found the highest comforts in their torments, the greatest liberty in their imprisonments, and in the midst of the flames the divinest ardours of love in their hearts, which, like a greater fire, put the other out. But he, poor soul, though always denying his own desires, breaking of his will in pieces, lying upon a rack, and fast nailed to the cross, where the body of sin was bleeding to death, yet found his spirit in horrid torments, and deprived of those divine delights which cheered the bright souls of the blessed martyrs, and made them shine with a greater lustre than did their fires. But since I cannot express the soreness of this agony in which he a long time lay, I shall only add that it was so great, that one day, being quite tired and spent, he fell into a kind of trance, and remained as immoveable for some space, as if he had been dead. And a blessed occasion this was, though all his acquaintance that were come to comfort him imagined he would then have expired, for he thought he saw a man coming to him with a very smiling aspect (as though he knew him), who bade him get up, and go as fast as he could to a certain oratory that was not far off, and in his way, where he should meet with some relief."

While engaged in fervent prayer, the pilgrim has the comfort to find himself again attended by the venerable man who had first instructed him respecting the journey to Jerusalem. They travel on together, meeting various characters, and encountering such dangers and obstacles to their progress, as might be expected on such a course. Like Bunyan's pilgrims, these too have their occasional controversial struggles with the strangers whom they meet. Thus they had just been listening to a wise and pleasant discourse on the Christian virtue of contentment, " when suddenly they heard the noise of a horse's heels behind them, which, causing them to turn their eyes back, a proper man, well mounted, presented himself to them, issuing out of another road upon the left hand, and falling then into that wherein they were. When he was come up, and had joined himself to them, he asked presently the common question, Whither travel you? They were not shy of making him a true answer, but told him that they were going to a place called Jerusalem. You are well overtaken then, replied he, for that is the design of my journey also, and I shall be very glad of your company. But I must tell you, that if you have still held this road, you are very much out of your way, or else all my knowledge fails me, for it lies a great deal more on this hand (pointing to the left), and here we must now turn again, and leave this wherein I find you, unless we mean to miss of our aim, and be led to some other place. Let me be your guide, if you please, for I am so well acquainted with the way, that it is impossible for me to mistake it. You may trust me, for I am confident, though I should shut mine eyes or go hoodwinked thither, I should not mislead you.

" He spoke very gracefully, and was witty in his conceits ; excellent company also by reason of his pleasant humour, and, withal, of a carriage very civil and inviting. But they observed that he had a sword by his side, and a pair of pistols before him, together with another instrument hanging at his belt, which was formed for pulling out of eyes. This they thought was none of a pilgrim's habit, and they viewed him so carefully, that they concluded he was one of that brood who, if they cannot persuade travellers into their way, will drive them into it, and then carry them blindfold for fear they should forsake it. Whereupon the father said to him, Sir, do not think me rude if I be so plain with you as to speak in the style of our usual proverb, and let you know that we had rather have your room than your company. We are strongly possessed against those who would make us believe we cannot see our way unless we let them pull out our eyes. Nor will you ever be able to invent so many good words as to reconcile us to them, who, when they find men in courses contrary to their own, are not content to labour by reason to bring them to their bent, but shoot them to death if they stiffly refuse, as if they were but rogues and thieves. And you will have a great deal to do to persuade us that you are not one of that number. We see what weapons you are provided of, and we shall never be convinced that they are innocent. We dread you more than the banditti and all the lawless men in the world. We had rather fall into the hands of Turks and barbarians than live under your tyranny, for though they strip us of our clothes and spoil our goods, yet they will leave us our senses and our reasons, of which you intend to bereave us. We may believe our eyes, and trust our feeling and our taste, in their country, but in yours they have lost their credit, and are deprived of their use in matters of the greatest concernment; and therefore I wonder you are so confident of the way wherein you would guide us, since your eyes do not always report things truly to you. You shall not see for us, since you acknowledge your sight so deficient. We can be sure of nothing if such as you be our informers. Perhaps there is no such person as Jesus whom we seek, or he is asleep in his grave, and we shall never see him at Jerusalem; for though there are that have told us they saw him, and handled him after he rose again, by what means will you assure us that it was not an illusion? Our hands and eyes may deceive us, you say, in other cases, and therefore what privilege had theirs from being cheated? But besides, as I was going to say at the first, if you are so certain of your way as you pretend, I beseech you, why do you not make it good by better arguments than those that are made of steel? Why cannot you illuminate us without casting us into the midst of a fire? who more likely to be wrong than they who are confident they are in the right, and cannot prove it? It is a great sign you intend to cozen us, because you will not let us examine your ware. Since you vend it in a dark shop, where nobody can see it, we hold it in great suspicion of being naught; but if we do not like it, why will you not suffer us to let it alone? Why must we be forced to buy, or else pay for our refusal with the price of our lives? Is this the way to make Christians, never to consider that they are men? Is this the mark of being filled with the Holy Ghost, to breathe forth nothing but threatenings and slaughters? Methinks you transform the heavenly dove into the shape of a vulture or a raven. We have heard of her sweet nature, of her sighs and mournings, but we are strangers to her fierceness, and know nothing of her croaking for a prey. To give her claws, and arm her with talons and a bloody beak, what is it but to turn her into a monster? I cannot conceive, saith one of your own neighbours, but more ingenious than the rest, that they should be the Christian pastors who become butchers of the flock: and that the Church,

which was for so many ages in great persecution, should now itself begin to persecute. Or if you reckon us for those creatures that are without the fold, then we are sure to be worried by you. Though the Church be never so loving a mother to you, yet she hath no kindness at all for strangers. You tell us, indeed, that she opens her arms to us, but we doubt that it is to press us to death. Nay, her breasts, we see, do feed you with blood, and not with milk. Her children are cruel and ravenous, and therefore what would you have us to judge of herself?

"The gentleman, who seemed all the time to be much troubled at this discourse, here interrupted it, and told him that he was too vehement; protesting that he had no design to do them any hurt. We are as innocent people, continued he, as any in all the world, and if you would let us travel together, I would bring you to more good company, who shall give you all the assurance imaginable of our harmless intentions. Do but tell what security you desire, and I will undertake it shall not be refused. I know them all so well, that I dare engage my soul for their fidelity to their word. Undertake nothing, I beseech you, replied the father, for other folks. If you had engaged that pawn only for yourself it might be taken, because you seem a gentleman, and a person of good nature: but as for the most of your company, they can never give me the assurance which I shall desire. There is but one security which I can confide in, and that is the same which the Lacedæmonian demanded of one who offered to seal him his faithful friendship; viz., 'That if they have any will to do us any mischief, they shall never have any power.' There is none but this that is worth a rush. The rest are also vain and infirm, that none but fools will trust unto them.

" He had no sooner said this, but before there could be any room for a reply, they were all accosted by another man, of a quite different shape and humour from this; more sad and melancholy, more rude, and of a heavier wit also, who crossed their way upon the right hand. He making a stop awhile, as they passed by him, and hearing them talk of Jerusalem, made no more ado but chopt into their company, and told them, that if they were going thither, they held a very unsafe course; and should wander in by-paths for ever, unless they went along with him, in the way that he would show them. To be short, he pressed them so earnestly, with so loud a voice, and so much heat, that the sweat dropped down from his face. He did little less than thunder among them, and threatened them with eternal destruction if they did not hearken to him. And, in fine, he told them, that he had cause to be thus vehement, for he was sure he was in the right, and could not misguide them. I like you the worse for that, said the young pilgrim (who thought himself sufficient to deal with this Hotspur), and we should have believed you sooner if you had not pretended to infallibility, and withal been so uncharitable. We met with your elder brother just now, whom you see here, though perhaps you are not well acquainted with him. And if we could be moved at all with confidence, and the pretences of an unerring spirit, he had got the start of you, and you had come too late to beg our assent. You both set up an oracle, but his is the ancienter of the two; and more resorted unto, and far better customed than yours. I wish that both your pretensions were more modest. For methinks there is nothing so hateful as a man that gives us nothing but words, and is angry that we will not believe him. It would put a wise man into a passion, to see one use threatening gestures instead of arguments; and provoke him to think the use of speech a mischief, when he hears poor and simple stuff uttered in terms that carry the style of edicts. But besides this, I observe that as this man would have pulled out mine eyes, so you would pull away from me my guide. You would have me travel alone by my own fancy, and take myself to be as wise as the best. But for my part, I will always be of the religion which reverences the conductors of souls; and am glad with all mine heart that I have met with one both to teach and to watch over me. He would lead me as if I was a beast, and had no understanding, and you would have me run, like a madman, on my own head; but there is a middle between these, and that is reason, under the guidance of the wise. He would take away all judgment from us: and you would have us take it all to ourselves. I like neither; but would take some, and leave the rest to others. Do not think but that I will judge for myself; but yet I will take a director with me, as God hath appointed, that so I may see to judge the better. Give me my eyes, say I to him that lays his hands upon them; and yet I cry to my guide, when I see the clearest, lend me yours, for they are like to be better than mine own. A great many eyes are safer than one. Others may see that which I cannot discover myself. Interest, pride, passion, and prejudice have too great a hand in our own determinations: if I can find none that are quite void of them, yet I will consult with those that are like to have less than myself. And if I cannot judge according to their sense, yet I will never impose my own upon them. If I cannot follow, yet I will not presume to lead. If I cannot be so humble as to quit my reason, yet I will not be so arrogant as to take upon me to guide them, or to become a confident teacher of others. Modesty instructs me to think that if they may mistake, much more may I; that if they whose work it is to inquire into truth, are not secure from error, then I cannot claim that privilege who have many other businesses to attend. I will neither, therefore, contradict their opinion, nor deny my own. I will neither, for the present, become their follower, nor yet forsake their guidance.

"The stranger did not expect to be encountered with such an opposition as this, and so betrayed a little amazement at it. And, besides, he was the more confounded, when the pilgrim, espying a dagger by his side, and a pistol peeping out of his pocket, thus proceeded to discourse to him. But though you two are so different in your opinions, yet methinks you conspire too much in your cruel practices. That young weapon of yours, which I see at your girdle, doth make me start. Your dagger, I doubt, when it is a little fleshed, will in a short time grow to be a sword. You are of the same persecuting spirit with your neighbour, and will suffer nobody to be of a contrary mind to yourself; and it is the worse in you, because you have often pretended to liberty, and will give none. It is yourself, I see, that you love, and nobody else. You cry out of those burdens which you are ready to lay on other men's backs. You do that of which you complain; and desire only to change places with those against whom you perpetually murmur. If you could but agree in other things, it would be best for you to go together, and leave us to ourselves. Though we would willingly come to a fair accord, (being, I hope, the children of peace,) yet I doubt you are of the humour of those men who are so obstinate that they will not stoop a jot, nor bow their heads, though it be to take up such a blessed thing as peace. It is very sad indeed that there should be such natures found in the world, but it is so apparent that there are, that you will have a difficult task of it to clear yourself from the imputation of being of that wilful party. Though peace lie at their feet, and entreat them to condescend a little for its sake, they do not love it so well as to purchase it with the least abatement of their own desires. There is no way to divert their imagination from the object on which it is pitched: and if they be once resolved a thing must be done, all the world cannot change them from their aim. They are enemies to all accommodation, and so tied to the forms they prescribe themselves, that it is impossible to reduce them to any equity, or to render them capable to remit of their rigour. Nay, so far do some men forget themselves, that, as many who observe it have complained, they would rather fall, than descend and come down. They desire all or nothing; they seek death or else victory. As for peace, which lies between both, and which ought always to be fought for by the vanquished, and desired by the victorious, they nothing care—unless they may have it on their own terms and conditions. If you intend then to have our company, you must throw away this stubborn, stiff, and resolute disposition, which makes men lose peace for little or nothing. A yielding, compliant, and gentle nature is the great friend of peace, and the only soil wherein it will grow. For the preparing of which soil there is nothing so necessary as humility. It is pride generally that makes men so obstinate and pertinacious. A conceit of themselves makes them fondly imagine that everybody must submit to them, and they to none. This, therefore, is as great an enemy to our happy agreement as any the world hath. It obstructs all passages to it; it makes a man stand upon punctilios and formalities, as if they were of equal consideration to peace and unity. It prefers the least trifle which supports its grandeur before the greatest blessings that heaven can bestow. It makes men endlessly wrangle, when all that they can say signifies nothing but that they have no mind to yield. You are better skilled than I, it is to be presumed, in the history of ancient times, and you cannot well choose but remember something of a contest between the Athenians and King Philip, about an isle that he had taken from them, and had a mind to restore. But then you cannot also but call to mind, how learnedly one of their proud orators advised them, that if the words of the treaty did import that he gave it to them, they should refuse it. He would rather have them lose that which they could not get, than not have it by way of surrender and restitution to them. Was not this a strange foolery? What was it else but to prize the vanity of a word, before the solidity of the thing, as one hath observed on that story?—to stand upon a fancy and shadow of honour, when a real interest was concerned. But such is the nature of pride, which thinks itself disgraced if you pluck a hair out of its head; and takes itself to be undone, if it lose but a word. Pride would have it so; and that will be obeyed though men suffer soundly for it. And are not most of the controversies that divide the world about matters of the like high moment?—are they not in great part a scuffling about syllables, and a fighting with shadows and idols of our own imagination? Is there not very hot bickerings about hard phrases? and is it not thought enough to make a man be killed, if he do not believe a barbarous word? Consider whether your weapons are not like to be engaged in these doughty quarrels—whether you have not sharpened them to serve in the cause of words. I doubt those that I see you armed withal are provided to protect cobwebs, and to defend the idle dreams and phantasms of sophisters. But is not the world in a sad case in the meantime? Is it not very strange that it should be so much at leisure? They know very well sure how to live and how to die, or else they would find themselves something else to do. It seems God hath not told them enough to employ them, and so they invent words out of their own brain about which to fight eternally. Away, for shame, with this vanity and pride. Away with this conceitedness, which hath thus embroiled the whole earth, and seeks to draw heaven into the contention too. If you would have us join with you in anything, it must be in our prayers that God would give men such a right sense of themselves that they may become humble and lowly in heart. To this

we will say Amen, both for ourselves and all others. We will beg this day and night that he would incline men's hearts to peace, by inclining them to yield one to another. That he would bestow upon them a soft and gentle disposition of mind. That he would mollify their hardness, and smooth the roughness and severity of their spirits. That all may be willing to quit their particular desires for the general good. That self-denial may have as great a place in all men's hearts as it hath in our religion. And that all who call themselves after the name of Christ, may learn of their Master, who was meek and lowly in heart; who did not cry, neither was his voice heard in the street; who did not quench the smoking flax, nor break the bruised reed; who did bear with the infirmities of those that followed him, and is now such an High Priest as can have compassion on the ignorant and them that are out of the way. Of these things we can be infallibly assured, and if you have a mind to be as confident of other matters which we think either doubtful or false, trouble not the world with it, and we will not trouble you nor envy to you the height of your illumination.

"When the two champions, for so they esteemed themselves, saw that there was no ground to be won of these men, they thought it best to quit the field, especially since the night was coming on a-pace to part them. They made, therefore, but a short return to what had been objected to them, and then, both sides expressing all the kindness that might be towards each other, and promising to live in charity, they took their several courses."

Most of the old chroniclers of pilgrimages, whether actual or spiritual, delight in descriptions of Jerusalem. Scripture and the picturings of human imagination are curiously intermingled in these accounts. Most of them exhibit some trait of originality; some feature or tone of colouring derived from the writer's own character and aspirations. Both Patrick and Bunyan were well acquainted with what had been told or dreamt of Jerusalem by preceding authors. Neither the one nor the other was independent of the impressions which these spiritual topographers had left on their minds. But each was original in his way; and the following account of the pilgrim's "fair sight of the heavenly Jerusalem" may claim a meed of admiration even from the most ardent eulogists of Bunyan. The chapter in which it occurs succeeds a dissertation on pilgrimages undertaken in the old spirit of superstition.

"The young man was glad to hear him speak these words, because they looked like a conclusion; and therefore, pulling him by the sleeve, he prayed him not to wait for their answer, but leave them to muse of what he had represented so plainly to their minds. And I wish, said he, turning towards them, that, if you regard not his discourse, there was some such person here as St. Gregory, to whom you bear a reverence, that he might tell you what he thought of your intended pilgrimages to Rome, Loretto, and such-like places. No doubt he would inveigh more sharply against them than those into Palestine. Think, I beseech you, upon his words, and if you be not pleased to go along with us, yet forbear, at least, these needless though expensive journeys, and reserve your money for some uses that will turn to a better account. And so having civilly taken their leaves of each other, he and his guide held on their way to that holy place where Jesus himself now resides. Several things they discoursed of, and many good things they did as they went along, till at last, having gained the top of a high hill (which without some difficulty could not be climbed), they met with a knot of more excellent persons, who recompensed for the tediousness of that company into which they had lately fallen. The spectacle which presented itself was no less wonderful than it was new, for there they beheld sundry pilgrims like themselves, who had placed their bodies, though in several postures, as if they never meant to stir from that place, unless it was to be carried directly up to heaven. Some of them were fallen upon their knees, and, with their hands upon their breasts, their eyes elevated toward the skies, and a very smiling countenance, they seemed not so much to ask as to possess something that they dearly loved, and for which they rendered thanks to God. Others of them stood gazing upon their tiptoes, with their mouths open and their eyes so fixed, as if their souls were gone half-way out of their bodies to fetch in something which they hungered to receive ; and others also stretched out their arms to such a length, as if either they saw that thing coming to them, or else they thought them to be wings whereby they could fly to that which they looked so greedily upon. For this they observed, after a careful view of them, that every one directed his eyes the same way, as if they waited for the very same good to descend into their embraces. And therefore these two persons, being not so much startled as ravished at this strange sight, thought it was best for them to do so too, and to try if they could make any discovery of that which attracted all these eyes and hearts unto it. And they had not done so very long, but, by the advantage of this mountain and the clearness of the air, and the steadiness of their eyes, and the quiet and silence wherein they all were, they had a very fair prospect of the heavenly Jerusalem.

"Now, you may be sure, our pilgrim's heart skipped for joy, and he began to bless the happy day which brought him hither, vowing that it should be marked in his calendar for a holy day as long as he lived ; for he was not only assured hereby that there was such a place, but he discovered something of the felicities of it, which here met him with a delicious entertainment. It did not seem to be situate in a region like to any that he had as yet beheld, but in one so clear and pure that the sky is but a smoky vapour in compare with it. There was no cloud that durst be so bold as to come within sight of it, nor was there any darkness that could approach to sully its beauty. But as there was a perpetual serenity about it, so an everlasting day was one of the principal ornaments of it. The rays of the sun, he perceived, never hid themselves from it, if he judged aright when, by the glittering of the place, he thought it all gilded with his beams. But sometimes he conceited that the city was all built of such precious stones, that they supplied the place of the sun by those streams of light which issued forth from every one of them. Nay, the very garments of the inhabitants (which he could discern a little) were so glittering, that they seemed able of themselves to create a continual day to those that wore them. He beheld also some winged people (for such are they that dwell there) come flying from one of the gates of the city very speedily towards him, who told him that they accompanied him in his journey though he did not see them, and that they had been at Jerusalem to carry news of his travels thither, and to relate the constancy and resolvedness of his mind in this purpose ; and that they were sent back again not only to wait upon him, but to let him know that the lord of the place did wait very passionately for his arrival, and would be exceeding glad in safety to receive him.

"Into what an ecstasy he was cast by this relation, especially when he heard a little whispering noise (for it was no more) of the music and the melodious airs which those choristers of heaven make, it is altogether needless to tell you. His soul was almost allured out of his body by this sight, and was held in by so very small a thread, that two or three sharp thoughts more of that happy place would have cut in two that slender tie. He verily thought that this was Pisgah, and that he was gone up to die there ; and when he saw that he must still live, yet he could not but say to his guide, Let us build us a tabernacle or two in this place, for it is good to be here, until those winged ministers shall be at leisure to come and fetch us away to heaven. Surely, said he, it cannot be long before they do us that favour. Let us sit still awhile and see if our longing souls, in the posture wherein they have been, cannot invite them to give us satisfaction and transport us thither. But his director (to whom he ever used to hearken) told him that this was a thing which a man might rather fancy than desire, for it could not be permitted that they should sit always gazing there ; neither was there any hopes of arriving at the desired place unless, by their own diligence in such things as God would have them employed, they still endeavoured to creep nearer and nearer unto it. And methinks, added he, it should be sufficient to content you that the rest of your way carries the face of such pleasure, and promises so much ease and facility to you in your passage, as you will discern if it please you but a little to turn your eyes from your journey's end to behold the path that leads you to it.

"With that the young man's eyes began to fall

a little from those lofty places whereon they had been fixed, and to cast themselves upon the ground which lay below under his feet, in which he was at present to make his abode. But he did not lose his pleasure by taking his eyes off from Jerusalem, for the road which lay thither appeared now so plain, so fair and smooth, so free from briars and thorns, and all that had molested and galled him before, that it proved the beginning of heaven to him. The earth he saw was everywhere ladened with so much plenty, that nothing troubled him but only that he could not see travellers enough to gather it. On every side of him there were so many beautiful flowers, that he could scarce tell whose invitation to accept when they seemed to desire to be plucked by his hands. The very stones had lost the hardness and roughness of their nature, and did soften and smooth themselves when the feet of pilgrims came to oppress them. And all the way likewise was so quiet and still, that if a leaf wagged, it was by the sweet breath of those musicians which sat among the branches. One could not speak so much as a word but an echo from the vault of heaven would repeat it, as if she had a great desire to learn, or was much in love with that language. Yea, all the mountains which they were still to climb seemed of so easy ascent, that they differed nothing from the plain ground; and the very trees which grew upon them were so straight and tall, that they seemed to lift up themselves above the clouds to beg the heavenly bodies that they would send their pure and unstained influences on them before they had lost anything of their innocence, and were defiled by their passage through our unwholesome air to the bosom of the earth. Many a mile one might pass through a forest of nothing but myrtles and laurels, under the shade of which a traveller might sweetly repose himself, and dream that he saw the crowns and garlands which were wreathing for him in Jerusalem. Every wood also (of which some stages wholly consisted) appeared like a goodly orchard, where an infinite variety of lovely fruit saluted them that passed through it; and though the courteous apples, with all the rest, seemed to bow themselves to kiss the pilgrim's hands, yet, by their fragrancy, one would judge that they were not of a mere terrestrial growth, but fed by some invisible roots above, from which they derived the refined nourishment of celestial juices, from the surplusage of which also it was (as one would be tempted to think) that the balm and all other aromatic liquors dropped, which had no other use in that place but to anoint the heads of them whom those trees overshadowed. In short, this way that he had now to pass was called by some poetical fancies the laughter and smile of nature; by others, a monopoly of pleasure; by others, a world of sweets that live in fair community together, neither envying nor contemning one the other, but contributing every one to the beauty and delight of the whole. But none of these names gave him any satisfaction, nor could it

please him to hear it called anything else than the Entrance of the Paradise above. And, indeed, when he came to taste of the fruit, he could not but conclude that he eat of the tree of life in the midst of the garden of God; and when he felt those distillations on his head, he could think of nothing else but the unction from above. All the things in this description were but so many pictures whereby his fancy represented to him the happiness of that life which hereafter he hoped to lead, wherein he thought to find everything to his desire. The difficulties of his journey seemed now to be overcome, and every step he saw would bring him to a new pleasure. There was nothing to be done but what promised to gratify him with repeated joys, and to reward his labours with abundance of content in the doing of it; and there was nothing to be suffered which threatened any harm, but seemed to have lost its prickles and thorns, and to court men into its embraces. Now he thought he should be so happy as to live more above, and hold a constant communication with heaven. He expected to surmount the clouds wherein he had been wrapped, and to live in a purer light, and enjoy a greater serenity of mind. Now he hoped to pass his time in sublimer meditations, in a steadier faith, in a more ardent love, in more comfortable expectations, in quicker tastes of the good things to come, and so in more perfect peace and joy in the Holy Ghost; in short, he discovered on all sides both present satisfactions and future hopes, with larger assurances also that they would not make him ashamed.

"Being thus, then, spurred by the admonitions of his friend, and the invitations of the way, on he went again (together with the happy companion of his travels), sometimes casting his eye upon Jerusalem and sometimes upon his way, which now became more easy and more delightful to him than ever before. But having descended a little from the head of that lofty hill, where they had stayed thus long, the young pilgrim observed that he had lost that fair sight of Jerusalem which he so much admired, at which he began to be surprised with a little quivering and coldness in his body, till his old Comforter told him that this ought to be the cause of no troublesome thoughts: For the whole way, said he, to that place consists much of hills and dales; and as now you are going down from the heights wherein you have been, so shall you advance again in due time, and be presented not only with a fresh, but with a fairer sight of it. He told him also how impossible it was for any traveller to remain long upon those mountains, where the air is so quick and piercing that it would make them quit their earthly mansions; and, withal, he discoursed of the advantage of those valleys, and showed him the silver brooks full of the waters of life which ran in those humble places, together with all the pretty flowers wherewith the verdant banks of those streams were crowned. In fine, he represented to him that they were so far from descending now into any dismal shades, that they were but going to ease their minds with a little variety in these cool levels, which were almost spent and exhaled by so long a sight of Jerusalem in those superior regions, not omitting also to let him know that it was not so impossible as he imagined to meet with something of it in those low meadows into which they were now entering, which spread so goodly a carpet for their feet to tread upon, that the hill which they had left seemed to bow its head to look upon the richness of it; and thereupon he showed him how those crystal waters which he heard murmuring, and inviting his thirst to quench itself in their streams, came down from a spring on the brow of that mountain where they had lately been. And can you believe, said he, that anything can flow from thence which brings no tidings with it from Jerusalem? Taste and see if their relish be not such as tells you from whence they come, and makes this place happy which flows with such contentment. Believe not me, but yourself (if it be not too much for you to stoop down and drink), that these valleys are watered from above, and receive at second hand what the more rising ground at the first enjoys.

"The young man heard him very obediently, and soon satisfied himself in the truth of what he said by tasting of the waters, which had a strong tincture of Jerusalem; for the rays that come from it, and beat continually upon that aspiring hill, had endued the whole body of it with some of their virtue, which might constantly be communicated to the neighbouring though lower places. He was immediately inspired, I mean, with a great heat of divine love, in which he found not a little of heaven. He saw that meditation, prayer, and such-like holy employments do but dispose the will to acts of charity and doing good to all, according as God hath done to us. The clearer sight he perceived that any one hath of the glory to come, the more powerfully is his heart touched with a fervent desire and endeavour to be thus employed. This is the natural issue of a right belief of what Christ hath promised. There is nothing so naturally flows from it when raised to its highest pitch as an easiness and pleasure in doing good, than which nothing can come nearer to the life of them that dwell above. He saw now that Jerusalem might be found in the houses of the sick, in hospitals, and the meanest places where humility and charity can find themselves any work. If he met with a poor stranger that moved his compassion, it was as if he had met with an angel; if any differences came in his way which he could compose, it was as if Jesus had spoken peace unto him. When the orphans and widows gave him their blessing, it was as if he had received one from heaven. And all this gave him the greater satisfaction, because he was afraid he should have met with it nowhere else, save only on such mountains as they had newly left."

The lesson which follows is one of practical experience. Were it not for occasional elevations and joy of spirit, most of the pilgrims to the Celestial City would either sink on the way, or be tempted to turn back. But it has ever been found necessary to warn them, in the earlier stages of their progress, that the cessation of an ecstacy, the lessening of the sudden splendour, brightening for a time the present as well as the future, is not to be regarded as a withdrawal of the divine favour. The unusual manifestation of heavenly love was to be an evidence of the truth, as comforting when remembered as it was elevating in immediate enjoyment. There is much wisdom in the guide's discourse to his companion.

"But his guide, who was better acquainted with his duty than himself, thought it best to bring him out of this rapture, because he saw that he would immerse himself too far in the pleasure of this contemplation, and likewise thought it was not safe to gratify themselves with too much of this honey at once. He prayed him therefore to lay aside this discourse a while, and to divert himself with the observation of some of those flowers and plants wherewith they saw the earth strewed as they went along. For sure, said he, these were not made for us to tread upon, nor only to feed our eyes with their grateful variety, or to bring a sweet odour to our noses; but there is a more internal beauty in them for our minds to prey upon, did we but let them penetrate beyond the surface of these things into their hidden properties. You are a Christian it is confessed, but doth that make you cease to be a man? You read the gospel of our Saviour, but must that give a discharge to all our rational inquiries into the book of nature? Doth the new creation intend to destroy the old? Or because we behold God in the face of Christ must we look upon him nowhere else? No such matter; there is a more ancient obligation upon you to study the works of God, of which you ought to quit yourself while you study his word. It is an honour to the school of Christ when his disciples are skilled in all wisdom. He is such a Master as would not have us know other things the less, but the more, by knowing him. And so they began to pry into many curiosities, which several of the creatures they met withal presented to them; not without a great astonishment at that infinite understanding that was the contriver of them. And having once tasted of this kind of learning, he often wished that it was in his power to understand more of his own body; or the motions of the sun, moon, and other stars; with many things besides in this great fabric, wherein he knew God had hid great treasures of wisdom, and engraven a fair image of himself. Yea, he conceived the whole world sometimes a great temple, and himself one of the priests that God had placed therein to offer up the praises of all the creatures, and acknowledge his wisdom, his power, his goodness; which are conspicuous in the frame of them. And though he could acquire but a very small knowledge of some of them, yet it was a great pleasure to see that there were many more intelligent priests than himself, and more acquainted with nature's mysteries, who rendered to God continually better praises, and called upon all his works in all places of his dominion to bless his holy name.

"And now would you think after he had gone thus far that he should be troubled with such an odd fancy as this, that he did not profit at all in virtue? Yet so it was, that one day he seriously told his friend, he could not perceive that he had done anything worthy of himself, or made any proficiency in the school of piety wherein with so much care he had been bred.

"No, said his companion? Nothing at all? That is very strange indeed, and you must pardon me if I tell you that it is a melancholy conceit. For have you overcome so many temptations, and yet done nothing? Do you love God and your neighbour so much as to have an infinite desire of doing good, and yet not at all bettered? Have you suffered such a long martyrdom, and yet been lazy and idle? Have you had so many sights of Jerusalem, and yet made no progress in your journey? Was not the last prospect which you gained of that place fairer than the former, and did not it seem nearer and closer to you? How should that come about, if you had stood still and not gone forward towards it? Away with these black thoughts which the fumes of melancholy and nothing else do breathe into you. For my part I think you have profited so much, that I please myself to look upon you no less than a gardener doth to behold the trees which he planted when they bring forth fruit; or a father rejoices to see the children of his cares grown up to the stature of men and women. I desire only that you would cherish an honest emulation of yourself, and cast a jealous eye on your own worth, lest you should not be so good as yourself. Do but labour not to come behind nor fall short of your own virtue, do but keep up close to your own example, and I shall think you such a proficient that I shall glory in the name of your instructor. But for the present, come along with me, and let us refresh ourselves a little in yonder fair bowling-green; that we may excite those natural spirits which I see are heavily oppressed by that grim enemy, I just now named, of all pious souls. And you shall soon see better thoughts in your soul, when you have better blood in your body.

"With much ado he persuaded him to consent to this motion, and though thereby he received some relief, yet the same dejected humour too much continued. For his mind being strongly impressed with those conceits, they could not so soon be discharged and blotted out. Besides the continuance therefore of that exercise, and the use of some physic, he thought good at seasonable times more particularly to remember all that the gracious God had done for him; bidding him to take great heed lest, under the guise of this humility (as it is esteemed), he proved unthankful for his favours, and by studying to depress himself, he withal depressed the bounty of his goodness. He let him know also that the perfection which he aimed at (the want whereof might possibly be the root of this new trouble) was not to be attained by such violent, passionate, and impetuous motions, but by leisurely, quiet, and silent steps unto it. Did you mind, said he, the flowers as we passed along, how some were hidden in their green cups; others were half-born; and the rest newly disclosed? Or have you never marked the rose how it swells into small knobs or buttons, which when they are full grown, do rive by little and little until they have discovered all their treasures? Suppose you should unbutton it as soon as it swells, or go about suddenly to rip it up when it is opening itself, would you not endanger the spoiling of its beauties, and deprive yourself of that wholly, which you desire too soon to enjoy? Your own case is nothing different; and if you will not be content to grow leisurely, you may miss of the happiness at which you would so speedily arrive. You must not make so much haste, as I have often told you. You must give yourself leave to ripen; and allow a fair time for your proceeding to perfection. And in the mean season be not so unreasonable as to think you have nothing, because you have not all that is in your desires. It may seem strange perhaps at first sight, but it is certainly true, that the desire of much virtue may prove inordinate. Though you may think that it can never be too passionately pursued, yet assure yourself your desires are undue, when such an affliction of spirit attends upon them, as is wont to accompany the desire of other things. If the violence and fierceness of them rend your heart, there may be as much hazard in it as there is in tearing up a rose when it is in labour to bring forth its leaves. That is, you will never be so good as otherways you might, nor obtain so much by your own eagerness as would come of itself in a course of nature. I do not intend to quench your zeal, nor is all this said to make you less fervent in your study to become more pious, or to move you to leave all to God's will without your own industry. But my meaning is, that just as you take order in your worldly affairs, so should you manage yourself in those of your soul. We must be diligent in the pursuit of such things as are needful for our bodies; yet we ought not to afflict ourselves with the anguish of cares and fears, and such like passions, but quietly put the issue of our labours into God's hands, and patiently expect what he will bless them withal. Even so must you bestir yourself with as much industry as you can for the good of your soul; yet with this condition, that if you cannot acquire all that you would, you do not suffer your heart to fall into a fit of impatience, vexation, and fretting at your present estate; which must needs be joined with a great distrust of God. By this means while you would avoid one fault you run into another. And you keep yourself with such violent hands from compassing your desires, that you seek for perfection by the means of the greatest imperfection; and would redress your disorders by constantly living in them. You must thank God therefore for what he gives, and patiently wait upon him for more when he pleases to bestow it. And I am apt to think that humility and patience in the company of our imperfections, when we do our best endeavour to outgrow them, is as acceptable to God as the nobler improvements of others that complain of no such imperfections. For the one is the gift of God as well as the other; and he that gives them to be without such defects, gives you grace to bear them meekly when they cannot be helped.

"I would have you, my friend, not to cease to follow the bravest examples; and when you cannot be master of all you desire, yet still to continue your desire. But be not disgusted at yourself, I beseech you, that you are in a state of desire, and not of perfect enjoyment. Let not this take away your peace, that you are not in the foremost ranks of those that are marching to Jerusalem. Be not cast down and sorely afflicted within yourself, that you do not advance so fast as you would. Do not follow your Saviour with a sour heart, dejected looks, and fallen wings, as many are wont to do, who perpetually lament their faults, and cannot yet amend them. But render him most humble thanks that he hath given you the knowledge of them, and an earnest longing to be without them, and a study to shake them off, together with good hopes that they may be cured; or that as some go to heaven in the height of virtue, so others may accompany them with as much as they could possibly attain. All have not the same temper, the same diversions, nor the same businesses in the world; and therefore be content with that degree which your condition will permit you to rise unto, and resolve not to vex yourself unreasonably about that which is not in your power to remedy. You have often heard, I believe, that there is no peace to be had here but by patience. And in my opinion he said true, who told one of his disciples, that it is no patience when a man is content to bear with his neighbour, if withal he be not content to bear with himself. Not to the end (as I told you), that he should indulge himself in idleness, and not strive to grow better; but that all the pains he takes to be so should not end in sorer pains and greater torments because he is yet no better.

"Many other things he added to the same effect; and at last prayed him that if he was fallen into such a dislike of himself as to be weary of long discourses as well as of his condition, yet at least he would observe these three things, not unworthy of his notice, though they were the advice of heathens. Hecaton had this saying, Askest thou wherein I have profited? I have begun to be a friend to myself. Such a man hath gotten very much. He will never be alone, but always hath a good companion with him. And he that is a friend to himself, will not fail to be a friend to everybody else. I believe you cannot deny that you might have made this answer to the same question. You have begun to take a great care of your soul. Nay, you have a long time made it your business to do it good. And if you ask other men, they will tell you that you are a friend to them, and have done them also a great deal of good. How came you to grow into this familiarity with your soul? What made you to let it have so much of your company? Sure it is a sign of some proficiency, that you are so well acquainted with it. And this brings to my mind another mark of your increase in virtue which is visible even in your complaints. It is an argument (saith Seneca) of a mind that is changed for the better, when it is acquainted with those faults which it was ignorant of before. To which I may add a third, do you not will and nill always the same things? Are not those things the matter of your choice to-day, which yesterday you desired? This is a testimony of your profiting, to be constant to yourself. And therefore take heed I beseech you of this sour loathing of yourself; for in time it will breed a dislike of your duty too, and spoil your appetite to anything that is good. While you are inordinately troubled that you cannot do as you would, you will not do what you can. And in a multitude of confused desires after a better condition you will waste the time which ought to be spent in doing your best in your present estate.

"With these good counsels and other remedies, too long to be related, he recovered the poor man to a better state of health, and brought him to conceive a better opinion of himself. And yet his health was not so confirmed, but that afterward he fell into a little distemper, and languished under a new trouble, very near of kin to this, and which it brings to my mind. It was a great despondency arising from the observation of some weaknesses he felt in his soul, which bred in him a diffidence and distrust of his own constancy, and a fear that he should never hold out in his journey, but at last sit down short of Jerusalem. This made him exceeding pensive, and to go drooping a great while, because he thought that every mile would prove his last, or at least that he should never be able to travel so long till he had finished his course. Which jealousy discovering itself by some means or other unto his friend (though he did what he could to conceal it), he was moved with a great deal of pity towards him, and beseeched him earnestly not to let every suspicion of himself which started up in his soul make such a deep impression there, before he had advised whether there were cause to entertain it or no. For if you had asked me about this matter as soon as you moved the doubt, I could soon have made you give yourself satisfaction, and laid such a scene of new thoughts in your mind, that you should have remembered the former no more. For tell me, I pray you, who brought you thus far in this long journey wherein you are engaged? Was it yourself, or was it somebody else? If it was yourself, you know upon what reasons it was begun; and if they were worth anything, they may make you to go on. And it should seem also that you have more-strength than you imagine, if you have travelled so many leagues, without any support, upon your own legs. But I perceive you so ill opinionated of yourself, that you are inclined by that, if there were no other reason, to ascribe your happy progress to some higher cause. Thither let us go then, and ask of God if he uses to forsake the work of his own hands, and to lose all that he hath done already, for want of doing a little more. Will he now forsake you after you have served him so many years? Will he disown one that hath been so long a client to him, and still seeks for his wonted protection? Doth he love his friends no better than to shake them off when they grow old? If I would at all have suspected his constancy, it should have been in the beginning of our acquaintance, and not now that he hath been tried for half an age. Was there any reason at first why he should bear a good will to you, or was there none? If there was none, then there needs none to move him now to continue his love. If there was any, then there is a greater reason now, because he hath loved you so long, and you are also more worthy his love. Do him the honour, then, that you would do a friend, to believe that he is not fickle and inconstant. Or do but justice to him, and think that he is not unfaithful, but true to his word; and then, as long as your Lord lives, you shall live also. And he that hath begun a good work in you will perfect it, no doubt, till he come to give you his rewards.

"I know you will tell me that you do not question his faithfulness and steadfastness to his friends, but you have been unkind to him, and so have forfeited his good esteem and love. And let it be so, since it is your pleasure, that you have not behaved yourself so gratefully as you ought; but is he of such a disposition that he can never be won to a reconciliation? I pray have a care what you say, for fear you make good men better than God, who are wont to forgive their brother when he repents, not only seven times, but seventy times seven. And say, I beseech you, hath he not pardoned you heretofore very lovingly when you humbly and obediently entreated him to pass by your offences? When you were one of the world, did he not then draw you to himself without your desire, and over-matched your sins by his infinite omnipotent goodness? What should hinder, then, his kindness and clemency towards you now that you are become a man separate from the world? If the mire and dirt wherein we wallowed could not hinder, but he would needs take us in his arms, and place us in his bosom, will he shake us off, and throw us out from thence now that we are washed and made clean? Will he not rather wash off a speck of dirt that hath light upon us than cast us down into the mire again? Can you think that he who took in strangers to his house, and gave them kind entertainment, will turn his children out of doors? After we have done him so many services, and laboured for his love, will he thrust us out in an heat of anger, and quite cashier us his family? O absurd suspicion! A jealousy unworthy of such an excellent Father, and unbecoming sons that have so nobly and tenderly been brought up by him. If you were to treat with a person like yourself, you must first think him very bad, or else you would not be so injurious as to harbour such thoughts of him. You must judge him very froward who will fall out with you upon every slight occasion, and never return with you into grace any more. Do not impute, then, a thing so unnatural unto God, nor so much wrong his infinite goodness, as to take him to be of so harsh a disposition, that we must never expect his favour more, if we chance but to offend him. No, if you can but believe that he loves himself, you need not fear that he should thus abandon you. You have cost him too much that he should so easily part with you. He hath bought you at so excessive a rate that you may be assured he will not willingly lose you. The breeding of you hath stood him in so much care, that he will not spare a little more to keep you.

"And if you are thus secure of God's love, I pray tell me what you think should separate you from him? Can you really think that you yourself shall have a mind to leave him, and return back to the world from whence you came? You cannot, I am confident, remain two minutes in this persuasion, if you be not forsaken of your reason, and left to the impostures of fancy and wild imagination. For what is that can dissolve that league of friendship that is so solemnly and religiously sworn betwixt you? Is there anything in him that can disgust you, and make him seem less amiable in your eyes? Can you fear that his conversation may grow tedious, and prove a burden to you in the conclusion? or what prejudice can you receive by loving of him, seeing you believe that all good is in him, and that he calls us to his own kingdom and glory? I am verily persuaded you think that you cannot cease to love me, to whom you profess yourself so much beholden. And yet what am I in compare with him, or what obligations have you received from me that can be so strong to hold you as those that he hath laid upon you? I may change, and not be so good as I am, or not so full of love to you. Some damage may appear that you may be in danger to receive by loving me, which I can never be able to repair. But there is not so much as a shadow of turning in him. He is always the same fulness and the same love, infinitely desirous of our happiness; and as for any loss that we may possibly sustain for his sake, it cannot be so great but he can make us a recompense for it incomparably greater. Do not hold yourself then in such suspicion, unless you can think that you have taken a wrong measure of him, especially since you are of opinion that you cannot but love me to the end, and also have so lately told me that you was satisfied the love of me would teach you to love God the better.

"I should proceed to remember you also that the ways of virtue which you have to tread are so pleasant, that you will not be inclined to relinquish them, and divert into any other path, and that you can never think fit so to disparage this noble life as to leave it after you have made a very long trial of it, and that you will not endure to retreat with so much shame as you will necessarily draw upon yourself by abandoning a course which you have so highly commended. All this I say, and much more I should call to your mind, but that you seem to discharge me of that trouble, by the cheerfulness which I observe to return into your countenance. I see that you begin to believe that you shall persevere, and that you recover your ancient comfort—that stronger is he who dwelleth in you than he who dwelleth in the world. The devil begins already to fly from you, and by the light of these truths we have chased away the cloud that hung over you. Carry them therefore, I entreat you, ever in your mind, and let me hear no more of these dejections of spirit, which are as unreasonable as they are uncomfortable both to yourself and others. I'll say no more of this matter after I have told you a story of an ancient pilgrim in the way to Jerusalem, to which therefore you had best attend. It is St. Peter, I mean, who you know had a mind to walk with our Saviour upon the water, which was no easy thing to do, and yet, by the power of his Master, was endued with such a virtue as to tread safely upon that yielding element. He went a pretty way while the face of the water was smooth and even, and it seemed nothing different from the solid earth. Until the wind began to be loud, and the plain way upon the water was turned into hills and dales, we hear of no shrieks, but then he cried out, and his heart and his feet began to sink together. But was there any reason to fear drowning after he had walked half a furlong? or to imagine it would not bear him up the next half as well as it had done the former? None at all, sure. The winds that blew, and the rough waves that began to lift up themselves were no less subject to that power which upheld him than the smooth and quiet surface of the sea. It was as easy to walk upon a billow as upon the still water. The blustering wind had no more power there than the silent air. Whence, then, proceeded this change, that the man who lately trampled upon the sea, and gloried over the deep, doth now feel himself slip into the bosom of it, and is in danger to be swallowed up by it? The firm ground which he thought was under him is gone, and he is left to the mercy of the angry waves. Was not the change within before his feet felt any? Did not a violent fear lay hold upon him, and did he not let go his hold of the hand which before sustained him? Yes, this was the business. If his faith had been as strong as once it was, his condition had been as safe in the midst of the storm as before it was in the calm. When this anchor broke, the waters began to suck him in. They challenged him then for their proper goods, because his faith was in a manner already shipwrecked. But did his gracious Master so part with him? Would he lose a servant because he was weak, and wanted confidence in him? or did he delay to help him, and only hold him up by the chin when all his body was in the deep? No; when he cried for relief, and beseeched to be saved, he instantly put forth his hand, caught hold of him, and rescued him from the jaws of death. He only chides him because he doubted, but neither lets him sink into the belly of the waters, nor stays his succours till he was in greater need of them. He straightway lends him more power, and chooses rather to encourage a little faith than let him perish because he had no more."

The main characteristics of Patrick's *Pilgrim* may be understood from these extracts. But it is a work well deserving of study. Its merits are not to be looked for in the occasionally controversial language of the author. Some of the discourses introduced might well be spared; but neither the spiritual teaching, nor the ingenuity of so excellent a writer, aiming at the same objects as Bunyan, will be unvalued by Bunyan's enlightened readers.

PILGRIMAGE OF MAN.—PILGRIMAGE OF THE SOUL.

THE careful study of Bunyan may be no less incidentally than immediately profitable. It is the case with most great authors and master-minds, that they open tracks of inquiry which, sooner or later, lead to the discovery of treasures of thought and learning long forgotten or neglected. Few readers of this age would have ever heard of Guillaume de Guileville, but for the connection of his writings with those of Bunyan.* This early French poet was born in Paris towards the close of the thirteenth century. Having assumed the habit of a monk of St. Bernard, in the royal abbey of Chalis, he attained, in time, to the dignity of prior, but has left no other record of himself except the simple intimation that he was led to write his poem by the study of the *Roman de la Rose.* The work to which he owes the preservation of his name is entitled *Le Romaunt des trois Pélerinages.* Of these three pilgrimages, the first is, "De l'Homme durant qu'est en Vie ;" the second, "De l'Ame séparée du Corps ;" and the third, "De Notre Sauveur Jésus Christ."

Guillaume de Guileville died in 1360, that is, about twenty years before the birth of our English poet, John Lidgat, who became a monk in the monastery of St. Edmund's Bury, and acquired equal reputation both for learning and genius. By him the poem of De Guileville became known to English readers, and afforded even Chaucer himself suggestions for some of the most beautiful passages in his writings. It is next to impossible that Bunyan should have been unacquainted with this once popular book ; it is still more so, that, having read it, he should fail to derive from it the ordinary advantages which men of genius enjoy through acquaintance with the writings of men of like mind and purposes.

The monk of Chalis begins his narrative with a dream which he had, at noon, in his monastery, when, he says, "he was avised in his sleep."

"Excited eke, and that at noon,
To Jerusalem for to goon,
Greatly moved in my corage
For to do my pilgrimage."

Then follows a description of the heavenly Jerusalem, as seen "in a mirror, large and bright." But he has no sooner resolved upon setting out on his pilgrimage, than he recollects the necessity of providing himself with a scrip and staff. Not knowing where to find them, he is greatly distressed.

* See a very interesting volume, entitled, *The Ancient Poem of Guillaume de Guileville, compared with the Pilgrim's Progress of John Bunyan.* Edited from Notes collected by the late Mr. Nathaniel Hill. London, Pickering, 1858.

"For which I went complayning
Out of myself tryst and weaping,
Searching tofour, and ek behynde,
Sherpe and bordon for to fynde.
And while I did my besynesse,
A lady of full gret fairnesse
And great noblesse, soth to say,
I did meet upon the way.
For God would I you behete
Sone that I should her meet,
Of grace for my owne prowh
Thereof I hadde joy enow ;
And my heart great gladness,
For she, as by lyklynesse,
Was daughter of some emperour,
Some mighty kyng or governour,
Or of that lord that giveth all
Which is of power most royal."

A description of great poetical excellence is given of this lady, whose name is Grace-Dieu. Seeing the pilgrim in deep distress, she inquires the cause, as Evangelist of Christian. He answers—

"Certys, quoth I, I may well weep,
For if ye lyst to take kepe
My joy, my mirth, and my plesaunce,
Mine health, and all my suffysaunce,
Bodeynly me han forsake.
I may complain and sorrow make,
For whilom above the skye
I was wont to flee full hyhe,
And had also full glad repayre
With bryddis flying in the aire,
In my most lusty fresh seson,
But now I am avalyd don,
And find by great adversity
All that is contrary unto me."

He then states that his body is like a clog to him, and exclaims—

"A body corrupt, it is no nay,
Grieveth the soul night and day,
Keepeth him in captivity,
It may not go at liberty,
Neither waking, nor asleep,
For which certys I may well weep."

Grace-Dieu comforts him with an assurance of help, if he will follow her instructions.

"To pilgrims, day and night,
I enlumine and give light,
To all pilgrims in their way,
As well in darkness as by day,
So they lyste toward me,
And lyste that I their guyde be.

And if they erryn in their way,
Again I do them well convey.
I will them helpen and redress,
For I am she in sothfastness,
Whom thou owest seek of right,
In strange land with all thy might."

Warning him of the difficulties he is about to encounter in seeking the heavenly Jerusalem, she adds—

"As thou goest to that city
Thou shalt have oft adversity,
Great mischief and encombraunce,
Empechementys and dysturbaunce,
Which thou mayst not, in no degree,
Pass nor endure without me.
Nor that city ever attain,
Though thou ever do thy pain,
Without that I thy guide be."

In the following passage, Grace-Dieu, summons the pilgrim to follow her to her house, founded thirteen hundred and thirty years, that is, at the time when God's grace established the Gospel. The pilgrim contemplated the building with awe and astonishment.

"And for the fairness and beauty
I had great will that house to see,
Abaysshed, for it was so fair,
For it hung high, up in the air,
'Tween heaven and earth stood the place,
As it had only by grace
From the heaven descended down.
So stood that heavenly mansion,
With steeples and with towers high,
Freshly arrayed to the eye,
As a place most royal,
Above all other, principal,
Which stood up on a fair river,
The water thereof wholsome and clear;
But there was nor passage in that place,
Nor ship whereby men myhte pass."

This river, emblematical of spiritual purification, or of the water of baptism, terrifies the pilgrim; and Grace-Dieu asks him—

"What meaneth this? what may this be?
That thou art now, as seemeth me,
So sore adread of this river,
Which is but light, smooth, and clear.
Why art thou fearful of this stream,
And art toward Jerusalem,
And mustest of necessity
Passen first the great sea,
Or thou come therto hersel,
And dreadest now this river smal."

A long dialogue follows. The pilgrim acknow-ledges the truth of what Grace-Dieu asserts, but laments that he cannot pass the river by his own strength or skill. An advocate then appears, and becomes sponsor for the troubled Guillaume, who being plunged into the river, passes it, to his great joy, in safety. Then Grace-Dieu—

"Led me forth in my repair,
To a place right inly fair,
And never she made me to-fore,
So good cheer syth I was bore,
Nor was so benign of her port,
Unto me to do confort.
Now, syth, quod she, that it is seen,
Thou art washed, and made all clean,
And art passed the river,
Without a peril or danger,
Thine enemy fled out of thy breast,
Where he afour had made his nest,
I shall thee shew of great delight
Full many thing for thy profit."

In the house of Grace-Dieu the pilgrim meets with other persons engaged in the same travel, and many things are explained to him, in the same manner as to Christian in the house of the Inter-preter. Thus he is present when a bishop inquires of Reason, why the mitre is horned, and the crozier is hooked? Even Nature herself appears, and enters into discourse. She is rebuked for some presumption by Grace-Dieu, and asks mercy. Re-pentance and Charity are next introduced, the former, it is worthy of notice, bearing not only a hammer and a rod, but a broom. Thus, she says—

"I go to every place;
Now here, now there about I trace,
By very plain confession,
Without fraud, or deception,
There may nothing me 'scape fro,
For Grace-Dieu will it be so,
For she ne will nowhere abide
But it be clean on every side.
Whose chamber, and whose mansion,
Dwelling and habitation,
Is truely without offence
A very cleane conscience."

A scrip and staff are provided the pilgrim, and with these he would have been content. But he is told that armour is needed, and Grace-Dieu will-ingly provides it.

"Come near, quoth she, and ha no dread.
Look up on high, and take good heed,
Upon this perche the harness see,
Wherewith that thou wilt armed be;
Pertinent to thy voyage,
And needful to thy pilgrimage.
Then saw I helmys and habergeons,
Plate and mail for champions.
Gorgets against all violence,
And jakkes stuffys of defence:
Targets and sheldys large and long,
And bucklers also that were strong,
For folk to make resistance
To all that would 'em do offence."

The pilgrim has no wish to bear the heavy armour provided him, and thinks that he may give it in charge to his attendant, Memory. He is warned against such negligence, and eventually suffers greatly from not obeying the advice thus given him. After having gone some way on his journey, he comes to a spot where the road divides. On the one side sits Industry, employing herself as a net-maker; on the other, the daughter of Idleness. Each answers the questions of the pilgrim according to her nature, and Bunyan, without copying, might well learn a lesson from this sweet poet and early master in the art of spiritual allegory. Happily for him, the pilgrim avoids the left, or by-path of Idleness, and pursues the road pointed to him out by the net-maker. Gluttony, and other vices, meet him on his path. These he effectually overcomes; but still has to encounter Wrath and Tribulation. The latter says of herself—

> "Some like leaves I whirl away,
> Which by the ground full lowe lay.
> But thoro my commission
> I ha turned them up side down.
> And many another eke also,
> With my trouble and with my wo,
> And with my tongs I 'em chace,
> Against the Lord when they tresspase,
> That I cause 'em for to flee
> To God on them to have pity:
> And some I have ek caused oft
> To flee up to the stars aloft."

Trembling, but leaning on his staff, Faith the pilgrim goes on his way, and enters a forest.

> "I fell anoon in my passage
> In to a wood full savage.
> Methought the way perillous,
> And by to pass encombrous.
> I knew not what was left to doone,
> For in a wood a man may soone
> Lose his way, and gone amiss,
> But be beware, and thus it is,
> As pilgrims know well, each one,
> That on pilgrimage gone,
> Passage they find narrow and straight,
> Brigands lie ek in await,
> And wylde bestys many one,
> T'assail pilgrims where they gone."

Avarice and Necromancy were familiar characters in the writings of mediæval poets and romancers. They were favourites with Guillaume de Guileville in their imaginative shape. But he was a churchman, and a religious teacher. Hence we find him introducing personages of a much less poetical nature. Dame Idolatry, Heresy, Gladness-of-the-World, appear as the enemies of the pilgrim, and rouse in him the proper qualities of resistance. But he is in great distress while struggling with these determined foes. A wide, deep stream of water rolls by his feet, and he seems in imminent danger of perishing. Suddenly, a valiant Christian knight places himself by his side, and fights for him; and soon after Grace-Dieu herself appears. She purifies him with water out of a rock; and then offers him shelter, according to the fashion of the times, in any of the religious houses rendered famous as abodes of sanctity. The poet represents the pilgrim as selecting that of Cisteaux. There he rests for a time; but, in no great while, is visited by two aged women, who, dressed in emblematical costume, announce themselves to him as Infirmity and Old Age. He suffers terribly from their chastisements. They warn him that death is also at hand. Unable to help himself, he is ready to sink with alarm, when Mercy comes to his succour, and opens to him the plans of divine grace, and methods of salvation. Grace-Dieu also appears; but the poetry here is far better than the theology. A sad confusion may be discovered between the notions of penance and redemption, of justification and purgatory. Such errors, however, do not enter into the main design of the work; and there is great beauty in the contrivance that the pilgrim should awake from his dream just as he supposes Death has pierced him with its dart, and he doubts whether he be dead or alive, till he hears the sound of the convent bell, calling him to matins.

Thus ends the narrative of the "Pilgrimage of Man." But De Guileville regarded this as only part of the subject of which he had to treat. The soul, when separate from the body, was still, in his view, on progress and pilgrimage.[*] Bunyan evidently felt as strong an inclination as the old French poet to follow it on in its sublime and mysterious path, when across the bourne. No doubt can be entertained that, had he deemed it lawful to obey this impulse, he might have written a work on the intermediate state of surpassing interest. That he did not stop at the moment of conducting his pilgrim to the side of the river, is a proof of his tendency to believe that more may be known of man, both in and after dying, than is commonly supposed. Had De Guileville been prevented, like Bunyan, by questions of doctrine, from following the soul in its separate state, the "Pilgrimage of Man" would probably have had a different ending. Connected with the after-plan, it was enough that the narrative should carry the pilgrim to his place of earthly repose, and there leave him to await the summons to a further stage in his progress. The difference between the two authors, in this respect, is worthy of remark, as illustrative of the combined influence and constraint which every important religious doctrine exercises on the imagination. Christian is at once in peace and glory, having passed the cold river. De Guileville's pilgrim has still to encounter enemies and alarms.

---

[*] *The Booke of the Pylgremage of the Sowle*, translated from the French of Guillaume de Guileville, and printed by William Caxton, an. 1483. Edited by Katherine Isabella Cust. Pickering, 1859. This is a very valuable reprint, and is edited with equal piety and ability.

"As I lay, on a St. Lawrence night, sleeping in my bed, me befell a full marvellous dream, which I shall rehearse. Methought that I had long time travelled toward the holy city of Jerusalem, and that I had made an end, and fully finished my fleshly pilgrimage, so that I might no further travel upon my foot, but needs must leave behind my fleshly careyne. Then came cruel Death, and smote me with his venomous dart, through which stroke body and soul were parted asunder. And so anon I felt myself lifted up into the air, seeing myself departed from my foul body. Which, when I beheld lying all dead, without any moving, seemed me so foul and horrible, that had I nought right late before issued therefrom, I would nought have supposed that ever it had been mine. Then came there to this body the noble, worthy lady, Dame Misericord, and covered it, lapping it in a clean linen cloth, and so full honestly laid it in the earth."

While he thus contemplated his earthly frame, so lately left, he saw Dame Prayer hastening to heaven on his behalf, for the "foul, horrible Sathanas was coming toward him, cruelly menacing him, and saying"—

"I have here long time abyden thee, and privily for thee lain in wait ; so it now befalle that I have not failed of my purpose ; for now art thou taken with me, and now must thou wend to myne habitacyon, condemned by right wise judgment of the sovereign judge. For now hast thou lost that lady that was thine helper and thine counsellor, Dame Grace-de-Dieu. It availeth thee nought for to look after her. Now art thou my prisoner. Cast down thy scrip and thy burden, for all thy pilgrimage is comen to a jape. Thou shalt full soon be brought in such a cage where thou shalt no talent have to laugh nor to sing ; but well might thou well say, ' Alas ! why, and to what purpose, had God formed me but to be encumbered with so much mischief ?' And when I saw this, and heard, full grievously had I been discomforted, had I not seen a fair youngling of full huge beauty, that me always accompanied.

" And at the last he approached me, and soon I perceived his person and his office. He began to speak, and said to this Sathanas, Thy malice, quod he, and thy cursydnesse is ever prest and ever ready for to tarye and deceive simple souls, with which thou hast nought at all to meddle ne entermete : but wonder wickedly wouldst thou treat them, if so were that no wight would help them ne defend. Flee thy way fast; and go; claim thy right in other place, for with this soul thou shalt nought have to meddle. Then said this Sathanas, with a despytous chere, Flee thou fast hence, quod he, for thou hast nought to withsaye me of pilgrims that misgoyn, which by their own misgovernance forlettyth the right way of virtue, and take my way. I ne claim nought there thy right is : no more ne claim thou there mine is. For what time that the sovereign king had banished me out of his blissful presence, and cast me down

into this misery and mischievous estate that I now am in, gave me this license at the lefte. He hath me suffered to do much thing to engendre and to portray figures to my resemblaunce, the which I clepe mine own creatures, as Envy, Treason, and such other, with all the generation of these old vices, that walkyn by the world in my name, for to let pilgrims of their way."

A long dialogue follows, the issue of which is, that the soul of the pilgrim is led to judgment, " between the angel and the foul Sathanas."

" So was I led between them both, and fast was I lift up into the air, the angel upon my right side, and the foul wight upon the other. But to this gentle angel full oft cast I mine eye, for dread of that other which me loathed so much, and was of him hugely in doubt. So then I beheld downward for to see the earth, and soothly me seemed the sea and the earth altogether no more but as it had been a little town or castle. And yet seemed me much more near than it was before. In this air saw I many a marvellous, wonderful, and diverse. The earth seemed me all clear and transparent, so that I might see clearly all that was within.

" Then beheld I the centre, even in the midst, which was wonder dark in itself, and was about environed by other of less dark matter and less, so that the overmost of the earth was most clear, and alway the clearness lessening downwards, by very formal process, anon to the centre, that was very dark, without any parcel of clearness; nought for they all was transparent, right as glass to the manner of my sight, which was that time all other than was my fleshly sight, while that I lived in earth. And right as the flitting air giveth place to the flight of birds, or as the flowing water to swimming of fishes, right so was all this earth passable to spirits.

" And also thick they passed to and fro on every side, as moats fleetyn in the sunbeam, as well in the air above, as in the earth beneath, wending alway to and fro without any ceasing. These spirits also in themselves were diverse and disparayble, both in their persons and in their wonderful occupations, of which I had full great marvel. For the sight of some things that I saw gladded much my heart, and the sight of some other things discomforted me hugely; nor such things would I nought have trowyd, if I had nought seen it myself. But this fair youngling, mine angel, he tarried nought at all, but hastily he hied to bring me to my judgment, toward a full marvellous place, which I beheld afar before me, bright shining, enflamed with huge light. To this place he led me, nought within, but made me abide without, where was a huge multitude gathered, and were abiding for the same cause, like as I was. This angel, my warden, left me there without, and went himself within. This company that was without cried busily to Saint Michael, each for his party, with high vows, and said, Michael, provost, deliver us our prey, and our prisoners. Mine enemy, this grisly ghost, also began to cryen, whereof I was full greatly annoyed, and in full high discomfort.

"But then I looked after my warden, to see what he would say, or do for me, beholding inward as far as I might. Then saw I many seats, royal and wonderful, more clear than any crystal polished; and much marvellous light I saw of dissemblable matter. Some seemed green, and some red; some like to gold, and some to silver; and other of more rich and noble colours than ever I saw flower, or any precious stone. Then saw I sitting on the seats huge plenty of people, which I had no time distinctly to beholden. But the wonderful clearness of this company was so glorious, that all manner of examples of resemblance that may be remembered in earth, be no more sufficient to declare the beauty, than is a clod of black earth for to representen the resemblaunce of any fair creature, in manner of a mirror. There was never creature that might see this sight, that he ne should fully be glorious, as me seemed; but it endured me but a moment, for smertely was my sight darked, by over drawing of a great curtain between my sight and that, that I might ne more see clearly that I saw before. But well I heard the voice of my warden that was within, that began to speak for me."

Preparations for a solemn judgment are now made. Michael ascends his throne. Satan pleads hard for the condemnation of the soul of the pilgrim. His guardian angel answers the adversary with bitter rebukes and sarcasms; but he paused for a while, when the trembling soul fell into great agony, being told that it must reply for itself, or find some sufficient advocate.

"Glorious God, Jesu! so great dread then and heavyness had thorough pierced my heart, so that I wist not what to do or say."

His perplexity was increased by the feeling that he had not, in his lifetime upon earth, served any saint in particular. Happily for him, he resolved, in this distress, to appeal immediately to Jesus. In his hymn to this only all-sufficing intercessor, he acknowledges the worthlessness of his scrip and staff, and whatever else had formerly given him a notion of merit and deserving. The judgment is carried on through many stages of argument and inquiry. It ends with the temporary banishment of the soul from heaven. In due time, it receives the joyful intelligence that the celestial mansions are open to it, and the description of its journey thither is well deserving of perusal.

"Full soon, said his guardian angel, shall I lead thee thither, for I have leave of the provost and all his assessors, that there be present with him. For now be Misericord and Justice accorded together; and so be as well Reason, Truth, and Equity, without gainsaying. All they ben one, and of one will.' When I thus had abiden awhile, and seen many things, that is to say, the elements, and all that was within, angels also I saw fleen to and fro; and Sathanas full busily by sea and land, and in the air aboven. I saw him full oft flee hither and thither, for to espy pilgrims' by-paths and by-ways. So, at the last, mine angel took me by the hand, and said to me thus: Now go we up into that sovereign city, without more abiding; for ben ended the pains and torments, and fully a-determyned. Now sing we, mount we, flee we upward, as fast as we may. For full nigh is the joy which we abyden: we ben full nigh to that rest that we have long desired, that never shall failen nor be ended. And thus singing, he led me forth, and shewed me the firmament. But in this point, I saw great foyson of byrdes, in every side about, that sang in the air nothing else, saying, but ever, Jesu! Jesu! without any ceasing. What may this be? quod I to my angel. Where have these byrdes learned thus to sing so readily, and lustily to hymn this blissful name Jesu! It is great joy and solace to hear them, and for to see them also is a pleasant thing. Certes, quod my angel, thou shouldst nought ben abashed, for thou hast seen them ere this; but thou art not avised thereof, now at this time, nor hast before this time taken but little heed of their sweet song; and that hath hindered thee greatly. And great dole it is when that mortal folk taketh none heed to their own advantage. These ben the byrdes that God Almighty made to that intent, that mortal folk should take their example to done as they done. These ben cleped larkes, which that in Latin have the name of praising, and of worshipping, and ben cleped *Alaude* nought withouten cause. For why? They rysen, and mounten far fro the earth, and spreden their wings preysen God with their mery song, and all their disport and play is to syngen Jesu!"

Few readers will fail to discover a strong resemblance between the general tone of this passage, and that which characterises some of the most admired descriptions and similes in Bunyan. The view of the heavenly Jerusalem is given with a large mixture of mediæval learning, somewhat lessening the pathos and poetical beauty of the chapter; but the picture is drawn with masterly power; and had Guillaume de Guileville, the monk of Chalis, been less of a scholar, or Bunyan more of one, the resemblance between their pilgrimages would have been still more striking.

LONGLANDE AND HAWES.

EARLY English literature is not less rich than that of France in illustrations of the taste for pilgrimages, and the habit of moulding all kinds of moral or religious truth into the forms of allegory. Thus, Robert Longlande, who wrote his famous *Vision of Pierce Plowman* towards the close of the fourteenth century, was in some respects the Bunyan of that age. He tells us that, after wandering about on the Malvern Hills, he at length fell asleep. In his dream, he saw the various classes of men struggling with the vices and follies to which they are characteristically subject. The clergy are chief sufferers at the hands of this keen satirist; but there is enough both of genuine poetry and elevated thought in his verses to render the *Vision of Pierce Plowman* worthy of popularity on broader grounds than that of its merit as a satire. "Robed in russet," says the poet, "I roamed about a whole summer long, to seek Dowel," that is, Do-well. While asleep, a person, the image of himself, came to his side, and called him by name.

"What art thou, quoth I tho, that thou my name knowest?
That thou wost wel, quoth he, and no wight better.
Wot I what thou art? Thought, seide he thanne:
I have sought thee this sevene yere."

Thought is then asked where Do-well may be found, and he answers that, not only Do-well, but Do-better, and Do-best, may be traced out by proper diligence.

But in the reign of Henry VII. appeared "*The Passetyme of Pleasure; or the Historie of Graunde Amoure and La Bel Pucel, contayning the Knowledge of the Seven Sciences, and the Course of Man's Life in this World.* Invented by Stephen Hawes, Groom of Kyng Henry the Seventh, hys chambre."* This remarkable poem, finished in 1506, abounds in all the varieties of personifications and allegorical incidents which a fertile genius could heap together. It must have been as well known in Bunyan's time, as Johnson's *Rasselas* and Goldsmith's *Vicar of Wakefield* are in ours. We impute no plagiarism to Bunyan by stating these facts; but it is assuredly interesting to know that his real greatness consisted not in originating, but in successfully adopting, a form of composition never before employed to so good a purpose.

The *Passetyme of Pleasure* opens with the appearance of the hero, Graunde Amoure, walking in a beautiful meadow. Through this, a path leads him to a glorious image, whose outstretched hands point to two highways—the one, the path of Contemplation; the other, of Active Life, conducting to the Tower of Beauty. Our hero chooses the latter. He overcomes several temptations to take first one, and then another by-path, and, continuing on the direct road, discovers at some distance another

* Warton: *Hist. of English Poetry*, vol. ii. sec. xxviii. p. 404.

image, bearing on its breast the inscription, "This is the road to the Tower of Doctrine: he that would reach it must avoid sloth." But by this time the night has overtaken him, and falling asleep at the foot of the image, he is awakened just before day, by the sound of a horn. A lady of great loveliness, seated on a palfrey, swift as the wind, and encircled with tongues of fire, approaches him. It is Fame, attended by her two greyhounds, milk-white, and on whose golden collars are inscribed, in letters of diamond, Grace and Governaunce. She tells him that her palfrey is Pegasus; that the tongues of fire indicate her office, which is to preserve illustrious names through countless ages; and that she knows one lady especially, of matchless beauty and excellence. This is La Bel Pucel, who inhabits a tower, built on a beautiful island, but which can only be reached through many dangers. The tower is the Tower of Doctrine. In it dwell the Seven Sciences; and in the Chamber of Music might be had the first glimpse of La Bel Pucel. Fame now leaves Graunde Amoure to be led by her two greyhounds to the castle. He finds it on a craggy rock. It is built of burnished copper; but the sky becoming somewhat clouded, he can look at the dazzling walls and turrets, richly emblazoned with various emblems in gold. The portress, Countenance, admits him; and he is conducted to a delicious fountain in the court of the castle, whence flow four rivers, clearer than any in the world. Reason is the marshal of the castle, Observance the sewer, Temperance the cook, Liberality the high-steward. Graunde Amoure is then allowed to inform Doctrine of the purpose of his pilgrimage. She entertains him at a solemn feast, and introduces him to her seven daughters. Grammar, the first of these damsels, shows the importance of her science in relation to all the other branches of knowledge; Logic follows with a very sober address; but Rhetoric appears with a laurel crown, her stately chamber being strewed with flowers, and garnished with the mirrors of speculation. She explains the five divisions of her art in eloquent language, and then dismisses Grande Amoure to her sister, Arithmetic, the walls of whose chamber are decorated with the three chief rules of her science emblazoned in gold. The pilgrim is at length admitted to the Tower of Music, built entirely of crystal. Music herself was seated before an organ, a solemn assembly listening with raptured attention to her strains. But among the hearers is a damsel, "more beautiful than Helen, Proserpine, Cressida, Queen Hyppolita, Medea, Dido, Polyxena, Alcmena, Menalippa, or even Fair Rosamond. This is La Bel Pucel. She leaves the chamber with Music. Graunde Amoure follows her, and declares the passion with which he is inspired. Music re-awakens the powers of harmony, and explains its principles. When the pilgrim retires, he is met by Counsell, who conducts him to a stately apartment, in which he is left to repose. Counsell attends him in the morning, and they seek La Bel Pucel in the palace garden. Courtesy, the portress, tells them that she is sitting in an arbour, weaving a garland. His vows, after some show of resistance, are accepted; but he is told by La Bel Pucel, that their union cannot take place till he have endured a long and hazardous discipline. He leaves her with many tears, and resumes his pilgrimage by visiting the Tower of Geometry, and next, that of Astronomy. Guided by his greyhounds, he afterwards traverses a vast plain, covered with flowers, and at the distant extremity of which he discerns a tower, high over which shines a flaming star. This tower is built on a beetling precipice of steel. It proves to be a mighty fortress. At the gate hang a shield, a helmet, and a horn. The pilgrim, seizing the latter, blows a blast which seems to shake the tower. A knight appears, and inquires his name. On being told that he has just left the Tower of Doctrine, he is cordially welcomed, and informed that the fortress is the Castle of Chivalry. On rising the next morning, he is led by the porter, Stedfastness, into the lower court of the castle, where he beholds a variety of emblematical devices, calculated to instruct him in the duties of war and chivalry. Soon after leaving this castle, he is met by Godfrey Gobilive, in the costume of a fool, or jester, and who addresses him at great length on the falsehood of women. Sapience comes up. Between the two he is betrayed into error, and is overtaken by Correction, who tells him that Godfrey Gobilive is False Report; and the next morning shows him the caitiff closely confined in a deep dungeon kept by Shamfastnesse. As he journeys on, he comes to a fountain, near which hang a shield and a horn; on the former is an inscription, informing the traveller that he is on the direct path to the house of La Bel Pucel, but that if he should venture to blow the horn, he will be immediately assailed by a giant. The knight defies this threat; blows the horn, and finds himself instantly in the presence of a monster, twelve feet high, and with three heads, from each of which floats a streamer, inscribed, Falsehood, Imagination, Perjury. A furious conflict follows. The knight cuts off the giant's three heads, with his sword, Clara-prudence. Vanity, Good-operation, Fidelity meet him. In their castle, to which he is admitted by the portress, Observance, he rests awhile. Perseverance is his next companion. She tells him, that Strangeness and Disdain had persuaded La

Bel Pucel not to love him, but that Peace and Mercy had arrived in time to thwart their plans, and that it was by her wish she now brought him a shield, and invited him to lodge for the night with her cousin Comfort, who lived hard by in a moated manor-house, sheltered by a wood. He accordingly passes the night in a chamber called Precious, and breathing of the richest perfumes. Perseverance and Comfort guide him on his way the next morning. He arrives at a lordly castle. It is guarded by a giant with seven heads. They are severally inscribed with the titles, Dissimulation, Delay, Discomfort, Variance, Envy, Detraction, Doubleness. The trees around are burdened with the shields of conquered knights; but Graunde Amoure undauntedly attacks the giant and slays him. Immediately appear five ladies, who congratulate him on the victory, and inform him that they are Stedfastness, Amorous-purveyance, Joy-after-sorrow, Pleasaunce, Good-report, Amitie, Continuance. They rode on white palfreys, and having been wiled from La Bel Pucel by the influence of Disdain, had been kept prisoners a whole year in the castle by the giant with seven heads. These ladies and the pilgrim now pursue their journey together. After traversing a wide and gloomy wilderness, abounding in savage beasts, they discern a tempestuous sea; but far on amid the waves, a charming island, with a stately castle. "Yonder," exclaimed Perseverance, "is the Palace of Pucel." But a horrible fiend here presented itself. It had been framed by Strangeness and Disdain, to terrify La Bel Pucel, when she banished them from her castle. Patience now sends a ship, named Perfectness, to receive the whole company, and convey them to the island. Graunde Amoure slays the monster made by the witches. He enters the castle, and is received by Peace, Mercy, Justice, Reason, Grace, and Memory.

Like the Moral Play to be hereafter noticed, the *Passetyme of Pleasure* traces the course of man's life to its end. Graunde Amoure grows old. He has spent many years of happiness with La Bel Pucel, and enjoyed whatever riches and high station could afford. One morning he is unexpectedly visited by a mysterious looking stranger, who, striking him on the breast with his staff, tells him that his name is Old Age, and that he must be obeyed. Policy and Avarice come soon after, and Graunde Amoure now loves money as much as he before delighted in pomp and pleasure. Death arrives. Contrition and Conscience appear. The career of Graunde Amoure is ended; but Mercy and Charity attend him to the grave, and Remembrance and Fame agree together to preserve his name to distant ages.

SPENSER AND BUNYAN.

BUNYAN's writings, like those of his immediate predecessors, abound in references to ideas and customs connected with the history of Jerusalem. The allusions thus made are not in the way of transient illustration, but with the strong feeling which impresses men concentrating their affections on one particular locality. A history of pilgrimages and crusades, written with a view to the illustration of religious poets and allegorists, would be the best commentary on many of their works. Few people can read the narratives of the early pilgrims without being deeply impressed by their simple pathos. The Empress Helena, Constantine's mother, performed an act of graceful homage to pious recollections when, at the age of eighty, she endeavoured to discover some traces of the spot where our Lord died and was buried. Her example was followed by numerous other pilgrims, who had nothing to induce them to undertake so painful and hazardous an enterprise but sentiments of affection and reverence. It was not till a later period that the idea of merit, of penance, or atonement, was attached to these journeys. But whatever the notions of the pilgrim, every stage of his route, and all the circumstances by which he was surrounded, might furnish subjects for a homily or a poem. Dangers and privations were his daily discipline; and though superstition and licentiousness were often seen side by side with the later travellers to Jerusalem, many returned to their homes well instructed in the practice of humility and self-denial. Equally welcome as such men would be at the fireside of the peasant, in the baronial hall, or hospitable monastery, their narratives supplied not only suggestions which an active fancy might work into useful lessons, but the lessons themselves. It was these which descended in various forms to the fifteenth and sixteenth centuries. Their origin had then long been forgotten. The poets changed them into what shape they pleased, and hence we have not only such productions as those above spoken of, but the more refined transformations of pilgrim records and morals by Tasso and Spenser. It is absolutely impossible that Bunyan should not have been well acquainted with the latter author. It is equally improbable that he did not read him frequently and studiously. The supposition that he voluntarily remained ignorant of the greatest of moral poets, writing in good plain English, is far more injurious to Bunyan's credit than any jealous notion of his originality is likely to advance it. The annotators on Milton have discovered innumerable resemblances between some of his finest passages, and expressions, or thoughts, to be found in other writers. These resemblances are accounted accidental or designed, according to the temper of the critic. In some instances, Milton has been charged with wholesale plagiarism. It would be difficult to disprove the fact of his imitating, or borrowing, to a much greater extent than would be endured in a modern author. But no reader of Milton regards his genius with less admiration because he had this command of the entire expanse of human learning, and all the tributary streams of thought. Such would be the case were Bunyan subjected to the same test of comparative criticism. If Bently, Bishop Newton, or Archdeacon Todd, had deemed it worth his while to edit *The Pilgrim's Progress*, not a page would have been wanting in parallel passages, or proofs of imitation. How vast is the difference between tracing some of the ideas of a great author to early and extraneous suggestions, and denying him the praise of originality, is strikingly illustrated by Lauder's forgeries. As long as any credit was given to the assertion, that the substance of the *Paradise Lost* could be found in some old Dutch Latin poems, Milton's fame remained in suspense. It could not be denied, even by his most enthusiastic admirers, that if he had borrowed so much, he deserved comparatively little honour as an original poet. The confession of Lauder himself put an end to this controversy. But Archdeacon Todd's huge collection of apparent imitations is still known to most readers of Milton. They prove, beyond any reasonable doubt, that this greatest of poets was largely indebted to his acquaintance with the schools of earlier genius for much which was best and brightest in his own mind. The discoveries thus made are to be reckoned among the noblest triumphs of patient learning. They body forth the sympathies of great intellects—show how they depend upon and help each other—illustrate, in fact, the divine economy in the communion of mind, as, for still higher purposes, it is exercised in the communion of spirit. To endeavour to exalt a man of genius by isolating him from his kind, is like praising the virtues of Simeon Stylites because he stood alone on his pillar. Originality does not consist in the exercise of thought and fancy, free from all congenial influences, but in individuality preserved, and held distinct, amid either these or conflicting powers. This was Shakspere's originality: it was that of Spenser and Milton. It was equally that of Bunyan, whose simplicity, with all the other admirable characteristics of his writings, was as little the fruit of ignorance as was that of Homer or Herodotus.

A reader with sufficient leisure and taste for such a task, would be well repaid by the pleasure and edification which he would receive from a comparison of Spenser and Bunyan. The latter would suffer no loss of fame by having the former for his commentator; and the student of both these great authors would gain a clearer, a more impressive knowledge of the nature of allegory, of its aims and uses, than either alone would give him. It is not for us to enter upon this task, but the following passages will show how well Spenser could teach the same lessons as Bunyan. The Red-cross Knight, after encountering many dangers, at length finds shelter in the House of Holiness, to which he is thus conducted—

" Wherein his weaker, wandring steps to guide,
  An ancient matron she to her does call,
  Whose sober looks her wisdom well descried :
  Her name was Mercy, well known over all,
  To be both gracious, and eke liberal :
  To whom the careful charge of him she gave,
  To lead aright, that he should never fall,
  In all his ways, through this wide worldes wave,
That mercy in the end his righteous soul might
    save.

" The godly matron by the hand him bears
  Forth from her presence, by a narrow way,
  Scattered with bushy thorns and ragged breares,
  Which still before him she removed away,
  That nothing might his ready passage stay.
  And ever when his feet encumbered were,
  Or gan to shrink, or from the right to stray,
  She held him fast, and firmly did upbear :
As careful nurse her child from falling oft does rear.

" Eftsoons unto an holy hospital,
  That was foreby the way, she did him bring :
  In which seven bead-men, that had vowed all
  Their life to service of high heaven's King,
  Did spend their days in doing godly thing.
  Their gates to all were open evermore,
  That by the weary way were travelling.
  And one sat waiting ever them before,
To call in comers by, that needy were and poor.

" The first of them, that eldest was and best,
  Of all the house had charge, and government,
  As guardian and steward of the rest,
  His office was to give entertainement
  And lodging unto all that came and went :
  Not unto such as could him feast again,
  And double quit for that he on them spent,
  But such as want of harbour did constrain,
Those for God's sake his duty was to entertain.

" The second was an almoner of the place :
  His office was the hungry for to feed,
  And thirsty give to drink, a work of grace :
  He feared not once himself to be in need ;
  Nor cared to hoard for them whom he did breed :
  The grace of God he laid up still in store ;
  Which as a stock he left unto his seed.
  He had enough, what need him care for more ?
And had he less, yet some he would give to the
    poor.

" The third had of their wardrobe custody,
  In which were not rich tyres nor garments gay,
  The plumes of pride, and wings of vanity,
  But clothes meet to keep keen cold away,
  And naked nature seemly to array :
  With which bare wretched wights he daily clad,
  The images of God in earthly clay.
  And if that no spare clothes to give he had,
His own coat he would cut, and it distribute glad.

" The fourth appointed by his office was
  Poor prisoners to relieve with gracious aid,
  And captives to redeem with price of brass
  From Turks and Sarazins, which them had staid.
  And though they faulty were, yet well he weighed,
  That God to us forgiveth every hour
  Much more than that, why they in bands were
    laid.
  And He that harrowed hell with heavy stower,
The faulty souls from thence brought to his hea-
    venly bower.

" The fifth had charge sick persons to attend,
  And comfort those in point of death which lay :
  For them most needeth comfort in the end,
  When sin and hell and death do most dismay,
  The feeble soul departing hence away.
  All is but lost, that living we bestow,
  If not well ended at our dying day.
  O man ! have mind of that last bitter throw,
For as the tree does fall, so lies it ever low.

" The sixth had charge of them now being dead,
  In seemly sort their corses to engrave,
  And deck with dainty flowers their bridal bed,
  That to their heavenly spouse both sweet and
    brave
  They might appear, when He their souls shall
    save.
  The wondrous workmanship of God's own mould,
  Whose face he made all beasts to fear, and gave
  All in his hand, even dead we honour should.
Ah, dearest God, me grant, I dead be not defould !

" The seventh, now after death and burial done,
  Had charge the tender orphans of the dead,
  And widows aid, lest they should be undone.
  In face of judgment, he their right would plead,
  Nor ought the power of mighty men did dread,
  In their defence ; nor would for gold or fee,
  Be won their rightful causes down to tread.
  And when they stood in most necessity,
He did supply their want, and gave them ever free.

" There when the elfin knight arrived was,
  The first and chiefest of the seven, whose care
  Was guests to welcome, towards him did pass ;
  Where seeing Mercy, that his steps upbare,
  And always led, to her with reverence rare,
  He humbly louted in meek lowliness,
  And seemly welcome for her did prepare.
  For of their order she was patroness,
Albe Clarissa were their chiefest foundcress.

" There she awhile him stays, himself to rest,
That to the rest more able he might be :
During which time, in every good behest,
And godly work of alms and charity,
She him instructed with great industry.
Shortly therein so perfect he became,
That from the first unto the last degree,
His mortal life he learned had to frame
In holy righteousness, without rebuke or blame.

" Thence forward, by that painful way they pass,
Forth to a hill, that was both steep and high :
On top whereof a sacred chapel was,
And eke a little hermitage thereby,
Wherein an aged, holy man did lie,
That day and night said his devotion,
Nor other worldly business did apply.
His name was Heavenly Contemplation :
Of God and goodness was his meditation."

By this sage old hermit, Contemplation, the warrior Christian is led, by a difficult and narrow road, up a lofty mountain—

" From whence, far off, he unto him did show
A little path, that was both steep and long,
Which to a goodly city led his view ;
Whose walls and towers were builded high and
    strong,
Of pearl and precious stone, that earthly tongue
Cannot describe, nor wit of man can tell :
Too high a ditty for my simple song.

The city of the great King, hight it well,
Wherein eternal peace and happiness doth dwell.

" As he thereon stood gazing, he might see
The blessed angels to and fro descend
From highest heaven in gladsome company,
And with great joy into that city wend,
As commonly as friend does with his friend.
Whereat he wondered much, and gan enquire
What stately building durst so high extend
Her lofty towers unto the starry sphere,
And what unknowen nation there empeopled
    were."

Soon after the season of rest and consolation thus enjoyed, the Christian soldier, who bore " on his breast a bloody cross "—

" The dear remembrance of his dying Lord "—

had to encounter a dreadful dragon. This monster, and the fight with it, furnish a description which, if Bunyan read anything, must have been familiar to him long before he wrote his own account of the battle between Christian and Apollyon. The same sort of resemblance exists between some other striking descriptions in both authors ; and, on the whole, it may be safely concluded that, though Bunyan was destitute of what is technically called learning, he was ignorant of nothing which could be taught him by books or traditions in his own language.

MORAL PLAYS.

AMONG the resemblances to be traced between Bunyan's inventions and the works of earlier writers, few are more striking than those which exist in the old Moral Plays, as compared with his allegories. In one of these may be found the probable groundwork of the *Holy War.* It is entitled the *Castle of Perseverance,* — and is followed by others, named, *Mind, Will, and Understanding — Mankind.* According to Mr. Collier,* this ancient drama was one of the most popular of the kind. A week's notice was given the inhabitants of the town or village in which it was to be performed. The messenger who made the announcement blew a trumpet, and then pronounced the following verses :—

> " Grace if God will graunte us of his mykyl myth,
> These percell in propyrtes we spose us to playe,
> This day sevenenyt before you in syth,
> At N. on the grene in ryal aray.

> " Ye, haste you thane thedyrward, syrs, hendly and hyth,
> All good neybors ful specyally we you pray,
> And loke that ye be there by tyme, luffely and lyth,
> For we schul be onward by underne of the day."

It is understood by the concluding line, that the play commenced with the earliest dawn, and as the performance took place on the village green, or in some other open place, no obstacle existed to its becoming a popular entertainment. According to Mr. Collier's analysis, the first scene represents Mundus, Belial, and Caro discoursing with each other on their several characteristics. Then enters Humanum Genus the representative, that is, of mankind, and as just born ! He says—

> " I was born this nyth in blody ble,
> And nakyd I am, as ye may se."

Scarcely have these words been uttered, when a good and a bad angel appear, and claim him by turns, as rightful property. At length, the unhappy Humanum Genus consents to the bad angel, when the " mynstrells pipe up," to proclaim the conquest. The victor leads his captive to Mundus, then in deep converse with his associates, Stultitia and Voluptas. They are directed to attend upon Humanum Genus. Detractio is another of his tutors, and he is next made acquainted with Avaritia, who leads him to the six other Deadly Sins. After a course of iniquity, Humanum Genus yields to the earnest efforts of the good angels, and is placed under the care of Pœnitentia and Confessio. He inquires of them, where he may find a safe abode ? They answer, " in the Castle of Perseverance," stronger, it is added, " than any in France." The seven cardinal virtues accompany

him to the castle. But he has scarcely entered it, when Belial besieges it, leading on the seven Deadly Sins, whom he severely punishes for allowing Humanum Genus to escape them. Mundus, on his part, is equally wrath with Avaritia. Belial exhorts his soldiers before they begin their assault on the castle, and the whole proceeding reminds us of the circumstances attending the siege of Mansoul. The assailants are defeated and retire. But Humanum Genus is not yet safe. He grows " hory and colde," and his " back gynneth to bowe and bende." Avaritia reappears at this juncture. He steals under the castle walls, and his persuasions overcome all the prudence at first opposed to his wiles. Humanum Genus leaves the castle ; has huge riches ; but in the midst of his success, a representative of the youth of the world appears. Avaritia and Mundus assist in despoiling him. Then come Mors, or " drery Death," and "Anima." The latter summons Misrecordia to her aid, but in vain ; and the Bad Angel, taking Humanum Genus on his back, disappears, exclaiming,—" Have good day : I goo to helle."

The earliest of printed moral plays, according to Mr. Collier, is entitled *Nature.* Man appears upon the stage having,, at first, for his companions, Nature, Reason, and Innocency. He becomes the victim of Pride, and all the other evil passions, who speak and argue like real persons. In one part of the play Gluttony enters armed with " a chese and a botell." He is challenged to fight, but refuses. Pride ceases to enjoy the favour of man ; but " Covetise " still exercises some power over him. Man and Reason then discourse together. Meekness, Charity, Patience, Good Occupation, Liberality, Abstinence, and Chastity successively enter. Man is introduced to Repentance, and receives a promise of salvation.

Another moral play bears the title of *Every Man,* meaning the human race. This curious ancient drama begins with a soliloquy, in which the Almighty deplores that mankind have forsaken Him, and " use the seven deadly synnes damnable." Death is summoned, and charged with a message to " Every Man," who is ordered to appear before his Maker, and bring with him his " book of counte," and any friend who may be willing to assist him in this great need. An admirable piece of moral satire follows. Every Man first meets with Fellowship, and begs him to afford the required support, but in vain. Kindred is next sought, but

> " They all at last do Every Man forsake,
> Save his good deeds there do he take.
> But beware, for and they be small,
> Before God he hath no help at all

* *History of English Dramatic Poetry,* 1831. Vol. ii. p. 279.

None excuse may be there for Every Man.
Alas! howe shall he do than?
For after death amends may no man make,
For then Mercy and Pity doth him forsake.
If his reckoning be not clear when he do come,
God will say, *ite Malediciti in ignem eternum.*
And he that hath his account whole and sound,
High in heaven he shall be crouned.
Unto which, please God, bring us all thither,
That we may live body and soul together.
Therto help the Trinity:
Amen, say ye, for Saint Charity."

The good works of Every Man are personified under the name of Goods, who refuses to follow him to the judgment. Good Deeds is seen lying faint on the ground, and can only point to the blank in the "books of works and deeds." Knowledge is introduced; she leads him to Confession, and then Strength, Discretion, Beauty, and Five Wits promise to be his companions on the long journey. But, as his weakness increases, he finds himself at the edge of the grave, and immediately calls upon these friends to fulfil their promise, and enter with him. Beauty instantly refuses. Five Wits, Strength, Discretion, equally break their promise. Knowledge follows their example. In the end Good Deeds alone attends him on the way.

The *Marriage of Wit and Science* is a moral play of later date, and of different aim, but the names and relationships of the allegorical personages can hardly fail to remind the reader of passages in the *Holy War*. Thus Wit, the Son of Nature, becomes enamoured of Lady Science, the daughter of Reason and Experience. His mother gives him a servant, Will, and tells him that if he wish to gain the lady he must use labour and perseverance. The parents of Lady Science, who is very bashful, persuade her to listen to the addresses of her suitors. Wit is introduced by Reason to Instruction, whose servants are Study and Diligence. Science at length agrees to marry Wit at the end of three or four years. But she makes it a condition that he shall become her knight, and enter into mortal combat with her known foe, the great giant Tediousness.

COLERIDGE AND MACAULAY ON "THE PILGRIM'S PROGRESS."

THE genius and honesty of Coleridge are eminently displayed in his *Notes on Bunyan*. No man ever sought to express his thoughts more earnestly on all matters of profound or refined criticism ; and it would be difficult to name either churchman or politician more likely, by his principles, to attack such a book as *The Pilgrim's Progress*. How interesting it is then to hear this great poet and philosopher thus speaking in defence of Bunyan. " It disappointed, nay, surprised me," he says, " to find Robert Southey express himself so coldly respecting the style and diction of *The Pilgrim's Progress*. I can find nothing homely in it but a few phrases and single words. The conversation between Faithful and Talkative is a model of unaffected dignity and rhythmical flow."

In Southey's *Life of Bunyan* occurs the following passage :—" ' We intended not,' says Baxter, ' to dig down the banks, or pull up the hedge, and lay all waste and common, when we desired the prelates' tyranny might cease.' No : for the intention had been under the pretext of abating one tyranny to establish a far severer and more galling in its stead. In doing this the banks had been thrown down, and the hedge destroyed, and while the bestial herd who broke in rejoiced in the havoc, Baxter, and other such erring though good men, stood marvelling at the mischief, which never could have been effected if they had not mainly assisted in it."

" But," says Coleridge, " the question is, would these erring good men have been either willing or able to assist in this work, if the more erring Lauds and Sheldons had not run in the opposite direction ? And as for ' the bestial herd,'—compare the whole body of Parliamentarians, all the fanatical sects included, with the royal and prelatical party in the reign of Charles II. These were indeed a bestial herd. See Baxter's unwilling, and Burnet's honest, description of the moral discipline throughout the realm under Cromwell."*

Again Southey says : " They passed with equal facility from strict Puritanism to the utmost license of practical and theoretical impiety, as Antinomianists, or Atheists, and from extreme profligacy to extreme superstition, in any of its forms."

Coleridge exclaims: " They ! How many ? And of these how many that would not have been in Bedlam, or fit for it, under some other form ? A madman falls into love or religion, and then, forsooth, it is love or religion that drove him mad."

Southey says : " In an evil hour were the doctrines of the gospel sophisticated with questions which should have been left in the schools for those

* Literary Remains, vol. iii. p. 391.

who are unwise enough to employ themselves in excogitations of useless subtlety."

Coleridge asks : " But what, at any rate, had Bunyan to do with the schools ? His perplexities clearly rose out of the operations of his own active but unarmed mind on the words of the apostle. If anything is to be arraigned it must be the Bible in English, the reading of which is imposed (and, in my judgment, well and wisely imposed), as a duty on all who can read. Though Protestants, we are not ignorant of the occasional and partial evils of promiscuous Bible readings ; but we see them vanish when we place them beside the good."

On the first line in *The Pilgrim's Progress*, " As I walked through the wilderness of this world," Coleridge writes : " That in the Apocalypse the wilderness is the symbol of the world, or rather of the worldly life, Bunyan discovered by the instinct of a similar genius. The whole Jewish history, indeed, in all its details, is so admirably adapted to, and suggestive of, symbolical use, as to justify the belief that the spiritual application, the interior and permanent sense, was in the original intention of the inspiring Spirit, though it might not have been present as an object of distinct consciousness to the inspired writers." Here it may be observed that these remarks would have commended themselves at once to most readers, if instead of " a similar genius," " the same spirit" had been the expression used. On the passage beginning, " Did you ever see your sins, and feel the burden of them," Coleridge remarks : " Most true. It is one thing to perceive and acknowledge this and that particular deed to be sinful, that is, contrary to the law of reason, or the commandment of God in Scripture, and another thing to feel sin within us independent of particular actions, except as the common ground of them. And it is this latter without which no man can become a Christian."

On the sweeping away of the dust in the Interpreter's house, he observes : " See Luther's *Table Talk*. The chapters in that work named, ' Law and Gospel,' contain the very marrow of divinity. Still, however, there remains much to be done on this subject, namely, to show how the discovery of sin by the law tends to strengthen the sin, and why it must necessarily have this effect, the mode of its action on the appetites and impetites through the imagination and understanding, and to exemplify all this in our actual experience."

An interesting specimen of criticism, equally illustrative of the tenderness and acuteness of the philosopher, follows. It is on this passage : " Then I saw that one came to Passion, and brought him a bag of treasure, and poured it down at his feet;

the which he took up, and rejoiced therein, and withal laughed Patience to scorn; but I beheld but awhile, and he had lavished all away, and had nothing left him but rags."

Coleridge observes: "This is one of the not many instances of faulty allegory in *The Pilgrim's Progress*; that is, it is no allegory. The beholding 'but awhile,' and the 'change into nothing but rags,' is not legitimately imaginable. A longer time and more interlinks are requisite. It is a hybrid compost of usual images and generalized words, like the Nile-born nondescript, with a head or tail of organized flesh, and a lump of semi-mud for the body. Yet, perhaps, these very defects are practically excellencies in relation to the intended readers of the *The Pilgrim's Progress*."

On the passage, "The Interpreter answered, 'This is Christ, who continually, with the oil of his grace, maintains the work already begun in the heart,'" he says: "This is beautiful, yet I cannot but think it would have been still more appropriate if the water-pourer had been a Mr. Legality, a prudentialist offering his calculations of consequences as the moral antidote to guilt and crime; and if the oil-instillator, out of sight, and from within, had represented the corrupt nature of man, that is, the spiritual will corrupted by taking up a nature into itself."

Bunyan says, in the character assumed, "I left off to watch and be sober. I laid the reins upon the neck of my lusts." The commentator observes: "This single paragraph proves, in opposition to Edwards, that in Bunyan's judgment there must be at least a negative co-operation of the will of man with the Divine grace, an energy of non-resistance to the workings of the Holy Spirit." "But," he adds, "some persons divide the regenerate will in man from the will of God, instead of including it."

On the argument, "Thou art but in the way, who, as we perceive, came in at the gate, and we are also in the way, that came tumbling over the wall," he observes: "The allegory is clearly defective, inasmuch as the 'way' represents two diverse meanings—first, the outward profession of Christianity; and second, the inward and spiritual grace. But it would be very difficult to mend it. In this instance (and it is, I believe, the only one in the work) the allegory degenerates into a sort of pun, that is, in the two senses of the word 'way,' and thus supplies Formal and Hypocrite with an argument which Christian cannot fairly answer, or rather one to which Bunyan could not make his Christian return the proper answer without contradicting the allegoric image. For the obvious and only proper answer is, 'No, you are not in the same "way" with me, though you are walking on the same "road."' But it has a worse defect, namely, that it leaves the reader uncertain as to what the writer precisely meant or wished to be understood by the allegory. Did Bunyan refer to the Quakers as rejecting the outward sacraments of baptism and the Lord's Supper? If so, it is the only unspiritual passage in the whole beautiful allegory—the only trait of sectarian narrow-mindedness, and, in Bunyan's own language, of legality. But I do not think that this was Bunyan's intention. I rather suppose that he refers to the Arminians and other Pelagians, who rely on the coincidence of their actions with the gospel precepts for salvation, whatever the ground or root of their conduct may be—who place, in short, the saving virtue in the stream, with little or no reference to the source. But it is the faith acting in our poor imperfect deeds that alone saves us; and even this faith is not ours, but the faith of the Son of God in us. 'I am crucified with Christ, nevertheless I live; yet not I, but Christ liveth in me : and the life which I now live in the flesh, I live by the faith of the Son of God, who loved me, and gave himself for me.' Illustrate this by a simile. Labouring under chronic bronchitis, I am told to inhale chlorine as a specific remedy. But I can do this only by dissolving a saturated solution of the gas in warm water, and then breathing the vapour. Now what the aqueous vapour, or steam, is to the chlorine, that our deeds, our outward life, is to faith."

How delightful would it have been to hear Bunyan and Coleridge converse together on these themes, each recognising, with love and profound respect, the other's spiritualized genius.

"One thing," says the dreamer, "I could not let slip. I took notice that now poor Christian was so confounded, that he did not know his own voice; and thus I perceived it. Just when he was come over against the mouth of the burning pit, one of the wicked ones got behind him and stepped up softly to him, and whisperingly suggested many grievous blasphemies to him, which he verily thought had proceeded from his own mind."

"There is a very beautiful letter," says Coleridge, "of Archbishop Leighton's to a lady under a similar distemperature of the imagination. In fact, it can scarcely not happen, under any weakness and consequent irritability of the nerves, to persons continually occupied with spiritual self-examination. No part of the pastoral duties requires more discretion, a greater practical psychological science. In this, as in what not, Luther is the great model, ever reminding the individual that not he, but Christ is to redeem him; and that the way to be redeemed is to think with will, mind, and affections on Christ, and not on himself. I am a sin-laden being, and Christ has promised to loose the whole burden if I but entirely trust in him. To torment myself with the detail of the noisome contents of the fardel, will but make it stick the closer, first to my imagination and then to my unwilling will."

We add to this testimony of the greatest of

modern philosophers, in praise of Bunyan, that of the most popular of modern critics. Lord Macaulay says, in a review of Southey's edition, published in 1830, "The characteristic peculiarity of *The Pilgrim's Progress* is that it is the only work of its kind which possesses a strong human interest. Other allegories only amuse the fancy. The allegory of Bunyan has been read by many thousands with tears. There are some good allegories in Johnson's works, and some of still higher merit by Addison. In these performances there is, perhaps, as much wit and ingenuity as in *The Pilgrim's Progress*. But the pleasure which is produced by the Vision of Mirza, the Vision of Theodore, the genealogy of Wit, or the contest between Rest and Labour, is exactly similar to the pleasure which we derive from one of Cowley's odes or from a canto of Hudibras. It is a pleasure which belongs wholly to the understanding, and in which the feelings have no part whatever. Nay, even Spenser himself, though assuredly one of the greatest poets that ever lived, could not succeed in the attempt to make allegory interesting. It was in vain that he lavished the riches of his mind on the House of Pride and the House of Temperance. One unpardonable fault, the fault of tediousness, pervades the whole of the *Fairy Queen*. We become sick of cardinal virtues and deadly sins, and long for the society of plain men and women. Of the persons who read the first canto, not one in ten reaches the end of the first book, and not one in a hundred perseveres to the end of the poem. Very few and very weary are those who are in at the death of the Blatant Beast. If the last six books, which are said to have been destroyed in Ireland, had been preserved, we doubt whether any heart less stout than that of a commentator would have held out to the end.

"It is not so with *The Pilgrim's Progress*. That wonderful book, while it obtains admiration from the most fastidious critics, is loved by those who are too simple to admire it. Doctor Johnson, all whose studies were desultory, and who hated, as he said, to read books through, made an exception in favour of *The Pilgrim's Progress*. That work was one of the two or three works which he wished longer. It was by no common merit that the illiterate sectary extracted praise like this from the most pedantic of critics and the most bigoted of Tories. In the wildest parts of Scotland *The Pilgrim's Progress* is the delight of the peasantry. In every nursery *The Pilgrim's Progress* is a greater favourite than *Jack the Giant-killer*. Every reader knows the straight and narrow path as well as he knows a road in which he has gone backward and forward a hundred times. This is the highest miracle of genius, that things which are not should be as though they were, that the imaginations of one mind should become the personal recollections of another. And this miracle the tinker has wrought. There is no ascent, no declivity, no resting-place, no turn-stile, with which we are not

perfectly acquainted. The wicket-gate, and the desolate swamp which separates it from the City of Destruction, the long line of road, as straight as a rule can make it, the Interpreter's house and all its fair shows, the prisoner in the iron cage, the palace, at the doors of which armed men kept guard, and on the battlements of which walked persons clothed all in gold, the cross and the sepulchre, the steep hill and the pleasant harbour, the stately front of the House Beautiful by the wayside, the chained lions crouching in the porch, the low green Valley of Humiliation, rich with grass and covered with flocks, all are as well known to us as the sights of our own street. Then we come to the narrow place where Apollyon strode right across the whole breadth of the way, to stop the journey of Christian, and where afterwards the pillar was set up to testify how bravely the pilgrim had fought the good fight. As we advance, the valley becomes deeper and deeper. The shade of the precipices on both sides falls blacker and blacker. The clouds gather overhead. Doleful voices, the clanking of chains, and the rushing of many feet to and fro, are heard through the darkness. The way, hardly discernible in the gloom, runs close by the mouth of the burning pit, which sends forth its flames, its noisome smoke, and its hideous shapes to terrify the adventurer. Thence he goes on, amidst the snares and pitfalls, with the mangled bodies of those who have perished lying in the ditch by his side. At the end of the long dark valley he passes the dens in which the old giants dwelt, amidst the bones of those whom they had slain.

"Then the road passes straight on through a waste moor, till at length the towers of a distant city appear before the traveller; and soon he is in the midst of the innumerable multitudes of Vanity Fair. There are the jugglers and the apes, the shops and the puppet-shows. There are Italian Row, and French Row, and Spanish Row, and British Row, with their crowds of buyers, sellers, and loungers, jabbering all the languages of the earth.

"Thence we go on by the little hill of the silver mine, and through the meadow of lilies, along the bank of that pleasant river which is bordered on both sides by fruit-trees. On the left branches off the path leading to the horrible castle, the court-yard of which is paved with the skulls of pilgrims; and right onward are the sheepfolds and orchards of the Delectable Mountains.

"From the Delectable Mountains, the way lies through the fogs and briars of the Enchanted Ground, with here and there a bed of soft cushions spread under a green harbour. And beyond is the land of Beulah, where the flowers, the grapes, and the songs of birds never cease, and where the sun shines night and day. Thence are plainly seen the golden pavements and streets of pearl, on the other side of that black and cold river over which there is no bridge.

"All the stages of the journey, all the forms which cross or overtake the pilgrims, giants, and hobgoblins, ill-favoured ones, and shining ones, the tall, comely, swarthy Madam Bubble, with her great purse by her side, and her fingers playing with the money, the black man in the bright vesture, Mr. Worldly-Wiseman and my Lord Hategood, Mr. Talkative, and Mrs. Timorous, all are actually existing beings to us. We follow the travellers through their allegorical progress with interest not inferior to that with which we follow Elizabeth from Siberia to Moscow, or Jeanie Deans from Edinburgh to London. Bunyan is almost the only writer who ever gave to the abstract the interest of the concrete. In the works of many celebrated authors, men are mere personifications. We have not a jealous man, but jealousy; not a traitor, but perfidy; not a patriot, but patriotism. The mind of Bunyan, on the contrary, was so imaginative that personifications, when he dealt with them became men. A dialogue between two qualities, in his dream, has more dramatic effect than a dialogue between two human beings in most plays.

" *The Pilgrim's Progress* undoubtedly is not a perfect allegory. The types are often inconsistent with each other; and sometimes the allegorical disguise is altogether thrown off. The river, for example, is emblematic of death; and we are told that every human being must pass through the river. But Faithful does not pass through it. He is martyred, not in shadow, but in reality, at Vanity Fair. Hopeful talks to Christian about Esau's birthright and about his own convictions of sin as Bunyan might have talked with one of his own congregation. The damsels at the House Beautiful catechize Christiana's boys, as any good ladies might catechize any boys at a Sunday school. But we do not believe that any man, whatever might be his genius, and whatever his good luck, could long continue a figurative history without falling into many inconsistencies. We are sure that inconsistencies, scarcely less gross than the worst into which Bunyan has fallen, may be found in the shortest and most elaborate allegories of the *Spectator* and the *Rambler*. The *Tale of a Tub*, and the *History of John Bull*, swarm with similar errors, if the name of error can be properly applied to that which is unavoidable. It is not easy to make a smile go on all fours. But we believe that no human ingenuity could produce such a centipede as a long allegory in which the correspondence between the outward sign and the thing signified should be exactly preserved. Certainly no writer, ancient or modern, has yet achieved the adventure. The best thing, on the whole, that an allegorist can do, is to present to his readers a succession of analogies, each of which may separately be striking and happy, without looking very nicely to see whether they harmonize with each other. This Bunyan has done; and, though a minute scrutiny may detect inconsistencies in

every page of his tale, the general effect which the tale produces on all persons, learned and unlearned, proves that he has done well. The passages which it is most difficult to defend are those in which he altogether drops the allegory, and puts into the mouth of his pilgrims religious ejaculations and disquisitions better suited to his own pulpit at Bedford or Reading than to the Enchanted Ground or to the Interpreter's Garden. Yet even these passages, though we will not undertake to defend them against the objections of critics, we feel that we could ill spare. We feel that the story owes much of its charm to these occasional glimpses of solemn and affecting subjects, which will not be hidden, which force themselves through the veil, and appear before us in their native aspect. The effect is not unlike that which is said to have been produced on the ancient stage, when the eyes of the actor were seen flaming through his mask, and giving life and expression to what would else have been an inanimate and uninteresting disguise.

"It is very amusing and very instructing to compare *The Pilgrim's Progress* with the *Grace Abounding*. The latter work is indeed one of the most remarkable pieces of autobiography in the world. It is a full and open confession of the fancies which passed through the mind of an illiterate man, whose affections were warm, whose nerves were irritable, whose imagination was ungovernable, and who was under the influence of the strongest religious excitement. In whatever age Bunyan had lived, the history of his feelings would, in all probability, have been very curious. But the time in which his lot was cast was the time of a great stirring of the human mind. A tremendous burst of public feeling, produced by the tyranny of the hierarchy, menaced the old ecclesiastical institutions with destruction. To the gloomy regularity of one intolerant Church had succeeded the license of innumerable sects, drunk with the sweet and heady must of their new liberty. Fanaticism, engendered by persecution, and destined to engender persecution in turn, spread rapidly through society. Even the strongest and most commanding minds were not proof against this strange taint. Any time might have produced George Fox and James Naylor. But to one time alone belong the frantic delusions of such a statesman as Vane, and the hysterical tears of such a soldier as Cromwell.

"It was through this Valley of the Shadow of Death, overhung by darkness, peopled with devils, resounding with blasphemy and lamentation, and passing amidst quagmires, snares, and pitfalls, close by the very mouth of hell, that Bunyan journeyed to that bright and fruitful land of Beulah, in which he sojourned during the latter period of his pilgrimage. The only trace which his cruel sufferings and temptations seem to have left behind them was an affectionate compassion for those who were still in the state in which he had once been. Religion has scarcely ever worn a form so calm and soothing as in his allegory. The feeling which predominates through the whole book is a feeling of tenderness for weak, timid, and harassed minds. The character of Mr. Fearing, of Mr. Feeble-Mind, of Mr. Despondency and his daughter Miss Muchafraid, the account of poor Littlefaith, who was robbed by three thieves, of his spending money, the description of Christian's terror in the dungeons of Giant Despair, and in his passage through the river, all clearly show how strong a sympathy Bunyan felt, after his own mind had become clear and cheerful, for persons afflicted with religious melancholy.

"Mr. Southey, who has no love for the Calvinists, admits that, if Calvinism had never worn a blacker appearance than in Bunyan's works, it would never have become a term of reproach. In fact, those works of Bunyan with which we are acquainted are by no means more Calvinistic than the articles and homilies of the Church of England. The moderation of his opinions on the subject of predestination gave offence to some zealous persons. We have seen an absurd allegory, the heroine of which is named Hephzibah, written by some raving supralapsarian preacher who was dissatisfied with the mild theology of *The Pilgrim's Progress*. In this foolish book, if we recollect rightly, the Interpreter is called the Enlightener, and the House Beautiful is Castle Strength. Mr. Southey tells us that the Catholics had also their Pilgrim's Progress, without a Giant Pope, in which the Interpreter is the Director, and the House Beautiful Grace's Hall. It is surely a remarkable proof of the power of Bunyan's genius, that two religious parties, both of which regarded his opinions as heterodox, should have had recourse to him for assistance.

"There are, we think, some characters and scenes in *The Pilgrim's Progress*, which can be fully comprehended and enjoyed only by persons familiar with the history of the times through which Bunyan lived. The character of Mr. Greatheart, the guide, is an example. His fighting is, of course, allegorical; but the allegory is not strictly preserved. He delivers a sermon on imputed righteousness to his companions; and, soon after, he gives battle to Giant Grim, who had taken upon him to back the lions. He expounds the fifty-third chapter of Isaiah to the household and guests of Gaius; and then he sallies out to attack Slaygood, who was of the nature of flesheaters, in his den. These are inconsistencies; but they are inconsistencies which add, we think, to the interest of the narrative. We have not the least doubt that Bunyan had in view some stout old Greatheart of Naseby and Worcester, who prayed with his men before he drilled them, who knew the spiritual state of every dragoon in his troop, and who, with the praises of God in his mouth, and a two-edged sword in his hand, had turned to flight, on many fields of battle, the swearing, drunken bravoes of Rupert and Lunsford.

"Every age produces such men as By-ends. But the middle of the seventeenth century was eminently prolific of such men. Mr. Southey thinks that the satire was aimed at some particular individual; and this seems by no means improbable. At all events Bunyan must have known many of those hypocrites who followed religion only when religion walked in silver slippers, when the sun shone, and when the people applauded. Indeed he might have easily found all the kindred of By-ends among the public men of his time. He might have found among the peers my Lord Turn-about, my Lord Time-server, and my Lord Fair-speech; in the House of Commons, Mr. Smooth-man, Mr. Anything, and Mr. Facing-both-ways; nor would 'the parson of the parish, Mr. Two-tongues,' have been wanting. The town of Bedford probably contained more than one politician who, after contriving to raise an estate by seeking the Lord during the reign of the saints, contrived to keep what he had got by persecuting the saints during the reign of the strumpets, and more than one priest who, during repeated changes in the discipline and doctrines of the church, had remained constant to nothing but his benefice.

"One of the most remarkable passages in *The Pilgrim's Progress* is that in which the proceedings against Faithful are described. It is impossible to doubt that Bunyan intended to satirise the mode in which state trials were conducted under Charles the Second. The license given to the witnesses for the prosecution, the shameless partiality and ferocious insolence of the judge, the precipitancy and the blind rancour of the jury, remind us of those odious mummeries which, from the Restoration to the Revolution, were merely forms preliminary to hanging, drawing, and quartering. Lord Hategood performs the office of counsel for the prisoners as well as Scroggs himself could have performed it.

"'*Judge.* Thou runagate, heretic, and traitor, hast thou heard what these honest gentlemen have witnessed against thee?

"'*Faithful.* May I speak a few words in my own defence?

"'*Judge.* Sirrah, sirrah! thou deservest to live no longer, but to be slain immediately upon the place: yet, that all men may see our gentleness to thee, let us hear what thou, vile runagate, hast to say.'

"No person who knows the state trials can be at a loss for parallel cases. Indeed, write what Bunyan would, the baseness and cruelty of the lawyers of those times 'sinned up to it still,' and even went beyond it. The imaginary trial of Faithful, before a jury composed of personified vices, was just and merciful, when compared with the real trial of Alice Lisle before that tribunal where all the vices sat in the person of Jefferies.

"The style of Bunyan is delightful to every reader, and invaluable as a study to every person who wishes to obtain a wide command over the

English language. The vocabulary is the vocabulary of the common people. There is not an expression, if we except a few technical terms of theology, which would puzzle the rudest peasant. We have observed several pages which do not contain a single word of more than two syllables. Yet no writer has said more exactly what he meant to say. For magnificence, for pathos, for vehement exhortation, for subtle disquisition, for every purpose of the poet, the orator, and the divine, this homely dialect, the dialect of plain working men, was perfectly sufficient. There is no book in our literature on which we would so readily stake the fame of the old unpolluted English language, no book which shows so well how rich that language is in its own proper wealth, and how little it has been improved by all that it has borrowed.

"Cowper said, forty or fifty years ago, that he dared not name John Bunyan in his verse, for fear of moving a sneer. To our refined forefathers, we suppose, Lord Roscommon's *Essay on Translated Verse*, and the Duke of Buckinghamshire's *Essay on Poetry*, appeared to be compositions infinitely superior to the allegory of the preaching tinker. We live in better times; and we are not afraid to say that, though there were many clever men in England during the latter half of the seventeenth century, there were only two minds which possessed the imaginative faculty in a very eminent degree. One of those minds produced the *Paradise Lost*, the other *The Pilgrim's Progress*."

EARLY PICTORIAL ILLUSTRATIONS OF BUNYAN.

HAD Bunyan been the friend of Albert Durer, or Hans Holbein, *The Pilgrim's Progress* would have been illustrated with designs answering to the very spirit of the author. The artists of the fifteenth and sixteenth centuries understood well that there is a standing-place both for poets and painters, between the world of dreams and the actual world. They made it their observatory. The distinct shapes of the one were not lost sight of in the golden mists, or grotesque confusion of the other. They discovered that there is an absolute and fixed relationship between the two states of existence ; and when the artist entered either into the real, or abstract meaning of the poet, the design which he drew was as distinct in outline as it was large in application and idealism. This is the case with some of the earliest wood engravings in existence. The illustrations of the *Biblia Pauperum*, published in 1432, exhibit many traces of original thought and power. Holbein's Bible cuts, and his illustrations of the Dance of Death, which appeared about a hundred years after the *Biblia Pauperum*, are still more remarkable as indicating the originality of genius, when dealing with objects recalled to existence by its spell. Even Cranmer's *Catechism*, a book intended entirely for the people, was ornamented with designs strongly marked by the features of genuine art. It is a fact, indeed, well worth remembering, that the woodcuts said to exhibit the greatest ability, were most of them produced about the year 1538, just ten years, that is, within the death of Albert Durer.

The least critical lover of art who has the means of comparing any of these early works with the original illustrations of Bunyan, cannot fail of surprise that so popular a book was not better treated by the artists of the day. It is not to be pleaded that the work was mainly circulated among a humble class of readers. Tindal's *Translation of the New Testament* had been expressly printed for the use of the people ; the *Biblia Pauperum* was certainly, in earlier times, not intended to please the vanity of the rich ; Archbishop Cranmer's *Catechism* had mainly children for its readers ;—but, in all these cases, the designs had, at least, some traits of artistic ability in their execution. They might generally be looked at with interest, not because they were free from grotesque violations of perspective, or other absurdities, but because, though roughly, they made truth visible.

A decline in any branch of art is connected with many important circumstances in the state of society. It especially indicates a loss of respect, on the side of the artist, for the class of people which he has to please or instruct. The first attempt to illustrate *The Pilgrim's Progress* was made with the fifth edition. It seems to have been simply a speculation of the publisher. The set of plates might be had separately for one shilling. It would be interesting to know how much the bookseller paid the artist for the designs, and still more to discover from what source the latter derived his notions of the pilgrim, and the scenes through which he passed. In a bibliographical point of view, these earliest pictorial illustrations of Bunyan are well deserving of a place in any complete edition of his works. They indicate the notions entertained by booksellers of the class of readers to whom they might look for a sale, and the rapid decline in artistical feeling, or respect for the people, which marked the early part of the eighteenth century. In the latter point of view, the history of the arts deserves much more attention than it has hitherto received. What was the actual mental state of the humbler, or the middle classes, when Albert Durer and Hans Holbein ministered to their taste for pictures ? What was the condition of their minds when the publisher of the fifth edition of *The Pilgrim's Progress* could tempt them to pay a shilling for the prints offered as illustrations ? The inquiry, properly pursued, would lead to the discovery of many interesting facts. We learn from Mr. Chatto's valuable and amusing *History of Wood Engraving*, that some of the best specimens of the art were produced in England between the years 1590 and 1610, just, that is, at the period when foreign artists were the least successful. Singular enough, the season of most violent popular awakening in England was so abundantly fruitful in such wretched prints, that it might have been supposed the nation was lost to all enjoyment of art. But what was the real case? Neither books nor pamphlets could convey with sufficient rapidity the thoughts, on the communication of which men supposed the assertion or security of their liberties depended. The rudest design, the worst executed engraving, might effect, in the way of suggestion, what a book by itself would never accomplish. Hence the reign of Charles I. was one of the most prolific in the production of wretched prints. But the greater number of them had a purpose and a meaning. Their low character, artistically considered, might be attributed to the fact, that nothing further was contemplated by either designer, engraver, or publisher, than the explanation to dull minds of some pressing interest or duty. In the observation of works of art, it is always of great importance to determine whether their defects be the result of an urgent, practical, homely necessity, or of slothful carelessness. We fear the latter was the case when the designs with which we are now con-

Copied from an edition published in 1692.

CHRISTIAN LOSES HIS BURDEN.

Who's this? the Pilgrim. How! 'tis very true,
Old things are passed away, all's become new.
Strange! he's another man, upon my word,
They be fine feathers that make a fine bird.

Copied from an edition published in 1692.

CHRISTIAN IN THE ARBOUR.

Shall they who wrong begin yet rightly end?
Shall they at all have *Safety* for their friend?
No, no, in headstrong manner they set out,
And headlong will they fall at last, no doubt.

Copied from an edition published in 1692.

CHRISTIAN AT THE HILL DIFFICULTY.

Difficulty is behind, *Fear* is before,
Tho' he 's got on the hill, the lions roar;
A Christian man is never long at ease,
When *one fright 's* gone, *another* doth him seize.

CHRISTIAN LEAVING THE PALACE BEAUTIFUL.

While *Christian* is among his godly friends,
Their golden mouths make him sufficient 'mends
For all his griefs; and when they let him go,
He 's clad with northern steel from top to toe.

CHRISTIAN'S COMBAT WITH APOLLYON.

A more unequal match can hardly be,
Christian must fight an Angel; but you see,
The valiant man, by handling sword and shield,
Doth make him, tho' a Dragon, quit the field.

THE VALLEY OF THE SHADOW OF DEATH.

Poor man! where art thou now? thy day is night.
Good man, be not cast down, thou art yet right,
Thy way to heaven lays by the gates of hell;
Cheer up, hold out, with thee it shall go well.

Copied from an edition published in 1683.

DOUBTING CASTLE.

The Pilgrims, now, to gratify the flesh,
Will seek its ease; but oh! how they afresh
Do plunge themselves new griefs into!
Who seek to please the flesh, themselves undo.

Copied from an edition published in 1692.

SHEPHERDS IN THE LAND OF BEULAH.

Mountains delectable they now ascend,
Where shepherds be, which to them do commend
Alluring things, and things that cautious are;
Pilgrims are steady kept by faith and fear.

Copied from an edition published in 1682.

THE ENTRANCE TO THE HEAVENLY CITY.

Now, now, look how the holy Pilgrims ride,
Clouds are their chariots, Angels are their guide:
Who would not here for Him all hazards run,
That thus provides for all His when this world's done?

Copied from an edition published in 1692.

CHRISTIAN AND EVANGELIST.

Christian no sooner leaves the world, but meets
Evangelist, who lovingly him greets
With tidings of another : and doth show
Him how to mount to that from this below.

Copied from an edition published in 1692.

CHRISTIAN MEETS MR. WORLDLY-WISEMAN.

When Christians unto carnal men give ear,
Out of their way they go, and pay for 't dear;
For Master *Worldly-Wiseman* can but show
A saint the way to bondage and to woe.

Copied from an edition published in 1692.

CHRISTIAN AT THE GATE.

He that will enter in, must first without
Stand knocking at the gate, nor need he doubt,
That is a knocker, but to enter in ;
For God can love him, and forgive his sin.

Copied from an edition published in 1708.

CHRISTIANA SETTING OUT.

Copied from an edition published in 1708.

MR. GREAT-HEART AND PILGRIMS.

Behold here how the slothful are a sign
Hung up, 'cause holy ways they did decline:
See here too how the child doth play the man,
And weak grow strong when *Great-heart* leads the van.

Copied from an edition published in 1687.

DEMOLITION OF DOUBTING CASTLE.

Though *Doubting Castle* be demolished,
And Giant *Despair* too hath lost his head,
Sin can rebuild the *Castle*, make 't remain,
And make *Despair*, the giant, live again.

VANITY FAIR.

Behold Vanity Fair! the pilgrims there
Are chained, and stoned beside:
Even so it was, our Lord pass'd here,
And on Mount *Calvary* dy'd.

CHRISTIAN AND FAITHFUL BEFORE THE JUDGE.

Now, *Faithful*, play the man, speak for thy God
Fear not the wicked's malice nor their rod:
Speak boldly, man, the truth is on thy side;
Die for it, and to life in triumph ride.

THE BURNING OF FAITHFUL.

Brave *Faithful*, bravely done in word and deed;
Judge, witnesses, and jury, have instead
Of overcoming thee, but shown their rage;
When they are dead, thou'lt live, from age to age.

cerned were produced. There was no urgent, pressing call for pictorial illustrations of Bunyan. All who could read him understood his meaning well enough. But the artist and bookseller suddenly bethought themselves that an additional shilling might be gained by the publication of prints. They soon appeared, and it is well that they have been preserved, as a very curious monument on the road between the days of Bunyan's executors and the age of Stoddart, Martin, the Art-Union, and Selous. A greater contrast cannot exist than that which appears between many of the illustrations in the present edition, and those first produced. There was an engraving of St. Christopher and the infant Jesus, well known in the fourteenth century. The accompaniments of the chief figures defied all pretensions to perspective; but St. Christopher himself might be regarded as a study for Michael Angelo. It is strange that, after more than two centuries of progress, no true artist could be found, or no bookseller of sufficient liberality, to employ an artist of genius to illustrate such an author as Bunyan. When we compare the prints of 1692 with those of the earliest foreign books, it is at once discoverable that the latter were the product of loving, thoughtful men, while the former were the work of mere hirelings. The three designs representing "Christian and Evangelist," "Christian meeting Mr. Worldly-Wiseman," and "Christian at the Gate," are utterly destitute of merit. But for the titles and verses at the foot of the print, it would be difficult to assign any character to Christian except that of a common tramp. He carries a pack, and, as far as the expression of his countenance is concerned, carries it very easily. The circle over Evangelist's head plainly indicates his saintly dignity; but there is nothing in his look or attitude to illustrate the striking language of the author, who describes him as pointing to a small distant object and glimmering light, discoverable over the wide field. But indifferent as are these first three designs, the next three are worse. Bunyan's pathetic narrative of the cross and sepulchre is turned into a wretched travestie by the absurd figure of the bundle, and the box-like modern tomb, into which it is falling. Were it not for the unmeaning appearance of Christian in a frame of basket-work, called an arbour, the terrified looks of Danger and Destruction might create a momentary interest. The hill Difficulty, with its lions, has little trace of the gloom which covered it as the sun went down, or of the shadowy terrors alluded to by the pilgrim's fear of "doleful creatures because of his sinful sleep." If anything can be said in behalf of the artist, it is that the figure of Christian himself at the "hill Difficulty" is not so absolutely ridiculous as that of the gentleman in the arbour. The next three plates exhibit "Christian leaving the Palace Beautiful," his

"Combat with Apollyon," and his passage through "The Valley of the Shadow of Death." Nobler subjects could hardly be suggested for the exercise of artistic genius, but a worse attempt to describe knightly heroism, whether real or spiritual, was never made than that which is here displayed. Neither the warrior nor the fiends could ever have appeared in any vision to the artist as they appeared in Bunyan's dream. One glimpse of them in the mirror of the author's imagination, of his solemn, earnest thoughts, would have been sufficient to save the engraver from these violations of common sense as well as taste. Of the next three plates only one bears the date of 1692, but it is the best of the three. "Doubting Castle," with Giant Despair at the gate, is inferior to most of the pictures in books for children. "The Entrance to the Heavenly City," where the pilgrims are shown riding on clouds, is even worse than the worst of all the rest.

There are two plates with the later dates of 1724 and 1727. They are united with one of the earliest designs, dated 1681. These are all rude enough both as to invention and engraving, but there is more meaning in them than in any of the rest. "Vanity Fair" is not without humour. Faithful pleading before the Judge has an honest, intelligent look; and there is a simple pathos in the picture of his burning, which makes us suspect that it was borrowed from some early martyrology.

The three illustrations of the second part of *The Pilgrim's Progress* are much better than any of those in the first. Both the single figures and the groups are easy and graceful. This superiority may be ascribed to the circumstance that in these plates there is no attempt to embody any allegory; and the artist had fewer difficulties to encounter.

Worthless as these early pictorial illustrations of Bunyan are, merely as prints, they are useful and interesting, as we have already intimated, when regarded in connection with the history of his times and writings. The booksellers must have had little respect for the taste of those among whom *The Pilgrim's Progress* was then circulated. They could have had as little hope of recommending it to readers of a higher class. A great change, in both respects, has taken place within the last thirty years. Publishers and artists have found that Bunyan's genius is now as well known as his piety. No talent for illustration is thought too great to be employed about his works—no expense is spared in recommending them to the most refined taste. The humblest class of readers look for a corresponding improvement in the editions which come within their means of purchase, and severe would be the disappointment of a publisher who should trust to illustrations no better than the designs above described.

INDEX.

Difficulty, hill of, ii. 25, 93.
Divine emblems, poem, iv. 445.
Dog, Satan under the form of a, ii. 83.
Door, shutting of that of the ark interpreted, iii. 422.
Doubters, army of, raised to attack Mansoul, iii. 77.
Doubting castle, ii. 55. Demolished, 121.
Dove, lesson taught by that of Noah, iii. 428.
Drunkard, story of, iv. 19. Drunkenness, evils of, 20.

E.

Ebal and Gerizim, iii. 471. Poem on, iv. 435.
Eber, the next after Shem to maintain religion, iii. 448.
Eden, garden of, iii. 379.
Elders, patriarchs and apostles so called, iv. 282.
Election, founded in grace, and the unchangeable will of God, i. 419, iii. 271. Whether the non-elect can receive the gospel and be saved, 282. Eternal and absolute, iv. 322.
Emmanuel, his address to the town of Mansoul, iii. 105.
Enchanted ground, arbour on, ii. 127.
Enemies, those of God's people; believers should learn to pity them; not to be grudged present enjoyments, ii. 301.
Enoch, son of Cain, iii. 403.
Ephesian-sinners, highest sort among the Gentiles, ii. 464.
Esau, Bunyan compares himself to, i. 28.
Euphrates, that which was the face of the kingdom of Babylon of old, iii. 379.
Evangelist, gives directions to the pilgrim, ii. 12.
Examination, use of, ii. 240, iii. 325.
Experience, receives commission in the town of Mansoul, to be captain over a thousand men, iii. 60.
Extortioners, who to be so called, iv. 45.
Ezra, directions given to by Artaxerxes, iv. 137.

F.

Fair-speech, form of, ii. 49.
Faith, what to be understood by it, i. 405, 421. Efficacy of, ii. 166. Opposed to unbelief in twenty-five particulars, 239. True and false, described, iii. 527. Doctrine of justification by, defended, iv. 220, 251. The cure of heart-trouble, 363.
Faithful, Mr., tempted, ii. 37. Put to death, 49.
Falls, spiritual, dangerous, but not a certain proof that they who suffer them were not coming to Christ, ii. 201.
Family, duties of the master of a, ii. 169.
Father, the name as applied to God, ii. 192.
Fear of God, treatise on, ii. 403. Several sorts of fear, 409. Effects of 414—422. Benefits produced by it, 431. Who have it not; twelve sorts of persons, 437. How to grow in this fear, 445. What hinders it, 447.
Fearing, Mr., his troublesome pilgrimage, ii. 107. His boldness at its close, 109.
Feeble-mind, Mr., in hands of Giant Slay-good, ii. 114. His history, 115.
First-born, offered to the Lord, sinners by imitation, iv. 9.
First day of the week, Sabbath reasons for observing, iv. 209. Breaking of bread, and charitable collections proper to, 210. The Lord himself with his church on this day, after his resurrection; the treasures of heaven broken up, 213. This day, while other days lie dead, is especially nominated in Scripture, 214. The Christian's principal manna day, 215.
Flight from persecution, whether lawful, considered, ii. 302.
Flood, Noah's, a type of three things:—1. Of the enemies of the church; 2. Of water baptism; 3. Of the general overthrow of the world by fire, iii. 416.
Footman, The Heavenly, spiritually considered, iv. 177.
Forgiveness, what is understood by, iv. 241.
Formalist, Mr., his conversation with Christian, ii. 25. Characteristics of a formalist described, 398.
Fowler, Mr., answer to his "Design of Christianity," iv. 222. Accused of contradicting the articles of his church, 267.
Freedom, duty of believers to live in sense of, as given by Christ, iii. 461.
Free-will, whether there be such a thing, questioned, iv. 249.
Fruit, some never ripe, hasty, ill-tasted, wild, ii. 252.
Fruitless professor, death of a, described, ii. 269.
Fundamentals, those of Christianity, primary and secondary, notions respecting, controverted, iv. 256.

G.

Gaius, an honourable disciple, keeps an inn for pilgrims, ii. 111. His spiritual interpretations at supper, 113.
Genesis, Exposition of first ten chapters of, iii. 369.
Gentiles, their concern with the Sabbath, iv. 199.
Giants, Grim, ii. 95. Maul, 105. Slay-good, 114. Despair, 121.
Gifford, Mr. Bunyan's early friend and instructor, account of, i. 17. His preface to "Sighs from Hell," 127.
Gnostics, some modern teachers compared to the ancient, iv. 403.
God, a spirit, eternal, infinite, incomprehensible, perfect, the Father, the Son, the Holy Ghost, iii. 369. Light, love, 370. Our God, iv. 83.
God, the Father, revealed to us by Jesus Christ, in his own person, iv. 239. Thrones of, 272.
God-head, how made known by light of nature, and how by Scripture, iv. 247.
God's-peace, a new officer in the town of Mansoul, iii. 66.
Golden altar, prepared by God for the prayers and tears of penitents, ii. 243.
Golden anchor, given to Christiana, ii. 100.
Goodwill, opens the wicket-gate to Christian, ii. 19.
Good works, promoted by doctrine of justification by grace, ii. 183. Two sorts of, iii. 297. Reward of, not to be doubted, 466. Help to render a death-bed easy, 471.
Gospel, six reasons why not received, i. 410. A sovereign remedy, provided by God through Christ, iii. 181.
Grace Abounding, i. 5. The sinner saved by, ii. 138, 144. Suffereth not a man to boast, 343. Considered in reference to election, iii. 284.
Grace of the Father, ii. 145. Of the Son, 146. Of the Spirit, 147. Who saved by, 148. Signs of being past— 1. God's patience abused; 2. The sinner left to himself; 3. The heart impenetrable, 266. Throne of, iv. 273. How to approach it, 286. Reasons for coming to it, 291.
Graces, imperfections of, ii. 505.
Great-grace, the king's champion, ii. 62.
Great-heart, Mr., sent by the interpreter as a protector to Christiana, ii. 91. Fights with Giant Grim and Giant Maul, 105.

H.

Half-priests, their character, neither can nor dare teach the people the whole counsel of God, iii. 307.
Haman perished because engaged against the queen, as Satan will because engaged against the church, iv. 322.
Heart-trouble forbidden, iv. 361. How to be prevented, 362. Faith its proper cure, 363.
Heaven, what to be enjoyed there, ii. 14. The imperial heaven, 493. God, necessary to the enjoyment of, 498. Heights of, reached through Christ, iv. 79, 91. Its glories described, 428.
Heedless and Too-bold, asleep in the arbour, on the enchanted ground, ii. 128.
Hell, sight from, i. 126. Torments of, 141. How many, iii. 197. State of those who perish there, iv. 431.
Hidings of God's face, a thing more bitter to the soul than death, ii. 494.
High-priest, his office, iii. 263. Christ our high-priest, 507. Effects of his sacrificial offering, iv. 296. His qualities as high-priest, 301.
Holiness, negative and positive, ii. 323. Definition of "a healthful complexion of soul, &c." disputed, iv. 222. Three things essential to inward and evangelical holiness, 228. Holiness of Adam, consistent with ignorance of Christ, not given him by promise, but by creation, 231.
Holy Ghost, sin against, i. 15, 24, ii. 488, iii. 114. His part in the work of our salvation, 141.
Holy life, beauty of Christianity, iii. 294.
Holy-man, Mr., his account of things requisite for pilgrims, ii. 119.
Holy, and most holy parts of the temple, iii. 254.
Holy War, iii. 4.
Hope, distinguished from faith, ii. 492. Excellency of, 495.
Hopeful, Mr., account of his life before conversion, ii. 65. His experience, 67. Keeps Christian's head above water in passing the river, 72.
House of the Forest of Lebanon, a type of the church in the wilderness, iv. 113. Of what materials built, 115. Porch of, 130.